Arthur Cohn

The
Literature
of
Chamber
Music

Volume 2
Eggermann
to
Kyurkchiisky

Hinshaw Music, Inc., Chapel Hill, North Carolina

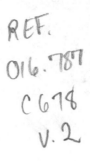

Library of Congress Card Number 95-2008
ISBN 0-937276-16-2

Printed in the United States of America

Contents

Volume I

Volume II

Volume III

Volume IV

Eggermann, Fritz (1898–)

DUO

- *Six Sketches* for Violin and Viola

With quasi-didactic persistence, Eggermann individually plots each of his half-dozen pieces. The preoccupation with formal detail, color, metrical detail, and so forth, for each piece holds its ground very well, supported totally by dodecaphonic treatment.

Double stops to enlarge the texture and fully define the harmonic content, plus use of inversion of the material, are found in the opening Andante. In addition, in all but one of the eighteen measures the meter changes. The second piece emphasizes meter differences also, with alternating measures of 3/4 and 2/4. The coloration is totally that of plucked sound. The third piece is a Lento, completely set in septuple meter and once again distinctively timbred— the violin plays throughout on the G string, the viola matches it by also playing totally on its lowest (C) string.

And so the formalistic statistics continue. A single melodic line (chromatic, of course) is continually broken up between the two instruments in number four. Save for the final measure, a three-voice Adagio in 11/8 constitutes the fifth piece, and the opus finishes with motoric music. Three chords employing the eight open strings of the two instruments are the signature for this twelve-tone origination.

Eggleston, Anne (1934–)

QUARTET

- **Quartet for Piano and Strings (Violin, Viola, and Cello) (1955)**

A catalogue description of this work begins: "The four movements, although not connected thematically, have in common the relationship between the piano as an individual and the strings as a group." This is used in bits but is especially important to the third movement (Lento). Elsewhere, the balance of the description applies: "These two elements are either united or contrasted." In any event, this point is generally applicable to any piano quartet.

Breadth of statement concerns the first movement. In the Allegro scherzando rhythmic punch is intensified by the constant interjection of foreshortened measures into the basic lengths— the latter 6/8, the former in 4/8. Fugal data is used to power the finale.

Egk, Werner (1901–83)

QUINTET

- **Five Pieces for Wind Quintet (Flute [alternating Piccolo], Oboe [alternating Oboe d'amore and English horn], Clarinet [alternating Basset horn], Horn, and Bassoon)**

(If the oboe d'amore and basset horn are not available—preferred instruments but not mandatory ones—the oboe substitutes for the former and the clarinet for the latter. In that case the only alternating instruments are the piccolo with the flute and the English horn with the oboe.)

Variety is, truly, the very spice of this work's makeup. Five different types of designs are matched by various timbre assortments, providing all the alternating instruments are used. The usual instruments of the wind quintet (flute, oboe, clarinet, horn, and bassoon) are called on in movements one and three, but even there a subtle difference exists. In the first piece a B-flat clarinet is used, in the third piece an A clarinet is required.

The flute is in full command in the opening "Monolog," the others truly accompany. Movement two is a Choral that is activated rather than proceeding with vertical sound hangings. "Mobile" is rhythmically organized for ready action. Part four stresses a "Dialog" with uneven participation; one instrument is mostly responded to by grouped instruments. The Finale is racy before and after a quiet interruption.

Colorful music, this. Music far from the usual patter and lighter affectations of so many wind quintets. Egk's pieces are of tougher fiber and individually colored; a welcome addition to the literature for the medium.

NONET

- **Polonaise, Adagio, and Finale for Four Wind Instruments (Oboe, Clarinet, Horn, and Bassoon) and String Quintet (Two Violins, Viola, Cello, and Double Bass)**

The Polonaise is a paraphrase on the dance design—not for dancing, this somewhat Stravinskian music. There is long solo first violin passage, but for the greater part the five string instruments move in a block-scoring procedure. (It may have been this compactness that decided Egk to indicate that the string quintet may be multiplied. No total given, simply that it can be used "in chorus.")

There is far less Stravinsky influence in the central slow movement. More of the string scoring cohesiveness here, though strong linear data are detailed in the winds. Also, a long cadenza flourish for the clarinet. The Finale again reminds one of the elastic neoclassical gestures in Stravinsky's ballet scores. Vital rhythmic motility in this work. And big sounds from Egk's instrumental nonet, but solid and meaty, minus any fat.

Ehle, Robert

QUINTETS

- **Partita for Two Trumpets, Horn, Trombone, and Tuba, Op. 3**

Freshly tonal music, with charm and variety and a well-balanced demeanor between purpose and the formal plan chosen. The vertically disposed Overture—"In the Manner of Handel" is followed by a compact Chaconne, with the ground-bass basis appearing seven times in all. Linear strength in the third part (Sinfonia); a Chorale and Pavane are next. Contrapuntalism is also the prime method for shaping the finale ("Fantasia in the Manner of Bach"). Ehle's detail avoids any academic programming.

- **Quintet for Brass (Two Trumpets, Horn, Trombone, and Tuba), Op. 28**

The Fanfare avoids any standard proclamatory-outlined brass phrases. Ehle's setting is packed with combined voicing or antiphonal swinging between paired instruments playing in thirds in a bitonal relationship. Movement two (Canto) colors its urgency with asymmetric detail. In the final movement ("Fugue on Jazz Riffs") metrical fluidity plays an important role as well. A colorfully convincing statement.

Ehrlich, Abel (1915–)

DUO

- *Testimony* **for Two Flutes (1961)**

Ehrlich's music is a general translation of a specific, searing incident. Thereby, subjective intention is realized by objective detail. The musical imagery does not depict the facts in a phrase-by-phrase parallel.

The event is derived from evidence given by

a witness at the famous Eichmann trial. Deportation raids were being made in the Warsaw ghetto. A woman saw her three sons placed in a truck with others to be taken to the gas chambers. She pleaded that her three children be freed, but the Nazi officer agreed to let her take only one. "The three boys were stretching out their arms to her, as if imploring—'take me!'" Unable to choose, the mother was forced to watch as all of her children were carried away to be murdered.

Although Ehrlich indicates the piece is based on three motives describing the cry of each child, the motivic material is acutely similar. The entire eight-minute composition consists of tightly meshed cellular depiction and development. The pitch movement is narrow in range, with pinpointed inextensile chromaticism. The lines are heard with intense fricative combinations: minor and major seconds, augmented and diminished octaves, minor ninths, and so forth.

Ehrlich states that his *Testimony* carries the message that "unless mankind can put a stop to the unending chain of hate begetting hate, the whole human race may be extinguished as were the innocent victims of the past."

Eichenwald, Philipp (1915–)

OCTET

- *Aspekte*: **Kammermusik für acht Spieler** (*Aspects*: **Chamber Music for Eight Players) (Flute, Clarinet, Violin, Cello, Harp, Piano, and Two Percussionists [Xylophone, Vibraphone, High and Low Cymbals, High and Low Tam-tams, Small Drum, and Five Wood Blocks]) (1958)**

Clearly detailed twelve-tone writing. As a result, the dimension of technical directness (simplicity, it might be called) gives considerable meaning to the music. This brings a reminder of the beautifully executed dodecaphonic music of Wallingford Riegger.

After four introductory percussion rolls, the tone row is introduced and spread through the instruments. It then appears constantly in new colors and new shapes. Examples: a statement of the entire row in the piano; then fragmented single pitches combined with the wood blocks; the row presented by the solo violin; prolonged pitch declaration begun by the harp and passed to the cello, clarinet, violin, flute, and piano; and a ten-part statement with the remainder contained in a retrograde thrust of the piano.

Einem, Gottfried von (1918–)

DUO

- **Sonata for Violin and Piano, Op. 11**

Tonally expansive—the polarity of the outer movements is A, the middle one, D—Einem's duo sonata is most telling in its textures and rhythmic disposition. The first movement covers 115 measures entirely in septuple time. Its concentrated length has the demeanor of a sonatina. The Larghetto is muted in the string instrument, subdued as well in its contents. A scalic theme is presented over pedal tones. It is then slightly varied with an ostinated piano counterpoint featuring the longest sound lengths off the pulse points. Syncopation is the principal consideration of the fast finale. Nothing is concealed in this extroverted event.

QUARTET

- *Laudes Eisgarnenses* **for Four Horns, Op. 58**

A two-movement piece based on the chorale "Es ist genug" from Bach's Cantata No. 60: *O*

Ewigkeit, du Donnerwort. The movements are contrasted by slow and fast tempos. Both are in three-part form, the first with a literal da capo recapitulation, the other presenting on return a developed form of the first part.

Eisenmann, Will (1906–)

TRIO

- **Divertimento for Two Clarinets and Bassoon**

Straussian *Expressionismus* set forth in neoclassic linear detail describes this three-movement piece. The light quality of movement one develops variationally. Movement two is no less weighty in its texture, though the content is dancelike and elegant in its phrases. And in firm balance with the first movement, the final Arioso also derives its contents from extension by development.

An important statistic: In movements two and three trio scoring never ceases for a single measure. In movement one, with a total of 55 measures, the three instruments play in all but 11 1/2 measures. Indeed, Eisenmann believes in keeping his performers fully occupied.

Eisikovits, Max (1908–83)

DUO

- *Images chassidiques et Rhapsodie chassidique* **for Cello and Piano**

The usual augmented intervals that mark the greater part of Orthodox Jewish music (which includes that of the Hasidic sect) fill the measures of this two-part piece. In the Elegie et danse (Images) there are both magisterial invocation and somewhat restrained rhythmical action. Still, the expression of religious rapture

that marks Hasidic dances is present. Present also are some harmonic supports that equate contemporary mannerisms, especially those pertaining to small cluster framework.

The Rhapsodie contains declarative, exclamatory, and incantational detail. There is continual change of tempo, but always returning to the general animato and appassionato temper of the movement.

Eisler, Hanns (1898–1962)

Eisler's output divides into three widely differing aspects, not separated and marking particular periods of activity but intertwined throughout his career. He wrote a number of works based on the Schoenbergian aesthetic; in direct opposite style are a large number of very tonal songs and music dealing with social content; and last, he was one of the most important creators of motion-picture music. In the last field he was able, when the opportunity offered, to integrate twelve-tone composition as the basic technical background for the score of an otherwise ordinary film. Furthermore, his treatise on motion-picture music, *Composing for the Films*, is considered one of the most authoritative in existence.

DUO

- **Duo for Violin and Cello, Op. 7, No. 1**

Eisler's string duo, written in the twelve-tone system, tends to revolve around dance rhythms (although these are of nonsymmetrical pulse), contains a certain amount of grotesquerie, and is in original form. No compromise is made for the performers because the work bristles with difficulties. The first movement begins as a minuet type, exposes that form in the initial section by way of ternary apportionment, then moves into a waltz section, recapitulates the opening theme, and terminates with a coda. A free rondo design constitutes the second movement.

The two instruments are scored with careful regard for sonorous objectives. These give varying colors and densities within the designs and are characterized by a type of virtuosity that invigorates the unaccompanied string duet—a difficult medium for the composer due to its confined instrumentation.

TRIOS

- *Präludium und Fuge über B–A–C–H for String Trio, Op. 46*

Eisler's piece is subtitled "Study on a Twelve-tone Row." And it is documented with the clearest projection. The *Präludium* begins with combination of the twelve-tones in the three instruments, the row constructed from three four-pitch groups, each duplicating the intervallic content. Accordingly, the "Bach" portion is B-flat (equals B) to A (a half step down), up to C (minor third upward), and completed by B (equals H) (again a half-step descent). The next group begins a minor third higher and repeats the intervallic arrangement, and once more this plan is used to complete the entire row. Thus the name "Bach" has been used thrice in different pitches.

From this point on full use of dodecaphonic technique applies: transposition, retrograde, and so forth. Syncopation is the driving force within the first part; a repetitive pitch "head" is basic to the fugue.

- **Sonatensatz for Flute, Oboe, and Harp, Op. 49**

The first movement of a full-scale sonata Eisler planned to write. Chromatic tonalism is the basis for the piece, which is classically structured with a repeat of the expositionary material. No lushness in this trio; the instruments are handled without any striving for special effects.

QUINTET

- **Divertimento for Wind Quintet, Op. 4**

The spirit of Schoenberg is very strong in Eisler's two-movement quintet. Indeed, the influence of the teacher on the pupil is evident in this case, but with the orderliness and flow of the music a double compliment is forthcoming.

Though the first movement is an Andante con moto, there is decided rhythmic vitality in the lines. Six variations on a widely arched theme and a coda make up the other movement. For the greater part, Eisler concentrates on a heavy textural affirmation. All to the good, though divisional definition does become slightly blurred.

Eisma, Will (1929–)

DUOS

- *Affairs II* for Alto Recorder (alternating Soprano Recorder) and Harpsichord (1963)

Additive structuring in the first of the two parts of Eisma's duo, titled "Report." The disclosure is one of free chromatic pitch action covering the total spectrum. Part two, "Phrases," is unmetered, proportionally notated. Of course, with this Dutch avant-gardist the harpsichord is not used in a standard manner. Its embellishments and ornamentations are those of tone clusters, glissandos with a pencil on the strings, and plucking of the strings. Ad lib choice of sounds is used in the recorder part; the performer also "plays" the harpsichord by touching its strings. Colorful displays indeed—music of modernistic panache.

- *The Light of the Cold, Still Moon* for Cello and Piano (1971)

A surrealistic coolness moves within this heated score. Eisma creates sound surfaces that pitch in and out, up and down, minus meter and pulse, but define clearly a type of impressionism as realized by avant-garde pigmentation. The instruction "Libero" ("Free") is noted six times within the score. There is also, significantly, a large section marked "Do not listen to each other!" Even if the players were to consider each other's sounds the result would be the same. No problem. Cohesion would disrupt this music of fragmented fragments.

- *Small Protocol* for Violin and Cello (1966)

A duet in which there is unified action as well as antiphonal-type responses, plus sonorous polyphony made from chunks of sound and swiftly projected pitch rows. The music zigs and zags and retains its general cubistic delivery of fractured fragments for about eight minutes.

QUARTETS

- *Archipel* for String Quartet (1964)

Archipel has the usual materials of the avant-garde (playing behind the bridge; quarter tones; notes to be played as quickly as possible, the number and pitches decided by the performer; and so on) and also employs a special mute, the "Tonwolf" described as a "sordine with lead." This is used as a contrast to the customary mute. Further, the four instruments are in scordatura, each altering the tuning of one string: the G string is lowered to F on violin 1, the D string on violin 2 is moved down a half step, the viola's C string is tuned to B, and the cello's A string is dropped to G-sharp.

Proportional notation rules, with time sig-

nals determining the span of action. Sustained sounds and clustered compacts are principal. The work ends with a *fortissimo* statement derived from graphic graffiti.

- *World within World* for Oboe, Violin, Viola, and Cello (1966)

No pastoral strains strain through the measures of Eisma's piece. This is a quartet of heated, mostly aleatoric detail, with jabs of pitches; whacks behind the strings; the squash of ponticello; the thrust, swing, and lunge of sounds. The devotion for these assorted sonorities, plus bits and pieces, remains fixed throughout the 10 1/2 minutes. Strong stuff that needs no pulse regularity to register a dramatic result.

Eler, André Frédéric (1764–1821)

QUARTET

- **Wind Quartet in F Major for Flute, Clarinet, Horn, and Bassoon, Op. 6, No. 1**

Two movements, with the greatest interest pointed toward the second of the pair. It is a theme with variations, but the old structural body is infused with some new formal vitamins. After the fourth variation an Adagio is inserted that sounds improvisational. Then follows a restatement of the theme of the movement. But it is in Allegro, whereas the initial thematic statement is in Allegretto. A vivid and active definition of sonata design, with the usual contrasts, opens the quartet. No tempo is indicated in the score.

Elgar, Edward (1857–1934)

Just before World War I, English music was star-studded with only two names, Purcell and

Elgar. And these widely separated temperaments were the leading lights in a period of over two centuries. In Elgar, the zenith of the English classic-romantic-nationalistic schools was reached. His style, however, was not an amalgam but a concentrate that furnished pure English qualities—serenity, propriety, and carefully balanced workmanship.

Elgar was a composer who gave the English the start of their musical revival, a composer who first broke with the cap-and-gown past; almost their creative raison d'être, their answer to the sarcastic and critical barbs that came from Germany, Italy, and France. Too often there had been dismissal of Elgar's work, with no acknowledgment or appreciation of his real talent.

Elgar had no formal training. His was the study by the eye and ear, without scholastic direction. It was a hard-boiled, practical knowledge that took root. A rare background, twice rare in that it led to a doctor's degree from Cambridge, at the age of 43. But this was merely the forerunner of a series of honors heaped on Elgar, from knighthood in 1904 to the highest honor possible for a musician in England—being named Master of the King's Musick in 1924.

Elgar's productivity was anything but slight. The numbered works reach eighty-seven, with this total almost duplicated by shorter, unnumbered items. His important chamber music is represented by three large works—a violin and piano sonata, a string quartet, and a quintet for piano and strings. Each of these is an important contribution to the literature, and all were written in quick succession between March 1918 and April 1919.

DUOS

- **Duett for Trombone and Double Bass (1887)**

This little-known musical savory (first published in 1970) was produced in one day: August 1, 1887. It's a bright little thing of forty-nine measures, in duple time, at allegretto speed. Equal time for the instruments, equal time for sequential writing, and equal time for stylistic imitation.

The London *Times* wrote that Elgar's duo was "a good piece for a school concert." But not so limited; professionals will find that while the music is "a piece of cake" performance-wise, it is, at least, worthy of encore status in a formal concert setting.

- **Sonata in E Minor for Violin and Piano, Op. 82**

Elgar's hallmarks were the spun melody ennobled by majestic profile, a vigorous and resolutely determined type of writing in the fast movements, and a warm romantic urge in the slower-paced sections. It takes temperament as well as a fine creative ability to form a theme with the beautiful proportions of the one that opens this Sonata. As an answer to criticism of Elgar's being mainly scholastic, it should be indicated that in this opening theme the home tonality of E minor is not stated immediately. The wide leaps and the ascent–descent on a nonsymmetrical basis are exhilarating writing and most enjoyable. Further to be noted is the modal spirit over Bach-like figurations for the string instrument in the middle section.

The second movement has the generic title Romance, since such designation can define anything in ballade style or in small form, preferably in slow or moderate tempo. In this instance, the music seems to turn on itself. (This Romance is not short, covering a six-minute span of the twenty-one-minute length of the Sonata.) It begins improvisationally, and it takes considerable time before the general idea of undulating figures settles into a theme made of quartal and quintal intervals. The extemporized outline returns to form an A–B–

A pattern of figurational rhapsody and placidity.

The tonic major to the home key's minor dominates the last movement. Within it a significant movement link is made by quoting a section from the Romance in augmented rhythm. The curvilinear sweep and warm rhythmic definition of the movement are Elgarian, but of suburban, not urban, flavor.

QUARTET

▪ **String Quartet in E Minor, Op. 83**

Though the quartet was commissioned by the Worshipful Company of Musicians, it actually was written without such impetus; it was added to the organization's list of commissions in view of an earlier invitation to Elgar for a string quartet he never wrote. When the quartet was published, the Worshipful Company of Musicians felt it was so worthy of being included in its list that it did so—substituting the noncommissioned work for the noncomposed commissioned opus!

The quartet is in E minor, a key that permeates two of Elgar's three significant chamber works (with the odd one also in a minor key). Even the cello concerto that followed the triple succession of chamber compositions is in E minor, an example of stylistic affinity and of a generating creative impulse that carried from one work to another. Further synthesis of compositional processes is manifest in the chamber works, each concentrated in three movements, with no minuet or scherzo to give contrastive lightness to the outer movements.

The main clue to the quartet is the 12/8 meter chosen for the opening—a broader concept of four pulse units per measure than the affinitive 4/4. The former is more articulatively majestic and close to the essence of this composer, with his often-met instruction *nobilmente* (though the quartet is more vernal than it is noble). The opening is somewhat ecclesiastical, but soon moves into full emotional drive, balanced with pastoral overtones. The middle movement concerns itself more with defined feeling than with the projection of a certain speed rate. The tempo is just a shade less than moderate, whereas the score's Italian indication piacevole means "pleasant" or "agreeable," denoting mellow performance requirements in full keeping with the attributes of this composer. Such reticent and intimate nonassertiveness is carefully carried out from the very beginning when a string trio sets the mood. The lively, warm vivacity of the last movement has excellent proportional form; it ends with the general classic affirmation of the related pivotal tonic home key (here E major in relation to the opening E minor). The sonata drama of two subjects is taken through various-paced situations, and all is on the sunny side, save a very short inferential use of colorplay, where the eeriness of ponticello creates a foil of contrast.

QUINTETS

▪ **Music for Wind Quintet (Two Flutes, Oboe, Clarinet, and Bassoon [or Cello]), Op. 6**

Young Elgar music, composed in 1878 and 1879. Twenty-two pieces are included, one of which is in four movements.

All of the material remained unpublished until 1976, then was issued in a performing edition made by Richard McNicol, who clarified inconsistencies of notation, dynamics, and the like. The music is divided into seven parts (called "volumes" by the editor, not by Elgar). As a unit identification this is all in good order. However, it is important to realize that only five of the seven parts of *Harmony Music* (*see* Volumes II, III, and IV *below*) were published. Part VI *(Harmony Music 6)*, consisting of an Allegro molto and an Andante arioso (composed May 7, 1879), and Part VII *(Harmony*

Music 7), consisting of an Allegro and a Scherzo–Allegro giusto (the only work composed later than 1879—on April 14, 1881), remain, as of this date, in manuscript. Further, the Four Dances comprising Volume VI were not given such title heading by Elgar, each being written as a separate piece, all in 1879.

There is disagreement as to the opus designation. McNicol makes no mention of it anywhere, simply identifying the works by dates of composition. Diana M. McVeagh in her book on Elgar specifically lists the compilation as "Opus 6—Quintets and Short Pieces." On the other hand, in Percy M. Young's detailed study of Elgar he states that Op. 6 can be applied to any of the wind quintet compositions, "but not [so] specified by Elgar."

It was for a domestic group in which he played bassoon that Elgar wrote these compositions. This explains the absence of the horn from the usual wind quintet instrumentation— the scoring fitting the combination at hand in which his brother Francis Thomas (Frank) played oboe. Elgar doubtless shifted to the cello at times since the manuscript material from which the published edition was made included cello parts for several of the pieces. (Elgar was a good violinist and had a working knowledge of the cello.) On that basis the alternate choice of bassoon or cello appears in the published edition. In most cases the part is the same for both instruments, in a few places the cello part is slightly expanded chordally.

(The discussions below follow the volume sequence as published. This logically finds the music composed in 1878 in the first volume and the balance, composed in 1879, distributed throughout the other volumes.)

- **Music for Wind Quintet (Volume I):** *Six Promenades* **(1878)**

Only showmanship (salesmanship?) can explain the affixing of titles to half of the total set. The second piece is named "Madame Taussaud's," the fourth one "Somniferous," and the sixth "Hell and Tommy." Rhythmic incision marks the first and last of these, the only difference applies to a moderate pace for "Taussaud" and an allegro basis (oddly dichotomous in being headed Allegro maestoso fuoco) for "Hell and Tommy." (How to play in a majestic manner and simultaneously with fire one leaves to performers to solve!)

Naturally the "Somniferous" (fourth) movement is in a slow tempo—here andante. Certainly it is far from being soporific music, so again, the ploy of gaining extra attention by use of a picturesque title. It enjoys excellent use of imitative details in the writing.

- **Music for Wind Quintet (Volume II):** *Harmony Music 1* **and** *Harmony Music 2* **(1879)**

Both are single movements and both have bustling geniality. A lighter surface is to be noted in the second of the pair, which emphasizes connective legato phrases, whereas the first one stresses articulative eighth-note continuity.

Conventional sonata form involves both; the tonalities are, respectively, G and F major. The instruments are handled with well-kept balance.

- **Music for Wind Quintet (Volume III):** *Harmony Music 3* **and** *Harmony Music 4* **(1879)**

Harmony Music 3 is incomplete. (The published score titles it "Fragment.") It is a spirited piece in A minor that breaks off at the end of measure 119 with a few notes indicated in the following measure-to-be.

Harmony Music 4 is a large-scale sonata package, perhaps too well ordered in its repetitive ideas. It bears the title "The Farm Yard," but this gimmick, similar to others in the series, is explained by one of Elgar's biographers as nothing more than "Schumannesque eagerness."

▪ Music for Wind Quintet (Volume IV): *Harmony Music 5* (1879)

An attractive, full-measured, four-movement quintet. There is an easy flow of expression as the music proceeds through standard formal channels.

Two of the movements have the fancy titles that appear attached to many of the pieces in this collection. The tag "The Mission" applies to the first movement. It is a flowing allegro moderato sonata construction, absent any revivalistic meanings. Movement three is titled "Noah's Ark." This rests firmly in a 6/8 andante in A minor. The other parts of the work are a Menuetto and Trio (movement two) and a Finale.

▪ Music for Wind Quintet (Volume V): Five Intermezzos (1879)

Elgar considered this set the best conceptions within the wind-quintet pieces he had composed. He wrote that he liked all of them, "on the whole," but that the Five Intermezzos were "mine own children."

In each case the forms are clearly bounded by rondo or ternary-totaled enclosures. Number one has the subtitle "The Farmyard," but is minus any rustic mimicry. (The same title, in three-word form ["The Farm Yard"] was used in connection with *Harmony Music 4* in Volume III of the series—*see above.*) Number three is also subtitled—"Nancy." She is delineated as a soft-spoken allegretto character.

▪ Music for Wind Quintet (Volume VI): Four Dances (1879)

At age 22 Elgar was not about to disturb formal matters by any fussy, far-flying ideas. Accordingly, these dance designs are exact and with-out surprises, but more importantly, they are most attractive.

The order of the dances is: Menuetto, Gavotte ("The Alphonsa"), Sarabande, and Gigue. As noted in the introductory commentary above, the dances, while published as a unit, were produced as separate items, and Elgar did not combine them under any principal title. (He later transferred the Sarabande to his unfinished opera *The Spanish Lady*, where it formed part of the first scene in the second act.) The heading Four Dances is a posthumous publication decision as is their internal sequential arrangement.

The editor (Richard McNicol) suggests that the dances "can be combined advantageously in performance with the longer movement of the *Harmony Music* to form more substantial and satisfactory works." One assumes one of the movements from *Harmony Music 1* and *2* or *3* and *4* is meant by this unclear suggestion, since each of these consists of a separate movement, whereas *Harmony Music 5* already encompasses four full-size movements.

(The published score notes the date for the Menuetto as 1878, with 1879 as the date for the other three movements. Elsewhere, 1879 is assigned the date for the Menuetto.)

▪ Music for Wind Quintet (Volume VII): Adagio cantabile *("Mrs. Winslow's Soothing Syrup")* and Andante con variazione *("Evesham Andante")* (1879)

The Adagio cantabile is, indeed, well named. Its principal tune is sweet (Elgar emphasizes this by his dolce expression mark).

Explicit variations, six in number, are detailed in the "Evesham Andante" (a fancy adjective that means nothing more than being fancy). The simple theme is never hidden, and the variational language concentrates on rhythmic synonyms for registration: eighths in the first variation, a long- and two-short-pitch figure in the second variation, triplets in the third, etc. What is engaging is the use of a two-measure ritornel that appears after the theme and then constantly reappears, separating one variation from the next. To tie up the entire matter it also forms the pithy coda, now expanded to three measures.

➤ Piano Quintet in A Minor, Op. 84

Most of Elgar's music is concerned with the grandness of man's faith in his own country. His music is of a spiritual quality that is optimistic though not happy-go-lucky. But in this quintet Elgar writes with restraint, expressing a type of creative mystery. The work is overcast and brooding, fraught with an introverted quality rare in this composer's output. In spite of this, or because of it, this quintet is one of the masterworks in the piano quintet medium.

The octave theme of the opening movement, to which mutterings are applied by the strings, is a motto used in the last movement in open harmonic spacing—an order giving remoteness by triply augmented rhythms. (One senses an unexplained programmatic significance in the opus.) This motto introduces the first Allegro, before which comes a passage for the strings (likewise used in the last movement), and after which comes the lightest theme in the entire quintet—a subject in thirds that suggests dance movement. This is the stuff of which Elgar's piano quintet is made. One does not insist on any specified meanings, merely because of thematic transference from first to last movement. The implications of sternness and tragedy, of a new form of musical speech, in a composer who had not written in that manner previously, demand some explanation. Unfortunately, other works cannot be studied to solve this precedent, for the reason that, although Elgar lived sixteen years after he wrote this work (in 1918), the death two years later of his wife practically brought a halt to his creative work. The answer may be that Elgar

was almost on the verge of a new style; a deep, introspective period analogous to late Beethoven.

But changes of style rarely affect certain deep-seated habits of a composer. Elgar's last movement contains his favorite score indication, nobilmente, as well as his restrained direction *con dignita*. In spite, however, of such carryovers from past works, and regardless of a rich and moving slow movement, based on a viola theme heard in the web of solo string quartet tone that opens that section, there is troubled thinking within the quintet. This makes it Elgar's "enigma" in the field of chamber music.

Elkus, Jonathan (1931–)

TRIO

■ *Five Sketches* for Two Clarinets and Bassoon (1954)

Sketches, but with their meaning clear. Only in the Alla polacca is there the sense of a single (one-piece) construction, and in that case a rhythmic cell is a glued escort for the material. Binary formations are present in the Notturna and pert Burlesca; a type of ternary design covers the Intrada. In the Recitativo–Capriccio, the formal split personality is matched by definitive data: separated, expressive figures for the first portion, zestful sixteenth-note sets for the other.

Elling, Catharinus (1858–1942)

QUARTET

■ Quartet for Piano, Violin, Viola, and Cello

Classical forms, all clearly articulated and all

sensitively balanced, are contained in this thirty-five-minute work. The materials are all admirably clear, warm-blooded, and always written with built-in playing comfort for the instrumentalists. There is no need to juice up the music and define it by special interpretative bargaining. Elling's piano quartet is accomplished, tonally defined music.

Sonata relationships are based in the first movement, with the keys of G minor and its relative major being involved. In the rondo-framed finale the G-minor tonality eventually (as expected in this style) matures into a concluding G major. The slow movement is developed variationally.

Elling's creative beat shows dramatically in the third movement (Presto). Built from shifting phrases (mostly of six- and eight-measure lengths), the music never yields as it courses through 824 measures of 3/8 time, pulsed one beat per measure. And in the central section of this scherzo-propelled music there is no lessening of pace, but rather intensification, with the instruction *ma con passione*.

Elliott, Lionel

DUO

- **Four Bagatelles for Cello and Piano**

Title modesty in this case. Elliott's pieces are examples of an unfussy approach to music, but certainly in size and content they are not the trifles indicated by the title. Nor are the pieces in the Beecham-named category of musical "lollipops." Even as to length, each of the four is longer than the usual "short" piece of music.

"Rococo" is a moderately moving, just slightly majestic, type of prelude. Key change, from major to minor, and color shift, from bowed to plucked sound, mark the central part of its ternary design. The third piece is titled "Restlessness," with a subtitle: "A Study." No

argument in this case as to proper titling. The music is a continuity of quadruple sets of triplets per measure, picturing the main title and confirming the subtitle, both by their insistence and consistence. The last of the bagatelles is "Evensong": richly harmonized, mainly antiphonally communicated, and eloquently communicative.

The title of the second piece is "A Spring Serenade," with the parenthetical indication "based on a song by Florian Pascal." This use provides an interesting twist and relationship. Elliott's work was published by Joseph Williams, Ltd. (the music was copyrighted in 1919). This London firm was established in 1808 by Lucy Williams. Her son (Joseph William Williams) succeeded her, and, in turn, his son, Joseph Benjamin Williams became the head of the firm in 1883. This Williams was a composer as well and for obvious reasons used a pseudonym: Florian Pascal. Williams/Pascal died in 1923, but the long life of this publishing house continued as a family company well into the 1960s when it was purchased by an American firm.

Ellis, David Graham (1953–)

TRIO

- ***Time-Trip* for Flute, Violin, and Piano (1975)**

A short science-fiction tale is to be read aloud before the start of Ellis's trio, but if it isn't, no harm pertains (in this writer's opinion).

Sharp, frictioned chords are motivally detonated throughout the piece. Between these are sections of piled-up weighted material. These consist of polyphonic-packed tremolandos and full-textured but dynamically low-keyed polyrhythmic ostinatos (three against four against five against six, five against seven against eight against ten, etc.). Strong athematic music, this, devoted to the smash of rhythmic color.

Elovaara, Toivo (1907–)

TRIO

- **Sonatina in F Minor for Two Violins and Cello (1937)**

Nice variety and vitality are present. So is the key of F minor. All four movements are in that tonality, with a shift to the tierce de Picardie made only at the end of the third movement.

Simplicity and a straightforward approach are represented. Tonal music of this kind always "sits well" in all respects. Sufficient reason, therefore, for accepting the work.

QUARTET

- **String Quartet in C Minor (1929)**

Elovaara's early-period quartet (written at the age of 22) is peppered with polyphony. The opening is defined by imitation and leads to an Allegro in fugato form. These two elements are then developed, and contrapuntalism is always prominent. Movement two (*attacca* from the first) is a Fuga, so the wholesale application of polyphony continues. There is less linear emphasis (but still imitative-style strength) in the finale.

Elton, Antony (1935–)

DUO

- **Short Sonata for Two Clarinets**

Equalized lines, in the sense that neither of the instruments is kept in a subsidiary position for more than a couple of measures. Partnered activity is the axiom here. A prime example is

the middle Adagio, where the two lines constantly push against each other, mostly with one voice moving a quarter of a beat after the other voice.

In the rhapsodic format of the first part, scherzo zeal (in 3/8 meter) later combines with a broad statement in 3/4 meter, the former further changed inwardly so that its accentuations form patterns of 2/8 + 1/8 and 1/8 + 2/8. The last movement is mainly an interlock of motility and a sustained stentorian line. This finale concludes with a wild Presto.

Emmanuel, Maurice (1862–1938)

DUO

- ***Suite on Popular Greek Airs* for Violin and Piano (1907)**

Emmanuel based his four-movement violin and piano suite on material obtained by Hubert Pernot during his folkloric researches in 1898.

Number one, indicated in Pernot's collection as "Khasapikos," is a twirling, Allegretto-paced music, leaning on the augmented interval for its special color. Some modal material filters through the fourth piece, derived from "Boulgarikos." A pair of *Chansons dansées*—"Marmaro et Amadès"—provides the fundamental of movement two. "Pyrghi" identifies the song Emmanuel used for constructing the third movement.

TRIO

- **Sonata for Clarinet, Flute, and Piano (1907)**

Solid writing, yet with complete textural clarity. The creative decisions here show tonal wisdom applied to carefully drawn designs.

Movement one shapes its material so that diatonic quality is contrasted to chromatic quality followed by a return to the diatonic. Wide-spanned triple pulse covers the Adagio; the temporal phrasing is in 9/4, but the measures are each exactly divided into three sets of three pulses. The music of the finale breathes with full scherzo health.

Emmert, František (1940–)

DUO

- **Sonata for Violin and Piano (1973)**

Powerful creative temper here. The majority stress of dissonance (augmented and diminished octaves, minor ninths, and the like) carries over to the music itself—aggressive, shifting in both its pace (fourteen times alone in the first movement) and metrical disposition. No Schoenbergian calculus here, but a type of updated Scriabinish text. This moves into almost free-ordered recitative style (movement two), confirmed by the great amount of violin-without-piano writing.

Emmert's Sonata is always powerful, its prose panchromatic, a music that is almost with emotional detachment. This is most apparent in the finale.

End, Jack (1918–)

QUINTET

- *Three Salutations* **for Brass Quintet (Two Trumpets, Horn, Trombone, and Tuba)**

A miniature survey of jazz speech in slightly formalistic dress. In the first of the set there's some warm bop. Part two is related to the blues, and the final piece is a brisk representation. Yes, some clichés are incorporated, but the writing by this composer–dance-band conduc-

tor is wise and classy.

Enesco, Georges (1881–1955)

Three decades after his death, Enesco, a romantic-nationalist, remains the great man of Romanian music. Those composers who followed him display, in the main, a mixture of French-like preciseness and elegance with symbolic, native characteristics. Lately, however, the exploitation of national musical topics has been somewhat smothered under the cloak of international tenets. While such neoclassic, neoromantic, serial, and aleatoric musical speech reveals good craftsmanship, it conceals indigenous feelings. It is in the work of Enesco (and in a few instances the music of Marcel Mihalovici) that the most illustrious examples of Romanian music exist.

DUOS

- **Cantabile et Presto for Flute and Piano (1904)**

In 1904 Enesco was requested by the officials of the Conservatoire de Paris to write some pieces for various instrumental combinations. This resulted in the above work, as well as the Allegro de Concert for solo chromatic harp, a Konzertstück for viola and piano, and Legende for Trumpet and Piano *(see below)*.

In the Cantabile et Presto contrastive pace is the creative strategy. The low register of the flute is featured in the initial part. In the Presto, variational twists, underscored by articulated figures, carry forward the music. Sensitive seamlessness in the construction adds strength to the conception.

- *Legende* **for Trumpet and Piano (1906)**

Enesco is here a master of understanding trumpet luminosity without resorting to brassy brashness. Tempo choices and timbre controls are governed beautifully. Set in ternary form, most of the piece is in slow tempo and concerned with stately thematic material. The middle portion has a rhapsodic thrust, but its extroverted manner is of subtle relationship to the previous totally introverted statement.

- **Second Sonata in C Major for Piano and Cello, Op. 26, No. 2**

Dedicated to the great Pablo Casals (who described Enesco as "the most amazing musician I have met in my whole life"), this sonata is all meat and muscle. Totally eloquent—Enesco's language is here of expansive neoromanticism—it bears the imprint of systematic concern for the instruments. They team up with a vengeance. In the Allegro moderato ed amabile there are 124 measures, only 8 of which find the cello silent. Broad meters of 6/4 and 9/4 predominate, with a variety of pulse divisions for the former. A sense of constant development surrounds the music. Again, in the 242 measures of movement two (most in 6/8 time, with the tempo heading Allegro agitato) the horizon is crowded, the gestures huge, the instruments in constant juxtaposition (in only 2 measures is the piano silent; the cello plays in all but 8 measures). The restlessness and the textural interplay provide intensity and a charged tensility to the whole.

In the large, somewhat freely designed slow movement the music builds from solo cello to a huge five-voice structure, then declines into the close. The range from a simple recitative projection to sumptuousness is telling.

The rhythms become sharper, the intervallic conditions closer in the Final à la roumaine. Portamentos, glissandos, and pizzicatos (even a single quarter-tone use) are important in this stylized music-in-constant-motion. It is a rhapsody, another honest-to-Enesco *Romanian Rhapsody*. (Enesco, like so many composers with best-seller pieces, mentioned in a letter how "sick and tired" he was of his pair of *Romanian Rhapsodies* for orchestra, "particularly of my first one.") In this sonata the native conduct and moods are rich, vital, a parquetry of sounds and colors, highlighted with use of the augmented step. Here, too, the instruments (save the initial measure for cello alone) never go to the sidelines. This lack of differentiation is curious and arguable in the other movements. Here, it is dynamically proper.

- **Sonata [No. 1] for Violin and Piano, Op. 2**

Enesco's early duo sonata is written with romantic parlance of sentiment, but with exceptional harmonic clarity. Romanian flavor is only slightly indicated, for the most part, in the final movement. There are three corporated matters in the first movement: a short motive, its extension into scherzo-spirited jollity and a long, legato-spun theme. Contrast is obtained in the slow movement by two themes and through a subtle change of the color scheme. While this movement's first section is related to the second by the alternate use of muted and unmuted tone, this is reversed on recapitulation. The suavity of moving thirds is paramount in this section of the work. There is some counterpoint in the last part of the Sonata, but most of it is bright and unserious.

- **Sonata No. 2 in F Minor for Violin and Piano, Op. 6**

Enesco's second violin and piano sonata is brooding and restless and only partially avoids being on the stormier side in the last third of its total. Cyclic formation is the technical pin that clasps the composition together. Its detail stems from the initial winding theme in F minor—the decisive dependency for the whole. It begins in the broad triple pulse of 9/4 time, eventually appears in duple arrangement and faster pace in the opening movement; it is in different tempo and form, but very recognizable, in the second movement and makes its final appearance in a fluid but assured F-major manner in the concluding movement. Unity of temper is equaled by thematic unity.

Enesco was not the type of composer who stubbornly stated his cyclic facts. He reiterated but colored his arguments. Accordingly, the main theme recurs in the opening part, but the backgrounds change. The melancholy gypsy air of the second movement marks the Romanian climate. In this case the principal topic is reviewed in rondo fashion and in the coda is heard in triple *piano* tremolo action by the violin. The coda is peaceful, of distant sound, a quiet string monologue. Sonata style is utilized for the final movement. Enesco's meanings are fully clear; similarly, the writing for the instruments, to be expected of a composer who was an expert on both the violin and the piano as well as a first-class conductor.

- **Sonata No. 3 in A Minor for Violin and Piano, Op. 25**

The clue to this work is its informative subtitle: "in popular Romanian character." It is chock-full of it, as expressed by melancholy curves and brooding, restless colorations.

Very few composers go to the trouble of furnishing an analysis of their work. Enesco has provided a précis. Movement one (marked Moderato malinconico) he states, is "mainly one of plaintive melancholy." Its themes "are all treated in free rhapsodic style, with many elaborations of cadence and subtleties of nuance." The first part of movement two (Andante sostenuto e misterioso) "is that of a nocturne." It then "gradually becomes more elaborate, with vague, fanciful figures." The music builds to a big climax, and "the movement ends almost as calmly as it began." Movement three (Allegro con brio) "is in free rondo form," which includes variational depiction of the main theme, described as a "jaunty freakish

little tune."

QUARTETS

- **String Quartet No. 1 in E-flat Major, Op. 22, No. 1**

(Though contained under one opus number, Enesco's two string quartets are separated by a span of thirty-one years. The initial quartet was written in 1920, the second quartet *[see below]* was completed in 1951.)

Rhapsodic detail is of major proportions in every one of the four movements. In the opening part of the quartet, tempos and dynamics are fervently contrasted. (The agogic particulars are of multitudinous totality in this composition.) Movement two (Andante pensieroso) has lyrical agitation. The music's intensity is of such nature that individual timbre and dynamic changes often accompany repetitions of a single pitch.

The scherzo movement is a music of thrust and release, and a music excited and disturbed. Significantly, Enesco constantly indicates *senza rigore* (without rigorousness) for a short rhythmic figure. No mildly melodic Trio interrupts this conception filled with metrical change. The finale is no less dramatic.

- **String Quartet No. 2 in G Major, Op. 22, No. 2**

A brooding, magnificent essay that has the depth of late Beethoven, the soul stirring of Mahler, and the exquisite workmanship of Mozart. There are no native (Romanian) synonyms in the quartet's vocabulary. It has the sober design of classical ancestry, but not once does Enesco follow the academic line of least resistance. Balances apply to the sonata, song-form, scherzo, and rondo designs, but the feeling persists that the quartet is a durchkomponiert conception. Thus the grand line, which never once departs from the dark-colored mood of

Enesco's *Quartetto serioso*.

OCTET

- **Octet in C Major for Four Violins, Two Violas, and Two Cellos, Op. 7**

The string octet medium cannot avoid simulating the symphonicism of a string orchestra since it is formed from a double string quartet. Any composer is hard put to do otherwise. Enesco complies with the sonorous instrumental fact proposed by eight string instruments and shapes his themes with big and bold character. Intimate charm is substituted by a chamber music pageant guided by dramatic flourish. The Octet is cast in one movement, but with four different sections clearly exposed. These indicate a broad first part, a scherzo type, plus slow and finale (waltz tempo) divisions.

Since orchestral scoring factors dominate and are unavoidable in eight-part writing, there is need for patterned groups to stabilize the crowded amount of voice movement. Clarity must be exhibited if octet manners are to show good breeding. This rule is very evident in the broad opening part of the work, one balanced and commanded by a full-scale sonata pattern. At the end of this, almost as a formal road sign, the second cellist tunes down his fourth string in order to sound a short pedal octave on B. The next section, marked aptly Très fougueux (very fiery), is certainly a heated division, metered in the quickly delivered duple accentuation form. Contrast then follows by the octet's slow portion and the concluding waltzlike rhapsody. The theme of the latter resembles that of the Très fougueux situation. In the last movement the principal subject begins as a ninth, descends an octave, moves up a second and is followed by double-octave depiction; while in the former case the contour is exactly the same save that it begins with a less tense octave leap in place of the ninth.

Enesco's Op. 7 is a very rich work, worthy of inclusion in the limited group of string octets that are of value. These can be listed without difficulty of choice. Only those by Mendelssohn, Svendsen, Glière, and the Two Pieces of Shostakovich's early work period can be considered of similar high rank. Enesco's contribution considerably strengthens the literature for eight string instruments.

Engel, Carl (1883–1944)

DUO

- **_Triptych_ for Violin and Piano (1920)**

Carl Engel was a man of many musical talents. He was a composer, writer, bibliographer, librarian, editor, and publisher. In these capacities he championed the work of many American composers, especially Charles Martin Loeffler and Ernest Bloch. Their stylistic influence shows in Engel's *Triptych*; Loeffler's by chromaticism and mysticism, Bloch's by fervor.

The *Triptych* (Engel's sole large-scale chamber work) is dark colored, deeply emotive, tragically striped. The opening G-minor subject appears over eight times, in each instance with differently developed backgrounds, plus changes of tonality and mood as well. The repetitions underline the music's intensity. Related ideas, one capricious, the other relaxed and divided into a pair of contrastive sections, are set in the work's middle panel. A large sonata form is employed in the final movement.

Engel, Lehman (1910–82)

DUO

- **Sonata for Cello and Piano (1945)**

A work for cello and piano poses problems of balance. The thicker, lower strings of the cello can be smudged in their articulation if not given room in which to sound (thus, if accompanied by fat sonorities on the piano, partial obliteration and confusion take place). On the other hand, overuse of the higher gamuts will fail to realize the potentials in the rich baritone register or the sonorous bass portion of the cello. The composer must treat the heavier piano with understanding of its dictatorial strength (as so often he does not, further being at the mercy of pianists who become visionless by the allure of the pedal that alienates musical explication). In music written for cello and piano, artistic farsightedness can result only if the piano part is cut down to the size of its string companion. This work is an excellent example of the how and why of such dicta. The texture of the piano is a delight. Companionship between keyboard and string instrument is equal, without either submerging the piano's individuality or losing that of the cello. The harmonic idiom and melodic lines are just as successfully clear, potent, and pleasurable.

The shifting mood to be noted in the development of the first movement (wherein the recapitulation is practically identical with the exposition) is a carryover from the great amount of functional work Engel had accomplished (for the Broadway trade, he had written music for *Hamlet, Macbeth, Henry VIII, Murder in the Cathedral*, etc.; composed works for many dancers; and written incidental music for many documentary films). The marchlike and waltzlike sections therein have the quick change that is part and parcel of such musical work. The same shift of mood is present in the slow movement (wherein especial significance is attached to a half-step progression), exemplified by the Alla marcia that forms the middle section.

The Scherzo (marked Allegro giocoso) uses a scale that is thrown up and down, together with a pitter-patter that is just short of being a waltz. More trenchant melodic portions are interlaced rather than separated deliberately to form the Trio of this form. Aside from two measures, the entire final movement is in the uneven meter of 5/8. Although there are two themes, the resemblances of these are such that the movement must be considered monothematic, but in an ever-changing presentation. These darting moods have the same affinity as the previous movement's change of pace. Engel's work is sharpened with correct balance in all departments. Clarity is the hallmark in instrumentation, form, and content.

Englund, Einar (1916–)

DUO

- **Sonata for Violin and Piano (1979)**

Tonality lives in this late 20th-century duo sonata. And so does appealing romantic temper. (Interesting statistic: The final cadence of the first movement is in E-flat major, the other movements end in unisons: C, D-sharp, and E-flat, in turn. That the outer movements match gives further stability.)

Germinal development marks the Preambulum. There is twinkle-in-the-eye character in the Intermezzo. This 3/8 metered Allegro giocoso music shoots beats over the bar lines, glides some pitches, sets two against three within certain measures, has a suave section in muted timbre, and uses plucked sound to add an acerbic slant to the whole. Shostakovich and Prokofiev come to mind in this place. Ternary form for the Elegia, with some juicy thirds reconfirming the romantic color of the Sonata. Rhythmic dash (what else?) in the finale.

QUINTET

■ **Piano Quintet (1941)**

Englund is a gifted pianist, and this makes the writing for the instrument in the quintet (his first official opus) intensely clean and telling. The scoring is not overdrawn, and there is a good balance registered in the four movements (the last two linked).

Sustained momentum in the F-minor initial movement. It ends with a slowed-down tempo and softly. This is paralleled in the Finale, which after a vigorously spirited presentation slows to a majestic peroration that runs in a declining dynamic level to a final F major. Between are Scherzo and Adagio movements. The latter starts softly and builds impressively. All of this music is handsomely accomplished.

Enriquez, Manuel (1926–)

DUOS

■ *Díptico I* **for Flute and Piano (1969)**

A great deal of the construction of this work is to be done by the performers. Ah, yes, the world of chance—the world wherein considerable creation as well as total re-creation is in the hands of the performers. According to Enriquez, the interpretation "must be ambivalent and of equal importance."

Score reading of a work of this type by a writer or a critic can only result in a single person's conjecturable findings. The composer, however, wishes *two* performers to be totally involved so that the re-creation provides "a 'double' work of art." Accordingly, the use of a recording of Enriquez's duo gives evidence that one solution provides a strong sense of instrumental individuality as well as an interplay of fractured and bent sound dabs together with percussive punctuations.

■ **Suite for Violin and Piano (1949)**

Early Enriquez music, composed at the age of 23, long before he studied with Stefan Wolpe, who inspired him to write in "a very contemporary language."

The six movements seethe with colors, and that descriptive word includes the use of chromatic diction. A six-pitch motto directs the first movement. Thirds in the violin and heavy chordal movement in the piano combine in the second piece. In the third movement the emphasis is on parallel motion: of thirds, fourths, and fifths; the violin is muted, the effect nocturnal. In comparison, movement four is cross riveted with dance accents. Motival detail holds the fifth piece in place; the play of duple and triple punctuations within the same time spans motivates the nationalistic tang of the final (sixth) piece. The violin is indulged: cadenza, portamento, up-and-down continuous four-string pizzicatos, and glissandos. Contemporary string-instrument virtuosity is the label. Truly effective music.

Eppert, Carl (1882–1961)

QUINTET

■ *A Little Symphony* **for Woodwind Quintet (Flute, Oboe, Clarinet, Alto Clarinet, and Bassoon), Op. 52**

A three-movement chronicle wherein the chromaticism, with its pitch pendulation, affects the formal factor. Each movement is a rhapsody. The third, for example, consists of 186 measures, in which seventeen major tempo changes with differing material take place. Similar conditions are present in the first two movements. The outer movements are, in general, fast-paced affairs; the middle one seeks a scherzo objective.

To be noted is the special instrumentation of

the piece. In place of the usual horn, an alto clarinet is used. It does stress that in this case the woodwind quintet group is purely made up of five woodwind instruments and not the standard four winds plus one brass.

Epstein, David (1930–)

TRIO

- **String Trio (1964)**

Contemporary syntax need not interfere with a classically derived structural solidity. It doesn't in this instance. An intensely dramatic and colorfully select (but never outré) four-movement work for violin, viola, and cello, Epstein's opus is a dynamic example of such crossbreeding.

Clear textures are an aid to the formal documentation. These make possible an affiliative retrograde method obtaining aural recognition. It is used partially in the first movement, while in the third movement the last sixteen measures are a cancrizan of the initial portion. The sustained and rhythmic elements, especially the former, relate to each other in this pair of movements, though the first is quasi-toccata mannered, the other a type of impressionistic *Anhang*. But no pastiche because of these differences. The two parts relate to each other in the same ratio as the second and fourth movements, so that subtly and consciously (?) the balance Epstein wishes is a 1–3, 2–4 situation.

Driven on motoric triplets, movement two emerges as a large ternary frame of reference, with a central slower and lyric division. (This analysis differs from the composer's viewpoint that the music is "roughly shaped along the lines of sonata form, though with a brief development and truncated recapitulation.") The difference is not that disparate. Epstein's key words are "roughly shaped." In the compositional process the tripartite definition be-

came stronger.

No analytical ambivalence exists for the Passacaglia fantastica. Though unbound from strictly measured lengths, which are basic to the form, the architectural clarity is undisturbed by the mensural differences of the permutations. It is a cogent blend of passacaglia shape with a fantasy inlay and overlay.

QUARTET

- **String Quartet [No. 2] (1971)**

Epstein's quartet is stuffed with content, purposefully overstuffed (as will be explained), with its systemization an all-embracing one. Cast in three continuous movements, each of the first pair is followed by an Interlude, and the quartet concludes with an "Epilogue."

The principal purpose here is concertolike virtuosity without traditional concerted rapport. The four instruments are considered as four individuals, although there is some consolidation, but of minor totality. The opening clues the ear as to the shape of things to come: The viola begins alone at ♩ = 50 and minus time signature; the first violin, also free of time signature, enters at ♩=112–116; and their material is completely different. It is quartet dialogue that is the objective, during which the instruments "respond *to* one another and at other times play *against* each other, almost as if unaware of the others' thoughts." Listened to without this premise of individuation, utter confusion reigns. Heard (rather overheard!) as several simultaneous conversations the musical sense becomes clear. And Epstein's sense brooks no nonsense in his definition of instrumental characterization (akin to Elliott Carter's method of assigning specific intervals or colorations to the instruments so that differentiation is acute and amalgamation nullified).

Music of this type is primed with specifics to solidify the content no matter the utter freedom of linear procedure. Pitches, timbres, intervals, dynamics, and methods of attack are measured carefully—all to make certain the paradox of total unity by way of instrumental individuality. The forms of the movements are as free as Epstein's handling of the quartet medium: a type of ternary design, sonata form liberally considered, and a loose kind of rondo can be ascertained in the three parts of the quartet. The Interludes are "somewhat like recitatives," and "comment upon the musical ideas of the preceding movements."

Inconsistent with the expected unity of string quartet procedures, Epstein's opus will seem problematical on first hearing. Its formulations require repeated exposure to become clear. Regardless, no one can doubt, or argue, that this quartet is a work of independent inquiry.

Erb, Donald (1927–)

DUO

- *Trio for Two* for Double Bass and Alto Flute (alternating Timpani) (1968)

A collage of strikes, glides, zigzagged tones, and even some human-voice shouts, providing a jazz-percussion hybrid. Nothing representational, simply direct color effects that, as they occur, create a sense of expectancy for the next one. In that regard, quite successful.

TRIOS

- *In No Strange Land* for Trombone, Double Bass, and Electronic Sounds (1968)

Erb's title is the title of a poem by Francis Thompson. His music reveals nothing about that affiliation, but it fully reveals a colorful and sensitive application of electronic ideas in connection with instrumental timbres. The degrees of sound are superbly contrasted. For example, in movement one of the total four the qualities are glutinous; in movement three they emerge as velutinous. Form is of elasticity; the trombone and double bass spit and spurt, enter and depart in a rhapsodic continuity. Some vocalism is tossed into the sound mass.

The integration of the material is virtuosic. In adding electronic synonyms to his vocabulary Erb is a masterful speaker in the instrumental-tape medium.

- String Trio for Violin, Cello, and Electric Guitar (1966)

Virtuoso use of the electric guitar, and probably the first time the instrument has been used in such an intimate combination. Splendid idea. There are some touches of jazz that match the hybrid instrumentation by combining guitar licks with weird string glissandos.

Such an odd-ball combination indicates that Erb is clearly his own man. His structural design is excellent and his conception interesting.

QUARTET

- *Phantasma* for Flute (alternating Alto Flute and Piccolo), Oboe (alternating English horn), Harpsichord, and Double Bass (1965)

Erb states that he is uninterested in any pertinent style and avoids any specific system. He is quoted as writing "what by instinct appeals to me."

Here his instinct leads to a swatch card of various chunks of material; the sum and substance form a catalogue of effects. A somewhat thickly populated score, but one that holds the interest.

QUINTET

- **Sonata for Harpsichord and String Quartet (1962)**

Three movements, each containing a rhapsodic content of diversification, balanced by the use of clear continuity. Throughout, there is a strong sense and feeling of relationship between one portion and the next.

Still, Erb's amazing use of color fantasy makes a listener get caught up immediately in his unique timbral world the moment the music begins with glassy sul ponticello fragments, two plucked sounds, and then a snapped-off-the-fingerboard pizzicato. And woven into the sonata's fabric are all types of sound dyes, including a semi col legno, combining the use of the wooden part of the bow with "some bow hair."

SEXTETS

- *Mirage* **for Flute (alternating Harmonica, Water Goblet, and Soda Bottle), Bassoon (alternating Slide Whistle), Trumpet (alternating Harmonicas in D and A-flat, Water Goblet, and Soda Bottle), Trombone, Keyboard (Piano, Electric Piano, Harpsichord, Electric Organ, and Harmonica), and Percussion (Vibraphone, Chimes, Marimba, Tam-tam, Bongos, Timbales, Bass Drum, Suspended Cymbal, Timpani, Harmonica, and Soda Bottle) (1977)**

From the instrumental array listed above it will be obvious that a sweatshop of activity applies to this eight-minute piece and that no berceuse is being gently sung. By all means the instrumentation of this "sextet" expands the meaning of the term "chamber music." More is to be expected. There is a luxuriant expansion of sound sources. Just a few: In the flute there are

multiphonics and key clicks; the bassoon flutter-tongues and sings a perfect fifth above the sound produced on the slide whistle; the trumpet sings glissandos while playing, improvises, and plays on the mouthpiece into a mute; masking tape is torn from a roll placed across the piano strings; and so on and on.

The *Mirage* score is not a spoof of far-out techniques. It represents a rhapsody of colorative, collective, and contrastive actions. All of it is planned with conviction and all of it sounds convincing.

- **Three Pieces for Brass Quintet (Two Trumpets, Horn, Trombone, and Tuba) and Piano (1968)**

The peak of the work is the witty, snide, and meaningfully distorted contents of the opening movement. Erb says it all by describing this section as using "many things one can do with a brass instrument without actually 'playing' it." Meaning: fancy-Dan breathing, percussing, and other weirdly wonderful effects that serve as superb aural stimulants. These include tapping the mouthpiece as well as the bell of the instrument, kissing into the mouthpiece, hissing into the instrument, hissed glissandos, free-pitch mouthpiece buzzing and choked sounds, and no-bones-about-it yelling into the instrument to produce "quarreling sounds!" As for the piano, aside from a single cluster, the keyboard is never touched in the opening movement. The sonorities come out of the instrument's guts, including rubbing a bottle up and down a low string, raking the strings, slapping the hand on them, and so forth.

In the middle piece, compressed intervals and short-spanned ones are intensified by the languid tempo. Microtonal shifts are employed; disjunct details are hardly present in Erb's fragmented lyricism.

A two-part finale that has jazzy densities contrasts moderate-paced with fast music. Both are intensely constructed. The first is tightened with frictioned intervals and fluttered sounds, the other is brightened by repetitive sounds and tone clusters. There is no mystery to Erb's sextet. Neither are there any barricades as he explores, clears, and plows his timbral territory.

SEPTET

- *Dance Pieces* for Violin, Trumpet, Piano, and Four Percussion Players (Percussion: Timpani, Two Small Triangles, Snare Drum, Tenor Drum, Temple Blocks, Maracas, Two Large Suspended Cymbals, Police Whistle, Gong, Large and Small Wood Blocks, Castanets, Bongos, Ratchet, Xylophone, Chimes, Glockenspiel, and Vibraphone) (1963)

Although he uses a huge number of percussion instruments, distributed among four players, Erb does not stop at that point with his emphasis on color dynamism. Like a chain reaction, the piano is heard with an ashtray placed on its heavy strings (which gives a meaningless pitch), delivers fist clusters, and is played Cowellian fashion by strumming the strings inside the case. The trumpet, in addition to different mutes, uses half-valve sounds, glissandos, and indulges in a lip smack against the mouthpiece. These polychromic points are concentrated and distributed in a variety of scoring in the three pieces: The piano is tacet in movement one; the violin and trumpet step aside for the second movement; and only in the third of the set is the full septet used.

Aided by metrical change, "Levels" has a consistent motoric presence. "Venetian Boat Song #3" is anti-barcarolle in its fantasy. In "Vortex" the sound particles become gradually heavier until they are flung into a revolving rotary motility climax of two free-choice cadenzas; the following eleven measures are akin to a relaxed coda.

(One percussionist plays the timpani and small triangle. The other three percussionists cover the remaining instruments.)

OCTET

- *Antipodes* for String Quartet and Percussion Quartet (Piano, Celesta, Claves, Temple Blocks, Glockenspiel, Two Large Suspended Cymbals, Two Snare Drums, Bongos, Police Whistle, Finger Cymbals, Timbales, Maracas, Large and Small Wood Blocks, Vibraphone, Xylophone, Tenor Drum, Large Tom-tom, Gong, Timpani, Bass Drum, Chimes, and Small Triangle) (1963)

The traditional and the new join hands in this octet's makeup. And in the sense of handling the string quartet Erb blends the new with the new. The strings strive incessantly to lose their "quartetish" identity. In movement one glissandos are constantly thrust into the picture—short, long, bowed, and plucked, plus a continuous type that covers six measures (eighteen beats) of ups and downs. Col legno is a preoccupation in movement two. In one place thirteen consecutive measures cover the wood taps—a matter of thirty-nine beats. The block writing and massed tremolando found in the Alla marcia third movement are further evidence of the coloristic virtuosity of Erb's concept. He proves that opposites do attract each other and work well together. *Antipodes* has creative virtue in its three contrasted movements.

A point in terms of the percussion: One player is actually concerned with piano and celesta, instruments rarely placed in the percussion class, no matter that hammers must strike strings in the former case and steel plates in the other instance. The other three percussionists handle no fewer than twenty-three instruments. In terms of this array one can state that chamber music instrumentation has become unfettered.

Erb, Marie Joseph (1858–1944)

QUARTET

- **Quartet in F Major for Two Violins, Viola, and Cello (1915)**

A dramatic cast hovers over Erb's string quartet. Not unexpected in the case of a composer who turned out nine operas. Though the forms are classical (sonata, ternary, minuet, and rondo), the treatment is individual and romantic. Erb's Quartet is inquisitive—thus refreshing.

There are constant shifts of tempo and ideas in the freely sprung sonata structure of the first movement. Within the twenty-seven major tempo changes an elemental strength courses through the four-part writing. The opening figure is pertinent. It becomes the fundament of the material: melodic and accompanimental. In the slow movement an unusual type of central section is of expressive range, by use of a funeral march. Once more the stimulus comes from a rhythmic figure (first heard in the cello).

The greatest action occurs in the third movement. Here, the tempo shifts from moderate speed to vivace, the pulse from triple to a tighter double total. Nor is Erb satisfied with a strict A–B–A frame. A coda adds color despite the reduced speed of its measures. In the finale, once again a rhythmic figure (heading the principal subject) is crucial to the design. Its exploration is restless.

Erbse, Heimo (1924–)

DUOS

- *Four Lyrical Pieces* for Viola and Piano, Op. 39c

The setting is twelve tone; the writing has aesthetic decorum and a neatness of scoring.

With minute changes for the string or wind instrument, but with no changes for the piano, Erbse made other versions: for bassoon and piano, as Op. 39a; for cello and piano, as Op. 39b; for bass clarinet or clarinet and piano, as Op. 39d; for English horn and piano, as Op. 39e; and for alto flute and piano, as Op. 39f.

- *Seven Sketches in the Form of an Old Suite* for Violin and Piano, Op. 34

The expressive possibilities of twelve-tone style applied to dance forms are explored in Erbse's seven-part suite. There are contemporized Bachian moves in the Präludium and then, in turn, a Forlano, Gavotte, Polonaise, Menuetto, and Air, plus a final jocose dance piece titled Badinerie (the form was used by Bach in his B-minor Suite for flute and strings).

Everything in the dances is clear, but none are tied tightly to formal coding or squared by metrical or rhythmical rigidity. Plentiful solo divisions for both instruments are also utilized.

(This is one of three versions of the work. The other two are for violin and chamber orchestra and violin with strings and piano.)

Erdmann, Dietrich (1917–)

DUOS

- *Dialoghi per due (Dialogues for Two)* for Cello and Piano (1969)

Erdmann does not follow any "ism." His duo is

in general (call it neutral) contemporary dissonant style. Each of the structural features of these four dialogues is clear, as is the give-and-take between the instruments. Nothing rigid—the loose formalism is held in place by the structural units around which each piece is built. Thus, the triplet swing of the third piece with chordal interjections; the repetitive tones, trills, and glissandos of the final one. Probably undisclosed subject matter in these chamber music conversations, but it is unnecessary to be informed; the dynamic effect of the music is sufficient.

- **Sonata for Oboe and Piano (1965)**

A very odd but still effective type of balance exists between the final part of the work and the opening movement. Erdmann's finale consists of a theme with four variations. The essence of the last variant has the same shape and feeling that pervade the initial movement of the duo sonata. Further, both are principally in 5/8 meter and both include other pulse measurements with an eighth note as the basis. Though the opening part is slower in speed, it does not deter a similar reflection regarding the conclusion. Even if this relationship is coincidental, it is good compositional strategy.

The theme of the variations is for unaccompanied oboe, but, oddly, its principal birthmark—a minor-seventh rise and a diminished-octave descent—is not utilized in the transformations. In line with equal partnership, the solo piano is given the first variation. Variation two has some slow waltz allegiance; vestiges of siciliana profile are to be heard in the third part of the movement. Like much of Erdmann's music, the Adagio (movement two) is free formed, equating a single ongoing gesture.

- *Tre pastelli (Three Pastels)* **for Violin and Piano (1970)**

It is generally conceded that musical pastels are calm and soothing. The chromatic, freely dissonant strands of Erdmann's set display darker tints—the moods are disturbed ones. The opening and closing movements are in slow tempo, a Vivace is in between. Both of the former are of the through-composed type; the second one extremely free: a kind of recitative-cadenza hybrid, though precisely metered.

Erdmann's pieces have a profundity that one does not expect from their title. The thought and expression strongly suggest a revamped impressionism—of heavy-laden category.

TRIO

- **String Trio**

If Erdmann's compact trio for violin, viola, and cello does not quicken the pulse, it does offer neatly conceived, well-organized neoclassic music. No additives in the form of instrumental effects.

The three movements are paced in the standard fast–slow–fast manner. They are played without pause between them. The stress is on linear dispositions with placement of tutti rhythmic blocks for control and contrast. The finale is vivacious. It is also the most sophisticated of the three movements. Set in 6/8, it contains a good amount of accentually distributed measures that provide triple pulses in the same time span as the duple.

QUARTET

- **Divertimento for Four Woodwinds (Flute, Oboe, Clarinet, and Bassoon)**

Just a bit more formal in its content than the title heading would imply. Movement one is bipartite, with a moderately moving division related to an apportionment in tarantellalike tally. The slow movement gives equal time to first the oboe and later the bassoon for thematic highlighting. In the final part of the quartet there is fast music. Then, circularlike, the work concludes with the first part of the opening movement.

- **Improvisation for Four Woodwind Players (Flute, Oboe, Clarinet, and Bassoon) (1967)**

Curiously, Erdmann uses the singular form in his title though there are actually three "improvisations." True, they are to be played in succession as a unit, and with each in a through-composed style the result is *like* a single improvisation. Yet, lacking any apparent relationship between the individual parts of the set, the total is certainly three and not one.

Pursuing the argument, the first (an Adagio) concludes with a reminder of the movement's opening; the second is an asymmetrical scherzo, with the persistence of its disposition producing an organized balance if not a thematic one. It is only in the final part (again an Adagio, thereby forming a divisional equality of pace that further negates single improvisation count) wherein the inquiry and exposure of extemporization is determinedly felt. Two points emphasize this: the ornamental formation of the voices and the fourteen-measure cadenza for the oboe.

The premise of the above is not meant to be a negative minority report. Title arguments notwithstanding, ample musical means are found in these short movements. They are nicely scored, neatly dissonant, and processed with craftsmanship.

- **Variations for Four Woodwinds (Flute, Oboe, Clarinet, and Bassoon)**

Nothing amiss, with total consignment of variations minus individual allotment. Still, defined variation apportionment has better signification. Whatever process, and even in the nonseparative type of variation (though to a lesser degree because of the desire not to sectionalize), variation identity is crucial.

Erdmann's plan is acutely clear. The theme is for oboe and clarinet. Variation one is for flute, oboe, and clarinet; variation six is a duet for flute and clarinet. The other six variations are for the entire quartet. However, further identification is made by beginning each one with a partial grouping. Of the six variations involved four have different instrumental entrances. Examples: variation two calls for oboe and bassoon; variation three for oboe, clarinet, and bassoon; etc.

Erdmann, Helmut W. (1947–)

TRIO

- **Trio II for Three Flutes (1973)**

The first pair of sounds in the work are a triple unison and then an octave sound, but thereafter Erdmann's piece is a banding of seconds, sevenths, ninths, clusters, and a paean to fricative harmony and polyphony. Of course, the percussiveness is lessened by the suavity of a tri-flute timbral total, but then it is cut into by the use of key clicks and embouchure manipulation.

The 120 measures stay metrically fixed in quadruple-pulse totals. (There is a bit of proportional notation that is free of beat rigidity, and this sometimes is allied with strict pulse arrangement.) These 120 measures are set in nine sections, each of different metronomic total, ranging from $\math<200b>d = 60$ to $d = 120$.

OCTET

- ***Raumkomposition (Spatial Composition) for Eight Flutes (1969)***

Sharply pitch pointed so that there is a constant clusterized sonority mist to the music. The lines move in and out, most often following a method of contrapuntalizing chordal sets. These linear shifts provide a polyrhythmic texture. Densities change often in this athematic music, and in a few places the voices join in a rhythmic tutti as quasi cadential points. A fascinating musical script special to flute literature.

Erickson, Robert (1917–)

DUO

- **Duo for Violin and Piano (1959)**

Full-stacked serialism with full-blooded attention to rhythmic unrest and metrical modulation, virtuosic manipulation of the lines for both instruments, and intense motival development. There are two movements, but in a sense the general character of movement two is a second consideration of the same (initial) objective, since there is practically no contrastive setting.

QUINTET

- **Ricercare á 5 for Five Trombones (1966)**

Erickson's super-duper avant-garde trombone essay is performed either as a quintet or with the "soloist" prerecording four of the parts and then performing with those parts heard on tape via loudspeakers.

As pertains to the form there is imitation aplenty and contrapuntalism aplenty, set forth by familiar trombone sounds and loads of new ones, including what Stuart Dempster, who commissioned the work, terms "funny" sounds. And there are as well improvisation, simultaneous singing and playing, whistling, whining, and bellowing into the mouthpiece of the instrument, imitations of percussion sounds, glissandos, and a variety of pitch peppering. Not for the fainthearted to play, but fun to hear.

Erkanian, Erwand (1951–)

DUO

- **Three Recitatives for Flute and Piano**

The Soviet avant-garde is represented here. And the style is the same as found for a long time in the music of composers from other countries. Meterless, fractured figures, piano plucking, and piano clusters. And, of course, athematic. It all works well, but at this point of creative stock taking, Erkanian's music may have been scandalous and shocking to the Soviets but not to us. Worth hearing, nonetheless.

Eröd, Iván (1936–)

TRIOS

- **Trio [No. 1] for Violin, Cello, and Piano (1976)**

Contrastingly styled affections in the first movement. It begins with a mix of plucked sound (even one on a piano string), tremolando, and coloristic flourishes. This leads to the major section, an Allegro vivace that has a further mix of duple and triple pulses within the same time spans. Unison writing is a prime ingredient, pitchwise and rhythmicwise. Confirmation of the premise takes place in the coda, with the first twenty-two of the total twenty-five measures in a trio-tight *fortissimo*.

More of this unison clarity is exposed in the third movement. This part exemplifies syncopation and includes separated cadenzas for the cello, violin, and piano. Chromaticism juiced with thirds is combined with lyrical content in the middle Adagio. There is urgency there.

- **Trio No. 2 for Violin, Cello, and Piano (1982)**

The gestures are big and utterly convincing. In the first of the two movements the materials are vehement and propulsive, despite their threnodic, funereal declarations. The music then shifts into a fast zone and thereafter moves away and back in its dynamic action.

Part two is defined by variational development. Rationally organized thought is in evidence, and likewise integration. As an example, in the sixth section of the music the cello repeats the piano's bass line of the first section and the violin repeats its first-section theme an octave higher.

QUARTETS

- **First String Quartet (1975)**

Polarity tonalism is used in Eröd's quartet, with the outer pair of movements moving from, around, and out of the pitch A as the focal point. The second of these is linked to the middle movement, consisting of a theme with four variations. Glissando markings are included in the second and third variants.

Eröd has stated that his creative attitude is "friendly, both towards performers and listeners." This is borne out by the uncomplicated flow of his initial string quartet. It also includes a friendly gesture in the first movement, where four names are woven into the text with pitch equivalents. Each of these appears once (the first three in succession), and no further affinity with the score is apparent. Inside stuff, no harm.

- **Four Pieces for String Quartet (1958)**

Superbly clear serial music, its security factored by Bartókian style, meaning rhythmic and linear lucidity. This is a healthfully lean music.

Everything is concentrated. What has to be said is said, minus attenuation and postscripts. Thus, miniature in size (34, 79, 54, and 57 measures, respectively, for the four pieces), but not miniature in statement. The Lento thrives on imitation. The Allegro energico (half the tone row is heard three times in the violins and the other half is added in the viola and cello) zips along in 3/8 time, its scherzo concept intercepted at different phrase points by an expanded 4/8 measure. This gives a dramatic punctuation by arresting the persistent one-in-a-bar drive. In the Moderato, ostinatos prop the melodic line, with block-chordal writing providing contrast.

The finale is a fugue, with inversion used in two of the answers to the subject. Its conclusion is distinguished by dynamic and textural extinguishment. One by one the instruments drop out until the viola ends alone. Thus a diverting fugal representation without the need for the usual stretto pileup for climax.

- **Ricercare ed Aria:** *S.C.H.E.* **for Flute, Oboe, Horn, and Bass Clarinet (1965)**

An example of an elegant compliment to a fellow Austrian composer, Karl Schiske, marking his fiftieth birthday. Thus the four initials in the title signify the letters in Schiske's name that can be (and are) equated by pitches.

The opening measure announces the sonic motto (E-flat equals S, C, B equals H, and E) in the horn (two ascending intervals: a sixth and a fourth). Later it is heard in imitation in combined ascending and inverted form. It then provides the springboard for full development in the Ricercare, a heavily delineated conception in four-voice counterpoint, its measures repeated, followed by an ending matching the quality of the beginning. In augmented form, the motto opens the Aria in the principal oboe voice; the music sings in its expansive continuity. The four pitches equal praise for the dedicatee, and they also bring praise to the dedicator in the manner in which the music has a distinctive chromatic cohesion.

Escher, Peter (1915–)

DUOS

- **Divertimento for Two Instruments for Flute and Violin or Two Violins, Op. 85**

Diverse moods in this romantically processed music, but with a serious quality that goes further than the title indicates.

Searching tempo changes are paramount in the untitled first movement. The "Serenata nuziale" ("Nuptial Serenade") is betrothed to a simple three-beat song, beautifully balanced between plucked accompaniment and the principal tune. Motival demonstration, marked by a quartal rise heard at the very beginning, colors the entire Scherzino. There is more to the fiery Finale than its tarantellalike motility. Quotations from the previous three movements are interlinked, that from the first movement set in much slower speed.

- **Duo for Two Clarinets, Op. 120**

Nice tunes and carefully ruled formal compartments. All in all, the music poses no problem and has solved the artistic objective of neatly saying what it wishes to say.

In movement one rhapsodic turns lead to the main material—a slow waltz assessment. The former then reappears with some development, the quasi waltz returns compressed in size, and the rhapsodic data plus some of the introductory music preceding the waltz close the movement. A carefully drawn blueprint, certainly.

Movement two is a "Dialog." Its strict antiphony first lives up to the assigned title after which the voices move against each other. Again, this exemplifies an exact measurement

of formal procedure. Some of the dialogue appears within the vivacious finale—and so does a bit of the rhapsodic turns of movement one. Escher's formal dogma remains clear and cannot be argued as to its recalls used for the sake of total balance and integration.

- **Seven Small Duos for Two Clarinets, Op. 122**

Music instantly recognizable as being of candid unpretentiousness. The tonal system reigns supreme, and there are no performing difficulties in this set, all being exceedingly modest efforts.

Interestingly, only one fast movement is included (number six—Gaîment). Expectedly, only flat keys are used, none repeated; the first five pieces of the work are in the major mode, the last two in D and F minor, respectively.

Escher, Rudolf (1912–80)

DUOS

- **Sonata for Two Flutes (1944)**

A rhythmic pattern serves as the introduction to the first subject, announced in the fifth measure; its tonal zone circumscribes A-flat. The second theme is placed in the tangential curve of G-flat and is in canon form. There is a slight combination of these two in the development that precedes the reprise, wherein the second theme's interstices (again in canon, which helps to distinguish one subject from the other) moves up a step into A-flat, the basic mark of the movement's tonality.

Antiphonal single melodic lines, which make a total binary situation, are used in the Adagio. The alternation of these lines (occasionally combined) forms the last section. In this case Escher gives further evidence that the truly systematic uses of tonality by contemporary composers are not the superficialities so many critics still persist in calling them, since the use of the tonal center of E-flat is the dominant relationship to that of the first movement. A racy presto tempo is used for the final Fugue. Double balances are forthcoming in this instance: with the first movement by the similar tonal center of A-flat; in regard to the chosen contrapuntal form by inversion of the fugue's subject as well as stretto.

- **Sonate concertante for Cello and Piano (1943)**

Formally measured, the initial movement is in circular shape. A short Allegro agitato, with much rhythmic motion; an Allegro, with swinging lilt; and a decisive section, once again an Allegro (each of the Allegros becomes progressively faster) convey a total trisectional stipulation. The meters of each of these are, for the most part, distinct from one another—namely, 4/8, 6/8, and 3/4—and are additional directives to the plan. After the complete development of the last Allegro the movement runs backward. In regard to color, a full assortment is served up: ponticello melodic lines, specially vibrated methods of pizzicato, glissandos, tremolandos played in normal manner and with snarling effect (the bow close to the bridge), col legno, and sliding harmonics. None of these are solely technical intoxicants but germane to the music as a whole.

There is a fairly brooding slow movement. The last movement moves sectionally through various channels. This finale contains an opening Lento, an Allegro that is moderately developed, followed by a section devoted to an uneven rhythm which consists of divisions in balance to each other (10/8; divided into 3:2 and 2:3), a return of the second section (somewhat changed), and a coda.

TRIO

- **Trio for Oboe, Clarinet, and Bassoon (1946)**

Although Escher's woodwind trio is in four movements, the last of these has the same material as the first, only the instrumental treatment being varied on the second presentation. The title, Pastorale, is retained fore and aft, and though of improvisatory character, the music is based on a defined theme. In prelude-epilogue fashion the twice-told tale is a tie that binds the suitelike character of the Trio.

The Rondeau that follows the opening part almost immediately (only a short pause intervenes between each of the first three movements) is cleverly handled, each of its three themes being expressed by different forms and colors. The coherency of individual relationship pertinent to total unification is thereby made plain instantly, and just as clearly secured by the use of archform, a favorite of this Dutch composer. The themes are arranged A–B–C–B–A, a method where the symmetry is related clockwise and spun backward rather than having the themes alternated for total balance. Theme A is very contrapuntal, while the B subject is denoted by employment of two instruments in invention form (texture is therefore contrasted but not polyphonic sequence). The third portion of the Rondeau is a series of solo recitatives. On the return of part B the invention is this time played by oboe and clarinet, compared to the exposition, where it was formed from clarinet and bassoon colors. The reentry of the first theme completes the formal circle. The penultimate movement of the Trio (just before the return of the recolored first movement Pastorale) is a straightforward Fugue.

QUINTET

- **Wind Quintet (Flute [alternating Alto Flute], Oboe d'amore, Clarinet [alternating Bass Clarinet], Bassoon, and Horn) (1967)**

Aside from the expansion of the five timbres by alternating the flute with an alto flute and the clarinet with a bass clarinet, the coloration of Escher's work is special in the use of an oboe d'amore throughout.

Though chromatically full scale, tonal centers are quite apparent. The continuity is comprehensive, and yet after the first time signature no fewer than 258 metrical changes take place in the total 381 measures. Part of this pertains to metrical modulation. In addition there are eighteen major tempo shifts. To have meaningful flow while the material is rhapsodic (there is a continuity of development) and grained with color fantasy proves the expert craftsmanship of this Dutch composer.

SEXTET

- *Le Tombeau de Ravel* for Flute, Oboe, Violin, Viola, Cello, and Harpsichord (1952)

As Ravel commemorated his predecessor in *Le Tombeau de Couperin* (in a six-movement suite for piano and later in an orchestral version of four of the movements), so Escher commemorates his predecessor in a seven-movement sextet. (Title coincidence: Arthur Benjamin had produced in 1949 a set of waltzes for viola or clarinet and piano titled *Le Tombeau de Ravel*.)

Finite instrumental balance pertains to Escher's work. The first, central, and last movements are for the entire ensemble. Movements two and three are for a solo instrument and a quartet, respectively; movements five and six are the same, in reversed order (quartet and

solo). Further, each of the solo settings is different, as are the quartet combinations.

Swirling within the textures of this colorful work are the breezes of impressionism, but the materials are often firmly contrapuntal. One prime example is the combination of three themes in the finale. This provides a cyclic touch to the work, since the themes are drawn from the first movement. And this technical act reflects the music's combination of a sonata structure (with development of material) with that of a suite.

Movement one, "Pavane pour une maison déserte," equates the exposition. The "deserted house" used in the title refers to the house in which Ravel lived in loneliness. Movement two is an adagio-paced Air for cello. The first of the two quartets is a Forlane for flute, viola, cello, and harpsichord. Then follows a Sarabande and the second quartet—a spirited Rigaudon for oboe and string trio. The second solo is a substantial Air for flute. Movement seven, representing the recapitulation, is a Hymne.

Eshpai, Andrei (1925–)

DUOS

- **Sonata [No. 1] for Violin and Piano (1966)**

A one-movement composition, with its developments stemming from the material presented at the beginning. The initial theme has some tertial movement, but it principally has a conjunct basis. This line direction is decidedly maintained in the balance of the Sonata and is one of the factors that tightly knits Eshpai's work. The other is the mesh of rhythmic ostinatos. Similarly shaped figuration and stepwise linear progress are consistently presented in the twice-as-slow Andante that follows the opening Allegro molto agitato. A short bridge passage (related to the opening) precedes the next section (Adagio), which again displays the repetitive syndrome, with eighth notes filling every measure in the piano. Next comes an Allegro molto, and once more the twins of conjunct melodic action and ostinato join hands.

Constructively there is no argument that Eshpai has obtained a harmonious relationship between the divisions of his work. Nevertheless, true contrasts are arrived at by tempo rather than from the materials. The coda is based on a dancy tune that seems completely fresh at first. But, here again, repetitive procedure rears its head.

■ **Sonata No. 2 for Violin and Piano (1970)**

A one-movement affair in which chromatic bite is of great influence, together with sharp rhythmic detail. Eshpai is of Mari extraction, and that nationalistic identification colors the work.

This duo sonata has a sizable unaccompanied violin opening. From its conclusion there is a high-fantastical personality to the music, which could be termed a "rhapsody" sonata without falsifying its identity.

Esplá, Oscar (1886–1976)

DUO

■ **Sonata for Violin and Piano, Op. 9**

This Spanish composer's music was always conceived in a grand neoromantic manner, usually of large scale (the Sonata is of more than fair length) and with a definite liking for thick and lush sonority. While Esplá's music is nationalistic to the core, it is far different from Falla's or Turina's. Esplá's compositions pay less attention to the precise and particular rhythms so quickly identified as being of Spanish origin. To a certain degree affinity with Spanish musical speech is found in the scales Esplá employs (in this work and in a few others); these are coded from musical characteristics indigenous to the eastern Levante region of Spain. One of these scales, a nine-tone affair (counting the duplication of the tonic at the extreme), flats all but the first and fourth tones and duplicates the third in both flatted and natural state. A slight modification of this pattern is used here.

The four movements of the composition are of extremely shifting, semirhapsodic character. Two principal motives form the working base of the entire work—one contains a melodic rise and descent, the other is a little rhythmic item. Together these make a type of cyclic cover that embraces the Sonata. If the auditor considers the facts as in a state of perpetual reevaluation, he will understand Esplá's method.

d'Estrade-Guerra, Oswald (1892–1980)

DUO

■ **Sonatine pastorale for Oboe and Clarinet**

Music of amiability and optimism. Music that is clear and unproblematic in its tonal sophistications. Movement two is like a chant. Movement three is divided into slow and animated sections, the former in the character of an improvisation.

QUARTET

■ **String Quartet No. 3**

Peppered tonalism marks this composer's work. There is impressive confidence in the writing and fluency of speech. The style does not avoid lively dissonance. The final chords in movements one and three are bare fifths, with an added sixth in the former, and an added fourth in the latter. The concluding chord of the quartet is a brazen *fortissimo* eight-part cluster that embraces an impacted major seventh.

Intervallic spans are emphasized to balance the content. In movement one the width is a third, in the finale it is a seventh. The middle movements are linked, a scherzo type (Fantaisiste, avec humour) moving to a Modéré. The latter movement is totally in muted timbre, and even more compressed since many sections are marked to be played without vibrato.

Etler, Alvin (1913–73)

DUOS

■ Sonata for Bassoon and Piano (1951)

Etler's work shows excellent concentration of resources. Mainly a study in black and white, this sonata's four movements are illustrative of musical objectivity, its structure the 20th-century façade of classical cognizance. The lines are long-breathed; the music sings. Indeed, this description confirms Etler's viewpoint of his duo sonata that "it is not intended for virtuoso display" and that "melodic directness and simplicity are the touchstones."

■ Sonata for Oboe and Piano (1952)

No imposing of modish notions in this man's sonatas. There is a total passion for the classic method applied to 20th-century enlargement. And both textures and pace are carefully and sensitively applied in relation to the materials shaping the movements.

The opening is short and slow paced. (Etler posits the speeds of his opus by metronomic denomination—the reading for the first movement is ♩ = c. 60.) Syncopation moves through-

out this part of the Sonata. Consistent use of thirds in the harmony colors the second, very fast (♩ = c. 192) movement. Again syncopation appears, this time for use with pedal pitches, in the second (again short) slow movement. The pace here is ♩ = c. 52. A dynamic finale follows, with block figures and soaring lines set in a speed five times faster than the previous movement (♩ = c. 132). A marvelously realized piece for the medium.

■ Sonata for Viola and Harpsichord (1959)

Updated classic style and therefore classic-type strength for this duo sonata. Fine tonal organization with a B pitch polarity for the first and fourth movements. The tonalities of the inner movements are not directly related to the outer ones, but they each revolve around a strong pitch center: D for movement two and E-flat for movement three. And in some respects textural weights follow suit, with the heaviest used in the outer, fast movements.

■ Sonata [No. 1] for Clarinet and Piano (1952)

Generous Hindemithian neoclassicism marks this well-crafted four-movement piece. Tempos are regulated so that sharp contrasts pertain: movement two is more than three times faster that movement one; movement four is a bit more than five times faster than movement three.

Important is the motivic identity that marks the first slow movement. (Etler does not use tempo designations in this work, but only metronomic speeds, which in this case is ♩ = c. 50.) Just as telling is the thin texture used in the finale (♩ = c. 112).

- **Sonata No. 2 for Clarinet and Piano (1969)**

Use here of the full-scale chromaticism that entered many of Etler's late works. This made for some complex formulation of writing but never was permitted to interfere with textural lucidity. One thing leading to another of the same kind, the chromaticity spills over into the first movement and produces rhapsodic content.

Modified toccata momentum carries the second movement, a music almost totally detailed by eighth-note motility.

An interesting point concerns the third movement. The editor of the published edition, Paul M. Shelden, indicates in his prefatory note that Etler requested that this third movement "be performed without a sense of 'phrasing.' " From the superb linear flow one can understand how Etler's objective can be achieved. And also one can enjoy the achievement of the rhythmic brio and virtuosic bravura of the finale.

TRIOS

- **Sonata for Oboe, Clarinet, and Viola (1944)**

The four movements are concentrated, with the tempos in direct contrast of slowest, medium fast, moderate, and fastest. Rhythmic pointedness is the credo practiced in the first, second, and last movements. In the opening, rhythm distills a secondary, lyric theme. In the second movement, rhythmic cadence is the important element in the perkiness of the main theme. Though intercepted by transitory and contrasted material, this principal subject is never dropped sufficiently to take a secondary place. And, again, rhythm is the distinguishing mark of the final movement's two alternative themes. Only the third, moderately paced movement is not fired by metrical effect.

- **Three Pieces for Recorder Trio (Two Trebles [Altos] and Tenor Recorders) or Other Treble Instruments (1959)**

Tonal refinement sounds through every note. All short, with "Pileated" a jogging rhythmic conception and "Pica Pica" emphasizing an anapest (two shorts and a long) rhythm. Between these two is a minor key-tinged "Mourning."

QUARTETS

- **Quartet for Oboe, Clarinet, Viola, and Bassoon**

The specialness of this wind-string quartet is found in its rhythmic wit. All the shaggy hairs of Etler's music are in place, colored by sliding chromatics derived from popular music.

A three-part design is used in the first movement. A flowing idea provides the monothematic impulse for the second part of the Quartet, with development derived from the latter portion of the theme. Grace-note decoratives add further rhythmic spice. In comparison to the slow movement's horizontal setting, that of the finale is as square-cut as can be. There, a merry duple-pulse music is run off without requiring any intellectual probing.

- **String Quartet No. 2 (1965)**

From the initial slowly sustained *pianississimo* sounds, played without vibrato, to the conclusion, twenty minutes later, consisting of tapping the back and bridge of the instruments, Etler's quartet is doused with special colors. Pizzicato types, col legno varieties, and microtones fill the textures. Above all is the use of glissando. In the totally muted third movement the gliding vocabulary is used in more than half of the total forty-six measures. And in places the glissando is continuous throughout a ten-measure span, making a pitch contact and moving away immediately to reach another and then still another, etc. The effect is hallucinatory.

Etler's late-period music became increasingly chromatic. It did not, however, use the special avant-garde sonorants that are packed into this score.

QUINTETS

- **Quintet for Brass Instruments (Two Trumpets, Horn, Tenor Trombone, and Tuba) (1963)**

Virtuosic promulgation is here applied to brass-instrument identification. Not a hint of pat fanfarric calls, lip service to militaristic sound charges, and the like. Etler's brass quintet is styled so that while it fits the brass instruments it avoids all clichés. Indeed, there is socked-in virtuosity, and the music calls for superb technicians.

A free chromaticism applies, tightly applied. In the first movement minute pitch sets are used which then develop. In the finale the chromaticism is emphatically secundal, and the music rides on ostinatos. The material preceding the slow movement equates a violent scherzo, with the quintal meter split into 2 + 3. High color parallels the music materials with various types of mutes, flutters, and the special quality obtainable from half-valve sounds.

This is contemporary brass chamber music that registers a high point in the literature. The plotting, balances, and relationships are magnificent.

- **Quintet for Piano and Strings (Two Violins, Viola, and Cello) (1950)**

The forms of the three movements are fantasia, ternary, and rondo, but all are modified with Etler's contemporary classical designations. He was never an academic. The textures follow suit so that the heaviest pertains to the opening movement, the middle movement is strengthened by contrapuntalism, and the finale is open to allow for a free-driving atmosphere. Proof again that solid musical designs do not become yellowed with age.

- **Quintet No. 1 for Woodwind Instruments (1955)**

Etler knew his winding way with the woodwinds—he was a first-rate oboist. Most of his earlier music has cheerful temper; this work is much more seriously propounded. It has intense colorations and glistening liquidity; its sonorities are a constant joy of fresh discovery. Above all, it bypasses the generally predictable chit-chat that marks so much music for the wind quintet.

Motival development is used in the first movement. The tightly textured second movement has been cogently described (in an unsigned record liner note) as "terse, clipped, insistent." In the concentrated slow movement (Lento) special attention is given the horn. A tarantella-type "let-go" music forms the finale.

- **Quintet No. 2 for Woodwind Instruments (1957)**

Sterner, stronger soundstuff is used in this Quintet than in the first woodwind quintet Etler wrote two years earlier. Total chromatic range and no nonsense, to the extent that the area of serialism is almost entered. The effect is decidedly athletic, even in the initial Andante con moto. Like many of Etler's slow movements, the material is concentrated in the third movement Adagio.

- ***Sonic Sequence* for Brass Quintet (Two Trumpets, Horn, and Two Trombones) (1967)**

Etler's chromatically laced music moves in small spans, the result of the development of a quadruple-pitch pattern that embraces the span of only a tone and a half. There are no smiles in Etler's grim, tone-cluster-style music.

Sonic Sequence was composed for recording purposes (to companion another Etler work on the disc). It represents, therefore, the rare instance of a musical composition receiving its concert premiere *after* being heard via a recording.

SEXTET

- **Sextet for Oboe, Clarinet, Bassoon, Violin, Viola, and Cello (1959)**

There is effective use of the mixed timbre combination chosen for this work. In the fantasialike structuring of the first movement, split between slow and fast music, a good amount of playing off the wind trio group against the string trio group takes place. In the fugal Lento, the winds are solely used in the outer sections, with full partnership of strings and winds taking place in the center. A more unified totality of scoring provides a third method in the happy, charged finale.

Evangelisti, Franco (1926–80)

QUARTET

- *Aleatorio* for String Quartet (1959)

Music in perpetual change (this, to the ultimate single note, where, for example, a pitch may be played by decision of the performer in five different ways). This is proposed with a concentration and a freedom that is the badge of the post-Webern sound draftsman.

Just sixteen measures to the score, divided into totals of 4–8–4. The order of these groups and the sequence of their repetition are in the hands of the players. There are many rules pertaining to the entire production (common

with aleatoric scores), but the main points are that the sequence of measures in any group remains unchanged and that the entire presentation of "no more than 2 per concert" should each be limited to five minutes. This music of motivic fractions has been termed "a precious and disarming gem." Those with open ears will agree.

Evans, David Moule

DUO

- *Moto perpetuo (Perpetual Motion)* for Viola and Piano

All the toccata ingredients are present. But Evans updates Perpetuum-Mobile tactics by inserting a section that shifts from the basic 2/4 time to an uneven 3/8 pulse. The change is dramatic, with unexpected suddenness, moving from *fortissimo strepitoso* (noisily) to *piano leggiero* (lightly). Three minutes of presto excitement. Made to order for the encore area.

Evlakhov, Orest (1912–)

QUINTET

- **Quintet in F Minor for Two Violins, Viola, Cello, and Piano, Op. 33**

Evlakhov's piano quintet displays a tight emotive waist throughout. Set in one movement, the usual four sections of a compound work are quite clear. So is polyphony, particularly in the fugue that defines the second part of the piece. The entire exposition is scored only for the strings. Its wide intervallic shape matches the fanfaristic outlines of the theme of the preceding (first) part.

Linear contraction is used for contrast in the Andante sostenuto section, colored by muted string timbre. Finale optimism follows, where, again, disjunctive detail is emphasized.

Evseyev, Sergei (1893–1956)

TRIO

- **Burlesque for Clarinet, Bassoon, and Piano, Op. 70**

A deft portrayal of a scherzo, following the fixed and true standards of the form. The tempo is presto; the central section is slightly slower in pace and broader in meter. To clinch matters there is an eight-measure coda, in faster than the presto basis. The technical requirements for the performers are minimal.

Ewald, Victor (1860–1935)

See also under **Collaborative Composers**

Variations sur un thème populaire russe

QUINTETS

- **Quintet [No. 1] in B-flat Minor for Two Trumpets, Horn, Tenor and Bass Trombones, Op. 5**

Unproblematic music, bathed in Russian-scented waters. Ewald's complacent acceptance of traditional formulas produces, of course, tuneful, reasonable, and lightly relaxing music, with well-balanced writing for the brass instruments.

The outer movements proceed in Moderato and Allegro moderato tempo, delineating sonata and march-type conceptions, respectively. The central movement is a tripartite structure. The outer sections are marked Adagio, the central section is an Allegro vivace of scherzo character, set in quintuple meter.

(A recording titled *Symphony for Brass*, by Ewald, minus any tonality heading or opus number, is the same as the above work. The title is certainly not an authentic one.)

- **Quintet No. 2 for Two Trumpets, Horn, Trombone, and Tuba, Op. 6**

Simple formality, as pertains to all of Ewald's output, set forth in romantic style. The brass instruments are used for presenting solid themes and their development. No technical acrobatics. Three movements: sonata and rondo style in the outer representations, a theme with six variations plus coda in the center.

(The edition reviewed is published by G. Schirmer in its Empire Brass Quintet series. However, one is certain that the choice of the tuba was purposely to duplicate the instrumentation the Empire fivesome use in their performances. Other Ewald brass quintets call for a bass trombone as the lowest-voiced instrument. It would be safe to say that the scoring for this Quintet is similar. Accordingly, substitution of a bass trombone for the tuba could not be criticized.)

- **Quintet No. 3 in D-flat Major for Two Trumpets, Horn, Tenor and Bass Trombones, Op. 7**

As in Ewald's other brass chamber music pieces, the writing is extremely effective and totally concerned with the integrity of romantic style. There are four movements: a sonata Allegro, an Intermezzo in minor tonality with a central section in the opposite mode, a slow movement (Andante), and a Vivo finale. There are a few folklike touches in the work, simply as flavor adjuncts to the romantic melos of the composition.

Eybler, Joseph (1765–1846)

DUOS

- **Sonatas for Two Cellos, Op. 7**

  - No. 1, in G Major
  - No. 2, in D Minor

These sonatas followed a pair of sonatas for the same combination, each stylistically specified, one "in Stylo parlante," the other "in Stylo fugato." The sonatas of Op. 7 are, for the most part, big display pieces, in the usual four tempos: fast–slow–minuet–fast.

In the first duo sonata Eybler casts entire sections in contrasted tonalities. The G-major tonality of the first movement is opposed to the flatted submediant key of the Andante; in turn the middle part of the latter's ternary design is in E-flat minor. The large rondo design of the G-major Finale (Vivace) also has a large portion in G minor.

A chromatically colored introduction in adagio tempo precedes the first movement proper (Allegro) in the second (D-minor) Sonata. Considerable conjunct-pitch passages are used in the Finale.

- **Sonatas for Violin and Piano, Op. 9**

  - No. 1, in C Major
  - No. 2, in F Major
  - No. 3, in B-flat Major

Eybler was a friend of both Haydn and Mozart. His music follows suit, with more of the former, and still more of Haydn's less advanced writing.

These sonatas show Eybler's light-faceted creative side. They also illustrate his penchant for precise formal duplication. All the sonatas are in three movements, each opening with a sonata-structured Allegro (Nos. 2 and 3 add the qualifying "moderato"). The second movements are in andante tempo: the first a swinging Siciliano; the second a Romanze. In the finales Eybler uses a theme and variation format for the first and third pieces, with exactly the same total (six) of variants. A difference in the endings, however. The first sonata is completed with a 6/8 zippy Presto variant; the third sonata with an Andante setting, totally in double stops for the violin and with a Coda that maintains the slightly heavier texture. The finale for the second sonata is a Rondo.

No masterpieces, but thoroughly enjoyable for what is attempted.

Ezaki, Kenjiro (1926–)

TRIO

- *Concretion* for Violin, Viola, and Cello **(1961)**

From the title of Ezaki's string trio one would expect athematicism. The language of this music is expressed by a growing together of its disparate sound symbols. These are represented by the fractured contradistinctions of glissandos, undulating tremolandos, plucked and bowed sounds, and so on; played on the fingerboard, near the bridge, past the bridge, plus some distinct percussive timbres (example: knocking on the body of the instrument with the finger). In addition, in part two, there are breath sounds (Ezaki terms them "noise") by the uttering of "hu," "shu," "ku," "ha," "ka," etc.

The materials not only concretize but erupt into disconnected pieces. The totality provides a flexible metrical structure, sometimes specifically meterized, most often the material to be played is defined by lengths in seconds. For example, the first of the three divisions within part four (the last part of the work) has this sequence: 2, 1, 6, 1.5, 5, 2, 3 seconds, followed by 4+1/2 /4 (one measure), a six-beat fermata

Ezaki

measure, and then 2 seconds of silence before the second division begins.

Aural identification of the four parts of the work is well-nigh impossible. Not only is there similarity of idiom but the silences occurring *between* the four parts (8 seconds between parts one and two, 5 seconds between parts two and three, and 4 seconds between parts three and four) cannot be differentiated from the silences interlocked *within* the progress of each of the four parts. Ezaki has overlooked identificational security, but he has not overlooked colorful, concretionary organization.

Fairchild, Blair (1877–1933)

DUO

- **Sonata for Violin and Piano, Op. 43**

Granting the use of the standard forms, the field is always open for freshness in the contexts. Fairchild is quite inventive in his four-movement opus, cogently written for the instruments (the work was dedicated to the American violinist of Polish birth, Samuel Dushkin [1891–1976]).

In the sonata-formationed first movement the first theme (in E minor) is constructed from two three-measure phrases; the second theme is no less unsquare in its build, consisting of two five-measure phrases. The scherzo element is portrayed in a movement tempoed slower than relates to the metronome indication: Allegretto vivo ($\downarrow$ = 192). Here again, pat process gives way to alternating material in two different meters (3/4 and 4/4), tied together by the use of syncopation and offbeat stress. Chromaticism is another form of stress, used in the C-sharp-minor slow movement. In the short final recapitulation the color is changed to muted timbre. The freshness of Fairchild's writing continues in the final movement—a music of energetic detail, principally set in septuple time, and including a *pas sec* fugato.

Fairchild's music is also caressed with romantic reflections which mark the details. There are dozens of rallentando, ritard, allargando, and cédez indications. All four (with their different shades of meaning) are used by Fairchild. They add further credits to his sensitively conceived duo sonata.

SEXTET

- *Concerto de chambre (Chamber Concerto)* **for Violin, Piano, and String Quartet (with Double Bass ad lib), Op. 26**

Fairchild was an American expatriate who was born in Massachusetts and spent the last twenty-eight years of his life in Paris. His most important chamber music work is this *Chamber Concerto*, modeled (with the proviso that a double bass may be used ad lib) after Chausson's great work for the same combination. But there is none of Chausson's harmony, nor is there the integrated attention of equality that may make a work brilliant but still fully in chamber style. The principal violin does not coalesce in many portions of the first movement, a two-theme affair, including a solo-violin cadenza and a long section for the two principal instruments.

However, throughout the three movements, the themes and their announcements are exposed simply, with definite clarity. The music is tonally clear, finding its stylistic source in the theorem that to have a strong foundation tonal relationships must exist.

Falaro, Anthony (1938–)

QUINTET

- **Suite for String Quintet (Two Violins, Viola, Cello, and Bass) (1971)**

Falaro's Suite (it may be performed by string orchestra) is a study in textural situations. Voices move, counterpoint is an important process, rhythm is continuous pliability, but there are no set themes, formality is free. The devices in the music's makeup all pertain to the structure, and the structure is the texture. Falaro's creative obedience is to a special objective. (His *Cosmoi*, for example, calls for a fifty-six-part string orchestra, the music based on a graphic design made by the composer and then realized in musical terms.)

The Suite has three distinct sections, with contrasting tempos: moderate, very slow, and fast. These can be played as a total unit or each section can be performed separately. Interestingly, each section is shorter than the previous one at a precise two-minute ratio (part one is 5 1/2 minutes, part two covers 3 1/2 minutes, and the last section totals 1 1/2 minutes). The sections are blocked off by sustained solo-instrument sound (viola at the end of part one, second violin at the end of part two).

The sound of things to come is made evident at the very start: three instruments enter in staggered form and total a chord of paired minor seconds. Prominent in part one are minutely moving glides. The pitch movement is sometimes so long spanned as to progress almost unnoticed. One such example: twenty beats to move (glide) a half step! The result is often a minuscule blend-into-a-pitch change rather than a specific (even-slower-than-slow) glissando or portamento. Falaro also uses in the latter part of the first section precisely defined pulsation counts for finger vibrato. Here, too, the differences are so minute as to be almost undistinguishable. One such example: five pulsations per beat covering five successive beats, followed by six pulsations each for ten beats and then nine beats played with four pulsations per beat. Both the glides and vibrato count are excellent coloratives, but for significant, recognizable registration they should be, in the case of glides, sufficiently concentrated in length. and in regard to vibrato, severely contrasted in totality.

Six different sets of cluster chords portray the entire second part. The last two sets are opposite in dynamic *(forte* and *piano)* and vibrato (intense and none). The final part of the Suite is a consideration of concentrated secundal, dissonant counterpoint. For the most part only some of the instruments are used. Of the forty-seven total measures, twenty-seven call for only three instruments. Thick movement and close-packed linear combinations prevail. Quadrate rising lines, matched by dynamic increase, bring Falaro's work to a conclusion on a solid unison. This reversal is novel and surprising in relation to what has preceded.

Falla, Manuel de (1876–1946)

SEXTET

- **Concerto for Harpsichord (or Piano), Flute, Oboe, Clarinet, Violin, and Cello (1926)**

The title of Falla's work has led to severe differences of opinion as to whether it is a solo vehicle accompanied by five players, or a work for six players in toto. In form, content, and instrumental style, the conception harks back to the days of the sonata da camera or concerto da camera, that is, a chamber work in sonata or concerto form. The Concerto is certainly ensemble music, not only because it is limited to six players but because the composer has indicated that all are "soloists" (read: "equal to each other"). Furthermore, although more grandiloquent speech is given to the keyboard instrument, the balances of the piece are those of chamber style.

Falla's three-movement work is less Spanish than broadly neoclassic. The composer lives in the 20th century and muses in retrospect. Notwithstanding the formula of free tonality and shifting harmonic roots, with some chordal brushing that uses the paints of combined keys, these deliberations do not interfere with the refined quality that cannot be termed other than classic. The Concerto becomes as much a hybrid of means (in harmony, form, and color) as is its title.

The basic compositional style can be recognized at the very start. The harpsichord plays in clear D major, but its rhythm is complicated by two rates of combined periodicities. To this, sharp string chords are pinned, one instrument being in the distinctly opposed key of E-flat minor. Thus tradition mingles with modernity as the music progresses in a sonata format. The principal theme is a 15th-century Castillian madrigal, "De los álamos vengo, madre" ("From the Poplar Woods I Come, Mother").

The slow movement was completed on the morning of Corpus Christi Day, but Falla has stated that this important religious festival had no significance to his music. (But the fact remains that at the end of the movement in the score this chronology and event are mentioned.) While the tempo is on the slow side, the conception is ornate, replete with arpeggios, grace notes, and swift-swept passages, all redolent of days past. The fact that the entire movement is, with few exceptions, concerned with *forte* and *fortissimo* dynamics gives a type of medieval sumptuousness.

In the final Vivace (in rondo form), a pertinent Spanish rhythm is employed, combining duple with triple patterns. Casting such rhythmic binomials in an 18th-century tonal setting shows the neoclassic hand at its best. Falla connects his own art with those of his forebears in a composition singular in his entire output.

Farberman, Harold (1929–)

TRIO

- **Trio for Violin, Piano, and Percussion (Two Bongos, Two Snare Drums, Two Tom-toms, Twelve Antique Cymbals, Triangle, Six Suspended Cymbals, Sizzle Cymbal, Gong, Tam-tam, Bell Tree, Two Tambourines, Four Wood Blocks, Xylophone, Glockenspiel, Vibraphone, and Small Bass Drum) (1963)**

Lots of action and lots of color, but they are always in partnership with clear thematics and rhythmic patterns. Lots of percussion (thirty-nine instruments that can be covered by a single percussionist, though the composer prefers two percussionists), with the special colors being drawn from a dozen antique cymbals embracing the total chromatic range, graduated sets of cymbals and wood blocks, and a Chinese bell tree.

Special to the structuring of the piece are two cadenzas. One is for violin, linking the first and second movements, the other is for piano, linking the third and fourth movements. Sharp contrast takes place by the total *pianissimo* level of movement four, followed by the consistent *fortissimo* delivery of the finale, à la March.

QUINTET

- *Five Images* **for Brass Quintet (Two Trumpets, Horn, Trombone, and Tuba) (1964)**

Highly chromatic music, rich in coloristic variety, and sensitively balanced in its structure. The odd-numbered movements are rhythmically driven, tightly banded and controlled (as noted in movement three) with "no ambiguity in basic pulse." The even-numbered movements have principally unmetered looseness, athematicism, and timbral transformations dealing with vibrato, glissando, pitch fracturing, and breathing into an instrument minus sound production. For total binding, most of the fifth movement is the same as movement one and includes a healthy quote from movement two.

SEXTET

- *Three States of Mind* **(for Six Musicians) (Violin, Cello, Trumpet, Flute, Piano, and Percussion [Bells, Xylophone, Ratchet, Dance-Drum Set, and Tom-toms])**

Music derived from a composition originally written for dance presentation. *States of Mind* is set in three movements, its materials rhapsodic and nervous. It is full of sound jabs and fragments, weaving in asymmetric rhythms, very much alive—not music for relaxation.

Farina, Carlo (c. 1600–c. 1640)

SEXTET

- *Capriccio stravagante (Outlandish Caprice) a 4*: *"Kurtzweilig Quodlibet" ("Diverting Quodlibet")* **for Two Violins, Viola, Cello, Bass, and Harpsichord**

This is a curious item. It combines program music of the most elementary character with some important historical documentation. The last pertains to the violin, made by Farina, who can be considered the first virtuoso of the instrument. His acknowledged enlargement of the violin's technical possibilities is substantiated in the initial use here of harmonics, pizzicato, staccato, col legno, and sul ponticello. (The Capriccio dates from 1627.)

Simply because of their naïveté, the programmatic portions of the work (containing fourteen illustratively specified sections) produce a humorous response (no yaks but smiles). The continuity is a real mix, thus the use of the term quodlibet.

A rhythmic beginning is set in D major (a tonality that is used for the greatest part of the piece—another example of stylistic unsophistication). A Presto conclusion leads to "La Lira" (a 15th-16th–century type of violin with drone strings), the section heard without harpsichord. This connects with "The Piper," which is linked to a variation of the "Lira" material. (Both these are also for strings alone.) Seven short sections with as many tempos precede the next pair of descriptions: "La Trombetta" (a small trumpet) and "Il Clarino" (a high-register trumpet). Both are in fast tempos, the former a mere six measures.

A series of concise portions follow: in turn, dealing with castanets, a hen, and a cock. Ponticello use for the first violin helps mark "The Flageolet," and later, muted strings depict "The Tremolo." The next part combines the picturing of piping by the soldiers with military drum beats (ponticello color for the former, pedal tones in the harpsichord for the latter).

Animals appear next: "Il Gatto" ("The Cat"), with continuous glissandos passed around the violins, viola, and cello and "Il Cane" ("The Dog"), its bark described by the use of successive downbows. The final descriptive section deals with "The Spanish Guitar." Pizzicatos, of course, for this. An Adagio division closes the work.

Farjeon, Harry (1878–1948)

QUARTET

- **String Quartet No. 4 in C, Op. 65**

Farjeon's three-movement work breaks no new ground whatsoever and, in fact, walks over well-trod traditional terrain. However, the conservative idiom does not prevent the use of some catchy tunes, especially the folk-dance turns delineated in the finale, where the greatest interest lies.

The material in the first pair of movements is distinctly expressed. In part one there are the usual contrasted themes and their development in sonata disposition, whereas emphasis on the first violin marks the slow movement. The virtues of the quartet are its clear thematic data, including a good supply of sequence. Only purists or pedants would be annoyed, since sequences, while stereotyped, are part of the logical actions of the classic-romantic school and cannot be denied.

Farkas, Ferenc (1905–)

DUOS

- **Quattro pezzi (Four Pieces) for Double Bass and Piano**

Though of a small frame of reference, each piece avoids a mundane, run-of-the-mill chronicle. Large-scale works have been composed for the double bass, but it functions best when its heavy sound is placed in concentrated arrangement. The thick timbre of the bass also presents a problem of balance, but Farkas has overcome it by retuning (scordatura) the bass a whole tone higher and by an open and thereby clarified type of piano writing.

The result is a spontaneity that is refreshing, set forth by conservative language. In the Intrada

(Introduction) a sixteenth-note figure carries the musical freight, supported principally by quintal harmonies. Rhythmic restraint marks the middle portion of the Scherzo, but even without any tempo shift the formal plan is clean and clear. In "Petit poème" ("Small Poem") a plain binary design is declared. The simplicity is compelling: the double-bass melodic line is set against constant moving thirds in the piano, supported by an undulating bass. Speed marks the final Rondo, stimulated by being mostly a three-voice affair.

- **Sonata a due for Viola and Cello (1961)**

The combination of viola and cello was once a chamber music curiosity. Contemporary composers have revised that situation; the Farkas opus being another fine addition to the literature for low-timbre string-instrument partnership.

The Introduction is followed by a large-scale sonata concept in which rich contrapuntalism is the primary developmental force. In the slow movement polyphonic pertinence is maintained. So are coloristic conditions, with ponticello, syncopated four-part tremolandos, and sweeping arpeggios. Muted color defines the end section of the movement. Its concluding portion complements the personality of the music, with the final cadence defined by pizzicato, glissando, and col legno taps. Stylistic warranty is, indeed, a firm factor in Farkas's music. It can be noted in the finale, which again develops from contrapuntal detail. The ending of the duo brings a recapitulation of the Introduction and a snippet from the finale's contour.

- ***Sonatina Based on Hungarian Folk Songs* for Double Bass (or Bassoon or Cello) and Piano**

Unqualified nationalism. The source is certified, the method of application is via Bartók in his relaxed and lighter demeanor, as in his

Rumanian Folk Dances. Accordingly, catchy tunes with no heavy makeup applied to them for all three movements. These follow the usual fast–slow–fast tempo layout, each section containing the type of rhythmic variety that proves their native authenticity and their Bartókian reliability at the same time.

■ Sonatina No. 1 for Violin and Piano (1930)

Basic to the first movement is a rhythmic motive. This F-major music has real dash. Movement two is in the relative-minor key, and its formation covers statements of the single theme in the three instrumental possibilities: first in the piano, then in the violin supported by the keyboard instrument, and last in the violin alone. This repetition is stimulated when played in the octave higher alternative setting that Farkas prudently offers. The final Presto has duple-pulse perpetual-motion projection. Ponticello and bariolage-bowing passages shade the music.

■ Sonatina No. 2 for Violin and Piano (1931)

The bright key of A major is used for the outer movements. A waltz conduction is prevalent in the first of these, minus the static rhythmic support of the dance, however. The other movement is a Scherzando. Its zip is aided by a combine of duple and triple pulses (the well-utilized join of 6/8 and 3/4 patterns). A broadly set Andante—most of the measures are in 8/4 meter—offers excellent contrast. It also offers a neat registration plan. The violin stays in its low gamut, moves gradually upward, slightly recedes, and then concludes in its initial B-minor region.

■ Sonatina No. 3 for Violin and Piano (1959)

Key determination in the first movement begins in the dorian mode, moves slightly away from this basis, and eventually settles in D major. The subordinate theme retains full chromatic action. A similar modal condition is used at the beginning of the slow (second) movement. Here, too, key fluidity applies, with the movement concluding in A major.

Consistency is to be credited to Farkas. Accordingly, the key signature for the final movement denotes G major, but the music firmly revolves around its dominant, confirmed by the final D-major chord. Therefore, firmly tonal music throughout, but avoiding any academic posture.

TRIOS

■ Notturno for Violin, Viola, and Cello, Op. 2

The 18th-century notturno form was the equivalent of the divertimento, serenade, and cassation. Farkas's 20th-century use of the design is shorter than the ancestral parallel, consisting of a pair of movements rather than three or more.

Movement one divides into precise halves, the only change being a tonality shift as the music progresses in the second division. A dance concept guides the other movement, set in sonata form. Metrical change is paramount in the opening movement, a constant duple pulse guides the second part of the work, tinged slightly with folk sensibility.

■ Serenade for Flute and Two Violins (1940)

(Farkas completed his trio in 1940 and revised it twenty-five years later; it was published in 1968 by Editio Musica, Budapest.)

The Serenade is totally focused light music,

romantically warm and tonal to the nth degree. Sensitive to the chosen medium, Farkas's piece runs through a lightly asymmetrical fast movement, a Marcietta that is slightly proclamatory, a very fast Scherzino, an Intermezzo (the one slow-paced item in the opus), and a Rondo that represents the speediest music of all five movements.

- *Three Dance Paraphrases* for Flute, Viola, and Horn (1972)

Hungarian folk material viewed through re-creative bifocals. The music is expanded and then amplified by instrumentation. Number one is in triple time consistently decorated with mordents. At practically the same speed the third piece is set in duple time and moves in and out of polyphonic territory. Number two is principally for the viola, its material slightly thickened by the use of double stops.

QUINTET

- Serenata for Flute, Oboe, Clarinet, Horn, and Bassoon

Farkas has never been concerned with contemporary fads and fashions. Though he has written works in twelve-tone technique, these are so molded as to become simply more chromatic elaborations of his tonal style. There is always fine workmanship in his music, with beautifully crafted textures drawn from first-class ideas. The imagery is always fresh. Conservative it is, but because it has immediacy and comprehensibility to the listener it does not signify music of sleight weight or value. The Serenata is a prime example of Farkas's abilities and his creative genuineness.

There are three movements, each with a particularly clear shape. The opening Allegro is in sonata form, with a pert initial subject and a more lyrical second theme. The developmental process is compact and minus any abstruse considerations. Ternary form is used for the slow movement; the finale is a Saltarello. Constant triple pulse guides the Italian dance through a rondo format.

Fasano, Renato (1902–79)

DUO

- Sonatina for Cello and Piano (1942)

Pitch stability anchors this work. The style is open; a light, athletic content is involved. Mixed in are some folksy turns, but not tunes.

The first part sits on D and then B major for a considerable amount of time. A cadenza for cello follows. In turn, there is an "Alla ninna nanna" ("Lullaby") episode, also supported totally on the D pitch. The final section alternates between an Allegro alla marcia and material twice as slow though marked Allegro vivo! Everywhere there are D's sounding (example: beginning with the "Lullaby" and into the concluding part the bass line solely sounds D for fifty-nine measures!). There are plenty of thirds, but just as many fourths, in the melodic line and harmonic framework.

Fauré, Gabriel (1845–1924)

Of the entire French school of composers, Fauré best typifies that cross-mingling of the super postromantic and the infiltration of the then new "cleansing" impressionistic technique. Fauré's work was a perfect combination of classic and romantic meanings that showed the musical world a new, noble French style. It is a cultured music that has a freshness that never stales. It is the language of a French Beethoven, with the same perfection of detail and form combined with the most individual of melodicism; treading not the paths of "tunes" but the architectonic line, which has more probity than so-called melody. Because Fauré's themes are not easily whistled, they are no less perfect.

His career parallels that of so many other composers with latently observed talent—the usual study, performance in the role of a church organist, and teaching. His pupils, including Enesco, Koechlin, Ravel, and Florent Schmitt, virtually constitute a Blue Book of French composers. He produced more than 130 works, the last work with actual numerical indication being the string quartet.

A composer who appeared during the transition in French music, Fauré left the world a heritage of great music that can be defined as a new form of classicism. This is neither the starched polyphonic type nor the later Stravinsky type, but a poetic classicism as perfect in its way as Beethoven's dramatic classicism.

DUOS

▪ Fantaisie for Flute and Piano, Op. 79

Two-sectioned in tempo (slow and fast) and laced with the usual Fauré lyrical largesse. The second part is colorfully balletic. This is the only composition Fauré wrote for the wind instrument.

Sonatas for Cello and Piano

▪ Sonata [No. 1] in D Minor for Cello and Piano, Op. 109

The reflective austerity of this Sonata is due mainly to the fact that Fauré refused to use a baritone instrument in mezzo-soprano regions. As a result, the music is given a grave quality by the color of the cello homophonically singing its way throughout (save in the last seven measures). There were no Straussian *Don Quixote* supercilious supererogations in Fauré's makeup. He considered a cello sonata as a

vehicle for an instrumental baritone-tenor to sing his poetry. One must realize that to assign a coloratura style to a cello is as ludicrous as some composers' attempts to make a concerto from a chamber work. Fauré was not misled.

Two themes form the procedures of the first movement: one in the composer's favored displaced rhythm of syncopation, the other lyrical. The slow movement is restrained. It takes certain advantage of placing the cello both as a bass symbol and as the leading voice under the piano's material. This contradicts (happily) the usual manner of majority soprano position for an instrument when it is allied with the keyboard instrument. After the most prevalent minor tonalities in the preceding movements, the major key of the final section emerges like sunshine. The cello sings again, and a long canon is superproductive for textural contrast.

▪ Sonata No. 2 in G Minor for Cello and Piano, Op. 117

The tonality is set immediately, but it is not rigid, shifting between the major and minor modes. In the opening movement the piano writing is exceedingly thin—a value that permits the cello to sound through the texture comfortably. The details are persuasively clear. The two principal themes have different contours: One ascends; the other basically descends; each is marked by specific harmonic data, the first framed by offbeat rhythms, the other by way of legato-warmed arpeggios.

A large ternary plan is used for the C-minor slow movement. It contains the Fauré brand of vocalization that floats into the ears with artistic simplicity. Vincent d'Indy considered it to be "a genuine masterpiece of expressive sensitivity." (It is little known that the slow movement is a transcription of the *Chant funéraire* that Fauré had written for the band of the Garde républicaine, in the previous year [Op. 117 was composed in 1922], to commemorate the centenary of the death of Napoleon I.) In the finale a pair of thematic propositions are developed and contrasted further to a chordal chorale subject.

(The dedication of the Sonata honors an American composer—Charles Martin Loeffler.)

Sonatas for Violin and Piano

- **Sonata [No. 1] in A Major for Violin and Piano, Op. 13**

If one word were required to describe Fauré's music, most especially this work, that word would be "elegant." But together with this is the most demarcated clarity and sense of unified style, uncommon in a composer's early music (this Sonata was the first of Fauré's chamber music compositions). Balanced proportions, immaculate translation of spiritual values into music, make this a light composition, but one never bordering on a state of triviality.

One of the primitive binding characteristics of musical composition is the sequence—an idea repeated on varying tonal levels. But this is a short cut to the ideal of balance and cultivation of the section in which it is applied. In many portions of this joyful work, Fauré seemingly sets up sequences, but they are not that at all. They represent a rhythmic monitoring that has tacit agreement and thus resemblance, but they are not shaped into compressed sections forming rhetoric by repetition. It is this factor that so capably blends the first movement with warm and long-mannered lines. The musical program Fauré presents is expressive and simple—two themes and their development are persuaded to climax by the rationale of the rhythm. This same proposal is used in the slow movement, first the pulsed flow of the theme is short–long, throwing the beats off gravity; later reversed and substituted by the more usual long sound on the loop of the strongest accent.

The Allegro vivo has the scamper of a scherzo, is metrically neither duple nor triple, but one pulse per measure, with occasional change by offbeat accent. The Trio is Schumannesque, seductively anticipated by breaking in on the Scherzo's course before being given its full head. The last movement flows with the same constancy as the opening section. The seed of all Fauré's music lies in the beautiful poetry of this violin and piano Sonata.

- **Sonata No. 2 in E Minor for Violin and Piano, Op. 108**

Excitement in music finds varied means of portrayal—the loud storm of brass, the violence of unadulterated percussion, the strettos of the contrapuntal "pileup," etc. But the much more refined means of syncopation is as telling. How it can be formed for splendid effect may be observed in the last part of this three-movement Sonata. It is retained with its quality of impatience; even the contrasting theme uses the device. And when canonic treatment is resorted to, the temper and temperature are maintained. Fauré's ability to use a single poised action, blunt with similarity, is proof of his excellent craftsmanship. Furthermore, when one instrument uses a more durable rhythmic theme and the other may ally the main theme in augmented values, the syncopation still persists. Thus, a movement rapt with one particular remains constant with inspired fury.

To a similar degree, the first movement has these same split rhythmic values, including imitative work in a perfect partnership between violin and piano. In the slow movement there is a magnificent example of thematic accompaniment. Over the inspirational beauty of the fully simplistic harmonies winds a mildly chaste theme. The entire movement emerges from it, disclosing dignified warmth.

TRIO

- **Trio in D Minor for Piano, Violin, and Cello, Op. 120**

The durability of sobriety, of tempered writing, relaxed and yet grounded with as much strength as any work making thrice the sound, is to be heard in this expressive Trio. Short in duration, it is a considerable work in Fauré's classical effusion. His stylistic, rhythmic habit—to be indulged in only by those who can carry off the difficult matter of cloistering the metrical impulse—is heard throughout.

Practically every section of the three movements is devoted to organic totality via a unitary idea. In the first movement, the eighth-note accompaniment reflects the inflection of a long-spun melodic line in the gentlest 3/4 meter, running in the most moderate of speed rates. Rhythmic life is maintained by syncopations, stretched ever so slightly (these are not syncopative scrubs that tear into a music's cloth). There is dialogue, but it is in the manner of a reticent tête-à-tête. The second movement has a more lacy theme (Fauré shows his romantic hands), in three-part form. The last movement is a Scherzo, announcing its directness by a string-unison theme of breadth and a nonsymmetrical, perky, sophisticatedly harmonized topic by the piano. Antiphonal address is used first, then the instruments join hands. Fauré preaches his classical sermon with the pithiness of the mature composer, never once losing his refined French ancestry. It is the cultivation of the most cultured type of chamber music. One need not be a Frenchman to understand this speech.

It is noteworthy that three of the greatest instrumentalists of all time gave the first public performance of this outstanding piano trio: Alfred Cortot (piano), Jacques Thibaud (violin), and the master of the cello, Pablo Casals. Fauré's work deserved this blessing.

QUARTETS

Piano Quartets

- **Quartet No. 1 in C Minor for Piano, Violin, Viola, and Cello, Op. 15**

The authoritative rhythm that opens this quartet not only fixes the key but sets the pulsatile outline and thematic modus operandi for the first movement. There are the usual contrasts and episodes, but the rhythmic idea permeates the total movement. For those who still think of Fauré as a cool, detached composer, the rebuttal lies in this movement. The Scherzo is delicate, formed from sensitive combinations of binomial and trinomial divisions within specific beats or in their nonsymmetrical assortment within the measures. Scherzo lightness is stabbed with these, to which color is applied with plentiful applications of string pizzicatos, plus the use of mutes to confirm the impressionistic Trio section. (The critic Alan Rich has picturesquely described this movement as "a veritable dance for moonbeams.")

The short Adagio has a rhythmic relationship to the opening movement, an indication that rarely does a composer dispose his several movements in as isolated a fashion as one might believe. In the last movement, there is the same matter of rhythmic kinship (without any manifest monotony) with contrast by Chopinesque wide-spanned lyricism.

- **Quartet No. 2 in G Minor for Piano, Violin, Viola, and Cello, Op. 45**

A unison opening matches the same textural plan in the companion work (*see above*). The contrasting, flowing second theme not only has its own flavor but through its difference increases the intensity of the dramatic first theme. Sonata form is the device of the movement, which finally pulls into the like-named major affinity of the home minor tonality. Again, as in the first piano quartet, pizzicato helps color the second-movement Scherzo, in which the main theme sounds syncopatively over a "noodling" repetitive Alberti bass, never quite deciding whether it will swim in duple or triple metrical channels. There is no Trio, but there is communal use of the first-movement theme, affording a rare illustration of the cyclic system in this composer's music.

In the slow movement, curious bell-like passages keep appearing in the piano and finally disappear. Against this is an introductory recitative, which builds eventually into a sicilianolike theme, one engendered with the warmth and delicacy of a *great* melody. This movement is one of the most expressive in the entire Fauré literature. The finale, which begins in minor and ends in the reverse tonality, is fluent and well crafted, but suffers a bit from rhythmic redundancy.

- **String Quartet in E Minor, Op. 121**

Fauré's lone string quartet was written in 1923 and 1924, during which time he was so ill that he required oxygen to maintain life. His deafness made it impossible for him to hear the work on completion, just short of two months before his death. He gave the finished manuscript to a pupil, Roger-Ducasse, with the request that the work be played privately for a few friends (including Dukas) and that it be published only "if it were found worth playing." This supremely modest statement is another example of Fauré's intrinsic honesty and sincerity. Worth publishing it most certainly was, and deserving of performance it surely is!

The poetic diction and certain of the techniques one observes, for instance, in Schumann's string quartets will be felt in this Frenchman's quartet. The use of syncopation, which instigates a quiet drive without recourse to frenetic allegro writing, and a gentle, semi-sad, romantic quality combine with the *élégance* that is French. The harmonies are a bit removed from classical style regulations. These, by their slightly astringent form, free the lines from vertical rigidity and stimulate the inner contexture.

There is always a definite indication in the works of the *important* composer that shows (especially in his latest works) a striving within the aesthetic, which is picked up by a later generation and then propelled and matured into a "new style." As Beethoven's last quartets touched the brim of the free tonality scheme that later marked the style of Berg, so Fauré's quartet presages the harmonic simmering that finally is fulfilled in the neoclassic works of Stravinsky. The harmony is free yet held in check by regularity of chord calculations. But the sideslip, the escaped resolution, and the gingery appoggiatura are all present to embellish and prove that classical usage does not deter contemporary feeling. This quartet also proves that the 79-year-old man was not only looking ahead, but doing so with wisdom.

(In 1878 Fauré began a violin concerto, indicating it as Op. 14. He first composed an Andante movement, then an opening Allegro movement. Although the two movements were given a premiere performance Fauré never finished the work and the torso remains unpublished. In place, he took the two themes of the Allegro movement and reused them in the first movement of his String Quartet.)

QUINTETS

Piano Quintets

- **Quintet [No. 1] in D Minor for Piano, Two Violins, Viola, and Cello, Op. 89**

The gestation of the first of Fauré's two piano quintets covered a nineteen-year span. Initially (in 1887, the year following the composition of the second piano quartet), it was envisaged as a third piano quartet. Four years later (1891) Fauré changed the sketches for the piece to the piano quintet medium and then put the materials aside. He resumed work on the quintet in 1894 but once again fell short of completing the score. Finally, in 1903, he recommenced, this time recasting the entire composition. It was completed in 1906, a few months before the first performance, given in Brussels, on March 23.

Fauré's first piano quintet is dedicated to the famed violinist Eugène Ysaÿe, to whom so many other French and Belgian creations were dedicated, and who was responsible for many a first performance of works now staples in the chamber music repertory. A second, no less important, feature is the fact that the Quintet was published by the American firm of G. Schirmer, an exceedingly rare instance of a foreign composer's work obtaining publication in the United States. (The intermediary that brought this about was his friend, Charles Martin Loeffler, the Alsatian-born, American composer.)

Logic is the image of this quintet's life. The inherent correctness of the sequence (the bane of many composers' existence) can serve only when it has expressive logic. Empty repetition of musical phrases may be correct, but musical design must convey more than mere patterns. The last movement is a good example of the propriety, the musical intercourse, that makes Fauré a master of his craft. A simple, yet vocal, four-measure idea is used eighteen times in succession. However, by its unlabored treatment it becomes diffused and elevated into an effusion of truly articulate meaning. Since there are only three movements, this basic regularity of phrase takes the place, to a certain extent, of the absent Scherzo, as it is integrated within the last movement. Therefore, the more sustained and serious second subject of the movement (italicized by octave leaps) takes on the premise not only of a related theme but a "fourth"-movement idea which combines with the gayer and lighter statement. This is nonscholastic music as carefully prepared for the auditor as any academic communication.

The first two movements are formed in Fauré's usual poetic manner; the first one contrasts two main themes, the second of which is announced by the strings alone.

- **Quintet No. 2 in C Minor for Piano, Two Violins, Viola, and Cello, Op. 115**

Fauré returned to a four-movement plan for this work (the first piano quintet had only three movements—*see above*), written when he was 76, three years before his death. (The composition is dedicated to Paul Dukas, composer of *The Sorcerer's Apprentice*.)

Pulsed identity traveling as the companion to a theme can compactly delineate its intrinsic design and raison d'être. In the opening movement kinetic sixteenth notes are used with a vigorously sustained subject; contrastive vigor through blocked string-instrument motion, as well as gently pulsed curves, provides the legato style of the second theme. Later, the rhythms interchange and become combined—development is taking place.

Mixtures of chromatic and diatonic scale lines pace the second movement (Scherzo). After the expressive slow movement, the finale is the most transparent. It is well worth noting how the first theme, with its large spread, covers at first the territory of an intervallic twelfth, then a tenth followed by a double octave; later, climaxed carefully by the largest tonal width, that of a seventeenth. From this there is developed a sonata-constructed movement displaying strength and power.

Favre, Georges (1905–)

DUO

- **Sonata for Violin and Piano**

Innate romanticism. And plenty of thick, chromatically intensified harmonies. The textures are generous. All these do not negate a firm chamber music document detailed around tonal centers.

The first and third movements are marked "animated," the first of the pair slightly slower (Modérément animé). The middle movement is a rondo-formationed Lent et expressif music. Its coda is a colorful ten-measure exposition of harmonic timbre for the violin with nubby-totaled chords for the piano. The theme of this slow movement is twice partially quoted in the finale.

TRIO

- *Gouaches*: **Suite for Oboe, Clarinet, and Bassoon**

Favre's musical parallel of the gouache painting method is to utilize polytonality. That technical discipline is close to the opaque colors basic to gouache style, since key mixture removes the clarity (transparency) found in the use of a single tonality.

The Pastorale is polyphonic—a bit different from the flowing homophonic simplicity found in most pastoral pieces. In the Intermède (Interlude) form is fashioned from contrastive tempos and qualities; the outer parts are light and sprightly, the middle is slower in speed and thereby emphasizes the thicker voice movement. The Grave is a truncated mini-fugue. It opens with the clarinet stating the subject in D-flat, answered by the bassoon in G. The flute covers but 1 3/4 measures of the 6-measure subject in C, with the balance of the very short piece freely formed.

Favre favors polyphony throughout the suite, even in the final Danse. Contrapuntalism adds interest to the concluding choreographic concept, but it also makes its flow a bit heavy laden. To balance matters, a snippet of the opening Pastorale is used in the coda.

QUINTET

- *Métope* **for Wind Quintet**

The opening portion serves as a ritornel for the piece, appearing twice more and just before the conclusion. In between are rhapsodic, chromatically encased sections in varied tempos. It is by this variety of disassociated materials and by the ritornel that *Métope* is, respectively, stimulated and sustained.

Felciano, Richard (1930–)

DUO

- *Spectra* **for Piccolo (alternating Flute and Alto Flute), and Double Bass (1967)**

Felciano's title is explained by him as referring "to the broad frequency spectrum which this particular combination of instruments makes possible." There are five sections, with three duets (one for each of the flute types with the string instrument) and two solo sections for the latter. In terms of the instrumentation, color was paramount in the conception, and color remains the principal factor in the assortments heard in the piece. The transformations are fascinating.

OCTET

- *Crasis* for Flute, Clarinet, Violin, Cello, Harp, Piano, Percussion (Two Tom-toms, Sand Block, Marimba, Very Large Gong, Timpani, Tambourine, Cymbals, Two Suspended Cymbals, Wood Chimes, Five Temple Blocks, Glass Chimes, Ratchet, Guiro, Vibraphone, Tubular Chimes, Two Bongos, Wood Block, Glockenspiel, and Snare Drum), and Electronic Tape (1967)

This is an attempt to simulate the sonorous climate of a Japanese Noh drama, hence oscillating, gliding, and wail-like sounds punctuated and criss-crossed by ictus jabs and explosive thrusts. By themselves, without any philosophical or imitative objective, Felciano's sound shapes are fresh, mobile, and inventive.

Felciano explains his choice of title thus: "As the work progresses, the relation of the live instruments to the electronic sounds proceeds from complement to fusion, hence the title (crasis: the joining of two vowels into one)."

Feld, Jindřich (1925–)

DUOS

- **Five Inventions for Two Flutes**

Bach comes to mind in the anapest rhythm of the Prélude. Part two, "Mouvement contraire" ("Contrary Motion"), takes place in the imitation of one flute's figures by the other. Contrapuntal style is maintained in part three (Canon), part four (Passacaille), and a final Fughette. The forms are as clear as the pitch polarities of each movement.

- **Sonata for Oboe and Piano (1982)**

The stylistic semaphore immediately appears. In the first measure, the oboe alone, in rubato and with a final ritard, states the tone row, which comes to rest on an A-flat. This is linked to measure 2, where the twelve tones are rhythmically stated by the piano. Within the first movement there is emphasis on pulsed detail framing lyrical lines, canonic conversation, and some short cadenzas for the oboe, which thereby balance the initial unaccompanied statement.

Movement two is a Scherzo, its format the usual balanced tripartite one. The Finale stresses quartal and quintal chordal arrangements, touches base with canonic detail, and meticulously pays attention to the oboe's articulative ability. The music of this last movement might be termed "busy," but it has clear rhythmic denomination, pulse demarcation, and metrical steadfastness.

- **Sonata for Viola and Piano (1955)**

Intervallic spans of quartal and quintal widths are the prime element in the opening movement. There is an introduction to the first movement proper (Allegro), in which tighter rhythms parallel the faster tempo. Movement two is ternary with the theme (within the total concept) passing from the violin to the piano and back to the violin. In the finale's rondo depiction Feld includes a sprightly Czech-flavored dance melody. Contrasted to it is material bound to percussive cluster harmonies.

- **Three Pieces for Oboe (or Flute or Clarinet) and Piano**

On the lighter side of the composer's catalogue. The pieces have a sophisticated tinge and will provide aural pleasure. There is bitonal and secundal alliance in "Playful," syncopation and chromatic crawl in "Melancholy," and cluster contacts in the vigorous pace of the Burlesque.

TRIOS

■ *Petit divertissement* **for Three Flutes**

Good atmospheric coloring in the set of three pieces. This represents Feld's tonal style, the stylistic simplicity a far cry from his dodecaphonically stimulated compositions. There is first a Quasi marcia, then the tranquillity of a Berceuse, onto the duple punctuations of a vivacious Scherzino that completes the compact divertimento.

■ **Trio for Flute, Violin, and Cello (1963)**

Feld's twelve-tone style embraces music neither very simple nor very complex, but nicely between the two. All four movements expose the tone row in its varied forms (original, retrograde, inversion, and retrograde of the inversion, plus transpositions) used in standard structures.

Three-part form begins the work, the textural content paralleling the thematic differences. Ternary form again is used for the slow movement, different in the employment of canon for the outer sections. Movement three is a Scherzo, and in the finale canonic procedure is again utilized.

QUARTETS

■ **String Quartet No. 4 (1965)**

Feld's quartet is divided into two parts, each including two movements. In the initial division, an Adagio of intensely dramatic long-phrased lines, often supported by driving rhythms, leads to a rhythmically dynamic Allegro. In the second division, a Scherzo, far less chromatic than the other parts of the work, is linked to another Adagio, creating a clear total structural balance. The logistics are worked out from dodecaphonic plans.

■ **String Quartet No. 5 (1979)**

Serial procedures are included. But not with overheated stricture. Sometimes openhearted (the pyramidal opening, which spells out the row, inverted canons, and the like); sometimes completely free of dodecaphonic rigidity. Mixed in are the ingredients of the post-Webern school: playing the highest pitches possible on a string, striking the instrument's body, microtones, and ad lib rhythmic distribution.

In the first movement polyphonic controls are contrasted to flying glissandos, sometimes in paired contrary motion, other times in tutti delivery. Movement two is a fusion of free rhythmic action (the row distributed between the four instruments), some ponticello inserts, a snide Waltz, and a Scherzo that covers considerable color ground, from col legno, to plucked, to bowed sounds.

The final movement is a fusion of tight lyricism and rhythmic unrest. Even in its more relaxed sections the music is percussively minded. While there are no instrumental discoveries in Feld's fifth string quartet, neither are there stale rhetorical gestures.

QUINTETS

■ **Capriccio for Wind Quartet (Flute, Oboe, Clarinet, and Bassoon), and Guitar (1964)**

Fun music, fit for concert purposes, though it was originally planned for presentation at educational concerts by the Prague Wind Quartet.

The music begins like Haydn's *Farewell* Symphony in reverse, with the musicians appearing singly rather than departing one by one. The guitarist is onstage and starts the composition. Then, in turn, the bassoonist, oboist, clarinetist, and flutist enter after first preluding backstage. Their introductory sounds are improvisations of their own, then at a specific point they are guided by the composed score. (Feld's title for this part of the work is "Introduzione all' entrata dei musicisti." He offers a translation that reads: "Welcome Introduction.")

Movement two is an "Interrupted Serenade." At first the solo bassoon is accompanied by the guitar, with ostinated polyrhythmic interjections by the other instruments. The music takes on a waltz context, moves into an Allegro section, and then returns to the initial part of the movement. "Merry music" is Feld's description of the one-minute "Intermezzo of Reconciliation" that follows. The work concludes with a jazzy "Twist Finale."

- **Quintet for Two Trumpets, Horn, and Two Trombones (1972)**

Dodecaphonic spit and quasi-tonal polish combine in Feld's four-movement brass quintet. Of course, in such a procedure motivic manipulation pertains, and, as with Schoenberg's music (though Feld has much brighter rhythmic interlocutions), the music's progress is within serious territory.

Felderhof, Jan (1907–)

TRIO

- **Trio for E-flat Clarinet, Clarinet, and Bass Clarinet (1968)**

Music that is rather blunt, serious stuff and somewhat heavy in its makeup. There is a good supply of ostinatos, which does clarify the data. The second movement is a Scherzando effectively registered by way of asymmetric detail. The last two movements are linked; the first one a short slow bit, the other a restless statement that will be even more fitful if the performers follow the instruction in the tempo heading: Moderato ma con moto e rubato.

QUARTET

- **Divertimento for Two Trumpets, Horn, and Trombone (1950)**

Dissonance becomes doubly candid when expressed by brass instruments. Here it provides music of powerful sonority related to tonal pungency.

The Entrata is not of irrelevant character nor of only parenthetical report in reference to a form more commonly used in earlier eras. It has proper "introductory" style and blocked fanfare writing, the opening motive being of the most importance. The second movement is texturally thick, the timbres dulled with the use of mutes. This contrapuntal Imitazione contrasts with the movements that precede and succeed it. Movement three (Melodia) is flowing for the most part, while the last piece (Alla marcia) is dynamic.

Feldman, Morton (1926–87)

DUOS

- *Durations II* for Cello and Piano (1960)

See below: Durations.

Durations

- *Durations I* for Violin, Cello, Alto Flute, and Piano (1960)

- *Durations II* for Cello and Piano (1960)

- *Durations III* for Violin, Tuba, and Piano (1961)

- *Durations IV* for Violin, Cello, and Vibraphone (1961)

- *Durations V* for Violin, Cello, Horn, Vibraphone, Harp, and Piano (alternating Celesta) (1961)

Meterless, pulseless music; the instruments "begin simultaneously, and are then free to choose their own durations." Only the sounds are designated in these pieces (one duo, two differently constituted trios, one quartet, and one sextet) in which, Feldman states, "each instrument is living out its own individual life in its own individual sound world."

The timbral combinations differ, but all five pieces are typical Feldman, meaning they are all flat surfaced and totally restrained. This is music without skin and bones, and only the marrow showing.

- *Extensions I* for Violin and Piano (1951)

The usual Feldman leanness of stuff and substance is found in the first of his four pieces with the *Extensions* title. (Number three is for solo piano, number four is for three pianos, and number two was withdrawn.) The music is mostly soft; loud designations are in the great minority. These strengths represent a black-white effect, since there are only *piano* and *forte* designations. There is consistent metrical application (all in triple pulse). Speedwise, the pace moves upward until it reaches its highest point, recedes a bit, and then remains fixed at that point for the remaining two-thirds of the duo.

- *Piece for Violin and Piano* (1950)

One can consider Feldman's duo a suppressed scherzo. And suppressed in length also, consisting of but forty-eight measures. And subdued in dynamic, with three isolated *forte* sounds, the remainder all *pianissimo*, and further subdued by muted timbre for the violin.

- *Projections IV* for Violin and Piano (1951)

See below: Projections.

Projections

- *Projections II* for Violin, Cello, Flute, Trumpet, and Piano (1951)

- *Projections IV* for Violin and Piano (1951)

- *Projections V* for Three Cellos, Three Flutes, Trumpet, and Two Pianos (1951)

All three works are conceived in graph notation. (There are two other works in the *Projections* series: *Projections I* is for unaccompanied cello; *Projections III* calls for two pianos.) This places the pitch choice in the hands of the performer, since only pitch areas of "high," "middle," and "low" are noted. Duration is indicated by the amount of space covered by square and rectangular shapes. Feldman's objective, he explains, is "to project sounds into time, free from a compositional rhetoric."

Dynamics are depressed. This is further emphasized in *Projections II*, with the trumpet, violin, and cello all muted. The same pertains to the trumpet and cellos in *Projections V*. All, a music of sounds with no relationships involved between them, thus totally abstract in all its dimensions.

▪ *Spring of Chosroes* for Violin and Piano (1977)

The duo is named for a sumptuous carpet, supposedly made for the Sassanian king Chosroes I, who lived in the mid-6th century (531–79). Feldman's music is silken soft, never rising above the *pianississimo* level, and including *pianissississimo* and *pianississississimo*, almost inaudible strengths. A special constant dynamic decline marks many pitches which start in triple *piano* and are followed by a decrescendo. Plastic metrical lengths give the music a motility that contrasts to the unclothed timbral level.

▪ *Vertical Thoughts II* for Violin and Piano (1963)

Nicolas Slonimsky's description of Feldman's music as being "on the threshold of audibility" could not be more accurate. With Feldman, the few sounds here and there amount to an anticlimax. Bits appear and disappear. Musical line has been flushed away like waste. The delicacy and reticence are powerful in their ability to function by understatement.

Here there are some "vertical thoughts," but there are also a good number of individual unmetered sounds, freely depicted always since one instrument does not play until the "preceding sound" of the other instrument "begins to fade."

(Four other *Vertical Thoughts* are in Feldman's catalogue. Number one is for two pianos; number three is for soprano, flute, horn, trumpet, trombone, tuba, 2 percussion, piano alternating celesta, violin, cello, and double bass; number four is for piano; and number five is for soprano, tuba, percussion, celesta, and violin.)

▪ *The Viola in My Life (3)* for Viola and Piano (1970)

The (3) after the title is explained by the use of the same title for a series of four works. The first two are for solo viola supported by a small group of instruments. Number four of the set is for viola and full orchestra. Only number three is in the chamber music category.

Some of Feldman's titles have flat factualness (*Chorus and Orchestra, Pianos and Voices*), others cover a total nonsignificance to the musical content (*Madam Press Died Last Week at Ninety, Rabbi Akiba*). *The Viola in My Life* title has no specific relationship to Feldman's career, but it is, at least, pertinent to the instrumentation of all four works and certainly is thus part of his (creative) "life."

Pulsatile repression is locked into this piece. It is another example from Feldman's world of many silences and few sounds, expanded a speck over a time space of six minutes. Though tones are repeated, the repetitions do not define a structural function but serve as reminders. Balance and formal organization give way to a total concept that avoids development and retains a single mood, undisturbed by any formal compartmentation.

Although everything is to be "extremely quiet," minute dynamic rise and fall surround nearly every viola sound. On the other hand, the dynamic plane is rigid in the piano part. Two qualities are braided. The viola (always muted) has sustained sounds, a little movement, and a twelve-note figure heard near the beginning. The piano totally produces chords, either softly punctuated or sustained. All these induce, with the reduced motility, the equivalent of a hypnotic stasis.

TRIOS

- **Durations III for Violin, Tuba, and Piano(1961)**

See above: Durations.

- **Durations IV for Violin, Cello, and Vibraphone (1961)**

See above: Durations.

QUARTETS

- **Durations I for Violin, Cello, Alto Flute, and Piano (1960)**

See above: Durations.

- **String Quartet [No. 1] (1979)**

This is the shorter (!) of Feldman's two string quartets, with a performance time of about an hour and forty minutes.

Athematicism doesn't come close to being applied to this piece. Feldman's quartet is practically all chords, and these are always those of pitch collision, mainly clustered. (One example is sufficient: A–C-flat equaling B–G-sharp–A.) This dissonant constancy results in a sonorous, superjunctioned superfetation. Interesting and fascinating, but be warned that a small amount goes a long way.

As usual with this composer, most of the time the dynamic level is close to being inaudible. A *pianississississimo* level (quintuple *piano*) is in the great majority, and sometimes this tremendously suppressed dynamic is followed by a decrescendo! An extreme dynamic for single pitches is *mezzoforte–pianississimo*. Quick change sometimes occurs so that a series of four connected sounds will be played, respectively, *forte–pianississimo–mezzoforte–forte*. Rhythms are highly charged, discharged from incessant vacillating metrical order. In a

set of fourteen measures (4/16, 5/16, 3/8, 7/16, 5/8, 3/2, 2/2, 7/16, 3/4, 5/8, 2/2, 3/8, 5/16, 3/16) there are nine different time signatures derived from four different denominators. Further, pulse straightforwardness is dissolved quite often so that in 3/8 there are four pulses, five within 4/16, three in 2/8, etc.

In its total lack of line writing, Feldman's quartet is almost machinelike in its repetitive production of pitch formations related one to the other only through their dissonantal unification. Direct dynamism here. Feldman's quartet gives up its secrets very quickly.

- **String Quartet No. 2 (1983)**

Without argument the longest piece of chamber music of all time. Just after Feldman's completion of the piece there were rumors that the work's length was anywhere from three and a half to five and a half hours. Then, after its first performance, a newspaper report mentioned "Feldman's four-hour string quartet." The publishers (Universal Edition) indicate the timing as three hours and forty-five minutes. The composer disagreed and indicated to the author that the performance time was five hours and fifteen minutes. Enough said—Feldman's opus, therefore, is a half-hour longer than the combined lengths of the first four symphonies of Gustav Mahler or the total performance time of eight Beethoven symphonies Nos. 2 through 9)!

Feldman's creative goal is the clinging to reiterative patterns and repetitive segments that endeavor to persuade and implore over and over and over and over again. These constitute an overwhelming exploitation of *concordia discors*. A severe technical ritual surrounds the music.

The relation to Feldman's first string quartet *(see above)* is absolute. Here, in addition to chords, there are multitudinous concentrated rhythmic figures, none elaborate. Enharmonic notation is acutely avoided. Thus, one example for the two violins reads F-flat–D–E-sharp–E-flat–G-flat–F for violin 1, simultaneously E–C-double-sharp–F–D-sharp–F-sharp–G-double-flat for violin 2. Considered *enharmonically* the passage for the two violins sounds E–D–F–E-flat–F-sharp–F, but Feldman wishes this to be projected otherwise. If performed with minute exactness, an extremely subtle breakdown of unisoned sounds takes place and mini-microtone pitches are projected.

Measure after measure is repeated, passage after passage is repeated. (One wag has stated that this is the simplest way of making a four-hour piece from a thirty-minute one!) But also chunks of repeated measures are a factor. For example: two measures of 3/8, the first played nine times, the second eleven times; then two measures of 1/4, the first played three times, the other four times; followed by twice alternating 7/16 and 5/16 measures, the former played three times, the latter four times. (This mechanical maximization of repeating a single measure reaches a total of thirteen within the work.)

Silence plays an important role in this jumbo production. In one twenty-seven-measure segment, there are fourteen measures of silences that alternate with the sounds.

- ***Structures* for String Quartet (1951)**

Music wrapped in a dream state, within which some textural contrasts apply. However, even when the sounds are more active they are singularly lightweight.

Intense luminosities are absent in the closet impressionism that styles Feldman's piece. For six minutes not even slight conversion takes place. Every measure is in 3/8 meter, all in the same unmodified tempo. Throughout, the four muted instruments play minus any dynamic change from the instruction "soft as possible."

Feldman's piece consists of 317 measures. 78 of these have no sounds whatsoever, and 63 of the total contain but a single pitched sound.

An example of positive unpositiveness.

QUINTETS

- ***De Kooning* for Horn, Piano (alternating Celesta), Violin, Cello, and Percussion (Large Vibraphone, Chimes, Bass Drum, Medium Tenor Drum, and Antique Cymbals) (1963)**

Durations in this quintet are determined at the moment of playing. With the usual Feldman style of a minimum of attack in sounding the pitches, and with very low-zone dynamics, the main thrust is a shifting from one timbre to another. Combined timbres are of much less total. Michael Nyman has described the process beautifully in his monograph *Experimental Music*: "As the sound of one instrument fades and decays so another instrument takes over: a kind of slow-motion tag game."

- ***Instruments 1* for Alto Flute, Oboe, Trombone, Celesta, and Percussion (Timpani, Xylophone, Glockenspiel, Marimba, Vibraphone, Crotales, Chimes, Triangle, Cymbals, Wood Block, Temple Block, Side Drum, Tenor Drum, Bass Drum, Tam-tam, and Maracas) (1974)**

Gloved sounds, as customary with Feldman. These are divided into sustained qualities for the two winds and the single brass, a few of the same but mostly lightly punctuated chords for the celesta, with additional timbre decorations and fills by the percussion.

A type of ritornel occurs three times (the last of these just prior to the concluding three measures of the piece). It is defined by polyrhythmic–polymetric detail. Within over three hundred measures of quiescent music (there are no dynamic signs, simply minute crescendos and decrescendos that emerge from the sounds guided by the "extremely quiet" expression instruction) this textural triarchy is almost of exotic color.

(There are three other works in Feldman's *Instruments* series. Number two is for flute alternating alto flute and piccolo, oboe alternating English horn, clarinet alternating bass clarinet, trumpet, trombone, tuba, percussion, harp, piano, and double bass; number three is for flute, oboe, and percussion; and number four—subtitled *Why Patterns*— is for violin, piano, and percussion, with a second setting scored for flute alternating alto flute, piano, and percussion.)

- *Projections II* **for Violin, Cello, Flute, Trumpet, and Piano (1951)**

See above: Projections.

- *Three Clarinets, Cello, and Piano* **(1971)**

The title is not missing from the above heading. The instrumentation *is* the title.

A full flood of isolated static sounds marks Feldman's eight-minute piece. The dynamic level is, as expected from Feldman, mainly triple and quadruple *piano*. This music of quiescence occasionally has slight upward dynamic pushes, but these are like minute vibrations to the monosyllabic sounds. Within the total 173 measures there are but 3 measures of *fortissimo* (clarinets and cello at measures 29, 30, and 31).

Feldman's music has an unmethodical listing of sounds so widely diffused that they are of total imbalance. It is this imbalance that produces Feldman's formal balance.

- **Two Pieces for Clarinet and String Quartet (1961)**

Aleatoric documentation. The pitches are indicated, but once the initial sound of all five instruments is produced the players are in control of durations. Each instrument is given specified silences. Dynamics are indicated to be "very low throughout."

SEXTET

- *Durations V* **for Violin, Cello, Horn, Vibraphone, Harp, and Piano (alternating Celesta) (1961)**

See above: Durations.

- **Two Pieces for Six Instruments (Flute, Alto Flute, Horn, Trumpet, Violin, and Cello) (1956)**

The Feldman trademarks: a completely stationary dynamic of "very soft," and a completely fixed metrical state. The progressions are fragile, the plotting minimalistic, but this has no relationship to minimalist style. These two short pieces can be termed superintrospective music. No emotive agonies here, just the sounds themselves reflecting total asceticism.

SEPTETS

- *False Relationships and the Extended Ending* **for Violin, Cello, Trombone, Three Pianos, and Chimes (1968)**

There are two groups within this total septet. One consists of piano, violin, and trombone. The other comprises two pianos, cello, and chimes. The two groups are independent of each other. However, the static use of sound patterns (as in Feldman's other music, there are no perceptible melodic progressions), in Feldmanish sounds of choked vibration, makes it impossible to distinguish one group from the other.

The dichotomy continues in terms of time proportions. For the silences there are exact time lengths; for the timbre projections the durations are to be in free, slow time. As is standard with Feldman the dynamic level is gloved—"very low throughout."

- *For Frank O'Hara* for Flute, Clarinet, Violin, Cello, Piano, and Percussion (Two Players: Glockenspiel, Xylophone, Vibraphone, Chimes, Gong, Triangle, Two Snare Drums, Bass Drum, and Timpani) (1973)

Feldman's memorial piece (for O'Hara, the great New York poet who died after being struck by a car) is not for those who like their music strong and direct. Like almost all of Feldman's music, it is stated at an extremely low dynamic level, recognizable musical time is in absentia (time signatures are used but only for eye convenience; the music avoids pulse demarcation), pitches are arranged in abstracto, and sounds *as* sounds are the total construction. Since there is no dynamic pulse the emotive condition is found to exist completely in the intellectualization.

If one agrees with that viewpoint, the late Alfred Frankenstein's remark that Feldman was "the great monotonist of modern music" is unacceptable, even though that famous critic wanted this read as meaning "high praise."

- *I Met Heine on the rue Fürstenberg* for Flute (alternating Piccolo), Clarinet (alternating Bass Clarinet), Piano, Voice, Violin, Cello, and Percussion (Vibraphone, Tenor Drum, Chimes, Temple Block, Glockenspiel, Timpani, Wood Block, and Triangle) (1971)

Since Heine died in 1856 the initial reaction to the title is that Feldman's piece is descriptive of an open-air ghost visitation. No! This is simply another example of Feldman's habit of listing an enigmatic title that perversely misrepresents but colorfully draws attention. Feldman's choice of title came about while he

was in Paris, where, he relates, he found himself on the rue Fürstenberg early one morning. "I was thinking a lot about Heine because of my situation (I found myself more or less in voluntary exile for a few years). And then I was writing, and in the middle of the piece I just wrote down the title: *I Met Heine*." And thus, fantasizing turns into association.

I Met Heine is in Feldman's flat-surface style. There are contrasts, but they are restrained. The music is wrapped in a dream state, described by the tempo heading—not one of speed, but of mood: Very Quiet. And quiet it is, minus dynamic indications and with only a few crescendos.

Feldman's scoring dismisses linear agitation. The piano has only chords; the percussion is active, but it is not aggressive. The textless voice part includes tremolandos (confirming its instrumental demeanor). Special in the Feldman output is the use of doubling—in this case, the voice. Fourteen times this occurs (really extraordinary for this composer), and just before the conclusion, the fifteenth instance covers a four-measure span for voice doubled by vibraphone.

- *The Straits of Magellan* for Flute, Horn, Trumpet, Amplified Guitar, Harp, Cello, and Double Bass (1961)

Don't try to fathom the title. It is, like most of Feldman's, decorative—quite often an acknowledgment of a friend or an event (a backdoor method of dedication?).

The Straits is music in which the performers become creative participants; the pitches are unspecified, though the durations are. Register and choice of pitches are for the most part free, with occasional indications as to the zone to be used (high or low). Special timbral qualities are defined, such as flutter-tonguing and harmonics; the dynamics are to be, per the usual Feldman dictum, "very low throughout."

NONET

- *Projections V* for Three Cellos, Three Flutes, Trumpet, and Two Pianos (1951)

See above: Projections.

Felix, Václav (1928–)

DUOS

- **Sonatina for Violin and Piano, Op. 20**

A programmatic tinge covers the middle movement, a variationally developed conception that was the result of impressions Felix obtained while walking across snow-covered land. Within the music is a fifty-measure quasi cadenza for the violin. (It may be cut if so desired.) Sonata form is used in the first movement; rondo form in the last. Chordal smash is basic to the latter.

- **Sonatine for Double Bass and Piano, Op. 1**

Felix's Op. 1 was begun in 1950, completed the following year, and totally revised in 1959. It is a music strong in both tonality and melodic substances.

March contours are disclosed in the F-major first movement. The E-major tonality of the second movement enriches its light dance aspects. Nice syncopative twists, juicy thirds, and some birhythmic combinations all brace the final movement in the F-major home tonality.

Distinctive scoring for the string instrument aids the coloristic effect. These include pizzicatos in the first movement, perfect-fifth pedal points in the middle movement, and high-tessitura sections in the final movement.

TRIO

- **Trio No. 2 in C Major for Violin, Cello, and Piano, Op. 5**

Felix appreciates the traditional law of four-movement design in his piano trio, written in 1956. The thrusting ascent of the initial theme's shape helps personalize the first movement, with the second theme, formed by conjunct movement interfused in two places with a span of a fourth, just as positive in its identity.

A compact ternary slow movement includes instrumental give-and-take; the initial theme is scored for the violin, in the recapitulation the theme is reannounced by the piano. Deprived of its chromatic gear and its asymmetry, the third movement would have been a polka. Ostinato patterns support the Presto finale.

Fellagara, Vittorio (1927–)

OCTET

- **Octet for Wind Instruments (Flute, Oboe, Clarinet, Bassoon, Horn, Two Trumpets, and Trombone) (1953)**

Fantasy detail, stuffed with chromatic shapes, sonorously integrated with the two combined quartets: one of woodwind makeup, the other of brass. There is as much action in the slow movement as there is in the first movement (Allegro moderato). A "Military March" completes the work. It runs a bit pompously, but not in strict meter. Plenty of trills help stimulate the contents.

NONET

- **Serenata for Chamber Group (Flute, Clarinet, Bass Clarinet [or Bassoon], Percussion [Three Cymbals, Three Drums, and Three Temple Blocks], Piano, Two Violins, Viola, and Cello) (1960)**

(This work is performable either in a nine-instrument setting or by multiple strings. In the latter instance the totals are to be four each of violin 1, violin 2, viola, and cello.)

Fellagara's opus has all the earmarks of the fractioned-fractured-rhythm and intervals-out-of-their-sockets dodecaphonic school, but it will be found that his total organization (not only of pitch but of dynamics, durations, color, and register) has jelled into emotional sense. Of course, no sentimentality is left for Tchaikovskian thinkers. That Fellagara's music is of an unsentimental type does not bring disfavor. (Performance time: eight minutes.)

Fenigstein, Victor (1923–)

DUO

- *Vortragsstück in Form von vier kurzen Berichten (Recital Piece in the Form of Four Short Statements)* **for Flute and Piano**

Expressionistic moods, with a sense of violence hanging over some of the proceedings. Fenigstein's four-part *Vortragsstück* has a performance time of 5 1/2 minutes. In that short span of time there are heavy harmonic punches, chromatic jabs, and colorful sparring. All these total aesthetic justification for the intense incidents of the work.

The entire first half of the second piece is exceedingly soft, with the flute totally concerned with harmonic tones. A figure of a broken triplet followed by a broken quintuplet appears in most of the measures of the third piece. Throughout, the dynamic indicators are minutely defined, and many are of successive dramatic difference.

TRIO

- *Seven Miniatures* **for Flute (or Oboe or Clarinet), Cello, and Piano**

Fenigstein's *Sette Miniature* are like fugitive sketches from which a stream of creative consciousness becomes operative. While each piece is balanced by its individual mood, no squarely measured forms are used. Each of the seven pieces is continuous and firmly sustained in its setting.

The character of each piece is explained, parenthetically, in the tempo/expression headings. In the first piece (Molto teneramente) the rhythmic situation of the music partially eradicates the "tenderly" definition. Number two (furtivamente) relies on surreptitiously disjunct short phrases, rhythmically disjunct as well. The third piece (allegramente burlesco) compares fast figures with spread ones. Number four (Molto grave) begins with dramatic decisiveness and then shifts into scherzo character.

In the fifth of the set (non espressivo, molto uguale), save for a three-measure matter of trills in *fortissimo*, everything is at a *pianissimo* level, which is decidedly expressive in its equal apportionment. The sixth miniature is termed Con cuore ardente. The music's "passionate heart" is shown by antiphony, explosive minute phrases, and metrical unrest (one measure is set in 9/8, divided into 2/4 + 3/8 + 1/4). The final piece is described as Molto semplice. The "simple" character applies to the short passages in octaves for the piano; the other instruments are much more active in their pitch contrast.

Fennelly, Brian (1937–)

QUINTETS

- *Evanescences* for Violin, Alto Flute, Clarinet, Cello, and Tape (1969)

Electronically generated material combines with a quartet consisting of paired winds (alto flute and clarinet) and strings (violin and cello). Interplay of the tape music with the instruments, as well as both units heard alone, provides the music's environment. Naturally, music of this type doesn't live in a diatonically furnished household.

By the action and play-on and play-off of the musical characters, Fennelly's finely crafted piece can, in a sense, be considered as chamber theater totally concerned with sound.

- **Wind Quintet (1967)**

Twelve-tone organization, detailed by extremely rhapsodic formal totality. Especially potent are the relationships of changing speed ratios and the simultaneous different tempos.

Fennelly has indicated that "the musical gestures incorporate more 'direct' configurations associated with past music, injecting moments of reminiscence or tinges of nostalgia, as well as those which project the complex energies of today. In general, linear, timbral, or dynamic considerations predominate over the projection of harmonic elements, which are essentially static."

Ferenczy, Oto (1921-)

QUARTET

- **Music for Four String Instruments (Two Violins, Viola, and Cello) (1947)**

Music the result of interest in the styles of Stravinsky and Bartók. (Some of this Czech's compositions also show the influence of Schoenberg and Webern.) This work was written in memory of Bartók (it was revised much later, in 1973).

The opening Sonata is developed from the contrastive point of compact and large phrase lengths. Movement two is an Intermezzo that strongly typifies Bartókian colorations, beginning with the opening, which combines arco, pizzicato, and col legno over a sixteen-measure length together with asymmetrical order. The imagery is sharp and severely contrasted in the Fantasie. A music of good fiber and colorfully scored without special effects.

Ferguson, Howard (1908–)

DUOS

- **Four Short Pieces for Clarinet (or Viola) and Piano, Op. 6**

A miniature in the chamber music field. The largest of the four sections is just a bit over fifty measures in length, but size is no determinant of value. Just because Ferguson's pieces lack substantial development, does not mean they cannot be considered strong music. The actual magic of these conceptions is conveyed swiftly, each brought to a focus and, therefore, of clear image.

Romantic vision shows in all four pieces. In the Prelude, very slight imitations remove staticness from the continuous arpeggiated flow.

The Scherzo is fast, a bagatelle representative of the form. Imitations also abound in the undulating scene of the Pastoral, precisely beamed rhythm in the final Burlesque.

- **Sonata No. 1 for Violin and Piano, Op. 2**

Music of romantic expression, but without any of the fussiness of that school. The outer movements are, respectively, sonata designed and fantasy impelled. Although the final movement is marked Quasi fantasia, it is not a loose assortment of material but a resurvey of materials that appeared in the two previous movements: Molto moderato and Allegro furioso. The latter is certainly a most interesting music, defining a fast-tempo, hearty and hardy rabid scherzo representative.

- **Sonata No. 2 for Violin and Piano, Op. 10**

The novelty of this Irish-born composer's music is its essential lack of experimentation. The clear directions and purposes of his output are certainly proof of creative health.

There are Brahmsian reminders (but only in summation, not technical resemblances). Ferguson's work has the 6/8 drive of Brahms's D-minor violin and piano sonata; its Adagio is a modern counterpart of that work's slow movement. The lyrical impulses and the engaging rhythm make this Sonata its 20th-century memoir.

All three movements employ a half step for the start of their themes (compositional cohesion that might mark the composer as one endeared to chromatics, but Ferguson is not). The first two descend; the last ascends. Thus, the theme of the second movement is a reply to that of the opening movement. The lyric secondary theme of the first movement is related to that used in the last movement. This integration is a prime essential of the highly compact formation of the work.

- ***Three Sketches* for Flute and Piano, Op. 14**

Fine atmosphere, clear detail, and a succinct approach. The first of the set has calm flow; the second is slower in tempo yet more active in its presentation of detail. The charm of the work reaches its greatest pertinency in the third piece (Con moto), which is based on a Hindu melody: "Koyaliňya bole ambuvaň" ("Cuckoos Sing in the Mango Tree"). And sing they do, with the familiar descent of a minor third, included in neatly smooth asymmetric arrangement.

OCTET

- **Octet for Clarinet, Bassoon, Horn, Two Violins, Viola, Cello, and Bass, Op. 4**

Ferguson's Octet matches the instrumentation of Schubert's famous eight-instrument work. It can certainly stand next to that masterpiece, what with its completely alive, natural, and flexible expression, splendid thematic identity, and richness of tonality.

Movement one is derived from the prime clarinet theme that begins the work. This theme is reintroduced, with different background, in the concluding part of the final movement. Motivic detail and syncopative adjuncts are the principal elements in the second movement (Scherzo). A flowing Andantino serves as the slow movement. The finale has the same saltarello punch that is found in the concluding movement of Mendelssohn's *Italian* Symphony. For relationship to this part of quadruple-meter material (Allegro feroce, to be played molto marcato) there is just as forceful duple-pulse data. A bit of lyricism creeps into the movement, but by far this is music with the throttle wide open.

(Ferguson composed his Octet in 1933. In 1948 he produced a Serenade for Chamber Orchestra, noted as "after the Octet, Op. 4.")

Fernandez, Oscar Lorenzo
(1897–1948)

DUO

- *Três Invenções—Seresteiras (Three Inventions—Serenades)* **for Clarinet and Bassoon (1944)**

Fernandez was not purely nationalistic in these three inventions patterned in the style of serenades. He effected a compromise between the basic restraint in music for two homophonic instruments (requiring contrapuntal feeding to stay in existence) and folk-style rhythmic spice. The possibilities of sonority and color are exploited further in the effective combination of two woodwinds—one high, the other low, one almost sweet and warm, the other more tonally desiccated and grayer in color. Indigenous folk rhythms are evident in the linear aspects of free counterpoint, which are, regardless of 20th-century impulse, tied to the garment strings of Bach. The year of composition, 1944, is a far point from the date that Bach conceived his invention form, but his spirit is present in most apparent fashion. Here, the very old musical world touches the new.

Each of the inventions is in three-part form. The first exploits the frictions of dissonant seconds, two clarinet flourishes separating the sections as well as the short coda. The first piece sings; the second is much more languid; while the third is a scherzo type.

Fernandez spread and nurtured his dedications, each being a personal acknowledgment to different Brazilians: the first to Villa-Lobos; the second to the musicologist Luiz Heitor Correa de Azevedo; and the last to another important writer on musical subjects, Renato Almeida.

TRIOS

- *Duas Invenções—Seresteiras (Two Inventions—Serenades)* **for Woodwind Trio (Flute, Clarinet, and Bassoon) (1944)**

A companion work to the set of *Three Inventions—Serenades* for clarinet and bassoon (*see above*) and composed in the same year. The play of the first is linear, as would be expected; but is contrasted to melodic indentions in lush thirds. An elaborate flute solo then makes homophony shove polyphony completely away. This attention to the flute is a doffing of the hat to the dedicatee—the musicologist, as well as flutist, Carleton Sprague Smith, once chief of the Music Division of the New York Public Library.

The second tripartite invention (similar to the individual movements of the companion set of pieces) is dedicated to another person—Mário de Andrade, the Brazilian musicologist. He doubtless appreciated, more than others, this excellent example of absolute polyphony, with far more dissonance than one is presumably permitted to use, if styled in classic counterpoint. But this is the 20th-century type, with more care given to seconds, sevenths, and fricative points than the mellifluous thirds and sixths of Bachian format.

- *Trio brasileiro (Brazilian Trio)* **[No. 2] for Piano, Violin, and Cello, Op. 32**

A difference exists between the composer who idealizes folk materials, using them as undertones that give insular flavor, and the composer who takes actual songs, dance tunes, and the like and directly quotes as well as develops them. The second category is demonstrated in this truly Brazilian chamber music composition. Even the themes, which are Fernandez's creation (five of the eight that propel the work are original), are of Brazilian inference. Thus, the major premise, an artistic effusion of folklore, is proven and not interfered with.

This was Fernandez's second work for the combination and was awarded first prize in a competition held by the Sociedad de Cultura Musical of Rio de Janeiro in 1924.

Cyclic technique is used. The first theme (heard at the beginning of the opening movement) makes thematic symmetry when it appears as a contrapuntal associate in the last movement. In addition, a third theme of the first section becomes transformed in rhythmic diminution in the Scherzo. The usual duo elements of a sonata *pronunciato* are available in movement one, by a vigorous minor mode theme and a lightly dancing one. Toward the end, the popular Brazilian tune "Sapo jururú" is used. A Canzone declaims first a song of the Ceará region of the composer's country, contrasted to an uneven rhythmic, slow-dance subject. The Scherzo is more a dance than a musical "joke." The transmuted theme (mentioned previously) appears in distinctive colorful harmonies of quartal spacing. In the finale, the material is indigenous to the hilt, a theme of the countryfolk in the region of Cuyabá (Matto Grosso), bracing the form in a climactic, though short, movement.

QUARTET

- **String Quartet No. 2 (1946)**

No restrictive formal orthodoxy applies. In every movement themes are compared, with episodes lined in, and then the comparison begins again. Movement one is typical. A short chordal introduction is developed in agitated tempo, followed by an interlude and a Scherzoso section. The introduction and agitated parts are restated, linked to the Scherzoso, now developed into a Quasi fuga. Some episodic data follows, and then introduction and agitated material are heard for the third time, succeeded by a cross-accented three-voices-against-one

final part, derived from the Scherzoso.

Triple sections mark the second movement, restated in the second part with slight changes. Rondo outline marks movement three, the material inculcated with folk-derived themes. The method of steady divisional statements applies to the Presto finale. A good amount of tutti rhythmic blocking is used. The concluding twenty-five measures reconfirms this.

QUINTET

- **Suite for Quintet of Wind Instruments (Flute, Oboe, Clarinet, Horn, and Bassoon), Op. 37**

All nationalistic music has its specific identity, its musical visiting card—the polka of the Czechs, the waltz of the Viennese, the jig of the British. The Brazilians have, akin to other countries, various rhythmic plans in their songs and dances. One is especially predominant, the modinha, a moderate sentimental song with a rubbery rhythm, mainly evident in groups of short–long–short sounds within one pulse. Such infiltration is used in the impressionistic-Brazilianistic quality of the opening movement of this quintet. This movement (as well as the other three) is titled, but the titles are less programmatic and more statements of mood (implied impressionism). The first is called "Pastoral Twilight in the Jungle." The technique employed vacillates between the bedding of French style and the cover of Brazilian embroidery. There are, as well, some jungle-bird fripperies in this semipastiche.

The short fugue that follows is for four voices (strictly woodwind color with the horn eliminated). Its subtitle, "Sacy-Péreré," is described as "a little supernatural being who appears in the jungle at evening, according to a Brazilian folk legend." The diminutive character makes the fugue take on a very gay face, far from the visage of most such contrapuntal expositions.

An unstated folk tune is quoted in the "Chanson—Song of the Dawn," and the work ends with a Presto in scherzo fashion ("Morning Gaiety"), including brilliantly stated and excited rhythms.

Ferneyhough, Brian (1943–)

DUOS

- *Coloratura* **for Oboe and Piano (1966)**

Do not expect the stereotyped ornamental documentation because of the title. Ferneyhough's piece has all the makin's: rapid passages and runs, trills and roulades, and multibravura. But these are not connected to tonal, carefully balanced melodic materials. The floridity is put to service for dismembered athematic lines, rhythmic splintering, and fractional phrasing.

There are eleven connected sections. The stylistic point is akin to the freest type of variation, but standard variational processes are totally absent. *Coloratura* is a set of peripatetic dissections that can be classified as variations minus a theme.

- *Four Miniatures* **for Flute and Piano (1965)**

Ferneyhough instructs the performers to obtain a "high degree of flexibility." With that the objective is to be "a continually fluctuating nervous intensity."

The twelve-tone generative ingredients to obtain this are made available through a variety of fixed and unfixed notation, multitudinous quick-change dynamic arrangements, and timbral distinctions (including glissandos, flutter-tonguing, vibrato differences, etc.). Compared to Ferneyhough's twelve-tone music, Schoenberg's sounds creamy smooth.

QUARTETS

- **Second String Quartet (1980)**

Like his earlier work for string quartet (*see below: Sonatas* for String Quartet), Ferneyhough's shorter quartet is hyperexpressionistic. Its resemblance to *Sonatas* is found in its density of material and the frenetic activity within each pulse, which in turn is exceedingly varied and fractured to form secondary pulse designs. None of the linear detail (all of it of super specificness) is decorative. With full equality, each pitch forms a part of the total fabric.

Ferneyhough's style is to organize, as he has stated, "a multitude of intersecting constructive and destructive currents." By "destructive" he means the freeing of material for reformulation and, thereafter, further reformulation—thus, a constant development.

Included in this controlled expressionistic fantasy are microtones, degrees of vibrato, and several forms each of col legno, pizzicato, and glissando. The instructions are numerous and meticulous. (One example: "From bar 156 onward begin all lower-string, double-stop glissandi 'sul tasto'; thereafter make a continuous transition to 'col leg. tratt' whilst remaining 'sul tasto' so that 'pure' wood [no hairs!] is reached at the moment this type of material ceases.") The result provides a decisive vitality to the sounds themselves. All of this restricts performance only to super-singular quartet teams.

- *Sonatas* **for String Quartet (1967)**

A huge conception of twenty-four movements of assorted size. Without considering the multitudinous metrical shifts, the total measures of these movements range from the minute: three and six; to those of medium length, such as eighteen and twenty-six; to the largest, with fifty-one as an example. The amount of silence between the movements is precisely indicated. Thus, between parts three and four, two seconds; between four and five, none; between six and seven, a mere breath; between sixteen and seventeen, three seconds; etc. (The total performance time is about three-quarters of an hour.)

With the constant evulgations of the quartet's stylistic demeanor it is simply impossible to realize the finalization of one movement and the beginning of the next. Purposefully so, since this meets the composer's objective that the effect of the work be "one long continuous movement." Nonetheless, to be identified in various places is a four-pitch shape and three cadenzas that can clue in the listener as to which section of the twenty-four is being presented. The viola begins movement six alone, and though the other instruments then join it, the tenor voice remains prominent, emerges alone again, and in the concluding part acts soloistically against the other voices. Movement twelve is practically for the two violins alone. When the viola and cello enter in the latter part of the movement they are defined in either a sustained or accompanimental manner. Movement eighteen is totally for the unaccompanied cello.

Ferneyhough's music totals a superfetation of events and fragments that proceed simultaneously on a vertical and horizontal basis. There is a certain amount of total serialistic procedures included that merge into or are smashed against free-loaded expressionistic devices: various produced pizzicatos; percussive bow attacks; glissandos and portamentos; and an array of harmonics, tremolandos, and bowing varieties. In all, Ferneyhough's *Sonatas*, with its immenseness of action in regard to all elements and with its vast coloristic displays, has a convulsive energy that bursts out and away from any specific formal boundaries.

SEXTET

- *Prometheus* **for Wind Instruments (Flute [alternating Piccolo], Oboe, English horn, Clarinet in B-flat [alternating Clarinet in E-flat], Horn, and Bassoon) (1967)**

Sharply detailed fragmentation, micro sound chips, and spidery and flowery assimilations constitute Ferneyhough's wind sextet. This style is a far cry from the chirpy French works for winds by such as Ibert and Milhaud or the caustic German types by such as Hindemith and Fortner. Because of the linear jaggedness and extreme panchromaticism a reminder of Schoenberg's wind quintet (Op. 26) will come to mind, but Ferneyhough's is far more colorful and much more freely organized and developed.

The music is marked off by cadenzas, and these are so placed as to provide structural balance. The composition begins with fluctuating tempos on the slow side (the instrumental action is, however, the very opposite). A long B-flat-clarinet cadenza follows and prefaces a section of slightly faster tempos, again of constantly changing denomination. At its conclusion there is a substantial cadenza for piccolo followed by a return to the metronomically slower-paced units. The conclusion is a surprise, in the form of an extended cadenza for E-flat clarinet. Obviously, there is a secondary balance provided by the colors of the cadenza triptych.

OCTET

■ *Funérailles (Obsequies)* for Seven Strings and Harp (alternating Crotales) (Two Violins [Violin 2 alternating Stones], Two Violas [Viola 2 alternating Maraca], Two Cellos [Cello 2 alternating Claves], and Bass [alternating Wood Block]) (1980)

The string septet is divided into two groups: one violin, one viola, and one cello (termed "solo trio") and a "tutti quartet" of violin, viola, cello, and bass. (Regardless of terminology all the instrumental forces are equal.) The "tutti quartet" plus harp amplifies its role by playing percussion instruments. Placement of the string instruments is to be made so that each group's individuality is realized without stressing antiphonal arrangement.

As usual with Ferneyhough the textures are heavy, the air thick with complex sounds, the rhetoric forceful and not flowing out with tonal milk and diatonic honey. The objective of this compositional involvement is not a public ritualistic celebration of mourning but (quoting from Ferneyhough's preface) "channeling the entire associative complex into an imaginary—a mythic—dimension. A rite taking place behind a curtain, or in the far distance." As usual the sonorous complexes are as exceedingly special as they are complex. Included are quarter tones, pitch inflections, very light bow pressure, half harmonics obtained by combining lowered bow contact for use over the instrument's fingerboard, and vibrational degrees ranging from zero to exceedingly intense.

Funérailles is scored in two separate versions. The material in the first setting is described as "dictating its contextual disposition," and in the second setting particular elements are separated, broken down, and reworked. This two-dimensional concept is not to be considered as either movements to be performed in succession or as a pair of distinctly different compositions. Both versions must be played but separated by performance of some other music. Ferneyhough stresses that neither version may be performed separately.

Fernström, John (1897–1961)

TRIO

■ Trio for Strings (Violin, Viola, and Cello), Op. 90

Romantically traditional but impeccably constructed and efficiently organized. With this Swedish composer's music one finds solidly based information rather than innovative guidance.

Nonetheless, no scholasticism. There is a keen coherence between homophonic and polyphonic style in the first movement. Short phrase structuring marks the slow movement. The Scherzo follows rule-book form but is diverting with the use of cross accentuation. The vigorous Finale is strongly colored by col legno ostinatos.

Ferrabosco, Alfonso (c. 1575–1628)

QUARTET

■ Fantasia for String Quartet

Famous as a composer of music for masques, Ferrabosco was also one of the most prominent composers of music for the viols. For that medium he wrote no fewer than forty-seven fantasias, most of which remain in manuscript. With the obsolescence of the viols, the only option for performance of the richly polyphonic music is on modern string instruments.

Ferrari-Trecate

Ferroud

This Fantasia was made so available in an edition by Sydney Beck, transcribed from a manuscript partbook in possession of the New York Public Library.

Ferrari-Trecate, Luigi (1884–1964)

QUARTET

- **Quartet for Strings in 3 Tempi (Two Violins, Viola, and Cello)**

Three tempos and three contrastive realizations. But there is total stylistic unity. Ferrari-Trecate's string quartet is tonally bound and mildly chromatic, a traditional concept that, nevertheless, holds the interest.

The first movement is sonata structured, prefaced by a sustained imitative statement and concluded by dynamic speedy music. Flaming contrapuntalism is the driving passion of this movement. The Adagio has linear vitality, but of the type developed from ornamentalized harmony. Color is the poetic release of this music. The first and extremely short third parts are muted, the second section the reverse, with the composer stressing that there be a marked difference in timbre, additional to the built-in contrast already provided by muted and unmuted tone. The third movement is a Presto a canone. Canonic and other imitative information never cease to be supplied in this huge movement, not for a single one of its 577 measures, all in 3/8 ("one-in-a-measure") speed.

Ferroud, Pierre-Octave (1900–36)

DUOS

- **Sonata in A for Cello and Piano (1932)**

Extroverted music (properly styled, purposefully or not, to validate the dedication of the opus to Prokofiev). The open textures are uncommon to Ferroud's other music, the motility of the lines perfectly balanced. And most of the lines in the first movement (Capriccio) avoid chords in both instruments. In movement two, a flowing Intermezzo, this is even more the case. There are 108 total measures. In 9 of these the cello has a sustained pedal in fifths, and in the same number of measures the piano has some chords; otherwise there are three clear lines: one for the cello, two (soprano and bass) for the piano. A snappy Rondo completes the piece.

- **Sonata in F for Violin and Piano**

Vertical aspects applied to linear writing occupied this talented composer. His music can be appreciated only if acknowledgment is given the doctrine of free tonality working its way around a basic center. Ferroud was a neoromantic in that he thickened the texture with chordal movement, was more disposed toward the harmonic combination than the polyphonic. The rhythm is free, with shifting flux, but not nervous; everything spins and spreads in the romantic sense of phraseology.

The slow movement combines a purely simple melody with ostinated rhythms that move hand in hand with this composer's penchant for designing densities as his backgrounds. Only the final movement (Rondo) becomes less opaque. It is in scherzo style with vacillating meters, has Bachian clarity in its middle section.

TRIOS

- *Pas redoublé (Doubled Step)* for Two Pipes in D and Piano (1934)

Not only march pace here, not only rhythmically marked measures, but doubled music all the way for the pipes, which, save for a half beat here and there, are rhythmically combined, first note to last. No doubt one of the peppiest pieces ever produced for the bamboo instrument.

- **Trio in E for Oboe, Clarinet, and Bassoon (1934)**

Mystical coincidence affords an interesting sidelight to this composition. Ferroud had dedicated his wind trio to fellow composer Filip Lazar. Lazar visited Ferroud's grave, contracted pneumonia, and, as a result, died less than three months after Ferroud had been killed in an automobile accident.

Many compositions indicate a tonality, but one must not always expect the major or minor definition. The "in E" of Ferroud's Trio is simply a gravity point, only a small amount of nailed tonality is displayed within active rhythmics and fat lines (thinned only by the fact that, even in combination, three wind instruments do not create thick sonorities). Ferroud's wind trio is free tonally, bound texturally. The instruments are *en bloc* in practically every measure of the three movements. The last of these is a quasi tarantella, a little lightened in horizontal movement, but in the vertical sense solidified as usual.

QUARTET

- **Quartet in C for Two Violins, Viola, and Cello (1936)**

Marked "in C," but that tonality is not reached until the second theme of the first movement. And even there it twists in and around the subdominant area as well. Among Ferroud's teachers was Florent Schmitt, and this opening movement is especially styled with the harmonic activity favored by Schmitt.

Ferroud's string quartet has precise textural differences set in balanced arrangement. Movements one and three (Allegro and Grave) retain a density throughout. Movements two and four (Scherzo vivace and Allegro giusto) are lean.

Fesca, Alexander Ernst (1820-49)

SEPTET

- **Septet No. 1 in C Minor for Oboe, Horn, Violin, Viola, Cello, Double Bass, and Piano, Op. 26**

Clear music and nicely colored. There are four movements. The first of these has been described as having a brilliancy similar to Weber. The central movements are an Andante in E-flat and a vivid Scherzo. Coloristic recitative passages are included in the finale. All of the aspirations of balanced designs are met in the first of Fesca's two septets; the inspirations are professional, even if not awe-inspiring.

Fesch, Willem de (1687–1761)

DUO

- **Sonata in D Minor for Cello and Basso Continuo, Op. 13, No. 4**

Interesting chromatic turns in the bass lines of this Flemish organist's duo. A broad Largo is followed by an Allemanda. This dance, which first appeared in the mid-16th century, is registered in its usual duple pulse, but it stands here in allegro rather than in the more usual moderate pace. A pair of Minuets complete the work, with the first one in D minor, the other in D major, and with the repetition of the initial dance serving for the regulatory da capo. The chromaticism is considerably lessened in this three-part finale.

Festing, Michael Christian (c. 1680–1752)

DUOS

- **Sonatas for Violin and Basso Continuo, Op. 4, Nos. 2 and 3**

According to the celebrated English music historian Charles Burney, Festing's sonatas showed him to be a composer with but "a feeble hand, little genius for composition, and but a shallow knowledge of counterpoint." However, another celebrated English music historian, Sir John Hawkins, thought otherwise, indicating that, particularly in music composed for the violin (Festing's instrument), "the nature and genius whereof he perfectly understood, he had but few equals."

The truth lies in between these verdicts. With only a figured bass to work from (sensitively realized by the editor, Gwilym Beechey), whatever counterpoint is heard is Beechey's. The violin writing is finely balanced, and where it is in two voices (movement one of Op. 4, No. 3) it is apt and colorfully sonorous.

The first of these duo sonatas is in C minor and has four movements; the second of the pair is in E major and has five movements. The tempo sequence is slow–fast in alternation, with an additional fast movement, an Aria with two variations, serving as the fifth movement of the second work. Certainly, the slow–fast–slow–fast–slow order of the first movement of Op. 4, No. 3 shows a contrastive unity that gives Festing creative credits, contrary to Burney's statement.

The third part of Op. 4, No. 2 is but a two-measure Adagio. The editor suggests amplification and offers a five-measure preliminary for that purpose.

Fetis, François-Joseph (1784–1871)

DUO

- **Five Sonatinas for Horn and Cello (or Bassoon)**

It is as a theorist, historian, and critic that this Belgian musician has an important place in musical history. Very little of his output as a composer remains in print, and what is available is hardly ever performed. Of the chamber music this set of compact pieces, first published in 1981 by Gérard Billaudot, warrants attention.

Each of the five pieces consists of a single, compact exposition. Thus: a twenty-two-measure piece, Allegretto non troppo, in cut time (number one); a twenty-measure total for the second of the set, Andante, in quadruple time; etc. All the pieces are in F major to accommodate the F horn.

Fetler, Paul (1920–)

DUO

- **Three Pieces for Violin and Piano (1952)**

Music invested with classical clarity and rhythmical resolution. The latter does not, by its pulsatile play, disturb the former but enhances it.

Movement one is titled "Essay." Its sentences move within duple and triple meter but with fluidity. The Air is colored by concentrated spans in the violin as compared to the spatial widths that mark the piano's part. In the outer sections of the Caprice the expressivity is found in the byplay of equal pulse measures (2/4) as compared to uneven ones (5/8). The central part of the piece has no such inner punctuation, moving steadily, at a slower and heavier pace, in straightforward 2/4 time. The scoring is of the open type (high piano far above the violin for example) with plenty of quartal harmonies.

Fibich, Zdenko (Zdeněk) (1850–1900)

DUOS

- **Romanza for Violin and Piano, Op. 10**

Title notwithstanding, Fibich's Romanza falls within sonatina dimensions. All themes are presented equally by both instruments. Substantial textures in this full romantic conception, but a sensitive and telling balance is obtained by beginning and concluding the piece in *pianissimo*.

- **Sonatina for Violin and Piano, Op. 27**

Fibich composed this Sonatina when he was 18; it was published 18 years later. The last report is that the duo has been reprinted more than a dozen times, certainly an imposing statistic. This success stimulated the publisher to bring out a transcription for viola and piano.

Movement one is in D minor, but the coda is totally in the opposite mode. A gentle G-major slow movement precedes the finale, which dances gaily through D major and is deftly decorated with grace notes.

TRIO

- **Trio in F Minor for Piano, Violin, and Cello**

Fibich, a most distinguished composer, produced more than six hundred works, but, considering such a total, not many in the chamber music medium. In comparison to Smetana and Dvořák he stands as a relatively minor Bohemian nationalist. His first chamber music work (and his only composition for piano trio) was composed at the age of 22, when his bent for the indigenous spirit was still uncultivated. The Trio (published without an opus number) is a full romantic expression, simple in presentation.

The slow movement is extremely short, consisting of but thirty-seven measures, a mild miniature but with telling moderate chromaticism in its harmony. This movement separates two fast ones. The first of these is based on a hurtled motive that skips vigorously through the fifth and octave of the key, plus a Schmannesque lyrical, second subject. The last movement is quasi modal, bright, with a recollective imprint inserted from the first movement. The nationalist pot is still not at a boil in this piano trio, but it is an excellent example of this composer's warmth and musical product.

QUARTET

- **Quartet for Violin, Viola, Cello, and Piano, Op. 11**

A richly scored work of three movements, which the Czech writer on music Josef Bartoš (1887–1952) termed Fibich's *chef d'oeuvre*. There is no doubt that it deserves a high place in piano quartet literature, especially for its thematic clarity and formal strength.

Ascending push marks all five themes of the work. In the first movement the initial theme in E minor is announced by the piano. The second theme, in G major, is first presented by the violin, its part indicated con passione, though the general expression instruction is dolce (sweet). A single theme in A major serves for the Tema con variazioni second movement, consisting of eight parts and a coda. Again, the piano presents the first theme of the third movement, and then the strings together detail the second theme. As in the opening part of the Quartet the keys for these are respectively E minor and G major. A subtle scoring matter is to be noted here—the kind that obtains a minute, sensitive point of balance. The second theme of the third movement is stated under a pedal trill in the piano, while the quartet's opening theme is announced below a tremolo plus sustained pedal point in the strings.

The final part of the third movement represents all these themes, beginning with a segment of the variation's subject. A direct matter of balance is obtained in this instance by the cyclic conclusion.

QUINTET

- **Quintet in D Major for Violin, Clarinet, Horn, Cello, and Piano (or Two Violins, Viola, Cello, and Piano), Op. 42**

Fervent Czech romanticism is displayed in this Quintet, originally scored to combine string, wind, brass, and keyboard instrumental colors. The second setting (substituting a second violin for the clarinet and a viola for the horn) was evidently made at the request of the publisher for commercial reasons. Certainly a more poetic result is produced by the initial setting.

There are four movements: the first is in sonata form, followed by a Schumannesque Largo, a Scherzo with two Trios preceding the recapitulation, and a Finale. The concluding part of the slow movement, a Maestoso statement, forms the basis (in a freely stated manner) for the concluding section of the Finale; the tempo there is Grandioso; the related section thus serves as a binding element.

The score, published by Editio Supraphon, was edited by Antonín Pokorný and Karel Šolc. There is a lengthy preface, unsigned but presumably by these men. They strongly suggest there is a program for the work, though "not directly authorized." For whatever value it may have, they state the first movement is "something like" a self-portrait of Fibich. The second movement is supposedly a musical portrait of Anežka Schulzová, with whom Fibich had a long affair, leaving his second wife to live with the poetess. Movement three is "a dialogue between [the] two lovers," and the concluding part has "erotic coloring." The evidence offered for all this is quite flimsy. One prefers to listen to Fibich's colorful and mature composition without giving heed to these suppositions and the editors' closing purplish statement that the Quintet "is a unique artistic medallion of the love of Zdeněk Fibich and Anežka Schulzová."

Ficher, Jacobo (1896–1978)

Ficher is an example of the musical evolutionary process that has taken place in many Latin American countries; namely, by a musician's birth and education in a European country (Ficher came from Russia to Argentina in 1923). This makes possible the placement of the old techniques into the musical stream. But at least several generations must pass before such amalgamation can be filtered down to a clear, national musical speech, or as pure a strain as might denote a nation's music. However, Ficher is a modernist. He has spoken with a Russian tongue, and his Hebraic ancestry shows in some of his works. National forms are rarely drawn on for his resources.

DUO

- **Three Pieces for Violin and Piano**

Nationalistic touch is present in the second piece of the set: "Canción de Cuna." The mood is intensified by maintaining the unyielding length of the four-measure phrases of the song, the repetitive rhythmic support, and the violin's muted timbre. The Allegro festivo is powered by detached passage data (sometimes these are weighted by consecutive fifths), plus chordal pomp and repetitive circumstance. In close respect the Preludio (the first piece) is similarly "festivo," with its proclamatory range of expression.

TRIO

- **Sonatina for Piano, Trumpet, and Alto Saxophone, Op. 21**

The odd combination in this trio, of a trumpet and saxophone with piano, is not used at all for color individuality. Triple timbre distinction is called on only to accentuate the linear writing, which is freely dissonant in a semirhapsodic style.

The music is formed by means of nonconcentricities of dissonant textures, in a "three-movement-in-one" design. The first movement is fast, and the composer does not frown (nor do others who write in a free, vigorous style of musical frictions) on the building of chords by seconds and fourths, rather than euphonious thirds and sixths. A short Lento in three-part form is followed by a Presto, in which alternating harmonic and contrapuntal sections occur in almost religious order. The counterpoint is in imitative style, but never strictly in set contrapuntal forms.

QUARTET

- **Quartet for Four Saxophones (Soprano, Alto, Tenor, and Baritone Saxophones)**

Regardless of aesthetic objectives, certain potentials must be utilized to obtain and realize balance in a musical composition. One or more may be stressed. Coherence by rhythmic weights is Ficher's choice in a work warmed by late-romantic-style tone combinations.

The dynamic force of rhythm clearly plots the quartet's story line. In the opening movement a dactyl (one long and two shorts) pattern

(a Bachian favorite) is contrasted with and opposed to an anapest unit of two shorts and a long, thereby complete affiliation since the later is a retrograde of the former. The spread of these into an equalized four sounds per pulse provides further affinity to the plan. Three-part form is used in the slow movement. Here, the simplest division of the quarter-note unit marks the outer divisions, a greater amount to denote the central section. (Tempo distinction follows suit.) Some slight harmonic counterpoint makes the compound duple-flung Scherzo flexible, with block chords affording contrast. In the finale the prime rhythmic manifestation is a triplet. Lesser totals per pulse are combined for tension or used separately for distinguishing the secondary theme of the design.

Though there are a large number of saxophone trios and quartets, conceived for the commercial marketplace, there are not too many solid and artistic examples, proper for the concert hall. Ficher's contribution is a worthy one. There is always the danger that an overburdened texture will result from combining similar instruments in ensemble. In his choice of compositional materials and their layout, Ficher has effectively avoided this.

Fickenscher, Arthur (1871–1954)

In certain respects Fickenscher is the American counterpart of the Czech Hába. For years Fickenscher experimented with the matter of pure intonation in contrast to tempered types and in 1912 culminated his labor by the invention of the Polytone. This instrument split the octave into sixty parts. While Fickenscher's music is practically unknown, the piano quintet discussed below is one of his best works, deserving of study and performance. It employs the use of nontempered pitch in connection with string instruments, partnered with the tempered, thus fixed, pitch of the piano.

Fickenscher's tonal dispositions are not as

absolute as Hába's measurements. The microtones are approximate, politely made rather than positively formed. They are divided into four forms: "somewhat higher" and "somewhat lower," together with "much higher" and "much lower." All these directions are to be followed in relation to the sounds measured off by half-step location in the twelve-part division of the octave.

QUINTET

- *From the Seventh Realm*: **Quintet for Piano, Two Violins, Viola, and Cello (1939)**

Nicolas Slonimsky has traced the background of this Quintet. It is thus described: Fickenscher's "major work was the *Evolutionary* Quintet, evolved from a violin sonata and an orchestral scherzo written in the 1890s; the manuscripts were burned in the San Francisco earthquake and fire of 1906; the musical material was then used from memory for a quintet for piano and strings, in 2 movements." The second movement, *From the Seventh Realm*, eventually became a separate work.

The plan of the work is the presentation of two principal themes that are freely developed. Although the quintet is formed by polyphonic continuity, Fickenscher's scoring does not result in thick-ordered sonority. The part writing is clear and of reward in establishing the many tempo changes of the quintet. The cello announces the first theme and the entire string group the second subject. While nontempered pitch is used very discreetly in ratio to the whole, it is employed where the melodic movement and scoring are such that the minute differences of pitch are heard clearly.

Although Fickenscher's use of nontempered tones is of relative and not exact measurement, the sounds are basically microtonal in quality. In result, they point more toward a color objective and not the complete reediting of the musical sound language that was Hába's microtonal goal. Fickenscher's sparse use of the microtones makes for ease of performance but still avoids truly breaking down the semitonal barrier. However, this does not interfere with the value of the quintet. Nor should one overlook the composer's idea in the matter of color. At the conclusion of the composition a second pianist is required to pluck the instrument's strings like a harp. If this is not feasible an ad lib scoring reassigns these sounds in the form of a string-instrument pizzicato. Again the goal is approached by a halfway measure, but one must grant Fickenscher his broad outlook and his creative courage, despite its restraint.

Field, John (1782–1837)

QUINTET

- **Quintet for Piano, Two Violins, Viola, and Cello**

Field's place in history as the composer who prefigured Chopin's style is just a bit in evidence in this composition. Practically the entire output of this Irish-born composer is for the piano (seven concertos, four sonatas, eighteen nocturnes, and so on), and, accordingly, the keyboard instrument is featured in the few chamber works he produced. Thus, for example: the First Divertissement in E is for piano and string quartet *ad lib* (italics mine). The same description pertains to a work titled *Le Midi Rondeau*, as well as the Sixteenth Nocturne. Actually, the only instrumentally full-scale composition is this A-flat-major piano quintet. Here, though, there is but a single movement (Andante).

The thematic material is announced by the string quartet alone; the piano follows, also in solo form, slightly elaborating the previous material; the strings then re-enter, again without the piano. This type of alternation is maintained as the music is developed in free concerto form.

Filippi, Amedeo de (1900–)

(Filippi also published compositions under the name of Philip Weston.)

DUOS

■ *Axioms* **for Two Clarinets**

A set of four pieces in twelve-tone style. Pithy conceptions (the performance times are, respectively 1:20, 1:20, 1:00, and 1:30). The logic is obtained mainly by motivic construction (for example: sixteenth-note patterns in the second piece; short–long rhythmic figures in the third). There are some repetitions and some partial imitations. A type of cool musical documentation.

■ *Bicinia dodecafonica* **for Two Trumpets**

Filippi bridges the centuries with his title choice. Bicinium is a 16th-century term for a vocal composition in two parts; dodecafonica describes of course, the twelve-tone technique of the 20th century.

The only slow-paced section occurs in the first movement. It is constructed in tripartite form, with the outer sections moving in a deliberate pulse with the central part energetically contrasted. The other three movements are in the moderate-to-fast-tempo range. All of the opus displays a nicely inventive consideration of contrapuntalism.

■ **Prelude, Air, and Fugue for Two**
   Trumpets

A constant alternate tightening of the basic meter applies to the Prelude. It starts with triple-pulse total, then moves into a smaller duple total. This contrastive pairing occurs three more times, and then the music concludes in the initial trinally measured form. A tonally stylish, richly counterpointed Air (in adagio pace) is the central piece. A neoclassic pursuit of balance is fully obtained in the final Fugue. It has solid qualities, formal definition, and is fittingly written for the pair of brass instruments.

■ *Seven Modes* **for Two Flutes**

To clarify: Actually these seven are church modes on which Filippi chose to base his music. In the widest sense of the word, "mode" signifies an arrangement of pitches used as the fundament for a composition; thus there is a major mode, a minor mode, a whole-tone mode, etc.

The first piece of the set is "Dorian." This modal form has half steps between pitches two and three and six and seven. Here the tonic is on F-sharp (the scale thereby is equal to A major plus D-sharp). A secondary opposed line projects a bitonal result, formed on a consistent ostinato basis that the composer marks as "automatico." Movement two is "Lydian." The half steps in this case fall between pitches four and five and seven and eight. The mode is transposed here to start on G (the scale equal to G major plus C-sharp). (Similar procedures follow for the other modes.)

However, only one other mode is presented in total pristine form: the "Mixolydian" (movement four). Shifts from the mode appear in "Phrygian" (movement three). The other modes—"Aeolian" (movement five), "Locrian" (movement six), and "Ionian" (movement seven)—are each intertwined with a different key statement.

■ **Twelve Inventions for Violin and Cello**

While all twelve are, as usual, short, linear

pieces (the average is about twenty-seven measures in length), only two (numbers three and six) have an announcing voice answered by the same material. Little matter, since the form is not fixed.

Filippi's inventions are chromatically sharp, artistically acrid in their polyphonic travels. Color in the way of pizzicato is liberally applied; two of the set (numbers four and eleven) are totally presented in muted timbre.

TRIOS

■ *Corydon Suite* **for Flute, Clarinet, and Bassoon**

English dance tunes—eight of them, and totaling a ten-minute performance time—make up this suite for wind trio.

No harum-scarum tactics are applied to the tunes. Filippi lets them stand in their natural nicety and flow and tonalizes sensitively.

Numbers two and seven are in well-known forms, respectively, Rigadoon and Hornpipe. The others are "Maggot" (number one), "Cushion Dance" (number three), "The Spanish Lady" (number four), "Light o' Love" (number five) and "Sibel" (number six). The final piece is the allegretto-paced "Sir Roger de Coverley," the name of an old English dance tune, long used as the finale for a ball, and still in use.

■ **Serenade for Three Flutes**

Formal fidelity but not pedantic piousness. The shapes of the March, Scherzino, Pastorale, and Rondino are clear, colored by light chromaticism. There is a vivacity of rhythmic detail. In the Pastorale a murmuring effect is obtained by combining the second and third flutes birhythmically (triplets together with paired eighths).

QUARTETS

■ *March of the Little Tumblers* **for Woodwind Quartet (Flute, Oboe, Clarinet, and Bassoon)**

A short sketch depicting the "agile movements and flip-flops of midget acrobats." Cute certainly. Very effective encore material for light chamber music concerts.

■ *Quadrivium* **for Two Trumpets, Horn, and Trombone**

Filippi's title is the Latin term that defined one of the arrangements of the liberal arts in the medieval system of education. These arts were divided into two groups: the trivium (consisting of grammar, dialectic, and rhetoric) and the quadrivium (consisting of geometry, arithmetic, music, and astronomy).

A picturesque title, doubtless. But its use here is simply to indicate, as its translation, *Four Ways*, shows, a set of four pieces for the four brass instruments. The style is twelve-tone, the approach not rigid, the result effective.

Fine, Irving (1914–62)

DUO

■ **Sonata for Violin and Piano (1946)**

The prosody, the development scheme, and the essential tonal clarity of this duo sonata find their roots in Stravinsky. The neoclassical attitude of that composer renounced all posturing, and Fine was as true a disciple as one might find.

An introduction to the first movement is a foreshadowing of forthcoming matters—a section that is truly preambulistic and not just a warm-up. The descent of the first two sounds and the rhythmic figure that follows are the elements of the main theme: the violin's suave entrance, its antithesis. Tertial curvatures of the melodic lines are related to the harmonies that inclose them. There is a further element in the first movement that ties together the logistics of this superbly educated music. The stress points within phrases are formed from the intervallic span of a seventh, and this device is also used considerably in the movement that follows. Bridge passages, the structural joints so easily identified in classical-vintage music, are absent. Precise and definite tonality made such explanatory haltings (for they were time markings, in a sense) easily identifiable. Here, the flow is maintained, even though one idea moves to another. But the balanced contour of a full-scale sonata (in its broadest sense) is evident.

Variational technique is expounded in the second movement, including the tie-in of a return to the flowing cantabile theme by exactly reversing the colors; the violin now plays what the piano played before, and vice versa. Integration of the movements is formed whereby the second theme of movement one emerges as the principal idea of movement three. This is surrounded with the previous elements of intervallic sevenths en route (intensifying tonal stability by inner incitation) in toccatalike formality, energized by asymmetric changes. This is a music of bravura, free of the unessential or the bright lights of frothy entertainment.

TRIO

■ Fantasia for String Trio (1957)

Fine's Fantasia represents a hybrid of dodecaphonic technique applied to free tonality; the two meet successfully. The outer movements are in slow tempo, the first lyrical (Fine termed it a "kind of fugato"), the other starting freely imitative in style, shifting to a rhapsodic state in the middle, and concluding "with the same quiet reflective quality of its beginning."

The middle movement (marked Scherzo but of mordacious content) is nervous, driven by cross accents, an example of virtuosity in motival crisscross.

The composer told this writer that all the melodic and much of the harmonic data are derived from the opening viola statement. The passion that drives the music proves Fine's inspiration.

QUARTET

■ String Quartet (1952)

Twelve-tone technique essentially is not far removed from the architectural soundness that marks Beethoven's towering musical structures. The motival unfolding of the classic master is matched at its analytical peak (no emotional premise is being considered) by the unity and variety of serial procedure. Fine's quartet furnishes important evidence to support this statement.

His use of dodecaphonic technique takes on new meaning, for his twelve tones are clothed with the royal purple of classic design. And within his music there is the necessary freedom that must be enjoyed by good art, unless it is to be a mere laboratory report. On top of all this the quartet has a tonal center. The twain have certainly met and embraced each other! Fine's heady rhythms are not bounded by a serial blueprint; they hammer the spikes into the quadruple lines, strengthening and thereby clarifying the work as a whole.

Though these formal purposes would seem to be served by eclectic choice rather than true serial technique, the facts are the opposite. Fine's quartet has clear positiveness; it is his own music, exhibiting a codification of rare sensibility and sensitivity.

There are two movements; the first is a propulsive, stamping, rhythmic music with an upward leaping motival unit linking varying sections. As the lines move horizontally they become tied vertically with ostinatos. The principal secondary element gives contrast by slower speed, more relaxed quality, and chordal movement, mainly in three parts. The second movement is governed by recitative potentials. These are either tonally repetitive or of broad tutti declaration. Again contrast is quite determined—by tripartite movement of the upper voices supplemented with a tonally similar pattern within which the rhythmic design constantly changes. All elements within the structure are in sensitive balance as Fine's quartet moves down from its initial high-pointed dramatic proclamation until it reaches a sonorous recession at its conclusion.

QUINTETS

▪ Partita for Wind Quintet (1948)

Fine's Partita tends mainly to use this generic title in its truest meaning; although the word *partita* is used frequently to identify a miscellaneous group of movements in suite form and of that character, it actually means a set of variations. The first three and the last sections of this work are definitely in the variation category, while the penultimate part is only subconsciously related to the variation principle. Regardless, the five movements establish a specific unit in one stylistic groove, especially in the neoclassic manner, refined (if one may be permitted the pun) with crystal-clear workmanship and a neutral (black-white) viewpoint of instrumental colors. There is no attempt at establishing a basic timbre design; the instruments share equally in promulgating the essentials of the work. The organic instrumentation of the music's 18th-century ancestry is in direct opposition to any pictorial or decorative luxuriance.

The first movement is an Introduction and Theme, of rhythmic gaiety, contrasted with an expressive, long-spun legato theme. Movement two, titled simply Variation, is an embellished

development of the preceding section, related very closely—especially in the use of the intervallic scope of a seventh and ninth with which the theme was concerned. The Interlude that follows is choralelike, but is variational in that it digests the rhythmic and syncopative properties of the theme. Movement four is a Gigue, with the compound time characteristics of that dance form (but interlaced with extensions into triple-meter measures). While there are no fugal sections, imitation and running passages are set forth. The concurrences of the fourth interval and the boundary of a seventh relate this movement to the thematic precepts of the first section. There is also first-movement resemblance in the Gigue's second theme. The Coda uses augmented forms of thematic portions. Fine described this final movement as having "the character of an epilogue and solemn processional."

▪ Romanza for Wind Quintet (1963)

One of the pair of works that Fine wrote for this medium. The Romanza has an engaging sonority plan, set as it is in a syntax whereby the intervallic elements of twelve-tone technique are reconciled to quasi tonality. A fresh approach, this, with a refreshing aural result.

Fine, Vivian (1913–)

DUOS

▪ Divertimento for Cello and Percussion (Cymbals, Tambourine, Wood Block, Snare Drum, and Timpani) (1951)

Fine's duo combination is no longer to be classed as an oddball chamber music medium. In 1951, however, it was a rare example, exemplifying the magnetism of percussion for the 20th-century composer. It is to be noted that with the five percussion instruments required (the tambourine is to be struck with a beater, the snare drum is minus the brittleness of the fundamental snare), metal, wood, and pitched and unpitched membranous colors are represented in the pulsatile palette.

Dissonance is the primary condition in the Divertimento. The linear spans of the string-instrument voice are an expressionistic concept. A more intense lyrical situation serves as contrast, but throughout the development the quality of the music remains one of contemporary malleability.

▪ **Duo for Flute and Viola (1961)**

Fine's wind-string Duo has linear compactness with angularity and dissonant bite. The music is sectionally specified. In turn it projects rhapsodically within a slow speed, becomes nervous in a faster tempo, and then bursts forth toccatawise in presto. A short flute cadenza leads to a recapitulation of the beginning of the work, and the finale is in moderate allegretto tempo but becoming accelerated for the conclusion. Fluidity is an intensifier of the material. Though rhythmic groupings are specified, metrical apportionment is withheld.

▪ **Four Pieces for Two Flutes (1930)**

The product of a 17-year-old composer exhibiting considerable talent. Vivian Fine's set of pieces was her first chamber work. One composition preceded this in her output, *Solo for Oboe*, composed in 1929. (The length of the two works is practically the same: 5 minutes for the flute duo, 4 1/2 minutes for the oboe composition.)

Fast but flowing music marks the first piece; a Lento tristo definition parallels the asymmetric flow of the second one. The third of the set is marked Stridente, and here more than in any other place the dissonant counterpoint that styles the entire work provides the most dynamic artistic activity, especially when the rhythms

slap against each other. The final piece relies on canon for its binding. In this place the intervallic contacts are milder than previous.

Finger, Godfrey (c. 1660–c. 1723)

DUOS

▪ **Sonata in C Minor for Treble Recorder and Basso Continuo, Op. 3, No. 2**

Editorial puffs sometimes need to be considered and checked very carefully. However, the remarks by Arthur W. Marshall, editor of this work (published by Nova Music in 1979), are truly on the mark. He considers Finger's C-minor piece his "finest recorder sonata" and that the work is "one of the greatest ever written for the instrument, with a remarkable power and grandeur not commonly associated with recorder music."

There are five movements: Adagio–Allegro–Adagio–Vivace–Presto. The music has splendid contrasts and features disjunct lines in the recorder part that add a no-nonsense richness to the composition.

▪ **Sonata in D Minor for Flute and Piano**

▪ **Sonata in G for Flute and Piano**

Both works (the piano parts arranged from the original figured bass for harpsichord) exemplify a more modern type of sonata, rather than the suitelike and contrapuntal formations of the late baroque composers. There is some separation of movements in the D-minor opus. In the G-major work the movements flow one into the next.

- **Sonata in B-flat for Two Oboes (or Violins or Recorders) and Basso Continuo**

Music completely alive to the need for contrast of texture. The first Andante has a bit of imitation but opts for mainly vertical disposition. The second Andante is totally homophonic. Both Allegro movements (numbers two and four of the piece) are Handelian fugues. Impressive evidence of the talents of this little-known composer, described by Peter Holman, the editor of this work, as the "best composer of chamber music between Purcell and Handel."

Finke, Fidelio Fritz (1891–1968)

QUARTET

- **String Quartet No. 1**

Polyphony is the thesis and antithesis of Finke's quartet. Even when a *Scherz* section is used, the lines are in a weave. Throughout, there is a sense of a contrapuntalistic anthem being sung in various ways.

The work is in one movement, beginning with a fugue that returns in the concluding part of the quartet. Bithematic material, all developed in linear application, applies to a large Allegro division. Later, the Scherzo is detailed, which also returns in the final part, after the fugue recapitulation.

The polyphonic passions of the work remind one of the textural constructions of Max Reger. For that matter, the robust romanticism of the music leans on that composer's style as well.

Finney, Ross Lee (1906–)

DUOS

- **Sonata No. 2 for Violin and Piano (1951)**

The pitch material is serialized but retains a polarity on E. Finney's twelve-tone process is not the rigid one that defines most twelve-tone composers. Pitches are repeated, and there are plentiful thirds, fifths, and octaves. As one critic once mentioned, Finney gives the illusion of pure diatonicism in his serial works. But, indeed, there is no discrepancy between serial procedures and plotting them within the forceful contours that have served composers prior to the Schoenbergian dictum.

In turn, the movements are tranquil, capricious, slow paced (marked "tenderly, but with passion"), and a concluding division indicated "tranquilly."

- **Sonata No. 2 in C for Cello and Piano (1950)**

Finney's last composition before he turned to "a more systematic 12-tone technique." The "in C" is a key polarity that stabilizes the duo—Finney's expressive and dynamic piece is fully chromatic but remains firmly and pertinently tonal. It also remains beautifully written for the combination of cello and piano, a medium always beset with balance problems. Noteworthy is Finney's structure, anchored at its extremes with slow-tempo, pensive statements (the first marked Introduction, the other Conclusion).

TRIO

- **Piano Trio No. 2 (1954)**

Serial pitch organization and a decided interlock throughout the work. Thoroughly detailed lyricism in the first movement. A permutation of the row produces a duple-pulse and triple-pulse combination (both within the same time span) for the fast second movement (Finney terms it "a somewhat zany statement"). Another permutation brings forth a tenderly expressive slow movement. The conclusion is of march directness, with a quiet coda. Persuasive piano trio music.

QUARTETS

▪ Divertissement for Piano, Clarinet, Violin, and Cello (1964)

Finney indicates this work, composed in Paris, is "nostalgic of feelings and experiences I had as a student there in the 20s." More so, especially, this is reflected in the timbral matters of hitting the strings of the piano with the flat of the hand, plucking the piano's strings, touching a piano string with the left hand and playing the pitch on the keyboard with the right hand, scraping the strings with a hard metal object, and so on. More pertinent to these juicy sound joys are the improvisational cadenzas and aleatoric actions before the final movement is heard. These may be omitted but portray Finney as he is never heard—a representative of the Ives-Cage school.

Rows control the music. It has a slow movement, but most of the quartet stays in the fast zone.

▪ String Quartet in E (1950)

Despite the heading, this is not a tonal work. It represents Finney's first composition "using a more systematic twelve-tone technique." There are three rows presented in the tranquil Introduction, and within the work these perform different functions; for example: the first one gives a sense of "triadic sonority" and the third row provides "scalewise momentum."

The forms are in the classic area, with a sonata-structured Allegro, Scherzo, Intermezzo,

and Fugue, prefaced by a short Adagio. As Finney has done elsewhere, the work ends with a short, quiet movement marked Conclusion.

▪ String Quartet [No. 1] (1935)

Conservative music in that Finney does not seek to regulate a specific system but works along the very intelligible channels of specific tonality, with sideslips that give flavor. This type of tonality moves within strong pitch centers rather than mere triadic establishment. Thus, the opening of the first movement is in the key of F minor, but it begins with a related tonality, the home key entering in the third measure. Accompanying this are colorful and exciting rhythms, offbeats, syncopations, and dramatic silences. The elements are not too far left of center, yet they are allied to the composer's hypothesis of contemporary speech.

Ornateness contrasted to an initial nervous type of legato line forms a potent ternary pattern for the slow movement. Germinal promulgation of the opening fiery measures is the main attribute of the last movement. There is a great deal of layered writing by dividing the quartet into units of two voices each. Finney obtains motor drive in this fast movement by generally packing the voices.

▪ String Quartet No. 4 in A (1947)

The entire first movement stems from the give-and-take, the play and development of a generating motive. The motor drive of Hindemith and the infiltrated, circumambient accents of Bartók propound the third movement. Fugal entries begin (and later reappear in) this fast-paced Scherzo. These are in the 20th-century manner, rising by minor thirds to form other than the usual associated points of tonic and dominant departure that mark the standard fugal form of the 18th and 19th centuries. Finally, the last entry is by way of the augmented prime. This fugal start furnishes the thematic wires on which the movement's apparatus is strung, leading to a thirty-three-measure section in dynamic unison in faster speed and with increasing loudness. The entire spirit furnishes an excellent foil to the movements that precede and follow.

The slow movement derives from solo lines that are designed, as the composer marks, "oratorically." The braced boundaries of these lines are formed by the pointedness of diminished octaves, major sevenths, and ninths, affording dramatic play to such utterances. The last movement, exceedingly short (only twenty-seven measures in length), is in chorale style, with a subdued peroration that ends in the combined modal anonymity of both A major and minor.

- **String Quartet No. 7 (1955)**

Finney's analysis indicates that the quartet is written "as one skates a figure 8." This is explained thus: "The central point is the Sostenuto, which is the beginning, the middle, and the end of the work. The first movement moves away from the center and after reaching its apogee returns to the center. The second movement does the same thing, but its moods are opposite from the first movement. It reaches its apogee . . . and reverses and returns to the central point."

QUINTETS

- **Piano Quintet [No. 1] (1953)**

The first two movements of the work were originally written as a string quartet. Not satisfied with the resultant sonority, Finney rewrote the work for the different (enlarged) scoring.

No academic use of twelve-tone style in this quintet (nor in any other Finney dodecaphonic composition). It is amazing and a delight to recognize a Schumann-Brahms overtone in Finney's twelve-tone music. (Other writers have remarked that the work represents loose romanticism, and that it is a setting of Brahms and Bruckner with contemporary data.) The quintet has a searching quality, a determined positiveness that is truly exciting.

The movements are a fantasy set similar to sonata form but minus any recapitulatory section. The Scherzo is in a modified rondo format. A Nocturne and full-fledged sonata structure mark the final pair of movements.

- **String Quintet (Two Violins, Viola, and Two Cellos) (1958)**

A one-movement work, organized, Finney states, "somewhat like a long lyric poem such as Milton's 'Lycidas.' " Row formationed, the work begins and closes with a Finney trademark—two slow divisions that complement each other, both set in adagio cantabile tempo. In the first of the two major parts of the quintet twice there are paired "Statements" and "Episodes." In the second major part there are Intermezzi: Nocturne in adagio and a scherzoish Capriccio, followed by "Restatements." As is usual with Finney, the hybrid style of twelve-tone with tonal character is made apparent throughout the composition.

Clarity of formal function is successfully depicted; the lyrical outgo is never repressed. Row-permutative involvement does not negate a tidiness in regard to rhythmic emphasis and direct melodic depiction.

Finzi, Gerald (1901–56)

Finzi's reputation has been brought about by his beautiful song settings and an excellent cantata, *Dies natalis*. His chamber music is just as refined and contains the vocal-type lyricism so important to the medium. The chamber output is small in total since Finzi not only worked very slowly, but was extremely self-critical.

His music is without floridity. Diatonic simplicity is paramount. Finzi was a composer devoted to classicism in the large sense, with perceptive regard for the progress of harmonies. Only a pedant would object to his chordal garnishes.

DUO

- **Five Bagatelles for Clarinet and Piano**

These Bagatelles should not be considered in terms of the French meaning of the word, i.e., "trifles," but in the pure musical sense of a set of short pieces. All five of the conceptions are compact but not of small importance.

The classical composer very rarely formed his themes from tonal montage; the broken triad and the conjunct diatonic line were the main sources. Finzi's relationship to this style is to be observed in the majority portions of this work. A plain C-major scale starts the theme of the Prelude, and the seven sounds are its main resource. There is refreshing tonal contrast in the statement, which is in three-part form, the same design used for the Romance, which bends its lines in changing meters. The Carol (there is no specific designation as to whether this is an Easter, May, or other type of carol, but the celebrations of the music are like a gentle Noël) is haunting, with a beautiful, modally formed section that divides into periodic half and complete cadences. Part four concerns the dotted rhythmic gracefulness of a Forlana, breathing a quiet spirit into this Italian dance. A free Fughetta gives an opposite expression.

TRIO

- **Prelude and Fugue for String Trio, Op. 24**

Usually, the intercommunion of a prelude followed by a fugue is only retained in title marriage. The musical content is sanctified by separation. Not in this case.

The Prelude is colored by muted tone; the opposite pertains to the Fugue. Alternating horizontal and tightly vertical ideas are used in the former. This thesis–antithesis serves more than contrast. The antithesis (the chordal item) becomes the spearhead for the fugue subject. Thus Finzi interlocks his two components. To seal the document he brings back the beginning of the Prelude at the end.

QUINTET

- **Interlude for Oboe and String Quartet, Op. 21**

An Interlude in title, submissive to pastoral warmth. Even when the pace hastens or the figurations become expansive the quintet emphasizes impressionistic lyricism.

Only the strings are used in the introduction and are retained without the oboe for a good part of the first section of the tripartite work. Finzi considers the form freely so that there is development within the divisions, and returns of sections are freshly presented. The coda is a quiet signature to this piece of vocalistic chamber music.

Fiorillo, Federigo (1755–1823?)

DUOS

- **Concertante duos for Two Violins, Op. 14**

  - No. 1, in G Major
  - No. 2, in A Major
  - No. 3, in B-flat Major
  - No. 4, in C Major
  - No. 5, in E Major
  - No. 6, in A-flat Major

Every violinist knows this composer's name, since he must find his way through Fiorillo's thirty-six studies (*Études pour violon formant*

36 caprices) as well as those by Kreutzer and Rode. And in his early days of practice he may have played Fiorillo's elementary duets. Of the large amount of chamber music Fiorillo produced practically nothing survives in modern reprint. The six duos listed above, published in 1972 by Edition Kunzelmann, deserve attention by violinists.

Of course, the second violin is mainly the lower voice, but in no way is the part subsidiary. These are truly equalized duets. All six are of two-movement total; the forms are sonata and rondo.

Features: the driving passages in movement one of the second duo and the scalic scurry of its second movement; the tempo shifts in the second movement of number three, in turn allegro, largo espressivo, allegro again, and a final presto; the large scale of the writing in the fifth duo; and the rhythmic kick in the final movement of the last duo.

Fišer, Luboš (1935–)

DUO

- **Sonata for Cello and Piano (1975)**

A seven-minute work, significantly or coincidentally limited to a group of seven pitches (B-flat–B–C–C-sharp–F–F-sharp–G). (*See below*: Trio for Violin, Cello, and Piano for another Fišer work based on a similar type of restricted pitch prearrangement.)

Seemingly, the form is a patchwork of sections. But there is persuasive perspicuity in the manner in which the music is structured. The opening is for solo cello. This material returns at the end, changed a bit, with slight piano support. The second section is a series of increasingly dynamic chords for the piano. These chords reappear later, this time crossed by an ostinato in the cello. Other interlineal relationships are similarly represented. Fišer's duo

sonata is sectionally arranged, texturally assorted, but free of any primitive nebulosity.

And only at the very end is another pitch permitted entry. The duo concludes with three C-major chords, in the extreme lower register of the piano, in triple *piano*.

TRIO

- **Trio for Violin, Cello, and Piano (1978)**

Fišer's three-instrument work is entirely based on a row of seven pitches: B-flat–B–C–D-flat–E–F–G-flat. "Row" does not mean serial application of these sounds (if so, one could then, facetiously, call the style "chip-off-the-old-block dodecaphony"). Further to this choice of sounds, for approximately the first half of the piece the E pitch is not used. Thereafter, it appears but rarely. It must be emphasized that Fišer's piano trio is not serial; it is simply pitch-confined. Thereby it produces a special sound quality, similar to any work that has a specifically limited pitch spectrum.

The music is divisionally structured, reflecting a variational inner- and inter-play of the pitches, in vertical, horizontal, chordal, and polyphonic engagement.

By the chromatic crawl of the opening the pitch boundaries of the piece are stabilized and emphasized. Derived from this generating material the next section consists of powerful double octaves in the solo piano, then a rubato portion for the unaccompanied violin, a return to the piano's octaves, and another rubato section, this time for the cello alone. A variety of graphic divisions follows, including one combining differently articulated ostinatos for each of the three instruments.

A return to the chromatic opening ushers in the concluding part of the work. The tempo on this recap is slightly slower, and this time the violin and cello are muted. Minus the E, the pitch "row" is heard in the cello, then repeated by the violin. A portion of the "row" follows.

And then, with gentle dramaticism, the Trio surprisingly ends with repeated C-major (!) chords. (This chordal conclusion is a harmonic duplicate of the ending of Fišer's cello and piano sonata—*see above*.)

QUARTET

■ *Testis (Witness)* **for String Quartet (1979)**

Twenty-five sections joined together. But no mishmash. The material is calculated to mesh, even though the structure is compartmentalized, by the use of a special restriction. *Testis*, like other of Fišer's works *(see above)*, is concentrated in its pitch budget. The music is based on a nine-tone total, with D, E-flat, and G-sharp not used.

In certain manner *Testis* is a free dissertation minus a theme (perhaps it is meant to be searching for one). As it progresses it constantly varies tempos, textures, and dynamics. It keeps in balance because of the deliberate use of less than the complete pitch potential. This brings an inner compactness that controls the sectional diversity.

Fisher, F.E. (18th century)

TRIOS

■ **Trio Sonata 7 in G Minor for Two Violins and Basso Continuo, Op. 2, No. 1**

■ **Trio Sonata 10 in B-flat Major for Two Violins and Basso Continuo, Op. 2, No. 4**

The only pair of works by this composer published in modern edition (by Oxford University Press). In a signed prefatory note by Stanley Sadie (the editor is Richard Platt) the statement is made that "little is known for certain" about Fisher. Two sets each of six trio sonatas are indicated as having been published: Op. 1 "in about 1756" and Op. 2 "about 1760." On the basis of the two examples discussed below all twelve deserve publication.

The G-minor sonata opens with a spirited movement that is linked to a strong double fugue. A March completes the work.

Imitation plays an important role in the Allegro con spirito beginning of the other (B-flat major) work. A keenness for phrase identification marks the middle Andante, with a descending sixth important within the construction. The entire movement is to be played at a *piano* level. Gigue content completes the opus.

Fisher, Stephen (1940–)

QUARTET

■ **String Quartet No. 1 (1962)**

Serialistic virtuosity. There are no pat summations. Fisher is mindful of not calling back all old dodecaphonic yesterdays in his extremely colorful treatment. The difference between his type of string quartet writing and the classical demeanor of Schoenberg's style is immediately recognizable.

Approximately of twenty-minute length, the quartet consists of two linked parts. Each of these begins at the slowest speed ($\downhalfnote = 54$) of the total variety of tempos within the piece. The first part is titled "Statement" and consists of three sections, with the first and third of these each further subsectioned three times. The second part consists of two sections and is followed by two codas.

Juxtapositional formal structuring derived from the row fundament solidifies the rhapsodic network of the composition. The textural variety is as prismatic as the assortment of pizzicatos, bowings, vibratos, and timbres. It is therefore meaningful that the final coda represents the simplest, most unelaborate part of the quartet. It begins with the row announced by the cello, with each of the six measures progressively faster, exactly specified by metronomic indication—the quartet note equaling, in turn, 54, 63, 72, 81, 90, and 99. (It will be noted that each increase is nine degrees.) (This brings immediately to mind the same process used in the sixth variation of Elliott Carter's *Variations for Orchestra,* written in 1955, also consisting of a six-measure thought, with each measure exactly increased in metronomic speed.) Three times this six-measure phrase is stated, each time with additional voicing. The speed is further increased and then pulled back to the tempo ($\quarternote = 54$) that began each of the two parts of the quartet, thus binding the total concept by concluding the work in the pace at which it began.

Fishman, Marian (1941–75)

QUARTET

- *Six Studies in Sonorities* for Four Woodwinds (Flute, Oboe, Clarinet, and Bassoon)

Add the adjective "compact" to the title. The first of the group is a Presto timed at thirty-five seconds. No other timings are given, but the fourth piece is a Lento of eleven measures that (following the metronomic indication) is of thirty-four seconds' length. The textures are of parallel tightness, enclosing frictioned combinations. Nothing new or experimental in Fishman's music. Her woodwind quartet represents standard modern-style sketches, totally avoiding any suggestion of lavender and old lace.

Fitelberg, Jerzy (1903–51)

DUOS

- **Concertino da camera for Violin and Piano (1951)**

Fitelberg's glowing neoclassic piece (commissioned by the Koussevitzky Music Foundation) opens with a Toccata—a toccata with a slight difference. It begins with asymmetric measurement set in moderately fast speed, the material ornamental in concept. Then follows the expected hammered fast music and, in turn, by a changed presentation of the moderate-tempo section, followed by a return to the faster speed.

Sobriety applies to the Elegy, excited by recitando detail. The final Rondo has a variety of ideas, each definitely standing on its own and yet related to define a total balance.

- **Duo for Violin and Cello**

In this duet, Fitelberg is concerned with copying techniques initiated by Stravinsky and Hindemith. A maximum sonority is obtained by minimum means; tonality is stretched; keys mingle as well (note the beginning with the jogging of a G-major theme on an F pedal point). The dissonances are constant; the total amount of music makes these frictions repeat themselves.

A loose sonata plan is used in the first two movements. The last movement is more unified. It begins with a long introduction in which the rise of an octave is most important. This interval plunges the Allegro that follows into a vigorous drive that emphasizes the principal theme. The coda, formed also from the octave essential, is in constantly decreased tempo.

- **Serenade for Violin (or Viola) and Piano (1943)**

A one-movement composition, with a lyrical legato-type introduction followed by the principal Allegro. Fitelberg's usual light astringency of neoclassic harmony is used together with a wide-ranged development of the thematic material in the principal section of the duo. Coolly restrained music at times, but totally informed music.

- **Sonatina for Two Violins**

Fitelberg's work was of the orthodoxy that complied only with absolute music. Not only is this objectivism illustrated in the second movement, but his tendency for writing lengthy ones. This Tema con variazioni (Theme with Variations) consists only of four portrayals of the theme. Whereas most composers (even with a theme of thirty-two-measure length) would convey their variational unfoldment in divisions somewhat close to that total, Fitelberg lets himself go to such an extent that the third of the variations is 111 measures in length, while the shortest is the second (55 measures). It will be apparent that these are not so much variations as rhapsodies that develop different poses. Such procedure serves to nullify the form somewhat. Further, the first two variations (with varying intercessions in each) are in the same tempo; the third is of minutely faster pace, while only the fourth (with march implications) can be determinedly distinguished from the other three. Though also quite free, the opening movement is much better designed; it has the composer's usual dissonant style, smoothed with Stravinskian neoclassic oil.

QUARTETS

- **String Quartet No. 2**

There is this about Fitelberg's second quartet—it is a proportioned whole, though the subject matter does not overly contrast. The motor that makes the rhythm operates unceasingly; the quartet is gripped by febrile excitement. Attention cannot wander with this continuity, even if but awaiting the relaxation of the pulse. When melodies of longer contour enter, they are underpinned by the hum of similar previous rhythm. This power feeds harmonies associated more with urban motivity than rural serenity.

The quartet is in one movement, with a slow section braced against two outer Presto formations. An anthology of 20th-century masters is to be heard—Stravinsky (rhythm), Hindemith (ostinato), Honegger (counterpoint), and Tansman (continuity). It is a worthy compendium and such eclectic choice *is* choice. Its representation of contemporary temper does not lower the quality of Fitelberg's quartet. Rather, its values are increased by such assimilation.

(Fitelberg arranged his second quartet for string orchestra, titling it Concerto for String Orchestra.)

- **String Quartet No. 5 (1945)**

Tonality is emphatically present in this quartet, but not the type of previous eras; rather the kind that is pertinent to the present day; tonality far removed from the diatonic weave of the classicists or romanticists; intonations with keyed centers, but premised on the fact that, with logical forward motion, tensions, and releases, and the like, concrete dissonant adaptation is just as valid. Such is this composer's style, with a penchant for the semiverbose, the ever-constant movement of all voices.

In the opening movement, a type of motto rhythm keeps reappearing, engendering the almost nine minutes of the movement. The structural form is as free of dogmatic inferences to stated sonata design as is the harmony.

The second movement is a set of variations,

the thematic basis deploying only slightly triadal confirmation. The first two and last variations are short, and, though fairly free, the thematic relationship is not too divergent. In the third of the set, complete independence is manifested, not in thematic advance but in length. This division appears as though separated, devoted to what might be an individual scherzo conception, set apart from the other three variants. The last movement is mainly in a speedy tempo, leaning somewhat on Hindemith.

QUINTET

- **Capriccio for Flute, Oboe, Clarinet, Bass Clarinet, Trombone (or Bassoon) (1947)**

(The Capriccio is a revision of a Wind Quintet, scored for the standard combination of flute, oboe, clarinet, horn, and bassoon, that Fitelberg composed in 1929.)

Mostly gay, just a bit serious neoclassic music. The score is intensely balletic, even in the slow-moving portions. Fitelberg's large ternary initial movement belies any small-scale divertimentolike anticipation; its central portion is totally developed. The Scherzo is minus any condensation or telescoping. There, precise classical form matches contemporary classical language. The music's basic effervescence also keys the finale.

Most of the quintet's spirit makes the choice of a trombone in place of a bassoon seem less than ideal for balance. There is one section in the final movement, however, where the use of the trombone brings benefits. This consists of a forty-seven-measure spread during which the trombone doubles the flute at a three-octave distance. This is color power at its best.

Fitzgerald, Bernard (1911–)

DUO

- *Four Gaelic Miniatures* **for Flute and Piano**

Simple melodies propped up with trim, tonally pat harmonies. Gaelic music is little available; this small suite is, therefore, doubly welcome.

The music thrives on repetition of phrases. "Rinnce fada" ("Meadow Dance") moves swiftly in one-in-a-bar direction. "Ceo ne maidne" ("Morning Mist") is slow paced, its lines clarified by triplet figures. "Port Coeil" ("Jig Tune") dances in duple pulse, and "Piobaire" ("A Piper") is likewise a dance, in fast triple time.

Flackton, William (1709–98)

DUOS

- **Sonatas for Cello and Basso Continuo, Op. 2**

  - No. 4, in C Major
  - No. 5, in B-flat Major
  - No. 6, in F Major

The second group of three of a set of six sonatas; the first group of three is for viola and basso continuo (*see below*).

Fluently musical, assured, and always entertaining compositions. There are none of the dull padded sections that all too often fill out the forms of 18th-century pieces. Flackton's music is balanced but always genuinely enlightening in whatever its formation may be. The first and third sonatas have similar designs: slow–fast–slow–Minuet, with a variational section dividing the initial part of the Minuet from its recapitulation. The second sonata is shorter, with only three movements. It begins with a Siciliana; an Allegro follows; and it is completed by a three-part Minuetto, the central section being a Variazione.

- **Sonatas for Viola and Basso Continuo, Op. 2**

  - No. 1, in C Major
  - No. 2, in D Major
  - No. 3, in G Major

The first group of a set of six sonatas, three each for tenor violin (now known as the viola) and cello. (The latter group is discussed *above*.) In a preface to the set Flackton indicated he "intended to shew that instrument [i.e., the viola] in a more conspicuous Manner than it has hitherto been accustomed." Further, he hoped to "establish a higher Veneration and Taste for this excellent, tho' too much neglected, instrument." Certainly, an important objective, since, as Renzo Sabatini, the editor of the contemporary edition (published by Doblinger), states, these were "the first original sonatas for the viola in England."

Each sonata begins with an ornamental slow movement and continues with a moderately polyphonic fast movement. The D- and G-major works are completed with a pair of Minuettos, the second one in a different key and at a slower pace, with a return then made to the first Minuetto. The concluding sections of the C-major piece have a Siciliana before the Minuetto and the second Minuetto is preceded by two short variations on the initial Minuetto's theme.

- **Sonata in C Minor for Viola and Basso Continuo, Op. 2, No. 8**

This Sonata was first published in 1776 in London. It was headed "Two Solos. One for a Violoncello and One for a Tenor, Accompanied either with a Violoncello or a Harpsichord, being a supplement to the second Edition of Six Solos, three for a Violoncello, and three for a Tenor Composed by William Flackton." The "six solos" ("sonatas") mentioned are discussed *above*. (The other of the "two solos"—that for cello, Op. 2, No. 7—remains unpublished.)

This modern edition was made by Antony Cullen in 1953 and published in 1955 by Lengnick. The design follows that used in the C-major viola sonata (Op. 2, No. 1) (*see above*), consisting of an ornamental Adagio, a vigorous Allegro moderato, a flowing Siciliana, and a finale embracing a Minuetto, with a Variation, and the usual da capo to the Minuetto proper.

Flagello, Nicolas (1928–)

DUO

- **Burlesca for Flute and Guitar (1961)**

There are hints of folk sounds here (the guitar can well breed this type of reaction even if it is not true). Neat scoring that is a compelling, constructive part of the piece. It shows that Flagello never postures, never attempts to write for the sake of mere effect.

Formally a shift between slow, recitativelike lines and a fast yet controlled music. The alternation proposes a rondo format.

QUINTET

- ***Philos* for Brass Quintet (Two Trumpets, Horn, Tenor Trombone, and Bass Trombone (or Tuba) (1970)**

Contrastive tempos, but parallel moods. The heart and voice of this piece are concerned with dark-toned sentiments. Flagello's music is definitely tonally based but colored and stimulated by chromatic adjuncts. These provide the tensions that are not released until the conclusion.

Basically, *Philos* is depicted in a binary structure, with slow-paced material compared to a faster Alla fuga division. Both return, tremendously truncated, to complete the quintet.

SEXTET

- *Lyra* **for Brass Sextet (Three Trumpets, Horn, Tenor Trombone, and Bass Trombone (1945)**

A short piece that effectively inserts some bitonality within its basically tonal style. Tonality is the fundament of Flagello's method, but it is never of academic retrocedence. *Lyra* is lyrical in its statement, begins and concludes softly, starts in the E-flat-major zone and ends on B major.

SEPTET

- *Prisma* **for Seven Horns (1974)**

Well made, nothing adventurous (which is not to imply a negative report), utilitarian classification. The music has scherzo spirit and pep, with shifts between and combinations of duple and triple pulses within the same time span. Ternary format.

Flanagan, William (1923–69)

Death by a suicidal act (an overdose of barbiturates) ended the career of this sensitive creator. Flanagan stated his total concern was with the "sound of music." This is set forth in music of expressive flowing lyricism, tonally designed, with formal transpicuity. Preoccupied with music for the voice, he produced only two works in the chamber music category: the Divertimento for String Quartet (1947) and the seven-minute Chaconne for Violin and Piano (*see below*).

DUO

- **Chaconne for Violin and Piano (1948)**

The slow-tempo, neoclassically oriented Chaconne is "for David Diamond," the last of Flanagan's six teachers. Sufficiently free so that it is not stunted by academic restrictions, the music is clearly chronicled. A nine-measure statement by the piano is followed by a dozen variations. Unification is strong, with no sequestering of any section. The continuity is marked by developed metrical change in the fourth part, repetition of the soprano line of the theme by the violin in the fifth part, and graphic embellishment in the ninth section. The tenth variant concludes with a violin cadenza.

Fleming, Robert (1921–76)

TRIO

- *A Two-Piece Suite* **for Two Clarinets and Bass Clarinet**

(A bibliographic listing of this composer's works indicates this trio can also be played by oboe, clarinet, and bassoon. The published score by Leeds Music [Canada] Limited makes no mention of this.)

The word is cute and the other word is pert for this pair of rondo-formationed pieces, one in moderato tempo, the other in slow (andante) pace. Tonal but freshly pitched. Woven within are French-Canadian folk songs: "Alouette," "Au clair de la lune," and "C'est l'aviron." Also a nine-measure ostinato of the opening measure of the famous Kreutzer violin etude. Here, harmonized in thirds, it is set against a rhythmically augmented-diminished chip of the "Alouette" melody. Just another enjoyable part of this totally deft composition.

Flosman, Oldřich (1925–)

DUOS

- **The Dream about the Violin: Sonata-Fantasie for Violin and Piano (1962)**

In the absence of any explanatory note, listeners to Flosman's one-movement work can exercise their own imagination in regard to his title.

Sectionally structured, with the opening portion for piano alone returning in modified form together with the violin twice later. A variety of ideas are used, with a lyrically fast extended section in A major set as the fourth and concluding parts of the duo. Rich and spacious music and also some rhythmically contrastive music. Flosman's dream certainly was not a troubled one.

- **Highwaymen Sonatina for Clarinet and Piano (1952)**

Descriptive title because of its influence from Czech folk-song materials. Flosman's work is totally a romantic item in the conservative category.

Finesse marks the handling of the materials in the first movement. There, rhythmic aliveness and inserted single-beat measures (1/4) color the lines. Song form is used in the middle slow movement. Quintal-built chords are used as ostinato framework in the outer sections. Dance expressiveness and rhythmic punch combine to provide the balances in the finale.

QUINTET

- **Dances for Harp and String Quartet (1961)**

Native idiom is not completely subsurface in this set of three pieces, romantically styled, sonorously scored. The first dance is slow paced and has breadth. The second dance is developed from an eleven-measure theme announced by the cello. Its tempo is moderately fast. The finale (minus a set metronomic indication in contrast to exact specifications for the previous two movements) is energetic but controlled, with pointed indented rhythms.

(The score includes a double-bass part to be used if the work is to be performed by a full string orchestra.)

SEXTET

- **Sonata for Wind Quintet and Piano (1962)**

Conventions are not smashed in this sextet, but neither can it be termed a conventional work. No avant-garde spill, simply an avoidance of cut-and-dried formulae for the usual sequence of fast–Scherzo–slow–fast movements.

The Allegro moderato has fantasy infusion in its sonata-proportioned form. Movement two (Allegro vivace) has a grotesque dance quality. Intensity is paramount in the Adagio. Penetrative dissonance is the main sap and impulsive force of that movement. In the finale, fugal definition surrounds the total rondo framework.

NONET

- **Nonet No. 2 for Flute, Oboe, Clarinet, Bassoon, Horn, Violin, Viola, Cello, and Double Bass (1962)**

Flosman cultivates the neoclassic garden, which is still a flourishing one. The style retains its good flavor. Here the evidence is in three movements: the first in sonata form but with some freedoms not according to the academic books; a slow movement set forth in variational style; and a fugally disposed finale. Flosman's writing is on the expert level—this is a finely arranged and fine-sounding Nonet for the traditional wind quintet plus one each of the string family.

Flothuis, Marius (1914–)

DUOS

- *Cantilena e Ritmi* for Alto Recorder and Harpsichord, Op. 48, No. 2

There are seven movements in Flothuis's duo "per flauto dolce alto e clavicembalo," but there is firm stability in its structure. The opening Cantilena is used for a Variazione della cantilena in movement four. There, the variational action is in the wind instrument; the keyboard instrument responds with eleven inserts of arpeggiated chords. The duo is firmly brought into balance with the concluding Ripresa della cantilena; the recapitulation is a literal one.

Movements two, three, five, and six are each a Ritmo (Rhythm). In every case the materials are developments drawn from the Cantilena and firmly balanced by a sequential use of meter: Ritmo 1 is in 5/8, Ritmo 2 is in 6/8, Ritmo 3 is in 7/8, and Ritmo 4 is in 8/8. At the conclusion of Ritmo 3, Flothuis has indicated "Omággio alla Grècia." This "Homage to Greece" pertains probably to the use of septuple meter, a rhythm used in a considerable number of Greek songs and dances and which has been described "as natural to perform" by the Greeks as a "western European does 2/4 time."

- **Sonata da camera (Chamber Sonata) for Flute and Harp, Op. 42**

Slow and fast tempos alternate in this modern setting of the late-17th- early-18th-century design. But, of course, only speed specifications duplicate the old form. Flothuis's music within the total structure is dissonant, conveyed with his usual fastidious craftsmanship

and maintenance of style.

Binary formation marks the initial movement, which is linked to a scherzolike Vivace, set in an A–B–C–A sequence. With a ternary total and a rondo format for the second pair of movements it will be noted that Flothuis manages to distinguish individually the shape of each of the four parts of his compact duo.

- **Sonata da camera (Chamber Sonata) for Flute and Piano, Op. 17**

Though the contents of the old sonata da camera and sonata da chiesa (church sonata) were stated differently and each included engaging variances so that formal fashion was not a steadfast routine, the patterns of the movements for both were in alternated speeds. The basic proposal of dance rhythms as compared to the matter of more placid rhythmic types differentiated the secular quality of the chamber sonata from the religious substance of the church sonata. This difference was a technical compromise that made for secure obtainment of two instrumental forms, each with distinct advantages. Flothuis's modern sonata da camera has tempo alternation (free, lightly fast, slow, and fastest) and compares four styles. The title is nothing more than a modern recollection of the historic.

A Cadenza forms the first movement that leads into a Sonatina. The latter is somewhat of earlier-century style in the matter of its constant imitations of figured patterns, and then follows a Lamento (steady quarter notes in the bass of the piano imply a processional chant). The duo concludes with a gay Rondo alla francese. Tonal centers are stipulated in this Rondo in the French Manner. But the harmonic articles are the type of commodities which would make sonata da contemporaneo a better title for this two-instrument package.

- *Three Encores* for Violin and Piano,
  Op. 53

Flothuis means what he says. The music is "intended to be played as the last item of a program or actually as 'encores.' In the latter case each of them can be played separately."

Strategically, the pieces are of short length. The first is a ternary item, built around quartal ascents in the melodic line. Slow tempo marks the second piece, constructed on a unitary basis. The third of the set zooms in very fast speed—a perpetual-motion depiction of continual triplet figures.

- **Three Pieces for Two Horns, Op. 24a**

Nothing special, but clean, straightforward, simple writing is offered here. Still, no potboiler, as some might contend. The two instruments are continually joined in the Marche. In part two, a descending fourth ostinato supports the Musette. A swift Rondo completes the short suite.

TRIOS

- **Nocturne for Flute, Oboe, and Clarinet,
  Op. 11**

Perfectly balanced arrangement for this short trio. It begins with a theme set forth in two parts, followed by a variation of the second part and then a variation of the first one. A coda ties up matters.

- *Trio serio* for Viola, Cello, and Piano,
  Op. 38, No. 2

If only for its unusual instrumental configuration Flothuis's work deserves attention. This changes the piano trio medium by moving its timbral character into a darker area. (The title of the work follows suit.) The second movement is mostly muted, and its coloration is further confirmation of the composer's objective. This division is a scherzo conception; it is followed by a fugue.

QUARTETS

- **Concertino for Oboe (alternating Oboe
  d'amore or English horn), Violin,
  Viola, and Cello, Op. 70a**

Of single construction, but with cogent variational development of the opening unaccompanied oboe theme. It is shaped with defined intervallic enlargement. In measure 1 the ascents are a minor third and a minor second; in measure 2 the moves are a perfect fifth and a minor second; and in measure 3 again a perfect fifth, but moving onto a major third.

In turn, the music is vivacious, with a spastic division of 8/8 meter into 2 + 3 + 3, and 5/8 time split into 2 + 3, then set forth in an asymmetrical Lento, and back to a Vivace section. The conclusion of the quartet sets the oboe as leader shifting to the oboe d'amore (preferred, rather than the more usually available English horn).

- **Four Inventions for Four Horns, Op. 64**

Specific specifications mark and control each of the pieces. In "Signals" motival transfer and combination meet the objective. Part two is "Harmony." This homophonic piece will bring to mind, according to the composer, one of Debussy's piano preludes: "Les Sons et les parfums tournent dans l'air du soir" ("The Sounds and Perfumes Swirl in the Evening Air").

The third piece, "Colors," contrasts open and closed timbres. In the finale Flothuis moves into the dodecaphonic area, with a fugato (the movement is titled "Polyphony"). The subject is constructed of eleven tones, with the twelfth pitch appearing in the response.

QUINTET

- **Quintet for Flute, Oboe, Clarinet, Bassoon, and Bass Clarinet, Op. 13**

Speed is the major characteristic property of scherzo form. Whimsy there may well be, even dramatic irony, but above all the assets are those of hustle and bustle. Brahmsian scherzos are at times rather gloomy, Beethoven's are bronze in color if placed alongside the silvery sparkle of Mendelssohn's. Nevertheless, it is the rhythmic factor that is the mouthpiece of the form. Therefore, if the rhythmic plan is too smooth the scherzo becomes somewhat make-believe, while a nervous pulse transmits a more retentive, insidious type. But a composer cannot simply produce his scherzo by a plan of nonsymmetrical measures, there must be much more—the organic applicability of the direct pulsatile stimulant.

The second movement of Flothuis's Op. 13 provides an untitled scherzo. Although marked Commodo this instruction is somewhat canceled by the composer's metronome marking, which means a faster performance than the leisurely pace defined by the Italian term. Nevertheless the rhythm takes full custody of the formal intent, and no defection from true scherzo depiction is made. Measures fly past in 5/8 time, in most instances the last beat kicking away from the duple pulse of the first four-fifths of the measure. When the contrasting middle section is announced the previous rhythmic unevenness continues in a seven-beat course, further engendered by the use of syncopation. There is no rust on the foundations of the scherzo form; it sparkles with Flothuis's new polish.

On the other hand, variation technique has many possibilities, derived from either high-lighting a theme or paradoxically burying it. Variation may be applied in sectional, piece-meal statement by thematic embellishment, or the theme may be fully developed to its last iota

of possibility. Yet variation can be so free as to use it only as an introduction to other discoveries. A composer is proud and greedy of his principal subject or else, having utilized it, deserts it as he proceeds elsewhere with little past memories of his thematic servant. In addition there is the type of variational masked ball, in which the theme is disguised, in turn, as a personality, a dance, a march, a nocturne, and the like.

Flothuis chooses a method concerned with weight and defined color. Each variation (the theme is for one instrument alone) calls for more players. Thus the first is for two instruments, the second variation is scored for three players, the third employs a quartet, and in the fourth variation the entire quintet is heard. Then subtraction of instruments is the reverse but complementary device that marks the remainder of the movement. Four voices are used in the fifth variation, three in the sixth, while a duet serves for the seventh variation. Perfect retention of the plan is marked by the next section when one solo instrument, the same one that began the movement, restates the theme. A five-measure coda, significantly for all five instruments, completes the movement and the work itself. Such mathematical contrivance may well seem like stiff technical arbitrariness, but in this instance it mirrors the particulars of the variation recital most graphically.

No less artful is the first movement, where development of the opening Grave proceeds in four differing sections; the Grave returns, in ritornel system, twice during the movement.

SEXTET

- **Divertimento for Clarinet, Bassoon, Horn, Violin, Viola, and Double Bass, Op. 46**

A number of loosely connected movements marked the 18th-century divertimento form.

(There was little difference between it and the serenade and cassation.) The general musical tone was one of not too serious a representation.

Flothuis's 20th-century example (composed in 1952) has ancestral ties. It is in six movements. Each of these goes its own engaging way, and the demeanor is certainly not hard crusted. The opening movement is an Entrata, a stately but decisive Introduction. There are two Scherzos separated by a Canzone (Song). To define the Scherzos the first of the pair is scored exclusively for clarinet, bassoon, and horn. The fifth movement is a Rondo, preluded by a Grave section.

The finale marks a full contemporary touch to the divertimento arrangement. It is a "Congedo" ("Leave-taking"), consisting of a succession of short cadenzalike passages for each of the six instruments in turn, each prefaced by a pithy chordal passage.

Foerster, Josef Bohuslav (1859–1951)

DUOS

- **Impromptu for Violin and Piano, Op. 154, No. 1**

A cup of romantic tea is served in this small duo; the brew is strong and flavorsome. The music begins in G minor, and the tonality changes five times before returning to the initial key. It later changes once more to G major. Uniformity of expression holds the music together regardless of its key shuffles.

- *Malá suita (Little Suite)* **for Two Violins, Op. 183**

And reduced in pitch scope. Only three notes (each quite separate from the others) are beyond the first position. Tonal to the nth degree and restrained in modulation.

Four movements, contrasted in all respects. The third (Adagio) is three voiced (chords in the second violin) and muted throughout. Splendid *Hausmusik.*

(A different setting of this work was made for three violins—*see below.*)

- **Sonata for Violin and Piano, Op. 10**

Quite often the manner in which a composer handles many musical forms presupposes a doctrinal attitude on his part. Any deviation, therefore, not only is an aid in gaining interest but is a creative credit. In the third movement of this duo sonata Foerster takes his scherzo-style music and dresses it polyphonically, commencing at the onset with a clear, unembellished three-voice fugal announcement that becomes the material for development. The contrasting section slows the music's speed and has the flux of varied stresses, not by percussive accentuation but by the subtle and comparative weight of different sound lengths.

Otherwise, Foerster's violin and piano duo is in reserved style. The first movement is set forth by sonata design; the slow section is a simple song type in three divisions, while a ritornel basis takes care of the final movement.

Foerster's opus is an early product; nevertheless it exemplifies, for the most part, the style of his total output. Foerster was less a Czech nationalist composer and much more a Czech composer who had a wholehearted romantic viewpoint.

- **Sonata No. 2 for Cello and Piano, Op. 130**

Easygoing and spacious romantic music. Unsentimentally romantic. Foerster's duo sonata is unscathed by the slightest impurity of that style.

Foerster's habit of manifold tonality and tempo changes is fully represented. These are especially prevalent in the third (final) movement, where, after a half-dozen speed differences, the music reaches its peak (Allegro risoluto). It then progresses downward in animation until a Pesante solenne point and continues reduction in tempo until the concluding Adagio. In terms of key Foerster chooses such colorful changes as G minor to C-sharp major and E major to G minor. The forms of the three movements are, respectively, sonata, binary, and rondo. Another type of balance is obtained by concluding each movement on a very soft dynamic level.

- ■ *Sonata quasi fantasia* **for Violin and Piano, Op. 177**

As indicated by the title, form is somewhat unleashed in Foerster's duo, written in 1943. And tonalities follow suit. In the first movement, which begins and concludes in F minor, there are nine tonality changes. That sense of rhapsody applies to the other two movements as well, and so do key shifts. There is also a mix of the light and lyrical and rhythmic seriousness. A cyclic touch (as though to pin down the fantasy finally) is the four-measure quotation (in augmentation) of the sonata's initial theme, just before the coda (Vivace) of the final movement.

- ■ *Zbirožská Suite* **for Viola and Piano, Op. 167**

Clear demarcation of form in the second and third movements. In the former, the initiatory statement is a lyrical one, solely for the piano. This is contrasted to an energetic section for both instruments, and then a return to the first section's material, this time the piano repeating its statement combined with a secondary line for the viola. The third movement is also ternary shaped, with push and shove via syncopation and with a restrained middle section.

Movement one is sectional. Textural variety marks the romantic climate that surrounds most of this Czech composer's music.

TRIOS

- ■ *Malá suita (Little Suite)* **for Three Violins**

Originally Foerster wrote his suite for two violins (*see above*). Fifty-eight years later he expanded the scoring to the three-violin total. And three is the figure for the number of movements. Everything is lightly scaled, the pitch range not going beyond the first position. Three-part form in the first piece, small rondo format in the Adagio, and imitational procedures in the final Allegro.

- ■ **Trio [No. 1] in F Minor for Violin, Cello, and Piano, Op. 8**

On the basis of this early work, written at the age of 24, it was apparent that Foerster was a figure to be reckoned with. Most of the piano trio was composed while he was a student at the Modern School in Prague, but its clarity and directness belie that it is the production of a novice,

There are Schumannesque moves throughout, but these do not interfere with genuine individuality. In the first movement the play of duple and triple accentuations within 6/8 meter is colorful. The Scherzo is lightly flowing, of giocoso temper. The most intense music is found in the final pair of movements, tempoed in the usual slow and fast manner. In the latter a short quotation is made of the slow-movement's theme just before the coda.

(The Trio bears the following dedication: "A Monsieur Edvard Grieg.")

QUARTET

- **String Quartet No. 4 in F Major, Op. 182**

A three-movement work in a traditional, romantically conservative idiom (matching Foerster's other compositions). There are additional special details, however.

The composer tells us that both the first and last movements, and the central part of the middle movement, represent his pleasant reactions after being present at a performance in a small town of his opera *Eva.* (Foerster had finished that work in 1897.) The quartet was completed in 1944 during the time the Nazis occupied Czechoslovakia. That tragedy is reflected in the outer parts of the quartet's middle movement, an Adagio framed and pulsed by rhythmic ostinatos in 6/4 time. Foerster describes this music (some of it taken from his Suite for Two Violins, Op. 183a) as picturing the fear he had that resulted from experiencing war.

QUINTET

- **Quintet for Wind Instruments (Flute, Oboe, Clarinet, Horn, and Bassoon), Op. 95**

Slovakian melorhythms are combined with Germanic formalism and procedures in Foerster's wind quintet. The melodic materials display warmth, but excessive bravura is avoided.

Within the sonata formulation of the first movement more attention is given to the initial theme—this, without upsetting formal balance. Tempo change (slow and sustained compared to fast) shapes the slow movement. Movement three is a capricious Scherzo, and this is followed by variational development of a chorale-shaped idea that designates the final movement.

NONET

- *Variations on Two Themes:* **Nonet for Flute, Oboe, Clarinet, Horn, Bassoon, Violin, Viola, Cello, and Double Bass, Op. 147**

The two themes are, as to be expected, dissimilar—one is conjunctly rhythmic, the other is a curved, connected idea. There are seven variations (movements), mostly separated, with the exception of the paired first and second and the paired third and fourth variants. Playing no favorites, Foerster varies the order of the themes in his developments. There is also variational borrowing: A suave idea in variation three is used in wholesale form in variation five (Scherzoso e fantastico).

Foerster's substantial work of twenty-five minutes was dedicated to the famous Czech Nonette, which gave the premiere performance. This ensemble began its life in 1924, and about two hundred compositions have been specifically written for the organization.

Fogg, Eric (1903–39)

QUARTET

- **Quartet in A-flat for Two Violins, Viola, and Cello**

Key enrichment, not academic tonal dogma, confirms Fogg's string quartet. The music is fluid, swinging in and out of its home tonality. There are no jolts, and all alterations are maintained with suave line control. In the middle division the voices pass to a pivotal (nonclassic) dominant, and from this section in E proceed to A-flat via A minor. Within, imitative snippets are contrasted with the harmonic devices and chordal figurations.

The latter are to the fore in the whirlwind Scherzo. In the Finale it is pillared polyphony that is first in the line of duty. Fogg showed a lusty, dramatic voice in his music, and it is emphasized in this string quartet. The Rhapsody (quasi recitative) is exultant and proclamatory, differentiated by soaring lines. Though in the majority, the last give way to a warmed type of neutrality, which, in turn, is completed with music of a plaintive quality.

Folprecht, Zdeněk (1900–61)

It is an unfortunate part of artistic history that some creators remain unknown save in their insular territory. Despite the instantaneous communication potentials of the present day, there continue to be composers of definite high rank who are isolated from the international stages. It requires a fair amount of time for those who have only superficial brilliancy to fade before the excellence of those who have shunned such showmanship (an exhibitionism quite different from honest and artistic experimentation) is recognized. (The artistic stalwarts prove themselves, are recognized, and maintain their place.) The worthy unknowns remain to be discovered by the re-creative researchers. It is a necessity to seek and find. And find one can. Folprecht is a vital example. Seemingly unknown, save in his native land (Czechoslovakia), and even there not totally recognized, he is a voice of creative accomplishment.

Folprecht's music does not challenge accepted practices. It is romantic in style, classically oriented in its structures. But the blend is beautifully made, with a freshness that proves that the classic-romantic viewpoint is not exhausted. Defined melody and colorful harmony with chromatic pigmentation are the basics of Folprecht's work. Above all, his music has profile; it evidences a personality.

QUARTETS

▪ **String Quartet No. 2, Op. 31**

The chromatic urgency in the slow-tempo introduction is the coalition for the initial movement. The phrases constantly move upward, descend, only to rise again. These lines finally burst into an Allegro energico in which the chromatic lines are intertwined with a rhythmic insistence on a two-short–one-long figure. Development follows, and the process of slow and fast sections is recapitulated and compressed at the same time. The constantly declining dynamic level at the end is as dramatic as projected sound ten times heavier. It also prepares for the threnodic slow movement. Entirely muted, that music is shaped by a contrastive, somewhat pedal-pointed Pastorale as the second of the three parts of the movement's design.

A chromatic-scale idea generates the third movement. This is a scherzo-fashioned conception, but minus any relaxed tempo relief. It maintains its persistent drive, additionally stimulated by syncopation, to the end. In the concluding portion the dynamic force is lessened (thus, the first three movements conclude in triple *piano*), but the excitation remains. The finale picks up the quiet conclusion of the third movement and starts softly. It is folk flavored, and its dance measures have a variational flair. This music defines a happy ending to a probing string quartet, and, of course, this time the movement ends forcefully.

▪ **String Quartet No. 3, Op. 35**

One commentator has described this quartet as "full of the joy of living and of an unclouded optimism." Everything being relative, this view can be accepted. However, the third string quartet by Folprecht also includes a large amount of severity that nullifies any thought that it is a mere happy-go-lucky composition.

The brio of the first movement, in sonata form, is unmistakable, and the triplet drive exemplifies a dramatic objective. The Largo is textured like a chorale; the vertical aspects are retained with rhythmic insistence. This slow movement is completely muted, and the darkened color emphasizes the intensity of the single *fortissimo* passage. (Paradoxically, greater emotive introgression is obtained by muted-string timbre rather than from the unmuted quality.)

The Scherzando never ceases its one-in-a-bar pulsation, but its moods vary: brilliant and rhythmic, grazioso, cantabile and expressive. A majestic introduction is the preamble to the main portion of the finale, a motoric Allegro vivace. The introduction returns as the preliminary to the extremely foreshortened recapitulation of the principal material.

NONET

- **Concertino for Flute, Oboe, Clarinet, Bassoon, Horn, Violin, Viola, Cello, and Double Bass, Op. 21**

Three consecutive years mark this composition. Completed in 1940, it was awarded a prize by the Society of Chamber Music in Prague in 1941 and was first performed in 1942 by the Czech Nonette, to whom the work is dedicated.

The "Concertino" designation supports the objective that each instrument is of solo strength within the total mass. Individual highlights there are, but for the greater part Folprecht enjoys the scoring comforts of doublings and blocks of sound derived from an orchestrational blueprint. In no sense is Folprecht's three-movement opus (approximately sixteen minutes in length) a pocket-size concerto. It concerns, however, by its scoring detail, a pocket-size orchestra. There is little doubt that nine instruments extend the chamber music body to the utmost. The sound becomes (in chamber music terms) heady. But everything is clear, and no mud clings to interfere with instrumental balances.

The Toccata drives constantly with rhythm. Only at the end is motoric emphasis discontinued. Ternary headway concerns the Intermezzo. The initial twenty-two measures of this movement reoccur in the concluding section, note for note, instrument for instrument, neatly completed by a seven-measure coda. Minus any explanatory title the Finale is just as much a "toccata" as the opening movement, as well as its parallel in terms of its formal ingredients. A disjunct, rising, thrusted theme is all-important throughout.

Fontana, Giovanni Battista (?–1631)

DUOS

- **Six Sonatas for Violin and Basso Continuo**

These six sonatas (enumerated sequentially as prima, seconda, terza, quarta, quinta, and sesta) are from a set of eighteen Fontana wrote for "il Violino o Cornetto, Fagotto, Chitarone, Violoncino o simile altro Instrumento." They were published in 1641, ten years after Fontana's death. Modern editions of the first six and three others (*see below*) were published by Doblinger in 1962 and 1976, respectively, both sets edited by Friedrich Cerha. Cerha's updating lists the first six sonatas for "violin and piano," but, of course, it should be understood that performances could be made in basso-continuo fashion, with instrumental support of the bass voice.

Indeed, the modern edition notwithstanding, other instruments can be used in substantiation of Fontana's heading. One example is a recording of these six sonatas by Gerard Schwarz on the trumpet, with the addition of a bassoon to the harpsichord's continuo. The performance of these works on modern trumpets (Schwarz used the C trumpet for the first, fifth, and sixth sonatas, and the D trumpet for the other three) can be disputed only by musicological scholiasts. The validity of the music is not lessened by such deviation from stern instrumental truth.

There are plenty of virtuosic opportunities in these early baroque pieces, each containing slow-tempo, polyphonic, and dancelike sections. (The virtuosity is of the type that refreshes the ears of jaded listeners.)

TRIOS

■ **Three Sonatas for Violin, Bassoon, and Basso Continuo**

Three sonatas from the set of eighteen Fontana produced (*see above* for details). In these sonatas, numbered nona (nine), decima (ten), and duodecima (twelve), the music is set differently with the melodic material shared between soprano (violin) and bass (bassoon) instruments and if so desired an additional bass voice giving support to the continuo. It will be noted that the editor here has not translated the continuo for piano as he did in the first six sonatas (discussed *above*). The formats of these three compositions are the same as in the other works in the set.

Fontyn, Jacqueline (1930–)

DUOS

■ *Filigrane (Filigree)* **for Flute and Harp (1970)**

Most flute and harp duos have a gentility about them, even in their dramatic moments. This is not found in Fontyn's rhapsodic amalgam, which covers a wide span of speeds, meters, colors, and effects. Form is free of form in *Filigrane*. Music that exists by intensive assortment does not need thematic interrelation.

Here, the improvisational reasoning of the design of the music (but the content itself is *not* improvisational) offers sufficient equilibrium. And an underlying sense of variation negates any incongruity.

The commitment in *Filigrane* is to total chromatic musical lingo. In the way the score includes an unconventional approach to the harp it brings a reminder of the use of colloquialisms within formal speech. These timbred incrustations give the music a propulsive facture and are basic to contemporary instrumental-type *verismo*. If heard within a strictly tonal ambience such effects would equate vulgarisms.

■ *Mosaïques (Mosaics)* **for Clarinet and Piano (1967)**

A half-dozen pithy pieces with panchromatic logic defining the individual specifics throughout the set. The total measures range from eighteen (the first piece) to thirty-three (the second piece), with running notes in the third movement, for example; fragmentation in the fifth, etc. No serial prejudice here, though the effect makes the music kin.

(The final piece may be omitted, reducing Fontyn's little suite to a five-part total.)

Foote, Arthur (1853–1937)

DUO

■ **Sonata in G Minor for Piano and Violin, Op. 20**

Rich, romantic expressions here, and sensitively stated throughout. The home key of the opening provides a type of tonal dramaticism. However, the stimulant of the minor key is balanced by the temporal use of 9/8 meter—akin to the pulsatile broadness of a Brahms Allegro.

Movement two is an Alla siciliano. No new

mintage, but neatly conveying the dotted 6/8 rhythm derived from the Sicilian dance. Key and tempo changes define the ternary structure, with D major contrasted to F major, and the latter (the central portion) at more than twice the speed. A tripartite plan also frames the slow movement. The intervallic octave ascent marks the outer portions of this Adagio; the middle part is less intense, becomes agitated, and then recedes.

In the finale the determinative aspects expected are present. However, strategically, it is the second theme that becomes principal to the design and provides the piece's peroration. At the age of 37 Foote knew how to create dramatic suavity.

QUARTET

- **String Quartet in D, Op. 70**

The lyrical flow that relates to Brahms is present. No clamor of dissent can rise for such richnesses. There are four movements: Allegro, Scherzo capriccioso, Andante espressivo, and a fast-paced Finale (Allegro non troppo), introduced by a section in slow tempo.

It is a truly romantic and easily digested string quartet. Although Foote's "no hair out of place" manner of writing makes one wish for a little sweat among the notes, there is no denying the warmth and breadth of his composition.

QUINTETS

- *A Night Piece* **for Flute and Strings (Two Violins, Viola, and Cello) (1923)**

This essay (also performable with multiple strings plus double basses) is a recasting of an earlier (1919) orchestral work titled Nocturne and Scherzo. Once reworked, the initial setting was abandoned, even though it had already achieved performance.

Foote's quintet is a beautifully turned out, romantically controlled conception, with a warm continuum of melody. Conservatively styled music, indeed, but not in the dull academic class.

- **Quintet in A Minor for Piano, Two Violins, Viola, and Cello, Op. 38**

Despite his American training, Foote wrapped his music in Germanic paper. It reminds one of Daniel Gregory Mason's remark that "Music hath Brahms to soothe the savage breast." Principally so, in the case of Foote, though the Scherzo has some Mendelssohnian distillations. The preceding movement, an Intermezzo (there is no slow movement), especially shows Foote's full-nurtured romantic style of writing.

In both the Intermezzo and Scherzo movements the designs include the usual comparative Trio section. While balance and symmetry are thereby covered, contrastive temporal consideration did not escape Foote's attention. The Trio of the Intermezzo is in faster tempo; in the Scherzo the Trio's speed is decreased. Tonalitywise the Trio of the Intermezzo makes an engaging and colorful modulation to D-flat major from the home tonality of F major. In the Scherzo the key change from the principal section to the Trio is one of mode: from D minor to D major. Dramatic quality is present in the two end movements, both Allegros. Both are thickly scored.

(Foote's Op. 38 was dedicated ["in Freundschaft gewidmet"] to the Kneisel Quartet, an organization that made chamber music history by being the first permanent group of its kind in America. It was formed in 1886 and continued in existence for thirty-one years.)

Forbes, Sebastian (1941–)

QUARTET

- **String Quartet No. 1 (1969)**

The titling of Forbes's quartet is not patly followed in the structures of the three movements. One would expect a threnodic point of view in the Elegy (movement one); a driving attention to figuration in the Toccata (movement two); and variations, of course, in the Chaconne (movement three). The opposite takes place.

Though there is ternary form in the Elegy, there is considerable rhythmic rhapsodizing and a theatricality in the central open-timbre part (the outer sections are muted). The Toccata shifts gears a number of times (a sectional arch form is used). There is dynamism, but there is also segmenting of the figures and split scoring of the instruments. And sectional formation applies to the Chaconne as well, which is minus a ground-bass declarative.

Fordell, Erik (1917–81)

DUO

- **Sonata for Violin and Piano, Op. 52**

The hothouse of superchromaticism, frequently reaching into the zones of polyharmony and polytonality, styles this music. It is the sort of writing that often has moved a composer to systematize his materials by use of the twelve-tone method. Here, procedures are, indeed, of heavy meshwork.

In the first movement the violin line increases compactness by conjunct detail. A rondo construction is used for the slow middle movement, a freer sonata shape is chosen for the last movement. Although movements one and two are each concluded with combined tonalities,

the last movement draws back into a final G-major chord. It does not fit appropriately with what has preceded.

QUARTET

- **String Quartet No. 4, Op. 50**

Very logical formations, balanced and emphasized by repetitive sections, are found in the three movements. The forms are, in turn, sonata, large song, and rondo. Fordell has no reticence regarding chromaticism. Oddly, however, the soprano and bass lines are often contrapuntally and disjunctively pitched, while the two inner voices move in parallel thirds—a join of the sweet and the tart.

Fordell's quartet keeps the players very active—there is heavy textural weight as a result. There is also a good amount of rhythmic unrest.

Fornerod, Aloys (1890–1965)

DUO

- **Sonata for Violin and Piano, Op. 11**

Fornerod is at his best when his musical discussions have a partial descriptive commitment—"partial" in the sense that there is no programmatic intent at any time. (The work discussed *below* [*Concert* for Two Violins and Piano] is another prime example of this approach.) Although there is conventional definition—the forms are all nicely and neatly packaged and need no probing—the contents are always fresh. (The tonal catalogue has never been and will never be completed.)

The four movements run their course with a polished exactitude that makes the auditor realize not another measure is needed and not an extra measure is included. (Saint Benedict's advice to his monks can be paraphrased: "He who overwrites cannot avoid error.") The Prélude contrasts a majestic theme with a chantlike idea. Both rely on intervallic descents to make their points. Movement two, "Air vif," is vivacious but lightly explained and underpinned with the hop-skip-and-jump of broken chords as a toccata personality unfolds. This "Fast Song" is in sharp contrast to the third part of the duo sonata, "Tender Song" ("Air tendre"). A caressing tune is the major item in this D-sharp-based music. The finale is a Rondeau, a music of truth-telling tonalism and formal finesse.

TRIO

- **Concert for Two Violins and Piano, Op. 16**

This Swiss violinist-composer's work in great part rivals the beauties found in Ravel's *Le Tombeau de Couperin*, which it resembles, especially in its first two movements: Ouverture and Courante et Musette. There is more Ravel (and some Fauré) in the third movement (Air), as well as in the final part of the opus (Tambourin).

That Fornerod's work is imitative in no way lessens its haunting appeal. The imagery is superb; the artistry of this little-known musician is striking. Combining, as he did, the formations found in the French baroque school with the suave spontaneities of Ravel and the graceful charm of Fauré, Fornerod has produced a small masterpiece.

Forst, Rudolf (1900–73)

QUARTET

- **Quartet for Strings (Two Violins, Viola, and Cello) (1936)**

Forst came into prominence with this work,

which was awarded the third prize of $250 in the National Broadcasting Company's Music Guild Contest, held in 1936. Four years later, the composer made an amplified version for full string orchestra under the title *Music for Strings*.

There are four movements rolled into one without pause. Forst is of the semi-free-voice school that is enmeshed in a type of chromaticism that falls short of becoming thick only by its rhythmic urgency. In this respect, of course, he deals with musical eclecticism; but that is no composer's shame, unless it is downright imitation.

The first portion is exceedingly rhapsodic, divisional in its change of moods. This section ties into the Scherzo, a spirited triple-meter division that has change of pace without slowing down the fundamental speed. This is managed by decreasing the sound spread per pulse, using two beats within the span of previous three, or by combining double and triple pulsations. The Adagio sostenuto is a chamber music counterpart of the Wagner-Reger-Strauss school. This postulate is completely turned around in the final portion, wherein free, fugally fueled motor rhythms give an excellent dramatic sweep to the music. It is a sure-fire conclusion to a work not completely individual but of lean directness.

Förster, Christoph (1693–1745)

DUO

- **Sonata in C Minor for Oboe and Basso Continuo**

The striding bass of the Largo compares beautifully with the pitch movement of the oboe line. Movement two also neatly distinguishes between the soprano and bass locations, with conjunct passages in the oboe and significant octave spans in the bass. There is nothing unusual in the final Gigue, but the six-measure unaccompanied oboe section in the preceding Adagio is a refreshing and unexpected matter.

Förster's oboe sonata doesn't need virtuosity. Its clean and clear depiction is the type of writing that can get the attention of jaded listeners of late-baroque music.

Fortner, Wolfgang (1907–)

Fortner is one of the leading composers in Germany, a creator devoted to classical solidity both in his earlier works and in those in twelve-tone style.

Polyphony, one of the most essential parts of musical science, is decisive in Fortner's work. It is a contemporary link to the magnificent polyphonic heritages of Germanic musical history. Important, however, is that Fortner's contrapuntalism is neither labored nor belabored. He does not write the inevitable academic and crabby fugue that appears in so many German composers' works. His fugues have purpose and uncontested dramatic values. The polyphony is natural, makes solid the individual lines when they need such musical lacement. At times the textures of Fortner's music are somewhat brittle; however, the use of dissonance, which tacks the harmony together, prevents any cracking.

DUOS

▪ Sonata for Cello and Piano (1949)

The forms used in this cello and piano sonata are classical in origin, but the composer is not insensitive to the fact that forms long overused may well be the device for soporific music. Fortner reshapes them to meet the demand that structural patterns must evolve, not devolve, from past practices. Although the first movement is marked by sonata design, it should be noted that rondo variation infiltrates, and, there-fore, ordinary treatment of the former method is discarded. The first theme of the movement is stated twice (in between a lighter, more rhythmic section occurs) and is then developed with heavy accents. This is followed by a rhythmic development of the secondary subject and a recapitulation of the movement's opening. The Scherzo proceeds on the set lines of ternary form, but again, its content is of newer thought. This movement's main theme exhibits the subtle alliance between harmony and melody. The former of these is secundal, the latter has its progress of short conjunct steps deflected in turn by disjunct skips from each. A long cello line placed over ostinato rhythm distinctly separates the Trio division.

There are four variations on the theme of the final movement—titled Ballata ("Variations sur un thème de Guillaume de Machaut"). This 14th-century polyphonicist's melody is treated with respect, if not imitation of his style. The second variant is initially for the piano alone; then that instrument retires and permits the cello to complete the section. Low, lightly struck intervallic seconds, in the final variation, show Fortner's careful regard for harmonic affinity between movements. A restatement of the theme, with primitive-type octaves (two voiced, one set for each hand) for the piano, makes an effective close for a resolute and beautifully controlled composition.

▪ Sonata for Flute and Piano (1947)

Though titled a "Sonata" none of the four movements of Fortner's duo are written in sonata form. The closest to sonata form is found in the second movement, fittingly titled Sonatine. "Divertimento" or "Suite" would be a more suitable title for this flute and piano composition.

Rhythmic specifics are important to the outer movements. In the Prélude it is all solo flute and accompaniment for the piano, which has a half-dozen chords and nine times that amount of a single rhythmic figure. In the final Fugue most of the activity is concerned with triplet groups.

Movement three is a set of continuous Variations. The theme is brought back at the end in reshaped form. It brings balance to a mostly ornamental movement, though scherzando-determined in its middle part.

TRIOS

■ Serenade for Flute, Oboe, and Bassoon (1945)

Light in content, serious in structure, and a total delight. Fortner's wind trio covers a lot of territory but is creatively unified.

The Intrada kicks off polyphonically, and its initial C-natural in the flute against a C-sharp in the bassoon indicates what's tonally afoot. A flowing Aria is in second place—a quartal melodic span most important within the polyphony. Movement three is a quintuple-meter Caprice. It deserves a place in the untitled book of musical records. With the exception of isolated quarter notes and quarter notes tied to eighths, practically all of the sounds in every one of the three instruments is marked staccato. Considering that fifty measures are concerned, that's a massive amount of staccato!

Part four is a "Partita zu einem Abschiedslied aus dem 16. Jahrhundert ("Partita Based on a Farewell Song of the 16th Century"). The song is stated in alternate progression with other types of short movements. Further, each time the "Liedsatz" ("Song Movement") is heard it is featured in a different instrument, in turn: flute, oboe, and bassoon. The contrasting movements are an Invention (totally *pianissimo* until the closing measures), a Kanon a 2—the two-voice Canon scored for oboe and bassoon—and a closing Sinfonia.

A vivacious Interludium, constantly interspersed with measures that lengthen the basic duple totals by half a beat, is the next-to-closing part. The finale is a Fuga a 3. Fortner's three-voice Fugue is *Scherz*-toned and related somewhat to the fourth movement "Partita," since the fugue subject is derived from the "Lied" theme of the former.

■ Trio for Violin, Cello, and Piano (1978)

Central to Fortner's piano trio is the active pitch movement. A bravura attitude applies to the use of the total chromatic spectrum. Maximum meaning is drawn from this, translated into a virtuosic handling of the instruments in their sound statements. The music is always alive and active, even in slow-tempo passages; the declaration of harmonic conduct is made in the very first sound—a ten-pitch combination in *fortissimo.*

The rhythmic accents, the rise and fall of linear data, are very flexibly detailed in the first of the two movements: "Lyrische Bewegungen" ("Lyrical Emotions"). Within are a constant interplacement and interweave of repetitive-pitch figures. These, at times, break out into ostinatos. Fortner's type of lyricism is expressionistic, dark colored in its fantasy.

The titling of movement two gives precise explanation of its structure: Caprice-Elegia—Caprice-Elegia. Apposite tempos apply, with fast and slow speeds, respectively. Nothing remains static with this composer. The second Caprice-Elegia uses inversion of the original lines and often simultaneously transfers the initial instrumental role (the cello's line in part one given to the violin, the violin's line assigned to the cello, as well as reversal of the upper and lower lines of the piano part). Further, the Caprice is shortened considerably in its rerun, and to achieve further relationship the Elegia is lengthened in its second appearance.

■ Trio for Violin, Viola, and Cello (1953)

The mathematical blueprint of Fortner's trio

for strings produces a vivid example of discoid music. The formula utilized bears out the theorem that the ending is the beginning.

The Trio is in five movements. Having reached dead center (the middle of the third movement [Kanon]) the music goes into reverse. At the end of the twenty-sixth measure of the Canon the sounds are heard palindromically until the end of its fifty-second measure. There is no stop to the process. The music is kept locked on its retrograde track. Parts three and two of the second movement are heard in reverse until the initial section is reached. At that point, in place of reversal, the triple-timbred polyphony is observed by opposite reflection—upward original motion is now inverted downward. Then, with only a slight deviation here and there, the first movement is retraced, sound for sound, from its original end to its initial start.

QUARTETS

- **String Quartet [No. 1] (1929)**

The opening movement of Fortner's quartet (when published it was not numbered) achieves a type of Gothic musical architecture; its flowing lines are contrasted to granite-shaped, leveled lines. The gargoyles may be considered as represented by the counterpoints, which are demarcated from the rigid geometric arches illustrated symbolically by block writing and stern unisons. Crystal clarity of form results regardless of this metaphorical analysis. Contrapuntal magic is displayed in the second movement, which consists of three sections, entirely fugal. The first of these develops one subject; another idea is stated in the second section, this time a double subject, both placed simultaneously in exposition; then the subject of the first part combines with one of the second's pair to form a peroration of fugal conative power. Fortner furnishes an example of polyphonic writing that eliminates any me-

chanical or mere intellectual consideration; the music is thrillingly alive.

The contrapuntal feast continues in the Scherzo—a rarely used method for picturing musical deviltry. But Fortner does not harm the piquant ideal of the Scherzo with dry polyphony. It further illustrates the exemplary art of this young composer (he was 22 when he composed this quartet) in endowing the most intricate forms of counterpoint with significance. There is a further point of importance. This type of composition records the tenets of many contemporary German composers, marks them as totally antiromantic. Chromatic harmonic divertissements are not for them; in place they seek historical associations, but in a truly creative musicological manner. Fortner's work in the third movement can be termed neo-protopolyphony. He uses a "four-in-two" canon (the first violin and viola playing one of the pair, and the second violin plus cello the other) for practically the entire Scherzo. Only at the end is the canonic skein spooled together. Then, after a measure of pause, a coda in fugal order is added with complete partnership of style. The Trio's contrast is defined as expertly. It begins in a noncontrapuntal manner, but soon the double-canon technique is again resumed; this time the partners change, with the first violin and cello matching each other against the second violin and viola. The effect is compelling because Fortner manages requisite contrast and yet does not depart from a fundamental embracing style. And above all, the entire movement, without loss of power or individuality, has true scherzo feeling.

It would be expected that with such attention to the matter of counterpoint the finale would evidence a similar use. Fortner does not disappoint. The Fuga is huge, its chromatic complexities set forth with all the verve of a Bach. It is prefaced by an Introduzione concertante in which the first violin represents the concertante by the solo prominence of its recitatives and cadenza flourishes. The past centuries resound in the halls of this work.

▪ String Quartet No. 2 (1938)

Four-movement classical composite form most generally balances the outer movements by employing fast tempos and encloses within these slow and scherzo (or one similar to the latter) divisions. Fortner follows this classical weight distribution by having fugal movements as the end sections, with an Air, Scherzo, and Intermezzo placed in between. Thus, by having two slow movements enclose a fast one, a large three-part design securely anchors the quartet in the middle. Further, there is a relationship between the outer movements and the exact middle section of the total centrality, since in the latter counterpoint (canonic investment) is the main principle observed. Moreover, the interpolation of the secondary (Scherzando) theme, drawn from the first movement, binds the work into a tight unit. Nor does the more reticent subsidiary theme of the last movement (though contrapuntal) lack a flexible relationship to the quietness of the expressive Intermezzo. Similarly to be considered is the consanguinity of the Scherzando's homophony in movement one to the fast-paced but nevertheless quiet duopolyphony (less active only when compared to quadruple-voice fugal flight) of movement three. This dialogism of divisions forms a structure so knit as to equate the most germane response of movement to movement, with balance and contrast, total objectives and individual features all clear. Such authoritative credit is generally available only for the elect composers of Bach-Beethoven stature. Accordingly, there is no question that Fortner is a creative master.

There are additional fresh cultivations that add intense interest to the basic, clear interpretation of each of the forms in the quartet— again testimony of the composer's communicative creativeness. The first movement is a sonata with fugal properties. The fugue holds the central position, its subject of legato, whirled, rhythmic figures followed by a springing line taken literally from the quartet's first two measures. This introduction foreshadows the contrapuntal type of framework that holds majority place in the movement and returns at the end. Thus we have fugal development based from without and a circular return made from within. The subsidiary Scherzando theme occurs twice. Its second appearance (before the recurrence of the introductory subject) is thus illustrative of a total redesigned sonata plan in which the fugue is a part of the overall architectural elaboration.

In the third movement the Trio is as pure a vertical formation as is the precise horizontal order of the canon that appears first. Probably realizing that the texture has been several-stranded in the previous movements, Fortner unblushedly composes the Intermezzo as a violin solo with triple-chord accompaniment. The Fuga moves through a large rondo pattern, and once again the novelty of placing polyphony in a mold usually filled with homophony, as well as the reverse, is to be noted. Thus, a fugue is found exceptionally in sonata form (as in movement one of this work), likewise the homophonic patches in the contrapuntal territory described by this final movement. The simpler contrapuntal subject that contrasts to the main fugue indicates the third party in the total argument. If it is represented as C, with the fugue coded by the letter B and the opening listed as A, the composer's rondo outline of A–B–C–B–A–C is made clear—one of classical balance. If Fortner's quartet is heard attentively one will realize a formal significance of the most impressive originality.

▪ String Quartet No. 3 (1948)

Mid-career found Fortner moving away from neoclassicism and some neoromantic colorisms to twelve-tone writing. But Fortner was in no hurry to bury his past aesthetic, as will be heard in this quartet, which represents the first of his twelve-tone compositions. Clearly portrayed forms, sharp rhythmic declarations, and nonrigid row doctrines give special meaning and expressive individuality to the work. The analytical moral here is that the strict dodecaphonic composer supports the method with his materials, whereas Fortner absorbs the method into his materials.

Sonata form is followed in the first movement. There is a sharp use of contrastive textures and, as well, a good amount of repetitive pitches. A full-fledged, exactly erected Scherzo follows. It has a slower-moving Trio and a da capo instruction that gives exact duplication of the main part. It also offers in the muted Trio "Wienerisch" dance qualities by up and down glissandos that are used in almost half of the measures.

Combined with the contrapuntalism of the slow movement (Largo) is the pulsed ambivalence that sets forth the six total beats in both duple and triple form. The finale (Presto) is a fugue. An episode within it, set in homophonic style and quietly dynamic, is also used for the coda. The fugue subject moves in also in soft statement, and by such combination confirms the conclusion.

- **String Quartet No. 4 (1975)**

The fact that performance of this quartet is from scores is especially informative, meaning that strict mensural conditions are not always defined. Most of the first movement is proportionally notated with either long-sounding pitches or at-will figures, mainly with five pitches defined. Otherwise the first movement (Prélude) is athematic and fully polyrhythmic in essence.

Even the theme of the second movement (Variations) is set in proportional (frame) notation. Then follows a type of rhythmic unison to mark the first variation, succeeded again by a section in frame notation and concluded by a totally polyphonic Lento.

The Burlesque and Madrigal movements bathe mostly in these lightly aleatoric waters. The qualities that are basic (derived from the notation of the pitches in graphic manner and the sections in traditional notation) fulfill the titles. However, it is *senza misura* (without strict time) that really codes the details of this entire quartet.

QUINTET

- **Five Bagatelles for Flute (alternating Piccolo), Oboe, Clarinet, Horn, and Bassoon (1960)**

Serial processes, impeccably organized, and emphasizing, in the majority, separative presentations of the pitch ordering. There is this to say: Thematic substances are rarely repeated, and most of the pieces are unitary in their totalities. One can expect to be musically scraped, scrunched, and even vexed. But not bored. The rhapsodic action holds one's attention.

The piccolo is used in the second piece of the set. Its timbre emphasizes the articulation of a persistent rhythmic figure on F-sharp and another one on C.

Question. Why do publishers list instrumentations minus the alternations that may occur? Example: This score, published by Schott, reads: "für Flöte, Oboe, Klarinette (B), Horn (F) und Fagott." Why no indication that the flute alternates with the piccolo?

Foss, Lukas (1922–)

DUOS

- **Capriccio for Cello and Piano (1948)**

A frothy work, making the piano almost a subsidiary voice to the mosaic virtuosity of the string instrument. Foss does not peep into the salon; his music is of concert-hall variety, informally glancing at Coplandesque westernese style and New England square dancing. A fancy as lighthearted as a Haydn finale.

- *Composer's Holiday* **for Violin (or Flute) and Piano (1944)**

- *Dedication* **for Violin (or Flute) and Piano (1944)**

- *Early Song* **for Violin (or Flute) and Piano (1944)**

Music that predates the period when Foss moved into the avant-garde circle in a desire to shed his tonal past fully and reside in the territory of what he once termed "dangerous music." The former means music of neoclassic arrangement, fully tonal, of course.

In 1986 Foss revised these pieces slightly, without disturbing their original concept and format. In so doing he indicated that the pieces could be played separately or as a unit with the title *Three American Pieces* for Violin (or Flute) and Piano. He also made orchestral transcriptions of the piano parts.

Early Song has an A–B–C–B structure, with a sensitively quiet conclusion. Ternary design marks *Dedication*. There is push and punch and Americanese ardor in the rhythmic drive of *Composer's Holiday.*

- *Three American Pieces* **for Violin (or Flute) and Piano**

See above under: *Composer's Holiday* for Violin (or Flute) and Piano

QUARTETS

- *Divertissement "Pour Mica"* **for String Quartet (String Quartet No. 2) (1972)**

"Mica" is the name used by her intimates for the owner and directing head of the important French publisher Editions Salabert. It represents the Romanian diminutive for her given name, Eugénie. Formally, Mica is Madame Francis Salabert. Foss's short piece was composed for a private concert of premieres given at Madame Salabert's home in Paris in November 1971. (The other works given their first performances were by Xenakis, Constant, Malec, Takemitsu, and de Pablo.)

The pitches used in the *Divertissement* are at the players' discretion. Foss regulates only the registral ranges, dividing them into five specific areas. For the greater part all rhythms are precisely indicated. Special to the piece is the considerable amount of natural harmonics employed. These are expanded from the five available series possible in a string quartet by eliminating one (on E) and adding eight others. The latter are obtained by retuning the strings of the violins—one set a half tone higher and the other a half tone lower.

Color flashes are paramount. So is activity—none of the textures are thinned; the four players are always involved. The first nineteen measures are repeated in da capo strictness, but this is a paradox, for the pitch choices (unless steadfastly determined prior to performance) will differ on the repetition. So does the timbre quality, since the repeat is to be col legno, with the exception of defined plucked sounds.

The coda is solely visual activity; sound by the performers is *verboten*. Foss's instruction is unarguable: "jouer sans jouer" ("play without playing"). Some of this pictorialism occurs within the piece. In a *Divertissement* such "nonarco" arco (a bowed silence) is fitting!

- *Echoi (Echoes)* for Four Soloists: Clarinet, Cello, Piano, and Percussion (Timpani, Vibraphone, Chimes, Glass Chimes, Antique Cymbal, Anvil [or Metal Plate], Temple Blocks, Wood Blocks, Wood Chimes, Two Small Muffled Gongs, Suspended Deep Gong, Sand Block, Three Suspended Cymbals [Sizzle and Normal], Three Pipes, Bongos, Timbali, Triangle, Claves, Snare Drum, Bass Drum, and Garbage-Can Lid) (1963)

Echoi—a four-part work that covers almost a half hour in length—sounds serialistic (but is not) and improvisatory simultaneously. There is improvisation—but the controls are defined by the composer so that one hears both coordinated and noncoordinated rhythms—and a process of fade-out and fade-in in the textures. Foss does not relinquish his creative rights to the performers and does not opt for blatant chance. Importantly, the materials are controlled by invented symbols and by explicit footnotes in the score.

There are plenty of echoes: canonic, imitations, from a distance, and in the last few minutes of the work through the imitating of previously heard music by the use of prerecorded tape tracks. All the echoes are Fossian. In the first three parts the qualities are direct but a bit restrained. Here, within *Echoi III*, Foss has used a children's tune that undergoes developmental distortion that is of direct contrast to the enormous activity and climactic tension found in *Echoi IV*.

One writer has termed *Echoi* "one of the most significant works of contemporary chamber music." True. Foss, on the other hand, calls for "four soloists." That is not exactly the proper description of a chamber music piece. In the score's prefatory notes this is rectified, the direction reading: "*Echoi* requires four virtuoso performers."

- *Round a Common Center* for Chamber Ensemble (Piano Quartet or Piano Quintet or Piano Quartet with Mezzo Voice or Piano Quintet with Mezzo Voice) (1979)

Commissioned for performance at the Winter Olympic Games, Foss's opus became an all-purpose, many-possible-formationed composition. First it was to be for strings and piano (the former three or four in total) with voice optional. Then, since Yehudi Menuhin was to perform with the commissioning group (the Cantilena Chamber Players), Foss was asked to add an optional part that the violinist would perform (and did, though this part is naturally not included in the published material). For the premiere performance Foss added narration, using an Auden poem. (This was used only in a recording made of the opus; it is not included in the definitive published score.)

Round a Common Center is freely tonal. It is also freely proportioned in its slow–fast divisions. In the latter improvised portions occur, but with pitch-controlled methodology directed by the composer. Soundless action is also included, with fingering and bowing maintained for visual results only, though the player may insert "occasional accidental sounds *ppp*."

- *Solo Observed* for Piano, Vibraphone (or Marimba), Harp (or Cello), and Organ (or Accordion) (1982)

In 1981 Foss wrote an extended work for piano titled *Solo for Piano*. It is constructed from a twelve-tone motive pulsed in consistent eighth notes. Consistency leads to persistency. The music is a tremendous perpetual-motion conception that will remind one more of minimalist procedures than ostinato. However, Foss denies this reaction, baldly and boldly. It is not minimalist music, he states, "in spite of an insistent, repetitive element, because each repetition is also a change implying development, growth and forward movement." Whatever it might be, it grips the listener with its pitch and rhythmic anchorage.

In 1982 Foss enlarged *Solo*, adding three instruments. The first part of the new work used the first 276 measures of the piano solo and then continued with 121 additional measures, in which most of the piano part is a duplicate of the original solo piece. (Foss changed his apportionment of measures somewhat, none of which have designated meters—the eighth note being equal throughout, regardless of totals within any measure.) Thus *Solo for Piano* became *Solo Observed*, in which a different atmosphere reigns. Foss says of the piece that "it is as if a new plateau has been reached." Indeed, but the rhythmic vibratility, the music's undulatance remains.

This is not the end of the story of this composition. From the chamber version of *Solo Observed* a setting was made for a chamber orchestra consisting of flute, clarinet, bassoon, horn, trumpet, trombone, one or more violins, one or more violas, and one or more cellos, in addition to the still important part for the piano.

■ String Quartet in G (String Quartet No. 1) (1947)

This work followed productions that were initially influenced by Hindemith and then by Copland. The first movement (Allegro) exemplifies aliveness through moving lines, spiced with lyrical themes, assorted in a neo-Hindemithian fashion. But the stringencies here are less ascetic than Hindemith's. Foss filters his through a more luscious cloth. This initial movement is surrounded, prologue and epilogue, by a slow section that intersects the fast-tempo material three other times in a dispersed development of its own idea.

Movement two consists of a theme and variations. The variants are free, dovetailing, as it were, several movements in one; harking

back (only slightly) to the free form of late Beethoven—thus, a polyglot of variation form itself and slow–scherzo–fast form.

Foss's quartet was especially recognized, receiving one of the annual publication awards of the Society for the Publication of American Music.

QUINTET

■ *The Cave of the Winds (La Grotte des vents)*: Wind Quintet (1972)

There is this to say in praise of Foss: His eclectic vocabulary keeps increasing. The word *eclectic* is used in the broadest (but absolute) sense since his style and procedure are the sum and substance of the restless avant-garde compositional world that he draws into his own creative disquietude. His objectives are not vacillatory, however, but with the know-how that he knows what he wants (Foss has always been a maven of the most fashionable trends in writing music—a fact, not necessarily a criticism!) and wants to use what he knows. In each of his compositions he moves into the creative fray with a firm (and from 1960 onward, always new) battle plan, carrying it out to the letter. As a result there is within this period of work (Foss will doubtless change, he always has) a development that shows growth in terms of the special aesthetic if not a maturing into a recognizable profile. However, that which is immediately recognizable is the éclat that marks *The Cave of the Winds*.

A specific technical relationship exists between this work and the *Divertissement (see above)*, not in content or form. Both, of course, indulge in avant-garde methodology of writing. However, as the quartet piece digs into the intrinsic potential of the string instruments and expands their timbre territory, so the quintet emphasizes the newest findings for the wind group. Pointedly, the latter's most important point concerns multiphones, whereby two or more pitches (chords, therefore) are sounded simultaneously on a single wind instrument. *The Cave* swarms with these. The initial eleven measures of the piece consist entirely of polydissonant mixtures of three-, four-, five-, and six-part chords for flute, oboe, clarinet, and bassoon. Multiphoned chords occupy the end of the first part, are found in the middle, and in practically every measure of the concluding section. However, the technique is not as yet perfected, and the sounds produced are often not of top reliability as to intonation, control, and total balance within a chord. Embouchure and air pressure must be governed with microintensity and concentration, and what is achieved in one place doesn't work in another. The chordal sounds are brashly new, enticing and exciting, but a hit-and-miss factor still prevails. No matter—the general effect, if not the purity, is unique.

Foss explains that he loves these multiphonic sounds. They enable him "to evoke anything from ancient Japanese court music to electronic music." (The latter quality is especially brought to mind.) He also uses them so as to avoid "slipping into the inevitable 'pastorale,'" found in so much wind music.

The Cave of the Winds has three distinct sections. A variety of chordal polyphony leads to a mix of figuration, ad lib material, textural shifts, and the like. It is finalized by mass chordal patterns indicated "repeat (à la Morse code)." The next major section is some eight minutes of aleatoric material outlined and "controlled" by the composer. Foss describes it as "strident, pauseless, merciless." (So much for a composer's quasi-sadistic approach to wind-instrument performers!) The final part of the quintet returns to the slow tempo of the beginning, and thus classical ternary form rears its head! The writing for these thirteen measures is severely vertical, and in one place totally in unison with subtle *pianissimo* strength. Such an effect, coming among the "merciless" chordal corrugations, is like a sudden *Mutterakkord* crashing into an elementary Czerny C-major exercise.

Fourestier, Louis (1892–1976)

QUARTET

- **String Quartet** *(of Venice)*

Fourestier was a traditionalist, and his quartet stays in the line of French romanticism. The Venetian flavor is hardly noticeable, save in the second movement (Serenata e Barcarolla), and even there the tempo in the outer parts (a presto at ♩ = 168) is not made for musical swaying. In movement one (Appassionato) there is a rhapsodizing that has more French attachment than Italian.

Movement three is a thickly textured Notturno. Movement four is a fully developed Tempo giocoso, Canzone e Stretta. One sees the shadow of Florent Schmitt hovering over these two movements.

Fourestier was a conductor specializing in opera (he appeared at the Metropolitan Opera in New York in 1946, 1947, and 1948). The colors used in the quartet show a sensitive knowledge of string instrumentation. Bowing placements are thoroughly indicated (for playing over the fingerboard and in normal position), and exact string definition to obtain subtle timbre differences is precisely selected. Col legno plays an important part in the second movement, and for the last quarter of the third movement the fourth string of the cello is lowered to B-flat to extend the range, especially for pedal purposes.

Frackenpohl, Arthur (1924–)

DUOS

- **Ballad and Tango for Flute and Piano (with Optional Rhythm Instruments) (Guitar, Drums, and Double Bass)**

An example of crossover style (with or without the optional instruments) in terms of chamber music. The song and dance statements include flute passages that can be improvised (for which chordal outlines are given) or performed as written. The rhythm group sets up a constant resonancy: chords for the guitar with two short optional solos, brushes on the small drum in the Ballad, sticks used for the Tango, and a plucked bull fiddle.

- **Sonatina *based on Three Sonatinas by Friedrich Kuhlau* for Trumpet and Piano**

An example of a wonderful conceit. Long known as staples in the teaching studio, Kuhlau's Sonatinas offer some worthy music. Frackenpohl has dipped into this repertoire and used material from three of Kuhlau's piano sonatinas for his three-movement duo.

Nothing scholastic in this transfer-paraphrase. And much more than trifles. A march atmosphere surrounds the first movement (from Op. 55, No. 5). The central movement is slow paced and based on music from Op. 20, No. 2. The finale is the Rondo from Op. 20, No. 1, which is probably the best-known movement in the Kuhlau piano catalogue. Throughout, there is stylistic rapport and no sense of trying to register more than is contained in the basic material.

- **Variations *("The Cobbler's Bench")* for Tuba and Piano**

Trust the music of Frackenpohl to be vividly colored and always offering some interesting twist. Here the title gives no hint that the theme for the five variations is the well-known tune "Pop! Goes the Weasel."

The theme is preceded by a short introduction which returns at the end for codetta purposes. No mistaking the outlines of the variants, which embrace a full contrastive gamut from the fast waltz of variation three to the doleful, minor-key fourth variation. Following the final variation is a good-size cadenza for the tuba. Everything is musical and of contemporary flavor.

QUARTET

- **Three Short Pieces for String Quartet (1970)**

Neoclassic punch. The virtuosity in the Toccata carries over into the Fughetta (the third piece), its subject having a range of a twelfth and agitated by syncopation that adds excitement to the fast tempo. In between is an Arioso that also favors the healthy aliveness of rhythmic punctuations.

QUINTETS

- **Brass Quintet for Two Trumpets, Horn, Trombone, and Tuba**

Music wedded to tradition, updated with a bit of contemporary accent, in both harmony and rhythm. Frackenpohl can write a good tune, as can be heard in the Blues. The outer parts (March and Rondo) move smartly. The former is form filled but avoids academic interpretation by mixing a rhythmic format with legato-spun lines. The Rondo includes unequivocal balance with a da capo repeat of the initial forty-seven measures. A sensible, practical piece of music.

- *Flutes Four* for **Four Flutes and Piano with Optional Rhythm Accompaniment (String Bass, Guitar, and Drum Set)**

Another entry by this American composer in the field of crossover chamber music (*see above*: Ballad and Tango).

The music is described as "in the pop-rock idiom" and the scoring for the flute-piano quintet has a neat extroverted chamber music sound. The published score analyzes the formal side as comprising "an introduction and three choruses with each chorus in the form AABA."

(Another version of this three-minute piece was made by the composer for four flutes and band.)

Françaix, Jean (1912–)

DUOS

- **Divertimento for Flute and Piano (1953)**

Written for the eminent French flutist Jean-Pierre Rampal (who gave the world premiere with the noted French pianist Robert Veyron-Lacroix in January 1955, in Paris) Françaix added a few pinches of virtuosity to his score. This is quite apparent in the whirl and whip of the opening Toccatina and the vim and vigor (even though the music is mostly *pianississimo* and never above a *mezzopiano*) of the Perpetuum Mobile (Perpetual Motion) of part three. For the other side of the character coin there is a lento-paced Notturno and another slow piece (metronomically identified only), titled Romanza. Athletic prose and a sense of exuberant humor describe the Finale. The wispy final triple *piano* measures are a delight and just as dynamic as a *fortissimo* closer.

- **Sonatine for Piano and Violin (1934)**

Compared to Stravinsky's neoclassic discourse, Françaix writes limericks. His lines are ruled off, bisected. For example, practically the entire first movement is formed from two- and four-measure phrases in capricious language. There is the fullest confidence displayed as the composer conveys the jigs and joggles of his pert scherzo idea over and over again. It equates with minute outlined Stravinsky, decidedly *not* in the grand manner.

The short Andante is expressed by a plan of antiphonal scoring in triplex denomination. First, a passage in thirds cadences on an intervallic fifth and is replied to by chorale form in the piano; second, the instruments merge in the middle of the movement and again the piano states its folk-like vertical measures; third, for climax, the violin brings in its phrase together with the keyboard idea for the final cadence.

The last movement is a set of pithy variations (Thême varié). Here again structure and style are well defined. The chattery utterance with a light glance is present in the waltz (variation one); filmy slow monotone is heard in the second variant; the piano is profiled by ostinato and perpetual rhythm in the third variation. The triple-meter brilliance and quick-change management of the fourth and final (longest) variant will remind one of the opening movement.

TRIOS

- **Divertissement for Oboe, Clarinet, and Bassoon**

Music conceived in the tonal-yet-not-throttled technique of neoclassicism. This is music similar to an acrobat on a tightrope; he makes all the gestures of falling off, creates much excitement, but keeps everything under control.

The opening three-part Prélude, in pandiatonic D-flat major, connects to an Allegretto assai. Formal slickness and formal exactness are in the latter, with all the phrases four and eight measures in length. Part three is a long-lined Elégie. It was described perfectly by a reviewer when the score was issued in 1954, by Schott, as music of "a hushed, haunting atmosphere." A Scherzo completes a chamber piece of viability and intelligent style.

- **Trio for Violin, Viola, and Cello (1933)**

Tonal consideration is primary but not confined. Explorations of other key points are made, but not at the expense of unsettling the continuity and importance of the main key. Its authority and relationship to all conditions is maintained.

The C-major key of the first movement, together with its modulations, displays all the germane and definite gestures of tonality. But the swaying of the tonality is exciting; one expects collapse, a falling into a quasi-atonal net. Françaix, an expert neoclassicist, avoids it; he knows his harmonic ropes and how to sway on them. It is the suppleness of the system that gives, paradoxically, the essential, pivotal strength. The pandiatonic chords and polyharmonies are kept in absolute tension within the light, kinetic vivaciousness of the opening movement until the final three measures, when C major is fully confirmed.

The Scherzo, aided by offbeat entrances, is just as light. In the sense of the repetition of a theme, the slow movement, though not so designated, is as much a rondo as the final movement, which is so classified. The unserious last movement has verve and go, but also includes a very effective flux of dynamics and speed that says as much as the vigorous jabber of the three string voices. This is made by a section cut into the movement (preceded and followed by a whole measure of silence) entirely in *pianissimo* with ironic, slower tempo. And, not to be overlooked, is the triple *piano* dynamic of the last measures of the movement—a typical thumb-to-the-nose effect.

QUARTETS

- ***Petit Quatuor (Little Quartet)* for Saxophones (Soprano, Alto, Tenor, and Baritone Saxophones)**

Discerning divertimento detail. All three pieces show the hand of an expert. The first piece, "Gaguenardise" ("Sarcasm"), vividly illustrates Françaix's usual role as the bright boulevardier of the neoclassic musical lodge. It also applies to the concluding "Sérénade comique" ("Comical Serenade"). Fun, yes; the humor, possibly a bit forced, arrived at by a preponderance of slap tongue sounds—used in more than four dozen measures. The movement in between is a gentle, chordally strung Cantilène (Song). It gives great contrast not only by mood and tempo but by being scored as a trio for the three lower-pitched saxophones.

- **Quartet for English horn, Violin, Viola, and Cello (1971)**

Scored for an unusual combination but styled in the familiar arguments of neoclassic language. There are five connected movements, flexible in their divertimentolike actions. These alternate in speeds, beginning with an Allegro vivace and concluding with an Allegro giocoso. Metrical flow is consistent with Françaix's fluid and civilized tonally expanded music. In the final movement the alternation of 4/8 and 5/8 measures in several sections is an additional spark to music of hedonistic spirit.

- **Quartet for Flute, Oboe, Clarinet, and Bassoon (1933)**

Pleasurable easy-come, easy-go music in Françaix's bright neoclassic style. There are four movements. Three are in allegro tempo (movements one, three, and four), paced at the same metronomic designation of 120 per pulse. Movement two is a gentle, slow movement, but even in this case the feeling is a somewhat active duple stress within each measure. Utterly French music, down to the last flippant sixteenth note.

QUINTETS

- ### Quintet for Clarinet and String Quartet (1977)

Short up and down phrases preface the initial Allegro. It has grace-note energy and good amounts of blocked string writing. The Scherzando has Françaix's usual vitality and exuberance. It also contains lots of plucked string sounds. Classical design is attended to by this neoclassicist in the inclusion of the basic Trio division. Here it is slightly slower in tempo, but no less active than the material that precedes it.

Movement three (Grave) gives special attention to the color of the clarinet's lower register (the so-called chalumeau). The finale is a Rondo. Its ending is again special. The unaccompanied clarinet brings reminders of the previous music's character: one measure of Lento, four measures of Allegro, eight measures of Scherzando, two free measures, and then seven measures that relate to the Rondo. The concluding six measures are for the five instruments in speedy tempo (but più tranquillo), totally at a soft level. Very effective.

- ### Quintet for Flute, Violin, Viola, Cello, and Harp (1934)

As usual, Françaix cannot be accused of harmonic incuriosity in this work, but the probing is strictly within neoclassic boundaries. Tonalities (F major, D minor, G major, and G major again) cover the four movements but do not block a lightly paced freshness throughout

and, for comparison, a gentle expressivity. The swift and witty Rondo finale is Haydn dressed in smart 20th-century clothes. (According to Harry Halbreich's notes on the work the refrain of this presto-tempo music "recalls a fast folk-song of Ile-de-France.")

- ### Quintet for Winds (1948)

Mostly verve and go for this fellow, a member of the neoclassic group. Only the third movement (a theme with five variations) has a partially serious demeanor. There are assorted delights in Françaix's wind quintet, including the flippant moves in the first movement, and the snide clownish steps in the final Tempo di marcia francese. This sort of musical sweet is Françaix's speciality of the house.

His statement regarding the music he creates is relevant. "My desire is to communicate joy rather than sorrow. Why be sad when you live in Paris? It would amount to cowardice towards your neighbour. Leave sorrow to silly people—or to the truly great. Aim at simplicity in music, in science, even in politics. Simplicity is more than a virtue; it is a faculty. But it is a posthumous faculty, acquired through sacrificing one's life to it . . . ."

OCTET

- ### Octet for Clarinet, Horn, Bassoon, Two Violins, Viola, Cello, and Double Bass (1972)

The neatly shaped profile of neoclassic creativity. Françaix's music never surprises with a stylistic shift, but, nonetheless, it always satisfies. More than once in this piece one hears the formal ingenuousness that marked the early compositions of Les Six, since Françaix's Octet never moves away from its hedonistic Gallic simplicity.

Only the fact that there is a defined Scherzo as movement two prevents definition of the principal part of the opening movement as a scherzo. (It is preceded by an introduction of a folkish tune with plain chordal harmonies.) The final movement, though not so described, is developed in a variational manner. Despite the shifts of its tempo gears a number of times, it is basically a waltz movement.

The dedication is to the Octuor de Paris. More important is the note in the score that Françaix composed the piece "à la mémoire vénérée de Franz Schubert."

Franchetti, Arnold (1906–)

OCTET

- *Three Italian Masques*: **Concertino for Piano, Brass (Three Trumpets and Two Tenor Trombones), Percussion (High, Small, and Medium Drums, Suspended Cymbal, and Bass Drum), and Double Bass (1953)**

A puppet-show tale about a cuckolded husband is the springboard for this work. The first movement, consisting of a type of prelude, nine variations, and a Finale, starts with the "Introduction of the Masques" and then portrays the three characters: Arlecchino, "the thief of love"; Columbina, "the frivolous wife"; and Pantalone, "her jealous husband." Movement two is a Serenade (described as the "impassioned call of Arlecchino"), and the last part is "Imbroglio e Baruffa" ("Imbroglio and Quarrel").

Sprightly twelve-tone derivations are used in movements one and three. The squared-to-the-last-chord Serenade is in direct contrast, being set in E-flat major. Its tonal state— almost a prosaic one—cleverly serves to brighten and ready the ear for the truly rhapsodic ventures surrounding the Finale's total chromaticism.

Franck, César (1822–90)

Franck holds a unique place in musical history. Because of his individuality of speech and style, one can recognize a work by Franck as readily as one can identify the musical fingerprints of Bach, Beethoven, and Tchaikovsky.

This Belgian was a French naturalized citizen who rescued that country's music from complete absorption with operatic devices of Wagnerian hue. It is difficult to estimate how delayed the maturity of French chamber music would have been if Franck had not appeared on the scene. It is sufficient to say Franck pursued the ideal of pure instrumental music, was unconcerned with the heroics of Wagner's staged shows, or with the need for nationalistic suggestions. He worked studiously and assiduously. His music is not large in bulk; the chamber music total is very small. Yet each of the single examples he composed for violin and piano, string quartet, and piano quintet is a masterpiece in its own right, and by comparison with other great works in similar media.

Franck's harmony, counterpoint, and forms are traditional. They stem directly from Beethoven. One hears the word *mystical* in connection with Franck, but this thought is not due to the harmony per se but to Franck's treatment of the harmony. Franck's music is firmly ensconced in the major and minor tonal systems; it avoids the obvious by chromatic shifts and uses certain dissonant chords as representing their own rights—not transitories to simple diatonic elements. He uses form as a means of musical welding. The cyclic insistence that was hinted at by Beethoven and considered by the romantics becomes fully mature in Franck. The cyclic premise is that organic unity best exists by relationships of themes within movements and are then taken over into other movements, interlocked in every possible way by thematic transference or portional carryover (from one movement to another). This represents an intense belief that a work exists not in its separate parts but as a whole, no matter how many movements are concerned and regardless of thematic relationships. Unity is expressed thereby, first having been implied by contrastive materials and all exemplifications are placed in order. Franck, therefore, is only romantic in that he agglutinated set forms. Since classicism is defined by use of sonata, rondo, binary and ternary forms, the scherzo, and the like, deviations from these are still classically bound, but romantic in their subjective newness.

One reason may be proposed for Franck's cyclic decision. This originates from his work as a church organist for over thirty years, during which multi-improvisations were a necessity in the services. What better method of obtaining organic unity, in what might otherwise have been just aimless wandering on the organ keys, than development and reuse of material?

DUO

- **Sonata in A Major for Violin and Piano**

Franck's awareness that chords need not necessarily be tonic-built in order to represent stability is exemplified by the chordal opening: The tonic is equaled by a simple dominant-ninth chord (a favorite Franckian vertical combine). The use of a slower tempo than usual for the opening movement (Allegretto ben moderato) is based on a plan to expose the fastest speeds as alternates to slower ones. In this manner, the work ends in fastest tempo, rather than following the more general custom of inclosing the boundary lines with the speediest movements and placing the less precipitate ones in the center.

The first theme played by the violin is the quintessence of the mood of the movement, establishing it. It has all the beautiful trappings and substantiation of Franck's musical aesthetic. To this, the piano replies with the second

theme, of different footing, and from these the entire movement is built.

The first entrance of corporate thematic use occurs after the opening theme of the second movement (a surging, wild, chromatic ride that proceeds up for tension and releases downward). It is represented by a passionate delivery of the first subject of the opening movement. Usual development and recapitulation follow, plus a dynamic coda. The intervallic third—which marks the stability of the connective theme—appears once again in the third movement, a fantasy only in the sense of musical review. Material previously heard and themes that will appear later are imbedded in this Recitativo-Fantasia.

In the last movement one of the most beautiful canons in all of music occurs. The piano is strictly imitated by the violin in amazing technical skill that does not interfere with the artistic outpour of the movement. Thematic scenery from other movements will be noted, kinship and communal attraction are proven, but above all sings this gorgeous canon.

It is important to set the record straight. Neither the cello and piano version, which gets a fair amount of play, nor the viola and piano version, which is rarely heard, were the work of Franck. Bearing in mind sales potentials, the publishers of the Franck opus issued these transcriptions. Recently, James Galway (the Irish-born flute virtuoso) has been performing a setting for flute and piano (he also recorded it). This, too, is riding the profit wagon without any cost or any authority. And, of course, once again, this version was never thought of, let alone sanctioned, by Franck.

TRIOS

- **Trio No. 1 in F-sharp Minor for Piano, Violin, and Cello, Op. 1, No. 1**

Franck's first published work consisted of three trios, written at the precocious age of 18. Some writers tend to belittle those works. Of course, they evince immaturities. In any event, Franck's stylistic simmerings are unmistakably present (and in the very first measures of the first movement). Four times, the eight-measure, quasi-passacaglia bass line repeats and drums itself into the mind, recurring in portions until the second of the cyclic themes (an up-down scale) is heard. These bass and scale lines are the two factors—none else; repeated, trimmed, but never obscured. It is Franck's proclamation of how he will compose from then on.

The scale theme is disported first in the Scherzo that follows, later in the hammered motive that starts the Scherzo's Trio. Rhythm is somewhat stilted, but cyclic treatment is not. The finale follows without pause. And the two patterns are present once again, almost overdone, one might say. There are weaknesses here, a type of sectional piecework, but the point to realize is the significance of two themes spearheading, driving, and almost constituting the entire raison d'être of a three-movement work.

- ■ *Trio de salon (Drawing Room Trio)*: **Trio No. 2 in B-flat Major for Piano, Violin, and Cello, Op. 1, No. 2**

Franck's father was a hard taskmaster, wanting to capitalize on his son's abilities. Though apparently Franck had no intention of writing another trio after the F-sharp-minor example, under his father's order two more trios were composed. Franck senior had patronage in mind with this plan. To curry favor, therefore, not only the new second and third trios *(see below)*, but the initial one as well *(see above)*, were dedicated to Leopold I, then the Belgian king. Failure resulted—the music did not catch the monarch's attention.

The first movement is quaint, ordered on simple themes with simple accompaniments. However, instrumental equality is present. The second movement is set in barcarolle rhythm

and style. Those who wish can get a glimpse of the Franck to be in the last three measures of the introduction; the chromatic glides are the man of the violin and piano sonata and the quintet. A minuet shows how salonlike this work is. A rather plain quasi rondo forms the last movement.

- ■ **Trio No. 3 in B Minor for Piano, Violin, and Cello, Op. 1, No. 3**

The picture of the first movement is drawn by surging and dramatic means based on reiterative rhythm, powered by triplets. The form is very clear, as incisive as the rhythm surrounding it. No matter how greatly materials are varied in a rondo form, there must be the predominance of a focal theme. The very *relationship* demands the strength of the first theme be compared to a semisubsidiary idea in second place, with a full subsidiary item in third place. In the second movement, the plan is somewhat different, yet does not fully succeed because of the lack of precise relationship definition. Two themes occur twice in succession, then, to complete matters, an augmentation of the first one is followed again by the initial subject, this time in regular rhythm and with simple accompaniment. What began nicely ends flatly.

Motival treatment, represented in elemental state in the introduction, is used in the last movement, together with various changes of tempo for further relationships to the first speed. The plan is somewhat contrived, not fully convincing.

- ■ **Trio No. 4 in B Major for Piano, Violin, and Cello, Op. 1, No. 4**

Originally, this one-movement work formed the final movement of the third piano trio *(see above)*. On the advice of Liszt, Franck wrote a new finale for the third trio and revised his previous final movement, casting it into a one-movement trio, dedicated to Liszt. Liszt would like it—it bears the transformation of theme technique that he used in his symphonic poems. The *idée fixe* is the skin and bones of the musical body. Every change is in terms of this thematic demand. Tempos are nonuniform; keys shift, reiteration made in various guises. But, above all, inside the music is this theme in assorted means of communication. It is a fantasy on one theme; Franck's cyclic resources in one compact package.

QUARTET

▪ String Quartet in D Major

Franck was an organist, and the organ sound penetrated deep into him; it tempered the writing of many of his works. The opening of this quartet, built broadly like a gigantic musical arch, is obviously influenced by the organ. Throughout the entire work, there is a massed, pillowed use of the string instruments, at times in the form of thickly held chords over tonal movement play. The instrumentation principles of a string quartet require that parts be equal, and that there are movement and relationship without dismissing the fundamental of themes, accompaniment, and the like. But the terms of any instrumentation (provided there be no wholesale use of theme and mere sonorous support) must be considered in relation to the modus operandi of the composer himself. Brahms scored his quartets in *his* style, Beethoven in *his*. This should answer critics who claim Franck's quartet is thick, the sonority padlocked and forming only string-quasi-organ music. Essentially, it is Franck, every inch of its four-instrument way.

The first movement has two tempos related to two ideas. The slow tempo section (Poco lento) begins and ends the movement with a motto theme that is fully developed. The Allegro is built on a subject already used in the coda portion of the previous slow section, and forms the entire basis, with certain subsidiaries, of the first movement's fast section. Splitting the fast section in two is a fugal presentation of the slow theme. Franck, therefore, makes a rondo plan by combining two movements within one. The representative pattern, A–B–A–B–A, indicates the whole. (It can also be analyzed as a five-part lied form.)

The Scherzo movement is enhanced in its shadowy skipping and deft dancing by muting the instruments. It contains an element that gives perfect illustration of how much can be said by not saying anything at all. Twenty-four times during this Vivace there is absolute silence, frequently lengthened by fermatas. These form the most dramatic contrasts against the several Scherzo materials. And within the Trio of the movement the cyclic stamp is softly pressed in when the cello states the opening theme of the quartet.

The slow movement (a Larghetto in B major) sounds, notwithstanding its structural sections, all of a piece, restless in rhythm and pitch, almost improvisatory in its restiveness. Here there are five sections plus a coda, the fourth one refers to a theme in the Scherzo's Trio, continuing thereby the cyclic interlock already begun in the previous movement.

In the final movement the full principle of thematic reidentification and reorientation takes place. Built into the principal Allegro molto are themes boldly restated from the other movements, especially the first one. The rhythms remain the same, or are in augmentation. The movement announces and sums up. It is noun and verb in the final musical sentence of this majestic composition. Themes are specifically connected, particularly the first-movement subject, which moves restlessly, in distinct antithesis to its initial majestic proclamation. In addition, the third movement's theme now reverses itself; instead of being restricted in its dolce state, it here sings triumphantly.

QUINTET

- **Piano Quintet in F Minor**

This important work was dedicated to a fellow composer, Camille Saint-Saëns, who dismissed it summarily, thought it poor, disliked its warmth. After the first performance, in which Saint-Saëns took part, he refused to accept from Franck the manuscript on which his name appeared as the dedicatee. (It is odd that Saint-Saëns played the work at all—one wonders why.) Bewildered by Saint-Saëns's rejection, Franck left the manuscript on the piano, and it was not until a much later date that the score was discovered in a pile of scrap paper.

Franck's main technique was not drawn from the authority of contrastive thematic and tonal relationship. He founded his own architectural form by the connections of the cyclic device, either fully thematic, or, as in this work, by an intervallic condition. The first theme descends stepwise in the dramatic proclamation that opens the quintet. The Allegro is also formed from themes that use this same interval—a tremendous unison burst from the strings, an antiphonal response from the piano, a succeeding subject that clings to the half-step descent pattern, and still other themes. These, naturally, are chromatic, but all are of dramatic quality. We have many themes, but all in one relationship. The semitone is the father of this work.

The slow movement displays the same affinity. Franck is not musically narrow-minded or sterile, or merely repetitive. He uses permutates, as in this instance, where the initial theme recoils on itself, but when it does, the same half-step slip takes place. Thematic transplantation from the first movement occurs, as well, and will recur in the last movement. It is this constant reapplication of inner and interdevelopments that holds the music in place, with new ideas constantly codifying the central germinal idea.

This same small-scale step earmark will be noted in the themes of the final movement; in this way, cadential tone is given to a theme, for example, that starts with a leap of a fourth, then a third and is completed by the second. This last governs the direction, sometimes up, other times down. But it is not mere technique that makes this quintet important. It is the fact that all its means are entirely logical; the perfection of the architecture holds the music incredibly. In short, there is exemplified the great craft of a creative artist translated into terms of musical clarity. Franck's music, with its redaction and unity, is correlated music, dissimilar to any other great composer's. Its individuality has not only validity and logic, but expressive beauty.

Franck, Maurice

DUOS

- **Fanfare, Andante and Allegro for Trombone and Piano**

This composer bears a famous name but has no relationship with the celebrated Belgian. He deserves credit for avoiding the junky kind of writing that has been produced for the cylindrical-bore instrument with its telescopic slide. There are few good chamber music pieces for the trombone, though there are a great number of horrors that have been turned out, especially for the *concours* held in European conservatories.

The Fanfare jets out from a half-beat triplet figure, and the simple three-part design is vividly clear. So is the pronouncement of the theme in the trombone and then its repetition by the piano. Imitation technique is important here. So are quartal harmonies and some neat fricative combinations.

The Andante indicated in the title doesn't exist! Its tempo is Lent, and there *is* a difference between the walking pace of the former and the slow speed defined by the latter. A choralelike atmosphere surrounds this middle piece of the total. Again, the trombone and piano alternate in stating the main topic. The quartal chords of part one now are replaced by seventh chords as the principal vertical element. The last movement is a sprightly double-pulse music, set in a rondo frame. To round out the harmonic sampling the emphasis here is on triads.

- **Theme and Variations for Viola and Piano**

The variations are powered by a potent drop of a third that occurs in nine of the theme's ten total measures. The ratio is maintained in the variations since the cogent intervallic span is clearly integrated in six of the seven transformations. Splendid logic pertains.

Variation one is for the solo viola, with the material expansively noted in double and triple stops. In variation two the interval stressed is the sixth (again a synchronous point, since the sixth is the inversion of the third). Horizontal-formationed intervallic development is applied in variation three. Variation four shifts between color (harmonics) and speed (vivo in triplet rhythmic distinction).

In the fifth variation the binding interval is not used. The music is free, a bit ornamental, finally in cadenza format. However, the final pair of variations return to the binding and important third in a setting of perpetual-motion outline (every measure activated by constant three-pitch sixteenth notes) and a concluding lyrical one. Franck's opus is certainly a splendid entry in the literature for viola and piano.

TRIO

- **Trio No. 2 for Reed Instruments (Oboe, Clarinet, and Bassoon)**

A single kind of musical typography marks the four movements of this woodwind trio. Tonal breadth so that the harmonies are not sticky: the first movement weaves around G, movement two is in F, the third movement is built on A, while the finale moves about considerably but concludes in C. And partner to the harmonic type is French-style wind chamber music writing of the majority kind, which means rhythmic aliveness keyed to balanced scoring minus any cocky cockade of instrumental behavior. In a couple of words, this is clean music.

Three-part design is used for the first movement, with Adagios surrounding an Allegretto. What counterpoint emerges is of the harmonic type. The middle portion has two passages with the special color of dulled dynamics (*sans nuances*). A jostling scherzo music fills movement two; a rolling melody propped by rhythmic accompanimental scoops marks the third movement (Andantino). After a three-time alternation of slow and fast tempos the finale settles into the latter speed. The last includes a good portion of imitative writing. Nothing is fussy.

Francmesnil, Roger de (1884–?)

QUARTET

- **String Quartet in G Minor (1919)**

Clear formal conditions are represented. Francmesnil writes in terms of the French classical-romantic composers. Occasionally a Franckian turn of harmonic phrase slips into the music; this does not throw the contents out of style but rather adds a nicely pungent flavor.

A declarative sonata-formed first movement

is followed by the Scherzo. The latter is mainly in septuple meter but breaks down to units of four and three pulses in each measure. The Trio is represented by a muted slow section (Lent expressif). This creates a type of false (anticipatory) slow movement since the proper slow movement is in third place (Lent et triste). Here the instruments are not muted, and the music proceeds in ternary formation. The key plan is B-flat minor, with a shift to F-sharp minor, a return to the initial tonality, and a final swerve to conclude matters in the relative major (D-flat) of the home key. Fugal procedures contrasted to lyrical portions describe the final movement.

Franco, Johan (1908–)

QUARTETS

- *The Prodigal: Six Aphorisms* for String Quartet (String Quartet No. 6) (1960)

Terse formulations totally figure in Franco's piece. The main title refers, of course, to the biblical parable of the prodigal son (Luke 15:11–32) who squandered his father's money. The titles of the six movements also follow a capsule procedure. Thus, movement one is indicated "Younger son asks father for his portion." In the biblical tale the text is: "The younger [son] said to him, 'Father, give me now my share of the property.'" Franco lists movement two as "Wastes his substance." This covers the following in the story: "After a few days the younger son sold his part of the property and left home with the money. He went to a country far away, where he wasted his money in reckless living." "Famine" (movement three) in the score matches "He spent everything he had. Then a severe famine spread over that country, and he was left without a thing." Similar aphoristic enumeration covers the remainder: movement four, "Husks fed to the swine"; movement five, "Enlightenment—Return to his father"; movement six, "The father receives him—All rejoice."

Franco's detailing is just as pithy. There is no prodigality in scope whatsoever, with a total of 187 measures for the entire quartet. And no programmatic approach, but rather a general, absolute-music consideration, salted and smartened with dissonance and simultaneity of keys. The expected subjectivity is replaced by total objectivity. For example, movement five, marked Misterioso, is completely muted and is bolstered on a bass line of perfect fifths in the cello with a frictioned dissonance in the viola; the mixed-key counterpoint in the finale ends with a polytonality formed from C major, C minor, and E major, etc. It is apparent that the defined inspiration is to be realized but separated from the actual compositional method. Titles notwithstanding, Franco's *Aphorisms* are actually abstractions.

- **String Quartet No. 3**

Franco has allegiance to classicism in his formal cogency and the logical unfoldment of his materials. But other concerns are blended with these. Franco uses panchromatic harmony. Because of the result of plausible movement of any part of the total sonorous organization, this might, paradoxically, be termed "polyphonic harmony." It makes a sure blend. It also produces a very detailed documentation.

In shape and length, the third quartet of this Holland-born composer, who settled in the United States in 1936, equals a five-movement suite. The last part is a postlude related to the music immediately preceding it. Movement three is a fugal pizzicato presentation. It provides neat and effective color comparison to the string quartet pigmentations of the two previous sections.

QUINTET

- **Divertimento for Flute and String
  Quartet (1945)**

Though occasionally the flute takes full command, integration and balance between the wind voice and strings is maintained. A Prelude ushers in matters, swinging from declarative direction to rubato rhapsody. The set of pieces continues with a Fugato, the fabric free of "one-two-three-four" patterned squareness in regard to the linear stitching. The quintet is completed by a set of permutations and coda on a principally conjunct idea. It has a slight resemblance to the subject that began the work.

Francoeur, François (1698–1787)

DUO

- **Sonata in D Minor for Soprano
  Recorder (or Violin) and Piano**

(This note concerns the modern edition, edited by Fritz Koschinsky and published by Otto Heinrich Noetzel in 1959.)

The music of this French violinist has a nice balletic quality. Movement two is a Corrente as substantiation, but the final Rondeau also has the same type of chordal hop, skip, and jump. More serious content applies to the opening Adagio.

Frank, Alan (1910–)

DUO

- **Suite for Two Clarinets Unaccompanied
  (1933)**

Music for the clarinet-duet medium remains almost a curiosity (aside from pedagogical studies where the teacher can play with the pupil). Poulenc's Sonata was the only contemporary representative of any value until this composer's four-movement work appeared in 1934, having been composed in August of the previous year.

With the combination of similar, strictly homophonic, instruments, the composer must, of necessity, draw on differences of register, attempt to color as best he can; that is, unless such a duet is to deteriorate into mere cerebral counterpoint or the primitiveness of melody and accompaniment. The philosophy of contrastive use of low and high registers, equaling, therefore, soprano and bass instruments as far as the limits of tonal range permit, is one of the main characteristics of this work. The rhythm is enterprising, spurring the music out of its economical shell. A composer long concerned with chamber music, Frank has creative "know-how."

A short three-part Prelude is followed by the second movement, which combines a March and Rondo (the former not in goose-step rhythm but exhilarated by out-of-step-wise measures in 7/8 time). The Dirge shows the value of a high–low scoring plan, with spacious registration used for the most part, while a temporary closeness of the two-voice sound gives excellent contrastive effect. Thirty-one measures of pert Allegro mark the Finale.

Frankel, Benjamin (1906–73)

Frankel has been variously typed as a neo-Hebraicist, a flexible lyricist, and as an esoteric genius. But the almost bleak severity of his music, its demanding asceticism, marks him as probably the most introspective composer of the English school. He tended, as to be expected, toward chamber and symphonic music rather than the flamboyancies of music making. There is an affinity with Bartók in the uncompromising beauties that can be found in his works, but at that point the relationship ends. It is merely in the mirroring of nonromanticism, in the picturing of nonsheltering mellifluous, contemporary emotions, that he is partner to the great Hungarian.

Conventions are not smashed in Frankel's works, yet they are not conventional. He was a composer of persuasive elusivity; his chamber music works are perfected examples of how to treat the actual symphonic orbit of chamber music in the broad sense of meaning, not in terms of color or overscaled instrumentation.

TRIOS

- *Pezzi pianissimi (Soft Pieces)* for Clarinet, Cello, and Piano, Op. 41

Music under wraps; the dynamic level never goes over the *mezzopiano* mark. Music of pliable textures, and a miniature-constructed music.

Wide-spanned phrases in the first of the four parts. In the second of the set there is scherzo spring with 10/16 and 7/16 meters. A short slow-paced representation follows, and *Pezzi pianissimi* concludes with an unwrapped (in tempo only) waltz. Naturally, Frankel's trio ends in *pianississimo* (triply soft).

- String Trio [No. 1] for Violin, Viola, and Cello, Op. 3

While sonata form requires pace as well as depth, length as well as thematic identification, it is possible to compress one's arguments and discussions in the employment of this structural type. This can be accomplished just as cogently in fewer minutes than the general time taken for an opening movement in a large-scale work, without mummifying the structure to the extent of sonatina proportions.

The Preludio gives no prolonged examination of the fanfarelike first theme, or the winding legato of the second. These are stated,

hardly developed, yet the inner lines give formal sureness. It is a matter of knowing what to say and what to eliminate. The Andante is fugal; even the subsidiary song theme is accompanied by rhythmic imitation, while the Scherzo has corresponding unity by way of expelled triplets. The composer's fingerprints always leave distinctive marks. The Epilogo is mostly restrained dynamically. Frankel fully realizes that the gloved hand is as dramatic as the musical mailed fist. It is an epilogue that not only brings expressive rest to the previous turbulence but also fleetingly recalls, in very subtle fashion, the first theme of the opening movement; and contains as well the most isolated semblance to a rising-line theme from the Scherzo.

- String Trio No. 2 for Violin, Viola, and Cello, Op. 34

Twelve-tone music that has a special luminosity due to Frankel's reiteration of the basic row, which defines thereby, in its overall pitch coverage, a thematic type of responsibility. Pitch repetitions and cogent rhythmic patterns clarify each of the three movements.

The work is dedicated to Martha Graham. Prefaced to the score are three statements by the dancer, apparently as reactions to the music dedicated to her. In regard to the opening Moderato: "It concerns the restless pacings of the heart on some winter evening. There are remembrances of childhood, certain dramatizations of well-known objects, dreams of romance, hatreds bred of longings and madness." For movement two (Allegro moderato): "An American dance is not a series of new steps . . . it is a characteristic time beat, a different speed, an accent, sharp, clear, staccato." And for the finale (Lento, Intimo): "In secret life of the heart there are invisible actors."

(One takes for granted that the inclusion of these comments was not mere window dressing, since they form part of the published score.

Their inclusion certifies Frankel's agreement with this viewpoint of the inner substances of his three movements for string trio.)

QUARTETS

- **Quartet for Piano and Strings (Violin, Viola, and Cello), Op. 26**

Sharply contrasted moods are presented in the three movements. There is a fervent, Blochian character to the opening movement. It is a declamatory music, and though Frankel uses contrapuntal weighting, the real force comes from combined tutti action. The movement ends with sensitive quietness, as does the final (third) movement. There, too (in lento tempo), Frankel is oratorical, the music containing indications that read *con intensità* and *drammatico*. But Frankel gives careful attention to length and balance. In between these two movements is a hop-skip-and-jump scherzo item.

- **Quartet No. 1 for Two Violins, Viola, and Cello, Op. 14**

The usual sonata form of an opening movement is not used here. In place, there are four growths to a high point, instigated by rhythm and dynamics; a terracing of the form, which does not make it sectional but leads with almost determined inevitability from a sighing motive, which is always changed (equaling development), to climax. The Allegro brioso is a Rondo-Scherzo; the standard Trio division that pertains to a Scherzo is absent; instead, the rhythm quickens, the pace is hurried and becomes more brilliant. In one fell swoop, the composer has given his Scherzo its Trio, its foil, its contrast.

What makes the slow movement of interest is the very avoidance of classical procedure whereby harmony stitches the melodic line with neatness. Yet, with classical directness of form, Frankel achieves solidity with a very keen edge by revolving his melodic lines contrary to the harmony; he avoids, as a rule, duplicating any vertical tone in placed sound by horizontal tones in motion. It is a silent bow to late Beethoven, plus the initiated means of Bartók. The perpendicular type of block writing used in the final movement is also particular to the latter composer's method.

- **Quartet No. 2 for Two Violins, Viola, and Cello, Op. 15**

Within the five-movement plan of this quartet, its moods alternate as well as its tempos. Productively, gloomy lyricism is replied to by robust rhythms; shifting motives by martially brilliant potencies. The overall pattern shows definitely the influence of late Beethoven (the gaiety has sting, the harmonies are free), while the modus operandi of the quartet, its curves and full sweep are influenced by the work of Bartók.

The imitations of the first movement illuminate such contrapuntal unity by the use of various intervallic ascents; the cello skips a seventh, the first violin a fifth, and so on, thereby giving resiliency to the continuity. When the climax arrives in the center of the movement, it is approached by charged rhythm. This does not falsify the style, rather it attests that the weights of texture are an aid in forming balance.

The large three-section plan of the Gioviale relates triple to duple meter, severity to lightness. Frankel's Scherzo is suspended correctly with stability. While the next two movements are troubled, the last of these absorbed in a mysterious cadence of string harmonics and cello pizzicato, the final movement confutes this by a triumphal, emphatic quality. Composers have their measured mannerisms—Frankel's show in the last movement's declaimed fanfares, but their value is one of unequivocal strength.

- **Quartet No. 4 for Two Violins, Viola, and Cello, Op. 21**

Power lies more in dissonance than in consonance, but strength lies also in triadal harmony. In the first movement, these are combined resourcefully. Secundal intervals command as the viola intones the main D-major theme. The movement is one of friction, even maintained when the principal theme is played pesante (heavily) and in augmentation. While ostinatos can turn into mechanical robots that stiffen the move of a Scherzando, they are the very strength of the second movement. The composer's absorption in them is intrinsic to the gliding rather than skipping main theme. Thus, contrast serves for the correct demarcation of the ostinatos themselves.

The slow movement is threnodic; the intervals clash, they refuse merely to be set in a minor tonality. There are definite Hebraic overtones in this sensitive elucidation of a quartet movement written "in tender memory" of a person close to the composer. The last movement takes the theme of the slow movement and develops it. This is a second elegy leading to an emotional close. But the grief is not appeased—the final cadence (one of the most beautiful conceptions in contemporary string quartet literature) is expressed poignantly by C major and minor combined.

Franklin, Benjamin (1706–90)

QUARTET

- **Quartet for Three Violins and Cello**

Maybe spurious, maybe not. (The composition was found in Paris in 1941 and was published there the following year.) Although the score was not in Franklin's handwriting, he certainly could have written the piece. It must be recalled that Franklin was a music lover; a writer of music essays; played the violin, guitar, and harp; and, in 1763, invented the glass harmonica (a mechanization of the now-extinct musical drinking glasses so that the fingers did not have to be wet in order to produce the required friction on the glasses).

Two writers have discussed the authenticity of Franklin's piece. M.E. Grenander, in the *American Quarterly*, XXVII (1975), supports it. W. Thomas Marrocco, in *Proceedings of the American Philosophical Society*, CXVI (1972), takes the opposite point of view. Further, Marrocco, in his article on Franklin, in *The New Grove Dictionary of American Music*, states that a second quartet by Franklin exists, calling for the same instruments, use of scordatura, and performance solely on the open strings.

The quartet is musically primitive and musically amateurish. But if by the philosopher, writer, statesman, educator, and humanitarian, then its sheer curiosity value outweighs all other arguments.

But double curiosity is offered. Franklin's odd "string quartet" makeup is *totally*, from first sound to last, in F major, and all pitches are heard via open strings. Accordingly, retuning (called scordatura) is required of all four instruments, and no two are alike. The first violin is tuned C–G–C–F, the second violin's strings are pitched B-flat–F–B-flat–E, and the third violin is tuned A–E–A–D. The scordatura of the cello is B-flat–F–C–G. Thus, no sound in any one octave is duplicated by the tuning series, and only the tones of the key of F major are represented, each at least once in the entire gamut. Minus modulation or chromatic intercession (the fingers of the left hand are not used in a single instance), the composition consists of five movements. The first, untitled, section is followed by a Minuet (without Trio), a Capriccio, another Minuet (again without Trio), and a Siciliano. None of the sections were assigned tempos, but the proper speeds would be immediately apparent to performers.

Franklin's four-instrument piece is the first complete work in musical history using solely open strings. Regardless of its restricted artistic result, it is a worthy experiment.

(Three composers have transcribed Franklin's Quartet for string orchestra. Frank Clark included all five movements, Arcady Dubensky *[q.v.]* selected three. John Vincent *[q.v.]* enlarged the scoring, calling for string orchestra with obbligato for glass harmonica or any one of nine substitute instruments: flute, oboe, clarinet, bells, celesta, vibraphone, harp, piano, or violin.)

Franko, Sam (1857–1937)

QUARTET

- **Lullaby for String Quartet, Op. 3, No. 1**

Franko combined a career as violinist, pedagogue, and composer. *Lullaby* is a simple construction in which the tune is carried by the first violin and the other three instruments have supporting roles. At the turn of the century Franko's *Lullaby* proved to be a sales success so versions for string orchestra and violin and piano were immediately produced.

Frederick II (Frederick the Great) (1712–86)

DUOS

- **Sonatas for Flute and Piano**

  - No. 1, in D Minor
  - No. 2, in B-flat Major
  - No. 3, in B-flat Major
  - No. 4, in D Major
  - No. 5, in A Major
  - No. 6, in B-flat Major
  - No. 7, in E Minor
  - No. 8, in D Minor
  - No. 9, in E-flat Major
  - No. 10, in D Major

These ten sonatas are from a group of twenty-five that this important 18th-century patron of music composed, published by Breitkopf & Härtel in 1934. In the collected works that were issued of this composer the numbering coincides only in the case of the fifth sonata. That numbering applied to the B&H sequence is: 2–18–23–24–5–4–9–11–14–16.

The editor, Carl Bartuzat, has changed the tonalities of sonatas Nos. 1, 2, 3, 4, and 10. Originally these were C minor, A major, G major, C major, and C major, respectively. A final point regarding the B&H edition is that the piano settings for the first five sonatas were made by the German music editor Paul Grafen Waldersee and for the last five sonatas the settings are by the German composer Günther Raphael *[q.v.]*.

Tasteful and effective conceptions in all respects. Special individuality is not present, but certainly any statement that Frederick's music was dry and academic can be totally nullified. There is practically no attention to polyphonic detail; the sonatas are homophonically localized.

Freed, Isadore (1900–60)

The music of this composer deserves rediscovery. Freed was a learned, sensitive composer. He made no attempt to cater to public-appeal requirements but proceeded on his creative way, composing as a true artist, concerned only with shaping his materials in the most refined fashion.

His technique deals with the constancy of line movements, these in sober form—the eloquence derived from action that is neither fully polyphonic nor falls in the vertical category. The merging of the two affords long-run ideas, organic within themselves, that move with the absence of severe cadential impressions that cut into musical lines, causing partitionings. This avoidance is a paramount rule with his work, yet there is sufficient punctuation for breathing needs. Chromaticism is used, but more for activating the lines, less for harmonic coloring. Freed is a modern composer who combines the neoclassic with the neoromantic, mixing these with a robust hand. The amalgam produces music that is controlled, not ultrapicturesque but enjoying strength, solidity, and profile. It takes time for such productions to be recognized amid the welter of musical "isms."

QUARTETS

▪ String Quartet [No. 1] (1931)

Freed's first quartet lives on rhythmic sophistication. A casual examination of the score could make one believe the music would be all nervous-edged, what with the metrical variety. This would not occur because the lines, though exceedingly vigorous, are chromatically smooth. Decidedly, the quartet is a dynamic sonoric document.

The first movement develops from a motive announced at the start by the cello. Movement two is an Allegro, a distant cousin to a Scherzo.

In this example, slow-paced sections cut into the main tempo drive. Otherwise, the superstructure of the music is clearly three part, with a strict recapitulation and then a concluding coda. The linear intensity increases in the slow (third) movement, and the rhythmic intensity increases in the final (fourth) rondo movement. In Freed's quartet the music moves from strength to strength.

▪ String Quartet No. 2 (1932)

The instrumentality of the first movement is a motive of four tones. It appears consistently in various guises and becomes more direct in the fast tempo that follows the opening Moderato. From such means, the entire opening movement's plot is spun, coursed through with many metrical changes that produce more fluidity. The confirmations between the movements of a work (not cyclic, but germane considerations in the overall concept) are to be observed in the second movement. Again, a terse phrase is the potent resource. The middle section of this three-part movement gives contrast in regard to pace and mood but at the same time is related to the opening movement's motive—only, in this instance, its direction is opposite. The slow movement is almost as germinally patterned, somewhat monothematic, and is discussed polyharmonically. The final part of the quartet is nervous, percussed with angular musical adaptation, an antithesis to a merely joyful, sparkling finale; this is the present-day prototype of 19th-century Presto conclusions.

▪ String Quartet No. 3 (1937)

Many composers have been attracted to the rhythmic binding, the precision, and the clarity of the ostinato. It is this device that is the backbone of the first movement—appearing in practically every measure—as the springboard of short melodic jets that are formed from its rhythm, framing the wide-scaled main theme. In the second movement, there is retrogression from such driven specifications to more sober, detailed chronicles. Chromatic to begin with, the second item of this movement's agenda is marked by density, higher gamut, and more chromaticism, returning to the original facts for the final point. In the third movement, the same type of ternary design is unfolded by use of pizzicato and arco to distinguish the sections. There are rhapsodical means in the Finale, which opens with a ten-measure unison developed in a type of durchkomponiert fashion. Freed is athletic here, and the vigor and body contacts of sonorous lines are what one must expect and should enjoy.

- *Triptych* for Violin, Viola, Cello, and Piano (1943)

Art forms have their analogies in music not only by way of actual techniques (highlighting in orchestration, for example) but also in the use of titles with parallel depiction. The triptych form has become somewhat favored. The three-paneled painting concept, so often found on altars, with the two outer sides balancing the inner (center) piece, has been used by a good number of composers. Freed was partial to it, for this was his second use of this title—the other being a string-orchestra piece, written in 1932.

The title is followed in the sense of three structures, the outer ones being symmetrical to each other; movements one and three are therefore fast paced, the slow movement falling between. Further, the triptych idea is to be noted in the first movement. Here, the same factors of faster and resolute outer portions balance themselves against a more lyrical central core. Still further, within this movement's first section, the strings separate and alternate from unison considerations to part writing. This textural light and shade affords further color and contrast to the formal plan. There is

little change of tempo in the other (third) fast-paced movement. It is planned, however, on two forms of thematic propulsion. The first of these is direct, square cut, and vertical; the second is round, syncopated, and horizontal. Both dwell in a sonata-form structure. It is to be especially noted that the constant flow of voices (a noncadential means of speech, only subtly punctuated) is Freed's characteristic unitive technique.

Freitas, Frederico de (1902–)

QUINTET

- Quintet for Flute, Oboe, Clarinet, Horn, and Bassoon (1950)

Another contribution to the romantic music bank. A fair account that will draw good interest from auditors.

Freitas's structural concepts are straightforward but enriched with tasteful ideas. In the Andante (movement two) the horn is assigned a rhythmically defined cadenza. A home-grown (Portuguese) type of song is registered in the third-movement Intermezzo—a modinha—a minor-key, somewhat sentimental type, though its sentimentality is reduced (or controlled) in this case since quintal meter makes the material more active and less cloying. The final Fugue (Fuga) is also less rigid in its demeanor by the use of a scherzando subject.

Frensel Wegener, Emmy (1901–73)

SEXTET

- Sextet for Flute (alternating Piccolo), Oboe, Clarinet, Bassoon, Horn, and Piano

Bach-like drive and dissonant lines emphasize

the first movement's fast tempo. In the slow movement a signal point is established by the engaging use made of the flute. Its color is mostly called on for alto and tenor qualities rather than the usual soprano domination; a passage devoted to flutter-tonguing technique is also especially interesting. But more than any other part it is the pert Vivace, which shows the capability of this Dutch composer. She conveys a single theme with excellent creative strategy. Timbre is her man Friday, its variety plus contrast of the movement's weight in relation to the others is of vivid result. At no time is the total sextet placed into service—the fullest tutti is pegged at a total of four instruments, and trio formations are in the majority. This is chamber music instrumentation of sensitivity.

Although the title of the last movement is Fugato, it is actually a composite of the contrapuntal form plus a Presto of equal length, which is patterned as a type of development of the former. A modified augmentation of the subject will be observed in the Fugato as well as a complete sextuple-voice exposition. Brilliance, bite, and staccato stimulation are added to the final section when the flute is replaced by a piccolo.

Frešo, Tibor (1918–)

DUO

- *Malá fantázia (A Little Fantasia)* for **Piano and Double Bass**

The fantasy in this case is like that of a well-balanced dance turn. And nice rhythmic activity in support. No fancy-free action in terms of form, however. Frešo's piece is set in a large three-part design, with the third section a literal restatement of the first part. Neat, fast-paced coda.

QUARTET

- *Na dedine (In the Village)*: **Suite for String Quartet**

All goes well and undisturbed in Frešo's hamlet sketches. The music glows with tonal faith, and it is designed with simple sincerity.

"Ráno" ("Morning") begins quietly, picks up steam, but then moves back into calmness. Movement two, "V kostole" ("In the Church"), is choralish for the most part, stimulated by tremolandos and syncopation. Frešo's determination for acute balance regardless of the picture he is painting continues in "Medzi deťmi" ("Among Children"): vivified music in vivace tempo bound by C major, followed by pliant lyrical lento music in A-flat major, and then a carbon copy repeat of the first section. "Večer" ("Evening") is explained by the tinted timbre of muted instruments.

Fricker, Peter Racine (1920–)

DUOS

- *Four Dialogues* for **Oboe and Piano, Op. 41**

Fricker avoids laissez-faire liberalistic writing that may identify rugged technical individualism but thereby bypasses emotional strengths. His style is fully solidified (Op. 41 was produced in 1965, when Fricker was 45) with contemporary unification.

Each of the pieces has definite profile and shows a splendid realization of the capabilities of the wind instrument. The first piece is three part, the Lento in the first section chordal and rectitativelike in turn. When it returns after lighter material (significantly duplicated also with recitative data) the chords have added weaving material, and a long oboe line moves against these. Scherzo character bound with pedal rhythms and crisscrossed with phrasings that metrically counterpoint the rhythms defines the colorful second dialogue. Tight and light textures mark the free ternary detail of the third piece. No slam bang finale, but a Lento religioso that matches the first piece of the set in terms of tempo and a similar sense of declamation.

- **Sonata for Horn and Piano, Op. 24**

Twelve-tone themes for the first two of the three movements. End of serial exactitude. And though there are no esoteric maneuvers, formal exactitude is also negated in this opus.

Sonata relationship serves in the opening movement. In the Scherzo (which follows the initial movement without pause) there are two short contrastive sections, equating thereby a pair of Trios. The final movement (Invocation) is somewhat declamatory music, set in a somewhat sonata-detailed design.

There are many examples of music first written in an instrumentally neutral manner and then later shaped according to the instrumentation desired. Not this piece. It is certain the music was conceived from the very first note for the horn. The horn writing is smooth, suave, lyrical, cleanly rhythmic. There is a true, mellow, overall quality that is special to the brass instrument. The piano part provides a perfect partnership.

- **Sonata for Violin and Piano, Op. 12**

Interesting formal credentials for Fricker's richly textured duo sonata. There are three movements, and each gets slower in tempo. The opening Allegro is followed by an Allegretto, and the work is completed by an Adagio. Special color in the middle movement, which is marked "Come un' valse distante," and to accentuate this setting the violin is muted in the outer sections of the music. The dynamism of the Sonata is intensely charged,

but each movement ends in a soft dynamic.

Sonata detail in the first movement. The material there includes cross phrasing that counterpoints the counterpointed lines still further. For example, quintuple-total phrases in the violin are set against quadrated phrases in the piano, themselves filled with syncopation. Rondo design is used for the middle movement—a conception filled with scherzo overtones that supplement Fricker's "distant waltz" description. The final Adagio is set forth in the form of a da capo aria.

QUARTET

- **String Quartet [No. 1] in One Movement (1948)**

Of all the great contemporary composers who influenced younger men, Bartók, at first, attracted the fewest. This is understandable, since the techniques of the Hungarian were less blatant than the new system of Schoenberg, or the word-of-mouth advertising, the hue and cry that followed Stravinsky at every new step he took. Though Schoenberg and Stravinsky were honest composers, they did not preach humility. Bartók was a retiring man who built his technique and wrote his music akin to Beethoven, displaying constant creative growth. Many a composer joined the celebrations of Stravinsky's work, were caught like flies in the stylistic molasses regarding Schoenberg; in comparison, the little-sung work of Bartók drew the fewest partisans. Later, Bartók disciples became more numerous, especially in the ranks of Hungarian composers.

It matters little that Fricker's idiom may have been hastened into Bartókian semblance by his study with a Hungarian composer, Matyas Seiber, to whom this quartet is dedicated. The Bartók lines, the frictions, rhapsody, and uncontroverted flux of fluidic rhythms are all present to enjoy. There are tentative reservations that one can make critically, but the music is healthy; and where there is creative health, there is worthiness. Fricker is another mark in the ledger of solvent British music of today.

There are two main sections plus a coda to this quartet, played without pause. The first is germinally explained by constant knitting of a sustained, severe, disjunctly formed theme, which passes through diaphanous qualities as well as semitranslucent textures. The tempos shift as much as the counterpointed style exchanges places with the percussiveness of perpendicular harmonies. These interchanges carry over into the Vivo, a movement of scherzo quality that combines, alternates, and collides duple and triple meters.

QUINTET

- **Quintet for Flute, Oboe, Clarinet, Horn, and Bassoon, Op. 5**

The gaiety and wit in Fricker's pantonal work reflect both Hindemith's and Bartók's style. Well-stabilized and colorful polyphonic sections highlight the piece, but there is neither academicism nor padding. Fricker picks his sounds carefully and doesn't waste a single one.

The introduction (not a small portion, but an expanded one) fits into the mold of the main division—an Allegro moderato—and also returns as the epilogue after the run of the Finale. This action is less cyclic than it is a pointed total balancing of the music.

Movement two is a Badinerie & Musette. Fricker treats the 18th-century form expansively, which means romantically. The Badinerie is a bantering affair, but here it is more horizontally pitched than usual and updated by mixing a sextuple-pulse feeling within the specified total quadrated meter. The flute takes over the preceptor's role to the greatest extent in the Badinerie; the ternary form is precisely balanced, with the central part of the triptych being a Musette of leaping intervals, but with very little drone identification, followed by a return to the Badinerie.

Movement three (Canonic Variations) consists of a theme and five variants. Color force is decided. The theme is for solo horn. The first canon is at the distance of a fourth, but through the spatial choice of mid-gamut oboe and low bassoon the distance is in reality two octaves more than this span. Variation two is a canon between clarinet and oboe at the interval of a fifth; the horn is tacet. The third variation is a canon between oboe and bassoon at the distance of a second (plus an octave), with the flute and the clarinet remaining silent. The only speedy variation is the fourth, a Vivo, with the canon at the distance of a sixth between flute and clarinet. The final variant is a canon between flute and bassoon at the distance of a seventh. It will be seen that, including the theme, four scoring types are represented (one solo, one trio, one quartet, and three quintets). Five types of canonic formations are presented (the intervallic distances being a second, a fourth, a fifth, a sixth, and a seventh). The instrumental pairing of the canons is assigned equally between the flute, oboe, clarinet, and bassoon, each being represented twice. And, throughout, the basic theme is always to be recognized in the contrapuntal action.

The concluding movement (Finale) squints at twelve tones for its perceptive bounding subject. The use of 12/8 time is converted into a triple set of meters each of triple-pulse total within each measure, thus: 3/8–3/4–3/8. (If one considers everything in eighths, since 12/8 is the metrical definition, the division of the measure is 3–2–2–2–3.) By crossphrasing Fricker avoids metrical rigidity.

Frid, Géza (1904–)

DUO

- *Paganini Variations* for Two Violins, Op. 77

The theme is the famous one brought into existence by Niccolò Paganini. The initial set of variations was composed by Paganini as part of his Op. 1 set of Caprices for solo violin. There it is the twenty-fourth (and concluding) section of the work, and Paganini used the theme for eleven variations and a finale. Important composers and not-so-important composers have worked out their permutations on the melody, the former group exemplified by Schumann, Liszt, Brahms, and Rachmaninoff. The entry by Frid, a Hungarian-born, Dutch composer, deserves a high mark.

There is an "Introduction," followed by the Tema (with pizzicato support). Ten variations and a Coda follow. There is quasi glissando in variation one, actual glissando in variation two, and septuple pulsing in variation three. Packed chording (four-voiced moving to six-voiced successions) defines the fourth variant. Following the fifth part of the work, there is a muted Intermezzo. Variants six and seven are blood brothers in that the latter is an inverted depiction of the former. Saltando bowing colors the eighth variation, and scalic runs excite the ninth variation. The final variant (Allegro agitato) is a *sempre fortissimo* affair; the Coda is a mostly instrumentally unified close.

(Multiple violin groups can perform Frid's piece. For this purpose some divisi sections are substituted.)

TRIOS

- *Chemins divers (Various Roads)* for Flute (alternating Piccolo ad lib), Bassoon, and Piano, Op. 75

Colorful detail and instrumental democracy define the first part "Chemins tortueux" ("Winding Roads"). In turn, there are passages for the piano alone, then the flute, again for the piano, and after that for the bassoon alone. All three instruments complete the movement. Part two reflects "Chemins nocturnes" ("Nocturnal Roads"). The pitch action is in the wind instruments; the piano is a voice of chordal reticence. "Chemins similaires" ("Similar Roads") defines a more pertinent tutti scoring. Panache and scoring plushery in this wind-piano trio.

- *Twelve Metamorphoses* for Two Flutes and Piano, Op. 54

Frid's trio is based on arranging the full chromatic scale so that the first, fourth, seventh, and tenth pitches function as tonics (C, E-flat, F-sharp, and A); the second, fifth, eighth, and eleventh act as dominants (D-flat, E, G, and B-flat); and the other pitches are used as "underdominants," or subdominants.

From these there are a dozen variations after a Quasi cadenza introduction for the flutes alone. The divisions are decidedly clear, including such as figurations for the fourth variant, scalic detail in the fifth variant, and augmentation in the sixth part. The seventh metamorphosis is for solo piano, the eighth a canon for the pair of flutes, and the work is climaxed with a full-framed fugue.

(Frid's trio was written in 1957. In 1963 he made a second setting for ten instruments, calling for pairs of flutes, oboes, clarinets, and bassoons, plus horn, and piano, under Op. 54a.)

QUARTETS

- **String Quartet No. 2, Op. 21**

The subtitle to Frid's work is Fugues. Already a special point. Six movements, making an important point two. Now, six fugues in a row sounds treacherous and boresome simultaneously, but these are not square-toed and cloddish contrapuntal conceptions. Each has a special illumination, beginning with the first, which is an all-pizzicato movement. The second fugue is a flowing Andantino and includes augmentation. Fugue number three is piled up with trills and ornamental coverings for the subject, which is identified by a short glissando. At first this descends, later it goes the opposite direction.

Movement four is an imitation of Bach's solo violin sonatas and partitas. Everything is piled into the first violin in b*ravissima* soloism, the other instruments totally subservient. The Intermezzo hints at rather than depicts a fugue. The Finale is a double fugue, the second subject becomes inverted, and thrown into the movement is a rough-tumbly section marked "Quasi jazz." There is full developmental detail in the Finale. It concludes with a unison pizzicato passage to match the timbral content of the opening of the work, dropping degreewise from *piano* to *pianissimo* to a final *pianississimo*. Frid's opus is a superb contribution to string quartet literature. It deserves wide hearing.

- **String Quartet No. 3, Op. 30**

Frid is no stick-in-place composer. He is a formal eager beaver. Each work plows unusual ground. This one, subtitled Fantasia tropica, has four movements and includes two Indonesian melodies. One is in movement two, "La notta" ("The Night'), titled "Katjang boentjes," played by the second violin; the other is in movement three, "Il giorno" ("The Day"), played by the viola, titled "Dongèng-liedje." Wrapped around these two movements is "La sera" ("The Evening"). This movement appears, therefore, at the beginning and at the end, and both statements are exactly the same.

"La sera" drives at first in a 3 + 2 + 3/8 meter, but later is relaxed in quality and concludes in almost bare texture, with D-major finality. Movement two runs on an impressionistic type of track. There are rubatoed and mysterious sounds, short glissandos, and sprays of natural harmonics. Movement three is closely related to the opening movement, with the same tempos and meter. However, it moves out into development and is four times the length of the initial part of the quartet.

Fried, Alexej (1922–)

DUO

- *Sonatina dramatica* **for Violin and Piano (1975)**

Fried has had considerable experience in the jazz field, and in his compositions he has emphasized the fusion of jazz with classical designs. The emphasis on syncopation, the repetition of rhythmic figurations, and the consistent supple motility in the melodic lines are the procedures of such partnership and vividly displayed in this duo sonatina.

In the second movement there are the additional ingredients of an E-flat sustained pedal and a rhythmically syncopative pedal on B-flat that moves occasionally to B-natural. The combine is first heard in the fifth measure. In all, this binder is heard in more than thirty measures. A related device of reiteration is to be noted in the third (final) movement. There it is expressed especially, and considerably, by combining both instruments into rhythmic unison.

TRIO

■ *Moravian Trio* for Flute, Marimba, and Harp (1978)

There is a type of out-of-doors style in the first of the two movements. A healthy amount of consecutive-fifth passages, sometimes tinged by a shift to a minor seventh, is used in the harp. And there's plenty of ostinato as well, assigned both the marimba and the harp. Rhythmically, an inculcation of jazz marks this movement.

Ostinatos and jazz inflections continue in the second movement (in different tempo but of almost the same length as the first movement; the latter is timed at 6:20, the former is 6 minutes in length). Also maintained is soloistic attention. In movement one there is a fairly long solo sequence for the marimba. In the second movement there is one of even greater length plus a sizable solo spot for the flute. These are quite telling and as colorfully exciting as more expansive timbral interplay.

QUINTETS

■ *Guernica*: Quintet for Soprano Saxophone (or Clarinet) and String Quartet (1978)

A number of Fried's works deal full face with jazz, sometimes styled in the Gunther Schuller "third-stream" manner. (Examples: *Jazz Concerto* for clarinet; *Jazz Dance Etudes* for clarinet, doubling soprano and alto saxophones, with jazz band; *Solstice*, a Concerto for two jazz bands; etc. At least fourteen of Fried's works are written in this stylistic category.) Some of the same quality is woven into *Guernica*.

Already the use of a soprano saxophone implies the field of jazz. And, rhythmically, Fried runs that course. In movement one the pulsatile power is supported by strong bitonality. The same type of chamber music

slang surrounds the third movement, made cohesive by triplet packing.

A vastly different approach marks the middle movement, set slow in tempo (andante) and styled parenthetically Quasi recitativo. An expanded solo for the saxophone opens the movement, followed by a string quartet section, and in turn, by the solo saxophone again. The five instruments then proceed polyphonically only to break off again for still another solo saxophone statement, this one to be played Quasi cadenza. The close of the movement leans on the material played by the strings earlier in the movement.

■ *The Life of the Insects*: Quintet for Flute, Violin, Viola, Cello, and Piano (1979)

A fancy title, this, which deliberately cultivates and stimulates interest. But what midges, bugs, beetles, or what have you, Fried is describing in his quintet remains a dark secret. That the vignettes that pass in review are not identified is an annoyance—the music is charming, however.

There are four movements. In these there are some tone-cluster introductions, some melodic flurries, plenty of ostinatos, melodic twitterings, and, of course, a considerable amount of rhythmic detail. Each part of the work is sectionally apportioned. All of it has tonal allegiance.

Friedman, Ignaz (1882–1948)

QUINTET

■ Piano Quintet in C Minor

Tonality prerogative with romantic demeanor here. This is to be expected from a Hugo Riemann pupil and a concert pianist who specialized in Chopin and edited the piano works of Schumann and Liszt. The salutary influence of example cannot by overlooked, and it wasn't by Friedman.

Sonata form covers the first movement, with a dramatic principal theme and a rich song subject, drenched with thirds, for contrast. A set of variations follows (Friedman does not title the movement as such). It includes the triple swing of minuet style, the quiet sway of a barcarolle, and a touch of fugato. The concluding movement is marked Epilog and, in comparison to the first part of the quintet, is subdued in quality. In its final measures the Epilog has both a quotation and a bit of augmentation transfer from the variation movement.

Friemann, Witold (1889–1977)

DUO

■ *Quasi una sonata* **for Clarinet and Piano (1951)**

Chromaticism leads to modulatory fancy in this Regerian-stuffed duo. There is a fine thoroughness to the harmony, but the incessant translocation of tonality centers gives a rhapsodic (almost feverish) tone to the work. Only the final movement is different. Simplicity of detail and tonal stability surround this vivacious, ternary-structured conclusion.

Movement one begins in C minor, relates the second theme in F-sharp minor, moves into considerable other key territories until it terminates in B minor. The second movement parallels this aesthetic dogma. It begins in G-flat major, moves to E and then A-flat major, returns to the initial tonality of G-flat, and concludes, as did the previous movement, in a key (E-flat major) quite different from the basic tonality. In both movements tonality unrest is matched by capricious thematic materials and their development.

Friml, Rudolf (1879–1972)

QUARTET

■ *In a Classical Mood* **for String Quartet**

Although Friml is credited with writing a good number of light-scale piano pieces, what you don't read in his biographical data is that he tried his hand at chamber music. The result was this short piece, published in 1958.

It will not rival his highly successful and certainly worthy operettas such as *Rose-Marie* and *The Vagabond King*. Still, it is logically light-faceted music, nicely contrasted and neatly put together.

The music is moderately paced, in G minor. The first section is an example of horizontal four-part harmony. This leads to a faster tempo for dancing spiccato figures punctuated with pizzicato. A return is then made to the initial material, which is both slightly changed and considerably shortened, followed by a bit of the second section and a chordal coda.

Frohne, Vincent (1936–)

DUO

■ *Pendulum* **for Flute and Piano, Op. 29**

The dedication of Frohne's piece to Severino Gazzelloni is an intimation as to the style of the duo. Proven. The music is filled with the pyrotechnics that are the performance trademark of this Italian musician, a magician in handling the pitch acrobatics of contemporary flute music. It's all here: registral and compass extremes, huge leaps, fluttered pitches, microtones, key clicks, antipitches with the sounding of air only, and a violence of pulse distribution. The piano part follows in full partnership, especially emphasizing fully active polyrhythmic detail. It, too, demands a virtuoso for this music of 20th-century gusto.

QUARTET

■ **String Quartet I, Op. 28**

Juxtaposed elaboration of assorted elements, emphasizing intervallic progress in fourths and fifths in the fully chromatic materials. The lines follow suit with assorted multi-changes of timbral qualities. The restlessness of the music continues even when the tempo slows.

In the second movement the viola is in scordatura, with its range lowered a whole tone below its basic C boundary. Another interesting point is the use by Frohne of a new dynamic marking—*m*. This is a level that is to be in between *mezzopiano* and *mezzoforte*.

Froidebise, Pierre (1914–62)

DUO

■ **Sonata for Violin and Piano (1938)**

Froidebise's later interest in Schoenbergian methods and his attention to aleatoric communication do not show in this early work. Rich romantic rhetoric does.

In length the duo is more a sonatina than a sonata. But its nine-minute scope is one of resolute concentration. It comprises a single movement, beginning with Adagietto thematic material that reappears several times and from which developments take place. Interspersed is faster-tempo music, hard driven in character, impulsive in its rhythmic demeanor. Ultimately, this more frenetic music takes over, and the duo sonata ends with it in command.

Fromm, Herbert (1905–)

DUO

■ **Sonata in G for Violin and Piano (1953)**

(The date indicated above is the year of revision. Fromm's Sonata was originally composed in 1949.)

Fluid tonality, but tonality that is controlled by pitch centers. The openness of the melodic writing is paramount. This type of rhetoric leads to asymmetric ordering in the spirited second movement and a type of through-composed quality in the slow movement. Hindemithian vitality (as well as quartal and quintal progressions) is present in the finale. No pat summations; the development of material is strong.

QUARTET

■ **String Quartet (1957)**

A quartet with a divertimento slant, with five of its movements in variation form. These are preceded by a Ricercare as an extended introduction, followed by a ternary-shaped Theme, defined by precise tempos: andante–agitato–andante. The variational progress samples assorted designs: an Allegro marcato that is scherzo patterned; Recitative and Arioso; March; Introduction and Ländler; and a Rondo-Finale.

Fromm's quartet is clearly indited. It is serious music, minus floridity; a music devoted to classicism in the large sense, with perceptive regard for harmonic order.

Fromme, Arnold (1925–)

QUINTET

- **Three Short Studies for Brass Quintet (Two Trumpets, Horn, Tenor Trombone, and Bass Trombone) (1968)**

Free-formed material, most pugnacious in its harmonic language in the first of the set of three pieces. Motivic detail there, choralish in the second of the group (including a bit of imitation in inverted form), and with canonic bits distributed in the final piece.

Though the moods (tempos) of the first and last Studies are different—Allegro feroce, ma non troppo and Giocoso—the metronomic indications are similar ($\downarrow$ = 112). The central piece (Moderato) is slower ($\downarrow$ = 80). Measure totals decrease in turn, with 67, 35, and 26 respectively for the three conceptions.

Frommel, Gerhard (1907–)

DUO

- *Movimento (Motion)* **for Viola and Cello (1945)**

Despite its descriptive title, Frommel's piece is cast in sonata form. Most of the development concentrates on the active rhythmic portion of the first theme and proceeds in a freewheeling Pfitzner manner—meaning, rugged contrapuntalism and austere insistence on making each specific point.

The chosen string timbres are, of course, propitious for this representation of neo-Pfitzner style. And, gratefully, Frommel bypasses any attempt to make the viola part equate the soprano range of a violin. *Movimento* is definitely a worthy addition to the growing corpus of duos for viola and cello.

OCTET

- **Bläser Suite (Suite for Wind Instruments) (Flute, Oboe, Two Clarinets, Bassoon, Double Bassoon, and Two Horns), Op. 18**

Tonally secure music, presented in simple patterns and directly-to-be-recognized forms. For what it endeavors to say, Frommel's Op. 18 offers eminently listenable music.

The Intrada is in the usual majestic manner, while the Canzona sings with counterpointed voices. This movement is practically a septet since the double bassoon has but one pedal pitch of 4 1/2 measures' length. Movement three is a Ballett—an Allegretto in duple rhythm. The Minnetto (*sic*) has two Trios; both present contrasts to the main section by differential of speed—the second of the pair is faster than the first, and each is in swifter tempo than the principal section. Since the Minnetto is repeated after each Trio, a rondo cloak lightly covers the form. The Finale begins with a slow introduction and then moves into a gay, fast pace. Before the concluding coda the tempo slows again, this time not quite as decelerated as the initial part of the movement. Speed, in this case, aids the matter of thematic formal balance.

Froschauer, Helmuth (1933–)

SEXTET

- **Sextet for Flute, Oboe, Two Clarinets, Horn, and Bassoon**

The suavity and, in the fast-tempo sections, the jauntiness that applies to balanced romantic music conceived in the mid-20th century. There are crisp rhythms that control the finale and plentiful chromatic tinting in the opening movement. Tenebrous content in the central Andante.

Frumerie, Gunnar de (1908–)

DUOS

- **Sonata No. 1 for Violin and Piano (1934)**

Frumerie uses the diatonic palette in his duo sonata, emphasizing the special coloration of quartal harmony. The music contains both the vibrations of simulated bell sounds and the ruggedness of the dance. Especially these qualities are found in the second and fourth movements.

The latter has a fairly long preamble in slow tempo, but once the music moves into full-charged pace it maintains a kinetic flight of sounds against tintinnabulant fifths and primitive stomping rhythms. The end of the movement recalls a few measures from the cantabile sweetness of the Siciliano third movement, only this time these measures have majestic pronouncement and *fortississimo* weight.

- **Sonata No. 2 for Violin and Piano (1944)**

The clue to Frumerie's first movement is found in its tempo heading: Allegro affabile. Accordingly, the music follows suit with affable temper and gentility. Set in C-sharp minor, the movement unfolds in sonata form, beginning and concluding softly. Three-part form is utilized for the second movement, and here again a quiet, partly nostalgic mood surrounds the outer parts, with more fervency in the center.

The Presto has Griegian overtones, its Trio impressed by simple chords over which the muted violin projects graceful dance lines. Only in the final movement, by way of a two-section format, is the music permitted its head.

TRIO

- **Trio No. 2 for Piano, Violin, and Cello (1952)**

Describing his music, Frumerie has stated: "My feeling is for tradition, and I have taken my bearings, so to say, from the past to the future. In my youth I was influenced by Bach, Brahms, Debussy and the earlier Honegger." In this piano trio there is, indeed, a good amount of Brahms, with some impressionistic color, and the rhythmic demeanor (especially of the finale) can well be applied to Honegger. However, no pastiche; the music holds together. One other composer can be indicated, namely Prokofiev, who certainly was a strong influence in regard to the second movement, a Scherzo.

Movement one is structured from a tender chromatic descending theme announced by the piano. The third movement is a threnodic Andante doloroso. There is a constant use of an E pitch doubled at the octave. The piano intones this within two-thirds of the total measures, the violin for an additional total of fifteen measures.

Frumerie adds cyclic interlock in both the Scherzo and the slow movement. In the former it appears within the central section, in the latter in the concluding part of the movement.

Fuchs, Robert (1847–1927)

DUOS

- **Sonata for Double Bass and Piano, Op. 97**

The greatest riches of this double bass sonata are to be found in the middle movement, which offers music of clearly elucidated Viennese swing, even with its Allegro scherzando tempo heading. Fuchs makes good use of plucked sound in this movement, which has a good-size, flowing Trio that is tonally contrasted (G major) to the principal part of the movement (G minor).

Traditional (Brahmsian) details are followed in the outer movements. The piano's textures, therefore, make no easy road for the bass to travel.

- **Sonata in D Minor for Viola and Piano, Op. 86**

Fuchs consistently embraced romantic creative mannerisms in his output. The evidence of romantic scale is to be observed in the first theme of the work. There, within a ten-measure total the viola soars over a span of 2 1/2 octaves. The piano responds with an even larger registration—3 octaves this time. This exuberant melodicism is retained in the development process, though the movement settles down and ends quietly. (But that, too, is romantic thinking.)

There is no Minuet or Scherzo; no *actual* Minuet, that is. The Andante grazioso does have minuet temperament and shape, with full ternary design, including a Trio duplicate; the tonalities are, in turn, B-flat–D–B-flat. A spirited finale with plenty of articulation needs no pleading to prove its romantic robustness (and chromatic coloration).

- **Sonata No. 2 for Cello and Piano, Op. 83**

Three movements: a moderately paced Allegro, an Adagio (to be played "with sentiment"), and an Allegro vivace.

Key change (ever the romantic procedure) intensifies the first part of the Sonata. Though the sections have bits of modulatory moves, the tonality territory is principally marked as E-flat minor, F-sharp minor, and E-flat major. The pitch centralization in the middle movement is on B—major–minor–major, in turn. In the finale the rondo process would demand key

change, and the tonalities of E-flat, B-flat, and A-flat are used, with a final return to E-flat major, which reflects, classically, on the E-flat-minor key that began Fuchs's duo sonata. Indeed, all these steps define a tonal symbiosis that is both balanced and of romantic pronunciation.

- **Twelve Duets for Violin and Viola, Op. 60**

  - No. 1, in B Minor
  - No. 2, in D Major
  - No. 3, in D Minor
  - No. 4, in G Minor
  - No. 5, in G Major
  - No. 6, in G Major
  - No. 7, in A Minor
  - No. 8, in A Minor
  - No. 9, in C Major
  - No. 10, in C Minor
  - No. 11, in B-flat Major
  - No. 12, in D Major

An exhibition of inspirations derived from Brahms, and thereby his style, appropriated as a guide to taste and content. Brahms never wrote a piece for two unaccompanied string instruments. Fuchs's set, therefore, offers both rich music and Brahms sublimation.

Each duet consists of a single movement of moderate length. In addition to the variety of tonalities, further key territory is used: in the fourth piece the last section is in G major, the sixth (the longest of the set) alternates between G and E major, and in the tenth duet the coloration changes beautifully when the C-minor key shifts to the major mode.

Hemiola technique is used in the sixth duet, with precise staccato triple pulses in the viola while the violin outlines the theme in syncopative duple progress within the measures. Various moods are displayed, concluding with a Walzer (Waltz).

TRIOS

■ **Terzetto for Two Violins and Viola, Op. 107**

Music of generous sweep, in which Brahmsian lyric quality is paramount. A bittersweet flavor is found in the contents, especially in the C-sharp-minor outer movements. A further support to this disposition is the scoring, which has a tenderness (the best possible word of description) due to the absence of a true (full) bass register. (The viola's lowest pitch is one octave below middle C—a cello would cover an additional octave below.)

There are three other movements. Of these, the second and fourth embrace large trinal patterns with each of the central sections defined as a Trio. A smaller totality, but also in ternary design, marks the slow, third movement.

■ **Trio for Violin, Viola, and Piano, Op. 115**

It is not unexpected to find that Fuchs had composed a piano trio using the viola in place of the usual cello. (Fuchs produced a single piano trio with the standard combination of violin, piano, and cello. It is in C major and is his Op. 22.) He favored the alto string instrument, composing two sets of *Fantasy Pieces* for Viola and Piano—one a group of seven, listed as Op. 57, the other a group of six, indicated as Op. 117. There are three Terzetti for Two Violins and Viola, a set of Twelve Duets for Violin and Viola, as well as a viola and piano sonata. (For one of the Terzetti, as well as the Twelve Duets, and for the viola and piano sonata, *see above*.)

In the sonata-structured opening movement there is an abundance of rhythmic doubling of the string instruments. Some of this type of texture is to be found in the pair of central movements, a light and entertaining Andante

grazioso and a moderately paced Scherzo. The Trio of the latter is represented by an A-flat-major Vivace that emphasizes octaval intervallic spans. This tonality is in acute contrast to the main part of the movement in B minor. The architectural sense of the finale derives from motival deliberations.

■ **Trio in A Major for Violin, Viola, and Cello, Op. 94**

Romantic music, but not the same old story. Fuchs's single string trio for the standard combination of violin, viola, and cello (he favored the grouping of two violins and a viola, for which he produced three works) immediately offers a new look by the use of three themes in the opening movement. Movement two consists of a set of five variations on a Scottish folk song "O Cruel Was My Father." Each part is clear, with more emphasis on curvaceously spread permutations than on sharply defined rhythmic ones.

The third movement is a gentle, minor-key Minuet, contrasted by a more active Trio and a shift to a major tonality. In the final part three sections are connected, based on the material set forth in the first section (Adagio sostenuto). The cello's motival data is taken up and developed in the fugal Allegretto piacevole that follows and which, in turn, is further developed in the concluding Allegro vivace.

QUINTET

■ **Quintet in E-flat Major for Clarinet, Two Violins, Viola, and Cello, Op. 102**

There is true Brahmsian surge in the first part of Fuchs's clarinet quintet, with the romantic rhythmic confidences that spring from the broader swing speeds of 6/8 and 9/8 measures. In the C-minor Scherzo the pulse is duple, and there is considerable light, springy detail. Key contrast provides colorful give-and-take, with both the Trio and the Coda set in C major.

Stylized intensity of detail marks the slow movement. In the finale the intensity is found in the richness of contrast, with a legato principal alla breve theme leading to rhythmic development and then to a ländler conception in triple time. The former rhythmic outline returns for a bit, but the concluding part drives to the final double bar in *forte* and *fortissimo* with E-flat-tonality optimism, and again with triple-pulse energy.

(The listing advertising the early edition of this work noted that the clarinet could be replaced by a second viola. The modern edition, published by Wollenweber of Munich, makes no mention of this.)

Fuerstner, Carl (1912–)

DUO

- *Nocturne and Dance* for Flute and Piano, Op. 36

The *Nocturne* has hazy impressionistic curves. Contrastive and equalized expressivity is heard in the grotesque points of the *Dance*. Extremely well conceived for the instruments.

Fuga, Sandro (1906–)

TRIO

- Trio for Violin, Cello, and Piano

Music of a tearing quality, combining Verdi dramaticism with Puccini chordal speech. The middle movement reaches a high point in Italian chamber music, notwithstanding the fact that one cannot hear its opening chords without immediately realizing that Puccini has lived. Two themes are concerned; one is a twining

scale, the other consists of archaic harmonies. These alternate in a mood of mystic beauty. It is as if Fuga were preparing the listener for the funereal heaviness of the last movement, cryptically headed by "a P. (November 1939)." This concluding part of the Trio is of surging theme, with a timpanic rhythmed motive—a modern D*ies irae* in which block chords and measured pulses draft an outline, with the picture of death as the inference. The pedal formations used therein are also called on constantly in the first movement, a dramatic and fiery matter in C-sharp minor, with the opening organ point dynamically projected on the dominant pitch point.

In each case of the trio's three sections a strong image is expressed. First a canvas of spectacular listing, then a picture with quasi-religious overtones and, finally, a definition of demise colored with the petition of sorrow and acquiescence. This is program music, without line-by-line evidence, and no story is necessary for it to be understood.

QUARTETS

- Quartet No. 1 for Two Violins, Viola, and Cello (1943)

Without subscribing to any but standard practices, Fuga's first string quartet has imaginative individualistic invention. And coloristic detail minus special effects.

Pedal figurations are the heart of the first movement, its lyricism sung often with combinations of duple- and triple-pulse lines. In parallel fashion the tonality moves about, beginning in the distant area of F-sharp major and winding down to B-flat minor. Indeed, creative freedom without negating total balance of form is to be noted in the central movement, its material developed in numerous motival ways. However, in the movement there is a dramatic set of sixty-eight measures of tight tutti rhythmic combine in constant syncopation. (Sixteen measures are repeated later in the movement.) Thus, the impacted value derived from deliberate static detail. Finally, the last movement is akin to organ writing for four string instruments. The music shifts between chordal and contrapuntal disposition. The effect is commanding.

- **Quartet No. 2 for Two Violins, Viola, and Cello (1945)**

Fuga's favorite mix of chordal and polyphonic writing is present in this work. And so are pedal equivalents by the use of rhythmic repetitions. The last are of intense depiction in the sonata-scaled, dramatic first movement. And in the Capriccio, pulse division is used as a colorful contrapuntal adjunct to song lines. Often the rhythm swings into lightly detailed separations so that in an alla breve measure the units split into 3–3–2 eighth notes. Another pulsatile effect is obtained by dividing a 3/2 meter into four sets of slurred eighth notes, obtaining thereby quadruple accentuation within the triple total. None of this is forced but produces a very natural sensibility to the music's progress.

The finale begins with a sustained, vertically defined Introduzione and then moves into a very speedy Fuga all'italiana. Healthy, athletic music.

- **Quartet No. 3 (*Elegiaco*) for Two Violins, Viola, and Cello (1948)**

Fuga's *Elegiac* Quartet ("Alla memoria di Paolo Giordani") is in one movement. It sways and shifts between fast and slow and fast sections. The slow-paced sections, though intense, have no maudlin quality, but rather deep eloquence. The fast-paced sections are principally motoric in their impetus, constituting a music of charge and of clenched fists.

Fukushima, Kazuo (1930–)

DUOS

- ***Ekagra* for Alto Flute and Piano (1957)**

Fukushima's essay was inspired by a Chinese ideogram that symbolizes concentration. Serially derived, but in an extremely free fashion, its concentration is not one of mood but of intervallic movement. This varies between motile disjunctiveness and almost static slow-motion arrangement. (An example of the latter: thirteen measures where only the pitches E, F, and F-sharp are used, with a different rhythmic content filling each of the measures.) Repetitive chord combinations in the piano also relate to the duo's symbolization, which has traditional Japanese court-music style as an inlay to its contemporary chromaticism.

- ***Kadha karuna* for Flute and Piano (1962)**

Like *Ekagra* (*see above*), this piece is a musical consideration of a Chinese ideogram. In Sanskrit, *kadha* means "poem." *Karuna* is also a word in the ancient Indic language, representing "compassion." In Buddhist thought the title represents "Buddha, the Giver of Light."

Using twelve-tone jargon, Fukushima's work has triple-divisional identification. The outer parts are defined by rhapsody and fantasy, projected by the flute, with mostly percussive interjections by the piano. An eight-measure portion, repeated literally to form sixteen measures, marks the central part. It is faster in speed, expansive and excited in content.

Kadha karuna is a mood piece, candidly expressed in the usual fractured total chromatic style—once again a flute and piano pastoral manifestation, but one translated into nervous urbanism.

This duo is the second version of the piece.

The initial setting was written three years earlier (1959) and had twice the forces: two flutes, piano, and Japanese drum.

- **Three Pieces from *Chū-U* for Flute and Piano (1964)**

Concentrated in every respect. Pitch movement is restrained. (In movement two, for example, the first nine measures of almost uninterrupted flute sound do not go beyond a minor third.) Rhythms have a sense of arrested motion, with isolated chordal insets by the piano, while the flute line can be described as being mostly the equivalent of pulselessness, its formations curving in and out and around a pitch point. The textures are sparse. In movement two the piano is silent; in movement three the flute breaks up the pitches of a chromatic scale to cover over seven measures. It then retires, and the remaining six measures are for unaccompanied piano. While there is more motility to the dynamics, they, too, tend to a demarcative (i.e., concentrated) arrangement.

One is reminded in this music of the flat color washes of Japanese prints. The sounds project a sense of persistent immobility. With such constraint and the minuteness of pitch selection, nationalism (which so many Japanese composers have been attempting to bypass) is exemplified in Fukushima's pieces.

Fuleihan, Anis (1900–70)

DUOS

- **Duo for Viola and Cello**

Energy dominates the outer movements: in the first through the subtle polyphonic knitting of the lines; in the last through the alla breve vivace tempo and the more vertical incisiveness of the construction. In contrast is a graceful waltz that is constantly kicked by metrical change from the basic triple pulse to that of duple. The scoring produces sounds that tend to be big but are meaningful.

- **Four Preludes for Violin and Piano (1945)**

A sense of controlled virtuosity streams through the second of the set, an Alla marcia thickened with violin chords and disjunct line action. The fourth piece is a Presto that jumps and sings forth in turn. The other pair of preludes are fully lyrical.

- ***Pastoral Sonata* for Flute and Piano (1940)**

One realizes that the word *Klangideal*, used so often in avant-garde music, can well apply to music that carries on the traditions of the classic-romantic school. That concept embraces the creative balance of tonal power that sings through this duo sonata.

A flowing first movement is followed by an ariosolike middle movement. Fuleihan has given the flutist a substantial cadenza just before the concluding statement in the latter. The finale whirls around contrastive conjunct and intervallically open passages.

- **Three Pieces for Cello and Piano**

A different arrangement of these three pieces, rather than the usual balanced outer divisions and a contrastively paced middle movement. Fuleihan begins with a slow Prologue, shifts to a kinetic Presto for an Interlude, and in the Epilogue puts on the tempo brakes with a Molto moderato indication.

Triadic detail is important to the first two pieces; sharper linear writing, as well as metrical change, marks the final one. These details are confirmed by the unresolved harmony of the conclusion. The tonalities for the first two pieces are A minor and D major.

QUARTETS

- *Humoristic Preludes* for Woodwind Quartet (Flute, Oboe, Clarinet, and Bassoon)

Each of the five pieces in the set is published separately. Apparently this is an unstated invitation to perform the preludes singly or in any grouping.

The Overture is properly lively and carefully set forth in tripartite design. "Acrobatics" is an athletic, triple-meter Presto. The third of the group ("In the Barnyard") has plenty of grace notes to stir the motility. "Serenade for Judy" sings suavely in the outer sections, dances discreetly in the middle portion. There is no delay in "Exit," with its continual allegro vivace action.

- **String Quartet No. 1 (1940)**

The score for Fuleihan's quartet, published in 1963, does not bear any composition date. It is also absent of any of the important details contained in the original (manuscript) score.

Fuleihan finished his opus in 1940, indicating its title as Quartet for String Orchestra. He then changed the heading to Quartet for String Instruments, specifying that the work was for "solo quartet or string chamber orchestra without bass." (At no time were double basses included, even when the work was listed as "for String Orchestra.")

Fuleihan was concerned with the interweave of patterns in his composition. At this remove, in these days of superior quartet teams, it is ridiculous to suggest that this quartet would offer any performance difficulties. In 1940 there were questions (at least in Fuleihan's mind). For that reason he stated: "The technical difficulties . . . are such as to render performances . . . unsatisfactory—unless by a virtuoso group." He, therefore, permitted the quartet to be performed by a grouped mass of string players (a string *chamber* orches-

tra), which he felt could achieve results under a conductor not feasible with an ordinary string foursome. More than two decades later he changed his mind and, with the placement of a third title, all previous prefatory remarks were removed.

Fuleihan was born in Cyprus. That background, plus travel and study of the music of the eastern Mediterranean countries, has resulted in true Eastern music infiltrations into his music (as will be seen in this work). This is far from the type of musically-simulated-by-guesswork tablets that are synthetics chopped out by composers who know not of what sounds they make. There is an individual flavor in his music. A true Eastern endowment is given his musical structure. This is especially to be heard in the middle movement (the theme that is in dialogue between the instruments is contrasted to one festooned with embroidery).

The opening movement is designed from an initial motive, built into an Agitato section by gradually increasing the speed in four shifts of tempo. The motival impetus (short–long sounds) then furnishes the power for the main section of the movement. A change of mood brings the extremely concentrated recapitulation; the movement is not from the schoolbooks. The final movement is a fiery Vivo. A scherzo trademark shows in its triple, rhythmic stride. It blazes to a tremendous peroration, extinguished by great reduction in speed and dynamic.

- **String Quartet No. 2 (1949)**

The principal compositional devices in the quartet are variation and fugue, both favorite resources of this composer. The fugal material is heard directly in the second movement, a pert scherzo-formationed music, in skippy Allegretto tempo. It also opens the fourth movement Finale (an Allegro vivace that is linked to the previous movement). Variational data is the control for the third movement's septuple-meter theme. A further interlock is the appearance of this theme in augmented form within the Finale.

Movement one is structured from two ideas. Initiating the quartet is a motive announced in *forte* and to be played ferociously. This is developed in contrast to a conjunct, chromatically colored, lyrical idea. The opening movement, as is the balance of Fuleihan's opus, is a cogent realization.

QUINTET

- **Quintet for Piano and String Quartet (1967)**

One of Fuleihan's major productions. The music has symphonicism (what piano quintet avoids this textural result?) but is commanded by a rhythmic pilotage that carries through all parts of the work and maintains a just balance for the radiant romantic style.

Free sonata detail is found in the first part of the Quintet; the second and final movements are developed in a variational manner. Linked to the latter is a solo piano section split between two completely opposite tempos (Andante at $\quarternote = 56$ and Molto vivace at $\quarternote = 260$–300). Preceding the last is a free fugal movement.

SEXTET

- **Divertimento for String Sextet (Two Violins, Two Violas, and Two Cellos)**

Tonal reliability and good amounts of piquancy are to be found in this composer's music. In this four-part essay (which can also be performed by a string orchestra) modality plays an important part.

A broadly stated opening movement, titled Entrance, is followed by a tri-pulse Serenade in which pizzicato support is used in most of the measures. The Chorale does not follow mensural formula, being set in 5/8 time and

with considerable linear action. The last statement also describes the concluding Fugue.

Fulton, Norman (1909–)

DUOS

- **Introduction, Air, and Reel for Viola and Piano**

A three-in-one work, totally linked, and with transfer of the material making it sometimes difficult to understand which part of the duo is in play. Further, save for a few ritards and one small portion of seven measures, the entire work (lasting 5 1/4 minutes) is in one tempo, marked $\quarternote = 69$.

Integration, therefore, if not differentiation. The initial rhythm in the piano (dotted eighth and sixteenth) is used for the Introduction, within the Air, and supports the Reel. And within the Reel some of the Introduction reappears.

- **Sonata da camera for Viola and Piano (1945)**

Rich tonal stability and cyclic stability at the same time. The sonata opens with a fortissimo double-stopped introductory statement by the viola, with dynamic octaves in the piano. Thinned down to single voicing, the motive marks the coda of the first movement, carries over within the main theme of the slow movement, and also appears in the final movement.

Clear distinctions to each movement in terms of tempo and content. Sonata design in the Molto allegro (the prefatory cyclic announcement is marked Lento e appassionata), lyricism in the Poco lento, ma sempre ritmico (a chromatically flavored item), and a balletic, lighter-scaled, and lighter-textured finale.

Fürst, Paul Walter (1926–)

DUOS

- *Ars bassi* for **Double Bass and Piano, Op. 41**

Fürst's *Bass Art* weaves its way through expansive tonal style, with considerable attention given to ostinato patterns. An amphibrachic pattern (a long sound between two shorter ones) is used in the first part, tarantella rhythmic swing is reiterated in the second movement, a three-measure sequence is set forth six consecutive times at the start of the fourth movement. And there are many other repetitive bits.

The music is proclamatory, jestful, recitativelike in turn in the first three movements. A more episodic frame of reference applies to the final movement, making it free-designed to some extent. The so-called anti-forms of some composers do not apply in this case.

- *Emotions*: **Seven Duos for Viola and Double Bass, Op. 57**

A wide range of sketches in a light contemporary style.

Number one works out of a play on the sound of C—quite colorful. Scherzo tactics are used in the second and fourth duos. Number five is a fascinating all-pizzicato movement, in minuet tempo. The plucked sounds include double-stop glissandos. There is nocturnal atmosphere in the sixth duo, and both improvisation and ostinato in the first section of the concluding duo. Striking characterizations in all of the seven pieces.

QUARTET

- **String Quartet, Op. 34**

Romantic data in this piece, more developed and accordingly expanded than is to be found in this composer's other music. A tendency for compartmentalization is to be noted, but nonetheless the music is soundly formed.

Movement one seizes the opening two-violin triplet, and it becomes the motivating point of the music. A drum-roll type of figure moves within the Lamento. Movement three represents a mid-20th-century realization of scherzo design, here colored with glides. Fürst's fondness for sectional discourse fully appears in the final movement.

QUINTETS

- *Apropos Wind Quintet*, **Op. 49**

"Apropos" can mean "suitably," and that this seven-minute work turns out to be. The materials fit the medium; the former representing the through-composed, connective style of Malipiero and the late period of Chávez's work, the latter setting forth the wind group of flute, oboe, clarinet, horn, and bassoon in their very comfortable and responsive lightly rhythmic personality.

There are some ornamental observations, mainly for the clarinet and some for the flute. The latter has a number of flutter-tongued focuses.

- **Third Wind Quintet, Op. 29**

Fürst's style here persistently avoids flowing statements and development of theme, but splinters the material in linked sections. These hang together, though they are often severely contrasted.

Thus, in movement one (thirteen measures in length) there are some twirls and then a solo horn ending. The final ten measures of the second movement are a changed recapitulation of the beginning of the movement, and thus this part of the work is to be placed in the song-form category. Free fact-finding follows in movements three and four. The finale has no metrical caution as it most often shifts its vivacious data in three-measure sequences that represent, in turn, 3/8, 4/8, and 5/8.

Fürstenau, Anton Bernhard
(1792–1852)

DUOS

- **Concertante duo in E Minor for Two Flutes**

- **Concertante duo in F Major for Two Flutes**

- **Concertante duo in D Major for Two Flutes**

The tonality plan of the first duo divides the first and third movements into E minor and E major. Contrasted to these fast movements is an Andante in G major. A principal strength to the design of the first movement is the contrary motion of the two voices. Imitation is a focal point in the finale.

Fürstenau was a close friend of Carl Maria von Weber (he was the first flutist in the Chapel Royal in Dresden, functioning under Weber's direction). In the F-major duo the final movement is a set of three variations on the theme "Über die blauen Wogen" from Weber's *Oberon*. Preceding this movement is an Allegro moderato, brilliant in conception, and a Poco Adagio in which the principal role is given the first flute.

A scherzo quality is bound into the duplepulse flow of the opening part of the third duo. The slow movement is set in the subdominant of the D-major base key; as in the slow movements of the other two duos, the second flute is placed in an accompanimental position. The final Rondo moves with plenty of zip, aided by imitative designs.

Fürstenau, Wolfram

SOLO—QUINTET

- **Railway-Traffic for One to Five Guitars (1973)**

Already much is clear in the title line of this work, which indicates five different performing possibilities. *Trein-Verkeer* is what can be described as determined indeterminacy.

Small notated segments appear on the score page, in various shapes, and staff interlocked. They vary slightly: one is chordal, another emphasizes repeated sounds, a third covers a pithy melodic scrap, and so forth. They are identified as train types: empty, local, passenger, etc. (The names mean nothing whatsoever.) So much for determinacy.

Phrase choices, playing entrances and exits, and all procedures are in the hands of whatever personnel is involved, being bound only by the notated material. If, for example, the second player enters during the playing of the first performer, he can start at the beginning of the phrase already in progress or choose another one. In the meantime the first player can go on to any other phrase or repeat the one he just played. Once begun, a phrase is to be finished. So much for indeterminacy.

DUO

- **Orationen (Texts) for Organ and Guitar (1969)**

The title refers to the variable texts (*Oratio, Evangelium*, etc.) of the different Masses. As to the subtitles, each combines a locale with one of the canonical hours at which service is held in the Roman Catholic Church, plus formal definition of the piece. Thus: "Innsbrucker Matutin" (quasi Intrada), "Maria Plainer Laudes" (quasi Toccata), "Salzburger Vesper" (quasi Concertino), and "Oberndorfer Complet" (Epilog). Therefore, Austrian types, in turn, relate to services held at night, sunrise, sunset, and nightfall.

Expect no sacred, somber, and solemn representations. The medium already hints at the message. For glory to and praise of God one can use any instrumental combination, but in a duo one would expect that a different balance would be chosen than the thin-toned guitar and the stentorian organ. That is, if sacred, somber, and solemn music were involved. Not here, however. All four of these musical texts are violent unctions—as insistent on using hard-crusted dissonances and raw-frictioned harmonies as the concentration on unchanged pitch in the monotonic recitation of a liturgical text. So the choice of an organ and guitar is in proper keeping.

Save for the second movement, the formal designation is in some sense or degree only partially fulfilled. In the "Laudes," the Toccata titling is fair, dealing with a persistent sixteenth-note movement by the organ that travels minus bar lines, minus meter, minus any dynamic change from the single *forte* indication at a pace of $\quarternote = 100$. The sixteenths are grouped in sets of two, three, four, five, and seven, and there are more than five hundred of them. (The guitar does very little in this movement.)

There is no reason to expect that religious subjects (especially without text) must be dressed in tonal cloth. Some may consider the Fürstenau score a deviation from rectitude. But no need for reproach. *Orationen* is simply an unritualistic treatment of ritual.

Furtwängler, Wilhelm (1886–1954)

DUO

- **Violin Sonata [No. 2] in D Major**

Music by this great conductor will expectedly produce curiosity. What sort of music did he write? Well then, be prepared for massivity rare in the world of the duo sonata medium. This violin and piano sonata comes in at fifty minutes! One would not be surprised if cuts were made by performers.

Stylewise, the music binds late Beethoven in the middle movement (Lento, Andante e Cantabile) with Brahms (Allegro moderato for the opening movement, Molto allegro [Presto] for the concluding movement).

Critics are acutely divided in their opinion of Furtwängler's opus. M. Kraemer states that the work has "intensity and passion" and that it exemplifies "a great conservative mind and far surpasses everything that has been said in music so far." (This writer totally disagrees.) Abram Loft writes that the work is guilty of "extreme inflation" and that it is unreal to think "that a concert program will have room for so long a work." (The response is affirmative to the first part of this statement, negative in reply to the other remark.)

Fussan, Werner (1912–)

DUOS

- **Music for Flute and Piano, Op. 13**

The title of Fussan's composition confirms his objective viewpoint. This concentrated work of three movements is in the restrained and very telling manner of neoclassicism. Fussan's harmonies group themselves around and are guided by pandiatonic controls; the counterpoint is very reserved. There is a relaxed but not completely loose feeling to the music, which has a pastoral air about it. Sonata design is used in the first movement; the second is in ternary form, very much highlighted by quartal harmonies. The last movement is formed from rondo principles.

A discussion regarding the tonality balances of this work is in order. Since the neoclassic composers follow the logic of key relationships as clearly as did Beethoven, it is odd to find that no movement in Fussan's Op. 13 ends in the tonic. Though the keys have the swinging-out-of-orbit freedom of 20th-century music, nonetheless the pivotal basis of A is used in the first two movements, yet both are completed in the subdominant (D). On the other hand, although the last movement begins in F and veers very quickly to the key of B, this last tonality follows the music's flow easily; accordingly, the final cadence in B major is much more rational.

■ **Music for Violin and Piano (1949)**

Organized with neoclassic, Hindemithian discrimination. The outer movements are moderately paced, with a shade more breadth pertaining to the final movement. Fussan uses a good amount of quartal intervals, both in line movement and in harmonic detail. (The final movement is completed in the rare key of D-sharp major.) Ornamental coloring is found in the slow movement. But even there, as elsewhere, there is a crispness to the rhythmic figures.

Füssl, Karl Heinz (1924–)

TRIO

■ *Nachtmusik (Night Music) for String Trio*

The contents of *Nachtmusik* indicates heady chromatic writing together with sharply op-

posed tonalities. Füssl blocks out his material freely, massing and opposing its darks and lights to give the broadest and yet most pertinent expression to the colorful formal assortment.

And variety there is. The Intrada stays in concentrated boundaries, comprising a twelve-measure, mainly vertical Largo. Movement two is a Sonate, its five sections precisely repeated in each instance.

There is no sing-song in this composer's concept of a Ständchen (Serenade). Already the tempo heading, Allegretto capriccioso, clues in the creative demeanor, and the music accordingly thrives on contrapuntal capers. Individuality continues in movement four with a Ländler al rovescio. This Austrian dance is usually in the character of a slow waltz. Here it is paced in a range that moves from ♩ = 136 to ♩ = 150. There are two six-measure phrases, then a pair of Trios. The first of these (faster than the second) consists of a pair of eight-measure thoughts; the other is a twenty-measure unit. However, each of the five portions is repeated, and the antithesis in each case is in rovescio form—i.e., totally in retrograde motion. A firm da capo rounds off this interesting conception.

"Nachtmusik" ("Night Music"), representing movement five, is colored constantly with sul tasto (playing on the fingerboard), glissandos, plucked timbre, sharply contrastive dynamic levels, and pungent dissonance. It also hints at an undisclosed program. Measure 3 is to be performed "Like a cry"; much later an arpeggiated passage between the three instruments is described as "When I go to my house"; and a duplicated type of figure for the cello reads " . . . the moon shines so beautifully." Nothing to go on with these snippets, but the music does speak of mysterious dark and light conflicts.

The concluding movement (Finale, Perpetuum Mobile) zips along on triplets, most of them set within quintuple-total pulses per measure.

Futterer, Carl (1873–1927)

QUINTET

- **Wind Quintet (1922)**

This composition by the Swiss composer was edited from a draft of the score. Not a reconstruction at all, the editing consisting of the addition of a few notes in the flute part in the slow movement, plus a single note for the bassoon, and the balancing of the dynamic indications.

Futterer's quintet is classically entrenched creatively, though his vertical and horizontal pitch arrangements are reaching into full romantic style. Serious music writing throughout the four movements—fast–slow–Vivace (a true scherzo example)–fast—but no ascetic asperities.

Fux, Johann Joseph (1660–1741)

TRIOS

- *Concentus Musico-Instrumentalis*: **Partita in F for Flute, Oboe, and Basso Continuo**

Fux produced 405 extant works. Among this total there are 29 partitas, 7 included under the collective title *Concentus Musico-Instrumentalis*. Various headings were assigned the partitas (suites) in the *Concentus*, such as Rondeau à 7, Serenada à 8, Sonata à 4. The final one (number seven) in the set is this Partita in F.

Represented here is fluid and nicely inventive chamber music. Fux's ability as a contrapuntalist is proclaimed in the third part, where melodies representing Italian and French styles are partnered. It highlights a work that includes a three-part Sinfonia and two picturesquely titled movements, "La Joye des fidels sujets" ("The Joy of the Faithful Subjects") and

"Les Ennemis confus" ("The Enemy is Confused"). The former heading has some relationship to the triple-beat dance pulse of the music, but the other one, also minuetlike, is totally healthy and refreshing, and even gentle. Furthermore, there is no confusion as to the clear F major progress of the music. It is quite apparent that Fux's "confused enemy" is simply a humorous title tactic.

- **Partita a tre for Two Violins and Basso Continuo, K.V. 322**

A dramatic Ouverture in G minor begins Fux's five-part composition, with a bustling Allegro surrounded by two different Largo statements. Then follow a Lully-type Entrée (here the marchlike music is to be played "un poco Grave"), a Menuett, a Siciliana, and a Giga.

These movements fulfill the usual designs. However, the Menuett provides extra evidence of Fux's contrapuntal mastery. The technique of double counterpoint is used, so that the bass line of the Menuett becomes the soprano line of the Trio, and the soprano line of the Menuett simultaneously becomes the Trio's bass line. Two dances are thus made from a single material.

- **Sinfonia a tre for Two Violins and Basso Continuo, K.V. 330**

Three movements: a substantial Adagio linked to a Vivace, a Largo, and a Final Presto. Plenty of polyphony in every part of the piece. As succinctly described by the editor, Erich Schenk, there is "the spirit of the Roman-Venetian late Baroque" in the music's style.

- **Sonata a tre for Three Violins**

Further proof that nullifies any statement that Fux produced only dry, academic music.

There are separate pairs of slow and fast movements. Tagged on to the second fast move-

Fux

ment is an Adagio. Then follows another rapid movement, with an unexpected return to the Adagio, now a bit more than doubled in size. Contrapuntalism everywhere, always impressive, always rich; in the fast movements the polyphony moves with agility and sparkle.

- *Sonata pastorale a tre* **for Two Violins and Basso Continuo, K.V. 397**

Two movements that the editor, Erich Schenk, describes as "eine liebliche Weihnachtsmusik" ("a lovely Christmas piece"). There is a broad Adagio and a fast movement (Un poco allegro) that mixes the vertical with the horizontal.

Interestingly, Schenk states that the well-known "Silent Night, Holy Night" is a later variant of Fux's melody in the opening movement.

QUARTET

- **Sonata a tre in D Minor for Violin (or Flute or Oboe), Second Violin, Cello, and Basso Continuo**

A fugal directness begins Fux's chamber piece and then connects in turn with a stately Grave, a sharply polyphonic Presto, another Grave, and a concluding Presto. Mostly, the two upper voices (the violins) are accompanied by the two bass parts (cello and continuo). However, in some places this distribution is canceled and thereby shows independent cello writing as compared to linkage with the figured bass (continuo).

The editor, Willi Hillemann, indicates that substituting a flute or an oboe for the first violin "is completely in accordance with contemporary usage and in fact gives a charming effect because of the change of tone."

Gaál, Jenö (1906–)

DUO

- **Sonata for Oboe and Piano (1959)**

A duo sonata based on standard foundations of style. Logical, balanced, and contemporaneously conservative. Bearing in mind the values of a lyrical oboe voice, Gaál follows that line of reasoning. In the second movement (Largo) more rhythmic motility is used to compensate for the slow tempo as well as to contrast with the previous movement. Light material and swift pace concern the neat finale. There, as elsewhere, the Hungarian composer is never guilty of pedestrian formations.

QUARTET

- **String Quartet No. 3 (1962)**

Determined and earnest music, cut to fit form without special deviations. Fluent line writing and strong rhythms, with developed material running a rondo track in the first movement, followed by a tripartite center movement (Largo), weighted vertically, and a polyphonic finale. The material in the last movement is in search of a fugue, but it never goes beyond outlining the start of one.

SEXTET

- **Sextet for Violin, Viola, Cello, Flute, Celesta, and Percussion (Xylophone, Cybal, Cymbal, and Triangle) (1964)**

Gaál flirts with twelve-tone writing (the work begins with a twelve-tone row in the viola, then transposed and announced by the violin, and then inverted by the cello) but opts for more rhapsodic assortments in his five-movement piece. Mostly sparse scoring in music that in the long run settles into free tonality rather than

continuing as it started and taking a positive position in terms of serialism.

Gabaye, Pierre (1930–)

DUO

- **Sonatine for Flute and Bassoon**

Poulencian patter and lyricism, with all its intonations modulated neatly. Gabaye shows a vivid and intuitive imagination in his wind duo. There are three movements: Modéré sans lenteur, Andante, and Rapide et brilliant.

Gaber, Harley (1943–)

QUINTET

- *The Winds Rise in the North* for **Three Violins, Viola, and Cello (1975)**

Clustered sonority bands in constant, slow-moving discharge. Gaber's raw-blistered music—absent of melody, counterpoint, rhythm, related motion, and form, concentrating only on sheer staticness—derives from the composer's metaphysical approach, which he describes as "trying to reach an understanding of things." The macerated metamorphosis that results probes but does not produce a solution.

An LP recording of the work comes close to an hour and three-quarters in length.

Gabrielski, Wilhelm (1791–1846)

QUARTET

- **Grand Quartet in A Major for Four Flutes, Op. 53, No. 2**

(The published edition indicates the composer

as J.W. Gabrielski. The "J" stands for Jan or Johann, the "W" for Wilhelm. However, it is as Wilhelm Gabrielski that this composer is commonly known.)

This is the best of his Op. 53 flute quartets, the others being in the keys of G (No. 1) and E (No. 3). All three are subtitled "Hommage à Kuhlau," though the published edition (1956) makes no mention of this fact.

As stated by classical theorists, the exposition of the first movement is constructed of two tonally contrasting sections. Development is not without its superficialities, and there is considerable use of sequential data. Simple ternary form marks the middle movement in F major. The spirited finale includes a D major marchlike section that constitutes an interesting turn in the events of the otherwise A-major movement.

Gaburo, Kenneth (1926–93)

DUO

- *Ideas and Transformations* No. 1 for Violin and Viola (1955)

Read: "Themes and Variations." Actually, extremely free variations. There are three in each set, with the second *Transformation* divided into five parts, each bearing a different tempo; actually, then, variations within a variation.

Gaburo's fabric is woven by twelve-tone threads. Unit distribution is basic. At times a specific timbre brings more cohesion, as in the all-pizzicato third part of *Transformation II* and the decisive rhythmic sharpness of the fourth part of that movement.

QUARTET

- *Line Studies* for Four Instruments (Viola, Flute, Clarinet, and Trombone) (1957)

Gaburo's *Line Studies* for a truly mixed instrumental bag of flute, clarinet, trombone, and viola is dodecaphonic music with class and cogency. The divided translations of the basic row—fragmented, spatially redesigned, harmonically emphasized, and "as a simultaneous definition of the total space offered by the instruments"—are in constant reactivation, but the subject's core remains. No stunt man, this fellow. The sounds Gaburo has created are those of honesty and meaning.

Gade, Niels (1817–90)

DUO

- *Phantasiestücke (Fantasy Pieces)* for Piano and Clarinet (or Violin), Op. 43

The third part of this four-part suite bears the title Ballade, but for that matter that heading could apply as well to the other movements. Clearly colored material, well balanced in voicing (notwithstanding the placement of the piano first in the title heading), and sensitively concerned with romantic diction.

TRIO

- *Novelettes* for Piano, Violin, and Cello, Op. 29

While it is sometimes considered poor analysis to relate one composer to another, it is the only satisfactory method of explaining the eclecticism of this composer. His gentility was respectably modeled from the suave characteristics of Schumann and Mendelssohn, mostly the latter.

The first movement of Gade's *Novelettes* is a light Scherzo. The second has odd affinity in the "head" of its main theme with a passage for first violin in the quartet by Debussy. This is a mere coincidence, but nevertheless worth noting. The three-part form of this rather touching slow movement changes into a minor key and then speeds up, not by tempo but by the amount of sound activity. Schumann (via the beginning of his piano quintet) will be observed holding Gade's hand in the Moderato. The last two movements are again Mendelssohnian, not new mintage "in the spirit" of that composer, but in frank imitation. Gade did not mince matters, he equates Mendelssohn's Danish agent.

(An edition for piano, violin, and viola is published. This was not made by the composer but by one E. Heim. The only changes, and extremely minute ones, are in the transfer of the cello part to the viola.)

QUARTETS

- **String Quartet in D Major, Op. 63**

Thirty-seven years separate this work from the earlier quartet discussed below, but hardly any difference in style separates the two. Again, Mendelssohn is embraced, and it does no harm to Gade to adopt such aesthetic patronage.

The work is written beautifully for the strings and therefore sounds with the fullest coherence. Four movements, with Allegro tempo for the outer sections (the Finale is led into via a Moderato portion). A light Allegretto vivace represents the scherzo area. A slow movement precedes the final movement.

- **String Quartet in F Minor (1851)**

Totally Mendelssohnian-tinted and so regulated. The outer movements have introductions

before the fast-paced major divisions. In the central place Gade has an Allegretto and a playful movement. The latter, however, does not have the feathery travel of the great Felix. Otherwise, Gade is faithful to him and produces a worthy work.

OCTET

- **Octet in F Major for Four Violins, Two Violas, and Two Cellos, Op. 17**

Of course, every string octet is compared to the famous Mendelssohn example, which has never been equaled. But it is time to revive this work, which certainly would not suffer if programmed with the Mendelssohn. There are the standard four movements, the music always confident and charming,, and what it says it says in a romantically direct and clear manner. Movements one and four are in fast tempo, within these there is an Andantino, and, expectedly, a Scherzo. Eight voices but the line writing is lucid and never cluttered.

Gagnebin, Henri (1886–1977)

DUO

- **Aubade for Horn and Piano**

Proper formal attention is given this conception of "morning music." This means controlled depiction, with no dynamic epiphany. This does not mean, however, mundane simplicity. There are tonal command and colorful echo effects.

QUARTET

- **String Quartet No. 3 in F-sharp Minor (1927)**

Romantic substance with some formal variety.

Gagnebin begins with a Concerto. Its baroque solid drive is accompanied with tinges of concerto-grosso style as solo bits are intersticed in the structure. In a few places the soloism is expanded. The quartet terminates with an Adagio. There, each of the instruments has an opportunity to specify its individual color in the weave. An Intermezzo in ternary form (stimulated by changing duple and triple meters) and a Scherzo (minus the usual Trio) form the inside movements. The Scherzo has a little twist—its ending is in a quiet dynamic and is accompanied by a constantly thinned texture.

Gaigerova, Varvara (1903–44)

QUARTET

- **Quartet No. 2 in G Major on Yakutian Folk Themes for Two Violins, Viola, and Cello, Op. 17**

The greater part of this composer's output cultivated the folk materials of the various Soviet republics. Her music shows the study she had with Miaskovsky. There are commanding use of the instruments and clear textures marking the balanced forms.

The quartet has four movements with the standard sequence of fast–scherzo type–slow–fast tempos. What especially colors this work is a huge amount of grace notes, while the use of strong rhythms gives a mobility to the quartet without overburdening it.

Gál, Hans (1890–1987)

DUOS

- **Divertimento for Mandolin and Harp (or Piano)**

The adventurous element pertains only to the combination (a rare one) of mandolin and harp. (Even a mandolin and piano duo in serious music can be considered unusual.) What Gál has provided is a classical survey, embracing a Preludio, a fast Burla (some glisses for harp here), an Intermezzo that has some scherzo detail, and a Rondo. Though set in well-trodden formal territory, the timbral combination does provide (to mix the metaphor vigorously) a listen in unexplored territory.

- **Partita for Mandolin and Piano**

There is a place for the mandolin on the chamber music stage, and Gál's piece provides substantial evidence. The style is diatonic, beginning with a Preambulo, a nicely curved Aria, and an articulately figurated Capriccio. Movement four is a Marcia, and here Gál gives way to a concluding cadenza for the plucked string instrument, leading to the closing Gigue.

- **Sonatine for Two Mandolins, Op. 59, No. 1**

Pleasurable tonal essays, straight to the instrumental point—Gál made no contemporary imposition into mandolin techniques in the several works he wrote for the instrument (*see above* and *below*). Faithful forms here: the first movement is in sonata format, moving with tranquil pace; the second movement is a *Menuett*; and the finale is a Rondo. The last is supported in great part with open fifths.

- **Suite for Violin and Piano, Op. 56**

The actions here are dictated by a keen regard for form and structure. All the material fulfills that objective, without textbook stricture, which is always a triumph for mediocrity.

Bachian figurations are the talismen in the Preambulo. In a ternary setting, its moderate-speed surveyal includes a touch of imitation. The Capriccio alternates a pair of themes—one pert, the other opposite. An Aria and a Rondo make up the other pair of movements. The latter has the largest contrapuntal incidence of the entire work. It is also the only movement that ends above a *pianissimo* level.

TRIOS

- *Huyton Suite* for Flute and Two Violins

The combination used is rare, chosen because of special circumstances. Huyton was the place in England where Gál (an Austrian) was interned at the beginning of World War II. The only instruments in the camp for which he could create music were these, and Gál accommodated himself accordingly. And to splendid effect. (In an article on the composer, Roger Oliver termed this music "delightful and witty.")

The trio begins with an Alla marcia that moves with reticent boldness; the Capriccio is a fugal proposal of scherzo manners, including a homophonically presented Trio (Gál works with romantic influences).

Variations generally carry on the one mean of incessant thematic development. The use of a ritornel (almost a second theme for variation), in this instance, poses a slight modification on variational design. While the theme of the Canzonetta con variazione has four, very distinctly clear, variations, the secondary item (occurring immediately each time after the theme and variations) is not embroidered; it is repeated literally, merely refashioned with new voicing and sonority arrangement. This is the philosophy of variation without cerebral cant. The celebrations of the final Fanfaronade (the score misspells this word as "fanfaronnade") are neither boastful nor ostentatious. Fast march rhythms are naturally called on for holiday-spirited music.

- *Little Suite* for Two Violins and Cello (with Piano ad lib), Op. 49a

Gál's *Kleine Suite* was originally written for a trio comprising two violins and cello, and then Gál added a piano part in the character of an 18th-century continuo. Matching this concept are the classical forms of a March and a pair of dances: Minuet and Rigaudon.

Three settings are therefore possible: as a string trio for the instruments noted, as a trio for two violins and piano (the left hand part of the piano score is an exact doubling of the cello part so there is no loss of the latter in using this combination), and as a quartet for the three string instruments and piano. (Practical thought is maintained in the composer's approval of multiplying the string parts in any of the settings noted.)

- *Serenade* for Clarinet, Violin, and Cello, Op. 93

Gál's trio sings mainly in a voice registered in the harmonic counterpoint range. The lines are of post-Brahmsian poundage. There is a bit of sugarcoating in the Trio of the three-part Burletta and in the swing of the Intermezzo, which includes a short cadenza for clarinet just before the concluding measures. The initial movement is a Cantabile, the closing one a Giocoso.

- Suite for Three Mandolins, Op. 59, No. 3

Conservative writing dealing with exactly balanced designs, and appealing because of the intelligent handling of the medium. Gál begins with a "Marche mignonne" and continues with music geared to dances: Sarabande, Gavotte, and Gigue. It will be noted that these dances increase sequentially in their rates of speed.

- **Trio for Oboe, Violin, and Viola, Op. 94**

The "Trio" titling does not indicate the special suite structuring that Gál uses. In the center he places a pair of Intermezzo movements. One of these is described as grazioso, the other as agitato. The first of the pair is a strict ternary conception. The second has a sectional-rondo depiction, with some development, and is specifically identified by the string duo that preludes the movement.

Gál begins his Op. 94 with a Pastorale. While he agrees with and therefore outlines the form's suavity and flow, he does not permit mere singsong spaciousness. In place, the music has linear expressivity. Movement four is an Introduzione: "Meditation on a Scottish Tune." The melody is merely identified as a "Highland Tune." The sections ("Meditations") that follow it are a sequence of six variations, with only the fifth of the group in the fast area (Alla marcia). To conclude the movement there is a reworking of the first part of the Pastorale.

- **Trio for Piano, Violin (or Flute or Oboe), and Cello, Op. 49b**

Lightweight in contents and textures but with an active give-and-take between the three instruments. Everything is pleasantly diatonic; the outer movements (Moderato e tranquillo and Marche burlesque) are in G; the central movement is a Pastorale in D major.

- **Trio for Violin, Viola d'amore (or Viola), and Cello, Op. 104**

Of course, this is a decidedly unique combination and would have special effect if the fourteen (seven bowed and seven sympathetic)-string instrument were used. For this reason, since the open strings of the viola d'amore state D major, all three movements favor sharp keys.

Traditional romantic style applies here, but there is no overchromatic "gilding the lily" to obtain special color within the style. The Trio has considerable flow in its opening statement. In the Presto the quadruple pulse is peppered by a continuous rhythmic figure that never lets go. Movement three is a Tema con variazioni; the third of the set is a murmuring muted bit; the fourth is markedly contrapuntal; the final section is an Alla marcia.

- ***Variationen über eine wiener Heurigenmelodie (Variations on a Present-day Viennese Melody)* for Violin, Cello, and Piano, Op. 9**

Gál sets himself rigid boundary totals in the first five variations. Not until the sixth part do the permutations break away from the inflexible quantity of twice eight-measure phrases. Despite this structural hair shirt every portion brings maximal returns. In the third section, the bare theme is stated in octave pizzicatos by the strings. In the sixth portion, alternant 4/8 and 3/8 measures guide the variational vocabulary. Strict canon rules part twelve. Assorted treatment covers the thirteenth variation, climaxed by Maestoso affirmation.

QUARTETS

- **Quartettino for Two Descant, Treble (or Tenor), and Tenor (or Bass) Recorders, Op. 78**

Nice tonal deeds for the recorder family, each of the three movements in traditional forms. The first is an Alla Marcia, the second a Tempo di minuetto, the last a Gigue. The players are well served by the expert writing.

- **String Quartet [No. 1] in F Minor, Op. 16**

Gál spins his themes, develops them, catches in all their parts the not-yet-scarred-by-war Viennese spirit of 1916. He in no way reflects

Schoenberg of the same country. A romantic center of gravity is in this melodious work. It has a Schubertian tang in its first movement, especially the use of several themes all of which have vocal qualities. In the Molto vivace, the value of constant sixteenth notes controls the scherzo design. Not even in the first of two contrasting Trios (contrasted only in themes, neither the pace, style, nor sonority plan changes) do they cease, for even in the second Trio the sixteenth-note lilt is present. The intent is song and rhythm. A slight coloristic coda, with the quartet playing ponticello, provides infinitesimal roughage.

With the haunting beauty of the slow movement theme, which would do credit to any composer (and especially Brahms), it is not to be wondered that the composer keeps repeating it. Nor should one look later than Brahms for the insertion in the energetic finale of one of those lushly formed, typically romantic themes running on the course of rich, mellow thirds and sixths. It occurs twice in this last movement of a work eclectic, to be sure, but posing the values of romantic refuge. Gál's controls may be of the 19th century, but they sincerely afford music of beauty.

- **String Quartet No. 2 in A Minor, Op. 35**

Gál shakes loose a bit from assimilative influences in this quartet. The dissonances are freer, the music is much more chromatic. The tie with romanticism (as exemplified by the first string quartet) is the use of extremely clear form and a melody here and there which sings like the voice of Schubert.

Four movements are the average total for a large-scale chamber music composition, three being next in use. The five-movement design used in this instance is rarer, for though Gál links the fourth and fifth, the former section is not a mere introduction but a fully developed movement.

The Preludio combines the binary rhythm of two and three pulses (the romantic cultivation holds on); the latter quality is constantly to the fore in theme and accompaniment patterns. The Toccata subject exhibits the value of an Alberti bass in affixing a tonal pivot for root purposes, but here, its use does not have the stereotyped static quality of that sort of technique. Only twice is the touch-and-go of this virtuoso movement interrupted. After the Canzone, where the song repeats itself several times, one can observe the Viennese line of composition of the 19th century amid the closer-to-our-day themes in both the Intermezzo capriccioso and the final Rondo.

- **String Quartet No. 4, Op. 99**

A late-romantic temper is evidenced in this music. It is much more nubby in its textures than Gál's earlier string quartets.

The first movement ("Legend") begins with an Adagio section in B-flat minor; it is spliced in twice later, the first time in changed tonality, the second time as a repeat of the initial presentation. In between is the major layout of the movement, in Allegro speed, set in a chromatically bitten B-flat major. This heavier articulated harmonic scheme is used in the Elegy as well (movement three). A Burlesque replaces the scherzo statement. And strong contrapuntalism enters the picture in the finale (Capriccio fugato). It represents weighty but telling polyphony.

Galante, Carlo (1959–)

TRIO

- *Zefiro torna (Zephyr Returns)* **for Flute, Clarinet, and Piano (1981)**

The constant flux of arpeggiated figures, broken chordal passages, and the unflagging attention to rhythmic sweeps can be termed neoimpressionistic. Galante's predilection for trills, grace notes, flutter-tongued sounds, and harmonics is further substantiation of a relationship to impressionistic technique, as are the bits of motival memos and reiterations.

Galindo, Blas (1910–)

DUOS

■ **Sonata for Cello and Piano (1949)**

The lean textural style that Galindo favors is present in this three-movement work. And his habitual quartal harmonic combinations as well.

The cello sonata (written on commission by the Koussevitzky Foundation) has a rondo-defined opening movement. In the slow movement (Lento) balance is obtained by use of the unaccompanied cello in the outer sections. This coloristic separation provides a dramatic central core to the work. Theatric qualities continue in the finale (Allegro), stimulated by gutsy rhythms that constantly change pulse measurement. Galindo's duo sonata is black and white music, its constant ongoing gestures guided by percussive instincts.

■ **Sonata for Violin and Piano (1945)**

Most of this work is devoted to stark, flinty style. By majority use of thin textural totalities (most often only three voices in the first movement) Galindo sharpens the clarity of his music.

In the Allegro, chords are at a minimum. When used they signify a type of *single* sound force rather than one of harmonic meaning. Counterpoint is applied by rhythmic transversion, not by linear force. Rhythms stream over the bar lines so that a duple line is felt while a ternal one is under way. Strengthening all of this is the use of a basal sound palette, one of "whitened," accidental-free lines.

A different viewpoint is used in the middle movement. Here the music is tonal and rich, with an indigenous section set in the central part of the movement. But in the finale Galindo returns to his primitivistic province, focused there by raw rhythm that is statically indicated. There is a Cantabile intermediary section, but this merely emphasizes the principal material—music of direct and bare propulsion.

■ **Suite for Violin and Piano (1957)**

As in all of his music, Galindo uses tightly integrated forms and textures in this three-part work. The central harmonic argument is concerned with quartal facts. This self-imposed contained style does not prevent overall balance and necessary contrast.

The Danza is in duple meter but often breaks away from square-cut metrical depiction and moves over the bar lines, producing a 3 + 3 + 2/8 total over two successive measures. Movement two (Melodia en lento) begins with solo piano followed by solo violin. The merge then occurs, with the movement's conclusion again presenting solo voices; in reverse this time—first the violin and then the piano.

The finale is a rhythmically vital, allegro-tempo "Son huasteco" (a Mayan Indian dance). Here again bar lines are crushed at times by the basic 3/8 meter being split over the bar line, causing a continuous set of 2/8 units. The central part of the movement is coloristically outlined in unleveled 5/16 time.

Gallay, Jacques-François (1795–1864)

TRIO

■ *La Saint-Hubert* **for Three Horns**

Music by the famous 19th-century horn virtuoso and pedagogue. There are six movements, with polished smooth tonal writing for the horns (as would be expected). No slow-paced music whatsoever, and considerable block styling. The fifth movement is akin to a fast waltz. Throughout one should not expect any creative subtleties.

Galliard, Johann Ernst
(c. 1680–1749)

DUO

- **Sonata in G Major for Cello and Basso Continuo**

Not just another entry in the huge 18th-century catalogue of duo sonatas, where, in most instances, one is hard put to tell one work from another. Galliard's flowing phrases in the Affettuoso opening movement provide a delicious conception. There is an emphasis on sprightly rhythms no matter the tempo. Thus, striding basses in the second-movement Spiritoso, warm response in the duple-pulse swing of the slow movement, and stately decisiveness in the final Minuetto. A four-movement formation that is certainly well realized.

Gallon, Noël (1891–1966)

DUO

- **Récit et Allegro for Bassoon and Piano**

As to be expected, the bassoon carries the full weight of the recitative portion. The Allegro is a small rondo conception. Gallon's liking for specially characteristic tonalities is made evident by the B-flat-minor section within this second part of the duo. It is further colored by expanded chromaticism.

QUINTET

- **Quintet for Harp, Two Violins, Viola, and Cello**

Instrumentation affects content, of course. In turn, any major instrumental limitation can affect the shaping of the content. The harp, no matter how daring and demanding a composer may be, is chromatically restricted. In Gallon's Quintet the outer and inner motility of the string quartet is strong, so that both its linear and chromatic activity compensate for the narrower harmonic territory of the harp. This point of detail covers all three movements. The basic tonality of the final movement is C-sharp major—a key rarely used in string-instrument writing since it is not the most fluid and openly sonorous. On the harp, however, this tonality offers no problems.

Form is clear in the moderate, slow, and animated speeds of the three parts of Gallon's piece. Importantly, the textural weights are less transparent here than in most chamber music where the harp is more than a mere coloristic part of the total. The heavier atmosphere can be described as Franckian with Straussian flavoring.

Gambarini, Costanza (1954–)
and Gambarini, Giuseppe (1915–)

DUOS

- **Sonatinas for Recorder and Guitar**

  - No. 1, in F Major
  - No. 2, in C Major
  - No. 3, in A Minor
  - No. 4, in F Major
  - No. 5, in G Major
  - No. 6, in D Minor

Indeed, Sonatinas! More to the point, these are

tiny duo sonatinas by the creative partners. Although all, save the fifth, are in three movements, the individual movement size is as minute as 4 1/4 measures (Largo of the first Sonatina) and 8 measures for the Larghetto (of No. 3) and the same total for the Adagio (of No. 6). Otherwise, the movements are mostly of 16-measure length. A few are longer, providing the indicated repeats of sections are taken.

The music moves in four-square progress and is modulation free, save for a couple of simple key shifts in the second of the set. The word for these pieces is "elementary."

Gamburg, Grigori (1900–67)

TRIO

- Trio for Violin, Viola, and Cello (1945)

Total balance is neatly realized in Gamburg's string trio. A Moderato and an Allegro cover the opening and concluding movements. These confirm the tonal objective of the work. The first movement is in C minor, the closing one in C major; the former (Preludio) is principally homophonic, the other (designated Finale) stresses contrapuntalism. In between are a pair of movements, both in triple-beat form. Again, speed and structure are contrasted. Movement two (Scherzo) is spirited, conjunctively tight. Movement three is a slow-swinging Siciliana.

Gan, Nikolai (1908–)

SEXTET

- *Children's Pictures:* Suite for Flute, Oboe, Two Clarinets, Bassoon, and Horn

This is the kind of composition that can teach the kiddies that music is quite digestible. And adults can enjoy it as well, since Gan's seven-part affair is music for children of all ages.

It begins with a "Little March" and continues with a D-minor "Children's Song." Part three is a scherzo disguised with the title "The Rain Began." Movement four (without horn) is a moderately swinging item called "A Fisherman Sings." Part five is also for reduced forces—this time the flute and horn are tacet in the scoring for "In the Chicken Coop." Its sounds are properly cacklelike. A Meditation and a Dance conclude the suite.

Ganne, Louis Gaston (1862–1923)

DUO

- Andante et Scherzo for Flute and Piano

No dealing with subtleties here. Nice squared tunes and balletic pace are compared. The *et* is equaled by a flute cadenza. Encore category.

Gardner, John (1917–)

QUARTET

- Theme and Variations for Two Trumpets, Horn, and Trombone, Op. 7

A thorough delight and a complete success. Clear variations on an F-major theme, announced throughout its sixteen-measure total by the trombone alone. The spontaneity of the variations makes the music fully alive.

Special to the work are the scherzo twist of variation three; two marches (the fourth and fifth variants), one a "Marcia lenta," the other a "Marcia rapida"; and a Habanera (variation six) that has a twinkle to its glide. The final variant (number eight) also has a distinctive dance rhythm (tarantella) as the basis for its vivacious fugue setting. It is complete with stretto and a total soft-sell conclusion.

Gardner, Samuel (1891–1984)

QUINTET

- *To a Soldier:* **Quintet in F Minor for Piano , Two Violins, Viola, and Cello, Op. 16**

It is an unfortunate type of blessing when a composer becomes known by one of his shorter, casual musical morsels at the expense of his larger musical productions. This was the case with Gardner, whose healthy quibble of a violin piece—*From the Canebrake*—adorned for dozens of years the repertoire of every concert violinist. Mention Gardner, and that seemed to be the only work most musicians knew. Overlooked were the large orchestral work *Broadway* and the excellent composition discussed here. (These works are still overlooked.)

The F-minor quintet is dedicated "To the memory of David Hochstein, killed in action, France, 1918." Another grim reminder of the course of wars memorialized in music. Hochstein was a concert violinist whose career, presaging great things, was cut short by this tragedy.

There are four movements in this semiprogrammatic opus. The first is a Prologue—"La Vie" ("Life")—set in robust, declamatory fashion, with tragic overtones; it is based on two alternating themes. A Capriccio follows, formed from an introduction and two themes, both stated first by the viola, next by the piano, then developed. The speed is breathtaking. The movement most concerned with the dedicatee is the third—"Dans la forêt (La Mort)" ("In the Forest [Death])." The threnodic clouds of this funereal march rarely catch the sun of a major tonality. There is an

unstated program as well in the final movement (Epilogue) of this semidescriptive work. Proof is in the thirteen major changes of tempo and mood alone. There is interwoven (as in retrospect one speaks of the deeds of a deceased human) basic material from the opening proclamatory movement and the thematic surfaces of the slow movement. Thus, Gardner signified the relationships of the hopefulness of Hochstein's life, its fervency, its being, and the significances of his death. The four glissandos of the viola in the coda (sweeping each time through the space of a minor interval), plus the entire minor tonality of the conclusion, place the final black fringe on this work devoted to a dead musician.

Gárdonyi, Zoltán (1906–)

QUARTET

- **String Quartet No. 3 (1954)**

The sweep of Hungarian folk melodies is the integrated technical affinity in this composer's music. There is breadth and dignity, and there is a rhythmic directness of quantitative apportionment that supports it.

Textural fullness and rhythmic units of short–long figures mark the first movement. Appropriate chromaticism is used to color the Lamento. Movement three is a trisectional Marcia, its tempo a bit faster than the usual march pace. The finale is a Tema con variazioni. There are seven variants in all, and there are no perplexing arguments to mar the smooth progress of the music.

Garnier, François Joseph
(1755–c. 1825)

DUO

- **Duo concertant for Oboe and Bassoon (or Cello), Op. 4, No. 4**

The striking point of Garnier's two-movement wind-instrument duo is the total cohesiveness and the acute maintenance of instrumental equality. Passages in thirds and sixths are in the majority—submissive accompanimental measures are exceedingly few in number.

Both movements are in B-flat. However, there is contrast in terms of meter (4/4 and 3/4, respectively), tempo headings (Allegro moderato and Allegretto scherzoso, in turn), and structure (sonata and rondo, respectively).

Garovi, Josef (1908–85)

DUO

- **Fantasie for Clarinet and Piano (1973)**

Interesting idea—a three-part work, divided fore and aft with unmetered material using hop-skip-and-jump tactics and straightforward, clearly formed, duple-pulse, scherzolike music in between. Formal habits, indeed, die hard. If not beguiling, the music has passable merits.

Garrido-Lecca, Celso (1926–)

QUINTET

- **Divertimento for Woodwind Quintet (1957)**

Pungent pantonal style. Each of the four movements is objectively direct. Garrido-Lecca avoids symmetrical structures but obtains balance within each by proportionally related material; as an example, the third-part Nocturno. It begins with slow-paced, yet febrile, figurations, matches these with mostly soft, yet excited, linear motion, and returns to different figurations, just a bit less in motility.

Connected pitch statements are contrasted to rhythmically punctuative detail in the Introduccion. This preface is linked to a set of five Variaciones plus Coda. The movement begins with a preliminary total of seven measures followed by an eighteen-measure theme. Each variation maintains this length without deviation; the second of the set is canonic. To continue the precision of balance, the Coda matches the seven-measure length of the preliminary portion. Rondo divisional arrangement, including literal repetitions, is used for the fourth movement titled Final–Jazz. It's a bit heavy-handed, but it's jazz nonetheless.

Gassmann, Florian Leopold
(1729–74)

TRIO

- **Trio in D Major for Clarinet, Horn, and Bassoon**

The initial publication of this work was by Edition Kunzelmann, in 1982. It was edited by Kurt Janetzky from the original manuscript that had been held in a private collection. For his work the editor is to be thanked. Nevertheless, retaining (for musicological exactitude?) the clarinet's indication as "solo" and the horn's as "obbligato" does no good. The clarinet is *not* a solo instrument, and of course, the horn is obligatory. It is clear that the three instruments function with complete chamber music equality.

Good melodies and good enough workmanship. Binary form is used for the Andante, Adagio, and final Allegro movements. The

Minuet that follows the Andante is, of course, of ternary construction. No development to speak of and no modulation. D major clings to all of the music.

Gattermeyer, Heinrich (1923–)

DUO

- **Duo for Viola and Double Bass**

Plenty of effervescence in the outer movements, the first of the pair stimulated by asymmetry, the other (titled Finaletto) by rhythmic aliveness. Considering the heaviness of the scoring, the results are a delight of fluency and flexibility. The music between these two parts is a lyrical Larghetto. There are little colors that brighten its quality: ponticello partnered with harmonics and tutti fingered tremolandos.

TRIO

- **Wind Trio (Oboe, Clarinet, and Bassoon), Op. 62, No. 2**

Gattermeyer understands the value of light-fashioned material for woodwinds. All the grace and substance of such hedonistic style is made available in the outer Allegro movements (the opening one is prefaced with a short Adagio). Fine line writing and an enthusiastic demeanor are exhibited—also cross accentuations in the opening movement. The middle movement is a compact three-part Andante.

An interesting point regarding the final cadences—all three movements end on a perfect fifth: A–E for movements one and two, E–B for the finale.

QUARTET

- **Wind Quartet (Oboe, Clarinet, Bassoon, and Horn), Op. 81, No. 2**

Formal vigor exhibited here. In movement one the 6/8 meter moves freely between triple and duple pulses on top of which there is a good supply of syncopation that further widens metrical definition. There are also shifts between homophonic and polyphonic writing. The tempo heading of movement two describes the music: Andante ostinato, and ostinato it is. There is a five-pitch item spread repeatedly over quadruple-pulse measures so that the sounds on accent points vary.

Movement three is a Scherzo that projects interplay between 2/4 and 3/4 time. Measure lengths match these so that two measures fit the 2/4 meter and three measures match the 3/4 meter. There are only a few exceptions to this scheme. The finale begins with a Lento, continues with vivacious material that links to a minimal recap of the Lento, and finishes off matters with a succinct Prestissimo.

Gaubert, Philippe (1879–1941)

DUOS

- **Allegretto for Clarinet and Piano**

Chamber music essence is not substantiated in this case. The bald creative pursuit here is a clarinet solo with piano accompaniment (and so described on the edition checked). However, since a number of chamber music listings specify Gaubert's piece, it is included in this compendium.

Compactness rules, with eighty-six measures, all in 2/4 meter. Conjunct figuration is the working method, with some braking into triplets and some speeding into sextuplets. The piano chords its way, save for a four-measure solo spot.

■ **Fantasie for Clarinet and Piano**

Gaubert's piece is like a quilt made of many patches. Thus it is as much a rhapsody as it is a fantasy. And as much related to Debussy style as it is to fancy-coursed clarinet passages.

■ **Fantasy for Flute and Piano**

Show-off time for the flute here, but without unmusical flamboyance. A slow-paced, nice tune is surrounded with zippy roulades and the like and then contrasted to a Vivo of mainly scalic sum and substance. Perhaps superficial musical satisfactions, but Gaubert certainly had no special private passions in mind in his simple display piece. (The piano is just a bit more than an accompanimental appointment.)

■ **Nocturne and Allegro scherzando for Flute and Piano**

Modest aims, but totally clear and musical ones in these contrasted pieces. Gaubert knew his craft, but he also knew his creative forebears. Debussy is present in the Nocturne, and Mendelssohn is accurately assessed (with a bit heavier footwork) in the Allegro scherzando.

■ **Sonata [No. 1] for Flute and Piano (1934)**

Gaubert was more known for his flute playing and conducting abilities than as a composer. He dedicated this work to his teacher (also a conductor), the famous Paul Taffanel, one of the most important flutists of all time. Although Gaubert never studied with César Franck (he was 11 when the latter died), the spirit of that master stalks every page of this excellently written duo sonata. As is to be expected, the flute writing is superb.

Thematic modification technique is used in the first movement, in which a scalewise theme is contrasted immediately to a slow-moving line. This latter then becomes altered into a 3/8 meter in vivo tempo. Later on, the first (scale) theme is likewise redressed. The slow movement—a gentle song—is in three-part form and is followed by an almost direct imitation of the flow of Franck's violin sonata. One realizes that musical analogies are overused, but the closeness to the Franckian musical grammar and speech is too obvious to pass unmentioned. Finally, in order to give truly full observance to this stylistic heritage, Gaubert brings back the first theme of the opening movement, ending the Sonata with the clarity and orderliness of a subdued, then dying away, dynamic plan.

■ **Sonata No. 2 for Flute and Piano**

Gaubert's opening movement is headed "A l'aise, mais sans lenteur." The aim is clear: "With ease, but without slowness." The music follows suit, defines the parenthetical title of the movement (Pastorale) in its majority adherence to flowing two-measure phrases. The emotions of this music are collected in tranquillity. There is contrast, however, with diatonic coloration followed by chromatic tinting and basic sixteenth-note groups compared to slower-moving totals.

Sharper tonal jurisdiction applies to movement two (E minor to A-flat major, with each of these not fully tonally confined). A fast one-in-a-measure finale follows. Again the lines flow. This is flourishing, fluid flute writing. It bears out the comment made by Percy A. Scholes that Gaubert "was one of the finest composers for flute of recent times."

■ **Sonata No. 3 for Flute and Piano**

The stylistic contrasts among Gaubert's three sonatas for flute and piano are extremely minimal. This work has a good quota of the Franckian thumbprints found in the first work of the group. It also relates to the initial sonata in terms of textural weight. Of the three, Gaubert's second sonata is the lightest in data and harmonic impress.

As usual there are three movements. The first is an Allegretto arranged in Gaubert's favorite triple-pulse measures, set in G major (the same tonality will prevail in the concluding movement). Movement two is an "Intermède pastoral" ("Pastoral Intermezzo"). The harmonic course begins simply in the dominant key of the first movement but quickly moves away from D major into B major and then A-flat major before returning to the home key. The terminal movement (Final) zips along. There is no doubt as to its joyous substances or extremely skillful handling of the instruments.

Gaul, Harvey (1881–1945)

Gaul was very curious about musical folklore. Though he concentrated in the small forms (miniature sets and suite compilations), his output is just as communicative as many large-cast compositions.

Gaul's interest in Jewish music derived from conducting a YMHA (Young Mens Hebrew Association) and YWHA (Young Womens Hebrew Association) chorus. He delved into the music of the blacks, the Indians, and the fertile Stephen Foster. Casting his net wide, he did research in the regional music of Tennessee, his adopted state of Pennsylvania (Gaul was born in New York and settled in Pittsburgh), New England, and the mountain zones. The pieces discussed below exemplify some of the results of his investigations. Not great music by any means, still, because of their distinctive content and expert workmanship, they deserve their place and performance in the chamber music field.

DUOS

- *Two Ancient Noëls* for Viola (or Cello) and Piano

Gaul drew his themes from a collection of ancient noëls. (The noël is French in origin and dates back to the 14th century. Originally a popular Christmas song, much later examples included quasi-religious texts set to music of total secular style.)

Marked as "freely arranged," the paired concepts are so clearly original they cannot be considered in any way as transcriptions. Both concern the Christmas season. "La Vierge et les bergers") ("The Virgin and the Shepherds") has a short preface, followed by two renderings (the second time in muted timbre), completed by a large coda. In both this piece and the ternary-planned "L'Annonciation de la Vierge" ("The Annunciation of the Virgin") the style is mostly modal. A bit of oppositely colored harmony does not throw the music out of style. It simply serves to emphasize the sensitive beauty of the whole.

- *Two Impressions from Palestine* for Cello and Piano

(The Holy Land is the subject matter for three of Gaul's compositions. In addition to this pair of pieces, he wrote *Palestinian Peregrinations* for piano trio [*see below*] and for string orchestra a set of *Palestinian Pastels*.)

The first *impression* is titled "A Yigdal from Yeman." The yigdal is the liturgical poem sometimes recited, more often sung, at the start of the daily service in the synagogue. Gaul's transmutation offers a keen duplication. It covers the orthodox Jew's basic chant (via the augmented step) plus the elaborate melodicism equivalent to the cantor's seizing the phrase and elaborating on it, as he beseeches God in the name of those worshipping. To this come the responsorial comments of the congregation. Gaul's example rises in excitement and tempo and then returns to its moderate starting point. Ernest Bloch and his royal, stentorian manner will come to mind. In comparison, Gaul's is a condensation, a concentrated view, but it contains all the proper pathos.

"A Night Piece from Nablus" also spirals to its highest-pitched excitement in the middle of the music. There are almost as much cantillative elements in this piece as in the previous one. The style includes plangent and fervent fifths, fanfarric spurts, and blocked chordal rejoinders. This is no stylistic error on Gaul's part. In Hebraic music there often is a crisscross, and sacred style merges into the secular.

TRIO

- *Palestinian Peregrinations* for Piano, Violin, and Cello

Two pieces in this abbreviated suite: "Within the Shadow of Mount Hermon" and "A Nigun from Haifa." (Gaul's titles are always stimulating. One recalls a very enticing example: "Father Gallitzen Remembers Prince Dmitri," used for a string-orchestra work.)

In the first of the set the patchwork effect of sectional divisions gives the equivalent of a rondo design. Noteworthy are richly ornamental, coloratura scalic formations. Gaul's source for this music was a collection titled *Songs of the Chalutzim.* (The Chalutzim were the Zionist pioneers.) These were based on a very ancient mode, with Arabic derivations called the *Ta-Anit.* A Palestinian folk theme spurs the second piece, then the nigun (an age-old synagogal melody) is first developed, so that the basic tune does not appear until the twenty-fourth measure. Further mutations then occur.

QUARTETS

- *From the Great Smokies* for String Quartet (1935)

Mountain-region folk songs are the basis for this three-part suite. All the trimmings added to the beautiful tunes are neat and the harmonies apt. The themes are presented several times, each statement in different décor. "Barbara Allen" (a ballade) and "Sourwood Mountain" (a song) are of English ancestry. By ternary thematic disposal, as though outlining a refrain, verse, and a return to the former, the last part, "In the Great Smokies," has a different format from the first two.

- *Tennessee Devil Tunes* for String Quartet

Gaul explained his title by stating that in the bush gullies of the state of Tennessee the tunes he had employed were considered "worldly" and therefore "of the devil." (However, Satan's melodies are beautiful and have the effect of timelessness.)

The first, "Up Clinch Mountain," and the second, "Cumberland Gap," have opposite characteristics. The former is lyrical, the other balletic. "Chilly Waters" is a folk ballade. The tunes are transferred to the string quartet world with simplicity. The only changes made are in varying the instrumental colors.

- *Three Pennsylvania Portraits* for String Quartet (1935)

Historic facts are recalled in this charming compilation. "Franklin Rubs His Musical Glasses" has nothing to do with the field of optics, but rather Benjamin Franklin's invention (in 1762) of the glass harmonica; the sounds produced by light friction on the rims of different-size glasses filled with water. A few of Gaul's chords simulate the sound of this quaint instrument, though the harmonic side-slips are of a much later time period.

"Ole Bull Comes to Kettle Creek" is based on a tune by the famous Norwegian violinist Ole Bornemann Bull (1810–80). During one of his five tours in America, Bull visited Kettle Creek, a village in the northern part of Pennsylvania.

The final portrait is titled "Francis Hopkinson Goes about Germantown." It utilizes a Serenade by Hopkinson (1737–91), considered to be America's first native composer. Hopkinson (one of the signers of the Declaration of Independence) was very active in Philadelphia's musical life (Germantown is a northern district of the city).

Stylistically, all three portraits have 20th-century touches. Nevertheless, they bear out Franklin's definition of melody as "an agreeable succession of sounds," and of harmony as "the co-existence of agreeable sounds."

Gayfer, J.M.

QUINTET

- **Suite for Woodwind Quintet**

Only the third movement (Dirge) differs from the otherwise cheerful contents of the Suite. The other messages set forth in this score are those of traditional equations: Overture, Waltz, Interlude, and March. The Overture moves like a galop minus any hopping movements. The neatness of the phrases, the rich harmonies, and the solidity of the scoring remove the work from any assembly-line (read: commercial) music.

Gebauer, Etienne (1777–1823)

DUO

- **Duo concertant for Clarinet and Violin, Op. 16, No. 3**

This neat work has fine instrumental balance, evenly dividing the materials between the two instruments, in a pair of Allegro movements. The style is, of course, neutrally classical (some might term it "yesterday's" classical style).

Compositions for clarinet and violin without piano are in very short supply. While Gebauer's piece is not to be classified as a find, it does have its effective quality, even though it coasts along on the formulas of the time in which it was written.

Gebauer, François René (1773–1844)

DUOS

- **Duetto No. 2 for Two Oboes (or Two Clarinets or Two English horns)**

Standard forms, but with a neat consideration of rhythmic contrasts in the first movement. There, Gebauer compares eighth notes with triplets and with sixteenth notes, so that the melodiousness does not bog down. That movement and the other outer movement, a rather compact Rondo, are in G major. The tonic minor is used for the inner Adagio movement.

- **Duos concertantes for Clarinet and Bassoon, Op. 8**

  - No. 1, in B-flat Major
  - No. 2, in C Minor
  - No. 3, in E-flat Major
  - No. 4, in C Major
  - No. 5, in D Minor
  - No. 6, in F Major

Pleasantly unadventurous music. That is not to say that the pieces will not be enjoyed, especially by the performers. Or, put it this way: Gebauer's duos are light scaled but far from flimsy. Perfect for home performance.

All six works are in two movements, with similar forms used throughout. In the first movement the music moves to the dominant at the end of the first half and then sweeps back to the tonic. All the second movements are also in the home key, set in rondo form, with a shift to the relative minor in the center portion in Nos. 1, 3, 4, and 6. The middle change is to a major key for the pair of duos (Nos. 2 and 5) in a minor tonality.

TRIO

- **Trio for Bassoon, Violin, and Cello, Op. 33, No. 3**

An unusual combination in which the cello functions as the bass representative; the bassoon is given top billing with the violin. (Gebauer's reasoning is understandable. He had a distinguished career as a bassoonist, including twenty-five years as the principal bassoonist of the Paris Opéra Orchestra.)

As to be expected, Gebauer's writing is bound to classic standard procedures. The result is not musically negligible, especially with finesse shown in the handling of a variety of rhythmic figurations in the first movement (Allegro fieramento). The succeeding Rondo also exemplifies contrastive types of rhythmic strategy. The movement also offers a distinct surprise when it shifts from its ongoing duple-paced Allegretto into a good-size Tempo di valse in 3/8 time for the concluding part of the piece.

Geiser, Walther (1897–)

DUOS

- **Sonatine for Oboe and Piano, Op. 38**

Geiser combines the three movements of his piece into a unit, marking off the divisions by fermatas. The writing is neoclassic, minus any scholastic advice. Textures are thin throughout, but especially in the first part, where half the total is strictly two voiced in the piano. Siciliano swing is clearly established in the second part; a relaxed rustic flavor is found in the final part.

- **Sonatine for Viola and Organ, Op. 46**

Obeisance to concentrated textures is followed by this Swiss composer-pedagogue. In the fugal beginning there are four lines, with not a single double stop in the viola part and single voicing for the organ's manuals and pedals. With the aid of a tempo push in the final measure a link is made to the Deciso movement. This section has even less voicing, with once again no chords in the viola and with the pedals eliminated in the organ. A pedal line is brought into play in the final measures, which lead to a broad, long-line, severely slow conclusion.

Geisler, Christian (1869–1951)

DUO

- **Sonata for Viola and Piano, Op. 10**

Geisler spoke in a romantic tongue, minus any old-German accents. Within forms of classical vintage, specific clear devices both strengthen and differentiate the contents. Motives and imitations are found in the sonata's first part. Save for the contrastive Trio, the Intermezzo (movement three) is made from a strict canon, undisturbed by any additional voices. Movements two and four are, respectively, a Romance and a Fuga.

Geissler, Fritz (1921–84)

DUO

- **Sonata for Clarinet and Piano (1954)**

Plenty of coherence in the three movements, and plenty of differentiation and formal freedom within each. Several creative profiles emerge from the music.

A rhythmic nervousness, combined with melodic lines that espouse the chromatic romantic and chords detailed by seconds and sevenths, is found in the Allegretto. Movement two has Mahlerian depth. Its Mesto definition is applied to alternative qualities of line and texture. A repetitive figure is developed from single to double to quadruple weighting and ultimately returns to the single strength.

The finale is marked Scherzando. Snide it is—an element common to all the material—including glissando thrusts, a slow division (of length) that is a parody (Mahler in another stance) of a "slow Foxtrot," and a short clarinet cadenza.

NONET

- *Ode to a Nightingale* for Nonet (Flute, Oboe, Clarinet, Horn, Bassoon, Two Violins, Viola, and Cello) (1968)

An introduction and four connected movements in a general expressionistic depiction of the Keats poem. The style is freely twelve tone and contains a Bergian sense of ecstatic line resolve intertwined within it. The conception is a reaction to and not a description of the text.

Geissler's music is kin to constant changes of instrumental registration. The emotive ebb and flow of the text is portrayed, whatever the programmatic association one makes.

Gelbrun, Artur (1913–)

DUO

- *Nigun and Dance* for Violin and Piano (1954)

Gelbrun studied in Warsaw (he was born in that city), Italy, and Switzerland. He immigrated to Israel in 1949. The last country shows its influence in this short duo by way of the dissonantly touched folk outlines of the *Dance*. Gelbrun was a violinist, and this is noted in the slightly virtuosic violin details wrapped into the piece, plus a short cadenza for the string instrument.

A nigun is an old synagogue melody, and Gelbrun's simulation, leaning on minor intervals, is expressive and moving in its simplicity. The tonal polarity is around C, but the music finally resolves into a C–B-flat plus B-natural combination. The poetry of the piece is not removed by such pitch tension.

Geminiani, Francesco (1687–1762)

DUOS

- **Duet in A Major for Two Violins**

The facile style of the old Italian school of composers set forth in a flowing and well-ornamented Adagio and a brisk Allegro agitato. Chain of command rules here, the second violin remains in second place throughout.

- **Sonata in A Major for Violin and Harpsichord, Op. 4, No. 10**

Geminiani's duo sonata, the tenth in a set of twelve, was first published in London in 1729 in three-movement form. In 1739 a second version was issued (also in London), which included a second slow movement. The three-movement version has a long and lyrical opening slow movement, a brilliant Allegro and a Minuet, with a contrastive central section in a minor tonality.

(In most instances when this version is performed the second and third movements are reversed for greater effect.)

- **Sonatas for Violin and Basso Continuo, Op. 1**

  - No. 1, in A Major
  - No. 2, in D Minor
  - No. 3, in E Minor

The initial opus of this once-neglected pupil of Corelli's was preceded by another Op. 1, consisting of a dozen (also the total of the second Op. 1) sonatas for violin alone.

In these three sonatas there are some adventuresome items, such as the fugal second movement of the A-major opus, preceded by a movement where Adagio and Presto statements alternate. The final fast movement is preluded by a short Grave. The D-minor duo is in four movements; the E minor in two.

- **Twelve Compositions from *The Art of Playing on the Violin* for Violin and Piano, Op. 9**

These assorted pieces are drawn from Geminiani's violin method, which was first published in English in London in 1751. Published translations followed: in French, in 1752, and in German, in 1785. Geminiani titled his compositions *12 Pieces in Different Styles for Violin and Violoncello, with Thorough Bass for the Harpsichord.* The figured bass in this edition (published in 1959 by Editio Musica, Budapest) was realized by László Böhm, and being set for piano there is no need for cello doubling of the bass line.

Fluent and assured music is represented. The forms are varied, including a Corrente (No. 4), an *Air* (No. 5), a *Giga* (No. 11), a *Gavotte en rondeau* (No. 8), and three Fugati (Nos. 3, 6, and 12). Short, tasteful cadenzas are included in Nos. 1, 3, and 9. Single line writing commands the first six pieces, with rich double stopping found in Nos. 7, 8, 10, and 12.

The editors have arranged the compositions' chronology so that two sonata combinations are offered (though not so indicated, these arrangements are not mandatory). Thus: Nos. 7, 8, 12 (Andante, *Gavotte en rondeau*, and Fugato could be termed Sonata 1), and Nos. 9, 10, 11 (Andante moderato, Allegro moderato, and *Giga* could be termed Sonata 2).

TRIOS

- **Sonata in A Major for Two Violins and Basso Continuo**

Those who contend this composer is a stuffy conservative should give some attention to the structure of this trio sonata. In terms of material it can be regarded as a single movement divided into eight sections alternating slow and fast tempos and with no material within any one section repeated elsewhere. All of the slow portions are short (the opening Grave is but four measures in length, the Andante in third place is only seven measures, etc.), while the third and fifth Allegro divisions are of major proportions.

This is an alive score, minus square phrasing situations and without any pedantic rigor.

- **Sonatas from** *The Art of Playing the Guitar or Cittra* **for Guitar (or Violin), Cello, and Harpsichord (or Piano)**

  - No. 1, in C Major
  - No. 2, in C Minor
  - No. 3, in D Major
  - No. 4, in D Minor
  - No. 6, in E Minor
  - No. 10, in G Minor

Six of the eleven total works contained in Geminiani's compilation (published in 1972 by Suvini Zerboni in a modern edition with the realization of the basso continuo by Giuseppe Radole). Though not listed in the title, the choice of the violin was Geminiani's, who indicated in a note under the main title that "These compositions are contrived so as to make very proper Solos for the Violin" and accordingly notated lines in the score for guitar (or cittra, an ancient lute-guitar type of six doubled strings) as well as violin.

There is no lackadaisical routine in these sonatas, notwithstanding that the fundamental contents offer no surprises. The interest is maintained by structural variety. Three sonatas (Nos. 4, 6, and 10) have but two movements, and in No. 4 the opening Allegro moderato has a prefatory Andante. Sonata No. 1 has four movements, the second of the group has five movements, and No. 3 totals six movements. Assorted tempos with balanced designs rule throughout. Movement two in Sonata No. 3 is

an infinite canon at the twelfth, and the same polyphonic form is used in the second (final) movement of Sonata No. 6, where the imitation is at the octave. These perpetual canons are so constructed that they can be repeated as often as desired.

Genishta, Osip (1795–1853)

DUO

- **Sonata for Cello and Piano, Op. 7**

Music by a little-known Russian composer. Genishta was a pianist and cellist who produced a good amount of piano and vocal music and a number of short pieces for cello. The cello and piano sonata was written in 1837 and published that year in Leipzig. (A modern edition was issued in Moscow in 1955.) Schumann praised the work in the progressive journal *Neue Zeitschrift für Musik*.

Schematic simplicity marks the duo. The first and third movements are cast in sonata form. Barcarolle flow identifies the middle movement. Throughout, nothing complicated whatsoever. This is solid but never stolid music.

Gentilucci, Armando (1939–)

QUINTET

- *Cile (Chile), 1973* **for Flute, Oboe, Clarinet, Horn, and Bassoon (1973)**

The emphasis is on the shock and jar of secundal lines, sequestered and spaced. Together with this is a framework of polyrhythmic conditioning, which clarifies the frictioning. The textures are heavy. Twice the music is interrupted for aleatoric statements. In the first of these the pitches are given but no rhythms, in the second only a fast succession is outlined to last fifteen seconds.

A picturesque and somewhat poignant ending. The horn intones a slow, flexibly rhythmic questioning line over a sustained chord consisting of two pairs of ninths.

Genzmer, Harald (1909–)

DUOS

- *Dance Pieces* for Two Alto Recorders: Books I and II

"Dance" in a general sense, since three of the eight pieces in the second book are differently titled. The others reflect mostly fast tempos and thereby do fit the overall concept.

Number three (Melodie) is principally in quintuple pulse. The same meter is used throughout movement four (Intermezzo). The Ostinato of number five moves in two ways—between the instruments and in meter totals, one measure in 2/2, the other in 3/2.

Neoclassically idiomatic music, all of this. There is just as much flavorsome dissonance in the other five pieces in the second set. Included are a kinetically figured conception in septuple meter (number six), an energetically paced piece in quadruple meter (number seven), and a finale featuring contrapuntal pulse action.

There are nine pieces in the first book. Metrical assortment is used (only one meter—4/4—is repeated) and tempo headings vary as well (two are repeated—Allegro and Comodo). All music of taste, and within its parameters, meaningful.

- Eleven Duets for Soprano and Alto Recorders

Tonal chromaticism with more than a touch or two of Hindemithian logic is represented here. Recorder players are offered generous oppor-

tunities in this set of eleven pieces. Their size ranges from the first one (Moderato), lasting 20 seconds, to a Fuge (movement eight) and a Dialog (movement nine) each with a performance time of 1 1/4 minutes.

Other formal types are represented: Cantilene, Caprice, Melodie, and Scherzino. The last hops, skips, and jumps along on alternate 6/8 and 5/8 measures.

- **Introduction and Allegro for Bassoon and Piano (1966)**

Understandably, the Introduction is in a slow (Adagio) tempo. It is rhythmically rhapsodic in content and returns in part for solo bassoon (with only a pair of isolated arpeggiated chords in the piano) as a preliminary to the Allegro's coda. Persistent elemental pulsatile detail in the fast music, lots of pedal figures, lots of Hindemith.

- **Introduzione, Aria e Finale for Violin and Organ**

No mistaking the neobaroque climate of Genzmer's three-part duo. This is a discriminating work, with dynamic formal clarity. In a very restricted medium, Genzmer's opus is to be placed in the top category.

Timbre tints are already specially strong in the combine of violin and organ. Genzmer goes coloristically further by beginning his work with a theme in the organ pedals. It is repeated a fifth higher and later freely developed while the violin counterpoints this three-part Introduction with double stops. A Stravinskian adagio-tempo Aria is spun out by the violin, with parallel-fifth movement in the organ. The Finale is a fugue. Special timbre juice comes from pedal points intoned on the organ's pedals.

- **Konzertantes Duo for Trumpet and Piano**

Vigorous music throughout in Genzmer's forthright neoclassic style. (Daintiness is foreign to this composer.) This is especially marked in the toccata sweep and drive of the third (final) movement. It may be this quality that convinced Genzmer to make a second version of the opus, with a string orchestra replacing the piano, but this does not deny the chamber music ambience of the duo.

Movement one has brilliant and articulate detail; it begins with a Moderato for the piano alone before plunging into the principal Allegro material. This divisional concept is repeated later in the movement. Characteristic neobaroque writing is found in the middle movement, an Adagio that emphasizes repetitive pitches.

- **Sonata for Cello and Organ**

Granting the extreme rarity of works in this medium, one does not question the sonata's scoring specialization. Although there is sufficient duo writing, there is just as much soloism. In the arpeggiated fundament that frames the Allegro moderato, most of the first part and the coda are for cello alone. Movement two (Adagio) begins with introductory C-sharps by the cello and continues with a full unaccompanied statement. In turn, the Finale begins with a substantial solo organ section and links to a portion for solo cello. And there are more examples of one-instrument texture in the movement.

The quality of the Finale is of uncompromising fantasy. This compares to the tripartite outlines to be recognized in the preceding slow movement.

- **Sonata for Trumpet and Organ**

Hindemithian for the greater part, but with some extra pepper added for taste. Slow and fast music are alternated; the second example of the former is a Choral, the second example of the latter is simply titled Finale.

Plenty of rhythmic action in the trumpet part, but the organ is not wanting in this respect. In the Choral this type of material is assigned the trumpet in a poco rubato manner, with antiphonal response of chorale-style statements by the organ. Practically the entire movement remains at a *piano* dynamic level.

- **Sonata in F-sharp Minor for Two Flutes (or other Melody Instruments) (1944)**

A formal ordering of the usual total sonata standards, with some neat touches to brighten matters. As an adjunct to the sonata form of the Allegro moderato, good chunks of imitation are utilized. The slow movement (Andante) is followed by a Grazioso e giocoso that is a scherzo type with a softened personality. The finale is a Fugue.

It is apparent that Genzmer seeks Gebrauchsmusik acceptance, what with the free choice of instruments. This should not result in bias concerning the music. This is by no means a negligible work.

- **Sonata [No. 1] for Alto Recorder and Piano**

Functional neoromanticism arranged in an Agile–Quiet–Merry–Lively sequence. Nothing pedestrian. If not extraordinary; feeling, sonority, and musical organization are fully satisfactory. There is quartal-harmony coloring in the second movement (Ruhig), and pedal anchorage is used in the third movement (Heiter).

- **Sonata [No. 1] for Viola and Piano**

Genzmer's viola and piano sonata is romantically furbished music. It has two movements:

Fantasie and Thema mit Variationen. The former, unlike its title, is a binary composite piece, consisting of a somewhat embellished theme and a broader subject. These alternately pass in review.

The five variations are precise assemblages drawn *to* the theme, not evolved from it. In spite of adornments, the theme remains almost naked—the elements of piecemeal variation technique are followed strictly. In the first variant, ornaments are attached to the theme's features; in the second still more, this time shaped and bent slightly by asymmetrical meters (but which do not disguise matters). Next comes a variation in broad style followed by a slow and very lyric section where a change is made to triple beat for flow of line. The fifth and last section is a type of perpetual movement of sixteenth notes. Genzmer holds to the truism of restrained variation, thereby keeping his personality neutral in all respects.

- **Sonata No. 2 for Alto Recorder and Piano**

Plentiful pandiatonic clarity. And plentiful piano clarity, thinned and spaced to permit the light sonority of the wind instrument to sound clearly and with proper balance. Polyharmony occasionally for contrast, and a supply of polytonality in the Presto conclusion—alternate D and F major in the soprano part of the piano, a tonally opposed ostinato in the bass, and A-flat major in the recorder.

Substantial sonatas for recorder and piano are not in good supply. Genzmer's three-movement opus is a significant entry. It is most rewarding and signifies highly ingenious music.

- **Sonata No. 2 for Viola and Piano (1955)**

Sharp differences concern the four movements, though basically the style is neoclassical at its most fervent slant. The opening Allegro has

scherzo finesse, the texture scrubbed thin. Movement two is active with heavily beamed notes relating to groups such as sixteen sixty-fourth notes per beat—all denoting the neobaroque plasticity of the Adagio.

And it is texture once again that is the dynamism for shaping the third movement (Presto). The outer sections are fundamentally unified in rhythm, the central part contrasts the lines of the instruments. The point of the last movement is one of fantasy as the music moves from Tranquillo to Vivace sections and from polyphony to monophony.

- **Sonatine for Cello and Piano**

A choice example from this prolific composer. Each of the three movements has imaginative individuality. Movement one whips through at a one-in-a-bar pace, tightly pulsed, lightly textured. Movement two surrounds the Adagio's cello line with good amounts of secundal harmony. That Genzmer has direct balance in mind is proven by the textural thinness of the concluding Rondo and the final chord of the work, which forms a major second from the pitches of C and D.

- **Sonatine for Clarinet and Piano**

The clear, and, at this date, traditional architecture of 20th-century neoclassicism. This is represented by a Lento with ornate rhetorical statements by the clarinet linked to an Allegro that moves in sonata formation. Genzmer's habit of having a decorative, baroque-contoured aria to delineate the slow movement is followed here. Vivacious finale, stimulated by rhythmic pedals and lots of clarinet trills.

- **Sonatine for Horn and Piano**

Well-shaped and fluently written music in Genzmer's neoclassic style. He does not overlook instrumental possibilities. Thus, movement three, driven in Presto tempo and based on triplet figures, is dynamically intensified by the instruction for the horn: *schmetternd* (blare). And a different type of possibility enhances the Finale, which has a variety of rhythmic pedals combined with a variety of mensural totals.

There is a lightly rhythmic first movement, set in 3/4 time, one beat to the measure. In movement two the instruments are compacted by counterpoint—linear in the horn, rhythmic in the piano.

- **Sonatine for Trombone and Piano**

Even though the outlines of Genzmer's three-movement work are familiar, and even though the materials are likewise, nonetheless, the writing is finely tuned, sensitively considered in terms of the instruments.

Genzmer does not (here or elsewhere) live dangerously in regard to creative style. The music is neoclassic, the impress of Hindemith recognizable. Thus, movement one is a broad Allegro, with pulse patterns in the piano and broad lines in the trombone. The Adagio is ternary in design. Its harmonic substances in the first section are secundal, more expansive in the center of the movement, and again of secundal denomination in the return to the initial material. The start of the recap is a bit thunderous in *fortissimo* and then dynamically lowered. The Finale is balanced between balletic, syncopative, and declarative elements.

- **Sonatine for Trumpet and Piano (1965)**

An excellent illustration of Genzmer's characteristically clear syntax. And succinctness simultaneously—the Sonatine's three movements embrace only eight minutes of performance time.

Motivally developed material in movement one, with light rhythmic framework. Movement two is aria formationed, with tertial-banked harmonies. The finale is a Saltarello.

This 16th-century Italian dance is set in quick triple meter. Genzmer uses duple pulse. Little matter. The music flies past with appetizing impulse minus any brakes until the final three measures.

- **Sonatine for Viola and Piano**

Unpretentious music that has directness and freshness. Clear development in the concentrated first movement with its theme emphasized by unisoned depiction. The melodic line of the slow movement has baroquelike turns. The final movement is not only fast but of rhythmic attraction, with most of the material carried by alternating 3/4 and 7/8 measures. Music of such flux can never be flabby.

- **Third Sonata for Violin and Piano (1954)**

Romantic contemporaneity in the first movement, with the rhythmic plotting out of Hindemith texts. Movement two is a broad song, supported by strong chordal detail and by widely spaced line writing for the piano. The use of muted timbre identifies the middle section of the music.

The finale is an Allegro molto that moves in constant 3/4 time (a total of 352 measures). The music is exciting, made more so by the texture, most of which is devoted to lean three-line writing for the two instruments. Direct black and white values are offered when textural change is made.

- **Twelve Duos for Two Trombones**

Sounds didactic, but there isn't a single piece in this set that wouldn't receive good response in a concert situation. Technical dexterity and supreme contrapuntalistic know-how in a 20th-century sense control and color the music. The only deviation from polyphony is in number six (Prestissimo), which tosses repetitive pitch figures from one instrument to the other, and in the final duo (Adagio molto tranquillo), a slow, processional music that is almost totally chordal.

Expert contrast. And variety. The third duo is vivaciously tempoed, contrasting broad sounds with pointed ones, set within septuple meter. Number four is a strict canon from start to finish at the unison. Fanfarric thrusts are basic to the seventh duo.

TRIOS

- **Trio for Flute, Bassoon (or Cello), and Harpsichord (or Piano)**

Sharply focused conditions for this light-timbred Trio. (The alternate instruments are less appropriate, especially the piano in place of the harpsichord.) In the second movement (Andante tranquillo), save for three and a fraction measures containing a single sustained G pitch for the bassoon, the two wind instruments are joined throughout the total fifty-seven measures.

In the Finale, a music of toccata demeanor and rhythmic kick (and a bit of hemiola), scoring contrasts between the winds and the keyboard instrument are strong. The four-measure Lento bit before the coda, a carryover from the opening of the first movement, is the only interruption to the Vivo-paced neoclassic urgency. The rhapsodic turns of this Lento preliminary are also utilized within the first movement proper (Allegro). There is certainty that Genzmer was influenced by the use of the harpsichord in creating these ornamented passages.

- **Trio for Flute, Viola, and Harp (1947)**

Genzmer's music offers neither experimentation nor eclectic directness. A considerable amount of his work is neoclassic. Some, like this Trio, are a careful and accurate rendering of neoromantic musical prose. Also, in this case much more chromaticism than usual, which, of course, is proper to neoromantic syntax.

Even the Scherzo (movement two) is heavied with pitch shifts and has the same basic quality as the preceding Fantasia and the Notturno that follows. The final part of the work is a Thema mit Variationen über ein altes Volkslied (Theme with Variations on an Old Folk Song). The entire theme is announced by the solo harp. Four variations follow, the speediest the final one.

- **Trio [No. 2] for Piano, Violin, and Cello (1964)**

Genzmer's close identification with neoclassic style is tellingly revealed in this four-part piano trio. There is not only stylistic command and clarity (and purity) but there is aliveness to the matter of instrumental values so that the full coloristic aspects of trio scoring are utilized. There are innumerable instances of sensitive detail: using the violin as the bass to the cello, pizzicato imitation (movement one); consecutive triple-stop pizzicato passages for the cello, bold antiphony between piano and strings, the latter in quadrupled voicing (movement two); superb three-part writing (movement four). Above all, the scoring never spills over into mini symphonicism.

Sweeping dramatic constructions in the first and last movements. A stimulating and tonically poetic conception, always forthright in its statements, marks the slow movement. The Burleske has special rhythmic conviction with fast-paced music measured in 11/8 time for the greater part and with the contrastive middle section canonically processed.

QUARTETS

- **Musik für vier Bläser (Music for Four Winds) (Two Trumpets and Two Trombones)**

(Peters, who published this work in 1968, was a bit imprecise in its titling. In instrumental nomenclature *bläser* is strictly used for woodwinds and *blechbläser* for brass.)

Mostly vertical controls are used in movements one (Fanfare), two (Choral), four (Andante), and five (Finale). Movement three is a Fuge. There is a good amount of fanfarric writing in the Finale. Thus, structural balance, though a bit of redundancy, in this music of neoclassic style.

- **Quartettino for Four Recorders (Soprano, Alto, Tenor, and Bass Recorders)**

Dozens upon dozens of transcriptions for the recorder fill publishers' catalogues. Original works are few. Of these, restrictive orthodoxy (and scholasticism) plagues 99 percent (and more!) of the total.

Genzmer's three-movement pithy work is neoclassic to the core. It is especially marked by resourceful part writing and use of rhythm and metrical difference in the sectionally set final (third) movement. There are no shopworn formulas in this 5 1/2-minute recorder quartet.

QUINTETS

- *Quintet on Themes by Johann Pachelbel for Two Trumpets, Horn, Trombone, and Tuba*

Neoclassic syntax and polished scoring that provide a rich sonority. An Introduction is followed by the longest movement, Gavotte with Three Variations. Genzmer's variational powers are on display in this set concerned with vivacious, proclamatory, and speedy (triplet) permutations. A simple Sarabande and a snappy Fuge complete the work.

- **Wind Quintet for Flute, Oboe, Clarinet, Horn, and Bassoon (1957)**

Like so much of Genzmer's music, this work is representative of Hindemith's style, from whom Genzmer learned much. There is this to say: In the motoric portions (the first and fourth movements) the music always sings.

Binary form is favored. In the first movement an Adagio is followed by an Allegro molto and this format is followed twice. Movement three is likewise structured, with a Moderato in 5/8 compared to material set in measures of double length. In movement two tempo has strong effect, with sustained vertical writing followed by speedy virtuosic passages. The zippy finale is balanced by rondo detail.

SEXTET

- **Sextet for Two Clarinets, Two Bassoons, and Two Horns**

Four movements, and in good part the name of Hindemith springs readily to mind. (Genzmer never abandoned his loyalty to Hindemithian procedures.)

Slow music (largo) alternates with allegro music at the start. The former is pithy; in order, six, three, and five measures in length. Movement two is tripartite, the outer sections propelled by no-nonsense, long–short rhythmic figures. The Intermezzo has fugal contours. Tempo again is a regulatory force in the Finale, which begins in lento, proceeds to allegro molto, and concludes in presto tempo.

SEPTET

- **Septet for Harp, Flute, Clarinet, Horn, Violin, Viola, and Cello (1949)**

It is surprising to hear the sounds of this three-movement work, written just after World War II. Indeed, in view of its vernal and warmly pleasant romantic sounds Genzmer's composition could be nicknamed the *Spring Septet.*

The composition begins calmly and ends similarly. All three parts are in E-flat major, with the middle movement more flowery than the other two. An introduction of miniature proportions, but a totality unto itself, leads into a Lebhaft surging theme. Next there is a haunting flute-harp episode in G major, and the movement is completed with development of the principal material. The final movement is in scherzo style; its main theme is one of directness and spaciousness.

NONET

- **Capriccio for Oboe, Clarinet, Bassoon, Horn, Two Violins, Viola, Cello, and Double Bass (1963)**

The published score indicates the Capriccio is "for chamber orchestra," but a prefatory note states the composition has been planned so that it can be performed as a nonet.

Genzmer's work is contemporaneously romantic in its syntax, with structural proportions distinct and yet not old and trite. The principal device is duo thematicism, related and recolored in the first and third movements. In the latter, kinetic, squared metrical figurations are compared to slower-sounding asymmetrical sections. The second movement is a short three-part affair, colored by muting the string quintet. Variationen über ein altes Tanzlied (Variations on an Old Dance Melody) concludes the nonet. There are three variations, the viola featured in the first one. Lots of drive in this finale, but no bang or bombast.

George, Earl (1924–)

DUOS

- **Sonata for Trumpet and Piano**

Standard contemporary musical language with strong rhythmic framework. The music begins with a proclamatory section marked Funebre, and this is joined to an Allegro agitato. There is tonal lucidity in every phase of the piece, with a good amount of warmth, especially the dramatic temperature in the second part of the duo.

- ***Tuckets and Sennets* for Trumpet and Piano (1973)**

George's trumpet soundings and signal calls consist of eight pieces that can be performed as a suite or individually "or in any grouping desired."

A colorful set. After the Prologue there is a Rag, mostly for the trumpet, with the piano to be "raucous" and to sound "like a player-piano." Some improvisation is included. The fourth piece is a Blues that has nonsynchronized data between the instruments resulting from controlled chance operations. The ad lib manifestations continue in Rock. Slow-paced music, freely-flowing in its rhythm, details part six, "Cocktail Music." "Hamlet" is for trumpet alone. The final Epilogue (Cancrizans) is a slow-tempo declarative conception.

George, Thom Ritter (1942–)

DUO

- *Six Canonic Sonatas* for Two Flutes (1966)

Excellent representations that fulfill the technique of canon without deviation in each of the six sonatas. All are canons at the unison, with the consequent following the antecedent at a distance of either one or two measures.

The nicely woven polyphonic materials are distributed, with one exception, over three-movement settings. *Canonic Sonata* No. 2 begins with an Adagio that is followed by a Presto, and then an eight-measure second Adagio precedes the final (fourth) movement (Tempo di menuetto). Significantly, the second Adagio uses a small portion of the initial Adagio but with the melodic line inverted. The fifth work has a theme, four variations, and a repeat of the theme as the middle movement. Nonetheless, there is no break in the strict imitation as the music progresses through the six sections.

QUINTET

- **Quintet No. 1 for Two Trumpets, Horn, Trombone, and Tuba**

Contemporary tonalism and bright brass colorings give George's work a good sense of direction within its five-movement span (the last two linked). Neat rhythmic plotting in the majority of movements, with the drive and qualities obtained without any high-decibel spicing and use of effects such as flutter sounds, smears, and bent tones.

Movement three is the longest of the five and represents the single slow-paced music in the quintet. It has neomodal touches. Movement four includes some pithy cadenza patches. Exemplary scoring clarity throughout.

Geraedts, Jaap (1924–)

QUINTET

- *Small Water Music* for Flute, Oboe, Clarinet, Bassoon, and Horn (1951)

Of course, Handel immediately comes to mind, but the only relationship, and a remote one at best, is the use within the Dutch composer's wind quintet of a couple of old dance formations.

Geraedts bases his music on a Dutch children's song and considers it a "Divertimento in Four Rhapsodic Variations." There is a four-measure introduction, and the theme leads into the first variation (quite extensive in terms of variation form). Part two is in Sarabande format, the third variation is Gavotte shaped. The finale is a vivacious concept and has a saltarello personality.

Gerber, René (1908–)

TRIO

- **Suite for Flute, Oboe, and Piano (1948)**

Control and blending of the wind and keyboard colors in neat neoclassic statements by this Swiss composer. There are four expressive and idiomatic dances, each disciplined and responsive to the formal requirements. All the right touches are present in the Sarabande (including some light imitative activity), the Gavotte (which flavors the dance recipe with metrical changes), the Loure (codified by its stressing of accentuation of a short note followed by a long note) and the final Gigue (which further stimulates the fast pace by contrasts between 6/8 and 2/4).

Gerhard, Robert (1896–1970)

DUO

- *Gemini:* **Duo concertante for Violin and Piano (1966)**

The scoring of this substantial piece bears out the equality of the title's meaning (twins). There is a direct percussiveness in the violin's part, and this is matched by the various types of piano clusters and contacts made directly on the piano's strings, including glissando with a plectrum or nail file. Forceful is the word for *Gemini.*

The form is episodic, described by Gerhard as "more like a braiding of diverse strands than a straight linear development." Repeats of these episodes take place "in a different context"—structurally, therefore, further affinity with the title in a dissimilar twins sense.

TRIO

- **Trio [No. 2] for Violin, Cello, and Piano (1918)**

Though not so indicated, this is Gerhard's second piano trio. It was dedicated to his teacher, Felipe Pedrell, considered, as Nicolas Slonimsky describes him, "the leading spirit of the modern Spanish nationalist revival in music."

The opus is somewhat of mixed content, with some imitation of Ravelian mannerisms. However, Gerhard believed in the symphonicism of the piano trio medium; the sonorous impact is rarely moderate, mostly lush and sumptuous. Spanish-style pulse patterns are employed, the second subject of the first movement pointedly using an indigenous floating rhythmic arrangement of 3 + 2 + 3.

Movement two coloristically divides the principal themes. The initial one is assigned to the piano and then repeated in octaves by the violin and cello, the second subject is announced by the strings.

A rondo pattern serves for the final Vif. Here the metrical plotting tends mostly to shift between quintal and triple arrangement. Within this part there is a pervading sense of Gerhard's using the second movement of Ravel's string quartet as his model. As in the Ravel work the strings announce the principal theme in pizzicato. Additionally, the spraying arpeggios and subsidiary theme are imitative of the Frenchman's work.

QUARTET

- **String Quartet No. 2 (1961)**

Serialism guides this quartet, but Gerhard guides the serialism. Rigidity of technical system was not for him, and thus there is no technical stasis in the piece. This to such extent that movement distribution is abandoned in favor of a single movement, its sections linked.

Frictions are expanded to include the scrap and strafe of hitting the body of the instrument, playing between the bridge and the tailpiece, tapping on the tailpiece, as well as nail glissando. There are seven specified sections. The second is where the noise (abrasiveness, if one prefers) enters. Throughout there is a raw power exhibited—another example of the potency of twelve-tone speech.

QUINTET

- **Wind Quintet for Flute (alternating Piccolo), Oboe, Clarinet, Bassoon, and Horn (1928)**

Gerhard completed his quintet in 1928, at the conclusion of a five-year period of study with Schoenberg. Creative imitation might be expected from Gerhard's exposure to Schoenbergian dicta, but this is not the case. A reconciliation between tone-row employment (which is fundamentally a source of motives) and direct thematicism (which denotes melodic prominence) is evident, especially in the first pair of movements.

The opening measures present a seven-note series in the bassoon, and this winds its way throughout the initial movement (three times in the oboe, twice in the clarinet, once in the horn, and three times in the bassoon). In addition, its arched shape is a characteristic that is totally associative with the movement. And though linearality is prime to this music, contrapuntal insistence gives way to a sufficient amount of rhythmic coincidence to indicate this is serial music free of rigidity. The same seven-note series is the basis for a passacaglia that structures the second movement. Significantly coincidental, there are seven sections in this contrapuntal configuration: part five matches the first section, part six is derived from part two, and the final portion both matches and is an expansion of part three. Organic and formal balance is clearly realized.

Reshaped, the opening pitch series appears in the finale, binding the quintet's form, together with the rhythmically changed theme of the third movement (a scherzo manifestation). Gerhard's Catalanian origins and environment, combined with the Viennese background, are displayed in the finale—manifested by its coloristic sweep and insistent triple-beat propulsion.

(The first performance of the quintet took place in Barcelona, in 1930. Double credit applied to Gerhard, since he conducted the five instrumentalists.)

SEXTET

- *Libra* for Flute (alternating Piccolo), Clarinet, Violin, Guitar, Piano, and Percussion (Vibraphone, Xylophone, Glockenspiel, Small Wood Block, Large Korean Block, Medium and Large Cymbals, Bass Drum, Snare Drum, Tam-tam, Castanets, and Timpani) (1968)

Gerhard produced three works with astrological titles. In addition to *Libra* there were *Gemini (see above)* and *Leo,* a dectet scored for flute, clarinet, horn, trumpet, trombone, piano, violin, cello, and two percussionists. He had no outward programmatic specifics in mind. Gerhard pointed out in his prefatory note to *Libra* that he had "a certain weakness for astrology . . . and for horoscopes." Interestingly, Libra was Gerhard's birth sign and Leo was his wife's.

Further, while in *Libra* nothing is said in the prefatory note relating the sign to the musical content, in the preface to *Leo* (which means lion) mention is made of the characteristics of the birth sign, that Gerhard "wanted to pay homage to the . . . self-reliance of the lion and to its terrific fighting power" and that the work "shows the way I tried to do it." In *Libra* (which means balance) one can only assume that that element was sought in the writing of the work and possibly that the title can mean a subtle method of self-acknowledgment.

A still further point. When *Gemini* was first performed its title was Duo concertante. It is now the music's subtitle. When *Leo* first appeared it had the subtitle Chamber Symphony. When the score was published it was removed.

A final word regarding this astrological detail. Gerhard stated that he disliked referring to a composition by a number and found a title to be "a useful means of reference."

Libra is in one movement. Various textures and timbres provide the strengths to make the balances. These are in terms of blocks, rather than formed from thematic lengths. Clearly focused, the climax is the concluding part of the work, with a short melody in the high register (stated in separated repetitions) supported by a dark ostinato in the low register. Other materials (ostinatos themselves) are secondary to these as color adjuncts.

OCTET

- *Concert for Eight* (Flute [alternating Piccolo], Clarinet, Accordion, Mandolin, Guitar, Piano, Double Bass, and Percussion [Three Suspended Cymbals, Three Korean Blocks, Tam-tam, Claves, Maracas, Antique Cymbal, Tenor Drum, Bass Drum, Tambourine, Four Tom-toms, Vibraphone, Glockenspiel, and Marimba]) (1962)

Gerhard's preface indicates that it was his intention "to write a piece of chamber music in the nature of a Divertimento, almost in the spirit of the *commedia dell'arte.* The eight instruments are introduced somewhat in the manner of *dramatis personae,* but the play itself consists of purely musical events, and must not be taken as evoking or illustrating any extramusical parallels whatever. From the conventions of the *commedia* two have been adopted: that of extempore invention and, sometimes, that of disguise or masking—by which I mean unusual ways of playing the instruments. The piece falls into eight sections, which are played without a break."

The "invention" is only in interpretative terms, the serenade element dominates the music, and this is especially due to the use of instruments associated with the serenade, such as the mandolin and the guitar. In the timbral matter the colors flash in their new dress. Thus, in the first entrance of the guitar the instrument is played with a cello bow, the instrument held

on the player's lap. Among the other "disguises" are playing with a cello bow on the edge of a cymbal (producing harmonics), striking the guitar strings with the nails, playing with the wooden part of the bow on the double bass's tailpiece, etc.

NONET

- **Nonet for Flute (alternating Piccolo), Oboe, Clarinet, Bassoon, Horn, Trumpet, Trombone, Tuba, and Accordion (1956)**

The rara avis in this Nonet, which includes two quartets of winds and brass, is the accordion. Orchestration treatises avoid mention of the instrument; its appearance in an orchestral score is extraordinary, no less so in a chamber music group. While there have been some worthy pieces written for the pipes-bellows-buttons-keyboard instrument, these have been due to the propagandizing, promulgation, and commissioning efforts of accordion players' organizations. The prospect of composing for the instrument has not attracted serious, first-rank composers, unless money is placed "up front" for specified creative services. Sensible people finding nothing useless, composers such as Roy Harris, Paul Creston, Lukas Foss, and David Diamond have made valuable contributions and removed a smidgen of the stigma that clings to the instrument. It still clings, however.

There is really nothing poor about the sound of the accordion. Nor can anyone deny its individual tone color. In proper place and company it is as worthy as the tuba, the mandolin, or the saxophone, to cite only some examples. It is only that the accordion (like the saxophone) has suffered by the company it has kept. The accordion brings to mind the old vaudeville atmosphere, the honky-tonk climate of cheap theater, the instrument decorated and spangled for use in a nightclub act. As with any instrument, top-flight proficiency is given to only a few, but the many can learn the instrument much more rapidly (apparently) than struggling with string-instrument intonation or wind-instrument embouchure problems. Commercialism (by instrument manufacturers and teaching studios) has turned loose an army of poor players playing poor music. Little wonder the accordion has worn the insignia of instrumental repression.

But, given sufficient understanding by composers like Roberto Gerhard, the accordion will obtain its deed of release, vouchsafing another color for the acute and astute composer. Gerhard has used the instrument in another chamber work *(see above: Concert for Eight)*, in his second symphony, and in his large work for speaker, chorus, and orchestra, *The Plague*. In Gerhard's hands the special abilities the accordion has for crescendo and diminuendo are not bypassed. Other sonic benefits he realizes are chordal sustainment, the sharp, ictus thrust, and capsulized, fricative clusters.

The traditional total of four movements are not only differentiated by tempo headings—Allegro moderato, Allegro, Andante, and Allegro assai, con slancio (Very Quick, with Impetuosity)—but by specific rhythmic plans. In the first movement sets of thirty-second notes on and off the beat pepper the preambulistic tone of the movement. Eighth notes—single and isolated, or in sets, detached and connected—are paramount in the second movement—a music of scherzo direction. In movement three, rhythm is stretched into long-spelled lines that sing. Movement four parlays repetitive sounds into either duple or triple accentuations within the same time span. The rhythmic projection is also lessened (and contrasted) by smaller-total sounds within the finale's measures, but the drive of its contents is not.

Gerschefski, Edwin (1909–)

DUO

- *Statement, Aria, and Development* **for Violin and Piano, Op. 12**

When a form is lucid then the form is valid. A composer must realize his own visions, and if he is a professional the conception will have integrity. (Pretenders are often accepted but eventually are found out.) The lucidity of this work is apparent despite the total absence of any obedience to items listed in the formal catalogue.

In the *Statement* (formerly this portion was termed Prologue, and before that the entire work was titled Sonatine) Gerschefski presents a directive outline from which he will operate. In another sense it constitutes a freely disposed prelude. But out of it are drawn the sharp variegation found in the long cadenza for violin that initiates the *Development*, and the essence of the toccata-coated duet that follows. In the latter more kinship with the *Statement* will be recognized—the same picture taken from an acutely different camera angle. This type of refocusing on a similar surface will be recognized in the *Aria*.

QUARTET

- **Eight Variations for String Quartet, Op. 25**

Variational personality is indicated here by localizing each part of the composition and eliminating any individualization within it. Saturation of a technical condition, therefore, is applied to the quartet body rather than contrapuntal weave, thematic statement with accompanimental background, and so forth. The total resource *is* the variation. This abstract solidarity in each of the eight parts may be emotionally bloodless, but it is dynamically constructive.

The twenty-measure theme is entirely motile in its individual voicing. The same condition is maintained in the sixty-eight-measure initial variation. In variation two there is no dynamic change, all instruments playing at *piano* level. Consistent, persistent, and insistent eighth notes structure the next section—for the greater part at the beginning and in the concluding portion sounded col legno. An Allegretto, waltz metered and totally muted, forms variation four. The fifth variation is meshed in a mass of tremolandos and glissandos, with an ambivalence between ponticello and natural sound. Then, in its concluding part, trilled and sustained sounds take over. Variation six is concerned with pizzicato and tapping the backs of the instruments with the knuckles. Syncopative motility rules variation seven. Firmly unisoned rhythm applied to all four instruments governs the final variation. Everything is arranged in series: six measures of harmonics, ten measures of tremolando, etc.

Gerschefski's emphasis on one aspect, completing it and then presenting another is like a series of flat surfaces. Minus any effects of decoration or special pictorial values, its novelty is the complete absence of novelty.

SEPTET

- **Septet for Brasses (Two Horns, Two Trumpets, Two Trombones, and Tuba), Op. 26**

Gerschefski's one-movement work (lasting eight minutes) was commissioned for radio performance by the then functioning League of Composers in 1938. It is scored for the four members of the orchestral brass family—two each of horns, trumpets, and trombones, and one tuba.

While there are thematic sections and the form is in a broad, "determined-by-tempo" A–B–A (and certain themes of the opening por-

tion are used in a semibackward manner in the recapitulation), Gerschefski is more concerned with patterns shaped into fascination by use of ultravaried rhythms, cross-rhythmic ideas, and instrumental coloristic effects. He pursues blended mixtures of timbre with nonreticence. Use is made of three different types of mutes, the use of a hat for the same purpose, as well as special vibrato, together with flares (a short, skittish glide) and glissando. The hothouse of jazz produced all such; slowly they found their way into the symphonic halls, and now they rest their somewhat weary bodies in chamber music domains.

It is of interest to observe the percussion effects contained in a brass chamber music piece. To clap one's hands in specified rhythms and accents, as does the second trumpeter (for nineteen measures) is possible by any instrumentalist. But a brass-instrument player may be required, as in this work, to hold a horn in one hand and strike the instrument with a muffled mouthpiece (for ten measures). These are musical existentialistic earmarks. In place, as here, they are logical.

Gershwin, George (1898–1937)

QUARTET

- *Lullaby* for String Quartet

The name of George Gershwin immediately brings to mind such great successes as the jazz-classical hybrid *Rhapsody in Blue;* the opera for black singers, *Porgy and Bess;* and works for the Broadway orbit, containing tunes from musical comedies that will last forever.

Mentioning chamber music in connection with Gershwin would seem to be a factual error. However, in the 1960s *Lullaby* for string quartet surfaced, having been shelved since its composition in 1919 or 1920. (Ira Gershwin stated that his brother had used *Lullaby*'s opening theme as a portion of an aria in the one-act opera *Blue Monday.*) Otherwise, almost total silence surrounded the short piece until it was premiered in 1967 and published the year following. (Larry Adler, the harmonica virtuoso, somehow learned of the work and obtained permission to make a transcription for harmonica and string quartet. That version was premiered in 1963 at the Edinburgh Festival. A second arrangement for harmonica and full string orchestra was also made by Adler and Morton Gould.)

But, is this the whole story? This writer remembers that during the time he was a pupil of Rubin Goldmark's, with whom Gershwin had studied (in addition to Edward Kilenyi, Henry Corwell, Wallingford Riegger, and Joseph Schillinger), Goldmark proudly claimed that while Gershwin had been studying with him, Gershwin had "been working on a string quartet." Was there ever a three- or four-movement quartet composed, or is *Lullaby* an isolated piece? Is *Lullaby "the* string quartet", or is it a part of a full-scale work—hidden, undiscovered and forever lost? Goldmark never exaggerated, and as all of Gershwin's teachers are deceased (they might have been able to shed some light on the matter), the facts may never be revealed.

A Gershwin three- or four-movement work for string quartet is fascinating to contemplate, especially after considering the sensitive stimulus afforded by *Lullaby:* It is charming. Although its technical flame is low, it has compelling warmth. The methods are simple: a tripartite design, framed by an introduction and coda, with the central portion a bit more active in address. The colors are just as modest: pedal points, pizzicato, and some tintinnabulative harmonics.

Gerster, Ottmar (1897–1969)

DUO

- **Divertimento for Violin and Viola**

The tonal richnesses of thirds and sixths create the strength within this string duo, without overlooking dissonance as a fruitful part of the total conception. Gerster can be compared to Hindemith providing one adds the footnote that the former man is much more cautious.

The first movement has toccata motility; the Intermezzo is light and has a Trio of simulated Viennese swing. A study in dynamic contrasts is afforded by the Scherzo. Because of the racing prestissimo speed, the dynamics have no resiliency; they are either very soft or very loud. The Trio of this movement is two dimensional, determined by the C pedal point of the viola against which the violin moves in all directions. The Trio section returns in changed manner as the coda, but retains its previous design. The Improvisation does not completely live up to its name since it strikes the balances of tripartite shape. A Fuga is in last place. There is a kinship in its subject to that of the opening movement inasmuch as in both instances the first five pitches are the same.

QUARTET

- **String Quartet [No. 1] (1923)**

Classical form is used in this tonal quartet. However, the composer is not so absorbed in imitation of past formulas that he cannot shake loose from them. He does so nicely without losing structural solidity and damaging his production thereby. The opening movement is in D; the second is in the relative minor of that key's dominant (F-sharp), changed to conform to classical design in that a shift is made into the major mode at the end. Movement three employs the dominant of the home tonality (A major), while the last movement, though it begins in F, concludes in the commanding key of D. This outline of tonal stability is the gold within Gerster's quartet; its glitter is marked by the harmonic pull on the tonality itself, with its tensions smartening the lines and illuminating the structure.

Fugatos sprinkle the ground of the opening movement; the secondary theme by its motion in fourths is in compulsive counteraction to the triadal moves of the first theme. The emotional slow movement is followed by a lively Scherzo, with true classical spirit of light and fancy order. While the Finale does not neglect counterpoint and its representation by way of imitation between the instruments, it is mostly in the form of a homophonic dance.

Gerster, Robert (1945–)

QUARTET

- *Cantata* for Woodwind Quartet (Flute, Oboe, Clarinet, and Bassoon)

Of course, from the heading it is apparent, title notwithstanding, that no vocal use is included. The only connection with Gerster's fancy head caption is that the several movements found in a cantata are equated here, in connected form. The last, therefore, further ratifies cantata practice by matching its continuous narrative text with instrumental sectional connection.

That said, the focus here is on timbre variety, framed and supported by unison data. The first part is a flute solo over a long-held unison. This leads to a rhythmic flurry of material entirely devoted to unisons and pitch doublings. There are separate solo spots for bassoon and oboe (again, each is pivoted by unison sound). There are eight sections in all, providing splendid sensations of woodwind timbre, devoted to music of substance minus sensationalism.

Geszler, György (1913–)

TRIO

- **Trio for Flute, Guitar, and Cello**

Folk sentiments twined into music that never stays metrically put, applied to tonal lines that are complexioned with various-colored dissonances.

Two Allegros surround a Largo. Each of the central ideas is literally repeated. In the first movement this covers the initial seventy-one measures, and, in the total fifty-eight measures of movement two the first fourteen are repeated. Tight rondo detail in movement three parallels these structural moves.

Geszler's contrastive use of the guitar creates its own effect. In the first movement, practically everything is single voiced. In movement two, fat chords are the rule. These styles are joined in movement three.

Gewicksmann, Vitali (1924–)

QUARTET

- **String Quartet No. 2 (1963)**

Most of the quartet is in expressionistic language, some of it is less arcane in its speech. It little matters since the change in formal (stylistic) syntax is not made within any single movement but retained for a total movement. Importantly, there is a specific color quality that is stressed in each separate part of the quartet. It produces a properly temperatured control for the material.

In the Andantino the linear detail stresses the rise of a seventh. Later this increases to a ninth. In movement two the principal point is made by chain pizzicatos followed by syncopative thematic material, also in plucked timbre. It is only after textural weight has reached its heaviest that bowed timbre is used. The thin concluding measures are a surprise, but they prepare for a connection with movement three. Linear incorporations are stressed there plus emphasis on high registration of sounds.

Movement four is a dead-center Scherzo, though, of course, not deadened in pace. The finale is fugal and reaches a tremendous climax with a triple *forte* twelve-tone chord. The reuse of thin texture and high registration conclude the quartet.

Ghedini, Giorgio Federico (1892–1965)

DUO

- **Canons for Violin and Cello (1946)**

Within the very strict formulation of canonic procedure Ghedini produces a string duet that equals three-movement design, bounded by separate and increasingly faster tempos. The opening moves from adagio to a little quicker tempo and the composition is concluded in a moderate allegretto speed. In all cases the usual restraint brought to bear by use of a canon is avoided with astonishing skill. Ghedini defines his polyphonic form expressionistically, creates a brooding rhapsody, far from the simple examples that are most commonly met. And yet each of the canons is at a different periodicity in reference to the imitation. Thus the first canon's consequent occurs two beats after the antecedent; the reply in the middle section is at an eight-beat distance to the leader and in the last canon the width of the reply to the question is narrower, thereby maintaining diverse methods throughout and assisting the total form with more definition. Above all, the writing proves the excellent craftsmanship of the composer, none of the rulered guidances bog down into mere technical display.

The voices of the first canon are at the distance of a minor second, and, furthermore, the consequent inverts the original melody in its imitating reply. The more fluid second section of the duet has the instruments responding at a span of a sixth, and this time the motion is paralleled. In the final part the violin and cello interweave between straightforward and contrary-motion canonic types.

TRIO

- *Seven Ricercari* for Violin, Cello, and Piano (1943)

A modern interpretation of the form. There are seven continuously strung movements, each of which is formed from the free-spun investigation of a principal, germinal motive. Within, everything is direct; padding is eliminated throughout.

The first of the group has some imitations. In contrast, the second of the set has broad-striding quarter notes and twirling arabesques. The third section is rather unique; the piano, which intones bell-like chords, is antiphonal to the strings, which in turn are also pitted in antiphony. In the next part a toccata style is manifested wherein the piano begins alone and sets forth a passacaglia type. There are abrupt dynamic transitions and ultimately augmentation in this fourth part of the trio. A legato figure is developed in the fifth ricercare; Bach style is employed for expanding the basic motive in the following portion, while the final section is of fugal viewpoint.

QUARTET

- **First Quartet for Strings (Two Violins, Viola, and Cello) (1927)**

The sheer black and white contrasts of the music propose the balances of standard classic style. There are romantic patches, and these add warmth to the motility of the material. There is a spaciousness to the quartet, set forth in Ghedini's neoclassic style. Movement two is developed in a variational manner, and this movement is linked to the triple-pulse scamper of the rondo-designed finale.

QUINTETS

- *Concerto a cinque* for Piano, Flute, Oboe, Clarinet, and Bassoon (1932)

Tonal, and thoroughly so, in an updated manner. Darting through the music one can spot the personalities of such as Roussel, Honegger, and Stravinsky. It really doesn't matter. All these gentlemen have their creative nails carefully filed. Indeed, all is very eclectic here, but handled with the very pink of courtesy and a neoclassic polish that provide a music worthy of attention.

The initial Allegro has snap, the slow movement is a lyric, long-phrased statement scored as a trio for flute, bassoon, and piano. Instrumentation plays an important role in the fourth movement as well, where most of the material is for solo piano. Ghedini opts for continuity in his *Concerto a cinque*. There is a minute halt after the opening movement, but the remaining four movements are linked.

- Quintet No. 1 (Flute, Oboe, Clarinet, Horn, and Bassoon) (1910)

The date of Ghedini's woodwind quintet reveals the important fact that it was composed at the age of 18. And this is no juvenile bit, merely of historic interest in regard to his total output. The music has clear and pertinent form, its logic based on classical formations with some romantic flavoring.

Three movements embrace the thirteen-minute performance time. The opening one is developed from a basic motive. A Romanza follows; its meaningful flow tends to favor the clarinet. The Finale vivaciously moves through sectional proportions.

SEPTET

- Adagio e Allegro da concerto for Flute, Clarinet, Horn, Violin, Viola, Cello, and Harp (1936)

The Adagio is practically bereft of ornamentation as it proceeds with long-line phrases, mostly set in three-measure proportions. Nothing dull, however, in this straightforwardness. The pace of the Allegro has the assist of brilliance in its rhythmic settings. There is a natural spontaneity to the music that is many notches above conventionality.

Ghent, Emmanuel (1925–)

DUOS

- *Entelechy (A Concert-Piece)* for Viola and Piano (1963)

The title of Ghent's piece is taken from Aristotelian logic. *Entelechy* is defined as "the full realization of form-giving cause or energeia as contrasted with mere potential existence." Or, to put it another way, the body (the "vessel") is the potential and its soul (within it) realizes varying actualities.

The string and keyboard instruments determine the terms (the vessel) within which the music functions (in two huge sectors of instrumental timbre). The potentiality is the continuity of development of the pitch forms employed from the very start and their projection into a multitudinous assortment of results.

Entelechy is free from rigid technical designs or associations. The material is presented in a total empirical manner (the derivation, therefore, of the potentialities). Yet, even with the vastness of pitch and rhythmic disjointures, a certain adherence is present. The opening swerve of the viola is a premise that appears in variegated statement and placement and it is this sonic curvature that is a binder within the realization.

Measures in the literal sense of rhythmic and phrasing significance do not exist, but small, compactly varied divisional representation does. Repetition in this guise is therefore present in part—for example: divisions 40 through 55 are repeated in divisions 160 through 175; divisions 170 through 175 match divisions 176 through 181. Otherwise, within *Entelechy* there is an avoidance of convention and a fusion of musical language with an overlay of exciting rhapsody that proves itself by its totality.

■ **Two Duos for Flute (or Oboe) and Clarinet (1962)**

Left-of-center duet music, this. Ghent avoids form that has been exhausted and chooses symbolistic portraiture for his music. Characters from life and Greek mythology are pictured in an implied (not programmatic) sense. The short first duo (it may be lengthened by an optional repeat of all but the final pair of measures) is titled *Natasha.* This is the name of the composer's wife, but that fact covers a midget offshoot to fictional record at the same time. Natasha is an important character in Tolstoy's *War and Peace,* and it was after her that Ghent's Russian-born wife was named. Save for a three-measure mid-cadence, the music is defined in triple meter, but mixed rhythmic arrangements within the measures destroy any sense of static presentation. The choice of pitches follows suit; intervallic tension is decisive.

The characters of the companion duo are instrumentally specified. Pygmalion is represented by the clarinet; the statue of a woman with which he fell in love (who later came to life and married Pygmalion), called Galatea, is

delineated by the flute or the oboe. Content reacts upon form, in this instance. The initial quintally measured allegro phrase in the clarinet is developed and after several tempo shifts is heard in presto speed. The fluid (and fruitful) free discourse gives way to paired rhythmic ostinatos in the final seventeen measures. Of these, the first eight stay on fixed, undeviating pitches. The negation of any linear motion, however, prepares for a positive conclusion. And what had begun softly ends softly.

TRIOS

■ *Helices* **for Violin, Piano, and Tape (1969)**

The liner note of a recording of Ghent's piece contains a description of the work. In all probability this unsigned data received the composer's approval or may even have been written by him. It states that *Helices* "derives its name from the structural notion, admittedly metaphorical, of unfolding spirals in which the same material returns with each twist of the helix. Each new turn, however, is always different by virtue of its own structural development as well as its juxtaposition with other elements unfolding in helicoid manner. The detailed inner structure was conceived in a similar fashion leading to the overlapping and intertwining of helices of different orders."

There are finely balanced sound complexes that twirl in *Helices,* lightly colored by the electronic material. A fluency of tender tartness surrounds Ghent's work. There are a pair of surprises: the almost total section for violin harmonics and the same instrument's tonal pedal-point passage.

■ *Triality I* **("2 Studies") for Violin, Trumpet, and Bassoon (1964)**

In the performance of music that combines sections in separate speeds in a relative manner (such as pitting an Allegro against a Moderato and an Andante) a general compromise of effect is more or less possible. However, when undeviating multimetronomic controls are demanded, the inescapable problem of human limitations rears its head. The use of individual conductors for controlling each separate tempo makes no difference, since conductors have the same frailty in regard to mathematical authentication as do performers.

In *Triality I* the three instruments (each in contrasted timbre to obtain decisive apportionment) progress at different speeds. In the first movement (extremely active rhythmically) the violin moves at ♩ = 84, the trumpet at ♩ = 60, and the bassoon at ♩ = 72. The ratio is 5:6:7. In movement two (totally of soundblock counteractions—rhythmic dynamism is absent) the ratio is 15:17:19, with the trumpet at ♩ = 40, the bassoon at ♩ = 45.3, and the violin set at ♩ = 50.7. If desired this may be changed so that the metronomic basis is ♩ = 60, ♩ = 68, and ♩ = 76 for the trumpet, bassoon, and violin respectively. While the basic overall tempos may be changed the relationship that is indicated cannot.

Ghent offers a perfect solution to the performance problems of his *Triality I*. The music is played with the aid of pulse signals registered on a tape reel, with a different pitch level used for each tempo. These click-track-like signals are transmitted to each performer by the use of a tiny earphone. The player then simply follows the pulse tempo that concerns his individual part. With such precise definition each player can concentrate on performing his part of the trio with meticulous regard for its individual rate of speed. Thus, electronic science enters the chamber music field, and Ghent's trio becomes a quartet with the aid of a tape machine!

It is to be noted that the trumpet is always moving at the slowest rate of speed, the violin at the fastest, and the bassoon exactly midway between the two. The use of mechanical minis-tration should not interfere with the acute detail pertinent to Ghent's tridimensional music—a music that has organic unity in its intersectionalism and fantastic plastic content. That each line is made of "raw" (athematic) materials only adds to the strength of the whole.

- *Triality II* **for Violin, Trumpet, and Bassoon (1964)**

The same basic style and line freedom pertains to this work as to *Triality I (see above).* The differences are that the second work is shorter and has a single movement. Only one metronomic tempo is defined: a quarter note is to embrace a 50 to 60 unit of speed for the violin. At this rate the bassoon is to play at a time lag of one-quarter of a pulse *after* the violin and the trumpet is to play one-quarter of a pulse *after* the bassoon. Though there are no differentiated tempos as in *Triality I,* the effect is similar in total realization. Regardless of similar metronomic speeds for all three instruments, the separation of pulse placements produces a triple dimension. Accordingly, tempowise, each instrument shadows the other, linearwise the sounds are unmeshed from metrical steadfastness.

Though not "absolutely required," Ghent indicates that beat signals, prepared on tape, as for *Triality I,* "will greatly facilitate the performance of this work." Indeed! Without such mechanical assistance, players would be hard put to maintain their individual roles in the resultant triple montage.

QUARTET

- **Quartet for Woodwinds (Flute, Oboe [English horn ad lib], Clarinet, and Bassoon) (1960)**

A far cry from Ghent's usual aculeated, polytempo output. Tonal meaning is outlined, developed, and confirmed.

The generative force of the piece lies in the opening two measures for the flute: a conjunct line that ascends and descends. From this the music expands and renews itself in a free, variationally developed manner. Ghent firms down his tonal premise (nary an accidental blurs the D tonality, and in the first thirty-four measures there are only three chromatic pitches; the first not appearing until the eighth measure). Deviation from the polarity is always clearly defined, but the modulatory administration does not jumble meaning. (The final cadence confirms this by a seventh chord on the D base.) The unification of the principal idea shows sensitivity and subtlety as use is made of imitation, rhythmic diminution, enlargement and dismemberment, motival chipping, and combination with other ideas. To prove his argument Ghent repeats the opening measures in slower tempo at the quartet's conclusion.

QUINTET

- **_Dithyrambos:_ Quintet for Brass Instruments (Horn, Two Trumpets, Tenor and Bass Trombones) (1965)**

With few exceptions, Ghent's music of violent complexity is totally uncoordinated in speed, meter, rhythm, and line. Indeed, this is the practice of truth to material, for the material involved could have meaning only if stated in a nonuniform manner. These are hunks and chunks of figures, not spun thoughts. They are not conceived to be joined together. Like Ghent's _Triality_ pieces (_see above_) a mechanical signal to each player (by the use of minute earphones) is the only method of playing this quintet, and even then the difficulties are tremendous. Without such aid combinations of speeds (each related to a basic quarter-note beat) of 71.1, 53.2, 94.8, 42.1, and 53.3, for example, are beyond any performer's ability. _Dithyrambos_ does not permit even a minuscule

amount of assumption in regard to such matters.

So that density is lessened and that each instrument sounds within its own sphere, the performers are to be separated (the composer desires fifteen to twenty feet between the players). Indeed, the significance of the work is its entire quintally totaled individuality. In the single duplication of sounds (at the beginning of movement two, which is joined to the opening movement) the two trumpets are notated in unison. However, one is marked "molto rubato," the other "quasi rubato." The meaning is that, while being "faithful" to their lines, one plays essentially as written, the other freely weaves "in and around the other line, now advancing, now retarding." (A pre-echo and post-echo device.) The only compliances to simplicity are the occasional tutti chords in the second movement (which has a slightly lesser amount of inner linearity), the five chords that mark the end of movement one, and the thinning out and chordal prongs at the conclusion of the quintet.

By negating classified metrical controls and coordinates, Ghent registers a positivistic music. This texturally huge composite of contrapuntalism, polytonalism, and polyrhythmicism proves that there is compatibility in incongruous associations. It also carries out the impassioned, wild, irregular strain that describes a dithyramb.

(A second version was made by Ghent, calling for a double brass quintet, including a tuba. The scoring is for four trumpets, two horns, two tenor trombones, bass trombone, and tuba. A bass trombone may be used in place of one of the tenor trombones.)

Giannini, Vittorio (1903–66)

Because this composer was concerned with the wealthy, emotional concepts of music, he was a romanticist; in that his form and structure had qualities of the Beethoven-Brahms school, he was a classicist. Such paradox is possible. Giannini created unabashedly, writing fertile, frank melodies (his Italian heritage helped in this regard) with the support of fully tonal harmonies (which might be termed conventional). (The viability of diatonic harmony will never wear out.) But he was no neoclassicist of pandiatonicism, or neoromanticist aping the Mahler cult. He was, frankly, a 20th-century composer using the well-sharpened tools of the 19th.

QUARTET

- **Quartet for Two Violins, Viola, and Cello (1930)**

Giannini's romantic demeanor shows immediately in the ardent, passionate thrust of his opening theme. It is further reflected in the large sweep and loosened structure of the initial movement. The sonata principle is surveyed with expansiveness, and this carries over to tonal elasticity that finds the first part of the Quartet progressing from B minor to F major and then D minor, back to B minor, on to B major, and finally concluding in B minor. In between, the chromatic battering of key points marks further romantic address and brio.

Movement two (Scherzo) is also a huge structure built on a rhythmic figure stated at the start and immediately passed from one instrument to the next, with a slow division (equating the Trio purpose) in the center. In the latter the cello has a double scordatura, which permits a B–F-sharp (perfect-fifth) pedal sound to be played on the open strings in the low register. Further romantic evidence persists: in the slow section third beats are to be drawn out and played rubato. Two-theme definition is used in the slow movement. The finale is of symphonic proportions; it includes augmentation of the secondary theme.

There are no doubts as to the natural growth of each of the four movements. Their size is Brucknernian, though Giannini's language is much warmer. A truthful view of the work must include the matter of the instrumental weights. In this respect Giannini should have realized that to spare the texture is to spoil the music.

QUINTET

- **Quintet for Piano, Two Violins, Viola, and Cello (1931)**

Sonata form is the mold for the first movement. The first subject is contrasted to the second by key change, type, as well as metrical difference. Development and recapitulation are ordered by instrumentational methods which clarify the divisions. Subjective influences can be observed in the slow movement. The form is rather free, proceeding from an introductory chromatic slow line to the first broad E-major theme. A secondary theme shifts the key, and developments take matters further.

The architectural plans of the final movement are proof of the composer's craftsmanship. Three complete statements are made of the first (legato) idea; then three of the second (gay and disconnected). A subsidiary theme enters; development inculcates the materials in somewhat interwoven manner. After a tremendous climax in largamente tempo, the second subject enters alone. Finally, both principal themes are combined in perfect accord. This denouement is a fitting conclusion to a piano quintet that affirms uncomplicatedly the theorem of the classic-romantic—the ideology that Giannini practiced.

Gibbs, Cecil Armstrong
(1889–1960)

DUO

- *Lyric Sonata* for Violin and Piano,
  Op. 63

Armstrong Gibbs (as he was better known, and the form used for most of his published scores, though some have the initial C indicated as well) was a composer who rejoiced in the folk song. Its mellow modal melorhythms, its haunting beauty, its nostalgic ache, its bucolic bounce are embraced in his music. Classic settings enclosed his thoughts, clear and simple; the music sings, laden with native turns, regardless of whether the notes pass quickly in review or take their time coming into view.

The Easy Flowing ("slow—1 in a bar") tempo of the sonata's opening is a declaration of the music's future contents. Three themes are developed in this part, but it is the initial one that carries the most importance. Binary total with binary subdivision defines the slow movement, joined to a Vivace con brio. In that finale, there is no mistaking the Englishry of Gibbs's rondo-impelled dance music.

TRIOS

Country Magic
for Violin, Cello, and Piano, Op. 47

The Yorkshire Dales: Three Impressions
for Violin, Cello, and Piano, Op. 58

Children's and popular concerts are common nowadays in the symphonic world. In point of fact, in some cities these often outnumber the regular, formal presentations. It is also true that in the United States attention to chamber music for children has grown considerably (the Young Audiences organizations are responsible for this). Popular concerts of chamber music remain neglected, however.

There is a plenteous literature that fits both of these special categories, in addition to the standard literature. Above all, to "play down" to an audience of children serves no good and would be recognized, in the long run, as fraudulent. Still, some lighter fare, shorter items, and colorful pieces are needed for variety, for illustrative purposes, and for a balanced musical diet. These piano trios by C. Armstrong Gibbs offer decided fringe benefits, without any sacrifice of artistry and musicality. These compositions are actually hybrids, since they can also be occasionally considered for formal chamber music concerts, even if they do not approach in any way the scale of a Mozart, Beethoven, Schubert, or Brahms piano trio.

- *Country Magic* for Violin, Cello, and
  Piano, Op. 47

The dreamy timbre of muted strings is used at the beginning and end portions of "Siesta." No somniferous inattention to metrical conditions in this case. The quintal arrangement swings in ratios that shift from 3:2 to 2:3, or mixes them. "The Open Road" is a suburban vista that compares marchlike travel with soaring lyricism. The song in "An Old Song" is folk song.

- *The Yorkshire Dales: Three
  Impressions* for Violin, Cello, and
  Piano, Op. 58

Coincidentally or not, Gibbs's subtitles for this colorful piano trio are marked by apt alliteration's artful aid. The three vales described are "Walden," "Whernside," and "Woodale." Folk song saturates these pieces, clings to them, and sings freely within them. Simplicity of similar design strictly encloses them.

- *The Three Graces: A Light Suite* for
  Violin, Cello, and Piano, Op. 92

Conventional style, but apt in terms of the objective. Only "Jennifer" (the third piece) has bright spirit in these sketches. This is motivated by one-in-a-bar speed and a fair balance between the string instruments playing together and in antiphony. "Margaret" (the first piece) is marked "Dreamily," and she muses in waltz tempo. "Susan" is described in an easy, relaxed manner.

QUARTETS

- *Miniature Quartet* for Two Violins,
  Viola, and Cello, Op. 74

A work of simplicity, awarded the Cobbett Prize in 1933 (Cobbett did for chamber music in England what Elizabeth Sprague Coolidge did for it in the United States). Gibbs was a romantic, but a nonchromatic believer. This quartet, of sonatina proportions, is of pops concert variety. (When will lighter chamber music be presented specifically for audiences who would enjoy and appreciate such music?)

The themes are well contrasted; they always sing. The harmony is tertial, at times modal. The final movement, with effective use of a viola pedal point, is a scherzo type. While Gibbs's *Miniature Quartet* is not based on folk song, it is a national type of music that breathes derivations from the English countryside.

- **String Quartet, Op. 73**

Gibbs's music for string quartet is gently romantic, adumbrated with folk-song feeling (though no folk material is used, even in developed form). Indeed, when a fugue occurs in this work, the feeling of the outdoors, of clarity, limpidity, and serenity stays with the four string instruments. There is no turn in the lane he walks that does not pass through cheerful countryside. This quartet exemplifies a serious composer writing lightly. In short, Gibbs represents the creation of English suburban music— he sings "Londonderry Air" types.

A neo-Mendelssohnian content is displayed in the first movement, including two contrasting thoughts, one more serious than the other, the first used at prologue, intermediary, and epilogue places. Cross-current form is used in the second movement. In this, intervallic fifths lead from impressionistic color to a swirling Scherzo, combined with a slower section (Andante moderato)—both the introduction and the Andante occur twice. In the last movement, an improvisatory section leads to a fugue, the former outlining the beginning of the fugue subject. Gibbs composes his quartet with care, craftsmanship, and attention to recreational temper.

- **Three Pieces for String Quartet**

England as seen by an English impressionist. No chromatic acerbities disturb the parallel movement in "Above Blea Tarn." As viewed, the waters flow andante, its splendor relating to a faster, more fiery, middle contrasting part. "Winster Valley" is matched by elongated, fivefold meter, the form matched as well by da capo restatement. "Loweswater: Calm after Storm—An Impression" is quietly disturbed by both murmuring pedal points and G-minor anxiety.

QUINTET

- *Peacock Pie:* Suite for Two Violins,
  Viola, Cello, and Piano

This folklike work is in the composer's usual light-mannered style. It is a derivative from the compositional school where the creative practice is in terms of romantic harmonies, modal connotations, and ease of performance. In reference to production, Gibbs thinks along very practical lines; a third violin may be substituted for the viola, a double bass may be used ad lib, and, furthermore, the suite may be played by a full-size string orchestra with piano.

The title is taken from Walter de la Mare's poems of the same name, and they are basic to the first and third movements. There is only some consideration toward relating a specific story. Gibbs's piano quintet, therefore, falls in the less determined class of program music. Still, the listener should have some inkling of Gibbs's music in relation to the subtitles so no false anticipation results. It is better to know that the inspiration of the first section ("The Huntsmen") is based on the lines:

Three jolly gentlemen,
In coats of red,
Rode their horses,
Up to bed.

rather than expect a wild Franckian *Le Chasseur maudit*! In Gibbs's case the jolly men of de la Mare evoke just as jolly a music.

The second movement ("The Sunken Garden") is from the same poet's *Motley:*

Speak not—whisper not;
Here bloweth thyme and bergamot.

Mutes help the whispering content of a romantic and semichromatic slow-paced movement. The final ("The Ride-by-Nights") is similar in temper to the opening movement and is not very feverish. The de la Mare lines that stimulate the music are:

Up on their brooms their Witches stream,
Crooked and black in the crescent's gleam;
One foot high, and one foot low,
Bearded, cloaked, and cowled, they go.

But these witches are nice ones, and fly about with moderate speed. The very nature of Gibbs is to be indulgent with his spirits. The music of

Peacock Pie is gentle throughout, whether speaking of happy horsemen or those who ride by the broom.

SEPTET

- ***The Enchanted Wood: A Dance Phantasy for Piano and Strings (Three Violins, Viola, and Two Cellos), Op. 25***

The above listing is one of two settings Gibbs made for his work, composed in 1919. The second scoring is for full string orchestra (in which the first of the three violin parts in the chamber version is indicated as a "solo" part) plus piano, with the solo designation also being applied to the keyboard instrument.

No forcing needed for designating this piece as programmatic, since the score is prefaced with a "Scenario." Accordingly: "On Midsummer Night the Enchanted Wood awakes from sleep under the spell of the Nightwind who first dances herself." Modal progressions lead to the first dance, a lightly faceted affair with much impetus assigned to the piano. The story continues: "Spurred on by her example, the flowers and grasses hold quiet carnival, and they are followed by the more boisterous revelry of the forest trees." Clear detail follows. The former is delineated by a quietly paced dance, the latter by the reverse, preluded by a short recitative section for the first violin. Gibbs's tale concludes: "At the first breath of the Dawnwind, the magic dissolves, and trees, grasses and flowers resume their natural state, and the Phantasy ends in the same atmosphere of unruffled calm with which it began." A violin line propped by chromatic harmonies leads into material used in the beginning of the piece, and triadic harmonies moving in contrary motion bring the piece to a close.

Gibilaro, Alfonso

DUO

- *Four Sicilian Miniatures* **for Oboe and Piano**

Partially an affirmation of program music, Gibilaro's opus has a good melodic voice and the pieces show this advantage. Neither virtuosic nor profound, they appeal because of their clarity and forthright descriptions.

The initial piece, "Capriccetto," "suggests happy children romping in the school playground." (It has abundant sixteenth-note patterns.) Movement two is "Song at Morning (Mattinata)." It vocalizes in triple beat throughout, with "guitar-like chords and musical figures suggestive of chirping birds and rustling leaves."

"Sicilian Wagoners (Notturnino)," Gibilaro states, "is based on an old folk tune." As a young boy in southern Sicily Gibilaro heard the principal melody "sung by Wagoners as they, and their beasts, slowly wended their weary way home after the day's toil in the scorching sun." (Note the use of the diminutive form for the secondary title, matching the reduced formal length of the opening movement.) The final part, "Sicilian Pipers," set in duple pulse, is also based on an old folk tune.

(Gibilaro later also made a version of the work for orchestra.)

Gibson, Robert (1947–)

DUO

- *Three Sketches* **for Flute and Guitar (1980)**

Short and picturesque. No academic sympathy here. Gibson's music is involved with articulated and angular rhythms and open-hearted

dissonance.

The first sketch is titled "Restless," but that quality appears within the "Plaintive" second piece, and is no less present in the "Capricious" finale. Two examples of the rhythmic polyphony in the last: cast in 12/8 time, the flute's line is split into 3–3–2–2–2 groups against the guitar in a 2–2–2–2–2–2 grouping, and in another measure the flute is divided into four basic pulses while the guitar is split into 3–2–2–2–3 rhythmic sets. This type of linear conflict is in the majority.

QUINTET

- **Quintet for Winds (Flute, Oboe, Clarinet, Horn, and Bassoon) (1974)**

A one-movement work of 4 1/2 minutes' length. It opens with a nine-pitch line in the oboe that is developed in free fashion. The chromatic shape of the opening spreads into every part of the piece, with frictional sound combinations and extremely tight polyrhythmic figurations. The result is an unrelaxed and thereby intense representation.

Gideon, Miriam (1906–)

DUOS

- *Fantasy on a Javanese Motive* **for Cello and Piano (1949)**

Building a composition on outside source material is not an uncommon practice among the creative fraternity. Of course, the borrower can become a sour sorrower if the raw stuff is not turned into artistic advantage.

Gideon ranges far for her basic substance, using a gamelan tune from Southeast Asia for her four-minute short story. The result is definitely to her advantage.

The motive is a pentatonic affair, its scalic

arrangement being A-sharp–B–D-sharp–E–F-sharp. It is heard in the cello line three times in succession at the start; the flanked statements are similar, the middle one is metrically changed. Simultaneously, the motive is expressed heterophonically by the piano. In a rhapsodic, improvisatory way, development follows, then the generative idea returns again for three connected presentations. The first of these has a fresh slant, the second and third match the initial pair announced at the beginning of the piece. Stylistically, the music remains Gideon's, though the piano "is used to achieve the sonorities of the gamelan orchestra."

- **Suite for Clarinet and Piano (1972)**

Three movements in the dissonant nontonal style of this composer. Though these can be mistaken as residing in dodecaphonic territory, Gideon's Suite has no identification with the *paradis artificiel* of serialism. There is a sense of Schoenbergian spikiness in the duo simply because it is intense in tone—representing the category of American expressionism most significantly.

Tempos of the pieces are contrasted, and a dynamic impetus pertains to the metrical condition. In movements one and two the time signatures mainly shift between duple and triple totals. This pulse progeneration moves into high gear in the Allegretto (third) piece. Beginning with a 15/16 time signature, there are forty-nine metrical changes in the total sixty-seven measures. Half of the latter have the sixteenth note as the unit for the time divisions, embracing totals of 7, 8, 9, 10, 11, 13, 15, and 17 within the bar lines. It is significant that only two of these eight patterns cover even-numbered computation.

- ***Three Biblical Masks* for Violin and Piano (1958)**

Gideon's *Masks* concern the three principal characters associated with the Jewish Purim holiday. This celebration commemorates the biblical tale relating to the rescue of the Jews of Persia from total slaughter. The plan for extermination had been made by Haman, the first minister of the king (Ahasuerus), who was defeated by the heroic strategy of the queen (Esther) and the wisdom of her uncle (Mordecai).

No programmatic pose, no picture-painting pedantry are to be found in these short pieces, set in atonal musical prose. These are sketches, not studies in depth. Nonetheless, the profiles are clearly etched by their individual content. (Though the movements are simply identified in the score as "Haman," "Esther," and "Mordecai," Gideon has indicated that the full titles are actually "The Crafty Haman," "The Gracious Queen Esther," and "The Noble Mordecai.")

A curled half-step motive is basic to the first part. Muted violin timbre with a lyrical objective is contrasted to scherzando character in part two. Chorale sections intersect the declamatory setting of the "Mordecai" movement. All of these are communicated with a mildly aggressive chromaticism pertinent to the composer's dissonant style.

(In a listing of works by this composer the main title—similar to the difference existent in the subtitles—is noted as *Three Masks*. Also, Gideon made a version of the duo for organ.)

QUARTETS

- **Quartet for Strings (Two Violins, Viola, and Cello) (1946)**

Continual varied juxtaposition—a type of plastic transformation—keys Gideon's string quartet. Powered by dissonant lines, the material has no reliance on garden-variety procedure. The music is distinguished by motival engenderment, constantly explicative as it constantly develops. In its disregard for literal repetition within each movement's essay the process is unconventional, but Gideon does not follow a crash course of disregard for architectural balance in bypassing dead-center formality.

Meter and tempo are the regulators in the first part. The Appassionato (in 2/4) twice alternates with a Scherzando (in 3/8), the latter at a speed almost twice as fast as the former. The slow movement, with shorter-length components, becomes agitated and then returns to the initial premise. An imaginative rondo frames the last movement. Coded, it stands as A–B–A–C–D–A–C–A. A different speed rate is used for the four contrastive episodes, the dominance of the principal refrain emphasized by being distinctly separative in quality and in the fastest tempo. The B portion is marked by connected line writing and is exactly half as fast as A. Episode D is a Vivo pointed up by its asymmetry, its progress one-sixth slower than A. Color and weight emphasize the two C sections. The instruments are muted in both instances, and with very minor exceptions the texture is only for two and three voices. In relationship to A the tempo is again changed, this time one-quarter slower.

Gideon's heteromorphic distribution distinctly defines the finale but does not splinter it. It is further proof of solid and sensitive craftsmanship. But, more importantly, the creative action is eloquent.

■ **Quartet for Woodwinds (Flute, Oboe, Clarinet, and Bassoon)**

Gideon's wind quartet is incisive music. It has direct, dispatched dissonance; a music minus any frailty. (Before women's lib one would have stated that this composer writes like a man. Let it stand. The important matter is that

Gideon turns out music of red-meat strength, so what point is there to sexual identity?) The document is validated by the final chord—one of spread minor seconds.

In the opening, syncopation is the contrasting agent for balancing the principal, biting statement. Tripartite division is used in the Andantino. Change is maintained there, matching the metrical shifts that dot the way. Full-spanned development is basic to the final movement.

Giefer, Willy

DUOS

■ **Cadenza for Alto Recorder and Piano (1970)**

This is music of free, improvisatory style, and gives the performers equal (and combined) time to exhibit technical brilliance. But, titlewise, not correct, in the sense that there are four movements; thus, Cadenzas would be closer to the formal truth of this piquant duo.

Giefer uses the avant-gardist's notational curves, zigzags, proportional ruling, frame notation, et al., for his unmetrical (i.e., freer-than-cadenza) music. All of this is at the service of a conscientious effort to obtain action and contrast, color and kaleidoscopic joinery. (Don't expect thematic statements.) Strong stuff that will, of course, sound different at each performance.

(Movement three is for solo recorder.)

■ **Improvisation for Violin and Piano (1966)**

Well, not exactly. Giefer's piece will sound like an improvisation, but everything is notated as to pitch. Durations, however, are in the realm of the haphazard, with pitches to be played as quickly as possible, graphic indication of sound lengths, and so forth. There is no rhythmic or metrical guide but a pictorialized quasi relationship between short and long rhythms.

Properly, the title should read in the plural, since there are two movements. This antithematic music thrives on timbre variety.

Gieseking, Walter (1895–1956)

QUARTET

- **Serenade for String Quartet**

Gieseking was a distinguished piano virtuoso, but he wrote most comfortably for string instruments in this thirteen-minute, three-part work. And wrote with considerable dynamic restraint.

The tonality of A major is used in the two outer movements. The opening one of the pair is optimistic, but makes its points quietly; the majority dynamics are *pianissimo* and *pianississimo,* with the conclusion beginning in *pianissimo* and continuing in a decrescendo. The final movement is a bit more extroverted, but nonetheless soft sounds are quite common. (Example: the initial six measures with the pizzicato background of the violins and cello as well as the bowed theme in the viola all in *pianissimo.*) Again, the concluding measures (fifteen in total) are set in the lowest dynamic zone. Movement two is a three-part Presto with rolling lines contrasted to a section that swings slowly and simply in 6/8 time. A literal return is then made to the Presto. Once more, the ending of the movement is pulled back dynamically, duplicating the first movement exactly: with a *pianissimo* start followed by a decrescendo.

Gieseler, Walter (1919–)

DUO

- *Five Episodes* **for Violin and Piano (1968)**

Clear and uncluttered pieces, free of themes, full of little ideas linked together and free of form. Gieseler's suite of nine minutes displays energy, even when the tempo reads otherwise. So, fidelity to total metrical elimination in the last three parts. Number three has groups that are tossed about "as fast as possible"; number four emphasizes long-sounding pitches hammered into with chordal nails; and cadenza spans cover the last of the set. The bits in the first piece are emphasized by tone-cluster punctuations; the second (slow-paced) episode chromaticizes a jagged line that spans four octaves.

Gil, José (1886–?)

DUO

- **Sonatina for Violin and Piano**

The saying goes that in every French composer there is one piece of Spanish music. Proof of such national neighborliness is successfully displayed, for example, in Debussy's *Iberia,* Ravel's *Rapsodie espagnole,* Chabrier's *España,* and Lalo's *Symphonie espagnole.* Some homegrown music lacks the cogent insight of such foreign stylistic trespassing. When a composer takes his native material and does not probe beyond the surface, it is raw imitation—really a forged national document. The action produces music with outline but not imagination; it is affected rather than effective.

Gil's composition is very close to such a product. It convinces only from the point of salon style, because of its use of skeletal folk material. In the Introducción there are south-of-the-border, semipopular rhythms. Serving for the middle part of the work is "Cielito" ("Little Heaven"), an Argentinian air in fast triple time. A Rondo containing the inevitable combine of double and trinal pulses is the form of the finale. Much more a suite than a sonatina, Gil's piece is satisfactory only as light music. It does not light up serious Argentinian music style.

Gilbert, Anthony (1934–)

DUO

- *The Incredible Flute Music* for Flute and Piano, Op. 11

Not an idle boast. Still, hype is not solely the province of commercial television. Accept the title as the decision of a blithe creative spirit whose choice of a heading for his composition will not harm the box office.

The stylistic fact is that this flute duo is another yield from the avant-garde crop. Colors galore: a unison on the flute to produce two different timbres, singing a sustained pitch (on A) through the instrument while simultaneously playing an assortment of thirty-four pitches, finger tremolo via the instrument's keys, special pitches *below* the lowest of the flute's range, and sounds that are a minor third *above* the highest possible on the flute. Less sound tinctures from the piano: a little bit of string plucking at the end of the work and a passage to be whistled. Otherwise, the piano writing can be categorized as "son of Stockhausen."

All this is fully believable music, extremely effective music, and exceedingly virtuosic music. The solo flute occupies front stage for the first half of the first movement and concludes the movement alone. The piano ushers in the second movement (Prestissimo). The pitch combinations and formal agenda fol-

lowed by the two instruments give a totality of sonorous splendor. It is combined with kaleidoscopic rhythms that bend and twist and never stay in place for a second. The quality is that of improvisationlike sonic doodlings, but supremely artistic ones.

Gillis, Don (1912–78)

Most of Gillis's best works are conceived with a light touch. Though he had composed in a serious manner, his greatest successes have been with music whimsically free, instrumentally comfortable (and knowledgeable). His chamber music might be termed buffa (minus farcical plotting but containing some humorous characteristics and often illustrative of cute characters). The humor in Gillis's work is straight to the point, but never ludicrous.

Recognizably stuffed with Americanese rhythms and melodic turns, most of his output is the result of tuning the tunes with harmonies. The contrapuntal side is given very little attention, and when it appears it is mostly of the animated harmonic type. This language fits the material. It also fits the implied programmatic slant of most of his music. (Gillis's ability to fashion a stimulating title is a special talent. An example: his *Symphony No. 5 1/2,* thus named because it was written between his fifth and sixth symphonic essays! Two of the subtitles of this work, with its play on formal designations, make obvious the sharpness of Gillis's wit: "Perpetual Emotion" and "Scherzophrenia.")

Such breeziness is a welcome voice, even though it may be (to some) an obvious one. We have yet to enjoy series of chamber music pops—a matter reserved solely for orchestral fare. (The Popular Concerts given in England in the 19th century—1,602 were presented!— were popular only in the sense of admission cost. The programs were the same as at full-dress concerts.) When it is recognized that there is a place for such presentations, the music of Don Gillis will offer a number of juicy possibilities.

TRIO

- *Silhouettes* **for Violin, Cello, and Piano**

Sectional disposition rules this piece, which industriously changes tempo (quite often from "slowly" to "suddenly fast") thirteen times before it concludes very softly. There is a sense of rondo disposition, but mainly fast-change moods rule Gillis's *Silhouettes*. Lightly brushed dissonance (Nicolas Slonimsky would use the adjective "nontoxic") colors this trio affair.

QUARTETS

- **Sonatina [No. 1] for Trumpet Quartet (1943)**

There is no arguing that four trumpets make a big-band-category sound. There is also no rebuttal of the fact that any four brass instruments (of single type or assorted) make a chamber music team. Q.E.D., Gillis's Sonatina belongs in the chamber music category.

The gay opening movement is filled with parallel triads and rhythmically parallel passages, plus interposed fanfarric sprays. Movement two is totally chordal, totally in slow tempo. A march-tempo conception completes the work. It is filled with Gillis's favorite parallel chromatic movement.

- **Sonatina No. 2 for Trumpet Quartet (1943)**

Contrasting tempos and parallel-fitting material (slow and marked by bare fifths, fast and jazzy) describe the opening movement of the Sonatina. Three-part design, with slow and martial speeds defining the sections, covers the middle movement. The metrical plan is basic to a quarter-note pulse but shifts, removing

squareness, though the music is enmeshed with Gillis's habitual parallel rhythmic constructions.

The rondo characteristic of the Finale is underlined by a number of tempo changes. Nothing somber here, although there is a bit of quasi nostalgia in the slow-paced passages. Otherwise all is spittingly bright, including a number of lip glissandos in the first trumpet part.

QUINTETS

- *The Fable of the Tortoise and the Hare:* **Suite No. 1 for Woodwind Quintet (1939)**

Three movements that offer the general aspects of the well-known tale. When the long-eared, rodentlike mammal is in full action, the music follows suit. When the terrestrial turtle moves, the music properly slows considerably.

"They're Off!" is bright and gay, bouncy, full of syncopative slyness. Three times the emphasis is shifted (by tempo and rhythmic simplicity) to the tortoise. "Br'er Rabbit Dreams" begins and ends slowly, the character bestirs himself only in the middle portion. The denouement, "And Mr. Tortoise Wins the Race," twice pictures the hare's opponent, with simple long–short rhythmic measures. This figure is intertwined with the fast music that depicts the contest.

- *Three Sketches:* **Suite No. 2 for Woodwind Quintet (1939)**

The first sketch, "Self-Portrait," delineates the composer as a warm person, a moderate extrovert. (For anyone who knew Gillis the likeness in tones is a true and honest one.) The music is ruled by mellifluous thirds. "Shadows" is slightly dark-mooded. Tempo changes in good number help create the proper atmosphere. There are a few hymnlike sections in the final sketch, "Sermonette (Southern Style)." The reply to these is like a religious-exultant congregational response of agreement. Otherwise, this five-instrument expostulation describes a peppy delivery from the pulpit, laced with jazzy syncopations.

- *Gone with the Woodwinds:* **Suite No. 3 for Woodwind Quintet (1939)**

Pre rock 'n roll styles fashion the three parts of Gillis's hedonistic suite. (His cleverness in choosing both apt and intriguing titles is also illustrated.) In "Five Piece Combo" small-dance-band elements are on tap: bouncy and bountiful rhythms, with grace notes spliced onto syncopations. Within this—a rondo-type setting—the instruments are colorfully displayed, especially the clarinet.

" 'Take Five' Blues" includes the "blue notes" (flatted tones) that earmark this form. Long and short glides plus incantatory parallel-motion passages help supply a melancholic quality to the music. The finale is "A Frolic in B-Bop Major." (The title contains a triple play on the word "bebop"; the "Bop" an aphaeresis of the full word, the "B" standing for the prefixal vocable, and the implication that "B-Bop" is a tonality—which it is not.) Ostinato figurations and a large amount of offbeat stresses give the requisite velocity to the conception. This is raw, but vivid, American music, professionally set forth.

Gilse, Jan van (1881–1944)

TRIO

- **Trio for Flute, Violin, and Viola (1927)**

Gilse's wind-string trio is of interlaced quality, has divertimento overtones, but in the greater part of the first two movements is somewhat thicker than average trio sonority. The first movement is sectional, marked off by differing treatment of the three instruments. The middle movement is an Alla marcia and is similarly formed in piecemeal divisions.

Contrapuntalism is the technique utilized for the concluding movement—by far the most interesting of all three. Its fugal form cultivates a spirited dance manner and has an exceedingly long subject, consisting of some twenty-three measures. The ternary design of the movement is codified by a total recapitulation of the fugue's exposition, however, with cleverness, turned completely upside down. Since the movement of all tones now goes in the exact opposite direction from the original presentation, both inner and outer balance is the resultant prize.

Gilson, Paul (1865–1942)

DUO

- *Romantische Werkjes (Romantic Pieces)* **for Clarinet (or Alto Saxophone) and Piano**

Gilson's reputation stems mainly from his talents as a teacher (Marcel Poot, one of the most important of the Belgian composers, was one of his pupils), music critic, and writer. In his book *Le Tutti orchestral* he exposes a unique viewpoint pertaining to scientific orchestration. His harmony treatise is valuable, though strongly advocating Wagnerian tenets.

The little suite for clarinet or saxophone (Gilson wrote a concerto for the latter instrument) is a concentrated example of his romantic diction. The Prelude is concerned with figurations and a long-spread line—one loosely expressive rather than carefully organized and balanced. Some of this characteristic is found in the Barcarolle and even in the strictly da capo-formationed Alla polacca. In Gilson's Belgian translation of the polonaise rhythm there are more repetitive patterns than are usually found.

Ginastera, Alberto (1916–83)

DUO

- **Duo for Flute and Oboe (1945)**

Use of sonata and fugue forms, together with a movement in choral style, represents Ginastera in neoclassic light. The wind-instrument duo begins with a decisive first subject, with longer time spans indicating the related theme. In the recapitulation not only do the instruments shift places but the principal theme's shape is also reversed—the initial set of descending fourths, followed by an ascendant fifth, is replaced by a rising set of fifths and a descending fourth. Precise balance, therefore, in regard to melodic shape and color. The Pastorale calmly flows in ternary form; the Fuga proceeds in regular order including the inevitable stretto.

QUARTETS

- **String Quartet No. 1, Op. 20**

This gives a vigorous view of the norms of Ginastera's art as applied to the field of chamber music. The composer's interest in and cultivation of folkloric musical style are illustrated here by two main facets: dance rhythms and contemplative, somewhat brooding song. The open-air quality of the finale and the wild initial movement represent the first; the deep-throated, extremely moving slow movement, the other. The initial and concluding movements burst with rhythms equating the pungent rhythmic drive that marks the malambo, the Argentinian dance that permeates a considerable part of Ginastera's early-period compositions. This folk pulsatile source is wound into the second movement as well, though in a softer dynamic manner.

The slow movement is also illustrative of Ginastera's acute color intuition. It is swept with harmonic glissandos, bariolage, and the rough-edge of ponticello. The writing is extremely effective.

- **String Quartet No. 2, Op. 26**

A quartet mostly of heated and intense musical prose, magical colors, and in some parts of terrifying power. There is no doubt that Ginastera's opus is of striking originality.

There are five movements, with the use of an arch form. Thus: two outer fast movements and a central Scherzo embracing a pair of slow movements. The tempo sequence and specifications show the composer's coloristic dramaticism in another (subtle) light: Allegro rustico–Adagio angoscioso (Slow and Anxiously)–Presto magico–Libero e rapsodico (Freely and Rhapsodic)–Furioso.

Sonata form is used in movement one; the hammered rhythms of this music that includes cross pulses is a Ginastera trademark. Movement two is in five sections. It reaches a frenzied climax in *fortississississimo,* but this quadruple *forte* is not sufficient. The players are to "accent greatly," and to play "desperately and with the greatest force." Movement three represents a Scherzo with two Trios. But that statement does not indicate the amazing sonorous emollients that principally clothe this music. It is to be played completely muted in one firm presto speed without a single accelerando or ritard throughout its 265 measures in 6/8 time. En route the sounds are produced on the fingerboard, close to the bridge, normally, bowed, plucked, tapped with the wooden part of the bow, glissandoed, vibratoed and not vibrated, detached and tremoloed (including in the latter category "the highest indeterminate nonharmonic pitch which can be produced"), and with combinations of these.

The fourth movement is a theme and three

variations. Each part is set as a cadenza for one instrument with supportive action from the others. The theme is for the first violin, variation one is for the cello, variation two is for the second violin (antiphony plays a major part in this portion), and the final variant spotlights the viola. More color here, with the use of quarter tones in the thematic statement. The finale (Furioso) begins in a frenzied manner and never deviates as it delivers a toccata document within partnered duple and triple metrical measurements.

QUINTETS

- *Impresiones de la Puna* for **Flute and String Quartet (1934)**

A prime example of Ginastera's early-period creative style—impressionism combined with Argentinian folk-music resources. The first movement of Ginastera's pictures of the high Andean plateau called Puna are imprinted by impressionism; the other two are dancelike, folk utterances, though the harmonies stem from the impressionistic school. It amounts, in total, to coloristic nationalism.

Movement one is titled "Quena," the term for the ancient (small-scaled in range) flute of the Incas; it is excellently imitated in this quintet by that instrument's modern representative. This first movement has the same light-factured characteristic of the entire work, which is scored in featherweight style. The flute plays alone in the second section of the strict three-part design; while sections one and three are a stylization of the only pentatonic tones the old flute could sound (though Ginastera's music is *not* pentatonic, as it will be realized).

The second movement, Canción (Song), has, likewise, the simplest formal equality; the easy swing of the outer, faster sections is in contrast to the metrically changed, slower melancholy song of the Andean Indians (called a yaraví) used in the middle. The Danza of the

last movement is cast in the Argentinian duple dance rhythm of the hueya (not so indicated by Ginastera, but there is no mistaking its steady outline). The slight darker tinge of this dance is mainly in the hands of the flute, the instrument that is highlighted in the entire quintet.

- **Quintet for Piano and String Quartet (1963)**

A colorful assortment is used in the seven movements, which includes three differently scored cadenzas, a nocturnal conception, and a Scherzo. The arrangement is detailed with exact balance.

Movement one is an Introduzione with banked tutti material in the strings dominating the music. The dynamic level begins sempre triple *forte,* stays that way (Ginastera reminds the performers he wishes "the fullest force" and later that they play "il più fortissimo possible"). After a high point is reached (marked "exalted") the dynamic weight lessens continually until the music ends *pianississississimo.* Movement three is a dazzling "Scherzo fantastico"; the strings are muted, the qualities all dynamically smothered in a constant triple *piano,* the effect mysterious; the reaction chills the blood. Movement five is a "Piccola musica notturna," a mix of expressivity, bell sounds, and hard-core, impressionistically thrusted sonorities. Movement seven is a Finale that reverses the dynamic plan of movement one. Here, in precipitous tempo with a belted-in perpetual-motion quality, the music begins *pppp* and mounts to a thunderous outpour of *ffff.* Accompanying all of this is a sense of savagery. It is fully declared in the final twelve-tone cluster, spread over two octaves, consisting of packed sixteen-voice chords, repeated thirteen times, all to be played "violentemente."

Between these four movements are cadenzas. The first one is for viola and cello, the second is for the two violins, and the third of the set is for piano. The last is a real concerto depiction, beginning with loud and dramatic intensity, but to be heard with rubato fluidity, and ending with the sounds projected as fast as possible.

Gipps, Ruth (1921–)

DUO

- **Sonatina for Horn and Piano, Op. 56**

Triadic harmony reigns supreme in Gipps's music. The parallelisms will remind one of Vaughan Williams, with whom she studied. But these are much simpler—which doesn't nullify their validity. The forms are distinct and fitting, with modified sonata design in the first movement and a Minuet that follows. Slight metrical shifts are in the former, none, of course, in the latter.

Variations on a Ground serves as the finale. No deviations in this case, save three extra 5/4 measures to end the piece. Otherwise the ground bass is static: four measures in total (three in 4/4, one in 3/4). Fourteen permutations are displayed, and not until the thirteenth is the bass changed from its undeviating progress. It is then transferred to the soprano region. Variations on a ground bass are to be at the composer's will. Gipps's will is not only well grounded but produces well-formed music. Its roots in the past are apparent. One is not taken aback by such traditional response.

Girnatis, Walter (1894–)

DUOS

- **Sonata for Oboe and Piano**

Girnatis is a romanticist, and thus the materials of his Sonata are fundamentally consonant. But he does not avoid chromatic stuff and

substance to color and expand his syntax. In the Moderato the lines constantly move into and away from G major, concluding in a broad final cadence in the G tonality. In the Allegro scherzando the same principal applies, but the music ends with a sure-fire Presto with a tonic ninth signature.

Movement two is a simply phrased Andantino, spotlighting the oboe. The harmonic content is fifthy and with plentiful octave pedal points.

- **Sonatina for Cello and Piano**

Pleasantly effective romantic music. But not noisily accomplished. Sextuplet groupings propel the first movement. The Arietta is the full property of the cello, with piano arpeggios propping the material. A peppy Rondino rounds out matters. A convincing to-the-point duo of about seven-minute length.

- **Sonatine for Alto Saxophone and Piano**

Clear actions with romantic elan. The forms are almost duplicates of this composer's Sonatina for Cello and Piano (*see above*), with an opening fast movement, an Arietta, and a Rondino. A one-measure Grave and an extension to two measures at the conclusion bind the sonata-detailed Allegro. Marked rhythmic flow punctuates the Arietta, and pulsatile drive gives choreographic delineation to the final Rondino.

Girón, Arsenio (1932–)

QUARTET

- **Quartet for Flute, Clarinet, Viola, and Piano (1963)**

The panchromatic style of this composer is set forth in music of a tense aspect. The sounds are always on the move; there is an overall restlessness. It carries over to the three movements: Allegro, Largo, and Presto, which are to follow each other without pause. The music of the middle movement begins with piano alone and in vertical arrangement, but it soon crosses into the linear area that consistently marks this Quartet that combines wind, string, and keyboard timbres. And that area certainly is very busy.

QUINTETS

- *Disparities and Differences* **for Brass Quintet (Two Trumpets, Horn, Trombone, and Tuba) (1968)**

The motto for the work is "The disparities and differences [of men]—North," and the music lives up to this thoroughly.

Dissimilarity results from an instrument breaking away in accelerando or falling back in ritarded tempo while the others proceed in regular, measured detail. The first of these loosened lines is by the muted second trumpet. It plays slower than the others and ultimately reenters the ensemble. The second resultant two-dimensional effect is obtained by the trombone, which plays faster than the others—completing its three-measure phrase, it joins the others. And so on.

The "four-against-one" tempo differentiation marks a partial aleatoric process since pitches and rhythms are defined by the composer. Further, varied tempos for the ensemble are used in one section where the instrumental lines may be played in any order. And still further, another portion is to be performed at a very fast pace, but not all the instruments are to play at the same tempo. All these portray the "disparities" and the "differences." Otherwise, normal chromatic detail, in free-formed continuity, applies.

- *Vias* **for Flute, Clarinet, Cello, Piano, and Percussion (Vibraphone, Glockenspiel, Xylophone, Two Suspended Cymbals, Two Drums, and Five Temple Blocks)**

Panchromatic diction covers the two movements. Girón is a composer of solid sound details. There are no shock tactics. The materials function in an unrepetitive manner, unfold in wide arcs, are vividly disjunct, maintaining a type of rhapsodic continuity in the first part, which is in slow tempo. The second part is opposite: fast in tempo and concentrated in its pitch movement.

The percussion occasionally is used as a doubling agent. Other times it punctuates with an ictus or rhythmically fills an opening. However, for the greater part it functions as an equal voice with the wind, string, and keyboard instruments. A special percussion color detail is the sounding of a block of vibrational sound (a three-part chord on the vibraphone, for example) into which another timbre enters (a glockenspiel phrase, for example).

SEXTET

- **Sextet for Winds (Flute, Oboe, Clarinet, Bassoon, Horn) and Trumpet**

A two-movement work (Adagio and Allegro) scored for the standard wind quintet plus trumpet. Girón's panchromatic syntax is dynamic and styled tightly. And so are the tempos. There isn't a single accelerando or ritard in the music. Registral changes are constant, with many successive augmented and diminished intervals. Sevenths and ninths tone the material with their stresses.

Giuffre, Jimmy (1921–)

SEPTET

- *Naiades* for Clarinet Choir (E-flat Clarinet, Three B-flat Clarinets, Alto Clarinet, Bass Clarinet, and E-flat Contrabass Clarinet) (1969)

Giuffre's conception of nymphs is mainly of translucent homophonic progress. Twice a section marked "Chant" of total septuple-voice matrix is inserted after measures containing rich tonal material, itself much favoring block harmony. Short and sweet music, but always a tasteful music.

Giuliani, Mauro (1781–1829)

DUOS

- Divertimento for Flute (or Violin) and Guitar

An extremely odd title since Giuliani's Divertimento consists of a single movement in allegretto tempo. Pace and pulse, construction and concept, equate a minuet.

- Grosse (Grand) Serenade for Flute (or Violin) and Guitar, Op. 82

One of the very best (certainly the most important) of the compositions written by this Italian guitar virtuoso. Though no particularly strong personality is evidenced, there is craftsmanship and music of average merit.

Movement one (Grazioso) consists of a theme and three variations. The first of these features the guitar, the second and third, the flute. A Menuetto follows, its Trio a charming chordal conception. Virtuosity stands out in the sizable third movement. A majestic Marcia, exactly in balance with a Trio and recapitula-

tion, completes the duo.

- Grosse (Grand) Sonata for Flute (or Violin) and Guitar, Op. 85

Considerable motility throughout the four movements, but there is a bright and airy quality to the materials, especially in the Allegro maestoso. Movement two is slow paced, a Scherzo follows, and the opus has a relaxed final movement marked Allegretto espressivo.

Equality in the scoring. The writing for the instruments has a slightly virtuosic demeanor.

- Theme, Variations, and Minuet for Flute and Guitar

No pat give-and-take in the four variations. Plenty of action for both instruments in all of them, including the slower-tempo third variant. The Minuet is colored with consecutive thirds and pitch repetition by the guitar. No real depth to this music, but neither are there any dull moments.

Glagolev, Yuri (1926–)

DUO

- Sonata for Violin and Piano

Classical balance is followed, with D-minor keying movement one and the music ending in the major mode. The relative minor of the latter is used for the central movement, and D major is the tonality for the Finale. The syntax is romantic and the textures are strong and full. In these terms everything is integrated and provides a totally persuasive account.

There is no neutral standoffishness in Glagolev's writing. The materials modulate, and this influences the phrases, which are enlarged and never lapse into squared measurement. Only in the dance pulse of the last movement does the music stay in place. Whatever, nothing in this duo is fussy.

Glanville-Hicks, Peggy (1912–)

DUOS

- Sonata for Piano and Percussion (Timpani, Xylophone, Small, Medium, and Large Gongs, Tam-tam, Cymbal, Two Tom-toms, Bass Drum, and Snare Drum) (1952)

The percussion instruments are used in various ways: in taking the lead, supporting, counterpointing, giving antiphonal response, and as solo voices. The music has an Eastern flavor.

    Movement one is made up of simple tunelets and snips of motives. A consistent use of a gapped scale brings the effect of a Javanese orchestra. In the haunting middle movement there are large chunks of repeated chords, a good supply of arpeggios, and the oriental simulation that results from use of augmented intervals. Repetitive patterns are emphasized in the final movement. Its concluding measures provide a very incisive climax. Loud it is, but never cheap.

- Sonatina for Treble Recorder (or Flute) and Piano

Nicely adjusted and splendidly structured music. Glanville-Hicks avoids two of the cardinal sins: verbosity and imbalance.

    The three movements are sensitively balanced and properly differentiated. Movement one has pandiatonic prose with some parenthetical use of polyharmonies. In the Lento recitativo pure and limpid modality is used. Quartal harmony is the chief element in the final part of the duo.

    The scoring takes care of the "Mutt and Jeff" difference that exists between the undernourished, though sweet, tone of the vertical flute and the stable strength of the piano. In total, the work illustrates the use of classic disciplines blended with impressionistic interpretations.

TRIOS

- Trios Nos. 1 and 2 for Pipes (Treble in D, Alto in G or A, and Tenor in D)

Both are slow-tempo pieces, the second much more so. Three-part form for number one, binary design for the other. Warm and simple, nicely listenable music.

QUARTET

- Concertino da camera for Flute, Clarinet, Bassoon, and Piano (1946)

Music that caresses the ear with its nicely colored ideas and filamented textures. The surfaces are crystal clear; the style and disposition are typically Gallic.

    The tempo headings are Allegretto, Adagio, and Allegro for the Finale. Seconds, fifths, and consecutive triads in the last; neat use of alternative scoring (the three winds responded to by the piano) in the central movement.

Glaser, Werner Wolf (1910–)

DUO

- Six Pieces for Soprano Recorder and Piano

Capsule-size pieces, bare and primitive—illustrating a kind of naked Hindemith style by this German-born Swedish composer. There is little use of accidentalized pitches—none at all in number six, a single B-flat in number five.

Glass, Louis (1864–1936)

QUARTET

- **String Quartet No. 4 in F-sharp Minor, Op. 35**

A pupil of Gade's (*q.v.*), Glass writes in a chromatic style. But it is not the chromaticism of Reger's tonality viewpoint, nor does it have the flavoring purposes sought by composers of the classical school; rather, it is somewhat akin to the tonal sideslips and shifts of Franck and his disciples. It mixes the musical grammar to such an extent that at times it is folklike, and then modulates into Franckian dialect.

In this quartet, there will be heard the mintage of certain Danish folk qualities (not especially demarked by definite characteristics, such as to enable one to identify Spanish, Italian, or English folk tunes, but by an "open-air" dance quality moving in simple rhythms) which are evident in the Trio to the Scherzo movement and in many parts of the finale. Otherwise, the forms are designated in usual proportions. Especially to be noticed are the excellent means of supplying density contrasts by scoring which drops one or two instruments from the ensemble, with entire sections laid out in two or three voices. Such juggling probes the essential values of juxtaposing musical weights. A plan of blocklike quarter notes contrasted to a type of grace-note rhythm livens the Scherzo. The last movement is most specifically Danish in its style.

Glass, Philip (1937–)

SEXTET

- **Brass Sextet (Two Trumpets, Two Horns, Trombone, and Tuba)**

(Some substitutions are available: baritone or tenor saxophone for the second horn; bassoon or a second trombone for the tuba.)

This is Glass prior to his meeting up with Hindu ragas, North African melorhythms, and minimalism—the technique acutely described by Nicolas Slonimsky as "merciless, relentless, unremitting homophony." This is Glass as he wrote in the early 1960s: tame, tonal, tuny music. Movement one is a vertically disposed Hymn. The Ballad has more harmonic movement. There is some rhythmic zing in the Finale.

Glasser, Stanley (1926–)

TRIO

- **Trio for Two Trumpets and Trombone (1958)**

Pleasant entertainment in this set of three pieces. Each is cleanly scored and each is deftly constructed. The first of the set (Ruvido) emphasizes counterpoint on a two-to-one basis: paired instruments in the same rhythm, the other instrument moving against the twosome. In the Lamentoso a trinal apportionment is hinted at by the use of muted timbre in the outer sections and unmuted sounds in the center. The Semplice tempo heading of the final part defines pointed themes, rhythmic vigor, and all framed by pandiatonic diction.

QUARTET

- **Three Dances for Four Trombones (1961)**

Sectional apportionment is used here. Little is repeated save in the second dance of the set. Sufficient natural vitality (plus that which is supplied by the timbre of the big brass instrument) to sustain interest. That said, the point is made that none of the three parts of the work are in slow speed.

Glazer, Stuart (1945–)

DUO

- **Duo for Clarinet (or Soprano Saxophone) and Percussion (Bongos, Temple Blocks, Small Suspended Cymbal, Medium Suspended Cymbal, and Vibraphone) (1975)**

Fresh inventive feeling based on twelve-tone procedures, but not so rigid as to interfere with colorful and interesting detail. Sonata form is used in the first of the pair of movements. Some free metrical depiction in the percussion occurs in the development portion. This "Slow and expressive" music is contrasted to fast-tempo music set in tripartite form.

Glazer's piece (just under seven minutes in length) shows a modest personality but one that proves he has fluency.

(The score indicates that the piece may be performed by three players—meaning, of course, a division of the percussion detail. Interestingly, all the percussion instruments are to be played with soft mallets.)

Glazunov, Alexander (1865–1936)

See also under **Collaborative Composers**

Jour de fête
Les Vendredis: Set I
Les Vendredis: Set II
Quartet sur le nom B–La–F
Variations sur un thème populaire russe

Glazunov can be considered one of the most important of the pre-Soviet group of composers who continued their work after the Revolution. Such composers forged a chain to the present-day creators, a majority of whom have continued, in turn, to add additional links by drawing on the large reservoir of folk materials that abound in the Soviet Union.

Glazunov had an affinity to Mendelssohn, not in terms of aesthetic but in regard to a relaxed, well-to-do existence, and a composite of serenity and favorably disposed friends. As a result, his music kept straight on the tracks of specific form. Glazunov never attempted one change in compositional practices. While this unexperimentalism is not extraordinary, specialness described his personal status. Few composers are wealthy, few can sit back without need to battle in the art arenas for recognition and essential financial returns. While this does not interfere with affirmative creation, it can waylay productivity. But, in terms of output, Glazunov is not found wanting. His total of works refutes any question of laziness; it includes eight symphonies, over three dozen orchestral compositions, three ballets, and seven full-scale string quartets, plus two suites and a number of smaller pieces for the same medium. No opera was composed—Glazunov's concentration was on instrumental soundness.

The main features of his work are an unfailing melodic gift and an assured hand at interlocking the instrumental voices. In other words, his scoring, either for four strings or a robust symphonic group, is sure-fire, well sounding, well proportioned, and of brilliant logic. In chamber music, he is one of the most outstanding of the Russian composers. Though his works are not the masterpieces of a Beethoven, a Brahms, or a Ravel, they form a part of the repertory. There has never been doubt as to their worth.

QUARTETS

- ***Elegy (in Memory of M. P. Belaiev)* for String Quartet, Op. 105**

There was more than a patron-musician relationship between Glazunov and the much older Belaiev, truly called the Maecenas of Russian music. (For a discussion that includes the work of Belaiev *see above,* under *Collaborative Composers.*) Between the two men there was the bond of enduring friendship, from the day they met until Belaiev's death in 1904.

Glazunov honored his friend in many compositions: one movement in the quartet celebrating Belaiev's birthday (*Jour de fête*), two pieces in the *Les Vendredis* collection plus another written jointly with two other composers, one of the variations in the *Variations on a Popular Russian Theme* dedicated to Belaiev, together with the composition of the final movement in the *Quartet on the Name B–La–F.* (All these compositions are discussed *above,* under *Collaborative Composers.*) In addition, there is the isolated *Fugato on the Name B–La–F* that Glazunov composed in 1887.

And honor continued long after Belaiev's death. In 1928 Glazunov wrote this *Elegy,* memorializing Belaiev in music for performance at a gathering in Leningrad that commemorated the twenty-fifth anniversary of Belaiev's death.

The music is in constant motion until it bursts into an Agitato. It then subsides, and the ending is an Alla marcia funebre. Belaiev's name is delineated by the viola (with the pitches B-flat–A–F), in repetitive use forming the upper part of the chords supporting the funereal march theme.

■ **Five Novellettes for String Quartet, Op. 15**

Lighter pieces have their place in the scheme of chamber music, but, while many are written, few are chosen. One of the most important works in this category is represented in this instance.

The usual definition of a novellette is a short piece in rather free form, but here the generic noun of the title means a bit more than a miscellaneous set of short pieces. There is something of an affinity between all the movements, save one, in that they are dances—a type of ballet presentation by way of string quartet music. The forms of these four movements are the simplest: rondo types, set in a ternary idea of contrast in between repetitions of a main point.

The first piece is "Alla spagnuola" ("In the Spanish Style") using the demarcation of long–short, and short–long rhythms over constant ostinatos. The contrasting lyrical theme, however, is more Slavic than Spanish. The same excitement is obtained in the "Orientale" by the use of reiterative rhythmic patterns, further enlivened by combining duplets and triplets—a tried-and-true means of exciting the rhythmic facet of music. The dance is rude and vigorous. The fourth movement, titled Valse, embraces more than one waltz. Similar to a Johann Strauss orchestral waltz, this section is a set of several waltz tunes bound into one. "All' ungherese" ("In the Hungarian Style"), which completes the work, is also concerned consistently with pedal points, used not only for dance-style purposes (which require rhythm as a lifeline) but because Glazunov was in love with such a technical device in *all* of his works. The shifts of slow and fast speeds, the rubatos, the augmented scale step so patently illustrative of popular Hungarian Gypsy style are imitated nicely, even to a final cadence that dims into diminuendo on a bare intervallic fifth.

The only serious movement is the "Interludium in Modo Antico" ("Interlude in Ancient Mode"). This is a haunting and beautifully expressed slow movement, using D as the polar point in a section devoid of any chromatics, save an occasional F-sharp which changes, momentarily, the modal-archaic writing, innocent of romantic lineage. Thus, the use of the lone sharpened pitch serves not only as contrast but as a transitory modulation from an ancient mode to a modern tonality. The scoring is organic and *like* an organ, with special effect obtained by muting the three upper strings to permit the cello to sing, in the final section, a song derived from the Greek Orthodox liturgy. The Novelettes remain the most widely known of this composer's chamber music, and the "Interludium," especially, has become standard encore fare.

(Gerald Abraham, the erudite English writer on music, has indicated that Glazunov's Five Novellettes were first titled Suite. After the first performance of the work, the change in title was made at the suggestion of Hans von Bülow.)

▪ *In modo religioso* for Trumpet, Horn, and Two Trombones, Op. 38

Introspective, formulated on chorale precepts that give a full romantic cast to the music. Thematically, Glazunov's *In Religious Mood* consists of a single strand shifting between the instruments as it proceeds in E-flat major throughout ninety-three triple-pulse measures in andante tempo.

There are several editions of this composition, public-domain procedures being what they are. As a result it is not easy to recognize the original version. The edition made by Robert King (published by the Robert King Music Co.) enlarges the total to a brass choir, with undefined multiple players on each original single part. In so doing, King sets the single second trombone to be doubled in constant octaves. Other changes and substitutions are offered: the cornet is to be used rather than the trumpet, the cornet joins with or replaces the horn, in turn the horn plays with the first trombone or replaces it, and for Glazunov's second trombone the octave doublings are to be played by "baritones and tubas" with trombone added or substituted at will. A quartet of chamber music quality becomes thereby a brassy tribe.

Commercial method also dictates the edition made by Emil Kahn, though in this case,

the quartet total is maintained. In place of the four brass, three clarinets and bass clarinet are offered. Further, in place of the horn, a second trumpet may be used. The last is the least offensive decision. To the publisher's credit (Edward B. Marks) the parts that equal Glazunov's original are so marked.

▪ Saxophone Quartet (Soprano, Alto, Tenor, and Baritone Saxophones) in B-flat Major, Op. 109

Glazunov lived in France for the last eight years of his life. It was there that he wrote his only works for saxophone: a concerto and this quartet; the latter composed in 1932 in Paris.

The heart of the work is the central movement: Canzona variée. The theme is a Kremlinesque modal melody followed by five variations of which the first two are chordal and of the same length as the theme (forty measures in 2/2 time). The next pair are stylistic simulations: "A la Schumann" and "A la Chopin"; the former scalic and exceedingly ornamental, the other a poetic, barcarollelike affair. The final variation is a spitting Scherzo in presto speed, containing a constant spray of quarter notes. It covers over two hundred measures and in the latter part of the variation moves into prestissimo tempo.

A rich, romantic Russian text fills the first movement. Solid textural totals stock the measures. The Finale is no less weighty, but the contents have a French-style sparkle.

▪ String Quartet No. 1 in D Major, Op. 1

Glazunov's first quartet for strings was written at the age of 17. The control exhibited proves he was far ahead of his opus designation. Little, if any, creative adolescence shows.

The introduction (Andantino moderato) has a pithy subject with the rise of a second and a fourth as its "head." It provides the elements for the first movement proper (Allegro moderato). Fugato and development follow, with plenty of the ostinato absorptions that mark Glazunov's later works. The introduction returns in changed manner. In its recapitulation it is soft in place of loud, flowing instead of detached, and of different tonality. The coda is integrated, being based on the second subject of the movement.

The remaining three movements are a Scherzo (minus the customary Trio), an Andante (concentrated in its monothematic status), and a Finale (decidedly Russian in its melos). All three movements are coherently constituted, though there is more invention in the last of these movements. (Originally, Glazunov completed his Op. 1 with a fugue. He rejected it, replacing it with more fitting, less formally constricted music.)

- **String Quartet No. 2 in F Major, Op. 10**

There are, generally, fundamental characteristics of a composer's work that form a tied relay throughout the course of his entire output, from the early compositions to the later ones. Glazunov is no exception. This second work for string quartet displays the technical facility and ability of the man—a nonchalance that emits a polished prose with balanced emotional appeal and the posting of the general manifestations of classical form. And the habits that Glazunov formed early in his career also show in this quartet, especially in the finale with its dominating first violin in sopra position declaring itself technically and in somewhat virtuosic style. Similarly, in the richly larded slow movement (Adagio molto), with the very average means of two contrasting themes. Of such is this Russian's music—simple to understand and hear, not voicing any curiosity at all.

Of the first two movements, the second (Scherzo) is most charged with rhythmic interest; it is built on the union of two eighth notes working themselves in between the fastening

of the triple pulse, inflicting, as it were, a syncopation on the bond of the rhythm. (The metrical effect is one measure of 3/4 followed by one of 3/8.) After the slower-paced Trio, a return is made to the faster (initial) tempo, followed by a lengthy coda, which merely repeats previous material but with more vigor and the seasoning of thicker sonorities by pedal points—a technique Glazunov will often use.

- ***Quatuor slave (Slavonic Quartet):* String Quartet No. 3 in G Major, Op. 26**

Glazunov's penchant for the insinuation of programmaticism, as well as interlining the chamber music apparatus with the richer oil of the orchestra, is to be noticed in this vigorous four-movement quartet. The use of titles (in this case, in the last three sections) causes no comment. But the unrefuted textural poundage of this quartet's last movement has been criticized.

How to define musical thickness? It does happen here that instruments combine in triple stops and the like, more than doubling the four voices into octaval proportions. Compositional stability demands that textures be proportionate to the basic idea. If they are, the design benefits; if they are not, then the music is overthick, overladen. The countercharge could well be that chamber music ideas should be expurgated if they must, of necessity, be expressed with a supply of huge sound. To this the reply, By what law? The last movement *is* orchestral (the composer later did make a symphonic setting but never withdrew his original version!), but its rondo style, no more than a choice of dance portions, sustains the title— "Une Fête slave" ("A Slavonic Festival"). (It continues for a long time, however.)

The first of the previous movements is in ordained sonata form, but somewhat concentrated, with the Russian (or Slavonic) flavor most apparent. The Interludium is choralelike; the Alla mazurka is in moderate triple time, but is more a gentle exposition of a choreographic scherzo than the Polish dance the composer used as a guide to his thoughts.

- **String Quartet No. 4 in A Minor, Op. 64**

The connective link of thematic transference (rare to this composer) is used practically throughout the entire composition. This means of unification is at times most apparent, at other times it requires an analytical cross-check of the score pages. The boldest (and simplest, therefore) use occurs at the very beginning, where a slow and fairly long introduction is requisitioned for the Allegro proper.

The slow movement as well as the Finale clings tenaciously to the coat-tails of constant articulation and continual use of the four instruments. This forms a retrogression because of the constant preoccupation with moving all the voices, advancing all ideas, in quadruple interlocution. Too many people inhabit the houses of these movements. The Scherzo, exceedingly long, is a whirlwind of velocity, producing a kineticism that is highly exciting and is a delightful excursion for the performer or listener who would like some Paganini in his quartet diet. At first the Scherzo's accents refuse to be regular, appearing at all points in the duple-pulse measures. Thereafter, they perform regular functions.

- **String Quartet No. 5 in D Minor, Op. 70**

Glazunov composed this quartet as gainful rest from the labor on his *Raymonda,* a work in the usual three acts of early Russian ballets, occupying a complete evening's entertainment. (For a composer of Glazunov's ability, creating music for ballet was not even a challenge.)

Classic utilities dictate the form of this fifth quartet, dedicated to Leopold Auer (1845–1930), the famous teacher of concert violinists, including Mischa Elman and Jascha Heifetz (himself a quartet player for a period of time in

an organization bearing his name). D minor, the tonality of the first movement, is balanced by the usual shift to the like-named major key for the last movement. The latter is gay, brilliant, the first violin working mightily. The opening movement begins contrapuntally, then shifts into higher-geared speed, using the same thematic material.

The Scherzo is patterned on familiar models. The main body is in B-flat major, set in the usual triple pulse, with Allegretto as the tempo. The Trio section is in the submediant tonality and is less active tempowise and rhythmically. The coda moves into Presto tempo and then puts on the brakes for the concluding measures. The slow movement—marked Adagio (con licenza)—is introspective, formulated on rubato precepts in keeping with the tempo direction "with some liberty." The result is a full romantic cast to the music's direction.

- **String Quartet No. 6 in B-flat Major, Op. 106**

As Glazunov continued to add to his prolific catalogue no contemporary thought infiltrated. His Op. 106 string quartet was composed in 1921 but does not fundamentally differ from the two previous quartets, written respectively in 1894 and 1899.

The opening movement is of solid sonority. There is economy in the use of the working substances. All the voices are kept in motion, often performing a simulated manner of counterpoint, but of harmonic detail not of polyphonic proportion. Compared to the earlier quartets the sixth quartet is exceedingly chromatic, especially in the plaintive slow movement (Andante piangevole). Further, both in the first (Allegro) and third (slow) movements there is an absence of the otherwise constantly favored ostinato method. The emphasis is on lyrical rapport.

The knitted textural quality is maintained in the "Intermezzo in the Russian Style" (the translation indicated in the printed score; another writer has noted the title as "Intermezzo rusticano"). It is devoted to a sparkling, juggled rhythm with most of the 8/8 measures in triple-patterned groups of 3/8–2/8–3/8. A set of variations completes the quartet. The tenth of these serves as a finale within the finale. It is in ternary build plus coda.

- ### String Quartet No. 7 in C Major, Op. 107

Glazunov's final string quartet is in four movements, each bearing a specific title. It differs greatly from his previous quartet. The classical stability of Op. 106 is replaced by suitelike extroverted writing and results in the use of Glazunov's favorite chord-packed scoring and wholesale ostinatos. Indeed, as the Slavic modal ecstasies, processional chants, and sounds of simulated bells pass in review, it would seem that although he was writing in Paris, the composer's thoughts were totally of his native Russia.

Chromaticism and its traveling companion, key change (there are six such major tonality shifts), are emphasized in the second movement, "Breath of Spring." Special timbre quality, by the use of mutes in the outer sections, with unmuted color together with change of character in the middle part, marks the third (scherzo-proposed) movement, "In the Mysterious Forest." Glazunov handles the quartet apparatus in this division with Mendelssohnian deftness.

Movement one ("Reminiscence of the Past") begins with an Adagio in contrapuntal (fugato) alignment. This generates the first of the pair of themes in the major part of the movement (Allegro). These themes undergo development in piecemeal fashion with growth made by change rather than by thematic argument and disclosure. Modal harmony is basic to both this movement and the final one, titled "Russian Festival." The unison opening clues the kind of

music to follow. It is full-scale music of celebration, sturdily scored, climaxed with fervent twelve-part chords for the four instruments.

- ### Suite for String Quartet, Op. 35

Though the subject material of this quartet is generally light, its length is Tolstoyan. The corpus of the five movements is also plated with interlocked relationships; the final movement is like a short suite in itself; the fourth movement is treated similarly as a midget form in a suite with variational positivism. But Glazunov does not make thunderbolts in his musical sky. His string quartet Suite contains the milder materials of entertainment, served up almost with sugary themes, but all palatable, toothsome, and light. This is devised with rhythms that are more keystoned to heavy chamber music and a blend of the Russian melos festooning all of this composer's output.

The opening (Introduction and Fugue) is by far the most serious section of the whole. But profound as Glazunov may be, his textures in this work are lighter than those used by composers such as Brahms or Dvořák, with whom he may be compared. The two portions are closely related (the fugue subject follows, sound for sound, the theme of the introduction, though altered rhythmically). On the other hand, the two parts' metrical, tempo, and color horizons are altered; in turn: quadruple and duple, slow and moderately fast, muted and unmuted. The home key of C major is set forth most definitely, with assorted coloring chromatic pitches. Then follows a Scherzo, quite long in itself, and formed from the contrast of brighter keys in the center in relation to the main tonality (F major). There is no fussiness in the writing, but there are redundant ostinatos, a favorite cliché of Glazunov's. An "Orientale" (likewise an idea used in the other suite Glazunov wrote for quartet—*Five Novellettes* [*see above*]) forms the third movement. It is Tartaric and sonorous but is also belabored with repetitive rhythmics.

A theme with five variations forms the penultimate section, with each variation in set character delineation—Tranquillo (as flowing as the theme itself); Mistico (aided by subdued coloring and the use of tremolando); a Scherzo (wherein, as in all other sections, the theme is easily identified—Glazunov merely transforms his theme and refuses to follow variational obliteration); Pensieroso (quasi imitative, engendering a contemplative mood), which has the slowest pace of all the variants; followed by an Alla polacca with restless pulse, yet pinioned to the characterization of polonaise rhythm. The final movement (Valse) consists of four distinct waltzes and then a return to the first two, followed by a long coda. The myriad activity and change merely point up the essential diversional aspects of the entire work.

Glick, Srul Irving (1934–)

DUO

■ *Suite hébraïque No. 1* **for Clarinet and Piano (1963)**

When published in 1968, Glick's work did not bear a numerical identification. However, he has since specified the use of the number to clarify the composition's place in the sequence of others bearing the same title, each for a different combination. As of this date of writing, No. 2 of the series is for clarinet, violin, viola, cello, and piano; No. 3 is scored for string quartet; No. 4 calls for alto saxophone or clarinet or viola and piano; and No. 5 is for flute, clarinet, violin, and cello.

The work under discussion is represented in two other settings. Originally for orchestra (written in 1961), a version for string quartet was made in 1964. While both of these are colorfully viable, the choice of the clarinet timbre is especially depictive for the tradi-

tional Hebraic idiom that soaks the work.

Though the six movements (three of which are dances) are simple in content, there is a passionate veracity to the music's style. In the Cantorial Chant the process of cantillative writing is true-speaking, with rhythmic differences rung on a repetitive pitch or applied to conjunct pitch alternation. The minor-key thrusts of the dances (a Chassidic Dance in movement two, a Hora in movement three, and a final Circle Dance) are pure and undistorted ethnic auxiliaries. Part five is a "Dialogue" solely concerned with oppositional phrases. The previous movement (Lullaby) adheres to orthodox Hebraic musical style with its emphasis on the augmented interval.

Glick indicates that he composed the suite as a tribute to his parents. This is carried out in the dedication, which reads: "To Mom and Dad."

Glière, Reinhold (1875–1956)

Though Glière's music cannot be considered essentially individual, it has warmth and stability. He represents a reconstructionist, a romantic outpost in the territory of the present day. Glière's creative beat was in the same rhythm as the older Russian composers, such as Glazunov, Ippolitov-Ivanov, Borodin, and Gretchaninov. None of these men were startling creators but are of a group whose work signifies the beauties of pre-Soviet music. Let it not be overlooked that the old Russian school's contributions enlarged the wealth of music and retains an important place in the total repertoire.

Glière was one of the composers who did not alter his style after the Russian Revolution. He accepted the change in governmental order, retained his previous reasoning as a romantic nationalist to equal the viewpoint of a Soviet composer. What had been a major stylistic premise was assumed to be, because of its rational aspect, acceptable under the new order. Time proved Glière to be correct. His Russian-underlined work made him one of the leading composers in the Soviet Union, and one of its most important teachers.

Hearing Glière's full-knowledged music one recognizes its Russian core. There is no mistaking the melos which rarely quotes folk material. With Glière, there had never been any criticism of not writing typically national music. His music's simplicity and its acceptance throughout the world give proof that he meets the demands made by all types of musical consumers. Although his style is vigorous, it is restrained in moving into any new path. He was a discriminating expert in the management of mellifluous sonority, so typical of most Russian composers since the days of Rimsky-Korsakov. Though the spice and tartness of Prokofiev's output is lacking, Glière's music is not all milk and buttered toast. And it has beautiful warm hues. Glière's work is fully as representative of Soviet meaning as the music by composers of the national minorities whose themes come from the Tadjik, Usbek, and other defined regions.

DUOS

■ **Eight Duets for Violin and Cello, Op. 39**

The eight pieces for violin and cello are all in a pleasing and unconcerned romantic style. They have a value in being of contrast to the more serious examples in the repertoire, such as the violin and cello duos by Ravel and Kodály.

The entire basis of the Prelude is that of a simple melody plus accompaniment. The Gavotte has a proper drone-style Musette for contrast. Movement three is played with muted instruments in order to aid the tranquillity of a Cradle Song and is the only instance of a slight Russian flavor in the entire set. The fourth and fifth movements are somewhat in salon fashion; the total lack of counterpoint in the opus is especially to be criticized in this instance. These two pieces (Canzonetta and Intermezzo) are followed by an Impromptu, also a little monotonous in its flowing melody and consistent triplet passages. The last is not least in this composition, since the vivacious Scherzo is certainly the best movement of the eight; and in turn the final piece, Etude, is the most dramatic of the lot. To achieve excitement Glière forms his Etude from measured tremolando passages.

■ **Ten Duets for Two Cellos (or Cello and Double Bass), Op. 53**

Duets for two cellos are rare (a version of this work exists for cello and double bass, a still rarer combination). The matter of restricted gamut territory is an unfavorable condition, but Glière is able to solve this problem, if not in exciting fashion at least with snug and clear effusions. The absence of Russian character is to be noted, however. Glière needed his quartet and octet media, his orchestral palette, for confirmation of his traditional, national aesthetic. Here, the music moves through late-romantic (sometimes Chopinesque) channels with structural contrast, the surest persuasive weapon to eliminate monotony.

The first piece is in flowing style; the second is a light affair, with repeated sounds the principal factor; the third movement provides a broad duple-measure, à-la-Brahms type of music, while the fourth is in scherzo style. In the fifth duet the two instruments are expanded to a quartet sonority total, only a few measures lacking double stops for both cellos. The sixth piece relates polyphony to homophony; the seventh is again very romantically bred, while the eighth is written in a broadly styled quintal meter contrasted to material of pedal-formed spirit. A murmuring accompanimental figure bolsters the melody of the ninth duet, and the last of the set is a triple-meter Capriccioso.

■ **Twelve Duets for Two Violins, Op. 49**

In three instances, Glière was attracted to the medium of the unaccompanied string duet. Aside from the work under discussion, he wrote a set of eight duos for violin and cello, and a group of ten for paired cellos or cello and double bass. (Both of these compositions are discussed *above*.)

Without variety, a series of short pieces dies on the vine. Within an orthodox range of reference, Glière covers the assorted gamut of tonality, tempo, method, and meter in these dozen pieces for two violins. Twelve tonalities (seven in the major mode and five in the minor) embrace constructions set in eight different speeds that are distributed from the slowest, andante, to the speediest, vivace. Metrical differences are just as assorted, with three types of duple arrangement, two of triple plan, and one of quadruple pulsation.

Concentrated forms are utilized, all in balanced confirmation. Each of the duets grants total equality to the instruments. Each piece has a different personality. Practically the entire third duo is written in four parts. Ostinatos are the highlight of number five, arpeggios are particular to the tenth of the set, a scherzo designed music (with a slower central portion) concludes the opus.

QUARTETS

■ **String Quartet [No. 1] in A Major, Op. 2**

Glière's compass points to the land of Russia from the opening viola solo to the very last measure of this quartet. Native spirit is the total quality contained in the classic forms that hold the work together. In the first movement a compared difference exists between a long-flowing legato line and a pithy, rhythmically declared theme. The second movement represents the Scherzo, and calls on especially convincing syncopative technique. The Trio division of the movement moves by way of alternating quadruple- and sextuple-pulse measures, further varied by splitting the former equally and differentiating the latter so that short–long and long–short rhythmic blocks oppose and yet balance each other. The high point of the quartet is the Tema con variazioni (Theme with Variations). Color, rhythm, lyricism, and scherzo distinction serve to light up the four variants, with the coda a whispery bit which slightly overshades the theme by surrounded tremolandos. The resounding, dramatic Finale contains a lyric theme of the type one whistles postperformance time.

Glière makes no move to change the order of roundly preserved tonal music in his first string quartet. A profitable feeling of complete satisfaction exists in its teeming melodic beauties.

■ **String Quartet No. 2 in G Minor, Op. 20**

Glière's second quartet is somewhat hampered by its length. All particulars of form are observed to the letter. If working material is lengthy in its initial proclamation any literal recapitulation (due to an academic viewpoint in regard to form) overburdens the work's structure and adds nothing new. The G-minor quartet is somewhat stalemated by antiquated musical law and order.

Boldest and the most interesting is the finale ("Orientale"), music symbolized by the constancy of the augmented step. In this case, a motival announcement is developed from an introductory, slow-tempo prelude into an alla breve Allegro. The other sections of the work follow usual paths: sonata form, a plainly stated slow movement, and a Scherzo.

Compared to his first quartet, Glière's second example holds the same place in value as the number it bears. It is dedicated to Rimsky-Korsakov. Glière did not study with him but had fully absorbed his mannerisms and style through instruction from Ippolitov-Ivanov.

- **String Quartet No. 3 in D Minor, Op. 67**

In his later works, Glière moved away a little from pure diatonic matters to those more chromatic. It is not that his aesthetic changed; typical Russian atmosphere is still present, but the musical language broadens and gives more depth to the lyric geniality. Most illustrative of such advance is movement one of this quartet. Its main theme is of wide scope, and as a result, of dramatic and urgent impulse. Further, the construction is now more unified; both subjects of the slow and final movements are related to the chief theme of the opening movement. And besides this, the last movement (Fuga) is split into a second part (Coda), also derived from the germinal theme. The slow movement is enhanced by variation treatment and is preceded by music of syncopative scherzo snap. Only the latter is not concerned with the otherwise unifying theme.

It is of interest to note that Glière dedicated his Op. 67 to an organization bearing his own name (the Glière Quartet). While many quartet organizations have taken the name of their first violinist for identification, in the Soviet Union at least four composers have been honored by the use of their surnames to title quartet teams. Of these, veneration was accorded to Beethoven and to two other Russian composers (Taneiev and Glazunov) in addition to Glière.

- **String Quartet No. 4 in F Minor, Op. 83**

A beautiful theme opens this quartet. Superbly constructed, exemplifying Russian melos, the principal subject sets the home tonality without deviating into a single chromatic. Glière knew his craft. It is evident in every measure of this work.

Full-scale sonata form is detailed in the opening movement. Here the tonal spectrum is broadened to include chromaticism in the second subject and development. Indeed, while Glière considered music with a formal temperament, the slight modifications in this quartet exemplify a conservative composer, but one with mature wisdom. The second movement (Vivace) represents the Scherzo. The specialness of this part is the whispery, muted central portion.

The slow movement is in Glière's favored variation form, in this instance the theme is followed by ten variations. The principal idea has all the ingredients for variational success: a rising fifth and a pair of ascending sevenths. For the most part, these intervallic earmarks remain defined in the changes. (Glière's variational technique was never cryptographic.) In this case even the theme's length (ten measures) is maintained in the first four variations, as well as in variations six and seven. No character-piece types are included. Shifting concepts occur, but the continuity is supple. The sixth variant is especially delicate, reminding one, in its muted text, of the moonlight music section in *Verklärte Nacht*. Most contrapuntal of all is the final Allegro. It begins with a fugato, and Glière's formal evaluation maintains this polyphonic premise in the music's development, including a stretto toward the conclusion.

Glière's Op. 83 was awarded a Stalin Prize in 1948. It was his last string quartet. A fifth work in the medium was under way at the time of his death at 81.

OCTET

- **Octet for Four Violins, Two Violas, and Two Cellos, Op. 5**

Though there are certain symphonic substances contained in Glière's string octet, as a general rule he manages to avoid a thickly meshed sonority. Nevertheless, the textures are of sufficient resonance, calculated to serve a meritorious and typical Glière melodicism. The composer's uniform fondness for Russian style and character is immediately recognizable in the opening theme of the first movement. A light scherzo style is guided through the second movement: a ternary design serves the slow movement, while the last part of the opus is in sonata form. The latter is stretched out—a little overstatistical in formal enumeration but is driven to conclusion with a compact Presto coda.

Glinka, Mikhail (1804–57)

Although Glinka is known as the founder of the Russian modern school of music (in the sense that he formed the methods and showed the means of writing music of true heritage), in the field of chamber music his contributions are mostly of historical record. One must turn to other composers for the mature richness of Russian chamber music.

TRIO

- *Trio pathétique* for Piano, Clarinet, and Bassoon

Glinka's trio possesses interesting incidents worthy of performance. It is traditionally placed rather than an example of nationalistic composition. At the age of 23 Glinka had not yet dressed his music in Russian style.

In the edition of his collected works, the trio is prefaced with a motto: "Je n'ai connu l'amour que par les peines qu'il cause." ("I have known love only through the sorrows it causes.") Other editions (including the one edited by Fernand Oubradous, published by Editions Translatlantiques in 1958) make no mention of it.

An Allegro moderato opens the work—a conception more lyrical than dynamic. It is as though the usual, more songlike, second sonata subject has moved into first place. This movement connects with the Scherzo, in turn with the standard contrastive Trio in slower tempo, and a recapitulation of the principal portion of the movement. The coda is a four-measure Lento that bridges into the third part of the work. The last forms the slow movement, split into ternary instrumental settings. In Largo pace the first twenty measures are for clarinet and piano, the next sixteen measures are for bassoon and piano. Then the tempo heading changes to Maestoso e risoluto and the scoring is for the entire trio. Though the first three movements are connected, the finale is separate. And separate are its components as well. There is a very compact, triplet-sprung Allegro con spirito; a pithy nine-measure Presto; a still more concentrated, one-measure Lento (preceded and followed by single whole measures of silence), then a concluding syncopated division of entirely different material.

Sometimes Glinka's trio is performed in violin, cello, and piano form, and in that scoring has also been recorded. This piano trio setting is not original at all. It was made by the celebrated violinist and teacher Johann Hřimaly (1844–1915). (Significantly, neither of the editions mentioned above make note of this transcription.)

QUARTETS

- **String Quartet [No. 1] in D Major**

The interesting point regarding this youthful work (composed in 1824 but not published until 1948) is the fact that it lacked the final two-thirds of the concluding (fourth) movement. It was provided by Nicolai Miaskovsky, one of Russia's most eminent composers.

Glinka's Soviet biographers describe the quartet as simply a student's exercise in the medium, but there is a bit more to the composition than such a negative report. There is neat organization in the first movement; a Menuetto with a nicely figurated Trio serves as movement three; and a Rondo completes the work. Movement two is a Tema con variazioni. The rich ornamentation in variant three and the rhythmic push in variant four give this movement a special colorful character.

- **String Quartet [No. 2] in F Major**

Early Glinka, composed in 1830, when he was 26.

The standard four movements of this quartet are visible patterns of German models; well wrought, stated in a simple, nondiscursive language, the lineage stemming from Haydn and Mozart. The Menuetto is a somewhat fast dance, and the final Rondo very gay. It is music with exterior finish.

SEXTET

- **Sextet for Piano, Two Violins, Viola, Cello, and Double Bass**

Glinka's work dates from 1832. It was first published in the fourth volume of his collected works in 1958, and before publication required considerable editorial correction and clarification of the manuscript. The original and complete title of the piece reads: *Gran sestetto originale.*

Fluent, if eclectic, language marks the composition, with good continuity and fitting sonorities. Considerable attention is given the piano, and in the central slow movement (which is linked to the Finale) the keyboard instrument takes over solo status. The outer movements are of length (306 and 404 measures respectively). The first movement begins with an introductory Allegro that later becomes bound in the development of the movement proper (Maestoso). A type of rhapsodic sectionalism marks the finale, but the structural corners are turned with smoothness.

SEPTET

- **Septet for Oboe, Bassoon, Horn, Two Violins, Cello, and Double Bass**

The date of this work is approximately 1823, and indeed for a young man of only 19 there is a good command of cohesive structural thought. The composition unfolds in straightforward and direct action, with a type of Italianate context. There are two points to be noted regarding the instrumentation. First, the elimination of the viola in the string body, thereby stressing the bass zone by use of cello and double bass. Second, the attention given the oboe and bassoon in assigning highlighted portions for these instruments.

An introduction precedes the main opening sonata-form Allegro. The slow movement moves rather simply, with only a minimal amount of ornamentation and elaboration. Movements three and four are represented by a Menuetto and a Rondo.

Gluck, Christoph Willibald (1714–87)

TRIOS

- **Trio Sonatas for Two Violins and Basso Continuo**

  - No. 1, in C Major
  - No. 2, in G Minor
  - No. 3, in A Major
  - No. 4, in B-flat Major
  - No. 5, in E-flat Major
  - No. 6, in F Major
  - No. 7, in E Major
  - No. 8, in F Major

The first six sonatas are in three movements, with the sequence being slow–fast–Minuet (or quasi Minuet). All of it is music of extroverted directness. There is a nice give-and-take between the violins and there is a fair amount of imitative writing.

The design is different in the seventh and eighth works of the group. No. 7 proceeds in Allegro–Andante–Allegro order. The first movement is marked Symphonia, and with its correspondence to the Italian opera overture form the editor, Gerhard Croll, considers that this work may be the overture to one of Gluck's "early and since lost Italian operas."

Sonata No. 8 has but two movements, an ornamental Moderato ed espressivo and an Allegro. The former is based on a duet in Gluck's opera *Le Nozze d'Ercole e d'Ebe*. The beginning of the duet is developed, and then, Croll indicates, Gluck "continues more independently in a smooth and delicate manner."

Glushkov, Pietr (1889–1966)

TRIO

- *In Memory of T. Shevchenko:* **Trio No. 5 for Violin, Cello, and Piano**

Glushkov's tribute is to Taras Shevchenko, the famed Ukrainian poet and artist (1814–61) who attacked in his writings serfdom, Russian autocracy, and Russian domination of non-Russian lands. The work bears an introductory motto by Shevchenko that the Ukrainian people comprise a united family, forever free. Each of the four movements has a preliminary motto, the first quoting words from a folk song, the second and third dealing with lines by the poet concerning freedom, and the last taken from a poem about the greatness of Shevchenko.

All four movements are in minor tonalities, the first and last shifting in their conclusions to the major mode in classic-style order. Movement one begins in D-minor paeanic vividness, takes on chromatic appendages as it moves into faster tempo, is contrasted to a section in slower-paced E-flat minor, and then returns to the speedier portion, now fully developed. Folk turns are curved within the B-minor second and E-minor third movements. A choralish Largo setting opens the finale, which contrasts to antiphonally directed fast-tempo material.

Gnessin, Mikhail (1883–1957)

Gnessin fluctuated between the use of a whole-hearted romantic technique of quasi-Scriabin variety and the desire to write authentic Jewish music. His early work was fully marked by the former manner, which, to a great degree, infiltrates the latter as well. Gnessin eventually turned away from the composition of works in a Jewish vein to a thick, neoromantic style that endeavored to express more popular Soviet utterances. But these were handicapped by diffuseness, for he combined the style of Wagner with Scriabin and added a Reger-like musical diction. Since Gnessin's style had been formed before the Russian Revolution he could not effect any change in the works written after it. His Jewish bent is explained by the fact that he was the son of a rabbi, but that background was submerged for a fairly long period of time.

QUARTET

- *Variations on a Jewish Folk Theme* **for String Quartet, Op. 24**

The theme of this quartet is in D minor, but not in the quasi-exotic fashion that includes augmented steps. Most of the variations are sober, neither complex nor ornamental, but rather quietly stated developments in which the theme's shape is recognizable. It is not until the sixth variant that a decided dramatic point is reached—underlined by the use of a great deal of octave declamation in the violins. A light dance style embraces the seventh variation, while the final (eighth) part is somewhat ornate and has a partial vivo quality. A very short but positive thematic statement concludes the composition.

QUINTET

- *Requiem* for Piano, Two Violins, Viola, and Cello, Op. 11

This work was originally conceived for orchestra and chorus, but when Gnessin changed over to the chamber music medium he did not sufficiently reduce the texture. The quintet's sonorous density shows that Gnessin experienced some conflicts and thereby unwisely carried over a few of his original textural ideas in regard to the final draft.

Gnessin was a favorite pupil of Rimsky-Korsakov's (his idiom is a far cry from that of Rimsky-Korsakov, however), and it was in memory of his teacher that he composed this work, immediately after Rimsky-Korsakov's death in 1908. *Requiem* is in one movement, in free ternary form, and is principally derived from the opening theme with its poignant mnemonic of a rising seventh. The middle section is fugal and is succeeded by a return to the main theme. Sustenance of the quintet's primary mood is obtained by the quiet close.

Godard, Benjamin (1849–95)

DUOS

- Sonata No. 1 for Piano and Violin, Op. 1

Melodic ease runs through Godard's debut opus. The man has been denigrated by critics stating his music belongs in the "drawing room," but this writer disagrees. The duo sonata is neat, clear, tonally direct, and moves through four movements with as musical a sense as the work of Saint-Saëns, for example. Certainly that would place it out of the category of "drawing room music."

- **Sonata No. 3 for Piano and Violin, Op. 9**

The music is delightfully unmannered, interesting, and perfectly designed for the instruments. (The piano preceding the violin in the title heading has no relationship to instrumental chain of command. Godard wrote with equal partnership.)

There are plenty of juicy qualities. Inserted in movement one are some dabs of color for the violin in the form of plucked sounds and harmonics and a tad of a cadenza for the piano. Agogic weights are contrasted in the Scherzo. Between the slow movement and finale there is more triple-pulse music, slower than the previous Scherzo, in the form of an Intermezzo. The finale dances through rondo territory.

- *Suite de trois morceaux* for Flute and Piano, Op. 116

Sure, lightweights all three: Allegretto, "Idylle," and Valse. But the graciously songful "Idylle" adds to the small credits that Godard has on the books. The Valse is witty and in one place beautifully snide (a quote from Waldteufel's most famous waltz, *The Skaters*).

(A setting of this work for flute and orchestra is also available.)

TRIO

- **Trio No. 2 in F for Piano, Violin, and Cello, Op. 72**

Music that exhibits Godard's special lyrical gifts. The music is conceived in the evergreen romantic style. Pedal-point props are important within Godard's piano trio, but these are part and parcel of the style. Save for the scherzo-formed third movement, there is robust scoring (piano trioistic generosity, it might be called).

Godron, Hugo (1900–71)

DUO

- *Suite bucolique* for Flute (or Oboe) and Piano (1939)

The most picturesque part of Godron's four-part suite is the final one, a Fugato. It is gay and open, chirpy, and with some syncopative dips that stimulate the lines. Close to its import is the seriousness of the third movement, a recitative in Adagio, chordally supporting a free (no metrical measurement) wind-instrument statement. The first part of the work is a curvaceously phrased Cavatine. Part two is a dance in one sense (the heading reads Allegro: Tempo rigaudon) and precisely ternary in another, with the middle section an Andante tristezza, followed by a literal rerun of the Allegro.

Godske-Nielsen, Svend (1867–1935)

QUARTET

- String Quartet, Op. 14

Simply ordered structural sense rules this work by a composer noted as a "pupil and friend of Carl Nielsen." But no apparent influence by that significant Danish composer appears within the music.

A swinging triple pulse covers the F-major first movement, set in sonata form. Mendelssohnian moves motivate and color the B-flat-major Intermezzo. The same pitch in minor controls the chromatic lines of the slow movement. Lightness returns in the Finale, fully determined in its tarantella-type formation.

Goeb, Roger (1914–)

Goeb is a *professional* composer. The adjective distinguishes the few from the majority. The latter do not have the willingness (or the special ability) to produce music for varied, sometimes severely contrasting purposes, at differing levels of technical difficulty. Goeb, on the other hand, can create a complex symphony, equally meet the demands and restrictions of writing short pieces for teaching purposes, or turn out a suite with flexible instrumentation for utilitarian use. In this diversity he always has retained his style, including a masterful handling of whatever instrumental resources were being utilized.

DUO

- Two Divertimenti for Two Flutes (1950)

This two-movement, two-flute work is most illustrative of Goeb's ability to handle restrained timbre. The divertimenti juxtapose clear but not simply pat intervallic lines to create both strength and interesting instrumental pigmentation. The pieces are structured in terms of a fluid tonal center. In the initial piece arabesque detail moves to a section devoted to trills; the tonality pivot shifts. When this portion is released, again the key orbit follows suit. To obtain a specific quality from tonality is not easy when there are only two homophonic instruments. Goeb meets the challenge. This ability is especially noticeable in the contrasts within the second piece of the set.

TRIO

- Suite for Woodwind Trio (Flute, Clarinet [or Flute 2], and Oboe [or Trumpet or Clarinet 2]) (1946)

Goeb adopts a very practical viewpoint for his neatly formulated trio, originally scored for flute, clarinet, and oboe. By suggested substitutions it is possible to perform the composition in five other versions: two flutes and oboe; two flutes and trumpet; flute, clarinet, and trumpet; flute and two clarinets; or two flutes and clarinet.

Integrated style and fluid lines define this four-part piece. A single, lively subject commands movement one, set in varied color and detail. The theme is first stated by the oboe, then by the clarinet with contrapuntal dressing, and later in imitative assortment. Metrical aliveness does not make the music nervous; it gives it pertness. Movement two (tempo heading: Quiet Motion) also has a single theme and is contrapuntal throughout; its climactic point is neatly poised at the halfway mark. Movement three (Graciously) contrasts, and thus balances, a mix of vertical and horizontal detail. Polyphony then takes wing in the gay finale, with a fugato plus stretto pileup. Nothing pinched or restrained in Goeb's concluding movement. Asymmetrical and birhythmic arrangements remove any rigidity.

QUARTET

- *Suite in Folk Style* for Four Clarinets (1948)

Diatonicism is the keystone for the greater part here. It does not travel down to an academic dead end. Goeb's triadic concordance has counteringredients. These pitch condiments flavor the piece and produce a music of warmth, not only through the calid clarinet medium.

There is a modal overlay, especially in the second movement (Lullaby), a sensitive G-minor conception in flowing duple meter. The Folk Song moves in rondo form, its sonorous packing firm but not heavy. Movement three (Folk Dance) is rooted in B-flat major for the first twenty-six measures and even thereafter hardly departs from its home base. But tonal monotony is not felt in this jolly, jiggy music.

Opulent contrapuntalism is reserved for the final movement (Canon). While it is not easy to build a canonic structure, especially when confined by tonal specifications, this one has special attractiveness. The first clarinet leads with a twenty-one-measure line, and the other instruments follow at distances below it of a fourth, a minor seventh, and a minor tenth. Before this combine has run its course, the first clarinet begins another canon, also strictly constructed. Following this polyphonic game is exhilarating.

QUINTETS

- *Prairie Songs* for Woodwind Quintet (1946)

Although a version exists of this work for chamber orchestra, the quintet is the original conception. In most respects the latter is a better setting because its compactness is not burdened by extra sonorous tiers.

Goeb has indicated his music uses "rhythmic and melodic characters of American folk music without actually borrowing directly from . . . folk literature." Folksy it is, indeed. "Evening" is covered by a quasi-polyphonic section, followed by soloism backed up with accompanimental ostinatos. Syncopation and rhythmic tidbits brighten the Dance. In "Morning," flute roulades are a preliminary to a moderately paced dancelike expression.

- Quintet for Trombone and Strings (Two Violins, Viola, and Cello) (1949)

Goeb's Quintet is one of the few examples existing for this special combination. For the greater part, the trombone is spotted against the strings. It declaims in parlando style in the opening movement, exhibits its rhythmic and coloristic personality in the second part, which includes glissando and use of various mutes, and spins a simple but appealing line in the

Aria. Obviously, integration of heavy (though not blunt) brass tone and string timbre is not easily accomplished. Goeb's solutions are artistically satisfying.

Playful Americanese diction is in the middle movement, containing the vivid contrast of string pizzicato against the trombone. In the Aria, the basic backgrounds are breadth of sound by chordal movement and exuberant rhythms.

■ **Quintet [No. 1] for Woodwinds (1949)**

Goeb's initial quintet for flute, oboe, clarinet, horn, and bassoon, similar to his second work in the medium (*see below*), cuts totally away from the often-depicted light frolics of Parisian wind-music chatter. Nothing wrong with such instrumental conversation, save that it has been a creative redundancy. Goeb's wind music has messages but not sweet, cloying ones. What it says it says precisely, incisively, and seriously. The stylistic constancy and the scoring are impeccable.

Movement one is brisk and rhythmic, with darting figures framed by dissonant harmonies. A Scherzando follows, its extroverted pulse reminding one of the practices of Walter Piston. In contrast, the Lento is a deeply introspective utterance, dark-tinged in color. The finale is an Allegro that succeeds in making clear its vitality without lightly cast exuberances.

■ **Quintet No. 2 for Woodwinds (1956)**

A fascinating wind quintet. Goeb's conception is one of fluid regard for timbre conduct and shows an acute ear for sound choices. Instrumental distinction is called on to accentuate the dissonant style of the four movements, each concerned with rhapsodic imagery. In Goeb's hands form is also originated by instrumental handling. And his scoring is far from the pert French brand of saucy sauce or the brittle

Germanic type of acidic acuteness. Goeb's winds sound with resinous tartness and the tartness is very telling.

There are four movements and the usual plan of pace is certified; the outer divisions are moderately fast, the inner sections a scherzo type and a moody, dark-dampened slow music.

This is truly a special composition, one with its own woodwind writ. Wind quintet teams should be grateful, and so should listeners.

Goedicke, Alexander (1877–1957)

DUOS

■ **Sonata for Cello and Piano, Op. 88**

Unlike his two sonatas for violin and piano (*see below*), Goedicke's cello sonata has big size and weighty textures in the first two-thirds of its total. This is what fundamental romantic music is all about.

The style approaches simulated symphonicism for two instruments. In turn, it also opts for some soloism. In this respect the cello has a short, tranquil recitative-type passage in the first movement, ornamental and ad lib sections in the Largo (second) movement, and a full-spanned cadenza in the final movement. Still, precision clarifies all the moves and there is balance in terms of the emotive objective.

■ **Sonata [No. 1] for Violin and Piano, Op. 10**

Complete allegiance to the spirit and style of classical form, with slight romantic melodic impresses. The middle movement is a lyrical cantilena and maintains that state within the considerable development. The Finale is a rondo.

The above is not negated by the use of cyclic detail. The conclusion of the first movement begins with a violin cadenza and is followed by a final statement of the movement's principal theme. At the end of the third movement (Finale) this initial theme of the Sonata is reannounced in augmented values.

- **Sonata No. 2 for Violin and Piano, Op. 83**

The creation of a persevering composer. Hardly a trace of national flavor—Goedicke, a Russian, leaned toward classic identity. Naturally this does not detract from a duo sonata written with a constancy of design and purpose.

Four movements: fast–slow–Scherzo–fast (Finale). There is marked attention to textural leanness in the outer movements. The Scherzo interestingly shifts weights from the weakest part of the measure (the tempo is Allegro animato, the meter is 3/8) to the strongest.

QUARTET

- **Quartet No. 2 for Two Violins, Viola, and Cello, Op. 75**

The focus in the first movement is motival derivation. This is set in contrast to a lyrical subject. One follows straightforward and clear depiction of the substances in this D-minor movement. The focus in the G-major third movement is variational. While there is substantial weight in these two movements, and even more in the finale (the tonality is again D minor), nothing can be termed overwritten. On the other hand, the slow movement (in F-sharp minor) has a number of sections within it for two- and three-voice combinations. Throughout, there is a good balance between thematic materials and their development.

Goehr, Alexander (1932–)

TRIO

- **Piano Trio, Op. 20**

The modern scoring conception of the violin, cello, and piano combination, wherein trio totality is not in the majority. Goehr's instrumental handling (of virtuosic content) often blocks the strings against the piano. He also counterblocks the individual voices in the first movement, where metrical proportions are not always equalized. (His instruction reads clearly: "It is of the utmost importance that each player 'realizes' [expresses] his own metre and is unhampered by the needs of precise ensemble.") The movement is of sectional depiction, in a continuous developmental process that brings to mind variation technique, but this has no relation to the set-piece detailing of general theme and variation form. Additional color is obtained with the violin's lowest (G) string raised a half tone to A-flat. (One critic has called the first movement "akin to a *danse macabre*." This might have been influenced by Goehr's use of scordatura, though in Saint-Saëns's orchestral *Danse macabre* the solo violin scordatura is the exact reverse: it is the *highest* (E) string that is retuned and it is *lowered* a half tone to E-flat.)

The violence of movement one is contrasted to the generally slow quietness of movement two. However, the push-pull of the severe chromaticism does not lessen the tension of this piano trio.

QUARTETS

- **String Quartet No. 2, Op. 23**

If one is not seduced by the intellectualism of Goehr's quartet one will be seduced by its colors: dead and alive vibrato, muted and open timbre, ponticello tremolo, and slow, stretched-out glissando. Of course one will argue that these are integrated *materia* not set apart and therefore should not be so considered. But considered they should be, since they add vitality to the discourse, and to enjoy them gives the opportunity for increased discovery of the quartet's processes.

Those processes begin with a set of variations, with permutations within the permutations so that each section is intensely contained. In the middle of the movement is a section "without tempo," a huge quadruple-instrument recitative with each voice active in the declarative polyphony. The movement ends quite fast, much speedier than the second movement, which defines a clearly apportioned ternary plan equating a scherzo. The finale is choralelike in disposition, intensely sustained, moving to a full-scope climax in the center (with the loudest dynamic) and then receding.

- **String Quartet No. 3 (1976)**

Twelve-tone music that handles the technique so that it has within it the weights and relationships that prevail in tonality. Indeed, Goehr's third quartet is serial but written in a manner that parallels the classical formations used in the work.

Movement one has paired subjects, the first one marked with the subtle coloration of grace notes, the second more flowing. There is intense development and there is recapitulation. Literal repeats of the first section and again in foreshortened form after the second section, with a pithy three-measure coda, mark the second movement. This four-section design is as clearly direct and as balanced as a classical minuet or scherzo. A rhapsodic and virtuosic rondo (beginning with a Lento introduction) concludes the quartet.

SEXTET

- **Suite for Flute, Clarinet, Horn, Harp, Violin (alternating Viola), and Cello, Op. 11**

A rhapsodic opening is balanced by a similarly characterized Intermezzo, only in the latter the harp functions soloistically. Movement three is a Scherzo and Trio. No recapitulation, but a bare reminder of one, a mini-flash of one, presented in eight measures. Soloism again in the Arietta, this time by the flute. More of the same—much more, in the Finale-Quodlibet—and made more prominent by cadenza liberalization and letting the flute roam alone. A type of harp cadenza is also set forth in the Finale. (These solo portions are in perfect sequential balance it will be noted, i.e., harp–flute–flute–harp.)

SEPTET

- *Canonic Chorale for Igor Stravinsky* for **Flute, Clarinet, Harp, and String Quartet (1971)**

A pithy memorial tribute to Stravinsky, for publication in Boosey and Hawkes's *Tempo* magazine. There is line declaration in the flute, inserted responses from the clarinet, and ostinato-tempered pitch movement in the harp. The work begins with the first 4 3/4 measures of Stravinsky's Three Pieces for String Quartet, which abruptly break off as the other instruments enter. Another tidbit from the quartet is set in toward the end.

OCTET

- *Lyric Pieces* for Wind Instruments
  (Flute, Oboe [alternating English
  horn], Clarinet, Bassoon, Horn,
  Trumpet, and Trombone) with
  Double Bass, Op. 36

Goehr's six pieces sing with full serial lyricism. And they are all tuned with telling sound experiences, clearly outlining different objectives, though no title guides are offered. The firm sense of design and instrumental use again demonstrate Goehr's ability to produce twelve-tone music meshed with fine color development.

The balances of all the pieces are emphasized by the use of strictly repeated sections; direct data, therefore, rather than the application of developmental procedures. In the first piece, proclamatory material is the fundament. The sustained phrases of the second piece are of twilight suburban character. In turn, movement three, agitated by its dots and dashes, grace notes and flutters, is a music totally of urbanistic motility. (The English horn is used in this movement.)

Movement four features the trumpet; the scoring is block type throughout. In the fifth piece there is unremitting syncopation. Set in triple pulse, in moderate speed the music is kin to a waltz, but one that never glides.

The final movement is a set of variations. Significantly, the theme's dimensions of eight plus eight measures are maintained in every one of the first four variations. (The sections are repeated only in the thematic statement.) Variations five and six are single eight-measure statements, and only the final variant departs from this fixed form, and then only by one measure less. Instrumental colors are highlighted in this final piece. Thus: the bassoon in variation one (in the first half it is totally unaccompanied), the flute in variation three, and in variation five only the oboe and clarinet play.

Goethals, Lucien (1931–)

DUO

- *Triptique* for Violin and Harpsichord
  (1975)

One of the form-building techniques, considering the three movements as a unit, is the amassing of textural totals. In the Prelude a third of the measures are for violin alone, and there are a good number of measures where the piano provides a mere fillip or two of a sound. Partnership of the instruments increases in the Intermezzo, while the fullest-weighted conduct appears in the final Divertimento.

The pitch arrangement uses all the twelve tones, though *Triptique* is not serially processed. Considerable disjunctivity is used throughout; in the first movement large amounts of pizzicato are utilized, matching the sputtering pitch presentation. The major developmental process in the second movement is a variously arranged sextuple rhythmic figure. It zigs and it zags in large total. This fluctuation is paralleled in the final movement with constant changes (small though they may be) of metronomically detailed speeds, mainly $\quad = 50$ (more or less) and $\quad = 112$ (also more or less). These two, it will be noted, signify a difference of only twelve notches on the metronome counting in eighths. There's a great deal of nervous energy in the concluding movement; this tempo flux produces additional power.

TRIO

- **Fantasia and Humoreske for Two Oboes
  and English horn (1975)**

Both pieces offer plenty of rhythmic agitation. By the constant crisscross of entrances in the

Fantasia, pulse specification gets lost and a disjunct linear mixture is produced. If this is Goethals's idea of creating a fantasy world he has succeeded in all counts. Still, fantasy never did mean a wealth of unrest.

There is more combining of voices in the Humoreske, even though rhythmic depiction is extremely nervous, most often avoiding a start on a beat for a figure. Here, as in the Fantasia, frictions (decided ones: minor seconds diminished octaves, etc.) are the whole show. Special color is supplied by the use of harmonics in the Fantasia, but the principal color of these pieces is obtained from their fragmented texts.

Goetz, Hermann (1840–76)

DUO

- **Drei leichte Stücke (Three Light Pieces) for Violin and Piano, Op. 2**

The German word *leicht* can also be translated "easy." However, though these pieces are not technically difficult, it would denigrate their musical value to classify them as "easy," in place of their stylistic light contents.

Even though the music has no special individuality, it has a fine general romantic personality, is impeccably constructed and efficiently organized. The titles of the set—March, Romance, and Rondo—clearly define the objectives involved.

TRIO

- **Trio in G Minor for Piano, Violin, and Cello, Op. 1**

In 1893 a critic by the name of George Bernard Shaw wrote of Goetz that "He has the charm of Schubert without his brainlessness, the refinement and inspiration of Mendelssohn without his limitation and timid gentility, Schumann's sense of harmonic expressions without his laboriousness . . . shewing itself in the Mozartian grace and responsiveness of his polyphony, he leaves all three of them simply nowhere. Brahms, who alone touches him in mere brute musical faculty, is a dolt in comparison to him."

This quotation is worthwhile only because Goetz's stylistic influences are brought to the fore acutely. The critical invectives the illustrious G.B.S. summoned up are, at this remove, proof that it's easier to be critical than to be correct.

The piano trio begins with somewhat threnodic color, but overall, despite its G-minor tonality, it is more energetic and dramatic than doleful. The outer movements stand in absolute balance. Both begin with prefatory material, both repeat the expositions of their formal propositions. The choice of related keys plays its part in this balance as well: B-flat major in the Feurig (Fiery) principal part of movement one, G major in the Ziemlich lebhaft (Rather Animated) principal division of the fourth movement.

An improvisatory tone (a positive romantic element, this) is to be found in the Sehr ruhig (Very Tranquil) slow movement. The principal themes of this part of the Trio are announced by the piano. Next to the opening movement it is the Scherzo (marked Flüchtig, erregt) (Fleetingly, Agitatedly) that provides, in its Mendelssohnian lineage, the greatest amount of color and drive. The trio (Etwas langsamer) (Somewhat Slower) is in the major mode of the home (G-minor) key. Its syncopative slow waltz format offers not only sharp contrast but is again an illustration of romantic creative temperament.

QUARTET

- **Quartet in E Major for Piano, Violin, Viola, and Cello, Op. 6**

Dedicated to Brahms and fully worthy of bearing his name. Goetz's piano quartet is as rich and as technically wise as the three great piano quartets Brahms produced. In a liner note written for a recording of the work, Laurence Vittes calls Op. 6 "one of the masterpieces of the literature," and he is absolutely correct in his opinion.

Goetz's handling of form is far from prosaic. His scholarship is of classical-romantic order; it has expressiveness without running into ornate overstress. The emotive quality of the romantic syntax and lines is of balanced, integrated beauty. Goetz is always strong in his favored introductory contrasts as, here, in the melancholic preface to the driving finale.

The slow movement is structured as a theme and variations; the preceding, initial movement is full of scoring power in its sonata-formed presentation. In the third movement (Scherzo), counterpoint plays an important part, not only in the main section of the movement but in the cogent canon that is woven into the contrastive Trio.

QUINTET

- **Quintet in C Minor for Piano, Violin, Viola, Cello, and Double Bass, Op. 16**

Op. 16 marks the last of Goetz's four chamber music compositions. It cannot be termed a "piano quintet" since that rubric calls for a combination of two violins, viola, and cello, with piano. Here, Goetz has replaced the second violin with a double bass. In the total four movements the bass has but a single line of melodic importance, but it does add a good amount of dark color to the composition.

There are general romantic arguments in the Quintet, but they are never platitudinous. Movement one, defining the darkest mood of all four, has a Goethe motto to set the character: "Und wenn der Mensch in seiner Qual verstummt, gab mir ein Gott zu sagen, was ich leide." ("And when man in his agony is reduced to silence, a God gave me [the ability] to express, what I suffer.") The slow movement registers well in direct contrast. It is followed by a fast-paced movement but with the stipulation "quasi menuetto." Its contrastive Trio has the flow of a ländler. There is scoring massivity in the rondo-designed finale (very few quintets in which the piano takes part can escape this textural result). Keen use of contrapuntalism helps to sort out matters.

Goeyens, Fernand (1892–1965)

DUO

- *Suite romantique* for Trumpet and Piano

No surprises in this three-movement duo. Heard today, the result gives the effect of a romantic revival. The pleasures, therefore, are all the expected ones and expect full allegiance to tonality.

"Jour de fête" ("Holiday") is a brother to fanfare writing, but there is a supple amount of legato contrasts. Some inner modulation, yes, but by far the key of C proclaims the former and the key of the dominant, the latter. Movement two is a "Melancholy Air" ("Air mélancolique"). Proper colored dress for this part, with the trumpet muted and chordally juiced by the piano for the peroration. The finale is titled "Chant de joie" ("Song of Joy"), but the tempo heading is Scherzo. It runs the ternary course and has the necessary contrastive conduct in terms of dynamic levels. No special pleading is necessary for Goeyens's trumpet writing. It has enough flair to go over the footlights, and yet its brilliance does not negate, with the piano, average chamber music equality.

Goeyvaerts, Karel (1923–)

TRIO

- *Pièce pour trois (Piece for Three)* for Flute, Violin, and Piano (1960)

A series of patterns, constantly rhapsodic. One can readily describe this type of music as representing a stream of consciousness style. Aside from minute, lightly punctuated eighth notes (mainly soft and never stronger than a *mezzoforte*) that begin and conclude the piece and appear in a few other places, nothing is repeated.

All the thoughts breathe color. These include piano pizzicato on the strings of the instrument.

QUINTET

- Piano Quartet for Violin, Viola, Cello, Piano, and Tape Recorder (1972)

Avant-garde foibles and fashions on display.

To begin with, a recording is made of a news broadcast, preferably "from different radio stations and in different languages." Combined with this a performance is planned (to last from a minimum of ten minutes to a maximum of a half hour) concocted from seven separate pages of music material (plus instructions). Nothing is pat—one or more of the musical items can be omitted, any of the set may be repeated.

What the composer has provided are a series of chords, measures of eighth-note patterns, sustained and isolated pitches, and so on. These amount to snippets, almost equivalent to musical doodlings.

In a sense the entire procedure is a game. The many rules are indicated, but just as many opportunities are given not to follow them. One example makes this dichotomy clear: The performers are to play "medium level notes in random succession. Start successively: piano,

viola, violin, violoncello. (Piano chooses the moment where notes are added or left out, followed at distance by viola, etc.) Intermittent low piano clusters." This instruction is succeeded by "The last group goes with a fast diminuendo, less notes, more silences, staccato, no more piano clusters." It is just this sheer formal incomprehensibility that makes a chamber music happening of this sort totally comprehensible.

Göhler, Georg (1874–1954)

TRIO

- *Variations on a Theme by W. A. Mozart* for Piano, Violin, and Cello

The theme is a Mozart minuet, deployed and developed in a modest manner. As a conductor specializing in the works of Bruckner and Mahler, Göhler might have been expected to be influenced accordingly in his creative work. He was not.

All ten variations are clearly disposed, each marked with the upbeat of the Mozart original. Clear counterpoint is an aid in maintenance of interest, as are solo and duo combinations. Variation three presents one string instrument at a time, the next variant is for solo piano, and the sixth variation is for cello and piano. A fugal exposition (with later augmentation of the subject) climaxes the trio.

QUARTET

- String Quartet No. 2 in F Minor (1936)

A representation of the old suite form with one addition. There is a Präludium and four dances: Allemande, Sarabande, Gavotte, and Gigue (representing movements two, three, four, and six). The "extra" is movement five (Basso ostinato). And, a further affinity with baroque-suite procedure, all the movements are in the same key (F minor).

Vigor aplenty in the Präludium. Imitations aplenty in all the dances, with some colorful dynamic opposition in the Gigue. The ostinato movement lives up to its name to the fullest extent. Its two-measure bass (eight-beat total, beginning on the second beat of the first measure and extending through the first beat of the third measure) is announced thirty-five consecutive times by the cello. The next three statements are by the viola, second violin, and first violin, respectively. Then, twice more by the cello again. Above the ostinato Göhler rings variations derived from a syncopative subject. All of the lines are laced and inlaid with both articulated polyphony and colorful harmony.

(A second version for full string orchestra was made. Within it there are considerable passages for solo instruments as well as for the full ensemble. In that version the title reads: Suite in F Minor for String Orchestra with Solo Quartet.)

Gold, Ernest (1921–)

QUARTET

- **String Quartet No. 1 (1948)**

Composer of a number of successful film scores, notably *Judgement at Nuremberg* and *Exodus* (its theme song a gold mine of income still maintained thirty years after its composition), Gold wrote concert music totally opposite in character. It is austere, serious, devoted to large-proportioned formal definition.

The quartet (chosen by the Society for the Publication of American Music for its award in 1956—its thirty-seventh season) begins with a sonata design. Both of its themes have extensive scope, the "head" of the first one defined by a triple set of eighth notes, the other more

lyrical, marked by large leaps and mixing conjunct with disjunct progression. Activity—notewise and tempowise—marks the Adagio's central portion, thereby codifying its tripartite form. Matching the first movement, duo-thematic material is used for the structure of the quartet's final part. Here, more than in the previous movements, Mahlerian largess is noticeable.

QUINTET

- ***Symphony for Five Instruments* (Violin, Viola, Cello, Bassoon, and Piano) (1952)**

Gold's title is well chosen. This quintet is, truly, a nonintimate production. It represents a symphonic poem with an inlay and overlay of tragic meaning covering the almost half-hour span of the music. (Composed in 1950, the original form of the piece was as a Trio for Violin, Bassoon, and Piano. In 1952, Gold enlarged the scoring to include viola and cello and retitled the work as a *Symphony for Five Instruments*.)

The score is prefaced by a quotation from the Lamentations of Jeremiah: "Arise, cry out in the night / The joy of our heart is ceased / Our dance is turned into mourning." In general terms, each of the three movements outlines, in succession, the three prose lines.

Movement one is driving and impetuous, subsiding only at the conclusion. Its principal theme links the quintet, reappearing in the middle movement and twice more in the final one. In the second movement the "joy" which has "ceased" is delineated by a melancholy waltz, scored for strings and bassoon. It alternates with solo piano sections of a mysterious mood. Ultimately, the instruments combine, the waltz idea remaining dominant. The finale commences with a dirgelike statement that recurs several times. Contrast in the central portion of the movement is obtained by a forty-three-measure duo for violin and piano. Though lighter in quality, the general despairing mood is not removed. The last use of the main theme is for unaccompanied violin and concludes the work. It is intensely dramatic by reverse means. Now it is heard as a thinned, desolate statement—the original "cry" almost totally stilled.

Goldenweiser, Alexander (1875–1961)

TRIO

- **Trio for Piano, Violin, and Cello, Op. 31**

Persuasive Russianism in this two-part piano trio. The first movement is a fully developed sonata in E minor. All three instruments have equal opportunity, and there is a fine sense of color, including a section in the rarely used key of C-flat major.

Movement two is a large set of variations on a simple G-major theme. Rich romantic detail and rich tonality choices. Tchaikovsky it isn't, in power or depth, but fully related in its melos.

Goldman, Richard Franko (1910–80)

DUOS

- **Divertimento for Flute and Piano**

The modern divertimento is an assortment of sweets and tangy sours. In this instance, the package contains three absolutely different items, living up to the expectancy of the colorful titles. With few exceptions, the piano is concentrated to a two-voice maximum. Such crisp delineation aids the projection of the flute lines. This almost places the work in the solo, not chamber music, category. In addition there is a cadenza for the flute (two choices are offered, one much larger than the other, both possible of shortening at the will of the flutist). Nevertheless, the style of chamber music can be as assorted as these three pieces, and regardless of the fact that the flute is in first place. But it is not exclusively a solo.

Movement one, "Apéritif" ("Appetizer"), is a fast prelude, jauntily concerned and built from a springing theme that skips through intervals of the fourth. The outer parts of these pitch progressions form a seventh, which span is the main concern of the following movement ("Icy Pastorale"). Since the warmth of most rural scenes uses the more mellifluous intervals of "horn" fifths, lush thirds, and sixths, Goldman restricts the thaw of his winter scene by the use of astringent tonal widths.

The final movement is a Tempo di fado (Portugal—18th century), a popular folk form of song and dance heard in the taverns of that country. The simple, whistleable tunes that form this movement (in which the cadenza is interpolated) are mainly in the minor mode.

- **Duo for Tubas (or Bassoons) (1948)**

Three aspects of a tone row are presented in three movements. In the first movement the effect is almost like a fast-paced waltz. The same type of meter is used in part two, marked, to match the slow metronomic indication ($\quarternote = 56$), with the tempo Andante pessimistico. Inversion of the series is the basis here. Inversion again plus retrograde movement is the fundament for the final Vigoroso music.

Dodecaphonic relevance does not deter Goldman from stretching his technical boundaries a bit.

- **Sonata for Violin and Piano (1952)**

Each of the three movements is based on a tone row, but is no more rigidly calculated or coldly academic than if developed from a triadic theme. The forms are clear and the music has stuff and fiber. It also has heart and voice.

The textural detail in the first movement moves from moderate weight to heaviest and then back again to the initial totality. In parallel fashion tempo signifies the divisions of the middle movement (Molto adagio). Motival deportment is emphasized in the final movement (Molto allegro).

- **Three Duets for Clarinets (1944)**

Expectedly, the three movements are contrapuntal, helping, therefore, to deter the merging of the lines and thus, a loss of interest. The music is built on perky (close-spaced) and slowly unwinding (wide-spaced) themes. Goldman obtains the maximum of contrast, with boundaries of sevenths and ninths prevailing in style with the bipartite writing. The last movement is jumpy with rhythm and in strict canonic form for the first quarter of its length.

Goldman's opus was published in 1945 by Mills Music. (It is dedicated to Aaron Copland.) Much later the composition was recorded and released under the title Sonatina for Two Clarinets.

Goldmann, Friedrich (1941–)

QUARTET

- **String Quartet (1975)**

Each of the three movements, in different manner, is, to borrow Flaubert's phrase, "sustained by the internal force of its style." Weights, densities, textures, spacings, and actions (vertical and horizontal) are specifically maintained within a movement and then changed in the next one. The totality is balanced by the use of panchromaticism throughout. Thereby harmonic tension is a constant in Goldmann's work, as well as invention. And in the total blueprint there is no paucity of coloristic detail.

Movement one is set forth with rhythmic polyphony. Movement two is void of metrical setting. Defined rhythms are notated based on a specific metronomic unit of $\downarrow = 60$. In this disjunctive quadruple arrangement of pulses the instruments enter one by one, separated by long time gaps. The order is first violin, cello, viola, and second violin. Then, in a reminder of Haydn's *Farewell* Symphony, they are singly silenced. This sequence is greatly compressed but balances the first part since the instruments conclude in the same order in which they appeared. The final movement consists of 208 measures. Of these 40 measures depart from total rhythmic unification of all four instruments as they proceed in asymmetrical measurement.

QUINTET

- ***Zusammenstellung:*** **Musik für Bläser** (***Assemblage:*** **Music for Winds) (Flute [alternating Alto Flute and Piccolo], Oboe [alternating English horn], Clarinet [alternating Bass Clarinet], Horn, and Bassoon [alternating Double Bassoon]) (1976)**

Relentless textural shifts—though through the music's twenty-eight-minute length each of the sections is of sizable total—together with coloristic twists, govern Goldmann's somewhat expressionistic, polyphonicized quintet.

The beginning is a quintet grouping. Then follows a trio for bass clarinet, horn, and bassoon. Next, set into this metrically unified trio, is a metrically free running line for alto flute. It breaks away in solo form and then returns (metrically open again) entwined with an exactly measured duo scored for English horn and bass clarinet. And so it goes on throughout. There are duo, trio, quartet, and quintet groupings, nonmetrical material combined with precisely metered music, and large solo presentations for horn, bassoon, clarinet, and English horn. Thus, each member of the quintet has a place in the spotlight.

(The score indicates that the work can be performed as a wind quintet, meaning minus alternating instruments. However, there is no accommodation shown for pitches used by the alternating instruments that are not in the ranges of the basic instruments.)

Goldmark, Karl (1830–1915)

Throughout Goldmark's career he remained faithful to the ideals of Brahms and Wagner. Brahms's idiom was in majority place—only the arrangement of Wagner's timbres attracted him. Though violent creative change surrounded Goldmark in his later years, the notes on his music paper remained in place. In Austria and Germany, the art of composition centered around the Brahmsian tradition until the Viennese composers began to tear down the carefully built tonal house and substitute a more radical architecture. Goldmark's music was sentimentally concerned with the murmurings and whisperings of past voices and avoided the vociferations of the new era.

DUO

- **Sonata for Violin and Piano, Op. 25**

The Op. 25 duo sonata is very representative of Goldmark's chamber music output. Formal demands are met successfully and there are no aural problems to solve. The motival impetus of a triplet figure is almost dogmatically pertinent to the sonata's opening movement, and rhythmic sway is of influence in this part of the work. Variational invention is used in the third movement, and this technique is partially found in the final movement. The sonata's metrical plan is somewhat static, clinging (with the exception of the concluding portion) to triple time.

TRIOS

- **Trio [No. 1] for Piano, Violin, and Cello, Op. 4**

Powerful scoring and a certain heaviness of weight permeate Goldmark's piano trio prose in the corner movements. Rudolf Felber, in an essay on this composer's chamber music, properly terms the opus a product of Goldmark's *Sturm und Drang* period.

Quite a liberated activization concerns the second movement (Adagio). It is packed with arpeggio writing for the piano, which opens the movement alone. A declamatory section for cello and piano follows. Then, marked with a tonality change, the full trio is utilized. Toward the end of the movement the solo piano concept returns. The Scherzo (movement three) splits and mixes its 6/8 meter into duple and triple divisions and adds syncopation for extra flavor. Fugal action is the principal structural point.

- **Trio [No. 2] for Piano, Violin, and Cello, Op. 33**

Classical orientation mixed with romantic zealousness shows Goldmark as a true follower of Brahms. His second piano trio is another example of the hybrid-type composer who builds a classical structure with romantic tools.

Only the short third movement, which leads *attacca* into the final Allegro, is sensitized with chromatic sounds. Diatonicism prevails as the Trio begins in stormy E minor, then proceeds into a contrasting Scherzo, with a classically determined tonal mode relationship of G major. The central section of this movement is marked by homespun, Viennese-style triple swing. For the most part, whatever foreign harmonic tones are used are merely decorative rather than special colorations in the music's fabric. The fourth movement commences in E minor to balance the first part of the Trio.

Beginning with *forte* power, it runs its course and subsides into the epilogue. There the quality is somewhat meditative, aided by the warmer parallel key of E major.

QUINTET

- **Quintet for Two Violins, Viola, Cello, and Piano, Op. 30**

Goldmark's piano quintet is highlighted by a superb slow movement—an entrancing song-swept expression set in G-flat major. The opening section of the movement, with measured eighth notes in the piano and the cello singing above, represents peak romanticism.

In the first movement Goldmark uses more polyphony than is to be found in his other chamber music productions. This contrapuntalism not only covers small sets of imitations but full-fledged canonic episodes. The scoring of the initial part of the movement gives prominence to the strings as a unit against the piano. Still another polyphonic detail is the fugato in the final Allegro vivace, which moves along in snappy alla breve time. Apt use of augmentation is another credit within the movement.

The Scherzo is concentrated, its specialty to be found in the area of harmonic suspensions. These are further stimulants within a stimulating conception.

Goldmark, Rubin (1872–1936)

Three important facts concern Goldmark. He was the nephew of the better-known Austrian composer Karl Goldmark. Second, he held high rank as a teacher, heading the composition department of the Juilliard School from 1924 until his death. Among his many pupils were Aaron Copland and George Gershwin. Third, the piano quartet discussed *below*, the best of his three chamber music pieces and winner of the Paderewski Prize in 1909.

Goldmark was a traditionalist in matters of form. A little more license entered his harmony. This amalgam never changed, regardless of the subject that inspired him. Classical-romantic calligraphy was used in orchestrally describing the Herculean performances of *Samson*, in the concert overture *Hiawatha*, and in Americana such as *The Call of the Plains* and the *Requiem,* suggested by Lincoln's Gettysburg Address. The script remained the same in his other compositions.

QUARTET

- **Quartet in A Major for Piano, Violin, Viola, and Cello, Op. 12**

The piano quartet is amply proportioned but never overly thick. Scoring fluidness evidences a control that many a romantically minded composer overlooked. This comparison of texture is made by the quasi-symphonic proposition of the opening part—a fully realized sonata movement in the home key—and the thinner, more concentrated aspect of the Scherzo. The latter is preceded by a modulatory-minded slow movement and followed by a rondo-shaped conclusion.

Golestan, Stan (1872–1956)

DUO

- **Sonatine for Flute and Piano (1932)**

A strong intervallic imprint defines Golestan's Romanian background in this charming and beautifully conceived duet. Without being overfervent, but certainly most distinct, the augmented step (many scalic forms in Romanian music utilize this span) is primary to the first two movements and provides emphatic contrast in the third movement by its use in the middle section. This third movement is titled

Adagietto. To make certain that no one misunderstands the pace to be used (adagietto is somewhat faster than adagio) Golestan protectively tempos the music Non troppo lento.

Compact sonata form, with an engaging and spritely secondary idea, opens the duo. The Perpetuum Mobile fully lives up to its title. Not for once does the flute deviate from its sextuplet charge in this perpetual motion. This rhythmic regularity is spruced up by metrical shifts between quadruple, duple, and triple pulsations. The Rondo Final is light and yet tinged with some native-turned seriousness.

The duo sonatine has definite nationalistic identity. Golestan, born in Vaslui, Romania, was long a resident in Paris (for many years during that time he was the music critic for the important paper *Le Figaro*). However, while he may have been considered a cosmopolitan Parisian he was above all a Romanian nationalist.

TRIO

- *Petite suite bucolique (en forme de Trio) (Little Pastoral Suite [in Trio form]),* **for Oboe, Clarinet, and Bassoon (1953)**

Golestan completed his wind trio in August 1953. It makes clear that the age of 81 does not deter a composer from writing with youthful spirit.

The first and third movements complement each other, both substantiated by three-part designs. And both conclude with unison declarations that proceed with increasing speed toward the finishing lines. The Humoresque (movement one) is quieter in its whimsicality than the third movement, "Jeux" ("Games"), where the scenario is considerably controlled by a rhythmic figure. This symmetrical shape is strengthened by the second movement (Lamento), which serves as a middle pivot of two-ply contrast. The double control comes

from content and use of rondo form.

QUARTETS

- **String Quartet [No. 1] in A-flat (1923)**

A welding of folkloristic detail, poetic native data, and cyclic coaction is found in Golestan's initial string quartet, composed in 1923. Another significance is the monitoring of the introductions, the yield of the movements coming from the preliminary substances. Golestan proves the axiom that the worth of anything is what it will bring.

The second topic of the first movement is "based on a Romanian folk theme." Its melancholy sentiments stand sharply in contrast to the principal subject, not only by its pathos but through the counter factors of speed, tonality, and broader boundaries. This folk theme also serves as the governor for the metrically shifting Scherzando of the second movement. (The preamble of this movement depicts the theme in slower-scaled speed.) Again initially outlined, the theme of the final movement is later rhythmically compressed, tossed in animated form, and eventually stretched into augmented values.

Golestan was sensitive to the dramaticism of dynamic deployment. In the final movement the sound-volume intensity climaxes more than a hundred measures before the conclusion. At that point the tempo begins to slow down, the sonority scale dims, and the instrumental sounds are whispery. In its concentration, this, too, exemplifies forceful expressivity.

- **String Quartet No. 2 (1934)**

Use of subtitles in a multiple-movement composition may infer a suite compilation. In this quartet (completed eleven years after Golestan's first work in the medium), such image is removed by the symmetrical concept of thematic quotation. Thus, interlinking proves structural totality—the theme of the Preludium postscripting the Allegro final.

Native resource is skillfully utilized in the quartet. Despite major-key tonality, the prelude is tinged with the plaintiveness of the Romanian doina. Additional evidence of this characteristic is found in the Lamento (movement three). Testimony to a beloved colleague is fulfilled with intense emotion in that part of the work. (The second quartet is indicated "In Memoriam Paul Dukas," with whom Golestan studied, in addition to Vincent d'Indy and Albert Roussel.)

Movements two and four are dance jubilations. In the latter, a binomial design is made from a motive built from a scale line completed with a syncopative twist and a contrastive theme of simplicity. In the former, balletic demonstration is cast in scherzo style, with regional music properties. Golestan does not hide his citizenship—the title of the movement is Scherzo (Mărunțel-Danse).

Golovkov, Alexei (1918–43)

QUARTET

- **String Quartet No. 2**

Golovkov's posthumously published quartet (issued in Moscow in 1957, fourteen years after the composer's death) is of substantial size. The opening sonata-structured Allegro vivo movement runs 486 measures; the third movement (Presto scherzando) covers no fewer than 635 measures. Movement two is a slow-tempo music; the finale is a Presto vivace, introduced by a slight quote from the quartet's opening. The conclusion of this fourth movement is one of breadth, moving dynamically from *fortissississimo* to a final *pianississississimo*.

Regularity of form is defined throughout. Clear themes but much phrase repetition are fundaments of Golovkov's style. And so are

ostinato patterns and pedal points. However, a romantic passion colors the music, and it is that matter that compensates for the attenuated continuity.

Golubev, Evgeni (1910–)

DUOS

- **Sonata for Trumpet and Piano, Op. 36, No. 2**

A one-movement affair. Although there are the requisite contrastive sections, it is the initial definitive and declarative material that commands the piece throughout. The episodes are distinct, especially one for the piano alone, and another, a total legato statement for the trumpet, quite oddly marked Pietoso (meaning "kindly" or "sympathetic"), to be played either muted or with open timbre.

The material fits the personality of the brass instrument. This is a rich and clear depiction, minus the fanfaristic and militaristic modes that style so much trumpet writing.

- **Sonata for Violin and Piano, Op. 37**

The phrase "rhapsodic romanticism" chosen to describe this work might be translated in the pejorative sense, but that is not the intent. Golubev's music has the divisional aspect that pertains to variational documentation, and it is that which led to the choice of phrase used. The Sonata is busy and harmonically punchy. Its textures are lessened in a few places, with the use of unaccompanied violin passages in the first two movements.

The finale is a type of grotesque dance. It, too, has a short solo violin section. And it also presses for color credits with the use of ponticello and harmonics, plus pizzicato of both right- and left-hand types.

Golubev

QUARTETS

- **String Quartet No. 2, Op. 31**

Music moving in the mainstream of the romantic tradition, solidified and colored with Russian melos in the first two of the three movements. In the third movement there is more attention given instrumental blood and guts, with fistfuls of sonority and a stress on rhythmic doublings by pairs of instruments.

Movement one contrasts homophonic distribution with polyphony, including a fugato. The second movement is Golubev's *Sérénade mélancolique,* with the instruments muted throughout and with the tripulsed music beginning in G minor and concluding in E-flat minor.

- **String Quartet No. 3, Op. 38**

Romantic thrust and passion and heavy textures mark the first movement. The form is a free sonata, but the push and shove of the lines cover the structure with rhapsody. One example: a *fortississimo* octave declaration by the first violin and viola (instrumental pairing is a favorite device of this composer) with oscillating quadruple-voice rhythmic accompaniment (also in triple *forte)* by the second violin and cello. The same type of rhythmic doubling occurs in the finale, but the textures are thinner and more "quartetish."

The Presto second movement represents the Scherzo. The music constituting the Trio division is picturesque and dynamically different in tonality (fully chromatic compared to the D-minor principal tonality), meter (triple in place of duple), timbre (all the instruments are muted), pace (here a Tempo di valse), and playing style (marked Flessibile [Flexible]). Just as vivid are the variational moods that pass in review in the slow movement. This is fervid romanticism, many cuts above the tuneful type.

González-Zuleta

QUINTET

- **Quintet for Harp, Two Violins, Viola, and Cello, Op. 39**

Music that romantically impresses with the aid of some impressionistic devices. There are four movements, and subtle balances are utilized. Thus, the string quartet is totally muted in movements one and three, the longest movements are numbers two and four. And in traditional means the tempo sequence is slow–fast–slow–fast.

The sonic aspects divide the thematic material between the plucked string instrument and the bowed string group. Antiphony is drawn on to focus comparative timbre qualities. Golubev is a traditionalist in writing for the harp. He avoids any special effects. The score includes a short harp cadenza (in movement one), and there are the usual glissandos and harmonic sounds.

González-Zuleta, Fabio (1920–)

QUINTET

- *Quinteto 1960 (Abstracto)* **for Woodwind Quintet**

Chromatic detail emphasized in good part by contrapuntal distinctions. In the first two movements these are alternated freely with total rhythmic passages cluster-tuned in vertical combination. Movement three is scherzolike. Movement four again exhibits pure rhythmicity and passages of linear detail.

This Colombian composer avoids the slick stereotyped style often found in wind quintet compositions. He substitutes the very opposite: sonorous stringency. Of course, he makes clear his objective by the subtitle of the work.

Goodman, Joseph (1918–)

DUOS

- *Jadis III (Hommage à "La Sérénade interrompue")* for Flute and Bassoon (1972)

Retrospective inspiration (*jadis* meaning "in days of yore") tied in with the character of a Debussy piano piece. (*"La Sérénade interrompue"* is the ninth of the set in the first book of Debussy's twelve préludes.)

Goodman's wind duo (the third of a group with the title *Jadis)* is suave and vocal music, a music of uninterrupted poetic content even when it explores rhythmically.

(The parenthetical part of the title does not appear in the published edition, issued in 1976 by General Music. On the other hand, the recording of the work, released in 1975 by Crystal Records, includes it in its liner notes but not on the label of the disc.)

- *Music* for Two Flutes

The creativity and technical command of Goodman's *Music* (four movements) are of brilliant order, realizing completely exciting experiences. Of course, music for paired flutes would seem to eliminate any possibility of a special stimulating reaction, but the flavors, textural clarity, and variety of the opus produce it.

A Sostenuto, long lined and contrapuntally bittered in its two-voice combine, links to an Allegretto, rhythmically filled and thrust phrased. Quintuple stress is paramount. This is conveyed by measures of 5/16 and measures in 8/16, which are mainly pulsed in totals of 5 and 3. The Vivo equals a Scherzo (in strict tripartite form), while the final Molto allegro is motivally constructed.

TRIOS

- Five Bagatelles for Flute, Clarinet, and Bassoon

A sense of etudelike responsivity (and responsibility) pervades Goodman's set of five pieces. This is especially indicated in the second piece, which principally tosses fast figurations about. These are prefaced by an Adagio of four measures, which appears at the end and once inside the movement—there for a total of two measures. Etude character is also represented somewhat in the third piece, with a breakup of pulse by dividing each beat between two instruments, and further by the motility of a unified rhythmic figure in the fourth of the set.

The first and fifth Bagatelles are related in their general style, thus providing a neat balance for the suite. Plenty of chromatic steam in this music, and colorful harmonic containers. Goodman does not hurl any new musical axioms, but he is far from a decidedly reticent creator.

- Trio for Flute, Violin, and Piano

Goodman practices unity within diversity in this three-movement work, and practices it by the exceedingly dangerous (and difficult) method of structural fusion. He executes it with passion and urgency. Providing the listener realizes what formal shapes are being developed, then the plan is successful. Not being privy to the plan aural definition would tend to blend the materials, which blend they must in any event—this is not spatial music with three orchestras in three parts of the hall each playing different, unrelated material, à la Henry Brant.

In movement one there are triple "levels" (the composer's term). These project (in order of instrumental entry) a sonata form distinguished by the violin, an Etude and Trio outlined by the piano, and an Introduction and Rhapsody defined by the flute. In movement two the violin begins what is described as a Rondo à la tarantella, the piano then announces a very simple subject in bare octaves, and a theme and variations are then developed. When the flute enters it joins the violin in terms of building the rondo form. The final movement is a slow-tempo (Lento) fugue.

Planned specifically or not, an overall scheme is operative as well. In turn, the amount of formal levels exactly decreases in each part of the work. There are three in the initial movement, two in the following movement, and one in the concluding movement. Indeed, creatively, Goodman lives dangerously, but safely.

QUINTET

- **Quintet for Wind Instruments (Flute, Oboe, Clarinet, Horn, and Bassoon) (1954)**

Tonality that is free of traditional cultures is apparent in all three movements. Sonata style is also free in the first movement, though there are the usual pair of principal contrasting ideas. (Goodman does not write squared "tunes.") Within the development of these the return of the second, more-agitated concept is marked by revamped instrumental apportionment and a few touches of invertible counterpoint.

Movement two is shaped like a scherzo. It has a middle section in faster tempo with a purposeful, precise rhythm. The outer sections are sharply contrastive. Symmetrical in total pulses (eight to the measure), these are disclosed in a variety of beat patterns: 3–2–3, 2–3–3, and 3–3–2. Juxtaposition brings additional variety: a pedal point is designated with totals of 2–6, a rhythmic ostinato of 2–3–3 units is joined to a line divided into 3–2–3 beats. The rhythmic amounts are never predictable, and thus the music takes on an urgency and a refreshing tensility.

The metrical keenness of the middle move-

ment becomes exceedingly sharper in the final one—a set of introspective variations. Derived from Boris Blacher's variable meter technique, precise arithmetical progressions structure the music. There are six such sets, and each is formulated so that the totality progressively contracts. The first continuity subtracts one beat in each measure (5–4–3–2–1) four times; the next group finds each measure less two pulses (11–9–7–5–3), again repeated four times. The proportions of larger totality paralleled by larger decreases remain constant. In the next group, three beats are subtracted in each of the measures (15–12–9–6–3), once more repeated four times. The next pattern reduces each measure unit by four (in ten sets of five measures); and the ultimate is reached in the configuration of 23–18–13–8–3 pulses per measure. This five-beat contraction is run through seven times. Finally, the original formula is utilized of reduction by one beat per measure (5–4–3–2–1) ten times, and a freely changing metric scheme then marks the coda. Symmetry equates symmetry—as the variants progress in these different arrangements the tempo is quickened. Goodman's rhythmic exposition is strictly charted mathematically, but the musical results justify the act.

Goossen, Frederic (1927–)

DUOS

- *Clausulae* **for Violin and Piano (1971)**

Pantonal music with clear, dissonant grammar. The form is a neat connection of seven pieces separated by cadences—hence the title from the Latin *clausula,* meaning "close." However, this term applied to the cadential formulas of 16th-century polyphonic music. Here it has no linked significance.

The tempo assortment is miscellaneous; there is no attempt to alternate strictly the separate speeds of the pieces. Save for the last six measures, the violin is a solo voice in the sixth part of the work.

- *Temple Music* **for Violin and Piano (1972)**

Fancy title, but nothing exotic, or signifying any special picture. *Temple Music* was written for the dedication of a synagogue, Temple Emanu-El, in Tuscaloosa, Alabama, and thus the choice of title.

According to Goossen, the plan of his duo was modeled on Beethoven's Piano Sonata, Op. 53 (the *Waldstein,* in C major). There are three movements: a strongly rhythmic one; a slow movement in the form of a violin recitative with antiphonal entrances for the piano alone; and a final fugue (Allegro risoluto), introduced by a Pesante section. The textural contrast between the second and third movements makes this pantonal duo extremely colorful.

Goossens, Eugene (1893–1962)

Romanticism is always present in this supervirtuoso composer's music, but not the potboiler type of sliding harmonies or of the swing-song of cakes and ale. With Goossens, romanticism was of color sound, of musical tinting—a far cry from the hybrid, steadfast holding-the-line of Brahms or Reger. His romanticism was of daring spirit, consciously related yet not belabored. Goossens passed through different stages. He was quite young but active in the days of the *Sacre* scandal, was writing and conducting in the heart of musical life during the vital, volatile post–World War I era, and influences did exert their effect on the wide-awake young composer determined to run away from the ancient gods. He always cherished the visionary style, even though it turns out to be a cloak more picturesque than romantic.

DUOS

- **Sonata No. 1 in E Minor for Violin and Piano, Op. 21**

Goossens's duo sonata is romantic, but unscathed by even the slightest impurity of such style. Nor had Goossens lost touch with his English environment, despite his cosmopolitanism, his residence in other countries, and regardless of his slight use of folk material. English disposition infiltrates or is deliberately punctuated within his chromatic sentences; as in the middle of the slow movement, where a Hampshire folk song is bedecked with Goossens's usual harmonies. Both in its first, reticent introduction, and then its broadly soaring repetition, the entire maturation of folk-song composition is felt. The movement forms an alpha and omega of juxtapositional technique. The folk tune forms the second part to the first, one of fully original material; when part three occurs, the two themes are combined in a handclasp of perfectly amalgamated art and folk materials.

The outer movements are, respectively, of sonata and scherzo style. While it will be noted that lyrical qualities are completely subsidiary to ironic rhythms in the latter, the shifting and the freeing of the compound is another instance of the romantic viewpoint. Goossens writes effectively; there are no mere effects in this music; the substance is of real musical matter.

- **Sonata No. 2 for Violin and Piano, Op. 50**

The music is heavy. Goossens's creative verve is enclosed in rich chromaticism. The pitch flux is insistent, and the scoring produces consistent textural luxuriance. With only two instruments involved there are huge sonorous implosions and explosions.

All three movements have these stylistic imprints. This does not lessen in regard to the central Intermezzo, marked A la sicilienne but seething with weighted lines.

TRIOS

- *Five Impressions of a Holiday* **for Flute (or Violin), Cello, and Piano, Op. 7**

Goossens may not have related the exact events that stirred him to write his Op. 7, but the sure, depictive touch and the color pertaining to instrumental usage state a great deal. In his musical processes, Goossens does not demand a prejudicial story-following listener. If one wishes, the imagination can float along with these beautifully formed French-style musical aquatints. The *Impressions* will not be harmed.

These pictorial surveys begin with "In the Hills." The music of this movement is based on a rising theme which can equal the viewing of new vistas. "By the Rivers" is somewhat ornamentally written. Since a set rhythm of a pair of eighth notes predominates, these waters flow evenly. The third movement is graphically painted and is titled "The Water Wheel" (a favorite subject with many composers who sense the possibilities of kinetic rhythm to sketch this object). The wheel glints brightly in the sun of E-flat major, a tonality used, however, in a Ravelian fashion. A point of importance—the wheel eventually stops.

Movement four, "The Village Church," is very carefully drawn indeed. Clashing bells, in carillon style, are sounded by the piano as the flute and cello intone a chant. The ecclesiastical feeling is paralleled by modal writing. The final movement consists of very merry music; the sounds of crowds are depicted by slightly dissonant seventh chords as well as by more frictioned harmonies. This section, "At the Fair," is the most joyous of the five pieces, concluding with a very delightful echo cadence contrasted to a drum effect. Goossens has had fun!

- **Suite for Flute, Violin, and Harp (or Two Violins and Harp [or Piano]), Op. 6**

A composer who imitates can be successful only if he produces a work with technical finish. To imitate may be to re-create, but unless the composition shows more than a mere catching of the spirit, the seeming *mot juste* may become nothing more than a negative cliché. Goossens was only 20 when he wrote this work under the influence of the Debussy school. He was ready for compositional liberation, having progressed through academic teaching and training unscathed. His expert knowledge included virtuosity, not only in composition but on the piano and violin; in addition, he possessed first-class ability as a conductor. Such all-round knowledge would make any composer hearken to the call of handling instruments graphically. Drawn to the impressionists as Goossens was, it almost had to follow that a composition written under such attraction would abound with color. But the novel sound combinations of this trio (less so if played in the alternate version, especially if the harp is replaced by a piano, because the piano cannot produce chordal glissandos, and two violins merge, whereas one violin with a flute gives more contrastive resource of color) are not mere effects; they are the significant manners of impressionistic musical society.

The Impromptu is like summer-afternoon music; the sonorities in both that movement and the succeeding Serenade captivate but are restrained. In the Serenade, a night-music atmosphere persists, but is one that seems to surround lush, heavily covered gardens; the song that is sung eventually dies away. The final Divertissement communicates the pleasures of diversion; it is a dance of riotous color; four times it is embraced in the sweep of glissando sound.

QUARTETS

- **Concert Piece for Oboe (alternating English horn), Two Harps, and Piano, Op. 65**

This is a second setting of Goossens's opus. The original was for oboe (alternating English horn), two harps, and orchestra. However, Goossens designed his composition so that it could "also be played as a chamber work" with the scoring as noted above. Affiliation continues in the dedication, which is for his sisters Marie and Sidonie, both harpists, and Leon, his brother, the distinguished oboist.

Tertial determination styles the first part of the work in terms of thrusting subjects and harmonic coloration. Variational development is the device for the second movement. At its concluding portion there is a huge cadenza for the two harps that includes a quotation from the beginning of the work and which then connects to a long cadenza for the English horn. The last is linked to the finale, which dances its way through scherzo, waltz, and galop. It also continues the cadenza element with a short "quasi" type for the oboe.

- *Phantasy Quartet* for Strings (Two Violins, Viola, and Cello), Op. 12

This modern type (in its freedom of style and structure, related only very partially to the old fancy) has as many forms as the half-dozen spellings that have been used ("phantasy," "phantasie," "fantasie," "fantaisie," "fantasy," and "fantasia" all mean the same). It deals, as in bygone days, with the materials compressed to but one movement. However, it is not a resurrection of the past form but rather a modification of sonata form; a condensation of several movements into one, or a transformation of compact thematic resources; above all, a musical economy of organic unity. Its appearance, in the early part of the present century,

was symptomatic of the times. Rather than the sprawling affairs of the 19th century, conciseness was becoming an important factor in the programming of concerts. Listeners could give a work more attention if it became aurally simple to encompass matters at a single hearing, as it were, rather than relate several movements together. In a word, the fantasy was a middleman between the formal structures of regulatory sonata form in compounded movements and the fanciful whims of the romantic era.

Goossens's employment of the form is of both spontaneous thematic connection and compression of separate movements into one unit; all by a rhapsodic portrayal of chromatic yet impressionistic means, requiring a virtuosic organization to make clear the work's meaning. The opening unison Largo proclamation forms the motto from which the thematic material for two sections (divided further into colored developments) is derived—first, a vacillating series of mooded tempos and then a slow-paced part. An Allegro scherzando follows; the beginning (not the introduction) is recalled and the scherzo idea drives to conclusion. Goossens not only uses sectional depiction and thematic transformation but also permits himself the leisure of formal relaxation inherent in works of unchecked fantasy. He appropriates all factors in sight.

- **String Quartet [No. 1], Op. 14**

Contrary to the initials marking the variations in Elgar's *Enigma,* those in Goossens's quartet were immediately recognized. The "A.B.," "R.J.," and "C.S." prefacing the three movements signify the names of the composer's colleagues in the Philharmonic Quartet (an organization in which Goossens was the second violin for a number of years, before composing, conducting, and other activities made impossible his continuance as a member). While this is the type of musical work that sounds aloud one's thoughts in public (since it presumably conveys in each of its movements a type of musical portrait of a different friend), one need not know the musicians involved, similar to meeting Elgar's friends "pictured within"; in fact, it is rather stimulating to guess what a person's characteristics are through music partially descriptive of him.

The first movement denotes Arthur Beckwith, who was the first violinist of the organization, apparently a scholarly gentleman as befits the leader of a string quartet. It is contemplative music, containing parallel elements of fugato, and has a coda of sober quality. The cello holds the stage for the last twenty-seven measures—the last nine completely alone, playing with even darker register than usually possible, since the lowest string, C, is tuned down to B-natural preliminary to this section.

The slow movement (inscribed to Raymond Jeremy) pictures with excellent silhouette the person involved and the instrument he played. It is not only slow-paced but darkened by use of mutes—concomitants of viola timbre, which instrument, further, is featured by majority assignments of solo work. The last movement (Allegro giocoso quasi burlesca) concerns the cellist, Cedric Sharpe. No doubt Mr. Sharpe was quicker in humor than generally concerns music assigned to the instrument he played, for the movement is one of blusterous quirks and pranks. The opening motive is important, a type of thematic generator, which later receives augmentation and spearheads a fugato. That the quartet personnel is unified is shown by a return of the first movement's theme.

■ String Quartet No. 2, Op. 59

While Goossens created music during his exceedingly busy career (which naturally brought to bear many varying interests), he never discarded, as he passed from French impressionistic influence to a more individually cultivated style, the sense of the colorist. Nor did he forsake, for all other means, the love of folk song.

The second string quartet is one of Goossens's most important works. He composed it (in 1940) in the northeastern part of the United States, at a time of international shock, with political prognosis, so patently incorrect, that there would be no war in our time, since Hitler's hordes had a year before already run amuck in Poland. Goossens revealed his true self in turning to his motherland for the symbols to show his deep love for his country, and the material stimulus to express it. The second movement defines his feelings. The music is based on lines from Coleridge, written in 1798—"Fears in Solitude—During the Alarm of an Invasion" ("There lives nor form nor feeling in my soul—Unborrowed from my country!"). Is there need to emphasize the parallel of the composer away from his country in time of critical emergency? Further, to implement this emotion, Goossens bases the movement on the haunting beauties of the English folk tune "Searching for Lambs."

The first movement begins with an introduction, leads to a metrically uneven theme (mainly in septimal pattern), related to a very rhythmic accompaniment and another dramatic theme. A preliminary pizzicato subject to the second theme, the rhythmic accompaniment and the secondary theme itself all combine in unit deployment to form an important fugato. Relationship is thus commandeered by contrast and then assimilation. The second movement states the folk tune in three different instruments before a contrasting faster section enters. There, again, the theme appears several times, but over it there is variation by rhapsodic latchstrings, rhythmic fantasy, and color. An Alla burlesca in large ternary form, more sardonic than gay, leads to the concluding movement.

In the last movement (Epilogue), there passes in review the entire quartet's themes and spirit. This is conveyed amid the final movement's subject, which has somewhat the shape of the third movement's precipitate descent.

(The second movement was transcribed for string orchestra and published with the title Pastorale, with the parenthetical subtitle Andante con tristezza.)

- *Two Sketches* for String Quartet, Op. 15

Magnificent instrumental picture painting is represented in these two quartet sketches.

"By the Tarn" is the first of the two pieces. The muted quartet instruments sounding within and around a constant background of undulating rhythm (generally triplets against eighths to show the waters have some currents) picture exactly the lake being described. Goossens's atmospheric writing evokes a perfect image of introspective calm. Compared to this, the second piece, "Jack O'Lantern (Ignis Fatuus)," is a kaleidoscopic whimsy, of biting and tantalizing "Will O' the Wisp" variety. In this instance, the virtuosity and color drawn from the quartet are of hair-raising order. Although kept under sonorous wraps by the use of mutes, the music employs various string-instrument coloristic techniques, including a chromatic triadal glissando by the second violin. The fluorescence of this piece is that of a dance in half shadows—a witches' sabbath in dim light.

(A version of "By the Tarn" was published for clarinet ad lib and string orchestra.)

QUINTET

- Quintet for Piano, Two Violins, Viola, and Cello, Op. 23

The synthesis of this Quintet, gained by transmutationary technique, is almost of the Franck school. But it cannot be classified with the works that follow Franckian belief. Harmonically, Goossens's departures are as foreign to Franck as is his form, though its fantasy mold (compression of movements into one

segment, intercoherence of thematic relationship) is very close to cyclic accessibilities.

All the revelations of this musical scripture are to be found in the four-measure introduction, and its music determinedly "endureth for ever." It is genuine composition in the matter of complete development of a motival source. The Allegro shapes it rhythmically in diminutive and augmented fashion. The Andante tranquillo (marked by muted strings) relaxes its impetuosity, then builds it dramatically to fanfared state, dismembers and scatters it jocosely. Though it returns ultimately in grandiose octaval proclamation, these are but the highlights of this one-theme usage; its spectrum catches much more in the prismal colors of this piano quintet.

SEXTET

- Sextet for Strings (Three Violins, Viola, and Two Cellos), Op. 37

What makes this work of ordinary technique is only the means that Goossens so often used—fantasy form, wherein interconnected movements are spurred and developed from an initially stated, unifying central theme. But the use of three violins, one viola, and two cellos to form the string sextet is special, especially in thinning out the middle voices for the support of soprano tone. But Goossens rarely was a composer satisfied with normal and average color. This composition can be considered as still another illustration of his predilection for the virtuoso use of instruments.

The Sextet (composed especially for the Berkshire Festival of Chamber Music in 1923, under the sponsorship of Elizabeth Sprague Coolidge) runs in one movement, from an impetuous introduction to a little slower section; the thematic means are derived from the former, developed in the latter, then marked by an Adagio and a contrastive section leading to the final Allegro. The interchange of the theme's form is fairly apparent, though figurations tend somewhat to hide it purposely. A fugato marks the last portion of the work, with a sustained, four-measure final announcement of thematic outline preceding the five-measure close.

OCTET

- **Concertino for String Octet (Four Violins, Two Violas, and Two Cellos) (1928)**

This work is like a foreigner amid the composer's productions. It fuses modern style within the true baroque tradition—thus merging sophistication with Handelian clarity. The title may lead one to expect the split-off characteristic of the concerto grosso (wherein the "concertino," of two or three voices, was contrasted by its solo texture to the ripieni—the tutti reinforcement of the whole string body). Goossens's Concertino but rarely uses solo characteristics in any total amount of voices; they are in the great minority in the athletic galvanism and muscular swing of the work as a whole. (There are three sections played without pause, with the first returning at the end.)

In the first part, the opening theme is restated in rondo-ritornel fashion, sometimes changed but still with evident profile. While there are lyrical moments in the middle portion, and a light rhythmic swing to the third section, the opening theme soon intrudes on such romantic deviations, and the work is brought to order with the decided stamping and drive of the original subject.

This octet is the direct antithesis to the great work for the same medium composed by Mendelssohn. If nature, the sky, and the sun are reflected in that composer's work for eight strings, clean and rich soil cling to this one.

(The Concertino is also available for double string orchestra, with the same instrumentation as the original chamber music version plus double basses.)

NONET

- **Fantasy for Nine Wind Instruments (Flute, Oboe, Two Clarinets, Two Bassoons, Two Horns, and Trumpet), Op. 40**

This nonet gives a full representation of wind color, not only using the fraternal brass instrument (the horn) so often associated with wind or (better stated) woodwind groups but the puissant trumpet. The woodwinds are six in number (flute, oboe, two clarinets, and two bassoons), the brass three (two horns with the trumpet).

Goossens employs thematic conversion technique. All three movements stem from the opening horn call; though in the slow movement such material is more bound in as an interrelative and contrastive matter than the first section, where it is developed to a high degree. Subdued fantasy is derived from the slow section's conjunct lines, more potent for this mood than would be the case in using a disjunct, clarionlike subject. The final section is announced by the trumpet (thus, balancing the flanking movements by brass-color declaration of themes). It is a rhythmic Scherzo brought to conclusion by an ever-increasing rate of speed, the final cadence punctuated by the announcement of the basic motive (or rather its termination)!

Gordon, Philip (1894–1983)

DUO

- **Sonatina for Clarinet and Piano**

Most of Gordon's output is of the didactic type in addition to a huge amount of transcriptions of standard literature made for orchestra, band, etc. His music is tonal and simple, neatly turned, and well sounding. Within such boundaries no critical quibbles can be made.

The contrapuntal opening surprises. Plenty of scalic stuff in the first movement. Binary form is used for the slow movement, partitioned in the middle by a short clarinet cadenza. A jiglike theme treated with five variations completes the piece. Each of the variants is a clear, supportive realization.

Górecki, Benedykt (1899–1980)

DUO

- **Two Etudes for Bassoon and Piano (1943)**

No specific technical point is stressed in this case. Passage-work is found in the second part of the first piece (Andante cantabile). The second piece begins slowly and moves onto an Allegro, which has large spans in its first part. One is hard put to agree with calling these pieces "studies."

Górecki, Henryk (1933–)

TRIOS

- *Genesis I: Element* for Three String Instruments (Violin, Viola, and Cello), Op. 19, No. 1

The first in a cycle of three compositions; the second (written, as was the first piece, in 1962) is *Canti strumentali* for fifteen performers; the third (composed in 1963) is *Monodram* for soprano, metal percussion, and six double basses.

Genesis is a set of sound bands shifted, combined, opposed, and moving. There is sectional formation but not development, merely change. And this applies to pitch, sometimes specific, other times approximated by graphic distribution of the notation. In one section all the strings are to be tuned very flat. No spiritual messages are involved in this string trio but a vitally constant tension by the brutalized timbral clustering.

- *La Musiquette III* **for Three Violas, Op. 25**

Pitch detail is completely at the discretion of the players; they are instructed to tune down all their strings "considerably." This means that the forceful blocks of massed sounds *as* blocks are the basic objective completely without specific relationship in terms of sounds. No metrical order is applied; the pitch divisions are regulated by sound lengths (the first set, for example, based on a metronomic unit coverage of $\quarternote$ = 48–50 proceeds in totals of 11–10–3–16–9). Throughout, the interplay is dictated by repetitive one-line sounds and explosive tutti chords sometimes at a dynamic strength of *fortissississimo*. Strong primitiveness surrounds the work.

(More violas can be utilized providing the balance is maintained between the voices.)

Gorini, Gino (1914–)

DUO

- **Sonata for Cello and Piano (1939)**

An attractive representation of Italian neoclassicism. The open harmonic scheme reminds one of Malipiero.

Sonority balance is always to be heeded in the writing of a cello-piano sonata. Gorini is careful about this point, and when he wishes the piano to have its head he makes certain it plays alone (as in the opening movement). This type of writing is matched by the opening of the middle (slow) movement where the entire statement is for solo cello. The finale is rhythmically dynamic and has equal instrumental apportionment. There is a perorative conclusion: very slow, very sustained, and very sonorous.

Gossec, François-Joseph (1734–1829)

DUO

- **Duet in B-flat Major for Two Violins**

A representative chamber work by this significant Belgian composer. It is neatly melodized and balanced. Movement one is an Allegretto with thematic weights mainly placed on offbeats. Movement two is a full-scale Minuetto. Both movements are in the home key, the only major tonal change is to G minor, marking the Trio of the Minuetto.

Gotkovsky, Ida (1933–)

DUOS

- *Images de Norvège (Norwegian Pictures)* **for Clarinet and Piano**

Two short pieces, slow and fast in tempo. The designs are ternary in both cases, and a short cadenza is built into the second of the images. Neatly turned items in updated tonal style.

- **Suite for Tuba and Piano (1969)**

The greatest amount of individuality pertains to the medium. A proclamatory Introduction is followed by an Andante, and the duo is completed by a perky Final. The last is the best because it displays the big brass baby capable of alive action. Nothing very heavy here, but certainly nothing like a type of *morceau de salon*.

- *Variations pathétiques* **for Alto Saxophone and Piano (1980)**

Free variations spread over six separate movements, and a juicy compilation it is. There are plentiful saxophone athletics here, with cadenzas in the two outer movements and plenty of perpetual-motion content in parts four and six.

Movement two is a Scherzo in prestissimo tempo, with pitch action and clanging open chords. Recitative type in movement three, aria type in movement five. All cohesively contemporaneously slanted in a collected manner. Musically responsible and responsive all the way.

Gotovac, Jakov (1895–1982)

OCTET

- *The Dalmatian Shepherd Boy* **for Eight Recorders (Two Soprano, Two Alto, Two Tenor, and Two Bass Recorders)**

A charming delight by this Yugoslavian composer. This is homespun, innocent music producing a vigor of expression derived from folk song. The ingredients are the pat ones: augmented steps, consecutive fifths, light modality, and drone pedals.

The form is fittingly simple, namely, A–B–A–Coda; the recapitulation shortened. Tonalities and tempos follow suit: The first and last sections are in A minor and in allegretto; the middle portion is in A major and tempoed andante.

Music for eight recorders is not often found. Nonetheless, for proper balance all eight are necessary for Gotovac's piece, though it never calls for eight separate parts. Most of the time the music is in four parts, sometimes in five. Two measures split into six voices, a single measure requires seven. (The score indicates that the music can also be played by a "recorder group.")

Gould, Elizabeth (1904–)

TRIO

- *Disciplines* for Woodwind Trio (Oboe, Clarinet, and Bassoon)

Gould runs a tight creative ship in her *Disciplines.* The trio begins with a twenty-measure theme, totally stated at the unison by the three instruments. The melody passes through seven modes, beginning with the locrian, onto the phrygian, linked to the aeolian, etc., ending with the lydian. Then follow three connected modal variations and a Conclusion based on the theme and again passing through and combining all seven modes.

A compact work (4 1/2 minutes in length). The composer indicates the objective was "to make music as meaningful and interesting as possible while strictly observing a number of limitations." The finding is an affirmative one.

Gould, Glenn (1932–82)

QUARTET

- **String Quartet, Op. 1**

Cast in one continuous movement, Gould's quartet is of great length. The largesse of late Beethoven, Mahler, and Schoenberg is the essential of this work. From the first named, come the developed formal aspects; from the second, breadth; and from the last, chromatic framing. The music is just short of the twelve-tone area (the fugue in the principal development section, stated to be in B minor, encompasses all pitches but D-sharp). On the other hand, dodecaphonic technique becomes the musical internality, practically adjusts and governs the disposition of the sounds and the motival developments. Thus, Gould can be called a diatonically concerned, chromatically

determined Schoenbergian. The quartet is dark grained, dark colored, rhythmically tight.

Gould, Morton (1913–)

DUOS

- *Benny's Gig:* **Eight Duos for Clarinet and Double Bass (1979)**

The duos were completed in 1979, but the first piece was written in 1962, with the indication "celebrating Benny's 1962 Russian tour." Taking note of the instrumentation, it shouldn't be difficult to guess that the Benny in question is the famous Benny Goodman. Matching the commemorative point of the first piece, the last is signed "For Benny's 70th Birthday—May 1979." When it was sent to Goodman a note accompanied the manuscript signifying Gould's "affection and friendship and admiration."

And not only the first and last pieces but all the others belong to Benny. The bass is the backup, though its line is varied: tenuto bowed in number one, played with "snap" in number two, plucked throughout in number three, serving up an ostinato in number five, and so on. Whatever, it retains its second-fiddle status throughout.

Of course, jazz there is. Assorted; for example: slow and nostalgic in the first piece, metrically swung in the fourth, defining a "Calypso Serenade" in the sixth part, bluesy in the seventh, and with a jaunty syncopative outline in the finale, which begins with introductory finger snaps by the clarinetist.

- **Duo for Flute and Clarinet (1972)**

A six-movement suite that totals ten minutes of luminously styled music, innocent of any austerity. Understandably, since Gould's wind-instrument duo was written to celebrate the wedding of friends who played the instruments represented.

The first movement (Unison) shifts freely from absolute doubling at the unison to octave duplication, in a few cases expanding to a two-octave span. In the final measure the distance is three octaves. Much is made from little in that movement.

Movement two (Song) is followed by a briskly rhythmic March, with some metrical play in the Trio. A pair of dances follow: Waltz and Hora. For the finale (Lullaby) Gould chooses gentility for his musical celebration, not exuberance.

- **Suite for Violin and Piano (1945)**

Gould's duo suite is musically hedonistic. It begins with a "Warm Up" represented by a perpetual motion of kinetic eighths and chromatic jazz. The Serenade, in systematic 3/4 and 2/4, has a middle section that, in its brief moment, affords a very delicate contrast by use of 3/4 and 3/8 alternate measures, as well as by the use of pizzicato. The March is Gould by way of Prokofiev, the dissonances of concert-stage manners not of marching "two-step" feature. Here, the irony is implicit (as in Prokofiev) through the medium of violin glissando and ponticello. The Blues has the quiet rhapsody of that form, with the *forte* sections equaling fever spots that make the music's face rosy. The Hoe-Down is as spirited as the first movement, an excellent stylization of that American dance with incessant changes of meter.

Gounod, Charles (1818–93)

DUOS

- *Petite étude scherzo* **for Two Cellos (or Two Double Basses)**

This is a four-square bit in three-four time, and though it is a super-polite Scherzo it still gets a more-than-passing grade. (Granting that a bit of bias might exist because the composer is Charles Gounod.)

There is no Trio, but trisectional relationship exists. The first part is in D major, and the next one in D minor. The third part is in D major again but, interestingly, does not totally repeat the opening section. It uses the first eight measures of part one, then takes the first five measures of the D-minor section, transposes it into D major, and completes the work with new material.

The original edition of the duet was published by Lemoine (Paris). A 1968 edition issued by Doblinger (Vienna) changes the title to *Petit scherzo,* removes the two cellos and calls only for the two double basses. Apparently these decisions were made by the editor, Rudolf Malarić.

- *Six Original Melodic Pieces* **for Horn and Piano**

Lucid melodic invention, but rejecting any special personal quality. Most of the piano writing is of subsidiary systemization. Aside from an occasional coloration—the echo phrase that follows the initial one in the second piece, the wide range of the fourth piece—the horn writing is of traditional purpose.

NONET

- *Petite symphonie (Little Symphony)* for Flute, Two Oboes, Two Clarinets, Two Bassoons, and Two Horns

A diverting chamber music entry, mostly of airy content. Gounod composed his nonet for the Société de Musique de Chambre pour Instruments à Vent (Chamber Music Society for Wind Instruments)—an organization founded in 1879 by Paul Taffanel, the French flutist-composer-conductor. The first performance of the *Petite symphonie* was given in Paris, on April 30, 1885.

The opening movement is introduced by an Adagio that moves into an Allegretto. Within these two sections there is a pedal-point bridge—first syncopated, then set in eighth-note patterns. The symphony's general joyous quality is retained, but considered in a more placid state in the song contours of the Andante cantabile. There, Gounod is contrapuntally minded in a simulated manner. The harmonic writing is spread, organized into lines that merge and coincide, contrary to the forthrightness of true polyphony. Clear formal presentations, contrasted respectively by triple and duple meters, are found in the Scherzo and Finale.

Gow, David (1924–)

DUO

- *Three Miniatures* for Clarinet and Piano

Two of these short items are slow, the last is quite fast. The second piece, Berceuse, is cradled by an ostinato bass that sets and maintains the C-sharp-minor tonality. The first miniature, Idyll, is structured from two-measure phrases. The final piece, Danse grotesque, likewise depends on ostinato underpinning. It also relies on sequence.

QUARTETS

- Quartet for Flute, Oboe, Cello, and Harpsichord (or Piano), Op. 28

Gow's one-movement, thirteen-minute quartet (awarded the Hans Oppenheimer Prize in 1967) is basically a two-part work. The beginning Adagio is fully developed and then links to a Moderato con brio that undergoes integrated development as well. The materials are clear toned, heard in a stinging harmonic language that is deft in its fluidal verbiage. The polyphony in this Quartet avoids mass conflict—no messy, muddy linear situations develop. The scoring is neatly done and its colorings most appropriate.

- Suite for Four Trombones

The music is structurally paced clearly and naturally. All the details of the subjects are immaculately projected, making for eloquent evidence of Gow's creative abilities.

Decisive figurations are in the Prelude. The voices come together in rhythmic unison to underline the final measures. There are nine measures of 5/2 time in the Slow Dance, each measure subdivided into a 3:2 ratio. The Scherzo does not hide the first trombone as the solo character. It plays with open tone while the other three instruments are muted. An adagio-tempo Valse triste and a resolute Fugue complete the quartet.

Graas, John J.

QUARTET

- Three Quartets for F Horns

Actually what this work contains is three movements, rather than three separate multimovement quartets. "Contrasts" relies on two themes, the first comparing imitation of a conjunct line, the other juxtaposing different dynamics. "Pyramids" is also in trisectional form; the title is more fanciful than of musical simulation. The overall effect is efficacious, with a quasi-majestic middle portion.

What is odd about the third piece is the presto conclusion to a music titled "In Memoriam (P.N.G.)." As is so often the case, no explanation for this piece is given. Certainly such data doesn't fall in the category of "confidential information." The entire movement puzzles one in view of the title. It is resolutely contrapuntal, and it is just as resolute in its less-than-threnodic tempo indication ($\quad = 80$).

Gradenwitz, Peter (1910–)

DUO

- *Four Palestinian Landscapes* for Oboe and Piano (1946)

The distinguishing mark of Gradenwitz's compositions is that of atonality, somewhat demonstrating Schoenbergian manifestations. The four movements of this duo represent such technical deposition. They are all based on a fundamental theme formed from a twelve-tone row, developed, however, with free-sounding freedom. Gradenwitz does not deny himself the serious values of stylistic contrasting methods, although these do not revoke the requirement of a balanced piece of work or make a ragged potpourri of ill-assorted techniques. Thus, bitonality is described at the end of the third movement by the combination of E minor and E major, while the C-major sections in movement four represent the clearest picture of pure tonality.

None of the movements of this suite (composed in Tel Aviv, January and February of 1946) bears an "official" title. Each is written in a different form with a distinctive texture (movement two is for piano alone, while movement three is practically a section for solo oboe). However, landscapes are depicted by the composer—sketching the various surroundings of the Yarkon River, the Sharon Plain, Lake Kinereth and that of Galilee. These have, according to Gradenwitz, "a unity of atmosphere apparent in even such different surroundings." The conformity is expressed by the use of one basic tone series for all four movements. But the music is not programmatic, and again in the composer's words: "the listener is free to associate with the music whatever experience comes to his own mind."

"On the Banks of the Yarkon River" (the suggestive background of the first movement, and similarly all other titles are interrelated, not positive) is in the form of a prelude, contains alternating sections derived from the tone row and includes wavy figures which support the further explanations given the row. Movement two—"Orange Groves in the Sharon Plain"—begins as a waltz and then changes counteractively to a march tempo. The theme of the latter is varied, then followed by a return to the triple-pulse measures. This second time the waltz is highly ornamented and forms a preliminary to a section in hora (an Israeli folk dance) style, which, in turn, prefaces the coda. The third movement, "On the Shores of Lake Kinereth," mixes recitative with songlike sections; while "Gay Galilee," the last part of the suite, is in rondo form.

Graener, Paul (1872–1944)

The chamber music of this prolific and expert composer covers many media. In his later period of work, however, he paid little attention to chamber music, concentrating instead on operatic composition. Though much of his orchestral music is Wagnerian, his chamber music does not follow this worship; the sonorities are intelligently moderated. (The wisdom of his accepting an official music position with the Nazi government is another matter. In November 1933, Graener was appointed vice president of the Reichsmusikkammer, organized by the infamous Joseph Goebbels, to supervise "the aesthetic and racial problems" of German music.)

The string quartets discussed below differ somewhat from the chamber music produced in Germany in the early 1900s. Neither work is verbose nor of Brucknerian length. And, no concern with any "ism." Yet, without being experimental, Graener's quartets have individual contours.

DUO

- **Suite for Flute and Piano, Op. 63**

Classically oriented in terms of form, but free in its harmonic syntax. One writer has termed the music "modernized Bach," but there is much more romantic confirmation than Bachian delineation.

Above all, nothing approaching deadly academic procedures. Graener colors the metrical points in the Praeludium with hemiola. That part of the duo flows. The next, a minuet (not so titled, but the tempo—Tempo di menuetto— and ternary form provide the proof), tiptoes with rhythmic delicacy. A type of Handelian breadth permeates the Larghetto, and a balletic finale pins down a splendid work for flute and piano. Unpretentious music, but artistically assertive.

QUARTETS

- *Quartet über ein Schwedisches Volkslied (Quartet Based on a Swedish Folk Song)* **for String Quartet, Op. 33**

Graener does not present his folk-song choice at the start, but extracts a rising interval from it for preludial purposes. (The song is of common eight-measure length, its initial words being "Spinn, spinn, lieb Töchterlein" ["Spin, spin, dear little daughter."]) Having raised the curtain, he introduces the Swedish melody in the first violin, accompanied by simple harmonization. It is then restated by the viola, surrounded by embroidered voices, and the movement is rounded out by a return of the prelude.

In the succeeding three movements Graener uses thematic components to spin his string quartet material. In movement two the fabric is of fanciful design, but with ternary-threaded form. The variation on the permutative idea that begins this section of the work is bound by specific intervallic patterns. In movement three the first two measures of the Swedish tune are employed to organize a free Scherzo-Rondo. Unconventionally, the final movement is an Elegie, again based on details drawn out of the basic melody. It is presented in an exceedingly loose three-part scheme.

- **String Quartet [No. 3], Op. 65**

The quartet is divided into two sections, with no pause between. Not specific variations, but variational treatment of a compact idea (a descending quartal interval and a conjunct line pinned on to a long–short pulse pattern) is employed in the first part. In the second part, Graener states an Adagio theme and freely develops it. By dividing the discussions into two different tempos, the equivalent of slow and Scherzo sections is achieved.

Graf, Friedrich Hartmann (1727–95)

QUARTET

- **Quartet in D Major for Four Flutes**

A lightly stated example of music that does not abandon traditional structural concepts; in fact, stays extremely close to them. There are three movements: Andante, Adagio, and Minuetto. Everything is neatly indicated and precisely written. Very little modulation, and when it takes place it stays close to the home key.

Gragnani, Filippo (1767–?)

SEXTET

- **Sextet for Flute, Clarinet, Violin, Two Guitars, and Cello, Op. 9**

As a virtuoso guitarist, Gragnani produced a good amount of music for the instrument, including several mixed instrumental ensembles, seven numbered opera comprising guitar duos, a trio for three guitars, and a large assortment of duos for the guitar with another instrument. The mixed instrumental sextet represents his best work and was published in a modern edition in 1982 by Suvini Zerboni.

Of appeal in the first movement is the alternating equality of lines assigned the two guitars contrasted to their compact tutti-duo definition. The short Adagio non tanto is principally for the flute. A Minuet and a sharply rhythmic finale complete the opus. Of total interest is the odd combination and the oft-used splitting of the six instruments into paired totalities: flute, clarinet, and violin as one group; two guitars and cello as the other.

Grainger, Percy (1882–1961)

Folk song is the heartbeat of most of this composer's output, incorporated in tidbits which, by virtue of Grainger's uncanny harmonic and color abilities, become larger and more important than the trifles they seem to be.

He was a very free soul. His extrovertism was exhibited in many ways—from the popularization of music to new ideas about how to compose, orchestrate, notate, and perform it. He called a viola a "middle fiddle"; he wrote "louden bit by bit," instead of the more common poco a poco crescendo; he orchestrated and rescored thrice again the same work in varying versions; he structured a composition so that it may be played by three or four or two hundred instruments, in a method termed "elastic scoring." Small wonder, therefore, that a man with such unconstraint would choose to have an audience of over twenty thousand people to witness his marriage. (It was held in Hollywood Bowl.) For Percy Grainger was an incarnate musical hedonist. It is that factor that nourishes his compositions.

QUARTET

- *Molly on the Shore* **for String Quartet (1907)**

Among the multitudinous settings of folk music (which include Celtic as well as English folk songs, dance tunes, sea chanties, and morris dances) that Grainger had made for innumerable combinations, the first of the lot, *Molly on the Shore,* is undoubtedly the most famous.

The work is "lovingly and reverently dedicated to the memory of Edvard Grieg," a testimonial conveying more than it reads, for Grieg thought of Grainger with esteem and affection. Grainger was Grieg's choice to play his piano concerto at an important English festival (Grainger's interpretation of this work became considered the most authoritative). Furthermore, it was Grieg's love of folk music that gave Grainger the clue to pursue folk materials by research.

Molly on the Shore is a presto Irish reel, based on two tunes to be found in the Petrie Collection of Irish Music and is "set for string four-some" (Graingerese for string quartet). Two melodies are used, one called "Temple Hill" and the other bearing the same title as the work itself. The combination of the two tunes is a matter of expert counterpoint, and relates nicely to the constancy of the pedal points and ostinato used.

(Seven other settings were made by Grainger. These are for string orchestra, full orchestra, small [theater] orchestra, violin and piano, wind band, two pianos, and solo piano. Two other settings are "special"—one for pianola, the other made for a recording for orchestra by Leopold Stokowski.)

OCTET

- *My Robin Is to the Greenwood Gone* for **Flute, English horn, Violin, Two Violas, Two Cellos, and Double Bass (1912)**

My Robin Is to the Greenwood Gone is the second of the settings Grainger made of songs and tunes from William Chappell's *Old English Popular Music*. The subtitle is "a room-music ramble upon the first 4 bars of the old tune of that name." Grainger's original version was scored for flute, English horn, and six strings (violin, two violas, two cellos, and double bass); his rearrangements include solo piano and piano trio versions.

Though only the beginning of the original melody is used, it is impossible to know where the original ends and Grainger has stepped in, so artful is the folk quality of the entire piece. The first presentation of the "theme-bit" (if Grainger can coin words, one is compelled to do likewise to describe his technique) occurs after a fully muted string introduction. The violin then sings the theme in unmuted timbre, with the flute and English horn entering, in turn. Whether quotation is in use or not, the work breathes the style and spirit of English folk music from first measure to last.

Gram, Peder (1881–1956)

Among Danish composers Gram stood somewhat in the shadows. First, considerable time was taken up by his conducting and writing activities. (In the latter case he published books dealing with modern music and harmonic analysis.) Second, the younger composers were more active in their promotional efforts and thereby their contemporaneously colored music was given prime attention.

There is nothing academically crabby or stylistically reactionary in Gram's music. He represents one of the impressive older Danish composers who, one is sure, will be given rightfully deserving attention in time.

DUO

- **Sonata for Cello and Piano, Op. 14**

The interval of a minor third is the paramount melodic core in the first movement, the tempo heading Andante misterioso e narrante ("in a moderated slow speed, mysteriously, and in a declamatory manner") clearly defining Gram's objective. Considerable flowing detail marks the development, with the greatest textural weight placed in the central part of the movement. This gives meaningful solidity but does not mean heaviness, which squashes expressivity.

The tempo heading of movement two, Allegro inquiéto ("in quick tempo, restless, uneasy"), similar to the preceding movement, implies a descriptive scenario behind the notes. Though the latter part of the movement is considerably calmer and slows down measurably to state choralelike material, previously the music is feverish. The succinct theorem there expressed is constant activity in the piano, with the cello's melodic lines those of urgency; the parts are knitted tightly into the total sound fabric. There is emotional intensity and it is only later (as mentioned) that this intensity is removed. Either way there is vitality, and it is undeniably eloquent.

QUARTET

- **String Quartet No. 3, Op. 30**

The third quartet is dedicated to C.F.A.H. Graae, a coworker (Gram called him a "department chief") in one of the several governmental positions Gram at one time held. Graae's initials and surname are transformed into their musical equivalents ("H" is the German for "B," and "R" is, of course, eliminated) and become the basis for the second movement (Allegro). (Gram favored a two-movement structure—it is used also in his Sonata for Cello and Piano—*see above*.) The unaccompanied first violin states the motto, and from then on the music skims along without a care in a duple-pulse scherzo ambience.

The preceding movement does not give any attention to the motto. It does give full attention, however, to polyphony throughout its seven-minute span.

Gramatges, Harold (1918–)

DUO

- **Duo in La-bemol (Duet in A-flat) for Flute and Piano**

Gramatges not only studied with José Ardévol, the principal Cuban composer and teacher, but (just prior to the appearance of this work) with the distinguished American composer Aaron Copland. It may well be mere coincidence, but more likely it was the impress of Copland's individuality on this (then) young man, for Copland's typical idiom is followed in the first two parts of this three-movement duet.

Gramatges's diction is enunciated by way of Copland's transparent, pandiatonically

"spaced-for-the-air-to-come-through" harmonies. Thus, triads in a dissonant cloth soak the fast flow of the Allegro moderato and the ternary form of the Tranquillo e molto cantabile.

The last section veers from Copland to a slightly more insular fountain of resource—the study with Ardévol. In this case, the frictions are more incisive; passages run in parallel sevenths, the entire modus operandi being Ardévolian contrapuntalism. It is not a platitude to state that few young composers are exempt from the almost solemn use of their teachers' techniques. Gramatges may have been imitative, but he imitated with fresh touches. Consequently, he was current with the times, and his formulations were sound contemporary ones. And so they remain.

Grant, Parks (1910–)

QUARTETS

- *Brevities:* **Suite No. 3 for Brass Quartet (Two Trumpets, Horn, and Trombone), Op. 44**

Grant doesn't muddy the formal waters in his four movements. In the Prelude a six-measure tune successively appears in the trumpet, horn, and trombone. There is neat bridgework between these statements, then a complementary section and a compact, changed recapitulation. Totally neat, clear, and musical. The Canon movement is really a series of the device—five in all, each in a different two-instrument pairing. The conception is productive, not pedantic, with a flow that is maintained as one canon begins simultaneously with the completion of the previous one. All the imitations are at the octave, and the entire movement retains a 5/4 meter.

The melody in the Chorale is "Allein Gott in der Höh' sei Ehr'." Save for four measures of antiphony, the 1 1/4 minutes of the piece revisit

Bach. Grant's scoring strategy in the March makes for a finely calculated sense of growth as well as structure. All the instruments are muted at the beginning. In measure 25 the horn is *senza sordino;* the others unveil their timbre personalities one by one in measures 42, 46, and 49. Thus, the totally unmuted final twenty-six measures balance the completely muted initial two dozen measures. With integrated material and a constant quadruple beat, the March is of firm solidity throughout.

Grant doesn't explore any undercurrents in his *Brevities.* The moral here is that that which is presented naturally falls on the ear enjoyably. The objective is restricted, yes; but is not superficial.

- *Excursions:* **Suite No. 2 for Brass Quartet (Two Trumpets or Cornets, Horn, and Tenor Trombone or Euphonium), Op. 38**

In the miscellaneous setting of a suite there is no requirement to advance the plot as one must in a sonata. Still, Grant's *Excursions* shows a subtle use of association between the opening Prelude and the closing "Homage to J.S.B." (Prelude and Fugue). (Of course, no mystery applies to the initials in the "Homage," especially because of the formal definition that follows them!) The opening Prelude is paragraphed by alternating fugato fragments with vertical detail. In the "Homage" the same homophonic and polyphonic arrangement is used but unifically separated.

Movement two titled "Color—Melodies" is a mild consideration of *Klangfarbenmelodie;* the opening melodic dissection occurring several times throughout the movement. Part three is a "Study with Twelve Tones"; the row's permutations are quite compact and clearly detailed in the music's progress. Movement four is a Nocturne, with a tripartite simplicity of form.

All parts of the work are lucid, smooth, and assured. Grant, a Mahlerian scholar, does not imitate that composer in his brass chamber music. Nor does he indulge in any gimmickry. *Excursions* makes its effect without such need.

- *Laconic Suite* **for Two Trumpets or Cornets, Horn, and Tenor Trombone or Euphonium, Op. 31**

The virtue here is simplicity. Light-framed music with no intellectual ax to grind. The Fanfare is projected on two rhythms: dotted-eighth and sixteenth patterns and triplets. Dynamically, the strongest point in the "Pensive Waltz" is *piano.* The opposite holds for "Jubilation," a ternary-arranged music mostly at the *forte* level.

Gräsbeck, Gottfrid (1927–)

DUO

- **Sonata da chiesa for Violin and Organ (1979)**

The inner currents are from Regerian territory. Chromaticism is the force in the "Paenitentia," "Rogamus," and "Glorificamus" movements. However, these are completed with rather diatonic sections, bringing cadences in A, C, and C, respectively. Pulling punches in this manner does not contravene the strong textural interplay that preceded. In the "Adoramus" movement this simpler harmonic style applies throughout.

Graun, Johann Gottlieb (1703–71)

DUO

- **Sonata No. 1 in D Major for Violin and Continuo**

The first of a set of six, set forth in four movements, alternating Adagio and Allegro divisions. Graun's music has a powerful animation, especially in the first Allegro. Nothing in this work is fanciful, neither are there any emotionally portentous moments, but there is represented, as Abram Loft has expressed it: "The work of a man completely conversant with the style of his time, bringing to his musical awareness the ear and hand of the thoroughly accomplished violinist."

TRIO

- **Trio Sonata in D Major for Two Flutes and Basso Continuo**

One of the very best of the nearly 150 trio sonatas this composer (a senior member of the orchestra of Frederick the Great) wrote. A good number of these trio sonatas included the flute or were completely for paired flutes.

Graun's four-movement work alternates slow and fast movements, each faster than the previous one in the specific tempo category (thus: Largo and Andante are the slow movements' tempos). The sonata exhibits *galanter Stil* (gallant style), a light and elegant music that is opposite to the more elaborate constructions of the baroque.

Grebenshchikov, Oleg (1905–80)

DUO

- **Three Greek Dances for Clarinet and Piano**

Folk-firmed materials. The tempo heading for the first of the group ("Kritikos") is Allegro moderato; the meter is entirely defined in 5/8 time, each measure split in a long–short design of 3 + 2. There are some imitations for additional flavoring.

The second dance ("Kuluriotikos") is in Allegretto giocoso tempo and is also in odd-totaled (7/8) metrical order. In this case the pulse design splits this septuple total into 3 + 2 + 2. There is a tremendous-size cadenza for the clarinet. Number three of the set ("Haniomikov—Sirmos") matches the tempo of the first dance but has straightforward rhythmic patterns in 2/4 time. A peppy ending (which one expects) is provided for this colorful, endemic music.

Green, Douglass (1926–)

QUARTET

- ***Four Conversations* for Four Clarinets (1959)**

Lightly tonal, sophisticated instrumental talk. In the case of "Chit-Chat" the outer sections have vernacular accentuations with a variety of even and uneven meters. The last movement also is vernacularly represented by its "Bull Session" title.

All four pieces are in ternary song forms. "Gossip" (movement two) is a 2/4 bit of vivacity. In turn, the slow-curved lines of movement three, "Moonlight Colloquy," are guided by way of quintuple meter.

Green, Ray (1909–)

DUOS

- **Concertante for Viola (or Clarinet) and Piano (1941)**

Most of Green's music pulls you into a rhythmic world. It is vividly illustrated in the Presto Jig (the final movement) of this duo. There one expects rhythmic devotion. Less so, in the case of an Allegro fugato (the opening movement). But this contrapuntal piece is a festivity of continual pulsatile positivism. Eighth-note movement is basic to Green's fugal structure, and it somewhat takes on the role of a perpetual motion. Included are some polymetrical splits. The contrasting movement is an Andante pastoral. No bow to the conventions of the pastoral species is made. There is fine harmonic action in this case, defining the music's shape—quintal-formed chords in the outer sections, triadic arrangements topped with seconds in the middle portion.

Green made a version for viola and orchestra of his duo concertante. It does not negate the chamber music setting. Neither do the insertions of an unaccompanied section of moderate length in the Pastoral or a lengthy cadenza in the Jig negate the equality expected in a chamber music duet. It is simply additional evidence of Green's uninhibited consideration of the music he creates.

- **Duo concertante for Violin and Piano (1950)**

Stark, strong syncopative detail surrounds this composition. Plus an allegro energico tempo and cut-time-metered drive, there is a momentum that is truly exciting. As is habitual with Green, the rhythmic detail (especially a triplet figure) generates additional energy. Slower-paced material gives the necessary contrast but is, in total, somewhat subsidiary to the frenetic activity of the principal data.

As in some of this composer's other chamber music compositions, there is a cadenza. Its content includes the usual string-instrument brilliances: arpeggios, mixed bowings, double and triple stops. And, as in some other cases, Green has made a second setting. The Duo concertante has been translated into a version for violin and orchestra and its title revised to *Concerto brevis*.

QUARTETS

- *Five Epigrammatic Portraits* **for String Quartet (1933)**

There are no picture-painting prosaicisms in these portraits (originally titled Romances, but since the music is neither contemplative nor directly emotional, the rejection of that word was apt). Totally concerned with linear individuality (as to note arrangement and rhythmic contour), the pungent dissonance of the music packs a real wallop. Green says what he has to say minus fuss or extra detail. Each thought is expressed in the most concentrated manner. (Four of the five pieces are less than a minute in length; the first one just a little longer.)

The tightness of construction and cohesiveness of these midget-size creations (notated throughout without bar lines) is admirable. Thinned-out clustered harmonies predominate. Each piece ends softly, regardless of previous dynamic changes. Structurally, each consists of three distinctly determined phrases, mainly equal in length. All of this is achieved without use of any special string-instrument device; not even a single natural or artificial harmonic appears in the score.

- *Holiday for Four:* **Chamber Quartet for Viola, Clarinet, Bassoon, and Piano (1937)**

Musical hedonism is the doctrine of this work.

It is a holiday of music and instrumental use, as well as of title. There is a freedom here similar to that granted the performers of Ives's music (only in transference of instruments, though the cross accents which particularly concern this work are also similar to such Ivesian agogics). The viola may be replaced by a second clarinet; saxophones may be used in place of any or all the string and wind instruments called for. Only the piano is retained, regardless of any other instrumental substitution.

The Fugal Introduction is far less academic than its title. There is no long-winded exposition. Matters get to work immediately on a short, pert subject. Contrapuntal means are used, but the hairs on this fugue are made shaggy with the mementos of jazz and its palpitations of accent and syncopation. Formal doctrines give way to a pleasurable play on the form. Green uses, in this instance, adjunctive freedom rather than pedantic restraint. A "Prairie Blues" is the slow movement of the three total parts. While there are no portamentoed glides to help instill flavor in this truly American contribution to musical form, "barbershop" seventh chords are present; as is a steady, pulsed beat. But the slight contrapuntal workmanship shows that the westerner of the open fields has been somewhat urbanized by eastern, scholastic demeanor. Organized and spirited tunes, plus jazz-swept rhythms, are the essence of the last movement, titled Festive Finale. The outer sections are balanced by a central episode concerned with a chamber music parallel of the jazz "break"—in this case, the precisely written form of what sounds like an improvised cadenza for a solo instrument, passed from one voice to the next. The three-part form has been stated in Americanese.

OCTET

- ***Three Pieces for a Concert*** **for Flute, Two Clarinets, Two Trumpets, Trombone, Percussion (Snare Drum, Bass Drum, Cymbal, and Triangle; Timpani and Bells, ad lib), and Piano (1948)**

The first two of these pieces are a bit different than one expects from their titles. It would not be feasible to march to the March, since it is in triple time, and it would be impossible to do so unless it were played so quickly that an entire measure would be equaled by a single step. However, Green's tempo heading is Fast—Not Too! and plus the exclamatory warning, there is a specific metronomic indication of $\downarrow$ = 112–132. Indeed, this is, as applies to a stylized concert march, music meant for playing and listening, not playing and striding. Further, movement two, termed "Quiet Song," has more swing (although always smoothly connected in legato form) and syncopative thrust than placidity.

The final piece of the set says it all: "Piece to End." Green's title doesn't beg the question at all. It is music most fitting to conclude this entertaining suite. The tempo heading is Fast—and Busy (twice the speed of the March), the content truly active, jazzy, and cross accented.

(The octet represents the second setting of the work. Initially, the Three Pieces were for chamber orchestra, composed in 1947.)

Gretchaninov, Alexander (1864–1956)

DUO

- **Sonata for Violin and Piano, Op. 87**

The complexities of contrapuntalism are rare in the work of this composer. Gretchaninov is first a melodist; second, a formalist; third, a composer who mixes his music with the disguises of emblematic polyphony. His talents in the fields of song, church music, and choral music carry over into chamber music. His instrumental lines *sing*. While this is no criticism of his writing (in fact, an impulse lacking in some composers), nevertheless, the repudiation of the horizontal formation makes for a musical miasma that erupts in constant verticalism. The interest, therefore, as in the first movement, is mainly melody with accompaniment, somewhat foreign to the substances of a sonata document. Only a combination of the first theme (in 3/4 meter) with a subsidiary subject in the violin (in 2/4 time) illustrates the utility of contrapuntal alliance, but, in relation to the whole, it is short-lived and relatively unimportant in its double appearance.

In the slow movement, there are four variations on a theme. These are in simple exploitation (save for the last—a fugue) ending with a "peroration," but the earnestness of this tailpiece is rather subdued. Gretchaninov observes rather than proclaims his romantic message, not only in its closing paragraph but in previous ones. In the last movement, the motion of grouped eighth notes is constant. In such form, therefore, this section serves as a neutral, rhythmic element, compared to earlier divisions. There is vigor, but it is dulled by lack of sufficient contrast. Vocalises are in the composer's mind, rather than the firm and equal combine of a violin with piano. Gretchaninov's duo sonata is neither awe-inspiring nor cerebrally exciting. More to the point, it is a fairly well-made piece of music in the old Russian school tradition.

TRIOS

- **Concertino for Two Alto Recorders (or Two Clarinets) and Piano, Op. 171**

This piece was commissioned by Harold Newman, then (1944) the owner of Hargail Music Press in New York City. The commission resulted after Gretchaninov had expressed a desire to write for the recorder upon hearing Newman play the instrument. It was Gretchaninov's decision to make the work available for two clarinets, if so desired, and this was followed by an arrangement for strings in place of the piano.

It is a simple and engaging piece of music, symmetrically designed in ternary form. A tidbit for home playing. In the concert hall it would serve only as encore fare.

- **Trio for Violin, Cello, and Piano, Op. 38**

The tempo heading of the first movement (Allegro passionato) tells the story of that section, except for an overabundance of combining the instrumental resources. Use of tutti is an excellent weapon in fighting the difficulties of the piano trio's instrumentation problems, but an overuse of doubling negates the essential individuality of the medium. No matter how carefully the composer scores, he will have his troubles with the combination. The top-bottom of the two string instruments and the refusal of amalgamation by the piano with *any* string instrument are constant vexations. But the solution is not to be found by constantly joining the violin with the cello.

Compared to the first movement, which is built from a motive, the second movement treads different soil; it concerns itself with a long-lined theme in which the instruments share equally. In this instance, the instrumentation is skillful, the blocked-in constriction of the first movement is happily lacking. The final movement is dancelike, with proportional attention to simple melodic statement. There will be observed, in its form, rondo propriety. Though Gretchaninov is typed as a nationalist, there is little evidence of such in this piano trio. It is a chamber music composition with no basic national ideology.

(Gretchaninov's Op. 38 is dedicated to the greatly significant Russian composer and pedagogue Sergei Taneyev.)

QUARTETS

- **String Quartet [No. 1] in G Major, Op. 2**

Lushness, richness, and the principle of unification by related motives are the main factors of this well-written, sonorous quartet. It is not one of the really great quartets in the repertoire, or, for that matter, even of the Russian school, but it has determined, satisfying musical impulses. Great art cannot always be achieved, but the least to be demanded is good art. The latter demand is met by Gretchaninov.

The introduction states a synoptic motive, which is then used as the headpiece for the Allegro non troppo forming the first movement. It returns in the introduction to the fourth movement, and is again taken over for motival manipulation in the main portion of the final section of the quartet. In the first movement, its treatment is songlike; in the last movement, it is dynamic. It is as if Gretchaninov wished to exploit his material to the fullest. Dissection of the two main possibilities (flowing and connected, detached and separative) not only conserves resources, but affords logical balance. Further congress of thought may be observed (in its smallest use) when this motival idea is heard in a few measures of the third movement.

The two inner movements are a quiet, lyrical slow movement and a Scherzo, which only applies its brakes to form the contrastive purposes of the Trio.

Some writers have complained about the orchestral proclivities of the scoring. But, similar to the same criticism hurled at Mendelssohn's and Grieg's string quartets, the scoring of a chamber music composition is to be condemned only when it fails to realize the intent of the musical idea. Gretchaninov uses packed unisons, permits full sonorous aspects of his four instruments; but his ideas warrant such use. To decry the right of quartet color in

its fullest engenderment is to dismiss most of the post-Brahms string quartet literature. Gretchaninov's quartet must be accepted or rejected solely on its musical worth, not because of its unisons or heavy sonorous action.

- **String Quartet No. 2 in D Minor, Op. 70**

The composer of traditional product is not prone to consider musical conversation of curious matters. His favorite subject is the retelling of old tales, with little more than change of characters in the same settings. In this work, Gretchaninov's allure is the effacement of all but well-wrought flowing melodic lines (he is essentially concerned with the ritual of the melodic; the song for four strings, rather than the contrapuntal prying into their formations) backed up with ordered harmony and the joinery of rhythmic brick and mortar. There are composers who feel that the architecture of a Rubinstein or of a Tchaikovsky is all-sufficient for any edifice. Gretchaninov belongs to this school of thought.

The four movements are different only in that the opening is in a slow tempo, rhapsodic in treatment in comparison to the slow movement, which occupies third place within the total and is in song form with its ternary symmetry. Though the Scherzo has the contrastive Trio, there is no decrease of speed throughout the movement. Rhythm (mainly of a repetitive organism) is the value from which stems the entire adventure of the final movement.

- **String Quartet No. 3 in C Minor, Op. 75**

Time generally brings some alteration of style in a composer's output. In Gretchaninov's case, his third quartet (composed nearly twenty-five years after the first) shows no innovation other than freer instrumental use, while the musical speech shows no change or increase of vocabulary. Gretchaninov, in this and his other works, treads neutral soil. He is not concerned in the least with the fact that it is the year 1915, and the 20th century is indicated clearly on the calendar. His music is neither luxuriated nor bittered with the astringency of the more contemporary age; it is the discreet judgement of a man refuting the new in favor of the old. He is a musical neutral.

The slow movement is a set of five variations on a restless theme. In keeping with the original means, the working out results in rather free disport. The variations are fanciful, based on moods more than harmonic-contrapuntal thematic demonstrations. In this movement, Gretchaninov is the romantic. In the following Scherzo, he is the older classicist. The outer movements are fresh Allegros, neither exceptional in treatment nor going beyond the boundaries of regulated formalities. Only the opening has a long quasi-improvisatory introduction. Figurations (the means of giving action to the most average Allegro sections) are very much in evidence.

- **String Quartet No. 4, Op. 124**

Motival development is the ruling device in the first movement. A well-known motive it is, duplicating the one that Beethoven used to begin his famous fifth symphony. Even when the songlike second subject appears it is accompanied by the same germinal item.

Variational aspects are the backbone of the slow movement. The theme is constantly attended by new surroundings, new ornaments, new harmonies and rhythms. Monotony is ruled out even without derivable developments. The third movement is coquettish, rooted in Tchaikovsky. It is a Scherzo that fulfills formal dictates less serious than those used by Beethoven, from whom most all scherzo blessings flow.

To a certain degree, the last movement is also a scherzo in its décor, but far less symmetrical. The unit pulse remains even, but its division is not. The equations of two and three

are arranged in various means, so that the driving motion never becomes rooted in one basic rhythm. In this instance, rhythm feeds the material. There is excitement, therefore, instead of a mundane and ordinary final vivacious movement.

Grey, Geoffrey (1934–)

SEXTET

- **Sonata for Brass Sextet (Three Trumpets and Three Trombones) (1966)**

Intervallic focus is important to the first two movements. There is a basic division, subtle though it may be. The first part of the work is more disjunct (in tertial widths) than the second, which is tighter and conjunct in its moves. In the latter there is additional emphasis on close pitch succession, with a good amount of attention given half-step progressions.

A short Largo section is linked to the final principal section, directed by offbeat pulsations. A reminder of the first part of the work completes the sextet.

Grieg, Edvard (1843–1907)

It is commonplace to state that Grieg was a miniaturist and that his music in the larger forms gets minus points for its sectionalism. Because of this, his critics have insisted that his large works have substance but no craft. Nonsense. The freshness of the melodic spans, the creative rhythms, and the individuality of his harmonies are sufficient. It is the sectionalism that *is* Griegian and that makes him deserve his special creative place.

More to the point is that Grieg used the chamber music medium in which to write nearly all of his works in larger forms (the piano concerto, the piano sonata, and a concert overture are the only other large-design works). The chamber music part of his catalog totals six compositions: three violin and piano sonatas, a cello and piano sonata, and two string quartets (the second in a two-movement, unfinished state).

DUOS

- **Sonata in A Minor for Cello and Piano, Op. 36**

The general tone of mystery and moodiness and the gray atmosphere of the major part of this work was probably caused by feelings induced by the death of Grieg's brother, John, to whom the opus is dedicated. Much of the first movement will remind one of portions of Grieg's piano concerto (the important work that Grieg had written fifteen years earlier).

In the second movement, the main theme (first stated by the piano alone and then by the cello, framed with rolling piano arpeggios) sounds like Grieg's *Sigurd Jorsalfar* march. One would rather believe that this is not so much self-quotation as it is the composer speaking his own personal language.

The last movement combines an opening recitative (later heard in the movement) with a genuine supple dance. This is on the order of a heavy "troll dance" in turn somewhat similar to the halling, the Norwegian folk dance, which, to continue the parallels, resembles the Russian Cossack dance, performed by men in acrobatic style. Grieg's zeal for rhythm does not make him overtopple any of the balances in this climactic final movement. There, as in the previous movements, the cello is scored with such effect that it is never covered; no sonority mud effaces the clarity of this heady work for two instruments.

- **Sonata [No. 1] in F Major for Violin and Piano, Op. 8**

What will strike one is the absence of ostentation in this duo sonata, and the full cooperation of both instruments in setting forth the music. There is no overshadowing of the violin by the piano, or reverse domination. This democratic give-and-take overuses (only to a degree) the matter of imitation in place of integral development; but the effect is a rich relishing of all themes by both partners, especially in the first and last movements. The former, in sonata style, is gay, yet not completely unsophisticated in its harmony; it has, as well, a flavorsome spirit of the folk idiom that Grieg uses fully in the second movement. The music is romantic but not of pale-moon variety; its scope is rather of the stronger midnight sun. In the last movement, there is a subsidiary theme, first set forth by the piano, then the violin, finally becoming fully neighborly in its handling when displayed in fugato outline.

The brightest folk spotlight, aside from such disposition and quality in the work as a whole, is in the center movement (there is no "set" slow or Scherzo movement), which, marked innocently Allegretto quasi andantino, is nothing like a formal moderately paced movement; it is more in the form of a Norwegian minuetlike dance, stemming particularly from the springdans or springar used very frequently by Grieg in his works. Although always in triple meter, the rhythmic elements of this dance vary. In the outer sections, Grieg makes them equal, whereas, in the faster Trio section (Piu vivo), he provides asymmetrical accents. These, with bare fifths and semidrone effect, imitate the instrument usually called on to play such dance music, namely the hardingfele, which (like the viola d'amore) has sympathetic strings giving a sonorous layer of the bagpipe drone of fifths and fourths.

■ **Sonata [No. 2] in G Major for Violin and Piano, Op. 13**

If there were some romantic materials that ousted essential Norwegian elements in certain parts of the first violin and piano sonata, none are present in this sunny work, dedicated to Grieg's contemporary, Johan Svendsen.

Grieg's devotion to nationalistic musical syntax is manifested in this three-movement Sonata. Every one of the movements is in triple meter, the pulse of the most popular of Norwegian dances, the springar or springdans. The only exception is the introduction to the first movement (the only time Grieg used a formal introduction in any of his four duo sonatas), where the recitative quality slightly foreshadows the theme of the opening movement proper. This similarity of meter can be criticized, especially since such leveling gives a similar cast to the movements. But it is typical of Grieg's style— the posting of ideas that all work with sequential thought—and similar rhythm is sequential meter. Grieg poses no rhythmic conundrum. He communicates with cadenced neutrality.

In the second movement, the three sections are in symmetrical tonalities: minor in the outer portions, major in the center. The main theme is square in construction, a simple and most average total of eight measures, but the slight, rhythmic-warmed twist at the end of the first half is not only wise but extremely lovely, enhancing the gentility of the whole. The final movement stems, as is so often the case with this composer, from the springar mentioned above. The open fifths are reminiscent of the Norwegian violin that usually plays these dance tunes. Critics have stated that a sonata becomes distorted if completed by a dance movement, that a serious compilation should assert and climax matters. Despite the validity of such thoughts, it would be impossible for a composer intent on ridding the air of academic standards, and favoring a purely national music, to write in terms of the very system he was attempting to upset. Thus, a Norwegian work *could* end with a dance-style movement.

■ **Sonata [No.3] in C Minor for Violin and Piano, Op. 45**

Most opinions designate this work as the best of the three violin and piano sonatas. It is broadly dramatic in the three-movement scale Grieg favored for his sonatas. The work is best because Grieg was able to combine the richness of the personal idiom he was pursuing with the particulars of classic technique. However, he followed the latter rather rigidly in his recapitulations, which merely repeat, with textbook garrulity, the details of the exposition with "correct" changes of key.

The theme of the opening movement is not long, more of germinal impulse; immediately announced, it is at once spurred on by its inherent characteristics. Thus, Grieg does not belie either the value of classical heritage, or his determination to write true, authentic Norwegian art music. The second theme is small framed, but in comparison with the dramatic anecdotal theme there is great contrast. The development is well planned, including the augmentation of the opening theme into one of tenacity by quadruple multiplication of the original pulse values.

The Romanza of the second movement is in utter simplicity. First, the piano, then, the violin in equal statement have a try at the beautiful theme. The contrasting section is like the Norwegian halling, a folk dance in duple meter. Since Grieg was delving constantly into folk secrets, this use is no doubt a resultant solution. In the finale, there is a definite clue to Sibelius's style—that of not completely stating a theme but interrupting it before cadential conclusion. Imitation technique as well as syncopation guide the animated movement considerably. The resolutive quality of offbeats helps the vigor of the decided rhythmic mechanism of the whole movement.

QUARTETS

- **String Quartet in G Minor, Op. 27**

Discounting the unfinished (two-movement) quartet, Op. 27 represents Grieg's single attempt at four-string writing. At one time the work was subjected to abuse, with the word "orchestral" (an ugly term in quartet analysis) being bandied about. We are far from such nonsense. Dramatic the Grieg quartet is; at times it is also heavily scored. By translating the string quartet idiom into his characteristic language, Grieg is not guilty of any creative error, and to have his work summarily dismissed because of its textural weight is a critical misunderstanding of and indifference to his individuality.

If one wishes to criticize, one can point out that Grieg's music is based on the sequential pronouncement of thematic material, with a fondness for the small thought restrung and repeated, rather than developmental musical inquiry. In defense it must be stated that Grieg was a poet, not an orator. Melody and supporting harmony rather than contrapuntalism mark his music.

The full vertical definition of the quartet's opening statement is all-important. (This theme, which serves as a motto, represents self-borrowing. It is taken from the first song, "Spillemaend," in his Six Songs, Op. 26, based on texts by Ibsen. Spillemaend, meaning "minstrel" or "fiddler," is a song about the Hulder, a Norse legendary figure who gives the gift of song to minstrels but robs them, in return, of peace and happiness.) The motto serves as a connective device; by way of soft dynamic presentation as the contrasting subject in the first movement; as the coda in the same movement, where it is heard in augmented form in the cello's tenor register below ponticello tremolando of the upper three instruments, then followed by a Presto statement. It does not appear in the Romanze of the second move-

ment (two speeds, therefore two moods, form the essentials of this movement), but the first theme of the quartet (a restless one appearing after the motto) is the utility for the agitated section here. However, the motto is hinted at in the theme of the third-movement Intermezzo, the first of two successive dance movements. If a springdans rhythm haunts the third movement, its Trio is a portrayal of the other Norwegian folk dance, the halling, making triple and duple meters contrast and silhouette each other.

The determination of the opening statement both begins and ends the last movement; thus, Grieg chooses the cyclic needle to stitch the quilt of this work. In between, comes a wild Presto in the form of a saltarello. But this is not the Italian dance, merely its rhythm of two pulses per measure pounding away in bare musical lustiness. The substance of the entire quartet is that of Norwegian nationalism. No better evidence of Grieg's musical motives and habits can be heard.

- **String Quartet in F Major (Unfinished)**

Only two movements of this work were finished by Grieg in 1892, fifteen years before he died. Sketches for the final two movements were found and completed by a colleague, Julius Röntgen. Performances usually discount this completion, preferring only the original Grieg portion, no matter that it only totals half a full quartet.

An introduction is followed by an Allegro movement in sonata form that does not disturb Griegian nationalistic aesthetic and style. There are rhythmic crosscurrents that electrify the main, binomial rhythm by cutting in with triple pulsations. The other movement is marked Scherzando, but it is Grieg's Norwegian Scherzo, meaning the rhythm of his country's folk dance—a type of springdans. It has that popular Norwegian dance's penchant for shifting accentuations, lightly formed in the main sections, with speedier, yet heavier style and some cross rhythms in the Trio portion.

Griend, Koos van de (1905–50)

DUO

- *Small Suite* for Violin and Cello

The title notwithstanding, Griend thinks in big color strokes in his duo, which is far from small in its five-part total of movements. Sonorities are expanded: in a huge number of double stops using the open A string in the violin and skittering harmonics in the cello; plus combinations of totally muted and muted-open paired timbre in the Scherzo; by enlarged voicing in the Capriccio; and through compact use of chunky four-part chords in the Marcia.

While there is keen contrapuntal duetting in the Praeludium and Espressivo movements, the thrust of energy is paramount: in the Scherzo with its presto pace and its free interchange of triple and duple meters; with the perpetual-motion vivacity of the Fughetta; and by the rhythmic firmness of the Marcia. This is a stimulating presentation.

TRIOS

- *Play Music* for Three Soprano
    Recorders

Short and sweet, artistically simple and tonal. A March in C major and, of course, in march tempo ($\downarrow$ = 120), then a Fugue in F major and in allegro moderato tempo.

- Trio for Violin, Viola, and Cello (1946)

Griend's string trio is in essence charming, graceful, and bounces along with Frenchified flare. The question arises, however, when is a string trio not a string trio? Thickening of texture occasionally is necessary, no matter the minimal total instruments employed. However, in the slow (third) movement, trio writing is in the minority (fourteen measures), quintuple voicing is in the great majority (sixty-six measures), and quartet textures come next with twenty-five measures. Single measures appear each for one and two voices. In addition, Griend retains a great deal of rhythmic repetition in this slow movement.

The opening has Mendelssohnian bounce and colorful harmonics. It also has a great deal of pedal anchorage. Movement two is a waltz, the rhythmic accompaniment distributed between two instruments for the greater part. Pedal points again appear in large quantity in the finale. And so do ostinatos.

QUARTET

- Quartet for Four Horns (1949)

Formal simplicity and tonal breadth in Griend's piece. A short piece it is, consisting of a single 4 1/2-minute conception. The compact form consists of alternating repeated sections of contrasted tempos. Within is timbral contrast as well. The four instruments are constantly in a mix of open and stopped sounds.

Griffes, Charles Tomlinson (1884–1920)

QUARTET

- *Two Sketches (Based on Indian Themes)* for String Quartet (1918)

The *Two Sketches* is Griffes's sole published chamber music composition. (For string quartet there remain three separate movements: one in B-flat [1903], a Vivace [Allegro assai quasi presto], written in 1907, and an Allegro energico ma maestoso, composed in 1919.) The *Two Sketches* represent Griffes's attempt to combine his impressionistic ideas with an elementary postulate of Americanism.

Of the pair of pieces in contrastive tempos (Lento e mesto and Allegro giocoso), only the theme of the former is identified: "Farewell Song of the Chippewa Indians."

In the first piece, shifting rhythms stimulate the staid monotonous quality, a characteristic of so many Indian melodies. Slight effects are introduced to imitate drums, by low pizzicatos and ponticellos, although, in the latter instance, there is less percussion than sibilation. The second movement is a pure war dance, though not so indicated by Griffes. Rhythmic insistence, demarked with grace-note twists tied on to certain melodic sounds, is the simulation of war cries. Therefore, to a certain degree, Griffes changes in this latter movement from an impressionist to a realist, with his feet directly on Indian ground. In this case he is reporting rather than observing.

Griffis, Elliot (1893–1967)

DUO

- **Sonata in G Major for Violin and Piano (1931)**

Sonatas are not necessarily limited to quartal total. There have been sonatas in two, three, five, six, and even more movements. Some composers regard the four-part formation as almost sacred. (Dvořák was of that opinion. His conviction was that "three is too few," and that "five is too many.")

Griffis's quintuple total includes another uncommon exhibit in sonata design: a cadenza in the first movement. All the movements are structured from the sonata-form principle, with contrastive principal themes and developments. None of the material is squared to symmetrical proportions; the insistence of change is primary. Tonally, Griffis exploits the triadic sys-

tem, but not to its unrestricted consequence.

Grimm, Carl Hugo (1890–1978)

OCTET

- **Divertimento for Eight Flutes (E-flat Flute, Six Flutes, and Alto Flute)**

Typical tonal writing in late-19th-century Germanic style. Grimm's Divertimento is cast in a divisional, one-movement structure. There are repeats of the introduction and the second theme interlocked in the seven sections.

Of course, the nicest part of eight flutes in ensemble is when they pipe and when they skim about in fast consecutive chordal action. There is additional interest in this case in the use of the considered obsolete E-flat flute (Terzflöte), which is built a minor third higher than the standard C instrument.

Grisoni, Renato (1922–)

DUO

- *Suite italiana* **for Alto Saxophone and Piano, Op. 26**

Properly, an Italian Dance Suite, since, in addition to a Praeludium and an Aria, all the movements are dances of Italian origin: Pavana, Corrente, Siciliana, and Saltarello, and the little-known Ballu tundu (a round dance) and Ossolana (a dance from the town of Ossoli). The latter is in allegro tempo but reflects stateliness; the Ballu tundu scoots about in very vivacious speed and scalically moves along two-in-a-bar.

These are tuny, tonal translations professionally crafted. No stylistic posturing at all, and set forth with equal apportionment for the two instruments.

QUARTET

- *Für Sigurd: Albumblatt (Album Leaf)* for Saxophone Quartet (Soprano, Alto, Tenor, and Baritone Saxophones), Op. 60

For Sigurd means Sigurd M. Rascher, the famous saxophone virtuoso, born in 1907. Many important composers wrote compositions for Rascher, including Jacques Ibert of France, Frank Martin of Switzerland, Alexander Glazunov of Russia, and Henry Brant of America. The dedication of this work to Rascher also describes the important role he played as "the pioneer of the concert saxophone."

Grisoni's *Albumblatt* (a 19th-century term for light-faceted pieces) consists of a number of sections strung together that shift from a slightly serious slant to a sampler of light, perky tunes. The signature section offers a surprise. It is an episode in slow tempo, totally assigned to the solo baritone saxophone, with tutti responses from the other instruments.

Groot, Cor de (1914–)

DUOS

- *Bassoonerie* for Bassoon and Harpsichord (or Piano) (1962)

In 1962 elegiac music was not necessarily deeply threnodic. Groot's *Bassonnerie* (the spelling used in the score) has a second-movement Elegiata (already a different terminology), and he sets it as a slow waltz (Tempo de valse lente). Expansive tonality guides all three movements. The first is a rhythmically nervous Rondella, the third is a rhythmically exact Conga, the Afro-Cuban dance in duple pulse, highlighting offbeat stresses within the measures.

- *Sonatina pastorale* for Oboe and Piano (1961)

Urban-type metrical action is twined into Groot's pastorale duo. In the first movement (Allegro scherzando) the music is in the long–short unequal divisioning of quintuple meter. Movement three is a speedy Rondo, and here the pulse arrangement is principally septuple (in a ratio of 4:3 within the measure) or quintuple (in a ratio of 2:3 within the measure). There are other pulse settings (2/4 and 3/4), but these also alternate and thus add to the general snappy and corky atmosphere.

Settled and illuminative in its expression is the second movement (Tempo de lamento). It is arranged to contrast lyricism with more active material. A gem of a conception. This movement, as the others, is in Groot's tonal polarity style. The outer movements are pitched around G, the middle one around E.

Gross, Eric (1926–)

TRIO

- Trio for Flute, Oboe, and Clarinet, Op. 10

Tonal lights are not ever extinguished in this work, but they are shaded by chromaticism and project dissonant colors. Neither is there any preoccupation with slim textures. Gross treats the woodwind trio with respect, but shows its ability to make big gestures and a pungent sound without the Frenchified cuteness so habitual with this medium.

Forms are in the area of standard choice, with a sonata-determined opening, a ternary slow movement, a scherzo type, and a fugal finale. Consistency of style distinguishes this Australian composer's opus.

Grossi, Pietro (1917–)

QUARTET

- *Composizione 6* for String Quartet (1960)

A formal blueprint of precision is followed in Grossi's *Sixth Composition,* the abstract title already clueing in the style of the piece. No ornaments in this structure, no indulgence to enrich the sound façade. For seventy-two measures the quartet plays rhythmically in unison in various sustained lengths. Then the pitches are separated in a spread quadruple antiphony. Finally, the sounds join together in three instruments, the fourth voice preceding or following alone.

(Grossi indicates that his quartet composition has a performance time of 9:36.)

Grosskopf, Erhard (1934–)

QUARTET

- *Sonata 3* for Flute, Violin, Viola, and Cello (1967)

Tough and stark music, a series of four abstract constructions. The use of repetitive pitch figures helps to clarify the polyrhythmic combinations. A restlessness pervades the music even though none of the movements are in the fast-tempo zone. This restlessness applies to the pitches themselves, with the use of flutter-tonguing, small-coursed glissandos, and microtones. The music represents a composer of aggressive personality.

Grossmann, Ferdinand (1887–1970)

TRIO

- String Trio (1952)

Grossmann was better known as a choral conductor than as a composer. His greatest success was as director of the Chamber Chorus of the Vienna Academy of Music. His creative output was limited, but this trio for violin, viola, and cello deserves attention. It is extremely well written, slightly adventurous, and represents a solid piece of chamber music.

The key analytical word is "mix." The mingling begins by compounding several movements in one. It continues in the syntax used.

The clue to the composite method is heard in the first four sounds of the work. These (in triple unison) are in clear C major. The music then picks up chromatic steam and travels on twelve-tone tracks. The unison opening is merely an introductory bow, from then on contrapuntalism reigns in the form of fugal mobilization. After the fugue there is more polyphonic detail. A link is then made to a flowing slow-paced section, also contrapuntal and filled with the devices of imitation and inversion. Finally, a duple-pulse march that seems to announce a return to clear tonality and as clear homophonic detail. But mix there is, and it is maintained; the music shifts to full-spread chromaticism and full-stocked contrapuntalism. Throughout the trio the interfusion works since the writing is always smooth in all the lines and smooth in the various shifts.

Grosz, Wilhelm (1894–1939)

DUO

- **Sonata for Violin and Piano, Op. 6**

While Grosz's music is filled with Viennese gaiety, the tonality scheme is far from neutral. Stylistically, the harmonic language is like late-period Mahler. Op. 6 is full of enthusiasm for dance color, dance design, and dance freedom. Grosz's style later took on jazz connections (one work, for example, was called *Jazz Band,* a miniature piece, quasi chamber music in concept), and one can see this rhythmic concoction simmering in the violin and piano sonata.

A lively and rhapsodic treatment of the first theme serves for the opening movement. Contrastive material is used rhythmically only to highlight the recurrence of the theme, always presented in a different manner. The second movement is a light tarantella affair, with a Trio in *Walzerzeitmass* (waltz tempo)—affinity of the nationalistic and the free romantic impulse. Ternary design serves for the emotionalism of the slow movement, and a very gay finale dishes up a fanfare-type theme, with contrasting episodes in somewhat heavy-handed chromaticism.

Grovlez, Gabriel (1879–1944)

DUO

- **Romance and Scherzo for Flute and Piano**

Contrastive moods, of course. The Romance flows and runs with melodic circularity, unimpeachably tonal (D-flat). It is enhanced (or adorned) by a short flute cadenza (the opus is a Morceau de Concours du Conservatoire National Supérieur de Musique de Paris—1927).

The Scherzo is effectively fast, set in quintal pulse (15/8) and concludes in duple pulse. It is neat and compelling. Efficient music, this.

Gruber, Heinz Karl (1943–)

OCTET

- ***Three MOB Pieces* for Seven Interchangeable Instruments and Percussion (Flute or Oboe, or Violin, or Clarinet; Clarinet or Violin, or Trumpet; Trumpet or Clarinet; Trombone or Horn, or Bassoon, or Cello; Guitar or Keyboard; Violin or Clarinet; Cello or Bassoon, or Double Bass; Percussion: Suspended Cymbal, Large Tin Can, Small Wood Block [or Side Drum without Snares], Three Tom-toms, and Hi-Hat [or Maracas]) (1968)**

MOB relates to the name of an organization, MOB art & tone ART, that produced informal concerts. Gruber played the double bass in the group and explains that "everyone did a bit of singing and acting." The objective was "inventing new kinds of programmes and discovering new audiences."

These three pieces typify the music that was written for the MOB ensemble. The very fluid instrumentation illustrates the unstuffy attitude of the MOB group; the contents run parallel. Number one is "Patrol," which swings in a bossa nova tempo and is fully scored. The second piece is "After Heine," which Gruber describes as "a little tribute to the great poet Heinrich Heine, whose poems often begin in a very romantic and flowery way, but end in despair." There is a jazzy, cabaret touch to the conception as there is to the third piece, "Verse," with a tempo heading of Soft Medium Rock.

Grudziński, Czesław (1911–)

DUO

- *Miniatures* for Cello and Piano

Simple but stylish and idiomatic national representations. "Kołysanka" is pitched on D and contrasts six-measure phrases with short ones of two-measure length. An Aria follows, and, in turn, the vivo crack of a "Krakowiak," in duple beat and substantially syncopated in its rhythms.

Movement four is still another Polish dance, the triple-pulse Mazurek (the mazurka or mazur). A lyrical, G minor, slow-paced "Pieśń bez słów" ("Song without Words") completes the suite.

Gruenberg, Louis (1884–1964)

DUO

- Sonata No. 1 for Violin and Piano, Op. 9

In Gruenberg's middle work period, he was concerned in his music with the quixotic posture. This is a more commendable fault than the fear of exploring. But his earlier music (of which this violin and piano sonata is one of the best examples) is not a product of faint heart either. There is nothing timid about a composer who destroys some fifty works at the age of 30! Thus, the duo sonata, composed some eight years after the house-cleaning, is representative of a mature person who has already undergone the greatest test of creative courage—the probing for full integrity.

Akin to the Marxian law that poverty is a crime, Gruenberg believed that lack of melody was also criminal. He stated that melody is the "actual blood" of a work; that "even a trivial melody is better than none at all." The present work uses melody as the magnetic lodestone, but there is nothing trivial about its overabundance. Melody pours and gushes from the first movement. There are two huge blocks in contrasted tempo, though in their legato surgings they are a bit similar. Differentiation is brought about by the use of color (a prime technical adequacy in all of Gruenberg's music, though not of trick origins or outré handling of the instruments). The first clings to the highest string of the violin, the second is darkened by majority use of the instrument's lower strings. Each of these is developed successively, the coda bringing quiet to the passionate state, with the minor tonality dissolving into major.

The last movement's moves are as melodically drawn, but the hand of the architect is more apparent. A rondolike main theme keeps reappearing, bisected by a differing rhythmic kernel, which becomes developed later. A portion in the middle marked Sognando (in a dreaming manner) has recitative turns and recalls hazily the main, second theme of the first movement. After the return of the finale's principal idea, this link of the corner movements is established further when the first theme of the opening movement is stated in very slow tempo.

Five variations on a theme constitute the middle movement. The seven-measure theme is a Kafir war song, taken from Richard Wallaschek's *Primitive Music*. Wallaschek (1860–1917) was a German musical aesthetician and musicologist, and he produced this book in 1893. Gruenberg first extends the theme by 8 1/2 measures, and then exploits it—initially, by the use of decoratives in Presto tempo (contrasted to two violent speed shifts into Lento), then by lushly romantic chromatic tapestry followed by waltz connotations and scherzolike shapes, and finally by a religiously expressive slow section.

QUARTETS

String Quartets

Only the two published string quartet suites are discussed below. Gruenberg composed three string quartets without specific titles. The first of these is marked Op. 6, composed in 1914; a second quartet, indicated as Op. 40, was composed in 1937. No opus number was assigned the third of the group, completed in 1938. All three are unpublished. There are three suites (none actually bearing such generic title). *Four Indiscretions* and *Four Diversions* were preceded by *Four Whimsicalities,* Op. 13, which remains in manuscript.

While the two sets of quartet pieces are not jazz music as such, there is such matter in the musical overtones with which they are concerned. Some attention, therefore, must be given to the period of Gruenberg's work when jazz occupied first place in his creative consciousness, and when he believed that it had a specific place in the schematics of composition.

The wisecrack, the letting down of the musical hair of these quartet suites is part and parcel of jazz delivery. Gruenberg followed the theory of dexterous rhythms and musical slang in many works. None were tagged with hidden meanings to become known only as the property of the analyst but sincerely proclaimed as *Jazzberries, Jazzettes, Jazz Masks, Jazz Dances, Jazz Epigrams, Jazz Suite.* Still another work was *The Daniel Jazz,* for tenor and eight instruments, as well as *Lady X,* a jazz operetta, written under a pseudonym.

As for many another American composer (Gruenberg was born in Russia, but came to the United States at the age of 2), black music was also a source of inspiration. That source was not applied in the quartets discussed below, but it remains for the record that Gruenberg fashioned the black idiom into his amazing and very successful opera based on Eugene O'Neill's *Emperor Jones,* as well as in another work (which also uses jazz), for baritone and eight instruments, composed in 1925—the setting of a text by James Weldon Johnson, the black poet, titled *The Creation: A Negro Sermon.*

- *Four Diversions* **for String Quartet, Op. 32**

The first movement does not sing, it skips to rhythms that are always in play, mainly the pulsed liveliness obtained from a long sound followed by a short one. There is no set form to the twenty-five measures of the second movement. An extemporizational caprice is built as if it were one long extended jazz improvisation. There are delicately colored blues-song connotations in the third movement, which includes harp imitations for the second violin, supported by lollipop harmonies. The fourth of these pieces is an Allegro burlando, with a rhythmic ostinato. It is combined with a gay theme that runs up and down and has, as well, metrical juggling of similar, repeated sounds. The partnership is a real romp. Gruenberg's *Diversions* are diversified and frolic in the right places.

- *Four Indiscretions* **for String Quartet, Op. 20**

Glissando final cadences to the first and fourth of these pieces give a "finger-to-the-nose" grimace. The first has a very flip-jazzed viola theme, which is then tossed around in a sauce of rhythms and variegated colors. It has a broader central section. There are jittery grace notes in the last piece, including a trumpet imitation. Sliding chords are the main characteristic of the slow second movement and the delicately limping third *Indiscretion,* which constantly changes its tempo gears. The scoring is pyrotechnical, a mastery of string quartet means that should not be overlooked but fully enjoyed.

Grünauer, Ingomar (1938–)

QUARTET

- **Wind Quartet for Flute, Oboe, Clarinet, and Bassoon (1965)**

The titles for the first two movements are Italian words indicating a manner of performance; thus: Tranquillo (Tranquil) for movement one, and Con anima (With Spirit) for movement two. Far more unusual is the third movement's title, *Sforzato,* which is an accentuation term, practically always abbreviated *sf* or *sfz.* (Its translation is "forced.") In a book giving tempo statistics *sforzato* would probably weigh in at zero. On the other hand, Tranquillo and Con anima are used quite often either as a total tempo heading or as a qualifying part combined with a specific speed indication. One example: Moderato con anima. This would be read as "to be played in moderate speed but with spirited quality."

The tempos in the quartet are defined by specific metronomic figures: ♩ = 54 for the 3/2 time signature of movement one, ♩. = 72 for the 3/8 meter of movement two, and ♪ = 108 for the 3/4 time signature of the final movement. Interestingly, all pulse totals in the work are triple, and more emphasis on this control pertains to the fact that nary a single ritard or accelerando is indicated. Indeed, the threefold cord in this music is never broken.

Formational constraint is the musical premise. Twenty-six measures directed and focused by sustained sounds, with rhythmically overlaid and underlaid bubbles, make up the first movement. As soon as one sustained quality (generally in two voices) is completed, another begins. Movement two (Con anima) consists of a theme, six variations, and a coda. Thematic length is undeviatingly matched from start to finish. There are thirteen measures in the theme, thirteen measures in each of the six permutations, and thirteen measures in the coda.

The symmetrical setting of movement two is certainly no happenstance. Such planning of compositional detail gives an irresistible balance, as telling in effect as it is vivid in variational specifications. The controls show minute planning that goes further than one movement itself. Each part of movement two has thirteen-measure length. Movement one has twenty-six measures (thus 2 x 13, significantly). Further, it must be emphasized again, both these movements are in triple meter.

While movement three has a different blueprint, it also is based on matched proportions. It consists of six seven-measure phrases, all but one tightly linked to the next, plus a closing measure (also linked to the previous phrase). In place of sustainment and variations, the action is one of unrest, with a heavy pitter-patter of figurations. Contemporary passions, all of these, but all controlled by the composer. The result, as in the previous movements, is more than intellectually meaningful.

Grundman, Clare (1913–)

DUO

- *Puppets* for Two Clarinets (1971)

Light stuff, unstuffy and carefree. The caper and the dance of the lines are seasoned with slight bite. Contemporary tone emerges from the emphasis on quartal melodic spans.

Grunenwald, Jean-Jacques (1911–)

QUARTET

- *Fantaisie-Arabesque* for Harpsichord (or Piano), Oboe, Clarinet, and Bassoon

Grunenwald's quartet has two features in its

three-movement span (the last two of these connected): banked-in cogent dissonances in its tonal pilotage and a scoring system that fundamentally separates the winds from the keyboard instrument. This antiphony divides but has none of the aspects of the stereophonic objectives of the "space-music" composers.

Duo thematicism is found in the opening movement. The introduction (for winds alone) outlines the downward fall that is pertinent to the flowery first theme, totally assigned to the harpsichord, while woodwind scale lines and pedal tones frame it. Theme two is conjunctively contrastive. It is assigned to the clarinet, with figurations in the other winds and chords followed by running counterpoint in the keyboard representative. When the initial theme is assigned to any of the wind instruments, once again the harpsichord is discreetly heard. Conversely directed upward, the single theme (providing still another contrast) of the Andante con moto is handled with similar scoring. The winds are heard first, then the harpsichord with woodwind background.

Equipoise returns in the end movement, with a pair of themes. In this case the scoring is much more abrupt in its antiphonal shifts, matching the presto velocity of the tempo. Only in the latter part of the piece does a wholesale combination of forces occur. The final chord attests to Grunenwald's harmonic calligraphy: an E-major tonic with an added sixth.

Grüner-Hegge, Odd (1899–1973)

TRIO

- **Trio in B Minor for Piano, Violin, and Cello, Op. 4**

This composer combined creativity with an extensive conducting career (he directed the Oslo Philharmonic Society Orchestra from 1931 to 1961, guest-conducted in many European cities, and directed operatic performances at the National Theatre in Oslo). As a pianist his abilities made possible solo appearances, and the instrument is strongly favored in his compositions.

The B-minor piano trio is a massive, romantically stabilized piece, with an impressive synthesis of trio instrumentation. Though the piano is a potent voice, it never dominates. The proportions of equality represent ideal (i.e., traditional) chamber music identity.

More than once the introspective quality of the music brings Brahms to mind. The sweep is constant, the quiet moments have an inner agitation. Both spell out the essential dramatic-rhetorical objective. Though basically in three movements, a lengthy epilogue has the measurement of a fourth division—beginning with somber quality and building to a tremendously fervent *fortissimo* in optimistic B-major tonality. The content of the preceding portions is clearly disposed: sonata form in the opening part, ternary features in the slow movement, with a lively third movement. Not a trace of pedanticism, however, appears in this standard format.

There are actually two versions of Grüner-Hegge's piano trio. Though totally revised in 1968, the work was composed as far back as 1918 and published in 1923. The second setting has not been published, but it has been recorded. The two differ most vividly, without changing the formal hypothesis and verification. In the later edition, passages are expanded, counterpoints added (or revamped), octave placements shifted, and there is greater attention to linear detail. Nevertheless, the structural clarity and emotional climate are similar in both instances.

Guarnieri, Camargo (1907–)

DUO

- **Sonatina for Flute and Piano**

To describe this composer in a few words, it can be said that he is a neoclassicist with Brazilian overtones. The former is represented by the clipped yet masterfully projected sounds in a tonally dissonant frame; the latter heard in the rhythm that, if not immediately identifiable *as* Brazilian, cannot be termed European or of average (neutral) condition. It is a rhythm that is particularly national. Nationalism on the part of a Brazilian composer equals (in this instance) Brazilian rhythm. This is especially noticeable in the last movement, which has a samba-simulated intensity. The music is not blatantly Brazilian but a modern tapping of the soil of folklore. There is virtuosity, a clear three-part form, but there is also the jockeying of an indigenous dance. That it is the climax of the work, the most Brazilian, does not make Guarnieri less national a voice in the other movements, or, for that matter, less healthy a creative personality.

Nor is the slow movement, with its melancholy feeling, of less Brazilian native cast. Within this portion of the work, the piano (as in the first movement) mainly retains lean two-part writing, permitting the flute to sound through more easily. One could very well attach titles to at least the last two movements, as a Serenade and Dance.

QUARTETS

- **String Quartet No. 2 (1944)**

Guarnieri's second quartet won the 1944 prize competition held by the Chamber Music Guild in Washington. The total entries for the contest were over the three-hundred mark.

Neoclassical tonality procedures mark the three movements, the polarity for the outer (fast) movements being A, and for the central slow movement, D. Rhythmic vitality is present in the speedy movements, with percussive accentuations and glides adorning the second of the pair. The slow movement has Brazilian sentiments mixed in with its nostalgic colorations.

- **String Quartet No. 3 (1962)**

Three movements—a standard design for this composer in his chamber music compositions. Thus, fast movements embracing a central slow one. Guarnieri's neoclassicism is fully present here, there is no evidence of "Brasildad" (explained by Nicolas Slonimsky as "a syndrome that is Brazilian in its melody and rhythm").

The lustiness of the fast music (the movements are marked Violento and Vivo e ritmato) contains polyphonic elements in imitative style. These two movements hustle and bustle but never splutter. The slow movement (Lento) is long lined, tripartite in shape, modally enunciated. It is most persuasive music and is the high point of the quartet.

Gubaidulina, Sofia (1931–)

TRIO

- **Five Etudes for Harp, Double Bass, and Percussion (Marimbaphone, Tambourine, Snare Drum, Cymbal, and Four Bongos) (1965)**

The instrumental updating adds coloristic excitement. Among the special consignments are playing the harp with sticks, using these thereby for glissandos in one direction or in opposite directions; playing chords behind the bridge of the double bass; finger contacts on the snare drum; and striking the bars of the marimbaphone both above and below.

Gubby

Gudmundsen-Holmgreen

Fervent attention to rhythm marks the set of pieces. Of course, asymmetricality is the name of the style here. In some places metrical coincidence is eliminated. Thus, in the second piece the percussion plays a strict quadruple-beat pattern regardless of the various quintuple-pulse divisions of the harp and double bass. (The percussion here may also improvise and make instrumental choices at will.) In the fourth etude the bass goes its own way, rubato, disregarding tempo definition on the part of the harp and percussion.

So, a healthy type of fervored fantasy is in play. This is wrapped around repetitive rhythmic ride-outs in the first etude, motile figurations in the second one, and glides and ostinatos in the third of the set. There is hammered insistence in the fourth piece, the music to be realized in an allegro type of pace and to be played in a "desperate" or "rash" manner. Irregular rhythmic ratios are used in practically every measure of the last etude. Thus: two sounds to fit in a total of three beats, six pitches to sound within the regular time span of four, five within three, etc. All these purposely, therefore, obscure the fundamental pulses within the measures.

Gubby, Roy

QUINTET

- *The Great Panathenaea* for Brass Quintet (Two Trumpets, Horn, Trombone, Bass Trombone [or Tuba])

The composer does not withhold his meaning. Thus, in the score the music is given its programmatic précis: "Every year a great Procession wound its way up to the Acropolis of Athens, but every fourth year a special one took place, known as The Great Panathenaea, when a new cloak of glorious design and colour was set on a model ship, to form its sail, and then draped around the gold and ivory statue. / Everyone imaginable was in the Procession: the noble maidens who had woven the cloak, the successful contenders in the Games, musicians playing the flutes and lyres, and others carrying olive branches and guiding the sacrificial beasts up the steep path."

To carry out this scene Gubby mixes small fanfarelike thrusts and short lyrical phrases. It is not a cheap imitation. It is music for five brass instruments hung on to a descriptive text. It is totally disinvolved. It is completely tonally clear.

Gudmundsen-Holmgreen, Pelle (1932–)

QUARTET

- **String Quartet No. 4 (1967)**

The scenario is a hypersophisticated one. For a six-minute span three different rhythmic tremolo lengths are set forth by the first violin (totaling twelve per pulse), second violin (totaling eight), and viola (totaling six). In a nonmetrical setting, based on a metronomic beat of forty per pulse length, these instruments shift between ponticello and ordinary sounds. Their dynamic is an unchanged *piano,* quarter tones are employed, and the three instruments' pitches are polyphonically deployed.

Supporting this is an undeviating B-flat in the cello. Its only change is one of dynamics, as it begins *pianississimo,* moves up to *mezzopiano* at the thirty-second mark, returns to the triple *piano* strength at the one-minute mark, and so on. (A six-minute one-pitch pedal point deserves its rightful place in music's record book!)

Guerra-Peixe   # Guézec

QUINTET

- *Terrace in Five Stages* **for Wind Quintet (Flute [alternating Piccolo], Oboe, Clarinet, Horn, and Bassoon) (1970)**

The simplicity of persistent pitch repetition controls the music of the first movement (sustained sounds), movement two (polyrhythmic), and movement three (mostly syncopative). A more rhapsodic quality embraces part four, with the entrance of the piccolo and the use of noise sounds (via overblowing, loose embouchure, and unusual fingering). The conclusion is quiet, set forth in a linear division of the material.

QUARTET

- **String Quartet No. 1 (1947)**

The twelve-tone system of this work is applied to clear forms. Motival mechanism is the medium of expressing, in the first movement, a large, three-part structure. Since motival principles are also utilized in the second movement a somewhat monotonous effect is realized, but this is lessened by the more lyric content of the third movement and the impetuosity of the last. Counterpoint is vaguely suggested in this quartet. Guerra-Peixe rather veils his contrapuntal flights in the form of short imitations. The spin of canon and the drama of fugue are absent.

Guerra-Peixe, César (1914–)

DUO

- *Pequeño dúo (Little Duet)* **for Violin and Cello (1946)**

Twelve-tone music by this Brazilian. Importantly, Guerra-Peixe "returned to his Brazilian roots" (as Nicolas Slonimsky describes it) and turned away from dodecaphonicism three years after composing this string duo.

The first movement is in free form, a binding color device being the use of glissando. The Largo has an important violin-stated motive. It appears eight times in the total seventeen measures, and then a ninth time when it is doubled in rhythmic value. The last movement is sectional, although developed completely on a motival design that takes the short opening descending unit, repeats it in varying forms, and in both possible directions. A four-measure slower idea divides the movement into a tripartite design.

Guézec, Jean-Pierre (1934–71)

TRIO

- **Trio for Violin, Viola, and Cello (1968)**

Art interchange is not a new partnership. One recalls poets declaiming of paintings that could be heard and music that could be seen. Despite Debussy's dislike of the term impressionism, it was his rapport with that genre of painting that made him leader of that affinitive school in music. Thus, color and sensations take the place of romantic rhetoric and equate the paintings of Monet, Manet, and Renoir. Expressionism in music (again a transfer from the vocabulary of painting), with its subterranean soul searching, is exemplified in the music of Schoenberg (the psychological premise of his *Erwartung,* for example) and in the Freudian concepts of certain music of Berg (*Wozzeck,* for example).

More recently, the sculptured shapes first realized by Alexander Calder (his mobiles and stabiles, with their free motion set off by air currents) became musically transferred in the work of Earle Brown (*q.v.*). The concept of mobility is realized by innumerable performance possibilities of a composition's contents (the function, so to speak, of unpredictability equaling spontaneity).

Guézec's objective was also the musical translation of painting. He was always inspired by pictorialism: the titles of some of his works denote this (*Architectures colorées, Formes, Reliefs polychromés*). His special regard was for the objective abstractions of Piet Mondrian. (An orchestral *Suite pour Mondrian* was composed in 1962, six years before this string trio.) The style of the orchestral composition is carried over to this chamber work. The various, differently arranged shapes and patterns are paralleled by sound chunks projected in time, the colors of each of the equated patterns differentiated (though the textural complexity sometimes does not make the portions as distinct as the specifics on a Mondrian canvas).

The colorations used for this sonic equivalent of a painting technique are of finesse, yet the differences register with proper acuteness. There is a kind of energy in the shifts of each type of attack or timbre manipulation. The score is filled with quarter-tone inflections, both below and above each member of the total chromatic range. Quite often the microtonal shading is made within an uninterrupted prolongation of sound in static or tremolando order. Most pertinent are the shades of vibrato, defined in four categories: very fast, regular, medium, and slow. The opposite form of nonvibrato is constantly used as a dynamic antonym. Dynamics are minutely considered. As a result changes are infinitesimal and powerful when antagonistic (a pizzicato chord for the trio with two of the instruments playing double *forte* and the other triple *piano,* for example). Contrapuntal dynamic planes are almost constant. Plucked sound is dry and flat as often as it is vibrant and alive.

There are fifteen connected sections in the work (it covers approximately eleven minutes in performance time). Expressive in its progression, freely unified, the form of the Trio is its content. Items can be specified: section three, with one minor exception totally stated in unisoned rhythm; section nine, chordal clusters in glissando underneath a vacillating trill; and section thirteen, polyphonicized sets of quarter-tone trills and antiphonal, ambivalently alternating harmonics—not one of the rhythms matching the other and the total in a hushed dynamic level of triple *piano.* Nevertheless, it is the total sonic impact that arranges itself in the mind and ears. The powers of Guézec's string trio are truly inexhaustibly evocative.

Guidi, Ferruccio

QUARTET

- **String Quartet in D, Op. 3**

Guidi's work (written in 1923) fulfills the usual string quartet requirements but on his own special terms, and the results are significant.

The second movement (Adagio) begins "without color" and quickly (after two measures) shifts to a "declamando rubato" quality that surrounds the fundamental repetitive eighth-note figuration. A slow-paced dance follows and then a return to the eighth-note material. This is linked to a vivacious section that is to sound "like the rhythm of a distant mazurka." Such unspecified program music becomes exactly specified in the third movement ("Commiato") ("Leave-taking"), which is prefaced by the line: "Mia vecchio Padova, addio!" ("Farewell, my old Padua!"). Sectional flexibility marks the music, which culminates in a fugue. Truly, all very diverting and far from a scholastic survey of four-movement form. This individuality includes the opening movement, which contrasts passages of dramatic thrust with suave, expressive ones.

Guignon, Jean-Pierre (1702–74)

DUOS

- **Sonatas for Two Cellos (or Viola da gambas or Bassoons), Op. 2**

  - No. 1, in C Major
  - No. 3, in B-flat Major
  - No. 4, in G Major

The original set consisted of six works, published in 1737, "Avec Privilége du Roi." The modern edition of half of the group was published by Edition Kneusslin Basel and issued in 1974. In so doing, the editors, Dieter Staehelin and Fritz Kneusslin, moved the fourth of the original group into the second slot so that the modern sequence follows Nos. 1–4–3.

Guignon's duo sonatas are direct and uncluttered, straightforward characterizations with equal time accorded both instruments. Tidy classic coherence prevails, with four movements in the C and B-flat-major works, three in the G-major opus. Dance forms are used, with a pair of Minuets in the first sonata, and a concluding Gigue in the B-flat-major sonata.

Guillard, Albert Le (1887–?)

QUARTET

- **String Quartet, Op. 5**

Rhapsodic coil and recoil mark the three movements. A constant sense of unrest pertains to the music, certified by the choice of formal depictions: emphasis on the initial rhythmically active theme in the first movement, variational treatment in the central movement, and the fantasy proportions of the final movement. Meter follows suit and is changed frequently. So are pitch and pattern stability.

Guillard's music has a fair amount of supple lyricism and a good amount of characteristic sensations, but it also has a good amount of striving for more than a quartet of string instruments can supply.

Gunzinger, Josef (1912–)

DUO

- **Suite for Flute and Viola**

Harmonic piquancy derived from a polarity point styles the harmony. No matter how the dissonance becomes projected, the solidarity of a fundamental tone center is realized. One has the sense of Rousselian order, with perhaps just a little less of the Frenchman's preciseness.

In the first of the four movements, long lines are governed by legato. The rhythms are fluid so that the principal meter of 9/8 is never divided into its usual three sets of threes but most often indented in 4 + 3 + 2 or 2 + 4 + 3. The same pulse lubricity is found in the other meters that mark the measures: 7/8, 8/8, 10/8, 11/8, 14/8, and 16/8.

Movement two is equal to a Scherzo, with its skittish triplet figures set in triple pulse. A fresh and lively Canon at the ninth below is represented in the third movement. The flexibility of rhythm culminates with a finale totally without metrical markings. It frames a type of quiet, gloved declamatory music.

Gusikoff, Michel (1893–1978)

QUARTET

- **"Oh! Susanna" Variations for String Quartet (1942)**

When a theme is of common knowledge, the

use of variational treatment is more assured of success. Most variations are not attempts to hide the thematic identity, but rather to show off its capabilities of development while retaining its contour. Gusikoff's path, therefore, was not exactly strewn with rocks. The success of a work can sometimes be judged by the number of versions that exist (for example, Ravel's orchestral *Pavane pour une Infante défunte,* Rachmaninoff's piano Prelude in C-sharp minor, etc.). Four exist for this work, the quartet version being the original. Since there is a place in the chamber music album for the snapshot as well as the etching and painting, this work has logical entertainment value of imponderable order.

"Oh! Susanna" (the published score for this work spells this "O, Susanna") is one of Stephen Foster's most notable songs. It was composed in 1848 and became a hit tune during the gold rush of 1849. This composer's treatment of Foster's banjoistic tune consists of six variations, only the fifth one deviating from the happy major mode. In some instances, the variations merge into each other; in other cases, there is a slight halt for separation purposes.

Gutiérrez Heras, Joaquín (1927–)

DUO

- *Sonata simple* for Flute and Piano

Clinically clean in terms of tonality, this represents a light (simple, indeed) example of neo-classic writing, mostly triadically determined. A touch of nationalistic flavor permeates the three movements. Music to please performer and auditor by its compactness and directness.

The Mexican composer's objective is maintained in the flute part of his duo sonata. The wind instrument is kept in the first two octaves of its range, with the D two octaves above middle C as the highest pitch.

Guy, Barry (1947–)

DUO

- *Four Miniatures* for Flute and Piano (1969)

The style of microtones, glissandos, varying types of air pressure for the flutist, vibratos, flutter-tonguing, special piano pedaling, and so forth. A music of four statements without development, without rhetoric, only a continuity of figments and fragments. Colorful, of course.

Guyonnet, Jacques (1933–)

DUO

- *Polyphonie I* for Alto Flute and Piano (1963)

Blocks of atonal material with a process of segmented individuation for each instrument. Naturally this means a multimetric situation, here including, as well, total release of metrical order. And this also means a frenzy of violent changes of dynamic, register, and timbre. For example, a series of five pitches, two of which are grace notes, and set over two fast beats, will have four different dynamic strengths. Rhythmic vertigo is a constant. And ditto other parameters.

Guyonnet's conception deals with abstract aspects that are ultracomplex. Nonetheless, this musical complexity fascinates and has genuineness.

QUARTET

- *Polyphonie III* for Alto Flute, Viola, and Two Pianos (1964)

This quartet of unusual instrumental makeup

has the same substances as Guyonnet's *Polyphonie I* (*see above*). (*Polyphonie II* is for two pianos.)

Timbral variety is given good attention. In a number of places the paired wind and string instruments are contrasted to total quartet scoring. The viola has a vivid cadenza, and later on the two pianos are featured alone in a substantial section.

Polyphonie III ends with instrumental decrease. In turn, the first piano, then the second piano, and later the flute drop out, leaving the viola to conclude the piece with a *fortississimo* pizzicato on a G-natural harmonic.

Guy-Ropartz: *see* Roparts, Guy

Gyrowetz, Adalbert (1763–1850)

TRIO

- **Trio No. 2 in D Major for Flute, Violin, and Cello**

A representative piece by this prolific composer (whose works include some sixty symphonies, about as many string quartets, thirty trios, and about forty violin sonatas). The Trio is the second of a set of six, first published in Paris in 1790; the modern edition appeared in 1980, edited by Herbert Kölbel and issued by Heinrichshofen.

The work represents an absolute stylistic bond with Haydn's early productions. Sonata proportions in the first movement, an Andante in the subdominant tonality that doesn't languish, and a concluding Rondo. The cello is completely a bass-voice support.

Gyulai, Elemér (1904–45)

DUOS

- **Sonata for Violin and Piano**

The traditions of Hungarian music as created by Bartók hold fast in Gyulai's duo sonata. But the rhythms are much milder and so are the harmonies. Call Gyulai a conservative Bartókian and, as well, a conservative Kodály disciple.

The outer movements are in triple time: the first a relaxed Moderato, the second a steaming Prestissimo. One 5/4 measure breaks the metrical continuity in the Moderato; nary a single shift is made in the 415 measures of the Prestissimo. To obtain required contrast there is a transfer from diatonicism to chromaticism in the first movement; in the finale slight tempo modifications serve the same purpose. Canonic portions color the slow (middle) movement.

- **Sonatina for Flute and Piano**

Folk items run through the pair of short movements, and Kodály comes to mind in the stylistic dressing. In the second movement (Allegro) bimetrical conditions are used, with 2/4 and 3/4 combined. There are other light polyrhythms, such as two against five, four against seven, to add further flavor.

Haag, Armin (1884–1944)

TRIO

- *Divertimento in Kanonsatzweise (Divertimento in Canon Form)* for Recorder, Violin, and Viola

Gebrauchsmusik ("music for use") was one of the creative reactions to the *fin-de-siècle* caused by both superbloated romantic music (with its performance difficulties) and the type conceived deliberately and almost preciously "for the sake of art." Originating in Germany, Gebrauchsmusik was a music designed for the most practical use, not determined for the concert stage. But many a work written in such spirit has values far beyond those pertinent to the original "workaday-music" conception. Simplicity in art is not a trifle to be overlooked smugly because it is more readily comprehensible to the listener. If a composer's enthusiasm for Gebrauchsmusik negates virtuosic complexities, it does not remove the directness that nourishes his practical composition and in turn speaks in a language that relates the essential ideas. This is not to imply that all works in the Gebrauchsmusik category are recommended for public performance. But the letter of credit necessary for consideration on the chamber music concert program is furnished by this seven-movement trio for recorder and two string instruments.

Each movement is a canon for two voices, with the third instrument used as a free accompanying line. The three possible combinations of duo instrumental color—violin and recorder, viola and recorder, and violin with viola—are all called on at one time or another. In the last movement the effect is almost that of a three-voice canon. The movements display varying canonic types, using imitation at the unison and intervals of the second, fourth, fifth, and oc-tave. By the medium of intervallic adjustment, necessary in view of the modulations attendant to imitation, the tonality of the original voice of the canon is maintained. Alteration is an important substance in the technique of imitation. For example, a canon's subject in G major, if duplicated a major second higher, would move into A major and cause bitonality unless the voices are made to conform by chromatically altering their pitches.

A composition consisting entirely of canons can well be monotonous unless the forms differ. Thus the interest is heightened here by the use of a March, with the canon stated at the unison; then a Gavotte, the imitation this time a second higher; an Andante, the canon shared between the viola and the violin—the latter a fifth above; and followed by a Menuett, illustrated by a canon at the octave. The next movement is an Air, wherein the viola imitates the recorder one octave below; this is succeeded by a Bourrée (the canon is at the fourth); and the composition is completed by a very quick Gigue, the duple meter outlining the easiest type of canon for both composer and listener—that at the octave.

Haan, Stefan de (1921–)

SEXTET

- Suite for a Brass Sextet (Three Trumpets, Two Trombones, and Bass Trombone)

No hidden meanings. The music says what it indicates it will say and says it in a bright, tonal manner. Clear and direct materials and, of course, brassy, but not mini-brass-bandy, stuff.

Some pyramidal scoring in the Introduction. An American dance of the early 20th century, the one–step, furnishes the quick, duple-meter moves for the Parody. Truthful meaning in the third part, False Relations, with chromatic changes deliberately made in two successive voices (rather than maintained by single-voice smoothness), adding flavor to the chords. Brevity and horizontal voicing define Counterpoint; speed stirs the Waltz; and dynamic identity marks the Finale. A bit of the opening movement ties up Haan's brass package.

Haas, Joseph (1879–1960)

DUOS

- **Kirchensonate (Church Sonata) in F Major for Violin and Organ, Op. 62, No. 1**

- **Kirchensonate (Church Sonata) in D Minor for Violin and Organ, Op. 62, No. 2**

The church sonata (in Italian, *sonata da chiesa*) in Haas's tonally secure 20th-century hands retains its dignity but not its distinctive movements. Each sonata, heard in continuous total order, is clearly sectional in disposition.

There is no doubt that Haas's viewpoint is one of general mood rather than of duplicating specific form. There is no fugal fast movement or dance-design finale as there was in the examples produced in the late 17th and early 18th centuries. Both sonatas are basically in slow tempos and when they speed up they never pass the moderate zone. There are some dynamic passages of impact, but the specific objective is restraint. Thus, the first work ends in triple *piano*, the second in quadruple *piano*. Since there are few concert halls that possess the organ necessary to present these works it is obviously a church locale that must serve. Haas has styled his work to fit such an environment.

Sonata No. 1: The initial solo violin phrase spells out the Latin "Jubilate." In the section

that follows, the organ spells out a parallel: "In dulci jubilo." Variational development is employed, with a return of the violin opening assigned to the organ for the final portion. Though the string instrument is muted, it is in this part of the Sonata that the textural weight is heaviest. This lessens in the final measures to match the declining dynamic level.

Sonata No. 2: As in the first sonata of the pair (*see above*), Haas places words beneath certain lines in the score. These are simply mood specifics, not programmatic designations, and serve as formal landmarks. Thus, the opening *forte* organ statement in D minor is set to the word Kyrie (from the Mass). It is immediately followed by a triple *piano* passage (again in the organ, simultaneous with a contrapuntal line in the violin) continuing the phrase: "eleison." The next *forte* statement is over the word Christi, and again the response in the contrasting dynamic completes the line with "eleison." This germinal procedure is used four additional times in the Sonata: the middle two are softly stated; the first and last are in the dynamic levels loud and soft respectively.

In the middle of the work Haas quotes a secular tune and underlays its text. The passage begins with *fortissimo* organ chords supported by a striding bass and a doubled unison pedal in the violin. With the violin muted, the section is completed with reduced dynamic intensity. Preceding and succeeding it are the main divisions of the Sonata, structured by developmental variation and linked by the sextuple use of the motto phrase.

- **Sonata for Horn and Piano, Op. 29**

The use of repeated sounds in the first movement fits the character of the horn precisely. Similar fanfarelike spurts adorn the lighter quality of the spirited Finale. The lyrical contrasts show off the singing quality of the horn at its best. As a result, the usual Regerian style of the composer is softened, even in the case of the keyboard instrument. The style is less mollified in the chromatically enriched, elegiacally contoured slow movement in F-sharp minor.

(Included in Schott's published edition of Haas's Op. 29 is a cello transcription for the slow movement. No mention is made *anywhere* that this is included, so one discovers this music, minus explanation, tucked inside the horn and piano parts. Strange.)

- **Sonata in B Minor for Violin and Piano, Op. 21**

A four-movement composition set forth according to Max Reger. Thus, sumptuous textural formations in the first movement, based on a theme that covers a good amount of territory in its intervallic detail. The second theme of the sonata construction is exactly the opposite, being tightly contained in its pitch movement.

A strictly designed B-flat-major Scherzo represents the second movement, with a lyrical centerpiece in the subdominant key. The slow movement, in ternary form, is profound and deeply moving. A high degree of dramatic intensity is reached when the initial theme (announced by the violin on its lowest string, *piano*) is restated two octaves higher in a *sempre fortissimo* outpouring. Nothing startlingly new about this procedure, but its effectiveness is undeniable. The Finale is a Rondo capriccioso, which, because of Haas's Regerian style, tends to be more dramatic than capricious.

Haas, Pavel (1899–1944)

QUARTETS

- *From Monkey's Mountains* for String Quartet (1925)

When a composer intends to evoke a natural setting, the listener expects descriptive guidelines. While Haas's four-part work is no vast and super-detailed musical travelogue, like Strauss's *An Alpine Symphony*, it nonetheless stirs auditory attention by the titles of the movements. But no indication is given as to what these represent.

Only the second movement, "The Coach, The Coachman, and the Horse," does the descriptive subtitle provide a program for the music: the continual glissandi presumably depict the movement of the vehicle, and shorter glides probably represent the squeaking of the lurching coach; the fast rhythmic movement of sixteenth-note patterns likely denotes animal motility. End of conjecture. In the other provocatively titled movement, "A Wild Night," the fourth, there are beams of activity (fast tremolandi; sudden, violent single-beat measures; "hurry" patterns), but what is being pictured—devils, witches, ogres, an orgy, whatever—is anyone's guess. The music does have interest—it would have much more if provided with identifiable relationships.

In the first and third movements—"The Landscape" and "The Moon and I . . . "—the descriptive subtitles are vague, atmospheric. There is impressionistic detail in both cases, aided by subdued rhythmic punctuations combined with long-phrased melodic lines in the first movement and suave chordalism in the third. But the ellipses at the title's end raise still another question.

These remarks obviously show incomplete knowledge of Haas's objectives, but nonetheless the music is interesting as a whole: colorful, expressive, varied, neat in every detail–and quite brilliant. None of this praise is meant to be faint.

Those who examine the score must not be confused by the 1961 date following the final double bar. This is a mark of arrogance on the part of the copyist, denoting the day, month, and year he completed making a fair copy of the score. It is worthless information. As noted above, Haas composed his quartet in 1925. He died on October 17, 1944, at the hands of the Nazi monsters in the concentration camp at Auschwitz (Oswiecim), Poland.

▪ **String Quartet No.3, Op. 15**

Haas studied for two years with Janáček at the Brno Conservatory. Some critics have stated that no one has ever attempted to imitate the renowned Moravian composer. Patent nonsense, that. The first movement of this quartet has the folklike quality, the vitality, and especially the palatable rhythmic ideas that parallel in great part the mature music of Janáček.

These qualities appear in the Lento as well, but to a lesser degree. The theme is a study in accelerated motion, moving from quarter notes to eighths to sixteenths. In related manner, the development leads to textural toughness where three and four different rhythmic patterns mesh tenaciously with one another. A Theme with Variations and Fugue describes the form for the final movement. The variations are tightly linked, with considerable freedom in the transformations. Tying the two components together, the theme of the variations appears in the concluding part of the fugue in augmentation.

Haass, Hans (1897–1955)

DUO

▪ *Mixtura* **for Clarinet (or Alto Saxophone) and Piano**

Despite the title, a neat and compact set of four pieces. If no masterworks, they are genuinely composed and balanced through in each case, using free tonal style.

The opening Preludio features broken triads with a shift made to quartal harmonies in the Scherzino. Again a change of basic chordal color is made to voicing and chording in fifths

in the Sarabande. Lean and tight texture certifies the spirit within the final Rondo. Not counting repeats, there are 52 measures (104 would be the total if the two large sections of the movement were repeated as indicated). Of these only 31/4 measures are four-voice, all else is maintained at a strict three-voice total.

Hába, Alois (1893–1973)

Microtonal Music

Microtonal (or microtonic) music is not of 20th-century newness as some think. Three examples: It is part of the pitch vocabulary of Arabic music; the Hindu scale systems include microtones; proposals for the use of quarter tones date back to the 17th century.

Some composers, such as Bloch, Bartók, and Copland, have included a small number of quarter tones simply for coloring purposes. Many of the post–World War II avant-garde fraternity have utilized microtonality as part of their enlarged timbral inventory.

As a total style, neither the microtonal output of the Russian composer Ivan Wyschnegradsky (1893–1979) (he produced some thirty compositions) nor that of the Mexican composer Julián Carrillo (1875–1965) should be overlooked. However, practically all of these compositions remain in manuscript, untested. Also to be recognized are the microtonal pieces of the American composer Ezra Sims (1928–) and the music of some Dutch composers, including the eminent Henk Badings (1907–), all of whom have employed a thirty-one–tone scale.

But for the creation of a literature of proven stability and viability—a music of prime importance and artistic effect—the credit belongs to the Czech composer Alois Hába, whose output includes a quarter-tone opera, six quarter-tone string quartets (for Nos. 1, 2, and 6, *see below*), and thirty-seven other works in the quarter-tone system. He also produced one string quartet in fifth tones *(see below)* and a total of seven works in sixth tones (one of these an opera, three are for string quartet [*see below* for the third quartet]). Instruments able to meet quarter-tone requirements were manufactured to his specifications, including pianos, clarinets, and trumpets, and Hába had a sixth-tone harmonium built as well. Hába taught microtonal composition to a large number of students and published two books dealing in depth with the fractional technique; one book covered quarter tones, the other third, sixth, and twelfth tones.

(Hába's creative inventory was not limited to works using fractional pitches. He wrote some fifty compositions in the standard twelve-pitch range.)

QUARTETS

- **Quartet for Four Bassoons, Op. 74**

A wind quartet of the same instruments such as this one offers problems that, naturally, do not concern the balances brought by a quartet of complementary timbres (such as one for piccolo, two flutes, and alto flute). Hába is moderately successful in solving his self-made scoring problem.

Predominantly chromatic syntax is used in all three movements. While the middle movement has ternary-form organization and the final movement relates to rondo procedures, the first part of the Quartet includes a continual run of thematic substances. Since counterpoint is not in first place here such thematic enthusiasm at least keeps matters interesting and avoids any blur in the textures. Plenty of nimble exercise for the four performers.

- **String Quartet No. 2 (No. 1 in the Quarter-Tone System), Op. 7**

This quartet does not completely break away from tradition and follow the espousals made by Hába in his later work (nonobservance of thematic continuity and no basic connection between movements). Opus 7 is in one continuous movement, containing the usual elements that bind most large-scale compound compositions. It is based on two themes used in a cyclic manner.

The composition opens with an Allegro non troppo, risoluto which is developed on a motival premise. This is followed by a transitory slow portion very closely allied to a division in the main Allegro and leads to a Scherzando. Here, the motive that began the quartet is employed but in a different meter and manner. After a one-measure pause the slow section begins. This is a continuation of the episode that bound the first and scherzo-type sections together. The final section (Allegro agitato) is, in turn, still another cyclic evolvement of the opening subject. It moves into a short division dealing again with the theme used first as an episode and later as the slow section. Hába then restates the opening of the quartet to conclude his composition.

Quarter tones mark the advance of practically every sound. Only a handful of progressions concern half- and whole-step distances. Such dogmatic insistence on microtonality was necessary at this stage of Hába's work in order to prove the value of its special speech and its very telling accentuations.

- **String Quartet No. 3 (No. 2 in the Quarter-Tone System), Op. 12**

Hába's second quarter-tone quartet is absorbed in fantasy and, therefore, without rigorous form. However, it is balanced inwardly by tempo design together with an extremely creative use of quartet sonority entwined with the composer's colored scale of quarter tones.

The quartet has two movements. Beginning slowly and becoming increasingly faster, the rhythm of the opening part is somewhat restrained in its patterns. Full rhythmic stride is reached through the music's constant evolutionary unfolding, obtained by indicating its thesis-antithesis through lines in transit, not by the specific action of themes per se. A brake is applied to the tempo for the next portion of the movement, an Allegretto that traces color on the music's outline by the viola's muted tone underneath the full timbre of the other instruments. The special value of this effect is to be gathered from the use of the viola in a long section during which it performs microtonic sixteenth-note figurations. The remainder of the movement is as freely formed as the first part.

In the second movement, Allegro scherzando, the mood is more volatile. Hába draws quite often on the pedal function. A section toward the end is especially noteworthy in reference to fractional harmony. In this instance, the first violin has shifting octaves—those formed by a pair of three-quarter tones—as well as the frictional secundal type whereby one sound of the pair is a quarter tone higher than the other.

- **String Quartet No. 7, Op. 73**

Pitch polarities are the harmonic stabilizers in the three movements. The first is based on D, the second moves about but settles on F, and the final movement works around the A pitch. A short–long motive is in command in the first movement, a sense of folk dance atmosphere colors the Finale. The middle movement includes fragments of Christmas carols, and for this reason, after its premiere performance, the piece was nicknamed the *Christmas* Quartet.

- **String Quartet No. 8, Op. 76**

A considerable number of Hába's works are constructed in a nonrepetitive fashion, and are lacking, therefore, in any thematic development. One of the exceptions is this quartet, composed in 1951.

Two main considerations distinguish the resolute tempo of the first movement: a short-long-short rhythmic idea and a compact scalic theme initially heard in the first violin and then in octaves in the viola and cello. Syncopative slants are featured in the Allegretto, which has the effect of a slow scherzo. Chromaticism attached to sharp, constant rhythmic play and interplay provides an exciting finale. Nonrepetitive style is certainly absent from this opus: In the final movement repeat signs surround an eight-measure phrase!

- **String Quartet No. 9, Op. 79**

Linear strength in this work, especially in the middle movement, where Hába uses his style of nonrepetition, though there is close identity between certain of the materials. In the opening movement there is a clear disposition of sonata design with direct repetitions avoided by way of slight pitch changes.

The Finale is an Allegro agitato. Instrumentally speaking, the approach is somewhat neutral, but the rhythmic coloration is powerful, with a constant array of patterns: off-beat sound weighting; syncopation; one group in sixteenths, another in eighths, others in triplets; and permutations of these. It is enunciative and declarative music. Three-quarters of the way through the movement the music slows to a Tempo di polka. Not a real polka at all, but a nervous one that serves both for contrast and for making the return of the principal tempo doubly exciting.

- **String Quartet No. 11 (No. 3 in the Sixth-Tone System), Op. 87**

Of course there is a ferment of microintervallic activity in the three movements of Hába's sixth-tone quartet, which divides the octave into thirty-six different pitches. (The eleventh of Hába's sixteen total string quartets was composed in 1958. It followed two other string quartets conceived in the sixth-tone system:

No. 5, produced in 1923, and No. 10, written in 1952.)

The formation of the three movements is in the traditional disposition of outer fast-paced tempos (Allegro energico and Allegro agitato) surrounding music of slow pace (Andante misterioso). But, as so often occurs in Hába's music, the structures are not the standard types of song form, rondo, and sonata. A constantly enfolding formal continuity involves the music. Most of the figurations and rhythmic patterns are made from sixteenth notes, even in the middle portion of the otherwise lyrical slow movement.

- **String Quartet No. 13, Op. 92**

This three-movement work, as does the greater part of Hába's output, follows the tenet of nonrepetitive construction. There is no motival development, no balancing of phrases, only a free and ever new unrolling of music in a variety of moods. The unity Hába obtains from such disparate means is undisputable. Moveover, in the first movement there is a flow between tonal and atonal character and in the other two movements there is use of a twelve-tone row. However, Hába treats his row formation as freely as he treats the formal shapes of the movements.

- **String Quartet No. 14 (No. 6 in the Quarter-Tone System), Op. 94**

Six short movements (the performance time is 101/2 minutes), each in Hába's style of nonrepetition of material and minus any development. Still, each movement of the work has divisional shape, so that movements one and three are each in two parts, movement two has four parts, and movements four, five, and six have three parts each.

Hába wrote down his creative impressions regarding this quartet; these give a unique insight into the psychological processes that combine with a composer's actual technical analysis. *(The translation is by Jan Machač.)* Movement one: "The flashing of an idea (suggestion) and its being seized upon by the consciousness." Movement two: "The pleasure in the idea, reinforcement of the creative self-confidence." Movement three: "The study of the idea and the desire for its development." Movement four: "The effort towards realization; overcoming obstacles." Movement five: "The feeling of love of creative work; satisfaction." Movement six: "The pleasure in a successful realization."

- **String Quartet No. 16 (in the Fifth-Tone System), Op. 98**

This represents Hába's single work in the fifth-tone system, embracing a thirty-one–pitch division of the octave. The music is concentrated into a set of eight pieces, each short, each reflecting a mood and without any development or recapitulation.

The first is a mainly Andante concept titled *Klidně—Calmo* ("Quietly"). Movement two has Allegro vivace tempo, and though headed *Vzrušeně—Con affezione* ("With Affection"), the score indicates a translation of "agitato." Antiphonal scoring is dominant in *Nerozhodně—Indeciso* ("Indecisively"). Movement four has the title *Tvrdě—Duramente* ("Harshly") and a subtitle *(Melodia cantabile)* ("Singing Melody"): The latter consists of short phrases, the former is denoted by pithy, forceful responses. Vivacity, scherzo style, with plentiful repetitive pitches, characterizes *Snivě—Sognando* ("Dreamily"). Movement six is in slow tempo, titled *Soustředěně—Con concentrazione* ("With Concentration"). An energetic four-voiced statement defines *Pevně—Fermamente* ("Firmly"). The eighth and last movement has three tempos in its sections, with the concluding one moving continually faster to the final measures, fulfilling the designation *Vesele—Allegramente* ("Brightly").

NONETS

- **First Nonet for Flute, Oboe, Clarinet, Bassoon, Horn, Violin, Viola, Cello, and Double Bass, Op. 40**

A one-movement conception, delineating six different sections. The third and fifth of these are on the slower-tempo side, the others are all fast, with the fourth a presto-paced Scherzando. Opus 40 is written in Hába's through-composed, style. One division merges into the next with certain demarcations used. Before the fourth section (Scherzando) there are sustained chords, *pianissimo*. The faster-paced, lighter-detailed music begins with short pizzicato pitches in the strings; the final part of the work outlines a duple-pulsed folk dance.

- **Third Nonet for Flute, Oboe, Clarinet, Bassoon, Horn, Violin, Viola, Cello, and Double Bass, Op. 82**

Hába's four-movement work embraces, in turn, fast music, scherzo definition, lyrical material, and a buoyant rhythmic finale. There is balance within each movement but also a good amount of formal freedom; for example, the first movement, which contains five short divisions. Throughout, the quality of Moravian folk material flavors the piece.

The Czech critic Jiří Pilka writes that Hába composed the work to express, in sound, gratefulness for the life he had led, stating that what he had accomplished was "a source of joy and gratitude to me."

Hába, Karel (1898–1972)

TRIO

- **Trio for Violin, Cello, and Piano, Op. 24**

One idea moves into the next in this Trio,

maintaining Karel Hába's basic style. However, the result is no pastiche. There are balances. The first movement, which begins with a four-measure phrase for the piano, is equaled at the conclusion with a similar phrase for the violin and cello. An ascending figure is fundamental to the variety encompassed in the middle movement. Further, while no exact repetition of material is used in the final movement, the layout provides a clear ternary design.

QUARTET

- **Second String Quartet, Op. 5**

No preoccupation with stated themes and their development here. Karel Hába, younger brother of the more famous Alois Hába, followed Alois's stylistic method. The freshness of the content remains clear as it moves from one section to the next. In the opening movement contrapuntalism is linked to a scherzando conception, followed by a Menuetto that retains scherzando quality, and then there is a return to polyphonic exploitation.

Linear, supple content marks the second movement. A timbral balance is evident in the use of total muting of the quartet for a section after the beginning of this movement and its conclusion. Similar divisional apportionment pertains to the third movement, which includes good amounts of polyphonic stratification.

Haber, Louis (1915–)

DUOS

- *Six Miniatures* **for Violin and Flute**

Precise silhouettes, pungently dissonant, cleverly colorful, but without a single *outré* instrumental effect. Vital symmetry is important to a March. Haber's has it, with acidulated major sevenths prominent in the "bass" line of the violin. The "Intermezzo" is a graceful touching of bases with bitonality. Shipshape parallel harmonies and two-voice contrary motion move the "Barcarolle" (the violin is muted). Kinetic energy, kicked along with cross accents and syncopation, drives the "South American Dance." Miniature No. 5 is a slow-tempo Prelude (the violin again muted). An impetuous "Perpetual Motion" is pushed by sixteenth-note patterns. A few times the action slows to eighth notes, but these are merely a contrast within the rhythmic industry. Haber's little pieces are a treat for a combination practically minus any literature.

■ Sonata for Violin and Piano

Brevity is the soul of this work, more a suite (and a baroque one) than a sonata. The opening Grave is but twenty-seven measures in length; the Adagio, which occupies third place, is three measures less in its total. If it were not for the binary-conditioned repeats of the other pair of movements they would also fall in the condensed classification. The outer parts recall the Golden Age of the suite by the ornate figurations that carry the voices in the Grave and the fast-tempo Gigue that concludes the piece.

But the hierarchy of Haber's harmonies and the practices of his chromatic disengagement go beyond any neoclassic relationship. Confirmatory proof is found in the cadences—the stylistic signature of a man's work. Haber's first movement ends with a frictional fifth (combining both perfect and diminished forms); the third movement is less tense, but still dissonant, being completed by a diminished fifth. The second movement concludes with a *fortissimo* powered *diabolus in musica* violating the D-major tonality beneath, and the Gigue ends with an open D–A percussively polluted with a D sharp and a G sharp.

TRIOS

■ *Parade, Blues and Allegro* for Flute, Violin, and Piano

Similar to his other chamber music discussed here, Haber's trio is compact and to the point. And he knows how to interplay the qualities of the instruments and create fresh touches with contrasting and stimulating effects.

The *Parade* swings along, but not with squared-off meter. Mainly 2/4, it broadens (but does not slow) to 3/4 several times, and the inclusion of a number of 1/4 measures adds zip to the proceedings. Tone clusters and ostinatos predominate in the rhythmic right of way. Repetitive patterns are also the underpinning for the *Blues*, in which the piano serves only as support; all the melodic contributions are made by the other two instruments. The final *Allegro* is pert, persistently partial to an anapestic rhythmic cell. Altogether, music that is a pleasure to play and hear.

■ Trio for Flute, Violin, and Piano

Light material presented with serious formality: a bit of padding and a bit of sectionalism. Yet it is sufficiently colorful to deserve occasional hearing.

Movement one is a Toccatina. Not short, however, with a performing time of 7 1/2 minutes. A mix of styles is included, with both tonality and twelve-tone represented in the material. A ternary Aria and a Rondo follow. The latter quotes the twelve-tone row used in movement one.

Hadamowsky, Hans (1906–86)

TRIO

- **Variations on a Folk Song for Two Oboes and English horn**

The German folk song Hadamowsky uses for his group of a dozen variations is "Treue Liebe," which not only introduces the trio but is repeated at its conclusion.

Skillfully executed variants, each clear in format, each clear in its tonal dress. Persistent triplet figuration by the English horn against juicy thirds and sixths in the oboes marks the second variation. Imitation moves the third variant, dovetailed and tutti triplets hold the fourth variation in place. Variation five has the quality of a fast waltz, variant seven has a three layer rhythmic plan (it is the heaviest of the variations). Ariosolike ornamentation is used in the eleventh part, scalic material is the principal element in the concluding variation.

Haddad, Don (1935–)

QUINTET

- *Encore '1812'* **for Wind Quintet and Double Bass (optional)**

A fast-paced sketch. Light fare. The music, in quintuple meter throughout, takes the partial outline of a melodic shape from Tchaikovsky's *1812 Overture* and jiggles it about. Later the same borrowing applies to part of a rhythmic figure.

SEXTET

- *Blues au vent* **for Woodwind Quintet and Percussion (Dance Band Drums)**

The main title and the subtitles, "Three by Four," "Twist," and "Ad Libitum," tell the tale. Not disco stuff, but clean jazz of the pre-rock days, far from rewarmed cold turkey. A few seconds short of six minutes in playing time.

Hader, Widmar (1941–)

DUO

- **Duet for Trumpet and Trombone (1968)**

There is nothing casual about Hader's worship of diminished octaves, major and minor seconds. These intervallic combinations form the significant stylistic link of the entire work. There is this to say: Hader balances these in regard to the linear travel of the two instrumental lines, most of which mark off conjunct progress.

Alternate fast and slow tempos regulate the total four movements. Compact music: the timings given are 1:45, 0:56, 2:3, and 1:2.

Hadley, Henry (1871–1937)

QUINTET

- **Piano Quintet in A Minor, Op. 50**

Only the minutest deviations from accepted standard romantic practice are found in the four movements of this work. The inner pair have special values: one a poetic slow movement, the other a piquant yet restrained Scherzo (with the usual contrasting central section in broader tempo). The outer movements are in the expected allegro speeds, the first to be played energico, the other, con brio.

Best of all, Hadley does not try to storm symphonic heights with his piano and four string instruments and always retains a chamber music ambience.

Hagerup Bull, Edvard (1922–)

DUOS

- *Mouvements brefs (Brief Movements)* for Alto Saxophone and Piano

Compact, but not exactly brief. The first movement, an Allegretto, runs more than a hundred measures. Slow and fast movements complete the work.

The hallmarks of the composer's style are to be heard—melody and rhythm are in constant change. The sense of the work is in the motival interplay, heavied by the texture but thoroughly developed both vertically and horizontally. In this reference, much is made of a falling third in the first movement. Music composition is rife with clear-cut formulas. This composer avoids these in favor of controlled rhapsodicism.

- **Sonata for Clarinet and Piano (1951)**

Three movements, with two Allegros surrounding an Andante. This may lead to the thought that a conventionality of design is at work. In general, yes: with sonata structures for the outer movements and a three-part form used for the central movement, titled Transition. However, the constant change of materials removes any rigid structural declaration. At the heart of the music is classicism being infused by postromantic pigmentation.

TRIO

- **Concert for Trumpet, Horn, and Trombone (1966)**

Concerted polyphony in great amounts in the three movements. Plenty of rhythmic energy and motion reminiscent of the style of Hindemith, but with textures that are heavier than the German composer's. (All three instruments play in every one of the seventy-nine measures in movement one, and there are very few places in the other two movements where fewer than all three voices are in action.) There are also more melodic progressions in intervals of sevenths, diminished and augmented octaves, than one finds in Hindemith's work.

Muscular and active neoclassic music by this Norwegian composer. Colored by the use of mutes, even the middle, slow movement is especially motile.

QUARTETS

- *Ad usum amicorum (For Use of Friends)*: Quartet for Flute, Violin, Cello, and Piano (1957)

Arabesquelike material permeates the four movements of the work, leading to tempo shifts within the movements that regulate the formal balances. There is no preoccupation with pat patterns or tunes. Hagerup Bull works out his music from motival data derived from large intervallic spans in both the third and fourth movements. In the latter, tighter rhythm prevails in the network of voices.

The second movement is an Allegretto that has dance flavor. According to the Norwegian musicologist Bjarne Kortsen, the principal part of the music "is plainly inspired by a Halling, as is clearly evident from the melodic/rhythmic structure and grouping of two and two bars." The music indeed does bear out the turns of the Norwegian folk dance, which ranges from the intentionally clumsy to the truly dynamic.

- *Quadridge* for Four Clarinets (E-flat Clarinet, Two B-flat Clarinets, and Bass Clarinet) (1963)

Chromatic syntax is the chief resource in the quartet. It is matched by rhapsodic turns and development of the material in each of the first two movements. There is less chromatic activity in the Leggiero finale.

Hagerup Bull's writing for the clarinets is full, intense in detail, and demands highly honed technique. The music speaks with authority, though without much color change.

QUINTET

- *Marionettes sérieuses (Serious Puppets): Capricci* for Five Wind Instruments (Flute, Oboe, Clarinet, Bassoon, and Horn) (1960)

No pink-pilled programmaticism in the quintet's three movements. Hagerup Bull indicates the title "alludes solely to the musical character of the work."

Basic to the structure as a whole is the opening motive in the oboe, which is developed and reshaped in both linear use and as a harmonic component. Movement one (Allegro) and two (Adagio) are tripartite, but with the contents not measured off for compartmented definition. Tempo changes are aids in establishing the balances. The third movement is in rondo form. As usual with this composer, tonality is full-blooded—chromaticism is not on holiday in this quintet.

Hahn, Reynaldo (1874–1947)

There are a number of composers, now deceased, whose work seems to have been interred with them. Fashions being what they are, the chamber music of Reynaldo Hahn, a sensitive French musician (he was born in Venezuela and was brought to Paris at the age of three), remains buried for the time being. Good art, however, always surfaces. In Hahn's case we look for the unjust inattention of the present to fade and allow us to rediscover the proven past.

Hahn was as superbly vocally minded in his chamber music as he was in his songs, some of which are fully the equal of Fauré's and Debussy's. The forms he used were unpreten-

tious. But nothing more was required to frame his lyricism. Sibelius's statement about Arnold Bax fits Reynaldo Hahn: "Thank God he can write a melody." Gide's comment also applies: "The classical artist tries to avoid a 'manner'; he seeks the 'ordinary.' "

DUO

- Sonata in C Major for Violin and Piano

The initial C-major theme has Mozartian purity. It is contrasted by a calmly contoured idea, delayed in total presentation by partitioned announcement. Both the opening and outer movements have a relaxed quality, even the more chromatic, sometime septuple-meter final one, which balances the diatonic personality of the first movement. Teutonic *kolossalismus* was foreign to Hahn's French-style clarity and flexibility. There is no belaborment in any part of the Sonata, which is summarized cyclically in the finale by material from the opening movement.

Toccata velocity vitalizes the second movement, for which Hahn included a slightly enigmatic parenthetical heading: *(12 C.V.—8 Cyl.— 5000 tours).* This is not a cryptogram but an abbreviated statistical report. It means twelve horsepower (C.V. standing for *cheval-vapeur*), eight cylinders, and five-thousand revolutions. Considering the speed of the music, this is Hahn's witty way of describing open-road travel by means of his automobile.

QUARTET

- String Quartet in A Minor

All the earmarks of the full melodist: A cantilena runs through the entire quartet, even in the speedy movements; and there is exemplary structural logic as well.

The first pair of movements have introductory sections. In the opening movement not only is it of substantial length but it returns totally at the end of the movement, providing a clear balance to the music. The introduction is in moderately slow speed and in triple time and it encloses the principal fast-tempo music set in quadruple time. The latter is given full development. Movement two's introduction, in slow tempo, is short, leading to the refreshing sound of folk-music depiction, paced one beat to the measure, identified by the title *Récit et Chanson de Provence*. The instruments are muted.

Movement three (Andantino) highlights the viola. This warmly focused conception is followed by a rondo-structured concluding movement.

QUINTET

- **Quintet for Two Violins, Viola, Cello, and Piano**

A favorite device in piano quintets is to state the principal theme in solid unison. This unfussy statement of fact is used to open Hahn's Quintet. Compact scoring is maintained. Either the piano or strings are heard alone, or one is featured with the other supporting.

As a whole, polyphony is hardly utilized in the work—in the opening F-sharp minor movement, not at all. The second part of the Quintet is in da capo aria form. The word *aria* is appropriately descriptive. Traditional rondo design is used in the final movement, its primary theme of folk character. There is a haunting, somewhat nostalgic flavor to this part of the Quintet, further evidence of Hahn's sensitive, poetic music.

Haidmayer, Karl (1927–)

DUO

- **Sonata I for Viola and Piano (1964)**

A lively and interesting work, tonally spiced

with dissonant ingredients but always properly proportioned in terms of the harmonic recipe. More interesting is Haidmayer's insistence on repetitive harmonies. Some examples: in the first movement the minor third, B-flat–D-flat, appears on each beat of the first 51/2 measures, is heard in three later measures; and fills every pulse in 101/2 measures in the recapitulation. A dozen consecutive measures are totally harmonized with the major second G-A, and so on. Eventually this spreads into full-scale ostinato, so that thirty measures in the final movement consist of the same harmonic pattern. Still, Haidmayer's music moves with pep and has a fine-threaded texture that makes it quite acceptable.

Movement two is a recitative announced by the viola—the piano merely rolls out a few arpeggios. The finale has a picturesque tempo heading: Presto romineasca ("Fast in the Roman style"). It presses forward at the requested rate of $\downarrow$ =200 and often mashes three-pitch rhythms in the viola against two in the piano.

Haieff, Alexei (1914–)

DUOS

- *Eclogue* **for Cello and Piano (1947)**

The clarities of neoclassicism are here displayed. The melodies Haieff distributes are delicate and durable, savory and succinct. Two tempos regulate the design: An Andantino marked by cello pizzicato opens the work and appears in the penultimate position in shorter form. The principal material, with a pronounced white-note quality, is in Allegro. It is also used for the concluding measures of the duo, also in very small amount.

- *Three Bagatelles* for Oboe and Bassoon (1955)

Since homophonic instruments are being used, Haieff's three-part set (begun in 1939 and completed in 1955) is naturally contrapuntal, with lightly salted dissonances helping to deter the merging of lines and increasing aural interest. Mainly perky, close-spaced items, they are examples of musical hedonism.

The music is also playable, as scored, for either solo harpsichord or piano.

QUARTET

- **String Quartet No. 1 (1951)**

Although some neoromantic air sweeps through the second movement Largo, consisting of a music set in fantasy form, the rest of Haieff's quartet, with its tonally leveled dependency and marked rhythms, relates it to the Stravinsky of the pre–twelve-tone days. No romantic dilly-dallying, just persuasive architecture: sonata form in movement one and rondo form in movement three.

Haigh, Morris

DUO

- **Serenade for Flute and Piano (1953)**

The clarity and precision of neoclassic style. And with decided thrust, even in the curling, wraparound rhythmics of the opening Prelude.

Movement two (Capriccio) is tenacious in its asymmetry. Lean texture here and tangy line writing. The Finale is a formal blood relative, though in this case the meter stays in one duple location (save for one measure). However, hocket process is used, most often partnering duple and triple pulse in the same time span. The third movement is a richly lyrical, chro-

matically intersticed Intermezzo.

Haik-Ventoura, Suzanne (1912–)

TRIO

- *Un beau dimanche (A Lovely Sunday)* for **Violin, Clarinet, and Piano**

Depictive titling is a principal point in this four-part suite. Descriptive headings are not limited to the four movements but are used also within each of the six sections of movement two, a theme and variations. The music's programmatic colorism places the trio squarely in the neoromantic orbit. Inculcated are especially vigorous metric structures, emphasizing irregularly ordered pulse groupings.

In *Tout en valsant* ("While Waltzing"), movement one, the harmonic restlessness is matched by the restive meters, which begin with 5–5/8 and later include such formulations as 5–5–6/8, 6–2/8, 4–5/8, and 6–5/8.

Movement two, *L'Évasion (Thème varié)* ("Escape [Theme and Variations]"), consists of six exceedingly free, rhapsodic variants derived from a two-measure idea that is more motivic than thematic, despite the parenthetical heading to the contrary. The first of the set (*Vers la gare en fredonnant*) ("Toward the Railroad Station, Humming") moves quickly along trirhythmic lines, with a relaxed conclusion. Variation two (*Le train de Chaville [bringuebalant et cahotant]*) ("The Train to Chaville [Shaky and Bumpy]") is twice as fast, is also trirhythmic, and likewise terminates with less linear activity. There is ambulatory harmony in part three: *Promenade dans les bois* ("Walk in the Woods"). This is in contrast to the suspended, nonlyrical sounds of variation four: *Au fil de l'eau* ("Drifting down the Stream"), framed by 5–5/8 metrical measurement. The violin is muted in variations three and four and continues its compressed timbre in the fifth section, *Retour en fiacre* ("Home in a Hackney Cab"). The pictured vehicular return is matched by a return of trirhythmic detail. Slow waltz swing is maintained in the *Dernière valse* ("Last Waltz"). Though the meter is 6/8, the sense is of paired 3/8 meters within each measure.

The restless specifications of movement three convey the *Solitude—Colloque* ("Solitude—Colloquy") title heading. There are variational responses in this movement as well as the restive meters used in the first movement. A rondo form with aggressive rhythmic detail marks the pictorial intent of the final movement, *Heureux projets* ("Joyful Plans").

Haines, Edmund (1914–74)

DUOS

- **Desvelo *(Night Vigil)* for Cello and Piano**

The music is based on a poem by the Spanish lyric poet Juan Ramón Jiménez (1881–1958). The translation follows: "Night departs, black bull / —great flesh of grief, terror and mystery—; / who roared terribly, immensely, / with the sweaty dread of all the fallen; / and day comes, fresh child, / asking trust, love and laughter, / —a child who, there far away, / in secret places where / beginnings and ends meet, / played a moment, / in some unknown field / of light and shadow, / with the bull who fled."

Haines uses an arch form (A-B-C-B-A) to freely transmit his response to the text, and that response is an expressionistic type of music. But the duo is no totally enmeshed, *angststricken* expressionistic essay. There is a spaciousness and outwardness in the music and only a minimal amount of morbidity in the dark colorations that flit through the measures.

While there is a strong relationship between the A sections, in that some repetition of material occurs, there is considerably less correspondence between the other sections, which are each, in turn, depicted by general type and exact tempo. The B divisions have breadth and are a bit slower in tempo than the C division, which has sharper impulses. The slowest tempo is reserved for the A sections, both also without specific metric measurement.

- **Modules *for Tuba and Piano (1972)***

The joys of performer choice are to be found here since the five sections of the piece can be played in any order. And more. The ritual of chance is included in the fourth part, a rather slow, free-measured *Dialogue*. Each performer has ten fragments that can be played, once again, in any order, but in exact alternate succession by the two instruments. And still more. The performers "may omit some fragments, transpose them, or improvise on them, keeping the character of the section."

Of course, instrumental interchange (each emphasized by being a solo segment) describes this fourth section. The others, though less easily identified, are each marked by a primary function of communication. Section one is improvisational in effect. The second part is quite fast in speed, nervous in rhythm, often mixing a 3-4-5 set of eighth notes in successive measures. Part three is the slowest of the sections; with its note values free, the stylistic sense is one of recitative. The final (fifth) section is in fast tempo; the tuba has a few flutter-tongued sounds, and the two instruments are purposefully uncoordinated in the latter part, though they do become joined in the final measure.

Modules is quite different from Haines's other music. In his free move to the creative left, with all the aleatoric analogues, the special effects and procedures are not used for their own sake but are chosen for their direct musical expressions.

QUARTETS

- **String Quartet No. 4 (1957)**

Haines's fourth quartet has a romantic center of gravity that spins in a contemporary orbit. Melodic juice gives a tang to Haines's ideas, which are intent on song and rhythm. The composition is structured on a variational basis. The grouping of its ten parts is made so that sets of variations provide the composite parallel of a movement. Thus the Theme, together with the Pastoral and Air (the last is optional), represent the opening movement; the next three variants (Dance, Second Dance, and Scherzo) make up the second movement. Movement three presents the opposite moods and tempos of a Soliloquy and Toccata, and the concluding part is represented by a Finale and an Epilogue.

Nice color is used in the scoring. This includes an all-pizzicato timbre for the Scherzo division. The seminal source for this, is, of course, Béla Bartók's fourth string quartet.

- **Toccata for Two Cornets, Trombone, and Baritone**

Haines's early music generally displays a poetic side and a racy rhythmicity and thrust that mark him as being in tune with the gusto of the times. The Toccata has none of the former, but plenty of the latter, and is fresh and invigorating even when the dynamic level is relaxed. It has bite—the opening chord is plugged inside with a second and marks well the harmonic language that will follow. Ternary framework holds Haines's music in place, the first twenty-nine measures being repeated later sound for sound for formal symmetry and then vigorously completed in a triple *forte* postscript.

The choice of instruments for this brass quartet represents esoterica in the chamber music catalogue. There are few works that call for cornets and fewer still for the baritone brass instrument.

Hajdú, Mihály (1909–)

DUO

- **Sonata No. 2 for Violin and Piano (1973)**

A colorful opening, with bitonal fifths in the piano over which the violin in a whispered dynamic plays tremolandos, glissandos, and ponticello. Then the music breaks out with Hungarian display, twice interrupted by a return of the prelude. The Andante blends a recitative line with quartal harmonies and small clusters. A Presto music with razor-edged definition of pulse that is either quintuple or sextuple, marks the finale.

TRIO

- **Trio for Wind Instruments (Two Flutes and Clarinet) (1958)**

The Hungarian nationalism that permeates most of Hadjú's compositions is central to this Trio as well. The dance push of the finale, set in an easygoing manner (mostly two- and four-measure phrases), is a prime illustration. There are some little bits of Hungarian motives also in the first movement, a light, swinging conception that has C major as its tonal home base. The middle movement is monothematic, with the theme passed around the instruments and also set in imitation.

Halaczinsky, Rudolf (1920–)

QUINTET

- *Epitaph for Five Winds* (Flute, Oboe, Clarinet, Horn, and Bassoon)

In Halaczinsky's wind quintet mostly direct dissonant harmonic formations are braced by a framework of sustained sounds and colored by repetitive pitches. There is always an inner push toward release, which finally takes place in a violently crammed, explosively individual pair of passages containing unmetered, uncoordinated music. The first of these lasts ten seconds; the second, eight seconds. Liberation having been accomplished, the music returns in shortened total to its initial state. Avant-garde style notwithstanding, clear, standard, ternary balance is thus established.

The use of silence as an aspect of music provides a subtly cohesive touch. There are seventeen measures in which silences—some lasting as long as four beats, others as little as two seconds—provide the source from which the music issues.

Halévy, Jacques-François-Fromental-Elie (1799–1862)

TRIO

- **Petit caprice for Three Oboes**

The celebrated French opera composer (*La Juive*) produced this single chamber music work: a fughetta of sixty-five measures in length. According to the editor, James Brown, Halévy's piece was written in the vistor's book of Gustav Vogt (1781-1870), professor of oboe at the Paris Conservatoire from 1816–1853. Its publication by Chester (in a volume of oboe trios, released in 1979) is doubtless a first.

Halffter, Cristóbal (1930–)

See also under **Collaborative Composers**

A Garland for Dr. K.

QUARTETS

- **Quartet No. 2 for Two Violins, Viola, and Cello (1970)**

Music vividly organized through an avant-garde concept. Aside from the doctrinal dictates of sound production of the post–Webernian school (which is to say: unfixed sounds as high-pitched as possible, percussive pizzicatos, rhythmic improvisation, playing on the mute attached to the bridge, etc.), Halffter superimposes in three different places one instrument's line on another, each free unto itself, without relationship to any other. This depicts a collage of qualities that rejoices in its unshackled understanding. Such pluralistic string pyrotechniana is a reminder of expansive, grandiloquent improvisation, controlled in this case, however, by specifically defined data. These three passages also demarcate the content, separating, and thereby stressing, different aspects of the sound objects.

The determined violence of Halffter's work is clear. It speaks of rebellion, deposing form for a formlessness that creates its own structure. It relates to an unindicated program basic to the work, since catalog listings give a subtitle for the Quartet, as "Memories, 1970." (The score does not indicate this secondary listing, however.)

- **Third String Quartet (1978)**

At one time, Halffter sought to infuse his writing with a blend of specific serialism and Latin melorhythms. Some of his works successfully accomplished this objective (for example: the *Cinco microformas* for orchestra). But that was in 1960. Nearly two decades later, Halffter's music, as in this quartet, represents a juxtapositional method that blocks disparate items together. A certain degree of relationship does exist (here based on the scurrying passages that begin the quartet), but this is a far cry from the developmental procedure that is to be found in rhapsodically styled tonal music.

In this ceremony of avant-garde style, polyphony is constant. It boils. It is detonative, since each of the four voices has strident energy. The voicing is further individualized by sections where each player performs independently of the others and passing synchronization is sheer luck of the draw.

SEXTET

- *Oda para felicitar a un amigo (Ode to Congratulate a Friend)* **for Alto Flute, Bass Clarinet, Viola, Cello, Piano (alternating Celesta), and Percussion (Suspended Cymbal, Gong, Glass, Triangle, Vibraphone, Xylophone, and Padded Drumsticks) (1969)**

Halffter's short piece was written to commemorate the eightieth birthday of the well-known publisher Dr. Alfred A. Kalmus, who ran the London affairs of the famed Universal Edition.

The music starts with isolated patches that particularize pointillistic lyricism, then the six instruments merge into motility, and all ends with extreme quietness. The conclusion—wherein the alto flutist blows into the instrument without producing a defined pitch and the violist draws the bow across the mute on the instrument's bridge—emphasizes the esoteric coloration that is particular to the work as a whole. In the percussion this adventuresome use of instruments is maintained with a violin bow drawn across the cymbal's rim, across the vibraphone's plates, passed over the triangle's surface, and so on. The piano ceases to sound its normal self when a bow is used to produce the sonorities, and the strings are plucked.

Of course, such unaccustomed procedures are the habitual custom of the avant-garde. Here, they form both an ode to the avant-garde's instrumental aesthetic and to a supportive publisher.

SEPTET

- *Antiphonismói (Antiphonal Modes)* **for Flute (alternating Alto Flute), Oboe (alternating English horn), Clarinet, Violin, Viola, Cello, and Piano (1967)**

One composer and seven assistant instrumentalist-composers are at work here. There are some actual improvisatory passages. But where the details are spelled out they become improvisational equivalents. This, via the entire arsenal of proportional notation, free sounds, tremolandos and glissandos pictured but not pitched, and so forth. A music of this type may seem faceless, yet its aural appeal is not to be denied. What is removed is a general, underlying pulse content. Specified time extent is mixed in with free-time coverage. In a sense, Halffter's design objective is, paradoxically, nondesign. It is successful since the actions, regardless of how they are obtained or notated (or specifically performed!), produce the effect of a total improvisation.

It is worth noting that the beginning and ending balance. Both outer points contain the esoterica endemic among the avant-garde. Meaning: nontonal sounds in the winds by blowing through the tubes and nontonal sounds in the strings by bowing on the wood of the instruments. Not antimusic. Simply sonic opportunism.

Halffter, Rodolfo (1900–)

DUOS

- **Pastorale for Violin and Piano (1940)**

First, what Halffter's piece is not: a float-along item that imitates the music of shepherds, their shawms and their pipes, or has idyllic plotting.

This Pastorale has a trenchant, virile viewpoint. It exercises the rhythmic element by maintaining the same measure lengths but mixes up the pulse accentuations so that sometimes the result is triple (measures 1, 4, 6, 8, 9, and 10, for example) and other times the total is duple (measures 2, 3, 5, and 7, for example). Gentility also gives way to strength with the use of strong chordal progress in the piano plus considerable double and triple stops for the violin. Special color is offered in the form of double trills and double harmonics for the violin.

- **Sonata for Cello and Piano (1960)**

Neoclassically shaped but with astringent inculcations within the harmonic materials. And bitonal as well. Movement one is illustrative of the last, beginning and concluding in F and A combined (the former containing both major and minor forms). Mixed tonalities are the confirmed endings for the other two movements as well, a Siciliana and a Rondo.

The blend of instrumentation is on the exhibitionistic side. This bears out a favorite instruction Halffter uses: *con espressione intensa.*

QUARTET

- **Quartet for String Instruments (Two Violins, Viola, and Cello) (1958)**

Powerfully rhythmic in each of its four movements. Established designs are used with a Sonata and a precisely cut-to-fit Scherzo (movements one and three, respectively). The former has Halffter's favorite accentual shifts between duple and triple in the same time lengths.

A Cavatina is represented by a large, five-part rondo structure and rondo design is also used for the finale, titled Fanfare. Tonality is expansive as pertains to this Spanish neoclassicist's harmonic style.

Hall, Pauline (1890–1969)

QUINTET

- **Suite for Five Winds (Flute [alternating Piccolo], Oboe, Clarinet, Bassoon, and Horn) (1945)**

Neoclassic contours and French spirit. The character is that of Poulenc (but less pungent) and Françaix (but more pungent). There are six movements: Alla Marcia, Rondeau, Polka, Pastorale, Tempo di Valse, and Epilogue.

Some nice touches of humor. The coda to the first movement is three times halted by 1/4 measures of rest. The first seven measures of the Polka consist of a duet between piccolo and muted horn. A snippet of the waltz appears toward the end of the otherwise serious Epilogue.

Hall, Richard (1903–82)

DUOS

- *Five Epigrams* **for Cello and Piano**

Chromatic statements. To the point, of course, with timings that are, in order: 11/2, 2, 11/2, 3, and 2 minutes for the five parts. In the fourth and fifth instances the *Epigrams* are significantly undersigned by literal recapitulations. Although all the pieces have considerable pitch movement, the realizations are direct. And successful.

- **Suite for Violin and Viola**

Standard forms are paraphrased in this duo. As a prime example there is the second-movement Scherzo which is designed as a rondo. Further, this is no lightly figured affair set in triple pulse, but a 5/8 concoction compared to a slower-moving 3/4, with the latter containing an even slower section. Another example is the Ostinato (movement four). A few times there is a consistent pattern: a three-measure, duple-pulse idea repeated five times by the violin and a four-measure duple-pulse idea repeated three times by the viola. However, more attention is given nonostinato data, conveying pastoral-like material.

The Prelude has fantasy flamboyance, as does the third part, Intermezzo. Notwithstanding, the last-named stays strictly within ternary boundaries. Sharp metrical differences highlight the final Rondo. These give a nervous edge to the music. Nerves in this case are of tonic effect.

■ *Two Diversions* **for Flute and Bassoon**

The music deals with positive matters: a blend of classical procedure with total chromatic freedom. (Twelve-tone writing is just around the corner.) In each piece there is bold, energetic presentation. In good part the first of the pair inhabits the polyphonic world of imitative technique. In the second piece there is the sense of an updated gigue—hard to contain in pulse order and so there is considerable metrical change.

Halldórsson, Skúli (1914–)

TRIO

■ *Moon Silver*: **Trio for Flute, Cello, and Piano**

Modal language for this short (four-minute) piece. The direction is thoroughly harmonic and no polyphonic inserts are used. Only a tinge of variational process is applied, but the compactness makes what is done sufficient.

NONET

■ **Theme and Variations for Flute, Oboe, Clarinet, Bassoon, Two Violins, Cello, Double Bass, and Percussion (Triangle, Vibraphone, Snare Drum, and Cymbals)**

Noninvolved, simple music, with a seamlessness that provides a formal bonus. The theme, presented by the flute accompanied with some light triangle punctuations, is as elementary as can be. It covers eight measures and consists of three pitches: G–A–B-flat. There are ten connected variations. In number four the theme appears in the major mode. The final variation restates the theme, this time with full nonet declaration.

Haller, Hermann (1914–)

DUO

■ *Sechs Inventionen (Six Inventions)* **for Flute and Harpsichord**

Bach's polyphonic inventions were each developed from a motive or subject of one-half measure to four measures in length and emphasized imitative counterpoint. Haller's are of different coinage. There is nothing fixed, and counterpoint is replaced by motile harmonic functions. These are taut and acrid, with a large supply of secundal clash. There is a small amount of free imitation in the second piece. In the fourth of the set there are segmented solo portions. Otherwise, there is a sense of free-flowing but controlled improvisational content.

Haller

TRIO

- *In Memoriam*: **Five Pieces for Piano Trio**

Alternating tempos bring fast-paced music for the second and fourth pieces. These speeds do not betray the intensity of the suite, doubtless to be regarded as a depiction of protest within the memorial point of reference. Haller's threnodic passions carry over to lines that surge back and forth in tempo and, in the third piece, to trills that move about in their pitch combinations. Frictional harmony is a stylistic fundament.

QUARTETS

- **String Quartet [No. 1]**

The sound materials are those of emancipated tonalism, with strong final cadences that conclude the four movements in C, D-flat, B minor, and C. Rhythm is quite dynamic and a constant. The twirling patterns of the first movement (divided between Adagio and Allegro) are important for setting the tone of the second movement (a scherzo kind of music) at its beginning and ending; in between, hammered eighth-note patterns prevail. Following the short slow movement it is again conjunct rhythmic figuration that carries the material. Such emphasis brings balance to this well-ordered neoromantic string quartet.

- **String Quartet No. 2**

Other chamber music compositions by this composer exhibit contemporary tonal expansiveness and a liking for abrasive harmonic formations. Still, over all of these works the general identification is that of the neoromantic.

The same applies here, plus an important juicing up of the composition by stylistic deflection. The four movements are linked: Adagio—Allegro energico—Lento—Allegro molto e deciso. The quarter tones that color the harmony of the Lento provide a small stylistic shift. A bigger one takes place just prior to the slow and tranquil muted coda, a music of unmetered plan, cadenza thrusts, and zigzag speeds that concludes with an aleatoric tinge. The last concerns figurations to be repeated at will within specific time spans.

Hallgrímsson

Hallgrímsson, Haflidi Magnus (1941–)

DUOS

- *Five Icelandic Folk Songs* for Cello and Piano

Modal harmonic climate warms this set of pieces. The music is totally idiomatic in its natural characterization. No more need be stated. And as a fine cellist, Hallgrímsson writes for the instrument with communicative sensitivity.

The second piece is a "Hymn" in which the theme becomes rhythmically augmented for contrastive purposes. Considerable bare fifths color the "Evening Song" (number three). The fourth part is a peppy "Song about the Animals"; dynamism marks the concluding "Song about the Light." No translation is offered for the initial piece of the suite, titled "Bi Bi Og Blaka," presented in a variational format.

- *Verse I* for Flute and Cello (1975)

Unmetered music that defines late 20th-century impressionism. The phrases flow with built-in rubatos. The bravura is held within the sounds—an ingredient that is in itself a color within the music's colors. Included in the sonic pigmentation is a section where the flute sings one octave below the pitches played. The duo is motivated by prefatory lines that read: "Waves

Hallnäs

of sea and time wash away memories of love."

Hallnäs, Hilding (1903–)

DUO

- **Sonata for Viola and Piano, Op. 19**

Traditional methods are employed in this duo. The outer movements are in D minor, the central one in the dominant relationship. Hallnäs sails with the classical winds, including a good supply of sequential ballast. The instruments share equally in presenting the thematic substances.

Sonata form is used for the opening movement; an A-B-A setting balances the design of the second movement; and a rondo formation is used for the conclusion's gay ambience.

QUARTET

- **String Quartet, Op. 32**

There is a world of difference between this work and Hallnäs's earlier viola sonata (see above). If the latter is comfortably traditional, this opus is restlessly modern. The quartet has sharpness of line and detail; it does not bubble blithely but demands dogmatically.

A pithy quartal caption wends its way through the first movement. It is present in both the principal and secondary themes and binds their development. Contrapuntal and fugato methods are fully utilized to increase the developmental detail. The Variazioni are very free, tangental ruminations, eight in number, but so formed as to imply a single piece of music without divisions. In the final movement an introduction outlines the principal idea of the Allegro agitato—again one of successive fourths, thereby defining the intervallic symmetry of the opening and concluding movements.

Hambourg

Halvorsen, Johan (1864–1935)

DUO

- **Konsert Caprice over Norske Melodier (Concert Caprice on Norwegian Melodies) for Two Violins**

Among the string-instrument performing fraternity Halvorsen's name is held in high regard for his brilliant setting of a Handel Passacaglia for violin and viola or violin and cello (see below).

This duet deserves similar recognition. It shows off the instruments colorfully. In turn, there is an introduction, a G-major tune followed by a pair of variations, an E-major melody, and a final halling, a Norwegian folk dance with movements that range from the intentionally awkward to the truly violent.

Hambourg, Charles (1895–?)

QUARTETS

- **Introduction to Chamber Music**

  - No. 1—String Quartet in D
  - No. 2—String Quartet in F

Planned as a didactic musical tool, Hambourg's two quartets can certainly find occasional use in home performance.

Everything is uninvolved, conforming "to the style and form employed by . . . Haydn and Mozart." Thus, each quartet is in four movements in a fast-slow-Minuet-rondo sequence.

Hambraeus, Bengt (1928–)

QUARTETS

- *Invenzione I* (Quartet III) for Two Violins, Viola, and Cello (1964)

Athematicism applied to its oft-met harmonic partner—secundal arrangement with allied sevenths, ninths, and the like. *Invenzione I* has length and retains an inner balance by close chromatic movement, made clear in the opening measure where a cluster chord is stated by the first violin and viola and the second violin circles inside it. Solidly banked sound segments progress through the quartet and there is considerable polyrhythmic action.

Similar to a number of this composer's works, *Invenzione I* can also be combined with three short pieces by Hambraeus, one each for piano, harpsichord, and percussion. The "solo movements can be performed" singly or in "combinations made up to a septet" (the three instruments mentioned plus the quartet). However, the quartet is "the framework" in such aleatoric designation. Hambraeus emphasizes that the quartet "retains its unity . . . and the other compositions are adjusted to it."

- *Transit II* for Horn, Trombone, Electric Guitar, and Piano (1963)

An intensely vehement set of sound patterns. The tempo is "violent," with the additional instruction of "fast and impetuous." There is considerable retention of a single pitch in the brass, with unflagging rhythmic changes, equivalent to variations, being rung on the unchanging pitch; for example, in the first twenty-three measures the trombone has only an F, which is articulated in more than fifteen varied rhythmic settings. In another place the same F pitch is imbedded in seventeen measures with similar rhythmic permutations. And so on. And the same for the trumpet. Assorted chordal thrusts occupy the piano and guitar.

Transit II can also be combined with Hambraeus's *Transit I* for tape, or as a concertino group in Hambraeus's orchestral *Transfiguration*. Double dimensional music results since the materials are mutually exclusive.

Hamerik, Ebbe (1898–1951)

QUINTET

- Quintet for Flute, Oboe, Clarinet, Horn, and Bassoon (1942)

Too often, woodwind music is concerned with "busy" pattern work and cloying, bucolic sonorities. These clichés are avoided here.

The Quintet timbres are well exhibited and given individual contours in the first movement, which is divided into five episodes. In the second part ten variations are developed from a folklike theme assigned to the bassoon. In the sixth variant, Morten Topp (in a note made for a recording of the piece) states that "the theme is changed step by step and transformed into the Danish folk melody 'Roselil og hendes moder.' " In this part of the Quintet Hamerik at first displays varying textures by way of different duet and trio combinations as well as several quartet groupings. These give coloristic force and conviction, with the full resource of the five instruments reserved for use later in the movement.

Movement three (Adagio) obtains contrast between a long melodic line and ornamental phrases. Two themes are used in the final Presto and later they are combined in fugato. Polyphony and polytonality stir within the music.

Hamilton, Iain (1922–)

DUOS

- *Five Scenes* **for Trumpet and Piano (1966)**

The management and command of Hamilton's suite are drawn from the dodecaphonic system. Linear movement is clear and textural density is avoided. Although artificial academic rigidity is absent it is not replaced by vacillating style. And no vacillation as to the technical objectives. This work has razor-edge Paganinish virtuosity.

Alternately fast and slow, the movements are, in turn, "Wild," "Nocturnal," "Declamato," "Nocturnal," and "Brilliant." Key titles and positively descriptive ones. Color is achieved by the use of cup, harmon, and straight mutes. Sonic variety comes from the keyboard instrument as well, which provides bell tones, tone clusters, and sounds both pointillistic and percussive. And virtuosity as well in the asymmetrical definition that underlines the varying moods of the suite.

All of which shows technical marksmanship together with musical mastership—very exhilarating. There is no doubt that Hamilton's *Five Scenes* are an illustrious addition to the top drawer repertoire of the trumpet.

- *Serenata* **for Violin and Clarinet (1955)**

The disciplines of twelve-tone technique but minus any academicism, which is equivalent to creative incompetence. Everything is compact: a flowing Grazioso first movement, a slow movement comparing small rhythmic cells with long lines, and a bright Allegro. Rhythmic vigor combined with some syncopation in the last.

- **Sonata for Clarinet and Piano, Op. 22**

Hamilton wrote this duo sonata specifically for a series of recitals he gave in Europe in 1953 with the British clarinetist John Davies. They premiered the work in Paris in 1954.

Four movements: a flexibly moving Andante in first place; sweeping passages in Presto pace in second place; and a vivacious fourth movement that has balletic tingle. Movement three is a set of merged variations, based on a tartly lyrical theme. These variants first move in delicate arabesques, and then in an Alla marcia that segments the theme, counterpoints it, and supports the material with moving fifths and sixths. In turn, the next variant is virtuosically molded, and the movement concludes with a tranquil Coda, colored by pedal framing.

Tonality is basic to the music, but in Hamilton's consideration it is quite kaleidoscopic in its setting and in no sense classically styled.

- **Sonata for Flautist and Piano (Flute, Piccolo, Alto Flute, and Bass Flute) (1966)**

Why this title? Why not simply, "Sonata for Flute" or, simpler still, "Flute Sonata" ? Because these would be imprecise, incomplete titles. This is a sonata for a flutist (or, as Hamilton would have it, flautist), a virtuoso who has mastered all the members of the flute family. (But, Webster's unabridged dictionary notwithstanding, this writer bridles at the term *flautist*, derived from *flauto*, the Italian word for the instrument, when there is the standard, fully descriptive English word *flutist*. After all no one prefers *fagottist* to *bassoonist*.)

The Sonata has nine sections, with breaks between in order to permit a smooth change of instrument. There is full use of huge disjunct pitch order and flutter-tonguing in the flute, and plenty of clusters (with the hands, the palms, and the forearms) and frictional harmony for the piano.

Section one is for the flute alone; section two is for flute and piano. The piccolo and later the alto flute are used in the third section. Balancing the initial part of the work, there is a solo piano cadenza in the fourth section. The flute and piano combination is used in the fifth part. In the next the bass flute is displayed. In case this unusual instrument is not available the regular flute is to be used. For parts seven and nine the duo is for flute and piano, in part eight the music is for piccolo and piano.

■ **Sonata for Viola and Piano, Op. 9**

The composer has indicated to this writer that not only is this "a large-scale work" but that it has "a solo part more like that of a concerto than a sonata." The beginning is proof of the last statement. More than a dozen measures of the opening Lento potente are hammer-driven triple and quadruple chords for the string instrument. The Allegro feroce, with which this preface is linked, is likewise intense and lives up to the fierceness indicated in the tempo heading.

Some of the intensity carries over into the slow movement, with a parallel expression via pitch denoted by the use of quarter tones.

The finale is again music of power and excitement until the concluding thirty measures. There an Alla marcia funebre changes the character considerably. Within this portion Hamilton quotes the Nürnberg motive from Wagner's *Die Meistersinger.*

■ **Sonata [No. 1] for Cello and Piano (1959)**

A "remarkable design," is one writer's description of the unique form that supports Hamilton's first duo sonata for cello and piano. Of the seven connected sections, four are descriptively defined cadenzas and three contain music of a more structured character. The units are balanced to perfection. "Cadenza 1 (Bizarro)" is scored for both instruments, "Cadenza 2 (Fantastico)" is for the cello, "Cadenza 3 (Passionato)" is for the piano, and "Cadenza 4 (Tempestoso)" is once again for the duo. Between these four cadenzas are the three movements: Allegro, Con moto, and Lento. (Some writers claim the final movement is marked Placido, but that word does not appear in the published score.)

This orderly arrangement of alternating structural types replaces symmetricalness based on thematic documentation and its development. Hamilton's Sonata is a serial work and thus minus tonality. As he notes, the music does not deal "with interrelated thematic or motivic material but rather with intervallic relationships."

■ **Sonata No. 2 for Cello and Piano (1974)**

Energy is the paramount point of the outer movements. This factor is differentiated so that the first movement is less nervous (its tempo heading is Fluente) than the third. In the opening there are cascades of ninefold pitches; these later change to totals of eight and they command the rhythmic demeanor. In the final movement sextuplets are a constant pulsatile projection and there is added to the Presto tempo colorations of ponticello timbre that excite the textural issue. There is an arioso quality with a rhapsodic undercurrent to the central, slow movement.

■ *Sonata notturna* **for Horn and Piano (1965)**

Hamilton's duo carries out the essence of the prefatory quote from Baudelaire: " . . . Le ciel / Se ferme lentement comme une grande alcôve / Et l'homme impatient se change en bête fauve." (" . . . The sky / It closes slowly like an alcove / The impatient man changes into a wild beast.")

There are eight sections played without a break. In turn these are a Lento, an Allegro, once again a Lento, then a Brutale, punched with packed seconds and some clusters. A muted horn Largo follows and a Lento in which the horn is unmuted. A Scherzando and once more a Lento complete the piece. Material is recurrent with transformations taking place.

There is careful discrimination of the use of varying textures and moods to define a composition within which tensions are constant. The sounds smolder with deep-bass filaments and horn exudations. There are also rhapsodic thrusts and cadenzalike tremors. The conflict of dark melancholy with passionate rhetoric produces a bold, exciting music.

- **Three Nocturnes for Clarinet and Piano, Op. 6**

As the winner of the Edwin Evans Memorial Prize, in 1951, Hamilton's three-part work became his first published composition in the same year.

Although the general concept of a nocturne is that of music in a somewhat melancholy or languid style, the opposite takes place in the second piece of the set. It has nightmarish mystery in its fast-pulsed Allegro diabolico tempo. The other two pieces are more in keeping with the general concept of the form, though there is a bit of rhapsodic urgency in the middle of the first nocturne.

TRIO

- **Trio for Violin, Cello, and Piano, Op. 25**

The three movements (fifteen minutes in performance time) are full of the neat dissonances that signal the accents of neoclassic speech. The part writing, especially in the first movement (Allegro giojoso) is somewhat weighty, but the contemporary tonalism makes certain that clarity obtains. (Hamilton considers this work "the most tonal" of all his compositions.)

The textural condition of the other two movements is lighter. In the Intermezzo the principal theme, stressing an iambic rhythmic figure, is contrasted to a flowing subject. The piano writing is extremely economical and its registral spacing provides a special color. As colorful in a different manner is the finale, a Presto of rhythmic vitality and high spirits, the most contrapuntal of the three movements. Lean music, this, with no thick, fatty substances.

QUARTETS

- **Quartet for Flute and String Trio (1951)**

The outer movements have a sparkling quality that contrasts with the darker writing for the flute in the central, slow movement. As in many of Hamilton's compositions, cellular development is the prime point. The Quartet is tonal, not in the classical sense but in the sense of pitch polarity balances.

- **String Quartet No. 1, Op. 5**

Hamilton's quartet, written as his degree thesis at the University of London, which he attended concurrently while studying at the Royal Academy of Music, won the Alfred Clements Prize in 1950, at that time the most important chamber music prize in Britain. It deserved this award. The quartet is superbly detailed. Hamilton's instinct for musical ebb and flow is beautifully expressed. Admirable poise and shape of phrases together with coloristic flexibility are all found here. Atmosphere, brilliance, and great technical élan are other particulars that bring enthusiastic response.

A complete chamber music virtuosity is present—a virtuosity of instrumental interplay and formal detail, not the shock effect of pyrotechnical pitch production. Development of motivic material is the paramount technical device in all four movements. Within these, considerable use of canonic and fugal writing is made.

Movement two is a vividly toned affair. In very quick tempo, with a middle section in sharply contrasting Andante molto pace, it is completely set in muted timbre. Dulling the sonority in this fast music provides an acutely increased level of excitement.

- **String Quartet No. 2 (1972)**

A three-movement opus, written in 1965 and revised, with a new middle movement, in 1972.

The contrastive tensions of rhythmic dismemberment, stressing plucked sounds, and vertical impingement, fill the thirty-seven-measure opening movement.

Movement two is a music of whirlwind tempo (Presto possibile) and whirlwind fantasy. A ritornel controls the musical shape. This refrain consists of a three-measure rhythmic counterpoint on a single pitch (D), with all instrumental moves coming off the quadruple beats. It begins the movement, concludes it, and is heard three times in between. In the middle of the second of these statements (therefore the middle of the total inner ritornels as well) Hamilton makes a strategically sensitive color change that produces formal finesse. The four instruments switch (also contrapuntally!) from muted to unmuted sound. This action splits the movement in neat halves.

In movement three this composer's favorite cadenza device is used. Consisting of restless, nervous, fantasy-impelled materials, it defines and thereby balances the structure. Each of the instruments is assigned a cadenza: the first is for the cello, the second for the paired second violin and viola, and the last for the first violin. The solo—duo—solo arrangement of the cadenzas provides an inner, textural, balance.

QUINTETS

- **Quintet for Brass (Two Trumpets, Horn, Tenor Trombone, and Tuba) (1964)**

One of Iain Hamilton's creative habits is the use of cadenza material. It is a pivotal rod in this work, unifying and balancing the entire structure. At the conclusion of the first movement a cadenza for the first trumpet leads into the second movement (Presto), in which the entire quintet is muted. That movement concluded, a horn cadenza provides the link to the third movement (Lento). In turn, at the division's end, a cadenza for the trombone moves into a second Lento movement. At the end of this slow movement, the tuba's solo turn becomes the bridge to the fifth movement (Presto). Finally, a short cadenza for the second trumpet ushers in the concluding (sixth) part of the work.

There is also additional balance within the total formal balance since the cadenzas form their own equipoise. It will be noted that the trumpets perform the first and last cadenzas and that the inner ones are assigned the other instruments in order of exact descending gamut: horn, trombone, and tuba.

- **Quintet for Clarinet and String Quartet (1947)**

Two "firsts" are represented by this clarinet quintet. It was Hamilton's initial chamber music piece and the first of his compositions to be performed in public.

Free chromaticism rules. Throughout, cellular data are expanded and "continually contrasted with additional material as the movements progress." The outer movements are fantasias, the central one (in fast pace) is described by the composer as bearing "certain resemblances to Bartók's use of sonata form."

- *Sonata for Five* (Flute, Oboe, Clarinet, Horn, and Bassoon) (1966)

The quintet begins in a serial-pitched cloud of tutti voicing, with sextuple rhythmic units combined with quintuple, and a few quadruple. Out of this mass the clarinet emerges. From that point on the clarinet in combination with another instrument alternates with the tutti. The last permutates the tone row.

There are four other movements. These feature in turn the oboe, horn, bassoon, and flute, but now minus the tutti. It is motival promulgation that binds this virtuoso composition for the wind quintet.

SEXTET

- Sextet for Flute, Two Clarinets, Violin, Cello, and Piano (1962)

Criss-crossed relationships provide an architectural stability to this work scored for three winds and piano trio. There are five movements: The first is a Prelude, the third an Interlude, and the fifth a Postlude. Developed from the same working (fully chromatic) material, each of these parts is in slow tempo: Andante, Adagio, and Lento, in turn. The central part of this triality is embraced by two Prestissimo sections, also concerned with the same basic material. This structural plan thereby alternates slow and fast sections with absolute balance obtained within each tempo group.

Compellingly contrapuntal style informs the work. For coloristic contrast there are short cadenzas in the two fast movements. In movement two these are for the flute, violin, paired clarinets, and piano. In movement four the paired clarinets appear again as does the cello. Further balance therefore: maintaining the cadenza bits only in movements in the same tempo and realizing an inner, subtle, balance by using the two clarinets in both movements and all the other instruments but once. The

logic is clear and artistically effective.

Hand, Frederic (1947–)

DUO

- *Four Excursions* for Guitar and Flute

It's not as easy to write for the guitar as it may seem. But Hand, a concert guitarist as well as a composer, has succeeded admirably in this set of four engaging pieces, alternating slow and lyrical definitions with faster and more rhythmic conceptions. Formal fitness in each case with balanced structuring.

Handel, George Frideric (1685–1759)

DUOS

- Sonatas for Flute and Continuo, Op. 1

- Sonatas (Hallenser Sonatas)

  - No. 1a, in E Minor
  - No. 1b, in E Minor
  - No. 2, in G Minor
  - No. 4, in A Minor
  - No. 5, in G Major
  - No. 7, in C Major
  - No. 9, in B Minor
  - No. 11, in F Major
  - Hallenser No. 1, in A Minor
  - Hallenser No. 2, in E Minor
  - Hallenser No. 3, in B Minor

Handel's Op. 1 consisted of *Fifteen Solos for a German Flute, a Hoboy, or Violin, with a Thorough Bass for the Harpsichord or Bass Violin*. Actually, there are sixteen sonatas in the set since there are two versions of the first work. However, the movements in the 1a Sonata are used in the various later sonatas in the opus so that performers tend to bypass it in favor of the 1b duo. Six of the sonatas are for violin *(see below)* and two are for oboe *(see below)*.

The seven other sonatas in the opus are further divided into those for flute *(Drei Sonaten für Querflöte und bezifferten Bass)*: Numbers 1a (1b), 5, and 9, and those for recorder *(Vier Sonaten für Blockflöte und bezifferten Bass)*: Numbers 2, 4, 7, and 11. (The other three works listed above are separate early sonatas for *Querflöte und bezifferten Bass*). Since the two instruments are so allied, and interchange of compositions is made between them, the listing above has used the flute rubric for indicating the medium.

The number of movements in the Op. 1 group shifts between four and five save for Op. 1, No. 9, which has seven. All three Hallenser Sonatas are in four movements: slow-fast-slow-fast (the finale of the second "Halle Sonata" is a Minuet).

- **Sonata in G Minor for Oboe and Continuo, Op. 1, No. 6**

- **Sonata in C Minor for Oboe and Continuo, Op. 1, No. 8**

The two oboe sonatas in the group of fifteen that Handel wrote, the others consisting of six for violin, three for flute, and four for recorder. Both are cast in *sonata da chiesa* form with two pairs of alternating slow- and fast-tempo movements.

- **Sonatas for Violin and Continuo, Op. 1**

  - No. 3, in A Major
  - No. 10, in G Minor
  - No. 12, in F Major
  - No. 13, in D Major
  - No. 14, in A Major
  - No. 15, in E-flat Major

All six sonatas consist of four movements, alternately slow and fast. There is always breadth of line in the former; in the second slow movement the arioso quality is paramount. (In the Op. 1, No. 3, the third movement Adagio is a mere five measures, serving as a link between the fast movements.) The finales have a pronounced rhythmic character.

Nowadays, the usual performance of these works finds the violin with a piano, less often with a harpsichord, and still less often with further continuo support. Whatever way, the sonatas represent superb Handel.

TRIOS

- **Trio Sonatas for Two Oboes and Basso Continuo**

  - No. 1, in B-flat Major
  - No. 2, in D Minor
  - No. 3, in E-flat Major
  - No. 4, in F Major
  - No. 5, in G Major
  - No. 6, in D Major

All six works are set in the four-movement form of the church sonata *(sonata da chiesa)* established in the late 17th century by Corelli. The opening movements are slow paced and preludial in tone; the second movements are fast paced and in fugal style; the third movements are again in slow tempo, more arioso in concept than the initial slow movements; and the finales are fast in tempo and dancelike in character.

- **Trio Sonatas for Two Violins (or Two Flutes or Two Oboes) and Basso Continuo, Op. 2**

  - No. 1, in B Minor
  - No. 2, in G Minor
  - No. 3, in B-flat Major
  - No. 4, in F Major
  - No. 5, in G Minor
  - No. 6, in G Minor
  - No. 7, in F Major
  - No. 8, in G Minor
  - No. 9, in E Major

It is important to realize that the order (and therefore the numbering) of these sonatas varies among the editions that are available; for example, the Schott edition lists the two F-major works as numbers three and five, whereas in the above grouping, which follows the Eulenberg edition (1978), edited by Basil Lam, these sonatas are numbered four and seven.

In Handel's day it was common practice to use a pair of similar instruments in trio sonatas. Thus, the three possible pairings noted above. However, in some instances a contrast of timbre was indicated (though not necessarily to be followed). In numbers one and four the original indication is for flute and violin with the bass.

The first six sonatas were first published not earlier than mid-1721 and not later than the first half of 1722. Later three more sonatas were found in Dresden in manuscript by the famous Handel scholar Karl Franz Friedrich Chrysander (1826–1901) and became known as the Dresden Trio Sonatas. Chrysander changed the numbering of the sonatas at the same time. Further, for the first sonata of the group (in B minor) he substituted another version he had found, set in C minor, and differing only in the order of the tempos for the slow movements (Andante and Largo in the B-minor opus are reversed in the C-minor work). (The Eulenberg edition prints both versions.)

Eight of the nine sonatas are in the four-movement format of the *sonata da chiesa*, with a sequence of slow-fast-slow-fast tempos. (The second of the fast movements tends to be lighter in content than the first of the pair.) Number four adds an additional Allegro to make a five-movement total. The *da chiesa* style means there are no dance movements and plenty of contrapuntalism. There is not a single movement in the collection that is of minor quality. In the slow movements depth, lyricism, and poematicism are detailed. In the fast movements one finds wit, energy, and linear strength. To this one can add Romain Rolland's words that these sonatas are "some of Handel's purest creations . . . their sophisticated feeling and urbane simplicity are a rare refreshment for the mind and the heart."

- **Trio Sonatas for Two Violins and Basso Continuo, Op. 5**

  - No. 1, in A Major
  - No. 2, in D Major
  - No. 3, in E Minor
  - No. 4, in G Major
  - No. 5, in G Minor
  - No. 6, in F Major
  - No. 7, in B-flat Major

Variety is a constant in this set of seven sonatas; there is no set pattern in the arrangement of the various formal types. As the editor of the edition, Siegfried Flesch, mentions: "One finds the pairing of a slow movement with a quick one, such as is typical of the Italian church sonata, but this also occurs in the style of the French overture." Indeed, it is a mixed bag and, as such, always colorful. There is fugue represented and there is the chaconne as well, but, no less effective (and charming) there are also the dance forms: allemande, saraband, gigue, gavotte, minuet, and so on.

In habitual baroque practice, Handel borrowed materials from his own music. Parts of numbers one and seven are from the Chandos

Anthems; the Gavotte in the A-major opus was originally in the opera *Ariodante*; and the Minuet in the B-flat major sonata is from *Terpsichore*.

Handel, George Frideric (1685–1759)—Halvorsen, Johan (1864–1935)

DUO

■ **Passacaglia for Violin and Viola (or Cello)**

A chamber music transcription standby. And deserving, since it's a real beauty. The scoring is magnificently planned and the effect is fully sonorous.

The duo is based on the sixth (final) movement of Handel's Suite No. 7 in G Minor for Harpsichord. Halvorsen expanded the size of Handel's original by rescoring some of the variations. The sound is fully baroque, and duo string performers have always been grateful for this contribution to the literature. Handel would have approved, one is certain.

Hannivoort, Hendrik Willem (1871–?)

QUARTET

■ **Quartet for Two Violins, Viola, and Cello**

It is quickly apparent that the data in Hannivoort's four-movement string quartet have all been heard before. Still, a sense of freshness covers the music because of its Haydnesque quality.

The first two movements begin their themes with the descent of a fifth. Both end quietly. In exact balance, the last two movements end

vigorously, but the intervallic fifth rears its head again (this time ascending) to earmark the principal theme of the Finale.

The tonalism falls nicely on the ear. Further, there is no trace of academic longueur in this creative document.

Hanson, Howard (1896–1981)

QUARTET

■ **Quartet in One Movement (Two Violins, Viola, and Cello), Op. 23**

Hanson's output covered all forms, but he was especially prolific in the fields of symphonic and choral composition. Opus 23 is his single entry in the string quartet medium and represents the most important of his very concentrated total of chamber music productions. Compactness is also evident in the quartet's form, with six changes of tempo based on three combinations of slow and fast speeds providing a unique balance.

Dual thematic evolution is the fundament of the composition. The two ideas are clearly presented in terms of contrastive mood and tempo. Alternative representation follows, each time varied in thematic presentation, background, and coloring. A light liturgical character surrounds the work.

The quartet was commissioned by the Elizabeth Sprague Coolidge Foundation for performance at the 1923 Coolidge Festival, at the Library of Congress in Washington, and was composed during the time Hanson held the first American Prix de Rome.

Hanuš

Hanuš, Jan (1915–)

DUOS

- *Sonata quasi una fantasia* for Oboe and Piano, Op. 61

The score is prefaced with a familiar quotation from Saint Paul's Epistle to the Corinthians: "When I was a child, my speech, my outlook, and my thoughts were all childish. When I grew up, I had finished with childish things. Now we see only puzzling reflections in a mirror, but then we shall see face to face."

In the outer sections of the first movement, Moderato con fantasia, there is strict rhythmic delineation but the music is without barlines. A portion of this unmetered material is repeated within the energetic second movement. Further, there is a resemblance between the central part of the first movement and the pitch shapes of the second movement. The latter movement especially bears a relationship to the score's motto.

- *Suite after Pictures by Mánes* for Violin and Piano, Op. 22

Five pictures by Josef Mánes (1820–71), the Czech painter and illustrator, furnish the program for Hanuš's duo. The music has an engaging tonal clarity. There is no lushness at any time and no disturbing musical opacity. Music of such description holds warm promise for a listener.

A rondo sequence is used in "Morning Song." Part two, "Love Song," doesn't meander in its rich lines. "Dance" follows, and its brio has Dvořákian temperature. Part four, "Lullaby," is muted in the outer sections, and the Suite is completed with an "Epilogue," most of which is a snappy, polka-style affair.

TRIO

- *Frescoes*: Trio for Violin, Cello, and Piano, Op. 51

The title provides no clues to the constitution of Hanuš's four musical pictures, which are in alternating slow and fast tempos. However, there is this to say: The two fast movements have a chamber music percussiveness that is just a bit more texturally impressed than mere motility of the sound material. The first of the fast movements, Fantastico e feroce, persistently projects variously accented rhythmic figures; the second, Molto e tempestuoso, has some of the grotesque formations found throughout Hanuš's music. Toward the end, this finale moves into slow tempo, drops significantly in dynamic power, and ends quietly on a two-pitch (C and E) combination spread more than six octaves apart.

QUARTETS

Fantasie for String Quartet, Op. 6

Hanuš's Fantasie is a tabloid presentation of the services of four-movement compound form, liberated in the outer sectors. While there is no slow movement, the contrasts of the two Intermezzos afford the variety of tempo necessary to the proper pace of any work taking almost twenty minutes in performance time. The two middle movements, titled Scherzo and Feroce (respectively subtitled Intermezzo 1 and 2), are in simple ternary form, the mood of the first lighter than the substantial pronouncements of the second. Ternary patterns are used for the first and fourth movements as well (titled Introduction and Finale), but, in both instances, thematic contours are shadowed in advance; then spatial liberation permits the thematic ideas to emerge, discharging them into free development. In both cases, the recapitulations are not subjected to symmetry of means, but rather musically translated so that blocked-in form is avoided. A trend of Czech music is thereby exhibited that has its roots in Smetana and Dvořák (rhythm of the dance) but does not sink into the canopied bed of romanticism.

- *Meditations 1959 on the Motives of Aeschylus' Prometheus:* **Dramatic Suite for String Quartet, Op. 46**

The 1959 in the title is the year Hanuš composed his five-movement piece. The music does not delineate the plot of the tragedy but represents the composer's reactions to the details of the tale. (The story of Prometheus intrigued Hanuš. In 1953, after nearly three years of work, he completed his opera *The Torch of Prometheus*, premiered in Prague in 1965.)

Despite the scenario (a peripheral kind of programmaticism), the forms of the movements are solidly balanced rondo or ternary arrangements, further balanced by use of alternating tempos. Movement one, "The Rebel," is a symphonic view for the four instruments, full of drive and rhythmic drumming, with special attention to col legno coloration. "The Chained" (movement two) is a lament. "Vultures" (movement three), set in a ferocious tempo, contrasts strongly with the fourth movement, "Io," of which the composer-critic Karel Šrom says: "It sings of a deep compassion on the part of Io, the favorite of Dios, hunted by the jealous Hera throughout the world, until her meeting with Prometheus, who is chained to the rock." The finale, "The Torch," recapitulates material from some of the previous movements.

QUINTETS

- *Domestic Suite* **for Wind Quintet, Op. 57**

For "domestic" read "Czech romantic." Hanuš's opus represents music we have heard before, but its sheer romantic prose does not date the music and thereby destroy it. Ideas and sonorities are skillfully handled, designs are clear, and the light flavors applied to the tried and true formal recipes add zest to the results.

In the Prelude there are both combination of and contrast between duple and triple pulses in the same temporal space. Movement three is a vivacious Scherzino set in octuple metrical measurement. However, not once is there equal divisional portions of the total beats. Varying ternary metrical references are utilized—3–3–2; 3–2–3; 2–3–3—providing a polite aggressiveness to the sounds.

There are wide-spanned principal lines in the "Meditation," most being earmarked by a cogent descent of a seventh. While the Finale has the ease, flow, and rhythmic keenness one expects of a concluding movement, the preceding movement, Nocturne, is not of average content. Although it proceeds in slow tempo, Adagio (non troppo lento), it contains much more activity than usual and a fair amount of tension as well.

- *Turmusik (Omaggio a Bohuslav Martinů (Tower Music [Hommage to Bohuslav Martinů])* **Quintet for Two Trumpets, Horn, Tenor and Bass Trombones, Op. 88**

Hanuš's title reflects the fact that Martinů was born in a church tower. (Martinů's father tended the bells of a church in Polička, Czechoslovakia, and the family lived in the tower for a number of years.) The movements' subtitles also depict this location.

The formal contents are Fantasia, Scherzino, Notturno, and Rondo. The first movement, subtitled "Horizons," opens and closes with sustained, slightly figurated materials that surround energetic contrapuntal formations, principally imitative. "The World Below" is the subtitle for movement two; the view is simulated by uneven pulse patterns of 2 + 3 and 3 + 2. Movement three, Notturno, is considerably calmer, but this is a polyphonicized placidity, representing the serenity of "The World Above." The Rondo, termed "The Returns," is spirited for the greater part and in some portions draws on material from the previous movements.

Haquinius, Algot (1886–1966)

QUARTET

■ **String Quartet**

A close-knit work, favoring the minor mode. The opening movement and closing set of variations are principally in A minor. In the variations only numbers four and five deviate from A minor, and even there the latter of the pair is in F-sharp minor. Only the fourth variation employs the major modality (A). The slow movement is in C-sharp minor, and the Trio of the otherwise D-major Allegretto is in B minor.

The textures of the Swedish composer's quartet are forceful—for the greater part not heavy but very active. Short measured tremolo figures are a characteristic device.

Hara, Hiroshi

DUO

■ **Sonatine for Flute and Piano**

Hara displays a fine neoclassic hand in this duo and provides a couple of clever surprises in his designs. Movement two, Berceuse, is cradled in neat duple-pulse measures, andante in tempo. In the middle, the music shifts into a "Danse rustique," set forth in gavotte tempo. A four-measure bit of this dance is also used as a *pianissimo* coda. In the finale, Rondo, the sweeping scalewise lines suddenly move into a four-voice fugue, and at its completion shift

just as cleanly back to the vivacious conjunct material. Open and clear sonata balances are present in the first movement.

Harbison, John (1938–)

QUINTET

■ *Incidental Music for Shakespeare's The Merchant of Venice* **for String Quintet (Two Violins, Viola, Cello, and Bass) (1971)**

As a concert piece the twelve sections are played without pause; for stage presentation the music "serves as preludes, fanfares, songs, and backgrounds."

Prelude: Act I, with its sharply opposed pitches, "suggests the darker aspects of the play." Syncopative unrest marks "Venice, a Street." "The Golden Casket," part three, is colored with harmonics and pizzicato tinged moving rhythm. It is preceded by a short, fanfarelike set of four measures (headed "The Caskets, Fanfare, Morocco"). In turn, these measures (titled "Fanfare, Arragon") are repeated after the first (Golden) casket scene and lead to "The Silver Casket," also timbre sensitized with harmonics but minus the pizzicato.

"Portia's Song" follows. It is sung only in stage performance. In concert performance the vocal line is doubled in the violins in combined bowed and plucked qualities. Section eight is "The Leaden Casket"; section nine, Prelude: Act IV is a repetition of the opening. Stately chordal music describes "Venice, a Court of Justice." The work concludes with Prelude: Act V and Epilogue ("... and draw her home with music ..."), the latter polyphonically voiced in the violins, continuously sounded in the viola, and supported by a sustained, ostinatolike line in the cello and bass.

Harbison's work is also performable with "a large string orchestra."

Harding, Kenneth (1903–)

DUO

- **Scherzo *(Enigma)* for Violin and Viola**

What this work's "enigma" is one does not know, for this short (four-minute) duet is of light character, composed with very definite form, in modal folk-tune style. The puzzle's solution will not alter these facts—that the composer uses the tonality of E (in neither major nor minor mode), introduces a theme that has contrasted episodes between its appearances, and which then leads to a more lilting, duple-measure section, with a return to the exposition. The theme is then augmented and tonic chords complete the work. Five fermatas occur during the piece. These may have nothing to do with the enigma, but they do stop the nice flow of this homespun, gentle string duet.

QUINTET

- **Phantasy on a Welsh Air—"Hobed o Hilion": Quintet for Two Violins, Viola, Cello, and Piano**

Fantasy equals phantasy equals the term adopted for competitions and commissions limited to English composers, made possible by the sole benefaction of the famed English chamber music philanthropist Walter Wilson Cobbett (1847–1937). A large number of successful works resulted, including compositions by Vaughan Williams, Bridge, Ireland, and Howells.

The form is free, but always in a single movement. At times it is a tabloid of the three or four movements of a sonata; other examples are free of sonata structural affiliation. The objective of moderate length with changes of mood—unity in diversity—has been the most satisfactory outcome.

Harding's *Phantasy* is much more concentrated, in its fewer than 150 total measures, than other compositions with that title. Nevertheless, in terms of its being organic and having variety, it fulfills all requirements of the form. Moderate in tempo, conservatively mannered, and favoring block constructions, its variational conduct will create no furrowed brows.

Hardisty, Donald M. (1932–)

QUINTET

- **Pisces of the Zodiac for Woodwind Quintet**

According to the composer, this work "was inspired by the phenomenon of small flying fish seen late one February evening. The imaginary marine images were viewed to be distinct characters in an outer-space aquatic drama." It is important, in this reference, to realize that Pisces is the astrological sign of the composer.

No one should underestimate such mystical or zodiacal influences. Neither can anyone deny the sovereign power of inspiration, be it derived from Messiaen's birds, Rudhyar's astrological controls, Strauss's homelife, or, as in this case, colorful imagery.

Hardisty's *Pisces* is in five sections (A–B–C–A–B), each marked by mostly specific metrical definition: 9/8 (triple pulse), 6/8 (duple pulse), and a variety of measured totals with the quarter note as the denominational basis. In terms of qualities these sections are basically articulative, flowing, and sharply rhythmic.

Harper, Edward (1941–)

QUINTET

- **Quintet for Flute, Clarinet, Violin, Cello, and Piano (1974)**

Harper's Quintet for piano trio and two wind instruments is highly organized; meaning, it has logical continuity. It opens using serial techniques and moves into a free handling of the chromatic range combined with loosely plotted, unsynchronized instrumentation.

The entrance of the piano is marked *molto libero*, indicating that its relationship with the other instrument playing (the flute) is "only approximate," thus anticipating the partial dropping of metrical binding and definition a little more than a dozen measures later. There, the flute and clarinet are totally independent of the other instruments. The free focus of material develops still further with the complete abandonment of meter and with all action determined by time-measured lengths (in seconds) until the conclusion of the piece. The ending counterbalances the beginning of the Quintet, where specific time signatures prevail. The continuity embracing the pulse changes is subtle and supple, never over obvious.

Harris, Arthur (1927–)

QUINTET

- *Four Moods* for Brass Quintet (Two Trumpets, Horn, Trombone, and Tuba) (1957)

This work consists of a chorale setting of "Komm süsser Tod," a Waltz, followed by a "Lyric Piece," and a spirited Finale. The music is nicely brushed with refined dissonance.

Harris, Donald (1931–)

DUO

- **Fantasy for Violin and Piano (1957)**

Harris's first opus utilizing the twelve-tone system. He describes his work as "lyric and romantic," a combination of an expressionistic sensibility with the dodecaphonic technique. Despite the many changes of tempo and mood the duo narrative (almost 7 1/2 minutes in length) is direct.

QUARTET

- **String Quartet (1965)**

Serialism, with the materials set within a single movement ten minutes in length. There are sharp differences within the textures, which display the nervous rhythms characteristic of much twelve-tone music. The colors include slowly and quickly arpeggiated sounds in both directions, glissandos, and struck and drawn col legno.

Harris has stated that "each instrument is employed both as a solo related only to itself and as part of a heterogeneous whole." The soloism in this case is in terms of a small phrase, a coloristic thrust, a wide registral contrast, and so on.

QUINTET

- *Ludus II* for Flute, Clarinet, Violin, Cello, and Piano (1973)

As Harris notes, the title, derived from the Latin, "refers to play or games." And the game here is prime instrumental virtuosity of the brightly brash contemporary type: multiple sonorities for the wind instruments, key slaps and key clicks, and the familiar sul ponticello and col legno effects. All this is projected in an uncompromising prose using serial syntax, polyrhythms, and hardcore asymmetry.

Harris indicates that "the death of someone close to me suggested the inclusion of a chorale, which begins with strict four-part writing." This is for flute and clarinet and is heard in the bitter dissonances of wind-instrument multiphonic resource.

Harris, Roy (1898–1979)

Certain creative figures seem to inspire the formation of cults, which propagandize for their heroes. Praise of Harris did not elevate him beyond his actual value. In fact, by now the music of Harris is of proven importance, greater than the limited ramifications that result from cultivation by a small group. The tremendous talk about this man (for which there were excellent and demanding creative reasons) proved that he, who was once the most-publicized composer ever to work in America, was worthy of such adulation. The literature concerning him was huge, at one time of proportions equaling the outpouring of a commercial press bureau. Now Harris is little written about, but his maturity has brought with it acceptance without purple prose to prove the point. Harris is to be reckoned with, whether he meets with full approval or not. (Like all people of importance, he has both those that are for him and against him.)

His style is immersed in old forms. His harmony calls on the modes (seven distinct scale formations, two of which are the common major scale and the so-called natural minor scale), which he uses separately, modulates by superimposition and the like, or forms into polyharmonies. The modes are assigned coloristic and mood values intended to help orient the inner meaning and shape the rise, fall, climaxes, and other differentials of each work. Harris based his speeds on whether or not they were faster than the normal human heartbeat;

creating thereby excitement or repose for the listener. Chromaticism is superficially incidental. Harris is clearly a diatonicist, aided by modified counterpoint, for his lines are more moving harmonies than steadfast individualities that move against each other. The lines of a Harris work are long-hewn, similar to his forms, which grow and spread from musical cells, not from contrasted and developed themes. He considered the material in one of his compositions to equate a theme fifty-five measures in length; the passacaglia subject in his Quintet for Piano and Strings is twenty-eight measures long, a far cry from the eight-measure dimensions of baroque vintage!

Harris's music is lean and angular. It avoids folk tunes, jazz, or any part of popular American trends. Folk ingredients are present, but not in their raw state; they have been fully polished as Harris uses them. His melting pot is a spiritual mixture that defines Americanism objectively, in terms of breadth and scope, not by the subjective use of material from any group or locale of the country—from its blacks, its Indians, its metropolitan Lower East Side or Upper West Side. As mentioned earlier, Harris's melodicism is most individual; it does not tread the path of "tunes" but of the architectonic line that has more inner depth than "melody." The fact that Harris's themes are not easily whistled does not make them any the less perfect. And while the functional, architectural means of composition are precisely tabulated, they never interfere with the total freer beauty of the music.

DUOS

- ***Four Charming Little Pieces* for Violin and Piano (1942)**

Harris's little suite was derived from a ballet *Namesake* composed in 1942. Oddly enough, the score calls for only violin and piano. (No record can be found of any performance of the ballet.) In 1943, parts two and three of the suite were published, parts one and four were published the following year.

Melodic temper is paramount and the sonorous combinations are discreetly pungent. Each piece has Harris's usual open-breathed, strongly lyrical statements.

A six-pitch persistent quarter-note phrase in the piano's bass frames the "Mood" that opens the suite. Slow swing surrounds the "Afternoon Slumber Song." There is heavy textural body to the piano in the "Summer Fields" conception, but this is contrasted colorfully by muting the violin. "There's a Charm about You" is a Harrisian folk song that moves in fast waltz time.

■ **Sonata for Violin and Piano (1942)**

Spontaneity is difficult to achieve in set forms, yet, with an outpouring of noble themes and a balance between lyricism and virtuosity that doesn't negate proper chamber music instrumental equality, each of the four movements gives the impression of complete freedom.

Harris described the first movement (Fantasy) as "a fantasia to illustrate the freedom of melodic qualities on the four different strings of the violin." Movement two, Pastorale, is a free adaptation of the English-American folk song "I'll Be True to My Love, If My Love Will Be True to Me." Long-line sustained statements mark the Andante religioso (third) movement, begun by a sixteen-measure section in very slow tempo for piano alone. The finale, Toccata, varies and combines duple and triple accentuations; has portions in long-short, nervous quintuple meter; is persistently kinetic; and explodes toward the conclusion in a hefty cadenza for violin.

The Sonata, one of Harris's most inspired works, was composed in 1942 and first performed in the same year at the Library of Congress, with violinist William Kroll and the composer's wife, Johana, as pianist. But there is a confusing history to this work. At first, Harris's duo was not published as a complete sonata, but in single movements, and only in the first and fourth movements are the titles the same as Harris had indicated. Although the composition has been recorded twice (in 1950 on the Columbia label, with Joseph Gingold, violin, and Johana Harris, piano [and with the label copy incorrectly titling the second movement a Scherzo grazioso!], and in 1964 by Contemporary Records with Eudice Shapiro, violin, and again Johana Harris), no mention is made of the fact that the first movement was originally published in 1945 as *Fantasy for Violin and Piano*, or that the second movement was published the previous year (1944) under the title *Dance of Spring*. Movement three also had a different title when issued in 1944: *Melody*. The finale, the only movement that showed a relationship to the Sonata, was published by Mills Music (publisher of the other movements) in 1953(!) as *Toccata—Fourth Movement—Sonata for Violin and Piano*. It will be noted that the earliest publication date of any of the four movements is two years after the premiere. Why Harris permitted piecemeal publication, variance in titling, and elimination of any relationship to the Sonata as a whole remains a mystery. One can understand the later gathering of separate pieces into a single work, but here the opposite took place! Moreover, in 1974, the complete four-movement Sonata was published by Belwin Mills. This did not end the confusion surrounding the work. There were no titles for the four movements and no explanation given for their elimination.

There are these final observations: In the second recorded edition of the Sonata there are some cuts and modifications in the first movement *(Fantasy)* and slight changes are made in the other three movements as well. And, given the publishing history of the work, one takes for granted that performance of the movements as separate pieces is permissible.

TRIO

- **Trio for Piano, Violin, and Cello (1934)**

The opening sixteen-measure theme exhibits stark strength (a constant characteristic of this composer) by exclusive use of various octaval arrangements (only one chord is used). Tension is formed nonharmonically, by leaps, and the excellent device (in fast movements) of changes from triple to quadruple meter. When the strings enter, they too are in unison and octave arrangement, save for an intermittent double-stop against which the piano crosses in a bold second layer, similarly in octaval distribution. The theme is constantly and logically expanded, shifted, and molded (not developed in the form of bits taken out and then exploited), incessantly changing its meter and pulse. This is the entire focus of the opening movement. Standard sonata-form techniques are not at work here; instead, thematic materials are developed rhythmically, by expansion, turns, and twists.

The slow movement is based on the continuity of the violin theme, which is presented in different guises (not variationally, but by expansion). Harris illustrates the principle of sustained form without resorting to recapitulation even in the broadest sense. The texture grows at the same time, culminating with the strings accompanying one another as well as the piano with left-hand pizzicato. In the coda, there is an expert ten-measure canon for the two strings alone, designed so that imitation occurs at the distance of an eighth note—a supreme difficulty of canonic work that is dramatic.

A double fugue forms the final section. In the span of the first subject, there are several different rhythmic patterns, a device of considerable effectiveness in fugal unfoldment, since greater clarity results when the other voices enter. While Harris was not an adherent of the Franck school, the exposition here is followed by exact quotation of sets of 5/4 measures from the first movement, accented unsymmetrically to form a series of measures in 10/8, and denoting the second fugue subject. The first subject works in with this and leads to the stretto section, with considerable blocklike movement within the moderate rate of speed.

QUARTETS

- **String Quartet No. 3—Four Preludes and Fugues (1937)**

A work made up of only preludes and fugues may seem like unconditional surrender to academic principles, but such systematized sequence is not the case here. There are ordered terms, but not checked, chalk-dusted music. The Bachian concept suggested by the title is not present; instead, Harris offers a revival of medieval means in a modern setting.

Mode-based, rather than key-based, scales and harmonies are used, providing sound flavors unavailable in the major and minor keys and a purity of line due to the diatonic quality of the modal scales. Harris uses different modes in the movements, one serving for each of the preludes, (in turn: Dorian, Lydian, Locrian, and Ionian), two being combined for the fugues (in turn: Dorian and Aeolian, Lydian and Ionian, Locrian and Phrygian, and Mixolydian and Ionian). Thus, differing qualities arise, rather than those of key levels. Since one mode is followed by combining two, modality is succeeded by bimodality, further logically enhanced by balancing a prelude (all of which have canonic impulses) with a fugue (the highest ordered form in polyphony); and ordered still further, in that the fugue's bimodality uses, as one of its two modes, that contained in the prelude! Musical syntax of perfect planning, yet not merely congealed modern academicism. The modes give (as do major- and minor-scale differences) degrees of luminosity or darkness, so that the four sections (divided, as noted, into eight by one and two modes-in-combination for each section) have the non-conformity which removes static tonality. There is a freshness in combining modes, since such polarity junctions relate to bitonalities formed from pitting two keys in partnership. The counterpoints that dominate every measure are modified by the harmonic textures that exist in superimposed form from the shaping of the polyphony. This quartet displays Harris's harmonic-contrapuntal method. He is not fully concerned with rigid line writing, but with conjunctive harmonies formed from polyphonic operations.

Absolute polyphonic discourse does not negate differences beyond those discussed above. In the first fugue, the subject is later inverted; in the second prelude and fugue, the instruments are muted. There is also the lightness of rocking pizzicatos and a thinned-tone coda in this second set. The third prelude extends textural totality to six-part writing for the four instruments in ten of its twenty-four measures; the third fugue also displays its subject in inverted form as it progresses. In the fourth fugue, the outer portions are in unison, and augmentation of the subject provides a strong effect.

(In 1939 Harris arranged the first pair of the set as Prelude and Fugue for Strings and Four Trumpets. The trumpet parts constituted fresh material.)

- **Three Variations on a Theme for String Quartet (String Quartet No. 2) (1933)**

Harris's quartet is dedicated to the esteemed patroness of chamber music Elizabeth Sprague Coolidge (q.v.). The variations are based on a two-pitch motive derived from Mrs. Coolidge's initials: E.S.C. (*Es* is the German for E-flat). This motive (E-flat–C) is heard at the beginning of each of the three movements; each derives its entire conception from the motive. Importantly, one should not overlook the difficulties in planning a work that is to be served by

the simple downward skip of a minor third.

As mentioned, each movement is a grand working out of this musical unit. It is only natural that, with such restricted means, the composer's imagery must be somewhat free and rhapsodic. The woven polyphony is stimulated by counterpointed rhythms; melodic items stem from the compact thought. The skip of the third predominates, down (as original), reversed upwards, inverted to form the interval of a sixth. While there are other tonal spans, of course, this representation of a person's name is given greatest importance. In order to project the form, mutations occur in the individual movements. In the second movement, the theme is followed by contrapuntal treatment and faster pace, succeeded by chordal changes in still faster tempo, then by rhythmic accompaniment (chords outlined by tertial movement at the top) to a cello line, completed by four other extensions. While the form is free, it is bound by woven lines that stem from the initial unit. The same plan can be followed in the declamatory third movement. This includes a short fugue, perorated with a slightly more than fifty-measure section in block chordal form, occupied continually with triform melodic outline that is colored, changed, and shifted in its vertical dress.

(This work illustrates Harris's addiction to self-transcription. Thirty-two years after completing the second quartet he transcribed the three movements for string orchestra, titling the piece *Rhythms and Spaces*. Dan Stehman, in his detailed study of Harris, describes the setting as: "An arrangement, with some new material in I. and III.")

QUINTETS

- *4 Minutes—20 Seconds* **for Flute with String Quartet (1934)**

Nothing ambiguous or mystical about this title. It means what it says! The running time of this work is (give and take) the time noted. In 1934, before long-playing recordings, the Columbia Phonograph Company recorded Harris's *Symphony (1933)*. One side of the last record in the set remained blank. Harris was, therefore, requested by this firm to compose a work to the specific maximum time limit of a twelve-inch disk (namely, four minutes, twenty seconds). The result was this quintet, written for functional commercialism, whereby purchasers would receive their full money's worth and not find a blank side in the album of records.

Why not such creative limitations? The architect plans with definite restrictions; the TV-script and film music composers do so, as well the muralist. Functional art can be a restrictive to one who cannot control his technique, but, to one who can, there is no reason why works should not be founded within specified boundaries. Harris was again faced with time limits in connection with a radio work and composed a six-movement piece *(Time Suite)*, wherein each movement was written to precise timings.

The music of this short work is meditative, a pastorale. A single theme is used with concentrated variations made on its components. Slight contrapuntal means move the lines. It is scored antiphonally, moves into a full climax, and returns to the quietness of the beginning. It is a little more than four minutes of modal lyricism.

- **Quintet for Piano and Strings (Two Violins, Viola, and Cello) (1936)**

Harris's full-measured involvement with contrapuntal methods is vividly displayed in this large-scale work, consisting of Passacaglia, Cadenza, and Fugue (actually a triple fugue), to be performed without interruption. This virile Quintet, both a landmark in Harris's career and one of the most important contemporary examples of the medium, has as the root of all matters a twenty-eight-measure opening theme stated in octaves by the highest and lowest string instruments. The other string voices enter and depart to create varying densities and dynamic subtleties without disturbing or enlarging this bare declaration of the essence of the whole. The extended theme (melodic breadth was particular to this composer, continual thematic growth was as natural to him as the precise, eight-measure minuet theme was to Haydn) is divisible into four units of seven measures each, with climactic rise held in abeyance until the last of the units. There is clever use of the complete chromatic range, though there is no affinity with the twelve-tone system—the total sounds are coincidental. The predilection of the passacaglia form for triple meter is maintained; in fact, it is the only matter maintained, for the rhythmic patterns are nonsymmetrical. The movement is in two sections; developmental processes place the subject in new light by interweaving voices and then by ultrarhythmic usages presaged by diminution (measured reduction of note values in speedier statement).

The Cadenza (properly "cadenze," since there are four separate ones) develops the Passacaglia theme. It will be observed that organically the movement continues the general atmosphere (sufficient, therefore); furthermore, its placement gives a general contour of balance between the two outer, resolute movements. There is deliberate use of pyrotechnically ordered virtuosity. This instrumental style is common to much modern chamber music, but not in the use of cadenza interpolations in the infrastructure of a work. The quadruple cadenzas are as carefully planned as the Passacaglia that preceded—planned as to their individuality; in regard to the string instruments, planned as to their pitch-range order (in succession: violin, viola, cello, and piano); also planned as to entrances and departures (all save the violin enter as part of the texture, and each finally shakes off as a lone voice). There is no cadenza for the second violin, since its color is already represented in the multiple array. Programmatic ideas may come to mind with each aspect of this instrumental resource, but what Harris had in mind was development by colored virtuosic declaration of the main theme.

The tenets of a triple fugue require that, at some time during its course, there be a combination of the three subjects. If this is not followed, it is not a *true* triple fugue, but a fugue with three different subjects. Here, the three subjects are distinctive: The first bears some resemblance to the Passacaglia theme; the second has a jiglike contour; the last is formed from wide legatos. The final movement, though titled simply Fugue, embraces the complete spectrum of both a double and a triple fugue. There are all possible partnerships of paired subjects: first and second, then second and third, and finally first and third. It is in the final section, preceding a short coda that restates materials from subjects one and three, that the triple combination takes place with subject one further developed, subject two in the strings in diminution, and the third subject in the piano, heard in vigorous dynamics.

(Harris also made a revised setting for piano and full string orchestra, minus double basses, changing the title to Concerto for Piano and Strings.)

SEXTETS

- **Concerto for Piano, Clarinet, and String Quartet, Op. 2**

Though this title may seem self-contradictory, it is actually correct. The term *concerto* usually signifies a work for a solo instrument with orchestral accompaniment, but it may be more truly defined as a competition, the pitting of one voice against others. The forces are unequal, so the solo voice is highlighted to make up for its lack of totality force. In any event, concerto style is met with rarely in the field of chamber music. However, there has been a revival in the use of this classic form for smaller combinations, especially when the movements are designed in linear fashion, or in the neoclassic vein. Harris's straight-lined writing is not that of the usual neoclassic assumption. He substitutes his own type of polyphony (quite often a counterpoint of blocked voices working rhythmically against each other), which makes the use of the "concerto" locution not out of place at all, though one will find full equality of the six instruments, as is to be expected in chamber music.

Though this work is an early production (composed in 1926), it has all the ingredients and means of Harris's later works—his usual long-swept lines and free polyphony. It was this work that catapulted Harris into prominence, and it still is, more than a half century after its composition, a fresh and worthy piece.

The opening Fantasia lives up to its titled freedom. The solo viola theme near the beginning is nurtured from introductory material and, in turn, builds into the never-repeating sense of the form. Movement two is the scherzo representative. There is no Trio, the two parts of the movement being separated by a Lento (in the uncommon time of 12/2), with the meter usually shifting and, when it does not, being marked by fluctuating phrase lengths. The clarinet has an important role, colored by the piano working octavally above and below it. The spirit is of the Scherzo; the form is free.

Although there are monothematic characteristics in the slow movement, the use of imitation is applied to the chromatic vacillation of the movement's main motive. The variances of the lines are aided considerably by withholding the timbre of the piano until last; that of the clarinet until the midway point. The strings are brought in separately and assist further by muting the upper three voices against the unmuted cello. The removal of mutes creates a still different color. The Finale is a very free fugue, with a long preliminary statement and a development into varying metrical divergencies of the very important short (sixteenth) notes in the subject.

- **String Sextet (Concerto for Two Violins, Two Violas, and Two Cellos) (1932)**

The elements of thematic construction, as such, are not to be found in the first movement, Prelude. A three-note figure is the entire marrow of the music's bones. It is developed, extended, twisted, imitated, thrown about, and changed rhythmically in order to make the movement's growth comprehensible. Leanness, hardness, and grand austerity are the predominating features. The crusty sound blocks (most are of sextet total) of this movement represent the earlier Harris style. Crags of sonority are developed, rather than the relating of a thematic tale and a spinning of its plot.

The material of the slow movement, Chorale, is first fully harmonized with somewhat chromatic reflections, then varied continuously in its melodic, harmonic, and rhythmic aspects. No sectionalism results, but a type of arch form, whereby climax arrives at a section of broken pizzicato and arco treatment, and recapitulation with the choralelike scoring of the changed theme, still a recognizable cantus firmus.

In the Finale, Harris dips wholeheartedly into the field of polyphonicism. (He prefaces this eight-minute movement with a technical analysis and further marks [in the score itself] almost sixty places concerned with the emplacement and working out of his material.) A huge fugal edifice is defined by this movement. A vigorous asymmetrical theme is introduced first, taken through fugato, some variation, and leads to the second theme (bearing a faint resemblance to the second movement's chorale subject). The two themes are then treated to an arrangement of multitudinous combination, variation, and fugal argument. The circle is gradually and finally completed when the shape of the opening first movement's motive joins in. There are rough edges to this formidable structure, but the polyphony should be enjoyed for its massive contour rather than for its beams, girders, and other parts of its innerness. The importance of the movement lies in its tremendous contrapuntal power. This provides total stability without resorting to recapitulatory balances.

(The Chorale movement can be performed by a full string orchestra, minus double basses. Another transcription of this second movement was made in 1969 [for solo organ] by a former student, George Lynn.)

Harrison, Julius (1885–1963)

DUO

- **Sonata in C Minor for Viola and Piano (1945)**

In some of his music, this English composer-conductor made use of folk-song material. That element is not included in this romantic duo sonata, the major chamber work Harrison produced.

To some the word *romantic* is a term of abuse, but this applies only to fanatical doctrinaires (as the composer Cyril Scott classified them). Harrison's viola and piano sonata is music full of expression, with a breadth of detail that has the tonal openness of style and treatment that can only be termed romantic. And in that respect it is beautifully managed instrumentally.

A five-pitch motive is a commanding point in the first movement. Movement two, robustly ornamented in its Andante, starts in C-sharp minor and moves to G major and F-sharp minor before returning to the home tonality. The concluding movement is a full-scale, fully developed Scherzo-Finale. A cyclic bit is placed in the coda by twice quoting the opening five-pitch motive.

Harrison, Lou (1917–)

See also under **Collaborative Composers**

Party Pieces

DUO

▪ **Suite for Cello and Harp (1949)**

Economy of material makes for a lightweight texture. Harrison slightly colors his work with some brassy and xylophonic sounds for the harp and binds it by making a literal repeat of the initial movement as the finale (part five). A subtle change in timbre is made by muting the cello on the da capo statement.

The effect of the duo is exceedingly fresh. Movement one (Chorale) and two (Pastorale) were derived from a score composed for a film dealing with the prehistoric paintings in the caves at Lascaux, France. (However, Harrison's music was not used in the film.) Harrison's objective was, in movement one, to depict "an old man plowing in the ancient manner behind the immemorial ox" and in movement two to show "the willowed, rivered landscape of the valley of the Dordogne where the caves were discovered." In movement one pitches are ordered so that each instrument is limited to a set of four: the cello uses D–E–F-sharp–G, the upper line of the piano has A–B–C-sharp–D, and its lower line uses D–E–F-sharp–G. Movement two is described as a "cumulatively decorated rondeau."

Movement three (Interlude) was originally for unaccompanied cello. The harp part was added by the composer-cellist Seymour Barab, who premiered the Suite with harpist Lucile Lawrence in the fall of 1949. Much of the harp part consists of rhythmically differentiated C pitches braced against the cello's line. Movement four is a rearranged section from Harrison's Symphony on G. It is "a strict twelve-tone" music, though "tonally centered."

TRIO

▪ **Trio for Violin, Viola, and Cello (1946)**

A one-movement piece (totaling 111 measures) of polyphonic interplay, with most attention given to a motive that descends a second and then a third. Development takes place and a type of ternary form results with a repeat toward the end of the first fourteen measures, pitched differently. Even with its chromatic knitting, the Trio is a flat-surfaced music, but always alive in its sonorous purity.

QUARTET

▪ **Suite No. 2 for String Quartet (1948)**

Harrison's poetic prosody, flavored by a neobaroque style that he favors, is not only expressive and superbly structured but always inventive. Here, in a three-movement total, the stylistic essence is that of secundal counterpoint, contrasted in both a diatonic and a chromatic manner.

A slow-paced opening is followed by sweepingly spaced lines set forth in canon. Movement three is kin to a Purcell Fantasia. Harrison says this finale is constructed from "a small motive of ascending fourths, which in the course of the movement inverts, expands to descending fifths and undergoes decoration."

(The work is also playable in a string orchestra setting.)

Harsányi, Tibor (1898–1954)

DUOS

▪ **Duo for Violin and Cello (1926)**

Harsányi's Duo (aside from some very slight Hungarian-rooted ideas, of minor total participation) shows a cosmopolitan composer at work, drawing his spiritual and mental charges from the findings that the greater contemporaries, such as Hindemith, Kodály, and Honegger, had made available. The musical trends of this century were present in the work of a man like Harsányi, who served to picture the best qualities in terms of quantitative apportionment. In short, Harsányi was an empiricist.

Harsányi studied with Kodály. Both the free spirit and refinement of his teacher's work can be heard in this duet, as well as melodic lines that move with Parisian lightness. Counterpoint is essential in a duet scored for homophonic instruments in order to avoid dullness. Accordingly, polyphony is the chief style of the three movements and most apparent in the fugato that ushers in the slow movement. Curiously, however, the subject of the fugato never appears later in imitative state. In the final movement, parallel writing is contrasted with lines that run against each other.

▪ Sonatine for Piano and Violin (1918)

Neoclassicism is represented here, somewhat thick in its textural arrangement. The melodic lines are always interesting; the harmonies that surround them squeeze hard, though their tightness does avoid undue chromaticism.

The Scherzo is formed from a scalewise theme with some imitation between the two instruments. Theme one of the last movement is encrusted in a welter of harmony, while theme two is dancelike. Developmental processes proceed in ordered patterns, but are sometimes blocked by their thickly textured expression. One is not surprised that the Sonatine was produced by a twenty-year-old composer. It serves to represent the young Harsányi; it also serves as a vehicle for a performing duo team that prefers heavy music styling.

QUARTET

▪ String Quartet (1925)

Plenty of fancy, plenty of sharp structural difference, and plenty of pointed dissonance in this four-movement String Quartet. Unity is not shattered by this approach and certainly interest is maintained. The principal feeling is one of unrest.

Mostly fast action in the first movement, a sonata formation with three themes. There is constant metrical volatility, with measures fractionally pleated: 4/4 + 1/8 is a pertinent example. Fluctuation continues in movement two. A pair of themes alternate in Lento and Allegro tempo. A third pairing smothers the lengths so that each is reduced to but two measures. The Lento section then follows and the movement concludes with (once again) a two-measure bit in Allegro.

Vertical and horizontal style are blended and contrasted in the third movement. Divisional detail marks the form, confirmed by a thirteen-measure Allegretto (each measure with a different time signature) and a Presto of principal concern. The movement ends with an exact repetition of the initial thirteen measures. The Finale does not deviate from this belief in change. There is a Grave that mixes three mini cadenzas into its materials and then there is a Vivace that twirls and dances about and has full-scale rhythmic briskness. But there is also a fugato before the quartet ends with some light pizzicato chords and a one-measure rhythmic unison bowed and played in *fortissimo*.

Hartig, Heinz Friedrich (1907–69)

QUINTET

- *Composizione per cinque (Composition for Five)* for Flute, Oboe, Violin, Viola, and Cello, Op. 50

Tight, technical systems often produce hermetic results. Though Hartig's *Composition* (the title already will put many on edge awaiting a cold and crabbed, rigorously ordered, abstraction) is in serial style, it is no rebarbative work. There is a complexity of detail, but color, rhythmic enthusiasm, and virtuosity are offered as well.

These items are put to work within linear soloism that is equally distributed among the five instruments and most often simultaneously exposed. Forms are free: the first movement split between moderately-paced music and a swinging, scherzolike concept (linked by a solo cello statement). Movement two is in quintuple meter, but the 5/8 frame is often loosened by duple and quadruple totals occupying the measures. Like the first movement, the last is divided between slow-paced and moderately moving material (the latter introduced by col legno and pizzicato timbres).

Hartley, Walter S. (1927–)

DUOS

- *Four Sketches* for Flute and Piano (1964)

The succinct theorem of the work is constant activity, the parts knitted tightly into the sound fabric, with plenty of chromatic yarn. And succinct in time scope as well, the four movements timed at 6:44.

Tripartite formations in the Prelude and Scherzino. The Nocturne is compact in structure, pitch-sprinkled in its latter part, where the flute has a cadenza in set tempo. Simplest and speediest is the Finale, which shifts between conjunct detail and quartal spans.

- *Poem* for Tenor Saxophone and Piano

Romanticism that has immediate accessibility is present here. Ternary format, with suave lines predominating. Music of directness minus any petty padding.

- Sonata for Tuba and Piano (1967)

A vigorous (even in its slower sections), sonorous duo conception, replete with blocked counterpoint and motile part activity.

There are four movements, the last two linked. There are serial slants in the first movement and fugal fibers in the final movement. Vitality and eloquent scoring for both instruments. An interesting point: In the third movement (an Adagio based on double-dotted rhythms) there is a brief quotation of the opening theme of the first movement, set in augmented time values.

- *Sonorities II* for Horn and Piano (1975)

A free-form, five-minute essay organized so that emphasis is on dark, bustling, bass-zone ostinatos and percussively packed clusters in the piano and dyads in the horn (two-pitch combinations obtained by playing one pitch and singing another). Further for the horn are chromatic lines and glissandos. Indeed, sonority stipulations are paramount.

- *Sonorities III* for Trombone and Piano (1976)

A five-section work that sharply color-contrasts free chromatic material. The tempos alternate in slow and fast succession and the data within each portion are both broad and vigorous. What ties up Hartley's sonority sampler is the use of trombone glissandos in wholesale quantity, in all divisions, save the initial one.

In section three the trombone is given an ad libitum opportunity to sing a short D pedal while simultaneously performing glissandos in the three measures that are involved. The pedal tone (if sung on pitch) produces additional sounds in the form of overtones. The beginning of the final five-measure section is signaled by a *fortississimo* cluster in the piano's bass zone.

TRIO

- *Tricinia: Four Pieces for Three Trombones* (Two Tenor Trombones and Bass Trombone) (1977)

In all four pieces line writing with good amounts of imitation is the dominating point. Of course, flowery figuration in a work for trombone trio is not to be expected, and this is replaced by the cohesiveness of the instrumental planes. Positive trombone eloquence is displayed in this seven-minute work.

Hartley indicates the Latin title means "three-voice pieces." The group of four pieces represents a second setting ("re-composition" is the descriptive word used) of vocal madrigals in Renaissance style that Hartley had written at a much earlier date.

QUARTETS

- *Quartet for Reeds* (Oboe, Clarinet, Alto Saxophone, and Bassoon) (1977)

A vigorous and pithy (91/2 minutes) six-movement divertimento that contains a contemporary bit of vertical and horizontal combinations. No fancy scoring or effects until suddenly, in the fifth movement, metrical elimination, multiphonics, and chance action take place. Save for multiphonics in a few measures for the

saxophone and bassoon, the previous clearly-punched style returns in the following movement.

- *Solemn Music for Brass Quartet* (Trumpet [or Cornet], Second Trumpet [or Cornet or Horn], Horn [or Trombone or Baritone], and Trombone [or Baritone or Euphonium]) (1968)

Conventionally tonal and open-hearted in terms of its instrumentation—the latter reminiscent of the instrumental ad libitums that are packed into the music of Percy Grainger. Not in Grainger's style, but following a warm, slightly chromatic process in the Prelude, with a more chordal status in the Anthem, and a fanfarric contour in the majestic Postlude.

For this four-minute work the quartet can be optionally stretched to a quintet by use of a tuba. Other possibilities are the use of multiple instruments and performance of the piece by a brass choir.

QUINTETS

- *Orpheus* for Two Trumpets, Horn, Tenor Trombone, and Bass Trombone (1960)

A fine, "white" sound covers this fully tonal piece conceived as a madrigal; one would never guess it wasn't from the 15th century. Music of the utmost clarity, balance, and expressive euphony.

- *Quintet for Brass* (Two Trumpets, Horn, Trombone, and Tuba) (1963)

Hartley's quintet sets forth standard (safe and sane) formal patterns. Short-long rhythmic figures and long-phrased passages, including some imitation, are in the first movement. Movement two has a scherzolike personality; the third movement flows; and the finale depends on rhythmic, syncopative drive. Tonal music, but pungently developed. Secundal pitch conjunctions are basic to the composition.

Hartmann, Erich (1920–)

QUARTET

- **Quartet for Double Basses**

Romantically updated in style. Definitely worthwhile unsophisticated music that even sophisticates will like, and completely cut away from mundane academicism. Rather solid textures, but the lines are poised and well integrated. The finale is a Saltarello, with the 16th-century Italian dance set in presto and stimulated by use of birhythmic (two against three and three against four) combinations.

Hartmann, Johan Peder Emilius (1805–1900)

This composer (note the one "n" in his given name) is not to be confused with his grandfather, Johann Ernst Hartmann (note the double "n" in the Christian name) (1726–93), a violinist-composer. J.P.E. Hartmann, as he was known, and as he is identified on his published scores, was the son of August Wilhelm Hartmann (1775–1850), an organist-composer. To complete this family tree mention should be made of Emil Hartmann (1836–98), the son of J.P.E. Hartmann, also a composer.

Niels Gade (q.v.) and J.P.E. Hartmann were the most important of the Danish romanticists. There is a further link between the two—Gade was Hartmann's son-in-law.

In Hartmann's work there is craftsmanship, conveyed in the then prevalent Germanic spirit and style of Mendelssohn and Schumann. Danish music history records that Hartmann's contemporaries often found his work rather abrupt and unmelodious. From this remove, of course, such criticism is only an amusing historical footnote. Robert Schumann would be expected to know better. He found Hartmann a master of form and one who understood "how to touch and fetter our interest throughout."

DUOS

- **Sonata for Flute and Piano, Op. 1**

Hartmann was only twenty when he produced his first work with a formal opus identification (in June of 1825). It gives a fair preview of his future output. More intensity appeared in the later chamber music, as well as more detailed development, but the general style is already determined.

In the classical turn of the first movement each of the instruments has a short cadenza. In the Scherzo the use of a 6/4 meter holds the motility a bit in check, providing a music of breadth rather than breeziness. Throughout, the orderliness and appositeness cannot be criticized—all key changes function in relationship to the home B-flat tonality.

- **Sonata No. 2 in C Major for Violin and Piano, Op. 39**

The initial piano figure in the introduction and the succeeding sustained line of the violin are the basic material for the movement proper that follows. The rhythmic figure is fundamental, the other idea is subsidiary, with bits interwoven within the development material. In the song design of the slow movement, key and speed changes mark the contrasting section. It has been said that Hartmann lacked the elegance of his colleague, Gade. The music of this slow movement denies such a view.

There is Mendelssohnian lightness in the Scherzo, but there is urgency as well; the force of contrary motion keys this. An interesting link is used to preface the Finale, in Allegro molto tempo, by employing the same octaval thought that bridged the initial part of the Scherzo to its central, more-relaxed division. Schumann's statement concerning Hartmann's formal ability comes to mind (*see above:* introductory essay).

Hartmann, Karl Amadeus (1905–63)

QUARTETS

- **First String Quartet *"Carillon"* (1934)**

This quartet does not strive to imitate the sounds of bells. The title is the name of the chamber music organization in Geneva that awarded Hartmann's quartet the first prize in its 1935 competition. Indeed, the sharply pointed ideas doubtless made an immediate impression on the star-studded jury, which included the Swiss conductor Ernest Ansermet, and composers Albert Roussel of France, Gian Francesco Malipiero of Italy, and Henri Gagnebin of Belgium.

Bartókian influence is apparent in the first movement, which has a consistent upward drive in contrast to the Langsam introduction that moves (plus glissando) in a descending form. The off-beat rhythmics and syncopative formations of the third movement also relate to Bartók. The central movement is totally muted and filled with harmonic-timbred pitches. (Thought: Were these bell-quality sounds deliberate on Hartmann's part, in view of the competition sponsor's name, or were they a psychic anticipation of his being awarded a prize by an organization known as Carillon?)

- **Second String Quartet (1946)**

Bartók's influence has been noted with respect to the first of the two string quartets Hartmann

produced *(see above).* The same creative impulses drive the incessant, motoric Presto that completes this quartet. Interesting point: There are two different conclusions: one of 96 measures, the other, marked *"virtuoser Schluss"* (*"virtuosic ending")* of 146 measures. Aside from length it is difficult to see any difference between the two.

However, in the richly scored, extremely passionate, and vividly energetic first movement (with a fair-length preface in Langsam tempo) the model is very clearly Hindemith. The rhythmics are direct, colored by 1/8 pulse tics that precede 2/4 and 4/4 meters, the polyphony open and wholesome.

In the middle movement (Andantino) the textural variance from vertical to horizontal shapes the design. The intensity is maintained but the climax withheld significantly (and strategically) until fifteen measures before the end of the movement.

Hartmann, Thomas de (1885–1956)

DUO

- **Sonata for Violin and Piano, Op. 51**

In a type of fantasy filled with a positiveness of brilliant writing, the music for the first part is warm with modalism, parallelisms, consecutive fifths, and full-scale sonority. In movement two Hartmann's heart belongs to his native Russia, as qualities of Russian Orthodox chant and folk tune fill the measures.

Movement three is a slashing dance. Toward the latter part there are large sections in turn for unaccompanied violin and then solo piano. The music has virtuosic rewards in its chamber music setting.

Hartwell, Hugh (1945–)

QUINTET

- *Matinée d'ivresse à.r., 1872 (Rapturous Morning)* for Clarinet, Violin, Cello, Piano, and Percussion (Vibraphone, Tubular Chimes, Hi-Hat, Crash or Splash and Rivet or Sizzle Cymbals, Gong, Dinner Gong, Two Bongo Drums, Two Timbales, Tom-tom, Bass Drum, Timpani, Triangle, Bamboo Wood "Chimes," Temple Blocks, Large Wood Block, Maracas, and Tambourine) (1966)

Toccata action in the piano, large amounts of detail produced from a healthy total of percussion instruments (using sixteen total beaters of sextuple variety), and a full chromatic syntax set forth a music of muscle and vitality. No sensuousness in Hartwell's score, but neither is there any *Weltschmerz*.

The climax is arrived at in a series of four *senza misura (without strict time)* sections: in order, lasting, in total seconds, 30–35, 15, 20–25, and 10–15. Musical "flying objects" are involved: continual glissandos, repetitive clusters, rolls on the piano's strings using timpani mallets; all loud and furious, and with percussive violence. From this triple *forte* state the music wheels down into triple *piano*. All in all, a powerful, evocative piece.

(The "à.r., 1872" in the title might represent "to R," a dedication.)

SEPTET

- Septet for Two Clarinets (Clarinet 1 alternating E-flat Clarinet), Bass Clarinet, Horn, Violin, Viola, and Cello (1969)

Twelve-tone music, structured in one movement, unified by its linear coil and recoil, and by the rhythmic figure heard in the initial measure. Freely formed, Hartwell's music is clear and lucidly stated. It does have a rough-edged staying quality as if to emphasize that any change to a lighter contrastive portion might nullify the stylistic purity.

Hartzell, Eugene (1932–)

The Workpoints Series by Eugene Hartzell

Hartzell studied composition with Hans Erich Apostel; the latter had studied with both Arnold Schoenberg and Alban Berg. In parallel fashion Hartzell adopted the creative style of the Viennese twelve-tone school. *The Workpoints*, a series of duets for the instruments of the wind quintet, are representative of his work.

Hartzell states that the title is owed "to the English writer Lawrence Durrell, who, at the end of his *Alexandria Quartet*, lists a number of workpoints, that is, threads of the plot which could perhaps be further elaborated. For me, the 'plot' is a series of three wind quintets, to which at least *Workpoints I* refers, namely, to various aspects of the basic tone-row which had not yet been taken up." . . . "All of them have one thing in common: the attempt to take a single idea—whether it be melodic, rhythmic or row-determined—and make a variegated piece out of it."

(*See below* for *Workpoints 1–6*.)

DUOS

- *Workpoints 1* for Flute and Bassoon (1977)

Fluid line writing without the use of metrical definition, though all pulse arrangements are precisely detailed. The initial statement reappears in changed surroundings three other times in the duo. In terms of pitch activity the structure can be considered ternary.

■ *Workpoints 2* **for Oboe and Clarinet (1977)**

Sectional distribution structures the music. Most sections partake of the huge disjunctiveness that is made clear at the start, with the clarinet descending a sixteenth and shortly moving through three pitches just short of three octaves higher. The second section places the voices closer; they become quite ornamental in the next (Molto lento) portion. In the following section, strict antiphony rules the scoring. The disjunctive element governs firmly in the last pair of sections.

■ *Workpoints 3* **for Flute and Horn (1977)**

A varied set of qualities colors *Workpoints 3,* bound (but not tightly) to an important intervallic span of a fourth. The music begins with marcato incisiveness but then shifts to a lyrical conspectus. Rhythmic material comes next; a bravado portion, this, with rhythmic criss-cross and horn glissandos. The balance is fairly fast paced but calm. It has an expressive, somewhat intimate manner.

■ *Workpoints 4* **for Flute and Oboe (1978)**

A four-section duo with the divisional tempos precise. Section two is three times the speed of the opening section, and section three twice its speed; the fourth (final) part of the work reverts to the pace and quality of the opening part. Save in the faster portion, the interval of a seventh is a prime character in the pitch depiction.

■ *Workpoints 5* **for Clarinet and Horn (1978)**

Hartzell's *Workpoint* compositions avoid set forms such as ternary, sonata, and the like. Still, in the variances of each work there is neat balance and an absence of free, rhapsodically

loose framework. Here, the sectional detail moves from an active repetitive pitch point in the soprano (the clarinet repeating the same sound via the use of alternate fingerings) set against horn phrases, to running figures and antiphonal duetting. Later, a short reprise finds the repetitive pitches now in the horn as well as a restated bit of the antiphony. There are no radical challenges in the *Workpoints,* but the further elaborations that are the composer's objective are certainly explored to the full— and artistically successful.

■ *Workpoints 6* **for Oboe and Bassoon (1979)**

The first three sounds of the duo are in total unison, but from that point on the music travels with direct, well-turned and well-sounding cross-rhythmics in part one. Long oboe lines and supportive bassoon figures are used in the second section; the roles are reversed in the following portion. A bit of the initial pitch unification returns toward the concluding part of the duo, this time at the octave. The ending is "As fast as possible" and the *fortissimo* final contrary-motion cadence is a true quip.

QUINTET

■ *Projections* **for Wind Quintet (1970)**

This American-born composer has been a permanent resident of Vienna since 1960. Before that time, from 1956 to 1958, he studied privately with the Austrian composer Hans Erich Apostel (1901–72). To honor his mentor, Hartzell dedicated his Capriccio for unaccompanied flute to him to mark Apostel's sixty-fifth birthday. *Projections* provides further testimonial, the dedication commemorating Apostel's seventieth birthday.

Apostel wrote in twelve-tone style, with some mix-in of chromatically tonal configurations. Hartzell follows suit in his *Projections,* and such technical connection makes the dedication to Apostel doubly appropriate.

Textural differences consistently mark the three parts of the work. These are formed less from the amount of total qualities and much more from considerable linear activity contrasted to less lively linear progress. Hartzell's conception always shows attention to timbre differences and their essences. These secure the polyphony with which the score is filled. Coloration is also obtained by interbinding: In movement three the start of a solo line is cut into by pithy rhythmic interjections. A different type of coloration is provided by Viennese swing: the Tempo di Ländler detail that twice concerns the third movement, including the give-and-take of slowing and speeding the basic comodo speed rate.

Harvey, Paul (1935–)

DUO

- **Sonata for Clarinet and Piano**

Warm, responsive romantic writing, with inbuilt formal restraint that gives proper structural balance. There are interesting colorful touches. The ending of the first movement totally relaxes the music's previous action, preparing for the following part's initial cantabile quality. Movement two combines slow movement and scherzo in one large three-part structure. The finale is peppy and jazzy.

QUARTETS

- *The Harfleur Song* for Saxophone Quartet (Soprano, Alto, Tenor, and Baritone Saxophones)

The melody is prefaced by an introductory section and is then variationally depicted with episodic sections in between. The entire matter is presented with a one-in-a-bar pulse and covers about two minutes in performance.

- *Robert Burns Suite* for Saxophone Quartet (Soprano, Alto, Tenor, and Baritone Saxophones)

Three pieces inspired by lines by the Scottish poet.

"My Wife's a Winsome Wee Thing" has engaging legato swing. "My Love Is Like a Red Red Rose" defines its design by textural build and then its lessening. The finale, "Bannocks o' Bearmeal," is fugal and includes a fascinating imitation of a bagpipe. The three lower instruments sustain an A pitch simultaneously very flat and very sharp to simulate the drones, and the soprano saxophone, representing the bagpipe's chanter, presents the melody.

Haslam, Herbert (1928–)

DUO

- *Haiku Set*: Eight Duos for Viola and Cello

Intermingling of art forms is represented in this sensitive work. Haslam's interpretations of the wispy, four-line Japanese poems, which range from eleven to fourteen words, are evidence of subtle, expressionistic transmutation into musical images. The potency of the music is doubled: These short pieces have emotive power without considering their Haiku stimuli.

The outer lines of the first Haiku read: "Ballet in the air . . . / They meet, they mate." A lightly splayed dance figure is announced; its antithesis is a long-short conjunctive rhythm. These are detailed, and the second one joined in the two instruments at the end in rhythmic coincidence. The second Haiku begins: "Dead my fine hopes." A Lento, ternary framework is used; the outer parts in fivefold meter. Again, the outer lines of the poem are basic in number three: "Wind blown, rained on . . . / Narrow path indeed." An ostinato figure embracing four diatonic pitches is pertinent to this quintuple-pulsed music. Pizzicato timbre colors these. In the fourth of the set, the words of lines two and four—"Long shadow / Reaches to the road"—are conveyed by extensive instrumental phrases (the first one has a two-octave span), intermingled voicing by fragmenting a phrase, and by glissando spread.

An Allegretto, mainly in pizzicato, with varied accents sprinkled throughout, is basic to number five. This Haiku begins: "Winter rain deepens." In the following piece the outer poetic lines serve a primary purpose: "Grey moor, unmarred / A bird . . . November." The misty tremolandos and avian viola calls are most representative. The seventh of the set is marked Arioso. It has complete separation of the two instruments, duetted voicing does not occur until the concluding measures. The response is linked so that the finishing pitch of one instrument becomes the starting pitch for the other. This division aptly (if perhaps only subconsciously) fulfills the Haiku's initial line: "Fever felled half-way." And, three-fourths of the final Haiku—"Roaring winter storm / Rushing to its / Utter end . . ."—likewise is matched by the contrapuntal disturbance and the ongoing tempo of the music.

QUARTET

- *Antimasque for Brass Quartet* (Two Trumpets and Two Trombones) (1960)

The virtue in the formal construction is powerful pulsatile action. Birhythmic combinations are contrasted to unified settings. In the latter, a repetitive pitch figure is motivally developed. Another position of strength is obtained by splitting the quartet into pairs and obtaining a contrapuntal texture. No scholasticism anywhere, just plenty of brass muscle.

Hasquenoph, Pierre (1922–82)

DUO

- *Sonata espressa (Expressive Sonata)* for Clarinet and Bassoon

There is no neutrality regarding contrapuntal activity in this duet. Even in the Scherzo, where it would be least expected, polyphonic conditions are paramount. With this linear stratification, bundled chromaticism prevails.

The outer movements are in the form of large binary designs. Both are fast-paced, both asymmetrically coursed, the Final a bit more than two-thirds faster than the initial Allegro. Large ternary forms structure the second movement Adagio and, of course, the third movement Scherzo. In the latter, squareness is obviated by a number of 2/8 measures set within the fast-moving 3/8 measures.

QUINTET

- *Sonate a cinq for Brass Instruments* (Two Trumpets, Horn, Trombone, and Bass Trombone [or Tuba]), Op. 32

An objective demeanor is proposed here—which means firmly sectional, variationally patterned details, balanced textures, and reliance on rhythmic mixtures. Thus, the last, with such as four against five against six or two against three against four, when moving into five-voice quintuplets or five-voice triplets, are keen examples of rhythmic tension followed by resolution.

Hasse, Johann Adolf (1699–1783)

TRIO

- **Sonata a tre in D Major for Two Flutes (or Violins) and Basso Continuo, Op. 3, No. 6**

The editor, Erich Schenk, writes that the music has "all the charm of the musical Rococo; in it Hasse proves unmistakably that he is mediator between Pergolesi—whose fondness for a three-movement structure with fugal Finale he shares—and the Classic era, whose musical language is anticipated by quite Mozartian turns of phrase."

Some neat imitation is built in the first movement, Allegro moderato. The central movement is, of course, in slow tempo (Andante amoroso), and, as indicated above, the finale is a Fuga, colored with syncopation and trills.

Hastings, Frank Seymour

DUO

- **Theme and Variations for Cello and Piano**

Romantic melorhythms confirm the period of composition; but Hastings's very effective piece is not a dated affair (it was published in 1914), even though a little bit of old lavender and lace cling to the theme.

Overall balance is achieved by repeating the initial variation, note for note, at the end. Its whirling figuration is a faultless way of getting the variations under way and bringing them to climax. The section preceding the repeated variant is an expansive Tarantella. Prior to that section, two mood depictions are compared, a Tempo di valse and a solemn, funereal setting.

Hatrík, Juraj (1941–)

DUO

- *Contrasts* for Violin and Piano (1963)

A one-movement work that has some nine divisions within it. This does not mean a range of styles is posited. Hatrík is aware of and sensitive to matters of unification. Cohesiveness is obtained by clear juxtapositions. Tempo and mood shifts, underlined by timbral and textural differences, reflect one on the other and simultaneously provide the needed contrast for a strong totality.

The plotting begins with quintuple-meter lyricism. Here the violin is muted, with thin, ostinato-layered lines in the piano. Development follows, with the violin now open-timbred and fat piano chords featured. A tempo shift leads to a mini cadenza for the violin. The fifth section is the principal one, carried along by Bartókian velocity. A second cadenza for the string instrument is next—in measure totals, it is nine times the length of the initial one. There follows a sizable episode that is attached to a changed return of the duo's opening—the violin again muted. A very simple and bare Adagio of about twenty seconds' length completes the piece.

Hattori, Koh-Ichi (1933–)

QUARTET

- *Two Movements for Strings (From the Southern Air)* for String Quartet (1974)

The "Southern" in the parenthetical title pertains to Japanese climate. It is reflected in the second movement, where Japanese folk melodies of the southern district are used "in nearly their original form." The first eight measures of this second movement are an exact duplicate of the first eight measures of the first movement, where Hattori imitates the intonation of the dialogue in *Bun-Ra-Ku*, the traditional Japanese puppet show.

In the first movement there are glissandos, which are further depictions of the sounds of Japanese speech. In a few places in the second movement a denatured sound is used by eliminating vibrato.

(*Two Movements* can also be performed by a string orchestra. All the parts are duplicated, the only change being the addition of the double bass.)

Haubenstock-Ramati, Roman (1919–)

See also under Collaborative Composers

A Garland for Dr. K.

SOLO/DUO/TRIO

- *Interpolation, Mobile for Flute (1, 2, and 3) (1958)*

The key word in the title is "mobile"; it immediately describes the aleatoric condition of the music. There are six melodic hunks (a classier word is "formants") with variants. These are to be performed according to certain rules and score directions. The first setting is by a single flute. This is then combined with realizations of the same half-dozen items by a second and then a third flutist. Two flutists can cover the total of three, or, still more insular, one flutist can play all three "solutions" by superimposition on previously recorded sections.

Whereas one performer is more economical, this does not give as free a conduct of the music as when three are concerned. However, in the long run, it really doesn't matter in music of this avant-garde conventionalism (read it as

"unconventionalism").

The version for a single flute is not to exceed four to five minutes. The version for three flutes should not go beyond twelve minutes.

Multiple 1, 2, 3, 4, 5, 6

- *Multiple 1 for Two Players*: Two String Instruments ad libitum (1969)

- *Multiple 2 for Seven Players*: Three String Instruments, Two Brass Instruments, and Two Woodwind Instruments ad libitum (1969)

- *Multiple 3 for Six Players*: Two Woodwind Instruments, Two Brass Instruments, and Two String Instruments ad libitum (1969)

- *Multiple 4 for Two Players*: One Woodwind Instrument and One Brass Instrument ad libitum (1969)

- *Multiple 5 for Two Players*: One Woodwind Instrument and One String Instrument ad libitum (1969)

- *Multiple 6 for Two Players*: One Brass Instrument and One String Instrument ad libitum (1969)

Each of Haubenstock-Ramati's *Multiple* pieces calls for a different group of instruments. Although four of the six are duos, there is no duplication of the instrumental combinations. The multitudinous possibilities make each version, in turn, of mind-boggling totality. Fair timbre affinity can be selected, for example, for the fourth of the set by choosing clarinet and horn. On the other hand, violent contrast can result in choosing piccolo and tuba. Et cetera. Et cetera.

The performance times vary between the pieces and in some cases within a single work.

Multiple 1 is indicated as running nine minutes; *Multiple 2*, the longest, has a twelve-minute performance time; the others are all eight to ten minutes in length. The variance of the last is due to the style of this set of pieces: a mix of indeterminacy, chance, and aleatoricism derived from and directed by graph and art notation—kaleidoscopic symbols spread over the score pages that mark the avant-garde composer.

(The pieces were composed in 1969. A gremlin in the publisher's print shop was let loose, apparently, since the fourth, fifth, and sixth pieces of the set are indicated as having been written in 1919—the year the composer was born!)

(For individual discussions, *see below* under Duos for *Multiple 4, Multiple 5*, and *Multiple 6*; under Sextet for *Multiple 3*, and under Septet for *Multiple 2*.)

DUOS

- ### *Multiple 4 for Two Players*: One Woodwind Instrument and One Brass Instrument ad libitum (1969)

As in the other *Multiple* pieces (*see above* and *see below*) changes to related instruments are possible for the woodwind representative selected initially. Thus, if an oboe, the transfer can be to English horn or oboe d'amore. As free as the notation is within the score, two places are indicated for the woodwind instrument to make such changes, but they can be bypassed, of course.

Colors galore. To mention a mere few: the wind instrument has the opportunity to make noiselike sounds, as well as "destroyed" and "deformed" sounds (i.e., not normal). If a flute has been chosen the player will, more than once, whisper into the instrument. And similar data apply to the brass instrument used.

The piece is purposely distorted in its sound complexes. Its excesses are related to the gurglers, rufflers, and stridors introduced in 1914 by Luigi Russolo, the futuristic composer who invented the *Intonarumori* ("Intonators of noise").

(For an ad lib use of electronic equipment pertaining here only to the woodwind instrument *see below: Multiple 6*.)

- ### *Multiple 5 for Two Players*: One Woodwind Instrument and One String Instrument ad libitum (1969)

Multiple 5 continues in the same manner as the previous example in the series (*see above*): mostly indeterminate in its pitch statements, disordered in its ordered freedom of disintegrated pulse arrangement—rampant and constant aleatoric characteristics. The score itself (from which the instruments play) looks like a chart of electronic responses to a piece of equipment showing its on-axis totals, impedance, and the like. Not even one standard notational item is used. Just one example relating to dynamics: *piano* is represented by a small dot, *mezzoforte* by a thicker dot, and *forte* by a "bullet"-size dot.

The woodwind instrument is treated as noted in *Multiple 4 (see above)*. The string instrument is required to perform all the usual techniques and a good number of unusual ones. These include a growing trill that expands from a single to three total half tones, a nervous tremolo (made with a quivering bow), scratching bow sound, placement of fingers on strings without any relation to pitch measurement by holding two, three, or four fingers very closely together, respectively over two, three, or four strings. The main emphasis is on noise. It is as if there is a hostility to anything that would resemble a clearly pitched, clearly shaped phrase. Still, that would be impure and would abruptly throw the music out of style.

(For an ad lib use of electronic equipment *see below: Multiple 6*. For this *Multiple*, however, the possibility applies to *both* instruments.)

- *Multiple 6 for Two Players*: One Brass
  Instrument and One String
  Instrument ad libitum (1969)

Adherence to the specifics used in the previous
Multiple pieces is maintained here: The special
sonorities and noises described in *Multiple 4*,
the string techniques mentioned in *Multiple 5*,
and the general comments made concerning
both of these pieces (*see above*).

One can add that electronic sound results
seem to be imitated in more than a few places.
Haubenstock-Ramati emphasizes this facet by
stating that the string-instrument performer
"may also use—in agreement with the other
performer—electronic modifiers and amplifi-
ers; these may be employed for the duration of
the piece or only in particular places."

TRIOS

- *Concerto a tre* for Piano (alternating
  Celesta and Electric Piano [or
  Organ]), Trombone, and Percussion
  (Large Tam-tam, Timpani, Cymbals,
  Vibraphone, Marimbaphone,
  Metallophones, Bongos, Congas, Two
  Low Cylindrical Bells, Glass Chimes,
  Crotales, Small Siamese Metallic
  Chimes, Jazz Drums, and Two or
  Three Low Drums) (1973)

Graphic notation functions here, with its lines,
swirls, ovals, squares, dots, dashes, and multitudinous graffiti. Of course, it is each of the
performer's task to set this notational house in
order, using both a stream of consciousness or
a translation-transmittal code of his own making. It must be remembered that in regard to the
last the re-creative truth is not being practiced
since where there is graphic notation the meanings should change from one performance to
the next.

There are four large "score" sheets.
Haubenstock-Ramati's instructions are very
general, and mainly pertain to instrumental use
rather than convey formalistic explanations.
For example, for the trombone in regard to the
first score sheet: (1) "Very slow glissandi:
normal and distorted sounds: muted, guttural,
stammered." (2) "The order of elements and
structures in the various play-throughs should
be strongly varied: solo actions." There are
pithy statements that do give minimal guidance, such as "This movement is a kind of
'guided improvisation': guided by the graphic
signs. It is pointillist, transparent and rather
'slow' music." Whatever results must take
place within a time space of nine to twelve
minutes.

- *Ricercari* for String Trio (1950)

The trio begins with 105 measures regulated by the tempo of Allegro inquieto.
This music is decidedly "uneasy." Its measured total should not lead one to think of
even moderate length. The meter is the rare
1/4 time, further splintered by the singular time
signature of 2/3, meaning exactly what it
says—a measure two-thirds the length of
the single pulse within a 1/4 measure. Exactly
103 beats and movement one is completed.
Movement two consists of an 18-measure
Lento, and the final movement is an Allegro
molto of 34 measures.

In the sense of the definition "to seek out,"
Haubenstock-Ramati's *Ricercari* fulfills its
obligations in a free dodecaphonic manner.

In movement one the opening *fortissimo*
tremolo moves upward with rhythmic drive to
mark the beginning, the expositional end, and
the start of the coda. Thematic examination is
free, a dissolving of the row in various ways
until it coheres as a strict vertical statement. In
that form it appears at the start of the development, at its conclusion, and in the coda.

Movement two is devoted to intervallic contrasts with the largest spacings used just past
the music's midpoint. The final movement, in

binary form, opens with a double ostinato (the violin and cello pitted against the viola) derived from a portion of the row, and then a rhythmic plunge states the entire tone row. After development, the ostinatos return, followed by a series of colorful chordal projections, a restatement of the rhythmic item, and a concentrated coda.

QUARTET

- **String Quartet No. 2 (1977)**

Carefully formalized, there stride through this work fixed and unfixed data, a catalogue of aleatoric and contemporary color procedures that boggle the mind (and ears). Haubenstock-Ramati has unbounded imagination (and vivid modernistic technical recall).

Movement one, titled "Bittersweet, 'Viennese,' " consists of four sharply contrasting sections. The first is for the second violin and viola, playing from graphic notation (minus time signature, of course), in the style of a "slow waltz"! Part two is a succession of "whispered" chords, separated by pauses. Part three is a tremolo bit (a reminder, the composer states, of Viennese waltz introductions). Part four is the climax of the movement: a four-instrument sonic mobile, free of intervallic equilibrium or affiliation. The purposeful chaos makes neatness from the un-neatness.

The five-section second movement has definite balances. The open and closing are related by their tremoloed definition, and sections two and four likewise by the parallel unrhythmic scurry of successive pitches. With the assorted detail in the center, an arch form is projected. But more. The final section is exactly duplicated four times in the last (sixth) movement. Thus anticipation becomes a cyclic device—for composers of the avant-garde, considered an unthinkable procedure!

Movements three and five consist of rigid isorhythmic canons. The pitches, however, are different for each instrument. As the first canon progresses each portion, in turn, is coloristically changed. Thus, the first portion is all pizzicato, the next one is tremolando sul ponticello, etc. In the other canon, while the pitches also change sectionally, the color process (of harmonics) remains the same.

The fourth part of the quartet is marked "Violente" and violent it is. It represents a string symphony of clusters: glided, chorded, polymetered, and pyramided in their contacts, and only texturally thinned in the concluding portion of the movement.

Movement six is considered a "Valse triste." In turn, each instrument has a chance at the "verse" and all four join in the "chorus." (The latter is the music already heard as the final section of the second movement.)

SEXTET

- *Multiple 3 for Six Players*: **Two Woodwind Instruments, Two Brass Instruments, and Two String Instruments ad libitum (1969)**

The ad lib for *Multiple 3* is controlled by the composer. Not just any two instruments of each group can be freely chosen, but, rather, a choice made within designated pairings. Thus, for the woodwinds there are three choices: flute and oboe, flute and C clarinet, and oboe and C clarinet. In each case the instrument alternates with others in the same family: the flute with alto flute and piccolo, the oboe with oboe d'amore and English horn, and the C clarinet with B-flat, E-flat, and bass clarinets.

There are also three choices offered for the two brass instruments: trumpet in C and horn, trumpet in C and trombone, and horn and trombone. The alternation process is continued in this group with the C trumpet always alternating with the B-flat trumpet.

The string instrument partnership is either violin and viola or viola and cello.

As in all of Haubenstock-Ramati's *Multiple* constructions the notational materials offer fantasy through their vivid symbology. The fantasy continues in the net product—one that is as much composed by the performers as by the composer; thus, this type of avant-garde music, formed from music minus form(ality).

SEPTET

- *Multiple 2 for Seven Players*: **Three String Instruments, Two Brass Instruments, and Two Woodwind Instruments ad libitum (1969)**

Without negating the ad lib opportunities Haubenstock-Ramati suggests that whatever instrument is chosen from the woodwind group, related members of its timbre family can be used. Thus: if a flute is selected it can alternate with piccolo and alto flute; if an oboe, the alternating instruments could be oboe d'amore and English horn. The clarinet would have the largest number of choices, with E-flat and bass instruments as well as the various saxophones. (No bassoon or double bassoon is mentioned in the instrumental possibilities.) The use of any one of these instruments would be acceptable as well as a lesser number of the alternating instruments. Nothing is mandatory and no specific indication for changing to another instrument is given.

The score of *Multiple 2* is highly organized—overly organized, some might say—with an extraordinary amount of instructions, graphs, and codes for the players to use in their translation of the symbols. The interpretative schedules are a blend of the rigorous and the free. No matter—Haubenstock-Ramati sets his own type of intense song for seven instruments. In the long run it amounts to extremely harsh and articulate in-and-out-of-control improvisation.

Haubiel, Charles (1892–1978)

DUOS

- *Nuances* **for Violin (or Flute) and Piano (1947)**

Not only title stimulation in this group of five pieces. Haubiel's shades of expression are never nebulous—all are to the point.

"Still" is dynamically subdued (only a three-measure *forte* disturbs the hush). "Fear" is created by a fast tempo and apprehensive broken chords. "Gentle" supports a caressingly arched line with amiable triadic harmonies. "Plaintive" (in which the violin is muted) is in a wistful 6/8 legato, with some discontent introduced as the dynamic intensities rise and fall. "Jocose" is developed by a waggish, stop-and-go rhythmic idea.

- *Pastoral* **for Oboe and Bassoon (1933)**

A combination of divisional structuring with variational application marks this duet. The effect is one of total smoothness, even when the music is rhythmically active. The lines are seemingly permitted to go their way and this naturalness makes the piece eminently successful. Of course, with this composer, one can expect total tonal lucidity.

- **Sonata in C Minor for Cello and Piano (1944)**

Classical designs—sonata, song form, and rondo—are used by Haubiel, but his language is expressively romantic. The growth and unity of each part of the work register clearly and immediately. Haubiel's craftsmanship is strong.

- **Sonata in D Minor for Violin and Piano**

Haubiel was never unconventional in his compositions. Still, there is a very odd place here in the first movement. Following standard academic practice, the sonata's exposition is marked to be repeated. Then, blithely, in a footnote, Haubiel says: "The composer advises against the use of the repeat." !!!

Long-line lyric expression combines with romantic thrust in the first movement. The tendency is toward virtuosic writing for the violin. Variational sequences are used to develop the slow movement's material. The setting of the finale is in the perpetual-motion category. It is packed with sixteenth-note figurations.

TRIOS

■ *Athenaeum Suite* **for Brass Trio (Trumpet, Horn, and Trombone)**

Haubiel's title is a fanciful allusion to the theoretical stance taken in his brass trio. Six of the seven movements are set in the church modes; the other is based on a more modern (melodic-harmonic minor) scalic arrangement. The ratio is maintained in regard to the forms: six are 17th-century dances; the other, a slowly spun Air. Use of total brass timbre produces a fitting baroque patina to the suite.

■ *In the French Manner* **for Flute, Cello, and Piano (1942)**

For "French" read "balletic." Even in the slow (middle) movement the materials are dance-soaked. And the structures have romantic radiation. In movement one considerable attention is given to alternating sections — one devoted to clipped rhythmic figures, the other to fast waltz action. There is less attention to development and more emphasis on motival repetitions in the finale. The slow movement is designed with textural distinction: first a long duo for flute and piano, then one for cello and piano, with all three instruments used thereafter as a unit.

■ *Romanza*: **Trio for Piano, Violin, and Cello (1932)**

Though the Romance, or Romanza, is generally fairly short, Haubiel's version is of substantial size, totaling fourteen minutes in performance time (cuts may be made, reducing the length to a little over eleven minutes, still an ample amount). It lives up to the formal designation, however, in terms of its emotional, somewhat sentimental, tone and narrative overlay.

The trio was made from incidental music Haubiel wrote for a play, *Will Shakespeare of Stratford-on-Avon* (by Margaret Crosby Munn). The play was produced in New York City in 1934, with the title *The Passionate Pilgrim.* Haubiel's reassembled redraft is a worthy, most successful, project.

The music is representational (the loves in Shakespeare's life), dominated by a theme, as fundamental in its delineative purpose as a Wagnerian leitmotif. It is heard immediately after a solo piano introduction, stated by the violin, reannounced by the cello, and then once more by both string instruments. The C-major lyrically and poetically expressive theme portrays Shakespeare's ideal love, the Dark Lady of the Sonnets. It is followed by a tenebrous (F minor) theme, descriptive of his wife, Ann Hathaway. In the next section, joyous C-major-framed music pictures the carefree ladies of London and the brilliant life at the court of Queen Elizabeth. The trio is concluded with a perorative fourth section (the Dark Lady theme) marked by a slow and soft extended coda.

(*See also*: *In Praise of Dance* for Oboe, Violin, Cello, and Piano.)

QUARTETS

■ *Echi classici (Classic Echoes)*: **String Quartet in C Minor (1936)**

Though standing by itself as a totality, Haubiel's

opus (the first movement was completed in 1922, when Haubiel was studying with the eminent pedagogue Rosario Scalero, and revised fourteen years later, immediately followed by the composition of the other three movements) was conceived as the first of three quartets to represent a stylistic survey. The cycle was to be named *Vista storica (Historical Vista)*. The second work was planned as *Momenti romantici (Romantic moments),* and the third was to have the title *Tendenze moderne (Contemporary Tendencies)*. The plan never went beyond the first-third mark.

Haubiel imitates nobly. The quartet is a faithful classical rewrite. Movement one begins with an introduction that sets the home tonality and moves into an Allegro moderato with strong fugal overtones. A more settled theme (in the dominant key) serves for contrast, and after the recapitulation the music swings into the more optimistic parallel major tonality at the terminal point.

This very typical equivalence is maintained in regard to the other three movements and their place in the total design. Movement two is constructed by way of a theme and five neatly distinguishable variations. The conformable-to-rule Minuetto fills the third slot and exemplifies total recall. Though here much more chromatic, its blood relative will be found in Haydn's *Quinten* Quartet (Op. 76, No. 2), with the same division of the quartet (violins pitted against the viola and cello) and with the same method (strict canon). Haydn's contrastive Trio is lightweight in texture; Haubiel's is not. It retains canonic treatment—this time for two instruments, with a pair of free added parts. As might be expected a Rondo serves for the finale and in the expected Allegro tempo. Unexpected, however, is the variational characteristic of this movement. However, such nonconformity does not shift the focus away from the classical terrain Haubiel surveys.

- *In Praise of Dance* for Oboe, Violin, Cello, and Piano (1932)

Much utilitarian-designed music rises to the surface and then disappears. When the stage play, the motion picture, the ballet, etc., for which it was composed is no longer presented, the musical auxiliary dies with it: End of run, end of music. For much of this type of creative pairing no mourning is necessary. However, like a gathering of significant fugitive articles and essays for a published collection, the compilation of such practically planned items into concert music individuality is a worthy project, providing the material has the stability to exist on its own.

The scoreboard shows that, in most instances, composers have shown good sense in choosing to make such transfers. *In Praise of Dance* represents such a decision. Originally part of the incidental music for the play *The Passionate Pilgrim* (the original title was *Will Shakespeare of Stratford-on-Avon),* produced in 1934 in New York City, six of the dances, the material elaborated, have been fashioned into a pair of suites: Partita and *Masks*.

(*See also: Romanza*: Trio for Piano, Violin, and Cello.)

Part 1: Partita

In this set, Haubiel groups three classical-period dances to match properly the present-day understanding of partita as a suite. The Minuet swings along, minus any contrastive Trio. Movement two is a Pavan. Its basic quadruple-beat measures are lengthened at many phrase endings into sextuple-beat totals. This contemporary modification colors the dance without disturbing its balance. Both duple and triple time patterns are utilized in the Gigue. Varying single meters have been used for this dance: 3/8, 6/8, 6/4, and 12/8. Here again, Haubiel considers the matter with 20th-century eyes and chooses a pair of meters for contrastive purposes.

Part 2: *Masks*

An established difference covers the second suite. While rhythmic definition is paramount, the materials are structured in a less formal manner. No dance stylization (as pertained to the first part) is considered. *Masks* is a set of romantically imagined pictures, absent of over-fancy objectives.

"Specters" flits in seven-beat speed, with a great deal of triadic color. "Fauns" is in triple meter, with graceful staccatos and legatos in the beginning and less restraint in the later portion. It leads into the last piece, titled "Witches," a lightly grotesque affair, highly actioned in concept.

QUINTET

- *Five Pieces for Five Winds* (Flute, Oboe, Clarinet, Horn, and Bassoon)

Haubiel's suite is a modern divertimento, formed with as much regard for the precepts of each individual form as were the 18th-century divertimentos, with their minuets and Trios, dances, and the like. There is apt attention to polyphony, a matter that was always of primary importance to this composer. He thought classically, but that did not deter the inclusion of a 5/8 movement (the second one, titled "In Five-Eight") or a 7/8 section (the fourth movement, titled just as simply "In Seven-Eight"), neither of which are exactly meters used by Handel or Mozart. The first of these is a scherzolike movement, with alternated ratios of 3:2 and 2:3 giving effective differences of long–short, and the reverse, metrical patterns. The second one is somewhat of the same plan, but with a thickness of voices for which Haubiel had a penchant. The third piece is a fairly free Canon with added voices.

SEXTET

- *Ballade* for Brass Sextet (Two Trumpets, Horn, Baritone horn, Trombone, and Tuba)

Haubiel's *Ballade* has a medieval, somber cast, set in a gloomy G-minor key. Everything remains foreboding, in the nature of a processional. This includes the broader-metered middle part. The instrumentation follows suit, with emphasis on the lower brass (the baritone horn, having the same range as the tenor trombone, reinforces the tenor gamut).

A compelling point is the two-measure scalewise refrain in the tuba. It is heard seven times in the first part, returns four times in the recapitulation. Then, doubled by the trombone, an octave higher, the ominous observation is heard five more times in succession—transposed, lengthened, and in augmented values. This insistence illustrates keen dramatic insight.

Haudebert, Lucien (1877–1963)

QUARTET

- *Bienvenue à Claudie (Welcome to Claudie)—Poème* for String Quartet, Op. 9

Haudebert's short essay is prefaced by lines from *Colas Breugnon* by his contemporary, Romain Rolland (1866–1944). ("Le charme de l'enfance est comme une musique: elle entre dans les coeurs plus sûrement que celle que nous exécutons.") ("The charm of childhood is like music: it enters our hearts more surely than the piece we play.")

The chromatic detail is constant, well blended within a continual change of key, meter, tempo, and material itself. With all instruments muted, an ornamented free design is made from this basis, until a section sets forth a fugato. The digressiveness then returns. At the conclusion of the piece, marked by unmuted timbre, the beginning is reviewed in shortened form.

Hauer, Josef Matthias (1883–1959)

Tropen Music by Josef Matthias Hauer

Hauer's tropes, or tone-constellations, consist of a twelve-tone series split evenly into sets of six pitches, with the sets arranged in complementary order. A shift from one trope to another, therefore, is equivalent to modulation. Although Schoenberg's formulation of the twelve-tone method has had wide acceptance, Hauer's tropen system of twelve-tone music has remained to this day (as the Austrian writer on music, Willi Reich, observes) "a purely private and personal matter, whereas Schoenberg's has not only been adopted" but has "in different ways [been] developed, by other distinguished composers."

There is an important and basic difference between the twelve-tone method and the tropen technique. The former is a generative device within the composer's pitch structuring and does not demand recognition by the listener. In the latter, to quote Reich again, "the transition from one trope to another forms an aesthetic element of which the hearer must be conscious."

In considering the objective of obtaining musical order without key relationship, Hauer was as much a pioneer as Schoenberg and at one time was very friendly with him (one of Hauer's books was dedicated to Schoenberg). But in later years, Hauer became very bitter, claiming among other things that Schoenberg had not only learned from him but had stolen his ideas. This was patent nonsense considering the differences of the techniques described above. Further, if one uses fully tonal music as

the basis for description, then Schoenberg's dodecaphonic music sounds superdissonant, while Hauer's tropen music is totally opposite.

Zwölftonspielen (Twelve-tone Games)

Hauer's huge output contains a great number of orchestral works titled Zwölftonmusik für Orchester (Twelve-tone Music for Orchestra). Some seventeen works bear this heading, each with an assigned opus number.

In the later part of Hauer's life, practically all of his compositions are of short length and use the generic identification Zwölftonspiel (Twelve-tone Game). A few bear numbers, but none have an opus designation. Virtually all of the pieces are identified with the month (most often with the day as well) and year of composition as part of the title. The instrumental media are of large variety: orchestra, chamber ensemble, chorus, vocal, piano, and multivaried chamber music settings. Roger Gustafson, in his superbly detailed catalogue of Hauer's compositions, enumerates no fewer than 135 Zwölftonspielen.

DUOS

- **Zwölftonspiel (Twelve-tone Game) for Violin and Harpsichord (August 26, 1948)**

The music is based on a twelve-tone row by one Emil Weidinger. Hauer's duo consists of twenty-five measures in 3/4 time and is to be played "not too fast, not too slow, not too loud, not too soft." It is entirely three-voiced, save for the final measure.

- **Zwölftonspiel (Twelve-tone Game) for Violin and Harpsichord (August 28, 1948)**

Arpeggiated context with certain pitches stressed in the harpsichord part; the violin is straightforward in melodic statement. There is no tempo or dynamic given this triple-pulsed music.

- *Zwölftonspiel (Twelve-tone Game)* for Violin (or Flute) and Harpsichord (August 31, 1948)

A slightly heavier texture marks this duo in comparison with the other two using the same medium *(see above)*. Using a flute in place of the violin would not make much difference. Pitchwise, the violin is contained within the span of an augmented octave (B flat above middle C to the B natural one octave higher). As usual, the violin line has no double stops. The only deviation here is an ad libitum final fifth. (In the duo dated August 26, 1948 *[see above]*, there is a single exception; the final measure of the violin part calls for a perfect fifth double stop.)

- *Zwölftonspiel (Twelve-tone Game)* for Violin and Piano (September 2, 1956)

The majority of Hauer's tropen compositions are texturally unchanged, the instruments in constant action. Similarly, here. And, often, neither tempo nor dynamic indications appear. However, this duo is an exception. The tempo is marked as ♩ = 80 and separate, but single, dynamics apply to the violin *(mezzoforte)* and the piano *(mezzopiano)*. There is continual rhythmic activity, with a marked use of two sounds opposed to three in the same pulse.

QUARTET

- **String Quartet No. 6, Op. 47**

Hauer's tropes (grouped together in blocked-off planes) are not of exclusive function, though of individual formation. They exist as designs by themselves, entities that need no special assistance like the harmony that supports a melody. This is illustrated by his String Quartet No. 6 since the four instrumental parts are the same as the string parts for Hauer's *VI Suite for Orchestra*, Op. 47. Taken out of context, the tropes retain their own force and are complete within themselves. Contained and retained with certain doublings they serve as well in the orchestral work.

The first movement is in jazz tempo; the four instruments play incessantly, each concerned with a different trope formation, each voice a counterpoint to the others. Movement two is slow in speed. While there is just as much contrapuntalism and nonstop use of all the instruments in this case, a little amount of vertical arrangement takes place in the form of rhythmic duplication. The same theory is followed in the third and fourth movements, concerned, respectively, with waltz and march concepts.

There is the complete sense of a neutral timbre spectrum. In Hauer's sixth string quartet not a single instrument stops playing in any one measure of the four total movements.

QUINTET

- *Zwölftonspiel (Twelve-tone Game)* for Piano Quintet (June 2, 1948)

In a few instances Hauer based his tropen compositions on another person's twelve-tone row *(see above: Zwölftonspiel* for Violin and Harpsichord [August 26, 1948]). In this instance the row was formulated by Wolfgang Kammerlander.

The material in the strings principally changes from sustained sound to sustained tremolo, furthered intensified to rhythmic shapes and then repeats the process. In the piano, chordal data mainly lead to tripleted ostinato measures, and this plan, too, is repeated. The total texture is one of solidity.

(This quintet is not included in Roger Gustafson's catalogue of Hauer's compositions *[see above: Zwölftonspielen].)*

NONET

- *Zwölftonspiel (Twelve-tone Game)* for
  Woodwinds, Strings (Flute, Clarinet,
  Bass Clarinet, Bassoon, Two Violins,
  Viola, and Cello), and Piano
  (April, 1951)

One of the longer tropen pieces Hauer produced, with the music divided into an *Erster Teil* and a *Zweiter Teil* ("First Part" and "Second Part"). There are no tempo or dynamic indications for any portion of the music. The rows go their assorted ways, with the piano (played without pedal) sounding bare octaves (save for a chordal final measure in each part), regardless of note lengths or rhythmic figures. This rigidity applies in a different manner to the strings. Whenever their voices move in rhythmic settings, octave doublings take place between the violins and others between the viola and cello. Otherwise, there is free line writing for the strings' sustained passages as there is totally for the woodwinds.

(The work is not listed in Roger Gustafson's catalogue of Hauer's compositions *[see above: Zwölftonspielen].)*

Haufrecht, Herbert (1909–)

QUINTET

- *A Woodland Serenade* for Woodwind
  Quintet

Haufrecht's interest in folk music and the educational field have been primary in his work. Always attentive to the needs of the music consumer, he attracted considerable attention with a piece for children's and pops' programs: *The Story of Ferdinand* (for orchestra with narrator), which achieved a large number of performances. However, his more serious music is nicely crafted, and its optimistic turns and clarity are its strengths. As are the aforementioned derivations from American song and dance.

The latter permeate the three movements of *A Woodland Serenade*. The opening Pastorale is no dreamy deal. Though it has flow, it mostly has drive—its marchlike tempo faster than one expects from the title. At the same time, the music has an easygoing sense of the blues in its coverage, the main tune marked by a long–short rhythmic cell. In the middle movement, the music lives up to the Nocturne designation. A modal overlay covers the measures that include a lumber-camp song "A Shantyman's Life." Another folk item is quoted in the final Rondo: "When McGuinness Gets a Job." This part bustles along with reel-like gaiety and real go. There is no doubt that Haufrecht's suite comprises a music of common sense and plain dealing.

Hauksson, Thorsteinn (1948–)

QUARTET

- *"a"* for Three Cellos and Double Bass
  (1975)

"a" is a quartet registration that alternates total chromatic pitch segments with ostinatos. The first of the latter are all on E. The next group brings F into the picture via polyrhythmic distribution. In conclusion, the A pitch is used for the final fifteen measures, set in quadruple rhythms.

Hauksson is stage minded. He indicates an arrangement of platforms for the performers and specifies special lighting: "The only lights on the stage or the audience should be brown spotlights, placed above each player (if possible)."

NONET

- *Mosaic* for Wind Quintet and String Quartet (1975)

DUO

- Sonata for Flute and Piano (1967)

A compendium of segments, most often opposed in pitch and rhythm, and including a variety of noises (an example: "blow very hard into the flute with the lips over the lip plate [the mouth covering it completely]) and aleatoric freedom. This type of sonic alchemy is a specialized music. It must be heard and considered on its own terms.

The score is prefaced with the statement that "an orthodox or rather classic three-movement style was maintained in the overall composition, but contentwise, spontaneity was emphasized." Yes and no. Hayashi's duo is neither orthodox nor classic, but it does have the traditional moderate-slow-fast tempo sequence of movements. The music certainly does not suffer from labored technical manipulation and shows exact but artistic plotting.

Havergal, Henry

TRIO

- *More Variations on a Theme of Handel for Flute and Two Clarinets*

Music for an off-beat trio combination, offering a fresh and nippy total timbre. Havergal's opus is light in content and entertaining in its variational approach. His well-assorted package of sweets is based on the thematic recipe of "The Harmonious Blacksmith." That title is not by Handel, though he is given credit for it. The gratuitous, yet quite fanciful, title was attached to the air Handel used for a group of variations (in his Harpsichord Suite No. 5 in E).

After the thematic entry, a pair of polyphonic considerations appear. There follow a rhythmic view in a minor mode and a turning of the thematic material upside down. Three vividly disparate scannings then come into view: a triple-swinged Waltz, a solemn quadrate-pulsed Dirge, and a two-to-the-measure English Jig.

Chordal ostinatos prevail in the first movement, as does antiphony. There is a somewhat odd point in the opening movement's structure. The initial four measures for solo piano are reused to conclude the movement, but while retaining its original repetitiveness the soloistic idea is stretched into a total of seventeen measures.

Movement two is a moderate-size ternary affair, with the central portion devoted to a flute cadenza supported by a series of five piano tremolandos divided for the two hands, with the right hand ascending and the left hand descending in turn for each of the entries.

The final movement is based on a Japanese folk song which is set in a rondo design and appears four times. In each case it is backed up in the piano with a canon. There are a number of sections for solo piano. It is all a finale music of fresh invention—a delight to hear.

Haydn, Joseph (1732–1809)

The stylistic gap that separates Bach and Haydn is not so great as one might think, if due credit is given the Mannheim school of composers who worked from twenty odd years before Haydn's birth through the late 18th century.

Whether Haydn was fully acquainted with the works of the Stamitzes, Holzbauer, Cannabich, and the others is immaterial. But the Mannheimers had already introduced the Minuet, formulated the sonata plan, had begun to eliminate, if but gradually, the basso continuo, and were drawing their musical shapes from a less fugal style than defined by the great Bach. It remained for Haydn to work toward the new goal, especially in the development sections of his works, and to achieve the requisite maturity of the style, becoming the first master of classicism, which reached its zenith in the works of Beethoven.

Haydn's chamber music output is bulky, but it is the string quartets that give him standing as a colossus in chamber music history. It was through these compositions that the cornerstone, and then the edifice above it, of authentic, mature chamber music came into being.

DUOS

- **Duet in D Major for Violin and Cello**

In the opinion of some, this work is not by Haydn. Spurious works were as common as the plagiaristic methods of many 18th-century composers. Music had to be turned out in quantity, and borrowing an idea, or part of a movement, was quite the thing. Furthermore, the practice of rearranging one's own works in order to meet deadlines was not looked down upon. Another device was to jump on the bandwagon of a well-known composer by writing a work under his name and selling it to a publisher who would also profit by such chicanery. Separating the wheat from the chaff has occupied musicologists for a long time, and their task may never cease. Nonetheless, when doubts arise as to authenticity, one must look to the music itself.

In general a worthy piece. The only point that can be questioned is that, throughout, the D-major key is stationary. Give-and-take occurs between the two voices in the opening ornamented Adagio, an energetic Allegro, and a final set of three variations on a Minuet theme.

- **Sonatas for Flute and Piano**

  - in C Major, Op. 87
  - in G Major, Op. 90

Transcriptions (extremely valid ones) of two Haydn string quartets without the minuet movements: Op. 87 is from the Op. 74, No. 1 quartet; Op. 90 is drawn from the first of the pair in Op. 77. Whether Haydn actually prepared the transcriptions is arguable. If he didn't, he deserves credit anyway.

Sonatas for Violin and Piano

Published editions of a set of eight violin and piano sonatas are available. Only the first (in G major) can be considered an original work *(see below)*.

At best these Sonatas are excellent for fiddling-piano use, a type of Gebrauchsmusik. The second, third, fourth, fifth, and sixth are arrangements from piano sonatas, the violin part as if pasted on to the piano as accompaniment to the latter. The last two (Nos. 7 and 8) are transcriptions of the two penultimate quartets (Op. 77). To stay within the limit of three movements (some of the works consist of but two), in the case of the latter sonatas, the minuet sections of the original are eliminated. The violin adds color, but the primary versions are naturally best, either as piano compositions or, in the matter of numbers seven and eight, as the beautifully mature string quartets.

- **Sonata No. 1 in G Major for Violin and Piano, Hob. XV:32**

Presumably, this is the only original sonata Haydn wrote for violin and piano. But there is a great deal of haze about the work, even with its official Hoboken catalogue identification. First, it remains unresolved as to whether it actually is a Haydn original or a Haydn transcription from an unidentified piano trio. Whatever the answer, the musical value of the duo cannot be downgraded.

- **Sonatas for Violin and Viola**

  - No. 1, in F Major, Hob. VI:1
  - No. 2, in A Major, Hob. VI:2
  - No. 3, in B-flat Major, Hob. VI:3
  - No. 4, in D Major, Hob. VI:4
  - No. 5, in E-flat Major, Hob. VI:5
  - No. 6, in C Major, Hob. VI:6

The duet form (without keyboard instrument) was not too favorable a medium for Haydn. One can find numerous duets attributed to him, but most of these are the handiwork of transcribers, ranging from such items as the violin duets, published as Op. 99 but naught more than a *reductio ad absurdum* from the quartets, Op. 17, to other rigged-up affairs, or one should say rigged-down! These violin and viola duos, however, are authentic.

The six sonatas are a throwback to early style. Specifically marked "with accompaniment of viola," the premise is a solo sonata for the violin voice, with a functional bass supplied by the viola. The viola is given a "handout" rarely; otherwise, it fills in. All the Sonatas are in early three-movement style, with ornamental and semivirtuosic filigrees in the violin carrying the full brunt of the musical messages.

TRIOS

- **Cassation in D Major for Flute, Violin, and Basso Continuo, Hob. IV:D2**

Variety in the instrumentation marks the several cassations Haydn produced. Most are for larger groups such as the G-major opus (Hob. II:G1) calling for pairs of oboes, horns, violins, violas, and one double bass. The D-major work for three instruments is typical of the style.

As far as can be ascertained Peter's publication of this work in 1973 (edited by Frank Nagel and with the bass realized by Winfried Radeke) represents a "first." It was prepared from material held by the Kungliga Musikaliska Akademiens Bibliotek, in Stockholm.

Light as a breeze in all movements save the slow one. The former consist of a pair of allegro-tempo movements and a pair of Minuets. All stay within the base tonality. The slow movement is in the subdominant tonality and is colorfully ornamented.

- **Divertimenti for Two Violas and Cello, Hob. XII:19**

One of the huge number of works of Haydn's that included the baryton. In this modern edition, published in 1977 by Wollenweber (Munich), violas are substituted for barytons. An alternate exists for the title as well: Cassations.

There are a dozen pieces in the set, all short, for the most part, binary in formation with each section repeated. Nos. 5 and 11 are Minuets, number eight is a Polonese. Conventional Haydn in scope, special in regard to the scoring, whether the top pair of voices are barytons or violas.

- *Eisenstädter* **Trios for Two Violins and Cello**

  - No. 1, in A Major
  - No. 2, in D Major
  - No. 3, in C Major
  - No. 4, in A Major
  - No. 5, in C Major

Only the third work of this set is in four movements, the others are in three movements. (The first two are arranged in slow–Minuet–fast-tempo order; the fourth shifts everything so that the sequence is Moderato–Adagio–Tempo di Minuetto; while the fifth abandons any slow movement and stands thus: Allegro–Menuett–Presto.) Movement three's formal difference is already suspicious, and one is not surprised to learn that Karl Geiringer considered the work spurious.

Transfer of medium is the case here. Nos. 1, 2, and 4 are arrangements of Nos. 8, 11, and 10 of the Trios for baryton, viola, and cello.

Suavity and suppleness constitute the name of Haydn's trio game. Plenty of flair for the violin; the others are supporting characters.

- *Leichte (Easy)* **Trios for Two Violins and Cello, Op. 21**

  - No. 1, in G Major
  - No. 2, in D Major
  - No. 3, in A Major
  - No. 4, in G Major
  - No. 5, in B-flat Major
  - No. 6, in E-flat Major
  - No. 7, in D Major
  - No. 8, in G Major
  - No. 9, in A Major
  - No. 10, in D Major
  - No. 11, in A Major
  - No. 12, in D Major

This collection of *Twelve Leichte Streichtrios,* published by C. F. Schmidt, is indeed "light," but certainly the other *(Eisenstädter)* string trios *(see above)* are only slightly more technically difficult than those in this set. The first violin holds the important role, the second violin and cello are completely subsidiary. The principal point is that the range of both violin parts stays completely within the first position.

That Haydn was unlikely to have designated these pieces "easy" remains fixed in the mind. Still, even the venerable *Cobbett* lists this work

without questioning its authenticity or that it might be a set of arrangements from other Haydn materials, regulated in technical terms by the editor, one F. May.

In the eighth trio the Andantino and the following Adagio find both the second violin and cello playing monotonous accompaniment patterns. Other situations duplicating this type of writing are, fortunately, few. There are some nice variations in the group and a special credit applies to the Pastorale that begins the eleventh trio. Mark the set as bland Haydn and music strictly for the pleasure of amateurs at home.

- **Trios for Baryton, Viola, and Cello**

For this combination Haydn produced a flood of 125 compositions (also called divertimenti). There was a definite reason for this—a demand for creative product from Haydn's patron, Prince Nikolaus Esterházy. The prince played the baryton, a basslike affair of six strings supplemented by an unfixed number of metal strings sounding in sympathetic vibration.

Haydn followed a general blueprint: three movements and always a Minuet therein, sometimes as the central movement, other times as the finale. All of it is bread-and-butter music, for general and comfortable top-surface playing and listening.

Trios for Piano, Violin, and Cello

There should be no autocracy in the trio medium. But one will find in Haydn's trios that the main role is taken by the piano. The violin is permitted intermittently to hold the stage, but only in restrained form, while the cello steadfastly thickens but does not even enlarge the bass section of the keyboard voice. It is fully the piano's servant — its role can be described as a basso continuo hangover.

We have proof that there were good cellists in the orchestras for which Haydn wrote and which were under his command during his

Esterházy days; so lack of technical abilities by cellists was not the reason for Haydn's reticence in dipping into and expanding the trio's resources. It was rather due to his following the prevailing practice of structuring the piano trio without instrumental equality. The published editions spelled out the matter truthfully. Haydn's piano trios were "Sonates pour le pianoforte avec l'accompagnement du violon et voloncelle." The odd point is that the trios were composed in Haydn's late work period. In place of his constant progressiveness Haydn reverted to being an ultra conservative.

Nonetheless, his trios contain much better music than the usual pigeonhole of "historical significance" would allow. The wealth of ideas and functioning of the organism of full creation make it impossible to shunt them to one side. The listener must bear in mind the lack of string-instrument freedom and resultant misproportion of the trio totality, but he can dwell on the overall thematic and harmonic beauties as a substitute. Briefly, the handling of the medium is false, the ideas true Haydn.

▪ No. 1, in G Minor, Hob. XV:1

The texture of this trio is thicker than is usual in Haydn's trio design. This is due mainly to the liberties granted the violin. In most of the trios, Haydn's restraint (and one continues to wonder at such reticence in handling his trio forces, in contrast to the balanced instrumentation of his quartets and symphonies) brings an unchangeableness to his material. Permitting the piano to turn from a solo voice into partnership with the violin increases the line energy and activates matters. Note the very beginning with a double line of lightly fashioned counterpoint. The give-and-take of voices is resorted to throughout in a duet in which the cello, as usual, merely doubles the bass line of the piano.

A Minuet serves as the middle movement. To obtain the greatest retention of contrastive-color advantages, the violin serves as a solo voice in the Trio portion, with simple and very elementary accompaniment in the piano. A Presto in simple style finishes off matters.

▪ No. 2, in F Major, Hob. XV:2

One of the shortest of Haydn's trios; it is one of the most communicative, notwithstanding a simplicity that eschews the erudite complexities of late classical style. The opening theme is seven measures long. Deftness of transference of the theme from violin to piano, plus the gentility of imitation, makes the first movement almost elfin in quality.

The Minuet, serving as the middle movement, is a wonder of construction. The main body of the dance proceeds to its midpoint in quickening note values — from quarters to eighths to triplets to sixteenths, a ratio, therefore, of 1–2–3–4 per pulse. Then the reversal of this handy method takes place with lesser rigidity. The method of pushing further and further, however, is caught at the midpoint and then relaxed when the Trio section enters. Fully different ideas take place there, with swirling triplets incessantly in the atmosphere, pinpointed by constant string pizzicato. Haydn's imagination produced such *healthy* music!

For the Finale, there is a theme with four variations. The only lack is the participation of the cello. Its actions are in the usual manner of holding the left hand of the piano.

The variations are as delightful as the previous two movements, with the key nonchanging, the theme always to the fore, and the filigrees suave and well mannered.

▪ No. 3, in C Major, Hob. XV:3

There are some points worth noting. Haydn's third piano trio has but two movements. The first begins with a unison introduction in Adagio tempo, followed by the most unruffled and relaxed of allegros. The writing is bare, thin, leisurely, almost sprawling in its rather lengthy proportions, and minus coloristic chromatic pitches. Thirty-two measures pass before one slight F-sharp is used in the C-major key, in order to introduce the dominant key relationship, and thirty-two more measures pass, with only the F-sharp in view, before an additional chromatic pitch is called on.

The second movement is a Rondo, but formed not so much from thematic interplay as from tempo contrast. The main theme is an andante, an adagio intervenes, a return is made to the andante, then an allegro follows, and finally the principal andante again. The flux of tempo asserts the form. To a certain extent, the bareness of the opening movement is continued in the Rondo.

■ **No. 9, in A Major, Hob. XV:9**

Haydn uses the rarer two-movement form for this trio—an Adagio followed by a Vivace. The first of these strives toward freedom of the instruments, if not individually, at least to wean the strings as a team away from the piano, functioning as one color opposed to the keyboard instrument's color.

In the second section, however, a return is made to the more shackled system of binding the cello to the bass line of the piano, and rarely permitting the violin to be a free voice. Nonetheless, the movement is full of musical health, with the usual nonrestraint of Haydn's finales. Concerned with the pithy total of one-octave boundaries of the main theme, Haydn contrasts this thesis with the antithesis of the wide leap, ranging from the spread of a seventh to that of a ninth, and later to the extent of a tenth. Leaps by themselves are not an important element in musical design, but when contrasted to pitch-concentrated themes they are a choice that stimulates.

■ **No. 12, in E Minor, Hob. XV:12**

The opening movement is determined and powered by the minor tonality that lends not only excitement but the force of clinging strength. Major keys are buoyant, to be sure, but the effect of any minor key gives strong support, so to speak, through its shadows. A special touch concerns the conclusion of the first movement. Rather than the standard shift to the major mode, the minor tonality is retained.

The color of pizzicato helps to brighten the usual instrumentation of Haydn's trios—the bland doubling by the cello and scholastic adherence of the violin to the piano. These pizzicato touches relieve and point up matters. The final Presto is in the form of a rondo. Thrice, the main theme returns to follow the dictates of this symmetrical form.

■ **No. 15, in G Major for Piano, Violin (or Flute), and Cello, Hob. XV:15**

■ **No. 16, in D Major for Piano, Violin (or Flute), and Cello, Hob. XV:16**

■ **No. 17, in F Major for Piano, Violin (or Flute), and Cello, Hob. XV:17**

Ever so slightly different from the textural weight of the other Haydn trios when a flute is used instead of a violin. (The designation reads *oder Flöte* ["or Flute"]. In the critical edition edited by H. C. Robbins Landon, published by Doblinger, Nos. 15 and 16 list only the flute. In No. 17 the heading reads: Flute or Violin. This variance makes no difference whatsoever.)

The three works are easygoing Haydn, with no special manipulation of the trio form. Number 17 is in two movements, the remaining two in the customary three-movement plan. One oddity is the last measure of Number 15. The violin (or flute) plays a legato set of three notes. The cello and piano state a chord underneath this, but since its value is equal to only two of the three melodic notes, there is one note in the upper line that sounds *after* the final chord. If the players are exact in prolonging the harmony it will stop short of the final melodic note, thus making a very untidy ending.

- **No. 18, in A Major, Hob. XV:18**

There are strong modulatory colorations in the first movement, Allegro moderato. The other Allegro (movement three) has typical Haydnesque vivaciousness and rhythmic thrust. Listeners will relish the balletic atmosphere of this rondo-designed music . It is captivating. (The final part of this trio became so popular that Haydn made a version for solo piano.) The middle, slow movement offers strong contrast between the home tonality and its tonic minor key.

- **No. 19, in G Minor, Hob. XV:19**

This is a rarity among the trios since it has four movements. It might be argued that the second one, a very short Presto, is merely an extension of the opening movement's double variations (on a theme which has a large sweep that moves just a bit over two octaves). However, Haydn's directive to move immediately *(attacca)* into the Presto is not an indication that this movement is part of the previous section. It is a juxtapositional method to obtain a more dynamic movement relationship.

- **No. 20, in B-flat Major, Hob. XV:20**

The spacing of the piano in the first movement is interesting. Separation of voices is not usual with Haydn; in fact, one must look to the Beethoven piano sonatas for such textural perspective. Together with width of spacing are certain intervallic jumps, adding agility to the music. The slow movement begins with a solo for the piano, to be played by the left hand alone, followed by the unfoldment of varia-

tional simplicity. The one-hand solo returns later, but if pianists use two hands it will not interfere in the slightest with the sound of the music. However, one can only wonder whether Haydn did not have in mind the usual, weaker effect of the left hand alone, and desire this to compress the energy of these passages so that they would be less weighted than would be the case if two hands were used.

The finale is in triple meter, with the theme first handled by the piano, later in the violin without any keyboard aid. With the main pulse occurring at each measure the effect here is lilting, with a "one-in-a-bar" feeling, equivalent to that of a fast minuet.

- **No. 21, in C Major, Hob. XV:21**

A short introduction leads to the first movement proper. The key plan in this trio is such that only a composer of Haydn's caliber could manage not to bore his listeners by reiterating one fundamental tonality framed by one intrinsic rhythm.

The middle movement, variational in concept, takes advantage of the instrumental resources, whereas the previous movement does not. The first theme is given to the violin. On the repetition of the theme (slightly embellished), the piano is used in solo vein. Once again, the keyboard instrument announces the theme with different decoration; this time the strings accompany. The fourth announcement of the theme is in the violin, with courteous byplay on the part of the piano. This plan continues, and it is wondrous to realize that the theme does not change, its treatment not too unshackled, yet freshness is ever present. The final Presto bounces along on a basic rhythm of sixteenth notes.

- **No. 23, in D Minor, Hob. XV:23**

The main characteristic of this trio is the succession of two slow movements. Both of these use variation technique, and the overbalance of similar types of musical language is saved by the fluidity of Haydn's approach. Haydn's variation treatment is far from any dazzling system. The theme stares one constantly in the face. To enlarge upon it modestly, without causing monotony, demands the most subtle methods of changing its frame, its refurbishment, its mode of existence. Haydn is not found wanting. A finale in fast tempo (sounding like a concerto with two string-instrument accompaniment) serves for the third movement.

▪ No. 24, in D Major, Hob. XV:24

This work is judged to be one of the best, if not *the* greatest of all of Haydn's trios. The opening movement is in sonata form, with robust themes almost symphonically displayed. The slow movement is very short, a preamble to the final Allegro, which bears the additional reminder of *ma dolce* ("but sweetly"). The slow movement, therefore, prepares the mood of the outer movement not only by contrast of key (D minor, followed by like-named major) but also by the gentle insistence of its drooping pessimism. This factor of preparation, in order to generate a certain retention of mood and yet smooth the way for the final effort, is not haphazard. The very outline of the last movement's theme furnishes the proof. Whereas the slow movement had a constant down-leafed theme, that of the concluding movement is optimistically lifted in the other direction.

▪ No. 25, in G Major, Hob. XV:25

The finale has achieved the household popularity plane, with resultant transcription of large total. A Rondo all' ongarese (known commonly as the *Gypsy Rondo*) is dance-lighted and most Hungarian in its minor-key episodes, where constantly moving eighths delineate a Haydn "Hungarian Dance." The hurry-scurry is al-ways delightful, and rhythmic simplicity is kept constant. The changes from major to minor are sectional, cut to size, easily managed and identified. (In the first edition, published in London, the finale was marked "in the Gypsies' stile.")

The opening movement is a set of variations, with much filigree work for the soloistic piano voice. The slow movement (in three-part form) sheds its light by the piano's theme with string accompaniment, after which the next section of this simple music is assigned to the violin. As usual, the cello merely supports. The return of the first theme is again given to the piano.

▪ No. 26, in F-sharp Minor, Hob. XV:26

There is a square-toed preciseness apparent in the opening movement. A verticalism surrounds the F-sharp-minor tonality, in spite of the widened territory occupied by arpeggios that spread harmonies out of their laced jackets. While it is axiomatic that keys and rhythmic designs should contrast in the separate movements of a large-scale work, this does not hold fully true in the second movement. (Haydn used the material from the Adagio of his Symphony No. 102 for this slow movement.) The tonality is at the same location, merely shifting from minor to major mode, while the rhythm still shakes hands with that of the preceding movement, being concerned in the majority of instances with similar six units per individual pulse. The finale continues the F-sharp tonality. It is set in minuet formation as to rhythm and lilt, but not constructed in that dance form.

▪ No. 27, in C Major, Hob. XV:27

Haydn concerns himself with the grace note in this work. This embellishment can ignite the stable tonal quality to which it is attached, keep matters alive when sonority is weak, or be used as coloristic embroidery. It is the last that holds true here. The movement is in sonata form, followed by a set of implied variations with the theme plainly audible, and it is quite apparent that the technicalities do not interfere with its simple unfoldment. A very short piano cadenza is an unusual addition to the coda portion. The last movement scampers rondowise in Presto style. In many of Haydn's finales, words cannot capture the happiness expressed. This closing movement is a perfect example of his buoyant cheerfulness as well as his ever-present humor.

- **No. 28, in E Major, Hob. XV:28**

In several parts of this work, Haydn attempted to move from the narrow course of his trio formation. The introduction of string pizzicato is a step in the unloosening of the style. (It is doubled by a pizzicato quality in the piano's bass line.) At least this affords individuality of color, if not of harmony or voice leading. There is, in the first movement, one of the most elaborate development sections in all of the piano trios.

The second movement is a short E-minor Passacaglia, with wholesale elimination, almost at the start, of the two string instruments. It is well to point out how Haydn would move, in many of these trios (as in the last movement of this one), in unassuming fashion from major to minor, without even the semblance of modulatory piquancy. The resultant shift, for example, from E major to the coldness of E minor is not covered in the slightest. Bare white-black color is thus signified.

- **No. 29, in E-flat Major, Hob. XV:29**

Ternary form is used in the first movement. A minor tonality marks the central section, and, in place of straightforward recapitulation Haydn utilizes variational treatment. A substantial coda concludes the movement.

The second movement begins in B major and passes into E-flat major, where it ultimately settles on an unresolved chord to prepare for the immediate entrance of the last movement. Its tempo is a rare one for any composer in the classical school—Andantino ed innocentemente. The speaking quality of the general dynamic setting bears out this *desiderata* of romantic intent.

The last movement is still another Haydn rarity—an Allemande, but when passed through the Haydn wringer its shape changes measurably. Even after its amalgamation as a stylized dance, the tempo of the Allemande was moderate. This speed was retained although the meter was reduced from quadruple in the measure to triple. The tempo is a presto assai. All that remains of the dance is its upbeated beginning. All else is terpsichorean flight.

- **No. 30, in E-flat Major, Hob. XV:30**

What difference a medium means to a composer can be seen in comparing this work, excellent as it is, with the late quartets. (Haydn had composed almost his entire quartet output.) To a degree, the violin and the cello are breaking away from the confines of serving the piano hand and foot. The opening measures, where the violin moves in contrary motion to the piano, are an example of this freer concept; imitations in the last movement, scored solely for the two strings with accompaniment in the piano (an oddity in these trios), are another. But the scoring is a far cry from the maturity and equality of the instruments achieved in the quartets. One must listen to the trios for their general freshness, not expect individuality of color or the engaging interplay of three instruments.

- **No. 31, in E-flat Minor, Hob. XV:31**

This key freezes string sonorities, save in the case of the penultimate step of the scale that forms the tonality. Yet the mood and intensity of a many-flatted key has values not available in the freer and more "open" keys of C, G, F major, and the like. The subtlety of direction should not be overlooked in the theme of the variationally-set first movement. The opening (combined violin and piano) rises. Later, the rhythmic elements of this theme are practically identical, but the motion is in reverse. Such craftsmanship may escape the listener and be apparent only to the reader of the score. One wishes, at such times particularly, that music could always be followed understandingly by the eye, as well as caught by the ear.

The second (and final) movement is as bright as the first movement was dark. In this part of the work, the violin is given a chance to stop shining the shoes of the pianist and act freely, with the opening theme completely in the string instrument's hands. The freeing of the voice of the violin, in fact, continues throughout. Haydn's finale is one of gaiety and motility. However, performance is to be slightly restrained by way of the Allegro ben moderato tempo heading.

While completely balanced instrumentation is lacking, this trio has a maturity in its overall scope that marks it as one of the best and most profound Haydn produced.

■ No. 32, in G Major, Hob. XV:32

A small, two-movement affair, with a slow (Andante) movement and a contrastive quick (Allegro) movement. Unpretentious music, actually an arrangement of a violin sonata. As one writer has noted, "In view of the close relationship between the cello and piano parts, no great changes in the structure of the work were necessary."

■ Trios for Two Violins and Bass (Cello)

- No. 1, in G Major
- No. 2, in D Major
- No. 3, in A Major
- No. 4, in G Major
- No. 5, in B-flat Major
- No. 6, in E-flat Major

While a little bit is tossed to the second violin, these six trios (edited by Karl Marguerre, published by Schott) give creative devotion to the first violin. Still, the music has standard Haydnesque effusiveness.

Only the first and fourth trios have three-movement structure. (The fourth trio has a supplemental movement—Adagio non tanto—published as an appendix within the edition. If used, it would serve as the third movement, followed by a fourth movement Allegro.) The other four trios are in two-movement form, a Moderato formation contrasted with a Tempo di menuetto shape. Two of the latter (numbers 3 and 6) progress with variations.

Though lacking in the special blends of the quartets, these trios have more than plausible values. The major affirmative point is the easy smoothness of the writing; there are no creative risks in any of the six works.

■ Trios for Violin, Viola, and Cello, Op. 53

- No. 1, in G Major
- No. 2, in B-flat Major
- No. 3, in D Major

More of two settings of the same music—in this case by Haydn. These are entertaining and well-wrought versions of the numbers 40 (E-flat major), 41 (A major), and 42 (G major) piano sonatas. All are a feast for the violin with sonorous submission by the viola and cello. What has not been resolved is which came first, the piano sonatas or the string trios. No matter, both are to be enjoyed and have rightful place in the Haydn canon.

- **Trio No. 2 in B-flat Major for Violin, konzertierende Viola, and Cello, Hob. V:8**

The most substantial movement is the opening one, with a set of six variations on an adagio theme. All the action is in the upper voices; the cello repeats its bass line for the theme persistently throughout all the variations. Obviously the key does not change. It clings to the B-flat-major home tonality throughout the two parts of the theme and the matching two sections of each variation (each section repeated and maintaining the same eight- and ten-measure lengths). Clarified substantiation of the variants. Examples: imitation in variation two, prancing triplets in the fourth variation, syncopation in variation five.

Affirmatively crafted forms for the remaining movements—with a Minuetto, and a quick-triggered Presto as the finale.

QUARTETS

- **Quartet in G Major for Flute (or Violin), Violin, Viola, and Guitar (Cello ad lib), Hob. II:1**

Early Haydn (the opus is number 5; this, the fourth work of the set), but super Haydn. The guitar functions in a continuo role, and it is probably for that reason that the cello part was issued by the publishers as an ad libitum support. (There is no mention of this, but what is certain is that the decision was not Haydn's.)

First there is a Vivace filled with voice interplay. Movement two is an Andante moderato that, again, has full instrumental participation. Movement three is a Menuetto; the contrastive Trio places the viola in a featured role. The finale is a Fantasia con variazioni. Each variant is for a solo voice with guitar

accompaniment: in turn, the violin, followed by the viola, the violin again, then the flute, and finally the viola. Thematic repetition (in unison, as when first stated) concludes the Quartet.

String Quartets

Haydn's initial efforts for two violins, viola, and cello were not the sure-fire mature works represented by the late opus numbers. The beginnings were tentative, the conception still embryonic. At first, five movements constituted the quartet structure, and the assorted qualities of divertimento stimulus were much in play. Slowly, but surely, the form became definite. The style of writing at the start was a complete reversal from the democratic partnership of contrapuntalism—being based on a solo-plus-accompaniment plan with lopsided significance. However, before Haydn had finished one-third of his quartet output, the first violin's prima-donna tactics were subordinated. The melodic impulse was assigned to other voices, and the materials became at times hybrid, with harmonic counterpoint edging into what was previously the exclusive field of homophonic dictatorship. After Haydn had composed thirty-six quartets, he remarked, in 1781, that he would compose in an "entirely new special style" ("Ganz neue besondere Art").

The first thirty-six quartets (embracing Opp. 1, 2, 3, 9, 17, and 20) are in a basic structural manner. Then comes the first big move. The string quartet palette is multichromaticized and the form manipulated. There is much invention, a striving for the greatest type of originality and a probing of possibilities. The modern string quartet becomes born of equality of voices, full development of themes. Just one year after Haydn had completed his set of six quartets, Op. 33, Mozart began to write the famous six quartets which he dedicated to the older man. Mozart showers affection on the father of his quartet "children," telling Haydn that he has taught him, Mozart, how to write quartets. From this point on, the two pace each other, each learning from the other. The communal democracy of this friendship has no equal in music.

Every quartet in the mature period of Haydn's work is individually organized, regardless of the fact that a single opus will contain a group of works. It is this responsibility, as it were, to the ideal he was pursuing that also marks Haydn as a superb genius. The constant and pointed differences of the form, the modulatory schemes, and the instrumentation become more and more carefully deployed, and point to the goal Beethoven was to realize later—namely, the fullest possible concentration of musical materials in an equalized musical medium.

The Actual Number of Haydn's String Quartets

It has been found that, through the untrustworthiness and unconscientiousness (lack of conscience applies as well) of his publishers, three of Haydn's string quartets are not string quartets in actuality. Op. 1, No. 5 is in reality a three-movement symphony that includes oboes and horns, and Op. 2, Nos. 3 and 5 are sextets for strings and two horns. Obviously, at this remove, it is apparent that the stripping down of the symphony to only strings makes little or no difference and the work is viable in its "new" four-string setting. A similar situation pertains to the sextets.

Accordingly, in all of the discussions that follow pertaining to the string quartets these three works are included. It is a fairly simple matter regarding any analysis or mention of these three works to realize that the *technical* commentary would not change in relation to a different scoring. The same would pertain to any *general* or *aesthetic* commentary.

But there are other reasons for retaining these "non string quartets." They *can be* played

as quartets, they *have been* played as quartets, and one can be assured they *will be* performed as quartets. Further, there are multitudinous copies of the scores and parts in use throughout the world, in the hands of individuals, performing organizations, libraries, music dealers, etc. And then, there is the permanence of recorded performances.

In *The String Quartet* (Thames and Hudson, 1938) Paul Griffiths closes his discussion of Haydn's early quartets by saying: "The only thing we can be sure of is that for two centuries Haydn's Opp. 1 and 2 have been played and enjoyed as string quartets." To which it can be added that as string quartets they will continue to be played in the years ahead. That said, there is still the matter of the *exact* total of Haydn's string quartets to consider.

Until 1930, it was generally agreed that Haydn's quartets numbered eighty-three. Then musicologists Marion Scott, of England, and Karl Geiringer, of Vienna, independently (and simultaneously) discovered another, making a total eighty-four to date. Nonetheless, the total of eighty-three remained fixed, despite the authenticity of the newly discovered work, which is considered the *first* quartet. It was not disbelief that continued to compute the Haydn quartets at eighty-three; it was merely a matter of tradition.

On the other hand, the *actual* quartets are seventy-six (seventy-seven, of course, with the discovered work), since seven of the total are taken up with *The Seven Last Words of Christ*, Op. 51 (originally composed for orchestra, later scored not only for string quartet but for voices and orchestra). Since Haydn considered these seven works *as* quartets they fall outside the field of transcription and have always been considered as absolutes in the quartet category. However, this writer makes this point: Op. 51 is *actually one work!* In all editions, the score lists each *movement* with a number (similar to a suite which consists of several sections included as one opus), thus Op. 51, No. 1; No. 2;

No. 3; etc. By this system, six works should be eliminated. Accordingly, the true total should read seventy-eight.

The Nicknames of the Haydn String Quartets

There is a vast difference between a composer's pictured intent of a work, manifested by a specific name attached to it or any movement within it, and the sobriquet fastened to works or sections of such by practitioners of music. Fondness for a piece of music will often be displayed by a personal title, which means nothing to anyone other than its manufacturer. But compositions in bulk are frequently an excuse for such nicknames—one speaks of Beethoven's Fifth, not of the Symphony in C minor. (How far this practice has taken root can be illustrated by the late conductor Pierre Monteux, who called his wife Eroica, because she was his third!)

Rarely does one find a nickname describing the technical difficulties of a work of music. On the other hand, a number of works have received their nicknames through historical association or facts of creation: Scarlatti's *Cat's Fugue does* sound like a cat scampering across Domenico's keyboard; Elgar's *Enigma Variations* are baldly true, even though the original title includes the noun, but without the illustrative adjective.

Above all, the auditor must not confuse programmatic intent with the nickname which is often a heavy stone around the neck of the work, causing imageries far from the true essence of the music. Mozart's Quartet in C major, K. 465, is an excellent example. Too often the parenthetical *Dissonance* is added after the title. Mozart's work is no more dissonant (in the general meaning of the term) than it is consonant. That a troublesome passage for the theorists caused the nickname is no excuse for the public to be burdened with a malapropism. If one is careful to distinguish between a nickname and an actual name, no harm is done by use of the former—in fact, it becomes serviceable. It may be difficult to remember that Haydn's sixty-eighth quartet is in D major, and that it is Op. 64, No. 5. On the other hand, the nickname *(Lark)* at least identifies it and may well help to recall its opus and number, as well as key.

Frown as purists may, nicknames have come to stay. Realizing this, it is well to reiterate that the listener must differentiate between a composer's title and a coined caption.

The list that follows is inclusive to such an extent that a few of the names indicated find exceedingly rare usage. They have been included for the sake of completeness.

If the reader knows the nickname, he need only refer to the alphabetical list, which will give him the opus number and the number in the opus (due to observations made regarding the total number of quartets—*see above: The Actual Number of Haydn's String Quartets*—the number the quartet holds in the total quartets is not given), together with an explanation of the cognomen. If the reader knows only the opus number, he can find if there are any nicknames attached to any work in the opus by checking the opus list, where he will be referred to the alphabetical list for details.

Alphabetical List of Nicknames

Apponyi Quartets—(Opp. 71, 74). So named because the six quartets (three in each set) were commissioned by Count Anton Apponyi, a friend of Haydn's and related to the famous Esterházys.

Bagpipe—(Op. 3, No. 3). The Minuet's theme in the first violin, later in the viola, is over a constant drone tone sounding like the Scottish instrument.

Bell—see *Quinten*. (Sequential open fifths sound like bells. This name is rarely used.)

Bird—(Op. 33, No. 3). This name exists for three reasons. First, the Trio of the Minuet, for the two violins alone, makes a sound like two birds chirping and whistling at each other. Second, the first movement has a plethora of reiterative grace notes, very suggestive of the feathered tribe. Third, the final movement contains a persistent cuckoo call.

Churchyard—see *Largo*. (Not in common use. The slow movement, especially, is full of accidentals. These, when sharps, are called *Kreuz* in German, i.e., "crosses." No better visual parallel for these than the cemetery region of many churches.)

Cuckoo—(Op. 1, No. 4). Rather farfetched, due to some semisemblance to a cuckoo call in the opening movement between the violins, imitated at a lower plane by the other two instruments. Actually, the last movement of the *Bird* Quartet deserves this nickname much more.

Donkey—see *Quinten*. (Not too often used—stemming from very wide leaps made in the final movement by the first violin. The name is propitious.)

Dream—(Op. 50, No. 5). Complete mystery surrounds this. All writers merely mention its existence, due to the slow movement, but assign no reason. Tovey stated it was known as *Le Rêve (The Dream)*. The poco Adagio is mainly in block moving chords, and such placid outlines (though there are bustling triplets) might be considered "dream" music.

Dudelsack—see *Bagpipe*. (This word is the German for bagpipe.)

Emperor—see *Kaiser*. (Both mean the same thing, only the languages differ.)

English Quartets—(Op. 74). Not only a rare name, but an incorrect one. One might assume that the title indicates the place of composition, but the truth is that Haydn composed these works just *after* he had returned from his first trip to London in 1793.

Erdödy Quartets—(Op. 76). The six quartets dedicated to Count Joseph Erdödy, who had requested Haydn to compose a set of quartets.

Fantasia—(Op. 3, No. 2). Because of the opening movement, which is not the usual Allegro, but a set of variations—Fantasia con variazioni. A mere identifier, certainly lacking the programmatic affinity of most of the other nicknames.

Farmyard—(Op. 76, No. 1). Manipulated offbeats in the slow movement, high against low voices, together with vigorous unisons and octave leaps give clucky effects. Fortunately, not a commonly used nickname; it is too wide of the mark for proper christening.

Fifths—see *Quinten*. (The latter merely more "musical" in its translation of the former. Since German use preceded English, the *Fifths* designation is less often met with than the *Quinten.*)

Frog—(Op. 50, No. 6). The Finale has a helter-skelter speed and "go" about it, mainly caused by the technical use of violin bariolage. In this form, the same sound is made in fast tempo on two alternate strings. However, the *quality* differs considerably, and it is this scampering and difference of subtle color change on similar sounds that give the partial effect of frog croaks. Since the entire last movement is concerned with this, the name is apt. The pell-mell of the movement has made other names find their way to this quartet, cross-referenced below.

Gli Scherzi Quartets—see Russian Quartets. (An alternate name for the set of quartets because Haydn used scherzos—sometimes called scherzandos—in place of the more usual minuets. Therefore, the cognomen Gli Scherzi [The Scherzos], describes an important development in string quartet formal organization.)

Graveyard—see *Churchyard*. (More explicit in regard to the "crosses" which typed this quartet's Largo, but even less common.)

Great Quartets—see Sun Quartets. (Though better known as the Sun set, the group was known under this name by Haydn's contemporaries, and each one of the six works is "great." The fugal finales, the contrapuntal mastery, so different from the previous quartets Haydn had issued, were certainly something to be labeled, and the superlative nickname is very fitting.)

Grossen Quartets—see Great Quartets. (The German equivalent for the English word.)

Haydn's Visiting Card—see *Unfinished*. (Actually the only quartet that Haydn nicknamed. He called it his "youngest child," and though he hoped to complete it, he was not strong enough to do so. Thus, despairing, he put in place of a final movement a few measures as the subject for a canon, based on the words "Hin ist alle meine Kraft, alt und schwach bin ich" ["Gone is all my strength, old and weak am I"]. This is from his vocal quartet—*Der Greis*. The nickname is explained by the fact that Haydn used this musical quotation as a visiting card for friends!)

Hexen Minuet—see *Quinten*. (Although this nickname deals with a particular movement—the third, a Minuet, in which the Trio section begins very mysteriously and is therefore called *Hexen* ["witches"]—it sometimes identifies the entire quartet.)

Hornpipe—see *Lark*. (A queer appellation, dealing with the final movement, but in which the perpetual-motion kineticism is certainly not in hornpipe style. The *Lark* definition, dealing with the opening movement, is a better name.)

Horseman—see *Rider*. (A synonym—either name is used.)

House on Fire—see *Frog*. (Of infrequent use to define the bustling last movement. If one must employ a nickname, this pushes matters considerably.)

How Do You Do?—(Op. 33, No. 5). Quite often musicians will put words to a theme merely for musical horseplay. Others have used such mnemonics to help them define intricate rhythms, choosing the syllables of words to define the proper stresses and thus apportion lengths correctly. The first four pitches of this quartet are a short scale, with the lengths greatest at the extremes. These there-fore match quite nicely the phrase "How—do—you-do—" (if one can picture the rhythm in speech). Since the phrase rises, the question in the polite remark is manifested as well. European musicians know this nickname much better than their American colleagues.

Joke—(Op. 33, No. 2). An excellent name. At the end of the last movement the theme is broken down, with rests occurring between. Each time, one thinks the movement is over, but no, more follows. Then comes what seems, once and for all, the final cadence, and again we are fooled. When still again the theme occurs, we are sure more will follow with the same trickery of silence. This time *we* are fooled. Haydn has had his joke and a good one it is! First-class musical tomfoolery with no vestiges of low comedy.

Jungfern Quartets—see Russian Quartets. (Farfetched substitute title. The cover of an early edition included the picture of a young girl, similar to the cover art of the "Sun" Quartets, which had the sun as an illustration. Young girl equals *Jungfern*, equals the "Russian" Quartets.)

Kaiser—(Op. 76, No. 3). The slow movement, a set of variations, is on the theme "Gott erhalte Franz den Kaiser" ("God Preserve the Emperor Francis"). Haydn's melody became the Austrian national hymn.

King of Prussia Quartets—(Op. 50). This set of six quartets was dedicated to Frederick William II, king of Prussia, the monarch to whom Mozart dedicated three quartets. However, it is more usual when mentioning the King of Prussia Quartets to mean the Mozart triplet, rather than the Haydn sextuplet.

La Chasse—(Op. 1, No. 1). The opening theme sounds like a call to the hunt; the nickname is adequate.

Largo—(Op. 76, No. 5). The slow movement bears this tempo. Its superb beauties are the high mark of the four-movement work, and it is considered one of the peaks of the Haydn quartet literature.

Lark—(Op. 64, No. 5). Achieved its baptism from the opening phrase of the first violin, which, entering after introductory material of seven measures of simple antiphony, makes a graceful sweep to a high note which it then embroiders with appendages, ending with a distinctive trill. Not an imitation of a lark by any means—merely suggestive.

Lobkowitz Quartets—(Op. 77). The name identifies the person who commissioned the music, Prince Franz Joseph Lobkowitz.

Maiden Quartets—see Jungfern Quartets. (The English equivalent for the German word.)

Prussian Quartets—see King of Prussia Quartets. (A shortened identification.)

Quinten—(Op. 76, No. 2). Two groups of falling intervallic fifths set the style for the opening movement, and such fifths trademark the entire movement. "Fifths" is the translation of *Quinten*.

Railwayman—(Op. 64, No. 6). This name is rather forced. Only the last five measures of the first movement are concerned. These move forward in increasing rhythmic and dynamic stride; hardly, without overly vivid imagery, suggestive of a train moving into speed with attendant noise.

Razor—(Op. 55, No. 2). Haydn was shaving when visited by one John Bland, a publisher. The razor was blunt, causing the composer to exclaim that for a good razor he would exchange his best quartet. The publisher brought Haydn his sharp and excellent razors, and Haydn, in turn, gave him this quartet. (Such barter principles do not apply today in the field of music.)

Recitative—(Op. 17, No. 5). The slow movement is sprinkled with recitatives, in the parlando style of this technique, with chordal rejoinders. A true-to-the-point-and-mark nickname.

Rider—(Op. 74, No. 3). Beginning and ending movements were the cause of this cognomen. The opening moves forward like a "Tempo di horse-trot" stimulated with grace notes. The

rhythms of the last movement suggest the ups and downs of riding in the saddle.

Row in Venice—(Op. 20, No. 4). A complete mystery, and to a degree confused with the next nickname *(see below)*. The only analogy is that drawn from an occasional full unison in the last movement, followed by some very odd diminished fourths in the first violin alone. One can conjure a heated statement, followed by slight retort in the comparatives of the unison and slight chord, in *forte* and *piano* respectively. Best forgotten, and best unused.

Row in Vienna—see *Frog; House on Fire*. (Confusing *[see above]*, and also better typified, if it must be, by the *Frog* designation. The vigor of the repeated pitches suggests a brawl to a degree, but *only* to a degree.)

Russian Quartets—(Op. 33). Simple and correct. These six works were dedicated to Grand Duke Paul of Russia.

Serenade—(Op. 3, No. 5). The slow movement has become world famous, with accompanying hackneyed performances in every possible transcribed version. The pizzicato accompaniment of this section (quasi guitar) fastened the serenade term on this quartet, though the movement is labeled simply Andante cantabile.

Stormwind—(Op. 55, No. 3). Due to the many chromatic passages, but especially the whirling and presto tempo scales of the last movement. One of the rarely used nicknames.

Sun Quartets—(Op. 20). The publisher's trademark on the original edition was a picture of the sun. Not to be confused with the *Sunrise* Quartet. The sun itself shines through these remarkable works, nickname or not.

Sunrise—(Op. 76, No. 4). (Op. 76 contains more nicknames, it will be observed, than any other set grouped under one opus number.) The opening theme of this quartet, with its beautiful ascent in soft dynamic, has all the potency of the beginning of a clear day. The person who coined this nickname deserves congratulations.

Tost Quartets—(Opp. 54, 55, 64). An informative identification. All twelve quartets in these three sets were dedicated to Johann Tost, a Viennese merchant and violinist.

Unfinished—(Op. 103). Because Haydn's last quartet is exactly that; only two movements exist.

Virgin Quartets—see Jungfern Quartets. (Another translation for the German word *Jungfern*. Not worth using, but at times one does run across this mid-Victorian designation.)

Wait Till the Clouds Roll By—(Op. 77, No. 2). Of use only in England. One theme has a supposed resemblance to an English ditty of the same name.

- **Op. 1, No. 1**—see *La Chasse*
- **Op. 1, No. 4**—see *Cuckoo*
- **Op. 3, No. 2**—see *Fantasia*
- **Op. 3, No. 3**—see *Bagpipe; Dudelsack*
- **Op. 3, No. 5**—see *Serenade*
- **Op. 17, No. 5**—see *Recitative*
- **Op. 20 (all)**—see Great Quartets; Grossen Quartets; Sun Quartets
- **Op. 20, No. 4**—see *Row in Venice*
- **Op. 33 (all)**—see Gli Scherzi Quartets; Jungfern Quartets; Maiden Quartets; Russian Quartets; Virgin Quartets
- **Op. 33, No. 2**—see *Joke*
- **Op. 33, No. 3**—see *Bird*
- **Op. 33, No. 5**—see *How Do You Do?*
- **Op. 50 (all)**—see King of Prussia Quartets; Prussian Quartets
- **Op. 50, No. 5**—see *Dream*
- **Op. 50, No. 6**—see *Frog; House on Fire; Row in Vienna*
- **Op. 54 (all)**—see Tost Quartets
- **Op. 55 (all)**—see Tost Quartets
- **Op. 55, No. 2**—see *Razor*
- **Op. 55, No. 3**—see *Stormwind*
- **Op. 64 (all)**—see Tost Quartets
- **Op. 64, No. 5**—see *Hornpipe; Lark*
- **Op. 64, No. 6**—see *Railwayman*
- **Op. 71 (all)**—see Apponyi Quartets
- **Op. 74 (all)**—see Apponyi Quartets;

English Quartets
- **Op. 74, No. 3**—see *Horseman; Rider*
- **Op. 76 (all)**—see Erdödy Quartets
- **Op. 76, No. 1**—see *Farmyard*
- **Op. 76, No. 2**—see *Bell; Donkey; Fifths; Hexen Minuet; Quinten*
- **Op. 76, No. 3**—see *Emperor; Kaiser*
- **Op. 76, No. 4**—see *Sunrise*
- **Op. 76, No. 5**—see *Churchyard; Graveyard; Largo*
- **Op. 77 (all)**—see Lobkowitz Quartets
- **Op. 77, No. 2**—see *Wait Till the Clouds Roll By*
- **Op. 103**—see *Haydn's Visiting Card; Unfinished*

- **String Quartet in E-flat Major, Op. 0**

When this quartet was discovered through the research of Marion Scott and Karl Geiringer it was published as Op. 1, No. 1, confusing it with the long published Op. 1, No. 1. In order to identify this quartet properly (and retain old identities) there has been common agreement to call it Op. 0. For the first publication of the work, copies are still available and others are in use, but these do not indicate the Op. 0. The new critical edition, under the editorship of H.C. Robbins Landon (published by Doblinger), identifies it "officially" as Op. 0. In the Hoboken catalogue there is complete clarification: Op. 0 is Hob. II:6; the Op. 1, No. 1 quartet is listed as Hob. III:1.

The quartet is in the usual five movements that mark Haydn's first efforts in string quartet style. He is too close to the woods of divertimento practice and the like to see the freed bloom of the real quartet form. Twelve quartets (in addition to this work) were to be written before four movements would mark the commencement of the maturing of quartet writing. The opening Presto is single-themed. Two Minuets surround the third movement in slow tempo. While moves are made toward the slightest change of key, only the slow movement shifts out of the tonic E-flat major, and then just a little to the side of it—to B-flat. Accompaniment figures are simple; youthful crudities are there for the keen ear, but the musical air is far from stale. It *is* Haydn in gay, unhampered youth.

String Quartets, Op. 1

The six quartets in this group are all (save the fifth) in five movements. The overall form is based on a design of two outer fast movements, two Minuets, and in the center, the slow movement. Haydn is cutting his eyeteeth on a new form. It is not to be wondered, therefore, that the first works would be similar to general utility music of the time, divertimentos, cassations, and serenades, which consist of assorted movements bound under one title, with no regard for distinctions. To the listener, the relationship is that the quartet (in its most mature, classically ordered sense) is a four-movement work, balanced by key, modulatory planes, and rates of speed; whereas divertimentos et al., enjoy no such *fundamental* stability. Haydn had to feel and find his way. Already the sprawling number of movements found in many divertimentos and related forms was being reduced to five.

▪ No. 1, in B-flat Major

The twice-used opening horn call marks the first nickname to be encountered in the quartets—*La Chasse (alla caccia)*, i.e., "in the hunting style." The lower voices proceed hand in hand; there is no four-part freedom. Both Minuets work on the principle of splitting the quartet into equal sets of two instruments each—already a marked advance in texture, if not in kneading the form's dough. This system was not to be dropped by Haydn. One watches for full-voiced freedom in vain; but then (at least) one does not have direct simplicity and primitiveness of melody-plus-accompaniment save

in the slow movement, which is sung by the first violin with undiluted accompaniment of straitlaced sixteenths.

▪ No. 2, in E-flat Major

The opening theme is a motive, repeated twice then stretched into cadential repose. While Beethoven was to take such motival implication and prove his musical argument, Haydn is still a freshman in the school of quartet composition—his motive stays alive through repetition at different levels and occasional handouts to the second violin and viola. The two Minuets are in the usual early style, but it is well worth noting the smatterings of imitation. The slow movement moves in the melody-accompaniment realm.

There is too much talk, of course, too much belaboring the point that the early quartets are all first violin versus the other three voices. In the great majority, this holds true, but there is this observable exception: In the last movement, in two places, the first violin serves (by pedal rhythm) the syncopated importance of the second violin and viola. It is elementary yet neatly charming.

▪ No. 3, in D Major

The first alteration in Haydn's quartet structural plans shows in this work. The first and third movements change places; the slow movement begins matters and the fast opening (Presto) is shifted to the middle. Haydn's choice of commencing the quartet with a slow movement is a transfer of the *sonata da chiesa* format, with its slow–fast–slow–fast order of movements.

In the slow movement the emphasis is less on the solo violin and more on a two-violin texture (in the form of instrumental dialogue). The other movements follow the general simple plan, save that there is more freedom in the cello voice, which is permitted occasionally to rove the field with the second violin in duet fashion.

▪ No. 4, in G Major

This work is square-cut, made from the same cloth as the other early quartets. Key shifts are held in rigid place, yet (as in the first of the two usual Minuets) the moving from the major mode to the minor, or the reverse on the same tonic (here it is G major to minor) is as effective as its use in the most mature quartets. The Adagio, in somewhat old-fashioned clothes, stems directly from the days of figured bass, with much of it directed from simple moving eighth notes in the lower two voices, above which the ornamental designs of the cantabile music move on and around. Reiteratively flipped, two-tone figures in the opening movement, suggestive of a cuckoo call, have at times identified this quartet with such a cognomen.

▪ No. 5, in B-flat Major

Haydn scholars have proven that this was actually a symphony (including oboes and horns with strings), not a quartet. Yet when the first authoritative edition was published (with Haydn's approval), this work appeared under the indicated opus and number. Accordingly, we can only accept Haydn's verdict that he wished it to be considered a quartet. It differs rather acutely from the others in the set, containing but three movements.

Much of the writing, especially in the outer fast movements, is on a two-voice basis, each voice reinforced by its closest partner (violins against viola-cello). What is interesting in the slow, middle movement is the attention to the dynamic plan. The movement divides itself in two—the first section arrives at the dominant of the home key, the second begins at that point and ends, as expected, at the tonic. But each part stems from a *piano dolce*, and, with only

the slightest interruption toward the end, increases into a *mezzoforte* and then a culminating *forte*. That the dynamic scheme is heard twice does not remove the fact that the plan is neatly executed. To hold interest, the symmetry is smashed by disproportionate lengths of the two sections.

▪ No. 6, in C Major

A simple initial movement is succeeded by the interesting first Minuet. The early quartets are triolike in their makeup—the violins underpinned by the bass line of viola-cello. Despite the characteristic of homophony, there is still the residue of the basso continuo style, in that the four voices are not free unto themselves. But in this movement (counting all repeats of sections) the viola is the leading voice *ten times*—above the second violin when the first is silent, and even above the latter when it is used. Future technical behavior is being mirrored in advance.

The slow movement is also a new departure. For the first time, Haydn resorts to two timbres—the first violin is muted, and the remaining instruments are contrasted in weight by nonuse of mutes and deployed in color by playing pizzicato throughout. These techniques are simple but fresh, and were novel at the time they were utilized.

String Quartets, Op. 2

Historians have not been able to ascertain exactly when these were written in relation to the first set of six quartets. It is commonly understood, however, that they stem practically from the same period of composition. The form is still the five-movement blueprint. The order of the movements, with one exception, is still the same as the Op. 1 group. But certain developments, plus a generally broader viewpoint, clearly indicate that the experience of composing the six Op. 1 quartets had benefitted Haydn.

The proof is the growth of technique displayed in the six Op. 2 quartets.

▪ No. 1, in A Major

The black-white of dynamic difference, from *forte* to an abrupt *piano*, is not only at the start of the work but is used in several key places of the first movement, and also is the complete axiom of the Trio to the first Minuet. The slow movement again backs into the groove of melody being simply accompanied. In fact, the Trios to the two Minuets are the most interesting and worthy of attention. The second one uses the neatness of plucked strings for delicate accompaniment, and then melodically. (Did Beethoven receive "prenatal" creative influence from such use—as in his Op. 74 quartet?)

▪ No. 2, in E Major

After the ordinary Allegro opening, the distinction of the first Minuet must be noted. The first portion of the Trio gives most of the work to the first violin, as might be expected. (In the early quartets, so often the Trio sections offer the most interesting sidelights on the control and emergence of the form in Haydn's hands. This is rather curious, for one would expect new ideas to be tried in the larger areas of the other movements.) When the last eight measures occur (before the return to the Minuet proper), the cello is given this same solo line, with slight changes of pitch location. This duologue is certainly didactic. Haydn wanted to pull the instruments out of their rooted positions.

The slow movement is formed from triple-voiced accompaniment against the first violin, which vocalizes in true Italian style. The accompaniment, however, finds the second violin leading the group so that there are almost duo propensities to the movement's formation. The first violin is soloistic, even to the use of double stops.

Bariolage, a form of obtaining one sound with the finger and then immediately repeating the sound by playing on the adjoining open string, is used in the second Trio section. However, this effect is given to the second violin, in the less common form of alternating the sounds on two adjoining strings, neither of which is open. The technique is more difficult—the effect colorful. In contrast, there is a most primitive Trio. A nicety in the last movement is the wide-spread legato arpeggio leaps of the first violin. The torn-from-their-sockets intervals can be thought of as twelve-tone technique in its incubation period.

▪ No. 3, in E-flat Major *(Originally a sextet for strings and two horns)*

Horn calls are scattered through the first movement (one wonders that no one has christened this the *Horn* Quartet). The section has considerable vitality. The Trio of the first of the two Minuets displays the dynamic *forte-piano* so characteristic of Beethoven in his "looking-over-the-cliff" style.

Movements three and four, especially the latter, show a change in the Haydn formal manner if not the style itself. The slow movement requires mutes. Such a veiling of timbre creates a sweetness that nonmuted strings can never achieve. The constraint of muted string tone can be a problem; but when put to use in forming an Adagio song, with the most gentle accompaniment, as in this instance, tenderness removes any question of dull effect. The second Minuet begins with the impression that something will happen—and well it does! Full pizzicato alternates with full arco. A great deal of the Trio is formed from the light-dramatic of the unison. Then follow three variations, a rather remarkable idea, and oddly enough never duplicated in any of the other quartets. The variants are free, in their pitch manipulation, number of measures (though only in one instance is a change made from the usual minuet eight-measure pattern), and color. The first variation features the viola, and, in the last, equal attention is given viola and cello against the two violins. The variations provide a life line that extends this movement to larger proportions than any of the others. The finale that follows is almost anticlimactic in its brevity and simplicity.

▪ No. 4, in F Major

The highlight in this quartet is the use of a minor-keyed slow movement. Haydn had not as yet dipped into the darker-dyed minor keys for the principal tonality of his quartets. This was to come later. But the effect of this mournful movement, in relation to the spirit of the two preceding ones, provides dramatic contrast. Other bits of the developing composer come through the regularity of approach. In the first movement, key shifts are more adroit than previously. The art of syncopation—an excellent means of engendering drive, aliveness, and excited sensibility—is used in the last movement.

▪ No. 5, in D Major *(Originally a sextet for strings and two horns)*

Real sonata form, with the opposition of two themes—in style, key, and characteristics—was not used by Haydn until later in his quartet output. But one can already detect this basis in musical structure in the first movement. It is rather bold to insert a direct cancellation of the tempo and paste in, as it were, an Adagio (of only three measures) in the coursed plunge of a Presto. But the inference is clear that relationships must be conveyed by differences.

The slow movement's tempo may cause some misunderstanding, not to mention controversy, on the part of the performers themselves. It reads, "Largo. Cantabile alla breve." ("Slowly and stately, in singing style, with two pulses per measure" is the literal translation.)

But while the first portion is easily understood, the latter part seems to cancel the first and requires interpretation. The complete meaning of alla breve signifies there are four beats in a measure, with two main pulsations. In a movement where the temporal setting is slow-going, two principal pulses within a total of four might well quicken matters. Therefore, what Haydn has done is to post a warning that the tempo is *not faster*, but that the strongest stresses are not equally distributed over the four beats but spaced in two. The finale has the beginnings of what would later become full grown in the final movement of the *Lark* (Op. 64, No. 5) Quartet.

▪ No. 6, in B-flat Major

This is similar to the single quartet (No. 3) of the Op. 1 series that shifted the order of the movements so that the slow movement is placed first, with two fast movements splicing two Minuets. The slow movement does not regulate itself in the usual melody-plus-accompaniment style. Instead, there are four variations of the Adagio theme. These are more advanced than one would expect in early quartet writing, with considerable melodic ornamentation. The rest of the work runs the course of the straight and narrow path that Haydn plotted in the early quartets.

A Preliminary Note Regarding Haydn's String Quartets, Op. 3

In 1964 the Haydn scholar H. C. Robbins Landon together with Alan Tyson presented evidence that, in their opinion, proved that the Op. 3 quartets were not by Haydn. It was their view that the six quartets were the work of Romanus Hofstetter (1742–1815), a German cleric and composer. Other Haydn experts have turned in a split decision—some agree with the Landon-Tyson theory, others do not. As long as the issue remains unresolved, the six works in Op. 3 can stay in the Haydn catalogue.

String Quartets, Op. 3

In 1761, Haydn joined the service of Prince Paul Anton Esterházy. Less than a year later, Paul Anton died and his brother Nikolaus took over. There is not space here to discuss in full the problems that beset a court musician, and the patronage system in general. Suffice to say, however, that the golden years of Haydn's creative work were at the Esterházy estate. Composing large amounts of music to order, his output was anything but the mundane results of such a stimulus. The Op. 3 set of six quartets have no precise date in historical catalogues, but it is believed that they belong to the period soon after Haydn took up his work with the Esterházy family.

These quartets are much different from the previous two sets. Haydn's quartet approach is now not quite so formal. The old influences and early ideas are being redigested; there is definite experimentation, as one will realize in surveying the six works. Full maturity is still not in the picture, but the future horizon is certainly becoming much clearer.

▪ No. 1, in E Major

The five-movement thought evaporates in the first quartet of the set. The quintuple set of movements is now lost forever.

But if five movements are not called for, the meat surrounding the formal bones is of the same taste. The opening movement is still duoset, with the violins quite often opposed to the two lower voices. The Minuet has the color of pizzicato splotches to help matters. The slow section is baldly concerned with a solo setting over two-ply accompaniment. Both of the violins are muted, permitting a graceful song to be sweetened by the nonstop-serenade-style pizzicato of the lower two instruments. The movement pictures charm and nice manners, but there is a static quality that cannot be overlooked. The last movement shows the

maturing viewpoint. It ends in a *pianissimo* dynamic. The *music* is now more important than the fulfilling of a form.

▪ No. 2, in C Major

Three movements mark this quartet as exceptional, especially since the speed rate is ever-increasing, leading from an Andante to the dance lilt of a Minuet and the usual, final fast-paced section. There are five variations on the first movement's theme. No key shifts are made, and the variants are squared properly. The fourth variation is amusing in its handling of the viola, which is bounced through various gamuts. The resultant merry quality indicates that the instruments of Haydn's string quartet would not have to wait too long before being freed of first-violin captivity. The finale is a beauty of derring-do, headlong pace, and merry-all-get-out. There is no need to explain such; one need only move along with the tide. But just when all is to end well, the work is lengthened by an episode that cannot escape attention. It is rather chordal—a chorale type in speedy tempo. This makes the movement over-long, but does not interfere with the pace itself.

▪ No. 3, in G Major

The bagpipe drone at the beginning of the Minuet (there is now only one minuet in any quartet) achieves distinction by accounting for the nickname of this quartet (*Bagpipe* or *Dudelsack*). The style is usual—two outer fast movements, inside of which are the slow and dance parts.

Motival exploitation (in the Haydn repetitive sense, not the Beethoven developed method) is mainly the core of the first movement. The exploitation of the first violin is carried throughout the slow movement, an Arioso that is ornamented with the middle voices only at cadential points. The last movement also depends on the first violin's energetic fiddling of a stimulating theme which includes kinetic grouplets of sixteenth notes.

▪ No. 4, in B-flat Major

This is an odd work in the Haydn catalogue of quartets. Since the four-movement plan was adopted in the earlier works of the set, it is rather surprising to find an example that is in two movements (plus two Adagio fractions). Most writers profess to be mystified by this quartet. The keys are not rounded out in the sense that a four-movement work will bring back eventually the tonality of the opening, no matter what deviations occur en route. If one listens to this work as a quartet of short length— as a throwback to earlier design with later techniques—there is no mystery, there is only the situation of an Allegro and a Presto! Why not? It is strange, of course, to see the steady progress of Haydn's quartet form interrupted by such a "crippled" work, but the speculation that perhaps two movements were lost, or that a publisher merely grouped two incidental and isolated pieces together, does *not* explain this music's nonformality. Haydn did sanction its publication in the complete quartets. We can only follow his approval and not consider this work as related to the four-movement quartets, in which case something is amiss, but as his attempt to compress the form, in which case naught is amiss. In its particular way this quartet is just as complete in its balance as any of the quartets that were to follow.

The first movement uses the contrast of a light theme, having one-voice accompaniment, with that of the full-blown insistence of a unison. Otherwise, it is in the usual opening-movement style of Haydn's quartets. The final movement is in Presto tempo, which twice is bordered with a three-measure Adagio. Essentially then, the slow movement that is presumably lacking *is* present. It merely has been telescoped, forming in its concentration just as much relief of pace as when it occupies the space of a complete movement.

▪ No. 5, in F Major

This composition is solidly in the quartet repertoire, whereas the prior works and those to follow (until Op. 20) are exceptions to this fact. The slow movement, an Andante cantabile, has the unauthorized (but acceptable) title of Serenade, and has been the trial and tribulation of young tyros on every instrument, including the mouth harmonica. The usual method of Haydn in stating blatant soloism is used. The principal violin is muted, and is fully accompanied by pizzicato throughout. The nice melody makes one forget that this is not true quartet style, but style must take secondary place to beauty.

In the 1600s, it was the custom in dance movements to have the Trio section actually played by three instrumentalists. No matter what the number of instruments, three would be used in order to confirm the balance and differences of the contrasting portions of the dance. In the Minuetto, Haydn draws on this method. The viola serves nicely by silence while the first violin states the theme; the second violin, the accompaniment, and the cello binds with pizzicato. The last movement foreshadows the Beethoven scherzo. It is not that form as yet, but the scherzando marking shows that Haydn did not want yawns from his audience.

▪ No. 6, in A Major

This quartet is the weakest of the half dozen in the Op. 3 group. But there is little Haydn music that does not have some compensatory features. The Minuet, with alternate color and textural applications of pizzicato and arco, should be given attention, as well as the final movement which (as in the previous quartet of the set) is a Scherzando. The whimsy reaches to the final measures, which are in decreasingly soft disposition. Dynamic endings that are subdued can either be ultradramatic or, with fanciful and lightly free thoughts, cause the smile of approval and pleasure. Such is the case with this final movement.

String Quartets, Op. 9

One need not belabor the fact that each new Haydn opus brought advance. This set of six quartets shows more progress in relation to the Op. 3 group than that half dozen did in relation to the twelve works in Opp. 2 and 1. Haydn was very nearly at the halfway mark of his life. These quartets were composed in 1769, when he was thirty-seven. Forty years of activity remained—and what years they were to be! The four-movement plan was now set securely; the first violin remains dominating, but the other voices are enriched with more liberties permitted them. A purer net quality hovers over the six works. Haydn himself was quite conscious of this. He even requested his publisher to discard the previous eighteen works and list these as his first quartets.

▪ No. 1, in C Major

The more ornamental a piece of music, the more the tempo must be reduced to take care of the embroidery factor which spreads itself over and around the beats per measure, and can therefore only be heard distinctly if the tempo permits unfoldment. The Moderato of the first movement exemplifies this. Save for one section, which is bald accompaniment, the entire movement is free of primitive writing. The Minuet ends quietly, as if fed on the minor key drabness of the contrasting Trio. Haydn is working slowly but surely toward the emotional stress of maturity, which paradoxically clarifies one's work, yet makes it more stormy. In the light-scaled last movement the first violin, contrary to conditions in the earlier quartets, is not greedy.

▪ No. 2, in E-flat Major

Once again a Moderato is used to obtain tempo freedom for projection of a more ornate style. It should be observed how scale lines help develop this movement. After the regularity of the Minuet, the slow movement offers still another facet of new technique. The opening Adagio is introductory, and amazingly sets forth the technique that the "jazz boys" of the 1930s, and thereafter, were to use for many of their specially arranged endings. It begins in pyramidal fashion, the four instruments entering one after the other in bass-to-soprano fashion. The following section is the movement proper, a solo message sealed with simple accompaniment in the other three voices. Toward the end, a fermata on a trill can be used for an extemporary cadenza or not. The score is not explicit, but if one hears a cadenza no surprise should be evinced. If not (and it is just as well for purposes of style), the music can go forward to the very few remaining measures. As to the inclusion of a cadenza, it is hardly stylistically fitting, especially since there is a simple swirling arpeggiated imitation of such flourish earlier. The remaining feature is that the last movement is not the usual Presto, but a much more regulated-in-speed Allegretto in which spicy syncopations are admirably stated and handled.

▪ No. 3, in G Major

The slow movement contains two unfilled measures, suitable for cadenza interpolation. Today, one questions this hiatus. It may have been customary, it may well have been in style for its day, but a 20th-century cadenza is an artifice we can do well without. It is a matter for thought.

Brilliance surrounds the first movement. The first violin uses double-string work, ornate trills, grace-noted leaps, scales, and arpeggios. (The violinists of Haydn's day must have been good technicians.) Even the cello has one try at matters. But all this does not interfere with subduing or compressing the lower voices. The Minuet's Trio has cross accents, a matter to be later exploited by Haydn. His brand of fun is displayed in the final portion of the work. This exemplifies musical sly wit in the use of the movement's opening motive and is new coinage in quartet literature. Haydn's joke book never repeated any stale stories.

▪ No. 4, in D Minor

After twenty-one quartets, Haydn uses a principal minor key for the first time. And with a decided vengeance. The later gradational shift so that minor-based pieces would turn into optimistically carved major keys is not present as yet. The D-minor tonality is used for every movement save the slow one, which is in the brighter B-flat major. Only the bald change to D major in the Trio of the Minuet deviates from this norm. The Trio is frugally scored and voiced with only two instruments being used— the first violin in double stops throughout, with the second violin furnishing the bass.

Motival manipulation (the expertness of which is the key point of classical development sections in large works) is quite apparent in the outer fast movements. The slow movement has again the "short-life-ahead" of the ad libitum cadenza, indicated by the fermata over the trill, plus the tonic chord in the second inversion. Classical procedure generally approached a soloist's cadenza with this semifinal chord, which placement indicates the tonic, yet has inflections of the dominant. Such instability is then brought home to harmonic repose by the cadenza itself.

▪ No. 5, in B-flat Major

A set of variations forms the opening movement in place of a usual sonata in allegro or moderato speed. But, note well, the second of these variants (there are four in all) is assigned to the three lower instruments.

In dance forms, the placement of the stresses must, of necessity, bring to the fore the specific nature of the dance involved. In the minuet, the most important is the gracefulness of the upbeat, which is then followed by the normal stress of the first beat in the following measure. In this Minuet, attention to the upbeat is repulsed and dislocated by transference to first beats. No special stress is used, rather the subtle one of weight by action. Most of the first beats are grouplets propelled to a slightly held tone, with such fall (adding accentuated force by downward tonal gravity) helping to form a real departure from the old-style Minuet.

Both the slow and last movements are usual Haydn, with the latter ending in surprise *piano* quality. Mozart was not looking the other way when such plans were exposed—note his use of this very subtle dramatic method.

▪ No. 6, in A Major

Repetitive sounds at the same pitch level are difficult items in forming a theme. Unless such are used in a pithy motive, the similarity can well destroy any essential value. In the opening theme of the first movement, Haydn's method is a prime example of how to accomplish the reiterated sound method without starching it into insensibility. An accompanying arched pitch placement works hand in hand with it, as the top portions move to F-sharp, then to A, then back to F-sharp; meanwhile, the fifth of the key repeats itself constantly. The first movement marks a move toward the mature sonata form, with distinctness of themes related yet opposed, designing the necessary drama and requisite contrast. A subsidiary theme will be recognized by its barcarolle-like contour. To this, a third—an elaboration of the repetitional idea—adds further contrast. These three items are the arguments for the first movement.

The systematic regard, in the slow movement, for triplets in calculated progression is matched with the insistence in the final movement of sixteenth notes in speedy Allegro. Dancing about on the prongs of a scale, the whole last movement is a tossed-off musical bonbon with little to chew on. One merely relaxes.

String Quartets, Op. 17

The six quartets in this opus continue the objective of expanding not only the form itself, but the use of the instruments concerned. Advances are made; the quartets are larger in scale, the dramatic becomes more implicit. There is no doubting that Haydn's constancy in concentrating so many of his creative hours on the composition of quartets will bring success—it is as if he persevered in his quartet duty unstintingly.

The original manuscript of this quartet set shows Haydn the spiritual keeper and the devout believer. Above each quartet is written: In Nomine Domini. At the end of the manuscript there appears: Laus Deo et B(eatae) V(irgini) M(ariae) et om(nibus) S(anctis).

▪ No. 1, in E Major

Everywhere in his music there are touches showing Haydn's originality, his creativeness, and his growth to the stature of one of the world's greatest composers. For example: the second half of the first movement where the cello *announces* what was previously stated by the first violin. This was rare in music written in 1771, the year these quartets were composed. Further, the acute sense of perspective in the unfolding of the Minuet theme, which arches its back up a fifth, then an octave, and finally a large-spaced tenth, followed by smaller spans in the second half of the theme, with imitation in the second section of this dance movement. Or (to cite just a few of the master strokes), the weighted proportions as they are

planned at the start of the final movement— first the two violins, then the addition of the viola, finally the cadential stamp with all four instruments. Furthermore, the final twenty-three measures completely shrouded in soft dynamic.

▪ No. 2, in F Major

Brilliance marks the first and final movements, with plentiful octave leaps in the former for the principal violin. The shift to the relative minor, for Trio purposes in the Minuet, advances a method of coloring that clings to the work, acutely emphasized by Haydn's specific directions. It will be observed that the intensity shifts rather constantly in the Adagio. Color, in terms of the extremes of instrumental exploitation, was not for the scope of classicism (aside from a use made of such device in Beethoven's Quartet in C-sharp minor, Op. 131). It remained for the advanced order of thought of the impressionists and their followers to dip rigorously into the well of orchestral devices (not orchestral sonorities—the two are different) and frame their chamber music works with the silver, gold, steel, and bronze of the wood tappings, the hissings, and the other accouterments selected by Richard Strauss and then used by Ravel, Stravinsky, and others. In the slow movement, Haydn directs the overall dynamic to be a *mezza voce*, a speaking, mid-conversational voice; later, the instruction is *sopra una corda* (on one string), which in this case is the G or D string, the fatter-toned of the violin's four. This method continues throughout with a shifting digestion of color principles that is a diet on which the Adagio lives.

▪ No. 3, in E-flat Major

Variations form the first movement, and these are rather standard, the figurations being first tripleted and later set in quadruple form. As is so often the case in the earlier Haydn quartets, the Trio of the Minuet offers interest a little out of the ordinary; here the second violin has its turn in the sun. After the simple Adagio, still influenced by first-violin dictatorship, it is the finale that offers the most innate and beautiful calculations. Haydn resorts to a contrapuntal method of imitation far more than in any previous quartet he had composed.

▪ No. 4, in C Minor

The minor key, rare in Haydn's quartets, brings to this work an ardency of emotional content. The opening theme is formed from the home key's tonic triad, a device common to classical music, but there is no substitute for its directness. The ending anticipates Beethoven's similar use, with the direction *mancando* (dying off, failing). This is not merely a *decrescendo* but a subsidence of the timbre's vitality plus decrease of dynamic strength. Haydn anticipates the methods of the late romanticists in this fashion.

Syncopations play a part in linking the Trio to the Minuet, while the finale is most original. The violin is extremely brilliant, using entire series of double stops that approach concerto demeanor. In style, the music is early Beethoven; it also pertains to Beethoven's middle period of work in its minor-key intensity—if one can explain matters in terms of time reversal, rather than always relating a later work to the past.

▪ No. 5, in G Major

The fifth quartet of the Op. 17 set is most often performed in relation to the others. One can understand the nickname *(Recitative)* when listening to the slow movement, which, according to some, was a favorite of the great violinist Joachim. The parlando, in which the first violinist exchanges speech with the combined lower three instruments, is absolute recitative style, and so indicated by Haydn.

This occurs twice, with slight overtones apparent of operatic music design. The quartet has much brilliance in the first and last movements. In the former, it is one of technique, whereas in the latter it is concerned with speed spread. The two methods are both imbued with the most expressive intensity, but the textures differ. One is luminous, whereas the other is bared with transparency.

▪ No. 6, in D Major

The first theme of this quartet will remind one of many things in the composer's output, as well as in Mozart's. (But it is a cliché of the period; each period in musical history has had its tonal mannerisms.) In the Minuet, the first violin takes over the Trio portion completely. The accompaniment would not be out of place in Haydn's Op. 1.

Haydn's persistent use of double stops in the first violin continues in the slow movement. The last movement is handled with more maturity, and all the instruments take part in the chase with resultant well-being. The quartet ends with its ears tucked in but with its eyes as bright as ever.

String Quartets, Op. 20

Preliminary shadowing of Haydn's definite urge to change his style of quartet composition is seen in the six works contained in this opus. He makes it clear that he is concerned with the contrapuntalization of his quartet structure. Fugues make their first appearance in three of the works, and then disappear (only one other real fugue will be found in the later quartets). The writing is freer; the cello is permitted finally to join the other members of the quartet in full solo statement, although complete integrated four-strand freedom is still somewhat lacking.

When these quartets were first published, the title page showed the publisher's trademark—a picture of the sun. Since then they have been called the Sun Quartets (Die Sonnen Quartette), and this name also fits the golden glow and warmth of the music. Indeed, the sun of greatness shines through practically every page. The clouds are the fugues, but these are clouds of richness, not of storms that obliterate. Grossen (Great) was a favorite term of Haydn's contemporaries for these six works, and this cognomen is an apt one, too.

Contrapuntalism is the peak of music composition; it is (so to speak) the calculus of musical science. Not that one must write contrapuntally to effect the highest form of creative message, but there is a tremendous impact in combining individual qualities that are alive at every turn. The polyphony of the fugue (beautifully described by the English music scholar, composer, and pianist, Donald Francis Tovey as "the mutual pursuit of voices or parts") is exacting for the composer, and most exhilarating for the listener. The maximum power of these works will be found in the three finales in determined fugal form.

▪ No. 1, in E-flat Major

Already one may notice new experiences for the cello—for instance, the phrase it plays in duet with the second violin shortly after the first theme is introduced. Improvisatory quality hangs over this first section and nothing is parceled out of former quartet style. Themes are thrown hither and thither—the cello sings over the bass of the viola, and there are subtleties of imitation.

Most of Haydn's Minuets were formed with equal voices in the Trio section. Very few used the baldness of only three voices to achieve contrast. In this quartet, one can observe the amalgam of old and new. The viola is kept quiet until the return to the Minuet proper, binding the Trio with the Minuet, not only by an urgent dissonant chord, but with density.

The slow movement is quite different from the earlier slow sections. The first violin remains as soprano, but it will be noted that the voices all move in regulated order, one with the other. The feeling of *accompaniment* is lost. It is as if one were listening to an enlarged chorale, of which each line *was* the chorale itself. The superb part writing is worth the attention of any student of harmony. (It may be mere coincidence that Beethoven's first quartet—not composed first, but considered in that fashion in the published editions—includes the same word in the tempo indication for the slow movement as here—*affettuoso*, a term used for the first time in Haydn's quartets.) The requisite feeling desired by Haydn is explicit in his writing. One can neither play nor listen to this beautiful movement without experiencing a profound emotional response.

To the straightness of the theme of the last movement is added the foil of syncopation—over twenty measures' worth, an intense method of mirroring preciseness and drive in music.

▪ No 2, in C Major

For the first time in thirty-two quartets (including the present one), the cello is given an opening theme. The composer has moved far from his early works. Haydn's use of the cello in stating themes will always be rare, yet it is the impulse that is more important than the actual result. The cello is now absolutely free; it has no more relationship to the old bass function than Haydn had to Palestrina. The development of the first movement shows the form of imitative question-answer means, and in this the cello plays an important role.

The slow movement bespeaks the symphonic. The unison is used in many places to augment sonority, provide dramatic utterance, and balance melodic portions. These last are not solely for the first violin, but are equally in the cello. The movement is unshackled Haydn, loose with the knowledge of sureness in treatment. The slow movement does not even conclude, but moves immediately from its dominant chord into the purity of the C-major Minuet, built constantly on pedal points. Stylistic affinity occurs in the Trio of the latter, which is cello-starred and also texturally unisoned.

The first quartet fugue is labeled *a IV Soggetti*—i.e., with four subjects. But this is not the exceedingly rare form of a quadruple fugue that takes four separate subjects through their paces and then combines them. This is a fugue with four themes, that, as it were, accompany and jostle each other. The academic difference need not be explained here. It is sufficient to point out that it takes just as much contrapuntal mastery to expose a fugue containing four subjects as it does to have four or less separate expositions and then combine the subjects themselves. Haydn's mastery of contrapuntal creation is as deft as Bach's. The interlarding of the subjects is wonderful aural enjoyment, from the opening that immediately sets two of the subjects against each other. Midway, the fugue reverses itself and runs crabwise *(al rovescio)*. The logic of such palindromic work is apparent. Throughout, all is in the mid-dynamic that finds no *crescendo* or *decrescendo*. The entire fugue is directed dynamically by the rise and fall of the subjects, their opposition to, and combination with, each other. The one difference from the usual fugue is that the ending is drawn into the orbit of homophonic style, the writing becomes partly and then completely vertical. This shift in style is accompanied by a direct change into a loud dynamic.

■ No. 3, in G Minor

The theme of the first movement is widerscaled than many of Haydn's melodies and uses unisons to create the contrary analogy of texture. The use of the viola and the cello marks the slow movement as not in early style— similarly the previous Minuet, which ends quietly.

That Haydn was in a fugue-conscious stage is apparent in the last movement—while not a fugue, it partakes of polyphonic nourishment, including canon and quadruple counterpoint. The finale represents Haydn-to-the-full fast music. Short of using a presto tempo (fitting only for more playfulness than is represented), Haydn makes certain his instruction is for very fast performance. The tempo reads Allegro di molto.

■ No. 4, in D Major

One of the most popular Haydn quartets. The opening movement is crystalline, almost an "allegroed-first-movement" minuet. The slow movement is a set of four variations in the allied key of D minor. The variations are simply enchanting, and by far the most advanced writing Haydn had accomplished to date. For that matter, they are as advanced as he would be in his entire quartet creations. The first variation is intrusted to the second violin, the second variant to the cello, which sings from the tenor register to the extreme of the bass gamut. The ending of this second movement is a high mark in Haydn literature, representing intense music written by a superb creator.

It was not until the Op. 9 quartets that Haydn began to give tempo indications to his minuet movements. After that point, practically every one would be given its velocity-rate marking, most generally allegretto, a speed moderately fast, somewhat less than allegro. In this quartet the Minuet is Alla zingarese, showing Haydn's predilection for the Hungarian style, which overtones several of the movements in his catalogue of compositions, and which was fairly fashionable in his day. The gypsy quality is evident in the cross-beat accents that disengage the tried-and-true trinal flow of the Minuet. The "zing" peps up the Minuet's formality. Since these quartets were dedicated to Nikolaus Zmekall von Domanovecz, an important Hungarian court official, it is not too presumptuous to assume that Haydn incorporated this gesture in his honor. On the other hand, the Trio is non-Hungarian. There are folk and Hungarian qualities as well in the final movement, again dealing with scherzando properties, and so indicated in the full tempo (Presto scherzando). It is amusing to hear Haydn's use of a percussion effect (practically a snare-drum sound) twice in this movement.

▪ No. 5, in F Minor

The fugue appears for the second time in Haydn's quartets as the finale. This time it has two subjects ("a due soggetti"), in comparison with its first use in Op. 20, No. 2, where it has four subjects. The previous, similar plan of using a *sotto voce* is followed throughout the fugue's course, which not only includes a cancrizanic manipulation but a full-borne stretto, where the subjects pile on top of each other in the four voices. Fugue style is maintained at one level of strength—the qualities being as serious as nonpolyphonic Haydn finales are light, deft, humorous, and free of gray-bearded learning. Only in the last few measures of the fugue is the cadence built from the mortar of straight homophony.

The first movement is tragic, in the rare minor-key color. The melancholy is enhanced by the pulsation of the immediately stated, propped accompaniment. This pessimism continues into the Minuet, only being lightened by the change to F major in the Trio. The slow movement is pastoral in feeling and includes one section that foreshadows the rubato of Chopin. The figuration is written out, of course. But whereas Chopinesque figurations and the like are transported to the land of rubato at the will of the player, here Haydn's instructions—*per figuram retardationis*—mean that the figures are to be held back, or shifted at the will of the player, so that they are in and out of focus with the straightforwardness of the supporting harmonies.

▪ No. 6, in A Major

The fugue figures again for the last movement. This time there are three subjects, two of which are first heard in the violins without preamble. It is with the entrance of the viola that the third subject is announced in the first violin. From that point on, the fugal material goes through exposition, transition, and development and then returns in the stretto portion with the trimmings of pedal point and reshaping of the subjects in contrary motion. There is no doubt that this fugue is the most highly developed of the fugues included in Op. 20. The energy and workmanship here are a far cry from any scholasticism that so many fugues represent. On the other hand, the criticism of all-too-much first violin can be applied to the slow movement. Both first and Minuet movements are fresh and joyful, especially the Trio section of the latter; the viola is suppressed, and coloration obtained by three performers using only one string of their instruments.

String Quartets, Op. 33

The composition of string quartets occupied Haydn practically from the start of his career. In fact, his very last work is an unfinished quartet. His output therefore is interlarded with constant attention to the string quartet form. But no gaps in quartet composition of any noteworthy length occurred, save in respect to the nine years preceding this set. Nine years in the life of an ever-practicing composer bring change, and in this case they brought an almost violent shift in Haydn's quartet style. The results of Haydn's study were immediately apparent, without the clue given by his remark, famous in chamber music history, that he had now composed his quartets in "Ganz neue besondere Art." The four string instrument works, from now on, are most definitely in an "entirely new, special style." Equalization is now brought about by individualization, themes are in great contrast, sonata form is past its infancy, and all is proportioned in such manner that no quartet will appear in the future that is not one in its own right, possessing definite characteristics setting it apart from its fellow quartets. The Op. 33 quartets mark the real art form of the string quartet, invested with the greatness of Haydn's talents.

▪ No. 1, in B Minor

The opening with its mixture of keys defines this quartet as in new style and form. The beginning seems convincingly to be in a major key, but the clever shift of the workmanship shows it is in B minor. The movement wends its way through specific sonata form, arranging the structure from the material of the opening, which is refashioned rather than stated and repeated. Haydn's elimination of the Minuet in this set of works is more a change of title (Scherzando) than a new form. Real scherzos would await Beethoven. But the slow movement is actually two-themed and again (in the use of sonata form) shows the new attributes.

The final movement is similar to earlier examples. It must not be forgotten that the functional point of sonata form is in the first movement. The remaining movements are freer and generally planned in other forms. One could not desire any change in these Haydn finales. Direct contrapuntalism (thrice represented in finales of the Op. 20 set, and in one other instance in the later quartets) is not needed to supplant the homophonic gaiety always so refreshing.

▪ No. 2, in E-flat Major

The opening movement represents a milder use of sonata form, since the opening subject is used to a fare-thee-well, but the elements of working a theme motivally are here for examination and full approval. Aside from a cheery second movement in the new scherzo plan, the greatest interest is found at the beginning of the slow movement; a far cry, it is, from the early works. The viola and cello sing in duet form at the start; the first violin is, for a time, held in second place. This never occurred in the previous quartets.

Musical fun and humor run the gamut from writing pieces "in the style of "; burlesques; quaint programmatics, such as Schenk's *Oddities of the Gout*; to the carefully prepared witticisms that can be found in many of Beethoven's scherzos. But there is a refined sense of fun that gives off chuckles, permits laughs without too obvious a musical tickling. Many a Haydn finale possesses such characteristics, but none possess as much keen humor as the last movement of this quartet (and this in spite of the broad, specially designed joke at the end). Sufficient to say, therefore, that the last movement is one grand grin from beginning to end, with the use of rests (one is warned!) to prepare the listener for the point of the joke.

▪ No. 3, in C Major

Given the key of C major, one has access to a tonality that is pure, relaxed, and most gentle. Haydn combines such in his opening movement. The music is gently prodded in Allegro tempo, relaxed with its grace-noted dips, and clear from start to finish in its unfoldment of the sonata story. The Scherzando is more a fast-moving "slow" movement than one concerned with scherzo implements. A movement may not carry out its title; Haydn's Scherzando is escape from stylization; his thoughts are propelled otherwise. The Trio with the two violins chirping is the source of the nickname for this quartet—the *Bird*. The last movement is merry and heady with laughter, and contains Hungarian flavor. This Rondo moves like a dog chasing its tail.

- **No. 4, in B-flat Major**

Mention has been made of musical humor *(see Op. 33, No. 2, above)*, its methods and certain possibilities. But the usual mannerisms of a comedian become a personal cliché—he will pantomime exclusively in his own particular style. Change his style, and the humor frequently falls flat. But not Haydn, one of the best musical wits up to the 20th century. In his humorous moments he rarely repeats himself. Note the last movement, where wild leaps and the use of rests for tension create the proper stage setting for the real flippancy of the coda. In soft dynamic, the quartet suddenly ends with tutti-borne pizzicato. It took daring as well as ingenuity, since humor needs as much planning as serious extemporization. The other movements are standard in fashion. The Largo is especially expressive with a fully spun eight-measure thematic line.

- **No. 5, in G Major**

Motival forms are necessary for thematic development. The opening fulfills this need, containing a rising figure that has been interpreted to signify the phrase *"How—do-you-do—?"* "Fine," says this first movement (thanks to Haydn). However, the dramatic use of silence should not be overlooked in the relaxed beauty of the movement.

Of importance in the slow movement is its unison work—a dramatic scoring method that gives impulse to the music. Of all the scherzos in this set of quartets, this one comes closest to what Beethoven was to accomplish with the form. It has maturity and is far from the quality of the minuet, which Haydn did not eradicate, regardless of the fact that the minuets bear a different label. The finale relaxes slightly—a set of variations on a theme reminiscent of the one Mozart used in his D-minor quartet (the second of the set dedicated to Haydn). To gather the proper energy to close the quartet,

Haydn indulges in a Presto.

- **No. 6, in D Major**

While many thematic ideas of Haydn seem to be similar, it is axiomatic that the mark of the true creative artist is the ability to stay within style, not blend varying sources, and maintain continual interest. The opening of this quartet is a case in point. A plain 6/8 meter winds its way—rather jumps its way—through the simple tonic of D major. (What wealth this composer had, and how he knew how to spend it.) Compare also the width of the two themes: the first narrow, the second wide. It is these two elements of measurement (since the only difference is that of tonic to dominant) that perform the function of theme relationship within the first movement.

Following the slow movement and "scherzo" (the latter mainly with biting upbeats) is a set of variations. The criss-cross of shifting from major to minor to major effects an excellent device of engendering the form. Haydn's variations are still not a fervent exploitation of variational patterns. But from the viewpoint of the colorist, he is most informed and creatively shrewd. Both minor-key variations are made the responsibility of the brown-colored cello, which then is afforded aid (nonaccompanimental, however) by the lighter colors of the higher instruments.

- **String Quartet in D Minor, Op. 42**

Haydn's forty-third quartet is distinctive since it is the only quartet that occupies a full opus by itself. Six per opus is the general rule, there being ten opus numbers, each containing a half-dozen quartets. Four opus numbers total three quartets each, and one (Op. 77) but two—with no consideration given *The Seven Last Words of Christ,* which has certain other features. The last quartet Haydn wrote fills the place of a single opus, but we know that is was projected as one of a series of quartets, and since it remains unfinished—with but two movements—the honor of an entire opus for one quartet really belongs to Op. 42. Sets of quartets under one work number were traditional in the days when amateurs subscribed to receive new quartets the same way one subscribes to a magazine today. One subscription would include several works, i.e., one opus equivalent to six works, for example.

Not being cut to pattern, the work is referred to almost mysteriously, as if Haydn had to splice several works to form one opus. Such reasoning need not be discussed here, for the music itself is fairly representative of its place in the quartet picture. The opening movement has the romantic instruction *Innocentemente*, certainly projected by the nicety of the writing, which is in developed style. The second movement is a typical but matured approach to the minuet. The slow movement has chaste grace and uses the dramatic cunning of a receding dynamic plane that is intensified by the use of *sforzatos*. Those who claim this is an early work that somehow or other crept into the later opus numbers are referred to the last movement, which is laced with tinted contrapuntal treatment, sufficient to place this quartet nowhere near the early period. Additional evidence is the rewarding device of ending the last (fast) movement in softness.

String Quartets, Op. 50

These six quartets were dedicated to the King of Prussia, Frederick William II. Although Mozart, when he did the same with his three great last quartets, paid specific homage to the monarch by including solo passages for the cello—an instrument the king played fairly well—Haydn took little notice of this possibility. Not that the cello is submerged in elementary fashion; it is as individually important as the other instruments, but it does not make soloistic proclamations. The compositions continue Haydn's development as a quartet composer, and are all perfect examples of the *métier* they exploit.

▪ No. 1, in B-flat Major

Pedal point is used to begin the work, and this device brings, in true adherence to its technical function, a tightening of texture; it also helps clarify the surface of the opening movement. The use of triplets placed in conjunction with the theme should be noted. The difference creates a stimulating, tensile rhythmic construction.

A shift to the dark key of E-flat minor is made in the slow movement. When the major tonality returns (and Haydn manages his stage in quick-shift fashion), it provides a dynamic dramatic effect.

The untitled third movement is in minuet form. The last movement is gay, includes a short cadenza, the dramaticism of silence, and the thumb-to-the-nose of the final two measures. Watch for that last scale in the cello that locks the door and says "good night"—it's Haydn's wink again!

▪ No. 2, in C Major

Mixing metaphors is poor grammar. Similarly, in music, to mix styles is poor composition. But in the opening of this quartet, Haydn mixes his ways of musical speaking, and trots out metaphorical mannerisms of *both* harmonic and contrapuntal style.

The second violin receives a great deal of attention in the further process of democratization Haydn was carrying on from his earliest quartets. This instrument begins the slow movement and has its share in the Trio of the Minuet. The other instruments partake generously in the Cantabile of the slow movement, a somewhat flowery manifestation. The contrapuntal side again occurs in the last movement. Within this finale there is a coloristic infiltration by the use of a Croatian folk tune "Hajde malo dere." Although reshaped the outlines of this dance song are unmistakable.

■ No. 3, in E-flat Major

"Romanticism" in its early glory is in the second movement, which opens in two-part harmony. The entire movement is fluid with textural shifts in its variational turns, and it highlights the work.

The first movement displays the usual two themes, recognizable from the compressed mordentlike subject and the broader and more distended second theme. The Minuet (Haydn has dropped his scherzo attempts), in usual Allegretto, and the Finale, in usual Presto, proceed in standard fashion.

■ No. 4, in F-sharp Minor

In this set of six quartets, it is the last half that contains two of the "great" works—this is the first of the pair. In previous quartets, Haydn has tried the fugue form thrice; he now uses it for the last time in his quartets. Having tried, seemingly, all possibilities, of two, three, and four subjects, he now concerns himself with the ordinary, but with what unordinary results: a one-subject fugue. In his approach to this form he maintains the same proportions; the fugues are all announced, developed, and completed in a medium dynamic strength. Only at the end, when he shifts into a coda of contrastive homophonic hemwork, is the settled dynamic raised to a full-blown *forte*.

The first movement has surging power, obtaining its drive from the opening symphonic-like unison figure. Variations in a major-minor form serve for the second movement, with the most individuality showing itself in the minor-keyed sections. The use of a solid F-sharp major key for the Minuet serves as an excellent foil for the concluding fugue, considered by Tovey as the "quietest and deepest of all the

few instrumental fugues since Bach."

■ No. 5, in F Major

After the transparencies of the first movement, the slow section spins itself in a very gentle Poco adagio, christened the *Dream*, probably because of the chordal qualities that tighten the music so that there is neither bustle nor liveliness—yet the music *moves*. Haydn at no time permits individual line work to disturb, and yet there is no monotony. Harmonic powers can keep interest alive in vertical rigidity. Fanciful, lightly spotted triplets are interspersed for relief, the style staying always within the prescribed boundaries.

Haydn's intense concentration with design unity—something that he had no need to worry about, even with the "let-go" quality of the very early quartets—can be noted in the Minuet. In the early quartets, the Trio is disconnected by differences. While the change from major to minor provides a difference, nonetheless, the same attention given to embellishing upbeats by twists of triple grace notes functions as the intermediary which practically combines both Minuet proper and the Trio.

The last movement has gestures which are tantamount to some 20th-century music in sound. The theme at the start is chirpy and moves in bland F major on the highest strings. A tremendous leap to the antithesis follows, with the caution *sopra una corda*, i.e., on one string. Thus these articulate plans give the gold and brown, black and white opposites of color, of chord, and of design.

■ No. 6, in D Major

This quartet is well known because of the last movement, and christened by many names. A wonderfully gay movement, indeed, based on a bow-finger technique that endows the finale with spirit and wholesome joy by use of bariolage, possible only on string instruments (somewhat imitated by a different premise on the harp). This presents the alternative quality of two strings, adjacent to each other. Such alternation, especially in the most usual combination of one open string (giving unstinted sonority, because no finger interferes with the string's complete vibration) and one stopped string, to equal the open string's pitch or alternate in pitch with it, results in rhythmic oscillation and subtly contrastive timbre. It is a practice used for pedal purposes (Brahms favored it), and whenever it is chosen achieves substantial success because no other method can be so delicate, save by specific selection which takes note of the varying densities of the separate strings on any instrument in the string family. The bubbling quality of the movement is enhanced by the vividness of the technique, which is given mainly to the first violin, with the other instruments participating as well. Watching a quartet player toss off these allegro figures is ballet action!

The beginning of the quartet is anticipatory—tension in a happy frame. Not until the fourth measure does Haydn state the tonic of the home key. But even in working out his material, Haydn carefully shows, for all to see, how his quartet creation (he not only *founded* it, but *made* it) has progressed. The key of G minor is close, yet it is fairly distant from the key base of this work. The music moves to and away from such foreign element. For the second movement there are variations with beautifully conceived inner voicing, and for an added tang the "Scotch snap" or the short-long rhythm that surrounds the Minuet.

- **The Seven Last Words of Christ for String Quartet, Op. 51**

The Seven Last Words of Christ was composed for orchestral performance in the Cádiz Cathedral to serve as musical interludes between the bishop's seven sermons, delivered as part of the Good Friday proceedings. (The scoring was for woodwinds minus clarinets, and strings, with four horns included in the fourth part and trumpets and drums in the finale.) Haydn followed the initial setting with a string quartet transcription, and later a version for four vocal soloists, four-part chorus, and orchestra. Also, his publisher (Artaria) prepared an edition for the forte-piano, which Haydn approved.

An "Introduzione" is followed by seven Sonatas in lento, grave, adagio, and largo tempos, and a concluding "Il Terremoto" ("The Earthquake"). Admittedly, the last part is a little naïve, its delineation mainly set in unisons and block chords.

Haydn changes his keys, but the essential nature of the church requisite clings so closely that the movements cannot break away into secular, slow-paced style. Moreover, Haydn himself warned that seven slow movements would be rather fatiguing. Nevertheless, the music is of moving power and profound intensity.

String Quartets, Opp. 54, 55

The six quartets of these two groups were published in 1789, just prior to Haydn's retirement, with pension, from work at the Esterházy estate. Haydn was fifty-seven and in his full maturity. The quartets were dedicated to "dem grosshandler Tost." Tost was a wealthy merchant, also an amateur violinist, of Vienna, and if one is permitted a pun, he certainly should be toasted for the beautiful works that carry his name. The quartet style of Haydn is now fully in hand, and the works are all individually masterpieces.

- **No. 1, in G Major (Op. 54)**

The Op. 54 set opens brilliantly with a lively subject. The ideas are sprightly. Most attention is given to the opening theme, in contrast to which the second theme has syncopated outline, more legato than the staccato of the preceding subject. Thematic contrast, a requisite of sonata form, is now carefully attended to by Haydn. The general pace of the slow movement is quickened in this work, an Allegretto taking its place. This is formed by combining the moving accompaniment of straightforward eighths under an exquisite melodic statement.

Both the Minuet and finale are beautiful music, the former mixing the mode of key skillfully and changing the dance form into a larger-canvased concept. While the latter is semicontrapuntal, more attention should be focused on the delightful play that Haydn obtains by two simple eighth notes; from their immediate statement as the upbeat to the main theme, these cover every inch of the movement's ground, exemplifying what can be done with such motival material.

▪ No. 2, in C Major (Op. 54)

The finale consists of a double-theme Adagio which incloses a short Presto in between its extremes (the second Adagio is heard in greatly reduced form). Having had a previous Adagio (movement two), the effect becomes a bit checked; one expects the graced gentility and springboard drive of the usual Haydn finale. Only the Presto section provides it.

On the other hand, the brilliance and tremendous scope of the first movement are perfect, matched by the haunting ornamental beauties of the slow movement (Adagio). These qualities are no less acute in the Minuet.

▪ No. 3, in E Major (Op. 54)

Building the musical structure requires the organization of certain fundamentals. Once these are outlined, their shapes are then expanded and the composition takes on outward settlement and organic "innards." For example, there is the opening of this work—as great as any of the Haydn quartets. Motion is used to construct the first theme—upward in second

violin and viola, downward in the antiphonal reply of the first violin. This sense of contrariness in the goal of the musical line is taken up by Haydn consistently in the movement, a fast-paced, "two-in-the-bar" Allegro, to which the foil is used of escaped rushing triplets.

Good art is never the result of improvisational quirks. In the second movement, Haydn's creative dexterity is seen in the first theme. He shows how thematic plotting must consider matters of pace, push, and, above all, placement. When the first violin enters, it first hovers close to its beginning. Then it jumps higher, descends, and then pushes to its highest point, receding slightly for cadential purposes. This is merely the beginning, but sufficient to outline what Haydn has demanded of his theme, which he leads, rather than permitting himself to be led. Ornateness is used to embellish thematic development. The finale is reticent in its dynamic plan, most of it retained in a *sotto voce* speech, thus permitting the greatest dissimilarity for the full-blown *fortes*. A colorful effect is obtained by the fillip of displaced weights per beat in the Minuet, the shorter of two sounds occupying the initial portion of a beat, thus throwing the weight off balance and creating more interest by such counteraction.

▪ No. 1, in A Major (Op. 55)

In the Trio to the customary Minuet, the first violin is propelled into concerto regions. More and more, the form of this relaxed movement is being shaped by Haydn into one that will parallel in its intensity those of the slow and fast sections. The finale—a Vivace—is headlong with merriment and contains a fugato with accompanying subjects that one could well regard as of triple fugue shape. (Tovey, who described the Haydn quartets with superb insight, prudently safeguarded his analysis by stating the finale "begins like a rondo, and runs away in an excellent [unofficial] double fugue.")

The first movement is orthodox in treatment, but the final cadence is well worth all the previous measures. The second violin and viola rush away from each other in typical Haydnesque tomfoolery. Movement two is a monothematic Adagio contabile, which one writer indicates is an "*adagio par excellence.*" And, the last word describes the constructional stability of the slow movement.

■ No. 2, in F Minor (Op. 55)

The form of this quartet is stylistically similar to mature Haydn, except that in this work there is a shifting of places of the first two movements. A slow double variational movement begins, followed by the initial fast movement. The variations are longer than is usual with Haydn, with the ever-present and inexhaustibly fresh arguments he brings to the subject of variational development. The main item of the Allegro is the prefix of the grace note, a part of the theme and one used constantly throughout the development portion. The suddenness of long pauses (Haydn anticipates Sibelius) serves to hurl the key center off its previous path. Modulation that is alphabetically closest (musically speaking) is paradoxically furthest away. Shifting a key a semitone up or down without pause is already of strong effect. When it is planned to follow two measures of rest, as in this instance, the effect is doubly powerful, since the ear retains the previous key polarity, notwithstanding silence, and is not prepared for the tonality shift. It is a Haydn master stroke of proper placement of resources.

The Minuet is in the tonic major with the Trio set in the F-minor home tonality. Its textural changes provide special color. As most usual, the final movement is a package of undiluted Presto joy; the structure made from a motive of chromatic descent.

■ No. 3, in B-flat Major (Op. 55)

Two elements form the first theme—a unison

and then harmonic fullness. In later development, the unison is retained or dispersed by harmonic verticalism. The contrasting second theme, on the other hand, is dissimilar, being as chromatic as the opening subject is diatonic. Chromaticism can muddle a diatonic thematic line; here it is a color that wards off any static settlement. These chromatic elements are also contained in the Minuet, where the Trio section is identified by simple triplet rhythmics.

There are new essences in the slow movement. What seems to be a simple Adagio turns into both variational and imitatory linear methods, spinning the slow movement form thereby into a free association of varying techniques within the unified style. There is no stop to the energy of the Finale.

String Quartets, Op. 64

The six quartets of this set were composed in 1790, and, similar to the six quartets represented by Opus numbers 54 and 55, were dedicated to Tost, who certainly received his share of fame from such recognition. It was the year Haydn's patron, Prince Nikolaus Esterházy, died. Haydn had at first been engaged by his brother, Prince Paul Anton, in 1761. When Paul Anton died, Nikolaus continued to provide music of all types and forms at the family estate (then called Eisenstadt, later Esterháza). Haydn at first was an assistant, but on the death of his superior, Gregor Joseph Werner, became the first in musical command. Patronage gave Haydn the necessary base to compose, regardless of the many duties that took their toll in time, strength, and wearing down of the nervous system. Without the necessity for producing music of all types and for varying occasions, it is doubtful whether Haydn's productivity would have been quite so large.

The quartets in this group are of the greatest importance and show complete mastery. There is absolutely divine genius in every measure.

▪ No. 1, in C Major

The opening Allegro moderato is fully in so-nata-form. Rhythmic balance and opposition are contained within the movement. The Minuet, formerly almost taken for granted in its speed rate, is now defined most precisely. It is to be Allegretto, but ma non troppo (not too much so). All too often the tempo of a minuet is too fast, or, worse still, it is played without regard to its place in its growth as a musical form taken over from utilitarian beginnings. There is much difference between the speedy (allegro) minuet and the more relaxed (alle-gretto) performance. The former tends toward its successor, the scherzo; whereas the latter is more in line with its ancestral start.

By regulating the speed, Haydn makes it possible to get the more pert effect of his third movement, an Allegretto modified by the additional Scherzando. This is a set of variations in which, sometime or another, a variant is handed to each of the instruments. The theme remains uncomplexioned with new makeup, appearing with intertwining combinations each time.

The finale shows the mature composer. The contrasting themes are not baldly related in vertical order, but rather ornamented, with the supportive parts almost as important as the theme which they accompany. This is represented by the contrapuntal fixing of live inner voices, these so important to keeping material on the move, and which here even goes so far as to include the formal element of a fugato in the central, development portion of the work.

▪ No. 2, in B Minor

Purposeful harmonic indecisiveness adds interest. For example, note the beginning of this work. One is certain the key is D major; but with careful, shifted extension of harmonic vocabulary, we are in B minor. There are certain chromatic elements, colorations and contrapuntal flowerings, which stimulate the seriousness of this remarkable work.

The slow movement is in the extreme key of B major (for string instruments, the more one uses sharps and flats, the more technically difficult and the less the fullness of sonority), but with affinity to the home key, used also to end this work. Again, the function of key color and contrast form the principal plan of the Minuet, where the main portion is in minor, the Trio in major. The latter is Schubertian, or as similar to the Viennese composer as Haydn could be. The concluding movement does favor wit and humor but its sonata format has room for some serious sections. There is frequently a misconception about Haydn's so-called light-heartedness. Actually, he was deadly serious—his merry finales merely a taking off of the coat after the day's hard work.

There is an interesting aspect to the finish of the last movement. One and a half measures of rest occur after the ascending tapping of eighth notes, which end in widely separated regions, splitting the instruments away from each other. From a strict, formal viewpoint, Haydn balances his total number of measures and thus eventually has filled out the fractional measure which is at the start of the movement. But, in performance, these measures should be related in actual measured time, else the formality of the score is lost, the purpose negated. It is rather customary to be careful about lifting bows off strings, removing instruments from under the chin, et cetera, at the completion of a slow movement. The mood must not be lost. But in a fast-paced, agile finale, it may well seem out of place. Listeners should take cognizance of the measure-and-a-half rest that follows the last sound. The players must either show this silent time space in relation to the previous sounds by clearly concluding their performance after the silent section or at least make mention in the program of the fact. Silence in music is the golden aid to balance and dramatic byplay. (Silence, as the concluding measure[s] of a composition, *equal* in importance to the preceding sounds, has been used by several contemporary composers. Lukas Foss's score notation for the procedure is indicated "Freeze!")

■ **No. 3, in B-flat Major**

Design in the first movement is displayed to posit the opposites necessary in sonata form. The first theme concerns itself with eighths and diametrically different dynamics — full *forte* against pallid *piano*. The second theme, on the other hand, is a galloping rhythm of insistent ubiquity. It is a joy to follow this first theme with broader values, and the second theme with its fully moving, off-the-ground sixteenths.

Slow movements can be spun by development, or managed by the form of variation treatment. Still another device is that which uses the "song form" method of the simple symmetrical pattern of A-B-A. In elementary-school music books, this is worked over considerably. Yet none of them can explain how to treat this musical objective individually. It took Bach to write *most* of his fugues in forms that no book clearly describes. The scholar at first codifies rigidly, and thereafter dwells in a kind of stultified academicism. Note, therefore, how Haydn takes the rule book of the A-B-A and then treats it in *his* musicological manner. The opening theme is in major, to which there is an almost inferential dialogue and accompaniment made from the kernels of the theme itself in the first violin—it is all certainly of one piece. Then follows the relationship of the center section in the primitive minor. When the A portion returns, it is changed, ornamented, at first cautiously to show one what Haydn is about, and then turned into a completely new idea based on moving triplets. The action is responsive and responsible to the previous material. The slow movement carries its line from start to finish, and with wondrous evolutions.

The Minuet has a syncopating Trio of stead-

fast, folklike dance cadences. These syncopations also light the way in the spirited chase of the final movement, which several times lapses into simple, chordal movement—breathtaking before the pace goes into high gear again. This fluidal manipulation of a fast movement, which never loses its rhythmic fervor, is one of the most brilliant designs Haydn fashioned.

■ **No. 4, in G Major**

Music in the scheme of major and minor tonalities quite often has its themes drawn from basic chords that state the steadfastness of the key. The opening theme of this work is a case in point. But touches of contrapuntal invention are also drawn on (as in so many of Haydn's later works, where counterpoint becomes full servant to the homophonic style but does not lose any grace or rights thereby). Haydn makes use of democracy in his instrumentation; the first violin at the crucial points of division (and actual completion of the first movement) is below *all* instruments. This is an amazing device for its day, and far afield from the early quartets.

There is much to admire. For instance, the opening of the Minuet shows how to fashion and bring to climax a four-measure beginning to an eight-measure thought. Eighths to sixteenths give drive; a sustained, longer sound relaxes and defines a temporary resting point. The Trio is rather of the dim past, with full solo violin and simple, limpid, pizzicato accompaniment. The slow movement is in the form of A-B-A, balanced by major-minor-major keys and supplemented by embroidered content on the return to the first portion. The finale is saturated in thirds and sixths, to which reinforced and acclamatory unisons give contrast.

■ **No. 5, in D Major**

One of the most popular works in the entire set. The nickname of the *Lark*, from the opening first-violin melodic twist, is explained fully in the earlier discussion of the nicknames of Haydn's quartets *(see The Nicknames of the Haydn String Quartets).*

The entire opening movement, a moderate Allegro, uses the basis of charm and joyousness of a very bubbly quality. There is no turbulence—but more a mood of relaxation. One endeavor to wax dramatic is a four-ply unison, but this is the only sign disturbing the beautiful serenity of the music.

The second movement has warmth in its spun lyricism and stimulating harmony. For contrast, the second section—as in earlier works of this set—moves into the pivotal minor. When the main theme returns, a symmetrical A-B-A pattern results, with ornamental furbishings. It is worth noting that the lower instruments are little changed from the type of writing assigned them at the start. The first violin varies the main theme, but the movement does not become a set of variations.

The third movement is a typical Haydn Minuet, and the work is completed by a whirlwind finale. Of kinetic formation, this perpetual motion uses the same foil of black-white key shift, as followed in the second movement when the key moves from D major to minor. Subjoined for needed contrast, inasmuch as sheer repetition of the flying figures would not have sufficient significance, is the use of the contrapuntal device—fugato. The quality is maintained without losing sight of the overall athletic insistence of the *perpetuum mobile*. Finally, this propelled movement filters down to the point where only the first violin is playing. A bare chromatic shift is made with a dexterity that is perfection in its simple manifestation. The speed continues to the very end, with a veritable bombardment of peppered sixteenth notes. Haydn has rarely been so lightfooted in his mercurial moments. It is a tour de force of agile construction.

■ **No. 6, in E-flat Major**

Most Haydn fast movements have a textural density that is equal to the full use of the four instruments (with few exceptions, as in trios of the minuets, et cetera). Notice, therefore, the comparative thinness of this quartet's opening movement. It is a lightweight only in its instrumentation, however. The beginning of the development is two-voiced. Later on, it stays that way for some seventeen measures, a record for Haydn in any of the total quartets. This passage, during which Haydn tosses around a motive glued together with the insistent accompaniment of the second violin, is glorious writing and of an appropriate thinness.

The slow movement is again in triple-section form, with a necessarily foreshortened return of the first portion. There is a declamatory beauty and insistence in the center portion of this movement, where the rhythmic energy increases to match the violin's stentorian address. The Minuet is adorned with some skyscraper notes for the first violin; Haydn had admiration for his instrumentalists' abilities. Mix scurrying figures, fast tempo, fugato propellation, thematic bounce—add Haydn—and one has the last movement. (Reginald Barrett-Ayres describes the conclusion of the finale thus: "Haydn leaves Op. 64 with a laugh, for the last page of the Eb quartet is sheer buffoonery, albeit artistic to boot. Phrases broken off in mid-stream, pauses, soft staccato augmentations, and rushing scales are all mixed together to make a hilarious coda, ending with four fortissimo chords.")

String Quartets, Opp. 71, 74

These half-dozen great quartets usher in the last fifteen of Haydn. Although somewhat overshadowed by the following six quartets (Op. 76), their values are of no lesser importance. They show how, with the melodic impetus being fed from an inexhaustible source,

Haydn was able to mix the profound with the light, and how he continually tried his hand at the new. One can perceive features being added as his quartet artistry grew.

Opp. 71 and 74 were dedicated to one Count Anton Apponyi, and were composed in 1793. Age sixty-one, Haydn had just returned from his first trip to London.

▪ No. 1, in E-flat Major (Op. 71)

Introductory chords indicate the newest approach Haydn made to begin his quartets. The vigor of the call to attention is then transferred to a widely spaced theme. This focus of spread permeates the main outline of the first movement, even to the extent of nearly a two-octave jump in the first violin, plus violent changes as abrupt as *pianissimo* to *forte*. The symphonic surrounds the concept. After the appoggiatura-flavored slow movement, considerable interest is attached to the crossfire of cross accents in the Minuet, plus the canonic imitations of the Trio—that portion of the Minuet form where most of Haydn's creative talents were concentrated.

The finale is a rondo, with a theme that has an appended item of scalic outline. These scales are used for figuration points of departure, as well as certain contrapuntal episodes. Syncopations plus opposing accents help destroy any semblance of too rigorous, straight pulsations. Thus, Haydn prevents boredom.

▪ No. 2, in D Major (Op. 71)

An Adagio introduction gives this quartet a unique beginning, for the Adagio does more than merely summon attention. From the essentials of this introduction, the beginning of the Allegro proper will be found; the offbeat entrances are from the syncopations of the introduction, later expanded into scale entrances, as well as the intervallic span of a fourth pushed upward into resultant octaves and tenths. Leaps of intervals surround the first movement, insisting on their right as originally stated at the inception of the fast portion.

An aria-detailed music describes the slow movement. It is followed by the usual Minuet. For the first time, we are faced with a speedy movement in minuet design. The tempo is a full Allegro, but otherwise regularly coursed; almost waltz overtones appear in the Trio section. The plan of the last movement is divisible into a duo-dynamic system, each accompanied by its own rate of speed. Most of the movement (two-thirds of it) is restrained in strength and modified in speed, an Allegretto. After the movement has subsided temporarily on a fermata, Haydn proceeds to use the same material for an Allegro in unchecked dynamic, ending almost with a Rossinian crescendo to a climactic unison.

▪ No. 3, in E-flat Major (Op. 71)

The introduction to this quartet is short, merely one sonorous nod. A stiff chord of twelve total tones (not Schoenberg's!) sets the key. One measure of rest, and the Vivace sets in. This class of introduction is to the point but less dynamic than the type from which resultant proceedings are drawn.

It is odd to examine theories endeavoring to explain away certain unexpected spots in compositions—even those by Haydn, who certainly knew what he was about. This first movement has received its share of questioning and doubt; here, Haydn crosses his cello and viola, causing some unusual harmony for a temporary space.

The variations of the second movement are in the usual major-minor shift plan, the former in the majority. They contain one absolutely beautiful anticipation of Mendelssohn's scoring procedures—lightly patted notes in the high register. The Minuet uses the force of dynamic plan to contrast the Trio with the main body of the movement. The finale is a Vivace in swinging 6/8 meter, enriched by rushing sixteenth-note passages. A new matter here. The form is a rondo, with a contrapuntal twist in the form of a fugato.

■ **No. 1, in C Major (Op. 74)**

Contrast is the hallmark of this quartet. In the last movement, the relationship is manifested and yet made dissimilar by method of technique. The opening theme is legato, smooth as silk in the *mezzoforte* indicated. When development takes place in the more coloristic states of syncopation and polyphonic sport, the theme is expected to return to its placid setting; but, no, Haydn instructs that the theme be played staccato. The development has made its effect on the thematic material.

The same method shows in the Minuet. The closely related use of tonality is not in sight, even in its *relative* sense. Mainly, Haydn used the simplicity of like-named keys, changing the *modus* from either major to minor or the reverse (more rare). Here the Trio is in A major, by no means related to the home key of the Minuet, which is in C major. Besides, during the course of the Minuet the usual simplicity is lacking. Haydn is moving into regions of further probing the quartet's relationships in the matter of tonalities. Ultimately, he is denoting the course of late romanticism.

The opening movement is preceded with the usual introduction of this set of quartets, followed by the chromatic ascending initial theme, a bit unlike Haydn's other thematic partners. The strength of chromaticism is used almost greedily throughout the first movement. The slow movement is also a bit different from other Haydn slow-paced sections. It is swept by the breeze of a moving Grazioso. It is more tender than profound, but full of Haydn's wisdom.

■ **No. 2, in F Major (Op. 74)**

Long-spun themes have more natural life since they absorb more space. The opening theme of the first movement is ten measures in length, followed by two measures of simple cadence on the dominant of the key. A ten-measure theme is rare in the Haydn catalogue, and it is gratifying to note how he builds the theme to a point that seems in usual midway balance, and then, receding but a bit, he goes even higher. This art of pitch placement for purposes of making the line not only fluid but alive in all of its peregrinations is the stuff of which good music is made. The theme is prefaced by a full and rather lengthy eight-measure introduction, setting the key, and not a pasted-on preamble of material, since it hints at the first theme. The opening movement has the further richness of polyphonic writing.

In the slow movement, Haydn uses his favorite three-part construction involved with variational interplay, with the center in the mode of minor, during which time the second violin takes over the first's chair. Key change (a sign of late Haydn) in the form of wider sweeps from the home orbit are manifested in the Minuet (a fast allegro type) wherein the Trio moves severely apart from the main body in a key differential of D-flat against F. The final movement is dramatic and fast; combining both is not easy.

■ **No. 3, in G Minor (Op. 74)**

Identity is concerned, in the opening movement, with the effect of proportional strength placed on the last two beats of a 3/4 meter. It will be observed that Haydn is using the compositional method of deploying *one* idea that centralizes his construction. This is not only technique and craft, it is the genius of great art. From the opening, where grace notes rock the last two beats of every measure (thus known as the *Rider* or *Horseman* quartet) the many-formed emphasis gives off-balanced (and thus balanced!) rights to beats two and three. Entrances are after first beats of rest; melodic valuations lift toward the concentration on such pulsations. Then a further change in form is made; the minor movement has a coda that brightens at the end in the major key.

Grandeur surrounds the symphonic canvas of the slow movement. The music is large in the sense not only of line but of conception. Rarely is there a sense of accompaniment to a theme, and yet the music is *not* contrapuntal. To effect this neutral state, Haydn writes and scores with full sweep and large strokes. Full compact verticalism, dramatic lines, and the like merge all inherent devices into a broad panorama. A writer once called this a movement of "Miltonic grandeur"—the statement is as inspired as the music that gave rise to it. The third-movement Menuetto (in Allegretto tempo) is in sharp contrast to the Largo assai tempo of the previous movement. The minuet flows in legato, bound polyphonically; the Trio has darker outline.

The final movement is happy with its minor-key overcoat, later to be taken off for the topcoat of a major key—all is optimistic, whether minor or major. Rhythm is the life line of this movement. Every measure is particularly concerned with it. It supports, conveys, and springboards the tinge of the overcast caused by the minor key. And it is the rhythm which seems to force the theme to stop its worrying and burst into hearty laughter. The movement is one of the perfect gems in the entire jewel case of Haydn.

String Quartets, Op. 76

The Op. 76 quartets, written in 1797 and 1798, represent the culmination of Haydn's golden mature period. The half-dozen works are practically the last quartets he wrote; only two marked Op. 77 and the two-movement (unfinished) quartet of Op. 103 followed.

The six works are so full of freshets of inspiration that only a volume of commentary on the Haydn quartets could do them full justice. Haydn by this time had nurtured his quartet discovery into a form already used by Mozart, but, aside from further exploitation by Beethoven, the quartet form was now firmly set. Its shape was now defined with two fast outer movements inclosing slow and minuet (later scherzo) sections. But even within such quasi-rigidity, each of the quartets in this set is distinctive—each has something new to offer, each displays a new facet of inspired creation.

These six are the most famous set in the total Haydn quartets, and include more nicknames than any other group of his quartets. The compositions are all in Haydn's favorite major keys, save the second which is in D minor. (Oddly, the first two keys match the first two of Mozart's set of six quartets dedicated to Haydn.) Minor tonalities are not common with this composer; only eleven of the total quartets are in the somber key (excluding *The Seven Last Words of Christ*). Of course, there are minor touches, modulatory sweeps to the darker key orbits, and the like, but in the main the home key is major. The key selection of Op. 76 is interesting, showing the keenness of polarity shifts for the different quartets. In no instance throughout the entire Haydn quartet catalogue, is a key repeated in succession in any one opus. And in only one instance out of a total of seventeen opus groups (each of which contains three or six quartets, save Op. 77, with two quartets, in addition to Op. 42 and Op. 103, with one quartet each, and not counting *The Seven Last Words of Christ*) is the same key *used twice within* any one opus. Haydn was unquestionably key-sensitive to a very amazing degree.

The Op. 76 quartets are compositional treasure houses. There are no virtuoso tendencies for the first violin so current in the early works; the writing does not approach the full independence marking late Beethoven, yet the instruments are all employed actively in the design, not as superaccompanimental voices. The first violin becomes the workhorse. This is true for any quartet—the highest-sounding instrument will have majority powers, because most thematic statements, melodic variations, residual counterpoints, and the like, are mainly in the highest voice. But the use of lower voices to merely supplement or be slaves to the authority of the first violin is not found in the Op. 76 quartets of Haydn.

These six works are not quite so advanced in relation to the early Beethoven quartets. Yet, in their simplicity, they support the axiom that the finest creative messages are often the simplest. Haydn and Beethoven actually complement each other, notwithstanding the disparity of style and treatment, and chronological difference.

- **No. 1, in G Major**

The symphonic robustness of triple introductory chords ushers in this famous group of quartets. All previous traces of formal tentativeness have disappeared. Haydn directs the form and is not controlled by it; for example, the opening theme is assigned to the cello and not to the customary first violin. In previous quartets, a main theme was occasionally stated in other than the soprano voice, but in this instance, with the maturing of the form, Haydn uses the three lower voices before bringing in the first violin, which even then is counterpointed rather than displayed homophonically. There is an occasional return to simpler, early quartet style, with a pretty fiddle tune over the most gentle harmonies; but such portions are only contrastive foils to the use of independent voice writing. The contrapuntal side of Haydn, not often given proper recognition, is the focal design of the development portion.

The second movement is a magnificent song with much manipulation of offbeats, giving

rise to at least one nickname which has fortunately not stayed with the quartet—the *Farmyard*, because of its almost cackling effect. The third movement shows the infiltration of the scherzo in place of the usual minuet. Though not indicated as either, the presto tempo is far afield from minuet territory; but the Trio has the polite, fluid scampering of minuet style. It was customary to end the large form of a quartet or symphony in a major key if the first movement were in the minor. However, it is unusual to reverse the process as in this instance, where the pivotal minor serves for the last movement. The code of tradition, however, brings key alignment to the movement's frame, when, midway through the last movement, the tonic major returns. In its wake, a freshness of color covers the fast pace.

- **No. 2, in D Minor**

Two sets of falling, intervallic fifths have identified this work as the *Quinten* Quartet, and these fifths trademark the production of the first movement throughout, sometimes by inversion but outlined constantly. It is this type of motival manipulation that was to be taken over bodily by Beethoven. The flourishes made by the first violin are a play on the fifth-spanned motive rather than isolated material with accompaniment. The difference is one that must be distinctly understood. The second movement is variationlike but not fully in that form. What is surprising is the indecisiveness of the key at certain junction points.

The entire main body of the Minuet is written as a strict canon. A purposeful system of technique can well be a stumbling block. To repeat what has gone before in unaltered outline, to continue to make good musical sense, and, furthermore, to set the idea in a minuet frame is not the simplest operation. The result here is exhilarating. The quartet body is divided into two blocks (violins pitted against the two lower instruments) to form a thick-voiced duet. The Trio (in much lighter weight) is called the *Hexen* (Witches) due to its very wispy, mysterious opening, and is a tasteful concoction.

Classical style is marked by smooth (diatonic) intervallic action. When the intervals are yanked out of their sockets, 20th-century manifestations glimmer in advance. To a certain extent, this waywardness of the gamut in certain portions of the last movement is an extension (subconscious or otherwise) of the intervallic wideness of the opening movement's theme. But the jerky leaps are most exciting. If they were influenced by a donkey's bray (it is not easy to separate the apocryphal from the truth), then Haydn is the source for the same programmatic device used by Mendelssohn in his Overture to *A Midsummer Night's Dream* . Incidentally, the closing section is another example of the method used by Haydn in the first quartet of this opus. The final movement repeats the opening movement's D-minor key, but closes optimistically in the like-named major.

▪ No. 3, in C Major

The focal point of this work is its second movement which consists of four variations on the theme (initially given in full harmonization), "Gott erhalte Franz den Kaiser" ("God Preserve the Emperor Francis"). Haydn's song (of Croatian heritage) is a wistful reminder of past history since the melody became the Austrian national hymn. There is a spiritual quality to these variations, and, in every instance, they present the theme itself untouched but surrounded with new, rejoindering relationships. The theme thus becomes purposefully static, so that its exploitation is well heard and understood. Not one change of key adorns the new dress of the variants, and yet it is because of Haydn's creative superiority that the movement is not monotonous.

Rhythmic attributes of the first movement, with its dotted sixteenths and thirty-seconds, become part of the picture in the third movement when the long-short of such cellular material is reversed into a short-long, giving added brightness to the simple trinality of the dance form.

Because of the variations, the quartet has been dubbed the *Kaiser* Quartet, but, with the virtuosic propelling of the last movement, this could well be changed to the *Kinetic*. The finale is based on a triplet rhythm thrown about the four instruments on a winged presto tempo. The slower-paced ideas merely serve to show up the insistence of this dashing treatment. Once again, the last movement, similar to the final movement of the first quartet in this set, uses the pivotal minor; likewise, a shift occurs at the three-quarter mark to the brighter major hue.

▪ No. 4, in B-flat Major

Some of the nicknames identified with the Haydn string quartets push reason practically to the breaking point. But the cognomen bestowed on this work *(Sunrise)* is so apt that one might take up the lance in favor of nicknames when they are as correct as this. This name should not be confused with the Op. 20 Sun Quartets, so-called because the title page of the original edition had a picture of the sun, the publisher's trademark, as an illustration. The opening on a pedal chord, over which the first violin softly twines the upward ascent of the theme, is one of the most thrilling moments in any of the Haydn quartets. In its subdued quality, there is a glorious grandeur paralleling in intensity the moment of a day's beginning. When ultimately a true chirpy Haydn Allegro breaks into this tremulous romanticism, it is as if the sun has burst into full splendor.

In many slow movements of the classical school, when the importance is homophonic, the individual melodic line is assigned to a single instrument—any change of color in such display awaiting later composers. In this slow movement, there is a sort of joint ownership of theme in the series of dialogues between two instruments setting forth the import of the basic homophonic message. It is worth noting, inter alia, how Haydn's instrumentation principles have advanced. This continues even into the Minuet, where one instrument or a pair will act as a rejoinder to a previously stated idea. The persisting impulse to place a minor key on the façade of major tonality is to be observed in the last movement, which is more concerned with a motive than with a fully coursed theme. The movement is built on the principle of increasing rates of speed, the accelerando matching the energy of the material itself. A bridge passage is formed to increase the tempo; this then gathers itself up and proceeds into a tempo just short of a firebrand presto.

▪ No. 5, in D Major

Thematic manipulation can be formed by means other than taking out the essential kernels of a theme and deploying them in various guises, or reshaping the theme's physiognomy. It can be achieved by doing either or both of these simultaneously with compression or elongation in actual time values. And, without disturbing the notation, the same result can be obtained by temporal shift. This last is the blueprint by which Haydn plans the freely ternary basis of the first movement. The very opening theme of the Allegretto, with its swaying Siciliano-like lilt, becomes a steadfast "two in a bar" Allegro which contains variation within its part of the tripartite structuring. The dialogue principle and freedom of instrumentation are also definitely used.

In the second movement, we meet once more a nickname. This time it is derived from the indicated tempo—the only instance of such use in the large list of Haydn quartet names. Thus, this *Largo* Quartet, considered the greatest slow movement of the Haydn output, is

quite aptly baptized. The key of F-sharp is a test of intonation every step of the way. The movement has a fervored intensity, as if a threnody were being spun; and all of this is based on simple triadal construction, without the need of coloring accidentals. To be able to achieve such emotion merely by expertness of voice leadings and fundamental diatonic harmonies requires a composer of genius.

The sprightliness of the Minuet (an Allegro, just a bit faster than most minuets, although unfortunately the distinction between allegretto and allegro tempos in regard to minuets is too often overlooked) is matched by a typical Haydn perpetual-motion finale. There is no stop of any consequence in these cascading eighths and sixteenths. It is the most joyful movement in this set of quartets.

▪ No. 6, in E-flat Major

This is the strangest and least understood work in the Op. 76 set. The classical school believed in square-cut construction, save for an occasional short introduction which might cut into an opening movement. The first movement (freely variational) is again (as in the fifth quartet of this group) split into two tempo speeds for differential qualities. There is a great deal of counterpoint, thereby forming another parallel with Beethoven (whose late quartets reached further into this domain than his earlier ones). The Allegro portion of the opening section is a fugato, thereby bringing into full bloom the inherent flowery part writing gently indicated in the previous Allegretto portion. Development of kindred portions, therefore, is equaled by development of tempos. The slow movement displays contrapuntalism at its most Haydnish best, and, if it were not for the title (Fantasia) of the movement, one might question the sudden inclusion of new, rhythmic features at the very end of the movement.

The third movement (a Presto minuet) introduces still another new phase, in that the Trio is twice the usual length; it is marked Alternativo and uses pyramidal thematics. The subtle substitution for the Trio shows how a composer can take a simple scale (here in E-flat) with its eight notes, roll it down or up, and obtain a genuine theme. The rungs on this tonal ladder are then tacked with the niceties of side-lighted accompaniment. Contrapuntal tactics are the engineering tools of the last movement, and only rarely does the first violin take over the field of operations.

String Quartets, Op. 77

These two quartets were dedicated to Prince Lobkowitz, the same aristocratic patron to whom Beethoven dedicated his Op. 18 set. The two quartets are written with full maturity, and make it possible for an unbroken line to be drawn to the great Mozart and Beethoven masterpieces in the same medium. These were the last complete quartets; only the two-movement Op. 103 was to follow. Six quartets were contemplated, but Haydn could finish only two; he was failing physically, and perhaps had a premonition that only a few more years remained in which to compose.

Both works are massive, long, and detailed. There is no shortwinded, pithy fast movement serving as a finale. Haydn's music is now mature and powerfully dramatic. The minuets are gone forever; everything is constructed with proportions that make the quartet style intimate, with complete intensity in its refinement. Haydn had lived through an entire history of the string quartet form; he knew it well.

▪ No. 1, in G Major

The opening movement has march connotations. There is a marked quarter-note rhythm, with much use made of a motive consisting of a dotted eighth plus a sixteenth. Opposed to this are onrushing triplet passages of the great-

est brilliance. In the slow movement, the modulations are amazing—far from the simple methods of textbook outline. The profundity of the music itself is matched with astonishing technique. And all of this is built from a two-measure unison thought expressed at the movement's onset.

Presto tempo can be used for a minuet. One can utilize any manner of speed, but it does not necessarily mean that name and tempo type coincide with each other. In this quartet, the third movement is titled Menuetto (Haydn favored this spelling, which follows Italian terminology) and Presto. The result is a Scherzo—virile and wild. The matter of length follows suit, being longer than the mild-paced minuets of the earlier quartets. In the Trio, the ostinato quarter notes are as much related to those of the opening movement as they are to the frenetic dance idea of the Trio itself. Beethoven absorbed this movement, as one can see by comparison with his middle-period works.

How Haydn had advanced from phrased subjects to motives can be noted in the last movement. Everything—themes, development, and subsidiary material—all stem from the opening theme. It is cut apart and splintered for use in a formal movement, but the rondo quality is adumbrated by the absolute of a movement built on a motive. It is one of the most informative and exciting movements in all quartet literature.

▪ No. 2, in F Major

The scherzo distillation of the minuet is present in this work similar to its companion in the opus. But one modification takes place—the tempo is not to be "too fast." The slow movement partakes of an odd beginning, being written in two-voice form for twenty measures before the full quartet enters. Thematic unfoldment is first based on simple bass-line association, then to full harmonic dress, and finally stated with contrapuntal-harmonic additions;

the theme is heard in the tenor voice of the cello as well as the second violin.

The first movement is subtle, less vigorous than the more dramatic first movement of the other work in the set. The main theme is shown in various colors, its possibilities exploited not only in the soprano but in the darker range. The final movement is difficult, with extremely individual part writing. Its exacting demands are an index of what would be required from that time on of string quartet players.

- **String Quartet** *(Unfinished)* **in B-flat Major, Op. 103**

This was Haydn's last composition, another of the unfinished works in musical history. There are but two movements, an Andante grazioso and a Minuet in somewhat quasi-Presto form. These were planned to form the middle movements of the customary four-movement work. There are many key changes in the first section, from the opening in B-flat, to G, then to E, and finally B-flat. It lacks nothing in its bittersweet reminder that this great composer was approaching his death.

At the end of the quartet, Haydn placed his visiting card, which explained a work that was not complete. The words accompanying the music on the card read: "Hin ist alle meine Kraft, alt und schwach bin ich" ("Gone is all my strength, old and weak am I"). Six years after writing this composition Haydn died. His hand had never faltered.

SEXTETS

- **Divertimentos for Two Oboes, Two Horns, and Two Bassoons**

  - No. 1, in F Major, Hob. II:15
  - No. 2, in F Major, Hob. II:23
  - No. 3, in C Major, Hob. II:7
  - No. 4, in C Major, Hob. II:14
  - No. 5, in D Major, Hob. II:18
  - No. 6, in G Major, Hob. II:3
  - No. 7, in G Major, Hob. II:deest
  - No. 8, in D Major, Hob. II:deest

The Divertimento heading was used very freely by Haydn. It identifies several hundred works, embracing a considerable number of different instrumental combinations. The designation varied. Sometimes Serenade was used, other times Feld-Parthie (Field-Partita) even Parthia. The published editions have varied as well and some of the above are Divertimento in one place and Field-Partita in another. With such interchange one could apply the word Cassation and not be in error.

Whatever; this is jolly music, with decided bounce for the greatest part. All of these eight works are Haydn lightweights but Haydn delights nonetheless.

Plenty of structural variety with a good supply of minuets and presto-tempoed music. And sometimes a bit of virtuosity, especially for the horns. For example: the finale of the sixth of the set.

OCTET

- **Octet in F Major for Two Flutes, Two Oboes, Two Bassoons, and Two Horns**

Haydn's work for his employer, Prince Esterházy, included the writing of all types of music. Wind music was included in such products. The Octet is most representative of such—

a serenade type of entertainment music, now considered equal to pure chamber music style. Composed probably for outdoor performance, it is ours now for pleasure indoors.

The eight instruments are six woodwind and two horns. The latter combine aptly with both woodwind and brass groups. The two outer Allegros are simple, sunny Haydn. His scoring relies more on balanced tuttis than an inclination to cull individual instrumental color values. However, the variations aptly take care of such advantages. Every instrumental combine has an opportunity of fulfilling the goal of the variants and of displaying its own particular color potential. In the third (there are four variations in all), the horn has difficult passages; Haydn writes as treacherously for that instrument as Richard Strauss was to write much later. The Minuet movement has a distinctive arrangement, occurring three times in alternation with different Trios. This is a rondo-tinctured application to the form and serves to enlarge the movement to proportions equaling the three others.

Haydn, Michael (1737–1806)

DUOS

- **Sonatas for Violin and Viola**

  - No. 1, in C Major
  - No. 2, in D Major
  - No. 3, in F Major
  - No. 4, in E Major

A compilation of well-integrated duos. The forms are cut from practically the same patterns. All four duos begin with an Allegro with a sonata delineation, then follows an Adagio, and, in turn, another Allegro in rondo design. The single deviation is the end movement of the D major duo, which though in Allegro speed sets forth a set of six variations (the

movement is not so titled) which includes a Menuetto as the fourth variant, repeats the theme and finishes off with a piu Allegro coda.

Haydn strikes a good textural balance and achieves a flexibility to the music that is of warmth and freshness. The scoring testimony does favor the violin.

TRIOS

- **Divertimento for Viola, Cello, and Double Bass**

What makes this trio special is the scoring. On the other hand the double bass is kept rather in the servant's quarters especially in the opening set of variations. There the bass restates note for note its line for the two pairs of eight measures of the theme throughout the six variations. Each of these is repeated with no tempo modification. A Menuetto and a loquacious Presto finale complete the work.

Haydn's work was discovered "at the back of the violoncello part of a sonata" in the Royal College of Music in London. It was first published in 1971 by Yorke Edition.

- **Divertimento in C Major for Oboe (or Flute), Viola, and Violone, P. 98**

The option of either an oboe or a flute was arrived at during preparation of the trio for publication. Working from two sets of material, the editor, Werner Rainer, found that one called for flute, the other for oboe, the only difference being some octave transpositions in the final movement.

As is often the case, Haydn uses two Minuets and varies them (also a habit). Both are in C major, but the Trio of the first one (movement two) stays in that tonality, while the Trio of the second (movement four) is in F major. A slight touch, but to be noted. The slow movement between the pair of Minuets is an Aria, which, for the greater part, is a duo for the oboe and viola. Another slow movement follows the second Minuet. It consists of a theme and four variations, measured to the finite point, thirty-two measures for each unit, and directed variationally by the oboe and viola; the violone (double bass) merely gives bass support. Aliveness, of course, in the outer movements.

- **Divertimento in D Major for Horn, Viola, and Violone**

The violone is an ancient double bass type, but though the score makes no mention of it the part may well be played (for better balance, also) by a cello at noted pitch. If so, some arrangement of octave register will be required in places where it would sound above the viola. Still, playing Haydn's trio with a double bass will bring some rather special sonorities.

As for the horn, it is expectedly a neutral member of the cast, save for some six measures in the Adagio where it jumps through triadic pitches in triplet rhythm. A pair of Minuets surround this single slow movement; the first and last movements are in the usual quick-paced settings.

QUARTETS

- **Quartet in C for English horn, Violin, Cello, and Double Bass, P. 115**

When cello and double bass are both utilized the normal method is closeness between the instruments and, for the greater part, doubling passages in octaves. Here, the wide spacing between these two instruments must be understood to mean that the cello functions as a tenor instrument (replacing the viola) and the bass *is* the entire bass (assuming the cello's usual function).

In the final Rondo (paced presto) separate pithy cadenzas appear for cello, English horn, and violin. These are the editor's work (Werner Rainer), fulfilling Haydn's direction "al suo piacere." The ad libitum direction means therefore that Rainer's cadenzas can be replaced by the performer's own, but whatever, cadenzas must be sounded.

Haydn's choice of instruments is colorful. Additionally there is bariolage bowing for the violin in the finale, and the muting of the violin and cello in the second movement Adagio. A spirited Allegro ushers in the mixed quartet.

- **Quartet in F Major for Flute, Violin, Viola, and Cello**

Published for the first time in 1974 by Doblinger, the score was made from parts in the Thurn-und Taxisschen Hofbibliothek in Regensburg. There was a question as to which Haydn had composed the piece; the editor of the publication, Werner Rainer, decided it was the younger Haydn, based on stylistic reasons.

Two movements only. A motile Andante begins the piece, a gracefully turned Minuet completes it.

- **String Quartet in A Major, P. 121**

Sound dicta and classical procedure. There are four movements with a fairly standard sequence. First is a Presto (faster tempoed than is usual for the first movement); then a Menuetto, the Trio shifting to the home key's minor mode; a set of variations; and a Rondo. In the variations movement the theme and four variants are followed by a bit of a formal switch, with a development of the theme itself.

- **String Quartet in B-flat Major, P. 125**

A divertimento format with a six-movement total. The beginning sets the tone of the piece with a Marcia scherzando. In turn there are a fast movement, two Minuets separated by a Molto adagio e cantabile spun with decorative detail, and a presto-tempo final Rondo that has the quality of a perpetual motion. Minimal amounts of poetry here but sufficient brilliance compensates for its lack.

- **String Quartets**

  - No. 1, in B-flat Major, P. 124
  - No. 2, in E-flat Major, P. 118
  - No. 3, in A Major, P. 122
  - No. 4, in G Minor, P. 120
  - No. 5, in F Major, P. 119
  - No. 6, in C Major, P. 116

The numbers assigned this set of string quartets follow the published scores by Doblinger, although it does not seem that Haydn numbered the set. However, according to the editor, Helmut Zehetmair, the numerous manuscript copies of the works all included this group of six quartets (the original manuscripts or early published editions have never been found). On the other hand, the numbering made by Lothar Herbert Perger (indicating some of the other works in these discussions of Michael Haydn's music—*see above* and *below*) in his thematic catalogue of Haydn's instrumental compositions contradicts the theory that these quartets constitute a set of six in one opus. None of Perger's numbers are chronological and three numbers are lacking to fulfill an unbroken sequence (117, 121, and 123). (For a separate consideration of P. 121, *see above* String Quartet in A Major.) Finally, to support Zehetmair's argument the tonalities are different for the six works.

The younger Haydn approached regularity in these quartets. All are in three movements, and begin Andante—the exception is the fourth quartet which is marked Andante un poco Allegro. The middle movements are all Minuets, again the exception being the fourth quartet, where a full Andante grazioso concept fills the central position. One of these Minuets (in quartet number three) is to be performed in the French tempo, which means on the slower side. All of the finales are straightforward rondos,

save the special fourth quartet, which again furnishes the exception with a Minuet set forth in a series of variations. Formal symmetry of music therefore (discounting the fourth of the group), cleanly organized and sensibly detailed.

QUINTETS

- **Divertimento in B-flat Major for Oboe, Bassoon, Violin, Viola, and Double Bass, P. 92**

Symphonic stability here—one of Michael Haydn's strongest divertimentos. The man does show real and intensive creative juice in this four-movement piece (the title "Quintet" was in one of the several sets of parts used in editing the work for publication).

The opening movement uses three types of rhythmic figures for its structuring. Eighths, triplets, and a long-short, single-pulsed item are integrated, contrasted, and mixed together for a brilliant result. In movement two antiphony, pairing the two winds in dialogue with the two upper string instruments, plays an important role. Some of the same contrastive method is used in the Trio of the Menuetto. Keys provide the comparison in the minuet movement, replacing tempo change. The principal part of the dance is in B-flat major, the Trio is in B-flat minor. To move the finale Haydn uses repetitive pitch figures and scale sweeps.

- **Quintet for Violin, Viola, Clarinet, Corno di Caccia, and Bassoon**

Quintet in title and in instrumental total, but formally a serenade, or divertimento, consisting of eight movements.

Movements for the greater part are of standard makeup, but the opening is restrained in the form of a stately march. The penultimate part begins with a Largo, in which the strings are muted, and then is linked to a set of three Tedeschi (Dances) in fast triple time, with unmuted strings. These shift so that the order is 1–2–1–3–1–Coda. In the other movements the usual divertimento contents pertain: a pair of Minuets, fast and slow music, and a Polonese.

There remains to make mention of the rare chamber music use of the hunting horn. This instrument is pitched in E-flat, the tonality for all but the fourth (Adagio) movement, which is in the dominant tonality.

- **Quintet in C Major for Two Violins, Two Violas, and Cello**

An interesting sidelight in connection with Mozart concerns this Quintet. Leopold Mozart wrote his son that Haydn "is a man whose merit you will be forced to acknowledge," despite the fact that Leopold disliked Haydn's manner. And acknowledgment indeed, for Mozart, after hearing Haydn's C-major quintet, promptly revised his own B-flat-major quintet (K. 174).

There is motival action in the first movement and the tossing about of sixteenth-note figures gives an exhilarative quality to the music. A sensitive dialogue between the first violin and first viola carries the fully muted Adagio cantabile; the second violin and second viola mainly support with plucked accompaniment, the cello with a simple, steady eighth-note bass. A Menuetto and Rondo complete the piece. In the latter scalewise lines are prime, with trills and little accents coloring the lyrical portions.

- **Quintet in F Major for Two Violins, Two Violas, and Cello**

Startling differences between this string quintet and the other two discussed (see above and below). No four-movement compound form in this case, but obvious divertimento style with a total of seven movements.

Already the opening tempo marks a differ-ence. It is noted as Allegro aperto (literally, "open," hence a quick tempo to be projected clearly and distinctly). Within, registral shifts are prominent. And one section utilizing triplet figurations stands out because of its rhythmic difference. There are two Minuets (movements two and four) surrounding the single slow movement of the Quintet. Further, set in B-flat major, the latter is the only instance of a different basic tonality in the entire work.

Movement five is a set of six variations. The theme consists of two eight-measure phrases, each repeated, and this format is followed religiously in every variation save the second half of the final variation, which is extended by two measures. All the instruments save the cello have at least a single chance in the variational spotlight; the cello remains fixed as a bass support. Then follows a vivacious Finale: Rondo, but surprisingly it does not conclude the Quintet. A Marcia in andantino pace is in the end position. No doubt as to the Quintet representing a high-style divertimento.

- **Quintet in G Major for Two Violins, Two Violas, and Cello**

None of Michael Haydn's string quintets should be approached as music of epic dimensions but, rather, as music of congeniality which describes the opening and closing fast-paced movements of this work. The Adagio affettuoso has a bit more depth, and a fine balance is obtained between the song of the first violin and the support of the other voices. Midway, there is rhythmic elaboration for all four voices serving as contrast. The usual Menuetto is included; its tempo, allegrino, is the equivalent of allegretto.

SEXTETS

- **Divertimento in D Major for Two Oboes, Two Horns, and Two Bassoons, P. 95**

(Haydn's D major Divertimento for winds is also known as Divertimento à 6.)

It is the minuet form that is of special order in this sextet. The first Menuetto stands minus a tempo, thus of standard speed, the second one has the speed rate as allegro, a preview of the later transfer (or redress) of the dance movement, in the classical compounded form, into a scherzo.

There is no failure of energy in Haydn's wind music. The first movement is an Allegro molto thrusting with octave leaps; the Finale is a Presto with triadic robustness. And, motility, is paramount in the slow movement (Andante grazioso).

- **Divertimento in G Major for Oboe, Two Horns, Bassoon, Viola, and Violone, P. 96**

The eloquence in the slow movement is entrusted solely to the viola and oboe—sometimes in dialogue fashion, other times in duet style. There is the standard Minuet and a pair of fast-tempo movements which frolic lightsomely as is the usual case with this composer's serenadelike music.

- **Notturno in F Major for Two Horns, Two Violins, Viola, and Bass, P. 106**

Haydn's music designed to be performed as an evening entertainment is a fine blend of creative sagacity and high spirits. It will win friends immediately.

Both the opening and closing movements are duple pulsed; the former is a 2/4 Allegro and features the bounce of eighth- and sixteenth-note patterns, the latter is a 6/8 Presto and also has eighths and sixteenths but there are more of these per pulse than in the opening movement—a subtle effect that makes its point. The Menuetto projects the principal rhythmic element by way of the second violin, and, in the Trio, chains of eighth notes are distributed throughout the instruments.

The Adagio is for strings only. Haydn has an ensemble of rhythm within this movement that provides a stylistic coherence that exemplifies ripe authority. A sextuplet ostinato of paired triplets, the first one broken, appears in practically every measure. At the same time the melodic line floats and moves also with triplets, most of them antiphonally placed in relation to the accompanimental sextuplets. This cogent control does not precisely agree with the remark of the editor of the Doblinger edition, Alois Strassl, who states the music obtains "its charm from . . . the loosened leading of the instrumental parts."

Healey, Derek (1936–)

DUO

- *Five Cameos* **for Soprano Recorder and Piano (or Harpsichord) (1963)**

Genuine, utilitarian pieces, never guilty of attempting more than simple routines. Quadruple steps move the measures of the "Marche militaire," waltz sway describes "The Swing," and agitated ostinato figures speed "The Horsemen." The fourth and fifth vignettes are a languid-paced "The Shepherd Boy" and a bouncy-pulsed "Sailors' Hornpipe."

Heath, John R. (1887–?)

QUARTET

- *Serbian Quartet* for Strings (Two Violins, Viola, and Cello)

Folk material is woven into all of the movements, as are the plaintive pungencies of augmented intervals, which already appear in the very first measure of the quartet and continue to be heard and stressed throughout the work.

A lengthy introduction leads to the main part of the first movement. Sectional arrangement is used with a minute return of the introduction in the coda. A short duple-pulse slow dance is the index to the second movement. Movement three is just as dance-outlined, but speedy, in Presto. It begins in A minor and returns to it after a G-minor section in moderate tempo. Then, to seal matters, the tempo moves still faster in the coda. Movement four matches movement one. There is an Adagio introduction, followed by the principal movement material, in Allegro con fuoco pace, with again a plan of sectional apportionment, and reuse of the Adagio to conclude the quartet.

Hedwall, Lennart (1932–)

DUOS

- *Five Epigrams* for Flute and Clarinet (1959)

Twelve-tone music but with only a toehold on strict procedures. The imitative process is given full treatment, especially in the first and last pieces. In lento tempo, parts one and two of the first *Epigram* become parts two and one in the last *Epigram*. There is a certain amount of freedom but it does not blot out recognition of the transfer, giving extremely strong relationship and balance to the work as a whole. Differ-

ent moods identify the other pieces, with a pastoral flow to number three and a pulse-kicked scherzando to number four. Allegro thrust marks the second piece.

- **Sonatina for Flute and Oboe (1975)**

Nicolas Slonimsky's biographical note on this Swedish conductor and composer describes his music as ranging "from the traditional to the audaciously dissonant." The Sonatina falls in between, leaning toward the traditional zone.

Movement one (written in 1975 after the second movement had been completed in 1964) is a three-section affair, chromatically crusted and depending on imitations to make its point. Movement two, pert and vivaciously swept, has a concluding section that shifts meter and speeds the tempo. This results in a diminutioned rhythmic development of the principal material.

Heger, Robert (1886–1978)

QUARTET

- *De Profundis*: **String Quartet in F-sharp Minor, Op. 34**

This twenty-eight-minute document by the Alsatian-born German conductor and composer reflects Reger in its serious attention to linear detail and Strauss in its lyrical mannerisms.

The dramaticism within the "De Profundis," Psalm 129, (Ps. 130 in the King James version) has attracted a good number of composers. Heger's music reflects the general tone of the psalm: "Out of the depths have I cried unto thee, O Lord." There is urgency in all of the four movements. Each is codified expertly, yet none is based on cold creative investigation which negates expressivity.

Movement one is a huge binary affair, with the second division pitched a bit higher. The second movement features a pithy motive linked to an exact scale formation. It is modified and changed but never loses its specific identity. It reflects into the contrasting section as well, where conjunctly bound units support the lyrical line. This pitch concentration moves also into the third movement, a set of five variations on (again) a scalewise theme, where tight rhythmic actions control the music until the final variant. For the terminal part of the work a rondo design applies, with the music moving into a concluding A major.

Heiden, Bernhard (1910–)

DUOS

- **Five Canons for Two Horns (1971)**

Most often when a composer subordinates himself to a rigid and exclusive technique the restrictions spell academic cohesion but little (if any) artistic involvement. Heiden's contrapuntal conception is polyphony without tears. It is musically alive and expressive and still checks off in terms of technical rules and regulations. Quite a feat. There are also within the set coloristic and metrical flux and a variety of shapes.

The first piece is a canon at the fifth below, the accentual demarcation of the consequent different from the antecedent. A ternary structure is used in the second piece, which is a canon at the third. Number three is a canon at the unison, the rhythmic motility creating a colorfully subtle excitement. Canon number four is set in inversion; the final piece is structured so that the *comes* is first at the third above and later at the fifth.

- **Five Short Pieces for Flute and Piano (1933)**

Early Heiden (written when he was 23). Still, a

good portion of the style-to-be is in evidence. This can be recognized in the polyphony of the third piece and the contrapuntal gestures in the fifth one. Both the second and fourth pieces are in clear rhythmic style, harmonically framed. The former has scherzo propulsion, the other has waltz grace.

- **_Inventions_ for Two Cellos (1967)**

Heiden's lyrical talent is somewhat of the type one hears in Busoni's music and certainly in Hindemith's (with whom Heiden studied for four years). It is basic to the six parts of this duo.

Creative imagery in this instance tends to reflect variational procedures; that is, without drawing on a basic thematic resource a pertinent permutative process applies to each of the six parts of the work. Thus, in number three, the dynamism of the two lines is aided by the persuasive undercurrent resulting from the muting of the instruments. In number four there is metrical flux that frames the lines, with strict alternation between 3/4 and 5/8. The final piece maintains a driving reiteration of sixteenth-note sounds punctuated by pizzicato.

In the restricted literature for two cellos, Heiden's *Inventions* is a very important addition.

- **_Siena_ for Cello and Piano (1961)**

Fancy title—no meaning. Heiden clears the air with his note that in endeavoring to find a title for a piece written in "time-honored" two-part form he finally chose the name of his cat. He emphasizes that *Siena* "has nothing to do with the Italian city, nor does it have any programmatic meaning."

The meaning is structurally clear. *Siena* begins with a Lento that has a declamatory air and a Vivace follows. The effect of the latter is a tight scherzo, minus any twitchings and stabilized by a persistent triple pulse. Toward the end a full-fledged cadenza is inserted (probably because the work was dedicated to virtuoso cellist Janos Starker, who premiered it with pianist Leon Pommers in January 1962.) The music then returns to its energetic pulse and concludes with a lessening of both dynamic and tempo.

- **Sonata for Alto Saxophone and Piano (1937)**

While there are pertinent Hindemithian influences in the work, Heiden's music has validity. There is a source of natural energy in the three movements, and note-spinning is kept out of the picture. Fast tempos cover parts one and two and most of part three. The last telescopes both slow and speedy sections, not only in tempo but also in terms of relationship of theme, the Presto material a working out of the fluency of the Adagio. The two sections, therefore, interlock as one—an indication of musical-engineering efficiency.

- **Sonata for Horn and Piano (1939)**

There is a special identity with the chosen brass instrument in this compact, three-movement work. Heiden avoids neutral writing that would fit any instrument with equivalent range. Quartal and quinary intervals (kin to the style of Paul Hindemith, with whom Heiden had studied) as well as the warmer tertial intervallic span are featured throughout. Tight rhythms and repetitive pitches are other distinctions. But, gratefully, no hunting horn calls!

Movement two has minuet tempo and is close to the structure of that dance, actually a small rondo in format. The finale is specifically a Rondo, gaily kicked around (nicely and neatly) by metrical shifts. Interestingly, all three movements are based on a B-flat tonal polarity.

- **Sonata for Viola and Piano (1959)**

There is marked contrastiveness throughout the Sonata. Of course, Heiden retains his habitual (strong) use of counterpoint, but relates it to vertical dispositions. The slow movement is especially illustrative of this technique. There, one theme is polyphonically detailed; another is gracefully legatoed in the viola and framed chordally in the piano. (Neatly colorful is a quartal passage in the piano.)

The first movement is also expressively contrasted, with one theme curved in shape and another conjunctly tight. Movement three is a scherzo type. It is texturally thin (more dynamic that way) and twists nervously in shifting quintuple and sextuple meters. In the finale—with a Lento preface in declamatory style—the structuring is developed from a tertial interval. This span is used rhythmically in both directions and is maintained as the melodic width in the contrasting, more lyrical section.

- **Sonata for Violin and Piano (1954)**

Strong neoclassic details, as usual with this composer. No restrictive formal orthodoxy. Individual characterization marks each of the four movements.

Rubato motility is detailed in the first movement, as is an amount of high-spirited improvisational style. These serve as a splendid foil for the Molto vivace second part of the work, which is a perpetual-motion dynamo of 214 measures wherein the violin has unceasing sets of sixteenth notes. (A simple two-measure A-minor cadence follows.) Movement three is a set of canons in rondo form, each exploring a different aspect of the art of canonic construction including inversion. The finale uses (develops) a bit of this movement as well as the opening movement within its Allegro delivery. Here, more than elsewhere, the shadow of Hindemith is in view.

- **Sonatina for Clarinet and Piano**

Legato detail embraces the entire three movements. Even in the final peppy Vivace, ma non troppo movement there are no passages of detached sounds. Good enough. The objective is clearly defined for the lines to be settled in their statements. The Sonatina is a music of mellowness.

The interval of a fourth plays an important role in the finale. Many times a number of these spans are run in consecutive order. More conjunct detail marks the opening movement. A binary formation is used in the middle, slow movement, where, ever the contrapuntalist, Heiden restates the first theme in canonic form.

- **Sonatina for Flute and Piano (1958)**

The peak of Heiden's three-movement work is the finale, where, within the most evenly distributed textural activity, a series of canons are displayed. These are contrasted in terms of articulative and connected lines.

The first movement has triple-beat liquidity. It flows like a quick waltz. The following movement, also in triple meter, has the sustained intensity of an aria.

QUARTET

- **Serenade for Bassoon, Violin, Viola, and Cello (1955)**

There is no cancellation of conventional procedure in the serenade format used by Heiden. Nonetheless, for the greater part, there is a fresh tang within the sequence of movements.

The Notturno has a transmutative quality as it moves (save for a single measure) in the restive pulse of quinary total. There is rhythmic spring in the March, which is to be expected. But there is also a nice inlay of counterpoint that is special when used in this form. The reticence of the close of the movement is also

special. Further restraint is found in the Intermezzo, in terms of tempo, dynamic, and melodic flow. Part four is a Scherzo in far-less-than-usual quadruple pulse. The speed of the movement is exciting by itself; the pileup of repetitive pitches increases the excitement. Once more Heiden opts for a quiet conclusion. And that mood of moderation continues in the sustained style of the Epilogue.

QUINTETS

- **Four Dances for Brass Quintet (Two Trumpets, Horn, Trombone, and Tuba) (1967)**

No dance types are specified. The set is rhythmic, of course, and only one (number three) is in moderate tempo.

Interesting and convincing metrical depictions surround neotonal procedures. In the first dance quintuple and sextuple meters alternate. In the fourth one the principal pulsatile measurement is septuple. The second dance is a fugue, with a countersubject that outlines the ubiquitous B-flat–A–C–B, which spells "Bach" in German. Number three of the set is marked by block scoring and interplay of muted and open timbre in the trumpets.

- **Quintet for Horn and String Quartet (1952)**

The shadow of late, late romanticism falls heavily on Heiden's four-movement Quintet. That isn't bad at all, since it is, in fact, descriptive of music that is civil and urbane, and freely tonal. Heiden's work (a stunning muted Vivace must be stressed) may be in romantic dress, but it moves with the security that marks classical gait.

- **Sinfonia for Woodwind Quintet (1949)**

Heiden's ternary-shaped six-minute piece is

superbly neo-Hindemithian. No monkey business; it says what it has to say directly, cleanly, and holds the attention. It is the work of a craftsman who has something to relate even though with a borrowed accent.

- **Woodwind Quintet (1965)**

It has been common to relate this composer's work to the style of Paul Hindemith. Indeed, the creative accordance is there to hear and, without overprotesting, no negative result comes from Heiden's music sounding like Hindemith's. (One is reminded that Heiden studied with Hindemith at the Hochschule für Musik in Berlin from 1929 to 1933.) In this work, at least, the Hindemithian quality is rougher, more edged, even more dissonant.

The quintet is a fine example of Heiden's immensely accomplished consideration of form. The Variations are laid out in six sections, defined by tempo change (Lento–Allegro moderato–Allegro–Allegro vivace–Adagio–Lento). Movement two is a Capriccio which is a play on intervallic expansion. Metrical activity is paralleled by solo change in the Intermezzo. The thematic line passes from oboe to clarinet to bassoon, et cetera, and the structure itself moves from restrained rhythmic motility to peak liveliness in the center, followed by a return to the initial state. In the Finale inserts of metrically foreshortened measures (in 3/8) contrast with measures of equally totalled quarter-note pulses in twos and threes. The effect, together with syncopative detail, is a music of bracing vitality. Indeed, if this be Hindemithian it is welcome, and one wishes more of it.

Heider, Werner (1930–)

DUO

- *Dialogue I* **for Clarinet and Piano (1960)**

Juicy atonalism, juiced up with hammer and tongs chromaticism. The music is thick with pitch movement, and the motility is peppered with irregular metrical order plus bimetricality in a number of places.

The array of instrumental interlocution spreads over nineteen sections. To keep order there are repeats of formal types and snippeted recapitulations. Thus, the total conversation is kept under control.

A pitch-packed Risoluto moves into a quiet portion. Then appears the first of three Scherzandos (the sections where the bimetricality is used), followed by a clarinet cadenza (others for either instrument will follow). Next, in order: Scherzando II; a piano cadenza; Scherzando III; a tartly lyrical segmented portion; a reworking of the Risoluto material; a Toccata (distinguished from the preceding section by its crusted rhythmic figures); a *fortissimo* forceful lyrical item; and a short solo piano section (not designated with "cadenza" permissiveness).

The first of the extremely truncated repeated portions then is heard: Scherzando I, with a two-measure basis for the piano combined with different meters for the clarinet. The sequence from that point on is: clarinet cadenza, Scherzando II (two measures), clarinet cadenza, Scherzando III (again two measures), clarinet cadenza, and a terminal portion that has six tempo shifts within it.

Heilman, William Clifford
(1877–1946)

TRIO

- **Trio for Piano, Violin, and Cello, Op. 7**

No sophisticated stylizations can be expected from a composer who received his training in Germany at the turn of the century. Accordingly, this Trio leans heavily on Brahms. No negative marks, however. The music sings, is beautifully shaped, and there are no dry, pedantic areas in the score.

The first movement is in C minor. The last movement begins in that same tonality but moves (expectedly, according to Hoyle) into the opposite mode in the final section. Richness marks the middle movement in B major, its textures full and robust.

Heilmann, Harald (1924–)

DUOS

- *Katharsis* **for Cello and Piano (1971)**

The hothouse world of atonality, with the rhapsodic ongoingness of the music structurally organized by majority conjunct pitch movement.

In its unfolding, Heilmann's ten-minute duo is the musical equivalent of the technique of free association. The release from tension takes place at the close with the keyboard instrument set at a *piano* dynamic level and then at a *pianissimo* level. The cello settles down considerably and in the concluding seven measures shifts between C-sharp and D and then A and G-sharp pitches, all in harmonics. The final sustained chord of the piece is bitonal: B and F-sharp minor.

- *Sonata seria* **for Bassoon (or Cello) and Piano**

Neatly balanced forms parallel the neatly arranged alliterative title endings: Prolog, Monolog, Dialog, and Nekrolog.

One can relish the scrupulous sensitivity and sensibility of the composition's free tonal style. In the Prolog, compactness includes a literal restatement of the initial theme. There is no confusion as to the representation of the second movement (Monolog), which is totally for the bassoon (or cello) alone. Thematic give-and-take fulfills the Dialog and ternary detail applies to the Nekrolog. There is threnodic substantiation in the latter, with bold *fortissimo* statements in the outer sections, and soft-stated lines within.

Heinichen, Johann David
(1683–1729)

DUO

- **Sonata in C Minor for Oboe and Bassoon (or Cello)**

Most of Heinichen's vast output (which includes 63 cantatas, 30 concertos, and 16 masses) remains unpublished. On the basis of this fine duo some of his other compositions should be brought into print without delay.

There is more than formal routine in this work. The objective might have been of ordinary or even modest pretension but the writing goes beyond it. The Grave has a bold striding bass that carries and intensifies the oboe line. Imitations bind the Allegro. Vivaldi comes to mind with the strong duet link of the Larghetto e cantabile. There is dynamism in the final movement (Allegro) that comes from vigorous imitative voicing of the lightweight material.

Heinick, David (1954–)

DUO

- **Duo for Flugelhorn (alternating Trumpet) and Tuba (1978)**

Music of hard-crusted tonalism, angular lines, and intense color of fourfold difference. There are certain textural checks and balances. The first quarter of the duo is for the flugelhorn and tuba. Next, the tuba has an unaccompanied section, followed by a pairing with the trumpet. Then, the trumpet has a lengthy solo and the work concludes in duo formation. Quartal-spaced progressions are emphasized.

QUINTET

- *Variations on an English Round* **for Woodwind Quintet**

Tight, logical, and neat construction, supported by declarative and pungent harmony. There is connective structuring beginning with the introduction to the theme, followed by six variations and a coda that concludes softly, the exact opposite to the opening of the work. The last is initiated by a glissando sweep of the horn to the highest possible pitch. This move is another connective device, being repeated toward the end of the first variation, just before the fifth variation, and prior to the concluding measures of the piece.

The fourth variation consists of rhythmic fracturing. Variations five and six are, respectively, fugal and canonic. Until the last measure, the latter is entirely free of chromatics—a telling contrastive twist.

Heininen, Paavo (1938–)

DUOS

- *Jeu I (Play I)* **for Flute and Piano, Op. 42**

Free association of material, so that everything is in a state of constant flux. The fragmentary stipulation rules the duo, a process the very opposite of thematic argument proven by its growth and development.

Of course in music of this type of shuttling montage the aural surprises are many over a fourteen-minute span. The coloristic verbiage includes flute microtones, different speeds of vibrato, key slaps, tongue rams, sounds minus defined pitch, huge multiphonics, and harmonics; and for the piano, string glissando and plucking, clusters, and hitting the steel frame of the instrument. Special is the use of singing, speaking, whispering, and whistling. And that includes within these using the names of Szymanowski, Stockhausen, and a number of fellow Finnish composers such as Rydman, Meriläinen, Aho, and so on. A prime example of what can be classified as "free-lance" composition.

- *Jeu II (Play II)* **for Violin and Piano, Op. 43**

Music that is conceived in a stream of consciousness, in which, Heininen explains "all parameters are of equal value as directions of musical argument, and all their combinations are equally probable." This is the same philosophy that governs the style of *Jeu I (see above)*. (Both works were composed in the same year, 1980, and, as will be noted, bear successive opus numbers.)

Here, the pianist is required to pluck and rub the strings, as well as to place assorted items on them in various ways (by dropping a steel bar, by striking them with a steel spoon, etc.). In places, the violinist is required to play without vibrato, to use exaggerated bow pressure to obtain a snarling effect, and to touch a plucked string very gently with the fingernail to produce a different type of snarling sound.

QUINTET

- **Quintet for Flute (alternating Piccolo and Alto Flute), Tenor Saxophone (alternating Alto Saxophone and Bass Clarinet), Piano, Vibraphone, and Percussion (Bass Drum, Small Drum, Tam-tam, Bongos, Tom-tom, Two Gongs, Two Cymbals, Crotales, Claves, Maracas, Wood Block, and Cow Bells), Op. 7**

A primacy of intensity and timbre (especially as concerns the large percussion assemblage) over matters of pitch and duration exists in the Quintet. Importantly, it is the piano that solidifies the heavy instrumental weight and action of the percussion.

There are five major connected sections in the piece, the first three serving as the "Exposition," with the second of these termed an "Improvisation." The fourth division is "Evolution," and the final section an "Epilogue." Heininen's music is of contemporaneously varied amalgamation with constant development of the material. In tonal music this style was labeled "through-composed."

Heiniö, Mikko (1948–)

SEXTET

- **Ākāśa for Six Trombones, Op. 27**

Ākāśa (a Sanskrit word meaning "ether, which produces and carries the sound," according to a note in the score) has the montage splurge of the ultramodern composer.

Athematic, additive-formed, the music swirls and glides through pitches, and there are countless effects, such as blowing into the instrument minus sound, whispering into the trombone, talking into it, slapping the palm on the mouthpiece, etc.

If feasible, the instruments should be separated. The best result is obtained by "placing the players in a semicircle around the audience."

Heiss, Hermann (1897–1966)

TRIO

- **String Trio No. 1 for Violin, Viola, and Cello (1953)**

In its formal makeup Heiss's trio is far afield from other string trios (and other string combinations, for that matter). The three movements, especially the second and third, form a fantasy tapestry of implied programmatic shapes.

The work begins with a *Fantasia*, balanced by unisoned pithiness at the extremes. In between, the lines move out, around, and away and then converge several times into unification.

Movement two is marked *Drei Charaktere (Three Characters)*. The first "character" has a mixed personality with shifts of timbre. The second of the group is a fast-moving chap and is strictly chordal from first beat to last (the form is just as strict, with a literal recapitulation of the first part). "Character" number three has a contrapuntal shuffle.

The final movement is an *Opera brevis (Short Opera)* that opens with a tutti which will serve as a ritornel. Then an "Aria per il basso" is announced by the cello. The ritornel is used again, followed by an "Aria per il soprano" for the violin, which includes harmonics, trills, and a rubato recitative. Once more, the ritornel, with the "Aria per il alto" (for the viola) following. The ritornel is reannounced and the work concludes with a *Balletto*, with the ritornel bringing down the curtain.

Heiss, John (1938–)

TRIO

- *Four Movements* **for Three Flutes**

No simple structure applies here, wherein the three soprano winds disport themselves with flowerings, flourishes, birdlike roulades, and ornamentations drawn from ultrabright contemporary ground plans. The use of double pitches expands the trio to four-, five-, and six-part writing. Special harmonics widen the color range. And key slaps are principally of two types: a straight percussive effect and one that combines the key contact with pitch. Style matches this sonic pilotage.

Rhapsodic urgency climaxing in vigorous contrapuntalism is found in movement one. Kinetic and asymmetric conditions control movement two, with a unison sweep for the instruments marking the conclusion. The sostenuto of the third part is governed by comparisons of vibrato, nonvibrato, and harmonics. Cluster arrangements give an impressionistic patina to the whole. The finale is cleverly proportioned. Polyphonic key clicks lead gradually to normal sound projection, with the contrapuntal activity maintained. Paralleling this is a tempo increase from M.M. $\d = 60$ to $\d = 90$ to $\d = 120$. The first movement is then recalled and a rhythmically unisoned, frictionally pitched coda concludes the action. Heiss's trio is a brilliant achievement. His instrumental knowledge results in true creative action.

QUARTET

- **Quartet for Flute, Clarinet, Cello, and Piano (1971)**

Coloristic instrumentation is matched by the rhapsodic content of this seven-minute piece. Heiss's detailing of instrumental inventiveness (*see above: Four Movements* for Three Flutes) does not extend to any of the four instruments used in this case, but instrumental independence of consideration does. The four instruments rarely combine rhythmically; they pursue individual linear lives—and healthy ones. This composition is, indeed, for a quartet of equal instruments.

Tempos change; the intensity of detail does not. But this type of line writing is, within its highly complex rhythmic and chromatic temper, always a line of rebound and reflex. The entire approach is as elastic as the formal freedom. Several times during the Quartet partially free passages (as far as entrances are concerned) are cued by a conductor. The pitches are given, with repetitions also decided by conductorial control. The last of these dictated sections completes the work in a quiet dynamic state. These contrapuntal combines are not hit-or-miss, but arranged to create fluidic frictions.

Never is Heiss subservient to the performers' decisions. The creative arrangement is totally his. Indeed, the results deserved the award of the Bowdoin College Contemporary Music Competition of 1971.

Hekster, Walter (1937–)

DUO

- *Interpolations No. II* **for Violin and Piano (1967)**

There are no triadic joys in Hekster's angry and violent atonal duo. The music is thick with chromatics and movement. But there is positive clarity in the structure, which alternates soloism with duality of the instruments. There are eleven textural divisions. The solo violin opens the work, and is heard in the fifth, eighth (very short), and tenth places. The solo piano is heard in the third and sixth positions. All the others are duo statements.

TRIOS

- **Reed Music for Oboe, Clarinet, and Bassoon (1970)**

An ongoing sequence of merged phrases, consisting mainly of grouped pitches played as quickly as possible or in medium tempo, plus sustainments controlled by proportional notation. In the sense that athematicism is the ruling point and that total chromatic pitch insularism reigns, with no cadential definition, Hekster's piece has continuity. However, structural outlines are made by timbre changes provided by separated sections—solo for each of the three instruments and for the three possible duet combinations: clarinet-bassoon, oboe-bassoon, and oboe-clarinet.

- **Windsong II for Trumpet, Flute, and Alto Saxophone (1970)**

Hekster's trio is written in his usual style of graphic notation. The rhythms are metrically unzoned and aleatorically determined. The instruments are introduced singly. First there is a long portion for trumpet alone, followed by a lengthier duo for trumpet and saxophone. All three instruments are then combined. Later in the piece the flute and saxophone have solo spots and there is another duo, this time by the flute and trumpet. In *Windsong* the composer has made certain of both color and textural assurances.

QUARTET

- **Ambage (Circumlocution) for String Quartet (1970)**

A mix of proportionally notated material and the opposite. With the latter there are three sections that are *sans ambages* ("without beating around the bush"). The first of these is a section of col legno percussing for the quartet. The other two sections are linked, one straight bowed rhythmics, the other lightly fingered plucked rhythmics of indeterminate pitch. With the freely noted data there are the standard array of avant-garde sound sprays, including assorted glissandos and quarter tones.

QUINTETS

- **Pentagram for Woodwind Quintet (1961)**

Sketchbook-size movements. Examples: Number three consists of nineteen measures in Allegro con moto tempo; number four has a total of eleven measures set in Lento tempo. The atonal style is a good match for such pithiness. So are the rhythmic variances.

- **Relief IV for Woodwind Quintet (1969)**

The world of nonmetrical music, of music to be performed within specific time lengths obtained from proportional notation, containing pitches indicated but with their rhythmic disposition at the will of the performer, a music of anything-can-happen, but without harm. In other words, Hekster's piece is a full-steamed avant-garde composition of sound swirls and pieces. In this case form gives way totally to a consideration of quintuplicated sonorous activity.

Helfer, Walter (1896–1959)

QUARTET

- **Quartet in G for Two Violins, Viola, and Cello (1923)**

Helfer was in the American group of composers who wrote in the traditional, romantic manner. He was a composer who quietly did his work, was written about rarely (though he had won his share of prizes, including the Prix de Rome and the Paderewski prize for an orchestral work), performed all too infrequently, but who, nonetheless, produced well-wrought music. Above all, Helfer's compositions have melodic spontaneity, and such claim cannot well be ignored.

There is no pretense or labored contrivance in the first movement, which has an introduction (later returning to usher in the coda), a two-theme sonata exposition, contrasts of key, meter, and mood; followed by development and a recapitulation of the material. There are dance suggestions in the second movement as well as the last. There is no slow movement; the changes of pace in the last two movements substitute for it.

Helgason, Hallgrímur (1941–)

DUO

- **Sonata [No. 2] for Violin and Piano**

Helgason studied with a number of teachers including Paul Hindemith, and it is Hindemith that will be recognized in the textural layering of the slow movement. The tonal cogency and lucidity there are heard as well in the sonata's first movement and the sectional finale.

Heller, James G. (1892–1971)

QUARTET

- ***Three Aquatints* for String Quartet, Op. 1**

This composer was unique. Though music was only his avocation, he produced a fairly large list of choral, orchestral, and chamber music works. Heller was a rabbi, the only one of his profession writing serious music in the United States. His music is not avocationary in sound; romantic it is, professional as well. At one time, his vocations overlapped. He carried on religious duties both with his own congregation and in connection with national affairs; he composed and for a dozen seasons wrote the program notes for his hometown orchestra, the Cincinnati Symphony.

These three pieces are more akin to watercolors than etchings. The first is in barcarolle drift, short canonic branches marking the second part of the balanced three-section form. The second is of uncompounded theme—each presentation being slightly embroidered and embellished upon; not varied, merely refurbished. The last piece is a kinetic presto, dancing on repetitive sixteenth notes, with cross-beat accents. The sixteenths do not stop, but are slowed down, combined with a cantabile melody, and run legato to form the contrast within the triple-part form, which has *spiccato* energy at its outer parts.

Helm, Everett (1913–)

DUOS

Sonatas for Flute and Piano

It is not only the devil that is the author of confusion. Sometimes it is also the music publisher, aided (also sometimes) by the forgetful composer.

Helm wrote two flute and piano sonatas, one published by the Arrow Press, the other by Schott. Neither sonata was numbered. Fortunately, the total of movements in the pair of works differs, with three in one and four in the other. The numbers indicated in the discussions below are based strictly on the order of publication—presumably paralleling the order of composition, but not always the case.

▪ Sonata [No. 1] for Flute and Piano

The problem of composing a work for flute and piano without meandering into the superficial pyrotechnical inanities of so many a flutist-composer is not so difficult as one would imagine. The flute has manifold color capabilities, with differences of register from the soft low section to the volatile higher extremity; it has, also, a technical proficiency that can make energetic movements a delight. Its capacity for the sustained line is one of its most beneficial powers. It is that which Helm calls on, in a reticent work, yet one that does not turn its back on color differentials. And there is sensitive attention to balance. For even in the semipolyharmonies that so often dot the harmonic landscape of this three-movement work, Helm keeps in mind the fact that the opposites of flute and piano do not attract each other, that the former is often canceled out or blurred by the heavy waters of the piano.

A fifth (an "open-air" interval) is the motival base for the first movement. In its repetition, transposition, and extension (to a sixth or an octave), the movement has beauty of coherence. The same idea is used in the slow movement, spreading into a lush melody that has capricious moments before it returns to its home base. There is Mozartian lightness in the outer parts of the final movement, in which the piano becomes thicker (by more than one sound per hand) only in the retelling of the expositionary material. The pastoral middle section sings forth, contrasting, therefore, to the somersaulting figures that precede and succeed it.

▪ Sonata [No. 2] for Flute and Piano

The first movement, Allegro, revolves freely around the area of C major. The music rolls with flexibility, including the subtle flux resulting from a shift of quadruple and then duple pulse into the unequal proportion of 7/8. Movement two is a Lento, with a double specified point certifying that the conception is not of confined issue. The piano is marked "recitative," while the flute is to play "in declamatory style." Though the structure is ternary, the music's malleability is freed of squareness, with such sensitive coloration as merging a flutter-tongued passage into a trill.

Movements three and four are an Aria, in andante tempo, and a concluding Vivo. There is a relationship between the pair, since the theme of the former provides the thematic "head" of the other. Variational rondo treatment applies to the Vivo—a music of brightness.

▪ Sonata for Violin and Piano (1936)

Helm employs mostly polyphonic language in the first movement. Where harmonic elements are utilized fourths are combined with thirds. Fundamentally, there are two basic ideas set in contrast, both projected from an extremely strong rhythmic subject. This pulsatile power influences the motility of the more lyrical item.

Variational treatment is sensitively applied in the middle movement. The materials in the final Presto are duple-knit throughout; they are fugal and chordal, detached and connected, fast and slow, energetic and placid. Opposites do attract each other.

Helmschrott, Robert M. (1938–)

TRIO

- *Invention* for Clarinet, Trombone, and Bassoon

No relationship to Bach's inventions. This is serial syntax set into free coinage. Helmschrott is his own man. And, in so being, he constructs an interfusion of contrapuntalism which, for the greater part, lays out an active rhythmic (and metric) sonorous smorgasbord. Tempo unrest is also particular to this dodecaphonic rhapsody. Within five minutes the music traverses thusly: largo–presto–largo–presto–andante–allegro molto–andante–allegro molto–andante–presto–adagio–allegro molto–andante–presto. Within this hyperactivity the sounds come to a holding point (by way of fermatas) fourteen times. That this number equals the number of tempo changes is mere coincidence. Overall, it would seem that Helmschrott's *Invention* consists of a set of confrontations.

Helps, Robert (1928–)

TRIO

- Trio for Piano, Violin, and Cello (1957)

The forms of the three connected movements are as fluid as Helps's chromatic syntax. There are no symmetrically formationed ground plans in the work, which covers a short Mesto, a vigorous and speedy (and metrically assorted) Molto marcato, and a Maestoso. But if formality is not squared, it is minutely integrated, with the material in continual transformation. There is unity within each division and a subtle relationship in terms of the entire Trio by way of thematic pitch movement: the opening themes of the three movements begin with a

rising minor third.

Full-fledged trio scoring is operative, with special attention to texture marking the final eighteen measures. Within this portion not one measure finds the three instruments combined. Eleven measures are for the two string instruments; the concluding three are for solo piano. This knowledgeabilility of piano trio coloration is a continuation of the learned writing that marks the entire opus.

Hely-Hutchinson, Victor (1901–47)

QUARTET

- *Three Fugal Fancies* for String Quartet

Hely-Hutchinson's compositions are generally of light subject matter and detail. Even here, with the use of a serious contrapuntal form, he avoids being austere. Rich and ripe conservative sound combinations result in this triplex array of fugal style. In the first part the subject has fivefold pulse arrangement, with an alternating ratio of 2:3. Lyrical sustainment vitalizes the slow movement. Jig character is the propulsion for the third of the set.

(A string orchestra, with double basses ad libitum, can also perform the piece.)

Hemel, Oscar van (1892–1981)

TRIO

- Trio for Violin, Viola (or Cello), and Piano (1937)

Music that surrounds fluid rhythmic details with wide sweep and impressive vitality. In the first movement the pulses are triple, quadruple, and quintuple (the last split between three and two divisions). Ternary detail in the Grave movement. Its thematic ordering is strictly set for the string instruments. The Rondo-Finale is colored by using tutti detailing for the rhythmic passages and opening up the texture when the quality is lyrical.

QUARTETS

- *About Commedia dell'arte* for Oboe Quartet (Oboe, Violin, Viola, and Cello) (1967)

Three of the stock characters in the popular form of comedy that flourished in Italy from the 16th to the 18th centuries are the cast of Hemel's seven-part chamber music suite.

"Arlecchino" (also known as Harlequin) was the most famous of these characters, and a fair amount of music has been produced delineating his personality. His acrobatic ability is pictured in the first movement with rhythmic twists and tempo changes. Movement two introduces "Colombina" (generally spelled Columbine). Her music is of moderate scherzo temper. Movement three is a combination of these two personages: "Colombina e Arlecchino" (the music does not specifically reidentify them). Movement four brings in "Petrolino" (generally spelled Pedrolino). Described elsewhere as a white-faced, moon-struck dreamer, Hemel's portrayal follows suit with a quiet line in the oboe, supported by ponticello string timbre for the greater part. The other movements relate to "Colombina e Petrolino," in number five, all three characters in number six, and a concluding "Elegia per Colombina e Petrolino."

- *Donquichotterie* for Four Trombones (1962)

No musico-cinematic doings in this three-part suite. Hemel hid what he had in mind with this fanciful title, but it does bring up, desire it or not, the picture of the musical macho Don and his adventures.

The only link (a remote one, indeed) is the fact that Strauss's famous *Don Quixote* consists of an Introduction and Theme with Variations, plus Finale, and Hemel's third (final) movement is also a Tema con variazione. All five variants are on the motile side, the second of the set a Giocoso affair, the third a Mazurka, the fourth strictly chordal, and the fifth and final one an antiphonally rhythmic Presto.

Movement one is an exact tripartite piece with tutti rhythmic enclosures of the four voices in the movement's outer sections. Movement two reminds one of the cavorting details within the Don Quixote tale. It starts as a fugue then runs through pithy tossings of part of the subject, including diminution, and concludes with a short coda. Plenty in this music to maintain interest.

Hemmer, Eugene (1929–77)

QUARTET

- **Divertimento for Harp, Marimba, Celesta, and Piano**

No startling structural or thematic revelations here, but certainly some very inviting sonority exhibits. And just as certainly, the only example of such a quartet combination.

There is considerable vibrational content. Examples: the end of the Overture with polyrhythmic statement (two against three against five) of bimodal ostinato formations for all four instruments; pendulous thrusts by the full quartet at the triple *forte* conclusion of the Rondo, with the bitonality of C and D major declared in up and down glissandos.

Movement two is an Aria that gives most of the attention to the marimba. Sound sweeps in this movement are rather restricted.

Henkemans, Hans (1913–)

QUINTETS

- *Aere festivo (Festive Air)* **for Three Trumpets and Two Trombones (1965)**

While the opening phrase in the first trumpet (there are two trumpets in C and a small trumpet in D) is used as the basis for a bit of development, the unity for the composition is obtained from sectional ordering. This leads to a polymetric bit and still later a triple-instrument cadenza. The final cadence arrives at a mild cluster, with the adjacent pitches of E–F–G–A–B spread over more than three octaves.

- **Quintet No. 2 for Flute, Oboe, Clarinet, Bassoon, and Horn (1962)**

A double layout of material that is both alternated and combined. One set is highly active and fantasy-loose, the other is smoother, built on the motility of triplets. Woven in is a good amount of polyrhythmic and polymetric arrangement, techniques that are strong reminders of the style of Willem Pijper, with whom Henkemans studied.

This is an accurate music in the sense that the detail does not fudge the issue. In all the sections no attempt is made to highlight voices but to retain an emphasis on the textural mass. This type of writing is an example of a method that is, in its way, somewhat unconventional.

Henn, Randahl W. (1953–)

DUO

- **Duo Sonata for Clarinet and Piano**

There is some virtuosity in this Duo Sonata, but Henn is concerned mainly with solid music,

not soloistic specialties—a fact not always realized in music presumably of chamber music format. Tonalism is the stylistic pivot, but there is a full chromatic flavor that spices the lines. And in some cases there is decided key mixture.

The music is texturally compelling. (The first two-dozen measures are for the piano alone.) Three movements, the first and last imbued with a combination of lyrical and scherzo elements.

Hennessy, Swan (1866–1929)

QUARTET

- **String Quartet No. 4, Op. 75**

Melodicism of the fully tonal brand, for the most part devoted to lively and energetic music.

In the first movement a central vigorously polyphonic conception is prefaced and followed by slow-paced sections. Ternary plotting is used in the next movement as well. The Allegretto scherzoso is rondo patterned. Some light color is applied to the initial theme, which is presented entirely in pizzicato the first and third times it is heard and entirely bowed the second time. There is vigorous authority to the finale, which is also tripartite, though of larger measurement than the other parts of the work.

Henrichsen, Børge Roger (1916–)

DUO

- *Praeludium in C—Souvenir* and *Made in Germany* **for Piano and Bass (1946)**

Henrichsen wears many hats: leader of a dance band, pedagogue, composer of swing and jazz as well as etudes in jazz form (some of these in such demand as to require six printings!), and lawyer! He represents a highly individual composer within the many talents in Denmark, the only composer devoted to the juicy *trouvailles* of New York's nightclubs *cum* Copenhagen's Tivoli.

Still, Henrichsen's "hot and sweet" is somewhat dated in relation to later jazz-rock style—like comparing the first film sound tracks to present-day Dolby stereo sound. The Danish composer blues his chords and jolts his sevenths, but at best provides a secondhand type of jazz for presentation at a serious concert. Nevertheless, there is profit for the listener provided he does not become impatient with the chi-chi musical arbitrations of this set of pieces or bored by the string bass pizzicato throughout (it is worth noting that the set of pieces is "for piano and bass," rather than the reverse). However, it is still a novelty to find highbrow chamber music flirting, if not fully consorting, with rag and bop.

Praeludium is the longest, moving in moderate tempo, with the *Souvenir* contrastively styled as a slow blues in which the conception is more partial to the bass than in the opening piece. *Souvenir* is to be followed immediately by *Made in Germany*, which uses a modified boogie-woogie foundation. It is falsely advertised since its true manufacturing was done in Broadway nightclubs of the late thirties. The tempo marking is medium swing, but the first two pieces revert to traditional Italian directions: moderato for *Praeludium* and sostenuto for *Souvenir*.

(For no worthy reason, the published title reads: Praeludium in C and Two Other Pieces—Souvenir and Made in Germany.)

Henriques, Fini (1867–1940)

DUO

- **Sonata for Violin and Piano, Op. 10**

Henriques was a fervent romanticist: Big gestures, robust lines are found in his music; also formal respect, as is evident in the opening, surging movement. The main theme is in 5/4 in G minor, the secondary idea is in the relative major and in broader 6/4 meter. And the intensity does not lessen in the presto speed of the Scherzo. The contrasting, long-arched lines in that movement do not halt the forward motion—the fundamental duple rhythm projects the motility. In the Trio the base tempo persists, but the effect is quicker, since three pulsations occupy the same time space as the previous two.

Urgency, even at a lower scale, is retained always in the Sonata. It is found in the Moderato (third) movement, where an Allegretto forms the contrasting middle part. Syncopation is doubly important in this movement, for the accentual displacement is transferred and becomes the *force majeure* for the Finale, which is linked to the third movement. The potency is not lessened in this concluding part until the coda. In presto tempo, even the contrasted second subject (the music is in sonata-allegro form) is not uttered with a subdued voice. At the close Henriques reverses himself. The music broadens into *fortissimo*, slows and moves into a quotation from the Allegretto, and ends in triple *piano* in the home key of G minor.

QUARTET

- **String Quartet**

Some composers repeat their own aesthetic method and formal passions. Henriques did. The same energy and romantic sound-surge, which substitutes wholesale tonal transfer for subtle harmonic tensions, found in his violin and piano sonata *(see above)* exist here. And also use of the cyclic tie with a quiet close. Such conformity gives coherence and is no hindrance to an individual composition's value.

Voice action of nonintimate discourse is matched by tonal activity in the first part. Beginning and concluding in A minor, in between, there are defined sections (some of length) presented in seven different tonalities. And the tempo is, significantly, Allegro energico. Telescopic form is used to define the slow and scherzo positions. The latter is both within the former and balanced within itself with a contrastive *meno mosso*.

The Finale also has a significant tempo (Allegro con brio), illustrating again Henriques's penchant for musical drive. Relationship exists in the contrasting sections without denying this objective by means of constant sixteenth-note formations. The music then gets faster, comes to a temporary halt, and the Adagio is then quoted. A sudden one-measure presto *fortissimo* outburst, and the quartet ends with a four-measure adagio *pianissimo* cadence.

Henselt, Adolph von (1814–89)

TRIO

- **Trio in A Minor for Piano, Violin, and Cello, Op. 24**

The textural and textual facets of romantic scoring, with fully resonanced piano writing. (The piano figures in every work Henselt produced, including a single concerto.) Henselt's writing is intelligent and skillful, even though it breeds conventionality in its sometimes Mendelssohnian quality.

Four movements, as expected. The first is an Allegro; the slow movement an Andante. Exact contrast marks the Scherzo, with a punctuative first theme and a flowing second

theme. Some contrapuntal colorism is used in the propulsively directed Finale.

Henze, Hans Werner (1926–)

DUOS

- **Sonata for Violin and Piano (1946)**

The Henze of early conservative writing. Full romantic stirrings but never overstressed. A bold Prélude with the type of rhythmic drive that identified early Hindemith. The Nocturne begins with chasteness, proceeding on a one-chord-per-measure basis, but then becomes activated and is followed by a return to the initial state. The violin is muted in the Intermezzo, and the piano is operative, first measure to last, with strict two-part writing. There is a calm and very slow tempo coda to conclude the Finale. But otherwise, this final part of the duo represents the music of a bright and brash youngish composer.

- **Sonatine for Flute and Piano (1947)**

Henze's early opus emphasizes ostinatos, with good attention to bitonal and polytonal elements.

After a four-measure flute introduction the opening part moves ahead in Molto vivace pace and the ground-stamping repetitive rhythms take hold. However, Henze knows the value of directness. The movement is concentrated, with textural values highlighted by using solo colors for episodes. There are but twenty-four measures in the Andantino; its pastoral effect conveyed by light, arpeggiated chords for the piano and flute melodicism. Though the Presto is sectionally conceived it achieves balance by way of rondolike assistance.

TRIO

- **Chamber Sonata for Piano, Violin, and Cello (1948)**

Schoenbergian relevancy is found in Henze's compact piano trio. But no serialistic sectarianism, simply the strong syntax that relates to expressionism. Form and matter are here concerned with full chromaticism; there is total avoidance of pitch polarity.

The septenary spans, plus diminished and augmented octaves, found in the first part (Allegro assai) match the uneven 7/8 meter and busy rhythms within it. Like begets like. Even in soft dynamic passages the motion is jagged, nonrelaxed. The Epilogo that follows the fourth movement has, in its beginning, a slight relationship to this opening movement. The trio's close, however, has a calm, though fully chromatic, context.

A lyrical quality marks the second movement, with muted string instruments and parallel chords posing polytonality. There is no contradiction in terms of style—the linear jaggedness remains. And it remains in the following Lento, distinguished further by unmuted string sound. In the sectional rhapsodic progress of the fourth movement one perceives tokens of variational process.

QUARTETS

- **String Quartet No. 1 (1947)**

Early Henze, composed when he was just 22. Virile Henze, as to be expected. Eclectic Henze, also not unexpected. Regardless, an admirable work, precisely composed and excellently proportioned. (Timings are given at the end of each of the four movements. In minutes they are respectively, 5, 5, 3, 5. But Schott's editors were napping when they read proofs, since the performance time noted on an introductory score page is given as "20 minuten"!)

The opening motival figure and pungent sixteenth-note passages carry the first movement. As in the rest of the quartet, the music mainly brings Hindemith to mind, occasionally Stravinsky. It is rhythm that simultaneously anchors and projects the material. In the Andantino the first thirty-three measures move over a constant cello pizzicato with nine pitches per measure. (Every instrument has a chance at the principal fluid melody of the movement.) A muted, compact third movement is laid out in ternary form. Rhythm again and hard-nosed attention to motoric Hindemith is heard in the final Presto. Hammered triplets here—generous use, with no self-denial.

- **String Quartet No. 2 (1952)**

Serialism in a very elaborate state exists in Henze's composition. Not only do the instruments develop the basic row but they constantly project new twelve-tone successions. Structurally, solid use of retrograde marks the first movement and canonic inversion is emphasized in the second movement.

Basic to the entire quartet is the attention to meter and rhythm. Though the first movement is notated in 4/4, the rhythmic units within the measures are heard in constant motility and assorted size, such as 5/16, 7/16, 4/32, 5/32, and 10/64. The result is nervous, the detail complex. In the second and third movements Blacher's variable-meter technique is applied (a method of systematic metrical changes which sets a pulsed [secondary] design within the total material). In movement two, for example, one metrical network with an eighth note as the denominator and successive numerator totals of 5, 4, 3, 2, 3, and 4 is heard eleven times in succession. In the third movement one metrical design consists successively of 3/8, 5/8, 3/8, 5/8, and 3/16, another of 3/8, 2/8, 3/8, 2/8, and 3/16. The sense of rhapsodic improvisation that results is a colorful inlay to the serial ordering.

- **String Quartet No. 3 (1976)**

Totally preoccupied with polyphonic detail, Henze's one-movement quartet (370 measures long with a performance time of eighteen minutes) is in a fluently linear style, independent of thematic packaging and its development. Blends and balances of motival detail are given further commentary. Actually, there is only one repeated section in the entire quartet; that is the first six measures in ♩ = 66, restated beginning with measure 294 at a faster pace of ♩ = 92.

The voicing is active, and similarly active are the tempos, which change every dozen or so measures. (An example: at the beginning where the metronomic indication is ♩ = 66, then 80, on to 92, back to 80, and then slightly slower at 72.) Textures are weighty, mainly made by the use of all four instruments. There are two special exceptions, both by the viola alone. The first of these occurs well into the work, the other concludes the quartet in a total twelve-pitch span, extremely slow moving, and in a crushed dynamic plane that starts *pppp* and concludes *ppppp*, underlining the dedication of the work to Henze's mother ("in memoriam M.A.G.").

- **String Quartet No. 4 (1976)**

Considered as a unit, the four movements are a multi-hybrid. Four distinct styles are presented, one per movement, as if Henze wished to prove his mastery of the compositional methods being followed in the late 20th century.

Movement one is an eight-minute presentation that zigs and zags down the aleatoric highway. Save for two measures of 4/8 and four of 2/4 there are no metrical controls. To a listener the six measures will hardly register with pulse regularity, what with the snippets, snatches, sensations, silences, sonic spills, and splashes that constitute the music. Some attention is given to repetitive chords as a sort of ostinato, but again the mingling of the many

ideas almost negates their definition. All of the aleatoric attractions are used: tapping on the strings with half bow stick and half bow hair, passages to be played "as fast as possible," intense quarter-tone vibrato, sonic translation of graphic, Morse codelike notation, etc. There are microtonal pitches as well. The movement's conclusion masses the sounds into *fffff*. This is a music of aggressive totality.

Movement two is a gloss on a Pavana by William Byrd (1543–1623) using 20th-century chromatic harmony and counterpoint. The effect is thrice two dimensional. First, the viola is featured as an unmuted timbre while the other instruments are muted throughout. Second, quite often the violins and cello play with a glassy ponticello sound, while just as often the viola plays flautando (bowing lightly on the strings over the end of the fingerboard). Third, the Byrd music is basic (though varied and molded) to the violins and cello; the viola counterattacks, as it were, in a different style, with thrusted tonality and rhythmic detail in total conflict with the other instruments. The ending successively tempers the dynamic force from *p* to *pp* to *ppp* to *pppp* to *ppppp* on to the final *pppppp*. The total is a twelve-minute piece of raw beauty.

To some extent, the third movement is kin to a scherzo. It has an implied Trio, with lighter material, which moves in slower tempo. The outer parts are swiftly paced, with practically a different meter for *every one* of the 102 measures that begin the movement and as well for the recapitulation, its measures half the total. An acute balance relates this movement to the previous one. Here, again, three instruments are muted (first violin, viola, and cello) while the second violin moves into a solo spot, plays with open timbre, and is registered mostly in the soprano zone. The other relationship pertains to the dynamics, with a similar descent from *p* to *pppp*. The timing is given as six minutes.

It is impossible to give a time length for the

final movement (the previous three already totaling twenty-six minutes). Here, Henze goes the whole hog with chance technique, in an artistically stylistic struggle titled Rondo improvvisato. Indeed, the effect is rampant improvisation, though all the pitches and formations of the materials are notated, some with meters, some with metronomic indications. Marked sections denote a "beginning," a "center," and an "ending." The beginning is a "theme" of sixteen measures in the first violin, viola, and cello, but with twenty-four measures simultaneously in the second violin. Various "events" are then notated for each instrument, from which the choices are to be decided freely. A return to the theme, "or parts of it," is to be made "occasionally." The lead for all the gestures is the first violin. "It initiates each new turn and gives the mood (character, color, intensity) to create and the echo to make by the fellow players." An intense jam session results. For example, after the thematic statement, the first violin has fourteen events, three with specified metronomic indications, one guided by a tempo heading, before the "center" is reached. At the same time, the second violin has eighteen events, four of which have metronomic controls. The viola also has fourteen events; the cello, thirteen.

What makes Henze's scenario one of fantastic mastery is not the procedure but the stylistic unity displayed in the data for all the instruments. There is a beauty here as well—a beauty of structural logic. Verily, this is strong music by a strong composer.

- **String Quartet No. 5 (1977)**

A six-movement work, indicated "in memoriam Benjamin Britten." Only the first movement is minus a specific tempo or descriptive identification, merely listed at $\quarternote = 72$. Movement two is headed "Atemlos" ("Breathless") as well as "Wild"; movement three is designated "Herzschlag" ("Heartbeat"); movement

four is noted "Still, entlegen" ("Quiet, distant"); movement five is indicated "Echos, Erinnerungen, ganz von fern" ("Echoes, Remembrances, all from the distance"); and movement six is titled "Morgenlied" ("Morning Song").

Henze has mentioned that the quartet has the character of a diary. The seething continuity and high coloration of this twelve-tone music confirms it. In movement three the four instruments are muted. There is intense quality in the measures of sustained col legno in that movement and no less in its closing unaccompanied cello passage. Plectra are used by the entire quartet in the fifth movement in an eight-measure portion. The pitch spectrum is broadened by the use of quarter tones.

QUINTETS

- *Amicizia! (Friendship!)* **Quintet for Clarinet, Trombone, Cello, Percussion (Crotales, Three Cymbals, Three Tam-tams, Three Bongos, Four Tom-toms, Timpani, Marimbaphone, and Vibraphone), and Piano (1976)**

Stylistic assortment here. Rhapsodic conduct first, then some aleatoric ancillaries (instructions to the performers to "listen to the notes of the piano and wed your own notes to the piano"), followed by rhapsodic, fast, chromatic music ending with solo piano, then similar slow-paced music, ending with a long unaccompanied clarinet section. Linear intensity matches these tempo changes.

The conclusion is the other side of the tonality coin, with triadic harmony dominating. The twain do meet.

- *L'autunno: Musica per cinque suonatori di strumenti a fiato (Autumn: Music for Five Players of Wind Instruments)* (Flute [alternating Piccolo and Alto Flute], Oboe [alternating Oboe d'amore], Clarinet [alternating E-flat Clarinet and Bass Clarinet], Horn [alternating Wagner Tuba ad lib], and Bassoon [alternating Double Bassoon]) (1977)

Reading the instrumentation list it is apparent that instrumental color is sharply delineated in this five-movement, twenty-minute piece. If the Wagner tuba is used in the second movement, only movement three will be for the traditional woodwind quintet of flute, oboe, clarinet, horn, and bassoon. And indeed, within the instrumental totality individual timbres are highlighted in extended solo sections. These are for the clarinet, with a lengthy unmetered section that concludes the first movement; a thirty-measure statement by the horn to begin the third movement; a thirty-six-measure section for the bassoon that terminates the third movement; a twenty-one-measure solo, again for the bassoon, in the middle of movement four; and a thirty-six-measure section for the double bassoon that brings the fourth movement to a close.

There is chromatic supremacy in Henze's style, dipping into serial exploits but always free in its application. That elucidation is tied into metrical play that is extremely free and fluid. There is rhapsody in the first movement; a balletic contour to the second movement (Allegretto). The third movement is tripartite in terms of textures and colors; the complete quintet plays in the central part (marked "melancholy"), solo horn and solo bassoon define respectively the outer sections.

Intense, virtuosic detailed polyphony carries the Vivace fourth part of the work. Its texture thins in the movement's final portion, leading to the solo discourse by the double bassoon that terminates the movement. Only the final cadence is vertically disposed in the otherwise contrapuntal finale, marked "Quia respexit humilitatem ancillae suae" ("For He hath regarded the low estate of his handmaiden").

- **Quintet for Flute, Oboe, Clarinet, Horn, and Bassoon (1952)**

Free dodecaphonicism is blended with direct polytonality in Henze's woodwind quintet. A dark quality marks the opening, a theme and six variations follow. In the second movement sectionalism marks the structure. So does tempo. The sections move at a repeatedly slower pace: the first, "Sehr ruhig" ("Very quiet"); the second, "Noch langsamer" ("More slowly"); and the third, "Sehr langsam, schleppend" ("Very slow, dragging"). Sequential expansion accentuates this pulling back of the action, with a precise ratioed increase of the number of measures for each portion. There are twelve measures in the first, fifteen in the second, and eighteen in the last. Drollery with a sense of parody is exhibited in the finale, which concludes with a pithy Galopp.

SEXTET

- *Der junge Törless (The Young Törless)*: **Fantasia for String Sextet (Three Violins, Two Violas, and Cello) (1965)**

This constitutes a recycling of earlier material. Henze had composed the score for a film by Volker Schlöndorff, *Der junge Törless*, based on the novel of the same name by the Austrian Robert Musil (1880–1942). An adaptation of portions of the film music was then made.

Richly expressive music, this; somewhat sectional as well—to be expected of music tied to dramatic situations. There are four movements. The first of these links four sections, the second section twice the speed of the first, progressing to a portion in the tempo of a funeral march, and then moving into faster-paced material. Movement two has binary detail, designed in unequal lengths within its total. On the other hand, the third movement is balanced in its ternary form, with an Air and a Pastorale, and a return to the former. Again, partnership of unequal divisions is made in the fourth movement. It consists of a Vivace based on a constant sixteenth-note figure that fills every beat in each measure (by the third violin), completed by an adagio section titled Epilogo.

Herberigs, Robert (1886–1974)

DUO

- **Sonatine for Clarinet and Piano (1939)**

Light romantic syntax is used. The outer movements are vital and rhythmic and stress the motility of sixteenth-note patterns. There is more chromatic flexibility in the slow movement—distinguished by a reverential theme. Herberigs opts for the less usual four-movement design in his Sonatine, following the Andante cantabile with a flowing music of compact total. It could easily be called "à la minuet."

Hermans, Nico (1919–)

QUARTET

- *Impressieflitsen (Impressively)* **for Four Flutes**

Flute quartets tend to be clear and positive in style and best when the scoring is of the open variety. Hermans follows suit. And the aesthetic issue remains fixed homophonically. There isn't a measure of counterpoint in the five movements. Furthermore, a positive formal account—all the pieces are in tripartite design. Neat,

undemanding tonal music.

Hermanson, Åke (1923–)

QUARTETS

- *In sono* **for Flute, Oboe (alternating English horn), Viola, and Cello, Op. 12**

In part in minimal style, with incessant statement of sustained sounds. These are combined with a motival development that never expands into thematic length. Checked vitality here (a kind of frozen music) creating a texture of granitic contour.

Hermanson is very much his own man. In the aural fascinations of *In sono* it is as though the guts of a few sounds have been dissected and redissected into their manifold fractional elements and are "seen" through the ears.

- *Lyrical Metamorphoses* **for String Quartet, Op. 2**

Motival continuity rather than thematic contrast and development describes Hermanson's uncompromising, decidedly personal technique. The motive is separated, contrasted, and mixed in a criss-cross of polyphony. There is constant change in the kinetic snippets. One motive having been exhausted, another enters and the procedure is repeated. The second motive is more concentrated but the sound chunks that emerge out of the new generative item are set forth in similar manner: combined, contrasted, and opposed. All this produces a nervous content throughout the music's fifteen-minute length.

Herrmann, Bernard (1911–75)

QUARTET

- *Echoes* for String Quartet (1966)

A one-movement work in sixteen divisions, each having some affinity with a motto theme that opens (and concludes) the quartet. It appears incessantly, compulsively—sometimes slightly changed or compressed but always recognizable—a significant influence on the work. In all it appears eight times within the eighteen-minute span of the composition. Further, the sections alternating with it draw from its construction, which emphasizes minor seconds and thirds.

Herrmann states that "the term *Echoes* is meant to imply a series of nostalgic emotional remembrances." His confessional approach in sound gives special meaning to the work but is minus any clues.

Interspersed are a slow waltz, a cello solo on top of a sighing accompaniment, a speedy Allegro (could this agitated music, with mysterious ostinatos, be a memory of writing one or more of his sixty-one film scores?), an Adagio (sad-contoured and also structured with ostinatos), a Tempo di habanera section (sinuous with the repetitive rhythm of the viola), a veiled Presto (alternating between dark and snarling sounds), a Lento, and an Allegro (with elements of "hurry" music).

Considered in a different way, *Echoes* might be described as a set of free variations on a repeated (varied) theme. No matter the analytical decision, the quartet has authoritative materials, colorfully presented and conceived in a style that is easily grasped. It is a success.

Hersant, Philippe (1948–)

DUO

- *Klage (Complaint)* for Two Flutes

Short, but not necessarily sweet. No matter. Color-tempered by a number of quarter-tone passages for the second flute. Certainly there is no complaint as to the effectiveness of this piece.

Hertl, František (1906–)

DUO

- Four Pieces for Double Bass and Piano

Standard middle-of-the-road music, but nothing namby-pamby here. Quartal and tertial harmonies support the Preludium. Its rhythmic stability continues in the Burleska, which has a "Go, man!" quality in its vivo tempo and rhythmic continuity. Some light bitonality colors the Nokturno. A presto-paced Tarantella, with a slightly slower central section, completes the suite.

Hervig, Richard B. (1917–)

DUO

- Sonata No. 2 for Clarinet and Piano (1970)

Sectional depiction marks the two movements, as do agitated detail, dramatic outbursts, fractured rhythms, and registral athleticism. A percussive impact surrounds the music. Hervig's duo bristles, the pitches claw and jab. Exciting stuff it is.

Formal stiffness, therefore, is bypassed. In the concluding part of the first movement the instruments start together and both "play as fast as possible: it is not necessary to end together." Movement two is much freer. The clarinet begins unmetered, the piano's time of entry "is approximate." Later, the piano repeats a rhythmic passage in its own tempo, "disregarding" the clarinet. Ultimately a muscular toccata exhibit results, but even here birhythmic detail is included before the much calmer conclusion. A powerful opus.

Herzogenberg, Heinrich von (1843–1900)

DUO

- *Legends* for Viola and Piano, Op. 62

A three-part suite that, in terms of the basic creative conception, is always alive to the true understanding of viola timbre. That Brahmsian particulars weave through the work is certainly no negative finding. (Harold Truscott considers Herzogenberg's chamber music "among the finest and most individual in the nineteenth century." He has written that *Legends* is a "fine concert item . . . one more nail in the coffin of the false idea, so prevalent among violists, that the literature of the instrument is small.")

The Andantino keenly indicates viola spacing for the greatest effect. A darker voice is heard when the string instrument's lines are placed between the piano's treble and bass materials in comparison to the poignant timbre produced when it sings above the piano. Movement two, a shadowy ballade type with a considerable amount of piano arpeggios, is prefaced by a poem: "Pfeile, durchdringet mich, / Lanzen, bezwinget mich, / Keulen, zerschmettert mich, / Blitze, durchwettert mich, / Dass ja das Nichtige, / Alles verflüchtige, / Glänze der Dauerstern, / Ewiger Liebe Kern." ("Arrows, pierce me, / Lances, overcome me, / Clubs, smash me, / Lightening bolts, weather me, / That indeed the frivolous, / All evaporates, / Shining of everlasting stars, / Endless essence of love.")

Variational conduct is followed in the final piece of the set. The theme is followed by three variants, each sixteen measures in length. Variation four is almost twice that length. No energetic or virtuosic discourse. The third variation is slightly faster than the others, the final one stresses some embellishments.

TRIOS

- Trio for Oboe, Horn, and Piano, Op. 61

A music of poetry and in some parts (the first movement) pastoral gentility. It is romantic, indeed. In terms of its scoring Herzogenberg's opus floats into the ear with artistic simplicity.

In the second movement, a presto-scaled Scherzo, the tempo does not brake for Trio contrast; that effect is obtained by using sounds of slightly longer length. The slow movement is permitted to flow—ornate figuration is withheld. The pastoral relaxation inherent in the music is not found in the final rondo-shaped Allegro. In place the music is sunny bright. Throughout, Herzogenberg's Trio is a delight of apt stylization.

- Trio [No. 1] for Piano, Violin, and Cello, Op. 24

As good an illustration as one can find of this now forgotten composer, who produced a huge amount of music, including five string quartets; three violin and piano sonatas; three cello and piano sonatas; pairs of piano trios, piano quartets, and string trios; and so forth. Practically all of it is out of print.

The first of the two piano trios shows a great deal of Schumann in its style. Others see additional influences on this baron's music—specifically Brahms and Wagner, and Slonimsky mentions Max Bruch.

There are four movements. Interestingly, the Andante proceeds, though not so described, as a set of variations. It highlights the work. Another point of interest is the use of the first movement's opening material in Allegro as the basis for the Lento introduction of the finale. Eclectic music, indeed, and always attractive.

QUINTET

- **Quintet for Oboe, Clarinet, Horn, Bassoon, and Piano, Op. 43**

Brahmsian spirit, and, of course, there is nothing wrong with that. The imitation is precise, especially in the rhythmic elements.

Four movements in the usual fast-slow-scherzo-fast sequence. An interesting point is that, save for the Adagio, which is in unexpected B major, all the movements are in E-flat major. Wilhelm Altmann, the important German music bibliographer, describes the Adagio has having "an ethereal beauty of its own." The third movement, an Allegretto, is catchy, scherzo-spirited music set in sextuple time that swings in broad duple pulse.

Hess, Willy (1906–)

DUOS

- *Drei Tonstücke (Three Tone Pieces)* **for Flute and Harp (or Piano), Op. 79**

The compactness and content of these oddly titled "tone pieces" are the very reverse of music with the almost similar title of "tone poems."

A lighthearted affair throughout. "Elfenreigen" ("Elves' Round Dance") moves barcarollelike over simple arpeggios. A Rondo that clings to G major is the second piece, followed by a subdued ending: "Kleines Notturno" ("Small Nocturne"). This is modestly scaled.

- **Duo in C Major for Flute and Viola, Op. 89**

Tonal responsibility, with no lapse in taste, and clear formal objectives appear in this charming duo suite.

The first movement, with the lilt of a minuet but not in minuet form, has sonatina ingredients. A Fughette follows, and a novel one it is. The subject is announced by the flute, the answer given by the viola, and then fugal fashions are abandoned, though the piquancy of the basic idea is maintained. At the conclusion, back comes the fugue subject, truncated, set in stretto.

Movement three begins as a choralish Adagio, expands into curvaceous antithesis, and is attached to a final Rondo. All of this opus represents orderly and refined music and in its genre is a splendid success.

- *Fünf Tonstücke (Five Tone Pieces)* **for Basset horn (or Clarinet) and Piano, Op. 98**

No saucy insouciance in this five-part suite, but moderately sweet, romantic tidbits. Everything is balanced to the utmost, four of the pieces being cast in ternary form. The types alternate: Numbers one, three, and five are each a Romanze; number two is a self-descriptive Rondo, and the fourth of the set is a "Reigentanz" ("Round Dance").

- **Sonata in C Major for Oboe and Piano, Op. 44**

This music, as most of Hess's, is very much in the Austro-German manner. But there is nothing cheap about such stylistic alliance. There is full romantic allegiance to cheerful harmonic munificence and clearly identifiable diatonic melodies, free of disturbing chromatics for the greater part, contained in forms scrupulously faithful to standard measurements.

Sonata rule covers the opening movement. Thematic alternation, balanced by placement within a rondo structure, is used for both the slow and final movements. A pointed, staccato-colored Scherzo precedes the Finale. The former has a relaxed Trio, its gemütlich (easygoing) tempo in contrast to the *rasch* (quick) tempo of the principal part.

- **Sonata in C Minor for Viola and Bassoon (or Cello), Op. 78**

Clear, exact, and lyrical romantic-bred music. The sonata detail of the Allegro agitato is prefaced by a Largo of fifteen measures and balanced by a minute coda of two measures in adagio tempo. Two alternative ideas in contrastive tempo and rhythmic action illustrate the composer's romantic sensibility. Despite these important and defined elements, there is a type of undisciplined fantasy to the writing. This does not apply to the final pair of movements: a clearly poised Minuet and a clearly designed Finale–Rondo.

- *Sonatina brevis* **for Two Violins, Op. 66**

Hess's concentrated duo is clearly tonal and as clear in its formal settings. Oddly, all three movements are in G major. Modulations are kept close to the pivotal key, as in the Trio to the middle Minuet, which moves into the subdominant (C major). A large binary plan covers the baroque thrust of the opening movement, with rondo detail plotting the Gigue that concludes the piece.

- *Trauermusik (Funeral Music)* **for Basset horn (or Clarinet) and Piano, Op. 101**

A tranquil F-minor music that brightens a bit in the center, set in C major, and then returns to its initial tonal space. The rhythmic figure often associated with funeral marches—the dotted-eighth and sixteenth combination—is emphasized.

TRIO

- **Trio in G Major for Violin, Viola, and Cello, Op. 76**

A thoroughly attractive work, composed in a thoroughly tonal style. Formal simplicity summarizes the four movements. But this does not mean the Trio is lacking in dignity, notwithstanding the divertimento air that infuses its measures. Hess's harmonies are simple, yet fully alive; his melodic invention has engaging spontaneity.

An introduction in moderate tempo leads to a bright Allegro, moving at a march speed. The key is G major (it will serve for movements three and four as well). Movement two is a Theme with Variations that begins and ends in the relative minor key. There are sixteen measures to the theme, and that length remains in the first two variants (the second in the key of C major). Expansion of shape is used in variation three with a return to the E-minor home tonality. In the next two variations the lengths are again reduced and other keys used. The final variant is a fugue with partial thematic restatement to wind up matters.

No scherzo, instead a "Deutscher Tanz" ("German Dance"), representing a lively three-beats-in-a-measure dance with a contrastive Trio. A gracefully turned Rondo comprises the final movement. It begins with a Grave introduction, thus providing a formal balance with the opening of the work.

QUINTETS

- **Divertimento in B-flat for Wind Quintet, Op. 51**

Punctilious attention to tonality and elimination of irrelevant detail. The opening and closing movements confirm the home tonality, with the middle Minuet in the subdominant E-flat major key. Pithy sonata forms are used in the outer movements, the finale having an introduction that is totally concerned with the imitation of a motive.

- **Quintet for Double Bassoon (or Bassoon) and String Quartet, Op. 63**

Music for such a singular medium generally comes into existence not for the sake of publicity but to fulfill a commission. Writing at the request of the English bassoon virtuoso John Parr, Hess produced an Andante and Rondo for double bassoon and string quartet. In this form the work received a successful premiere on October 3, 1953, in Sheffield, England.

In 1977, at his publisher's request (Amadeus Verlag) a third part (i.e., the first movement of Op. 63) was added, consisting of an introduction in moderate tempo, followed by a sonata-designed Allegro non troppo. The original Andante and Rondo became movements two and three—the latter marked Tempo di minuetto.

While there is at times the sense of solo with accompaniment, the composition certainly falls within the chamber music category. Of course, it loses its specialness if a bassoon is used instead of the double bassoon. While the huge wind instrument has a somewhat gruff timbre, it nonetheless has a resourceful quality and is far more effective here than a bassoon would be. This is because Hess has adroitly tailored his light romantic writing for the double bass wind instrument.

A published version is available for double bassoon (or bassoon) with piano. In that format (less effective by far) the composer has not provided an alternate title. "Quintet" it certainly cannot be. "Sonata" would not be official (though it certainly would be correct). Obviously, the title must remain as "Quintet" with a note that the piano part is a transfer from the four string instruments.

Hessenberg, Kurt (1908–)

Hessenberg's music submits to the neoclassic tenets of tonality. These are engaged carefully, not overemphasized, but spread diatonically over the music's surface. At times the harmony is raked with chromatic teeth which dig the tonality out of its bounded fields and cover it with polytonal frictions. The melodic lines keep in motion but are more patterned blocks than continuous flow, whereby climax is obtained by rise and fall. Hessenberg's polyphony is sharp, of the "back-to-Bach" school, but occasionally it moves to the side as it makes its way to that destination.

Colorful fascinations, special effects, and odd formations are not present in this man's work. He composes strictly to scale, refuses the addition of footnotes to his essays. Accordingly, his music is fashioned from exactly measured models; its language is uniformity sustained by erudition, but sometimes with almost too cold logic. Nonetheless, his method of reasoning produces music of solid accomplishment.

DUOS

- **Sonata for Cello and Piano, Op. 23**

The sections of this one-movement Sonata are distinctly clarified by the composer. The opening subject sounds like a consolidation of Bach and Hindemith, contrasted sagaciously to a more romantic *zartheit*. Triplets are the rhythmic underpinning of the very slow-moving division (one particular passage, where the cello sings as a bass instrument supported above by the piano, is very effective). A cello recitative (Hessenberg calls on a kindred solo device in his violin sonata—*see below*) connects the slow-tempo portion with the final division.

The resultant change in texture is a gratifying way to denote separation without breaking the overall continuity. The excellent harmony of the final part of the Sonata shows a practiced hand and is matched by the neatness of the surrounding formal frame.

- **Sonata in B-flat for Flute and Piano, Op. 38**

Tri-divisioned like a suite. A Notturno and a slow-paced, emphatically lyrical Fantasia surround a peppy Rondo, which feasts on staccato and rhythmic detail. There are no individual departures in musical grammar—Hessenberg remains the responsive, responsible neoclassicist. Color, too, is restrained, forming a part of the total document and not as a specialized instrumental attribute.

- **Sonata in F Major for Violin and Piano, Op. 25**

Sonata form is utilized for the first movement. The second movement is mysterious, a type of dark intermezzo, supported by constant moving eighth notes with further adumbration contributed by the muted violin. Contrast is made certain by the violin cadenza in the center of the movement but causes a break in the mood. When the duo is resumed, there is little opportunity to sink into the initial atmosphere again.

The concluding movement combines a short three-part Un poco Adagio with the Allegretto finale proper, and in turn the second theme of the latter becomes the subject for a very long Presto. Though meant as a coda, the length of this speedy section almost totals a movement by itself.

- **Suite for Flute and Piano, Op. 77**

A sonatina is a diminutive sonata, with fewer and shorter movements than the larger form. Here, Sonatina is the title of the first of a group of four movements, maintained in concentrated total (eighty-eight measures). Hessenberg convinces that his title choice is proper.

Formal positiveness is the rule for the remainder: Ostinato—based on a two-measure unit; Fughetta—cleanly linear and unfussy; Andantino con variazioni—five of the last. All nonacademic considerations. All music of neoclassic personality.

TRIOS

- **Trio for Piano, Violin, and Cello, Op. 53**

Polyphony is the exclusive point of the second movement. It is also the primary technical device in the large first movement. There, imitation and fugato-sprung sections are paramount, with a counterweighted section in salterellolike rhythm as the secondary item. No rhetorical flourishes. An introduction, first and second thematic materials, twice stated in alternation, and a return to the introduction offer sufficient evidence of solid, neoclassically formulated music.

The final part of the Trio is a set of Variations. A four-paragraph theme (all but the first of thirteen-measure length) supported by string-instrument syncopation has a straightforward quality. In turn, the variations have a directness that avoids all excess and thereby relate to the generative theme. An all-pizzicato, all-string-instrument affair provides the first variation. Total trio forces in lyrical explanation mark the second variation. The third, completely concerned with moving eighth notes, is for the piano alone. Rhythmic considerations are next, succeeded by an Adagio (piano ostinato with violin prominence in the first part and violincello imitation in the second), and a culminating Presto. With most of this final part in lowered dynamic the impact is of a subtle kind.

- **Trio for Violin, Viola, and Cello, Op. 48**

Structural stability and structural equality. The first, third, and fifth movements are fast, balanced at the extremes via a heading of Vivace (both at ♩ = 152) with Presto as the speed for the middle of these three movements. Significantly, all are in duple meter.

Movement two is a Larghetto wherein pizzicato is the paramount timbre supporting the melodic lines. Movement four is a compact Lento, its lines intensified by imitation.

QUARTETS

- **Quartettino for Four Flutes (Three Flutes and Alto Flute), Op. 99**

A juicy amount of music in this Quartettino—seven movements in all. Clear forms. Everything is fresh and charming even to ears that may have been sated by music using neoclassic language.

Engaging vitality and contrapuntal skill are evidenced in the opening Präludium, second movement Invention, and sixth movement Kanon. A fine intensity marks the Elegie (part four), with the upper three voices playing against a bass line in the alto flute. The other three movements are two Scherzino pieces (the second one defined by a balletic metrical alternation of 3+3+2/8 and 4/8 contrasted to straightforward 2/4) and a final jaunty Rondino. There are all hits and no errors in this flute score.

- **Serenade for Wind Quartet (Oboe, Clarinet, Horn, and Bassoon), Op. 89**

One cannot argue against the lean and generally precise utterances that mark neoclassic syntax. Proof of Hessenberg's mastery of the style is given here in this six-movement work.

Staccato spit and peppery personality are found in the March, which has a softer textural center portion. Movement two is a Scherzo,

again contrastively supple in the center. Neat final cadence—dynamically restrained. (It is an old creative trick but it still sounds new.) The remaining movements consist of an Elegie, Intermezzo, Berceuse, and Finale based on a German folk song. Scalic drive in the last. Sharp formal perception in all cases.

- **String Quartet No. 2**

The interval of a minor third is the generator of this quartet. In the opening Lento its rhythmic declaration is later augmented and then taken over as the spur for development of the material in the Allegro molto. It is the fundamental pitch width in the Vivace scherzando and pertinent in the final Lento.

This is certainly inner structural coherence of the most cogent type. Though the material differs in terms of rhythmic shape, intensity, temporal arrangement, and placement of register, it is the minor third that controls and balances the composition.

- **String Quartet No. 3, Op. 33**

Classical orientation for this beautifully crafted work; decidedly clear formal sense, securely scored—the work of a sensitive composer throughout.

The A-major first movement works out from a motival basis. Movement two is a large-scoped G-minor Scherzo conception; the Trio portion one-third slower in speed and secured by ostinato. Though not so indicated, the Andante tranquillo consists of a D-major theme and five variations. The A-major tonality returns for the Vivace finale, which contains a fugato as part of its development.

- **String Quartet No. 4, Op. 60**

Hessenberg has never abandoned traditional structural concepts in his music. But nothing is simply squared and ruled in his output. Thus, the opening movement of the fourth quartet, which exhibits intense toccata drive with asymmetric controls. This division is prefaced by a three-measure Lento that reappears one hundred measures later, doubled in length, and once more still later in the movement, again increased in spread to a total of ten measures. The Lento also begins the third movement, a rhapsodic affair. Movement two is a Rondo with scherzo stimulation.

QUINTET

- *Das bucklichte Männlein (The Little Hunchback)—Paraphrase on an Old Song* for Flute, Oboe, Clarinet, Horn, and Bassoon, Op. 105

Hessenberg's "paraphrase" turns into a six-part variational set. As a constructive item, the continuity emphasizes the rhythmic idea heard in the oboe in the first two measures of the piece. It is used, for example, within the oboe and clarinet voices in the first variant, and serves there for expansiveness in the ornate flute line. It is slightly compressed in the second variant, and so forth. In its way this structural method is distinctly related to motival development. Above all, its absolute conjunct shape is of primary cohesiveness within the entire format of Hessenberg's wind quintet.

Hétu, Jacques (1938–)

DUO

- Four Pieces for Flute and Piano (1965)

Mixing styles may not be the best creative strategy, but if separated stylistically, as here, in suite form, impartial critical response would score the result as favorable. Indeed, the clue to Hétu's Four Pieces is that he is aiming for choice contrastive command. Juxtaposed and blended within a single composition, such stylistic conflict could only be a horrible failure.

The Récitatif is in serial style; the flute is assigned the recitatives and they are heated, the piano's actions are no less. The Scherzo is firmly neoclassical, fixed in exact ternary form. Its principal part drives ahead on eighth notes in duple measurement, the Trio is structured as a sustained lyrical line in adagio tempo. Movement three is an Intermezzo, chromatically juiced for neoromantic taste. There is just as much chromaticism in the final Rondo, but the syntax is atonal.

Heussenstamm, George (1926–)

TRIO

- Seven Etudes for Oboe, Clarinet, and Bassoon, Op. 17

Accomplished, thoroughly succinct, fertile settings, each devoted to a specific structural point. Some are projections of a rhythmic motive: number one, triplets; number two, sixteenths. Contrapuntalism is a strength: The third etude is a fugue; the fifth, a canon.

QUARTET

- *Tubafour* for Four Tubas, Op. 30

A mainly dark, somewhat turgid quality embraces this work. Within the instrumental limitations of the sonority chosen, Heussenstamm has resorted to a somewhat fragmentary style. Virility there is, though no gaiety.

QUINTETS

- **Brass Quintet No. 5 (Two Trumpets, Horn, Tenor Trombone, and Tuba), Op. 73**

Blocked formations make up this seventeen-minute work. But the constructions are so accommodated that there is no noticeable dislocation of the varied elements. Within, attention is given to solo lines, together with unrestricted temporal and aleatoric processes. Regarding the latter there is a huge section to be delivered "freely, heroically," and where "no strict vertical coordination [is] intended."

- ***Ensembles* for Brass Quintet (Two Trumpets, Horn, Tenor Trombone, and Tenor-Bass Trombone), Op. 58**

Ensembles is a continuous run of divisional yet kaleidoscopically knitted sections—thirty in all. Tutti statements are intertwined with solos, duos, trios, and quartets. The textural and timbral differences make for a clear balance through the force of consistency.

The music is coloristically braced with the use of mutes, playing through the unattached mouthpieces of the instruments, some aleatoric opportunities, and the usual flutters and glisses. In the concluding measures the horn plays off stage.

- ***Mini-Variations* for Flute (alternating Piccolo), Oboe, Violin, Viola, and Cello, Op. 25**

Mini-Variations, indeed. And in some cases, mini-mini variants, such as a two-measure total for number six, four-measure length for variation three, and a five-measure span for variation sixteen. But an ample variational survey with twenty-five in all.

The theme is a twelve-tone row spread over a three-measure Adagio. Texture and color

assist in projecting the permutations. Variation four is a two-voice canon for flute and oboe, using partial inversion. Variations four and five are quartets; the first does not include the flute, the other does not include the oboe. In variation nine the scoring is for the three strings, each specifically timbred: the violin playing harmonics, the viola in tremolando ponticello, and the cello muted. The piccolo makes its initial appearance in the dot-and-dash motility of variation ten. A different trio combination (flute, violin, and cello) identifies the eleventh variation. And so on, with clear portrayals throughout the quintet, including such a marked specification as the solo violin in variation nineteen.

SEXTET

- ***Set for Double Reeds* (Two Oboes [alternating Two English horns], Two English horns [alternating Two Oboes], and Two Bassoons), Op. 39**

Heussenstamm's sextet (the scoring listed above, of course, totals four oboes alternating with as many English horns plus two bassoons) has intense concentrated color. He scores with adroitness (a creative strategy) in order to nullify an overkill of one basic type of timbre and, simultaneously, to arrive at a clear balance of the materials.

After an introductory section the first movement uses a unit-blocked type of scoring—antiphonal implications result. In movement three the scoring is set forth on a vertical basis, and in movement five pyramided instrumental action is important. In this last part of the work nonvibrational sounds as well as trills are emphasized. In contrast are movements two and four. Both are quintet settings, the former for four oboes and the first bassoon, the latter for four English horns and the second bassoon. Thereby, perfect instrumental equality in these sonorous stimulations.

Hibbard, William (1939–)

DUO

- *Portraits* **for Flute and Piano (1964)**

A set of three pieces, with colorful serial details. Emphasis is on sonoric and rhythmic qualities. There are some breathy key taps for the wind instrument and a good amount of string plucking for the piano.

In the first of the set there are persistent pitch duplications. The second piece is constructed in large tripartite division. The last piece of the set is the shortest and contains tight lines.

Indeed, there are no sweet-looking profiles delineated in these musical portraits. The music is always dramatic and deeply emotive.

Hibbard's score is indicated thus: *Film version: Boston, Mass. August, 1963. Present version: Iowa City, Iowa. Oct.–Nov., 1964.* The initial setting was the result of a commission from the Boston Museum of Fine Arts to compose music for a documentary film devoted to the museum's collection of Old Kingdom Egyptian portrait sculpture. As Hibbard explains: "When composing the work, I had already decided to make a concert piece out of it as well." However, he found the music for the end of the film unsatisfactory as the conclusion for a concert work. Hibbard therefore composed new music for the finale of the nonfilm setting. Finally, since the film "was concerned with portrait sculpture," Hibbard "thought it appropriate to entitle the concert version *Portraits*."

TRIOS

- *Bass Trombone, Bass Clarinet, Harp* **(1973)**

The title of Hibbard's work is exactly as listed above. "Trio for" does not precede the named instruments.

The mode of free-formed communication is special, inventive, and telling. The trombone (using a variety of mutes) provides a direct impression of timbre, principally by emphasizing ictus quality for its entries; the more spontaneously quiet use of the bass clarinet is in direct contrast, and the harp inserts add fluidity.

- **String Trio (1964)**

Expressionistic music of almost violent activity. The serial syntax includes rhythmic particulars that are fractioned and fractured to the fullest extent, spreading to the metrical designations, which include such as $1^{3/5}/2$, $4^{2/3}/4$, $6^{5}/2$, etc. Layered on and within the work are coloristic detail (playing on the fingerboard and close to the bridge, col legno both drawn and struck) with percussive extension applied by tapping with the bow in various locations on the instruments in order to achieve high, medium, and low qualities.

An indication of Hibbard's stylistic direction and finesse appears in the very first measure. The violin is muted, the viola and cello are not. There are combinations of eight against six against five rhythmic totals with the violin and viola in *pianissimo* and the cello in *pianississimo*. Even here (and elsewhere) when the dynamic level is restrained the material is highly tensed. In fact it is exactly the nervous linear intensity of Hibbard's writing that makes his trio a creative achievement.

QUARTET

- **String Quartet (1971)**

Within the one-movement construction are Babbittesque procedures (rhythmic serialism) and Carterian processes (though not rigidly applied, specific personality character is assigned each of the four instruments). Though developed from ritornello data, Hibbard's work is constructed by tight serial structuring. A rational music it is, fully validating twelve-tone style.

Hidas, Frigyes (1928–)

DUOS

- **Fantasia for Clarinet and Piano (1965)**

Tonality rules, but Hidas opts for quartal harmonization. This flavors the peppy (somewhat jazzy) main subject set in septimal time. The clarinet is given special attention with virtuosic and cadenza-type material.

- **Introduzione e Fughetta for Two Trombones (1977)**

As expected, music short and to the point. The Lento dialogue of the "Introduction" covers fifteen measures. Then follows a jazzy Allegretto in which polyphony gives way to exact instrumental partnership throughout the central section. This makes the return to contrapuntal arrangement doubly effective.

TRIOS

- *Interludio* **for Three Trombones (1977)**

In addition to using the trombone in a variety of brass chamber music combinations, Hidas has given the instrument particular attention. For one trombone he has written a Fantasia and for the bass trombone a Meditation. For two trombones there is the Introduzione e Fughetta *(see above)*. As indicated, this *Interludio* is for trombone trio. Discussed below is a work for trombone quartet: Scherzo e Corale. Further, in 1980, Hidas, on a commission from the International Trombone Association, wrote a work titled Seven Bagatelles, calling for ten tenor trombones and two bass trombones.

The *Interludio* is a compact, tripartite piece, with the recapitulation shortened. Triadic writing marks the outer parts, the middle section is more linear.

- **Trio for Horn, Trombone, and Tuba**

Ternary design for this brass trio that has a majority of weighted timbres. The outer sections have a recitative-lyrical quality, the inner division is itself exactly split for binary contrast. The first of this pairing is fast and nervous, with Hidas's favored metrical shifts, the second is a motival built, swinging tri-pulsed portion.

QUARTETS

- *Chamber Music* **for Four Horns (1974)**

One of the most substantial of all the horn quartets in the literature. Hidas's scoring is both clear and colorful, but minus any fancy effects. Throughout there is liberated activization. And this especially pertains to the rhythmic detail. Though there is occasional metrical change in movement two (quadruple to sextuple), the pulse projection is most significant in movement four. The music there is fast-tempoed and entirely set in eighth-note measurement with shifts principally between 7/8, 10/8, and 11/8, plus normal and special accentuations. The result makes one sit up and take notice.

The first pair of movements defines majestic and jocose moods. Chordal shapes fill the third (Lento) movement. The finale (movement five) is a set of five variations. Hidas's theme is of length, but most of the variants are shorter. Variation three is completely in bound, tutti rhythm. Variation four (mostly set in 3+2/4 meter), save for the concluding five measures, is totally in muted timbre.

- **Quartettino for Brass Instruments (Two Trumpets, Trombone, and Bass) (1977)**

Hidas leaves open the instrument he means by the indication "Bass." The part seems best fitted for a tuba.

Clear, defined patterns serve the objective of this accessible music. There are five short movements, the first four in tripartite shape, the last a rondo. The style is homespun and lightly contemporary in its makeup.

- **Scherzo e Corale for Four Trombones (1977)**

Unity is obtained here by vivid opposites. The Scherzo dynamically pursues metrical agitation. It contains ten different pulse patterns (2/8, 3/8, 5/8, 6/8, 7/8, 8/8, 9/8, 10/8, 2/4, and 4/4), utilized so that there are eighty-one time-signature changes in the total 104 measures. Within this pulsatile plenitude the initial phrase of the piece appears five different times as a ritornel identification.

The Chorale, a twenty-one-measure lento-tempo, solemn statement, is linked to the Scherzo, but that is its sole affiliation. While the lines move, the metrical apportionment is tightly maintained in quadruple pulse.

QUINTET

- **Brass Quintet for Two Trumpets, Horn, Trombone, and Tuba (1973)**

Always clarification of detail, principally homophonic and chordal, in this compact one-movement piece. The form is clearly sectionally disposed with alternate slow and fast portions, this contrastive pairing occurring three times, plus a two-measure wrap up in andante. Hidas's lightly sophisticated music is beautifully textured and avoids undue special effects.

SEXTETS

- **Five Movements for Brass Sextet (Three Trumpets, Two Trombones, and Tuba) (1972)**

Fresh and clean, luminous brass writing set forth with interesting structural proportions. Hidas has produced a good number of brass chamber works (*see above* and *below*), but hardly repeats himself. In this instance he begins with a "Signal," which is still another entry in the fanfare world. Two scherzos are separated by an Interlude containing broad lyrical material. Scherzo 1 is developed from a short-and-two-long rhythmic figure; Scherzo 2 zooms out from a triplet unit. After all this activity comes a final movement of repose—a blocked, strictly vertical Chorale.

Scoring is important to the work. In the "Signal" most of the writing is in blocked timbres, with trumpets as one group and the trombones and tuba the other. A different assignment is used in Scherzo 1, with trumpets one and three joined with trombone two, and trumpet two partnered with trombone one. The tuba is withheld for a solo spot in the central part of the movement. In Scherzo 2 there is pyramid scoring, which, by its successive entrance of instruments, results in a dynamic intensification by way of textural weight.

- **Sextet for Brass Instruments (Three Trumpets, Two Trombones, and Tuba) (1972)**

Strictly ternary-structured music, with an opening section, a slower second part, a literal return to the first part (which is shortened), and then a coda.

Action, contrast, and development are achieved by using sound masses rather than concentrated thematic statements. Rhythm is a major credit in this type of music. It is interesting to note that a Hungarian critic considers the middle chordalized section "reminiscent of big-band jazz."

Hill, Edward Burlingame (1872–1960)

DUO

- **Sonata for Clarinet (or Violin) and Piano, Op. 32**

As much as this composer was a conservative romantic, he was not unaware of modern currents. His overall music is of pure diatonicism, but there are moments when the acid drips (if not harmonically, then rhythmically) into the mellifluousness. Thus, in the opening movement, where a single motive scans the entire design, the motive is cut into rhythmically on reappearance by the foreshortening of certain sections of the main phrase. The slow movement, lush in melody, is designed by its rhythmic changes so that it does not slip into inevitable monotony. The Scherzino is aided by syncopation; the final movement, likewise.

SEXTET

- **Sextet for Flute, Oboe, Clarinet, Horn, Bassoon, and Piano, Op. 39**

Hill was in his sixties when he composed this prize-winning work (selected by the Society for the Publication of American Music in 1937, after being commissioned by Elizabeth Sprague Coolidge); yet it definitely bears the mark of a young man, in the jazz shrugs of its opening movement, spliced with syncopation, especially in forming a 4/4 measure so that it has arranged pulsations of 11/2, 11/2, and 1. The contrasting theme is rhythmically straightforward. Hill's rhythmic ability has been generally overlooked in written estimates of his work, but it is one of the strongest parts of the musical structures he produced.

The first movement's germination carries over into the effectively wrought Scherzo, alive with movement, with each instrument sharing matters. There, the sextet's voices settle into choral states, and one feels the origination of the usual Trio section, even though the strong rhythm continues. But a surprise awaits, in that the chordalizing is but a preparatory foil to the actual Trio, which shifts the "one-in-a-bar" pulse to a duple 6/8 meter. Without change of tempo, pitch speed is reduced, nonetheless, by the fact that two sounds now occur where three did previously. With the return of the latter, the recapitulation of the movement is defined.

Hill was not an impressionist, but he more than glanced at the techniques of the style. The opening of the slow movement, with the spacing of hollow timbre (the bassoon two octaves below the oboe), is New England impressionism if not French. The Finale is gay, and includes the main theme expressed in fugato.

Hiller, Lejaren (1924–)

DUO

- **Sonata No. 3 for Violin and Piano (1970)**

Hiller tells us that the three movements are in C, F-sharp, and C, respectively. A sense of relationship to standard practice is thereby made. (The F sharp could be considered a lowered dominant.) He also indicates the Sonata has three movements: "a sonata allegro, a slow movement and a rondo finale." And, as he properly states, these total a "traditional" format. His description that the music is "crushingly difficult to play," and that "its mood is harsh and relentless" would not remove it from additional ancestral ties.

What does are the timbral revelations in the piece. The violinist scratches the bow roughly across the strings on the far side of the bridge, plays snap pizzicato, bows on the fingerboard minus vibrato, produces purposeful rough sounds by pressing the bow very hard on the strings, and performs both chordal and harmonic glissandos. The pianist produces clusters, plays chords with the chin while the two hands are busy with tremolandos, amplifies chordal spans by playing pitches with the elbows while the two hands play others, and displays a heavy percussive personality.

It's music of the late-20th century, no doubt. "Relentless" is the word, indeed. In movement two the violin has the same snap pizzicatoed minor second for forty-five consecutive measures while the piano weaves around a small pitch space with tone clusters and ostinatos and strikes the piano's strings with a tam-tam beater, all these in septuple pulse. There is pugnacious pulsatile drive in the outer movements. It thunderstrikes the ear. For this alone Hiller's duo sonata will not be easily forgotten.

QUARTET

- **String Quartet No. 5 (in Quarter Tones) (1962)**

A gigantic blueprint, minutely detailed, controls the structuring of this quartet. The conformation is certainly not of ordinary specifications.

Twice the usual number of pitches is available to guide the sounds, since quarter tones provide a twenty-four-pitch division of the octave. Serial technique is used, with four twenty-four-pitch rows related to each other. (Row two, for example, is formed by taking in succession every fifth note of row one, etc.) In addition to the full span of permutations—by inversion, retrograde, transposition, and so on—split rows are used.

The quartet is in seven sections. The first, third, fifth, and seventh present the four rows (thus variation form is represented, since the second, third, and fourth rows are derived from

the first row). Within these sections (each row or section is termed a Theme) are three four-part Variations. The first of these delineates the exposition, development, recapitulation, and coda of a sonata; the second set covers the formal outlines of a scherzo; and the third set equates a finale form. The last of this set of variations is "a quartet inside a quartet" with four movements combined in individual material, tempo, meter, and dynamic strength. The last word is descriptive of the architecture of Hiller's quartet. (It has its share of special colors as well, including rapping the instrument with the knuckles, producing squeaking and rasping sounds, and snap pizzicato.)

Hiller, Lejaren (1924–) and Isaacson, Leonard

QUARTET

- *Illiac Suite* **for String Quartet (1957)**

This, according to Hiller, represents the "first substantial piece of music produced with a computer." Of course, computer programming for musical composition just cannot be dismissed—it will not go away—but we are far from the nonexperimental stage, regardless of all the tracts, the explanations, and the copious theory. There is no positive stylistic identity to *Illiac* (an acronym for the name of the computer used: Illinois Accumulator). That is for the future. Whatever, the *Illiac Suite* is fantastically functional and beautifully braintrusted. It should be experienced.

There are four movements, each titled "Experiment." The first moves from monody to two-part and then four-part writing. "Counterpoint rules are progressively introduced" in "Experiment II." Chromatic harmony and tone rows are included in part three, plus modern playing techniques. "Experiment IV" is an example of music "dependent on probability and weighted frequency distributions." Academic procedures, indeed, but a process of composition to be given full attention.

Hilmera, Oldřich (1891–1948)

DUO

- *Con umore (With Humor)* **for Bassoon (or Cello) and Piano**

No belly laughs, but mild, lighthearted short stories. Each of the three items—"Groteska," Humoreska, and Scherzando is succinctly motival in its makeup.

Hindemith, Paul (1895–1963)

There are two pertinent remarks which well describe Hindemith's creative viewpoint, plus one he made himself. Paul Bekker said most cleverly, "Er komponiert überhaupt nicht, er musiziert," while Alfred Einstein called Hindemith "a musician who produces music as a tree bears fruit, without further philosophical purpose." Hindemith explained his credo thusly, "Composing for one's own satisfaction is probably gone forever . . . the composer and consumer ought most emphatically to come at least to an understanding." It must be understood, however, that Hindemith never devoted himself exclusively to music of utilitarian purpose, generically called Gebrauchsmusik. (This technical goal is discussed *below*, in relation to the chamber music works that fall in that category.)

Hindemith preached the universality of the musician; he must be able to teach and conduct, write for all type of audiences, and perform on all kind of instruments. Hindemith was the rarest of composers, one who composed with A to Z fullness, far from the thinking that only one type of audience existed.

Hindemith is not to be classified with the atonal tag so often incorrectly attached to him. With Hindemith tonality was a prime requirement. He was a direct descendant of the classic and romantic schools (the latter manifested quite often by the beauties that sensitize his slow movements, the former illustrated by his formal precision). He did not mimic these schools of thought but continued their arguments logically and inevitably. Accordingly, his early output was a further consideration of Brahmsian-Regerian doctrines. Hindemith's second period of work was based on free tonality, expressed purer thought, and avoided luxuriance by keenness (but not thinness). Harmonic compression would have meant an aesthetic retrogression itself, for there was but one way to go in that manner—a return to classic chordal vocabulary. Realizing this, Hindemith freed himself from romanticism and its packed harmony by the adoption of linear assembly. In so doing, musical strength was maintained (horizontalism moves on long phrases and is not clipped or punctuated with commas). There was dissonance holding first place, but all of Hindemith's work at that time was devoted to tonal release, not tonal discontinuance. Atonality, it must be repeated, was the complete opposite of Hindemith's approach.

The compositions from Hindemith's latest period synthesized all the elements of his previous work. His music was shaped by tonality in a special manner—a combination of his original romantic membership with his later employment of tonal freedom by use of tonal centers. However, these centers are not all equal to each other, but related by the measurement of one center in regard to other points which afford (depending on pitch distance) tension or repose, stability or motility. Furthermore, modulations from one orbit move to another, and, in turn, give a particular tensility compared to release. Thus, diatonic and chromatic selections combine, triadic and other types of consonant and dissonant chords are confirmed, all based on an obedience to rooted tonal points with all varieties of harmony moving within those positions.

Hindemith began his career by composing chamber music and, with only slight deviations in his total output, he remains one of the greats of 20th-century instrumental music. It is apparent that where a large number of works is concerned a composer's output will be uneven; no matter, Hindemith always has his compensations. The music is so well constructed, so lacking in any incorrect equipment, that even a second-rate Hindemith work has conviction.

Hindemith's instrumental writing is sure, based on knowledge gained from performing on many instruments himself. Hindemithian sonorities are neither ground down nor chiseled to conformed technical designs (embracing, for example, exactly fitting passages, mundane figurations that are the wholesale cheapness of hackneyed pedagogy or so-called violinistic or pianistic writing), all of which, and more, interfere with the truest manifestation of composition. He handled every instrumental voice with expert exploitation, but short of experimentation. This represented still another strength in the work of one of the most important composers of the 20th century.

Paul Hindemith and Gebrauchsmusik

Hindemith first came into contact with Gebrauchsmusik at Baden-Baden during one of the modern music festivals held there. The attempt to modify contemporary concert-hall music, with its terrifying newness and thereby nullify the usual stuffiness fed children in schools, was the prime impetus of the examples he heard in 1921. Teachers who persisted in following a syllabus of 1890s vintage naturally could not prepare younger people's ears to listen to 20th-century music. A new way had to be found. Gebrauchsmusik was the manner of approach, though as it developed it proved to be an additional and very important

benefit by its new premise. Not only was the composer aided by writing uncomplicated music which gave him larger returns materially and otherwise; not only were future listeners for his other compositions given a taste of things to come, but a new category of fine concert-hall music of different character was developed simultaneously. The hard-boiled adult audiences found in its simplicity and freshness (which did not give way to any mundane doctrine) a music they could enjoy as much as those for whom it was specifically written.

There has been some criticism that to translate the term Gebrauchsmusik as "utility music" is incorrect. It is and is not. When used to describe compositions written to order to meet everyday demands, the term is proper. For example, a number of German composers were asked to write operas for children, music for accompanying singing at a meal, marching music for political groups, etc. In the sense that the word "utility" may be restricted literally, the generic term is not so good a choice. Let it be understood, therefore, that Gebrauchsmusik consists of every type of specified music outside the general territory to which concert music, first and last, is devoted. It is music for children, for political groups, for schools, home and fireside; music for playing and singing or both together, or for the ad libitum fun obtained by the improvisational exchange and substitution of instruments in connection with any or all of the individual parts of a piece of music.

The technique of Gebrauchsmusik was one of simplification. Above all, the composer's idiom was to remain unchanged. The purpose of this educational propaganda was to quietly agitate for the acceptance of contemporary manners, but cut down to smaller-scaled technical levels, eliminating any virtuosic order. Music could remain in the lower string-instrument positions, or in the first position exclusively. (But this restriction is only one of instrumental range and technical boundary. In the hands of a mature player who shifts through a violin's positions as he sees fit, so as to achieve the highest artistic result, in some instances these simple pieces become the equal of others not originally written with any limit in mind.) The precept of all utilitarian-planned music was to teach by stimulation, to encourage the making of music, rather than passively listening to others. Active participation was the guiding rule—it was better to play the false note oneself rather than pay to watch someone avoid it.

Gebrauchsmusik was not new. Composers had written to order and had scaled down their musical semantics so that a pocket-size vocabulary was used in place of an unabridged one. But in Germany the movement took root with great rapidity in the 1920s. Many a composer went to work in the field of Gebrauchsmusik. The leader of the group was Paul Hindemith; Kurt Weill and Carl Orff were among the others. It bore out Hindemith's belief that understanding between the professional composer and the amateur consumer could only come through music directly, not indirectly via written or verbal promotion and propaganda.

Plöner Musiktag (A Day of Music at Plön) (1932) by Paul Hindemith

(Of the nine works in this series, three fall within the categories covered by this compendium. Discussions of these three compositions will be found below, in terms of the number of instruments used.)

The nine miscellaneous works which make up Hindemith's *Plöner Musiktag* came about in a very accidental way. The students of the Plön school had requested Hindemith to visit them and listen to their music making and he agreed to do so. During his visit Hindemith noted the wonderful spirit displayed by the students and promised to arrange a music festival for the school to take place in June 1932

and write music especially for it. Hindemith had not only found orchestral and choral groups at Plön, but other types of music work as well, even by the very youngest children who were capable of performing only on miniature-size recorders. Thus Hindemith overlooked no possibility in his commission since music accompanied every part of the school's activity, from lunch music to compositions performed from the school tower.

Hindemith never forgot the day he spent when he returned to the Plön school. He related how activities began at 7 A.M. and continued with dress rehearsals of a composition he had written for afternoon performance and of work on the music he had composed for an evening concert. Music filled every minute and was the exclusive consideration. It was a day that left all exhausted but filled with joy. This was the most satisfying definition of Gebrauchsmusik. Hindemith had not only written but rehearsed and participated in the performance of his music. From such a project, contemporary music made a tremendous impression on the students and faculty at Plön.

The music Hindemith composed comprises four sections, each for use at a different occasion during a day's full extent. The first is *Morgenmusik (Morning Music)*, a work for brass instruments to be played from the top of a tower. Though the ten-minute composition is basically written for massed instruments, it can be considered chamber music by eliminating any doubling of the individual parts *(see below)*. Section two, *Tefelmusik (Table Music)*, is a set of four pieces (titled March, Intermezzo, Trio for Strings, and Waltz) to be played at table during a meal. This suite of pieces calls for a string group plus flute and trumpet (or clarinet). The third section is a *Kantate (Cantata)* on Martin Agricola's words, titled *Mahnung an die Jugend, sich der Musik zu befleissigen (Admonition to Youth to Apply itself to Music)*, scored for chorus, solo voice, a speaker, strings, winds, and percussion instruments, lasting a little over a half-hour in performance time. The fourth part of Hindemith's "music for the entire day" is titled *Abendkonzert (Evening Concert)* and consists of a half-dozen works which total the proper assortment required for a full-size concert. These are first, an eight-minute Introduction for Orchestra, consisting of massed instruments playing in triple-divided parts; second, a flute solo with the accompaniment of multiple string instruments, and third, Two Duets for Violin and Clarinet *(see below)*. Next in order is a set of Variations for clarinet and combined strings; then a Trio for Recorders *(see below)*, and the "Plön" music is completed by a Quodlibet, again scored for a full orchestra of massed instruments which divide into high, medium, and low parts.

DUOS

▪ Duet for Viola and Cello (1934)

Hindemith's short duet (about 3 3/4 minutes in length) should not be confused with the Duet for Viola and Cello (also short) that begins the second of the three-part (eight-section) *Die Serenaden*, Op. 35, for soprano, oboe, viola, and cello.

Without preidentification, just hearing a few measures will make clear the profile of Paul Hindemith. Thus: succinct linear energy with metrically assorted rhythmic zip (the music is in an irregular variety of two, three, and four eighths per measure) color the motival underpinning of the three-part structure.

The background concerning the composition of the piece is interesting and explains the confusion that exists in referring to this work, incorrectly, as a Scherzo. It has scherzo quality, but that title is not the definitive one.

Hindemith produced this work to fill a blank side in a set of recordings he was making. (This was, of course, in the days before long-playing records had come into being.) At that time it

was titled Scherzo, with its premiere performance that of the recording itself (a short-play, 10-inch disc); Hindemith's instrumental partner was the famed cellist, Emanuel Feuermann. When preparing the music for publication, Hindemith removed the Scherzo title.

▪ *Fourteen leichte Stücke (Fourteen Easy Duets)* for Two Violins (1931)

More Hindemith for the educational trade (all the music is in the first position). But, as usual with this composer, charm, cleverness, and sheer good music result that go beyond didactic determination. In the hands of professional performers, the music is worthy of the concert hall.

Some of the highlights of the set follow. In number four, off-beat pizzicatos project the lively principal tune. Number six is a "Piece with Variations." The theme is set in constant metrical change; the two variations (in fast and slow tempo respectively) stay put in triple pulse, with a final chordal cadence in slow-paced, quadruple-time order. Number eight is a kinetic item; number nine has expansivity within its muted measures; the thirteenth is a lively Rondo.

▪ *A Frog He Went a-Courting: Variations on an Old English Nursery Song* for Cello and Piano (1941)

It certainly is planned coincidence that the theme and twelve variations of this work match the total of verses of the nursery song. Neither is it happenstance that, save for one additional measure at the end of the eighth variation, each variation consists of sixteen measures (even with tempo and time-signature changes), thereby paralleling the two-line total for each of the verses.

With a vivid imagination one can fit verse with music content. Variation five, for example, with agitated off-beat rhythmic figures, does clue into the fifth verse: "Uncle rat went galloping to town, / To buy his niece a wedding-gown." And the constantly busy, chromatically zigzagged lines of the cello for variation seven (a Jig) compare somewhat to the seventh verse: "The first [to] come in was the bumble-bee / With his fiddle on his knee." But the music is simply a tight, continuous set of variations. Though programmatically inspired one should not strive to hear it as a descriptive translation.

- *Kleine Sonate (Small Sonata)* **for Viola d'amore and Piano, Op. 25, No. 2**

This represents the first of two examples within Hindemith's massive catalogue that call on the rarely used string instrument. The other instance is its employment as the solo voice in Kammermusik No. 6 (Concerto for Viola d'amore and Chamber Orchestra), Op. 46, No. 1. Regardless of a fairly extensive literature by 17th- and 18th-century composers, and samplings by such men as Meyerbeer, Charpentier, Puccini, Strauss, and Loeffler, contemporary composers have given the highly individual viola d'amore scant attention. (Doubtless the principal cause is that there are few performers of the instrument.)

Though tunings for the instrument vary, the richest is an accordatura of D major, with the sympathetic strings that lie just behind the bowed strings furnishing a distinctive timbre. Hindemith takes advantage of a sure thing and makes this the key focus of the sonata, especially in the vigorous final movement, where the closely positioned D-major triad appears as a repetitive fanfare device some twenty-eight times. As usual, Hindemith is a master of the sonorous resource he employs. The writing offers a synoptic view of what can be accomplished by the viola d'amore, with sweeping, connected assorted thirds and fourths plus imaginative five-, six-, and seven-part pizzicato chords.

The first movement, which connects with the second one, is in the form of an invention (not so titled by Hindemith) on a three-measure subject. Regardless of octave doublings, chordal amplification, and string-instrument double stops, the music defines strict three-voice arrangement.

Movement two (Sehr langsam) has cohesive development that continues within the clear demarcation of an arch form outlined as: A–B–C–B–A.

In the final movement sharp rhythms and pulsatile chordal blocks enjoy a workout. There are two principal ideas, the second one representing the type of beautifully bittered lyrical themes so natural to this composer. Both are combined and form simultaneously a duple-triple metrical partnership. Few composers can carry off this type of learned levity as well as Hindemith.

- *Konzertstück(Concert Piece)* **for Two Alto Saxophones (1933)**

A Hindemith sleeper. This little known, full-size (three-movement) duo was completed on June 14, 1933, in Berlin. The work was written at the request of the German-American saxophone virtuoso Sigurd Rascher, though it was solely Hindemith's decision to call for two saxophones. Rascher had problems finding a proper partner to perform the work, resulting in more than a quarter of a century's delay of the premiere until July 29, 1960, when Rascher presented the work with his daughter Carina at the Eastman School of Music. Hindemith had accepted an invitation to hear the *Concert Piece* for the first time at a concert in Zurich on March 6, 1964, but he did not live to hear his composition, having died the previous December. Rascher copyrighted the composition in 1970 and it was published in 1976 by the New York firm of McGinnis and Marx.

The opening movement is vivace-toned (marked Lebhaft), its dynamism supported by favorite Hindemith rhythms (long–short and the trisyllabic unit of a long sound followed by two short sounds). A moderately slow (Mässig langsam) movement follows set in tripartite form. The finale is again lively (Lebhaft) music, spurred by cross accents, syncopation, and polyphony.

- *Schulwerk für Instrumental-Zusammenspiel* (*Educational Music for Instrumental Ensembles*), Op. 44

Op. 44 consists of four works that are a part of the music Hindemith composed for young people and for use in the home. All the compositions of Op. 44 are written for string groups. Although the fourth of the group is specifically for string orchestra, the other three chamber music works can also be performed by massed groups of players, each of which duplicates one of the individual parts in the total.

The first part of Op. 44 consists of *Neun Stücke (Nine Pieces)* for two violins, written for beginners, and is entirely in the first position; the second is titled *Acht Kanons (Eight Canons)* and is for two violins with a third, accompanimental part for either violin or viola. It is described as composed for "slightly advanced students." Part three is a set of *Acht Stücke (Eight Pieces)* for string quartet and was written with moderately advanced players in mind. (Parts one, two, and three are discussed separately below.) The fourth work is titled *Fünf Stücke (Five Pieces)* and is for technically proficient instrumentalists. It calls for a string orchestra with an important solo violin part to be played by the *concertmeister* and is therefore outside the scope of this compendium.

It will be noted that the compositions call for an increasing number of players and require increasingly higher levels of technical ability.

- *Neun Stücke in der ersten Lage (Nine Pieces in the First Position)* for Two Violins, Op. 44, No. 1

Though these pieces are "for beginners," the last five of the set can be given some attention. These, though small in scale, offer fair musical virtues. The first four should be bypassed as simply elementary exercises with no performance value.

Canonic bits and imitations are featured in the seventh and eighth pieces. In the final movement the music has breadth and fine polyphonic spirit.

The Sonatas of Paul Hindemith

Hindemith created a sonata for practically every important orchestral instrument. By such productivity Hindemith again manifested his mission of making music available to everyone. Moreover, the prime point is that all of the works are significant additions to 20th-century music and represent a special chapter in chamber music history.

These "serial" sonatas (the author's term) are in addition to the number of sonatas Hindemith wrote for violin, viola, and cello. The string group includes sonatas for viola d'amore and double bass. There is one for each of the principal woodwinds: flute, oboe, English horn, clarinet, and bassoon, and one work apiece for the brass members: horn, trumpet, trombone, and tuba, as well as a sonata for alto horn or alto saxophone. Another group contains three sonatas for piano; one for two pianos; a single example for one piano, four hands; three for organ; and one for harp. In addition, Hindemith produced unaccompanied sonatas for violin, viola, and cello.

- **Sonata for Alto Horn in E-flat (or Alto Saxophone) and Piano (1943)**

An extra added attraction, and indeed a special one, changes Hindemith's usual four-movement design (broad-tempoed, scherzolike, expressively slow-paced, and lively, in turn) into a five-part total. Before the final movement the instrumentalists speak lines written by the composer, which are an intrinsic part of the composition. Hindemith made two versions of his prose: one in German, *Das Posthorn (Zweigespräch)*, and one in English, *The Posthorn (Dialogue)*.

The English version of Hindemith's text is:

Horn Player:

Is not the sounding of a horn to our busy souls / (even as the scent of blossoms wilted long ago, / or the discolored folds of musty tapestry, / or crumbling leaves of ancient yellowed tomes) / like a sonorous visit from those ages / which counted speed by straining horses' gallop, / and not by lightning prisioned up in cables; / and when to live and learn they ranged the countryside, / not just the closely printed pages? / The cornucopia's gift calls forth in us / a pallid yearning, melancholy longing.

Pianist:

The old is good not just because it's past, / nor is the new supreme because we live with it, / and never yet a man felt greater joy / than he could bear or truly comprehend. / Your task it is, amid confusion, rush, and noise, / to grasp the lasting, calm, and meaningful, / and finding it anew, to hold and treasure it.

The Sonata is also playable, as noted, on an alto saxophone. (In that case, what is to be followed in regard to the dialogue, specifically directed toward the horn's character, is not indicated.) Hindemith had also stated that the work could be performed on the usual (F) French horn. Choice of this instrument is at the expense of the special timbre of the alto instrument. The saxophone version is certainly worthy as a substitute setting.

- **Sonata for Bassoon and Piano (1938)**

Hell, it can be said, is paved with pretentious music. Although a composer cannot be a meek personality if he wishes to turn out a competent work of size for bassoon and piano, he cannot display nonchalant disregard for the problem he faces. If the bassoon is asked to pit itself against merciless thick piano tone it can only mean a composer's defeat. The bassoon is not a timid instrument, but it is fragile in terms of sonorous density. Care must be given it, and Hindemith's work is exemplary in that regard. His overall plan is directed so that the more vocal-like sections become the principal strengths of the structure. There is no instrumental contradiction—the bassoon is used properly for the truly lyric voice it represents.

In the first movement and at the conclusion of the second, rustic feeling is predominant. In both instances this is indicated by a bacarolle-mannered pleasantness, swung along in 6/8 meter and signified exactly as a "pastoral" by the composer in the concluding section mentioned. The second movement begins in very slow tempo and is comfortably designed for its mood by use of a binary pattern. This part is followed by a March, one of Hindemith's formal identification marks. The March is neatly compressed in its rhythm and is a tightly knit totality. In addition, this movement includes a contrasting Trio and some polyphony as well.

- **Sonata for Bass Tuba and Piano (1955)**

Fantasy structuring marks the first movement of the work. There is a sense of improvisatory gestures in this part of the duo. Movement two is another Allegro that has scherzo quality. The finale is a set of variations, based on a theme that covers the total chromatic spectrum, but that doesn't mean Hindemith, the arch-opponent of dodecaphonic music, had changed his course. Contrapuntalism here aplenty. The Sonata ends quietly.

- **Sonata for Cello and Piano, Op. 11, No. 3**

Hindemith's first sonata for cello and piano shows a young composer breaking vigorously with the past. This is music with smash and recoil, full of violent reaction, compared with the smoother, earlier works that share the same opus number. The energy and drive of the first movement show an athletic composer pitchforking his sounds to propel them off the ground. When the music halts, it moves into a section completely removed in character (thus Hindemith creates two movements in one, similarly followed in the case of the movement marked by him as "II"). This is also lively music, moving in square duple meter, but gauged differently from the previous section by means of more concentrated sonority. The action and charge of the music are not released therefore; it is simply that the sounds are tightened instead of spread kinetically.

A three-part slow March occupies the first half of the second movement and progresses into the finale. Rhythmic action with free-conducted lines persists in this instance. In direct conflict, but with shrewd climax, the general dynamic level moves from a *forte* to a concluding triple *piano*. The force of the former is not of lesser account in the latter.

- **Sonata for Cello and Piano (1948)**

This, the second of Hindemith's two sonatas for cello and piano, was composed 29 years after the first one, completed in 1919 and designated as Op. 11, No. 3 (*see above*). The later sonata was the result of a commission from the great Russian cellist Gregor Piatigorsky (1903–76) who gave the first performance (with the pianist, Ralph Berkowitz) at the Berkshire Music Center (since 1985 known as the Tanglewood Music Center) in the summer of 1948. Piatigorsky is also to be credited with giving the world premiere, in Boston, of Hindemith's Concerto for Cello and Orchestra (with Koussevitsky conducting the Boston Symphony Orchestra) on February 7, 1941. Though no mention is made in the published score, this is Hindemith's second cello concerto. The first concerto, composed in 1915 and listed as Op. 3 was premiered in 1917. Unfortunately, both score and orchestral parts were lost in an air raid which damaged Hindemith's house in Frankfurt during World War II.

The opening Pastorale of Hindemith's second cello and piano sonata is best described as "dynamic," a word that may seem odd when used in connection with a pastorale. But the noiseless tenor of quiet music has its own predominant strength. Hindemith's Pastorale flows in a broad, uneven metrical manner, and obtains its boldness of simplicity through the explanations found in a free sonata style. It contains a fugue (already the sign of a Hindemithian idyll) as the central part. This movement has one of those touches only a great composer manages to evoke. The measures where the cello plays quadruple chords of the "head" of the fugue subject in deep bass-baritone resonant pizzicato, replied to by the piano in a higher sonority, are worth waiting for. Hearing them, one will realize why loud piping is of lesser effect when compared to the stronger enunciation of a softer voice.

In the sonata's middle movement a mildly fast type of music is combined with a slow-paced section. In the outer parts the treatment given is considerably varied. And again a master touch of spatial scoring enters the sonata picture. Hindemith's solution of an intervallic second is neat—a pronging of the dissonance with clever coloring, as he separates this friction at a four-octave distance.

A passacaglia is used for the finale. Again, "dynamic" is the proper word for describing this movement. The variants on the subject total twenty-four; the theme is a masterful arrangement devoted to an uneven phrase length of seven measures. This is as individual a passacaglia subject as possible, containing four descents; the first is of a minor seventh, and the last three are climaxed by extension of this measurement to an augmented octave. The movement ends with a fugato.

- **Sonata for Clarinet (or Viola) and Piano (1939)**

Within any large-scale work there are matters to consider aside from the logic of a particular movement's design or structure. The contribution made by a discriminating overall effect is more subtle; it is an objective on a plane secondary to the transmuting of one specific idea per each division of the composition. Notwithstanding four distinct and concrete patterns in this composition, there is an interlink that gives a duodimensional reality to the utilized balanced conventions of a four-movement sonata plan. The first, second, and fourth movements conclude in a *pianissimo* dynamic, the third in *piano*. The natural intensities of the fast, scherzo, slow, and pertly demeanored movements have minute but communicable effect on the general reticence of the final cadences.

The first part of the Sonata is hinged on quartal movement, both of melodic line and of the harmonic dressings that give it cover. When the clarinet in the last measures uses the intensity of octave ascent together with a contrary falling dynamic plane the effect is entrancing. Movement two (a scherzo concept), marked Lively, is bold, fresh, and also humorous; the third movement is a darkly colored song in very slow tempo, while the final movement is a Little Rondo.

(Hindemith permits performance by a viola in place of the clarinet, but warns that the effect will be different from what he intended.)

- **Sonata for Double Bass and Piano (1949)**

In this Sonata the string instrument is pitched differently from its usual accordatura. Each of the strings is raised a whole tone in order to achieve a slightly greater brilliance.

Hindemith, a composer who knew all instruments perfectly (he was able to perform on fourteen instruments!), realized that the scoring of a double bass sonata must be carefully plotted. He proceeded to take care that the deep bass tone was nurtured without becoming overly active and thus out of character. Virtuosity is possible, but is not the best profit to be derived from the double bass—a ponderous instrument is not the paragon for fiery pyrotechnics. Hindemith's Sonata is strictly in chamber music style. The piano writing carefully avoids smear in regard to the tonal features; the weighty bass does not struggle with distress.

In the first movement a sonata outline is used for detail. The melodic conclusion in this case is an expression of very fitting taste. Movement two is a Scherzo, movement three a Molto adagio set in semivariational treatment. Only a little bit of counterpoint is employed (a fugue for double bass and piano is not an especially propitious type of design). This movement leads into a Recitative and is succeeded by a thirty-two measure Lied (Song) consisting of a short ternary exposition that exhibits the tenor zone of the string instrument.

- **Sonata for English horn and Piano (1941)**

The Hindemith sonatas are of manifold variety; the number of movements varies, the forms differ, and, of course, the colors change. Additional service to these works is the fact that Hindemith always fits the instrument to his music (or the other way around, which is the same thing). His English horn sonata is not in the usual three- or four-movement style, but is a concentrated matter pertinent to the theme and variation principle and in which two basic speeds are placed in opposition. Though Hindemith does not belabor the most familiar use of the instrument (to depict pastoral facets of music, the shepherd's voice, and so on), neither does he miss an opportunity to expand it. He balances all possibilities so that a melancholic atmosphere contrasts with a more cheerful view. In addition, the spice of variety stems from the shifting commentary basic to variational procedure.

The Sonata is in six sections. The principal theme is exposed in the slow-paced initial portion, then contrasted to a *pesante* "one-beat-per-measure" Allegro, with the accents shifting from strong to weak beats. This part moves into a return of the slow theme not only accorded the value of new treatment but a change of meter. Section four is a Scherzo and variates the second part; then in succession there appear another translation of the opening theme and a slightly different version of the second portion. Hindemith's Sonata is, therefore, to be classified in the double variation category.

■ **Sonata for Flute and Piano (1936)**

Virtuosity is not lacking in Hindemith's music, but he never indulges in it for sheer pretentiousness. The use of the agile flute in connection with the exposition of a sonata might lead some to make such an error—Hindemith does not. The content explains the instrument's character and type of personality. It is not simply conventional but exercises proper discrimination for the charming wind instrument. Thus geniality and light niceties dot the surface of the music's conversation.

In the first movement the play of brightness against broadness is especially exhilarating. The development is integral, native to the material presented and includes the main theme in augmentation. A binary plan is employed for the slow movement, while the last two movements are gay and released in decorum. The first of these has a giguelike contour. Hindemith's fondness for the form in question is shown by the exhibit of the final March. The pulse of this homespun design is more than of minor importance to him; under his hands the march form is top-flight in value. Its crispness is still further evidence of his extreme fondness for rhythmic depiction.

■ **Sonata for Horn and Piano (1939)**

Most vital to Hindemith's horn sonata is the fact that the music does not in anyway sound as if it could be transferred to another instrument. The color is integral to the music itself and the technical account pertains to horn character. Brass vocalism pervades the entire atmosphere. It is a warm-blooded work with no lack of proper musical corpuscles. This is a further exemplification of Hindemith's special ability to attune his ideas to the personality of each instrument, not merely to write in symbolic regard for it.

The horn sonata's finale (third movement) is a combination of a moderately fast section of dramatic character (which contains certain imitative sections that make impressive block-line contours) together with the use of a timbral thesis-antithesis plan. This yields first to a slow section and then a developed manner of return to the principal portion. However, the latter's speed broadens toward the conclusion and this proposes a tempo balance, if not a thematic one. Within the sonata design of the first movement the conclusion is hastened by almost a fifty-percent rise in speed. Not only does this result in dramatic climax but when the velocity slows down in the very last measures it sets the mood for the moderate-paced second movement.

- **Sonata for Oboe and Piano (1938)**

In this Sonata Hindemith uses the motival principle to coordinate various movements. The opening theme, which rises a minor third and then moves from that point to an augmented step, is closely matched by the second movement's subject; this moves a whole tone and then a step and a half, and is still further ratified by the latter part of the second movement, where the end of this motive expands to the distance of a third. Control of the germinal material is thus confirmed in a most determined manner.

Rhythm is cleverly disposed in the first movement with the piano in across-the-barline triple pulses poised against the precise duple punctuation of the theme. Such invention is constant with Hindemith—in this case of aid to the cheerfulness of the opening section. The second movement divides into four parts. A total binary style twice is obtained by combining a slow movement with scherzolike liveliness and running through this twice with but one exception—in the recapitulation the "scherzo" changes clothes and appears in fugal dress.

The first movement follows Hindemith's fluctuating magnet of tonal polarity, the intimate principle of so many of this composer's works. In this part of the Sonata the orbit revolves around G, then to the F-sharp just below, and finally shifts to an A-flat tonality above. The slow movement has some chromaticism that seems to imply a Wagnerian glance, but with a decidedly cold stare. The Tristan-like measures which unfold within the movement may well be an ironic touch. Wagner is possibly dear to Hindemith—like a dear enemy.

- **Sonata for Trombone and Piano (1941)**

Hindemith's trombone and piano sonata shows the composer most worthy of his labor. It is not an easy piece to perform, yet does not indulge in fantasies foreign to the majestic breadth and stability of the most sonorous of all brass instruments. There is a firmness and a declamatory quality to this one-movement work, which is parceled into definite quadruple sections. (One must disagree with those who describe the Sonata as in four movements. Most significantly, Hindemith did not indicate movement numbers, separating the sections with fermatas, and withholding the use of the final, double bar line for the conclusion of the fourth section.) Wide-spaced intervals are used, giving the enthusiastic and healthy "well-to-do" quality of most brass-timbred thematics. In Hindemith's hands the trombone is like a prancing instrument (but retains its footing); it dominates and is resolute, it calls to order without any theatrical (artificial) manner.

The first section of the Sonata is concerned with a broad and nobly imposing theme. This movement is followed by a scherzo-styled division in which the trombone interrupts the piano's action four different times. The keyboard instrument presents its part, with little change made in its tonal or rhythmic plan. The humorous intent of the antiphonal reply is very noticeable, the trombone using varied rhythmic twists arranged in eighth notes, sixteenth notes, and triplets. Section three is based on an English tune ("Swashbuckler's Song"). The bravado of this movement is a fitting change of pace and character as compared to the return of the initial section. This recapitulation is not only presented for the effect of formal balance but as a confirmation that the main impulse of the work, notwithstanding its scherzo and folk style deviations, is one of declarative power.

- **Sonata for Trumpet and Piano (1939)**

Hindemith never completely eliminated the principles of Gebrauchsmusik from his thinking. In the preface to the score he states that a clarinet or any other instrument of approximate range, such as an oboe, a violin, or viola, may be substituted for the trumpet. He very carefully warns that this will cause "a makeshift substitute for the intended effect, and I do not advise such substitutions in public performance." Nonetheless, this offers a work for home use to the player who wishes contemporary materials.

The trumpet sonata has several noteworthy features, including defined effects of varied mood. Its first movement's thematic content engages the prime character of the brass instrument's quality by a rising, determined clarion quartal interval. In addition, short jets of simulative bugle calls give edge to the character of the movement set in a rondo style, with the principal theme stated three times. The second movement is exceedingly odd. It is cast in four sections which are paired in turn—the first and third match together as do the second and fourth with some varied change made in the second part of each twosome. But what is most interesting is the imprinted play in the theme of an apparent ironic view of "Ach, du Lieber Augustin." If Hindemith's theme is totally original and the shape of his tune is merely coincidental it remains just as special. If it is included purposefully, then it illustrates the gentle type of musical sarcasm.

In the last movement the music is fully of authoritative character. The first part is funereal (framed by quasi–*Mathis der Maler* sonority), titled "Music of Mourning," and leads to a very impressive statement of the chorale "Alle Menschen müssen sterben" ("All Men Must Die"). The effect is symphonic as the music rises from a soft dynamic plane to an imposing *fortissimo* and then dies down, with the trumpet proclaiming the theme and the piano concerned with ostinato rhythm. It serves to form one of the most dynamic parts of all the Hindemith sonatas for woodwind and brass instruments.

- **Sonata for Tuba and Piano (1943)**

A classic in the sparse viable literature for tuba and piano. Although there is sufficient activity assigned the tuba (the recitativelike penultimate variation in the final movement, where the line is constantly speeded and then reversed), the greater part of the work assigns short lyrical phrases and rhythmically pointed ideas to the brass instrument and figurations and motility to the piano. The most expressive and significant example of this arrangement of responsibilities is to be heard in the entire final part of the Variations.

Fantasy proportions define the opening movement (the tempo, significantly, Allegro pesante), with metrical synchronization also an important factor in its construction: thus, 6/4 in the tuba with 2/2 simultaneously in the piano, and 9/4 for the tuba with 3/2 for the piano. Movement two is akin to a scherzo in its demeanor. Then follow the Variationen, surprisingly developed from a twelve-tone theme. But serial music this is not. Rather, it illustrates Hindemith's concept of using the total chromatic.

Two points must be put straight. First, the word "tuba" always implies the *bass* tuba. Nonetheless, most writers, record annotators, and bibliographers list this work as a Sonata for Bass Tuba and Piano. Hindemith's title is definitely minus the adjective. Second, the same coterie date the work as of 1955. Again, an error. The published score clearly indicates that the *tuba* sonata was composed in *1943*, notwithstanding the much later copyright date (1957) that appears on the music.

- **Sonata for Viola and Piano, Op. 11, No. 4**

Within this Sonata one finds a Brahms and Hindemith partnership. Harmonically they clasp hands. In rhythmic and structural matters Hindemith is the senior partner. Amalgamation of movements takes place but not in the usual manner of combination whereby one type is formed and benefited by the contrast of the other (for example, a scherzo as the middle of a trisectional structured slow movement). Hindemith's formal telescoping is graphic and forcible, of a newness that achieves propitious unity. In the preface to the Sonata Hindemith states that no pauses should occur between any of the three movements. He goes on to say "The second and third movements, especially, must be so closely connected that the listener does not have the impression of hearing a Finale, but grasps the last movement only as a continuation of the Variations." By this, Hindemith gives pertinent information but does not tell all there is to tell.

The trick of pacing two-thirds of a work by two sets of variations is a difficult method of obtaining balance by the very contrary means of unbalance. Nevertheless, by the composer's use of a different method of "variating" in the third movement, the provocative excitation of matching movements and yet contrasting them, is accomplished. The second movement (titled Theme with Variations) contains another possession also to be observed; namely, the theme is concerned with folk song. Metrically speaking, the music is nonsymmetrical. To further matters its rhythm is in flux—of a meticulous inexactness. The four variations are ornamentational, capricious, flowing, and syncopated, but ostinato-controlled versions (with freed backgrounds at the same time). The partnered third movement (titled Finale [with Variations]) successfully negotiates combining sonata form with variation design, and further synthesizes the plan of the correlationship of the last movement to the preceding one by the variations which continue the previous set. The encasement of the entire final two-thirds of the Sonata is only part of the technical drama. There is further invention. Hindemith employs in the finale's development a casting of the sonata style's double subject species and typifies at the same time a

glimmered constitutional make-up of the variations of the movement itself (not to be confused with the variations of the previous movement) by the use of one variation in repeated form and a change in the backgrounds. It is quite a feat to do all this—include a fugato, round it all off with a wild coda and still make sense!

A few other points are also worth attention. The last movement consists of three additional variations to the four which are in the previous part of the Sonata. At all times the thematic generator is always clearly understood—just an additional difficulty that is solved. Of these three variations, the second is to be played "with bizarre ungainliness" and the last one begins the coda. The section most flattering to Brahms is the opening Fantasy, quietly eloquent and somewhat improvisational music, designed monothematically.

- **Sonata for Viola and Piano, Op. 25, No. 4**

Although the greatest number of Hindemith works were published soon after their first performances, some leftovers remained in manuscript—a matter too hazy to understand. This Sonata was one of them. Composed in 1922, it was not published by Schott until 1977, fourteen years after Hindemith's death in 1963.

Violent vitality springs forth from the first movement. The motoric definition embraces a plentiful supply of repetitive figures, especially in the bass. The lyrical phrases are that much more contrastive. The ending, with wide contrary motion in the piano against conjunct lines in the viola, is evidence of discriminative scoring.

The slow movement is short (38 measures of very slow quarter-note pulses) and is framed in ternary design. The Finale is just the opposite (174 measures of very lively quarter-note pulses) and is framed in rondo design. This is music of muscle and tone and exultant energy. It has wonderful pedals and a large number of ostinatos. Both of these techniques add to the excitement.

■ **Sonata for Viola and Piano (1939)**

The architecture of this work brings the first and fourth movements into equipoise at their terminal sections, notwithstanding that the prefatory divisions to these (in the broadest analytical sense) are different. In the first movement the bright and vigorous theme is contrasted to music of fugato type and then moves on to conclude in fugal style. The last movement (Finale mit Zwei Variationen) (Finale with Two Variations) uses a fugal basis for the second of the variants, its subject fashioned from the principal theme by assorted augmented rhythmic values. It is fascinating to hear how the tonal polarity basis permits Hindemith to chromaticize afield yet retain the most punctilious clarity of key center. The first movement bends and stretches, but does not fly off at a tonal tangent to destroy thereby key security. It begins and ends in F, in between very determinedly touching the regions of E and F-sharp, which lie below and above.

The middle movements include a dynamic scherzo representation, which is fully developed, together with a Phantasie. The first of these employs both vertical and horizontal assignments to give contrastive commentary; the other, a slow movement, is rhapsodic. A single theme is of sufficient content for this slow part, with its profile determined by a succinct, but powerful rising seventh. The movement contains some use of arpeggios that are not of academic brand, but in the Bach-translated-by-Hindemith category.

■ **Sonata in C for Violin and Piano (1939)**

Every one of the three movements of the Sonata in C has the patent nobility that shows real achievement. Each clinches a defined argument not necessarily of old standing and simply repeated in a new-fashioned demeanor. In the first movement the most cohesive stability is obtained by forming both of the principal themes from the same starting sounds, with most of the definition of these brought to bear by points of mood and dynamic. The second movement divides into three sections, with the slow chromatic theme changing to a very lively quintuple portion. By such insertion the matter of a scherzo movement is accomplished without need of separation. This division contains both a completely developed form and a full-fledged canon. When the slow theme returns, therefore, two types of musical conduct have been portrayed, tripartite-measured realization has been commandeered and the recapitulation has been of proper authorization, though changed in reference to part one of the movement. In this place the violin is given a facile type of ornamentation pinned to rigid, sextuple blocks as a frame for the statement of the theme in the piano.

The sonata's most demonstrative part is the Fugue. While fugues are often pretentious, they are more often of the academic variety. But Hindemith could muster a fugue that is always dynamic. The ceremony of contrapuntal composition is one he most willingly (and cheerfully) loved to attend. In this case the Fugue is actually a triple fugue. Three subjects are separately announced and then combined in an artistic manner. The fugue's climax is obtained by a fully fed augmentation of the first subject as the movement pulls into the terminal C major.

■ **Sonata in D for Violin and Piano, Op. 11, No. 2**

In his second sonata for violin and piano Hindemith surveys the back country of romanticism. The diagonal bend of semidissonance is prominent; linear aspects are definitely shadowed. Notwithstanding the point that the work pays testimony to its ancestral forebears—

Brahms and Reger—there is quite an amount of the young composer opening his eyes in it. No snug glance observes and blindly copies in this case. The result is a remarkably terse duo sonata that stands apart from Germanic postromanticism by absolutely separate definition.

Dance elements, the most clear-cut kind of pulse in the rhythmic list, are represented. The third movement (this work, therefore, differs in regard to totality of movements in comparison to the first violin and piano sonata, which only has two movements) is rondo styled—"in the tempo and character of a quick dance." The D-major key feeling is germinal to the movement as a whole and matches the spirit of the movement. The middle (slow) movement is in ternary form. Insofar as the opening portion of the Sonata is concerned, Hindemith again changes the conception of form somewhat. Most first movements generally outline sonata style, but without departing from this basis Hindemith's patterns undergo some change. The initial theme is in the restless moving-in, moving-out, focused-unfocused style used by Reger. However, Hindemith treats this idea in variational manner as it reoccurs to contrast the second theme—and change also is inserted for the latter. Secondary subjects are usually lyrical. Here, Hindemith's subordinate subject diverges from this viewpoint (though it still retains its contrastive relationship), as it flows in its rhythmic-stimulated stream. This type gives him the same effective value of a singing theme but with more pronged direction.

- **Sonata in E for Violin and Piano (1935)**

This Sonata has a relaxed manner, contains vernal qualities rather than the *Sturm und Drang* of the earlier sonatas. Even in the faster, concluding section the matter of flow is basic to the music. Throughout, there is a definite, connective principle that formally binds the work. This is brought about by the use of tonal centers in the first movement plus a small amount of cyclic assistance which brings the opening movement into some equivalence with the last. In turn, the latter is connected with the slow-tempo preceding part.

The sonata's opening subject is a mark of the precision and yet dimensional freedom of a tonal center. It is in E, substantially so, but neither bounded by major nor minor, embracing both. The second idea of the movement moves a half-step below this tonality location, while the recapitulation, stated in circular fashion (the second subject is announced first), steps beyond the initial tonal region and the movement concludes in the precisely defined key of E major. This fluidity of key, shifting at the distance of a half-step in each direction, proves the basic premise devoted to tonality but of oscillatory manner. The shifts from E to E-flat then to F and finally to E are in the overall an extension of the key dress of the initial theme itself moving inside and outside E. But all this is done so effortlessly and without fuss that the sonata's quiet emotional warmth is never lost.

Both the slow movement and the final movement are as one—by attachment with no pause intervening, and through the fact that the former cuts into the latter. The finale is concerned with tarantella-styled rhythm and pace further stimulated by shifting, alternating, and combining duple and triple pulses which equate 6/8 and 3/4.

- **Sonata in E-flat Major for Violin and Piano, Op. 11, No. 1**

Hindemith's first violin and piano sonata shows that he will have none of the diagrams proposed by dry and stuffy textbooks. Notwithstanding that Hindemith at this early period cannot be false to his love of Brahms, he begins to shake loose from him. The Sonata is short, only two movements. (This type of conciseness is later recanted by Hindemith, though he never deserts the role represented by the music's dynamic pithiness of expression.)

Further, Hindemith sticks little harmonic spikes into the romantic tissue of his duo sonata. As this is done it is accompanied by dance pulse actions. Stiff Teutonicism starts to vibrate from its hinges and such type of rhythm is also a manner he will never drop. In Hindemith's hands the rubato of romanticism also becomes a negated element.

While the first movement is in sonata style it is changed by a unique idea. The total development core is itself set in ternary division, being embraced on either side by the main theme. This results in a short and large form combined into one. A rondo style is developed in the second movement with tertial harmony used moderately in the majority.

- **Sonatine (in Canon Style) for Two Flutes, Op. 31, No. 3**

(The title above appears on the latest published edition of the work [1952]. When Schott [Hindemith's exclusive publisher] originally issued the composition in 1924, the title was *Kanonische Sonatine* [Canonic Sonatina] for Two Flutes, Op. 31, No. 3.)

Neoclassicism, in its fullest accepted definition, was not the technique practiced by Hindemith. His talents were not set to work in revitalizing older musical science by inculcation of contemporary originations. Hindemith's forward creative impulse was made in terms of tonality, but not with passivity. The chordal apparatus is swung about, given latitude. Although this is to be compared with, and is, a type of classicism, it cannot be described as "neoclassic." He was too linear minded to be included with the neoclassicists.

But the bandying of terms is of little import in regard to this work, in which Hindemith revives (as have a few other composers) a type of 18th-century construction—the unaccompanied duet for two flutes. But when Hindemith surveys this type of composition he shakes it free through his individuality of polyphonic direction. Hindemith's remarkable technique permits a complete technical control to function and yet not interfere with the inherent value of the music if considered apart from the method.

Canonic plan is used a great deal by Hindemith within short spaces or as the total condition of a movement. In this instance it serves for an entire composition. The yield from Bachian linear systems is natural to the composition of canons. In this case it is changed by Hindemith's creative spirit. In addition, the use of a concertante style strengthens the work by its unified arrangement which considers both flute voices of equal importance. Under Hindemith's adroit hands canonic composition results in artistic confirmation.

The three movements are devoted to canonic methods from start to finish. Each movement is varied in treatment—by a different interval of imitation, change in relation to the measured space of the answering voice, as well as speed, mood, and rhythm. The moderate-paced first movement has the comes replying to the dux at the distance of a measure and one-half and at the interval of a third higher. This section is mainly in 12/8 meter and displays a flowing manner. The second movement is a baroque-styled, ornamented canon titled Capriccio. In this case, the consequent enters at the sixth measure with its imitating interval a second below the leader. Complete formal balance, garnered by contrast of speed and style, is furnished by the final Presto. This movement has the stimulus of motor rhythm, an additional support to the thinness of flute tone. Here the antecedent is replied to by the consequent voice at a distance of three measures at the interval of a fifth below. Later on (in the middle section) the imitation is hurried in stretto manner with the consequent then entering only one beat later but with the same fivefold reply. After some shifts are made, the movement is concluded with the intervallic distance between the two voices that of a diminished octave.

- ■ *Stücke (Pieces)* **for Bassoon and Cello (1941)**

In Luther Noss' *Paul Hindemith in the United States* he gives the background for the creation of this work. Noss relates that "Hindemith dashed off" the duo as "house music" for performance on the bassoon in which he would be joined by his wife Gertrude playing the cello. Hindemith was a viola virtuoso but "could play all of the standard orchestral wind instruments and was especially proficient as a bassoonist."

Hindemith presented the manuscript of this duo to Karl Geiringer, the eminent Austrian-American music scholar and writer, in 1941. It was finally published by Schott in 1969. (Hindemith did not assign the *Stücke* title to his duo, the decision to do so was made by Schott.)

Four short pieces. Thus: a twenty-nine-measure Moderato with polyphonic give and take; a twenty-two-measure Andante with some imitations; an Allegretto of two dozen measures of scherzo quality; and a variationally conceived Allegro of fifty-six measures. As usual with Hindemith the material is organized with discrimination.

The publishers point out that Hindemith wrote his duo on a single staff "without indicating which part is to be played by which instrument." It is obvious that he may have had the possibility in mind that the instruments could exchange parts. Because of this basic equality in the voicing the editorial suggestion is made that "there is no good reason why two bassoons or two cellos should not be used." Certainly, if any change is made from the published score it is only fair to Hindemith to give all the above facts.

- ■ **Three Pieces for Cello and Piano, Op. 8**

In the Hindemith canon this work is of impor-

tance, since Op. 8 represents Hindemith's first published work, issued some two months before the composer had reached the age of 22. The Three Pieces display engaging and full romantic impulse; each is in a definite key and arranged sequentially. Number one is a Capriccio in A major, the second is a Phantasiestück with B-major tonality, while the Scherzo is in C minor.

It is noteworthy that having just reached his majority Hindemith acts as a composer freed a little from the heaviness of his pedantic handbag, which contained the works of Brahms, Reger, Schubert, and Schumann. The first piece is devoted to Hindemith's always-to-be-favored nonsymmetrical statement: while the unit pulse is basic, the measures are free as to the totality of beats in each. A ternary form is utilized with the cello muted throughout, giving special color to the matter of *fortissimo* pizzicato chords. The second piece is rather rhapsodic, and combines duple rhythms with trinal types. The Scherzo moves according to average scale.

- ■ **Two Duets for Violin and Clarinet (1932)**

The first duet consists of a Lebhaft in moderate, duple-measure pace, written in tripartite form with the initial section repeated literally. The second of the pair is slower in speed and also arranged in three-part form. Throughout, Hindemith's music is gentle in character and typically linear.

(To find the place this duet holds in a group of compositions, see above: *Plöner Musiktag.*)

- ■ *Zwei Kanonische Duette (Two Canonic Duets)* **for Two Violins (1929)**

Canonic technique, a matter not uncommon to musical composition, is nonetheless rarely called on as the substance for an entire work. The difficulty of writing a canon increases in direct ratio to the length the canon extends. To keep sounds moving in imitative regularity produces the very rigidity which the choice of canonic technique proposes to avoid in the first place. But the longer the canon the more difficult it is to maintain the first voice meaningfully ahead of the second, and, at the same time, preserve unity in the endeavor to match the second part with the initial one and conserve the continuous flow of both. The total result is very often nothing more than a dry, mechanical technical trick that at best has the temporary value of having gotten over the formal hurdle and once heard is immediately forgotten. There are not many canons that have the virtue of eloquent expression in place of bald artifice. In fact, there are so few, that they can be listed with little trouble.

The prime difficulty of the constant strict canon is to effect an endowed meaning of balance and design. As pointed out, the voices must duplicate each other and in so doing adjustments must be made in order to create contrapuntal sense. Most often these editings of otherwise static imitations destroy the line of the antecedent and ultimately do the same to the consequent. Most canons are, therefore, free rather than strict in style, not only in respect to the individual voices but in regard to the designs they display.

Hindemith illustrates the spontaneous gift he possesses in this work. He is able to write in defined formal structures of length and yet not be forced even once to break away from canonic strictness. The two pieces prove Hindemith's amazing abilities as a contrapuntalist. Both duets make good musical, artistic and technical sense, and possess emotional qualities as well.

The first duet is a three-movement affair titled *Kanonisches Vortragstück (Canonic Presentation)*. Each section is written in the free tonal Hindemithian manner (but let this not be marked as the reason for Hindemith's success in managing a long-term canonic policy; it is just as difficult to write a 20th-century-style canon as one in Bachian style). The first move-

ment is cast in ternary form (the initial motive appears four times, twice each in the outer sections) with the imitation made at the unison (save for one instance, this is the interval between the imitating antithesis to the original thesis for the entire two duets), at a distance of one measure. The middle movement is gracefully stated in strict scherzo style—i.e., three-part form with a Trio as the central core. The reply of the second voice to the leader is again at a one measure's distance. Rondo style serves for the fast, last movement, the consequent this time replying at a distance of three measures. The marvelous unity of the three movements represents creative primacy in canonic literature.

In the second duet the problem Hindemith sets for himself is even more difficult, since he works in variation form together with strict stylistic usage of design. Nevertheless, the canonic barrier does not block the road to expert and convincing music. The solution to the problem is bold. This is illustrated by the movement's theme, which is so managed that its last part balances the first. However, it must be noted that Hindemith realizes more than a simple equipoise of phrase. The second voice still imitates the previous material with unalterable exactitude. This is accomplished at the unison without any intervallic free exchange— the usual way that eliminates falling in the rut which always landscapes canonic territory. Although a measured thematic weight of the type Hindemith uses in this case almost subverts its possibility for imitation, it works beautifully in his hands.

Movement two of the second duet consists of five variations concluded with a Finale. The theme is recognizable in each variational part with the distance of reply strictly confirmed as well—the antithesis being spaced at a span of two measures. The only exceptions are (1) in the opening variation when the second section is quickly bridged into the first and the reply is then lessened to the space of one measure, and

(2) in the Finale. In the latter case the reply is withheld for a longer interval of four measures. Additionally, the original interval of imitation is changed from the unison to the fourth below as the movement runs its course in tarantella speed.

TRIOS

- *Acht Kanons (Eight Canons)* for Two
  Violins with Accompaniment of
  Violin 3 (or Viola), Op. 44, No. 2

The pitch range is limited to the first position and the music is designed for "slightly advanced players." Nevertheless, these boundaries do not interfere with valid artistic results. Once again the music illustrates that special Hindemithian chemistry that makes all of his music "work."

The use of canon in every piece is, of course, of technical exacting order, but there are plentiful differences and sufficient variety to block out monotony and attendant boredom. (The third voice is not canonic, though bits of the material being imitated creep into the accompanimental part of the eighth piece.)

The imitation is at the unison in numbers one, two, three, and eight. Number four is a canon at the fourth below; the opposite direction is used in numbers five and seven, with the imitation a minor second above. A distinct difference is utilized in the sixth of the set, which has the responding voice set in inversion. The tempos vary and so do the time spans between the first and second voices. However, special excitement is furnished by the final, very-fast-tempo canon, with the consequent moving in at only a single beat's distance from the antecedent.

- **Rondo for Three Guitars (1925)**

No instrument failed to interest Hindemith. The rhythmical moderately fast Rondo (con-

centrated in 114 measures of triple-beat music) was composed as a "musical intermezzo" and first performed on the Music-in-the-Home Day at the five-day Festival of New Music in Berlin, in 1930.

(A compression of the scoring for performance by two guitars was made by Wilhelm Bruck and Theodor Ross. It was issued in 1978 by Schott, Hindemith's publisher.)

- **Trio for Recorders (Soprano and Two
  Alto Recorders) (1932)**

This three-movement composition can be performed either as a trio or by duplicating each of the three parts to any desired total. By using one soprano and two alto instruments Hindemith obtains a wider tonal range and a timbre difference, though the latter is only of minor effect.

The first movement, Lebhaft, opens with marchlike character, is followed by a slower central portion and a revamped recapitulation. Even in the "workaday" aspects of Hindemith's music he refused the choice of the easy way of a literal repeat to balance a form. This refusal emphasized an important point in the educational purposes Hindemith sought since amateurs were to be given (according to the tenets of Gebrauchsmusik) the same plans relating to music composed for professionals. Formal advance, therefore, was part of the plan, despite the simplification of compositional technique.

Movement two is in a faster tempo than the first. Its rondo form also has march-music pertness as well as the concise Hindemithian aspect of rhythm. The concluding movement is a Fugato.

(For details concerning the place this Trio has in a group of works known as *Plöner Musiktag*, see above.)

- **Trio for Viola, Heckelphone (or Tenor
  Saxophone), and Piano, Op. 47**

The instruments in this Trio are a rare combination, even if the baritone-type oboe is replaced by a tenor saxophone, as Hindemith permits. The Trio is in two parts—the first in three sections, the second in four. Sequential instrumental strength marks part one: the Solo is for piano, the Arioso is for the heckelphone and piano, and, notwithstanding the subtitle Duett, the complete trio force is used in the third section. The Solo is fugal, with a pair of subjects. It is the second of these that marks the expressive line and its development by the wind instrument in the Arioso. Then, in the Duett the first fugal subject is heard with accompanimental rhythmic support by the piano. A two-voice canon at the distance of a minor second follows, using the second fugal subject. The Duett then turns into a true trio by full piano participation. Hindemith leaves no technical weapon unused. He combines the two subjects and concludes part one with imitation between the viola and the heckelphone.

Part two is a Potpourri. It varies a primary idea in a dozen different ways in its initial division and mixes and tosses three items in the second. This is followed by a duple-pulsed allotment, bounced and rocked by jazzy, irregular accentuation, and the opus is concluded by a Prestissimo presenting rhythmic propulsion and lyrical abandon simultaneously.

- **Trio No. 1 for Violin, Viola, and Cello, Op. 34**

A composition of transcendent power; the working material is handled freely, the horizontal impulse being the paramount objective.

Without careful design, polyphony totals sheer horizontal motion, a voiced thickness, a mushy bed of sound strands. But in no measure of the Trio does Hindemith fail. He achieves the most efficient clarity within the freshness that signifies his conception of modern counterpoint and in no lesser degree the forms employed are of effective invention.

The fourth movement is a fugue. It begins

with the expositional part wherein the answers to the subject are placed at tonal distances which equate a semiclustered sphere. This is determined by the initial E direction (while the lines are chromatic, the entering point can be considered the tonal axis), which moves to the viola's G-sharp and swings to the cello's F-sharp. A contrasting section follows, set in a binomial rhythm with the voices not combined in trio formation but in a two-versus-one disposition. This part of the movement is also a fugue, a secondary one, and by its departure from the ordinary furnishes quite a remarkable method of presentation. Then follows the re-exposition of the first subject (which may be considered a development) in turn succeeded by a Prestissimo. While a standard perspective of pedal point is used, Hindemith's contemporary type is much more angular, a geometric construction of hard lines. Hindemith's dramatic center of attraction is made by moving parallel nail-biting sevenths together as the two lower voices announce the second subject first and then the initial subject last and play it in canonic form. In one sweep Hindemith furnishes all parts concerned with fugal architecture: the tower of pedal point, the floors equal to the subjects, the underpinning of polyphonic concrete and the woodwork of canon. Completion of the movement then follows in antithetical style, with the first fugue subject stated in unison. No faint creative heart conceived this music and no delicate aural consideration can be applied, unless one wishes to miss the daring beauties of this gigantic creation.

Polyphony is major to the second (slow) movement as well, with a canon formed between the violin and the viola. The result is a Bach-Hindemith invention. Strength of color predominates in the third movement. Save for the last few measures (where the cello changes to bowed sounds), the three instruments are completely muted and fully concerned with pizzicato throughout.

The opening movement Toccata is a whirlwind of kinetic vigor, tied onto a solid and positive form of music. The instrumental motion streams and steams, does not stop even for a contrasting melodic section. Linear composition is maintained without letup. Three cadenzas are marched out in the coda—in turn, for the violin, viola, and cello. Equal partnership having been confirmed, two of the instruments then play a short cadenza, and finally an upbeat midget set of grace notes, also with cadenza impulse, reannounces the theme to bring the Trio to its conclusion.

- **Trio No. 2 for Violin, Viola, and Cello (1933)**

Hindemith's second string trio (dedicated to the famous microtonal composer Alois Hába) is based on exceedingly unconstrained tonality; but one is reminded that atonality is not Hindemith's way of work and is the improper term for this composition. There are composers who write with complete negation of tonality, do not at least "reinsert," as it were, a tonal zone to focus the ever-circling music. For such the term "atonality" is correct; for Hindemith, in spite of some opinions, the word would be of analytical falseness.

The music of Hindemith's Trio has a clear realization of tonal matter, but with plastic freedom. It recoils and leaps, tenses and relaxes, and forms its own kind of tonics and dominants. It is not glued to a key, but is a mobile tonality, made from seconds and sevenths, fourths and fifths, and diminished and augmented intervals—as motile as Hindemith's rhythms.

The first movement is extremely polyphonic, let loose by figurations and rhythms. Though disposed rhapsodically, it is nurtured by a generating motive announced by the violin in the first measure. The second movement, an untitled scherzo, is in classical design with an inner section of more lyrical character. This interlocking of fast and slow elements is fol-

lowed acutely in the third (final) movement. In this case tonal chromaticism and unshackled rhythm arc contrasted to a tighter direction of accidentalized tones and sharper cut pulse, plus a further deployment of black and white effect by moving from slow to fast speed velocities. The two sections are heard twice, varied in treatment upon repetition, and distinguished with an accelerando section furnishing additional drive to conclude the Trio.

QUARTETS

- *Acht Stücke (Eight Pieces)* **for Two Violins, Viola, and Cello, Op. 44, No. 3**

The eight pieces are a synthesis, a concentrate of Hindemith's early (but not initial) style. To listen to them is to hear a capsule version of Hindemith's art. All of his methods are detailed as a representation, a sampling of the larger works. Nevertheless, the small and precise settings of these pieces make perfect art jewels. True, the *Acht Stücke* are written to limits of the first position for educational purposes devoted to obtain the attention of younger players and secure performance from them. But this only limits the tonal compass, not the quality of the quartet. In any event, most performers avail themselves of other positions in order to obtain more pertinent color and dynamics and to give deeper meaning to the music as a whole. Important music can be formed within the most restricted means, providing the composer is sufficiently expert.

The first piece is cast in simple form and progresses from A minor to the finality of A major. The fast-running second item is square-cut, vertically designed and grim in character. Movement three vacillates between major and minor and concludes in the latter mode. Sardonicism is Hindemith's idea in this instance. Though only a minute part of the whole, it is the clever final cadence built on an odd scale formation that illustrates his frame of mind. The rondo style of the fourth piece is in lusty D major. Offbeat rhythmic patterns propel the action of the music and silence is an aid in the neat cadential flick of humor. The fifth movement is fast, a march type; the sixth is one of the longest of the entire set. Hindemith employs a song style plus a fugato in this part of the work. Movements seven and eight have affinity in two ways: grotesquerie of character and a decreasing dynamic plane for the final cadences. The second example of the latter is illustrated by an unaccompanied violin.

- *"Minimax"—Repertorium für Militärmusik (Repertory for Military Music)* **for String Quartet (1923)**

One can only guess at the precise meaning of the title, notwithstanding the clues found in the contents. (Hindemith left zero data and it was not until 1978 that Schott published the score.) It might stand for the abbreviated combination of "minimum-maximum," meaning a small instrumental setting of material that really only fits large forces (a transfer [far-fetched?] of the word's meaning in the field of mathematics: "the lowest of a set of maximum values"), or it could mean partnering minimal seriousness with maximum tomfoolery. Whatever, it is a gem of a burlesque for four string instruments. Truly, Hindemith proves the axiom that basic originality (military music for a string quartet!) provokes resultant originality (a matchless travesty of band style rather than a mere copy of it). Hearing this twenty-one-minute work will make believers.

There are six movements. The first is "Army March 606 (Der Hohenfürstenberger)." The title pays tribute to Prince Fürst zu Fürstenberg, sponsor of the important Donaueschingen Chamber Music Festivals, where Hindemith played an important role, first as composer and performer, and later as artistic director. Combining part of the title of a march which

Hindemith is mimicking, "Hohenfriedberger Marsch," with the prince's name, gives the mouth-filling heading. The "606" goes forward in C major, with Trio and recapitulation, plus an occasional sour and pungent D-flat by the cello.

Part two is an Overture to "Wasserdichter und Vogelbauer." But even minus the mock title ("Water Poet and Bird Peasant") the source of supply, Suppé's *Poet and Peasant (Dichter und Bauer)* Overture, would be recognized. The takeoff on Suppé's old chestnut includes the usual majestic beginning, the "hurry" allegro music, and the light galop-style particulars.

Part three is termed "Ein Abend an der Donauquelle" ("An Evening on the Danube")— Intermezzo for 2 Distant Trumpets. Of course there are no trumpets, but there are the second violin and viola, imitatively playing "from the distance." The "Evening" being described, after an introduction by first violin and cello, is entirely in the hands of the other pair of instruments, including a cadenza in which they have some snippety quotes from Wagner and Beethoven, and a yodel call.

The fourth movement is "Löwenzähnchen an Baches Rand" ("Dandelions on the Edge of the Brook")—Concert Waltz. The music consists of a chain of waltzes. Stylistically, everything is as it should be, with an introduction and three waltzes plus coda, primed with Viennese flavor.

The fifth movement is titled "Die beiden lustigen Mistfinken" ("The Two Merry Dirty People")—Character Piece, Solo for 2 Piccolos. Here again there are no actual piccolos. This is a takeoff, according to Erwin R. Jacobi, on a piece by Henri Kling (1842–1918) called "Die beiden kleinen Finken," Fantasie-polka for 2 Flutes or 2 Piccolos and Accompaniment. The twitters to imitate the tweets are formed by scads of harmonics in the violins. Lots of grace-note chirps, as well.

Movement six has the title "Alte Karbonaden"–March. And a march it is, but one that goes out of step in a number of measures. However, that's the proper type of march for this formal parody.

- **Quartet for Clarinet, Violin, Cello, and Piano (1938)**

As is so often the case, the use of the clarinet by Hindemith gives the Quartet a mellow quality. This fact is especially noticeable in the first movement, where a romantic glow (shining in the composer's style) suffuses the music, based on three themes and set in ternary form.

The middle movement is also obedient to ternary form, with the central section more ornamental in design and conveying within its rhythm a slight infiltration by the return of the varied first theme. The last movement is a diversified variational type, unburdened from rigid declaration of subject. It includes contrapuntal design and rhythmic augmentation; it ends with the principal theme's transformation into a fast duple kinetic section.

- **Sonata for Four Horns (1952)**

The quartet opens with a twenty-three measure Fugato in very slow tempo. Movement two (Lebhaft) is sonata designed, the themes carefully balanced. The first one is begun by upward and downward intervallic fourths from which a motive is drawn; the second theme descends a fourth and later ascends the same distance. The middle section of the movement is a fantasia type, based on the fugato's subject.

A set of five variations on a melody (doubtless chosen with forethought) titled "Ich schell mein Horn" ("I Ring My Horn") represents the finale. The permutations follow Hindemith's usual variation style of writing, including imitation, canon, ornamental rhythm, and pulsatile drive.

- **String Quartet No. 1, Op. 10**

Hindemith's very early quartet demonstrates the attempt of a young composer to cut away from imitative writing. The tendency to length is one piece of evidence that romanticism still breathes in Hindemith's ear. There is the additional point that tonality (notwithstanding the use of the stretching that Brahms and especially Reger had begun) is a determined factor; the quartet is based on F minor. Thickness of writing is still another sign that indicates this quartet is an early Hindemith opus. However, the astute skill of the instrumental writing shows the hand of a thoroughly imaginative string player.

Here and there one sees marks that point out that Hindemith's style will shift. The method used for fugato replies points to a later day. The imitations in the third movement are inserted at distances of a half step, such as E-flat, E-natural, and F and in the recapitulation by C, C-sharp, and D. Counterpoint is an important element in the quartet's structure and the seething, stamped-from-iron rhythms also show that Hindemith, though young, is bound to get off the old-fashioned scholastic chair in which he sits. The tail end of romanticism begins to vanish in this work; in Hindemith's next string quartet he departs for other regions.

The first of the three movements is in sonata form. The music arches a width of two octaves, has an important tensile point in between by a leap of a seventh and already academicism is being choked out of existence. Further, a fugato is substituted in place of a development section. Movement two is a Thema mit Variationen. The five variants are freely written, contain some special colors and are climaxed by a muted tone mutation in march tempo which the composer asks to be played "as music from a distance." The final movement is symphonic in scope, a designed sectionalism set forth with dancelike array. (Since the quartet does not contain a scherzo, this characteristic is, therefore, transferred into the finale.) The contrasting subject is as lush in sound as the opening one is rhythmic. Scordatura appears in one section of the movement when the cello's fourth string is tuned down and Hindemith employs a great amount of pedal and ostinato (technical blood brothers). The quartet ends with an energetic storm of sound that is a typical mannerism of the composer, moving from Prestissimo to accelerando and then to still another accelerated speed! (This is, of course, impossible unless the first Prestissimo is taken several notches below the terrific speed it represents.)

- **String Quartet No. 2, Op. 16**

Hindemith's second string quartet almost moves out from the area of romanticism. Only the slight shadow remaining in the slow movement shows that stylistic individuality has not been completed. The harmony within this quartet is based on melodic freedom. While the quartet's tonality is C, the opening movement's theme moves to numerous points of the tonal compass—to B-flat, D-flat, and elsewhere. Notwithstanding the similar freedom of the second subject, it rings itself around the point of G, representing the classical dominant of the home key. It is the axis of the principal key that provides the home station for the tonalities lying in the distance; this pivot is of sufficient power to control all other key positions and maintain them in proper relationship. The first movement ends in C, the second begins in the tonality of A (thus of close relationship to C since A represents its relative minor, changed here to major) and the last movement is governed by C as well. In the progression and evolution of tonality Hindemith proves the validity of both old and new methods to match up, compare, and be allied.

Melodic material does not have diffidence here. Hindemith uses motivally cast dynamic themes; he employs warm subjects rounded by song and has some lengthy topics plus several robust ideas in the quartet. Thematic wealth, indeed. One example: In the opening movement there are three secondary subjects; the first of these is very boldly dry and smart, while the second is a reiteration of the compelling initial idea, but in slower tempo and extended rhythms.

Chromaticism is a major point in the slow movement. In this case Hindemith's use of quartet color aids in avoiding entanglements.

The last movement is a long dissertation in which duple and triple rhythms alternate freely, and combine as well in a steady impulsed beat. One section of the movement is rather startling in effect and unique as a device. There, for fifty-three measures, the second violin continuously performs an ad libitum, nonmetered figure in ostinato-layered sound which equals a horizontal cluster, since one pivotal sound is incessantly circled by half tones above and below it. (This is akin to Hindemith's much later plan of tonality for an entire movement whereby the modulations to the prime key are related by moving stepwise above and below it.) During this time a dialogue exists between the first violin and the two lowest instruments and eventually all three are combined. The tempo of the fifty-three measures undergoes radical change fifteen times; in addition, there are four whole measures of rest together with fermatas. It is a wonderful inspiration—a bas-relief effect within the total sonorous frame of the quartet.

- **String Quartet No. 3, Op. 22**

Of all the Hindemith string quartets the third has a place of distinction in the confirmed repertoire. Stylistic synthesis had already begun in the third string quartet. Hindemith's mature manner of almost thirty years later is more solid but does not depart very much from the style and beautiful expressive quality of Op. 22. Nor was he able to go much beyond the individuality of the third string quartet.

This is the only quartet of the half dozen Hindemith produced that consists of five movements. (Of these, the fourth is compact in arrangement and serves as a prelude to the finale.) Each part of the work displays clarity of form and theme, plus melodic potency. All of the formal patterns are based on reconstituted classical ordering.

The first movement is a free Fugato, suggestive of combined keys since Hindemith uses his favorite measuring off of semitonal distances for presenting the subject by the various voices. The tonal planes are marked at the start by G (first violin), then by F (viola), a move to A-flat (cello), and finally F-sharp (second violin). Movement two is a total stream of power channeled through the most violent and barbaric type of string sonorous action. The music is scanned by irregular rhythm; it is not nervous in character but rather ultradynamic—an example of string quartet locomotiveness. This section represents the scherzo movement. Its driven force brings to mind a set of drums percussed by steel beaters.

The third movement is the most captivating of all. In muted loveliness, this movement progresses dissonantly but intimately, stimulated by repetitive quinary intervals. Although the key clashes are tensile they are of subdued manner. The music's nocturnal mood represents impressionism coded by bitonality.

Movement four is a wild toccatalike affair, improvisational in its course through free fantasy. Bariolage effects give an intense sonority scale as first the cello then the viola sweep over the strings. This movement proceeds directly into the final Rondo. There, Hindemith serves up a fugal movement of almost chaste quality.

- **String Quartet No. 4, Op. 32**

Polyphony, the reigning doctrine of Hindemith's music, was employed in goodly degree in his first three string quartets. In this one it explodes in every direction. All facets of composition bend the knee to horizontal severity. Contrapuntalism is no avocation in Hindemith's fourth quartet; it is its sole occupation. All of the music is tense with counterpointed moving and opposed voices, crowded with linear stimuli as harmony is eliminated and turned over on its side. The quartet glories in a parade of polyphonic forms and methods.

The first movement plunges into a fugue, then partakes of a second helping, this time of a double fugue with the pair of subjects announced together. A cadenza for the two violins then forms a bridge to the point where the ultimate into fugal inquiry is made. There Hindemith combines the three fugue subjects. He requires birhythms in order to do so, but proves his structural point. The substantiality of the fugal language, making complete sense at all times, marks the composer as one of the few great contrapuntalists since Johann Sebastian Bach.

In the poetic slow movement two techniques are drawn upon to distinguish the weaving voices. One concerns the formal measurement of counterpoint (by a canon between the second violin and viola which moves in an augmented octave antecedent-consequent fashion); the other is of baroque vintage (illustrated by the ground-bass pizzicato of the cello). (The polyphonic connections of the quartet go even further since this freely stated basso ostinato is the genesis for the fourth movement's Passacaglia.) An additional point is made by the free chorale-recitative section which cuts into the movement for the purpose of indicating the concentrated recapitulatory division. The next part, a "Kleiner Marsch" ("Little March"), gives the quartet a different contour and thus fosters the greatest type of contrast. The vivace, sempre crescendo tempo indication is fully descriptive. After the music moves from an initial triple *piano* to a triple *forte* the former dynamic is resumed and maintained by a literal repeat of the first nine measures, with the addition of a skeletal texture for the remaining measures.

The last movement is a tremendous chamber music declaration employing passacaglia and fugato. There are twenty-seven variants of the theme, the basic subject making its appearance, at one time or another, in every one of the four string voices. The fugato is in a tempo ("as fast as possible") that taxes even the best of virtuosos. It proposes the ultimate possibility inherent in the passacaglia subject, which is perorated by powerful six- and seven-part writing. And no one should overlook the one final master stroke of the composer. The first set of three tones in the initial fugue of the quartet's opening movement is equal to the foremost three rising sounds of the passacaglia theme, and in turn to the beginning tones of the fugato, and marks the coda as well. Hindemith's derring-do forms the perfect idea of integration within the richness of varied modern polyphony.

String Quartet [No. 5] in E-flat (1943)

A span of twenty years (the time between Hindemith's fourth quartet and the appearance of the E-flat quartet, not marked as number five, but taking that place in the chronology) is bound to bring change to any composer. In this work ("written for the Budapest String Quartet") Hindemith has become less dynamic in speech, but not one whit less in intensity or concentration. This quartet exemplifies a Hindemithian period devoted to mature deliberation. While polyphonic spinning continues, it is knitted with yarns of less bright colors. The tonality has been drawn a bit closer together, the total effect one of compactness—of Hindemithian simplicity.

But the first movement is still a sign that Hindemith is not concerned with changing his formal plan to meet any purpose save that of 20th-century character. It is a "very quiet and expressive" fugue, short in length and important in total application. Not only does the fugue serve for contrast to the next movement

but it gives the quartet's form an *entente cordiale* through cyclic-mannered use when combined inside the final movement. The second movement is full of Hindemith's gingered drive. A triplet and dotted eighth plus sixteenth serve as the binding rhythms and are also related to the fugue that preceded in the sense that the sixteenth note is the dynamic arsis of its prosody. Such interweaving is not new to Hindemith's work but is more clarified in this quartet, showing the essence of technical compact.

To a certain extent the title of the third movement, "Quiet, Variations," is confused. Set off by a comma, the word "quiet" is actually the movement's tempo heading but becomes (intentionally or not) mostly descriptive of its style as well. Hindemith goes about his variational field in a quiet manner, but the sound is certainly not of subdued total. Furthermore, the very integrated variants, all of which clearly establish and deploy the thematic premise, grow increasingly faster in tempo and accordingly initial quietness turns into later vigor and dynamicism.

The new and novel manner of the composer, when related to his previous work, is expressed in the last movement. First, a broad theme is announced and this moves into a fugato (as mentioned, the theme of the first movement is used within this portion). Hindemith then whisks off the mask of determination from the music and concludes the movement in a grazioso fast swinging triple meter derived from the fugal material. There is no doubt that a composer's mellowness is shown in such a finish to a string quartet.

■ String Quartet No. 6 (1945)

The speedy first movement is of fully realized voice movement with calm but elocutionary power. Hindemith's concentration on essentials carries over to the short length of the movement. A middle-placed fugato serves as the inner weight matched by the equilibrium of the outer sections. A quiet scherzo type is used in the second part of the quartet; it too is short. The thirteen-measure theme of the movement includes tonal ornamentation during its quite wide-pitched path and is stated three times: initially by the first violin, then the other violin, and last by the viola. Since there are only episodes between these thematic statements the movement exemplifies monothematic solidity. Movement three begins slowly and progresses into an exceedingly fast section which has imitations between the instruments, counter subjects, and some canonic duplication. The coda reflects a diverting aspect. First the tempo (but not the theme!) of the slow section is freely illustrated by antiphonal progression; then the subject of the very fast-paced part is superimposed over a pedal chord.

The most chromatic and polyphonic movement of the quartet is the last one—a canon. This is balanced in the flanked sections with the reiterative subject in the first violin and viola voices at a span of a perfect fourth and at a distance of two measures. With proper check for the classical order governing Hindemith's tonality principles (no matter their freedom), the quartet ends in the home key of E-flat.

QUINTETS

- *Drei Stücke für Fünf Instrumente (Three Pieces for Five Instruments)* **(Clarinet, Trumpet, Violin, Double Bass, and Piano) (1925)**

A mix of the four instrumental families: woodwind, brass, string, and keyboard. Plenty of color in this sonic democracy, therefore, with the tonal material handled in a pliant manner.

Two flipped intervallic spans are basic to the first piece, a Scherzando. Both are flung by grace notes, one up a fourth, the other up a seventh. Most of the second piece (in "slow eighths") belongs to the piano, weaving ornamental detail and repetitive pitches. Consider-

able syncopated accompaniment binds the material. The lively finale ends softly, as do the other two movements. However, in this case Hindemith sets his instrumental team into *piano* and *pianissimo* for six measures and then has a diminuendo covering six more measures. The balance of eight measures is soft and thin, and moves into a ritard. A neat, diverting contribution.

- *Kleine Kammermusik (Little Chamber Music)* **for Five Wind Instruments (Flute [alternating Piccolo], Oboe, Clarinet, Horn, and Bassoon), Op. 24, No. 2**

One of the most widely performed of all contemporary works for wind instruments, it is, without doubt, one of Hindemith's most charming pieces.

The quintet embodies humor, parody, and irony—some of the passages sound as though they were written with acid. The music's dancy attitude, displayed in typical post–World War I style, equals a chamber music hedonistic view of life presented in cameo fashion. The dissonant chordal bite of the very first beat outlines and sketches the type of aesthetic axiom that the composer will propound. Hindemith's tonal axis is announced by the combined seconds of C, D, and E—publishing the fact that the quintet's tonality is to be free, and friction harmony will persist.

All the forms are as concentrated as the harmony heard within them. No ostentatious display or looseness of construction is to be found. Severe, parceled contrast is the ruling principle, with no use made of sonata form, though partial elements of that design can be observed in the first movement. That part is a fast-paced affair tied together with a rhythmic cell that consists of an eighth and two sixteenths. Interlocution takes place when the more lyrical secondary theme is stabilized by an accompanimental background that contains this same rhythm. Since no other family of instruments can furnish the piquant articulation possible to woodwind tone,the spiculate aspect of Hindemith's first-movement music is considerably enhanced accordingly. The slower penultimate section is suggestive of a furrowed brow to which the final two measures give a cadential grin in reply.

In proper place, soft sounds have as much influence as the bombastic explanation. For example, it is a quiet dynamic use that implies the most concentrated and telling detail in musical parody. This fact is demonstrated in the second movement (Walzer), not related to any "Blue Danube." Ostinatos form the middle core of the slow movement that follows, designing the music, thereby, in divisional, ternary style. The intervallic condition pertaining to the thesis part of the theme is worth attention as it moves from a rising third to an ascending quartal width. The fourth movement is very short—only twenty-three measures. It contains solo passages for all the instruments save the oboe, with episodic alternations provided by a motto unit of two-measure length. Hindemith's creative trademark is placed on the final movement by way of its march quality.

- **Quintet for Clarinet (B-flat and E-flat Clarinets) and String Quartet, Op. 30**

Motoric motility in abundance here; the work was composed in 1923, when Hindemith was 28 and still in his "sehr schnell und wild" creative period. (It remains puzzling that the Quintet was not published until 1955; Schott, Hindemith's publisher, normally produced his works as fast as they came off the creator's worktable.) Even in quieter tempos within the five-movement work (the score sets the timing of the piece as eighteen minutes, the recording by the Musical Heritage Society runs 20:26) the stylistic immoderation comes through, as in the fourth movement Arioso (Sehr ruhig [Very Quiet]), where one glissando after an-

other decorates the solo violin's recitative, framed only by simple drummed pizzicatos. Very consequential scoring in this case; the first violin's line is played con sordino, the clarinet only has three low (snidelike) solo E-flats—responses marking the end of each section of the movement.

The second movement (linked to the first) is marked Ruhig (Quiet). It is a polyphonic nocturne, principally canonically structured.

There are other important features. Movement three is marked Schneller Ländler (Faster Ländler). The dictionary defines a Ländler as "an Austrian dance in the character of a slow waltz." Hindemith's Ländler exhibit is totally opposite. It is, as indicated, "fast," but more importantly, it is, for the greater part, brash, brazen, and blustery. Pointedly, it is in this movement that Hindemith uses the shrill E-flat clarinet to replace the warmer B-flat instrument. One section of twenty-five measures is built on ostinato detail featuring open-string use plus pizzicato. Another section, also somewhat detailed in terms of ostinato, stresses open strings and a bit of bariolage bowing. And, to cap matters, the first and fifth movements match each other to the finite point. This perfect formal symmetry is obtained as the finale runs through the first movement in precisioned retrograde (crabwise) fashion.

SEXTET

- *Morgenmusik (Morning Music)* **for Brass Instruments (Two Trumpets, Two Horns, and Two Trombones, [and Tuba ad lib]) (1932)**

Hindemith's composition for brass instruments calls for trumpets in two divided parts (flugelhorns, etc., may be added at will to each of these), and horns and trombones also combined in two parts, with a tuba ad libitum. Though conceived originally for a massed combination of performers, the three movements of the work are written strictly in four voices throughout. (To find the place this work holds in a group of compositions see above: *Plöner Musiktag*.)

In the chamber music category, therefore, this composition (a modern equivalent of baroque tower music) is to be classified as a sextet or septet for two each of trumpets, horns, and trombones, with a tuba ad libitum. There is a second point to consider additional to the fact that the choice or rejection of the tuba decides whether Hindemith's *Morgenmusik* is a sextet or septet. If use is made of only one horn and one trombone (and this is possible, since these instruments are combined in each of the two lower parts) the work can be performed as a quartet or, with a tuba, as a quintet. However, Hindemith's doubling of his third and fourth voices (uncommon in chamber music composition) is of different color and effect than if the voices are divided between one horn and a single trombone.

The Moderato first movement is proclamatory; the second is a Lied (Song) which is played through twice. The thesis and antithesis of the opening portion of the Lied is cleverly stated by rhythmic fluidity, with two measures of half notes in triple meter being followed by a single measure in quarter notes, also in trinal beat. Thus Hindemith slices one measure of the phrase's beginning in half to serve as the "codetta" meter at its end. Movement three is the quickest of the set. Its contrapuntal and antiphonal scoring effects produce music of triumphant character.

SEPTET

- **Septet for Wind Instruments (Flute, Oboe, Clarinet, Bass Clarinet, Bassoon, Horn, and Trumpet) (1948)**

The instrumentation of this work represents the modern composer's attention to variance of timbre in the larger totals of chamber music.

Exemplary regard for this especially colorful combination is shown in the first movement by the textural flux and the counterplay of density. These are substances that include the use of the full tutti to the specific dissimilarity of a trio formation, as well as the weaving and interlineation of voices usual to Hindemith's work. Two elements are most important to the movement. First, a combined tutti made of trilled and sustained tone, at one point into a whole set of measures concerned with moving trills and pedal sound and second, a very lyrical theme.

A very short Intermezzo marks the second movement. This is scored for a sextet, with the trumpet being eliminated, and contains improvisational-like sections with rhythmic emphasis concentrated off the beat. The elimination of the septet's brightest color in this part of the work serves well for heightened contrast when the trumpet pronounces the theme of the following movement (Variationen). The different hues of the seven instruments are, naturally, of great aid in lighting up the mutabilities pertaining to variation form. Thus the flute, oboe, horn, and bassoon are given opportunities to mark off variations within parts of the total design.

In the fourth movement, a second Intermezzo, Hindemith again silences the trumpet and thereby symmetrizes matters of form, color, and texture in alternate movements. The septet's balance is furthered by the fact that the style of this fourth movement is similar to the first Intermezzo, has the same extemporaneous quality and is even more engendered since the previous emphasis off the beat is now precisely on the beat. That all this is accomplished by the tour de force of perfect retrograde (crab) motion is analytically fascinating, but does not, in any way, hinder the value of the music's impression. Every sound and color, the entire score and rhythmic plan of the earlier movement, is run backwards so that the last measure of movement two becomes the starting point for movement four; and sweeps on, thereafter, by reverse repetition to the very end (equal, therefore, to the second movement's start). No more perfect symmetry is possible.

The final movement is a Fugue titled "Alter Berner Marsch." There are six entries of the principal subject. All the instruments, save the trumpet, are represented in this exposition, sometimes by doubling. Then come two other expositions concerned with a pair of new themes and eventually, with usual Hindemithian bravado (plus the necessary ability to manage it), the three themes are combined. But there is even more! From the start of the movement the trumpet's march tune appears constantly, weaving its way in and out of the polyphony. When the fugue reaches its maximum combination of subjects the trumpet tune disports with it as well. No composer could do better in regard to a so highly geared polyphonic creation. No better fugal bargain was ever driven home.

(It is rare, indeed, when a composer is given special recognition by music critics. Hindemith was so honored in 1952 when the New York Music Critics Circle chose the Septet as the "most outstanding" chamber music composition premiered in New York during the 1952 season.)

OCTET

■ **Octet for Clarinet, Bassoon, Horn, Violin, Two Violas, Cello, and Double Bass (1958)**

Semidiaphanous instrumental qualities predominate, with the darker, mellow winds (clarinet and bassoon) and horn associated with a string quintet of violin, two violas, cello, and double bass definitely pitched toward smoky colors.

The kinship of form and content integrates the richness of the composer's varied, masterful modern polyphony. Counterpoint is almost the whole means of regulating the expression, yet the linear bargain is not overdriven into

boredom. The contrapuntalism in each of the five movements has a different point to explain: a sonata-style initial part; variations; a slow-paced division; a gingered, dry scherzo description; and a novel twist to a fugue that intertwines "drei altmodische Tänzer" ("Three Old-Fashioned Dances") (waltz, polka, and galop).

(When Hindemith sent the score of the Octet to his publisher it was accompanied with a note that displayed both modesty and immodesty. He wrote: "A useful piece, though on account of its nature and form no world-shattering event. Still, there has been no piece since Schubert's Octet which the many existing more-than-quartet chamber music ensembles might like to put in their programmes.")

Hinton, Arthur (1869–1941)

DUO

■ **Sonata for Violin and Piano**

Romantic confidences (the work was published about 1910 and lacks an opus number) and Brahmsian habits are here presented. In the first movement there are juicy thirds and sixths, and in the final (third) movement there is a breadth to the phrasing, with 3/2 and 6/4 measures in molto vivace tempo. Both movements are in sonata form, and the components are structured with craftsmanship.

There is unrest in the middle (slow) movement, already hinted at in the initial theme which, in piecemeal sections, rises and then descends a semitone. The tempo shifts as a pair of subjects are developed and intertwined with yet a third idea. Subdued excitement throughout, but eventually resolved. It is again a creative romantic's exemplification.

Hirai, Kōzaburō Y. (1910–)

DUO

- *Paraphrase on a Japanese Folk Tune,
  "Sakura, Sakura" ("Cherry Blossom")
  for Cello and Piano (1953)*

Hirai has produced a good number of compositions based on folk melodies for orchestra, chorus, chamber combinations, and solo instruments. The melody used as the basis for this short piece praises the beauties of the national flower of Japan, its text containing words such as "bright" and "glorious."

The unadorned folk tune is purely diatonic and comprises fourteen measures. The entrance of the cello (after a four-measure prelude by the piano) states the first eight measures of the tune without any embellishment. A declamatory style is applied to the paraphrase, ending with a section marked Grandioso. Hirai mentions his attempt in the music to imitate the koto (a Japanese zitherlike instrument), considering the cello's "noble and singing tone" to have the most pertinent affinity.

Hirano, Jun-Ichi (1947–)

DUO

- *Distance for Viola and Piano (1974)*

Silken suavity and recitative richness are totally partnered in the first of the three movements. The form is free, though tempo and metrical order are firmly in place. Movements two and three are marked "without tempo" but paradoxically metronomically set at $\quarternote = 48$–60. (A part of the third movement returns to metrical and tempo definiteness.) In movement two there is impressionistic determination. In movement three the objective is rhythmic springiness mixed in with free repetitions

and ostinatos.

Hlaváč, Miroslav (1923–)

DUO

- *Musica Dialogica for Violin and Viola
  (1965)*

A revelatory use of the medium by the Czech composer, filled with considerable brio and sonority. All the details are presented meticulously. There is a sensitive interplay of the voices and a decided personality to the duo. Also evident is an enriched tonal style as the sounds are controlled by an A pitch polarity.

Double counterpoint is the ballast for the first movement. In the Larghetto cantabile color enriches the contents, with passages joining harmonics and plucked timbre and with sections of massed tremolando. The finale is a cross-accented, syncopatively swung Rondo. Truly, no *musica reservata* tendencies in this extroverted *Musica Dialogica*.

TRIO

- *Lyrical Praeludium and Capriccio for
  Flute, Oboe, and Harp (1964)*

In both pieces the means of alternation are constant. The separations of the ideas in the first part make possible the delineation of a balanced rondo design. In the *Capriccio* the two-measure Andante patetico that ushers in the movement gives way to the music's rhythmic principality, paced exactly twice as fast. However, the Andante, compressed to a single measure, steps in (twice as slow, of course, and *subito*) no fewer than nine times thereafter (twice with harp alone, the other times calling on all three instruments). This dictatorial dichotomy is indeed capricious, but it does shape the structural balance.

Heaviness is the descriptive term for the romantic harmony used. The same word applies to the textures. In the second part, all three instruments are in action for practically the entire time.

Hlobil, Emil (1901–87)

DUOS

- **Five Inventions for Two Violins**

"Workaday" music, easy to play and with a light touch. A rondo presentation begins the set, then follow a bit of slow music and a jaunty Allegretto. The fourth piece is a syncopative waltz contrasted by the fifth piece which is fast paced and held in place by ostinatos.

- **Serenata for Violin and Piano, Op. 12a**

The principal theme is split between a canon and rich romantic rhetoric. A considerable part of the piece consists of chordal movement with the melodic line doubled rhythmically. The Serenata can be described as highly charged music, even in the soft dynamic levels used at the beginning and end.

QUARTETS

- **Quartet for Harpsichord (or Piano), Violin, Viola, and Cello, Op. 23**

Classically controlled music, but romantically curved in most of its phrases. Hlobil's Quartet has crystal clear instrumentation, especially determined by the tonal ping of the harpsichord. (The use of a piano surrenders a good part of the composition's sonorous charm.)

The basic tonality is C for the outer movements, both in sonata form; the tonality for the central, ternary-balanced slow movement is E-flat. It is in the finale that a nationalistic accent underlines the musical prose.

- **String Quartet No. 5, Op. 81**

Chromaticism is used in this quartet on a more intense level than is found in Hlobil's other chamber works. This leads to vigorous detail but with plentiful pliant development of motives in the initial Allegro vivace movement. The shifting demeanor of that movement continues in the Larghetto division. While there is a more settled condition in the finale, nonetheless a sense of contextual struggle is apparent.

The tonality frame of reference is a certification of all this. The first movement begins with a saber-cutting eight-pitch dissonance; eventually the movement terminates in C major. The second movement has a bitonal beginning, but, once again, the music pulls back tonally this time to B-flat major. Significantly, however, the final chords in Hlobil's quartet sign off in C major/minor.

QUINTET

- **Quintet for Two Violins, Two Violas, and Cello, Op. 1**

Virility is expected from a young composer and it is illustrated in this one-movement work, the first opus of the Czech musician, written at age 24. Despite some episodic looseness and textural thickness the Quintet has a convincing strength and convincing romantic substances.

There is a single movement and the divisions produce a circular form. The opening Lento is contrasted by an Allegro, marked by disjunctive spans. There are tighter lines in the Adagio, which is linked to scherzo material. The music then reverses with the return of the Adagio, Allegro, and Lento sections. Literal repetition is avoided but not musical gusto, provided by rhythmic guts.

NONET

- **Nonet for Flute (alternating Piccolo), Oboe, Clarinet, Horn, Bassoon, Violin, Viola, Cello, and Double Bass, Op. 27**

A persuasive work that has romantic nuances with classical architectonics for firm balance in each of its three movements. Central to this work, as to others by the same composer, is a scoring that has textural fidelity without resorting to any special effects. (The piccolo is used only in the concluding eleven measures of the finale.) A nonet combination can pose a problem with the possibility of muddy textures splattering on motile passages. Not here. Hlobil's handling of his nine instruments offers a very rich and resonant result.

Hoddinott, Alun (1929–)

DUOS

- **Sonata for Clarinet and Piano, Op. 50**

The first movement is marked Cadenza. It has the heated action of such display but is kept within precisely duple-pulse measures. Angular music, this, with direct rhythmic impact. Part two is slower (Adagio) but the pitches employed and deployed are of no lesser intensity than the previous movement. The finale is a presto-delivered Moto Perpetuo. No question as to its rhythmic touch and go. It is shaped with the keenest percipience regarding instrumental balance.

- **Sonata [No. 1] for Violin and Piano, Op. 63**

A one-movement compilation that shifts tempo some eleven times with a range from adagio (four times) to presto (four times), with a single

maestoso and two allegros as well. The free structural development begins with asymmetrical presto non troppo music onto another speedy section of lighter content. A short adagio comes next followed by a division of mixed-metered material related to the opening.

The character of an Alla marcia marks the fifth section, succeeded by slow music, and then a full-scale cadenza for the violin. The next adagio pair is respectively marked by violin harmonics and contrary-motion piano passages. A kinetic presto (a reminder of Hoddinott's favored "perpetual motion" music) leads to the final maestoso totally for the violin alone save for the final two measures.

- **Sonata No. 2 for Violin and Piano, Op. 73, No. 1**

Those who know Hoddinott's music will probably recall his clarinet sonata (*see above*) in reference to this work. Both have first movements with a Cadenza title and both present a perpetual-motion movement. There are differences, however. The Cadenza in this case is an unmetered set-to and even contains some aleatoric pitch action. It also contains whole-tone colorations. The Moto Perpetuo is less rhythmically active than the earlier one referred to and includes tremolandos combined with sustained lines that reflect motival change rather than perpetual motion. The final movement, Episodi e coda, uses some bits from the opening movement. Hoddinott's consistent attention to symmetry of varying types in his compositions illustrates creative discernment.

TRIOS

- **Nocturnes and Cadenzas for Clarinet, Violin, and Cello, Op. 53**

In sequence the title should read Cadenzas and Nocturnes since three of the latter follow three of the former. There is sensitive cadenza balance that provides coloristic character. The cello cadenza that begins the trio is proclamatory, the second cadenza for the violin is a spiky and agitated type, the final one for the clarinet is marked Andante e mesto, with its mournful character leading smoothly into the third nocturne, a short Adagio.

The first of the night pieces reflects a Bartókian quality, the second one is speedy but held in a blanketed timbre with the violin and cello muted. Within these Nocturnes there is parallel symmetrical scale to the solo-voiced Cadenzas by the use of tutti scoring in all three and with a tempo plan of Adagio–Presto–Adagio.

- **Trio for Violin, Cello, and Piano, Op. 77**

Serial syntax, as clearly determined in its application as music conceived with steadfast tonalism. Such classical lucidity and poise applied to twelve-tone style provide an ordered continuity to Hoddinott's Trio. There are two contrasted movements, an Andante, with a somewhat introverted, brooding atmosphere, and an energetic Allegro molto. The close of the work reflects the beginning of the piece to provide a confirmed balance.

QUARTETS

- **Divertimento for Oboe, Clarinet, Horn, and Bassoon, Op. 32**

Formal equilibration that makes for immediate understanding of this Welshman's contemporaneously judicious music. There is a relationship in general character (the materials are different) between the outer movements—a pomp and circumstance type of Overture and a firm, two-stepped March. Parts two and four are a pair of Scherzos. Both are nimble, both are in 6/8 time, the first is in presto, the second prestissimo. The latter is in a steadfast *pianissimo* until the final measure which closes matters

with four *fortissimo* sounds.

The central part is a set of Variations. The symmetry surrounding the work is maintained. Both theme and the first seven variations are tightly eight measures in length; the final (eighth) variant is extended by an additional four measures.

- **String Quartet No. 1, Op. 43**

Dark music, intense in a spare sense. There are two movements, a Grave that contrasts lines with chords and an Allegro molto that has Bartókian breakaway rhythmics. Within the latter there is a central portion with wide-spanned doubling by the first violin and cello supported by inner-voice ostinatos. The rhythmic action then returns, followed by material based on the Grave section, plus a coda.

SEXTET

- **Sextet for Flute, Clarinet, Bassoon, Violin, Viola, and Cello, Op. 20**

Rhythmic punch, clean, however, not motoric or rigid, is principal in this early Hoddinott piece. It covers the opening movement, sweeps through the entire presto-tempo third movement (set in quintuple meter throughout), and is the basis of the finale. The last is the only part of the work that shifts its tempo setting from a beginning maestoso to allegro, a return of the former speed, then a short adagio episode, followed by the fast music again.

This completely alive work is naturally expressed. It has contrast in the form of a moderate-paced music (movement two) that swings in triple meter but that fluidly moves about, and a fourth movement Adagio that is texturally shaped to define a three-part structure. There, too, there is full evidence of spontaneity.

SEPTETS

- **Septet for Clarinet, Horn, Bassoon, Piano, Violin, Viola, and Cello, Op. 10**

Pertinent structural unfolding of the material for each of the three movements. And, as precise a denomination in each case. Thus: chromatic conditioning in the first movement (Moderato), ornamental definition of line in the second movement (Adagio), and scalic motility, rhythmic pungency, and syncopative unrest in the finale (Allegro assai). There is a driving potency in the opening movement, the ability to form long-line melodic statements in the central movement, and a vigor and vitality in the finale.

Mostly, Hoddinott's Septet is robust, strengthened by triplanal scoring in the majority: winds as one unit, strings as a second one, and the piano as a unitary, third voice. It is totally thoughtful and well-wrought contemporary music.

Hoddinott's Septet was commissioned by the B.B.C. (British Broadcasting Corporation) for the tenth anniversary of its Third Program. It was first performed by the well-known Melos Ensemble, on December 8, 1956.

- **Variations for Flute, Clarinet, Harp, and String Quartet, Op. 28**

Six character variations and a finale on a subject that the composer Edmund Rubbra described as "a 'theme' that sounds like a variation."

In turn there is a March, a Nocturne (the strings all muted), and a quintuple-pulsed Scherzo completely concerned with octave distribution; one set for the strings, another, smaller, set for the pair of winds, and with the harp inserting D octave accents here and there. Waltz curves are in part four; an Elegy is in part five, and a Pastoral (minus the harp) in part six.

The Finale is a vigorous and pithy Presto.

OCTET

- **Divertimenti for Eight Instruments (Flute, Clarinet, Bassoon, Horn, Violin, Viola, Cello, and Double Bass), Op. 58**

Not the conventional assortment of divertimento-character pieces. Hoddinott alternates three Scherzos with two contrasted formal types. In part two there is a clear Canzonetta, in part four there is a bracing Barcaruola. (The Welsh composer's use of the Italian to designate the familiar barcarolle spelling is also a diverting slant.) This boat song doesn't sway in moderate 6/8 time but is in 3/8 time with its pulse constantly cutting across the bar lines.

The Scherzos are set forth on the basis of tempo increase. The first is "fast and light," paced at a metronomic 120 per pulse. The second is an "alla marcia" pegged at 132 per pulse. Scherzo 3 begins presto ($\downarrow$ = c.184) then is pushed up to prestissimo, where the beat is to be at 240.

Hodeir, André (1921–)

SEXTET

- ***Osymetrios* for Trumpet, Tenor Saxophone, Trombone, Piano, Double Bass, and Drums (1960)**

One of Hodeir's few works that fit the chamber music category. This famous French music critic and jazz expert is better known for his books on jazz (*Toward Jazz, The Worlds of Jazz*, etc.), but the music he has produced deserves the fullest attention.

Osymetrios has, of course, a jazz-slanted scoring. The sextet is sequenced in fast-slower-fast proportions, all in cut time. Each of these three divisions is further sectionalized, so, for example, the middle one has no less than five sections. The scoring is very full, with constant action in the percussion, which has "fill-in" additions made at the will of the performer. Totally syncopative, totally chamber music jazz.

Hodge, M. Talbot

DUO

- **Sonata in One Movement for Violin and Piano**

Compressing the coverage of a sonata into one movement may be considered a dogmatic way of achieving formal definition. But Hodge's one-movement solution is anything but dogmatic. What seems to be the principal theme (it is heard a number of times in succession) turns out to be a long prelude that later becomes a shortened epilogue. These statements are in slow tempo, the material that is in between is the prime data, detailed in allegro moderato pace. Hodge negates an absolute tonic at the beginning of his tonal architecture. The supportable pedal utilized is dissonantly colored, resolved at the sonata's conclusion in a serene E major.

The allegro moderato tempo is confirmed by the combined meters of 6/8 and 3/4, the former first heard in the violin, the other the property of the piano. The instruments change metrical roles and just before the contrasting theme enters merge into the 6/8 definition. The second subject swings back and forth, at first between these two differently accented pulse totals, finally maturing into a definite duple swing. Full development takes place and the two themes are restarted before the concluding section.

TRIO

- *Three Sketches* for Flute (alternating Piccolo), Violin, and Piano

Miniatures that make their individual points without fuss. There is practically no stop to the third piece "The Merry-Go-Round," which goes around in quadruple pulse. Poetic substance confirms "In the Woods." Hodge's second sketch is titled "The Lake at Sunset." It is brightened to climax by coordinating four simultaneous harmonic lines. To stimulate the hobby-horse ride, the piccolo is used a few times.

Hodja-Enatov, A.

TRIO

- **Trio for Piano, Violin, and Cello**

Music that resembles the ballet scores of Aram Khachaturian, with melismatic touches in the lines and folk tunes filtering among the textures. Mostly set in three-part forms; development means restating the melody and adding a new background or harmonic line.

Not salon music, however. There are three movements, with moderate- and fast-tempo items surrounding a center piece that has a haunting demeanor in E-flat minor.

Hodkinson, Sydney (1934–)

TRIO

- *Stanzas* for Piano Trio (1959)

Instrumentation is built into the nine-part structure. Thereby, an alternative scoring plan carries out the formal *(Stanzas)* objective. The odd-numbered movements are for the total trio, the even-numbered ones cover four different settings, in order: cello and piano, violin and cello, solo piano, and violin and piano. It will be noted that only solo violin and solo cello are not used in the seven different voicings existent in the piano trio medium.

Generated by tone-row methodology, Hodkinson's trio is a disciplined and strongly knit piece, but is no technical polemic, dogmatically pursuing its dodecaphonic dogma. It has a quick-change personality with variety spicing the totality. Part three, for example, is a tightly rhythmic conception, slightly fragmented with coloristic touches, including some patterns to be played with a "slight jazz feeling." A sharp difference occurs with the next part; it is slow in tempo, made fluid by dispensing with metrical rigidity. And further illustrative of the heterogeneity is movement seven, where there isn't a tinge of counterpoint and the rhythmic violence is a rite that is kin to Stravinsky's *Le sacre du printemps* and Bartók's *Allegro barbaro*. It is such inventive detail, contained in a compact compositional mold, that makes Hodkinson's *Stanzas* several cuts above the ordinary.

Hoérée, Arthur (1897–)

QUARTET

- *Pastorale et Danse*: **Two Pieces for String Quartet, Op. 2**

Critic (he published books on Roussel, Stravinsky, and Honegger) as well as composer, Hoérée became known in the latter field by the performance of his Septet, in Zurich in 1926, at the International Society for Contemporary Music Festival. His musical productions are extremely small in total. Together with the Septet (which contains a soprano voice and is therefore excluded from this compendium), the *Pastorale et Danse* completes his

chamber music catalogue. The two quartet pieces date from 1923, were written in nine days, and shortly thereafter were awarded the Prix Lepaule.

Both pieces abound in color, including a pair of overstated devices. The glissandos that underpin the first measures occur in dozen lots, as do ostinatos. Within the measures the voice of Vincent d'Indy (one of Hoérée's teachers) is heard, as well as that of another famed Frenchman of different aesthetic cut, Maurice Ravel. D'Indy will be recalled by the use of a ritornel, heard four times in the *Pastorale* (the last one a link to the *Danse*) and once toward the end of the second piece. The Ravelian gestures are those of sparkling and sweeping harmonics, together with semi-exotic quartet colorings.

Choreographically inclined music needs pulse, of course, but static pitch pivoting can put a brake on forward motion. Hoérée's two-piece set is worthy, even if it is made temporarily insecure by being too secure. In one place, eighteen measures of the pitch C are rhythmically stated and passed around the quartet. Serving as a bridge to a thematic restatement these measures are somewhat, if not downright, dull. They represent the work's single blemish.

Høffding, Finn (1899–)

DUO

- *Dialoger (Dialogues)* **for Oboe and Clarinet, Op. 10**

Neatly frictioned harmony and fluidic lines are employed in this stimulating duet. Høffding delineates the programmatic situations so aptly that an auditor can come close to describing the conversational atmospheres without referring to the designations.

The "Simple Conversation" has both friendly counterpoint and dissonances. Part two is a

"Serious Conversation." Here, the lines are more probing and agreement is shown by the final E-flat octave sound. Deft humor is displayed in the "Altercation." (Worth noting for its onomatopoeic coloration is the Danish title: *Mundhuggeri.*) The obstinate retort of the clarinet "person," over and over again, no matter what the oboe "other party" of the dispute says, is prime artistic buffoonery. Further, the retorts get warmer and warmer until both disputants are embroiled pitchwise a minor second apart. Number four of the set is a "Sublime Conversation." This is formed without metrical involvement as one instrument holds the stage and the other merely replies monosyllabically. The last dialogue is subtitled Rondo-Finale. Its material is as light-textured as one would expect from the movement's main title: "Gay Conversation."

QUARTET

- **String Quartet, Op. 6**

Høffding's early opus shows the potency of late-romantic harmony, the drive and power of Hindemith, and in minor total, the rhythmic manners of Stravinsky and Bartók. Indeed, it is a derivative work, but not all of its fingers are in other pies.

Movement one begins with an Introduzione built from a thrusting triplet figure (Høffding marks this unit "Le terzine sempre deciso"). The movement proper is a motoric Allegro agitato which yields its drive only for a short, contrasting section.

Movement two joins duple structures. The first of these is in tripartite formation, exceedingly slow paced (♪ = 34!), melancholy, and darkened by chromatic sounds in its outer portions. The middle section is a swingy waltz set in lazy quarter notes. Part two of the movement is a "Rondo di Metamorfose," which sprints along constantly depicting new points of view. An inner link to part one is made by a return of

the waltz material just prior to the movement's coda. The last concludes with tight vertical formations in *forte* that are dynamically reinforced with plentiful accentuations.

Höffer, Paul (1895–1949)

DUO

- *Bratschen-Musik mit Klavier (Viola Music with Piano)*(1946)

Höffer's title implies piano accompaniment, but the music does not bear out this assumption. True enough, the viola announces the principal propositions of the first three of the four movements, but this does not deny chamber music partnership.

There are forty-five measures in the Moderato. The motival arrangement first heard impregnates every one of them, save the closing measure. A lightly legatoed theme ushers in movement two. It is of quartal facture, as is the piano's support, and fully possesses the music. However, a conjunctively lyrical contrast is supplied, framed for the most part by ostinatos. Baroque figuration (mainly emphasizing a pattern of a long note followed by two much shorter ones) is not surrendered in the Adagio. Again, repetitive structuring is basic—this single pattern appears in every one but the last of the total fifty-eight measures.

The final Allegro maintains Höffer's decisive use of single intrinsic identification for each division of his duo. In this case it is a two-ply rhythmic figure, consisting of either four sixteenths or a mixed rhythmic group of five pitches. This generator is used melodically, antiphonally, accompanimentally, and as a contrapuntal aid. And, once more it appears somehow, somewhere, in all the measures save the final two-measure cadence. While this type of technique firmly holds material together through its componential concentration it does neutralize any surprise factor.

TRIOS

- **Kleine Suite (Small Suite) for Oboe, Clarinet, and Bassoon (1944)**

Five helpings from the storehouse of Gebrauchs-musik, innocent of any modern-fashioned concepts such as polytonality, etc. Totally tonal and totally unsophisticated in his objective, Höffer varies the trio procedure by duet formations in movements two and four of the total five. The former is for clarinet and bassoon, the other for oboe and clarinet. Some imitation appears in part three, an Adagio. Alla marcia is the tempo that fully describes the end movement.

- **Thema mit Variationen (Theme with Variations) for Oboe, Clarinet, and Bassoon (1944)**

Music with the same utilitarian principles as described immediately above *(see: Kleine Suite)*. Only the form differs in this case. There are five continuous variations on the oboe theme. The third is pert, the fourth is marked by the only major key change. Part five combines variations within the variation. In its swing and meter the result parallels a chain of waltzes.

Hoffmann, Adolf G. (1890–?)

QUARTET

- **Prelude and Fugue for String Quartet (1935)**

Pairing a prelude with a fugue is, of course, traditional practice. Still, Hoffmann's substantial work (almost twelve minutes in length) is no hackneyed formal arrangement. In writing, definite assertions are basic to clear meaning; the

same demands apply to musical composition.

The definite assertions here are provided by contrast: the Prelude is muted, the Fugue played with open timbre; the Prelude is set in sextuple meter, the Fugue principally in 5/4 arrangement, though it changes its pulse apportionment as it proceeds. A slow tempo and a restrained dynamic plane for the Prelude, a moderately fast pace and a more pertinent dynamism for the Fugue are further contrasts. Principal to all these (and not so traditional) is the interspersion of preludial segments within the Fugue. Indeed, such clear plotting of the work not only provides proven intellectuality but artistice actuality.

Hoffmeister, Franz Anton (1754–1812)

DUOS

- **Duo in F Major for Violin and Cello, Op. 5, No. 2**

- **Duo in A Major for Violin and Cello, Op. 5, No. 3**

Music for paired instruments and using paired movements in each case. The F-major work begins Andante and then runs a Molto allegro course. The A major work has a fast first movement and a Rondo in allegretto tempo. All the music has a neutral emotive quality, the materials well held together.

- **Sonata for Clarinet and Piano**

This is the sixth of a set of sonatas in which Hoffmeister used various types of clarinets: C, B-flat, and A. This work calls for the last type. The title of the set reads: *Six Duos pour le Piano Forte et Clarinette*. Bearing out the titled chain of command the principal theme of each of the three movements is initially announced by the piano. However, overall, the instruments are equal, in a give-and-take manner.

- **Sonata for Piano and Violin (or Flute), Op. 11, No. 3**

Precise classic forms, of course (tonalities, for example: E-flat major in the outer movements, the dominant key for the central movement).

In the first movement there is constant interplay and intervallic partnership by the instruments that shifts freely between unison and octaves, thirds and sixths. Little antiphonal moves brighten the middle part (Andantino scherzando). Important to the finale is the moderate kineticism, obtained from long passages of eighth-note figures.

- **Three Duos concertants for Flute and Viola**

  - **No. 1, in G Major**
  - **No. 2, in D Major**
  - **No. 3, in F Major**

During Mozart's lifetime, Hoffmeister was the principal publisher of his music. Further affiliation applies, since in this set of duos he was probably imitating Mozart's pair of duos for violin and viola *(q.v.)*. It's a splendid imitation. Worthy, absolutely.

Each work is in three movements. In every case the initial movement is in Allegro tempo. The finales of the second and third works proceed in lighter-paced Allegretto cast. In the first duo there is no tempo for the final movement, simply the word Rondo. Its stylistic classification and duple-pulsed motility make it also fit the Allegretto pattern. Two of the central movements are, as expected, in the slow zone. In the first duo the marking is Poco adagio, and in the second duo it is Lento. A brighter atmosphere applies to the Romance in the third duo, which stresses a quickish tempo by its alla breve time signature.

There has been at least one recording of the first of these three duos, performed in a violin and viola version. No problem, providing it is understood that instrumental transfer is at work. The duos were published in 1789-1790 by the Hoffmeister Verlag and were titled *Trois Duos concertants pour la Flute-traversière et Viola*. Understandably, the compositions should be considered in terms of Hoffmeister's choice of instrumental combination.

- **Twelve Duos for Two Clarinets**

The title can well be misleading. These are not twelve duos, each in several movements, but a set of twelve pieces. The music is free-planned as to form, with some of the duos short and others of fair length.

Number four is a full-sized Menuetto with the usual Trio. Numbers seven and eight are Allemande conceptions, the ninth of the group is a Marcia. Nicely conceived items, producing a music that has both vigor and direction if decidedly low-key in dramatic content.

NONET

- **Serenade in E-flat for Two Oboes (or Two Flutes), Two Clarinets, Two Horns, Two Bassoons, and Double Bass (or Double Bassoon)**

Authentic classical forms, and what is to be expected takes place within such structures. There's a truthful ring to the work and a scoring solidity that is made evident in the opening slow-paced first movement, and this basis is maintained throughout.

In the Allegro a tertial descent is most important. The next movement is a Menuettino, followed by a contrastively metered and differently tempoed section and a return to the Menuettino. Fast and slow music follow, with a recapitulation of the former. A short clarinet cadenza then preludes the final Rondo.

Hofmann, Leopold (1738–93)

DUO

- **Divertimento for Flute and Bassoon**

Only in the first movement (Allegro) is there an opportunity for the bassoon to go beyond the boundaries of bass-line stability and rhythmic underpinning. In the Menuetto and final Vivace, although the bassoon does not simply act as an accompanist, the process of classic devotion is to look to the flute for first-voice decisiveness. Still, the flute is not flamboyant.

Hofmann, Wolfgang (1922–)

DUO

- **Sonatine for Viola d'amore and Harpsichord (1963)**

Special colors applied to clear formal conditions. In the first movement strict antiphony in the opening and closing sections contrasts a racy, asymmetrical Allegretto. A two-theme second movement includes, within its development, some scherzo segments. A productive production if not of special individual profile.

Hohensee, Wolfgang (1927–)

QUINTET

- **Wind Quintet in D**

Neoromantic loyalty is expressed here. And thematic parity, as noted in the pair of subjects used for statement and development in the opening Allegro rubato movement. The same method applies to the Comodo finale, which alternates its objective between fugal and lyrical ideas.

The finale is preceded by a short Recitativo, which displays the subdivisional climate of the work with a series of small single announcements each followed by just as short full tutti combinations. Movement two is a scherzo type.

Of interest is that, save for the Recitativo, each movement ends softly. All, nicely tuned conclusions.

Hoiby, Lee (1926–)

QUARTET

- *Diversions* **for Flute, Oboe, Clarinet, and Bassoon, Op. 10**

Music of agility and sparkle, its content spontaneous and natural. With Hoiby, the style is tonally balanced. Movement one is a moderately paced "Greeting." A fast "Waltz" follows. Parts three and four are a "Promenade" and a "Gambol," the former faster than the latter.

SEXTET

- **Sextet for Wind Quintet and Piano, Op. 28a**

(Another version exists for string quartet and piano [also listed under the unified title "Piano Quintet"], as Op. 28.)

There are two movements. The first, set in a sonata frame, emphasizes the lyrical side, set forth in the rich romantic syntax used by this composer. Movement two is a Theme followed by eight Variations. Some of these are linked, others are separate units. The third of the group is a Presto, quintuple-pulsed conception for three instruments (oboe, bassoon, and piano). The following variant is also for less than the six-ply total, calling only for the wind quintet, but even at that, most of the writing is three-voiced. The fifth variation is a broadly metered, but scherzando-tempoed, setting for the sextet, while the following variation is for the solo piano. Variations six and seven are linked and the last is also connected to the Finale, a compact, vivacious music, combining a scherzando quality with allegro speed.

Holbrooke, Josef (1878–1958)

Any discussion of the music of Holbrooke demands mention of the muddle that exists in regard to his opus numbers, together with the matter of resettings which again brought confusion as to opus identification and the like.

Kenneth L. Thompson (in his article "Holbrooke: Some Catalogue Data," in *Music & Letters*, October 1965) outlines the situation clearly: "Many works bore various opus numbers at different periods; conversely, an opus number can be found attached to several different works; and the identity of some earlier compositions, particularly in the realm of chamber music, is difficult to trace because of recasting and incorporation into new definitive versions."

As far as possible clarification as to opus and title are indicated in the individual commentaries that follow.

DUOS

- *Poeana: Dreams* for Flute and Harp

The music is in slow waltz format, its second section a bit faster. There is full ternary balance with the first and second divisions each repeated; the third is minus repetition. Just a bit sentimental but no sugary elements. Whatever one has said about Holbrooke (his refusal to modernize his style, though coloristically he was especially sensitive) in terms of craftsmanship, no one can argue his straightforward sensibility.

- **Sonata No. 3** *(Oriental)* **for Violin and Piano, Op. 83**

Holbrooke was a composer of Straussian aspects. Rarely did he desert vivid, picturesque, and descriptive explanations. Sometimes, his expressive intensity became limited by the pursuit of such an objective. Nonetheless, even when the description is merely implied, as in this one-movement work, it exhibits him at his best.

The pseudoexotic slant is accomplished by a constant use of fourths. Sonata indication notwithstanding, binary form is used. Introductory gonglike sounds set off the sections, which are bound up by a lengthy coda in very fast tempo.

TRIO

- **Nocturne:** *Fairyland* **for Viola (or Cello), Oboe (or Oboe d'amore or Clarinet or Flute), and Piano, Op. 57, No. 1**

Holbrooke's trio (plenty of instrumental choices are included) is based on Edgar Allan Poe's poem. A general mood is portrayed, specific programmatic conditions are not attempted.

The music is given balance by an augmented octave descent in the opening and closing of the piece. This delineates freely the lines "Dim vales and huge moons" and "They use that moon no more / For the same end as before." The animation in the middle portion of the work is a parallel to the line "soaring in the skies."

QUARTETS

- *The Pickwick Club—A Humoreske in Two Parts* **for String Quartet (String Quartet No. 3), Op. 68**

Program music virtuosity is exemplified in this

survey of characters and events in the Charles Dickens story. Divided into two expansive parts, and though one section is connected with the next, because of the demand for sharp contrasts due to the story line, the form of the work is extremely episodic. In fact, Pickwickian humor (in sonic translation) sometimes gets lost in the process. Nonetheless, the shifting arrangement of Holbrooke's music effectively translates the essence of the broad humors in the Dickens tale.

Without a doubt this quartet's specific series of depictions is one of the most elaborate pieces of program chamber music in existence. Other works may be concerned with either a set of movements, each singly descriptive, or a story (of complexity or not) related in a general way, whereas Holbrooke is totally decided in each and every one of his musical scrutinies—almost akin to Strauss's method in his *Domestic Symphony*. (In that work, everything from the bathing of a baby to the picturing of a family's relatives is described by sixty-seven identifiable motives.) In his "musicorama" Holbrooke does not attempt to suggest but to describe, as completely as he can within the limits of four string instruments, the personalities and maneuvers of Dickens's cast of characters. He uses eighteen specific sections to do so, continuously run and divided in two parts; ten in the first and eight in the second. (Bibliographic listings are incorrect in stating that thirteen is the total. George Lowe, the composer's biographer, also gives the same incorrect total.)

Part I: The main character, "Mr. Pickwick," is described by the opening unison theme. Straussian-like rushing scherzo rhythms plus the use of high string timbre picture "A Field Day" and lead to the section titled "Snodgrass and Winkle." Their personalities are more tranquil than those of the previous section, which returns after Snodgrass and Winkle's profiles have been outlined. Heavy and slow tempo, accented cello and viola sounds with a pizzicato frame above, delineate the next division—"Joe,

the Fat Boy." This is followed by "The Amorous Mr. Tupman," who is pictured by employment of the "Pickwick" theme together with lightly ornamented passages. For the mood of affection Holbrooke uses the folk tune "The Banks of Allan Water." A short pause is made preliminary to ushering in "The Picnic," a long portion during which many events take place. After a unison passage (the "Picnic" theme) an immediate tempo change brings a waltz-termed speed describing the personality and charm of "Miss Rachel"; later "They Ride" (cello imitation of horse's hooves and rhythmically marked disjunct leaps in the other instruments); and "The Horse Shies!" (heavy rhythm followed by pizzicato on the part of the three lower instruments while the first violin figurates in pedal fashion). A ritard is made and leads to a "Maestoso"—the horse and everything else is under control. Next comes "The Card Party" (which takes place at Mr. Wardle's house). This portion is in salon style, with a strict waltz accompaniment enclosing the four sectional refrains of the viola (playing "The Ivy Green"). Part I comes to a close with the reannouncement of the opening "Pickwick" theme.

Part II: The principal subject (merely because of its several appearances—there is no main theme in the formal sense) opens the second part and this time (though unchanged in form, but stated in a lower register) displays "The Romantic Side of Mr. Pickwick." This is fairly well developed until the "Picnic" theme from Part I makes a reappearance. Again Holbrooke employs a musical idea to cover more than one situation. This time (changed only in transposition) the "Picnic" theme represents "Sam Weller's Character." Clever scoring marks the next episode, picturing " 'Mr. Jingle's' (alias Trotter's) Character" by low strings and high harmonics woven in with a hymn tune, "There Is a Happy Land." A short pause then brings in a perfectly mad succession of musical jesting, descriptive of " 'The First of September' (Mr. Winkle and Mr. Tupman with the Guns)." Holbrooke's music travels with pyrotechnical aim, includes vestiges of the material employed for the "Field Day," in Part I, as well as for Mr. Tupman, who also bowed in during the earlier portion of the quartet. The "Mr. Tupman" theme is now signified by being written in harmonics. Just at the close of this episode Holbrooke introduces "Ye Gentlemen of England."

"Mr. Pickwick and Mrs. Bardell" then enter the quartet picture. As behooves "ladies first," her theme is played completely by the unaccompanied viola. "Mr. Pickwick" then joins her with his theme announced by the cello in a *pianissimo* dynamic. The music builds into real sport as Holbrooke employs "We Won't Go Home Until Morning" and follows it with a veritable quartet cadenza (in *furioso* runs). This is succeeded by the "Dodson and Fogg" episode described by tremolo sound in the upper three voices and an exceedingly high-gamut cello solo. The music again breaks loose to display "The Torturous Wiles of Mrs. Bardell." Within this portion the first violin part is written with Paganini-like abandon, requiring jumps from the lowest to the highest string, totaling close to three octaves, to be made ten times in either direction. But all ends very well. "Pickwick, His Dignity Unimpaired" is delineated by the use of his theme and the tune "Sally in Our Alley" is played with Holbrookian harmonies as the music draws to a very soft, high-register penultimate close. With two sets of triple C major chords Holbrooke concludes his uniquely picturesque work.

■ **String Quartet No. 1:** *Fantasie in D Minor*, **Op. 17b**

Holbrooke's observance of delineatory subject matter (but just short of picturing a definite story) is seen in this individually titled three-movement work (the first two run together). The quartet follows the same program as

Beethoven's Sonata in E-flat, Op. 81a for piano, with its movements titled "Les Adieux, l'absence et le retour." But while Beethoven's work was to commemorate the departure from Vienna of his friend, the Archduke Rudolf (the French entered Vienna eight days later), Holbrooke's "Departure, Absence, and Return" is merely imaginative stimulus—such events are, of course, common in life everywhere.

The three movements convey by key, tempo, and style the inferences of the titles. "Departure" is vigorous, mainly in D minor, is contrasted to a more tranquil, major tonality episode in sonata-styled form. "Absence," as to be expected, is plaintive, but with an ending of rosier complexion—apparently the departed one will return soon. Tchaikovsky, however, has a large hand in the early portion of the movement (Holbrooke dipped his pen into many colored inks, including the red of Strauss, the orange of Wagner, the black of Tchaikovsky). The last movement ("Return") is gay, a little unpolished but attractive—in an "all's well that ends well" fashion.

(Two points: *Cobbett* spells the title "Phantasy"; any listing of the opus as number 3 has been proven to be incorrect.)

■ **String Quartet No. 2:** *Impressions: Belgium, 1915; Russia, 1915*, **Op. 59a**

Stylistic musical homage is sometimes nationalistic, more generally in imitation of a specific composer. Holbrooke uses both types for the two movements of this quartet; the second of which appears in this instance in its third version among his works. At first, it was the fourth movement of a large string orchestra composition, then was rescored and amplified for large orchestra as a section in *Les Hommages*, a suite which paid the composer's respects to Wagner, Grieg, Dvořák, and Tchaikovsky. Holbrooke turned again to that work for material to capture a Russian mood, using the "Tchaikovsky" movement (somewhat changed, in part, in the quartet version).

The start of World War I drew Holbrooke to write these two pieces (also known as *War Impressions*). Belgium has no immediately identifiable nationalistic music such as Russia. Therefore, instead of the musical prototype exemplified by the second impression ("a Russian Dance—on a Russian Folk Tune"), a generic form is chosen to illustrate *Belgium, 1915*—that of a Serenade. The neo-Tchaikovskiana of the second movement is somewhat "Trepakian." It is introduced fugally, and has in the center a contrasting, more settled quality. However, Russia was not this calm or happy; nor was Belgium, in the year 1915.

(As with many Holbrooke works, a second opus number has been assigned to this composition: 58. This is as fully acceptable as 59a. However, titling this quartet, as one writer has done, *Song and Dance* is positively false. That title refers to the fifth string quartet only.)

- **String Quartet No. 5:** *Song and Dance—Folk Song Suite No. 2,* **Op. 72**

The published edition of this work will confuse and irritate since it bears the paradoxical heading of "String Quartet No. 2 (String Quartet No. 5)"!!! Holbrooke's fourth, fifth, and sixth string quartets dealt with folk songs and dances. Thus, No. 2 was meant to signify that this was the second of the three quartets dealing with folk materials and, at the same time, the fifth in regard to Holbrooke's total quartets. To clarify matters further: String Quartets Nos. 4, 5, and 6 are also respectively titled Folk Song Suites Nos. 1, 2, and 3, with the opus numbers, in turn, 71, 72, and 73.

Holbrooke speaks plainly of complete nationalism in this light composition. Three-quarters of the British Isles is represented: Scottish material in the first movement, Welsh music in the two middle sections, and Irish themes in the last movement. The treatment given the melodies is entertaining but not prosaic; the scoring engages the color of the string quartet in full fashion; the flavors of the songs and dances are not diminished by tense counterpoint, heavy harmony, or unclear forms.

Strathspeys ("Keep the Country," "Bonnie Lassie," "Tullochgorum," and "Cameron's Got His Wife") constitute the opening movement. The Scotch strathspey is to the reel as slow is to fast, but, for purposes of balance (so that the outer movements will compare in terms of speed to the two inner ones), Holbrooke makes his strathspey jog much faster. The vivace pace is retained unordinarily, but the Scotch snap (the short and long rhythmic combination) is represented with full heathered strength, as is the reverse rhythm (still snappy but "unscotched"). Both slow movements are made up of Welsh songs. The first is the "Song of the Bottle"; the second, the very well known "All through the Night." In these instances obbligato lines and varying harmonies weave around the melodies.

Though the jig was common to Ireland, Scotland, and England, the first-named country showed it the greatest love; so it remained to become the most popular of the Irish dances. Thus, "jig" and "Ireland" ("Irish") have become synonymous. Nine, run in succession, constitute the last movement. After a short introduction, "Garry Owen," "Irish Washerwoman," "Paddy O'Carroll," and "The Tight Little Island" are used. The composer permits the next three to be eliminated, if desired. Thus, "Roaring Jelly," "Paddy Whack," and "The Patriot" are optional. Finally, with full Irish eloquence, the last two are presented—"Go to the Devil" (in contrasted *pianissimo* and *forte*), followed by the very popular "St. Patrick's Day."

- **Symphonic Quartet No. 1** *(Byron)* **for Piano, Violin, Viola, and Cello, Op. 31**

Holbrooke was a strong admirer of Byron.

Other examples in his catalogue of Byronic inspiration include *Byron: "Ode to Victory,"* Symphonic Poem with Chorus ad libitum; the fourth orchestral poem, titled *Byron*; and *Marino Falerio*, music based on Byron's tragedy.

Though clearly subtitled *Byron* and listing lines that are the basis for the score, Holbrooke stressed his Op. 31 should not be listened to as program music. Rather odd that, considering the spelling out of all the text involved. Whatever, the composition (also listed as Piano Quartet No. 1) is formally constructed in a manner that makes sense, program or not.

The idea of composing this piano quartet came to Holbrooke after he had read some Greek history and was strengthened by examining Byron's translation of a war song, "Sons of the Greeks, Arise!"

There are three movements; the first of these is based on lines that begin: "Sons of the Greeks, arise, / The glorious hour's gone forth, / And worthy of such ties, / Display who give us birth... ." The main theme is one of violence, and contrast is obtained by marchlike material.

The slow movement follows, with the muted strings playing recitativolike passages over a constant tremolo in the piano. This relates to "Sparta, Sparta, why in slumbers / Lethargic dost thou lie? / Awake, and join thy numbers... ." The climax of the movement is exactly opposite dynamically to the beginning, a complete *fortissimo* being built from lines in packed intervallic thirds.

The finale has the greatest length. It has a merry tone, though based on a fairly serious pronouncement: "Leonidas recalling, / That chief of ancient song, / Who saved ye once from falling... ." Rondo form is used with a much slower tempo embracing an important subsidiary subject that occurs twice.

- **Symphonic Quartet No. 2 for Piano, Violin, Viola, and Cello, Op. 21**

Holbrooke's Op. 21 (also known as Piano Quartet No. 2) was composed "To the memory of my friend A. J. Jaeger." (Jaeger was also one of Elgar's close friends and has been described as his "friend, adviser, and champion." The "Nimrod" in Elgar's *Enigma Variations* represents Jaeger.) Originally the music was for piano, violin, and cello (representing Piano Trio No. 3) and was composed in 1898. Holbrooke recast the composition as a piano quartet in 1905. (His retention of the trio's opus number for this work is confusing. It results in a lower opus number for a later work [piano quartet No. 2] as compared to a higher opus number for an earlier work [piano quartet No. 1]. *See above under:* Holbrooke.)

A commemorative mood hangs over most of the composition, from the somber G-minor opening to the same tonality's use for most of the final movement. The slow movement is a Lament, has Celtic feeling, and is likewise in a minor key.

QUINTETS

- **Quintet No. 1 for Clarinet and String Quartet, Op. 27, No. 1**

Robust romanticism covers the two movements. Trust this composer to seek the graphic over the generic form. (Trust this composer to also vacillate in regard to opus identification. One can find this Quintet listed as Op. 15 without any explanation for the use of that number.)

Movement one is a Cavatina, fully lyrical in a quiet manner. The other movement is a Theme and Variations. The first variation is a vivacious Caprice; next is a slow Romance, followed by a Gigue. The fourth variant is a moving Elegie, succeeded by a Serenade, March, and Galop. The duple hopping of the last contrasts with the majestic quadruple pulse of the former. The eighth variation combines a very slight shadow of thematic contour with the melody of a sea song—"Tom Bowling." Then follow a Hornpipe and a Capriccio, wherein "Three Blind Mice" is intertwined with swirling passages. (Holbrooke is fond of this tune. It forms the base for one of his most popular orchestral works, a set of twenty variations. He is very partial to the matter of ringing changes on a well-known theme, illustrated by his variations for orchestra on "Auld Lang Syne" and "The Girl I Left Behind Me.") A Fuga forms the final variation, while a reannouncement of the theme plus coda concludes the work.

- **Symphonic Quintet No. 3** *(Diabolique)* **for Piano, Two Violins, Viola, and Cello, Op. 44**

No more "symphonic" in concept than most piano quintets. No problem, therefore, in that respect. The problem is that listings of this work vary. Some label the composition No.4 while an early published edition of the work identifies it as No. 1.

The subtitle stems from the movement titled Valse ("Diabolique"). This would seem to portend more than the signified, ordinary tempo heading: Valse grazioso. Sorry. Holbrooke's diablerie is an unleering Satan relaxing in carpet slippers. Though there is some agitation to the movement's content, no musical demonolatry is portrayed.

The first movement is in contrasted-subject sonata style. It ends with an unresolved chord that is an excellent suspension to the resolution brought by the E-flat major tonality of the following movement. That part is structured by double themes and a scherzando contrast. The Finale, shaped in the form of a rondo and including a fugal section, follows the waltz movement.

SEXTET

- **Sextet No. 4** *(In Memoriam)* **for Piano, Two Violins, Viola, Cello, and Double Bass, Op. 46**

Holbrooke was always interested in the furtherance of rarely used instruments. His orchestral scores abound with the use of saxophones, sarrusophones, euphoniums, concertinas, mushroom bells, and the like. While he had reticent regard for instruments in reference to his chamber music, the desire to extend its colors is evidenced in this sextet, as well as in a trio that calls for the oboe d'amore. Accordingly, the bass functions here as an individual voice, not as a mere straphanger in the cello car. The use of the bass represents a second setting. Originally, the work was Holbrooke's Piano Quintet No. 3, Op. 43. (first performed in 1903). The rescoring in sextet form took place in 1905.

As usual, Holbrooke manifests his penchant for the association of his music with some direct picture, or emotion. The title already signifies what is fully explained by the central movement, an Elegie *("On the Death of a Friend—Frederick Westlake").* This movement rises to tremendous emotional intensity. The opening movement is fraught with expressiveness as well; the main theme is a beautifully formed affair in F minor, with contrast in the brightness of a major key. The Finale, however, is of somewhat less threnodic character. Here, Holbrooke forgets tragedy in a duplemeter dance.

Hold, Trevor (1939–)

DUO

- *Variations on a Popular Song* for Two
  Cellos (1975)

Although most of the variations are connected,
there will be no difficulty in recognizing the
format of each. Hold's piece (the popular tune
is not identified) is a variational survey, using
dance types for the greater part. Thus, variation
one exemplifies Ragtime, the fifth variation is
a Sarabande (mostly four-voice and sometimes
five-voice for the two instruments), and the
sixth variation is a Polka, completely depicted
with plucked sounds. Variation seven is a
Charleston (the social dance that originated as
a solo dance by a black in Charleston, South
Carolina), the eighth variation is a swinging
Tango.

The other variants are a lyrical Antiphon,
styled in free imitation (number two), a Burlesque
(number three), a Scherzo that also utilizes
imitation (number four), and the Finale (representing the ninth and concluding variation).

All the styles are represented honestly and
there's none of that pretentious hamming that
is all effects and no music. Truly, a warm and
wise work.

Holden, David (1911–)

QUINTET

- *Music for Piano and Strings* (Two
  Violins, Viola, and Cello) (1937)

There is a resemblance to concerto grosso style
in the first movement, brought about by the
ritornel aspects of the main theme, which is
forthright in its diatonic build. Though the
neoclassic depictions of the present century
have used the Corelli-Vivaldi-Handel mold to
counteract the virtuoso flourishes of 19th-cen-
tury concerto form, Holden stands more or less
with his feet in both centuries, since the piano
has two sections, of fair length, wherein the
entire spotlight is on the keyboard instrument.

There is a curious mixture of styles and
forms, as though offering a little of everything
for everyone's satisfaction. The second movement, which leads immediately into the last, is
foundationally Rachmaninoff, also somewhat
"fifthy" in its harmonies. The last movement
begins in a neo-Haydn category, and then moves
into a very smart quotation and working over of
one of the most famous of all musical examples—"Sumer Is Icumen In" (dating from
the early part of the 13th century). The original
form of this last is canonic, but Holden with-
holds this device until later in the movement.
Then, the upper three strings and upper piano
voices play the rota (medieval terminology for
a round, i.e., a strict canon), while the lower
strings and bass piano voices perform a ground
bass in constant imitation. Holden runs a course
from the 13th to the 20th centuries, yet establishes structural and stylistic unification.

Holden's work received two prizes: the
George Arthur Knight Prize of Harvard University and the Society for the Publication of
American Music Award. Continuing the double
factor, *Music* is also possible of performance
by a full string orchestra, including the usual
double bass.

Holdheim, Theodore (1923–)

DUO

- **Sonata for Trumpet and Piano (1958)**

Holdheim teaches mathematics and physics in
addition to being a composer. There is no
carryover from the nonmusic activities to the
musical creative one. No geometric or alge-
braic systems enter into his compositions, no

consideration of such matters as the Fibonacci series, no sonorous representation of arcana. Instead, Holdheim deals with traditional compositional laws and processes of music in his work, with a little updating. It is most productive.

The forms are classical: sonata for the first movement, binary for the Grave division, and rondo for the finale. All messages are clear, including the precise repetition of the exposition of the first movement. So are the meters, but they move with contemporary measurement and change in the outer movements, especially the long–short and short–long division of quintuple meter in the final Allegro vivace. The tonal language is just as clear, permitted sufficient extension to always be fresh in sound, never allowed to be routine.

In the last movement there is a section of specialness. A B-flat-minor melody is introduced by the piano and then is given five successive simple variations with no change of shape, merely of detail. Both melody and Holdheim's harmony haunt the ear long after they have been heard. It is an inspired moment.

Holewa, Hans (1905–)

DUO

- *Kammermusik (Chamber Music)* for Cello and Piano (1964)

Dark-thrusted music. One does not need the composer's remarks to realize the pessimistic tone contained in the duo's lines. Holewa speaks of a "spiralling feeling of isolation. Isolation as a feeling of powerlessness, that is, despair." He points out that lightness of detail is limited to two very short phrases, both played by the piano: a scherzando item in the Calmo first movement and a grazioso bit in the Andante fourth movement.

Movement two is marked Alla marcia. Again

Holewa clues in the listener. Although denying any program for the music, he mentions that in his sketches for the movement he indicated a "kind of motto." This reads: "There is too much marching—even refugees march, and deported persons, and prisoners and doomed persons."

TRIO

- **Trio for Violin, Viola, and Cello (1959)**

Although each of the four movements portrays its own decided quality, formal distinctions are free. Full chromaticism rules. And so does athletic action. This is most noticeable in the contrapuntal charge (often trirhythmically detailed) of the second movement and the toccata energy of the finale. Holewa's pervasive intensity is not regulated in maintained mensural terms; septuple meter is split between 3/4 and 2/2 and there is a variety of other totals.

The first movement has rhapsodic exploration. Movement three surrounds various pedals with contemporary colored recitatives, some measured with bar-lined distinction, others without such control.

QUARTET

- *Miniatures* for String Quartet (1961)

Dodecaphonic orientation in this two-part structure (each divided into three sections). A further balance relates to the tempo distinctions in the first part with a pair of andante divisions surrounding an allegretto. In the second part the speed increases: adagio to andante to allegro.

There is a fair amount of difference distinguishing one miniature from the next, though there is no evasion of serially sounded aggressiveness. Clear-cut situations all—there are no effects and the only special colors (if they are to be called special) are plucked sounds, muted sounds, and harmonics. A single exception is the final pithy glissando for the entire quartet.

Holland, Theodore (1878–1947)

QUARTET

- **Quartet in C Minor for Two Violins, Viola, and Cello (1933)**

Holland was neither originator nor nationalist. He was part of the middle-of-the-road group who culled and resang the stanzas of the romantic composers. In this work, these are heard with a cyclic refrain, all three movements receiving their impetus and working instructions from the initial theme.

Development processes are used within the opening pair of movements. In the third part the thematic premise is translated into variational language. By the end of the tenth section the variational method is on the verge of being overrepetitive. When, therefore, the Finale of the set enters, its fast and nervous 5/8 meter is a welcome surprise. It clears the air. It also reconfirms the values of sharp contrast.

Hollander, Benoît (1853–1942)

QUARTET

- **Quartet No. 2 for Two Violins, Viola, and Cello, Op. 30**

Hollander likes to ride the melodic winds in his C-sharp-minor string quartet. He also likes to avoid conservatism without destroying the traditional logic of classical form. The themes are warm and long-spanned: The viola's opening eight-measure statement in the slow movement and the cello's expressive ten-measure melody, which begins the final part of the work, are but two examples. In terms of design the first part of the Quartet has a formal point of departure and yet is perfectly balanced. It is a two-part affair, the first half further divided. The movement begins with a fugal exposition and development leading to a homophonic section where a dialogue is maintained between the first violin and cello. The fugue casts a reflection on this part of the music since the principal rhythmic outline of the fugue becomes set into the cello line. Part two of the first movement is an energetic and fluidly dynamic scherzo. The motility of the music is invigorated by the concept of combining two and three sounds within one beat.

Another scherzo follows the solo-emphasized slow movement. The earlier scherzo emphasized thrust. This time the scherzo has more swing than thrust, though it contains cross-accents and cross-syncopative rhythms.

Two principal ideas are developed in the fantasialike final movement. Quite often Hollander retains the linear action of the music but checks its dynamic weight. However, this does not check the excitement. This creative strategy carries over to the coda, which is entirely in *pianissimo* plus the muting of the violins and viola.

Holliger, Heinz (1939–)

DUO

- ***Mobile* for Oboe and Harp (1962)**

A music of twelve events, each akin to improvisational sound graffiti. Holliger indicates the progress to be taken from one event to the next. There are three possibilities and these cannot be mixed. The total running of the course is up to the performers. They can play through the sequence once, twice, or three times. In each case the order of the events varies. As examples, the first sequence is: 1–3–10–11–7–9–4–8–2–5–6–12. The second possibility is: 1–6–3–9–4–5–10–7–8–11–2–12.

There is this to realize: Holliger's musical *Mobile* is lightweight only in terms of total instruments used. Its actions are weighted otherwise. The athematic-unrelated events total a multi-evocative form. This provides, from the internal force of the special style, its own type of balance. Also to be realized is the dazzingly pyrotechnical writing for the instruments, especially for the oboe—included are the rarities of harmonics and double harmonics. The technical resources of the wind instrument are taken to the limit (Holliger is a virtuoso on the instrument). Almost the same applies to the harp.

TRIO

- **Trio for Oboe (alternating English horn), Viola, and Harp (1966)**

Fantasy that mixes exact and free tempos in the first part. Part two moves in the aleatoric sphere. There are seven sections used by the performers; the sections are introduced by a *Signal* and can be cut into by a *Trope*. The last movement uses the English horn; it is a music of dark color.

The principal interest in this Trio is in the association and disassociation of the colors. Avant-garde performance virtuosity is a demand.

QUARTET

- **String Quartet (1973)**

Indeterminacy, chance, and much noise within a performance time that is between thirty and thirty-five minutes. Materials are strewn over time-block indications (there are no controlling meters), as the string foursome is changed into a group of percussive simulants. The disordered complexity boggles the mind, while it will clog the ears, since constant tension is maintained and there is relentless instrumental activity.

In Holliger's world normal actions are less common than abnormal ones. Thus, the production of harmonics stifled by insufficient finger pressure; notating natural harmonics that are impossible, thus producing squeals; playing on the tailpiece and behind the bridge; overpressuring the bow; and so on. In addition, every instrument undergoes scordatura during the course of the piece. One example: the first violin's A string is lowered to G, later to F, and ultimately to D. The D string is moved down to B, then to G-sharp, further on to F, and finally to E a seventh below. Etc. Save for the E strings of the violins and the A string of the viola, every string of the four instruments is manipulated downward.

At one point Holliger requests electrical amplification, "if possible." And, in the wild and woolly world of the avant-garde, Holliger adds a new twist: the performer is to inhale when playing up-bow, exhale when playing down-bow. And, "if possible," to use "a stethoscope microphone to amplify [the] breathing sound."

All of this produces a music of heated rawness and a freedom that champions chaos. Instructional notes make this clear: "All 4 players choose own bowing movements and style of bowing. Total independence among the players. As unsynchronized as possible... . Extremely excited, aggressive... ." Timbres are purposefully irritated—again quoting Holliger: "Bow in jerks, grating," and further, "press bowhair and stick. . . cracking noise by twisting bow. . . ." And, finally, in connection with the breathing matter indicated previously, there are specific instructions for the concluding part of the work that move into the field of theatrics. There is a verdict that Holliger's quartet tends to move extremely close to the world of antimusic.

QUINTET

- *"h" for Wind Quintet (1968)*

A script of eleven connected sections, some-times distinct in their differences, sometimes so blended as to be unrecognizable. Above all, in Holliger's virtuosic piece for flute, oboe, clarinet, horn, and bassoon, there is a unity arrived at from the divisional interlock of a few similarities and many disparities. Diversity in this case knits into a stylistically balanced totality.

The instrumental writing is intricate, of avant-garde coalition, requiring four large pages of instructions in the score. Included are such timbre pungencies as overtones sounding with actual pitches; and timbre purple patches such as quarter tones, vibrato differences, high and low tongue clicks, vocal noises ("ha," "tsch," "k," etc.), slap tongue sounds, air noises, instrumental key noises, and many more. There is a heavy refusal to use more than a minimal amount of standard detail.

Holliger's title is the German term for the B-natural pitch. A little of this sound filters into the 10 1/2-minute work. Most of the time (as in the very beginning) the pitch is deflowered with multiphonic application.

Some of the form-building particulars are especially marked. Section three, for example, is scored without bassoon. Section six is fully unmetered, a wild mix of sound garnishes on the part of all five instruments. In the following section (also unmetered) a tutti series of staccato pitches are played in a roughed quadruple *fortissimo*. The division ends with trills that continue into section eight. Section nine begins like the start of the piece (on the pitch B multiphonically stated by the oboe) and moves into en masse multiphonics for the entire quintet. Slap-tongued sounds indicate the start of the final section of this catalogue of avant-garde sonorities.

Hollós, Lajos (1923–)

SEXTET

- *Hommage à Muharay: Two Ancient Folk Songs* **for Brasses (Three Trumpets, Two Trombones, and Tuba) (1975)**

Freely disposed but not overfancied. The first part is a kind of "spoken" music tied in with rubato. This connects to a vivacious move-a-long music. Tonal, of course.

Hollós, Máté (1954–)

TRIO

- *Dúli-dúli:* **Trio for Clarinets (Two Clarinets [Clarinet 2 alternating Alto Saxophone] and Bass Clarinet) (1979)**

Hollós explains that the words "Dúli-dúli" are found "in Finno-Ugrian and Slavonic folk songs" and are mistakenly thought to be non-sense words. However, the word is derived from the Finnish *tuuli*, which means "wind"; therefore, "melodic lines accompanied by 'dúli' imitate the blowing of the wind."

Accordingly, much of this wind sound at the beginning and end of this short piece is imitated by way of a B-flat pitch. In between there is folklike material, but not flattened out in squared phrasing. The winds here are not wild but they certainly are active.

Holm, Mogens Winkel (1936–)

TRIO

- *Transitions II* for Flute, Cello, and Piano (1973)

An unabashed celebration of dynamic restraint that embraces eleven minutes in performance.

There are 300 measures in all. Save for six of these measures (played twice), in which a crescendo to *forte* is followed by a return to *pianissimo*, everything is dead *pianissimo*—without a speck of dynamic change. The cello is also sempre sul ponticello and sempre senza vibrato, the flute is to play senza vibrato, dolce, and the piano is also to play dolce.

Holm explains his intent: "A chamber work in *pianissimo*, and seemingly of the same nature throughout, like the sounds in grass or water—sounds that are pleasant to listen to if one only gave oneself the time... ." / "However, the work is not about grass or water, but rather—for each of the three instruments—a series of repetition and shifting principles and the effects of these in interplay. The music could perhaps be compared to three sonorous whirls or spirals that move, quietly interlocking, by turning about themselves a couple of times in slow motion."

There is, of course, shock effect in a music that moves with uncompromisingly dynamic singleness. The total avoidance of usual qualities of expressiveness (which would include contrasts) brings forth expressivity of a completely different kind. *Transitions* thus represents an exploration of sonorous objectiveness.

Holm, Peder (1926–)

QUARTET

- **String Quartet (1967)**

A slavish litany of rhapsodic facts is included in this one-movement quartet. The beginning mixes a pair of tone rows, the second of the pair broken into six, two, and four sounds. These are developed and lead into a repetitive pitch phrase (announced by the cello) followed by further developments. Next is a moderately fast, rhythmically unified section that has scherzo character, combined in turn with a tripleted figure, and finally a chromatically lush melodic idea, framed with material from the scherzolike section.

The various moves and interlocking of basic material remove a distinctive profile from the music. This is balanced, however, by convincing vigor and a good supply of instrumental color.

QUINTETS

- *Little Suite* for Five Cellos (1956)

Simple charm (and certainly concerned with a rare medium) that meets standard structural necessities. Three movements: a waltzlike piece stressing upbeats, a moderately snappy rhythmic affair, and a concluding Maestoso concept that begins chordally and moves into a contrapuntal phrase.

The music represents this Danish composer in a predominantly conservative mood. (The seven-minute suite can also be played by a cello orchestra.)

- **Two Pieces for Woodwind Quintet (Flute, Oboe [alternating English horn], Clarinet, Horn, and Bassoon) (1968)**

Short, free-formed pieces, one fairly slow, the other moderately fast. Holm is preoccupied with figures that are freely repeated and uncoordinated between the instruments. Solo situations add colorful paragraphs in the two essays. All of it totals the now familiar blend of straight and aleatoric stylistic conduct, but the effect is one of freshness.

Holmboe, Vagn (1909–)

DUO

- **Sonata for Violin and Piano (1935)**

Holmboe's interest in Romanian folk songs, the result of his stay in Romania in the early 1930s, filters through some of his later compositions, in this one it sheathes it. Accordingly, the special turns in the melodic elements, matched by slightly frictional harmony, together with racing rhythms.

Modal contours stream through the work. The Allegro is cast in the Phrygian mode and stays there without a solitary chromatic pitch for over 120 measures. Aside from an occasional B-flat, the same holds true for the slow movement, conveyed in a verbalized manner, each bar line representing a comma or a semicolon; the discourse backed by more than a dozen time signatures. Ostinatos anchor the last movement's structure.

QUARTETS

- *Quartetto medico* **for Flute, Oboe, Clarinet, and Piano, Op. 70**

No chamber music nostrums are put forth in this quartet. The only *materia medica* offered is the healing art of the sounds of chamber music; good for the psyche, good for the soul, to hear and to enjoy.

The title is due to the dedication, made to one Dr. Knud Mose. So Holmboe continues the play-ploy of titling in terms of his tempo heads. Movement one is Andante medicamento. Movement two is indicated Allegro quasi febrilo; the only thing feverish about the music is its rhythmic go-forthness.

Intermedico I, an interlude, is a fugue, and since only the winds play, the tempo, Andante senza pianisticitis, is on target—Intermedico II follows. Holmboe shifts to French for this subtitle: sans marais. The finale is tuny and for all the instruments, so all's well that ends well. It is described as Allegro con frangula (Fast with fringes).

- **String Quartet No. 1, Op. 46**

A rhapsodic preamble passes into an Animato set in Bulgarian rhythm whereby the four main pulses are sequenced in groups of 3 + 3 + 2 and also changed for fluidic contrast. The integration of the introduction into the movement proper tightens and unifies the structure.

An interesting concept of variation form is employed in the slow movement. The theme is developed into three free variations, the last of these the longest, far beyond average variation length. To complete the movement, Holmboe paraphrases a bit from the second variant, ties it to a bit from the first variant, and then reverses completely into thematic restatement.

Introductory material is again used to begin the final movement. It is of virtuosic delivery, has power, fantastic sonorities, and blazes with quartet color. The principal part is set in quintuple time, excited by gnashing accents. Pedals, trills, twelve-to-fifteen total part chords, antiphony, and hemiola distribution are all operative in the brilliant conclusion.

■ **String Quartet No. 2, Op. 47**

A five-movement work with fast and slow speeds exactly contrasted in alternate fashion. In the first movement the percussive color effect of dissonance (sliding tones with a pivotal static sound) serves as a pedal background helping to distinguish diverse ideas.

Movement three is wild in pace, built on the intertwining of duple and triple pulses. No less an amount of intensity concerns the finale (movement five). It is unsquared in its quintuple rhythms and unstinting in its regard for Bartókian style.

A declamatory motive haunts the first slow movement and becomes the prime contrastive point. The other slow movement differs by the use of muted timbre, conciseness, and textural quality. Thereby, a dark, somber, almost sequestered mood awaits the burst of the final movement.

■ **String Quartet No. 3, Op. 48**

Similar to his second quartet *(see above)* Holmboe's third quartet is in five movements. However, the tempo order is the exact reverse with the sequence here starting with slow tempo.

The central part of the quartet is a chaconne with a twelve-tone subject. There is clear projection of the permutations (including inversion and retrograde inversion of the row) and the movement ends firmly in a tonally defined C. The finale begins with a resemblance to the chaconne's subject and then recalls the opening of the work. That beginning is vigorous, of declamatory dominance which later develops into almost free parlando (especially by the viola). The two fast-tempo movements are defined, respectively, in scherzo style and motivally developed polyphony.

■ **String Quartet No. 6, Op. 78**

Tempo maintenance is a strong codification in the music. With the exception of two measures in the finale, marked sostenuto, this entire fourth movement progresses in Allegro spirituoso definition. (The use of mutes within this part of the work gives a mysterious excitation to the contents.) In movement two, a full-scaled Scherzo, the pace never slackens from the molto vivace tempo. Movement three combines set tempo with set dynamic gradation, with the heading Adagio e piano. There are some minute dynamic swells but they are quickly canceled by sonority compression; the tempo never moves away from its ♩ = c. 56. (The thin sound-weight of harmonics colors one portion of this movement.)

Although there is tempo change in the first movement, within each the same retentive coherence applies as in the other movements. An alternation of speeds is used: lento and allegro con fuoco, in an A–B–A–B–A sequence.

■ **String Quartet No. 8, Op. 87**

Five movements which cover the standard fast and slow divisions plus a scherzo equivalent. Thus movements one, two, three, and five follow the fast–slow–scherzo–fast sequence, with movement four a short fourteen-measure portion. The last is devoted to a rubato recitative totally in the hands of the first violin and linked to the concluding movement.

There are a variety of qualities in the piece, strongly compared but not losing the stylistic identity of this composer's incisiveness, depicted regardless of tempo or dynamic strength. The chimerical second movement is a case in point. But regardless of its phrase splitting, slow tempo, and reduced dynamic level, it is anything but a lightweight offering. Elsewhere there are Bartókian streaks, especially in the pivotal central movement (Presto volante et robusto). Throughout, the cellular developmental process particular to Holmboe's writing is fully defined.

■ **String Quartet No. 9, Op. 92**

Short phrases in the first movement and a persistent polyphonic demeanor. The action forms textures of varying density. The elements of this opening movement return in the fifth movement (finale) providing thereby a determined balance. (The tempo of the first movement is Andante determinato; that of the finale retains the andante and shifts to tranquillo for the character designation.)

Both the second and fourth movements are keyed to repetitive rhythmic figures; in the former in sextuplet totals, in the latter in quadruple totals. The central movement is a muted Adagio, and here too there is considerable inner stirring in the lines.

■ **String Quartet No. 10, Op. 102**

An odd entry in the Holmboe string quartet catalogue, since it consists of only a pair of movements. It begins with a cello theme which provides the generative material for the quartet, written in the metamorphosed style that identifies this composer's entire output. As usual with Holmboe, the power and meaning of the music come from straightforward scoring. Timbral gimmicks are not for this composer.

■ **String Quartet No. 11** *(Rustico)*, **Op. 111**

■ **String Quartet No. 12, Op. 116**

■ **String Quartet No. 13, Op. 124**

■ **String Quartet No. 14, Op. 125**

All four quartets exemplify Holmboe's technique of metamorphosis, which he has described as "an embryo which is unfolded in accordance with the conditions present." Totally meaning a stylistic plan of motival development.

One can hardly find any basic difference between Holmboe's eleventh quartet and the others. There is a bit more open texture in the *Rustico* quartet; the descriptive subtitle is further confirmed by the dance spirit of the finale.

The first movement in the Op. 116 (Allegro robusto) is colored in the first movement by a rhythmically unified motive delivered with successive down bows. There are sharp dynamic differences in the finale of this quartet that relate to the opening movement's essential dramatic character.

In the Op. 124 quartet especially to be noted is the third (totally muted) movement. Though Holmboe's style is basically a process of variation in the sense of germinal change and cellular permutations, etc., he has not been prone to use direct variational form. The sense of this movement, however, tends toward defined variations.

The fourteenth quartet is in six movements. It has a dark eloquence in its projection, especially in the first two movements, *both* played throughout with muted timbre. A different type of coloristic association is involved in the fourth part of the quartet, with a compact setting of moderately fast music totally in plucked timbre. Bartókian elements have never left the score pages of this important Danish composer.

QUINTETS

■ **Notturno for Flute, Oboe, Clarinet, Horn, and Bassoon, Op. 19**

Holmboe composed his wind quintet some seven years after a sojourn in Transylvania, where he had investigated Balkan folk music. The quintet gives off such folkloristic flavors mixed in with the Danish composer's very coloristic Bartókian procedures.

The first pair of movements consists of a Tranquillo, which is a rhapsody of melisma and fioritura, and a Scherzando that exists by way of a syncopative motive. Movements three and four have a certain relationship to the first pair of movements. The Improvvisazione (movement three) has less horizontal pitch freedom than movement one. What freedom there is is reserved for the outer portions of the movement. And in place of syncopation for the fast-moving Scherzando the finale (con moto) moves up and down on the rungs of eighth-note rhythms that brace the music's patterns.

- **Quintet for Two Trumpets, Horn, Trombone, and Tuba, Op. 79**

Development from motival material is the ruling method in this brass work. This pertains to the more serious slow movements as well as to the lighter and breezier fast movements. There is also the use of a special metrical outline. The entire third movement is in five time, its fifty measures totally muted. And the finale is principally set in septuple time.

An interesting point is that each movement increases in terms of performance length. Movement one (Poco lento) is about 21/4 minutes, movement two (Allegro) runs about 21/2 minutes, movement three (Adagio) covers a span of about 33/4 minutes, and movement four (Vivace) is about 41/2 minutes in length.

- *Tropos* **for String Quintet (Two Violins, Two Violas, and Cello), Op. 75**

Holmboe is not to be classified as a twelve-tone composer, even though he partly uses that technique in this two-viola string quintet.

It is in full swing in the second movement, Presto spirituoso. In the second slow movement there is further permutation, with most of the movement scored for reduced forces (violin and viola). A short fragmented music colors movement four, and Holmboe's favorite five-movement structure is concluded with an Allegro vivace. Here the row is rather negligible (it has not controlled all the material previously). The hybrid technique is convincing.

Holmès, Augusta (1847–1903)

DUO

- **Fantaisie for Clarinet and Piano**

The fantasy design has no formal standard. In the vernacular it is a sort of "do your own thing." Understandable, naturally, in music made from a number of linked-up and not thematically connected sections. There is no reason to argue that some fantasys, like this one, are equal to creative streams of consciousness.

Holmès's piece is easily divided into five sections. The second and last have an unusual relationship, even though they have different qualitative objectives; the former is a Marcia funèbre, the other a March minus specification. Tempo differences distinguish the pair, with the second one almost three-fifths again as fast as the first. What is a connective subtlety is the fact that both of these marches originate from three successive similar chords. In the funereal section the tonality is (expectedly) minor; in the other case the mode is in the brighter major orbit. The marches are separated by a section marked "like a dream" and a proclamatory division. A Recitative, mainly assigned to the clarinet, opens the duo.

While a fantasy, the thought persists that some program was considered when this piece was composed. No clue is given. The fact remains that the first section begins in C minor and the concluding one is terminated in optimistic C major. And furthermore, there are those two marches!

Holoubek, Ladislav (1913–)

QUARTET

- *Musical Scene* for String Quartet

A novel format. Holoubek presents a media sampler within the six movements and also balances the structure in arch form based on the instrumentation. Movement one is a solo violin piece; movement two is a Duo. Importantly, in regard to the last, the second violin has a solo slant, as it were, since it is scored above and plays above the first violin throughout. Movement three is a Trio I for the two violins and viola and is a Menuet. The full group plays in movement four, titled Quartet, the music set in fugal style.

The instrumentation totals now go in reverse. Movement five is an allegro-tempo Trio II, but the formation this time is for two violins and cello. Movement six begins as a duo (the second violin again above the other violin) and ends as the work began, as a solo for the first violin.

Holscsevnyikov, Vlagyimir

QUARTET

- **Quartet for Strings (Two Violins, Viola, and Cello)**

A big work, plastic and free in its consistent movement. In the background is Bartók and in the foreground are the post-Bartókian effects of nonmetricality, percussive sonorities, nonsynchronization, and the like. Lots of instrumental dazzle.

Following a short Preludio is a Lamento projected between exact pulse arrangement and free measures further loosened by rubato indications. The last formation opens the movement and occurs eight other times within it.

Movement three is a Scherzo capriccioso, jaggy and jumpy in its pulse ordering. The Notturno is filled with sections consisting only of detonations made by striking the instruments with the fingers, hitting the tailpiece with the bow, and trilling (!) near the F holes of the instruments by use of alternate finger contacts. The music is filled with polyrhythms. A sectional Finale (containing a review of the colors used previously) concludes the opus.

Holst, Gustav (1874–1934)

TRIO

- **Terzetto for Flute, Oboe, and Viola (1925)**

There are four very important points that concern this trio. First, it is Holst's only chamber music composition in a fairly big catalogue of works (two very early specimens were disowned, never published or performed). Second, the work has an odd history; it disappeared and turned up only after Holst's death, to be published ten years afterward. Third, the composition consists of but two movements. And last, and most important of all, is that the entire work is written polytonally (flute in A major, oboe in A-flat major, and the viola in C major; later, respectively, in E, D-flat, and E-flat).

Polytonality was not the usual technique for this extremely interesting composer. The trio is especially fascinating, and illustrative of what a composer concerned with a particular aesthetic can accomplish in a technique completely different from his own. As usual with Holst, the effect is stimulating. His entire career consisted of the composition of music with inventiveness, and an independence of vision that made of him one of the best composers of the English school.

Naturally, polytonality requires polyphony for its best registration. It is counterpoint that is used, therefore, in both the Allegretto and the faster second movement. A large ternary form is employed in the first movement, with some intersticed choralelike sections. The second movement is fugal, more relaxed intermediate portions giving flux and contrastive pace. The final measures are a gem. Each instrument runs arpeggiandos through its individual tonality's tonic triad (the flute in A, the oboe in A-flat, and the viola in C). The resultant entrancingly correlated polytonality has no better illustration.

Holst, Imogen (1907–84)

TRIO

- *Deddington Suite* **for Recorder Trio (Soprano or Alto, Alto or Soprano, and Tenor or Alto Recorders)**

Folk spirit throughout in four compact movements, guided by alternate slow and fast tempos. Modal character. The second movement (marked Quick and Light) delightfully breezes along on top of a five-pitch G-major figure that sometimes starts on the tonic, sometimes on the subdominant, and sometimes on the dominant. The finale (Quick), a three-voice canon, moves on to quote a bit from the preceding slow movement, and then returns for a foreshortened statement of the movement's initial part.

Holten, Willem Van

DUO

- *Sonata lirico* **for Flute and Piano**

And "lyric" means tuny and texturally lightweight. The music is full of soloism, though it has a good amount of duoism. Thus the entire first part of the exposition of movement one is for piano alone, many portions of the slow

movement are for unaccompanied flute, movement three plays with antiphony so there are further to and fro single timbres, and even the concluding measures of the final movement are for a single instrument.

The swing in movement one, set in triple pulse, removes any heaviness from the content. Movement three is colored by consecutive seconds. Incisiveness and dramatic wrap up are bypassed in the concluding part of the piece in favor of a simple lyrical Adagio.

Homs, Joaquín (1906–)

It was Wordsworth who said, "Like—but oh! how different!" That statement fits the proper indication of this composer's forename.

The published music itself offers no solution. In some places it's "Joaquim," elsewhere it stands as "Joaquin." The latter form is used by Arthur Custer in his article "Contemporary Music in Spain" (*Musical Quarterly*, January 1965). In the Vinton-edited *Dictionary of Contemporary Music* it is given as "Joaquim." In both Livermore's *Short History of Spanish Music* and the sixth edition of *Baker's Biographical Dictionary of Musicians*, edited by the ever-faultless Nicolas Slonimsky, the first name reads: Joaquín (with accent). The decision of this writer is to follow the ever-faultless Slonimsky.

TRIO

- **String Trio (1968)**

Freely applied architecture spells out a three-part plan for this one-movement trio. The aspects of the form derive from majority emphasis on sustained quality in the outer parts (in a very moderate tempo), and rhythmic declaration in the middle portion (in a moderately fast speed). The linear aspects of emphasis on the constricted interval of the second (and its inversion into a seventh) are matched by vertical deployment. With care accorded spacings there is no overburdening of density. In atonical music the disjunctive profile is usually very vivid. In Homs's trio for strings the outline is much more compact.

QUARTETS

- **String Quartet No. 6 (1966)**

Motival units drawn from the basic tone row give positive connection to the first movement (Allegro moderato). A scherzo climate permeates the movement, brought especially by the use of fast triplet figures. As a secondary point, a type of color balance exists between the ponticello passage that occurs midway and its timbral repetition throughout the concluding fifteen measures of the movement.

Flat-surfaced music, sustained and moving from *pianissimo* to *piano* and back again to *pianissimo* sets the slow movement (Andante). The row announcement takes twelve measures of quintuple meter to unfold, via staggered entrances of the instruments. This subdued idea alternates with more active material. The finale (Allegro vivace) has variational conduct as it proceeds from the thematic (row) announcement by the viola and then repeated by the second violin. It thereafter undergoes permutation, enlargement, and coloration.

- **String Quartet No. 7 (1968)**

Although septuple meter is no rare pattern, it is exceedingly unusual to cast an entire work of length in seven-beat division. Homs's one-movement piece (a favorite device of his) covers eleven minutes in performance time and not one of its 226 measures deviates from the 7/8 time signature. Neither is the meter the often-met convenience of combining quadruple and triple (or the reverse) pulse sets within measures. In the cases where one voice is so

fractioned it is canceled by another voice set in contrary disposition. A number of the measures consist of 3/4 (six eighths) plus an additional eighth, but here again, this is often disturbed by another arrangement of the pulses.

The quartet's septuple meter is consistently mobile, never regular. And the musical content follows suit. Nontonal, it alternately contrasts long-span materials with decisive rhythmic ones. As these types reappear they are changed (not developed from the previous ones). The dual actions are sufficient to give contrast and attain balance. This is *durchkomponiert* music.

OCTETS

- *Music for Eight* **(Flute, Clarinet, Trumpet, Violin, Viola, Cello, Piano, and Percussion [Timpani, Snare Drum, Vibraphone, Triangle, Cymbals, Suspended Cymbal, and Three Wood Blocks]) (1964)**

Homs's mixed-color octet consists of two movements. Twelve-tone ordering applies. In the Passacaglia, the subject is of fourteen-measure length. Much attention is given the head of the subject with its compact pitch arrangement (A–B–D–C-sharp). The music is cleanly scored, minus undue weight by pudgy doublings, and it is colored in assorted ways. Two of the variations that appear toward the end of the movement are of special note: one consists of pizzicato with flute fluttered pitches and muted trumpet, the other calls for vibraphone and string-instrument harmonics.

The second movement, "Derivaciones" ("Derivations"), is scherzolike music of speed and inner energy. There is no dodecaphonic restrictive orthodoxy applied as variational rhapsody reigns.

- *Octet de Vent (Wind Octet)* **(Flute, Oboe, Clarinet, Bass Clarinet, Horn, Trumpet, Trombone, and Tuba) (1968)**

Forms, in this three-movement serial work, are derived not from themes but from pitch propositions—extracted from the tone row. The musical arguments in each case are continuous and connected, not separative and disjointed as in moment form. Coherence is obtained from shapes, not from thematic sections in contrast and recapitulation. In the first movement (Moderato) sustained sounds are set in juxtaposed entrances. From these, short motives emerge and rhythmic elongation is made. And then, for balance, the sustained elements return.

Movement two (Agitato) fragments the basic material at the start. In the first five measures there are no combined entrances of instruments. From this the pitch play produces its own form. What seems to be a stylistic error (sustained qualities in the concluding part of the movement) is not that at all, but an anticipation of the finale, which is linked to the second movement. Marked Sostenuto, the finale is compact (twenty-eight measures lasting three minutes), and consists of unremitting long sounds.

Honegger, Arthur (1892–1955)

Generally, mention of Honegger brings to mind his *Pacific 231* or his *Rugby*—works now rarely performed but which, during the 1920s and the "verismo" period of musical composition, were heard frequently. A composer may be classified incorrectly through hackneyed short works or a *pièce d'occasion*. While Honegger's *Pacific 231* is one of the cleverest examples of musical programmatics, yet the true composer is seen in his *Le Roi David*, in the chamber works, and the late symphonies.

Honegger's music is athletic and lyrical. The former is best exemplified in *Horace Victorieux*. The lyricism is acrid-sweet, based on free, almost atonal harmony, but not concerned with any rigorous setting and placement of the chromatic spectrum. Because of clear contrapuntal leanings there is a Bachian evocativeness in all of his music; romantic rotundity and thickness cannot be found: Honegger is rather clipped and tight, partial to the tautness of 20th-century nervous energy.

Honegger's creative verve is enclosed in rich chromaticism (a derivative of Honegger's assimilation of Wagner, his certain interest in Reger, but excluding either composer's overluxuriance). There is, as has been said, free harmony, but the resultant polytonality is not generally the ordered setting of lines in separate keys against each other. Honegger's main musical grammar derives from contrapuntal juxtaposition, which, as it embraces specific vertical combinations of the diatonic system, adds up to a total of *chordal* counterpoint. These combines make the musical structure rock-ribbed with superpositioned sounds which place foreign elements on otherwise recognizable triads, seventh and ninth chords. Activity is constant, the parts interlaced and interwoven—a polycolored fabric.

That quite often Honegger's lyricism seems austere is due to the fact that he is not tempted to romantic excess. Musical architecture represents to him the requisition of fresh, modern materials, not the use of prefabricated leftover sections of others. His choice of the sonorous equivalents of chrome and steel shows full reflection in his music; his structural balance is unfailing.

Honegger's music exemplifies modern polyphony. Unless one accepts that fact, his music can neither be understood nor take effect. He sustains under contemporary conditions the tradition and philosophy of absolute music as practiced by Bach.

DUOS

■ *Intrada* **for Trumpet and Piano (1947)**

Honegger's *Intrada* was written in August 1947 as the required piece for the *Concours International d'Exécution musicale*, held in Geneva in the same year.

A majestic first part, with the theme climbing chromatically just short of two octaves, is followed by legato conjunct data and some fanfarelike articulations. A part of this material returns in a final Maestoso. Before it does there is a long section (115 measures) of crisp content. The music is waltz contoured but is not for the dance floor. This type of rhythmic concept is for concert exhibitionism.

■ **Sonata for Viola and Piano (1920)**

Honegger's music is implicitly chromatic, its ebb and flow are not only present in the harmonic conduits but cover the melodic shapes as well. At times, his music almost sounds completely atonal, though Honegger is not without key roots in his uncompromising polyphony.

When this Sonata opens, the spring of the piano's line immediately brings to mind the complexities of Honegger's harmonic thinking. Its tones are (in varying octaves) A–B-flat–B-natural–G-sharp, and before the measure has been completed the other eight tones of the possible twelve are sounded. This defines not only the free use of chromaticism but the fullest use as well. Yet the purpose is clear—to outline the design's features. Honegger shapes his sounds as he wishes, does not rigorously consider them only to latch onto one technique and never be unfastened. Without stylistic pastiche his works are each lit from a central system, but with individual regard for the drama to be enacted.

The shifting line of the Andante is related to the Vivace, which is based on a theme of two four-measure units (thereby forming the equal of the well-ordered classical eight-measure standard). Though this is of chromatic order, the atmosphere is lightened, and contrast is achieved by drawing two differing concepts from the same resource. Three times this correlation occurs—a gigantic binary idea in triple formation. The same binary conception (but with more tonally pinned harmonies) is used in the middle movement, this time twice. In the last movement, the design relates free polyphony and shifting keys in the larger center to the smaller outer parts in plain, though dissonantized, C major. The coda is like bells tossed by the wind; intervallic seconds predominate.

■ **Sonata No. 1 for Violin and Piano (1918)**

Honegger's first violin and piano sonata is the largest of his two-instrument chamber productions. As an early work (composed, one movement each, in 1916, 1917, and 1918) there is an overabundance of material. But Honegger already shows clearly the mark of the intuitive pathfinder—working with free polyphony, unconditional forms and rhythms. There is polytonality in the first movement, but it is thick and one considers it overdrawn. Only later works will show Honegger as the master of the glories of contemporary polyphony. There, one will observe sufficient instrumental leg room, and the air necessary for contrapuntal health.

In the second movement the means are more concentrated. Though the same language is used as in the opening movement, the music is not thickened by sound interlardment. The frisky subject of this part goes through many changes, is related to a lyrical section and to a fugato, and concludes in proper stylistic manner with F major pitted against other keys; only the final cadence obliterates any dual key capacity. But the last movement, enclosing a fast movement within adagio speed, is again very thick. It offers sonority engulfed en masse in complex tonal heaps. One argues that here Honegger's hand is too vigorous.

▪ Sonata No. 2 for Violin and Piano (1919)

In classical and romantic music a sonata movement was codified by thematic contrasts and development of these fundamentals. With Beethoven, however, the individual expressive needs of a work already demanded pushing beyond this form's boundaries. Sonata reasoning became freer through the years, but maintained its place as the first among all musical forms. Proof of the value of this classical definition was given by the retention of sonata design in the work of the most diversified composers. While many composers shifted their sonata scenes with abandon, some learned, as did Honegger, that it was possible to obtain a new significance to the old form without emphatically creating a brand-new one.

The first movement of this Sonata is a case in point. The broad theme is a swinging and sensuous "echt Brahms" item (in meter only!) fitted by 9/4 and 12/4 patterns. A fugato substitutes for the development section and combines partially with the material of the main subject before recapitulation. The slow section is monothematic; changes of the theme are merely designs woven around the main subject. In the finale, Honegger shapes his rondo prototype by introducing the two principal themes in the extreme bass zone of the piano.

▪ Sonatine for Cello and Piano (1922)

This is an alternate setting of Honegger's Sonatine for Clarinet and Piano (for details *see below*).

It works almost (two-thirds) as well for the cello as it does for the clarinet. It is the finale, with its gangbusters' activity, that comes off better with the wind instrument. However, the setting for cello and piano remains a fully official Honegger opus.

▪ Sonatine for Clarinet and Piano (1922)

This composition for clarinet or cello *(see above* for the latter version) represents relaxed Honegger. The compressed and concentrated three movements define a residue of true sonata form. There is such condensed depiction that if one is not aurally quick, the subtle Honeggerian order will pass by all too swiftly. In the first movement the composer uses a lazy type of theme, a short fugato (wherein the subject is heard in augmented rhythm), and a recapitulation. A synthesis of ternary form is employed in the Lent et soutenu. The finale consists of thirty-seven measures and includes some nimble jazz glides. Actually, this work is a "sonatinette."

▪ Sonatine for Two Violins (1920)

Proof that proper climax can be obtained even with the minimal means of two-voiced polyphony is ably presented in the opening movement of this work. Thematic relationship is made clear by alternating homophonically coupled statements, with four-part writing. Contrasts are also detailed by color (muted timbre in the middle movement). In the ternary form of this central (and poetic) part of the work, swinging arpeggios mark its second section. Fugal design defines the final movement.

The Sonatine was written in April and June of 1920. The premiere (in 1921) was certainly a historic affair, since two famous 20th-century composers were the instrumentalists—Honegger himself and Darius Milhaud, to whom the work is dedicated.

▪ Sonatine for Violin and Cello (1932)

A composer as fond of polyphony as Honegger would have been drawn to the possibilities available in combing homophonic instruments. In this duet suave contrapuntalism is linked with smart rhythmic ideas. As usual with

Honegger, there is tonal independence. Though the first movement begins in unisoned G major, assorted tonal interlacement quickly appears from within. Principally, there are two main motives, both in duple meter; one swings, the other plunges.

The large three-part slow movement starts in aria style, is followed by a fugal section (an ornamental development of the first part), and then returns to the initial manner. Whimsicality is found in the finale. The stop-and-go of some rhythms is somewhat Stravinskian, but the gay E-major theme is decidedly French.

TRIO

- *Petite Suite* **for Two Instruments and Piano (1934)**

A charming, beautiful bit of semi-whimsy; an odd item in Honegger's catalogue, also singular in several other ways. Not only in its simplicity is the work an example of French Gebrauchsmusik. The "two instruments" are not specified. Thus any choice can be made for the two parts. These are elementary, since their total range is from middle C to a minor tenth above, and only that wide in one instance; otherwise the compass is pegged at a ninth's distance.

Three categories of combination are used in the same total of movements. The opening movement calls for one instrument and piano, the last for all three players, while the middle section employs the two instruments without the piano. The music is tonal, served by a handful of chords, and only in a few measures of the last movement are bitonality and birhythm to be found. A drone effect predominates in that example of simple contemporary folk-like music. Of interest is the long–short unequal septuple rhythm used in the third piece.

Honegger composed his trio for his niece and nephew. Indeed, it is music for children to play and enjoy, but, as is so often the case, adults will also enjoy it.

QUARTETS

- **Rhapsody for Two Flutes, Clarinet, and Piano (or Two Violins, Viola, and Piano) (1917)**

This quartet's somewhat impressionistic cast represents Honegger in a different light (explained by the fact that it is an early work). Rhapsodic deference is present more by the curvatures traced by the tones than by the form, which is tripartite. The two outer portions are duplicates, in a way, of Debussy's and Ravel's style; while the central section is a more precise and direct type of rhythmic march.

Throughout, the meter is ruled by subdivisions. In the outer parts the pulse is based on the alternating scheme of 3: 2: 3; in the Allegro, quintuple rhythm prevails, not in specific ratio so that three beats follow two or the reverse, but by intermingling the accentuation points. Compared to other Honegger works his Rhapsody is a relaxation from formal stringency and harmonic astringency.

(Not indicated in the published score is Honegger's approval for playing this quartet by flute, oboe, clarinet, and piano.)

String Quartets

Honegger's three string quartets were composed in two different periods: the first in 1916–17, the other two in 1934–36. There is a marked design to these quartets, each in three movements. The first is largely contrapuntal, resulting in a thickly textured score. The second quartet is much more texturally refined, the structure displaying all-important clarity. The music's motor drive is truly exciting. The third string quartet shows complete maturity in a way that combines the best elements of the previous two examples.

▪ [No. 1] (1917)

Honegger's preoccupation with moving lines (his technique's strongest point) shows throughout the opening movement. The theme is not accompanied or supported; it is triple-stranded by the counterpoints produced by the first violin and viola while the second violin runs in fierce tripleted legato. From first to last the tight and close texture remains in this way. In the recapitulation, this nonpadded method is again evident; the counterpoints are now formed by the violin and cello while the second violin once more plays triplets; these are supported by the viola's strong octaves. Movement of line gives relationship to the themes; the main one surges upward, the softer second subject moves downward.

Honegger's love of Bach and his study of that master's works show in the Adagio, a section where part writing is contrasted superbly to huge sonorous rhapsodic creation. A fully dissonant and roughly vigorous final movement is completed by a *pianissimo* Adagio. The entire quartet is packed with harmonic tensility, addressed smartly with sonority.

▪ No. 2 (1934)

In the first movement, a folklike theme is contrasted to a more agile idea. Honegger's resolute rhetoric is shown by the main theme. Although the principal subject is in A minor, it is tied to the second violin's and viola's combination of minor and major seventh chords and the cello's pedal tone on D. The composer's fundamental methods are outlined: clarity within each key, and precise juxtaposition of tonality, equating thereby polyharmony and polytonality—but above all, discrimination in regard to proper place of all elements. This is as ordered a music as any composer's of the 17th or 18th century.

An aria-type line is utilized in the middle movement. The sections of the three parts have interconnection by employment of the first section's rhythmic cell as the basis for the vigorous rhythm and stormy sound of the central section. Honegger's ternary form outlines the factors of turmoil, strife, and repose. Rough and brutal music is depicted in the third movement. The triplet rhythm that begins matters is matched against a trumpetlike motive, then the two are combined. The incessant rhythm and tremendous sonority range do not make for capriciousness. The final movement of the quartet is contemporary music of urbanistic sound.

▪ No. 3 (1936)

It is interesting to trace the order in which Honegger composed this work—one actually written backwards; that is, the last movement was composed first, then the middle section, and finally the first movement. Polychordal style is present, as it is in all of Honegger's works. The forms are clear; both vertical and horizontal writing are in the most clarified state. There is a directness and vigor to the first movement which is very exciting and which treats the quartet almost like a minimal string orchestra. But the music is lean; no fat remains on its edges.

The individual, broad tripartite structure favored by Honegger in his other string quartets applies to the slow movement here as well. In the return to the initial section, the recapitulation combines both the first theme and introductory material. The textural differences in the outer sections thereby provide further contrast.

Honegger's craftsmanship is nowhere better seen than in the last movement. A simple bass line becomes blown into a vigorous principal subject in full unison, in turn becoming the rhythmic accompaniment to a very dramatic theme, first announced, also in unison this time, by the viola and cello. The entire movement is concerned with the deployment of the original bass line, the initial (unisonal) subject, its later emergence into a supportive figure, and combinations of these three. The unison subject appears on top and bottom until finally the three items are combined—accompaniment, bass line, and dramatic theme in compression. One might think that the final product would be mere mechanics. In the hands of Honegger, ultradramatic music results.

- **Trois contrepoints (Three Counterpoints) for Piccolo, Oboe (alternating English horn), Violin, and Cello (1922)**

Honegger dedicated one each of the three movements of this work to Maurice Jaubert, Jacques Brillouin, and Marcel Delannoy, all not only close friends but composers. Since composers were involved, was he in reality attempting to illustrate, by example, the true art of modern counterpoint? But let it be understood that these three pieces are not dry, polyphonic exercises. Most definitely they are concert etudes—chamber music in the contrapuntal forms of prelude, chorale, and canon. These are carefully arranged so that the medium changes, thus combining cleverly a duet, trio, and quartet in a single work, by the use of a different instrumentation for each *contrepoint*.

The first is a Prélude à 2 voix (Prelude for Two Voices), scored for oboe and cello. The movement is vigorous, and one should listen for invertible counterpoint and inversion as well. The second piece is a Choral à 3 voix (Chorale for Three Voices), in which the somber English horn is joined with the two string instruments. The wind instrument always intones the chorale in its four separate recitations, while the violin ornaments above and the cello plays a constantly conjunct-moving bass line—music that again finds Honegger en rapport with Bach.

In the last movement the full instrumentation is used for the Canon sur basse obstinée à 4 voix (Canon with Ostinato Bass for Four Voices). A three-part commentary (the first subject in canon form returns at the end) gives convincing balance to the design. Additionally, and of importance, however, are the canonic imitations in strict style, played, always at the octave, by the piccolo, violin and English horn; the order of entrance moves upward from the lowest voice or directly downward from the highest-pitched instrument. The cello matches its ostinato with the overall form; parts one and three are the same. The speed of the movement makes the interlocutions quite exciting.

Honma, Masao (1930–)

QUARTET

- **Poly Ostinato for String Quartet**

In both movements there are considerable ostinatos; most are short-lived, but are reborn in different guises. Above all, Honma does not spare the polyphonic positivity of his conception: a composite of linear activity, packing within it polyrhythmic settings, (though the basic meter is unitary) and polytonality.

Varying levels of vibrato are a special color within the work, ranging from none whatsoever to rapid and intense. One example is the opening E-natural for the first violin that begins the second movement. This pitch is repeated four times for a total of twelve beats. Within this total there is to be no vibrato at first, then a small amount, and as the pitch moves from its *piano* range to a *mezzoforte* the normal vibrato is applied and then advances further into a "molto" (intense) quality.

Though thick in content, Honma's work is an adjusted statement, its inflections primed for dissonance in regard to all elements, including the intermarriage of disparate tonalities, pulse arrangements, and colorations. The chordal clusters (one of eight pitches played arco, the other of four hard-driven pizzicatos in *fortissimo*) that conclude the quartet is a proper signature.

Hook, James (1746–1827)

TRIO

- **Sonata in G Major for Three Flutes, Op. 83, No. 4**

A choice example from the enormous output of this prolific English organist and composer. Op. 83 represents a set of a half-dozen sonatas for flute trio, published in 1797.

Traditional forms are used for the three movements, but are not four-square in anyway. There are three successive themes presented in the initial Allegretto. But the recapitulation in this sonata plan attends only to the third theme. Some cogent syncopation is a bonus.

The Andante is measured exactly (four times sixteen measures). But while this provides a precisely ruled ternary design, there are neat inclusions of interest: imitation and dynamic contrast in part A, contrastive rhythmic units and a bit of antiphony in part B. A small rondo form is used for the finale (Allegro vivace). The textural differences in the middle section of this movement prove further that no part of this work is without coloristic detail.

Hopkins, Antony (1921–)

DUOS

- **Fantasy for Clarinet and Piano**

Aside from two interludes in slow tempo Hopkins's piece is in the allegro orbit. A good sense of integration, brought by specific intervallic conditions, refreshes the music. The ini-

tial theme begins with the rise of a seventh, its antithesis also starts with a seventh but moving downward. As the development of these ideas goes forward similar wide spans occur at strategic places: a fifth upward, octave ascents, a seventh drop, and so on. Confirmation occurs in the recapitulation of the opening, which begins with an ascending seventh. This portion concludes the piece as it progresses within a decreasing dynamic plane.

- **Suite for Soprano Recorder and Piano (1953)**

Four short movements covering a five-minute span in performance. The second is a reminder of Benjamin Britten's *Peter Grimes* (one of the interludes). The comparison is not meant to be odious. Gaiety and spirit are here.

Hori, Etsuko (1943–)

TRIO

- *Two Movements* **for Three Flutes (Flute 2 alternates Piccolo, Flute 3 alternates Alto Flute)**

Precise structural strength in the first of the pair of movements. The outer sections are balanced by related slow-tempo material. Within these outer sections there is a ternary division, again with matched outer parts, both in moderato tempo. The central part of this ternary division is slow-paced. Hori further demarcates the quintuple total of the encased forms by using the alto flute as the third voice in sections one and five. Otherwise three flutes are concerned. (The final part is further marked by an introductory double-tongued-then-flutter-tongued cadenza by the first flute.)

Structural partitioning is also used in the second movement, where there are two tripartite sections in succession. The first is headed by a septuple-metered Scherzando theme, the second is marked by a motivally sprung peripatetic Presto. The first part of the Scherzando section then returns to complete the movement. Imitation technique plays a major part in this second movement in clarifying the chromatic imbrications that totally style Hori's trio.

(The published score has a serious tempo error at the beginning of the second movement. It reads: Adagio assai. . . .This should read: Allegro assai. . . .)

Horký, Karel (1909–)

DUO

■ **Sonatina for Clarinet and Piano (1965)**

The textures remind one of the scholarly work of the late-19th-century German composers. The harmonic language moves (emphatically so in the first part of the Sonatina), close to panchromatic style. These jointly make a basically conservative 20th-century piece of music.

The only exception to formal difference is the placement of an Andantino of fair length in the middle of the final, fast movement. All in all, Horký's Sonatina has fluency if not individuality.

Horneman, Christian Frederik Emil (1840–1906)

QUARTET

■ **String Quartet No. 1 in G Minor**

Horneman's work was composed between 1857 and 1860 and was edited and revised from the manuscript for publication by Paulus Bache. Edition Dania issued the score in 1945. (On the cover and title page, as well as in the editor's note, the name is misspelled as "Hornemann.")

Full classical identity. It is not academic—thus, movement two has a short Andante in the outer sections and a variationally developed Moderato in between. It is not timid—thus, there is full let-go in the Finale. A sonata-scaled Allegro vivace opens the quartet; a Scherzo controls the third movement.

Horovitz, Joseph (1926–)

DUOS

■ *Adam-Blues* **for Trombone and Piano**

The picturesque title is explained by the commission Horovitz received from *ADAM,* an International Literary Review. The music was for a celebration concert. (It was given in London on October 17, 1968.) To tie-in the concept Horovitz's music is based on a pitch succession of A–D–A–Mi (the last being the French and Italian pitch names for E).

Slow blues tempo, applied to consistent legato phrases, and depicted by use of a ternary structure. A sensitive occasional piece of music.

■ **Sonata for Cello and Piano, Op. 14**

Organized with discrimination and in a manner that reshuffles classic order. There is always a sense of *durchführung* (through-leading) in the first movement. In the Scherzo there is no relaxing Trio. This connects with the Finale, which begins with a pithy quote from the opening of the Sonata and then passes through a series of rhapsodic changes.

Horovitz's duo is to be placed in the neoclassic category. The harmonies are always subtle, colorful, and always fresh sounding. A finely styled opus.

■ **Sonatina for Oboe and Piano, Op. 3**

Music ignited by neoclassic activity, especially confirmed by the cleanliness and white-black quality of the writing for the instruments in combination. The textures are light and the total makes fitting the dedication to Nadia Boulanger, one of Horovitz's teachers.

There is a motivally engendered opening Allegro movement. The thematic material in the central movement (Interludium) is also organized from motival enlargement. A prancing, snapped rhythmic Vivo music serves as the finale.

■ *Two Majorcan Pieces* **for Clarinet and Piano**

Re-creative documentation of the folk music of Majorca. Horovitz presents a folkloristic essence; there is no direct quotation of Majorcan music, which he described as "Spanish with a difference." The duos are each named after a town in Majorca. "Paquera" oozes with calid curves; "Valdemosa" has a blood-warm beat. Horovitz avoids all effects and cleverness in his splendidly registered conceptions.

QUARTETS

■ *Brass Polka* **for Brass Quartet (Trumpet, Horn, Trombone, and Tuba)**

The Bohemian dance form set forth on the fast side. And in its middle section set forth with some zippy rhythms. Unmistakable color power here.

■ *Jazz Suite* **for Two Flutes and Two Clarinets**

A fully syncopative package of three items. Tonally styled, with march-pace swing in the Scherzando; slow-pushed legato phrases in the Blues; and rhythmic-bite detail in the "Owlglass Rag." Clear presentations. Scoring sonorousness is at its best here.

■ **Quartet for Oboe and Strings (Violin, Viola, and Cello), Op. 18**

Horovitz has no compulsion to bypass traditional format in his Op. 18. The tempo sequence is: Vivo, Larghetto, and Molto allegro. There is authentic balance between the oboe and the string trio without nullifying the fact that the oboe is a rich, singing quality. The wind instrument is given plenty of opportunity in the central movement—a music of full-blown lyrical disposition with chromatic fellowship.

Rhythmic authority and clarity mark the outer movements; the opening one running on rondolike rails, the other slightly heavier in content but always energetic.

■ **String Quartet No. 4, Op. 16**

In addition to the fundamental balance derived from adherence to tonality, Horovitz's three-movement structure achieves a tight cohesion by surrounding a vigorous movement with two slow movements, the second of the pair twice as slow in speed. (A further confirmation is obtained by the pitch points of the conclusions, in turn: C minor, A minor, and C. Still further, each movement ends in dynamic strengths of either double or triple *piano*.)

Quasi fugal proportions in the first movement, variational aspects in the other slow movement. The middle movement follows sonata form, but is never academically confined. Especially appealing is a consistent, unfailing concern for textural clarity.

■ **String Quartet No. 5 (1969)**

Horovitz indicates that "the emotional content" of his quartet was "deeply influenced" by his Viennese origin. (Born in Vienna in 1926, he was taken to England after the Anschluss in 1938.) The music shows that when Horovitz went home again his reaction was of a bittersweet nature. It is noted below.

"In this one-movement quartet the opening thematic material is deliberately based on the decadent chromatic gestures prevalent in early twentieth-century Viennese music. Healthier diatonic discords tear into these themes during a long development section, and, in a way, finally cleanse them. The melodies of the first section (statements) are entirely based on the intervals of the Third and Sixth, but with garish appendages of extra chromaticism (produced by means of bitonality between the upper and lower instruments). After the conflict these intervals emerge in their true and elemental role as essential pillars of a major key (E). For me there is a link between the survival of humanity and the constant affirmation of the tonal system."

QUINTETS

- *Folk Song Fantasy* for Brass Quintet (Two Trumpets, Horn, and Two Trombones)

Neat tonal item, compact and harmonically sure and certain. There are subtly contrasted episodes, juxtaposed without any feeling of incongruity. No special effects but fine textural balances.

- *Music Hall Suite* for Brass Quintet (Two Trumpets, Horn, Trombone, and Tuba) (1964)

Scintillating subjects given the proper pops touch, reminding one of Morton Gould in his younger days. Most colorful: the rhythmic play in "Trick-Cyclists" and the very effective brass-sound translation of "Soft-Shoe-Shuffle." "Les Girls" concludes the work in the form of a modernized Offenbachian galop. (The other

movements are "Soubrette Song" and "Adagio-Team." In the latter, the scoring is for a quartet, with the second trumpet tacet.)

Horusitzky, Zoltán (1903–)

TRIO

- **Cassazione for Two Trumpets and Trombone**

Total artistic Hungarian nationalism. Triple-pulsed swing in movement one, with some imitative voicing. Duple-pulsed aliveness in movement three—a dance that has velocity tempo, is texturally contrastive, and contains strategic measures of total silence. Movement two is an "Intermezzo bizzaro." Nothing especially eccentric, regardless of title, unless linear figures that move mainly in fourth spans and eight consecutive trombone glissandos are so considered.

QUARTETS

- **String Quartet No. 3**

Indigenous content surrounds this Hungarian composer's work. The folk resource is the prime element in the working materials, most often sprung from a motival unit.

In the first movement weights are heaviest (pitch lengths) off the beat. In movement two the method is reversed. Movements three and four return to the use of short–long rhythmic elements. The former movement is set forth in a large A–B–A–B formation, the latter indulges in a mild amount of polyphonic writing.

- **String Quartet No. 4**

As usual with this composer motival details solidify the structuring of the greater part of the work, in this case the opening and closing movements. A fanfarric idea is the generating item for the former, a sharp rhythmic unit is firmly developed in the other movement.

Especially noticeable is the Hungarian color of the music. In the central part of the quartet recitative substances for a single instrument mark the first and fifth sections, two-, three-, and four-part voicing define the declarative chantlike writing of the third section. In sections two and four there are chorale statements. Both are extremely soft dynamically and are heard without vibrato.

Horvath, Josef Maria (1931–)

QUARTET

- *Redundanz 2 (Redundance 2)* **for String Quartet**

(This is one of three works using the same title for wind octet *[see below]* and string quartet compositions written between 1966 and 1968. *Redundanz 2* achieved double honors. It was awarded first prize at the Composers Competition of the Austrian Youth and Music in 1967 and in the same year won first prize at the Composers Competition of the Fédération Internationale des Jeunesses Musicales on the occasion of the Twenty-first World Congress at Montreal.)

The quartet is immersed in blazing colors and effects. There are no themes in this music of explosive explorations, simply sets of timbral representations that cover a span of close to thirteen minutes. The opening moves immediately into this special world of sound with nine measures of muted, ponticello-bowed fractured pitches, each kicked off with a grace note. And onward later in related manner: nineteen measures of polyphonic harmonics; fingered (two-pitch) tremolo with intervals narrowing à la glissando, tutti tremolandos contrapuntalized so that the voices combine in totals of 4–5–6–

7, tutti distribution in polyphonic ostinato, and massive multiple glissandos traveling in all directions for twenty-five measures. The score is chock-full of special noises such as playing on the bridge and behind it, and a grinding, grating, scrunchy sound obtained by pressing the bow on all four strings.

Importantly, these sonic substances are never used as isolates, accompanimental or the like, but appear in total quartet application. The thesaurus of techniques is good to the last sound in the last measure. There, in soft dynamic, the upper three instruments polyphonically play a one-beat sweep combining col legno and sul ponticello.

OCTET

- *Redundanz 1 (Redundance 1)* **for Wind Octet (Oboe, English horn [alternating Oboe 2], Clarinet in E-flat [alternating Clarinet in B-flat], Bass Clarinet [alternating Clarinet 2], Two Horns, Two Bassoons [Bassoon 2 alternating Double Bassoon]) (1966)**

Athematic materials that are disposed in sectional form, quite often merged in polyrhythmic apportionment. Though mostly in moderate tempo there is, through the dispersion and fracturing of units, constant vigor and vitality to the octet. It has a charge as it vehemently and passionately goes its eight-minute way.

Horvath demands virtuosity on the part of the players, including flutter-tongued sound projections. Past the midway mark the oboes and small (E-flat) clarinet imitate the sound of a glass harmonica with the playing of harmonic-timbred pitches. In two places there are sprays of thirty-second notes, with each of the eight pitches in each beat assigned another instrument. This whirlwind of kaleidoscopic change is of hideous difficulty and almost impossible to achieve, even at a tempo of

♩ = 76. Horvath understands, of course, and he requests the performers to do their best. Even a partial achievement of these sections (thirteen measures in one place and much later seven more measures) would have to be considered phenomenal.

Hotteterre, Jacques (c. 1684–1762)

DUOS

- *First Suite of Pieces* for Two Treble Instruments without Basso Continuo (for Two Recorders or Two Flutes or Two Oboes or Two Violins), Op. 4

(The original title reads: *Premiere suite de pièces à deux dessus sans Basso continuo.* The key word here is *dessus*, which is an old term meaning treble. Thus, *dessus de viole* signifies a treble viol.)

Beautifully melodically tied music, with some imitations that add spice to the tuneful lines. Not the greatest example of French baroque music but certainly skillful representations. These begin with a two-part Duo, opening in slow pace and linked to music moving in fast speed. Part two is an Allemande, followed by two Rondeau movements in contrasted tempos, and a Gigue. The concluding movement, a Passacaille (Passacaglia), is the most dynamic.

- Sonata in C Major for Soprano Recorder (or Alto Recorder or Violin) and Piano

A five-movement work (the edition translates and combines the continuo into the single modern keyboard instrument, though one can substitute a harpsichord without criticism). As usual with Hotteterre, the work opens with a Prélude. This one is of breadth in its phrases. The Allemande in second place is the opposite in tempo terms. A Courante follows. The penultimate movement is an A-minor Grave. It is strictly chordal in every one of its triple beats per measure. A Gigue wraps up matters.

- Suite in C Minor for Flute and Continuo

The usual dance presentations with a prefatory movement. Following the Prélude there are an Allemande, a Sarabande, an extremely short Gavotte (about a half minute in length), and a Rondeau.

Typical music that exemplifies Hotteterre's fine craft. Throughout, the materials are especially marked by strong bass lines. These take on, thereby, an importance that one finds in the music of Bach and Handel.

- Suite in D for Flute (or Oboe or Violin) and Basso Continuo, Op. 2, No. 1

The alternate instrumentation is not the idea of the editor of the modern edition (David Lasocki), published by Nova Music, London (1979). Hotteterre wrote that "Although these pieces are composed for the flute, they could nevertheless be suitable for all the instruments that play the soprano part, such as the recorder, the oboe, the violin, the treble viol, etc."

The binary-designed Prélude (lentement and bright in tempo, with a short, second lentement of four measures inserted before a repeat of the bright section) is followed by a series of dances, each with a characteristically quaint and colorful title. (Such titles, one is reminded, give flavor but do not change the formal meanings.) Accordingly: a graceful Allemande—"La Royalle," a gay Rondeau—"Le Duc d'Orléans," a dignified Sarabande—"La d'Armagnac," a moderately duple-pulsed Gavotte—"La Meudon," a large double Menuet—"Le Comte de Brione," and a concluding Gigue—"La Folichon."

- **Suite in D for Flute and Continuo**

A composition exhibiting the typical light and charming style of this French composer, sometimes indicated with the surname "le Romain," doubtless due to his long sojourns in Rome.

Typical music of the very early part of the 18th century (the music dates from 1708), with a Prélude followed by four dance movements: Allemande, Courante, Sarabande, and Gigue. Unpretentious but exceedingly pleasing music.

- **Suite in E Minor for Flute (or Oboe or Violin) and Basso Continuo**

(In regard to the possibility of substitution of the homophonic instrument *see above*: Suite in D, Op. 2, No. 1.)

This is another example of the dance-form variety that marks this composer's output. (For the flute, Hotteterre published in his lifetime two volumes containing a total of nine suites. This E-minor suite is the fourth of the set of nine.) As was his habit, Hotteterre begins with a Prélude and follows with six fancifully designated movements, five of which are dances. The sequence is Allemande—"La Fontainebleau," Sarabande—"Le Départ," Air—"Le Fleuri," Gavotte—"La Mitilde," Branle de Village—"L'Auteuil," and a concluding Menuet—"Le Beaulieu." The last is actually two minuets, with each section of the pair repeated, followed by a repetition of the entire first minuet, minus repeats of its sections.

Hovhaness, Alan (1911–)

Hovhaness has a unique status among American composers, past and present. No other composer has identified himself so fully with Eastern music, especially that of Armenia (homeland of the composer's ancestors). Along with this, his music has an interlineation of medieval plus pre-Christian mannerisms. His picturesque ideas call for odd combinations and severely drawn forms. Modalism and Gregorianism are often present in his music; a tremendous number of reiterated figures and cross-rhythms are also used in setting forth his esoteric Eastern materials.

To some, all this translates as spiritual music and receives affirmative response, with others a bit of Hovhaness goes a very long way. His music is of such quality that it often makes heavy the concert-hall atmosphere, titillating and stimulating but somewhat enervating the listener. Hearing it is rather like visiting a Chinese theater, eating an egg buried for a hundred years, or making a trip through a strange house where words are uttered in a tongue one has dimly heard and yet not really heard at all. (Music is not always so international a language as one thinks.)

Nonetheless, Hovhaness's music shows the mark of a craftsman—one need not know the history of Coptic music or the Syrian modes to realize this. This knowledge and the ability to convey it are his chief strengths, whether one accepts or rejects his unusual music.

There is another matter to realize in Hovhaness's work. He renounced all the music he had written prior to 1940 (over a thousand compositions!) and presumably destroyed all of it. However, a small amount had been published and, of course, Hovhaness has been unable to control the use of such materials. Sibelius was a strong influence in this early period of work (Hovhaness dedicated both his initial piano trio and initial string quartet to the Finnish master). And polyphony was stressed.

(Of the compositions discussed below, the duets for wind instruments (Opp. 13 and 21), the Op. 3 Trio, and the Op. 8 String Quartet date from this pre-1940 period.)

DUOS

- **Duet for Violin and Harpsichord, Op. 122**

Hovhaness can boast of a prolific production—over the four-hundred mark as far as opus numbers are concerned—fifty-six symphonies at the time this is being written. Parallel with this is an astounding speed of execution. This duo is a case in point. It was commissioned on May 16, 1954, composed the next day, and two weeks later given its first hearing in Frankfurt, Germany.

Three short movements: a lightly tone-clustered Prelude, a three-measure (metered 5/2, 7/2, 5/2) "Haiku," and a majestic Aria. Lots of sustained violin harmonic sounds in the first movement, minute color crusts for the string instrument in the second movement, and static rhythm (persistent three chords per measure) for the piano in the last movement.

- **Fantasy for Double Bass (or Cello) and Piano, Op. 277, No. 2**

Sectional disposition. Hovhaness defines his instrumental characters without mixing them. The piano chordalizes and projects sweeping rhythmic patterns, repeated at length (repetition is a Hovhanessian habit). The string instrument is a lyrical voice and occasionally contrasts this with plucked timbre.

There is a relationship between several of the sections, but it is one of general outline, not one of development of the material.

- **The Garden of Adonis: Suite for Flute and Harp (or Piano), Op. 245**

The title is based on a canto from *The Faerie Queene* by Edmund Spenser (1552?–1599) that describes a garden of rebirth or reincarnation where souls appear as flowers.

And plenty of rhythmic flowers appear in most of the seven movements, principally by way of harp (or piano) swirls set within the melodic simplicity of the flute. Movement three, marked "like a solemn dance," has a pulse movement that prods the adagio tempo into hinting at a faster pace. It is completed, as is the following movement, with unaccompanied flute, and is represented by Hovhaness's favorite unmetered passage work *(senza misura)*.

- **Kirgiz Suite No. 1 (Composed on Three Kirgiz Motives) for Violin and Piano, Op. 73**

A work of inexhaustible patterns. Consider the Variations, which consist of a statement and two recastings based on a C-major scale plus F-sharp. This is maintained until the last section, when the piano shifts among three pitches: C-sharp–F–F-sharp. No bar lines are employed; the music walks within itself, free of the tyranny of metrical measurement. Color is twined into the restricted tonal basis. The violin never sounds the G pitch. When it plays the A pitch it is always approached by a leap of two octaves from a low B sound and is always heard as a natural harmonic. Ostinatos highlight the piano part. One consists of a three-note figure repeated forty-five times; another pattern is repeated twenty-five times.

Movement two is titled "A Kirgiz Tala *(4 + 4 + 3 + 4)*." (A tala is a rhythmic cycle in Indian music.) Here it is set in bare harmonic intervals while the violin chants. The same constant intervallic base supports the short, final, fast Dance.

Of such are Hovhaness's technical ecstasies. His music requires a listener's willingness to meet it on its very pertinent Eastern terms.

- **Prelude and Fugue for Oboe and Bassoon, Op. 13**

Exoticism marks both of the pieces (an early production, composed in 1937). In the Prelude the bassoon functions as a drone, sounding expanded fifths while the nasal wind instrument colorfully covers a two-octave scope with plentiful sounds pertaining to augmented intervals.

Timbre differences are made most emphatic in the Fugue by the spacing methods used. The final measures are quite individual with the oboe serving as the bass to the bassoon's cold soprano voice.

- *Shatakh* for Violin and Piano, Op. 73, No. 1

Unique music. *Shatakh* is the purest and truest duo possible for violin and piano. (The writer knows of no other in existence exactly like it.) The piano is heard in unitary voice throughout, playing repeated pitches or single, double, or triple grace notes leading to a sustained sound. There are no chords whatsoever. The notation for the piano in the second of the pair of movements employs two staves, but this still concerns but one sound at a time; the performer merely is asked to use two hands to make the single line more fluid. Hence, one violin line (also totally concerned with single pitches) and one individual piano-timbred line equal a duet of the strictest mathematical total. Unique music, indeed!

An Adagio in 4/4 time occupies the first movement. Melismas and tonal curves revolving around themselves are the principal features. Only a few accidentals intervene. Simultaneously, the piano ripples sixteenth-note figurations sounding like a Balinese or Javanese gamelan, or, for that matter, like a gambang (Japanese xylophone). When the violin moves to an extremely high tessitura the rhythm in the piano becomes more excited with groups of eight, nine, ten, and eleven intersticing the sets of four sixteenths each. A return is made to the opening section but it is then freely embroidered.

Movement two is in direct antithesis as to speed, meter, and content. The section is a Presto, with a pattern of three measures of 2/4 followed by one of 3/4. Not the slightest deviation is made from this mechanistic metrical cultivation. The music hugs itself. It takes considerable time before it moves out of a B to G boundary, with most of the action within that span in the area of D to G. It finally breaks away and ascends. But when it arrives at the upper gamut it settles in just as statically as it did in the lower level.

- Sonata for Trumpet and Organ, Op. 200

A triple hymn without words, with chant-contoured trumpet lines absent of marked rhythm. Hovhaness is in his usual evangelical manner writing music "which might be sung among high mountain peaks." The brass instrument "becomes the voice of the cantor, the messenger of God, who sings blessings and hope to the people."

Moving tertial chords and static cluster chords in the organ support the conjunct curls of the trumpet in movement one. It is barless and its *senza misura* codification covers most of the second and third movements. Pyramidic chord constructions are used for the organ in the second movement, constructed downward rather than in the usual upward manner. Cluster-harmony color commands the third movement.

- Sonata for Two Bassoons (or Cello and Bassoon), Op. 266

Mostly a quite serious affair, and not due only to the use of two bass-register instruments. There is no linear light levity and there are no bucking-bronco rhythms. The opening is a Fuga, its tempo marked "Solemn," the closing is a Largo, its conjunct-moving line occasionally including a mordent-type kick. The central part of the opus is where the fast music is and where phrase repetition prevails. The insertion in this movement of parallel-fifth progressions adds a bit of color change when it occurs.

- **Sonata for Two Clarinets, Op. 297**

A rather odd total structure, with an andante-paced movement titled "Malinconia" followed by two Fuga movements. There is a slight difference between the fugues, though both are in the fast tempo zone—the second of the pair has a decided gigue stance. Nonetheless, there is less formal comparison within the entire work since the first movement has a fugal and completely polyphonic décor.

- **Suite for English horn and Bassoon, Op. 21**

Hovhaness wrote this duo in 1937 for a very rare instrumental partnership. The opus opens with a fugue. However, its subject is of such length that it tends to lose its identity in part when the second voice enters and the music moves along. No counterpoint is to be heard in the second movement, but it takes on an important role in the final part of the work.

- **Suite for Oboe and Bassoon, Op. 23**

Music of specific detail in each of the ten movements, rather than music developed formally. This confirms Hovhanessian style.

Movements two, four, and five are Canzonas, each based on a mode: A, F, and C, in turn. Long phrases define the first and third parts of the duo, each without specific meter. A pair of Dances (movements six and ten), two more pieces based on modes (D and E), both titled Fantasy (movements seven and eight), and an Adagio (movement nine) complete the Suite.

- **Three Visions of Saint Mesrob for Violin and Piano, Op. 198**

Coloristic evocations. Exactly calculated but giving the opposite impression. It is as though the sounds are of improvisational conduct, and, liking what has been produced, the players therefore keep repeating the same idea.

"Celestial Mountain" and "Celestial Alphabet" (the outer movements) surround the violin with light, piano-formed bell sonancy alternating with softly stated clusters in the former piece and chromatic chord progressions in the latter one. The violin's curved lines in both cases are limited to a seven-pitch basis. The middle "vision" is termed "Celestial Bird." The songster is simulated with diatonic voice (save for one C-sharp and a pair of B-flats). The violin is metered in quintuple time, the piano is free of bar-line definition and plays rapidly "without rhythm." It is totally diatonic and represents the "twittering of celestial birds."

TRIOS

- **Firdausi for Clarinet, Harp, and Percussion (Indian Tambura, Two Laotian Drum-Gongs, Javanese or Balinese large, deep Gongs, Two Tablas, Two Darbukkas, Two Dumbeks, Two Mrdungans, Two Moroccan Drums, Two Chinese Drums, and Timpani), Op. 252**

Firdausi was a 10th-century Persian poet. Hovhaness delineates him as a "magical singer" who describes mystical and magical events. There are eighteen of these, beginning with an "Invocation," concluding with a "Love Song." In between there are four dances, three sections concerned with an avatar, etc. These short movements Hovhaness indicates as suggesting "verses and parables, festivals, processions of heros and animals, mysterious and strange combats and demons." The textures are fragile, the sounds mostly on the sweet side, the percussion restrained. Nonviolence rules.

Hovhaness's complete unpretentiousness makes his piece almost forceful in effect, despite the restricted and exceedingly rarefied instrumentation. In regard to this music of gentle-pulsed continuity it is important to understand that the percussion instruments detailed are not actually mandatory. Hovhaness states the percussion "may be freely chosen" from this list, or the choice can be made "from instruments of similar nature, or from invented instruments having mysterious sounds of evocative, poetic beauty."

- **Sonata for Two Oboes and Organ, Op. 130**

Two measures of parallel-fifth chords, otherwise only chordal fillers for the organ. The keyboard instrument is supremely subsidiary in this three-movement opus. Imitation, canonic details, and give and take between the wind instruments fill the measures as do long-drawn melismatic passages with their elaborative chanting detail. All very exotic and all very similar throughout the ten-minute span of the composition.

- **Suite for Violin, Piano, and Percussion (Celesta, Giant Tam-tam, and Xylophone), Op. 99**

Repetitive oscillatory patterns plus the effect of unending improvisation on and around the same sound-course typify this Eastern music in Western instrumental translation (save for the microtoned violin, which occasionally plays sixth tones).

The six movements of Hovhaness's Suite (Prelude, Pastoral, Allegro, Pastoral, Canon, and Allegro) contain many other devices: improvisatory and meterless designs, plus rhythmic patterns that range in cycles from as few as six beats to as many as fifty-nine. Color is paramount; the pianist simulates a gong by striking the bass strings inside the piano with a timpani stick, and in the fifth movement (Canon)

an effective sonorous impact is made by utilizing tritonality.

There is an oft-used instruction in the score which, at first glance, makes no sense; however, its meaning is disclosed upon hearing the music. This "hold pedal *forever*" (my italics) indication to the pianist does much to explain the static quality of Hovhaness's music and the effect it gives—the non-changing retracing of carbon-copied sounds, even though of original construction. (This writer does not pretend to understand the meaning the composer gives for this Suite: ". . . ancient religious concept of form in three arcs: supplication, revelation, and ascension into praise.")

- **Trio for Violin, Viola, and Cello, Op. 201**

In a considerable number of his compositions Hovhaness favors rhythmless murmuring. This consists of varied free figures. They are heard in part two (Allegro) from beginning to end, played pizzicato by the viola and cello. After some fifteen seconds the violin enters playing a modal melody and concludes some fifteen seconds before the murmuring ends. In part three (Lento) one of the three sections is again devoted to this murmuring sound, polyphonically figured so that a true blur results.

The opening Adagio is tricolored with pizzicato figures in the violin, arpeggiated pizzicato chords in the cello, and a melodic line for the viola. This returns in shortened form after a freely phrased (*senza misura*) section.

- **Trio I for Violin, Cello, and Piano, Op. 3**

The published score of this work lists the composer as Alan Scott Hovaness. This name was used for a number of Hovhaness's early compositions. Scott was his mother's maiden name; the single "h" in the surname is merely an altered spelling. The Op. 8 String Quartet No. 1 (*see below*) was also published with this self-styled designation.

The penetrating force of imitation is in charge of the development of the opening E-minor theme. The related technique of canon rules the slow movement. There, after the proclamatory opening, a double canon in the piano is banked against the strings. Another canon is used in the coda—single style this time.

The Fuga of the last movement is a jolly one. Some polyphonic magic is practiced in this instance, namely combining augmentation and diminution and making it work successfully. The usual stretto is included in the movement.

QUARTETS

- **Divertimento for Four Wind Instruments (Oboe, Clarinet, Horn, and Bassoon or Three Clarinets and Bass Clarinet), Op. 61, No. 5**

A good amount of polyphony in the seven movements. Clearly articulated imitation is in the Fantasy (movement two), Canzona (movement three), and another Canzona (movement four). Full-proportioned counterpoint rules in the fifth movement, Canon in Four Keys, and in the seventh movement, Fugue (Finale).

No special modes or colors here. This is somewhat a rarity in Hovhaness's vast catalogue. Neat homophonic statements replace the exotic manner in the Prelude (movement one) and in the Aria (movement six).

- *The Flowering Peach* **for Alto Saxophone (alternating Clarinet), Percussion (Vibraphone, Glockenspiel, Celesta [or Vibraphone], Tam-tam, and Timpani), and Harp (or Piano), Op. 125**

(Two percussionists are required.)

A seven-part suite representing music written for a play about Noah and the Ark by Clifford Odets. Some of the music is a complete movement used with the actual stage production. Other parts were expanded from the specifically timed sections which served within the play. Part six, "Sun and Moon," with the vibraphone written in *jhala* technique (melody interwoven with repetitive pitches—here all on G), was originally composed for the play but was deleted before the play opened on Broadway in December 1954.

The Overture sets the mood. Part two is divided between "Lifting of Voices" and "Building the Ark." The former accompanied a scene in which the Ark is being prepared, the latter is a "hammering" section which represented the building of the Ark itself. Part three, Intermezzo, suggests the lullaby of the Ark, with later a background of rainlike sounds (simulated by the glockenspiel).

"Rain," part four, served as an interlude within the play. The descriptive instrumentation of harp, glockenspiel, and timpani includes the *jhala* technique mentioned above. "Love Song" represents the love of Noah's son Japheth for Rachel, who later became his wife. Hovhaness describes the "Sun and Moon" movement as summing up "the atmosphere on the Ark when the two celestial bodies reappear after having been blotted out for forty days and forty nights." The final "Rainbow Hymn" first accompanied the death of Esther, Noah's wife, within the play. The chorale that follows is a hymn to the "beneficent rainbow of God."

- *Koke No Niwa (Moss Garden)* **for English horn, Harp, and Percussion (Timpani, Tam-tam, Glockenspiel, and Marimba), Op. 181**

Hovhaness's quartet (two percussionists are required) is the result of a commission by a Tokyo television station to create a musical tribute to the Moss Temple in Kyoto, called Koke Dera. The title of the work was predefined for Hovhaness as *Koke No Niwa*, which means moss garden.

Hovhaness's exoticism is made to order for this type of subject, including the almost rhythmically static statements by the English horn and slight punctuations by the four percussion timbres.

- **Quartet No. 1 for Flute, Oboe, Cello, and Harpsichord, Op. 97**

Though only the initial movement is titled Ostinato, all three divisions display this repetitive device for the keyboard instrument. The string and wind voices express the melodic force, confined within small areas, as Hovhaness likes to do. There is a skillful play of textural weights: solo, duet, and tutti combinations are utilized. In this reference, Hovhaness uses the raga (the Hindu scalic pattern bound in with certain regulations as to use) to explain his opus: "The path of a central raga is like a sun with planetary ragas or belts of meteorites of free sounds circling around the powerful center. The first movement circles around the oboe; the second movement circles around the flute; after a duet for flute and oboe the third movement circles around the cello and oboe." This précis should be applied to the actual textural content. Tutti weight is employed in the first movement. Movement two begins with the harpsichord alone and then becomes a duet with the addition of the flute. The finale starts as a duet for the flute and oboe and eventually becomes a tutti.

There is a fascinating condition to the structuring of the music. Each movement ends as if it is incomplete. In regard to this abruptness Hovhaness's keen sense of arrested motion is fully beguiling.

(The use of "number one" in the title is deceiving. Hovhaness has not written another work for this combination. The number is used to differentiate this quartet from another one *[see below]* that, save for replacing the harpsichord with a piano, is scored for the same instruments.)

- **Quartet No. 2 for Flute, Oboe, Cello, and Piano, Op. 112**

Coherence is obtained by the divertissement aspect of this opus. Usually one expects four movements, or at least three, in a "quartet." Hovhaness's use of the word applies strictly to the number of players participating. From the formal viewpoint the many movements are akin to musical aphorisms. They contain sensitive use of color, though the complete work tends to length (fourteen minutes). At least one or two of the sections have a sardonic, humor-fed cast.

(As with Quartet No. 1, *see above*, there is no other Hovhaness work for this medium. The number was used to make certain it is not confused with the other quartet calling for exactly the same wind and string instruments but another type of keyboard instrument.)

- **String Quartet No. 1, Op. 8**

Hovhaness apportions his quartet in precisely balanced equations of tempo and style—two andantes (both explained by the dark moods of *mesto* and *lamentando*) are spliced by a pair of fugues. Contrapuntal methods also seep into the slow movements, and further, the fugal divisions are of different type. In one swoop, the listener is offered compactness, stylistic affinity, and variety.

The Prelude features the viola in solo highlighting at the start. It is followed by a canon between the violins, and is completed by a return to the principal theme. Movement two is titled with the directional marker: Fugue with 4 Subjects. This is not simply an example of contrapuntal jugglery; the result has true musical zest. Oddly (but certainly a balanced procedure) the first pair of subjects are initially stated by the first violin, the last pair by the cello. In comparison, the other fugue (final movement) is rather unassuming. It is preceded by music of dramatic outline.

- *Upon Enchanted Ground* for Flute,
   Cello, Giant Tam-tam, and Harp,
   Op. 90, No. 1

The music, though of fairly enchanting character, makes no thematic gestures, avoids harmony as we know it, and diffuses its rhythms. Thus, with gentle-pulsed motility, Hovhaness defines his personal idea of Hindu music in a span of four minutes.

QUINTETS

- Piano Quintet [No. 1], Op. 9

In formal terms Hovhaness can always be relied upon to present unburdened particulars. His Op. 9 is no standard four-movement fast-slow-Scherzo-fast sequence. The movements are short and all five represent a stress on atmospheric color and a variety of instrumental conditions.

In the fourteen-measure Andante a viola melody unfolds with bits of pizzicato glissandos, col legno taps, and a short spray from the piano as accompaniment. Movement two is based on a gapped scale. Melody is again backed up with precise accompaniment (piano clusters) in movement three. The Allegro molto that follows is mainly a unison statement by the strings. The finale (Allegretto) has total delicacy. The strings are muted and there is tonal unanimity. Not once does the music deviate from pure C major and as a confirmatory seal the final chord (sustained for fourteen beats plus a fermata) is a seven-part cluster combining the total C-major pitches.

(Hovhaness completed his first piano quintet in 1927. He revised it in 1962.)

- *Sharagan and Fugue for Brass Choir*
   (Two Trumpets, Horn, and Two
   Trombones), Op. 58

The "brass choir" designation can turn away brass chamber music performers, but that's probably Hovhaness's method of indicating that multiple instrumentation can be used. Best, however, is the quintet total, which is just as official.

A baroque quality of sound is expertly set forth in this hymn (the meaning of *Sharagan*) and Fugue. Modalism is the technique, fully utilized, with hardly any Hovhanessian exotic overhang.

- *Six Dances* for Brass Quintet (Two
   Trumpets, Horn, Trombone, and
   Tuba), Op. 79

Hovhaness's faith in cantillative and Eastern exotic colors is maintained in this set of dances, scored for two trumpets, horn, trombone, and tuba. Imaginative music and imaged with the support of ostinatos.

Further support and bearing are supplied by the individual metrical conditions. The "Solenne" is set in 13/8 measures which move constantly in 4/8 + 4/8 + 5/8 division. Movement two (Allegro moderato) is quintuply metered, its beats split between 2/8 and 3/8. Movement three (Allegretto) unevenly breaks the measures into 3/4 + 3/8; in turn the 3/4 portion consists of three 2/8 units.

Movement four begins with a duet between the trombone and tuba. A spirited music, it is cast in septuple meter (7/8) with the measures divided between 4/8 and 3/8. Conjunctive substances fill the Moderato of the fifth movement with a meter of 5/8 + 4/8. In the finale (Allegro brillant) repeated pitches are of importance. This is the only movement of the six that has a straightforward pulse—the music moving in moderately paced 2/2 time.

- Wind Quintet, Op. 159

With the exception of the second of the four movements, sliding pitches are a constant quality. And again, in movements one, three, and four, *senza misura* sections contrast with defined metrical phrases.

In movement one the free statements are alternated with music of processional content. In movement three, pyramidally constructed chords have a somber effect with their progress in largo tempo and *pianissimo* dynamic. The rhythm is also quiet and static—whole-note designations; the *senza misura* here is then one of sharp activity. With its unmetered phrases, slow chordal progressions, and melodic lines the final part of the quintet is a compounding of the two previous (first and third) movements. Free of unmetrical ordering, movement two is regulated by alternating a short (always of two-measure length) dance tune with a single chord. A linked pitch from this chord gives single pedal support to the tune.

- ■ *The World Beneath the Sea No. I* for Alto Saxophone (or Clarinet), Timpani, Giant Tam-tam, Vibraphone, and Harp, Op. 133, No. 1

A type of musical world's record is set in each of the two movements of this quintet. In the first movement the harp rapidly repeats a three-pitch figure through a fermata measure and then through seventy measures of largo in 2/2 time. In movement two a three-pitch figure (of different sounds) is again rapidly repeated within a fermata, maintained through 270 individual beats in largo, and continued further into a five-beat measure with a fermata.

In both movements the saxophone chants its way. The percussion instruments reflect the harp's replications with ostinatolike detail. Apparently there is considerable passivity in the territory Hovhaness describes.

- ■ *The World Beneath the Sea No. II* for Clarinet, Timpani, Bells (or Chimes or Glockenspiel), Harp, and Double Bass, Op. 133, No. 2

The unremitting sounds of a repetitive figure by the harp in *The World Beneath the Sea No. I (see above),* is used here as well. It is only of slightly less total in this companion work—found in the opening, third, and closing (fifth) movements.

Only clarinet and harp play in the first two movements. Aside from the mysterious murmuring constancy of the harp, the melodic line is reduced in pitch change and marked by microtonal connections. The same style applies to the fourth movement. A type of slow march defines the final movement; the only fast music is in the third part of the quintet.

SEXTET

- ⬝ Sextet for Violin and Percussion (Five Players) (Timpani, Glockenspiel, Chimes, Celesta, Bass Drum, and Giant Tam-tam), Op. 108

Central to this work, as to so many others by this composer, is the element of timbre. Of course, with five percussionists this may seem to be a rather obvious statement. However, though there is represented the ordinary type of rhythmic percussive detail (movement three of the total four), otherwise there is the fresh fascinations of decrescendo by instrumental subtraction, combinations that are expressive though minus any pulse demarcation, and (in movement four) the plastic functioning of free-metered lines in triple and quadruple combination.

The shapes of the movements are independent, made from what might be termed sonic alliteration, as well as gliding, intervallically contained melodic segments. These are, of course, all in the violin; in small amount the timpani primitively parallel these with rolled glissandos.

In movement three a vibrational ostinato is set by the percussion against the violin's line. Movement four is marked Andante, celestial and bird-like. The violin commands this last movement with melismatic continuity.

Hovland, Egil (1924–)

DUOS

- *Cantus I* for Flute and Harpsichord, Op. 45

Screaming chromatic gestures do not support the title, but block harpsichord passages that are tightly dissonant but rhythmically in place do. The two colors alternate and shift about in solo statement, as quasi-ritornel, and in combined form.

Hovland's piece (timed at 5:45) starts slowly, retains that pace and concludes still slower by one-fifth. There are no meters. This goes well with the pitch looseness.

- *Cantus II: Variations on a Noël* for Soprano Recorder and Piano, Op. 83, No. 1

Continuous permutations and always defining the theme clearly. There are decorations, but none are abstractly fashioned.

The theme is announced unaccompanied by the recorder. It concludes the duo fully harmonized. Not a smidgen of counterpoint, but in the simple format of the work it is not needed. Two effects: In a thirteen-measure span the recorder player while performing sings a twelfth below, and shortly thereafter, in a syncopative sequence, the wind instrument is played with *rytmisk vibrato med store utsving* (rhythmic vibration with extensive amplifying effect).

- **Suite for Flute and Piano, Op. 15**

A type of neoclassic consideration that tempers the sharp points so that smoothness is fundamental to the music. Call it a mellow neoclassicism. And a colorful assortment without use of odd-ball effects.

There is type of relationship between the Intrata and the Finale by way of short upswept figures. Movement two is a pure Dialog, the piano represented by a single voice. The two instruments converse fugally. The *Meditasjon* (Meditation) is activated by syncopation, styled by quartal harmony.

- **Variations for Oboe and Piano, Op. 64**

Like playing with magic squares, a good part of the piece is based on specific systems. Criticism of creative trickery or gimmickery can be hurled at Hovland, but it matters little. First, the piece is dedicated to the composer's son, Per Egil. Accordingly, the basic working material is derived by taking the twelve pitches and matching the alphabet against them thus: C = A, C-sharp = B, D = C, D-sharp = D, E = E, etc. Thus the "Per Egil" is matched by D-sharp–E–F–E–F-sharp–G-sharp–B. Second, the first movement is one-voiced, the second movement is in 2/4 time, the third movement is in 3/4 time, the fourth movement is in 4/4 time, and the fifth movement is in 5/8 time.

The initial "Soliloquy" is for oboe alone. "Roundabout" matches the duple meter with two pitches throughout for the piano plus total bitonal procedure. Part three is a "Patter-Dance of the Tone-drops" structured in tripartite form. There is a Trio and it is set forth as a canon. Part four, "Fable," follows the quadruple meter with quadruple form (A–B–C–A) and the use of a four-pitch segment taken from the seven-pitch "name" motto. The finale, "Hoppity-Hop," is set as a five-part rondo form, and again the motto is drawn from for an important motive consisting of five of the seven pitches.

QUINTET

■ **Wind Quintet, Op. 50**

Seven movements that radiate from a combination of serial and aleatoric procedures. In the latter case Hovland samples a variety of chance offerings. In one place in the first movement all five performers choose their own tempo, each as fast as possible within the player's ability. Previously there is a passage to be played over and over for about thirty seconds and then is to come to a stop.

The individual ability of the players is the prime element in the work. For example, in movement two a measure is to be repeated "as long as possible in one breath." Dynamic improvisation is another process in the piece. In the concluding section of the third movement each instrument is assigned (for its unmetered music) a different metronomic tempo, the slowest ♩ = 60, the quickest ♩ = 100.

Obviously, form in a balanced sense gets squashed with the use of such freely disposed writing. What keeps Hovland's quintet together is the development of the basic tone row. Within, tempo, pulse, and dynamics shift and spin as in a chromoscope.

Howarth, Elgar (1935–)

QUINTET

■ **Variations for Brass Quintet (Trumpet in D, Trumpet in B-flat, Horn, Trombone, and Tuba)**

No ordinary variational run through. Each portion of this ten-minute piece: Introduction, Themes (the plural total is correct), four variations, and Chorale is thoroughly developed in a total chromatic (serially related) style that has intense vitality, virtuosic-styled sonorities, and individual contours.

Instrumentation is a cataloguing asset in defining the music's progress. The first variation, Fanfare, which has none of the old-fashioned ceremonial calls and all of the new-fashioned nervous rhythms and intervallic spread, is for the two trumpets and trombone. The second variation is a Nocturne for horn and trombone. Following an Intermezzo, the fourth variant is marked Capriccio, which is mostly a pyrotechnical cadenza for the pungent small D trumpet and trombone. The final Chorale negates linear shiftings but does not negate harmonic acridity.

Howe, Mary (1882–1964)

DUOS

■ *Interlude between Two Pieces* **for Flute and Piano (or Recorder and Harpsichord) (1942)**

The title of this work is both curious and quaint, reading as if it explained a one-movement total. But this is actually a three-section work, with only the middle one mentioned in the main title; the outer pieces have their own individual names. The instruments used are in equilibration, the new matching the old, since the predecessors of the flute and piano are, respectively, the recorder and harpsichord.

The Interlude is extremely free, a concentrated modern fantasia; the rhythmic vagaries of the keyboard instrument touch on quarter, eighth, sixteenth, and thirty-second notes, as well as triplets and quintlets in its off-axis introduction. The rhythmic flurries calm down considerably when the wind instrument enters. The "two pieces" are first, "Traits," a scherzo model over an ostinato sixteenth-note rhythm, and last, "Tactics," the conduct of which is semifugal, somewhat concerned with intervals of the fourth and fifth, and considerably unconstrained in the complete sense.

Sonata for Violin and Piano (1922)

A Sonata with romantic deportment, confirmed by the twists within the formal patterns. In the Lento recitative the E-minor tonality is not confirmed until the fifth measure. A relaxed quality surrounds the mensurally defined recitative sections, interrupted by the main objective, a lightly articulated scherzo expression. Both considerations return in the same order but are considerably compressed.

Contour changes are also found in the opening part of the Sonata. Contrasting material to the principal proclamatory theme takes on sectional deportment and there is no recapitulated material. In the concluding movement the connective medium is development by thematic metamorphosis. This is no blustery finale; the music sings even when it soars in a *forte*.

Sonata in D for Violin and Piano (1922)

The impulse of romantic chromaticism to embellish classical solidity of harmonic structure is manifested in the first movement. The basic tonality is stimulated, expanded, and deviations made from it. The main theme immediately shows tonal expansion, in that frictioned seconds are added to its triads. The final cadence affirms these incidents in refusing to settle into a pure tonic, but consists rather of an unresolved suspension hanging on to it.

Combining general forms in telescoped movements, reducing length, compressing and concentrating the meaning of a work stems from the late Beethoven quartets, with their vacillating shifts of tempo. Though the middle movement is harmonically non-Beethoven, the memorandum of opposing characteristic forms (and allied tempos) shows its ancestral link. A recitative-shaped Lento (in restrained, declamatory fashion) mixes with an Allegro scherzando. The latter triumphs. If chromaticism equals romanticism, the last movement provides evidence. Melodic shapes are clearly determined, the harmonies shifting these in varied directions.

TRIO

Suite mélancolique for Piano, Violin, and Cello (1931)

The basic principle of contrast and repetition surrounds most formal patterns, of which the ternary plan (used here in the first two movements—Prélude and Chanson Grave [Solemn Song]) is the most common in shorter pieces. Reshaping and shortening of the third part, so that the music shall not be too square, is followed. The form of the Air gai is developed from a unitheme so that the "Gay Air" almost remains constant. Elégiaque is represented by one of the "repetition" forms, in that the theme always returns in varied dress.

QUARTETS

String Quartet (1939)

To be able to extract movements from a compound work does not necessarily prove it is of "suite" compilation. If the movements do not have an inner-balanced relationship, however, then the suite connotation is on view, as is the case with this quartet. (Two movements—the first and third—have been recorded separately by two different quartet teams, and it is cogent to the argument that the titles listed are merely the lifting out of the tempo designations, without reference—or credit!—to their source.)

The harmonies of his work are most often the antipode of diatonicism; Howe has no reaction against fairly excessive chromaticism, for this is romantic music, at times of French flavor. This is very evident in the first and second movements. In the last one, the drive of the motor rhythm (and style is affected by this primitive source) channels the accidentals that jar the natural tones.

The first movement is in Allegro speed, in a free formal designation equivalent to a fantasy structure. Contrapuntal substances contrast to shifting harmonic elements; pizzicato colors exploit their timbre value against that of fat block writing. There is a balanced result, though without precise symmetry.

The second movement is based on lines by Leonora Speyer: "But this I know: The mist is stronger than these rugged hills—And when it wills They go." The music catches succinctly and aptly this spirit by chromatic movement and the sigh of well-spaced dissonance. Programmatic detail is a crutch of value. The final movement, save for a few measures of free recitative for the first violin, maintains the inflexibility expressed by the tempo, Allegro inevitabile. The recurrent decuple rhythm, divided into six and four eighths per measure, gives tightness then looseness in its rates of periodicity, and maintains, as well, driven obstinacy.

▪ *Three Pieces after Emily Dickinson* for String Quartet (1941)

A motto is sometimes used as the preface to a work or a movement within a composition in order to reset the inspiration or the mood the composer followed. There are two types of such motivation. The first is nonliteral—the general tone of the argument is the impulse. The second is demonstrative—planning the music so that it makes the translation of the motto one of plausibility. In the latter instance, program music will result, more or less. Quite often a composer will argue that music picture-painting was not intended, not even used. If that is the case then the subconscious spirit has filtered into the very intellectual consciousness with sequential allegiance to the motto, poem, or written phrase that forms the composition's preface. Howe seems to have been most heedful of the famed American poetess's ideas as she composed these three

movements for string quartet. With such attention her suite belongs in the scope of program music.

"The Summers of Hesperides"

> Except the smaller size, no Lives are
> round,
> These hurry to a sphere, and show, and
> end.
> The larger, slower grow, and later hang—
> The summers of Hesperides are long.

has an undulating figure that marks the music constantly until the coda, where the rhythm simmers down into restfulness. Not only the "hurry" and "end" of these lines are in the music, but the attenuated and relaxed quality of Emily Dickinson's words as well.

"Birds, by the Snow"

> Water is taught by thirst;
> Land, by the oceans passed;
> Transport, by throe;
> Peace, by its battles told;
> Love, by memorial mould;
> Birds, by the snow.

does not describe water, battles, birds, or the like. But it matches the rhyme, the delicacy of the concept by its muted color and its adherence to a monothematic concentration. The chromatic sway that haunts the music makes one appreciate the later settlement of the tonality, as well its picture of peace after battle. A reading of the poem is essential before the music is heard. Then, one will fully realize how definite Howe's music has been linked to Dickinson's beautiful lines.

The third movement is titled "God for a Frontier."

I am afraid to own a body,
I am afraid to own a soul;
Profound, precarious property,
Possession not optional.
Double estate entailed at pleasure—
Upon an unsuspecting heir;
Duke in a moment of deathlessness,
And God for a frontier.

The rhythmic conjunction that marks the first theme is contrasted to a lyrical, flowing subject. Fear, hope, and eventual faith are expressed by skillful, simulated musical expression.

QUINTET

- **Suite for String Quartet and Piano (1923)**

This piano quintet (the title is a bit misleading; the piano does *not* accompany the strings) uses defined forms, but changes them to suit individual purposes.

The opening movement, a Romanza, does not follow the sentimentality of that form, but does include its lyricism. The interlaced polyphony is far from sentimental symbology. The Scherzo shifts from triple to duple meter, and within the former there is additional interest obtained by sizing double pulses in the time space of three. The final movement is somewhat symphonic and thick. It illustrates an instrumentational situation that few composers can master when scoring for the combination of four string instruments and piano. The rhythm is as asymmetrical as in the previous movement.

Howells, Herbert (1892–1983)

DUO

- **Sonata No. 3 for Violin and Piano, Op. 38**

Impressionism is defined broadly as being of pictorial origin, suggested musically by instrumental color. But Howells was an impressionist only by way of his love for the outdoors, at times, the inspiration (but not the fully technical origin) of his music. This Sonata, said to be inspired by the grandeur of the Canadian Rockies, is, thus, a type of symbolistic outlook; its harmonic means are much more diatonic (in the modern sense of employing chords freed from rigorous application) and modal. In the latter instance, it must be said that the impressionists used modality, but their rhythms were quite observant of that type of chordal flow, and accordingly followed suit; whereas Howells most often frees his harmony from the rhythm. In total description, Howells is an impressionist-modalist, as well as a composer concerned with the semi-inculcation of folk song. But, with all these, he is free, using them as he wishes, for his sensitive textures form a very beautiful structure with a foundation on contemporary ground (the soil not crumbling, however, from any tendency to dig deep and discover new musical bedrock). Above all, his use of form is classic—something the impressionists considered but never truly accepted.

The first movement is typical of the composer—the beauty of his thematic creation, his limpid melodicism. The close of the movement (which is cast in sonata form) draws on the muted violin to give the last announcement of the theme. A clear-cut use of binary form is found in the middle movement. As the two themes recur, the background is given a different perspective; the second theme's last presentation neatly combines the flow of a triple meter against a duple-pinned ostinato. The final movement is energetic, again mainly of modal harmonies. At its close, the first movement's theme reappears and the reverberant chord of duplicated seconds that began the Sonata completes it as well.

QUARTETS

- *Fantasy String Quartet*, **Op. 25**

Modality wrapped around themes that have the basic folk song contours constantly found in Howells's music but are solely of his own making. Fantasy here means pastoral fantasy, for even when the music comes to its most dramatic moment (a *fortissimo* line in the first violin that covers three octaves in scope over pulsating sextuplets in the other three instruments working in opposite motion) the quality is not of urban turmoil but rather of a suburban wind in the willows.

Termed a fantasy, the structure (divisional though it may be) proposes a balance of the first part in moderate tempo with the final part in slower pace. In total, Howells leads his materials so that the sense of four connected (and related) movements is felt.

In the tag end of the 20th century, music of Howells's ductility may be an old-fashioned recipe, but only to those whose diet begins with Berio and ends with Xenakis.

- *Lady Audrey's Suite* **for String Quartet, Op. 19**

Howells's suite is a musical delight. His work is conceived as a genre painting for string quartet with very refreshing themes which contain whimsy and humor. Always the explorer of the delicate idea in music (without overlooking leanness of texture), Howells is represented as a semi-impressionist in this work. Symbolism, a modal harmonic plan, instrumental color paralleling the stipplers' school of painting, together with the use of high-lighted instrumental registers for individuality of timbre—all these are included in his musical sensations. Though there is a sense of folk songs in the quartet, Howells does not put these in as embroideries over his music, *Lady Audrey's Suite* is a truly English music. Regardless of the music's story, Howells sets its terms in pastoral shades of simmering loveliness and composes a specifically national music without defined extraction from such sources.

The anecdotal material of the suite was suggested to the composer by a little girl. In "The Four Sleepy Golliwogs' Dance" the opening motive of the second violin dominates the movement and the first violin's thematic line rises and falls—picturing the "poor, stiff" golliwogs. They "hated dancing, and they were so sleepy. But a spiteful 'magician' poked them with a prickly fork. So they danced as best they could, then bowed and ran away."

In movement two, the opening viola subject suggests the shepherd's pipes within "The Little Girl and the Old Shepherd." Vernal mood is first, last, and always in this part of the work, and a very effective subtlety marks the final change of key. The story is of the simplest— "In the fields and woods the little girl had little else than the flowers to think of, and the old lonely shepherd who piped the only scraps of tune he cared for. She often pitied his loneliness."

The third movement, "Prayer Time," is a set of six variations on a theme. Each variation describes a day of the week while the fundamental theme represents Sunday. It is played by the cello alone and is suggestive of plainsong (most apt for depicting the sabbath). This theme is used in shifting form to blend in all the other "day of the week" variations as a reminder that Sunday is the most important of the seven days when compared to all the others. Howells's principal subject represents the little girl going to church and hearing "the solemn things sung by the parson in a low up and down voice. So at prayer time each evening in the week she would think both of the parson's words and of the doings of each day." These are as follows: a chorale with muted upper strings as the full-timbred cello intones the theme below ("a lonely Monday"), next a simple scherzolike section ("a five-finger exercise") representing Tuesday, and then a sustained portion that describes Wednesday ("a tale of organs and saints"). The succeeding variation is a waltz with a muted-tone coda, which typifies Thursday ("a tea party and dancing"); this is followed by an ornamented variant ("a fairy tale on Friday"), and the movement concludes with a tranquil, final variation describing "a quiet Sabbath eve."

Movement four is titled "The Old Shepherd's Tale." ("Once the old shepherd told her a tale of himself and his friends that had happened years ago. Then he was not always slow going and lonely.") This is a very lively movement, with a triplet rhythmic figure paramount throughout the gay dance.

- **Quartet in A Minor for Piano, Violin, Viola, and Cello, Op. 21**

There are several odd facts concerning this piano quartet, one of the best of the composer's productions. It has specialness by its type of dedication ("To the Hill at Chosen and Ivor Gurney who knows it"), and therein lies the second matter. Although the work is issued without a program, and no titles mark its three movements, the composer has elsewhere described it with such poetic words as to imply a definite story. Yet, in view of its published form, the quartet must be considered at the opposite pole—a work in the "absolute music" category.

A composer's thoughts are often stimulated by nonmusical factors—the taking of a journey or the return from one; the beauty of a woman, or love for her; the thousand and one incidents that flash through daily life. Accordingly, if one were to consider all inspiration as descriptive, then only a small minority of works could be classified as "absolute music." At least, Howells has been fair enough to say what he had in mind; but such sincerity was the man's characteristic—it can be heard in his music. The remaining point is amusing. The first notes of this work were sketched while Howells's landlady kept him waiting nearly a half hour for a meal. Thus, hunger makes music; almost bears out (in a much less romantic sense!) the traditional attitude that composers wore dirty clothes, lived in attics, and composed best when their stomachs were empty.

But one need not know the composer's story to appreciate the rural English enchantment of the composition. The Gloucestershire hill (mentioned in the dedication) and the country of Cotswold and Severn that may be seen from it are conveyed impressively on this quartet's canvas. The beauties of modal harmony in the opening movement, with two themes contrasted to a more animated section, respond to Howells's images—a picture of dawn, the wind over the hill, the trees blowing, grayness melting into color, half light to full radiance, dawn to day. The middle movement is the hill on a day in midsummer, the thoughts of a man as he lies on the grass looking up into the vast vault of sky. Then, the surge of the final energetic movement (bound to the first movement by use of its second theme in augmented rhythm), considering the hill in the month of March, the winds of spring in riot.

It will be found that the music is gray and white in its colorations, that it is a picture and an abstraction of the effect of nature, that it seems to probe folk song and yet has none. It is all that and even more—a composition conveying tender emotions that produce a chamber music "pastoral symphony."

Hrisanidis (Hrisanide), Alexandre (1936–)

DUO

- **Sonata for Clarinet and Piano (1962)**

Debussy placed the titles of his piano Préludes at the ends of the pieces to warn that the descriptive headings were merely suggestive and not to be taken literally. Hrisanidis does likewise. Disregarding questions of compositional style, at that point all similarity vanishes in the case of Hrisanidis's second movement. The title, ". . . Variants," is exact, a technical truth. The similarity reappears with the other two movements. Martin Cooper has indicated that, in Debussy's case, "the scene or the sense-impression has passed through the composer's sensibility and emerges in a purely musical form." This concept could apply to Hrisanidis as well, though the use of ellipses in the titling supposes an affectation. The "sense-impression" is direct and without ambivalence in the last movement: ". . . Lament." In the opening movement, however, the clue is quite mysterious: ". . . Inscription on the Green Wood."

Monothematicism is the ruling austerity, with no corruptible deviations, in the sonata's opening movement. The subject is metamorphosed, shaken, juggled, given microanalysis. All in atonal accretions. Though athematicism is the contrastive rule of the closing movement, there are intervallic positives. In addition to tight major sevenths and minor ninths, emphasis is on the augmented second (or ninth) with the former's inversion, the diminished seventh.

Completely different and freest of all is the central part (". . . Variants"), for unaccompanied clarinet. Long in extent, luxuriantly detailed in its continual variation of a variation, the last based on a very ambiguously shaped idea (oddly enough of eight-measure length!), the movement is constructed in precisely closed form, but offers semi-open-form possibilities. There are seven solutions available to the performers. The first is without cuts; the others are with internal deletions while the outer portions remain intact. Thus, Hrisanidis's "Variants" can beget variants.

TRIO

- **Trio for Violin, Viola, and Bassoon (1958)**

Unlike Hrisanidis's later music, which includes considerable symbolic notation combined with both free and fixed structural components. Like Hrisanidis's earlier works, containing organic dissonant linear interchange, settled with strong vertical girders. This very rare trio combination has responsive rhythmic and metrical order, though it quickly departs from the chordal pedal with which it syncopatively begins.

Totally free of tonality, somewhat related to serialism by its plastic chromaticism, only the first of the three movements derives from a shaped theme. It is then fragmented, dissolved, and refragmented. The complex twice thickens into massivity. Short imitative units are important in these cases; the first leads into tutti strength, the other shifts away from it, just prior to the movement's conclusion. Athematic free variation applies to the second and third movements of the Trio. In the former instance, the final measures are a fine example of sensitive color, especially in the use of high viola timbre.

QUARTET

- *Soliloquium x 11* **for String Quartet (1970)**

Open-form composition triggers Hrisanidis's eleven-part discourse. His prospectus is complex, the data presented with instructions almost as rigid as the laws of Fuxian counterpoint, though the possibilities are as free as the turns of a roulette wheel.

There are eleven structures; six are "fixed" (nonetheless, notated with plentiful analogue and pictorial representation), and five, totally graphic in their detail, are termed "intermediate." The quartet must start with one of the fixed structures and be completed by choice of another. In between structures are to be used strictly in alternation, beginning with an intermediate one. The order of succession is in the hands of the performers, with the proviso that none of the structures can be repeated and there is to be no hiatus between them.

The intermediate structures are to be realized from documentation that includes geometric ideographs, tablatures, letters, arrows, numbers, assorted pitchless musical shapes, et al. While improvisation defies outlining in advance and resists written description, in general terms, the basis for the five intermediate structures follows. (1) Rapidly repeated sounds in varying totals. These include "uncontrolled" pitches played between the bridge and the tailpiece as well as on the bridge and in the ponticello area simultaneously. The dynamic level is soft. (2) Entry by specified chordal attack into total chromatic improvisation (but not scalic). Shifts to other improvisations begin with a sustained or spiccato or staccato quality. (3) Improvisation derived from minor-second intervals, including separation of the interval, clustering, trilling, glissandos, and appoggiaturas. (4) The material is activated by whole-note sounds then into glissandos; new pitch departures and glissandos are at will. The dynamic intensity here is a continuous *fortissimo*. (5) Totality of slow glissandos in a soft dynamic, always ending in tenuto. Mixed in are to be four (and *only* four) improvisations, of these precisely two are to ascend and two the reverse. These quadruple wavy depictions in the graphic structure were made by Hrisanidis from electroencephalograms (records of the electrical potentials in the brain). They are like counteractions within the general texture, to be

played in an *agitato forte; détaché*, and tremolando; "nervously and clearly"; and to sound "like so many forks of lightning."

The six fixed materials are directed and notated by the composer. However, since they include a large amount of free notation (the equivalent of controlled chance) they almost defeat the objective of being different from the intermediate (graphically determined) sections. Still, there are certain distinctions within the fixed sections. These are: (1) thirty-two seconds exactly of slow glissandos, interlocked near the start and at the conclusion by sustained sound bands. (2) Mainly clusters; an eight-second silence in the structure is prominent. (3) Instrumental glossolalia—dense and intense. Guitarlike pizzicatos are specialties within this portion. (4) A continuation of the glossolalia (*exactly* twice the length of the previous one: one minute and thirty-six seconds as compared to forty-eight seconds). In this structure hammered accentuations in triple *forte* are highlighted. (5) A short section, motivally engendered. (6) Begins with polyphonic tremolandos and with molto vibrato plucking a feature.

QUINTETS

- ***Directions* for Flute, Oboe, Clarinet, Bassoon, and Horn (1969)**

Another open-form composition by this composer, whose late works delegate the ordering of their component parts to the performers. Hrisanidis has stated that (at least in his *Directions*) he had in mind the embodiment of the plastic principles of Paul Klee. The exact inspiration or takeoff point is not indicated, but Hrisanidis doubtless had in mind a belief that the famous expressionistic Swiss painter included in his *Schöpferische Konfession*: "Pictorial art springs from movement, is itself fixed movement, and is perceived through movements." This view of the dynamic nature of art is transferred to Hrisanidis's musical concept, which produces "fixed movement" (transmitted by the composer in the organized component parts—the structures) and is then "perceived through movements" (by performance flux, through infinite rearrangement).

Directions has six structures, interchangeable at will (which include a good amount of free notational and improvisational pitch elements, designed so as to produce structural stability). These vary in length, ranging from 11/2 to 33/4 minutes. None are to be repeated, and if all are used the performance time is 151/4 minutes. (A variety of possibilities is suggested by the composer, but oddly none cover more than four of the structures.)

The scoring includes flute-sound oscillation while playing a pitch, blowing forcefully into the instrument without producing a musical sound (the effect gives the equivalent of "pffff" or "phhhh"), striking the horn with a ring or metal rod, and sharply tapping the fingers against the finger keys of the instrument (resulting in a "tzack-tzack" sound).

"Structure A" comprises intense sound blocks and whirling, multi-instrumental glossolalia. It is to be performed in a relentless *fortissimo*. The second (B) structure is concerned with polyrhythmy, climaxing in a riveting of five against six against seven against eleven. "Structure C" is identified by its pointillistic sonic dots. For just a little less than 21/2 minutes no instrument plays more than one sound, no two are connected. Dynamic consideration is free, but must range through five levels (*pianissimo, piano, mezzoforte, forte,* and *fortissimo*), to be presented in any order successively. Once completed the differences are re-presented, again with freedom of level-choice. The fourth (D) structure covers a polyphonic, polyrhythmic, and polyglot poly-referenced mass. The sound is akin to improvisational mixed media, though intensely controlled by the composer. Nonetheless, Hrisanidis includes free improvisation within his governed improvisation. The disorderly orderliness is

further stocked with the same dynamic variety included in the previous structure. "Structure E" is involved with silences that constantly break into a kaleidoscopic variety of sound substances. There are more special qualities and effects in this portion than in any other part of the quintet.

The final (F) structure begins with figures that merge into an assortment of trilled sounds. The structure *must* end with eight seconds of silence (there are other spans of silence, but none of this length). This, of course, separates this structure from the others, no matter where it is placed. If this structure is used to conclude *Directions*, the musicians are to hold their instruments in playing position for the eight-second duration to register that the silence is part of the composition. However, Hrisanidis considers a conductor "indispensable." (No metrical arrangement applies; the music is notated in precise one-second divisions, so that the conductor is instructed to beat each second as a part of a constant succession.) The conductor, therefore, can aid the final structural direction of *Directions* by retaining his beat while the players maintain a playing position.

- *M. P. 5 (Musique pour 5) (Music for 5)* **for Violin, Viola, Cello, Tenor Saxophone (or Clarinet), and Piano (1967)**

In the conventional sense, themes, metrical relationships, and subject contrast are not found in Hrisanidis's avant-garde quintet. Attention must pertain to the sonic blocks as they are promulgated in linear assortment. *M. P. 5* begins intervallically with the superimposition of three major sixths (in the three string instruments). This introductory structure is soon combined with other spans and eventually destroyed by a changing cluster harmony, as the music thickens and activates. Like a many-dimensional collage, the material depth of sound and its aural definition (akin to perspective) shifts. At times the clusters are packed close, other times less so. Hrisanidis's proposal in crushing specific pitch and interval identity (save in its totalled variance of textural density) becomes deadly clear at six minutes into the work, which in all covers just fifteen seconds short of sixteen minutes. At the six-minute mark all the strings of the violin, viola, and cello are shunted out of their normal tuning by fractional shifts of the string pegs in a wide variety of pitch dislocation, upward and downward. This "out-of-tune" apportionment of the instrumental total is maintained to the very conclusion.

Color figures as an intradimension. The saxophone is withheld until just a bit before the string retuning. Later on the saxophone is the sole voice, followed by entrance of the full quintet. The piano is then checked out for a considerable period of time; the quintet again returns, etc. This variety of timbre quality is constant and specific, not a passing coloristic incident. The setting-off of components—saxophone, piano, and string trio—is in the form of regulated cadenzas, the moods of these described by the composer "as varied as daylight, twilight, and the night."

Hrisanidis's sound world is a multivariety of contemporary complexions. In the strings all parts of the instruments are employed, including arpeggiandos behind the bridge, hitting in the sounding-board area, and so forth. The saxophonist strikes the finger keys without blowing; the pianist produces percussion effects by use of the pedal and the lid of the instrument. A large number of other special qualities are included in the sonorous catalogue.

Because of its complexity, *M. P. 5* can be performed only with the aid of a conductor or by means of a prerecorded tape that defines all the time references required. (There are no metrical definitions in the work. The spacings of the material are timed in totals of seconds, with subdivisions of the longer time segments.)

The "conducted" tape is not heard by the audience, since the players use individual earphones. Consequently, an example of a brand-new performance method involving new chamber music demands!

Hrušovský, Ivan (1927–)

DUO

- *Suita piccola (Small Suite)* **for Cello and Piano**

Small in size but dramatic in tone. There is a constant tension in the Praeludium, resultant from an unceasing rhythmic ongoingness in the piano, alternating between duple- and triple-pulse totals. Some antiphony in the Recitativo. In the concluding Gigue, lines collide and contrapuntal action on a one-against-one basis brings excitement. Neat, dance refinement is avoided in this instance.

NONET

- *Combinazioni sonoriche (Sonorous Combinations)* **for Nine Instruments (Flute, Oboe, Bass Clarinet, Trumpet, Vibraphone, Piano, Violin, Viola, and Cello (1963)**

Slovakian serialism. There is an Introduction that sets the row scene. This is followed by five linked "structures," developing the material. The second of these crushes the row into severely demarcated pitches; the third section emphasizes dynamic differences. The final structure is an aleatoric mix linked to a calm Coda. The latter concludes with a sustained single B pitch, matching the opening, which tossed the same pitch around the nine instruments over an eight-measure span.

Hubeau, Jean (1917–)

DUOS

- **Sonata for Trumpet and Piano (1943)**

Hubeau's set of three pieces (which he titles *Sonate pour Trompette chromatique et Piano*) are delightful depictions. Though styled with predictable accentuations, they register with sensitive artistry.

The first of the group is a Sarabande that includes a very minute, but extremely colorful, episode. The Intermède (Interlude) is fast and chirpy, its motivic point descending in tight half tones. A swinging tripleted background, slightly syncopated, backs up the melody of the Spiritual, illustrating this French composer's concept of the blues.

- **Sonata in C Minor for Violin and Piano (1941)**

Music exemplifying the school of classical-romantic scholarship. The forms of the three movements are standard: sonata, ternary, and a final Rondo; the tonalities are of decided contrast with C minor and C major for the outer movements and F-sharp major for the central one.

Serious music writing in all aspects, with special chromaticism to enlarge the six-sharp key in the Andante, but, significantly, minus any meanderings. Hubeau favors broad lines in all three movements.

- *Sonatine-Caprice* **for Two Violins (1943)**

A charming, decidedly tonal work of three movements, containing some slight dissonance. Hubeau uses the violins aptly in this semi-implied descriptive composition he wrote in August 1943 as "a souvenir for two violins from Montjoie (in the mountains)."

Musical acrostics (which most often favor the name of Bach by representing its four letters via matched tones) are used in the first movement's Berceuse. The names of "Michèle" and "Dominique" are formed from exact musical equivalents for all letters ranging from A to G (the letter H is, as usual, matched by a B, thereby taking advantage of the German translation). Those characters which do not fall within the musical alphabet after H are paraphrased—the next seven letters equal, one a piece, the seven that exist in the musical range of A to G, and similarly for the next seven, and so forth. "Michèle" appears for the first time in the opening measure of the first violin while "Dominique" can be heard initially in the fifth measure of the second-violin part.

The second movement is an étude—"Les Moustiques" ("The Mosquitoes"); these fly about in moderate scherzo style. The final movement is a "Caprice—La Fine!" ("Caprice—The End!"). This conclusion is in brilliant A major, is extremely sonorous and hardly moves away from its defined tonality.

QUARTET

- *Sonatine humoresque* **for Horn, Flute, Clarinet, and Piano (1942)**

Three pieces that move with surface lightness, consistently tonal, consistently repeating sections that enlarge the basic short forms utilized. A balletic point of view exists in the Ouverture, Sicilienne, and Tarentelle—the last two linked.

Huber, Klaus (1924–)

SOLO/DUO/TRIO

- *Oiseaux d'argent (Silver Birds)* **for 1, 2, or 3 Flutes (1977)**

Form as free-flighted as the winged personalities described in the title. And the contents provide a further analogue.

The duo formations can be arrived at by joining any two of the three separate flute parts. As for solo presentation, the performer can play one part after the other, or a suggested order of 3–1–2. However, to show how the composer wants to simplify matters, he notes that "nevertheless, any other order is possible."

No tempo and no meter are given, so coincidence within duo or trio presentation is pure happenstance. The first flute part is marked with a number of vibrato colorations. Flute two is motivally constructed on moving eighth notes and little grace-noted sweeps of pitches linked to sustained sounds. With few exceptions the third flute plays harmonics throughout. Colorful aleatoric intercourse no matter how it turns out.

DUO

- *Noctes intelligibilis lucis (Darkness of the Light of Intellect)* **for Oboe and Harpsichord (1961)**

A short motto, taken from the writings of St. Jean de la Croix, begins the duo (St. John of the Cross was a famous Spanish mystic who died in 1591.) Part I (a free consideration of "la Nuit des sens") ("Darkness of the Senses") is written in open form, with improvisatory elements within. Part II (a response to "la Nuit de l'esprit") ("Darkness of the Intellect") is pronouncedly static in conception. Both headings were taken from St. John's mystical vocabulary. His revelation was founded on the renunciation of the life of the senses and the intellect in order to be transported by faith. The two parts are separated by a fifty-second Vexatio (Tantalization) based on three different rhythmic progressions. This short portion returns at the conclusion of the second part of the piece in retrograde form, titled Eductio (Exit), described by Huber as music "in an unreal guise which barely oversteps the threshold of audibility."

The fascination of the intense luminosity of the oboe timbre, ranging totally over its pitch span, is matched by the harpsichord sounds, which are removed from the tinkly tingles common to this instrument. Among other things, hearing punched deep-bass clusters on the keyboard instrument is aurally fascinating.

In certain respects form is secondary to the dialogue undertaken by the instruments; the improvisationlike conversation animates and shapes the design. There is expert sensibility in this piece, and exquisite sensitivity.

TRIOS

- *Sabeth (Sabbath)* **for Alto Flute, English horn (or Viola), and Harp (1967)**

Huber's 6 1/2-minute *Sabeth* was composed for Günter Eich's sixtieth birthday and specifically for a broadcast performance in Switzerland (over Radio Zürich). It was Eich's radio play of the same title that "inspired" the writing of Huber's trio.

The music is to "express the irrational, magical world" of Eich's prose, which "derives particular effect from silence in its highpoints." To achieve this Huber dips into the slightly chancy bowl of proportional notation, traverses the approximate area of nonmetrical definition, and joins the aleatoric fraternity by use of free sequential production of specified pitches both within and without notated rhythms. Quarter and third tones are employed and a variety of coloristic condiments within the structural menu. Fragmentation joins hands with chattery ("busy") combinations, form is formed from bits and pieces that cling to Huber's objective of the "irrational." The "magical" quality is obtained from the velvety timbre of the dark-colored instruments employed.

- *Six Miniatures* **for Clarinet, Violin, and Cello (1963)**

The main precept that directs this trio is motival development. This applies to numbers one, two, three, and six. The fifth of the group is a three-part conception. Coloristic bravado holds forth in number four. There the clarinet rhapsodizes while the two string instruments respond with muted tremolo figures in the nasal, glassy timbre resultant from ponticello bowing, interspersed with some plucked sounds.

QUINTET

- *Drei Sätze in zwei Teilen (Three Movements in Two Parts)* **for Wind Quintet (Flute [alternating Piccolo], Oboe [alternating English horn], Clarinet, Horn, and Bassoon) (1958)**

Serialistic symbolism is built into Huber's piece, but he does not explain it. Still, the structural details are intricate, but clear.

Movement one, "Der kleine Bogen" ("The Small Arc"), proceeds through chromatically intense directions, and later the sound materials are run in reverse. Huber marks one section *Culminatio*, but this climax is actually only the second of three texturally heavy sections within the first movement. A *Transitio* is introduced in fugato, and with the entrance of the English horn the second movement, "Crux," begins. This is a seven-sectioned division, with one short measure of total silence falling between sections four and five.

Movement three, "Der grosse Bogen" ("The Large Arc"), which constitutes Part two of the quintet, is marked by the entrance of the piccolo. Retrograde action concerns this movement as well, thereby balancing the procedure of movement one. The movement is split by a Choral with the melodic line first set in two-octave spacing by the piccolo and horn and later in one-octave doubling by the piccolo and

clarinet.

SEPTET

- *Two Movements for Seven Brass Instruments* **(Two Trumpets, Two Horns, Two Trombones, and Tuba) (1958)**

Persuasive serialism. Cogent textural variety is exemplified as the music is developed. In both movements, the central portions are contrasted to the outer materials. In the first of the pair the content is more open, denoted with quieter tempo. In the second movement the pitch progress is agitated in the center (termed "Der Kreisel") ("The Top").

Hübler, Klaus-Karl (1956–)

QUARTETS

- **String Quartet No. 1:** *Hommage à Alban Berg* **(1977)**

Hübler's testimonial to Berg widens the pitch spectrum by the use of quarter, three-quarter, and third tones. No mere decorations, these, but of substantial majority. Expressionistic zig-zag marks the music, loaded with histrionic definitions: "hysterical," "with the most intense strength," "ecstatic," "with intimate feeling," and so forth.

Each of the sections (two in the first part and three in the second) has packed textural weight which decreases in each of the concluding portions. These provide a formal unity for the turbulent syntax that directs the work. The final (fifth) division (a Lento marziale) has short *pianissississimo* phrases for the first violin, viola, and cello, while the second violin in sharp *fortississimo*, colored by muting of the instrument, plucks a D pitch in ostinato. (The pattern covers three measures, each with rhyth-

Hübler

mic difference, and is repeated ten times.) And then, still further decrease of sound, with single pitches by the viola in each of seven measures. Hübler is intent on sonorous release—the final three measures consist of total silence.

- **String Quartet No. 2**: *Sur le premier prélude* **(1980)**

Five variations based on an unidentified prelude. (It could be by Bach or even Kreutzer, but Hübler's inspirational secret is of little concern.)

Direct monitoring applies to each variant. The first (Praeludium) consists of zigzagged phrases tossed from one instrument to the other. Variation II, is a Scherzo that shifts between single-voice segments and unified ones. Variation III is a ferocious Toccata, with huge chordal blocks again acrobatically moving between the instruments. A Notturno describes the fourth variant, one that avoids suavity in favor of fractured items. This leads into Variation V, which has measured tremolo figures punctuated by twelve-part *fortissimo* chords. The conclusion has four of these chords separated by silences that increase in exact double length from four beats to eight and finally to sixteen.

QUINTET

- *Riflessi (Reflections)* **for Five Instruments (Alto Flute, Violin, Viola, Cello, and Harp) (1979)**

A 6 1/2-minute projection of impressionism revisited. Harpistic husbandry: a few isolated sounds, some repetitive harmonics, not (gratefully) a single glissando. There are parallels in the other instruments—a sustained sound here and a repeated two-pitch figure there. The quintet has sheer musical concentration; its language is serially derived.

Huggler

Hueber, Kurt Anton (1928–)

DUO

- **Sonata for Trumpet and Piano, Op. 9**

There isn't the slightest doubt that Hueber's Sonata is not formally four-square. Each of the two pair of movements has sharp differences. The first pair consists of a Marcia funèbre (Funeral March) and another march, this one animated and very much on the go. Movement three presents a short, muted quasi-threnodic conception, while movement four is a peppy, one-in-a-bar setting that has waltz contours. Then to continue the extreme contrast, the final dozen measures of the Marcia funèbre return.

Hueber's most effective writing is always tidy and to the point. So is the fricative harmony that colors and supports the entire work.

Huggler, John (1928–)

QUINTET

- **Quintet for Brass Instruments No. 1 (Two Trumpets, Horn, Bass Trombone, and Tuba) (1955)**

Serial derived, Huggler's brass quintet thrives on juxtaposed qualities. In the first movement, an Adagio, with legatoed lines, moves into a fast, asymmetric section. This is followed by a lyrical portion, a short return to the sustained slow mood, with a concluding Allegro. It totals a looseness of formal arrangement that Huggler describes as thematic growth "couched in terms of sudden, sometimes brutal changes," with, at times, different moods "generated simultaneously." Thematic resemblances occur, especially in the second Scherzo movement (in moderately fast tempo) and the third (a fantasialike division). The lively finale is vitalized by imitation work.

Regardless of shifts, each of the movements has close-knit formal unity. Though serial derived the quintet can be classified as fully turned, fully tuned, classically proportioned music.

Hughes, Mark (1934–)

DUO

- **Sonata for Horn and Piano**

A restlessness of tonality and rhythm marks this work. Still, both fuel the dramatic drive of the music, most evident in the third (final) movement, Fugue and Cadenza, where the form becomes stretched to include, in addition to the basic opposites of contrapuntalism and display, a quote from the opening movement and a Coda of scherzoistic contour. In this final movement color is another important ingredient, with a nineteen-measure section for the muted horn and a six-measure portion for "echo horn."

Chromaticism and asymmetric detail mark the first movement, which concludes with the piano alone. Textural differences are of significance in shaping the slow (second) movement.

Hughes, Robert (1933–)

See also under **Collaborative Composers**

Party Pieces

DUO

- *Sonitudes* **for Flute and Cello (1970)**

The cellist beats the D and A strings of the instrument with a drumstick to begin the piece (pitch changes apply only to the higher string). Later the cello is laid on the floor and the same two strings are hit with the drumstick and also slapped against the fingerboard. The flute has no histrionics to match these actions, except blowing through the instrument to simulate what the composer terms a "wind shriek." This effect opens the second part of the work, a Recitative, which is linked to the first section, titled Scene and subtitled Introduction. A Serenade, with rubato as its principal essence (and with, as Hughes describes it, "free-sounding cross rhythms") and a peripatetic Caprice (the tempo designation is "As fast as possible") conclude *Sonitudes*.

Hughes explains that "the difficulty of the work gives it the aspect of an etude, yet the extension of its sonorities by the cello make it a serious concert piece, a sonorous etude, and hence its title, *Sonitudes*."

There's little been written of value for the flute-cello combination. Hughes's contribution is a fruitful addition.

Hugon, Georges (1904–80)

QUARTET

- **String Quartet**

First things come first. The initial pair of measures are the chapter and verse of Hugon's opening movement. Again and again these measures appear; in sequence, separate, or split off to be heard in one half of their total. Of course, such repetitiveness drives the meaning home, but there is a slight amount of overdrive in this case. The importance of the generative device is reconfirmed at the conclusion of the entire quartet when the two-measure motive appears in augmentation.

Movement two (Lent) is linked to movement three (Allegro). Both seethe with unrest—chromatically and metrically. Meticulous definition applies to the latter, so that measures such as 31/2/4 appear in the slow movement and carry over to the final part of the quartet with settings such as 11/2/4, 21/2/4, and 41/2/4. It is important to realize that Hugon does not break down these time signatures in terms of total eighth notes. A 21/2/4 measure, for example, is not equal to a 5/8 measure, but planned as a true 2/4 plus an extra half beat (or one eighth). The music for these movements roams, therefore, is somewhat breathless but always emotionally driven.

(Hugon's work is dedicated to his teacher, Paul Dukas, and to the Calvet Quartet.)

Humble, Keith (1927–)

DUO

- *Arcade IV* for Guitar and Percussion (Vibraphone, Marimba, Triangle, Crotale, Marimbaphone, Three Cymbals, Gong, Tam-tam, and Glockenspiel) (1969)

Arcade IV is one of a set of five compositions, each scored differently, written during 1968 and 1969. Its four-movement shape reflects an impressionistic avant-garde style.

The Introduction is a pithy, mainly softly disposed concept. There are recitative elements in the Dance. The most evocative and rhapsodically expressive portion is the Nocturne, which (after a very short introduction) is controlled by specific events that are structurally defined by the performers. This might be termed "determined indeterminacy." *Arcade* then concludes with an Epilogue in the majority use of slow tempo. In total, a coloristically convincing duo.

TRIO

- String Trio (1954)

A twelve-tone composition in which the devel-

opments follow a sectional classification rather than projected in repetition, continuation, or compound forms. The scenario is smooth, though it does continually change. One section is all pizzicato rhythmic bits, another consists of three-pitch groups in *pianissimo*, legato-phrased, another is a continuous massed syncopative segment, still another is a texture built entirely from col-legno tappings. And so on. The technical passions are clear in this Australian composer's chamber piece for violin, viola, and cello.

Humel, Gerald (1931–)

DUO

- Sonata *"Journey to Praha"* for Violin and Piano

Style and forms are quite clear. The former is twelve-tone, the latter define fantasy proportions in the corner movements and a scherzo atmosphere in the central one. What is special is the use of the Czech national anthem as the basis for the tone row that is the springboard for the work. Humel's piece is craggy but tightly formationed, and if its sentiments are not mellifluous, they are secure.

TRIOS

- *Arabesque* for Guitar, Cello, and Percussion (Snare Drum, Three Bongos, Low Tom-tom, Five Triangles, and Marimbaphone) (1977)

Humel prefaces his score with a general statement regarding his work. "The title has been derived from dancing. Arabesque is one of the basic positions in the formal, academic dance. During the period of the Romantic ballet it reached its zenith as the most expressive gesture of poetic high flight."

Humel's *Arabesque* is a substantial fantasy stuffed with chromatic shapes. The moods shift between lyrical and exultant. There is a highly individual feeling for color.

■ **Trio for Flute, Viola, and Cello (1964)**

Full-range construction, matching total pitch coverage via dodecaphonic means with heavy scoring. Nubby chords for the string instruments and virtuosic use of color. Two examples of the latter: seven consecutive measures in the first movement filled with viola harmonics, and in the second movement a considerable amount of flute pitches to be sounded in the novel manner of "quasi pizzicato." Humel's Trio exemplifies chamber music massiveness.

Hummel, Bertold (1925–)

QUARTET

■ **Divertimento for Four Violins (1968)**

Juicy sonorities and practically engaging all four instruments throughout the composition. Hummel's style avoids pitch decoration; it is direct and in respect to the Marsch opener and Finale the contents has a 20th-century casualness. The movement in between these is a Waltz. It runs as one would expect, save for the surprise neat twist of the final three measures.

(The Divertimento can be performed by multiple players and the work is then for Violin Orchestra.)

Hummel, Johann Nepomuk (1778–1837)

At one time an exceedingly popular composer, Hummel now is a rare name on concert pro-

grams. But, as is the case with many other composers, some of his compositions deserve revival.

Hummel's music has affinities with Haydn and early Mozart; he studied with both of these men, as well as Clementi. He also studied with Beethoven's teacher, Albrechtsberger, as well as with Salieri, who taught Schubert. This is all a very handsome and excellent background. There are further connections with Beethoven. Hummel was not only his friend, but dedicated his three Op. 30 quartets to Prince Lobkowitz, to whom Beethoven's first six quartets were similarly dedicated.

DUOS

■ **Sonata in A Major for Cello and Piano, Op. 104**

The greatest interest in this duo lies in the Rondo. For this final movement there was not the equality of partnership found in the first two movements. Accordingly, the renowned German cellist Friedrich Grützmacher (1832–1903) rearranged the movement giving more material to the cello. In the Oxford University Press edition of the work, published in 1978, the original version of the measures Grützmacher rewrote are set forth in an appendix so that one can opt for either version, or, for that matter, present both as a historical addenda.

Movement one is a broad 6/4 conception, set forth in standard sonata procedure. The slow movement is a Romanza. It has some ornateness, but that is assigned solely to the keyboard instrument.

■ **Sonata in C for Mandolin and Piano, Op. 37**

Hummel's work for this rarely heard combination will surprise. It is no run-of-the-mill, bland opus. Its three movements: Allegro con spirito,

Andante moderato (a siciliano), and a catchy Rondo (tempoed Allegretto più tosto Allegro) contain formal clarity and variety.

The Sonata shows full knowledge of mandolin technique, with tremolando chords and repetitive sounds coloring the material.

(Hummel's entry into music for the mandolin was not a one-time thing. He also composed a mandolin concerto for the Venetian virtuoso Bartolomeo Bartolazzi. It is also in three movements; with a fast first movement, a set of variations, and a rondo. While the work has formal respectability it is less striking than the Sonata.)

- **Sonata in D Major for Flute (or Violin) and Piano, Op. 50**

A fine example of Viennese classicism. This is music scrupulously devoted to material that fits the wind instrument like a glove, without negating equality to the keyboard instrument. And music beautifully structured in its three movements. The first of these is in sonata form and is colored by tonality manipulation. Ascending fourths are the generating matter for the slow movement, which is linked to a breezy Rondo-Pastorale finale.

Hummel's duo has enjoyed publication by a number of houses. Modern editions (for firmer commercial purposes) do not list the alternative instrumental choice noted above. This follows the original edition which reads: *Sonata pour Piano et Flute ou Violon composée par J. N. Hummel.*

TRIOS

- **Adagio, Variations, and Rondo *on "Schöne Minka"* for Flute, Cello, and Piano, Op. 78**

Creative strategy is as important as any other type. Rather than announce the simple, Ukrainian A-minor tune on which he will weave his variations, Hummel prefaces matters with substantial content. The seriousness and length of the slow-tempo beginning contrasts strongly with the half-dozen variants on the "Schöne Minka" melody. All the variations are pleasantly relaxed and unforced and clearly show their parenthood.

Strategy is also found within the musical action. The fifth variation, with tremolo background, is a clever move into quasi-romantic style. And what seems to be a dynamically soft ending is suddenly shifted to true conclusion with a set of three forceful chords.

Trios for Piano, Violin, and Cello

Hummel's trios for piano, violin, and cello were all composed after Mozart's death and in terms of scoring details and general aesthetic demeanor show Mozartian influence. However, in terms of expressive subject material and structural development, Hummel sits below Mozart at the piano trio table. This does not mean a pedantic result.

The mundane cello details of Haydn's trios are completely absent from Hummel's trios; the three instruments reflect a fine scoring *esprit de corps*. All seven trios (Nos. 1-4 are discussed *below*; the others are No. 5, in E major, Op. 83; No. 6, in E-flat major, Op. 93; and No. 7, also in E-flat major, Op. 96) are in three movements. None of them is a direct carbon copy of the others; the forms change slightly but sufficiently to avoid repetitively molded schemes.

- **No. 1 in E-flat Major, Op. 12**

This is Hummel's initial work for the piano trio combination. The piano sets the tonality and the violin anticipates the contours of the main theme. For the time being the cello is withheld from any thematic address and is only used for sundry instrumental anchorage. However, it becomes a full-fledged participant later in the work. The first subject is announced by the piano and the movement unfurls in a clear sonata depiction. There is an odd coda (in length, hardly one at all)—a glimmer of romantic cross-reference, consisting of a capsule (two-measure) arpeggio, quasi-cadenza.

A string duet procedure announces the Andante (second movement)—comparison is furnished by semi-bravura piano writing. The Finale literally flies on the push of triplets in presto tempo. Effective, absolutely. No less effective is the spare, wiry-strong writing for the piano, the texture consisting of only two voices.

- **No. 2 in F Major, Op. 22**

The last two movements employ colorful forms. The first of these consists of a set of variations of the "small-game" variety. This permits the theme to be maintained throughout the four permutations as well as the coda. The cello is given the entire spotlight on the trio's stage in the last of the variations.

A Rondo alla Turca, set in vivace tempo, constitutes the third (final) movement. This music "in the Turkish style" does not picture any whirling dervish. It is rather a gay, two-beats-per-measure music, with only a drum imitation now and then for ethnic effectuation.

- **No. 3 in G Major, Op. 35**

Use of two different rhythmic patterns distinguishes the exposition and recapitulation of the first movement from the development section. The basic, principal generator consists of paired eighth notes. Derivatives proceed from these, while in the development process a triplet figure is the spearhead. Nothing unique whatsoever in this plan, yet it clearly demarcates the design. A music of minuet character and a Rondo complete the Trio.

- **No. 4 in G Major, Op. 65**

In all of Hummel's trios counterpoint is practically nonexistent. A bit of imitation between the instruments does take place, but otherwise the music runs on the sound track on firm harmonic wheels.

Straightforward form as well. Here the music is set forth by sonata means, followed by a slow movement that has a slight variational tinge, and is completed by a vivacious Rondo. Pleasant and direct music. As with Hummel's other trios, the writing offers no special technical difficulties.

QUARTET

- **String Quartet in G Major, Op. 30, No. 2**

An oddity in this string quartet is the preponderance of high cello writing. The result creates a distinct color and flavor to the composition. There are Mozartian touches in the Minuet (in a tempo of Allegro con fuoco, verging on the Beethoven scherzos, which were developed from the dance form). Hummel knew his sources and, it will be seen, used them well. In the Trio to the Minuet, the key changes, and, over a pizzicato bass, there is a gentle melody treated canonically in its last section. Both the slow movement and the last are strictly in the Haydn manner. These are ornate and particularly highlight the first violin. In the final movement, there is the soloism of whipped-bowed bariolage and double stops for that instrument. These techniques stem from the early work period of Haydn.

QUINTET

- **Quintet for Piano, Violin, Viola, Cello, and Double Bass, Op. 87**

One tends to agree fully with Richard Franko

Goldman, who wrote in an article published in *The Musical Quarterly* (January 1967) that this Quintet is superior to the famous Schumann piano quintet. (Hummel's Op. 87 still remains to be rediscovered.) In regard to the instrumentation, Hummel's setting of the piano-quintet formation subtracts the second violin and adds a double bass. Looking at it another way, the medium he uses is the standard piano quartet plus double bass. This combination gives more solidity to the texture.

Catalogue listings indicate the tonality of the Quintet as E-flat. (The 1969 edition, published by Wollenweber of Munich, omits any tonality identification.) And, indeed, the key signature is E-flat major. But most of the work courses through the dramatic color of E-flat minor. The tonal virtuosity matches some of the pianistic floridity, with excursions to the keys of A major, D major, F-sharp major, and F-sharp minor, in the first movement.

Movement two is a Menuetto, set forth with Trio. But the tempo, Allegro con fuoco, shows the heading to be a mere disguise for a dynamic scherzo, start to finish. The Largo is extremely concentrated, decoratively concerned in the writing for the piano, and leads into the Finale, the most lighthearted and relaxed part of the entire work. It runs a rondo course.

SEPTETS

- *Grand Military Septet* in C Major for Flute, Violin, Clarinet, Cello, Trumpet, Double Bass, and Piano, Op. 114

The use of the trumpet indeed gives the Hummel work its name, there being no militaristic tone to the opus. The brass instrument is used sparingly. While it is excluded from the scoring in the Adagio it is the featured color in the closing cadence of the Menuetto, an incorrect designation for a speedy scherzo conception.

The outer movements are in the standard fast-paced tempo. In the finale Hummel colors the material with contrapuntal episodes. One writer has indicated that these do not subject the listener "to polyphonic complexities."

- **Septet for Piano, Flute, Oboe, Horn, Viola, Cello, and Double Bass, Op. 74**

(Hummel's Op. 74 is often termed *Grand Septet*. The score published by Peters is indicated as *Septett*.)

Most often, especially in the spirited, sonata-designed first movement, the piano is semi-soloistic, pitted against or answering the other six instruments, as well as embroidering their remarks with its own. There are, as in so many of Hummel's opening movements, sharp tonality moves.

In lesser degree the piano is restrained in the second part of the work, its quaint title Menuetto o Scherzo, with an Alternativo in the style of a Ländler. Still, Hummel was quite aware of his designation since the swing of the music falls between minuet and scherzo speed rates. It also defines a creative viewpoint that finds a place between classic and romantic style. The keys are contrasted here to mark the form. There is a minor tonality for the outer parts and major for the central portion. In the latter, the cello takes the initial lead and the piano ejects nicely reflected grace notes.

In the Andante con variazioni more attention is given the other instruments, but the emphasis is on ornamental piano writing. An active Finale is projected with vigorous scalic material and the development includes a decidedly chromatic fugato. The music in the Finale is heavier in texture, especially because there is no soprano voice in the string instrument group.

OCTET

- **Octet: Partita in E-flat Major for Two Oboes, Two Clarinets, Two Horns, Two Bassoons, and Contrabassoon ad lib**

The contrabassoon is an editorial substitute for the original serpent. Of course, that means nine instruments are playing an "octet." However, only eight voices are involved, since the contrabassoon merely doubles the second bassoon to give more bass depth.

Lightly conceived outdoorish music, even in its moderately paced inner movement in A-flat, which is in the style of a siciliana. The outer movements are in the expected fast tempo and both are in the E-flat home tonality.

Humperdinck, Engelbert (1854–1921)

QUARTET

- **String Quartet**

Though Humperdinck composed seven operas, eight sets of incidental music (five were for productions of Shakespeare's plays), a symphony, a pair of orchestral pieces, and a good amount of music for voice and chorus, he remains known only by his remarkable opera *Hánsel und Gretel*.

The String Quartet is his single piece of chamber music. The Wagnerian hand that guided the opera is not in evidence. Instead, a fresh folk expression, fully Schumannesque, unfolds in the three movements. Everything is cheerful, *gemütlich*, and tonally cleansed in the C-major Allegro, the commodious, Gavotte-like second movement, and the lively Rondo. The French have a word for such happy music—it is *dégagé*.

Huré, Jean (1877–1930)

DUO

- **Sonata [No. 1] in F-sharp Minor for Cello and Piano (1903)**

Huré produced three cello and piano sonatas, all oddly centering on the F and F-sharp pitches. The second work is in F major, and the third in F-sharp major. The 1903 work (in F-sharp minor) is the most direct of the set by way of its forthright material, shapeliness, and discriminating sense of scoring proportion. It is dedicated to Pablo Casals.

In a work by Jean Huré one expects the formal habit of combining movements. This expectation is satisfied here. A flowing theme is contrasted to enunciative material (fanfare-type rhythms coded by pitch repetition), passes on to triple-beat light and graceful music (a scherzo inference), is succeeded by long line positiveness, and the plot concludes with an epiloguelike section containing reminders of the opening of the Sonata.

TRIO

- **Suite sur des chants bretons (Suite on Breton Folk Songs) for Piano, Violin, and Cello (1898)**

Chamber music is an excellent agent for folksong translation or inculcation. The very essence of folk *materia*, with its simplicity, makes its emergence in chamber works propitious. There are few composers who have not, at one time or another, been stimulated to draw from the deep well of traditional song. Either (as in many cases) such ingredients are present, with or without defined quotation, or else the folkloristic musical covering is conveyed through the stylistic manner of the composer. (Some of Bach's chorales are an example of the latter.) As illustrative of the former, where the folk materials are first uncovered and stated, then enlarged upon, is Huré's suite for piano trio, also known as *Petite Suite en Trio (Little Suite for Trio)*.

The profile of Bretonic song is very strong in this suite; the composer wishes it to be. Rather than variate upon the tunes used, they are worked on, but never lose, thereby, their spirit or identity. (It was not the first time that Huré was attracted to this fountainhead of melodicism.) In the first two movements, the shift from minor to major tonality has the analogical primitiveness of folk song. In the first movement, it serves as a coda; in the second, as the middle section. In the fourth piece, the latter premise is again used, but reversed, the minor key balancing the outer major key portions. The third movement is a chorale impression for the instruments. The sonority is tucked in, allowed to lift itself, and then settles into a distant, quadruple *piano*. All of it has chant definitions.

QUARTET

- **String Quartet No. 2 (1920)**

Huré had a predilection for combining several divisions of a work in one-movement totality. There is actually little difference between the three- or four-movement work and the composition which unites such total in one unbroken movement. Save for enlarged thought in the former plan, similar basic goals pertain in both cases. Unless a composer is writing a fantasy or rhapsody, he will necessarily have to relate his composition in some defined form. The simplest, of course, would be an A–B–A design, really a "two-movement-in-one" idea with reprise. The single attribute in favor of compression of several movements into one is its balanced unity, when the objective is for nonstop music.

In this instance, the logic of the quartet is exposed by interlocked and interconnective features of the compounded three movements. The three sections are an Allegro, followed by a fugue, then a semislow section, including a fugato, and then a return to the Allegro. Freedom is, of course, used in the sense that recapitulations are dissimilar to previous expositions. Balance is obtained by chain-linked references to prior material. A theme in fourths haunts the work; it carries over into the second and last sections; in turn, trills and tremolandos carry over from the second to third portions, making a triple bargain of the materials Huré offers. Within this, folk-flavored themes from the first and third movements are intertwined. There is an open-air quality to this sonorous music, and a special preoccupation with the use of ponticello color.

QUINTET

- **Quintet for Piano, Two Violins, Viola, and Cello (1908)**

This is a one-movement work, a favored form of the composer, which includes within it a four-movement distinction, but with quite loose application. A pastoral mood is first established, however, the thick treatment of the Quintet almost stifles the liberated quality of the joyous major key. After subsiding, the key changes, and there is a long-arched development, succeeded by a return of the opening theme. A long episode follows in the freest type of writing—the violin declaims in extemporaneous fashion; the rhythmic accompaniment continuing to match each of the dozen successive phrases, with the harmonic plan changing at the beginning of each. The second part is detailed in sonata form. Set in the contrastive minor key, it is given full-scale development. With the return of the opening material of this section and an Andante in the home key of D major (titled Postludio), the four-section-in-one-movement plan is made clear.

Hurlstone, William Y. (1876–1906)

DUO

- **Sonata in D for Cello and Piano**

Tonal clarity, control, and contrast, especially the play of major versus minor tonalities, are the fundaments of this duo sonata. The shape of folk song winds through the measures of the first movement, its principal themes neatly placed in the home key and its dominant. No mistaking these thematic shapes; one is of agile turn, the other of lyrical voice. Development and recapitulation are according to standard measurement, with the latter concentrated and changed in its format.

The slow movement retains its B-minor-key poignancy until it is canceled by the concluding tranquil and tender measures in B major. There follows a light and fast Scherzo in sharply defined E minor–C major–E minor form. In the final Rondo, the relationship of principal and subsidiary triads within the D-major key provides an additional major-minor coloration to the thematic details.

QUARTET

- **Phantasie for String Quartet**

Walter Willson Cobbett (1847–1937), England's great chamber music philanthropist, sponsored a series of competitions for English composers that began in 1905, for the composition of a work in phantasy form. This was to bring a 20th-century revival of the old "Fancy," used frequently by many English composers of the late 16th and 17th centuries. The word means exactly what it says—the form to be at the will of the writer. Implied, of course, was that there would be a sense of formal balance. The first competition brought sixty-seven entries; the winning composition was Hurlstone's Phantasie. (Among the some forty-winners during the life of the competition were such important names as Ralph Vaughan Williams, John Ireland, Frank Bridge, Herbert Howells, and H. Waldo Warner.)

Hurlstone's piece is based on a pair of themes, one in A minor, the other in A major. The former has an ascending outline, the other is more jagged in its contour. Development of the themes takes place in terms of changed states, tonalities, and tempos, all without hiding the thematic outlines. Then, the themes are redeveloped, the first one swinging in triple meter plus ingrained imitations, contrasted to the second theme emphasizing dynamic and textural conditions. A short Andante sostenuto features the cello in a metamorphosis of the second theme, the Allegro vivace that follows is concerned with the initial theme. The pair are then mixed and the quartet concludes with an enthusiastic *fortissimo*.

Hurník, Ilja (1922–)

DUO

- **Partita in A for Flute and Piano**

A fancy-coursed Introduction is followed by a series of dances. Hurník is the classicist in this work, but no faded mementoes of baroque suite particulars enter the sound premises.

A bit of imitation finds its way in the Siciliano. This technique becomes full-scale in the Gavotta, which is mostly set in canon; its contrasting central section weaves its melodic line over broken chords in ostinato, with a very simplistic bass line. The Sarabanda is in triple time, as expected, but it has another slant in its requested performance instruction: Andante dramatico. Hurník omits the Trio from the fifth movement Menuet. In place there is a second Minuet, with a *da capo*, as usual, to the first of the pair. Matters are wrapped up with a Gigue, propelled in prestissimo.

QUARTETS

- *Esercizi (Exercises)* for Flute
  (alternating Piccolo), Oboe,
  Clarinet, and Bassoon (1958)

Not a set of etudes, but a six-part work, the title equaling the 18th-century term for suite.

There is an updating in terms of the formal content. The second movement Gavotta has quintuple-pulsed measures inserted in the principal duple-metered content. In the frenetic pace of the Fuga (part five) quadruple and quintuple meters jostle each other.

Full formal command in Hurník's contemporary romanticism, clearly depicted in the buoyancy and energy of the end movements. The central pair of movements are a scherzo type and a slow music that moves over a rhythmically steadfast bass projection. Fat creative credits apply to this wind quartet.

- *Sonata da camera* for Flute, Oboe (or
  Clarinet), Cello, and Harpsichord
  (or Piano) (1953)

Romantic gentility controls this four-part sonata, set forth with suite characteristics. A Czech critic has described the quartet as one of "smiling good humor," but this is not totally on target, since the second movement is a Quasi marcia funèbre. Otherwise, agreement, with a swinging light-faceted first movement, a triple-pulsed concept clearly defined by the tempo, Allegretto innocente, and a tarantella-type finale.

QUINTET

- *Die Vier Jahreszeiten (The Four
  Seasons)* for Wind Quintet (1952)

Nine subjects that are carried out with clear sonic direction. "The Feast" is a three-part march. Movement two, "The Cuckoo," is con-firmed by scattered cuckoo calls in the clarinet. Tarantella zip is used for "The Harvest Time"; a proper polka is chosen, of course, for "The Harvest Festival Polka." Part five is "At the Little Fire," and no flaming content enters the scene—the music sounds under wraps, never heavier than *piano* dynamically.

Off-beat kicks color "The Swallows' Flight" and these carry over, plus syncopation, in "At the Country Festival." A curvaceous theme describes "The Starving Little Bird," and crisp rhythms help move "The Sleigh Ride."

Hurum, Alf (1882–1972)

QUARTET

- **String Quartet, Op. 6**

A delight. Hurum's work, frequently played in his native Norway, is practically unknown elsewhere. But this sentient work is to be relished for its scrupulous sensitivity and sensibility. It is totally eclectic music—music without a measure of discovery, but complete with rediscovery.

There are four movements. The first is in sonata form with a majestic and forthright scalic A-minor principal theme. Movement two is a duple-pulsed, quite fast Scherzo. Its Trio is in slower pace—its sounds skip gracefully. Movement three is a Canzonetta. The Norwegian musicologist Bjarne Kortsen states that this music "bears the unmistakable stamp of having been inspired by Russian music, and by Tchaikovsky in particular (cf. the famous Andante cantabile from the D-major string quartet), though without any sign of direct influence." Its form is the ternary type plus coda, that of the finale is a rondo. The latter is in A major and energetically folk-dances its way through the measures. As in the other parts of the work, the materials here are fervently lyrical, with a splendid sense of line.

Husa, Karel (1921–)

DUO

- **Sonata for Violin and Piano (1973)**

Grim music and paramount tensility in Husa's Sonata. Strong medicine, indeed, and one of the bitterest pieces of music for violin and piano in the literature. The sound qualities of the instruments are used for continual attack even in the middle (slow) movement, with glisses, microtones, frictions, clusters, and percussive plucked sounds by both the violin and the piano. No one should expect affable and amiable tinkles from music "influenced—although not voluntarily—by some events of the past years, such as continuous wars, senseless destruction of nature" and the "killing of animals," as Husa explains. Truly, a gripping piece of chamber music.

TRIOS

- *Évocations de Slovaquie* for Clarinet, Viola, and Cello (1951)

Three settings of this work exist. The first is for the trio medium noted above. Twelve years later (in 1963) Husa reset his *Slovakian Evocations* for wind quintet (flute, oboe, clarinet, horn, and bassoon) and piano, and in another scoring for solo wind quintet with string orchestra, xylophone, harp or piano. These last two also underwent a title change and the *Evocations* were given the less colorful title of *Serenade*.

The externals of Slovakian folk material are here rekindled by stylistic preparation (thematic embellishment and metamorphosis) in the warmth (and heat) of Husa's creative oven. According to the composer, the instruments chosen (clarinet, viola, and cello) recall "some of the small dance ensembles used by the musicians of Slovakia." The product is a real fruit from the native vine.

The music is not directly descriptive but rather symbolistic. Movement one, "The Mountain," concerns nature; "Night" is metaphysical (Husa's term); and "Dance" deals with the people.

- **Two Preludes for Flute, Clarinet, and Bassoon (1966)**

In the now wholly familiar "traditional" contemporary style. No outlandish fancies for this composer. The Adagio projects repetitive pitch figures in fair number; it also has wide registral scoring and includes a flute cadenza. The Allegro is a bit more settled but no less dynamic.

QUARTETS

- **String Quartet No. 1, Op. 8**

Three movements in the standard sequence of fast-slow-fast. (The first movement has a prelude and epilogue in adagio forming precise balance.) Husa's passion for sonority is evident in the work as well as his liking for motility. The music is close to twelve-tone style but does not use that technique.

- **String Quartet No. 2 (1959)**

Bartókian technique remains a staple contemporary argument. In his second quartet Husa is heart and soul a Bartókian as much as Webern was a devout follower of Schoenberg, and Piston believed in the neoclassic Stravinsky. No folk material, however, in this rhythmically meshed, percussively driven composition. It is of composite order, of essentially primitive style but organic as a whole.

Form is obtained by the use of large sections, which is a far cry from classical practice. And so is the harmonic language, which is atonal.

- **String Quartet No. 3 (1968)**

As pertained to Husa's second string quartet *(see above)* there are Bartókian connections in this work, but much less in this case. Instrumental individuality invigorates the work, with featured spots given to the viola in movement one, to the cello in movement two, and to both violins in movement three. Movement four, Husa indicates, "is an epiologue, when all the instruments come together." To which must be added that motility and color effects are incessant, forming the quality of the work as a whole.

The quartet is based on a twelve-tone row, but strict dodecaphonic technique does not apply. Husa points out that he does not insist "on rules of [the] Schoenberg or Webern school. I repeat notes freely and do not always use all twelve tones before repeating the row. I write octaves, forbidden by Schoenberg. Also, the whole composition has a strong center on note 'd.' "

QUINTET

- **Divertimento for Brass Quintet (Two Trumpets, Horn, Trombone, and Tuba) (1968)**

Husa has made second (and even third) settings of a fair number of his compositions—the Divertimento is an example. The four movements are a transcription of half of his *Eight Czech Duos* for piano four hands, composed in 1955. Still another transcription of the Divertimento was made for brass (three trumpets, four horns, three trombones, and tuba) plus two percussionists. In this case the Elegy (movement three of the brass quintet version) was dropped and a new movement titled Song was substituted.

First, there is a vertically designed Overture. A duple-pulsed Scherzo is in second place. (It contains a single measure in 3/4.) All the instruments are muted in the recitative-sectioned Elegy. The finale is a zinging Slovak Dance. It takes one to make one, and Husa, born in Prague and living there until 1946, delivers the product with magnificent flair and gusto.

Huss, Henry Holden (1862–1953)

QUARTET

- **Quartet in B minor for Strings (Two Violins, Viola, and Cello), Op. 31**

Huss was one of the group of American composers writing in the 20th century who formed a link to the 19th century. While there are safe and sound academic overtones to his quartet, there is also a little "letting go" that sharpens the outlines. The work is in defined, very recognizable forms, but has certain features of note. Truly, Huss's Op. 31 gives every indication that it was composed much later than its 1918 date. (Special recognition followed in 1920, the date Huss was awarded the double prize of the National Federation of Music Clubs and publication by the Society for the Publication of American Music.)

Incisive chords that announce the quartet, followed by sustained harmony, are used, as well, to begin the fourth movement. The lowering of the tonic for the key of the second subject of the opening movement exhibits formal freedom. The vigor of exciting syncopation and full-throated lyricism are additional assets.

The use of mutes is not bound to any period. They are called on for the coda of the first movement; are used to distinguish not only the Trio of the second movement's Scherzo, but to give a completely varied color to the recapitulation of that movement; and finally are the means to vary the return of the main portion of the slow movement. While Huss never looked toward the schools of Ravel-Stravinsky-Hindemith, or any other of the 20th century, he took more than a glance at Franck of the 19th century, via his cyclic manner. Thus, another noteworthy feature is the amplification of the Scherzo's Trio as one of the main considerations in the last movement. Here, as well, the composer's vision goes back to the practices of the 18th century as the quartet ends in the major form of the home tonality.

Huston, Scott (1916–)

TRIO

- *Lifestyles* for Clarinet, Cello, and Piano (1972)

Instrumental simmerings, shifting tempos and meters are the particulars for Huston's four-movement opus. The first pair is termed "Introspective, Reflective: Calm and Cool," the second pair is again of combined title: "Nervous, Frustrated: Energetic, Unpredictable." The sonorities, colors, and textures are stylistic splinters from the Donaueschingen and Darmstadt workbenches. Huston puts them together fairly well, though his glue does not contain more than a bit of thematic substance.

SEXTET

- *Four Our Times*: Suite for Six Brass Instruments (Two Trumpets, Horn, Trombone, Second Trombone [or Baritone Horn], and Bass [Tuba]) (1973)

(The score indicates the sixth instrument as a "Bass." One takes this to mean a tuba, though the part can be negotiated by a bass trombone.)

General programmatics cover the three parts: "Brilliance of Bells," "Thoughtful Solitude" (which can be performed totally open-timbred or muted), and "Tempered Animation." Tempo situations (moderately, slowly, and fast, in turn) follow the sense of these titles, as does the broadly tonal syntax.

Huszár, Lajos

QUINTET

- **Brass Quintet (Two Trumpets, Horn, Trombone, and Tuba) (1980)**

What Huszár has done is to take standard forms and revamp them a bit—updating, as it were, without disturbing balances. The Toccata doesn't zip along, rhythmically clean as a whistle, but contains syncopations, fracturing of beats, and segmenting. The Scherzo is a nervous piece and, somewhat expectedly, has no relaxed Trio for contrast. In the final place is a Cantilena. Here too there is full change from the usual homophonic basis to use of both harmonic counterpoint and full-status linear disposition.

Huth, Gustav (1902–69)

SEXTET

- *Nights in the Jizera Mountains* for Six Wind Instruments (Two Clarinets, Two Trumpets, Euphonium, and Bass Tuba) (1951)

Since there is a Jizera river that descends from the Jizera mountains the composer offers an alternate title: *Nights at the Jizera River*. A third possibility by quite free translation of the original Czech title is *The Music of Jizera Nights*.

Whatever, this is folksy, simple music, set for a folksy instrumental combo—nowhere else duplicated. The music drips with consecutive passages chock-full of consecutive thirds.

The headings of the three movements help explain the parenthetical title the composer placed on his score: *Hudci táhli*, which means "The (Village) Musicians Wanderings." The short suite opens with an "Introductory Serenade." It continues with a "Sousedská," a slow, triple-beat Czech round dance. The last part is a

"Farewell March." Everything is tuny and tuneful, and in movement one somewhat sentimental.

Hüttel, Josef (1893–1951)

QUARTET

- **String Quartet**

The inheritances of Czech nationalism which have steadfastly avoided grandiloquent style are portrayed in every measure of this work. Hüttel utilizes contemporary harmonic qualities to define national expression. The quartet sings (in a very vocal sense) and is organized on the theory that melodic lines keep trim the musical body. While there are no novel effects of timbre, the sonorous material is expertly conveyed. Hüttel determinedly represents his allegiance to nationalistic factors, in distinction to the cosmopolite composer who avoids specific nationalistic concord.

The first movement is attuned to sonata form, the development begun by fugato. The beauties of the song fervencies of the slow movement are enhanced by shifting quartal intervals into those of sixths. In the last movement, a scherzo theme, in view of the absence of such a movement, is telescoped into the design, with the thematic sauciness used as a ritornel. The development of the compendious theme includes fugato, though essentially Hüttel is not a contrapuntalist.

Huybrechts, Albert (1899–1938)

DUO

- **Sonata for Violin and Piano (1925)**

This work won the 1926 Elizabeth Sprague Coolidge Prize of the Library of Congress, one year after its composition. Huybrechts was a partial member of the Franck school, having studied with Joseph Jongen, himself a disciple of Franckian policy. Lyricism that stems from Franck is present, especially in the exploitation of the short phrase; but the harmonic plan (especially in the first movement) extends the tonality so that polytonal inflections take place. The impulse is to combine keys almost blatantly, yet relate them; for example, B major and B-flat major are immediately stated at the start of the second movement, a Lento. On the other hand, there is a full grasping of Scriabinesque technique with chordal items which are built brashly in square-cut fourths. The rhapsodic second section of the slow movement likewise stems from the Russian mystic. (But quartal harmony sounds suspiciously like bitonality, and of this the listener must be aware—namely, what is being heard is less portrayed dissonance, more a preconceived specific of harmonic language that deserts the triad in favor of the quartal arrangement.) In the same movement, the shifting rhythmic plan also draws its resources from Scriabin.

TRIO

- **Trio for Violin, Viola, and Cello (1935)**

The slippery spots and skittish sides that embrace tonal chromaticism are very strong in all parts of this three-movement Trio. Of course, such vacillating harmonic color provides a special tinge to the music, made more brilliant when it is carried along with the rhythmic liveliness that identifies all of Huybrechts's work. (It is this pulsatile stimulus that eliminates the aural fatigue that results from incessant pitch movement.)

A substantial introduction (Lent e grave) prefaces the principal part of the opening division which is set forth in animated pace. This Animé in sharp rhythmic quadruple pulse begins pitchwise, with simplicity, but picks up chromatic steam as it moves along. Three-part form balances the slow (central) movement. Additional color is provided with pizzicato syncopation, progression in fifths, and a section in harmonics that appears before the recapitulation. The final movement matches the first in terms of pulse definition and consistency of action.

QUARTETS

- **String Quartet No. 1 (1924)**

Huybrechts's quartet (it won the Ojai Vally Prize for a String Quartet in 1926) is brilliantly scored, especially in its extended first movement. Juicy chord streams, declarative octaves, scintillating tremolandos, and tingling harmonics add a range of colors that produce a blaze of virtuosity and effect. The movement is structured to contrast wide intervallic movement (in Huybrechts's favored quartal depiction) with tighter-spaced pitches, the latter giving an effect of scherzo treatment within the movement.

The true Scherzo follows, as part of the second (and final) movement. This is a rondo-styled music defining quintuple-metered sections in relation to triple-pulsed sections. Trills, cross-rhythms, syncopations, and arpeggios orchestrate this four-string-instrument essay. A music of such colorful texture and maximum energy deserved the prize it received.

- **String Quartet No. 2 (1927)**

The first movement is a development of the initial boldly rhythmic theme, followed by a lyrical episode and a return to the measured idea. Block rhythms set in a fast pace have motor drive. If these are then furnished with varying off- and on-the-beat accents, in nonsymmetrical fashion, the excitement becomes doubly increased. This is the plan used in the second movement, together with more poetic portions.

The slow movement combines rhythmic flux in practically every measure, during which the last half of each is less active, in the sense

that fewer sounds occupy the portion involved. The last movement is a cheerful Rondo, in breezy "open-air" style. This movement, more than any of the others, matches Huybrechts's description of his second string quartet that "it radiates peaceful happiness."

Hvoslef, Ketil (1939–)

QUINTET

- **Wind Quintet (1964)**

(When this work appeared the composer's name was Ketil Saeverud. Composer-identification confusion was the result of Ketil being the son of the well-known Norwegian composer Harald Saeverud; accordingly, the son took his mother's maiden name in 1980. Of course, this decision may have been caused by the desire to be considered individually and not as the son of a top-rank composer.)

The quintet is in four movements and fundamentally consists of a pair of fast movements that enclose two slower ones. The first of the latter is an Andantino in broad 3/2 time but gives the effect of a scherzo with repetitive patterns a principal point. The following movement, Andante semplicemente, is in arch form. It consists of 119 measures and not a single one has the entire quintet playing. In fact it is only in the final two measures that as many as four instruments are used. This lightness of scoring is basic to the entire work. The outer movements are in sonata and rondo forms, respectively.

Hye-Knudsen

Hye-Knudsen, Joh.

DUO

- **Two Chamber Duets for Flute and Cello, Op. 4**

Intimate and concentrated to the greatest degree, the duet medium must depend on polyphony to register effectively. Of course, the more opposed the timbres used, the easier to effect this. Hye-Knudsen chooses soprano wind and bass string instruments and thereby coloristic contrast is assured. The other (contrapuntalistic) requirement is fulfilled in the pair of pieces that make up his Op. 4.

In the Prélude two themes are exposed and at the same time serve to introduce the instruments. The cello presents a twenty-measure C-sharp-minor Northern-flavored statement, the flute alone follows with an E-major rhythmically stimulated subject. In the twelfth measure of this section the instruments are joined. The give and take of imitation technique invigorates the piece, which is completed by balancing the opening via the enharmonic tonality of D-flat major.

"Song and Dance" would more pertinently describe the second piece, titled *Chanson*. In the outer portions the music does sing, mostly in canonic compactness. In the middle the music is balletic and moves at first also with canonic steps. In these pieces the basic criteria for a chamber duo are met without complexity, without monotony, and with full clarity.

Iannaccone, Anthony (1943–)

DUOS

- *Aria concertante* for Cello and Piano (1976)

Iannaccone's most serious work. There is a Mahlerian intensity in this composition, organized through serial as well as traditional motivic methods.

Beginning with a freely disposed Arioso the music expands into a Scherzo, with this first movement ending quietly. The latter mood continues in the second movement's Aria, which thenceforth parallels the first movement in its "gradual accumulation of tension and momentum." This forms the "Metamorphosis," which concludes quietly, corresponding to the first part of the duo. Thus, similar balances within each movement and thereby total balance.

- *Bicinia* for Flute and Alto Saxophone (1974)

In its segmentation, controlled by wire-thin connections, *Bicinia* (the 16th-century term for a vocal composition in two parts) has slightly nervous linear intensity. Part 1 is slow, the second part is twice as fast. The structures are sharply contrastive. In the first part the materials are free, sounding quasi-cadenza and quasi-improvisational. In the serially processed second part a strict A–B–A (da capo) arrangement is used.

- *Remembrance* for Viola (or Alto Saxophone) and Piano (1968)

Music representing this composer's preserial style. The logic of this short, intensely pensive piece is obtained by use of pitch polarity around the C-sharp area. There is well-registered use of textures and dynamics to obtain tension and release, or, as the composer has stated, "a pyramidal rise and fall."

- *Rituals* for Violin and Piano (1973)

Iannaccone's chamber music rite is both direct—rhapsodic and virtuosic—and symbolistic, incorporating a pair of chants from the ritual of the Roman Mass—*Victimae paschali* and the *Dies irae*. The latter are crunched into the texture with the related twelve-note theme of the piece. Though the spontaneous effect of the work sounds like improvisation, the expressive vitality and flux are strictly the consequence of Iannaccone's creative discipline.

- Sonatina for Trumpet and Tuba (1975)

The instrumental combination itself is sufficiently unusual to draw interest. But there is more. The music is a bit snide, has some sophisticated humor, and is aided by chatty, caustic counterpoint.

A one-movement structure, tightly developed from the opening six-pitch motive announced by the trumpet.

TRIO

- Trio for Flute, Clarinet, and Piano (1980)

Hearty, serial-style music, but always with freed detail. The composer explains that his Trio "reflects an attempt to join together a musical form of timbral continuities and contrasts with the more basic elements of song and dance."

Save for a central section of force, a delicacy pervades the Prelude. The Fantasy also begins and concludes quietly, but elsewhere it contains robustness and energy. In the Divertimento rhythmic rhapsody drives the music. When the basic meter is quadrate, the pulse is not only straightforward but arranged so that accents give eighth-note totals of 3+2+3 or 3+3+2 or 2+3+3, etc. Syncopative rhythms over the bar lines provide additional pulsatile stimulants. The same applies to the later use in the movement of shifts between duple and triple accentuations stated within the same time lengths.

QUARTETS

- *Anamorphoses* **for Two Trumpets, Trombone, and Percussion (Xylophone, Glockenspiel, Vibraphone, Marimba, Temple Blocks, Wood Chimes, Tubular Bells [Chimes], Tam-tam, Bass Drum, and Timpani) (1972)**

The raw material for this quartet (one percussionist handles all the listed instruments) is described by the composer as "a twelve-note row and two simple rhythmic cells." Avant-garde colorations include quarter tones, half-valved pitches for the brass instruments, and improvising on given pitches.

Virtuosic implications throughout. There are two movements: a ten-minute Scherzando and an eight-minute slow–fast–slow movement (indicated respectively, caloroso–semplice–caloroso). Everything is impelling and none of the material is rubbished with inconsequential staged effects. Importantly, the composer indicates that "some of the timbral and articulative gestures in *Anamorphoses* were influenced by the electronic music medium."

- *Four Mythical Sketches* **for Two Baritone horns and Two Tubas (1968/1971)**

There is no closed end to chamber music media. Special timbral combinations were few and far between until the 1920s. Since then the spectrum has become polychromized to the utmost. Anything and everything can be chosen, and is! Witness this brass quartet.

Iannaccone's suite was a response to colleagues "who complained of a lack of interesting literature for tubas." He has gone further than just music for tubas. Chamber music including the baritone horn (another name for the euphonium, present in most band compositions but a rarity in orchestral scores) is even of lesser total.

The movements are based on subjects from Greek mythology. "Hades," the abode of the dead, is ponderous and hellishly serious in its serialized pitch activity, its grave tempo of two-way meaning. "Pluto," the god of the underworld, is presented with rhythmic, scherzo-outlined quality. "Persephone," the goddess of fertility, Pluto's queen, has lyrical potency. The fourth sketch, "Poseidon," is fugally energetic, as befits music pertaining to the god of the sea. Special effects are used, concentrated solely in the "Hades" portion. These are blowing through the instrument without producing a defined pitch, nonpitched sound attacks obtained by use of the tongue, short quarter-tone distanced glissandos, and pitch obtained by singing into the instrument on the syllable "du."

Programmatic in a general way, the four pieces are balanced by their differing tempos and mood qualities. No intellectual frenzy is involved, but a solidity of brass instrument language. The first two movements can be performed separately. The third and fourth movements (connected without pause) can be performed only as part of the total suite.

(The split dates in the title heading are due to the fact that "Hades" was composed in 1968 and the other three movements were written in 1971. The last were later published separately by Presser as *Three Mythical Sketches.)*

- **String Quartet (1965)**

The propulsiveness of the final (third) movement stems from Bartók. But there are other influences in this early work, including

Stravinsky and Berg. But, if eclectic, Iannaccone's quartet avoids developmental dead spots and linear stolidity. The textural content is heavy, the coloration dark, the sonoric temperature chromatically heated.

QUINTET

- *Parodies* **for Woodwind Quintet (1974)**

Self-borrowing applies here. Movement one, a staccato-flavored Caprice, movement two, a Cantilena, and movement three, an active Intermezzo, are based on sketches Iannaccone made in 1959 for a woodwind quartet. In turn, the opening oboe melody of the Caprice (after a one-measure introduction) provides the thematic basis for the first two movements as well as the finale, titled "Rag." And—more transfer. The "Rag" itself is a revised setting from an earlier group of three, titled *Retail Rags*. Emphatically, this new viewpoint works well and offers evocative entertainment.

Iannaccone explains his title in detail. "The word *parody* is used to mean a 'takeoff,' evocation, and new interpretation of preexisting material, not unlike the Renaissance parody mass and parody motet. It does not denote caricature but implies both a calling forth of associations and a new setting of older material."

Ibert, Jacques (1890–1962)

Of necessity most composers must be typed only by consideration of their best efforts in preference to their entire output (which may show conflicting attitudes). The separation into time and style periods of activity, as applied to Beethoven, does not pose a classification quandary. In his case, growth is accompanied not by sharp change but by acute adaptation. Beethoven's technical action is variable, but his aesthetic deportment does not yield to it; it

is a solid pivot from first work to last. With Stravinsky, strenuous artistic change defies a defined compartmentalization of all his music. Ibert, however, was consistent, though not of Beethovenian intellect. There is no fleeting attention to the creative reasonings of others. The type and style of all his works are individually sensitive if not progressively reshaped with more vital and deeper thoughts. Ibert's music avoids empiricism as well as sensationalism. To know one of his compositions may well be to know them all, but the vigorous regard he had for the strict maintenance of idiom does not bore as one passes from one work to the next. His choice of synonyms not only avoids dullness but shuns patterned speech and also furnishes a pleasant surprise, notwithstanding the fact that the listener knows what to expect. There is no problem in typing Ibert as a master of sheer musical pleasure with plentiful "kick."

DUOS

- *Entr'acte* **for Flute (or Violin) and Harp (1935)**

The special coloring of certain instruments would draw a composer of picturesque intent to them. Ibert's short piece creates a definite mood of romantic poesy. It courses its way by busy figurations, its tunes creating the effect of an idealized dance.

(A recording of this duo for flute and guitar was probably approved by the publisher, the copyright laws being what they are, but had never been suggested by Ibert.)

- *Jeux (Games)*: **Sonatine for Violin (or Flute) and Piano (1924)**

Ibert's musical conduct always resulted in a product made with good taste. He was a composer of excellent aesthetic breeding—it shows in his creative manners and polished wit. Quite often the miniature forms tempted him, but, because of the subtle and pleasing refinements of which he was capable, none of these are mere trifles.

The two sections of this work exemplify the lightness of the composer and demonstrate how Ibert formed delicious sounds, here portrayed by animated and tender music. "Animé" is light and gay, written in tripartite style, jumping on the feet of quintuple pulse. "Tendre" is a vocal type, heard first with simple accompaniment, restated in canonic form. The ending is sensitive—the sounds in motion, vibrating in the suspended sonority of G-sharp major.

TRIOS

- *Cinq pièces en trio* **for Oboe, Clarinet, and Bassoon**

Ibert has been damned as a serious composer of light music and, flipping the coin, as too light in his serious music. Nonsense, confusion will arise and matters will never be sorted out until it is realized that even in meaningful musical matters there is a place for a sense of humor and that important connotations can be realized in the decor of bright instrumental declarations.

Rhythmic forwardness and jiggy style are found in the first piece, a bit more pulse precision is represented in the fifth piece. Number three of the set skims along. Catchy melodic framework with direct contrasts marks the pair of slower-paced pieces (numbers two and four).

- **Trio for Violin, Cello, and Harp (1944)**

In this Trio Ibert does not use long-strung classical forms, since his themes will not permit undue development. Excellent and impressive music results because it is placed in simple frames that match its character.

Measures containing extra beats inserted at strategic points in the thematic line give additional kick to the first movement. Compared with the outer movements, the middle one is rather serious. A breezy type of scherzo is called on for the finale. Ibert's magnificent sense of color is exhibited in this section. One example: Just before the recapitulation of the principal subject, the violin and cello whiz down in flying chromatic thirds, while the harp's banjolike sounds cause a new element to be associated with the re-entrance of the theme, heard at first in unaccompanied string duet arrangement.

QUARTETS

- *Deux mouvements (Two Movements)* **for Two Flutes, Clarinet, and Bassoon (1923)**

The pieces have the immediacy of improvisations. The forms are free, the timbres exhilarating. As is usual with Ibert, a mischievous quality is displayed. In both movements the main themes are announced by the clarinet— that of the second piece being prefaced by a ballet type of material with a contemporary outlook. A refreshing and captivating bit of chamber music.

- *Pastoral for Four Pipes* **(Treble in D, Treble in G, Alto in D, and Bass in G)**

Ibert's miniature is prefaced with the motto: "Annihilating all that's made / To a green thought in a green shade." Textures as well as themes provide balance for this pithy three-part piece. The first portion is for the two treble pipes, the second section is for the two lower instruments, and the third portion is a return of the initial material freshly set for all four instruments.

- **String Quartet (1942)**

The only example of the medium in Ibert's

good-size catalogue. Akin to his supple orchestration, the quartet is deft, yet retains a relaxed profundity throughout.

The first movement is a simple, large trisequestered idea with pulsations conveyed constantly by sixteenth-note rhythmic patterns. The key feeling is C major, but the deviations are many. Even the final cadence attempts to pull away from this prime tonality.

Although the slow movement (Andante assai) is songlike, there are hidden meanings within it. Ibert has stated that this section depicted his reaction to the Second World War—would always remind him "of this dreadful period of my life!" It is followed without pause by the third part of the work, a pyrotechnical pizzicato dissertation with no use of the bow by any of the instruments for the entire 251 measures, written in strict 3/8 meter. A little bit of pizzicato goes a long way, but it is surprising how the ear will not tire of over two hundred measures of such timbre, especially when it is heard in the up tempo used in this case. The final movement, very contrapuntal in character, contains the markedness of march rhythmics within its lines; the form is sonata-rondo, with much writing in compressed, duo-voice form.

QUINTET

- *Trois pièces brèves (Three Short Pieces)* **for Woodwind Quintet (1930)**

With the exception of Hindemith's *Kleine Kammermusik*, Op. 24, No. 2, this is the most favored contemporary work in the wind-quintet category. Ibert's tuneful themes do not require enlargement by argument. These pieces, for a delightful and frolicking pocket-size orchestra, are examples of true hedonistic music; they combine paprika with soda pop—a pleasure to the ear, a delight to play.

The two fast movements embracing a slow division are as balanced in total as they are individually. The first movement, of rondo character, is conceived on a more vertical basis than the third piece. Metrical shifts define the latter—the final cadence is as typical a snapshot of the composer's style as one can find.

It is worth noting that the middle piece practically amounts to a duet for flute and clarinet, written in free imitatory style. Only at the very end are the quintuple instrumental forces employed, providing a contrastive textural weight to define the coda.

SEXTET

- *Le Jardinier de Samos (The Gardener of Samos)* **for Flute, Clarinet, Trumpet, Violin, Cello, and Percussion (Military Drum and Tabor) (1932)**

Originally composed as incidental music for a play, the work serves just as competently as a suite for performance on the chamber music concert platform. A colorful assortment is packaged into the piece. Each of the five movements is for a different instrumental group, each calls for a different total of players, and variety marks the formal settings. It certainly was not happenstance that the five movements include a duo, trio, quartet, quintet, and sextet.

The trumpet carries the Overture with a brilliant tune. All six instruments participate in this opening. (The military drum plays in but two measures—the initial one and the penultimate one.) The Air de Danse is principally for the flute; the other instruments (violin, cello, and tabor [also known as tambourin]) are subordinate.

The Prelude to the Second Act and the Prelude to the Fourth Act are in sharp contrast. The first of the pair is a warm string duo. The second (scored for clarinet and string instruments) is active internally though the tempo is grave et noble. Ibert indicated this music was plotted in the style of a scholastic fugue. Accordingly, to subtly parallel this academicism the violin scrapes close to the bridge.

Movement five (Prelude to the Fifth Act) calls for the five pitched instruments. It has an unusual time signature: 6+3/16. This metrical arrangement bears out Ibert's fully gay, basic creative temperament.

Ichiyanagi, Toshi (1933–)

QUARTET

- **String Quartet No. 1**

In the early 1950s, Ichiyanagi, a student of John Cage's, became the first to introduce chance operations as a compositional technique into Japanese music. The quartet exemplifies this method.

There are minute events for each instrument. These have no tempo, no meter, no pulse division, no dynamic, and avoid cohesion with any of the other instruments. The music is a filling of the tone space with isolated sounds and noises.

The score may be played through once or twice, in the latter case the score is turned upside down.

Ikenouchi, Tomojirō (1906–)

QUARTET

- **Prelude and Fugue for String Quartet**

Decidedly, music of the late-romantic *(read:* chromatic) school. More than once the slippery voice action recalls Franckian properties. Within these, Ikenouchi exploits the full gamuts of the instruments. (One section in the Prelude is of especially high sonority.)

The Prelude develops into Bachian-invention contrapuntal circumstance, set in a contemporary environment. This portion has a

subtle relationship with the quartet's second part, via the ascending line of the fugal subject. The Fugue is worked out to the utmost, halts for an insertion of Prelude material, then returns to the stretto, augmentation, and inversion accessories of fugal fact.

Ikonomov, Boyan (1900–73)

TRIO

- **Trio in E for Oboe, Clarinet, and Bassoon, Op. 14**

Most woodwind trios are of lighter character than this one. The sobriety is matched by an insistence on total textural equality that does push color individuality to one side. Uniformity of meter is a parallel: totally triple in movement one, always duple in movement two, and constantly septuple in the final movement. In the latter instance the divisional pulse is dogmatically 2/4 plus 3/8. Ikonomov's musical detail is temperate, unextravagant, tempered by Rousselian neoclassicism. This makes patently clear the objectives of the three movements.

QUARTET

- **String Quartet No. 2 in A, Op. 16**

Honest vigor of invention gives a plus sign to this work. A little minus mark concerns the textural heaviness—a habit with this Bulgarian composer. Orthodox forms cover the fast–slow–fastest tempos of the three movements, with balanced tonality allegiance: A for the corner movements, E-flat for the central one.

Ikonomov breaks no new ground in his quartet, leaning on Roussel (with whom he studied; he was also a student of Nadia Boulanger's) to guide his trim neoclassical vehicle. Creative strategy, however, begins each movement a bit differently designed from what then follows. In the first movement it is fugato, in the second, a violin recitative, and in the final movement, a rhythmic ostinato tossed from one instrument to the next. Nevertheless, the characteristics these beginnings set are fulfilled by the materials to which they are linked.

Ikonomov, Stefan (1937–)

DUO

- *Burlesque* for Horn and Piano

A devotion to changing speeds marks the sectional order of the music. And no subtle implications. Thus, the first portion is an Allegro, where the quarter note is metronomically set at 280; this changes to a Lento, where the quarter note equals 40. And, so on. Such action does help the parody. So does the sharp-pointed harmony.

Iliev, Konstantin (1924–)

DUO

- Sonata for Clarinet and Piano, Op. 36

Animated by engaging themes and peppered with dissonance. Movement one chromaticizes around the key point of C; movement two mixes its keys and ends in A-flat combined with E minor; the finale floats around and is completed with the bitonal partnership of C and D-flat.

Form, however, is of less-contemporary formation. It serves, therefore, to make Iliev's harmonic content sharp and clear and places it in relief. The sonata-designed opening part is followed by two movements, both in three-divisioned total; the second of the pair much

bigger in scope. In the first of these, a leisurely flowing music shifts between duple and triple pulsations within similar time spans. In the other, the soundings are from the dance floor, with scherzo flippancy. The contrastive middle portion is waltz-toned.

Imbrie, Andrew (1921–)

DUOS

- Impromptu for Violin and Piano (1960)

A sizable work in three parts, which Imbrie describes as "essentially similar to movements of a brief sonata." Though it does not lack some direct dynamism, tension is the principal ingredient in Imbrie's close-to-fifteen-minute work. This tension is more the result of linear activity than vertical enunciation.

Imbrie conceived his duo as "a virtuoso piece for *both* [my italics] violin and piano." This instrumental equality brings the piece into the chamber music domain.

- Sonata for Cello and Piano (1966)

Classically refurbished materials will be recognized in the Sonata. Handling of the duo medium is colorfully alive, but there is no striving for auditory awe-striking. The concept is supple, sometimes austere, but tonally balanced.

Imbrie avoids fragmentary ideas. There are strong contrasts, but these do not interfere with or interrupt the overall continuity.

TRIOS

- Serenade for Flute, Viola, and Piano (1952)

Imbrie avoids light facets in his Serenade. Each of the three essays has a serious demeanor.

This includes the middle movement, a Siciliano that bypasses its traditional dance derivatives, but not its duple rhythmic reliance. It contains successive cadenzas for flute and viola. Another mark of special distinction is the last movement. No gay, flyweight affair, this. In place is an Adagio—exceptional as the concluding division of a serenade! Its introverted tone is the antithesis of the extroverted quality of the opening movement.

The formal logic of Imbrie's music stamps him as a neoclassicist. The textural tone and strong floridity of speech imply a dovetailing with neoromanticism.

- **Trio for Violin, Cello, and Piano (1946)**

Imbrie's piano trio was composed in the space of forty-three days (July 10–Aug. 21) in 1946, "for the Princeton Bicentennial," celebrated that year. (The university was chartered in 1746, opened the next year, and was rechartered in 1748.) Imbrie received his higher education at Princeton, graduating in 1942, which explains the creative objective.

The compositional style is neoclassic, set in a broad chromatic state. A sense of tonal center is retained in the freely functional harmony. In the first and last movements it is G; in the slow movement it is E-flat (the music ends in E-flat minor). But the range is strong. The Germanic sinew in this type of neoclassically styled music contrasts with the tomboyish quality found in its French-based relative.

No radical innovations mark the Trio, but Imbrie is cognizant of instrumental distinction within the medium. All three movements begin with piano alone, with the complete exposition of the slow movement also assigned to the solo piano. This is followed by a dialogue between the strings.

QUARTETS

- **Quartet in B-flat (String Quartet No. 1) (1942)**

This Quartet focused the spotlight on Imbrie and brought attention to his work. True talent eventually surfaces; rarely, however, is it quickly recognized. The B-flat quartet was Imbrie's senior thesis at Princeton, written during the time he was studying with Roger Sessions there (the Quartet is dedicated to Sessions). It was completed in June 1942, the year Imbrie graduated. The following season (1943–44) the Quartet won the coveted New York Critics' Circle award for chamber music. Imbrie was on his way. Deservedly.

A Lento quasi cadenza for the first violin introduces the Quartet and makes a pivotal return in the middle of the first movement (Allegro). It is paralleled by a Maestoso introduction in the third movement (Allegro), which reappears later. These tempo responses are not only contrasts but reference aids in fixing the designs. A further nicety occurs at the conclusion of the middle movement. Here, once again, there is a first-violin cadenza, which thereby relates to the opening of the Quartet in terms of method. Small-spanned, these cadenzas create a tempo rondo in the five placements made within the three movements.

Imbrie's work is seasoned with rhythmic salt. The drive of the sonata-formationed first movement is contrasted by a flowing subject and stimulated by double pulses bisecting triple ones. Off-beat voice changes spur the slow movement, in which the combination of major and minor harmonies plays an important role. And in the final part of the Quartet, which Imbrie describes as "a kind of sonata-rondo," the meter is of uneven quintuple total, but with fluid division of the beats.

- **String Quartet No. 2 (1953)**

The traditional neoclassic links to the past are here retained—clear, declarative form and the use of pitch centers as the basis for free diatonicism. In Imbrie's hands these substantially true and proven considerations are stylistically expanded, becoming bridges joining the past with the present. Tonality, laced with dissonant counterpoint and chromaticized with a no-nonsense diction, is now hardboiled. Imbrie is not endeavoring to charm. The string voices take the ear into custody and hold attention with rich polyphonic detail. This is a rhythmically stable music—not a single metrical change is made from beginning to end within each of the three movements, though the inner designs are of virtuosic order. Again, this shows a dovetailing of classic stability with contemporary activity. All superficiality is banished. The quartet is a web of enthusiastic detail.

In the opening movement (Alla marcia) a static rhythmic motive is let loose, but controlled. It inhabits the world of percussion without being percussive. From this germinal point, drum-stroke reverberations are contained in the music. Elongations and contractions are inherently related to the basic idea. And these are colored by a jazzy touch here and there. Motival data are also the rationale of the slow movement, which is linked to the opening part of the quartet. The first of these motives, displaying a rising fourth, is paramount. Four-part writing for the violins alone defines the contrasting section. Though the final movement is not attached to the slow movement, it is linked to it by intervallic tendency. The slow part ends with a B–D-flat–F chord in harmonics. The finale begins with these three pitches in succession as the opening motive, stated in octaves. A simple matter, but a congenial ploy for establishing continuity. This sonata-designed finale is refreshed by its perpetual-motion briskness. The sixteenth notes bounce, buzz, and bustle and boss the instrumental activity. And always classical action is the referee. Imbrie's second quartet begins in D. It ends similarly.

- **String Quartet No. 3 (1957)**

Each of Imbrie's quartets accepts classical synonymity in its structure. The second quartet expands tonal boundaries into panchromatic territory. The third quartet digs deeper into this area with dodecaphonic tools. For the greater part, row technique applies to the first movement, with portions of the system used in the other two divisions of the work. But as Imbrie adds, he also retains. Tonality is not dispossessed. It functions in certain areas as an overlay to the influence of the row. Since tonalism is chromatically administered, Imbrie has accomplished a neat combine of classical contours with a total chromaticism which is both twelve-tone controlled and the opposite. It makes for beautiful logic.

The design of the work is apron-stringed to balanced practices. The fastest music is in the center, surrounded by slower movements, Allegretto in front and Poco adagio at the end. Nonrigid sonata form is in movement one. Constantly engrossed in polyphonic detail, the plan has vivid textural contrasts in splitting the voices two against two, or in total rhythmic unification of all four voices. The Scherzo is three part, its triple beat insistence clarified and excited by the use of total silence or by textural thinning. The Trio is lyrical, but its quality avoids the often-met-with contrastive compromise. It swerves and curves, whereas the main material is vertically pinpointed. The aesthetic link to this music is found in Beethoven's scherzos. Sectional form marks the finale. There, a liedlike reflective music is followed by nervous, rhapsodic, explosively expressive ejaculations of the lines. The aesthetic link to this portion is found in Alban Berg's music. A return is then made to the initial material, and the quartet ends with short fragments drawn from the middle portion of the movement.

SEXTET

- **Divertimento for Six Instruments (Flute, Bassoon, Trumpet, Violin, Cello, and Piano) (1948)**

Only the Finale of this five-movement work for six instruments does not have a descriptive title. Its rhythmic élan matches and balances the touch-and-go of the opening "Fanfare." Though the trumpet (the single brass instrument of the sextet) is important in the "Fanfare," this is no run-of-the-mill set of flourishes. A key point is the trumpet's articulative figure that closes with a glissando, but the other instruments are given some fancy-dan opportunities for display as well.

The "Colloquy" is mainly commerce between sustained ideas and rhythmic ones, and the "Soliloquy" negates monophonic proportion for contrapuntal euphony. This is really a six-voice soliloquy since every instrument has a spotlighted chance. Movement four is titled "The Poet Has Spoken!" In this case soliloquizing speech is present. The bassoon is the "poet." He speaks with seven-beat scription throughout, maintaining his leading role regardless of rejoinders from the other instruments.

While divertimentos are generally light-faceted—and so, to a degree, is Imbrie's—there is more substance to this opus than usually pertains to divertimento creative tactics. Imbrie's well-knit, neoclassic-spiced free formulations are far from rote representations.

SEPTET

- *Dandelion Wine* **for Oboe, Clarinet, String Quartet, and Piano (1967)**

A short, expressionistic piece. The intriguing title is the name of a novel by Ray Bradbury, concerning memories of a boyhood spent in a small town. The tale describes the bottling of dandelion wine, with each bottle dated. Imbrie believes these bottles "become symbols of memory, since each date recalls a particular summer day and its activities."

Nothing graphic is included in Imbrie's *Dandelion Wine*. It is the essence of the novel's basis that is utilized. The musical ideas are presented in fantasy arrangement, and at the end certain of them are recalled "in new contexts to give, if possible, the effect of poignant reminiscences, all 'bottled' in a very brief container." The relationships of these recalls are rather free.

Though *Dandelion Wine* was written by Imbrie in Princeton, "at a time and place quite conducive to a mood similar to that invoked in the novel," no summer haze, lazy, relaxed quality, or nostalgia are to be found in the music. *Dandelion Wine* is an absolute piece of absolute music.

Inagaki, Seiichi (1935–)

DUO

- *Dialog* **for Violin and Piano (alternating Cymbals and Maracas)**

Bearing out the title, Inagaki's duo is a sublimation of sonorous searchings without thematic or motival recourse. The violin glides and glisses, oscillates and undulates, obliterating any tinge of pulse pointedness. The piano mainly has minute conjunct patterns and contact with the instrument's strings either by scratching them with the fingernails or brushing them with the fingers. Here again, specific rhythms are set adrift. In all these sonorous items microtones are either exactly depicted or heard within the sonic motility. Further color is, of course, obtained from the shaking of the maracas and using a cello bow to play along the edge of the cymbals.

Inagaki considers his piece "a spiritual dialogue, a touching of hearts." Thus, sentiment has not been forgotten in avant-garde music.

QUARTET

- *Catalysis* for Flute, Violin, and Percussions (Ancient Cymbals, Two Gongs, Three Suspended Cymbals, Five Temple Blocks, Bell, Tam-tam, Triangle, Three Tenor Drums, and Naruko [Bamboo]) (1974)

(For the percussion two players are required.)

Structure gives way to a knitting together of sound swatches. Most of the percussion timbres are of metallic quality and these furnish a high-heated quality to the score. Rub-off takes place, since the violin has such fricatives as playing with the bow hair between the bridge and the tailpiece as well as playing with the wooden part of the bow in the same "no-man's-land" area.

Action within this music is of the aggressive kind. Dynamic seduction is the result, the music's title notwithstanding.

NONET

- *Pulse* for Brass and Percussion (Three Trumpets, Three Trombones, and Three Percussion [Nine Suspended Cymbals, Glockenspiel, Xylophone, Six Cow Bells, Six Wood Blocks, Six Bongos, Gong, Six Timpani, Eight Tom-toms, Naruko ((Bamboo)), Three Pieces of Iron, Claves, Tam-tam, Marimba, and Maracas])

The twain do not meet in Inagaki's thirteen-minute nonet. Most of the brass writing presents flat-surfaced sounds; rhythmic articulation and motility come from the percussion trio. Featured in the brass scoring are noise

sounds obtained by pressing the lips on the mouthpiece and shaping "si," and "fo," or "ra," and "ri."

This is a brittle and sharply cut music. Fervor there is, but not of the poetic kind.

Inagaki, Takuzo (1940–)

DUO

- *Rocking Chair* for Viola (or Double Bass) and Piano, Op. 1

An unfortunate title for a neatly nondescriptive romantic duo. It's a three-part item, with F major followed by B-flat major, and then, of course, a return to the former tonality. Firmly rooted melodic and harmonic virtues.

TRIO

- *Home Concert* for Violin, Viola, and Cello, Op. 4

A set of four short tonal pieces, simple in content, without any unexpected derivations. Music for the home, truly, and music for moderately advanced players.

QUARTET

- *Contrast Suite* for Double Bass Quartet, Op. 5

Sketches that convey, by way of contemporary tonalism, specific moods in parts three and four, and precise dynamic settings in parts one and two. The former pair are "Impeto" ("Impetus") and "Sereno" ("Serene"), with ostinato drive in the first one and a tuneful arrangement in the other. Parts one and two are titled "Piano" and "Forte," but the dynamic headings should be read in terms of the rhythmic action (quiet and mostly active, in turn) rather than in the sense of defined sonorous measurement.

Inch, Herbert (1904–88)

DUO

- **Sonata for Cello and Piano (1941)**

Key coherence by way of key stability certifies this duo sonata. Every movement begins in D and concludes in D. And most of the harmony stays in D and the close surrounding tonal territory.

In the opening movement, the home tonality is departed from quickly, but one is aware that this is a temporary move; the wayward chords will return home, and they do. Especially formative is the opening theme, which is irregular, splashing its way in a zigzag course until it finally cleanses itself by a sweep down the orbited members of the C-major chord. The piece was composed when Inch held a fellowship at the American Academy in Rome, and one suspects 20th-century speech percolated into his studio, for the vagaries are of such manner. However, the second theme includes 17 1/2 measures before its pure C major is touched with an accidental.

A large three-part form dictates the middle movement, and the last is a type of gigue, but has more of the English-style "jig" about it, in view of its modal cast. The unevenness of the pulse (5/4) stimulates matters.

d'Indy, Vincent (1851–1931)

When d'Indy gave his inaugural speech as the president of the Schola Cantorum in Paris, in 1896, he stated that the most important function was the study of the classic forms—that music must be founded on principles "that are sane, serious, and trustworthy." These tenets are fundamental to his compositions, regardless of the media in which they are set. Careful attention to all matters, meticulous regard to scoring (someone said d'Indy was never guilty

of an unclean sonority), and a wholehearted acceptance of Franck's cyclical treatment of sonata form, with more than a passing acceptance of Wagner—these were Vincent d'Indy's operative tools.

He was a prodigious worker in all musical fields: composer of more than a hundred major works, conductor, teacher of many students (the most famous are Honegger and Roussel), writer (his biographies of Franck and Beethoven are very important, as is a remarkable three-volume general study of music—*Cours de composition musicale*—in addition to innumerable essays), musicologist (especially in regard to authentic editions of the works of Monteverdi and Rameau), as well as a lecturer, editor, and propagandist for music.

D'Indy's music is healthy, fully and completely organized to the last sixteenth note. The ideal of logic and craftsmanship was his first point in a creed that demanded rigorous attention to all details. Whether a certain freedom was lost in so doing, whether with such precision and rigid technique the essentially required meatiness and flavor have been negated, is an opinion that must be reached individually. Above all, his compositions demand respect. He is a reborn classicist (like Fauré), in the Franck tradition. Manifesting such attractiveness, his music is neither the blatant outpouring of a lush romanticist, nor that of an insular composer, French in manner though his refined musical productions may be. He is substantially an expressive composer—cool, studious, and learned. His place is assured. He should be listened to, carefully, with deep concentration.

DUOS

- **Sonata in C for Violin and Piano, Op. 59**

Henri Temianka, who has recorded d'Indy's single violin and piano sonata, calls the work "turbulent." Martin Cooper in *French Music* describes the Sonata as "a predominantly lyrical, meditative work." Another writer brands it "stern and austere." D'Indy's Op. 59 is very rarely turbulent (the score has very little sprint and abandon), but it does have a hint of inner vehemence. The music is roughly lyrical, with beakers of chromatic foam wetting the sounds. And it is indeed stern and austere in its obedience to the matter of restraint. Cooper's descriptive "meditative" is closest to the mark, with the heavy determination of d'Indy's writing to belong in the Franck classification.

No better evidence for the last statement than the opening of the Sonata, set in 9/8 time. The flow and curves of Franck's violin and piano sonata are immediately recalled, and though treatment of detail is different, the similarity of effect is simply startling. (The Franck is also in 9/8 meter.)

The interweave of the cyclic process colors the music. In both the second (scherzo-Trio type) and third (slow) movements material appears derived from the main theme of the first movement. Similarly, this takes place in the finale, a Très animé music set in a partnered depiction of sonata and rondo form. All of this is exactly the basis of d'Indy's compositional principia: to subordinate "the structure to certain themes, which appear in various forms . . . acting as regulators and making for unity."

- **Sonata in D for Cello and Piano, Op. 84**

A suite scenario is followed in d'Indy's four-movement Sonata. The "Entrée" compares a pair of subjects, both moderately spun in triple meter, the first in 3/4 and the other in 3/2. A combination of these takes place near the conclusion. Dance forms are used for movements two and four: Gavotte en rondeau and Gigue. A good part of the latter has rhythmic leaning, rather than vertical emphasis, with syncopations crossing the bar lines. Between the dances a contrastive slow movement appears—an Air in strict binary statement.

D'Indy's opus was begun in 1924, completed in 1925, and published in 1926. In the latter year a transcription for viola and piano, made by Armand Parent, the Belgian composer-violinist (1863–1934), was published.

TRIO

- **Trio in B-flat Major for Clarinet (or Violin), Cello, and Piano, Op. 29**

In this Trio, patent use is made of transformational thematic technique. While the theorem that music should be enjoyed for its own beauty is, of course, correct (regardless of exactly how, or even why, it is formed), nonetheless, the intellectual capacity and methods of a composer need to be brought out into the open. A composer wishes his music to be enjoyed not only for its purely sensuous and emotional values but for its command of speech and method of presentation as well. Finding the key to any artwork strengthens one's understanding of it.

The unison theme of the first movement is the musical dictator of this composition. It powers the Overture (a fanciful title for music that contains, however, the usual sonata-form ingredients) and serves as the theme for the Divertissement. The latter form is generally light and entertaining, but in this case it defines a scherzo type with two Trios each called Intermède (Intermezzo). The theme is in straight rhythm, with each note very short and precise in contrast to the legato aspect of its initial statement. The two Trios are in oppositional style, as is expected (syncopation is used in the first one, slower tempo in the second).

Color helps portray the devotional character of the "Chant élégiaque" ("Elegiac Song"); beginning by the use of the clarinet alone and then by presenting the cello alone, using two different themes. Although the thematic transference method is rather hidden here, d'Indy draws on the same source as previously for the theme stated initially in syncopative legato by the clarinet. Both instruments combine for a *fortissimo* peroration. The piano blends all these elements with ostinato character in each of the three sections that make up the "Chant." In the last movement, the transformational device is used for development purposes, including the augmentation of the theme's rhythmic values in various ways.

QUARTETS

■ **Quartet for Piano, Violin, Viola, and Cello, Op. 7**

D'Indy's A-minor piano quartet is considered his first chamber music composition, though before it was completed (it was begun in 1878 and occupied the composer until 1888) the Op. 29 Trio for Clarinet, Cello, and Piano had been finished (in 1887). (So much for the validity of opus numbers!)

Though only of marginal total, the cyclic signature of this composer is indicated. In the finale, a nine-measure insert of the previous part of the work (an expressive Ballade) is made. The finale itself is a vigorous achievement that relates two types of triple-meter material (9/8 and 3/4) with its opposite chronology. A different kind of vigor (fluid rather than mercurial) is produced by the opening movement of the Quartet. No grandstanding dramatic viewpoint is involved, but the music registers emphatically with romantic flush. Sonata form holds the music in place, including a complete repetition of the exposition.

■ **String Quartet No. 2, Op. 45**

It is somewhat amusing still to hear at this late point in time academic protests against the twelve-tone technique of Schoenberg and his followers. The system, it is said, is arbitrary; the results cerebral, nonemotional; anyone could write music in such "helter-skelter,"

senseless fashion. While this is not the place to counterargue such patent nonsense (since twelve-tone technique is as logical a method as Palestrinian polyphony), some points must be made here relative to the quartet to be discussed.

What difference is there between one system of organizing sounds and another, excepting the system itself? The argument that belabors the kind of method is false. Any plan that produces a musical structure is sound, if it has logic. Of course, different systems (and one must always follow some predicated method) will produce different sounds. An operative base will factor the musical arrangement; it will result in classic, romantic, or impressionistic style—or twelve-tone style! But one is as *correct* as another. Truly, no one style can be judged correct and others not.

In his Op. 45, d'Indy heads the score with a motto of four sounds, to be read in triple solution, based on the three different clefs that precede the motto. This gives a total of twelve sounds. However, through pitch coincidences the actual pitch differences total eight. These sounds, therefore, are the "row" of tones d'Indy indicates he will exploit by various means.

Now, no attempt is being made to compare d'Indy with Schoenberg. Still, while their temperaments and music are as wide apart as the poles, their general approach to the science of forming their music rests in the same skeleton of taking a row of sounds and permutating these in specific plan. The tonal result should determine the final judgment; but unless understanding of the music's formation is undertaken, it is impossible to judge correctly.

The entire quartet shows an industrious (and fully artistic) occupation with the three thematic tone threads. The related rows interlock, mix with each other, have varied rhythmic shapes, and become the technical tools for the most thorough exploration. This occurs in every measure in some fashion until the final cadence, which is a quadruple rhythmic augmentation of the third of the tone rows.

D'Indy's first row of four tones is announced in quartet unison, and immediately thereafter the other forms appear in literal statement or in transposed state. What is important is that there are four sound forms that constantly cut through the arrangement of the lines. Fugal exposition, development with resources of rhythmic manipulation, such as augmentation and so on, occur.

A scherzo movement is in second place, based on the second permutate of the row motto. It is formed in a combination of triple and duple meter, broken out from a quintuple setting, with occasional interpolations of a single-beat measure. Trio contrast is afforded by use of a songlike theme which is in sextuple, rhythmic shape. The slow movement, likewise, takes its impulse from one of the rows (the second, in this case). The last movement has several features—augmentation of the first of the tone rows, manipulation of the various components in melodic inversion, and the like, combining a legato theme with punctilious rhythmic life, as well as fugato.

QUINTET

- *Suite en parties* **for Flute obbligato, Violin, Viola, Cello, and Harp, Op. 91**

The title of this work is best explained rather than simply translated. *En parties* signifies "in variations," stemming from the fact that the French word has the same meaning as partita. Since, in turn, a partita is either a suite or a set of variations, the latter is obviously the correct definition. *(Parties* also means parts or voices, but neither is applicable here.)

All four movements stem from the theme of the opening section. Importantly, each theme's shape begins with the same outline, and each movement is structured by variational process. Further affinity with the opening part of the

Suite is derived by some variational treatment of its second theme. All together this defines cyclic transformation, emphatically carried over throughout, regardless of the form used for each of the movements.

Explanation is required in regard to the flute's obbligato nature. Contrary to some ideas, an obbligato voice is neither an appendage nor a subsidiary. The idea that, in emergencies, one can perform music calling for an obbligato voice *without* it, and be free from any general harm to the basic setup, is absolutely false. Such type of voice must be marked ad libitum, the antonym of obbligato, not its synonym! Actually obbligato means *obligatory;* i.e., a requirement to be observed. The flute has a very important role; it is the principal voice in the two middle movements and has, in addition, salient functions. Notwithstanding, the other voices are not just accompanying instruments.

The title of the opening movement, "Entrée en sonate," is a favorite of the composer's. It is used in several other works for describing the first movement. It signifies a prelude, somewhat of dance origin and character (of the era of Lully and Rameau), composed in sonata form. Three entries of the first theme of this movement are followed by the second theme, and development of these elements then follows.

The title of the second movement is lengthy—"Air désuet, pour flûte, avec les répétitions au nazard et tierce lointaine." This is an "Unused [or obsolete] Air" for the flute, with the air's repetitions referring to technical names concerning organ stops. The theme is of ancient, modal sound; it is introduced by the germinal skip of a fifth that surrounds all the main themes of the work, and is then stated by the flute above simple accompaniment. On the repeats of the theme, use is made of the "nazard et tierce lointaine" effect. These are so-called mutation stops on an organ, whereby one sound has its character changed by implantation of overtones produced by the stop or stops, which give synthetic sympatheticness (it is this principle of mixtures of stops, et al., that makes varying tone colors and timbre effects possible on the organ). The "nazard" and "tierce lointaine" are just two of very many. The former gives the twelfth above (when used with any fundamental sound); the latter, two octaves plus a third above. The result gives a triad which is shadowed by its third and fifth, essential in its root. D'Indy obtains this effect by interesting use of spacing of the pitches whereby the harp sounds the "nazard" with stopped vibrations; while the violin playing harmonics implies the "tierce lointaine" ("the third in the distance").

A "Sarabande avec deux doubles" follows. The "doubles" (variation of a dance theme by embellishment and filigree) are assigned to the flute; the first broad, the second faster and more capricious. Thus, variation within variation. The final movement is still another alterational form built on the general variation—"Farandole variée en rondeau"—plus placing, it will be noted, the variations in rondo form. In this case, the French dance design is not in equal binary meter, but in an unequal septuple condition of four, followed by three beats per measure. The march tempo heartiness used calls on the main theme four times as the ritornel, which is varied on each appearance. Further, the two significances of the form of the dance are validated with folk-character sentiment.

SEXTET

- **Sextet for Two Violins, Two Violas, and Two Cellos, Op. 92**

It has been often said that this composer was dry, sober, and avoided any deliberate attempt to draw on instrumental colors in chamber music; that he was not concerned with special sonority values and ingredients, per se, either.

In a word, d'Indy was a musical reservist, an austere graybeard. That d'Indy was concerned with deliberate order in his music is not to be argued; that some of his music deals only with grays, whites, and neutral colors is also not to be denied; but that all of his music is centered on nothing but architectural properties is not true. This Sextet is an example that proves in several ways this particular point.

The second movement serves aptly as an illustration. It is a Divertissement (and let it be noted how often d'Indy uses the descriptive title rather than a mere tempo designation), wherein the sextet is split into two string trio groups (each consisting of violin, viola, and cello), one using mutes, the other not. In two sections, this timbre differential is removed, causing further contrasted qualities. This movement serves as the light dance section of the composition (à la minuet, or scherzo). Color is exemplified still further in the movement's Trio, when triple harmonics are used combined with pizzicato. Throughout, the values of antiphony are called on, especially cogent since the colors are not parallel.

Classic forms were at the heart of d'Indy's principles, together with a love for the practices of the old French composers. Thus, the first movement is an "Entrée en sonate" ("Overture in Sonata Form"). Thereby, d'Indy follows classic lineage with the impress of the Lully-Rameau school. This Overture is similar to the subdivisional style of the other three movements of the Sextet. The exposition, development, and recapitulation follow sonata practice; the stately activity is related to the style of an earlier period.

A Theme, Variations, and Finale constitute the final movement, which illustrates a fascinating exploitation of both variation and cyclic form, plus an added attraction that is rarely used by any composer. The variations are of the fully developed type. Of these, the fourth one, featuring the first viola voice, is especially important. This variation appears again after the final section, thereby validating d'Indy's principium that absolute clarity can only be achieved by thematic transformation. The concluding section is led into directly from the variations (the last of which is a fugato) and is titled enigmatically (or incorrectly) in part as "Quodlibet alla Schumann." The meaning of the first of these three words is apparent, the last two not; for if d'Indy could imitate Franck, he could not imitate Schumann. Be that as it may, the "quodlibet," which is a kind of musical tossed salad (the Latin word means "what you please"), is in the tempo of a gay march, and consists of snatches of themes drawn from the first and last movements, together with other new themes, which are shifted, changed rhythmically, and thrown together in a very healthy manner, including a development of one subject from the Divertissement. Rather than attempt to classify the snippets and the promulgation of this planned extemporization, it is better to let the counterpoints have their horizontal say and enjoy the musical gaiety.

SEPTETS

- *Chanson et Danses* for Flute, Oboe, Two Clarinets, Horn, and Two Bassoons, Op. 50

This "Song and Dances" is termed a divertissement by d'Indy and is scored for the less common wind septet, including a horn. The first movement is in ternary form, with sensitive attention to the scoring, which permits all harmonies and countermelodic proportions to be heard very cleanly. The *Danses* are nothing more than terpsichoric considerations in rondo form. If each dance theme were to be identified by a letter, the plan is almost a symmetrical alternation of the first subject (A) with two others, the movement evolving into an A–B–A–C–A–B–C–A plan. The first statement of the third theme shows off the beautiful, haunting qualities of low flute tone, a matter of

which the French school of composers took advantage before any other group. Cyclic twist never is avoided by d'Indy, even in a light work, or a short one. The *Chanson* section returns to form a subdued coda.

- **Suite in D—*Dans le style ancien (In the Olden Style)*— for Two Flutes, Two Violins, Viola, Cello, and Trumpet, Op. 24**

Thrice unusual: in terms of the combination used—two flutes, string quartet, and trumpet—in regard to the appearance of the then rarely used trumpet in the field of chamber music (the septet was created in 1886), and last, exceptional, because the brass instrument d'Indy requests is a trumpet in D—an instrument of narrower bore, higher range, and more tensile color than the average trumpet used in the orchestra. However, though the type of trumpet tone will change somewhat, there is no reason to avoid use of the most common B-flat instrument, since the highest pitches called for will cause no trouble for the more standard instrument; and the color in the middle and low registers will not be affected. D'Indy treats the brass instrument with reticence, as well he should in a mellifluous combination of strings and flutes, and with regard for a work "in the olden style."

The style is, however, a modern counterpart of the old forms; the molds are recognizable as from the classical period, the contents late 19th century with resultant romantic tinge. The shortest of preludes is followed by the "Entrée," used here in the style of a "scene" in a ballet sense—a dance prelude after a prelude. This moderate and gay dance is in 2/4 time, with two slower contrasting sections. A Sarabande follows, somber with its minor-key definition, slowly dictated by its characteristic stateliness. The Minuet gives the trumpet an opportunity for displaying solo color, and the contrasting Trio section is based on duple incisions (formed by mild syncopations) into the body of the triple functioning meter. A "Ronde française" ("French Round Dance"), written in the forceful combination of light contrapuntalism plus variational treatment, completes the composition.

Inghelbrecht, Désiré Emile (1880–1965)

DUO

- *Sonatine en trois parties (in Three Parts) for Flute and Harp (or Piano) (1918)*

Inghelbrecht's music is permeated with the expressiveness found in Debussy's music, of which he was a conducting specialist. It also has links to the work of Ravel. No one can fault these models.

Peaceful lyricism, with motile modality—even in the more animated sections the music flows—are found in the Préamble (Prelude). Similar quality pertains to the Sicilienne that forms the middle movement. The conjunct arch of the main theme of this dance music contrasts neatly with the disjunct, downward-motion second theme. A repeat of the first two measures of the Sicilienne ushers in the finale, Rondes (Round Dances). The precept that good art results from balanced correspondence between form and matter rules here. Conspicuously concise, with shifting pulse divisions, this is typical strong music of light content.

QUARTET

- **String Quartet**

Inghelbrecht's knowledge of instruments was considerably strengthened by his work as a conductor (he was director of the Pasdeloup Orchestra and conductor of the Paris Opéra for five years). It shows in his scintillating scoring

of the scherzando middle of the second movement, which is surrounded by the slow music of the quartet. In the former there are flying right- and left-hand pizzicatos, rows of harmonics, massed col legno chording, and sweeping ponticello arpeggios. Rich color and excitement are produced.

Movement one has sonata specifications. Included in the development is a section in the extremely rare key of C-sharp major. The finale binds the quartet by quoting in its center material from the first movement and from both the slow and scherzo sections of the second movement.

Ioannidis, Yannis (1930–)

QUINTET

- *Actinia* **for Wind Quintet (1969)**

Atonality is hooked loosely onto a generative tone center in Ioannidis's piece, which opens and closes with a sustained F-sharp in the horn. Over this, a conjunct idea, desyllabilized as it were into disjunct identity, is announced. Then follow permutations—radiated variations—within which the F-sharp fundamental swims freely.

A pivotal pitch particular does not negate nor fuzz atonality. While it would not permit the absolute equality pertinent to twelve-tone composition, it does not interfere with atonal pitch independence, while retaining its position as a contrastive element. (Interestingly, Ioannidis's earlier works adhered to a great extent to Schoenbergian principles. His adoption of free atonality, he explains, gives just as much tone parity as dodecaphonicism, and insures an "unlimited number of harmonic combinations.")

Actinia relies, for the greater part, on quintet totality. Such mass scoring, however, does not negate linear neatness or blur the permutative aspects. All the sectional shifts are delineated with clarity. None are repeated, save the second section, which is exactly duplicated by the final section.

Ioannidis does not explain the relation of his title to the music. He merely describes *Actinia* as a "sound piece," which is totally vague. According to Webster, *Actinia* is a genus of sea anemones, which, though more picturesque, is just as vague.

Iordan, Irina (1910–)

QUARTET

- **String Quartet, Op. 10**

Classical order, neatly balanced between vertical and horizontal writing, describes Iordan's G-minor quartet. (Both corner Allegro movements begin in the home key and eventually settle in the same-based major mode.) The use of harmonic style to contrast the linear for formalistic purposes is significant.

Though the picturesque is not the ideal Iordan pursues, coloristic circumstances make secure the inner pair of movements. The Allegro scherzando moves over a twirling rhythmic figure that appears in practically every measure. The Trio for this scherzo music is concentrated and manifests a recitative demeanor. In the slow movement, its important outer portions highlight the unmuted first violin against the other three muted instruments.

Ippolitov-Ivanov, Mikhail (1859–1935)

TRIO

- ***Two Kirghiz Songs* for Oboe, Clarinet, and Bassoon**

The background for Ippolitov-Ivanov's mini trio is described by W. Alexander Jones, who edited the score for publication by the now-defunct American publishers, Mercury Music. "These two pieces for oboe, clarinet, and bassoon are based on melodies of the Kirghiz, a Turkic people living in the region between the Volga and Irtisch Rivers in Asiatic Russia."

Nationalistic eloquence is illustrated first by slow-paced music, defined *amoroso,* mainly involved with a descending melodic line. The second part is fast-paced and defined *humoresco.* It features a modal tune revolving around E, supported by jogging eighth notes.

QUARTET

- **String Quartet in A Minor, Op. 13**

Ippolitov-Ivanov's opus is featured by its middle pair of movements. Contrast in the presto-paced *Humoresca—Scherzando* is obtained not by the usual reduction of speed but by the lengthening of note values. Both this and the following movement, Intermezzo (a tripartite-designed pastoral conception), could well serve as excellent encore items.

The Lento introduction to the quartet is cut into the Finale, an ordinary, bustling type of music, found in large quantity among the output of the lesser lights of the Russian school. In the opening movement, this same Lento prelude reverses its position and serves for coda purposes.

Ireland, John (1879–1962)

DUOS

- *Fantasy-Sonata* for Clarinet and Piano
  (1943)

Ireland's somewhat rhapsodic work (bearing a
very natural relationship to the clarinet, an
instrument that possesses such inherencies
in its rather full gamut and varying color registers) sets forth the variety of three movements, but, in addition, is connected by primary
material. For example, the second theme of the
major first part serves as a cell from which
grows the second section's theme, and in the
last portion the opening subject is both augmented and changed ornamentally. As a result,
the work is a unit, even with its punctuated
fantasy. Freedom is conveyed by changes of
mood, but formal amalgamation is not left in
the lurch.

- **Sonata for Cello and Piano (1923)**

Ireland's Sonata is of the rugged-music type.
Logical shaping of the material is displayed in
the three movements (set forth in moderate
tempo, then in slow pace, and in a finale of *con
moto* depiction), with the details presented
without lushness or mere pursuit of luxuriant
sounds. Ireland's music never could be termed
of extravagant manner and this applies as well
to the direct, no twistings of this duo sonata.
The scoring is clear, so that the cello does not
fight nubby piano textures and overdetailed
material.

- **Sonata No. 1 in D Minor for Violin and
  Piano (1944)**

(The composition date following the title applies to the final revision. Ireland composed
this duo sonata in 1907, revised it in 1917, and
once again in 1944.)

While the sensuous side of music holds the
principal enthusiasm of many a listener, there
is as much stimulation available in the lesser
colored, intimate manners of composition.
Ireland's Sonata is of the neutral type. He knew
well all the current and most fashionable techniques (past periods of musical history have
had similar representatives), used them a bit (in
this case, rhythmic straightforwardness), but
was most concerned with the well-grounded
depiction of his substances so that the structures were clear.

Although the home tonality begins the first
movement (in sonata form), Ireland shows
postromantic freedom in starting his recapitulation in E minor. This is one mark of his not
being merely the cold logician, but one determined to be diverse in his music and not just
academic. The Romance is ethereal, colored by
the use of modal scales and harmonies, set in
ternary form. The final Rondo, recognizing
classical tradition, concludes in D major. It
thereby balances the D minor tonality of the
initial movement.

- **Sonata No. 2 in A Minor for Violin and
  Piano (1917)**

Ireland had won two prizes before he produced
this duo sonata. In 1908 he was awarded second prize in the Cobbett competition with his
Phantasie in A minor for piano trio *(see below),*
and in 1909 he was awarded first prize in
another Cobbett competition for his first violin
and piano sonata *(see above).* Ireland's composition was one of 134 entries. However, it was
this second violin and piano sonata that brought
him his reputation. Harold Rutland describes
the matter in *The Musical Times* of August
1959. "After its first performance by Albert
Sammons and William Murdoch on 6 March
1917, a publisher arrived on Ireland's doorstep
the next morning before he had had breakfast;
he also received a number of other offers. And
orders came in for the whole of the first edition

before it was even printed." A remarkable happening—not possible with contemporary music of any kind these days!

There are three movements. The first, a driving Allegro, grows out of an upbeat rhythmic figure. Movement two is defined by an unabashed lyrical outlook. The finale has glitter. It is based on what one critic has described as "a boisterous theme of unaffectedly popular type."

TRIOS

- **Phantasie in A Minor for Piano, Violin, and Cello (1906)**

Monographic means are used in this one-movement work, which has classical unity by way of thematic derivation. Although Ireland's trio is divisible into triple sections, they are, however, all very similar; it is speed deviation rather than thematic difference that tells the tale. The cello states the theme, which is then slightly developed. A quieter section deploys the same idea, relaxing its rhythmic impulsion. The last section is reached with the change to A major. The achievements are rewarding, even though the work is almost too dependent on the one theme rather than attaining contrastive independence from it.

- **Trio No. 2 in One Movement for Piano, Violin, and Cello (1917)**

Most composers have their artistic autographs showing clearly in the make-up of their harmonies; their creative habits are recorded in their allegiance to either homophony or contrapuntalism. In many instances, they will have, as well, their pet forms. Ireland's favorite chamber music design was the fantasy, the work in undivided sections, the compression of several movements into one. This type of musical journalism has one advantage: it gets quickly to the point, and emphasizes it by

headlining the main features and telling the full story in a few paragraphs.

While this Trio has variational style attributes, these are considered in the form of three-sectional tempos. All sounds proceed from the opening theme; all roads travel from its central point. After the somber minor theme, the speed is doubled for a type of march. The slow tempo returns, with the theme now figurated with some line movement. The final section vacillates between agitated and tranquil developments. It terminates, eventually, in a vivacious section which turns the home key's dark quality into an optimistic major tonality.

QUARTET

- **String Quartet No. 1 in D Minor, Op. Posth.**

Written in 1895, when Ireland was age 16. Publication by Boosey & Hawkes took place in 1973, eleven years after Ireland's death.

To deny this work because of its youthful imitations of Brahms would be false. Sonata detail is used in the first movement; the music moves nicely, flows organically. The Scherzo, which is also in D minor, with the contrastive Trio in D major, could be considered the strongest movement. A very short slow movement in A major contains the greatest amount of chromaticism in the work. The Finale supplies a vivacious D-major music, with straightforward sensibility of form.

Ireland's four-movement piece stands up quite well in its romantic coherences. There was no valid reason for his suppression of the composition.

SEXTET

- **Sextet for Clarinet, Horn, and String Quartet (1898)**

Ireland wrote his Sextet at the age of 19. Charles Villiers Stanford, his teacher, did not approve of the work, but nevertheless Ireland retained the score. He first heard it performed when he was eighty years of age.

At this remove one realizes that Stanford erred and that Ireland was wise in not destroying the piece. Yes, it is patently a Brahms imitation, but there's not a measure in the four movements of the work that would cause composer embarrassment. In turn, the tempos are fast–slow–allegretto (Intermezzo)–moderato. There is fine unity, and all the shapes have firm and healthy musical flesh covering them.

Irino, Yoshirō (1921–80)

DUO

- *Globus I* for Horn and Percussions (Vibraphone, Glockenspiel, Timpani, Triangle, Snare Drum, Tom-toms, Bongos, Tam-tam, Small and Large Suspended Cymbals) (1971)

In his other compositions, Irino is specifically contemporary in his speech and, at times, specifically dodecaphonic in his style. Much of the former and some of the latter are meshed in this duo plus the latest breakthrough in the chamber music world—theatricalism.

The use of "percussions" in the title raises a problem. Although "percussion" holds good for the use of any number of pulsatile instruments, "percussions" leads to the thought that two or more performers are required. For the sake of clarification of the various instruments, Irino uses three staves to set out the percussion. Though no mention is made of the number of players, it is apparent that with proper placement of the instruments a single player can handle the "percussions," intricate as the part in totality may be.

Metrical association is eliminated in *Globus I.* Each event, pitch succession, or phrase is designated to fit in a specific time span. Thus, in the very beginning a triangle sound covers five seconds. It is followed by five different percussion qualities—these also to total five seconds. The triangle reenters as prelude to the horn's entrance. These two sounds occupy five more seconds. A further example: Sets of horn phrases are each to be played in three seconds, a previous horn phrase is to occupy nine seconds. Some aleatoric dogma rears its head (repeating given pitches in ad libitum progressions). All of these actions are lucid and persuasive in their rhapsodic continuity, with the oppositional timbres dousing the music with color.

About midway the horn makes his histrionic move after a long uninterrupted vibraphone solo. The brass-instrument performer walks toward the audience and while playing walks through the hall, sings into his instrument, etc., and eventually returns to his position on stage. Musical rhapsody is thereby equated by a performer's motility. The sense of ceremonial attention brought by moving from stage to audience and back to the stage is simply another effect in the free franchise that marks the entire work.

Mention must be made of one rather silly note in the score. When the tam-tam first enters it is marked *pppp*. All well and proper. However, the instruction by the composer reads: "very weak, [so] that the audience can't hear." What value such canceled sound?

(In the same year Irino wrote *Globus II,* for marimba, double bass, and percussion. In 1975 *Globus III* for violin, cello, piano, harp, and shō, plus two dancers, was completed.)

Isaacson, Leonard

Illiac Suite for String Quartet

see: Hiller, Lejaren and
Isaacson, Leonard

Isamitt, Carlos (1887–1974)

DUO

- **Three Pastorales for Violin and Piano**

Succinctly dissonant music, joined to nationalistic materials. Isamitt's motion-seething suite
is kneaded and crusted from the free use of
pitch and chord, derived (as was most of his
music) from melodies by the Araucanian Indians (once living in the southern part of South
America, with few survivors at the present
time).

A distinction of the Araucanian Indians'
music is the adherence to a type of microtonality
which can only be expressed (if half tones are
the smallest fractional interval) in the moving
chromaticism illustrated by this work. Isamitt
studied this people's music and instruments,
and had written many articles about these subjects. It stands to reason that when a musical-
folkloric researchist composes as well (Isamitt
was no hobbyist in composition, having produced more than sixty major works), the joint
activity will carry over from one field to the
other. Thus, these rhapsodical pieces reflect
(rather than state) Araucanian themes, all three
conceptions being free in form and spirit, and
set in atonal frames.

Ishii, Maki (1936–)

DUO

- **Four Bagatelles for Violin and Piano
  (1961)**

Music as pithy as Webern's. No other resemblance, however. These pieces are short, each
covering a single process of reasoning, though
the total seven measures of the first movement
are repeated literally. The theorem that change
equals complete balance is followed in these
four miniatures. Each shifts its timbre particulars, tempos, and textures constantly. Though
the metrical definition remains firm for each
piece (5/4, 4/4, 6/8, and 2/4) the fluidity within
the measures negates distinct pulse. It is manifold detail that defines the individual structures.

TRIO

- *Black Intention II* **for Oboe, Clarinet,
  and Bassoon**

Music of deliberate overkill. Once begun, the
instruments provide constant sound over a period of about eight minutes. (Ishii warns that
"breath training" should be undertaken in order
"to execute the long and continuous rapid passages.")

The music is a continuum of pitch criss-
cross, minus metrical or rhythmical definition
for the greater part and with each instrument
going its own way. One example: twenty-seven
pitches in the oboe, to be played "as fast as
possible" in a type of continual glissando and
then repeated four more times before proceeding to the next segment. Just before this the
clarinet begins its glissando series of twenty-
six different pitches, and before that the bassoon has begun its set of thirty pitches. Nothing
fits together in these surrealistic sound assortments. Another section is a type of out-of-

focus heterophony, with each player independent of the others, and each making his own gradual accelerando. And so on.

Ishii's intentions are violent ones, though he terms his objective to be "black." No other word can better fit the close of the work. The screaming highest pitches of the oboe and clarinet together with the lowest pitch on the bassoon are to be sustained "as long as possible," without *diminuendo,* while playing *fortississississimo.*

SEPTET

- *La-sen [I] (Spiral:* **Music for Seven Players and Electronic Sounds (Flute, Oboe, Harp, Piano, and Three Percussion [Claves, Three Maracas, Three Large Suspended Cymbals, Sistro, Two Tam-tams, Temple Blocks, Marimbaphone, Two Bongos, Two Congas, Bass Drum, Snare Drum, Tambourine, Military Drum, Glockenspiel, Castanets, Five Cow Bells, and Xylophone]) (1969)**

Ishii's music is mainly devoted to combining the special timbres of Japanese instruments (Ishii was born in Tokyo) with the modern techniques of serialism and chance procedures. *La-sen I* (no number appears in the published score, but is required since a *La-sen II* for unaccompanied cello was written the year following) exhibits total fusion: instrumental and electronic sounds, old and new notation (just a bit of the former via pitch definition, with graphic and aleatoric details for the latter), and Eastern and Western elements.

This is a music of purplescent inflamed sounds. There are no themes, of course. Pulse is smothered since rhythmic figures are fractioned and fractured. One can term this a continuity of discontinuity. As Ishii explains it, the fusion mentioned above was applied to "the most varied traditional Japanese percussion and the oldest Buddhist prayer songs (Shômyô)." In addition, these two types were "electronically manipulated and used with purely electronically generated sounds."

NONET

- **Praeludium and Variations for Nine Players (Flute, Clarinet, Bassoon, Horn, Piano, Violin, Viola, Cello, and Percussion [Triangle, Claves, Antique Cymbal, Bells, Two Wood Blocks, Military Drum, Cymbals, and Tam-tam]) (1960)**

Serial language with effective sensitivity in spreading the pitch placement. The texture increases and then lessens in the Praeludium. Part two consists of seven variations on a theme; the theme is without pertinent shape, merely tossing the tone row around in the first two measures without use of the string instruments. Slow and moderate tempos are retained until the fifth variation, which is speedy and the following variant, which is to be played "as fast as possible."

Ištvan, Miloslav (1928–)

TRIOS

- *Refrains* **for String Trio (1965)**

Notwithstanding its title, Ištvan's opus for violin, viola, and cello is free of specific and direct relationships, save for a slight sense of variational processes for some of the figures that appear. *Refrains,* sharply post-Webern in its amalgamation, depends on assorted segments to sing its frictioned song.

In place of time signatures Ištvan adopts a one-second length for whatever material is noted between the dotted lines that serve as bar lines. This permits multitudinous pulse totals within the one-second time span, as well as fluid rhythms that float from one second to the next, plus varied sustained sounds and rhythmic poly-dovetailing. If performed exactly, the length of the piece totals six minutes and fourteen seconds.

Refrains was composed two years after Ištvan joined a creative organization that was dedicated to free musical experimentation. The music produced was to be "uninhibited by puritanically limited didactical regulations."

- **The Micro-Worlds Diptych (1977)**

  - *Summer Micro-Worlds*
  - *Micro-Worlds of My City*

These two picturesque suites can be performed as independent compositions or as a two-part totality, even though calling for different instrumental combinations. The first piece is for flute, harp, and harpsichord (composed Aug. 1975–May 1977), the other piece is scored for two violas, oboe, and clarinet (composed between Sept. 1976 and Sept. 1977). *Summer Micro-Worlds* is the longer of the pair, with a performance time of fourteen minutes; the other work is timed at eleven minutes.

In both pieces Ištvan seeks the special values brought by spatial distribution of the instruments (still a rarity in the field of chamber music). For the *Summer* composition either of two arrangements is to be followed. In the first setting the harp and harpsichord are next to each other on one side of the stage and the flute is placed as far as possible on the other side. The second setting spaces the instruments in three places: both the harp and flute are on stage, as widely separated as possible, with the harpsichord placed on the floor level beneath the stage. This instrumental separation is further accentuated by amplification of the harpsichord. In the *City* piece one spacing plan is to be followed: The violas are to be situated at the extreme far left of the stage and the oboe and

clarinet placed together on the extreme right of the stage.

The timbre differentiation in both works is also aided by the overall dynamic plan. For the greater part throughout, each instrument has its individual dynamic area.

- **Summer Micro-Worlds for Flute, Harp, and Harpsichord (1977)**

There are no halts to Ištvan's scenario. When there is a silence between sections it is exactly specified mensurally and is therefore to be considered as part of the ongoing material.

No guesswork applies to the objective of the trio. There are specific indications. The first part is marked Exposition I and is divided into four sections. The first of these is for the flute alone, a winding, fairly fast music describing "Grass and Wind." Section two is for the harp alone, with a majority total of measures of rest (some containing harp-string vibrational carry over) fulfilling the title: "Spirals of Silence." The entrance of the harpsichord marks section three: "Drops." There are interpenetrations by the harp, placed into perspective, as most of the combined materials in the work, by different dynamics and different metronomic speeds. The return of the flute, later interlocked again by the harp, signifies the fourth part of the first Exposition: "A Quiet Corner on a Path."

This connects to Intermezzo I in A, a scherzo-delineated music, very tonal and built on a constant ostinato A pitch—all for the harpsichord. Exposition II follows, divided into two sections. The first of these, "Designs of the Moss on a Stone," begins when the harp joins in opposition to the harpsichord, which continues projecting the material used in the Intermezzo. The flute enters and creates a third unit. The final nineteen measures of this portion are for the harp and harpsichord. When the flute enters again (on a flutter-tongued pitch) it defines the second section: "The Micro-World of Sounds."

Intermezzo II in A follows, again for harpsichord alone at first and later in polymetrical combine with the harp. This leads to free developmental material, no longer an illustrative adjunct, but simply defined as Metamorphoses I. The concluding portion is for flute alone and leads to Intermezzo III in A. This is, once again, quite similar to the previous Intermezzo material but enlarged in this case and calling on all three instruments. A harp glissando combined with a *forte*-impacted chromatic cluster on the harpsichord ushers in Metamorphoses II, the final part of the suite.

QUARTET

- *Micro-Worlds of My City* for Two Violas, Oboe, and Clarinet (1977)

The first part is a four-section Exposition. It begins with "A Paper Fluttering Alongside a Wall." The action is principally in the clarinet; the oboe dashes in and out, mainly with the same pitch; the violas provide sustained support. Section two is titled "A Lonely Street." The leading voice is now the oboe, its curvaceous triplets, at times rhythmically doubled by the clarinet, ride over the harmonic surfaces of the violas. Leading out of this quartet structure the violas take the spotlight for the first time, with polyphonic pitch detail and contrastive accentuations. This combination describes "A Quiet Corner Next to Dustbins." The clarinet is the principal voice in the final section: "Rainy Blues." There is no complaisant metrical order to this part of the work. The pulse detail changes constantly and in most cases the measures contain the extra kick of a fractional beat, thus: 4 + 1/8, 3 + 1/8, and 5 + 1/8.

A short central portion follows, titled "Interludium con sordini." The "muting" is obtained by the playing style, since the violas are not muted, but are to play "senza accenti, tenuto") ("without accents, sustained"). The oboe has a fluctuating two-pitch pedal in support; the clarinet enters only in the concluding measures. The final part is a Recapitulation and Coda. This is somewhat free but with sufficient recall to bring effective balance.

QUINTET

- *Homage to J. S. Bach* for Wind Quintet (1971)

One doesn't write a ditty in paying tribute to the great Johann Sebastian Bach. A polyphonic work is quite proper and acceptable. Ištvan bears this in mind but goes the further step by presenting a polyphonic multiplicity of elements in addition to contrapuntal procedures. These include polymeters, different tempos heard simultaneously, and indeterminacy combined with exact mensural depiction.

There are considerable fragmented units, with these set against each other in shifting rhythmic placements (further polyphony). Also stressed are a broad-lined subject and a repetitive perky rhythmic motive. The several appearances of these, after sections devoted to polymetrical play and aleatoric assortment, posit a type of rondo document honoring Bach.

Ito, Hidenao (1933–)

DUO

- *Apocalypse* for Flute and Piano (1965)

The revelations heard here indicate that form is replaced by function. And function relates to antiform, the abandonment of all traditional rituals. *Apocalypse* is super-post-Webernian data, a super-free play of sound durations, pitch assortment, dynamic conflict, and timbre terror. Jagged in its contours, the duo's yield is unyielding in terms of its concentrated sonic explosions.

A pithy introduction for flute alone is followed by four "movements" for the two instruments. The differences of these sections become dissolved in the manifold aleatoric detail, since meter, rhythm, and tempo cease to register as components and the entity is a soniferous salmagundi.

Each instrument has multiple choices within each of the four parts—the composer terms these "paragraphs." No matter the name, the result is derived from free decisions by each of the performers—alone and in combination with the other. Chance is bounded by defined notation, but the freedoms permitted effectuate improvisational equivalents. Pitch and register displacement are basic to Ito's piece. Nonetheless, the sonic dislocations are handled with a sense of refinement.

Ives, Charles (1874–1954)

At one time, Ives was considered an iconoclast, a composer who, together with a few individualists (such as Ruggles and Varèse, both now "accepted," having scored in the late innings, as it were), provided the pungent offering of ultramodernism in the catalogue of contemporary music. But Ives has come into his own. He has now been recognized; the famed Pulitzer Prize was awarded him; he is termed a great composer; forgiveness for critical sins is being asked. Wholesale acceptance of Ives has not been forthcoming—cannot, honestly, for there are aspects of his work that confound one with their musical illiteracy. It was part of Ives's method to be a finger painter, one who drew with the native strength and individuality of the primitive, yet who simply doodled from time to time. Endorsement is not complete, but the Ives cult is ten thousand times the very few that supported him in the early 1920s. That group depended on the courageous leadership of Henry Cowell and Nicolas Slonimsky, who constantly propagandized on behalf of Ives's music.

Ives was consistently casual about his music. Once it was written, he cared nothing about performances, was unconcerned about his scrawled manuscripts and piled them in closets, drawers, barns, and other storage places. Accordingly, some manuscripts are lost, others unidentified; the composer did not know where they were, and cared less. But this is an important aspect of Ives's character. It must be believed that his attitude was one of complete humility, not a pose.

He was a creative crossbreed—a combined Joycean, Proustian composer, with elements of the folk singer, the mountaineer, and the revivalist. He combined with seeming informality a huge criss-cross of compositional techniques—from four-part hymnodic harmony to twelve-tone inculcation—microtone usage, athematicism, and other "isms" as well. All these methods were natural to him, years before Schoenberg, Stravinsky, Hába, Stockhausen, and the like "discovered" them! One can find all these techniques in his works, plus pantonality, pandiatonicism, polytonality, and polyrhythms. The engineering facility of the man was staggering. Ives was more *creative* than any composer one can find among a hundred picked at random, for most composers imitate rather than truly create. All means are used as natural consequences in his music, often accompanied not by a defined but by a suggestive program (and indicated with ingenuous wit in the matter of marginalia, footnotes, and remarks in the scores). As a naturalist, the matters of dissonance were of no consequence to Ives. Musical materials existed, they were to be used; if a C-major chord was required, it was just as efficacious and valuable as a chord that amalgamated all twelve tones of the octave, plus fractional tones in between. It was not a matter of compromise with him, merely one of sound selectivity. It was this attitude that made his music uneven—of stylistic *varia*. One is accustomed to a defined style, of Beethoven, of Debussy, of Bartók. Given not one but many shifts, quite often, a critical impasse is formed. Apparently, the music is out of joint, impure, yes, even incorrect; yet, it is so often in place, pure and absolutely correct for Ives's ideas, purposes, and story line.

In the sense that a great deal of Ives's music consists in the setting down of his memories of younger days spent in New England, he is that hard-to-find "American" composer, writing that constantly hoped-for "American" music. Some of these recollections take the form of imitating two bands marching toward each other, with resultant quaking of tonality plus polytonality. Because, quite often his remembrances were those of out-of-tune and out-of-time playing, it is difficult for the critical fraternity (and listeners) to specify the type of his music. It may well be that Ives will be consigned to history books with a mere paragraph or two. The facts point in the opposite direction. He was one of the most daring and original of visionaries, a composer who ran far in front of the pack. If the facts are analyzed coldly, regardless of personal tastes, it must be admitted that some of his music is the most individual of all time.

Charles Ives's Chamber Music for Miscellaneous Groups of Instruments

Ives never took anything for granted. When he felt the need, he wrote different versions of his compositions—not out of dissatisfaction with the initial concept but simply to review his work from different angles. A heading from his catalogue is illuminating. Thus, "Ragtime pieces (about a dozen)—mostly for small theatre orchestra. Some of these . . . were used as scherzos in some of the piano, and violin and piano sonatas . . . later." Another item regarding a number of overtures for large and small orchestra indicates that "Parts of these were made into songs and shorter pieces." He allowed the same freedom to performers in the way of ad libitum passages, extra material they could but didn't have to use, secondary readings, or the aid of an assistant player either to enlarge a passage or reduce its difficulty.

Well then, overtures redesigned into songs and theater orchestra ragtime refurbished as chamber music scherzos! Of course, some of these were a complete redraft and a total cancellation of the originals. But exceedingly few. For Ives, composition was a creative–re-creative act. This is a far cry from making a piano reduction of an orchestral accompaniment to a solo work or an orchestral transcription of a keyboard work. The precept is unorthodoxy, and Ives was its key promoter.

This reexploration turned a number of pieces first composed for varying chamber combinations into works for voice and piano. Hardly any harmonic, melodic, or other changes took place, save accommodation in terms of the medium. Both settings remained viable. In some cases words were already in the instrumental score, not to be sung—though Ives wouldn't have minded if they were sung with (or even without!) the instrumental line that had the words indicated—but merely as prosodic compositional supports—syllabic transformations for *instrumental* declamation, guides to the performer to the inner meaning, and interpretative aids.

No such amount of double-pronged composition has been equalled in all musical history. It remains for some forward-looking organizations to follow this nonconformist attitude. Performance of both versions, in immediate succession, would serve pedagogic, historic, and artistic objectives. It would also serve to keep musical twins together, the pair being separated only by extremely delayed birth.

(These miscellaneous works are listed in the usual order of totality that pertains to all compositions discussed in this compendium. However, because of the several ad libitums concerned, not as instrumental substitutes but as "extras," the placement of each work takes no notice of the ad libs, though they are always indicated in the title headings. For example, a work, for five instruments with a sixth instrument ad libitum will be found in the quintet category, not among the sextets.)

DUOS

- *Largo* for Violin and Piano (1901)

This is the second of three settings that Ives made of his sixty-two–measure piece. The initial version (according to the Cowells in their book on Ives) was for violin and organ (solo stop). Ives then rewrote the *Largo* for violin and piano, making it the second movement of what is known as the *Pre-First Sonata* for Violin and Piano. (There was even a prelude that had been composed as part of a pre-*Pre-First Sonata*.) From this sonata movements were later incorporated in the four "official" violin and piano sonatas. The only exception was the *Largo*.

Ives decided he would write another second movement for his *"pre-"* sonata. He did not waste the music for the first exhibit but turned it into a trio *(see below)*, thus marking the third version of the piece.

It is important to realize that Ives made no changes in his material as he translated the *Largo*. Both linear and vertical data remained intact. The violin part in both the duo and trio representations remained untouched, down to the most minute diacritical definition. Only transfers from piano to clarinet (in the trio version) for highlighting purposes or for thinning the voicing of the piano part mark the differences of the two settings. Of course, color enlargement distinguishes and makes more effective the trio version.

(For a further discussion, *see below: Largo* for Violin, Clarinet, and Piano.)

- Sonata No. 1 for Violin and Piano (1908)

Rugged sound mixtures are basic to this Sonata, as is an introspective temper. Ives offers a feast of techniques that defies the creative law of stylistic integration. He makes his own individual style and it fits, though of conglomerate combine. Those who wish their music in apple-pie order must seek elsewhere. This is an American music, not only by virtue of having been written by an American but because native thematic backdrops color-frame the music's setting. The total truly shows a creative Connecticut Yankee serving in nobody's court!

In the Andante tonality stays rooted for only a fraction of time and then takes off on a ride of unhinged rhapsody. There is no pretense of specific dissonant arrangement in the music; the tensions intermingle, as do the rhythms, developing into a fresco of solid power. The movement turns into an allegro vivace that throws together the sacred (hymn-tempered) with the profane (ragtime-rhymed). With the return of the opening section, a large three-part conception is defined. In the middle movement, one can hear tune snatches, simply dressed or disguised, sneered or snickered at, sometimes fondly remembered. Thus: "The Old Oaken Bucket" (it opens the movement), a bit of "All through the Night," and the march silhouette of "Glory, Glory, Hallelujah." A hymnodic base is also the stimulant for the closing movement, plus an insert that is a full setting of "Watchman, Tell Us of the Night" for the piano alone. Ives indicates the words of this melody and traces the tune via cross-accented harmonies. Though the movement is called a "song without words unintended to be sung," the pianist might sing along as he plays—or get someone else to do it. Ives being Ives, the certainty is that he wouldn't have objected to this added attraction, despite his instruction.

- Sonata No. 2 for Violin and Piano (Second Piano ad lib) (1910)

A work that shows the true creative spirit of the composer, with a range from the very intimate to the most rollicking type of musical horseplay. A music of moods and fantasy, its expressive intensity makes it one of the great American sonatas for the violin and piano combination. Without giving way to any but his natural expressions and qualities, Ives's second violin and piano sonata is just a little less adventurous (the last movement's opening section is void of bar lines) than many of his other pieces. It was finished in 1910, but only received its first hearing thirty-six years later!

The opening movement ("Autumn") is thickest of the three, in changing tempos, with its allegro theme of defined folk quality. The mood is rhapsodic (there is both certainty and changeableness in any season of the year), but the form, while free in its unwinding, is cogent. The fast theme of the movement twice follows a slow introduction, and on its final appearance speaks maestoso-fashion. Fifths predominate in the ever-shifting harmony (a confirmed habit with Ives).

Movement two ("In the Barn") is, once again, an Ives example of creative transfer. (Ives wrote this music for a small theater orchestra in 1902. In November 1907, he revised the material for violin and piano.) "In the Barn" is a humorous fantasy that starts off in quadrille rhythm. There is pulsatile snap and much sonic sport. There are recollections of the whining tone and improvising, plus the "dips" and "scrapes," of the typical country-dance performer. (Tonal polish and impeccable bowing are better held back a bit here. For stylistic truth it is better to be a *fiddler* than a *violinist* in presenting this portion of the Sonata.) A semblance of a hornpipe is thrown in; the counterpoint is spotted with the *Till Eulenspiegel* motive and a terse quote from *Pagliacci*. There is a maze of syncopation, two-step dance snatches of "Old Zip Coon," variations on it, "Dixie," and "Marching through Georgia," etc. It is real sport to identify the music as it is thrown joyfully about the premises, but treated with careful consideration of style. These snippets are in place, not pasted on. It is such treatment that makes Ivesian folk quotations so enthralling. (During all this, the mood changes but then returns to the dance pace, with the last section improvisational and less concerned with the dance.)

It is in this second movement that the duo expands into a trio, if so desired. In the original manuscript a bass-drum simulation is suggested in the concluding part of the movement, to be played on the lowest pitches of the piano by an extra pianist. If used, it furnishes fuel to the ongoing musical fire. Again, it is an exemplification of Ivesian ear-stretching.

The haunting final movement, "The Revival," is slow, somber, set in a contemplative frame. Based on the hymn "Come, Thou Fount of Every Blessing" (used also in the first string quartet), the music builds slowly, finally heard in full exultation. The theme is ever called on, and the close is touchingly beautiful. Its simplicity is finished art.

▪ Sonata No. 3 for Violin and Piano (1914)

Structurally, Ives's third sonata is somewhat different from his usual music. A mood of vital seriousness pervades the work. The syntax is in great part triadic and polyharmonic, as well as modal and polymodal. Ivesian diction is retained, represented by syncopative, crossed rhythmic arrow points that move together, apart, and against each other.

The opening movement is developed from the old hymn tune "Beulah Land," by a specific sectional design, specified as "verse" and "refrain." Verse one is given to the violin, the second is assigned to the piano in augmented rhythm, the third verse is again stated by the string instrument—this time in broader statement—while the fourth and last verse is taken over by the piano and then the violin. In between these divisions there is a folk-style idea combined with repetitive piano chords and quiet bell sounds. In connection with this rondo proposal (a free association of hymnodic format), a sweeping chordal arpeggio in the piano always announces the verses—simultaneously serving as a summons to order and a spotlight. The refrain also appears four times. Save for the first of these, each is stated by the violin with vertical and horizontal supports from the piano. Basically, there is not much change in the refrains. Only a fast and then a slower (to be played with "swing") section interrupt their specific insertion.

In the second movement (in part, originally composed for small theater orchestra), there is a combination of old-style "rag" plus more modern representations of this rhythmic utilitarianism. An improvisational slant is illustrated in this case. Two different measures are to be repeated "if ragged," and two others are to be played "only if ragged."

Movement three is a sustained, lyrical division; the principal theme presented some seven times in a changing shape. The coda, concluding with a light, bitonal dissonance, exhibits a specially sensitive aspect.

- **Sonata No. 4 (*Children's Day at the Camp Meeting*) for Violin and Piano (1915)**

Although a great number of Ives's works have indirect narrative significance, this one has descriptive notes supplied by the composer. These are more of general essence rather than a series of remarks telling what takes place within the music and at what point.

The Sonata is sustained and vigorated by the salt and pepper of dissonance. These are used to illustrate the excitement of children at play, the singing of wrong pitches in hymns, the conflicts of hymn and march tunes when pitted against each other, as well as the impressionistic description of nature—of "distant voices of the farmers," and the enthusiasms of deacons who "roar, pray and shout."

In the opening movement, Ives imitates the singing and action that accompany the marching type of hymn tunes. The music is mainly contrapuntal, written in an improvisational quasi-organ style. The principal hymn used is "Work for the Night Is Coming" (by Lowell Mason [1792–1872], whose psalm tunes were at one time very popular). As the youngsters keep up their parading, during lulls in the separated outdoor services, a clash occurs since the person at the small organ being used practices and improvises at the same time. In addition, tempo difference adds to the polyphonic order of the whole inasmuch as the children increase their speed as the mood takes hold and the pace almost becomes that of a real march. Darkness, or the call for the next service, brings a halt to such proceedings, and the music resumes as quietly as it began.

Hymn tunes, as well, form the second movement's background. These are combined with "the outdoor sounds of nature on those Summer days—the west wind in the pines and oaks, the running brook . . . ." Ives describes this idea in the first section, via unbar-lined music set in free rhythm. Without warning, an Allegro (*con slugarocko*) interposes. This part of the Sonata is of full fun, though concerned with crushing dissonance. The Italian coinage of the parenthetical tempo expresses the boys throwing stones on the rocks in the brook. Such terminology is typical of Ives's earthy humor. Just as suddenly, the mood is reversed and a return made to the start of the Sonata. Now it is evening, and the distinct sound of an "amen" is heard in the last measure as the violin pivots between the widely separated tones of the piano. The final movement of the Sonata is the shortest of all. A hymn is sung ("Shall We Gather at the River" by Robert Lowry [1826–99]), but the harmonization is in full Ivesian style. This is followed by the young people marching, described with a tutti, all-congregational style of music.

TRIOS

- *Largo* for Violin, Clarinet, and Piano
  (1902)

(For the original version of this work and details concerning its relationship to this piece, *see above: Largo* for Violin and Piano.)

A true triple blend is used. The piano begins and is then combined with the violin. Again, the piano is heard alone and this time it is joined by the clarinet. Once more only the piano plays, followed by the total trio forces. The recapitulation matches the opening, starting with solo piano, and the *Largo* concludes as a duet for violin and piano. Texturally, the piece is just as precisely balanced. The writing is spare at the outermost portions, meatiest in the middle. This is paralleled by tempo changes: largo, succeeded by a faster speed rate that starts andante, moves into a ragtime-processed quasi allegretto, recedes into the andante again, and finally, to firm up the entire A–B–A form, returns to the largo tempo. Balance is the name of the formal game in all aspects.

The opus is an example of Ives's music in almost a stark-naked state: no hymn tunes, no march snippets, nothing but the sounds of strange voices, formed from mixed tonalities.

- Trio for Violin, Cello, and Piano (1911)

The combination of lines that give rise to pointed, honest-to-goodness counterpoint can only be achieved by acute independence. Such nonchordal, free-pitch polyphony clothes the opening movement. Totally in slow tempo, the movement has introspective, expressionistic content. In the first part the piano is the total soprano voice, the cello is the complete bass. Territorial space is never breached in this partnership. In part two the violin is now the soprano, the piano the bass. Only with three extremely minor exceptions are the instrumental areas crossed in this case. The final section

is for the total trio. Climax is thereby obtained by textural weight. The final coalescing factor is a surprising C-major triad.

Ives described the third movement as "partly a remembrance of a Sunday service," held on the Yale campus. There is a mixture of hymnodic materials, bell simulations, and rhythmic interplay that produce the habitual Ivesian collage. The "Sunday service" element becomes dominant at the very end with a quotation from "Rock of Ages" in the cello; the Trio concluding with a clustered, unresolved chord. (The section just prior to this is a literal recapitulation of seventy-one measures—an uncharacteristic Ives procedure.)

However, the central movement exemplifies a typical Ivesian robust bill of health. It is a fast, chirpy, gossipy Scherzo. The rock-and-sock-'em music is filled with the snippets of familiar tunes that are part of Ives's creative trademark. Among them is an augmentation of "My Old Kentucky Home"; another is a retempoing of "Marching through Georgia"; and still another is an Ivesian "disagreement" with "Rally round the Flag, Boys." There are more, including fragments of "Jingle Bells" and "Boys and Girls Come Out to Play." Ives titled the movement *TSIAJ* (the acronym stands for "This Scherzo Is a Joke"). (The music's secondary, parenthetical title, "Medley on the Campus Fence," reflects the use of the melodic bits.) Ives once stated that *TSIAJ* was a poor joke. Unacceptable. The music is superb sonic fun, including two unexpected adagio inserts, wide-ranging arpeggios toward the end, and a flippant final cadence as bonuses.

QUARTETS

- *"Ann Street"* for Trumpet, Flute,
  Trombone (or Baritone horn or
  Baritone Saxophone), and Piano
  (1921)

"Ann Street" is an example of Ivesian transfer.

The original conception was for voice and piano, as a short item set to a text found in the *New York Herald Tribune*. Scored for this pithy instrumental ensemble, it was planned to be the third in a *Set* for trumpet, saxophone, and piano. It is a music cross-sectioned with brashness and sentiment.

- **Scherzo for Two Violins, Viola, and Cello (1914)**

(*See also*: *Set* for String Quartet, Bass, and Piano)

Real raggy, flip, and funny are the descriptions of this fifty-measure item. It is ruled to precision: twenty measures in part one, a single measure to link the central (Trio) portion of seven measures, twenty measures of a literal recap of the initial section, and two measures to button up matters. The tail end of the first part is a musical yack—a canonic snippet quoting the famous (infamous?) hootchy-kootchy, that pseudo-Oriental, cheap carnival dance tune, that Ives begins with blatant perfect fifths (when read with a tempered pitch spelling). More subtle, but just as pointed, are the closing triple chords—beautifully noisy, via three sets of different augmented octaves combined with a major seventh. Ives thought of these chords as representing "three cheers!"

The central section is a scalic and rhythmic salmagundi. The first violin and viola run chromatically and the second violin and cello move conjunctively in C major. However, no decided partnership, since each instrument pursues an individual rhythmic existence. Each measure is a different complex; thus, measure four of this section pits twelve sounds against eight against three and against two. This pulsatile intoxication shows Ives at his baldest and boldest. In the manuscript this portion is properly described: "Practice for String Q't in Holding Your Own!" Such a remark finds proper place in this short and sweet-sour piece, which is brazen, musical sass.

(In Kirkpatrick's bibliography of Ives's compositions in *The New Grove Dictionary of American Music* the title reads: Scherzo: "Holding Your Own.")

- **String Quartet [No. 1]** (*A Revival Service*) **(1896)**

Ives did not number this quartet but titled it *Organ Quartett* (to be explained below). For a considerable time it was thought of as a three-movement work, until the original first movement was found in Ives's manuscripts after his death. It had become detached from the autograph score when Ives decided to make an orchestral setting for incorporation as the third movement in his Fourth Symphony.

The source materials that Ives used confirm the subtitle of the work. The third movement was drawn from an organ prelude, while another section is from a postlude for a church service. Other material was picked from various organ pieces and offertories played at what is only identified as "C.Ch." (meaning: Centre Church in New Haven), as well as a collection of chorale preludes and postludes indicated for revival service use. It is all this that caused the original title of *Organ Quartett* (the double *t* was used). At one time, it was Ives's idea to score the work for strings and organ, but the idea was abandoned. Finally, the title page declares, facetiously, that it is, "From the Salvation Army—Not Quite."

The spirit of the church service of bygone days is indeed reflected (with some unpious speaking) in Ives's quartet. In fact, basically, the harmonies are of the choir loft; few Ives issues are at stake as he rolls out his anthems for four string instruments. Simple, elementary, for the most part correctly resolved harmonies (some cutely clever inappropriate-appropriate voice leadings salt the texture) reflect Ivesian academicism. The first movement is one of the finest portions of the work. It is a superb Fugue, derived from the hymn "From Greenland's Icy

Mountains to Afric's Coral Strand." A later use is made of another hymn: "All Hail the Pow'r of Jesus' Name." Movement two is an allegro-tempo Prelude in tripartite form, which structure is duplicated in movement three, Offertory; the latter is based on still another hymn tune: "Come, Thou Fount of Every Blessing." The finale is a Postlude derived from a march-tempo hymn, "Stand Up, Stand Up for Jesus!" In this concluding movement the later Ives peeps out when combined triple and quadruple meters are used, one of the former for a theme drawn from the opening movement. The quartet terminates in correct cadential style, via a plagal formation.

- **String Quartet No. 2 (1913)**

Ives's heterodox formulas, his musical intensity and fervor (notwithstanding the fact that the basic reasoning may well seem that of madness, to some) belong to no fanatical school. One may call this quartet atonal, polyrhythmic, of linear counterpoint, built partly of folk materials, sarcastic, happy, moody, or even skeptical. It is all these. The resultant combination is Charles Ives, *his* style, and in that manner he writes purely.

In this quartet, the changes are many but combine to form integrated music. The expression is most personal, moving above the techniques that form the music. (Now such techniques can be labeled and identified. When Ives wrote his quartet in the early part of the 20th century, these matters were unknown to most.) Tonality, per se, does not exist, yet there is the decided factor of balance, tension and release, and drive to climax that form any art message. It takes several hearings of a performance of this work, to realize that, in spite of all of its harshnesses, its nullification of any technical compromise, there is a bracing musical philosophy that makes true sense. It is music that is sacred without dogma.

Though all three movements have titles, the work is not programmatic. "Discussions" (as the case with the other movements) has no suave melodies. The "themes" of this quartet are those of conversation expressed in the give-and-take of free counterpoint. The form is as unrestricted as any round-table talk or the town hall meetings of the composer's native New England. The instrumental voices erupt, cross over each other, jump, and clash. Occasionally, they discuss provisionally, at times, concurrently. A discussion reaches its most decided level, and then another begins. These are the elements of the first movement. Without any sense of tomfoolery, but one of a composer engrossed in his environment, quotations occur, in the early part of the movement, from "Dixie," "Marching through Georgia," and "Hail Columbia." Their significance can be translated in many ways, including popular integrations into an artwork, or as unstated programmaticism.

The following movement, "Arguments," is far less serious. The bounce of rhythms projects the pointed associations of voices disputing, rather than discussing freely. As befits the waywardness of no agenda, polyrhythms are developed, breaking down finally into a very sarcastic second-violin cadenza, simpering with its burlesque quality, and twice interrupted violently by the other instruments. Once more, the argument picks up speed, and quotations occur again, this time combinations from well-known symphonies (the march tune from Tchaikovsky's *Pathétique,* the choral theme of the last movement of Beethoven's "Ninth"), and "Columbia, the Gem of the Ocean." Such source material may be that of hellcatish origin, or an attempt to indicate that this contention is developing into the differing merits of popular songs versus symphonic music. Again, this is to be decided by the listener—he can make of it what he will. There is no doubt about the course of the methodical drive and the polyphonic rhythms that aid such excitement. The final cadence is based on the open strings of the violins, ending with two sharp chords which combine various tonalities. This "argument" has been unfinished, inconclusive.

The final movement is titled "The Call of the Mountains." It is mainly introspective, swept with varying moods (for there is no main theme or usual development). It is music of multi-lined aspect, of ecstatic pronouncement, with a tremendous climax toward the end, finally settling in the repose of an F-major tonality, but creased with a dissonant G-sharp. The vistas of this movement are impossible of harmonic resolution, just as one can never explain satisfactorily the how and why of nature, its breadth or its grandeur. There is no signified quality to this "Call," save the musical parallel of the spaciousness and granitelike immensity of a mountain.

QUINTETS

■ *Adagio cantabile* **for String Quartet and Piano (with optional Bass) (1908) (Alternate title: The Innate)**

(See also: Set for String Quartet, Bass, and Piano)

Similar to the first number in this *Set,* Ives made a vocal setting after the initial instrumental fact. The piano quintet (or sextet, if the bass is utilized) was composed in 1908. In 1916, the version for voice and piano or organ appeared with the title *The Innate.* (Oddly, it is this vocal title that appears on the first published edition of the *instrumental original,* issued in 1967.) The text of *The Innate* offers a meaningful clue to the original nonvocal opus. The first four lines of the total twelve give the essence: "Voices live in every finite being, / Often, undivined, near silence. / Hear them! / Hear them in you! in others!"

An increasing dynamic intensity is used for this emotional music, beginning softly, moving into a *mezzopiano,* and eventually into *forte,* seven measures from the end. The music then subsides, swiftly descending in 3 1/2 measures from *piano* to *pianissimo* onto *pianississimo* and then into total decay. A duo-dimensional plan applies. At first the strings are deployed against the piano; the former mainly in unison, the latter a polychromaticized opponent. Matters are then reversed. The strings move with intense chromatic detail and the piano has a simple line in bare octaves. For the ending all the lines blend with sensitive tonality opposition.

■ *Adagio sostenuto* **for Two Violins, Viola (or Violin 3 ad lib), Cello (ad lib), Solo English horn (or Flute or Basset horn), Piano (or Harp), Celesta or High Bell (ad lib) (before 1910)**

A solo listing in a chamber music opus seems to nullify the entire concept of the medium. Not in an Ives chamber piece. Certainly, not here. The wind instrument does not hog the limelight. It is more a principal voice—a *hauptstimme.* The other parts of the textural mass are far from accompanimental. While the wind color is emphasized, the instrument is not set off and drawn away from the others.

Substituting a harp for the piano constricts the harmonic content a bit. Due to the constant chromaticism, some editing for the plucked instrument would be mandatory. Together with the free choice of the celesta or high bell (merely used for six high Ds in place of the piano if so desired), and the other ad libs all this represents Ives's do-the-best-you-can-and-do-what-you-wish attitude.

An exact date for this work cannot be ascertained; the best estimate is sometime before 1910. In 1921, Ives, as so often the case, made a vocal arrangement titled "At Sea," using words from a poem by Robert Underwood Johnson. In the original version he termed *Adagio sostenuto* as "a song without voice." The later vocal setting can certainly apply to the instrumental one in terms of mood meaning, obtained from the opening lines of the song: "Some things are undivined except by love."

Most of the chordal content is friction-fuzzed, creating polyharmonies. However, there is a related balance between the opening of C major plus A minor and the conclusion consisting of the dominant of C major (G) and the retention of A minor.

- *The Innate* for String Quartet and Piano (with optional Bass) (1908) (*See: Adagio cantabile*)

(*See also: Set* for String Quartet, Bass, and Piano)

- *Allegro (the See'r)* for Clarinet, Solo Cornet or Trumpet (or Horn ad lib), Alto horn (or Horn or Trombone or Tenor Saxophone)(Second Alto horn ad lib), Piano, and Percussion (Snare Drum and Bass Drum) (? 1908)

Described as a "Scherzo" in certain listings, though no such title appears in the photocopy of the score given the author by Ives. The piece was reset by Ives for voice and piano, probably in 1913.

(It calls for five players, but the final three measures for the alto horn are indicated, with Ivesian nonchalance, "octaves ad lib." No great gain, but if followed it, of course, enlarges the piece into a sextet. An expensive undertaking, however, for the playing of four total sounds.)

The polyphonic complexity is framed at the beginning and end with more vertical qualities. This sets off the incisive syncopations that identify the piece. The concluding cadence gives a reverse, O Henry-like twist. (A recording of the piece produces a timing of forty-eight seconds.)

- *Hallowe'en* for String Quartet and Piano (Bass Drum or Drum ad lib) (1906)

This work for piano with four strings evokes the flashy humor of Hallowe'en by the sensations of direct and meaningful cacophony. It is a short composition, realistically atmospherical. Its fourteen measures are to be played three or four times, and it ends with a four-measure coda. Each of the string instruments stays uncompromisingly in one key; the first violin in C major, the second in B, the viola is in D-flat, and the cello in D. It will be noted that these keys are at the distance of half steps, forming a clustered tonality amalgam, furthered and enhanced by cross accents of every conceivable type. The piano has ultra-dissonant chords, as if it were banging away with no relationship to the string instruments. This is no musical gambol on the green!

Each "time around," the work gets louder and faster (from allegretto to presto, from *pianissimo* to quadruple *forte),* and, of course, funnier! Commencing with but violin and cello, more instruments jump in to build the bonfire as each section is repeated. This is hail music, well met (and meant!). Even a bass drum (or "a drum"—Ives did not designate the type) may be added, improvising as the performer wishes at certain places. According to Ives, this musical quip was written "for a hallowe'en party and not for a nice concert," but it certainly can be performed under the latter conditions. There is room for such raw musical caricature in the concert hall.

(*Hallowe'en* appears in a published edition as the first of *Three Outdoor Scenes.* The second "scene" is *The Pond,* and the third is *Central Park in the Dark.* The compilation is not authentic. Neither the main title nor the grouping was proposed by Ives. Sufficient confusion exists in the Ives catalogue without its being increased by a publisher's offhand and unauthorized decision.)

- *Hymn* for Two Violins, Viola, Solo Cello, and Bass (1904)
  (See: Largo Cantabile)

(See also: Set for String Quartet, Bass, and Piano)

- *In Re Con Moto Et Al* for Piano Quintet (1913)

The *Re* in the title has nothing to do with tonic sol-fa notation. Ives's "with regard to" pertains to five-instrument music drawn and quartered by the sharpest possible rhythmic knife. The sonic splinters build into one of the greatest explosions possible, the quintet sounding like twenty times its total. There is no piano quintet music like this one, which has nothing to do with its concentrated length of a little over three minutes, but much more would be too much. The specialness of Charles Ives's piano quintet music is its mallet-and-chisel style. Ives described it vividly as "studies in rhythm, time, duration, space, pulse, meter, accent, together and in various ways . . . ."

The metrical definition has no brotherly love for convention, with such arrangements as 33/8, 11/4, 33/16, and 15/16. Further, the more common measure separations are just as inner-competitive with cross accentuations plus such as five or eleven direct units to be set evenly across four beats. There are total pulse complications: of instrument against instrument, even when in the same meter, and in the polymetricality that exists between the total string group (already rhythmically in battle) and the piano.

In this work the climax is obtained by assault. The pent-up energy of the music is evident at the start and it doesn't take long to let loose. On the way one point is underlined, an eight-part fruitfully dissonant chord. It is heard thirty times, the fifth, sixth, and thirtieth appearances all in *fortissimo tremolando.* It is the sole item that has any relationship to motive,

theme, or subject. The quintet is completed with a nine-part unison followed by the special dissonant chord. This time (the thirty-first) it is lightly flipped in *pianissimo,* providing a masterful concluding stroke.

- *Largo cantabile* for Two Violins, Viola, Solo Cello, and Bass (1904)
  (Alternate title: Hymn)

(See also: Set for String Quartet, Bass, and Piano)

Ives composed this in August 1904. Seventeen years later, he transcribed the work (minus a few of the initial measures) for voice and piano with the *Hymn* title. The cello's line, designated as a "solo" voice in the first setting, is based on a hymnodic text noted in the score. It begins "Thou hidden love of God, whose height, / Whose depth, unfathomed no man knows," and continues for four more lines in the same vein.

No conventional four-square hymn format. Church deacons and ministers could be expected to state that Ives was in need of harmonic exorcism. Their mistake, however. The music is slightly, ever so slightly, touched with atonality. Mainly it is of late-romantic style, as the cello (simulating the hymnodic text) takes its soloistic place or floats within the texture. Solo designation notwithstanding, Ives's *Largo cantabile* (or *Hymn*) remains a sensitive piece of chamber music.

- *Largo risoluto No. 1 ("The Law of Diminishing Returns")* for Piano Quintet (1908)

Ives's enigmatic title is a humorous ploy. The developmental procedure that follows the first nine measures—a granity, rocky, super-dissonant quasi prelude—in its command and individuality, is creative money in the bank, with compounded interest. A more apt subtitle would be "The Proof of Profitable Returns."

The first three measures of the cello part (rhythmically doubled by the piano, as pertains to the entire initial nine measures) are the basic creative investment. These three measures are then announced by the piano alone in octaves, spearheading a section of imitation in super-rhythmic detail, made more exciting by polymetricality. Intermingled are percussive pedals. Ives wants to prove his point, so the section is repeated note-for-note. A fierce quantity of sound, this. But profitable.

(The published score omits the subtitle given in the heading above.)

- *Largo risoluto No. 2 ("A Shadow Made— a Silhouette")* **for Piano Quintet (1908)**

Unlike the subtitle for *Largo risoluto No. 1 (see above),* the explanatory title here is exact. The quintet is timbre-split. Thereby, the work is heard twice as a delineated outline with shadowed background. The first time the piano plays *forte,* the strings *piano.* (Ives indicated the latter "as if heard in the distance.") On the repeat (minus the last ten measures) the dynamic roles are reversed.

Ives uses a different pandiatonic base for both strings and keyboard instrument, thus simultaneously creating bitonal partnership (E-flat for the string quartet, A for the piano). Since chromatic change is fairly minimal, the chordal choices create a constant frictional harmonic compaction that makes for the best of both worlds since the *effect* within each unit (strings and piano) is a bitonal haze. The clash is not loosened until the end of the two-measure final cadence. There the strings conclude the piece with a pure E-flat-major triad, having combined in the penultimate measure with the just-as-pure A-major triad of the piano.

(As with the published score for *Largo risoluto No. 1—see above—* the score issued for this work does not include the subtitle.)

- *Scherzo ("All the Way Around and Back")* **for Clarinet (or Flute), Violin (or Flute ad lib), Bugle (or Trumpet), Middle Bells (or Horn), Piano (or Two Pianos)**

A unique combination. One doubts any other use of the primitive brass bugle can be found in chamber music literature. The limits of the instrument are further limited by Ives to the pitches of the C-major triad.

Ives's piece is a study in increasing pulse specifications within a 4/4 measure. It begins with one sound carried over 1 1/2 measures, onto one total sound in the measure, then in succession two, three, four, and five sounds within the bar-line separations. The total then jumps to seven for three measures and finally another jump to an eleven total. Naturally (this is Ives!), there are cross-rhythms against these, but the pulse increase is patently clear. The rhythms then are reversed in a slightly free palindromic arrangement. Having reached the ultimate point of return the piece is completed by a short, four-measure coda. No scherzo form, but a sort of scherzolike jest.

SEXTETS

- *Allegretto sombreoso (from the "Incantation")* **for Flute, English horn (or Trumpet or Basset horn), Three Violins, and Piano (? 1909)**

Another instrumental work that was refashioned by Ives into a vocal piece (in 1921).

Ives made no programmatic gestures in his instrumental transmutation of Byron's lines. Undoubtedly their sense was important to the instrumental interpretation, since they are set forth in the English horn's part in the score. However, while the lines are the creative guide, they are treated with almost total neutrality. ("When the moon is on the wave, and the glow-worm in the grass, and the meteor on the grave, and the wisp on the morass; / When the falling stars are shooting and the answered owls are hooting and the silent leaves are still in the shadow of the hill. / Shall my soul be upon thine, with a power and with a sign.") No "mickey-mouse" tactics are used to represent falling stars and hooting owls. Everything remains soft and flowing. Only the phrase "with a power" is illuminated by the climactic intensity of a *fortissimo*.

Metrically fluid, with many measures of 12/16 and 13/16, euphoniousness is maintained, the incantation a song without words with spellbinding effect. An arpeggiated ostinato is basic, formed from a ninth chord arrangement projected from a fundamental F. An important part of every measure, the F is maintained into the final chord, where it is braced above by an E-flat and below by a C-sharp.

- *"From the Steeples and the Mountains"* **for Four Bells (Two High and Two Low) (or Two Pianos), Trumpet (Trumpet 2 ad lib), and Trombone (? 1902)**

"From the Steeples and the Mountains" (only forty-eight measures in length) was probably composed in 1902 but remained unheard until 1965, when it was given its premiere in New York. Ives's tintinnabulous sound-picture calls for the inclusion of two pairs of huge bells arranged in scalar, sustained, and arpeggiated patterns. The clash of the bells is further intensified by the frictions derived from the combined, clustered tonalities of B, C, and D-flat. Against these, a trumpet (there are three notes at the very end for another trumpet if one wishes to augment the forces) and trombone are in opposition, each severely linear—rhythmic simultaneity is practically nonexistent.

The ending is sheer sonic liberation—a joy for those who don't wince at strong music. It bears out fully the motto Ives placed at the score's conclusion: "From the Steeples—the

Bells!—then the Rocks on the Mountains begin to shout!"

- **Scherzo** *("Over the Pavements")* **for Piccolo, Clarinet, Bassoon (or Saxophone), Trumpet, Piano, Percussion (Bass Drum and Cymbal), and Three Trombones (ad lib) (1913)**

A scherzo design, utilizing flavorsome polyrhythms, suggested to Ives by the hurry of city dwellers. The jazzy, nervous accents convey a Shavian-Ivesian humor.

Included is a thirteen-measure section, which is marked "Cadenza (to play or not to play)," though it is much more settled in quality then the rest of the piece. The tempo of this section is typical of Ives: allegro molto (or as fast as possible).

- *Set* **for String Quartet, Bass, and Piano**

  I—*See:* Largo cantabile *(Alternate title:* Hymn) (1904)
  II—*See:* Scherzo (1914)
  III—*See:* Adagio cantabile *(Alternate title:* The Innate) (1908)

The main title has been treated very loosely. Such confusion stems from Ives himself—cataloguing accuracy, titling precision, and finality of instrumentation were matters that little concerned this creative maverick. Though Ives often used the generic heading "set," rather than the more common word "suite," for a miscellaneous group of pieces or separate movements, he did not apply the "set" heading to this one. Although each composition is for a different combine, since all three pieces call for four or five strings, with one including the piano, Ives indicated the group could be performed as a unit or individually. It was the Cowells in their book on Ives who titled the compilation a "set."

Because of the differences in the approach

to the use and meaning of the bass instrumental voice in a variety of ways, the Cowells complete title reads: *Set for String Quartet, "Basso," and Piano.* On the other hand, John Kirkpatrick, the Ives scholar, designates the three pieces as *A Set of 3 Short Pieces.* The matter is made sticky by the separate scores that have been published, none of which make mention of the other pieces and their possible relationship as proposed by Ives.

(As mentioned above, each part of this *Set* may be performed separately. Accordingly, the compositions are discussed individually within the numerical total order that is followed in this compendium.)

SEPTETS

- *"Like a Sick Eagle"* for Flute, English horn (or Basset horn), Violin, Viola, Cello, Double Bass, and Piano, with Voice ad lib (1909)

Ten measures of intensely sensitive music, in largo molto pace. (This tempo designation formed the title when Ives originally produced the piece in 1909.) It was termed an "intonation"—another way of describing this dynamically restrained music that moves strictly between *pianissimo* and *piano.* When Ives made a voice and piano setting (probably in 1913), he dispensed with bar lines. Understandably, since *"Like a Sick Eagle,"* no matter its embellishments, is the projection of a single, principal theme of conduct. This is emphasized by the ad lib voice part, which is a note-for-note duplicate of the English horn part. Some Ives pieces denote an instrument as "solo," which nevertheless does not separate from the totality and therefore becomes accompanied. In *"Like a Sick Eagle,"* the English horn, with or without voice, is of primacy. Of the other instruments, only the violin maintains a special, obbligato-type role. The remaining instruments supplement—the flute adds a counterpoint in the last

four measures and the piano has only a pair of chords, with a slight voice change in the second of these. (Ivesian provisions are always casual. It is possible to use more than one double bass—the number is not given. An added tone is placed in the bass part's final measure, but is to be played "only if more than one bass." More than one bass would spoil the balance, and the added note is merely an octave doubling of a pitch in the piano part.)

Throughout in the violin and the ad lib voice, slides through microtones are requested, producing quarter tones between basic half steps and third tones between basic whole steps. Ives had an absorbing interest in microtones from his early days so their use here is not surprising. (In the voice and piano version, the voice follows the same method.) The microtonal objective is to obtain "a more desolate sound," and certainly is a stimulus to depicting the harmonic ache of the piece. It is also a potent colorific aid to the mood of the text, by Keats, its final part reading: " . . . I must die, like a sick eagle looking towards the sky."

- *"Luck and Work"* for Flute, Basset horn (or English horn), Three Violins, Piano, and Drums (1916)

Eleven measures of music, once noted as "Allegro Andante" *(sic!),* in two sections, the first Allegro con spirito, the other Andante. Ives made his instrumental pithy opus in 1916 having written the original setting for voice and piano in 1913. His instrumentation calls for comment only in terms of the "drums." The plural designation is probably a misnomer (always possible, of course, that it isn't and constitutes one of Ives's casual ad libitums). A simple part is given the instrument, with nine single-stroke sounds and one measure of two successive rolls. "Drums" could mean any member of the membraneous family; so, one drum (or more) is Ives again with an instrumental color that is chance-tinged.

Four measures in fast tempo are followed by four of andante, with the designation "slower and easily." Then, three measures of animando for conclusion. Based on words (by Robert Underwood Johnson) marked under the wind-instrument line, these speed divisions mark two persons with different approaches to life. One (Allegro) seeks "the magic four-leaved clover." The other (Andante) "will plant a crop to bear him double." Content delineates these opposites: complex rhythms for the first as a thesis, and a simpler pulse arrangement for the second, as the antithesis. The textures follow suit.

NONET

- ***The Unanswered Question* for Flute Quartet (or Oboe for Flute 3, or Clarinet for Flute 4), Trumpet (or English horn or Oboe or Clarinet), and String Quartet (1906)**

A popularity point has been reached by this piece far beyond any others in the Ives catalogue. This work, utilizing separation of instruments (stereophonic methodology), poly-tempo and aleatoric techniques, marks still another triple credit for the remarkable inventive mind of Charles Ives. Composed in 1906 (originally subtitled "A Cosmic Landscape," but eliminated later) *The Unanswered Question* is a godfather figure in the work styles of such men as John Cage, Henry Brant, Earle Brown, Karlheinz Stockhausen, and many others. In one fell swoop, Ives once again anticipated and defined systems a half century before the creative pack adopted them.

Most often the work is performed with a full (muted) string orchestra—permitted by Ives. He also indicated that a full treble woodwind choir could be used in place of the four flutes, but this is very rarely done. No matter this enlarged setting (in part or totally), there can only be a single trumpet. However, these are suggested permissions granted to performers. The work, in its basic state, is for nine instruments. Of these, the string quartet is always muted and to be either off stage or "away from the trumpet and flutes." The trumpet is muted, unless performance takes place "in a very large room" (or with a "larger" string orchestra). The oboe and clarinet substitutions for the brass instrument are permitted only if the instrument involved is not substituting for one of the flutes.

The Unanswered Question is program music, based on a philosophical essay. The string quartet represents "The Silences of the Druids—Who Know, See, and Hear Nothing"; the trumpet propounds "The Perennial Question of Existence," and the flutes attempt to give the answer but never succeed. The last group makes six separate entries in contrary, changing tempo—beginning very slowly and each time picking up the pace until a presto is reached. Against this the string quartet and trumpet steadfastly maintain a largo speed rate. The winds "need not be played in the exact time position indicated." Actually, because of the relative entry point for all sections, with only generally indicated tempos, they cannot.

As Ives conceived the piece, it is not to be performed with exactitude; tempos and meters are in opposition to one another. Thus, one group (the strings), playing in extremely slow tempo, and another (the winds), playing at ever-faster speed, and the declamatory trumpet, must be considered as separate entities meeting only by happenstance. The more the blend of these three instrumental components, the less effective the result. This is neither a joke nor a trick. With three different levels at work simultaneously, it is amazing how easily the tridimensional facts can be followed by the ear.

Ivey

Ivey, Jean Eichelberger (1923–)

DUOS

- *Aldebaran* for Viola and Tape (1972)

A semiprogrammatic consideration, noted by the composer as suggestive of the mood in which one "contemplates the sky on a starry night." Accordingly the title, "named after a star, whose name is Arabic for 'the follower.' " Fundamentally, Ivey's *Aldebaran* is built from impressionistic soundshots for the viola with similar partnership by the electronic tape.

- Music for Viola and Piano (1974)

A rhapsodic composition, its mood suggested by a quotation from the poet Sidney Lanier: "solemn spaces where the shadows bide." There is complete virtuosic thrust in this piece with the full resources of the instruments used as well as some special effects. One of these concerns the violist assisting the pianist in creating sounds directly on the piano's strings.

Jachino, Carlo (1887–1971)

QUARTET

■ **String Quartet No. 2**

Jachino came to prominence by way of this quartet, which was awarded one of the four prizes in the international competition held in 1928 by the Musical Fund Society of Philadelphia. The $10,000 prize money was the largest sum ever offered for chamber music works, and it was understandable that 643 entries were received from composers all over the world.

The contest was judged by men in various fields of musical endeavor: Fritz Reiner and Willem Mengelberg, conductors; Frederick Stock, conductor and composer; Thaddeus Rich, internationally known concertmeister of the Philadelphia Orchestra and chamber music performer; Samuel L. Laciar, composer, music critic, and writer on chamber music; and Gilbert Reynolds Combs, music educator. The first prize of $6,000 was divided between Bartók's Quartet No. 3 and Casella's Serenata and displayed the judges' uncanny discernment. Bartók's third string quartet is considered, without argument, among the most important chamber music productions of the present century. At this remove, Casella's Serenata does not receive the attention it deserves. This is undoubtedly due to its mixed instrumentation calling for two winds (clarinet and bassoon), one brass (trumpet), and a pair of string instruments (violin and cello). The $4,000 second prize was divided between Jachino's work and a piano quintet by H. Waldo Warner. Although these have lesser significance and have had few performances, their values are distinguished and far from the average run of faceless music that marks the entries in prize contests for composers.

Jachino's quartet departs from classical form, yet outlines certain of its features with lucidity. The aim is not only intelligible but individual. Although the first movement is very slow, this does not negate the use of another slow (much shorter) movement in third place. The most contemporary manner is found in the fast-paced second movement. There, the usual scherzo form has variety that announces a distinct freshness of creative approach. The music begins with bell-like combinations and then moves into regular scherzo style, which includes a broader (Trio) section in quintuple meter. Next a return is made to the tintinnabular portion, followed by a repetition of the Scherzo proper, with a cadenza leading to the initial section which serves as the movement's postscript. Thus Jachino applies rondo style within a triple-meter Scherzo. Oddly enough the same pulse total is chosen for the last movement.

Jacob, Gordon (1895–1984)

DUOS

■ *Five Pieces (in the Form of a Suite)* **for Harmonica and Piano**

An exceedingly rare and delightful instrumental combination productive of delightful music. This work is worthy for its special color alone.

There are frisky thirds and sevenths in the "Caprice." The former also soothes the "Cradle Song" and propels the "Russian Dance." A "Threnody" and a triple-pulse boisterous "Country Dance" complete the proceedings.

(Jacob also made a version for harmonica and string orchestra and in that form the work has been commercially recorded.)

■ *Miniature Suite* **for Clarinet and Viola**

Tonal detail with fresh flavoring. (Jacob was never an academic creator.) The movements are a pert March; Berceuse, cradled with moving eighth notes; Minuet and Trio; and a fully chromatic Fugue. The last has a subject of eleven-pitch total. Miniatures all, but serious stuff. (Jacob never produced salonistic tidbits.)

■ **Prelude, Passacaglia, and Fugue for Violin and Viola (1948)**

The temptation to achieve expanded sonorities in this restricted medium is avoided. Jacob controls his line writing so that the duo formation is paramount. There are three- and four-part voicings, but these are used to underpin cadences or to form a contrasting density. Classic forms are employed, and Jacob adheres to style, using chromatic tones only to moisten the possible dryness of set forms.

The Handelian opening is used at the end of the Fugue for unification, and is succeeded by a short coda. Not only are the molds of classic directness, but they contain similar techniques. In the Prelude, a pair of canons separates the majestic theme to depict binary conditions. The ground bass of the Passacaglia (five measures in length) is utilized nine times before it is stated twice in the violin, then returned to the lower voice. The Fugue subject illustrates how twelve tones can be used without validating these by dodecaphonic technique.

■ **Sonata for Cello and Piano (1957)**

Although there are sections that flow and are calm, the greater part of the music is of bravura detail, intense in its demeanor. Jacob's duo sonata represents romantic fervor set forth with a dramatic commando approach. This applies to the outer movements, though the initial one shifts gears into a quieter quality and a slower pace in its final part. The same drive, though not as heavy, describes the second movement, an allegro vivace Scherzo. The Adagio's strength is drawn from block-chord detail.

Jacob's piece opens *fortissimo* and concludes *fortississimo*. Movements one, two, and three terminate, as is so often this composer's

method, *pianissimo*. An interesting concept, in view of the overall alive and bright tone of the music.

■ **Sonata for Oboe and Piano**

Mozartian clarity is found in the refinements of this duo sonata. Strength and balance are detailed in the forms of the composition by the opposites of conjunct and disjunct lines in the first movement and short and long figures in the second movement. The latter is a scherzo and Trio conception, with exact recapitulation of the initial material. Both this part and the third movement (Adagio) emphasize seventh spans in the melodic lines. Sonata scale is projected in the finale, which moves swiftly and signs off with this composer's most-often observed signature: a *pianissimo–pianississimo* dynamic level.

■ **Sonata for Treble Recorder and Piano**

Conscientious attention to open textures and tonal clarification here. The first movement, save for a single measure, is in quintuple meter, and mostly free of chromatic pitches. Only the Largo furnishes a slight exception to the above. Movement two is a Scherzo; movement four has the hop-quick moves of a Galop.

■ **Sonatina for Two Violas**

Nothing pretentious, but extremely persuasive material that is set forth in equal distribution for the two players, with tonal certainty, and without any fancy effects.

A vigorous, motivally engendered first movement. Movement two is tempoed Adagio, but is a set of four variations on a simple eight-measure theme of continuous two-voice quarter notes that are phrased over the bar lines. The end movement is a kicked-rhythm affair, contrasted in the center with music based on the previous material slowed in pace and broadened in statement.

- **Sonatina for Viola (or Clarinet) and Piano (1948)**

Most often, music in sonatina form veers away from the very serious, and that applies to this duo. Joyful and gay material in the outer movements, the latter a Rondo, the former stressing conjunct lines. A tripartite central movement provides the additional balance.

- **Three Inventions for Flute and Oboe (1934)**

One writer has described this duo as "a lively set" of pieces. And that it is, of eight-minute length, with allegro vivace and allegro giusto tempos for the outer movements and a poco lento designation for the inner one.

Jacob follows the linear disposition of the form. There is plenty of imitation throughout. In the third part the invention turns into a fugue.

- **Three Pieces for Viola and Piano**

Although the subjects are of vivid difference, movement one (Elegy) and movement three (Scherzo) share the common property of quartal harmonization. They also share a somewhat repetitive use of figurations, though these define differences: emotive stress in the Elegy and peripatetic drive in the Scherzo.

However, reduplication in the most absolute, dynamic sense takes place in the second piece, properly titled Ostinato. There are fifty measures in andante con moto tempo. Save for the final (fiftieth) measure, each measure has the same succession of four triads: B-flat minor–G major–E minor–G minor. There is no bass line for the piano, and the viola's line moves below, in between, and above the ostinato sequence. The restricted harmonic setting, combined with the chromatically inflected viola voice, provides a vivid dramatic result.

- **Tuba Suite for Tuba and Piano**

Truly a mixed bag, a sampler of the tuba's ability to sing, articulate, and prove its virtuosic capabilities.

As to the first item, the documentation is the opening Prelude, the third-movement Saraband, and the seventh-movement Ground ("Jacob's Dream"). In the absence of any explanation one assumes it is the composer who is being identified. As to the second point there are three dance representations: Hornpipe, Bourrée, and Mazurka (movements two, four, and six, respectively). The last of these is prefaced by a "Brief Interlude" for piano alone, totaling fifteen measures. A good strategic move, this, both for color change and for granting the brass-instrument performer a chance to rest.

As to the third element the evidence is the finale (movement eight), a Galop (with cadenza). The pace is a furious presto that toward the end moves up several notches and concludes in a sixteen-measure prestissimo in *fortissimo*. The huge cadenza is set within the movement. This soloistic splurge may not be of chamber music regularity, but it matches the stylistic spirit of the entire opus.

- **Variations for Treble Recorder and Harpsichord (or Piano) (1963)**

Jacob was a contemporary classicist, but did not believe stubbornly that meaningful directness must be secondary to formal requirements. The ten variations on a Scottish-type theme (constantly shifting between 3/4 and 2/4 time) are all clear, and minus any bedeviled webs of mere technique called on to fulfill the design.

A colorful march quality surrounds the third variation. Number five is for the keyboard instrument alone. In the seventh variation both instruments play, with the fifth variant's soprano line now assigned to the recorder in totally inverted form.

The final part of the piece is a flying duple-pulse Presto.

TRIOS

- *Aubade* **for Two Flutes and Clarinet**

Generally, *Aubade (Morning Music)* compositions are in one movement. Jacob's contribution is full-fledged, with four movements. It begins with a rhythmically bright, slow tempo "Bon Jour" ("Good Morning") in C minor and neatly concludes in a more wide-awake C major. Two dances follow: Gavotte and Valsette. A carefree, pitch-connected concept completes matters with an "Adieu" ("Farewell") in polite C major.

- *Six Shakespearian Sketches* **for String Trio (1946)**

Jacob's little suite falls in the class of implied program music. (A rare type of music for the string trio medium.) The movement titles have a set description, the music simply follows suit in general terms. Even without titles, the general dispositions the half-dozen movements portray would be apparent to the listener.

Movement one is "How Sweet the Moonlight Sleeps on Yonder Bank." The instruments are muted; the play of fourths in the undulating accompaniment to the featured cello line gives archaic sweetness, and the colors of chordal harmonics add to the nocturnal mood. "Foot It Featly" is a triple-meter light dance, mostly set in chordal blocks. Movement three ("In Sad Cypress") is the most chromatic of this basically diatonic work. Its form gives the feeling of a single unit, though a binary build links its twenty-two measures.

The next part, "Grace in All Simplicity," is minuetlike; "And A' Babbled of Green Fields" continues the general vernal basis of the trio. The most energetic music is retained for the last movement, "Here a Dance of Clowns." It is certainly a dance of fun, with entrances off the beat, syncopation, and a merry all-get-out from start to finish.

- **Trio for Clarinet, Viola, and Piano**

Jacob's Trio had the unusual basis of being commissioned by a commercial organization—British Petroleum Company Limited. The first performance was given at this organization's BP House in July 1969.

This English composer's style of melodiousness and rhythmic ingenuity is authoritatively exhibited in the work. Interlacements are contained in the four movements. The opening movement and the third are both Adagios (metronomically almost identical, the first is marked $\downarrow = 36$, the other is $\downarrow = 40$). Open fifths support the Trio of the second movement Menuetto and the same interval serves as the foundational pivot for the concluding section of the second slow (Adagio) movement. A further link is the attachment of the last to the finale, a Presto assai that swirls up and down the pitch range. And one more link is the use within the finale of a partial quotation from the second Adagio.

- **Trio for Flute (alternating Piccolo), Oboe, and Harpsichord (or Piano) (1958)**

Jacob's tonal music is always fresh, tuneful, and brilliantly scored. And decisively clear in its structural arrangements.

Key motility brightens the aspects of the first part of the work. The Adagio is principally governed by antiphonal scoring that compares the two wind instruments with the keyboard representative. Movement three is a large ternary affair, with saltarellolike material in the outer sections. The motival finale uses a piccolo to further brighten the instrumental setting.

■ **Trio for Piano, Violin, and Cello (1955)**

The opening slow movement grows in texture and power, then subsides and is linked to a strictly structured Scherzo, with a Trio in contrasting tonality and tempo. An exact repetition of the main material completes the movement. Another slow movement follows. It is chromatically detailed and embraces all twelve tones in its main thematic line, but dodecaphonic process is foreign to this composer. The concluding movement has a tranquil section but is principally concerned with the touch-and-go representative of toccata format.

■ **Two Pieces for Two Oboes and English horn**

Tempo contrast, as is to be expected. The first part of the trio is a dolorous Adagio; the second piece is a whimsical Scherzo with bouncy rhythm. In both cases three-part form is used. The scoring changes in the slow-pace piece; the recapitulation in the second piece is a literal da capo.

Jacob's favorite reticent dynamic close is present. Both pieces conclude in *pianissimo*.

QUARTETS

■ **Quartet for Oboe and Strings (Violin, Viola, and Cello) (1938)**

The oboe quartet begins in C minor, turns to the like-named major, then to F minor, and finally to C major again. It will be noted that the modes alternate, and that, additionally, there is interlocution between the second and fourth movements, as well as a lifting-up of the tonal orbit a fourth in the third movement. Furthermore, homophony rules in the first movement, fugal distinction in the second, semi-contrapuntal means are the technique in the third, and forthright rhythmic stability in the last. Accordingly, one method pertains to the center

parts, another to the outer. These convey four bands in the packing of the work. Aside from varying tempos, the perfection of balance is more than suggestive. Such coordination supports the foundation that solidifies a composition and marks a distinguished work that more than satisfies.

It is said that to think is to act, but very often the functioning of the thought is less than eloquent. In this composer's case, there is not only the attempted deed but achievement in the avoidance of the "big sound"—the bargain attraction for the grandstand. Save for the second movement's final cadence, all others end in a subdued dynamic, and all four movements begin softly. Jacob was a sensitive composer. This shows in his workmanship, in his musical speech, manners, and in his sincerity.

■ **Scherzo for Two Trumpets, Horn, and Trombone**

Full formal scrutiny, but with special attention applied to the contrasting Trio, where the change of tonality and tempo is not unusual, but the use of total fugal procedures is, and is stimulating. Within, Jacob uses inversion and stretto as well.

■ **Suite for Four Pipers (Treble, Alto, Tenor, and Bass Pipes)**

Three dances for the recorderlike instruments. Fitting, light material it is, comprising a Gavotte and Musette, an expressive Pavane, and a vivacious Bourrée.

■ **Suite for Four Trombones (1968)**

Shakespeare's phrase "Come, give us a taste of your quality" comes to mind in the five-part disposition of this quartet. Majestic sonants are present in the Intrada, lyricism in the form of chordal statement is heard in the Sarabanda, and moderately speeded rhythm is exhibited in the Alla marcia. Part four demonstrates color. In this Spirituale all four trombones are muted; the first uses a cup mute, the others straight mutes. The finale shows the strength of contrapuntalism in a Finale alla fuga.

QUINTETS

- **Divertimento for Harmonica and String Quartet (1954)**

There are at least a good half-dozen worthy pieces for harmonica and orchestra, but that total is far from being equaled in the harmonica–string quartet medium. This is a most attractive entry.

In five of the eight movements the material is of light content, but polished, warm, wise, and classy nonetheless. These movements are the March, the triadically detailed Romance, the Scherzetto, the F-minor Slavonic Dance, and the concluding Jig. A more serious stance pertains to the remaining three movements. In the Siciliano only the viola and cello are used from the quartet group. The Elegy also calls for half the quartet team (this time the two violins, and thereby the movements that have reduced scoring are balanced). The third of this group is the Sarabande, antiphonally presented in the first two-thirds of its setting.

- **Quintet for Clarinet and Strings (Two Violins, Viola, and Cello) (1942)**

Aside from the opening movement, the other three enlist forms with explanatory titles. The second-movement Scherzo is very rhythmic, a dynamic type that makes its way more on the nondisputed response of motoric patterns than on pert delivery. In contrast to the dogmatic compulsion of the main section, a slower, almost lazy episode twice interjects. This serves as the modern form of a double Trio, as well as for coda purposes. The Rhapsody favors the clarinet, the only time the full balance that should exist in any chamber music creation is disturbed. But this "wrong" proves to be "right," since it permits a striking contrast to exist between the Rhapsody and the other movements.

The final movement consists of an Introduction, Theme, and Variations. The bouncy theme is moderate in speed and all the variations are direct in their various presentations. The third is a march type; the fifth (and last) a fugato communication. One will observe Jacob's predilection to end not only a work but all of its parts with reserve. All four movements are completed softly—the loudest being the last, which is in *piano*; whereas the other three are thrice softer.

- **Suite for Bassoon, Two Violins, Viola, and Cello**

Jacob always knew what he was about. This Suite for bassoon and string quartet (a medium that has a sparse literature) does not make a false creative step. None of this music will induce shut-eye in the listener.

The Prelude is a broadly expressive slow-tempo statement that combines muted strings with the declamatory-styled wind instrument (it also has an expressive four-measure "quasi cadenza"). The stimulant is in the metrical order that precisely alternates three-beat measures with two-beat totals. A scherzoish Caprice follows. Movements three and four are a chromatically detailed Elegy and a Rondo that has let-go atmosphere, barely interrupted by a few small ritards and a short molto meno mosso portion.

SEXTET

- **Sextet for Piano, Flute (alternating Piccolo), Oboe (alternating English horn), Clarinet, Horn, and Bassoon**

Homage to two musicians is wrapped around

this composition for piano and wind quintet. Jacob composed the work in memory of the great English French-horn player and teacher Aubrey Brain (1893–1955) for the Dennis Brain Ensemble, which gave the premiere performance. Shortly afterward (in 1957) Dennis (Aubrey's son, born 1921), considered one of the greatest of all horn virtuosos, was killed as he drove at high speed, at night, from Birmingham to London, and hit a tree. In his preface to the published score, issued in 1962 by Musica Rara, Jacob indicates that he regards the work "as a double tribute to the memory of father and son."

The pitches A, B, E, B, and A, taken from the name Aubrey Brain, are used as the thematic generator for all movements but the Cortége. There, Jacob explains the key is "B-flat minor and is therefore centred round the note B-flat (=B in Continental nomenclature), thus bringing into prominence the initial B."

In view of the above background, movement one is a fitting Elegiac Prelude, its tempo mainly adagio, the same pace for the Epilogue that concludes the work. A tripleted energized Scherzo marks the second movement. The Cortége follows. It begins with unaccompanied clarinet, which is linked to music "in the style of a slow march" that begins with English horn and octave support from the piano. A lighter-faceted Minuet and Trio and a vivacious Rondo with a contrastive Epilogue (mentioned earlier) are the concluding parts of this major chamber music contribution by Jacob.

OCTETS

■ **Divertimento in E-flat for Wind Octet (Two Oboes, Two Clarinets, Two Bassoons, and Two Horns)**

There's a hearty portion of enjoyment in this three-part Divertimento. And there's a healthy portrayal of technique.

Movement one is a March, in E-flat, of course, but with spiced harmony and with weights mainly placed on weak beats. The middle movement, Sarabande on a Ground, is a gem of variational statement. The subject (announced by the first horn) consists of four measures and is heard fifteen times in succession. Each instrument has an opportunity to present the subject, sometimes in combination with another. These sixty measures are then followed by a twelve-measure coda. Movement three is a fast-moving Rondo, set forth in mostly block-type scoring.

■ **Interludes from *Music for a Festival* for Trumpets and Trombones (Four Trumpets, Two Trombones, Bass Trombone, and Timpani)**

Solid writing for this vivid brass septet, backed up with a small amount for the timpani. A sense of outdoorish ambience covers the five movements.

The Intrada is completely *fortissimo*, presenting majestic triadic material. Part two, Round of Seven Parts, is an extremely skillful (and successful) follow-the-leader conception. Of course, to maintain absolute linear strictness the timpani is eliminated. In the adagio-tempo Interlude chordal sevenths shift back and forth to complete triads. The Saraband is structured so that the central section is for the trumpets alone. In conclusion there is a Madrigal (also minus the timpani) which is scored in antiphonal fashion with shifting homophonic and contrapuntal material.

■ **Serenade for Woodwind (Two Flutes [Flute 2 alternating Piccolo], Two Oboes [Oboe 2 alternating English horn], Two Clarinets, and Two Horns) (1950)**

A full-scale piece, eight movements covering twenty-four minutes. The forms are standard: March, Arietta, Gavotte, Interlude (Incantation), Toccatina, Sarabande, Scherzo, and Epilogue. All direct and transpicuous in their variety.

The textural plan of the Sarabande alternates the sextuple lower voices with paired flutes, and concludes with tutti assimilation. To give a silvery edge to the Scherzo, the piccolo is used. The English horn adds its garnet timbre to the Interlude and plays an important part in the Epilogue.

Jacob, Werner (1938–)

SEPTET

■ *Komposition 5/7 (Fünf Strukturen für 7 Solo Instrumente) (Five Structures for 7 Solo Instruments)* **(Flute [alternating Piccolo], Bass Clarinet, Trumpet, Trombone, Violin, Viola, and Double Bass) (1969)**

The key center (in its broadest, nontonal sense) is the total chromatic as applied to five movements. (*Structures* is a better word since the formative validity arises from minute pitch components rather than broad thematic details that contrast and balance in their horizontal determination.) Each structure has a purposeful shape.

The first is called "Antiphon," but the chants sung here consist of constructive dispersal of intervallic jets. "Static" describes individual instrumental movement, the sounds themselves are in constant action—a tossing from one isolated pitch to the next. "Culmination" (structure number three) has shapes that remind one of the "Antiphon." The continuous development (derived from pitch measurements one to the next) remains in "Fixation." The final "Acceleration" has threefold meaning. The tempo moves from slow to fast and simultaneously the rhythmic activity becomes acute and the texture thickens. With almost classic reserve, a

return is then made to the initial ascetic state.

Jacobi, Frederick (1891–1952)

DUOS

■ **Ballade for Violin and Piano (1942)**

A sizable work, lasting close to twelve minutes. Here, Jacobi uses romantic enlargement of harmony with a pinch of present-day salt. The resultant musical dish is an excellent one.

■ **Fantasy for Viola and Piano (1941)**

Illustrative of Jacobi's excellent craftsmanship, which denies mere academicism. The Fantasy is of high accomplishment in a neoromantic manner. The ultracontemporary will call it old-fashioned music, and the average contemporary's ears will not be shocked. Both should be able to recognize a creative voice very much alive and interesting.

■ *Impressions from the Odyssey*: **Three Pieces for Violin and Piano (1947)**

This was Jacobi's final chamber music work. The suite is of miniature size, dynamic in its tightness and enunciation.

Though dealing in turn with "Ulysses," "Penelope," and Ulysses' homecoming years later ("The Return"), the sections cling as a totality. Interlocution is obtained by intervallic expansion—the important declamatory second in "Ulysses" becomes a ninth in "The Return"—and by tonal span definition—stressing of a rising fourth in parts two and three. Save for the final cadence, Jacobi delineates the character of "Penelope" by strict three-voice writing.

QUARTETS

■ **String Quartet [No. 1] on Indian Themes (1924)**

Without the oft-used means of three classified periods in relation to a composer's work, it is easily possible to divide Jacobi's music into the small Indian-conscious group, the large corpus of music inspired by his Hebraic extraction, and those works that are not based on or devoted to either of these two. The Indian period of Jacobi's creative activities was passed through quickly, including two large works. Both are important in their respective literatures—this quartet, written in 1924, and the *Indian Dances* for orchestra, completed in 1928.

At one time, to compose "American" music it seemed necessary to draw from the heritages of the Indians or the blacks. We view this more maturely now and realize that all national extractions make up American folk art. Jacobi's initial quartet is to be considered as a result of his study of Indian music, not as an attempt to produce "American" music. Only the last two movements are based on authentic Indian thematic material. Themes for the second movement were found in Natalie Curtis's *The Indians' Book*. Within the instrumental foursome, solo voices are made prominent inside a fully muted sonority, with the conception based on love songs. In the last movement, there are incorporated ritualistic rain-, corn-, and war-dance themes heard by the composer during a stay in New Mexico. The general feeling is barbaric; the color of the quartet is exploited to equate Indian percussive and other instrumental sonorities (by left-hand pizzicato, successive down bows, striking by the ivory tip of the bow, playing with the wood of the bow); the rhythms shift in choreographic delineation. Although there are no quoted themes in the opening movement, Jacobi has caught well the very essence and outlines of Indian melodicism.

■ **String Quartet No. 2 (1933)**

The opening movement's main subject emerges from an almost vagrant introduction (but which sets the stage well for the robustness that will follow). The movement exemplifies tremendous string quartet power.

Ostinatos help the general introspective tone of the slow movement, mainly moving in the dark tonality of B-flat minor. The final movement can be considered a joint scherzo-finale, since the main theme of its rondo shape is both nervous and humorous. Three times total silence is used to heighten the dramaticism within this concluding movement. These general pauses also serve to mark points in the music's design.

■ **String Quartet No. 3 (1945)**

The shape of the first movement preserves the elements of sonata form, redesigned in terms of the present century. Jacobi cuts his recapitulation down to the minimum (a fairly long solo for second violin heralds this section, oddly enough, *not* for the first violin). The congress of intervallic movement shows craftsmanship of high order, using the half step in the thrust-out motive of the introduction (it begins, and then leaps, and returns, all on this axis of the semitone) as an important motion implement in the main theme. (Such is the orientation of the classical-Beethoven school.) Though double and triple (as well as quadruple) stops are not foreign to string quartet composition, the first type is used practically throughout the main theme, thereby increasing the density of the sonority.

The stepwise particular reappears in the remaining three movements, the last of which quotes the introduction of the first. The result of such chromatic leanings matches use of a rhapsodical rondo form in the slow section. The present-day fashion for using mutes in fast sections (a Bartók original) is followed in the

Scherzo. The final movement is bisectional; the first part is vigorous and once again chromatic; the last part, a rhythmically tripleted coda, relaxes the work into a tonality presaged by the cello's first rhythmic and later sustained pedal point on C.

QUINTETS

- *Hagiographa (Holy Writings): Three Biblical Narratives* **for Piano and Strings (Two Violins, Viola, and Cello) (1938)**

Jacobi's piano quintet is one of the best of his Hebraic creations. (The title is an equivalent of the Hebrew word *Hagada* and, in full, means "Holy Writings from the Bible.") Jacobi's other compositions in the Hebraic category are a Concerto for Cello and Orchestra (based on the Ninetieth, Ninety-first, and Ninety-second psalms), *Six Pieces for the Organ for Use in the Synagogue*, and a *Sabbath Evening Service*.

Jacobi's sacred chamber music subject is set in patterns that follow the classical and romantic three-movement plan of balanced (fast-slow-fastest) tempos. The first part is entitled "Job" and includes two principal subjects, both excellently contrasted and of more than usual length. The first of these is vigorous, constantly rising in pitch placement (illustrating the sorrows "piled high upon the head of the patient Job"). Job's resignation to what he must bear is brought out by the second theme. This is lyrical in concept and its tones move in a falling fashion. The themes are then developed, in order to show the advent of Job's friends and "his stormy argument with God and their final conciliation."

"Ruth," the second movement, is also built on a pair of themes. The first subject is stated initially by the use of bare octaves, then succeeded by a harmonization framed in simple organumlike pedal point. The other subject is larger in scope, thicker in weight, and more melodic than the first by tertial, parallel movement. These themes depict Ruth's idyllic nature. Tempo design is compounded with the three-part form. The music increases its speed and then returns to its andante base. The middle section of the movement found its inspiration from the biblical lines—"Entreat me not to leave thee, or to return from following after thee; for whither thou goest I will go; and where thou lodgest I shall lodge; thy people shall be my people, and thy God my God."

Movement three ("Joshua") begins with a decisively articulated rhythmic theme, supported by vigorous chords. The music is given full power, its drive and motion hardly slacken as the composer pictures the siege and battle of Jericho. It was a rare achievement on Jacobi's part to write so vividly with only five instruments. With an imitative blare of trumpets the music progresses to a presto—one not to be played overly fast, however. This final section is entirely concerned with a theme suggestive of a ritualistic dance of gratitude.

- **Scherzo for Flute, Oboe, Clarinet, Horn, and Bassoon (1936)**

The main characteristic of the scherzo is its large three-part form, two firmly rhythmical sections enclosing a more relaxed section (the Trio); there is the usual triple meter, vigorous punctuation, and a sly, pert drollery. The scherzo plan cuts more deeply than fast movements which have surface momentum. Jacobi's Scherzo follows this plan, especially being guaranteed more incisive tone through the power of woodwind-instrument articulation. He adds the contemporary means, however, of not squarely designing his phrases to exact proportions, so that equality of thesis and antithesis does not always occur—surprise number one. The second surprise (one that intensifies interest) is not only that of syncopation but of squeezing four pulses within the time span of the triple meter used to articulate this five-minute work.

Jacobi, Wolfgang (1894–1972)

DUO

- **Sonata for Viola and Piano**

Effective and functional Hindemithian music. The three movements are organized with discrimination. In the first and second of these there are two principal, antithetical ideas. In the former, toccata triplet passages are compared to a tranquil subject supported by quartal harmonies. In the latter, a fugato is contrasted with baroquelike double-dotted rhythmic figures.

Movement two is completed by a prestissimo, impetuoso twenty-four-measure passage for the piano, all in octaves. This segment roars into the finale, which is a big fugue.

Jacobsohn, Gabriel (1923–48)

TRIO

- **Adagio and Allegro for Oboe, Clarinet, and Horn**

Jacobsohn (Ben-Yaacov) was born in Berlin and died in his adopted country during the battle for the Old City of Jerusalem. Among the unpublished works he left was this very short Adagio and Allegro (twenty-eight and eighty-six measures, respectively), but in reverse order in the manuscript. In addition, there was a short movement of minuet character. The committee formed to edit and arrange the publication of Jacobsohn's music chose to shift the order of the two movements and omit the minuet, believing (because of its compactness) it was planned simply as an introduction to a projected finale.

Jacobsohn shows a good sense of tonal style in this pithy example. His form is clear, and his handling of dynamic qualities excellent. The Adagio is mainly subdued, rising to a *mezzoforte* level but once. Aside from the obvious matter of tempo relationship, this example of subtle dynamic reticence proves the decision to place the slow movement before the rondo-style Allegro to have been a sensible one.

Jacobson, Maurice (1896–1976)

TRIO

- **Suite of Four Pieces for Flute (or Violin), Cello, and Piano**

One can expect that music by a music publisher–composer will not break any lances for creative freedom or, for that matter, cast jealous glances at superadvanced techniques. Jacobson's music is trustworthy, tonal music, with sufficient interest for average auditors. (For the record, Jacobson rose in rank through the important publishing house of Curwen and became the firm's president. His trio, however, was published elsewhere—by Augener.)

No disturbing registrations or time-marking padding are found in the musical plots. Rhythmic detail is favored as are minor keys: C and G minor in the first and second pieces, A major in the last. The third of the set is an Adagio espressivo that begins in E minor and concludes in D-flat major.

Jacoby, Hanoch (1909–)

DUOS

- *King David's Lyre* **for Violin (or Viola) and Piano (1948)**

King David's Lyre is based on a Talmudic legend. (Jacoby indicates that the tale may be narrated before the music is performed.) Placed close to an open window, King David's lyre would sound by the play of the breezes on it, inspiring the king to compose psalms and other melodies: a shepherd's tune, a mourning song, and a dance of joy.

Jacoby's setting of this story is cast in theme and variation form and begins with an imitation of the aeolian harp. The first of the variations simulates the shepherd's tune. Its mood and style become changed to majestic contours in the second variation. Variation three is in slow tempo, and Hebrew words accompany the melodic line. (The composer makes no mention that they should be sung. One assumes they could. In any event they give programmatic underlining to the duo by relating the meaning of the melody.) Psalm 137 is the source of the text: "By the rivers of Babylon, there we sat down, yea, we wept, when we remembered Zion." A lullaby is represented in the fourth variation, the muted violin depicting a mother praying for the coming of the Jewish Messiah. Real Chassidic ecstasy holds forth in part five, in vivid contrast to the fugato that follows. The last draws its inspiration from the biblical prophecy that the House of Jacob will return to its native home. A Tempo di hora and thematic restatement conclude the piece. The words on which the final portion is based are drawn from Genesis 28:15: "And, behold, I am with thee, and will keep thee in all places whither thou goest, and will bring thee again into this land."

Oddly, the entire set of variations and finale is placed in an unyielding D-minor tonality. Nonetheless, the piece is emotionally powered, very colorful and dramatic. Coincidentally, Jacoby completed *King David's Lyre* on May 14, 1948, the date marking the official beginning of the state of Israel.

- *Persian Wedding Nigun* for Two Cellos (1971)

The ancient nigun was a wordless hymn, spontaneously conceived and rendered as a prayer in the synagogue by the rabbi. Its expected simple nature and just as expected repetitiveness are represented in this short piece. In a couple of places a slight modulatory gesture is made and quickly abandoned, and the music returns to its primitive D-minor state.

QUINTET

- **Quintet for Flute, Oboe, Clarinet, Horn, and Bassoon (1946)**

Music with neoclassic demeanor. In movement one a rhythmic unit taken from the initial statement is the core on which the development section pivots. Contrapuntal absence is purposeful, delayed to make its use in the following Adagio more vivid. The principal method there is the use of chordal pinpoints succeeded by canonic detail. This arrangement is both novel and expressive. Three-part strict regularity pertains, the sections filled by two separate canons, with a literal recapitulation, plus a coda of nonimitative facture. Within the movement's central portion linear monotony is avoided by the simultaneous use of the subject and its augmentation. Such polyphonic interweavement provides a dramatic lift.

Thematic variations conclude the Quintet. The placid and bittersweet quality of the theme flows within the first and second parts, with greater motion in the latter. In the next pair, eighth-note and triplet movement are contrasted. Variation five employs thematic segmentation. A faster tempo stimulates both the sixth variation and coda.

Jacoby's permutations are not too involved. Basically, they follow the principle of thematic embroidery, plus figurations that overlay and form the inlay as well. While this method does hold the material together, it can only be termed neutral variation style.

Jadassohn, Salomon (1831–1902)

QUARTET

- **Piano Quartet in C Minor, Op. 77**

A representation of the conventional sense that embraced this German composer-teacher-writer's music. The Op. 77 quartet for piano, violin, viola, and cello is one of Jadassohn's best works. Perhaps not profound, and certainly not of individual cast, but deserving of a hearing now and then.

The first movement has a short, declarative introduction and proceeds in a sonata conception, set in allegro agitato tempo. The triplet figure that is important within the second theme is given the most attention in the development. A Scherzo, also in the home tonality of C minor, follows; the Trio in A-flat major is kept in the same tempo but has slightly less action. In the remaining pair of movements the tonalities move into different areas—the Adagio is in E-flat and the Finale is in C major. All positive and tight tonality relationships, these. Ornamental harmony contrasts with the vertical writing of the slow movement, a fugato colors the concluding movement.

Jaffe, Gerard (1925–)

DUO

- *Variations on a Flippant Theme* for Flute and Piano

Jaffe's theme is animated, its flippancy derived from the use of 5/8 meter, which provides uneven beat distribution. (There is additional flippancy found in the score's prefatory note concerned with the composition's first performance. In that place the title of the piece is followed parenthetically by "In the Form of Two Matched Pears and a Tale." No explana-

tion, however, so flippancy is met with annoyance.)

There are four variations. A flowing consideration, then a rhythmically figurated depiction (neither in the basic quintuple pulse), followed by a variation devoted to canon and to the 5/8 measurement. The final variant is longer than the total of the three preceding variations. The rhythmic effect within its measures, which untethers eight pulses into units of 3–3–2, is striking. It also is a sharp reminder of (and relationship to) the flippant theme with its unit arrangement of 2–1–2.

TRIO

- **Variations for Alto Recorder (or Flute), B-flat Clarinet, and Piano**

Jaffe's transformations cling closely to the principal intervallic direction of his theme. The quartal descents there will be heard in part three (a moderately fast, incisive section), in the slow, sustained fourth variation, and in the succeeding three parts: in turn; bouncy, tender, and fast paced. In the second variation the intervallic span is expanded to a sixth or exactly inverted to a third.

Instrumental color is not emphasized in this trio combination. For clarity's sake (that is, to emphasize the variational decision) the timbres are in full balance.

Jakončič, Joško (1903–54)

DUO

- *Drei musikalische Gedanken (Three Musical Thoughts)* for Violin and Piano (1923)

Although the first of the three pieces is in E-flat major, all the "thoughts" are on the darker side of the spectrum. (The last item is titled "Melancholy.") Three other points of unanimity: All three pieces are in slow tempo, set in tripartite form, and are written in a chromatic-romantic syntax.

James, Philip (1890–1975)

QUINTET

- **Suite for Woodwind Quintet (Flute [alternating Piccolo], Oboe, Clarinet, Horn, and Bassoon) (1936)**

James was very partial to the Bachian era for the designs he used in this four-movement piece. He was an expert orchestrator, and his scoring for the work exploits beautifully the colors of the four woodwind and single brass instruments that constitute the "woodwind quintet."

It will be realized that James's music is a crossbreeding of the contemporary with the late romantic. The music is within, and encircles around, tonal polarities. Thus, it has its roots and freedom at the same time. This neoromanticism is evinced in the opening Praeludium, a short section germinated by the impulse of sets of sixteenth notes. Then follow a Gavot and Drone (the spelling of the first is purposeful, describing the dance and, at the same time, the name of the inhabitants from whom the dance is said to have been derived). But this is not a dance of a 17th-century ballroom. The Gavot's mood and rhythm are edged with the margins of the present century, the rhythms shift, including measures of 1 1/2 beats. The Musette is used quite often to furnish contrast to a Gavotte; in this instance, its parallel is called-on. The Drone is both single-pitched and chordal; it shifts between instruments, it has rhythmic movement, occasionally it stops. It is also musically photographed with present-day lenses.

An "Introspection" leads to the final and largest movement, Variations and Fugue ("On a Theme of Haydn"). The piccolo is called on in this movement, which uses the second part of Haydn's theme for the second movement of his Symphony No. 103 in E-flat Major *(Drum Roll)*. The four variations are somewhat free, ending with a short fugue colored by linear embroideries.

Janáček, Leoš (1854–1928)

DUOS

- ***Dumka* for Violin and Piano (1880)**

Dvořák is to be credited with introducing the dumka form into concert music, and it is Dvořákian character that marks this early Janáček piece. The dumka is an eastern Slavonic folk ballad that is alternately elegiac and gay. Janáček's piece begins con moto, moves into contrastive adagio, and then returns to the initial mood.

(The date assigned this work [1889] by the publisher, Artia, is incorrect.)

- ***Pohadka (Fairy Tale)* for Cello and Piano (1910)**

The basis of the three movements (two moderately paced and one fast) is a Russian fairy tale by A. V. Zhukovsky titled *Czar Berendjei*. This tells of the sadness of the czar, who had no children. However, in the course of a protracted absence a son is born to him, whom he pledges "to the Immortal Skeleton."

In any case, the materials are so disposed as to reflect a negation of programmaticism. Movements one and two are in rondo form, the final movement has sonata shape. All three movements are in G-flat major, with the concluding section of the first movement set in F-sharp minor. And, the basic tempo throughout is in the fast zone: con moto for the first two movements, allegro for the third movement.

▪ *Romance* for Violin and Piano (1879)

Composed during Janáček's study in Leipzig. The plan was to produce a cycle of seven pieces for violin and piano, with four of the group to be presented as "Czech Romances." Only this, the fourth of that projected set survived and was published (without number) in 1938 by Hudební Matice. It represents a young Janáček writing in romantic script.

▪ Sonata for Violin and Piano (1913)

The dating must be explained. The Sonata was written in 1913, revised during World War I, mingled at its start with the fears, as Janáček recalled, "when we were expecting the Russians to enter Moravia," and then finally completed in 1921. (According to some scholars, this is actually Janáček's third violin and piano sonata. It is so described in a number of catalogs. However, there has never been a trace of the manuscripts to substantiate the existence of two earlier sonatas.)

Janáček's primitive (but extraordinarily knowledgeable) style will be noted in the intense data of the piece. The opening movement, with abrupt changes from a single fast theme to a completely opposed tempo, conveys the musical translation of the subtleties of Moravian language. The Ballada that follows alternates two subjects, in unadorned style, with the final statement in ad libitum manner. There is no sense of *two* instruments; the combination is *one*. In movement three there is a special fascination in terms of rhythm. It is charged with elongation, contraction, and attendant irregularity. This is characteristic Janáček. The same thematics of language are used in the final movement, where a menacing motive is repeated constantly (always in sets of three), against a long-arched melodic line.

QUARTETS

String Quartets

There is confusion about the numbering of Janáček's quartets. He produced his first string quartet in 1880, during his term of study in Vienna. Unfortunately, the manuscript of this work has never been found. Accordingly, when the second quartet, finished in 1923, was published in 1925, it was designated as number one, and when the third and final quartet, completed in 1928, was published in 1938, it was designated as number two.

In order not to add to the confusion the numbering of the quartets discussed below follows the publication's numerical designations.

▪ String Quartet [No. 1] *(Inspired by Tolstoy's "Kreutzer Sonata")* (1923)

Janáček indicated the motivation for his quartet in a letter to Kamila Stössel, dated October 14, 1924. He wrote: "I had in mind an unhappy, tortured, beaten woman, beaten to death as Tolstoy described her in his 'Kreutzer Sonata.'" In no sense is there a scene-by-scene portrayal of Tolstoy's novel. What Janáček depicts are the furtiveness, cruelty, and passion of the tale. No line-by-line scenario is needed. The listener shares in a chamber music drama conveyed by the power of perfectly integrated music.

Each part of the work is terse, but alive with shifts of mood, pace, and intensity. There is the denominator of two relationships in each of the sections. The initial one has a melodramatic, motival Adagio and a folklike theme that is set over a weird drone. The two developments that follow are formed each from two additional themes. Scale lines and a subject developed from the folk idea are in the second movement, a declamatory point and a vigorous antiphonal suggestion are stated in the third, and the last is based once again on the opening Adagio motive. Sonata, song, rondo, and other standard designs are foreign to this magnificent, highly individual piece of music.

- **String Quartet [No. 2]** *(Intimate Letters)* **(1928)**

The quartet bears the subtitle *Listy důvěrné (Intimate Letters)* as the score has it, though on recordings this has been translated as *Secret Pages* and *Intimate Pages*. The work is a sort of Moravian *Aus meinem Leben* (Smetana's autobiographical string quartet), written as a declaration of love for the woman to whom Janáček turned in the latter part of his life: Kamila Stösslová (or Stössel), thirty-eight years his junior. He described his feelings in a letter to her: ". . . for eleven years you have been mine without your knowing it, all-embracing protectress. You have been everywhere in my compositions, wherever there are deep feelings, sincerity, truth, passion and love." (Originally the title of the quartet was *Love Letters*, but that manuscript score title was changed by Janáček since he did not want "to present his feelings for the discretion of stupid people.")

Thus movement one describes Janáček's impression of their initial meeting; the second concerns summer events at a spa at which they stayed; the merry third part includes a musical image of the woman; and the finale tells of Janáček's longing for her and its fulfillment. (Originally Janáček scored his work for a viola d'amore in place of the viola. The choice of this fourteen-string instrument, with its passionate timbre, underlines further the composer's feelings.)

The entire quartet is pervaded with transient thoughts and fleeting ideas, bound by determined pronouncements, articulations, and punctuations. Technically speaking, these are obtained by changing meters, dislodged accents, and other refractional permutations. (Janáček's music is as if seen in mirrors reflecting various shapes.) The dominating repetitive patterns are sometimes overemphasized, but such is the Janáček method. And throughout there is intertwined a *Tristanesque* emotionalism, but minus Wagnerian overtones.

SEXTET

- *Mládí (Youth)*: **Suite for Flute (alternating Piccolo), Oboe, Clarinet, Horn, Bassoon, and Bass Clarinet (1924)**

Youthful reminiscences set for a chamber music sextet. Ease and gaiety are the prime points, although one writer has indicated that the second part is a remembrance of less happy moments spent "under the restraint of strict regulations" when, between the ages of eleven and fifteen, Janáček was a choirboy at the Old Brno Cloister.

Movement three is based on a march Janáček had written for piccolo, glockenspiel, and tambourine or piano, which he had termed *March of the Blue Boys*, due to the blue uniforms the choirboys wore.

The only bow to musical form (in the classic sense) is the increasing speed of the four movements—but only in general terms, since the tempos constantly change within each section. Janáček's ideas of wind scoring are as far from the traditional as possible, including the rare chamber music use of the flabby-toned bass clarinet.

The 4/4 beat of the second movement, interrupted eight times and stretched an extra sixteenth, is a delightful rhythmic anachronism. And the catchy march, already mentioned, is a pert parody.

Janáček

SEPTET

- **Concertino for Piano, Two Violins, Viola, Clarinet in E-flat (alternating Clarinet in B-flat), Horn, and Bassoon (1925)**

Janáček originally planned this work to be a suite entitled *Spring*. It was written soon after *Mládí (see above)* and, as noted in the score's prefatory note, is "a sort of sequel in contents." However, while *Mládí* is reminiscent of Janáček's youthful ease and joyfulness, the Concertino reflects the composer's years of creative struggle, rejection, and fight for recognition. Understandably, the title *Spring* was not a proper reflection of the inner contents of the four-movement work.

A hybrid plan of concerto (prominence of the piano), chamber music (seven instrumentalists), and symphonic elements (despite the first movement calling only for horn and piano and the second movement only for the E-flat clarinet and piano) makes this work unique. The sound is expressly and expressively nationalistic with a tough accent—not by way of tunes and dances, but by naturalism in the lines, which are never cut to fit squared phrase lengths or smoothed to ordinary balances. A maximum sonority is obtained by minimal means. The frictions are mild but powerful. Janáček's Concertino is an example of Moravian musical philology set within an extraordinary concerto design.

Since Janáček's music gains if it is presented for the realistic substance it is rather than for the smooth-grained romanticism that it is not, a performance that is almost unrounded and slightly spiky is truer than one of graduate-school polish. Playing this music demands clear-cut roughage.

Janeček

OCTET

- **Capriccio for Piano (Left Hand) and Wind Instruments (Flute [alternating Piccolo], Two Trumpets, Three Trombones, and Tenor Tuba) (1926)**

Unusual instrumentation to begin with, and more so in the use of only the left hand for the pianist. The latter was to fulfill a request from the virtuoso Otaker Hollmann, who returned from the battlefields of World War I with his right arm completely paralyzed.

Originally the work was titled *Defiance*, with the explanation that the music defiantly mocked all conventions that were contrary to Janáček's affection for a married woman. The published score makes no mention of this but states that, according to letters and "authentic statements," Janáček's work "expresses a revolt against (the) cruel destiny."

The full scale of the four movements approaches concerto style but falls just short of it. Janáček's extremely odd coloration (a flute and alternating piccolo are the only woodwind representatives; the other instruments are all brass: a pair of high trumpets [in F], three trombones, and a tenor tuba) and his avoidance of virtuosity turn the Capriccio into a six-timbred sonata for concerted instruments. Thereby, it fully straddles the fields of chamber and solo-accompaniment music.

Janeček, Karel (1903–74)

DUOS

- **Sonata for Violin and Piano, Op. 21**

Laced with panchromatic harmonies, gingered with cross-accidentalized pitches, Janeček's one-movement piece tells an untold tale. Like the music of Leoš Janáček, whose name resembles his, Karel Janeček's is a criss-cross of moods, situations, and quick change.

In the eighteen minutes that cover this duo there are thirteen abrupt changes of tempo. All of these are approached and quitted with ingressive and aggressive immediacy. It is this tempo circumstance that seems to mark off points in a musical drama for two instruments.

The opening is majestically slow, arching up to a ninth, later appearance changes this span to an eleventh. Next, a short, three-measure Allegro, with grotesque data, then, two measures of the initial Adagio reappear, and the fast tempo returns, contrapuntally served, peppered with canonic condiments. Now lengthened, the Adagio is reintroduced and then succeeded by a Scherzando with a repeated regard for polyphonic partiality, imitations between the voices, plus canonic control. The complete cast of characters has then been made known and the music moves dynamically *forte* and *fortissimo* into and away from them onto a final perorative Andante in an optimistic D tonality.

■ **Sonata in G for Cello and Piano, Op. 33**

Prosaicness was not for this composer. His three-movement cello-piano sonata is coloristically and formally fascinating. Yet no new ground is traveled save that Janeček viewed familiar terrain with fresh vision.

This is evident in the first measure, with the main theme of the movement stated in cello pizzicato, supported by an octave toccata-type figure in the piano. The repeat of the theme is in triadic chunks for the piano, and the cello has the previous figuration of the piano. The form itself is A–B–A–B.

Movement two is a dynamically understated, muted cello Lento, titled "Nenia" ("Epitaph"). The finale is a set of eleven Variations, each compact and descriptive. The first is a Ricercar, the second is a Fugato, the third is a Scherzo, and the fourth an Aria. In the fifth variant the eight measures describe a "Ninna nanna" ("Lullaby"). In turn there are "Quinte"

("Fifths"), "Crome" ("Eighth Notes"), and "Semicrome" ("Sixteenth Notes"), respectively seven, six, and six measures in length. Each of these describe the piano's part. Variation nine is a Capriccio, variation ten is "Syncopated," and the concluding variant is marked Finale.

Janssen, Werner (1899–1990)

QUARTET

■ *American Kaleidoscope* for String
Quartet (1932)

At one time, Janssen was deeply involved with composition; in latter years, the field of conducting (wherein he had been very successful and had pursued an undeviating course of programming unusual works of all periods) had made the creative part of his activity take a very minor place. His music is of American spirit. It is most usually descriptive, the orchestral piece *New Year's Eve in New York*, for example. It partakes also of the spirituals of the blacks and jocular jazz rhythms.

Janssen does not tell what his *Kaleidoscope* represents. He merely conveys many moods, including song-swept blues, fox trots, sensuous southern inflections; cut-and-dried, down-on-the-ground ragtime, jazz, musical bunny-rolls, Charlestons, and other forms of popular music in one connected movement. The instruments are handled without kid gloves; all the stops are out. Pizzicato, mutes, glissandos, hitting the belly of the instrument with the bow, or with the hand, excessive vibrato—all these are used, and more, including the *outré* musical effect of making nonsensical sounds ("tchick") with the mouth. The first time for such frippery in chamber music and requiring no dictional aptitude!

Jaques-Dalcroze, Émile
(1865–1950)

Jaques-Dalcroze was the founder of the method known as eurythmics. This musical pedagogy was, in the words of its founder, "to create by the help of rhythm a rapid and regular current of communication between brain and body; and to make feeling for rhythm a physical experience." Rhythm, thereby, becomes an ordained part of musical projection. Responsiveness is more acute, decided, and flexible, rather than only estimated mentally. Further, the use of gestures in accord with rhythms and music makes a new plastic art. As a result, Dalcroze eurythmics are now studied in practically every country in the world (though, as usual, when first introduced there was little response).

As a composer, Jaques-Dalcroze naturally would be overly preoccupied with rhythmic aspects and their intricacies in his creations. But his rhythmic facets are complex only in vertical array and sequence, not in their inner-horizontal dispositions. Thus, the rhythm is like a seismograph of sensitivity; the more graphic its portrayal by the performers, the less neo-academic the results of this intense rhythmic concentration.

TRIOS

■ **Twelve Novelettes and Caprices for Piano, Violin, and Cello (1920)**

Jaques-Dalcroze's twelve trio pieces, divided into three equal sets (a second version, the pieces were originally for piano), were published in 1920 by Augener. (A second copyright was issued in 1924.) Strangely enough, therefore, when four of the dozen pieces were recorded more than a decade after his death and issued by the *Communauté de travail pour la diffusion de la musique Suisse*, the main title was reversed to read: *Caprices et Novelettes*,

and the numerical adjective was eliminated. There is no valid reason for this, and Jaques-Dalcroze's complete published title should be retained.

Further, no identifications of the three sets (again following the format of the published editions) are indicated for the four pieces recorded: Nos. 1, 5, 8, and 11. Naturally, the first of these is in Set I; Nos. 5 and 8 are the first and last items in Set II, and No. 11 is the penultimate piece in Set III.

■ **Set I: Nos. 1–4 (1920)**

There are constant changes of meter in the music of this composer, but the beauty of this technical procedure is that it is never forced, but always provides a natural continuity. In the first of the set these pulse shifts move between 2/4 and 3/4. The cohesive item in the material is a flippant rhythmic figure.

Number two of the set is kin to a moderate-moving waltz, its flow interrupted by shorter-pulse measures. Ternary form marks the third piece, a lyrical example. Mindful of contrast, the fourth piece illustrates music of a gutsy, dynamic demeanor, the motility a reminder of perpetual-motion sound affairs. Most of the beginning of this piece is in 12/8 and 10/8, the middle portion is principally in 6/8 and 9/8, with a return to the 12/8 furnishing a recapitulative balance.

■ **Set II: Nos. 5–8 (1920)**

Alternate speeds yield a fine compounded balance of the four pieces. The first one is an Andante (to be performed lightly and with simplicity). The second is an Allègrement, a bright and gay affair. In its first part every one of the sixteen measures is bound by a different meter. The central portion is more settled; the recapitulation is almost as metrically variable as the initial part of the piece.

The third of the set is slow again (Tranquillo

e soave). The final piece is an Allegretto marziale, with syncopative twists and a strident middle division.

■ **Set III: Nos. 9–12 (1920)**

Any discussion of this composer's music emphasizes his preoccupation with elastic and fluid rhythms and metrical ordering. One critic, Cynthia Cox, has stated that, in this work "this tendency is carried almost to excess." And in the syncopative framework of the first piece, this finding might be substantiated, since in the thirty-eight total measures, after an upbeat, there are twenty-one different meters, including such as 20/16 and 24/16. However, the composer's metrical sympathy and rhythmic concern do not interfere with the attractiveness of the music and its engaging flow.

The second and fourth pieces of the set have a determined impact, regardless of the constant metrical change. The tempos are indicative: *Deciso e robusto* for the former and *Violent* for the latter. Between this pair there is a legato-depicted musical exhibit, defined mostly in quintuple meter. The central part of this third piece of the set is texturally thick, thereby clarifying the divisional sections of a tripartite-formed music.

QUARTETS

■ *Rythmes de danse: Trois suites de pièces brèves (Dance Rhythms: Three Suites of Short Pieces)* **for String Quartet (1922)**

Jaques-Dalcroze tended to make varied versions of a work. This set of three suites is his own independent version selected from a piano composition of the same title, and, as such, cannot be considered as a mere transcription.

Each Suite consists of six pieces drawn in a new order from the piano version; thus, for example, No. 1 of the quartet set is No. 10 in the

piano version; No. 8 is the third of the keyboard group; while No. 13 is listed as No. 23 in the piano set. Only Nos. 15 and 16 of these eighteen pieces for string quartet have the same numbers in the first version. It is also of interest that nine of the quartet pieces were changed into still other arrangements for violin and piano.

■ **Suite I (1922)**

The first piece is sprightly; its design mainly concerned with emphasis by sound or silence on the third of each triple set of eighth notes—this, regardless of whether the measure is set in 3/8 or 6/8. The following piece is lyrical, in slow tempo; the pulsative background either syncopative or block chordal. The tempo of the third piece contains the indication *con finezza* (a subtle yet completely declarative estimate of the composer's lifework, whether as a teacher or as a composer); the music, free in form, is of waltz variety.

Rhythms that break down the bar lines by moving over and across them mark the next piece. The forms are (in most of the pieces in all three suites) in free distribution of an A–B–A plan; the fifth piece defines this very clearly with a songlike quintuple meter; as does the last, which is marchlike.

■ **Suite II (1922)**

A fast waltz swing permeates the opening; an additional beat in several measures causes rhythmic hesitation and is a delicate artifice. There is a certain dryness to the unceasing undulation used in the second piece. In the third part, waltz meter appears again; this time of slower pulse. Similarly pulsed connotations are used in the fifth piece, with contrast added by unitary- and duple-rhythmed measures.

It is in the catching of the rhythmic subtleties that these pieces (and those of the other two suites) have the highest interest for the listener;

musically, the pedanticism shows through, arising from the composer's engrossment with rhythmic plotting. The fourth piece is designed from one theme reworked six times, plus one subsidiary section. The rhythmic changes are nervous. In eighty-five measures, there are forty-four meter changes, using a total of nine different metrical settings (2/4, 3/4, 4/8, 5/8, 7/8, 8/8, 6/16, 9/16, and 12/16). A Scherzo serves as the finale (sixth of the Suite, twelfth of the total series of eighteen).

▪ Suite III (1922)

Kineticism in presto tempo opens this Suite, followed by a languid serenade type of music, with propitious muting of the full quartet and contrasted by very agile rhythmic snap. In the third piece, there is a semblance to tarantella rhythm, with a falling off of the rhythmic impulse at each cadential point. The fourth part is of gentle scherzo quality—constantly in eighth-note units, but shifting from duple to triple, quadruple to sextuple. But the flow is not hindered by the asymmetricality, rather the interest is heightened.

Three-part form is used for the last two pieces; one a simple Allegretto semplice of song character, the other an Allegro risoluto fully concerned with exceedingly sharp rhythmic distinctions.

▪ Seven Dances: Set I for String Quartet

Romantic harmony details are found in the two sets of dances that were published in 1927 (by Joseph Williams). (Set II is discussed *below*.) No lushness, however—Jaques-Dalcroze made his meanings known straightforwardly, the basic materials being colored by a sensitive use of rhythmic flux.

A flowing piece (marked *un poco misterioso*) begins the set. This mysterious quality is noted also in connection with the second dance, moving in Moderato tempo. The final music in the first set is a light scherzo essay, metrically set in quintuple pulse, with only a few triple-pulse measures to give some contrast.

▪ Seven Dances: Set II for String Quartet

As expected, the same style is followed in this set as in the first one *(see above)*. There is rather a settled rhythmic confirmation in these dances, compared to most of Jaques-Dalcroze's music. The Scherzando has a few shifts to 2/4 measures, otherwise it moves gracefully in the usual triple-beat form. There is no metrical change whatsoever in the slow waltz of the second dance. The binary format of the third dance (marked Lento funebre) has a 12/8 meter in the first part, with 9/8 plus 12/8 in the second part. The finale has respectable lighthearted sense, mixing its pulse arrangements, which adds sparkle.

Járdányi, Pál (1920–66)

DUOS

▪ Sonatina for Cello and Piano (1965)

As is basic to this composer's work, folk-song positivism is the element in control. In movement two (the finale), secundal tightness in the cello line, by way of double stops, grace-note attachments, and conjunct motion, is set against the open intervals of thirds, fourths, and fifths in the piano for effective contrast. Lyric cohesion marks the first movement.

▪ Sonatina for Flute and Piano (1952)

White-note music. Járdányi keeps the textures open, so the combination sounds free and the flute swings clear of any heavy-handed keyboard partnership. Tonalities are just as clearly defined. Movement one begins in D minor and concludes in D major; movement two starts in

B minor, shifts to the dominant, and finishes in F-sharp major. Though the finale has the key signature of G major, the music is firmly in the D orbit. Neat, simple, and convincing music.

▪ Violin Duos (1937)

Bartók's set of forty-four duos for violins, composed in 1931, has left an undiluted influence on Hungarian composers to this very day. Early on, Járdányi, at the age of 17, one year before he began studying composition with Kodály, produced a set of eleven that is a clone of Bartók's creation. Worthy in all respects.

A considerable part of the duos is straight out of folk-music land. Good amounts of bare fifths and modality are sprinkled throughout the textures. The first half of the second duo is polyrhythmic, with the first violin set in 3+3+2/8 and the second violin set in 2+3+3/8. Full-scoped quintuple meter drives the Allegro pace of the sixth duo. The final duo is a short theme with as short a set of three variations.

TRIO

▪ Variations for Two Violins and Cello

Not much attention is given this instrumental combination by composers, so the Hungarian's contribution is welcome. Doubly so, because of its neat, compact, and beautifully shaped presentation.

The variants are continuous, beginning with the theme in the violin and then transferred in a fair duplication to the cello to serve as the first permutation. In turn, there are a faster-paced, all-pizzicato variation, a richly chorded Largo, and a final scherzo-tinged division. By this time the tonality has traveled from the initial A minor to A major.

QUARTETS

▪ String Quartet No. 1 (1947)

Járdányi's nationalistic temper is tenacious in the first of his two string quartets. Formality there is, of course, but it bends and twists in the surge of Hungarian rhapsodicism that permeates each of the three movements. This pertains not only to theme and development but to tempos and their flexibility in terms of ritards, accelerandos, and rubatos. These variances total a pertinent color within the sounds themselves. Even in its quieter moments, there is no draw-off in intensity in this quartet.

▪ String Quartet No. 2 (1954)

The dedication reads: "In memoriam Béla Bartók," and the music sounds with full remembrances of the great Hungarian. There is considerable attention to lyricism in the first movement, though a bit of ostinato-layered rhythmic support is used as well. Movement two presents a B-minor theme that has four variations. The second of these is firmed up by trills supporting the ornamental permutation, the third variant is a march type bearing the Bartókian portamento trademark. In the finale the quality is outgoing. Toward the end the theme of movement two is recalled in augmented form.

QUINTET

▪ *Fantasia and Variations on a Hungarian Folk Song* for Flute, Oboe, Clarinet, Horn, and Bassoon (1955)

The separate proportions of fantasy and variational structuring merge in Járdányi's wind quintet. Formalism gives way to a bundling of material within various set tempos and then to a firing up of the sounds via melismatic rhapsodizing or sharp rhythmic contacts. Either way, the spirit of Hungarian nationalism is not dimmed in this music.

Jarecki, Tadeusz (1888–1955)

TRIO

- Trio: Fugato e Aria for Piano, Violin, and Cello (or Viola), Op. 11

Formal communication is simply obtained in this Trio of 71/2 minutes' length. The Fugato returns after the Aria, the recall defining a ternary structure. Polyphony followed by strongly chromaticized homophony and an agitated allegro followed by a sustained lento provide classification and tempo contrast. Compellingly clear music in all respects.

QUARTET

- Quartet for Strings (Two Violins, Viola, and Cello), Op. 16

This is a prize-winning work (the Berkshire Competition of 1918, sponsored by Elizabeth Sprague Coolidge). The jinx that unaccountably foredooms most musical compositions that have won competitions has clung to this one. It has been hardly performed, and for no valid reason. It is fine, impressionistically stained and sustained music, fully and absolutely deserving of rediscovery.

The second movement is muted and tranquil. It sings of the countryside and is permeated with the quality of, as the composer states, *un rêve* (a dream). The Presto interchanges a waltzlike theme with stress on second and third beats, while the other voices work in opposition (the concretely designed polyrhythm of the last movement is almost an extension of this principle) with a duple-pulse singsong that moves modally through triads. In the last movement, the combining of quintuple meters, one

marked by quarter-note units, the other by eighths, gives a rhythmic counterpoint of sharply etched opposition. A canon forms a further layer on this polyphony. To bind the work, the opening measures are used as the closing ones.

Jarnach, Philipp (1892–1982)

DUO

- Sonatine for Flute and Piano, Op. 12

Full romantic expansion of harmony. All expansiveness of material is formally controlled but permitted to roam expressively. This leads to a section marked Rezitativ, with the piano, in turn, linked to another "recitative" for the flute alone, which is more dynamized, in the manner of a cadenza.

(Jarnach's piece has also been issued as a Romanza for violin and piano.)

Jaroch, Jiří (1920–)

NONETS

- *Children's Suite*: Nonet for Violin, Viola, Cello, Bass, Flute, Oboe, Clarinet, Bassoon, and Horn (1952)

The world of the child set for listening in the world of the adult (of course, just as propitious for being heard by the young).

Jaroch's style does not reach back to the dim past. He carefully prepares his tonal sounds with a slight touch of contemporary flavor and colors the total with exhilarating rhythms. The three subjects are positively clear in their presentation: "Taneček" ("Little Dance"), "Ukolébavka" ("Lullaby"), and "Hra na honěnou" ("Blindman's Buff"). Totally enchanting.

■ **Nonet No. 2 for Flute, Oboe, Clarinet, Bassoon, Horn, Violin, Viola, Cello, and Double Bass (1965)**

The language is romantic, the formal conditions, especially in the outer movements, no hand-me-down. The first movement has a crawling half-step subject that is given free variational development. But what tunes up this conception is that as the music progresses the textures get heavier, activating the rhythmic corpuscles. Then the procedure is set in reverse. The final movement has a pair of ideas, one a chordal block, the other a rhythmically shifting single-pitch unit. These set off the areas in the movement. (Jaroch balances these in the overall concept with the chordal item opening the movement and the repetitive item closing it.)

The middle movement represents active, duo-pulse, neat, and well-turned fast music. It concludes in a *pianississimo* level, as do the other two movements.

Jaubert, Maurice (1900–40)

TRIO

■ **Sarabande for Violin, Viola, and Cello**

The slow, dignified expression of the 17th-, 18th-century dance is used for a moving piece that begins fugally, rises to a huge climax, and then extinguishes into a quiescent minor tonality. It is as if Jaubert anticipated his death, which followed on June 19, 1940, when he was killed in the last agonizing days of French resistance against the Nazis.

Jelinek, Hanns (1901–69)

Zwölftonwerk (Twelve-Tone Music), Op. 15

Jelinek's Op. 15 is prefaced by a slightly flowery, somewhat old-fashioned set of lines. It is "for the use of performers, / for the pleasure of [the] listeners, / for the stimulation of [the] teachers, / for the instruction of [the] pupils / written / and dedicated / to all friends and lovers / of compositions in [the] twelve-tone system." It has, naturally, important instructional value, but aside from the overall objectives the pieces stand strongly on their own feet as concert music. Such musicoeducational material brings a reminder of Bach's didactically planned compositions, such as the *Wohltemperierte Clavier (Well-Tempered Clavier)* with the explanatory note that it was meant "for the use and profit of young musicians who are anxious to learn, as well as for the amusement of those who are already expert in the art."

There are two series of pieces in Jelinek's *Zwölftonwerk.* The first one, of five parts—consisting of four two-part inventions, six small "character pieces," three "dance pieces," four toccatas, and a nine-movement suite—is entirely for piano.

The second series of four pieces (parts six, seven, eight, and nine) are chamber music compositions, each in a different form, and each calling for a different combination of instruments. In order, the series consists of a set of canons for two flutes, a Sonatina and a Divertimento for woodwind instruments, and a string trio. (Separate discussions of these four works appear below.)

The important point regarding these compositions is that all are based on a single twelve-tone row. As usual the basic set is also presented in its other three forms: retrograde, inversion, and retrograde inversion.

DUOS

- **Four Canons for Two Flutes: from**
  Zwölftonwerk (Twelve-Tone Music),
  Op. 15—Series 2, Part VI

(See introductory essay above: *Zwölftonwerk.*)
Variety within stability is maintained here. The tempos are balanced in the first and fourth movements (Poco adagio and Poco andante), with a Tempo di Ländler and Vivace in between. In exact parallel definition the meters are 4/4 for the outer movements, with further balance in the midsection movements. Both of the latter are in triple meter, the Ländler, of course, in the standard 3/4 (waltz) designation and the Vivace in 3/8 time.

Diversification is maintained in the canonic types. In movement one the canon is at the octave. In movement two (significantly, set in exact ternary form) the canon is at the unison. The interval of imitation in the third canon is a fifth below. In the final movement the canon is *per motu contrario*—"by inversion." And though there is less diversification in the use of the tone row there is commanding balance. The first two canons use the basic series, the other pair of canons the inverted row. Good choice, since this means that the canon by inversion is thereby based on the row in inversion.

- ***Olla Podrida* for Flute and Guitar,**
  Op. 30

A catchy title for a three-movement suite. A sense of parody hangs over the music, already hinted at in the titles of the movements: Capriccietto, Bolerino, and Rondoletto.

Each movement features a specific technical point of view. In the Capriccietto the entire structural scheme is colored by syncopative patterns, and the scoring is strictly two part (the guitar part is limited to single sounds plus some glides). In the Bolerino, though the triple-beat rhythmic patterns are far from straightforward, a basic bolero underlay will be noted. Virtuosity is let loose in the chromaticized finale. This is obtained by plenty of metrical play and a sizable cadenza for the guitar.

TRIOS

- **Sonatina a Tre for Oboe, English horn,**
  and Bassoon: from *Zwölftonwerk*
  ***(Twelve-Tone Music)*, Op.15—Series**
  2, Part VII

(See introductory essay above: *Zwölftonwerk.*)
Three forms of the basic tone row (with transpositions) are used, matching thereby the number of movements and the number of instruments. The one form of the series not used is retrograde inversion.

Repeated pitches are a constant in the opening movement. This provides freshness and also relieves the polyphony. The latter is most acutely demonstrative in the following slow movement. Metrical unrest is a coloristic aid in the perky finale.

- **Trio for Violin, Viola, and Cello: from**
  Zwölftonwerk (Twelve-Tone Music),
  Op. 15—Series 2, Part IX

(See introductory essay above: *Zwölftonwerk.*)
The last of Jelinek's series of works based on a single twelve-tone row contains a full mix of the forms of the basic tone series, and includes, as well, selective (derived) configurations, some mirror reflections, variants, and even a bit of an unrelated row.

A sectional disposition of the material marks the opening part of the work. It has the quality of a waltz-in-progress, swinging its way with Viennese warmth—another manifestation of how romantic music can be propounded without specific tonality. Sectionalism is also to be found in the slow movement, a music that contrasts moving fifths with chromatic sweep. The finale has rondo formulation.

QUARTET

- Divertimento for E-flat Clarinet, B-flat Clarinet, Basset horn, and Bass Clarinet: from *Zwölftonwerk (Twelve-Tone Music)*, Op. 15— Series 2, Part VIII

(See introductory essay above: *Zwölftonwerk*.)

The use of the fundamental twelve-tone row for this quartet, scored for instruments of the clarinet family, is described by the composer thus: "die Reihe in mehrere selbständige Gruppen zerlegt wird" ("the row is broken up into several independent groups"). The formal catchall of divertimento design fits the process exceedingly well.

A short, slow-paced but rhapsodically figured Introduzione preludes an Overtura piccola (Small Overture). Not exactly "small" (totaling 141 measures). That size fits the Intermezzo (totaling 34 measures). The repeated pitches and compact rhythms in the Intermezzo emphasize the vertical type of dodecaphony that is basic to this part of the work as well as to the Scherzino, a virtuosic example to be played "as fast as possible."

The Scherzino is preceded by a Capriccio and followed by a Notturno. Both of these movements represent, quite strongly, the neoromantic unrest of chromaticism, whether it be applied to serial style or not. But if unrest there be, there are unpedantic controls in Jelinek's wind quartet. The same pertains to the other parts of the *Zwölftonwerk* cycle, entirely based on a single twelve-tone row.

OCTET

- *Two Blue O's* for Celesta, Harpsichord, Harp, Glockenspiel, Vibraphone, Xylorimba (or Marimbaphone), Double Bass, and Percussion (Large and Small Drums; Large and Small Tom-toms; Large, Small, and Foot Cymbals; Wood Block, and Tam-tam), Op. 31

Dark and bright conceptions, matched by tempos indicated as very slow and rather quick. Jelinek does not mince matters in his descriptive sound materials. "Organ Point" is stitched by persistent pitch repetition on B as different patterns move about, with most attention given the double bass. This is slow-slithered but somewhat taut jazz stuff.

The "Ostinato" is based on a three-measure idea, and rhythmic patterns, rather than tunes, sail along with it. It displays the sincerity of café jazz style but is nevertheless somewhat mild mannered.

NONET

- *Three Blue Sketches* for Flute, Clarinet, Alto Saxophone, Baritone Saxophone, Trumpet, Tenor Trombone, Vibraphone, Double Bass, and Percussion (Hand and Foot Cymbals, Large and Small Drums, Tom-tom, and Tam-tam) (1956)

The title and the instrumentation, with its reeds, brasses, and rhythm section, make this a jazz nonet. Plenty of syncopation, cross accents, and raggedy rag. Also, plenty of solidly banked tutti. The one-man percussion section doesn't miss a measure in the medium swing opening, tempo contrasted (very slow) middle movement, and final part, marked not too fast. It's apparent Jelinek had not forgotten the time when he eked out a living playing the piano in silent-movie houses and cabarets.

Jemnitz, Sándor (Alexander) (1890–1963)

DUOS

- **Duo Sonata for Viola and Cello, Op. 25**

Jemnitz's study with both Max Reger and Arnold Schoenberg is reflected in this remarkably colorful duet, swamped with performance difficulties. When this work for an ebony-colored combination of instruments was published in 1927 (by Schott) it represented an extremely rare instance of use of the medium. That no longer holds true, though the literature for viola and cello in combination is still of small total.

In order to compensate for the lack of a defined soprano instrument, the viola scales the heights quite often. However, while the tonal gamut is thereby increased, the timbre of such extension of the viola is contracted to cutting thinness. Reger's rhetoric of hundreds of sounds is displayed as Jemnitz shoves his pitches about with rhapsodic abandon; the influence of Schoenberg is illustrated by tenacious, linear allegiance. Though expressionism is the ribwork of Jemnitz's morbid allegory, he is most certainly a Schoenbergian independent.

It is natural that the forms of a work of such character would be free. Dogmatic formal philosophy, always the stuff of stiff opinion, confutes the corollaries of an original thinker. Jemnitz guards and defends well his independent point of view in this pyrotechnical dissertation that demands a violist and a cellist who can deal with Paganini-like demands. There are four movements: the first is to be considered in ternary design; the second a Presto of scherzo shape, replete with color hysteria, the form definitely equaling an A–B–A partition. Jemnitz's writing reaches a total of six-part chords, uses mandolin pizzicato strumming, double harmonics, col legno, left-hand pizzicato, plus the additional wealth of string instrument techniques. In the Adagio, there is a persistent fivefold figure that aids coherence. Most of the final movement employs the dissonance of parallel minor sevenths, intervallic controls that claim attention through their abrasive effect. Only at the end do these dissolve into more euphonious spacings.

- ***The Letter* for Double Bass and Piano**

Jemnitz doesn't disclose the contents of his letter, but there is no doubt that most of it concerns some light and lively information (or as light and lively as a double bass can communicate it). Jemnitz does repeat himself (measures 1–16 are heard again in measures 36–51). The syntax is of late-romantic type. Certainly this is a good musical "read."

- **Partita for Two Violins, Op. 29**

In comparison to his other works, Jemnitz is almost a pure nationalist in this short composition. The sonorous and linear thicknesses that mark the points of Jemnitz's composition compass are eliminated in this instance. Concentration of resources is the directional guide that is of latent influence as the dissonances are posted on thin but incisive lines that are just as probing as massed layers of sound. The first of the three movements is Hungarian in spirit. It is influenced by the D harmonic-minor scale, with friction intervals predominating. The Lento is chromatic, and once again intervallic clash is the weapon of interest. A Vivo without a solitary pitch accidental completes the duet.

- **Sonata No. 1 for Violin and Piano, Op. 10**

Jemnitz's Op. 10 shows the influence of Reger, though it is somewhat refined. The music is clear, of late-romantic order. Counterpoint is neatly conveyed in the first movement; the second theme is in direct contrast by homophonic arrangement. The two inner movements are similar to intermezzos—one playful, the other serious; the formal scope of the second of the pair is a bit freer. A rondo type is utilized in the final part, thereby balancing the vigor of the opening movement.

- **Sonata [No. 2] for Violin and Piano, Op. 14**

In his second violin and piano sonata Jemnitz is still influenced by Reger, but is starting to shake loose from such faith. The harmonies lean toward consecutive seconds; the writing as a whole tends to rhapsodic conduct. Though Reger's music is complexioned with motile lines, they are strictly controlled, not permitted any of the extempore manners found in Jemnitz's Sonata.

A broad declaration of sonata form is discharged in the first movement, a gavotte method prevails in the second. However, the form of the latter is not literal. It has the characteristic upbeat, but the music is primarily occupied with more serious concert-hall speech, not the light directions that marked the "easy come, easy go" of 17th-century drawing rooms. A broad type of slow movement and a sprightly division, somewhat looking into the scherzo domain, complete the work.

- **Sonata [No. 3] for Violin and Piano, Op. 22**

Jemnitz's third violin and piano sonata compares to his first two as driving rain does to pure sunlight. In this work there is a brutal and unshaken belief in the expressionistic school of composition. The violin is heard as a febrile instrument on behalf of this now atonally minded and mannered Hungarian composer.

The difference between the third and the first two sonatas is of simple explanation. Before his Op. 22 Jemnitz had ended his study with Reger and had been under the tutelage of Schoenberg. However, this act did not deter Jemnitz's compulsion to write an ultra-Germanic type of music. With typical Regerian fondness for ascetic musical content, Jemnitz composed items for violin alone, cello alone, and even unaccompanied works for double bass and trumpet! But he had mastered all the prevailing technical considerations and his fully controlled gifts demanded to be fascinated by other methods. Very late German romanticism had arrived at a cul-de-sac, its creed outworn, whereupon Jemnitz warmed himself at the Schoenbergian blaze. From that point on Jemnitz's output was charmed with Schoenbergian accent but calculated to embrace an individual choice of words. Extreme expressionistic media marked the new period of work as if in expiation for past creative sins. The compositions denoted the nonmoderation that can mark instrumental combinations—a duet for saxophone and banjo, a quartet for four trumpets, a trio using guitar, and another three-instrument work that partnered two string instruments with a flute.

Violent extravagance is the dominating issue of the third violin and piano sonata. The first movement is somewhat akin to a sonata, and contains a surrealistic application of color sound, including polyphonic glissandos for the violin (a matter so difficult that one is certain that only a few violinists can truly master the technique). In the Adagio most of the expressiveness is given the violin, while the piano supports. The final movement is shaped in the form of rondo variations—the particulars of the variants ingrained, not baldly specific.

- **Suite No. 2 for Violin and Piano, Op. 60**

As applies to all of Jemnitz's music, the chromatic gestures here are continuous. This is basic, gut-level, mid-20th-century romanticism (Op. 60 was written in 1953). And it clearly represents Jemnitz's mature style—derived from Reger, inculcated from expressionistic Schoenberg.

Jemnitz does not tend to smile in his music, but there is a bit of hedonistic lift in the Intermezzo (movement two), with a Hungarian-like allegro conception twice following dramatic and passionate lento statements. Some of the same unfettered quality is to be found in the Burlesque (movement four). Also to be found is an unaccompanied section of virtuosic content for the violin.

Movement three is an Arioso. No sing-song in this music, but rich, rouladed lines. The opening movement has a picturesque title "L'histoire vraie" ("The True Story"). Although the tale is not described, its constructive truth is to be found in variational development.

TRIOS

▪ *Flute Trio* for Flute, Violin, and Viola, Op. 19

Jemnitz's trio has thickness of texture. The color pile is like encaustic painting—mezzotints are absent. By far the most striking representation in this respect is the Presto volante (movement three). For the first fifty-five measures the violin and flute are doubled at the unison. This creates a special mixture since the violin is muted and thus veils the flute's timbre while equaling it in weight. Against this partnership the viola employs its own form of pigmented power via col legno taps, homophonic unisons on two strings, and droned two-tone chords.

The third movement is a wild dance; its slower-paced middle section is improvisationally minded, simmering with chords, harmonics, propulsive grace notes, and arpeggios. (The quality of this section brings to mind Jemnitz's Hungarian heritage.) The recapitulation is thematically similar to the first part of the movement; the coda uses portions of the middle section as its prelude and the main theme as its epilogue.

Movements one and two are much more conservative: The first has some rhapsodic bends and glides set in a sonata frame, the second is balanced by the use of a large ternary design.

The last movement is a set of variations, though not so captioned by Jemnitz. The first of these is partially imitative, with the theme quite recognizable. A capricious variant follows, in turn succeeded by one much calmer but with decorative linear turns. In the fourth part the violin has the greater variational responsibility, while the fifth part is, by turns, chordal and polyphonic. Variation six is marked Vigoroso (Alla cadenza). It employs the viola in a dazzling display, with assorted ideas supplied by the supportive violin. A fiery 5/4 section and a fugue complete the variations. Jemnitz's choice of a slow and exceedingly quiet close is unexpected. Its translucency is especially effective.

▪ **Serenade for Violin, Viola, and Cello, Op. 24**

Panchromaticism propels Jemnitz's string trio. Only by the inculcation of pitch polarity does the music pull away from absolute atonalism; thus, the G area is involved in the outer movements and D in the central one.

A motival generator is basic to the first movement. It is immediately placed in imitation and is also employed to shape the secondary subject. The Lento is also formed from a cellular basis first heard in the viola inside the softly sonorous opening tutti and then developed by a process of expansivity, taking on a sense of variation. In the last movement the initial theme is constantly variated, counterpointed, and given imitative treatment. It leads to a second subject of close relationship, individualized by use of a Tempo di tango (even a bit of the actual dance element is introduced). The return to the opening section makes the movement only somewhat of ternary design. The exact divisional specifications of such design are not present through the variational aspects applied to the subjects.

(The Serenade was dedicated to three of the original members of the once-famous Kolisch Quartet: Rudolf Kolisch, violin; Eugen Lehner, viola; and Benar Heifetz, cello.)

- **Trio for Flute, Oboe, and Clarinet, Op. 70**

Concentrated linear stipulations with the major changes within the three movements those of tempo, in turn: Vivo, Lento, and Allegretto. Jemnitz opts for sober writing, dense with pitch shifts, with the ultrachromaticism wiping out any key adherence, even though D major is the key signature for all movements. The trio's textural weight reminds one of Reger's organ pieces.

Jeney, Zoltán (1943–)

DUO

- *Tropi* **for Two Trumpets (1975)**

Obvious quasi-didactic sternness that deals with constant sets of small pitch patterns. These *Tropi* continue for eighty-four measures, organized in moderate-pace, quadruple-pulse measures. Color impressions come from a variety of dynamic changes, directed within the totally muted trumpets, as well as occasional fluttertongued ejections on either the pitch A or B.

TRIO

- *Round* **for Piano, Harpsichord, and Harp (1972)**

Antithematic-style music in ametric arrangement. The pitches are isolated, to be played very short, the projection of each instrumental

part individually controlled by the performer so that a good part of the creative behavior is his. However, by his pitch arrangements Jeney is certain to obtain a quality of tight, restrained sonorities since all sounds are maintained within one octave. (The piano and harpsichord are scored for one hand only, and simultaneous pitches for each of these instruments are limited to three.)

Compression is matched by repression. There is to be no dynamic change, and all sounds are to be at the lowest level, "on the very borders of intelligible audibility." If the combined sound of the trio of instruments is too definite then performance should be with the instruments behind a curtain.

(Jeney indicates that the piano and harpsichord parts can be performed also on two prepared pianos.)

Jenni, Donald (1937–)

DUO

- *Musique printanière* **for Flute and Piano (1967)**

Most of the writing is percussive in tone. Jenni does not hunt with the hounds of flute tradition in their pastoral-nocturnal habitats. Accordingly, an individual approach to registral conditions is to be noted. For the first part of the piece (of four-minute length) the piano is approximately in the same range as the flute. In the later portion, the total ranges of both instruments are utilized.

Jenni explains that *printanière* means "both 'primeval' and 'having to do with springtime.'" Clearly, most of the former, with only a little bit of the latter.

QUARTET

- *Cucumber Music: Metamorphosis* for Four Players-Nine Instruments (Alto Flute [alternating Piccolo], Viola [alternating Toy Piano], Celesta [alternating Piano], Vibraphone [alternating Glockenspiel, and Two Tam-tams, medium and low]) (1969)

Completely minus meter indications and barline measurements, structurally Jenni's piece is loosely analogous to binary formation. Repetitive rhythmic projections are followed by quiet, moody data. White/black, extrovert/introvert, and thesis/antithesis come to mind with this chromatic network of duplicative reverberations. Jenni describes it differently. "Its structure projects a gradual focusing and stabilizing of events from initially active (though essentially static) blocks of animated, isorhythmic sonorities, through increasingly more intense heterophonic interplay, to an ultimate transformation into broadly arching single strands."

According to the composer, the title *Cucumber Music* "has no symbolic significance." Again, quoting the composer: "*Cucumber Music* was a working title which, somewhat in the nature of a nickname, has stayed with the work (and won it a certain amount of rapport on its tours of rural Iowa)". (Meaning, performance of the work on tours made by the organization for which the work was written: the University of Iowa's Center for New Music.) A different reaction from this writer. Actually, the title is a poor choice leading thoughts totally astray regardless of the composer's disclaimer.

(The subtitle indicates nine instruments are used by the four performers. However, two tam-tams remain as a total of two, and thus the explanatory title should read properly "ten instruments.")

NONET

- *Cherry Valley: An Ensemble for Nine Flutes* (Seven Flutes and Two Alto Flutes [Second Alto Flute alternating with Bass Flute]) (1976)

The little bits of ultrachromatic material that are tossed about give an athletic tone to Jenni's nonet. In the second part of the piece there is considerably more vertical cohesion. This latter is preceded by the first flute and the first alto flute performing "birdlike improvisation" on given pitches, with interspersion of silences, for a span of thirteen seconds.

There is dogmatic virtuosity here, and it would be best to have the baton of a conductor to keep matters straight.

(The bass flute is used only in the extremely soft closing portion of the work. If it is not available for the five measures involved, the composer has indicated a substitute part for the second alto flute.)

Jensch, Lothar (1916–)

QUARTET

- *Mouvement à quatre* for String Quartet (1960)

Serial music set forth in a businesslike fashion, maintaining its progress in unmetered detail, but with precise rhythmic definition. And just as precise metronomic controls. In the nine-minute span there are twenty-eight metronome markings.

The music embodies full rhapsody not only in its pace flux and energy but in its coloristic projection. There is consistent successive timbre qualification. One example: a quintuplet in col legno spiccato, then a sixteenth-note drawn with the wood of the bow, followed by a ponticello sound in *mezzopiano*, and concluded with a broken triplet that includes pitches in normal timbre and then plucked sound.

Jentsch, Walter (1900–)

DUO

- **Five Pieces for Alto Recorder and Piano, Op. 49**

Standard forms refreshingly presented. Bachian turns in the Präludium that opens the composition. More or less give-and-take in the Dialog. Part three is a Waltz, part five a Tarantella. In between these is a romantically pressed, ternary-totaled "Ausblick" ("View"). Conventions are followed in this music, but nothing is mundane.

Jentzsch, Wilfried (1941–)

DUO

- *Zusammengefügtes (United Together)* for Oboe and High-Hat Cymbal (1969)

Aleatoric style is unsystematized, therefore description of a composition using it is difficult to come by. There are no repetitions or sequences to hold material together, simply flashes of content, related only through their unrelationship. (The parallel of action painting, with its indeterminacy and irregularity, comes to mind.)

Three parts, with the last giving some faint reminders of the first. (So much for structural balance.) No meters—proportional notation is the guide, aided by indicated timing totals (in seconds) for sections. Thus, as an example, the first part has seven sections, timed respectively at 15, 9, 7, 8, 6, 12, and 14 seconds, for a total of 1:11.

The high-hat cymbal consists of two matched cymbals fitted onto a pedal. The bottom cymbal, face up, is in a fixed position; the depression of the pedal brings the face of the top cymbal down onto the face of the bottom one. In addition to this, Jentzsch uses different types of beaters for the cymbals: soft, hard, wood (or metal), and brushes. The yield from the cymbals is not only punctuation but a sophisticated, atmospheric touch that adds its poplike brassy qualities to the oboe's improvisational-like pitched qualities.

QUARTET

- **String Quartet (1972)**

Nonmetrical, nonthematic—a fantasy of shapes, isolated sounds, and effects, plus amorphous rhythmic patterns. The sonorities include innumerable glides, many produced in out-of-bounds territory (behind the bridge), and show a zeal for the rawest properties. Pitches of warmth to caress the ears are totally absent. The final nine-part tone cluster (G-sharp–A–C–C-sharp–D–E-flat–E–F–F-sharp) is heard over a thirteen-second span as it is divided (with some doubling) into three-part chords for the four instruments. Each instrument repeats its own chord: twenty-one times for the first violin against thirteen times for the second violin, eight for the viola, and five for the cello. With this intense rhythmic combine, stylistic certification takes place.

Jereb, Ervin

SEPTET

- *Copper Engravings* for Seven Brass
  Instruments and a Percussionist
  (Three Trumpets, Horn, Tenor
  Trombone, Second Tenor Trombone
  or Bass Trombone, Tuba, and
  Percussion ad libitum [Two Timpani,
  Small Drum, Two Bongos, Tenor and
  Bass Tom-toms, Tam-tam, Three
  Temple Blocks, Wood Block,
  Suspended Cymbal, Marimba, and
  Vibraphone]) (1977)

(Since the percussion may be omitted, *Copper Engravings* is listed as a septet.)

More concerned with color and effect than theme and material, Jereb's piece retains an impacted vehemence. There are seven movements, and even when the tempo is slow and the dynamics are subdued (the second of the set, for example) the vitality crackles. Among the timbral offerings are tonguing while breathing through the instruments without blowing, lip glissandos, and percussive sounds such as hitting the mouthpiece with the flat of the hand, valve clicks, and knee slappings. In one section within the sixth movement the first trumpet plays into the bell of the tuba and the second trumpet plays in the bell of the horn.

This scoring freedom carries over to sections that are without meter or bar lines and to the structure of the work and its instrumentation as well. Three of the movements may be omitted, cutting performance time almost in half, and though the title does not indicate it, the percussion can be omitted. (The indication of the percussion's ad libitum status is buried in the instrumentation listing.)

Jeremiáš, Otakar (1892–1962)

QUARTET

- Quartet in E Minor for Violin, Viola,
  Cello, and Piano, Op. 5

The romantic turns and values that permeate Smetana's music fill the measures of this Czech composer's work, written at the age of 19. There are no revelations, but there are poetry and solidity of harmony and form. The Quartet has three movements: Allegro moderato (with a coda that is very subdued in speed and dynamic); a central slow movement (Adagio molto espressivo); and a swinging, dance-flavored Allegro capriccioso.

The Czech critic Josef Plavec speaks of the music's "vitality, energy [and] optimism." He also mentions Jeremiáš's "uncommon lyric talent." It is the element of lyricism that is the strongest point in this piano quartet.

Jersild, Jørgen (1913–)

QUARTET

- *Fantasia e canto affettuoso* for Flute,
  Clarinet, Cello, and Harp

The second of three compositions using the harp, each in a different setting. The first is a solo work titled *Pezzo elegiaco. Parte seconda* is the work under discussion and *Parte terza* is a Concerto for Harp and Orchestra. (The publisher, Wilhelm Hansen, has issued the compositions under the rubric *Libro d'arpa*.)

The first part of the quartet is a *Fantasia sopra un motto*, based on the opening for harp alone. The second part is headed *Canto affettuoso con metamorfosi*. The fantasia concept notwithstanding, there is a fair chunk of recapitulation of the initial portion of the first part. The free variational essence of part two has just as much fantasy character as part one. The mix is colorful, and the use of the instruments takes heed of individual highlighting without upsetting balances. Where suavity and suppleness constitute the name of Jersild's chamber music presentation, it is so covered, and where there should be flair it is likewise fully accomplished.

QUINTET

- *Music Making in the Forest*: **Serenade for Five Wind Instruments (Flute, Oboe, Clarinet, Horn, and Bassoon) (1947)**

A light-spirited three-movement work. Unity is secured in each part by placement in ternary packaging. Simplistic rhythms are matched by tonally embraced melodic lines that have an impressionistic flavor.

Jesinghaus, Walter (1902–66)

DUO

- *Sonatina brevis* **for Violin and Piano, Op. 22A**

A one-movement conception, with basically two themes that are alternated and slightly developed. Jesinghaus uses a tonal polarity that circles around B major. The music is smoothly molded, unpretentious, and clearly defined, even though no special individuality pertains.

Jettel, Rudolf (1904–76)

DUOS

- *Concertante Sonata* **for Double Bass and Piano**

Tonal polarities bind the three movements of Jettel's duo sonata. The last is a double affair, with a full-size slow movement linked to an equally full-size Allegro. (The published Edition Eulenburg piano score indicates Andante moderato for the former while the double-bass part is marked Adagio. The metronomic indication is the same for both [♩ = 54].) Movement one is built around D and concludes in D minor. Movement two follows suit, being based on B and ending in B major. The last movement is the most chromatic and has a bitonal termination.

Jettel's composition (using a scordatura that raises the pitch of all the strings a whole tone) has color, but avoids special effects. (One reviewer has described the work as being in "bass-as-a-big-cello style.") It is vigorously rhythmic without asymmetricality; the vitality is built into the lines. This contemporary music has sufficient adventurousness but always displays good manners.

- **Sonata for Violin and Piano**

An interesting connection exists that exemplifies the chromatic clarity of the work. Bombarded chromaticism there is, and the cadential signatures of the first and third movements prove it. In the former case, the violin sweeps through a chromatic line to help identify and complete the movement in F-sharp major, which opened in the same key. In the third (and final) movement the same practice is followed for the F-sharp-minor tonality. Movement two is in C-sharp minor.

The middle (second) movement is intensified by specific use of the heaviest string of the violin, a short cadenza, and in the recapitulation by the weight of double-stop writing. There are lighter content and thinner textures in the concluding movement, as compared to the passionate energy of the first movement.

(There is no clue to solve the different tempos printed in the piano score for the third movement, since the same metronomic indication ($\downarrow = 144$) is given for both parts. The violin cue line reads Allegro moderato; the piano staves are headed Allegro barbarico. The separate violin part has the latter indication.)

TRIOS

▪ Theme and Variations for Three Clarinets

Music that fills the requirements of tonal style and taste. Within a sixteen-minute span there are eleven variations on a tripartite G-major theme. It is all plain sailing (but not plain music). The variants are not unduly elaborate and are not weighed down by academic devices. Thus, for example: Number one elaborates the material a bit; variant two places the ornamentation in triplets; the theme is clearly assigned to the third clarinet in part three; variation four is a Scherzo; imitation is used in variation five. And so on, with a vigorous march representing the tenth part and a heady conception marking the finale.

One special point: There is practically total use of the three clarinets throughout the piece.

▪ Trio in C Minor for Clarinet, Violin, and Viola

A good part of Jettel's warm-timbred Trio has romantic identification. There are sections that remind one of Brahms and other portions bring Reger to mind. But the music has sonorous juice and at times the writing is most inventive. (In one case it is somewhat restricted; namely, the constant four-square phrases in the first movement.)

There are five parts, tempoed fast and slow, in turn. Most of the movements are regulated by three-part structuring, with recaps always changed in color and shape but pertinently related to the initial statements.

QUINTETS

▪ Wind Quintet for Flute, Oboe, Clarinet, Horn, and Bassoon

The classic pursuit of formal balance with vertical and horizontal romantic writing is exhibited here, and successfully. There is some wit in this composer's music, but for the most part it has the solid qualities of moderately serious expression. In the medium of the wind quintet this is always welcome, what with the chirps and tweeps that fill so much of the music written for that combination.

Full development of two principal themes regulates the first movement. The slow movement encloses the Scherzo, which is set strictly in alternating long–short 3/8 and 2/8 meters. The finale has vivacity, emphasizes sound weights off the beat, and includes the hemiola process of combining triple and duple pulses within the same measure.

▪ Wind Quintet No. 3

Twentieth-century tonalism that landscapes the standard, light-faceted territory occupied by most woodwind quintet compositions. Good substances, however, and good handling of the instruments (all five are provided a cadenza in the last part of the work).

Three movements. The first is a sonata; the second a more serious conception with emphasis on legato phrasing; the third a sonata type containing a literal recapitulation of the entire first part of the movement.

Jež, Jakob (1928–)

DUOS

- *Pastoral Inventions* for Violin and Piano

Chromatic distillations and mainly devoted to motival processes. In melodic movement the spans of seconds and sevenths are favored. Jež's three pieces are all free formed. It is not surprising, therefore, that the duo ends with the violinist tapping his finger on the body of the instrument.

- *Stihi I–II–III–IV (Verses I–II–III–IV)* for Oboe and Viola (1966)

The freeway of the avant-garde as viewed by this Slovakian composer. Assorted technical tokens: Part one is metered, part four gives total pulses but the rhythms are only partially guided by the composer—the performers must do the rest. Color specification applies to parts two and three: the music is mostly for the oboe alone in the former, totally solo for the viola in the latter.

TRIO

- *Assonances* for Oboe, Harp, and Piano

The agreement among the absolutely remote details of these three pieces is found in the open-hearted, enthusiastic promotion of color. Even the long opening oboe solo draws on twisted rhythms that emphasize color rather than thematic formations. So, when the harp enters it plays a glissando with an iron rod. Clusters are as much a part of the scoring for the harp as they are for the piano. And a plectrum is used by the pianist, as well as fingers, for plucking the strings. And so on.

Actually, there is nothing new whatsoever in this trio. But the rich, turbulent instrumental ideas do communicate a discharge of vibrant timbres.

Ježek, Jaroslav (1906–42)

DUO

- Duo for Two Violins (1934)

Busy, motoric music, with its rhythmic flow hardly broken in the outer fast movements. Both resemble Roussel style with slightly cushioned harmony. Some nationalistic (Czechoslovak) presence in the central movement, marked by the fact that throughout one or the other of the violins is muted.

Jiménez-Mabarak, Carlos (1916–)

DUO

- Cinco Piezas (Five Pieces) for Flute and Piano

Twelve-tone style as perceived by this Mexican composer and directed toward picturesque settings. Slow, rhapsodically curved lines depict *Alegoría del Perejil (The Symbolism of Parsley)*. The tempo is quick and the asymmetry decided in *La Imagen repentina (A Sudden Image)*. The same applies to the finale *Danza mágica (Magic Dance)*. The movements preceding this dance are a Nocturno and one titled *El Ave prodigiosa (The Miraculous Bird)*.

Jíra, Milan (1935–)

QUARTET

- Five Impromptus for String Quartet

A fine range of expressiveness impresses the ear in this eight-minute work. In the first piece a jingly scherzo is presented, with busybody changes of meter, mainly quintuple and septuple. The second Impromptu is patiently devoted to stuttering rhythms and emphasizes glissando sweeps at the same time.

Ferocious attention to color continues, though not ferociously applied. In movement three the emphasis is on pizzicato ostinatos, principally detailing a minor-ninth span. Movement four relies on sustained sounds, its effect after the preceding movements one of slow motion exempt of rhythm. But snappy pulsations reappear in the final piece, riding full steam on warmly heated repetitives and tutti declaratives.

Jirák, Karel Boleslav (1891–1972)

DUO

▪ **Sonata for Viola and Piano, Op. 26**

Jirák's viola sonata is in one movement, combining sonata style with variations; the former is descriptive of the outer sections, wherein the recapitulation follows excisionary practice, with new material forming the coda. The music begins in G, shifts to the implied subdominant sense (when the viola enters), and then gravitates to the tonic orbit for the variations. The return of the first section then follows with the final chord stating C minor.

The variations stem from a theme embedded in parallel sevenths, a modal assertion not punctuated by a chromatic coloration. If Jirák rhapsodically pinched the first and third sections, he was careful to smooth the set designs of the inner variations. Each is set forth definitely: the first ornamented, the second a precise Scherzo (a two-note rhythmic unit is constant), the third a quasi tarantella (a three-note idea being preserved), followed by a return of the theme in outline form.

The piano serves as an intermediary, ending the first section alone, bridging into its return, and then, as at the beginning, announcing, as a solo voice, the sonata-form portion.

TRIO

▪ **Divertimento for Violin, Viola, and Cello, Op. 28**

Dependence on the polyphonic stimulant strengthens (and dramatizes) the first and last movements. There are motival developments, fugato hints, imitations, and use of inversion in the Preludio. Movement five, which concludes the opus, is an energetic and exciting Fuga. It includes augmentation.

There isn't a mundane moment in Jirák's trio. The Aria sings in all instruments, constantly supported by set, moving chords. A segment of the Aria is lifted into the otherwise driving Scherzo, containing a music that varies its meter considerably—and effectively. The Recitativo is strictly chordal in its outer sections. In the center there is a free solo for the violin over a four-part pizzicato ostinato in the viola and cello. This is a fine, vital, and powerfully colorful string trio.

QUARTETS

▪ **String Quartet No. 1 in C Minor, Op. 9**

Heated and intense writing are the elements of the first part of Jirák's one-movement string quartet. This leads to a decidedly individual Scherzo, which in its first part is fugally designed; the Trio section glides in slower tempo and then later is restated, also fugally. Finally, the music of the Scherzo is combined with that of the Trio.

The final part of the work begins with slow-tempo material, is followed by episodic data and then a return to the opening part of the quartet, with a Grave sostenuto-tempo conclusion.

A Czech writer has described the music as "a work of powerful inner crisis, with pain, longing and defiance as its emotional mainsprings." No further explanation is given, but this description is certainly an apt one.

- **String Quartet No. 3, Op. 41**

Jirák's quartet contains no hedonistic over-simplicities. This even pertains to the Scherzo, which hovers between A major and A minor. The outer movements are in C-sharp minor, and the principal tempo indications are clues to the content: In the opening movement (after a sustained introduction) the heading is Inquieto ed appassionato and in the closing movement the pace is immediately Allegro energico. The only somewhat relaxed section of the quartet is the Trio to the Scherzo, conceived as a Ritmo di polka to be played in moderate tempo and with intimate feeling. Movement two is an Andante con variazioni. There are four rather free variations.

QUINTET

- **Quintet for Two Violins, Viola, Cello, and Piano, Op. 50**

Late-romantic statistics and largeness of gesture are represented here. As occurs with so many piano quintets, there is considerable block writing, with strings set against the piano.

Balladic intensity is found in the first movement, cast in a sonata design. The slow movement, according to the Czech critic Karel Mlejnek, recalls the atmosphere that is found in the "funereal moods" of Josef Suk's music. Part three is a vivacious Scherzo with a gentle Trio that has polka outlines.

It is movement four that holds particular interest. A Tema con variazioni, the subject of the variants is an ancient Greek song that was carved on the tombstone of Seikilos (first century A.D.), discovered in 1883. Freely translated the words of the song are: "So long as you live, be bright; be not overly distressed. Life is but brief, the time demands fulfillment." Jirák's set of five variations is marked by attention to a rising fifth in the original melody (in its transcription in modern notation). The move-

ment is concluded by an antiphonally scored section that relates to the theme itself, entirely heard in a low dynamic plane.

Jirásek, Ivo (1920–)

QUARTET

- *Quattro Studi (Four Studies)* **for String Quartet (1966)**

Aggressive music that shadowboxes with twelve-tone (but is not serial) and Bartók styles. The textural play is interesting, moving in and out of instrumental quadrupling in total unification of block rhythms and complete polyphony.

Introduced in the first movement and used in the succeeding three movements are two types of glissando: slow (thus emphasizing a microtonal establishment) and very fast. Movement three has an engaging format. It is principally contrapuntal and then moves into a twelve-measure duet for the two violins which connects with a sizable cadenza for the first violin. The conclusion of the movement once again illustrates the quartet's textural duality: four measures of mixed voicing and three measures of *fortissississimo* in chunky tutti.

Jirko, Ivan (1926–78)

DUO

- **Sonata for Cello and Piano (1955)**

Jirko's two-movement Sonata is without floridity; the stability of diatonicism marks that refinement. In this duo Jirko is a composer devoted to classicism in the large sense, with perceptive sensitivity and regard for the progress of harmonies. Only a pedant would object to his chordal garnishes.

The tonal polarity is directly on E beginning with the initial sounds in the opening (Moderato) movement, which ends in clear E major. The conclusion of the Allegro, a music of toccata deliverance in its personality, is in E minor. Breadth of phrase (and meter) mark the first movement. Most of the pulse total is either 3/2 or 2/2—more of the former than the latter.

TRIO

- *Giuòcchi per tre (Games for Three)* for Violin, Viola, and Cello (1972)

Playful tossing of motives gives a light touch to the Preludio. The final measure, with its triple ponticello trill, is the confirmatory sign for this description. The second *Game* is marked Ballabile, a title occasionally given to dancelike pieces or ballets in the 19th-century opera field. In Jirko's example, the music is balletic to the hilt, but rhythmically ambivalent.

The Canzonetta sings soloistically, with large unaccompanied sections for viola, cello, and violin, in turn. Then, in the second half the full trio chromaticizes its song.

Most perpetual-motion pieces are frothy spittings of a repetitive rhythmic figure. Jirko's lively moto perpetuo musical travel piece is not such a sprint at all. Sixteenth-note figures are basic, but there is also instrumental diffusion, splitting of the rhythmic units, compression of time lengths per measure from 4/4 (equaling 16/16) to 12/16, and four-unit figures reduced to three. All of this is exciting stuff.

QUINTET

- Suite for Wind Quintet (1956)

A sense of serenade style permeates a good part of this quintet, especially the march bravado of the final movement, conceived in sonata style. Movement two also has the light dance touch

that is part of the serenade perspective (and of so many Czech compositions). In the first movement the solo colors of the bassoon and the flute are highlighted. In the Adagio more than once the stylistic device recalls Janáček.

Joachim, Joseph (1831–1907)

DUO

- **Variations for Viola and Piano, Op. 10**

History has recorded that Joachim was one of the greatest masters of the violin. He was no less a superlative chamber music performer, leading the famed Joachim Quartet from 1869 until his death in 1907. He was also a composer of outstanding gifts, but his career as a performer left little time for creative work. He concentrated on compositions for the violin. Most were made for virtuosos, but none tried to impress simply by the force of fiddling histrionics. Joachim was a great friend of Brahms's and Harold Truscott, the English writer on music, has pointed out that Joachim "contributed to Brahms's style many of the features which . . . are called Brahmsian." We are therefore faced with the premise that Joachim was a pre-Brahms Brahmsian!

Op. 10 is a set of ten variations (plus a coda of length) on a theme by Joachim. (This has led to listings of the work that are descriptively correct, though precisely not, such as *Variations on an Original Theme*.)

The theme is for solo piano; the variations are more or less continuous and total a cohesive structure. The "Brahmsian" (or, truthfully, "Joachimistic") element is powerful, the contrapuntal writing dramatic. Important is the equality of the scoring; the piano writing is of such expressivity and color that it brought the statement by Truscott of his "regret" that Joachim never "gave us a solo piano work."

The last two variations are, in turn, exceedingly ornamental (variation nine is marked "Rather slow, with deep melancholic 'Gipsy-like' expression") and contain a nationalistic tinge (variation ten is an Allegretto vivace al' ongarese). These are followed by an Adagio, which partly recalls (in different rhythm) the opening theme (again for solo piano), followed by a variational type of material. The closing measures match the opening measures with their quiet dynamic.

Joachim's work is truly a variational masterpiece. It deserves placement with the great examples of music written in variation form.

Joachim, Otto (1910–)

DUOS

■ *Expansion* for Flute and Piano (1962)

A rigorous expansion of material—both sounds and silences—builds the structure.

There are ten sections of serial-style, meterless music interspersed with nine sections of silence. The sections of sound material progressively increase as to length, with each about five seconds longer than the previous segment. In turn, after the first silence of one beat, each silence thereafter is rigidly expanded by a single beat, the second absence of sound embracing two beats, the third totaling three beats, and so on, with nine beats covering the last (ninth) silence. Truly, Joachim's duo lives up to its title.

■ *Quattro intermezzi* for Flute and Guitar (1978)

Joachim produced his four pieces in the space of two days (May 29–30, 1978), but they do not show anything less than sensitive, highly polished serial writing.

The set embraces six minutes, with clearly distinct dimensions for each piece. Number one is fantasy-scoped; a quiet triple-pulse waltzlike concept that insinuates duple accentuations within it follows. The third intermezzo has an improvisational quality. In the rhythmically vivacious final piece the guitar has trampoline-type ostinatos (used in all but three of the fifty-nine measures), and the flute is just as athletic in its demeanor.

■ **Sonata for Cello and Piano (1954)**

Joachim's work is described in a catalogue as being "serial with four mood-expressive movements which have considerable wit and warmth. Though the work is very short, it nevertheless retains a good deal of intensity."

More analysis is needed, aside from indicating the duration, which is honed to a precise listing of eight minutes and five seconds! The two inner movements are slow (Lento and Largo), surrounding fast-pace movements listed as Allegro moderato and Allegro scherzando. However, the first of the speedy movements has more playfulness than the movement marked "scherzando." There, one would expect to find some whimsy, but the contents are rhythmically uneasy. The finale's ending, however, is special; it is set in Largo, for cello alone. Its four measures (twenty-three beats in total) are completely concerned with a variety of double-stopped fifths, punctuated at the end with another five-pitch chord by the piano in *fortississimo*.

The first of the slow movements is thin-textured. It rigidly stays within the boundaries of the tone row, heard in assorted statements six times and ending with a quarter of the row as a *pianissimo* chord for the piano.

QUARTET

■ **String Quartet (1956)**

The key to Joachim's quartet is that while it partakes of serial technique, it does not use it exclusively. The fundamental row is announced by the quartet in alternation with the D pitch and is followed by its bare statement by the cello. Thereafter, it functions rather freely; somewhat strictly, other times partially, contrary to dodecaphonic discipline. No stylistic disorder, since Joachim manages to blend the twelve-tone style with other free tonal materials.

Classical form holds the work rather compactly. Thus, sonata structure in the opening; a lyrical rondo type as movement two; a slow waltz, preceded by a sizable fantasy-patterned initial part as the total third movement; and a variational-conditioned finale with steamy rhythmic drive.

Jóhannsson, Magnús Blöndal (1925–)

DUO

■ **Duo for Oboe and Clarinet (1954)**

The concern here is for contrapuntal utility, which binds the music rather strongly to Germanic style. Nicely put in all three movements, the writing of this Icelandic composer avoids note spinning and evidences craftsmanship.

Three movements, the center one a tripartite scherzo-monitored affair with a contrastive middle portion of more lyrical bent. The attempt to move away from key stolidity is made by consistent quartal melodic movement.

Johansen, David Monrad (1888–1974)

DUO

■ **Suite for Cello and Piano, Op. 24**

Romantic positiveness but without undue ef-

florescence. The lines in the music have fullness and, where necessary, impact, but there is no overgrowth to disturb clear statements.

The Fantasia shifts its pace and moods, but within is a good amount of imitative writing. Movement two is a Berceuse, but the quiet controls are removed for an agitated, nonslumbery middle section. Block chords and arpeggiated voicing are the supports that are used in the Dans. An Elegi follows, and the duo concludes with a Finale that has drive and power. Its presto close is preceded by a pair of miniature cadenzas for the cello. Lots of verve here, and, certainly in the quieter moments, there are no musty lavender-and-old-lace negatives.

QUARTET

■ **Quartet for Two Violins, Viola, and Cello, Op. 36**

The Norwegian composer's single string quartet, composed at the age of 81. It was a huge success at its premiere and in 1970 was awarded the Norwegian Composers' Society's prize as the "Work of the Year."

Importantly, the opening compactly totaled Agitato binds the Quartet. It appears four times within the sonata-form first movement and begins and concludes the finale. This last is a whirlwind tripleted drive in Presto, which is halted for the start of a fugue, then resumed in presto for three measures, and again tempo braked for the recommencement of the fugue, only to punch back into a short presto once more.

This concreteness and specificity carries over to the middle pair of movements. The first of the pair is a slightly unusual Scherzo, since the Trio is heard not only as the customary central portion but as the conclusion. The other is the slow movement, arranged in double binary song form.

QUINTET

- **Quintet for Flute and Strings (Two Violins, Viola, and Cello)**

Johansen's Quintet presents a persuasive argument for mixing of styles. Thus, the final movement (Passacaglia) crawls chromatically, and in so doing combines a C polarity with twelve-tone scope; the preambulistic permutated tone of the opening movement is somewhat paralleled by the variational basis of the last movement; and finally, the middle movement's strictly tonal music in ternary form is firmly related in its key strengths to the other movements.

Movements one and three are in slow tempo, thus the less usual method of balancing compound tempos, which, in the great majority of cases, will enclose a slow movement between fast-paced movements.

The rhapsodic flute cascades of the opening movement are somewhat soloistic in relation to the string quartet. Movement two is strongly nationalistic in its scherzo format, with a dance thrust that reminds one of the Norwegian halling. There are a dozen variations in the final movement, with the measurement of the variants strictly kept to the subject's eight-measure length or exactly doubled, in the case of the ninth and tenth variations. A coda (of seventeen measures) completes the Quintet.

Johanson, Sven-Eric (1919–)

QUARTET

- **String Quartet No. 2 (1948)**

A mix of strong Hindemithian sonorities and austere Sibelian qualities colors this work. The duality does not negate a resultant personality. The profile of this Swedish composer's quartet is clear and there are no false wrinkles.

Three themes are presented in the initial movement in exact increases of speed; first an adagio espressivo, then an allegro, half again as fast, and third, a presto twice as fast as the first section. The three divisions are run through a second time (there are some slight changes) with the proportions exactly the same in parts one and two, and with a shortened third part. Movement two has scherzo definition, constructed from motival stipulations, syncopated figures, and supportive ostinatos. Movement three turns away completely from harmonic patterning to a chromatic, dark-colored fugue. In the end movement Johanson uses the first movement's theme as the springboard for his main theme, and then, to support the argument, he brings back the opening of the first movement to usher in the coda. The formal focus of this plan provides not only a cyclic binder but dramatic immediacy.

Johnsen, Hallvard (1916–)

DUOS

- **Suite for Flute and Horn, Op. 41**

Titles can sometimes conflict with inner content. What is expected in the four parts of Johnsen's Suite through the movement headings is not exactly provided. These are not pat, standard formations—especially with the expressionistic colors derived from the harmonic style.

The Pastorale flows, but as it moves, built-in foliated rubatos form shadows on the sound horizon. The Elegy is certainly expressive, but it is just as certainly pitch-active, especially in the flute. The Humoresque gets involved with a rhythmic comprehensiveness that puts little kinks into the whimsicality. Nothing wrong with these concepts, but the governing (titled) depictions given the music are truly edited.

Only the final Canzona is permitted its song.

It ends with a minor sixth. The previous three movements conclude with dissonant pitch combinations.

- **Suite for Two Trumpets, Op. 33**

Although Johnsen uses small forms for his four movements, the recapitulations are considerably varied. These remove any tendency of squareness from the structures. Nor is there any squareness to the pungent, always chromatically energetic harmonies and counterpoints.

Each part of the duo is treated to varying degrees of metamorphosis. Slow tempos are found in the opening and closing movements; the faster-paced materials are in the center.

SEXTET

- **Wind Quintet with Vibraphone, Op. 45**

The repertoire of 20th-century chamber music is filled with unusual instrumental combinations. Sometimes these combinations are created merely for the sake of ostentatious display. But that's not the case here. There is certainly no attitudinizing represented in Johnsen's sextet—the striving for color that can cut against the timbre qualities (for the wind quintet the plural is correct) is a welcome idea. However, the vibraphone is given a subsidiary part at best. Still, its reserved role does not warrant the statement by Bjarne Kortsen, the important Norwegian musicologist, that "the vibraphone can easily be omitted without there arising any feeling of loss."

Johnsen has no inhibitions about stretching his tonalities with plentiful chromatic bends. There is also a good amount of thematic transfer within the movements, culminating in a healthy quotation from the beginning of the sextet as preamble to the coda of the final movement.

Johnson, Hunter (1906–)

DUO

- **Serenade for Flute and Clarinet (1937)**

Tonal materials, arranged with contemporary handling so that no clichés halt the flow and the interweaving of the two voices. Metrical fluidity prevails as well, especially in the central part of this freely formed three-part duo. Johnson's short piece is both good sounding and well proportioned.

TRIO

- **Trio for Flute, Oboe, and Piano (1954)**

Classical orientation does not lead to dogmatic propriety. The shifting and freeing of the materials in Johnson's three-movement work are illustrative of a 20th-century romantic viewpoint. No effects spoil the polished texture of Johnson's Trio; the substances are all musically (and stylistically) meaningful.

There is sonata detail in the first part of the piece. Variational transformations are the strength of the middle (slow) movement. The finale has punch in its balanced presentation of exposition, development, recapitulation, and coda. The activity of the Trio is always stimulated and supported by shifts of meter and tempo.

Johnson, Lockrem (1924–77)

DUOS

- *Sonata breve* (Sonata No. 2) for Violin and Piano, Op. 26

Composed in 1948 and revised twice afterward, Johnson's piece then won one of two prizes given by the National Federation of

Music Clubs in its 1949 contests (the other was for his Chaconne, Op. 29, for piano). He then proceeded to make still another (fourth) revision, in February 1953.

What is appealing and novel about Johnson's piece is its lean directness and its concomitant compactness. A sonata is a sonata is a 137-measure one-chunk totality as Lockrem Johnson perceived the form. An approximate six-minute performing time span brings thoughts of a sonatina, but this is a sonata, clearly specified as to length by the "brief" indication in the title.

Its tonal polarity is firmly in A, with which the music begins and ends. The progress and development within are constant. On the way contrasting data are picked up, but basically the music is of single projection, minus any monitoring by way of coded, prescribed design, minus the usual demand of recapitulation. Metronomically there are a great number of changes, the fastest toward the latter part of the work, but these are inner-speed developments within the total development. This is chamber music of sensitive impact.

■ Sonata No. 1 for Cello and Piano, Op. 33

One can trust this composer constantly to consider form in a new light. His initial cello sonata does not disappoint. In the first of the pair of movements a three-note motive lights the fire for an illuminating development. The close of the movement is like an O. Henryish unexpected twist. Each instrument is given a cadenza, and with perfect balance the piano adds little supports to the cello's major manifestation and then the tactic is reversed. Though freely detailed, the cadenzas are not mere displays—they bear a relationship to the previous material of the movement.

The cadenza impression carries over to the next movement, in the form of a dialogue; the cello is proclamatory, not virtuosic, the piano is given disjunct tremolandos. This entire section is an introduction to the principal Allegro con spirito, a gay, breezy, folksy music, with abundant sharp counterpoint, but sharply within the general style. Within the sonata treatment of this movement there is a passage of sculpted dissonance: the cello ascending in pizzicato, the piano descending in two parts. Since there is a recapitulation section, it is heard twice—and well worth it.

The difference between the two movements presents a stylistic bipartition. This ramification is no creative error. It is, once again, Johnson's consideration of fresh formal productivity, specifying an overall element that is in addition to the specialness of each of the movements.

■ Sonata No. 2 for Cello and Piano (or Harpsichord), Op. 42

Form is freed in this duo. There are contrasting themes in the opening movement, but there is avoidance of exact compartmenting of the music. Within the total the shapes are precisely detailed—the first theme tends to descend in its short paragraphing, the second theme is marked by sweeping legatos. In the middle movement an augmented interval acts as a colorative agogic punctuation among the pitches. In scoring almost the entire first half of the movement is for the piano alone. Pace moves with motoric regularity in the final part of the work. The surprise is that the motility suddenly turns into a Fuga burlesca.

The movements end quietly. Each movement is balanced and yet is never structurally predictable. This is further evidence that none of Lockrem Johnson's music is directed by rigid system.

■ *Sonata rinverdita* (Sonata No. 3) for Violin and Piano, Op. 38

There is no compact English equivalent for *rinverdita*, which comes from the Italian *rinverdire*, meaning "to make green again." (One writer states this means Johnson's work is "a sort of 'spring' sonata.") But there is a definite link to the form itself in reference to Johnson's choice of title. As in his second sonata for violin and piano *(see above)* Johnson refuses to belabor his points. He synthesizes his arguments and they become more potent thereby, runs the sonata course in about six minutes (the same performing time as his previous violin and piano sonata), and avoids the stuttering and stammering that so often embarrass musical action. All these comprise the meaning of *rinverdita* here—sonata form reassessed and revitalized, thus with a fresh ("green") attitude.

This turns out to be a structure of positive symmetry—a moderate-tempo exposition, a middle section twice as slow in tempo, and a da capo recapitulation. In this respect Johnson's new-look sonata seems to equal old ternary form. The difference is that the B section is not of simple contrast but full-scale. The other difference is the development and continuity disclosed in the A section. The plan has additional distinctions. There are a pair of themes in the first part; the piano alone presents the initial one, the violin enters with the second one. These thematic roles are maintained by the respective instruments. Eventually, in the latter part of the first section, they combine (and, of course, are heard again in the representation). In the middle section the string texture is totally different. Only there is the violin given two- and three-part chords, in a total that produces defined registration.

Johnson's sonata is beautifully iced with dissonance. Its sound is indeed a fresh one.

Johnson, Robert Sherlaw (1932–)

DUO

- **Sonata for Alto Flute and Cello**

All the bases are touched in the three movements of this Sonata for an exceedingly rare combination of instruments. Movement one is for the cello alone, movement two is for the alto flute alone, and both play together in the final movement.

Solo for Cello vividly simulates two-voice writing, with a good amount of contrastive registering, especially with the lower voice using the C and G open strings. *Solo for Flute* is also disjunctively written, but with plenty of suppleness. (The movement can be played as an entity. In that case a C flute can be substituted.) The third movement *(Duo)* has a relationship to the previous pair of unaccompanied solos. It is thoroughly tense, serious stuff, but heated by its rhythmic detail. Thus, a 5/4 measure is defined as 5+5+5+5/16, a 7/8 measurement is defined as 7+7/16.

QUARTET

- **String Quartet No. 2 (1969)**

A seemingly serial breeze moves through the score. But no technical crusading for dodecaphony is proposed. Johnson's writing deals with panchromatic data, and virtuosically so. Simultaneousness of rhythmic sets within a given time unit are mingled in with the contents, giving a linear vacillation that purposely erases any (monotonous) pulse regularity. These—such as 5:4, 7:8, and 9:8, mixed with metrical assignments such as 31/2/4 and 41/2/4 (Johnson indicates these as 3+♪/4 and 4+♪/4)—finally join together in polyrhythmy. One example: Two measures of 4/4 are partnered with single consecutive measures of 3/4, 3/8, 3/4, and 1/8, with the second and third of these further complexed by a 5:3 rhythmic simultaneity. Thus a second layer of virtuosity is placed on the music.

Sonata form is found in the first movement but not ordered in the traditional sense. There is contrasting material and total balance and that equates sonata form no matter how one approaches the design. A number of sustained sound layers joined with recitativelike passages mark the slow movement. In the final movement the principal technique is rhythmic interaction: soloistic, combined, and antiphonalized. Expansively wrought music, this—a music of nervous excitation that concludes on a soft dynamic level.

QUINTET

- **Quintet for Clarinet, Violin, Viola, Cello, and Piano (1974)**

Johnson's Quintet is full of dodecaphonic diction, abounding in extremely busy but always discriminative phrases. This especially concerns the final (fourth) movement, where there is considerable activity in the instrumental lines though the metronomic pace ($\text{\textquarternote}$= 76) is otherwise.

Although the twelve-tone soil is tilled in the same manner that many other composers have long since plowed it, everything is not barren, particularly the variational concept of the third movement. Movement one is developed from a pair of phrases that move in opposite direction. The force of rhythmic activity (emphasized in most of Johnson's music) embellishes the lines in the slow movement. Further, treatment of pulse (such as measures in 6+$\text{\texteighthnote}$/8, 4+$\text{\texteighthnote}$/8, plus a variety of metrical conditions) make the music supple. It is also quite muscular when the three string instruments are combined in tutti formation against other detail in the clarinet and piano.

Indeed, Johnson's piece has no smug dodecaphonic religiosity. The strength of the

music is its sober emotiveness. This is far different from a sober music governed by creative self-denial due to technical stylistic restrictions.

SEXTET

- *Triptych* **for Flute, Clarinet, Violin, Cello, Piano, and Percussion (Marimba, Vibraphone, Three Chinese Blocks, Three Cymbals, and Tam-tam) (1973)**

Johnson titles the first two pieces "Catenary 1" and "Catenary 2." The music only loosely matches (in both cases) a part of the definition of the word, namely: "the curve assumed by a perfectly flexible inextensible cord of uniform density and cross section hanging freely from two fixed points." The two end (read "fixed") points are reflected by the thinnest textures of each piece. In "Catenary 2" there is a direct equality of pitch selection between the first and final measures—the vibraphone's chords in the former case are horizontally spelled out by the flute in the latter case. (There is no valid reason for a composer not to explain the reason for the use of a special [thoroughly nonmusical] title. For that matter, one would expect that a publisher's editor would demand an explanation to be included in the score. Johnson and his publisher [Oxford University Press] are both guilty in this case for a total lack of information.)

The third part is a "Procession." Johnson's conception does not rhythmically picture a parade. Once in a while a rhythmic idea comes through, but mainly this is music absent of pomp and filled with rhapsodic circumstance.

Johnson, Roger (1941–)

QUINTET

- **Woodwind Quintet (1970)**

A one-movement conception, serially styled, though the row is far less than the entire twelve tones, but a four-pitch series. It is developed in three types of setting: chordal, linear, and *senza misura*. But Johnson is no academic graybeard. Included in his work are some aleatoric opportunities for the performers.

SEXTETS

- *Ritual Music* **for Six Horns**

For the greater part, Johnson's *Ritual Music* is devoted to the formulary of performer participation in the free choice of rhythms and pitch arrangements. Still, aleatoric attitudes are restricted since all the pitches used are defined by the composer. Though the composition's conclusions cannot be determined the tonal textures remain fixed. There is no doubt that the contrastive, precisely ordered measures will be fully recognized, since they cover decided chords and chordal polyphony. In no manner can the free measures result in this style.

No actual ritual is in mind; the composer requests an "air of severity and deliberation . . . a quality of solemnity."

- **Suite for Six Horns**

Johnson doesn't write like this anymore. Atonality, electronic instrumentation, and some aleatoric concepts are his current creative interests—all a far cry from this fresh tonalism.

So, no technical polemics are illustrated here. Johnson's three-movement piece is richly consonant and presents three formats. The first is totally a delicate two-voice canon (Prologue), the imitation always in echo (muted) form. The

Chorale is followed by a medieval-like Fugato that is concluded in homophonic style.

Johnston, Ben (1926–)

DUOS

- **Duo for Flute and Double Bass (1963)**

Lyric serialism that holds fast throughout the three movements—Prelude, "Interim," and "Flight." Strongly colored by the contrastive properties of the flute and double bass to begin with, the music provides additional sonorous sensation by the use of microtones.

Rhythmic variety in full. In movement one there are polyrhythmic arrangements and in the middle movement the patterns are based on durations drawn from proportional notation. Movement three is principally depicted asymmetrically.

- **Duo for Two Violins**

The pitch detail is totally opposite to the standard tempered tuning, with twelve equally divided pitches in each octave and duplicated in lower and higher equivalents. *(See below*: String Quartet No. 2 for further related commentary.)

A four-voice Fuga begins the Duo. Movement two is an Aria, totally muted and totally supported and colored by fingered tremolandos. A motoric, metrically changing Toccata climaxes the work.

Obviously, only the most dedicated violinists would spend the time to conquer the intonational makeup Johnston proposes. At least, through training, string players are preconditioned to some of the differences nullified by equal temperament. In the case of the sensitive performer such training means that all C-sharps and D-flats, all F-sharps and G-flats, etc., are not played identically. Johnston's Duo would certainly widen the performers' pitch horizon if they are willing to tackle its truly monstrous problems of intonation.

QUARTET

- **String Quartet No. 2 (1964)**

Johnston's quartet utilizes pure intervals (the opposite of the well-tempered dozen) plus minute microtones. Such pitch distinctions define a very lucid and bright new sound world. With this method, enharmonics (D-sharp equals E-flat, A-sharp equals B-flat, etc.) don't exist, and in fact, the term is a technical abomination. Fluctuations in intervallic movement create an intense quality, as in the finale's beginning, where a line curves up and down a quarter tone and then dips a three-quarter-tone distance. Pitches one-tenth of a tone below "normal" and sounds a fifth of a tone apart have a fascinating color, but these pitch choices are not decorative but integral to the music.

There are three movements in the close to fifteen-minute total of the quartet. The first is a whimsical, wispy Scherzo with extremely contrastive portions. Movement two sounds contrapuntal, but this is the result of vertical dismemberment. Fantasy rules the finale. It is in this division that the micropitches reflect their greatest impact.

Jolas, Betsy (1926–)

DUO

- **Remember for English horn (or Viola) and Cello (1971)**

Jolas's piece is a tribute to the French composer Jean-Pierre Guézec (1934–71). It concentrates its materials within a 41/2-minute total, is minus bar lines, and is guided by specifically indicated time spans. Most of it is dynamically downgraded and extremely atmo-

spheric. The last is carried out by dozens of consecutive harmonic sounds by the cello.

QUARTET

- **Quatuor III (Nine Etudes) (Two Violins, Viola, and Cello) (1973)**

A good-size sampler of string techniques that more or less adhere to the descriptive headings. The sequence is in nine parts: "Bowing," "Vibrato," "Aleatory Structures," "Frills and Bowed Tremolo," "Harmonics," "Multiple Stops," "Aleatory Structures around a held C," "Pizzicato," and "Summing Up."

Jolas indicates that part seven "is in memory of Purcell's *Fancy* on one note." There, as elsewhere, the zest is for a particular sound quality more than thematic detail. Still, the logic and rhetoric are positive within the patterned colors and lines.

Jolivet, André (1905–74)

DUOS

- **Alla rustica: Divertissement for Flute and Harp (1963)**

The divisional aspects of Jolivet's pithy piece are clearly detailed by mood and tempo. Part one is mainly a filigreed recitative on-go by the flute in adagio pace. This leads into a peasantlike dance in allegro aperto speed. The essence bears out the main title: *In a Rustic Manner*. The tempo definition likewise fulfills the style: *aperto* meaning open, frank, and straightforward, an instruction for energetic delivery of the music in strict time. The dance demands this, though there is plenty of *spumante* (sparkle) in the fundamental tune that sweeps through it. With a choice chromatic underpinning Jolivet peppers the dissonant tonalism that embraces the music.

Alla rustica is beautifully communicative. It is far different from the mystic incantational premises of a large part of Jolivet's earlier output. The only formula here is warmth and attractive directness.

- **Chant de Linos for Flute and Piano (1944)**

See below: Chant de Linos for Flute, Violin, Viola, Cello, and Harp (1944)

- **Sérénade for Two Guitars (1956)**

No pedantic response to instrumental demeanor or mechanical regard for form is to be expected from Jolivet. The Serenade addresses separate national styles in each of the four movements, but in directing his attention thus, Jolivet retains his own creative personality.

Only the first movement's heading gives any hint of the music's contents, a Praeludio e canzona that evokes Italy; the material is colored by harmonics. Movement two (Allegro trepidante) and movement four (Con allegria) are concerned with Spain and America, respectively. Both are percussive and dissonant; a borrowing from Manuel de Falla appears in the former, while the latter luxuriates in jazz. The Andante malinconico (part three) has a bittersweet cordiality toward French melody.

- **Sonata for Flute and Piano (1958)**

No lace cuffs on this sonata dress. Even with the rather languid moves of the first movement and the staid situation of the second there is an inner intensity, a chromatic massage that heats up the music. The duo is plashy at times, rich elsewhere, unshackled in other places, but always there is intensity.

The tempos are clear and descriptive of the contents of the sonata's three parts. Movement one is marked "fluid," and if it sounds somewhat pastoral and gentle the gentility is edged.

The second movement is headed "grave" and builds texturally from unaccompanied flute to nine-voice strength. Movement three is indicated as "violent." That it is. The music is a discharge of nervous energy, the chordal indents are percussive, the rhythms are nail-pointed in their determinative arrangements.

- **Sonatine for Flute and Clarinet (1961)**

Structurally speaking, no textbook outlines are followed here. Jolivet's duo is of unordinary format and contains colorful and responsive interplay of the two instruments in all particulars.

Movement one is a ternary-designed piece, its midsection devoted to a good amount of linear activity. Movement two's tempo is quasi cadenza. Quite odd, twice so, since the music is precisely metered, chirps along at a nice scherzo pace, rhythmically profiled and focused.

Individuality comes to the fore again in the last movement. It begins with an Intermezzo. This is not an entity, but a suave, legato-based idea, propped with short, trill-like figures that serve as a part of the finale, a Vivace in which the paired voices are pushed unceasingly. Eventually there is a speed-up and the music goes into presto, and to maintain the excitement another speed boost opens the throttle totally to a prestissimo. This progressively faster scanning of a sound landscape is fascinating, the more so in that it is accomplished by only a pair of wind instruments.

- **Sonatine for Oboe and Bassoon (1963)**

Like the Sonatine for Flute and Clarinet *(see above),* this duo also exemplifies a cut out of the ordinary in terms of its forms. It also shares with the flute and clarinet sonatine the same simplified creative attitude. Not that it is *light* music, but rather lighter in weight (considerably so) in comparison with Jolivet's symphonies and concertos. It is Jolivet with gloves on.

No loss in effectiveness occurs thereby.

Three distinct formations style this oboe and bassoon piece. First, an Ouverture, marked with increasing rhythmic activity in the final portion. Second, a Récitatif, wherein ornamental figures help project the instrumental soliloquy. The final Ostinato deviates from the general norm; it is not built from a persistent rhythmic figure but from rhythmic continuity. A general technical device, including metrical ambivalence, thus substitutes for single emphasis. The result is telling.

TRIOS

■ *Pastorales de Noël (Christmas Pastorals)* **for Flute (or Violin), Bassoon (or Viola or Cello), and Harp (1943)**

At first Jolivet's work completely rejected facile methods, had more than a kinship with expressionism, was devoted to almost cosmic, esoteric musical philosophy, a type determinedly atonal, a probing, as it were, of subconscious trauma. In his later compositions the style changed radically. There is such wide divergence between this work, composed in 1943, and the quartet *(see below)*, written in 1934 that it is extremely difficult to believe the two compositions did not come from different composers. The style in this three-instrument work is tonal, the textures thin instead of thick, the musical picturing of the recesses of semipsychoneuroticism are replaced by a partial theological viewpoint. But Jolivet composed his *Christmas Pastorals* in secular style; there is no beseeching his Lord, there is no preaching.

The *Pastorales de Noël* consist of four movements. "L'Etoile" ("The Star"), the first of the set, is restrained, written simply in a sectional manner; it waits for the very end before stating its climax. "Les Mages" ("The Wise Men") is scored with convincing regard for soloistic equality. The bassoon announces the theme;

the flute replies, while the harp accompanies with an ostinato. Movement three, titled "La Vierge et l'Enfant" ("The Virgin and the Child"), is in clear waltz style. Rhythmic plans, however, place most stress on second beats, which hold over to the third pulse—a suspended rhythm, therefore, rather than one of concrete definition. The consideration of the subject matter is happy, but not overly so—simplicity is maintained. The last section is an "Entrée et Danse des Bergers" ("Entrance and Dance of the Shepherds"). Jolivet weighs his balances in this case just as aptly. The supple introduction is in triple meter; the fast dance is in contrastive duple beat with one theme reappearing in slightly changed guise.

■ **Suite for String Trio (1930)**

The string-instrument landscape is full of action and involved counterpoint. The chromatic expansiveness is intense. This is fully represented in the inner pair of movements, Aria I and Aria II. For example, the opening of the former presents three different themes simultaneously.

Packed line writing pertains to the Prélude as well. The reverse is followed in the concluding part of the movement which is totally chordal and relaxed. But there is little relaxation in the other end movement, a Fugue en rondeau. There, polyphonic heaviness is emphasized as is soloism, with a sizable cadenza for the violin over a sustained G-sharp in the cello.

QUARTET

■ **String Quartet No. 1 (1934)**

Jolivet's quartet is not purveyed by the twelve-tone system, though very often the sonorities seem to be governed by such technique. The excursions of sound are exceedingly free—without tonality, but magnetized to specific double-tone (intervallic) orbits around which the separate movements fluctuate. The sections of the quartet depart from projections of a vacillating augmented fifth and arrive ultimately at the adduction of this same interval, lowered into a more simply framed perfect fifth. It is this spatial measurement that forms the denominator, the crux and axis of this quartet; just as a defined tonality is the pivot of a Mozart work; as a row of tones is the axle of a Schoenberg serial composition. Thus Jolivet's theoretical data are as carefully organized as the theorems of those who use pandiatonic orientation, as controlled a conception as that of composers who pattern their works by employing fluid tonality that sprays from a central source.

The first movement has a church music title, "Volontaire" ("Voluntary"), which is rather foreign to the music itself. It begins with a unison theme made from a horizontal triad. This poses an augmented fifth from B-flat as the longest-sounding tones on its extremes. Melodic movement is very complex, likewise all associates to it; but the augmented interval predominates (a set of chained-pyramided trills, for example, clutches this interval). When the movement moves to its conclusion, the perfect-fifth interval engages the cadence.

The second section, "Allant" ("Moving"), displays immediately the intervallic motto. The movement is in three parts; the beginning of the second of these is used for the final cadence. But while the chorale of the initial section is topped by the augmented interval, that of the recapitulation is lowered into the perfect fifth. The final section, "Vif" ("Fast"), again exhibits the fifth, around which other tones force themselves in opposition. Activity and motion are just short of the fatigue mark, checked by expert concentration on line and detail. In the final measures each instrument of the quartet sounds the important perfect fifth, forming a polysyllabic quintuple harmony of interlocked intervals in powerful dissonant sonority. Jolivet

has proven his thesis.

Style, in any art, must be in absolute manner if the conception, regardless of type, is to be one of clear and direct expression. If Jolivet expatiates with some tautology on the most concise of musical materials—a set of two sounds—he can be forgiven because he is serious and does not stray from the subject. Furthermore, he dresses his thoughts just as expertly—as well as with a type of overembellishment that parallels the rhetoric. The color potential is always used, sometimes gilded in effect. There are innumerable glissandos, some so small spanned that a specific, microtonal effect takes place. (Though all glissandos consist of the most minute demarcations of successive fractional sounds, when a glissando covers only the distance of a half tone the effect ceases to be that of a glissando, or even a portamento, and *implies*, instead, the sound of a quarter tone.) The glassy whine of ponticello is used in all forms, including trills and glissando. The opposite type (playing on the fingerboard—sul tasto) is also available in plentiful amounts. In addition the effect of poco ponticello is utilized. This half a portion of "catty" sound needs mathematical bowing on the part of performers, and, to be recognized, ears opened to the keenest point of sensitivity on the part of listeners. If Jolivet's quartet is heard and reheard sufficiently it will have its believers.

QUINTET

- *Chant de Linos* for Flute, Violin, Viola, Cello, and Harp (1944)

This work exists in two versions. Originally Jolivet composed the *Chant de Linos* for a competition at the Paris Conservatoire. It called for flute and piano. Later he reset the composition for the above quintet medium. Though the piece strongly emphasizes the flute the other instruments' participation in the proceedings is never mundane.

The writing can be classified as non-Germanic postromantic poematicism, but in Jolivetian fashion rhapsodic fantasy becomes the creative reasoning as the sections blend one onto the other. The piece moves from a cadenza-recitative into a "Funeral Lamentation" (the quintet's title is derived from an ancient Greek funeral ritual), which is followed by a portion described as "the mourning song interrupted by cries," another cadenza, a lively dance set in septuple meter, a condensed recapitulation of the opening themes, and a sonorous conclusion.

SEPTET

- *Rapsodie à sept (Rhapsody for Seven Instruments)* for **Violin, Double Bass, Clarinet, Bassoon, Trumpet, Trombone, and Percussion (Suspended Cymbal, Charleston Cymbal, Tam-tam, Tambourine, Small and Large Side Drums, Military Drum, Bass Drum, Triangle, Wood Block, Three Chinese Blocks, Cow Bell, and Sleigh Bells) (1957)**

The instrumentation of the *Rapsodie à sept* is the same as that chosen by Stravinsky for his *Histoire du soldat*, but the language of the piece is far different. There is some rub-off from jazz, but the facts are those of a roving commission of sound and fancy. There is no mechanical response to form, but rather composed improvisation—as in the last movement ("Incisive"). In the first two-thirds of the work ("Resolute" and "Hiératique") there is an insistence on gliding sounds, a link from one place to the next. Thus the material is unified despite Jolivet's various sound complexes.

Joly, Denis (1906–)

TRIO

- **Trio for Oboe, Clarinet, and Bassoon**

Joly's four-movement piece presents clear, contemporary classicism with interesting interplay that removes any academic mnemonics. The scoring is direct and there are no supercolorful effects or fallout that destroy meaning.

The Prelude is a bright, totally contrapuntal piece. Direct contrast is offered in the Scherzetto, with its pert rhythmic basis. Still, there is a good helping of polyphonic play in the movement. Movement three is a Madrigal, where again counterpoint rules supreme.

Joly's final movement is a Farandole. But this street dance does not stay in place. Persistently, its animated measures, in the dance's standard 6/8 time, are interrupted by quintuple-pulse measures, four times by lengthening of the metrical total to nine, plus single measures in 8/8 and 7/8. Contemporaneity embellishes dance solidity in this manner. And such stimulation is further enhanced, once again, by a heady amount of productive polyphonic writing.

Joly, Suzanne

QUARTET

- *Sequences* for **Saxophone Quartet (Soprano, Alto, Tenor, and Baritone Saxophones)**

A six-part programmatic assortment for an assortment of saxophones. Joly's sketches (the shortest is 1:20 in length, the longest is timed at 2:30) of the art world are gift-wrapped with attention-grabbing titles.

The quartet begins with a two-part portrayal:

"Générique-Atelier d'Artiste" ("Generic-Artist's Studio"). The generality of the latter's workplace is described by short solo lines via three of the saxophones (the alto remains silent). Lots of eighth-note work pictures the activity in the studio. A bit of the introduction is used for a coda. Then follows "Modèles et Rapins" ("Models and Art Students") who concentrate their efforts in waltz time.

Part three is a three-part "Mobiles," with flitting figures the principal point of the music's action. Part four is titled "Carrière" ("Career"), identified by combining a smooth line with the opposite (meaning accomplishment with simultaneous problems?). "Exotique" ("Exotic") presents a solo slithery line with three-pitched arpeggios split between the three other instruments. The finale is a "Cortège (Beaux-Arts)" ("Parade [Fine Arts]"). March tempo, of course; no oompah, but little fanfares and some flounce, frisk, and frolic.

Jonák, Zdeněk (1917–)

DUO

- *Mim (The Mime)* **for Flute and Harp (1965)**

Lightly gestured music that ping-pongs its way between the instruments. The contents are nourished by clarity and mini ostinatos.

An introduction gives separate cadenzas, the one for the harp swooping up and down in piquant fourths. In keeping with the title objective there are some tempo shifts from the principal allegro vivo. Another harp cadenza appears later and again includes consecutive fourths, this time in a scalewise run. Good show all around.

Jones, Charles (1910–)

DUO

- **Sonatina for Violin and Piano (1942)**

Jones's duo shows that he has reaped the benefits of the swirling tonal combines and rhythmic riches of Darius Milhaud. (Understandable, since Jones enjoyed a long association with Milhaud at both Mills College and the Aspen Music School.) This is a Canadian-born, naturalized American's view of French pantonality and rhythmic freedom.

Movement one is mainly in 6/8, but all types of pulsatile permutations are used as synonyms for it, as well as for foreshortening and lengthening the measure. The same implications of modern-differentiated rhythms surround the slow movement—three pulses mingle with and against two pulses in jointly combined rhythms of 4/8 and 12/16. The form is as free; the music sings, but the punctuations are few, what with this fluidic rhythm. These same calculations occur even more so in the final movement. There, but few measures contain duple or triple pulse regularities.

QUARTETS

- *Lyric Waltz Suite: Essays in the Poetic and Lyric Aspects of the Waltz* **for Flute, Oboe, Clarinet, and Bassoon (1948)**

Two sets of three lines each from Wallace Stevens's "Ideas of Order" preface Jones's woodwind quartet: "The truth is that there comes a time / When we can mourn no more over music / That is so much motionless sound." "There comes a time when the waltz / Is no longer a mode of desire, a mode / Of revealing desire and is empty of shadows."

There are four waltzes in the set, all, of course, in 3/4 time. After the fourth one the first waltz is replayed "in a somewhat faster tempo." Bearing out the explanatory title, Jones's waltzes consist of linear interweave, the voicing rounded, the 1–2–3 pulse pit-a-pat not present. A delight to the ear with its pandiatonic style. Movement three, with its principal line interrupted several times, is especially colorful.

- **String Quartet No. 2 (1944)**

Combined with a decided consideration of pandiatonic style are some bitonal elements as well as polytonal splicings. There is considerable attention to asymmetricality and rhythmic criss-cross. In the Moderato opening movement the combine of 3/4 (triple pulse) with 6/8 (duple pulse) tinges the material. Hemiola appears also in the final (fourth) movement. In the Allegro second movement bimetricality is used. Broad-pulse measurements are basic to the choralelike seriousness of the Adagio, which has 7/4, 4/2 (8/4), 5/2, and 9/4 meters. The stamina of this slow movement's substances is just as exciting as the more nervous moves of the other three movements.

Criticism is due for the production of the published score. Both the title on the cover and on the first inside page read "String Quartet (1944)." The quartet's number (2) is not found save on the top of the first page of music. Partial titling on a score's cover is unfair to the composer and misleading to the potential buyer.

- **String Quartet No. 6 (1970)**

Fantasy proportions in this one-movement, fifteen-minute work. The father of it all is neoclassic diction, but here extended into enlarged chromaticism and the use of jagged intervallic punctuations.

The music is acutely colored. Pizzicato is both normal and heavy and there are passages of flying left-hand plucked sounds. Jones calls for loads of harmonics, both natural and artificial. To obtain an open-string pizzicato sound on E-flat, twice the second violin uses scordatura, tuning the D string up a half tone. And, in one place, the first violin sounds pitches without the bow or plucking by applying strong pressure with the fingers of the left hand.

Jones, Collier (1928–)

QUINTET

- *Four Movements for Five Brass* (Two Trumpets, Horn, Trombone, and Tuba) (1957)

Hedonistic flavor marks many woodwind pieces, especially those written by French composers. A carbon-copy transfer of such style is represented here in a brass quintet composed by an American. Once known, this suite has all of the ingredients for instant and lasting popularity.

Jones's music has a saucy Poulencian vocabulary, jazzy jargon, and Stravinskian bite, all packaged with neoclassic clarity. A short, pert motive moves through the Introduction and March. In "Pretentions," chorale-type music is contrasted to unpretentious, pitch-static rhythmic passages. Asymmetric detail always brightens sonic syntax and it is of aid in the Finale–Allegro. It is doubly potent in the preceding Waltz. Only a few triple-beat oompah's are used in this conception of the dance, which two-steps and expands into quadruple beat as well. Jones's disregard of traditional rhythmic format is another example of creative light sophistication.

Jones, Kelsey (1922–)

DUO

- **Introduction and Fugue for Violin and Piano (1959)**

Rhapsodic bravura, and that description also applies to the Fugue, which bypasses staid contrapuntalism. This American-born, Canadian-taught (also by Nadia Boulanger) composer knows the way to invent exciting, brilliant sonorities, and to invigorate a form that is often broad and sturdy but plain and formulabound at the same time.

The Fugue is projected with rhythmic effervescence, and has two expositions, the second one presents the subject inverted. Between these a powerful violin cadenza cuts into the fugue's episodes. A vivid portrayal.

Jones, Richard (fl. 1740)

DUOS

- **Suites for Violin and Basso Continuo, Op. 3**

  - No. 1, in A Major
  - No. 2, in G Minor
  - No. 3, in D Major
  - No. 4, in B-flat Major

These four works are from the second of two collections of music for violin and basso continuo by this English violinist-composer. According to the editor, Gwilym Beechey, the Suites "were published about 1740 or just before." The heading for the set was "Six Suites of Lessons."

Faithfully executed music in baroque *sonata da camera* (chamber sonata) style. There are several unifying factors. Each suite is in five movements, each maintains the indicated tonality throughout, and each begins with a Preludio that features sixteenth-note figurations. While the order of the dances included varies from suite to suite, all four works contain a Giga and a Minuet. No forms are repeated save in the B-flat-major opus, where there are successive Aria depictions serving as movements two and three. Sarabanda, Gavot, and Corrente forms are represented, and in the D-major suite there is a March.

Jong, Marinus de (1891–)

QUINTETS

- *Aphoristic Triptych* for **Wind Quintet, Op. 82b**

Though quoting aphorisms by Klinger, Auffenberg, and Eliot (Christian names are not given so exactly which Klinger and which Eliot are being quoted are not known) as its basis, Jong's music is not precisely of terse formulation. (The performance time of the three pieces is given as about eleven minutes.)

However, the general sonic characteristic of each is clearly detailed. In the first, noted as a "Character Piece," the music is decisive and declarative, portrayed in a moderate tempo with resolute rhythmic markings. The Auffenberg quote is matched by a Scherzo. Set in the usual A–B–A format, it has a different type of coda. After the recapitulation a sixteen-measure quote from the B section and a six-measure snippet from the A section wrap up matters. The third aphorism is titled "Fata Morgana," depicted by a swirling, allegretto-paced music.

The idea behind the conception removes any type of routine from Jong's suite. It is certainly listenable music of worth without any technical complicatedness.

- *Humoristic Suite on Old Netherland Folk Songs* for Brass Quintet (Two Trumpets, Horn, Trombone, and Tuba), Op. 128

For "humoristic" read "light" or "gay," which is closer to the mark than to expect a farcical or even a drollish musical concoction. But quickly let it be said that Jong's opus has artistic taste and brass gusto in presenting its homespun facts.

The first three of the five movements each announces the folk theme and proceeds with a pair of variations. In the first movement, "Jan, mijne man, is altijd ziek" ("Jan, my man, is always ill"), the principal tune is steadfastly adhered to in the variations. In movement two, "Franse ratten, rolt uw matten" ("French rats, roll from your mats"), and movement three, "Als wij soldaten, te samen, te velde gaan" ("When we soldiers go down the fields together"), the first variation is somewhat demure and the theme stands out boldly and clearly. The second variation in each case is a bit more developed but without any brash departure from the thematic base.

Movements four and five bypass variational treatment. "Als de boer een paar kloefkens heeft" ("If when the farmer has a couple of horseshoes") and "St. Joris, oft den Reus" are accessible, lively expressions, both in duple (6/8) pulse, both tuneful delights. These Jong-seasoned folk tunes will positively charm the ear and brighten the spirit.

- **Wind Quintet No. 3:** *on Old Netherland Folk Songs,* Op. 157

Six folk songs are used in Jong's three-movement composition for flute, oboe, clarinet, horn, and bassoon. The folk melodies (no titles are given) are the product of research by Florimond Van Duyze (1843–1910), a Belgian music scholar and composer. Van Duyze published a number of collections of old Netherland vocal

music, the most important being the four-volume *Het oude nederlandsche Lied,* begun in 1903 and completed in 1908. It is from this compilation that Jong selected his thematic materials.

A type of sectionalism pervades the opening movement where two of the folk songs are used. The oboe states the G-minor theme for the set of six variations comprising the middle movement. Not until the final variation does the G-minor tonality change to G major. The final Rondo is built from three different folk songs. General jauntiness is the descriptive term for this part of the quintet.

Jongen, Joseph (1873–1953)

DUOS

- *Dance lente (Slow Dance)* for Flute and Harp (or Piano)

The presence and urbanity of Debussy is to be heard in this Belgian composer's piece. A duo in total instruments but practically a pure solo situation for the flute, with harp backup. The use of the more dynamic piano lessens the effectiveness of the music.

- **Prelude, Habanera, and Allegro for Double Bass and Piano, Op. 106**

The three pieces are linked together, with only a smidgen of a halt before the final Allegro. The Prelude is recitative-flushed by the double bass, with the piano held in second place. This inequality is not present in the sensuous, slow Cuban dance that is used in part two. Each instrument has a go at the main theme of the Habanera before proceeding to the Allegro. This final part has a rhapsodic, somewhat scherzando quality. Jongen does not hamper it with self-conscious formality.

■ **Sonata for Flute and Piano, Op. 77**

Jongen's work is cast in the usual four-movement mold but avoids academic confinement. The first movement, titled Prélude, has the moves and strengths of sonata form. Movement two (marked Très animé) spreads itself over rondo territory. It has a certain sprightliness of texture and, of course, of pace, and its phrases emphasize a forward-pushing quality.

The large, usual slow movement is replaced by music in moderate tempo. It is set in a large ternary format, with the outer parts flexible in pulse (most often alternating quadruple with duple meter), and is severely conjunct in its melodic lines. The finale is a Gigue.

■ **Sonata-Duo for Violin and Cello, Op. 109**

Jongen touches a number of bases in his one-movement string duo. Such variety of formal detail in no way detracts from the music's attractive coherence.

First come two separate canons, strictly constructed but fully musical. Then follow considerable passagework and figures held together by ostinato framework. The next part consists of a theme (stated in unison and of the most simplistic type) and six variations. The first two restate the theme exactly; combined, respectively, with syncopative and eighth-note progressions. Variation three is built on juxtaposed duple and triple figures. The fourth variant moves along on syncopative glides. Trills are important in the fifth variation's configuration, and, preceded by a mini cadenza, the final variational setting is energetic.

The concluding part of the duo consists of full-scale, fast-paced music in D-major tonality. Jongen pulls out the stops with octave passages and ripely totaled chords. Since the D and A strings of both instruments represent the tonic and dominant territories of the home key, the result is duo string music of brilliance and

power. It is all most convincing.

■ **Sonata No. 1 in D Major for Violin and Piano, Op. 27**

Jongen's Sonata was composed in 1903 (a second violin and piano sonata was completed six years later, indicated as Op. 34). The initial duo sonata preaches the good words of César Franck. Though Jongen's early compositions are bound to this creative ideology, all of them are finely worded, well organized, and containing a clarity that brings no negativeness to such imitation.

Op. 27 was dedicated to the famous Belgian violinist, composer, and conductor Eugène Ysaÿe. Interestingly, as a result, an interlock takes place between Franck the composer, Jongen his creative disciple, and Ysaÿe the violinist, when it is recalled that in 1886 Franck wrote his sole violin and piano sonata expressly for Ysaÿe.

Jongen calls his movements "parts," and each is of large size. The opening of the work recalls the startling organlike resource of Franck's string quartet (in the same key). A pair of contrastive themes, fully detailed development, and recapitulation mark the usual sonata form. The slow movement includes an engaging rhythmic background for the piano. It proceeds from half notes and occasional quarter notes to eighths, then in order come triplets, sextuplets, some syncopation, and finally, octuple sounds per beat. Franck's influence is at its greatest intensity in the final movement. All of the immediately recognizable Franckian mannerisms are heard: the melodic surges, the structural sequences, and the chromatic chordal dips.

TRIOS

- **Trio: Prélude, Variations et Final for Piano, Violin, and Viola, Op. 30**

Those that believe chamber music compositions should only relate intimate thoughts and restrained ideas would probably call Jongen's Trio pugnacious. Those that only limit the actions of chamber music to the basic sonorous strengths of the instruments employed would term this music symphonic. Whatever, Jongen opts for full-toned sonority. (A compensation for the fact that the usual piano trio combination is changed with the less powerful viola used in place of the cello?) An immediate notification as to sonorous weight is made in the Prelude. A seventeen-measure thematic statement is announced, doubled note for note at the octave by two instruments throughout. In the theme's recapitulation (shortened to eleven measures) the same weight applies. There is, in addition, a heavy totality of textural involvement by polyphonic figuration on the part of all three instruments plus a good amount of string instrument fingered and rhythmic tremolando. (The former is a type of detached trill.)

An extended introduction precedes the Variations; both the former and the theme of the latter are presented by the piano alone. The variational elaborations are the opposite of laconic. The scoring, however, is again styled with full voicing. Inner balance occurs with the repeated use of the solo piano to present the principal subject of the energetic Finale.

- **Two Pieces in Trio for Piano, Violin, and Cello, Op. 95**

Warmly romantic in temper, Jongen's paired pieces have the classic meticulousness of detail and this composer's native aristocratic profile. The first of the two pieces is an *Elégie nocturnale*, its breadth of phrases contrasted to the tighter-themed *Appassionato*, which is fully developed.

QUARTETS

- **Deux Sérénades (Two Serenades) for String Quartet, Op. 61**

In the early part of his creative life Jongen was a Franckian disciple. Then, in his early thirties, he moved away from Franckian style to a more fanciful, extroverted manner. The Two Serenades are the best examples of this later creative role.

The first, a *Sérénade tendre* (Tender Serenade), lives up only partially to its title. The outer parts are light, but the middle is a prancing scherzo, bisected with some deft rhythmic strokes that scratch the duple polish and are colored beautifully by impressionistic use of muted timbre. The wealth of sonority (after the return of the first theme, and preceding the coda) is far from an indication of tender sentiments.

The *Sérénade dramatique* (Dramatic Serenade) uses several devices to give effect—uneven rhythm, a solo violin declamatory line, a contrasting supple subject, imitations, as well as a quite colorful *pièce de résistance,* a fugato played pizzicato. In the year 1918 (the date of composition), this last idea was more novel than a listener of today can realize. A return to earlier material then gives requisite balance.

- **Prelude and Chaconne for String Quartet, Op. 101**

No simple preliminary is represented in the Prelude. It has size (223 measures in triple time) and exploits a dynamic bravura for the greater part. Full-scale totality also describes the Chaconne. It consists of thirteen divisions and is completed by a fugue and coda. The polyphonic detail included in the Chaconne is of strong substance and invention, especially the eighth variation, which shifts the tonality from D minor to D-sharp minor, moves the pulse denominator from 3/2 to 4/2, and works out the thematic development in augmentation.

- **Quartet for Piano, Violin, Viola, and Cello, Op. 23**

There is no mistaking the Franckian language of Jongen's piano quartet. (Creative attachment all around, since the work is dedicated to Vincent d'Indy, who was the foremost of Franck's pupils and became the leader of the Franckian school of composers.) The type of chromaticism that moves constantly between tension and release, chamber music opulence, and thematic transformation (cyclic means) are all to be found in Franck's works and are duplicated in Jongen's amply communicative four-instrument opus.

The Scherzo (movement two) moves under wraps. Save for a very short section, the string instruments are muted and a considerable part of the movement is heard in a restrained dynamic level. Throughout the four movements the scoring is always coloristically detailed and avoids the overuse of block writing.

- **Quartet No. 2 in A Major for Two Violins, Viola, and Cello, Op. 50**

In numbered works alone, Jongen's output reached a total of 137. (This opus number marked Jongen's final work, the *Trois mouvements symphoniques*, written in 1951.) Within this mass of music the Franckian-style compositions occupy a little less than half the total. In the second string quartet there are signs of moving away from this creative fellow countryman/father figure but they are of minor total. The work contains the scope, the full textures, and the chromatic imprint of the Belgian master.

The unification of the cyclic device, the leitmotiv method that binds is of prime importance. In the second movement (Lento) within the pair of sharply contrasted themes and their development there is additional development

applied to the initial movement's principal theme. In the final movement it also serves, with inner change, as the main theme. Thus, in the first movement it is rhythmically restive, in the finale its rhythm is flattened out and the sounds progress with straightforward regularity.

Jongen's string quartet leans on Franck. Granted. Still, there is enough sonorousness and sweep to persuade one to accept the work on its own imitative terms.

- **Quartet [No. 3] for Two Violins, Viola, and Cello, Op. 67**

Although the published score does not indicate a number, this is Jongen's third work for string quartet, composed in 1921. Eleven years later the *Two Sketches* for string quartet were produced, and, in 1934, a Prelude and Chaconne for the same combination, was written. (For the latter work *see above*.)

The third quartet is far less dependent on Franckian procedures than the second quartet, though cyclic style is utilized. Tying the work together is the opening theme, which serves as the generator for the four movements: Allegro non troppo, Tempo di scherzo, Andantino molto cantabile, and Très animé. Fully to Jongen's credit are the textural balances, the diatonically proposed harmonies (which do not bend chromatically too often), and the coloristic effectuation. The last is especially stimulating in a thirty-two-measure section within the Scherzo. It consists of first violin harmonics, fingered tremolandos played ponticello by the second violin and viola, while the cello takes the lead playing in territory usually reserved for the first violin. A further striking effect is the use of reverse arpeggiando pizzicato at the end of the same movement.

The chromatic fugato in the slow (third) movement is a return to Franckian methodology. However, the many pedal points that Jongen employs are not pertinent to the older

Belgian composer's technical processes.

- **Two Paraphrases on Walloon Christmas Carols for Three Flutes and Alto Flute (or Clarinet), Op. 114**

Jongen's approach to the tuneful pair of carols is neither prolix nor obscure. The melodies are dressed up, but not dressed to kill. In the first one, "Hoûte on pau . . ." there is a sense of development of the melody. In the second one, "Qui vout dire çoulá, fré Matî?" ("What does that mean, Brother Matî?"), which begins with an introduction, the sense is of variational treatment. Either way a pair of light delights, never excessive in their handling.

- **Two Pieces for Four Cellos, Op. 89**

Quite a number of quartets for four cellos have proved to be failures. The reason has been that the upper line should have a soprano quality but has resulted in such a strained sonority that it has nullified the values of the tenor-baritone-bass combination. Jongen watched his balances, and the result is a fine entry in the four-cello catalogue.

There's plenty of chromatic words in the telling of the *Légende*. The final measures include a very picturesque passage consisting of three-voice harmonics. The *Danses* are processed in a pungently rhythmic way.

QUINTET

- **Concerto for Woodwind Quintet, Op. 124**

A one-movement work but clearly divided into three main divisions with a final one summarizing some of the previous material. In terms of scoring this is a "quintuple" concerto, since the five instruments participate with complete equality. A touch of Debussy color wash is used in some places, otherwise Franckian orientation applies.

Jongen, Léon (1884–1969)

TRIO

- **Trio for Oboe, Clarinet, and Bassoon (1937)**

An example of well-scored and fully-scored wind trio music, composed in familiar techniques. Léon Jongen, the brother of the better-known Joseph Jongen, peppers his music with chromatic additives which place him rigidly right of center in the conservative camp.

Movement one, for structural purposes, gives full contrastive play to fugal and lyrical details. The second movement is responsible to the scherzo fraternity. However, while the speed is fiery (the music is in 3/4 time with a metronomic indication of a $\quarternote = 192$), the usual rhythmic pointedness is eliminated in favor of flowing phrases. (Symbolically, this scherzo wears galoshes on its feet.) Part three has a recitative type of music in andante tempo linked to a rondo distribution in Allegro giocoso speed.

QUARTETS

- **Divertissement for Four Saxophones (Soprano, Alto, Tenor, and Baritone Saxophones) (1937)**

A tonally chromatic scherzo representative. Jongen maintains rhythmic pressure from the beginning to the end. An interlude in the center relaxes the tempo somewhat, but it is only a pithy amount of speed decline and the music gets rolling again very quickly.

- **Divertissement on a Theme of Haydn in the Form of Variations for Violin, Viola, Cello, and Piano (1955)**

Jongen's eleven-minute piano quartet, dedicated "to the memory of my brother Joseph" (the eminent Belgian composer—*see above*),

Jongen

is a packet of variation delights. The Haydn theme is the well-known one from the slow movement (Andante) of Symphony No. 94 in G major (the *Surprise*). In a form of "Tel maître tel valet" ("Like master like man"), Jongen structures his music in a set of variations, imitating the formal outlines of Haydn's movement, which consists of four variations and a coda.

Sometimes ironic and caustic, sometimes "surprising"(!) as well, never dull, and always creatively brilliant, Jongen's variations have the additional attraction of always maintaining the thematic bloodline within them.

An introduction precedes the lightly harmonized thematic announcement, which is linked to the first variation with the theme in the piano. Among the variational processes are the theme in a minor key (juiced up with running chromatic thirds), rhythmic augmentation of Haydn's subject (agitated by string tremolandos), and a Debussyish *Nocturne pastoral* in D-flat. Later variations include a Tempo di marcia, the theme again shifted to a minor tonality, substantiated by rhythmic antiphonal counterpoint, a Lento section in E-flat major, with the viola singing the melody, surrounded by pizzicatos and gentle piano chording, a strong rhythmic portion riding on off-beat accentuations, and finally a vigorous Tarantella paced Vivamente. A two-part coda wraps up matters neatly and colorfully, one portion in slow tempo, the other in presto.

Certainly, the Divertissement represents one of the best works this composer produced. Its novel and rewarding contents would bring parallel success to any chamber music team that would perform it.

QUINTET

▪ **Quintet for Piano, Flute, Clarinet, Horn, and Bassoon (1958)**

Jongen displays creative intelligence in his Quintet for keyboard and wind instruments. Everything in the work is potently communicative even though it is not of startling originality.

The architectonics of the first movement, paralleled with a specific scoring plan, command the music. The principal theme is a long-lined, eighteen-measure affair that consistently moves to a higher pitch point. It is first announced by a three-part octaval unison, then reannounced in compressed total in a two-part octaval doubling. Imitative details mark the contrasting second theme. Slowed in tempo, it is used for coda purposes as well. Movement two has rhapsodic overtones. The finale is a vivacious Rondino highlighted by a folksy, diatonic theme and utilizing the stability of rhythmic ostinato patterns. A bonus in the formal depiction is the presentation of the main theme in augmentation toward the conclusion of the work.

Jora

Jora, Mihail (1891–1971)

QUARTET

▪ **String Quartet, Op. 9**

Although Jora studied in Leipzig with Max Reger, his quartet transmits Romanian messages in every one of its four parts. There are chromatic harmonies of post-Franckian dialect and at times the texture is of heavy German make, but these are subordinate to the native flavor.

Natural nationalism vividly occupies the music at the start, with a modal-like melody harmonized by off-beat, connected thirds. Added to this are the marks of indigenous information: the grace-note curve, the dance tap of wood on strings. The Presto displays the rhythmic "thematicism" of Bartók. Basically the detail is in sevenfold meter, but cadentially aligned phrases are made from a three-measure concept in the sequence 7/8, 4/8, and 2/4. Both the slow-tempo and final movements are also common to native melos. The former is in song form, the latter is freely realized, its principal concern a very decisive subject. It is climaxed in the vociferous coda, which covers twelve measures of string-quartet unison in triple *forte* and then concludes in a compact three-measure Largamente.

Jordan, Sverre (1889–1972)

DUO

- **Sonatina for Flute and Piano, Op. 61**

Although a considerable amount of national folk music was basic to this Norwegian's compositions, none of it is used in this richly tonal piece. There is an outdoor quality to the music with its neoromantic carpeting. Sharply contoured designs: with rolling pitched themes in the first movement, a gentle Romanza as the center piece, and a snappy rhythmic Scherzando to complete the work.

Jørgensen, Axel (1881–1947)

DUO

- **Suite for Trombone and Piano, Op. 22**

Fresh and clearly styled music. Tonal logic with sufficient modulatory relations to maintain freshness.

The trombone's trump card of characterization—joining the militaristic and the fanfaristic—is used in the opening "Triomphale" ("Triumphant"). The moves are in order, though the feeling of lightness is secondary, in the Menuet giocoso. The final part links a Ballade and Polonaise, with a further direct combination since the latter is set

forth as a theme and variations, polonaise powered. Only two variations, with the second one swinging back to include the first. Music that is not overly thick but certainly forceful and colorful.

Jørgensen, Erik (1912–)

DUO

- *Figure in Tempo* for Cello and Piano (1961)

Strong and strict dodecaphonic style put into balance within classic tripartite form. Proof again that negates the theory that the two styles cannot blend. And an impressive blend it is.

The initial section is recitativelike, lyrical, but not relaxed in its probing lines. In the second section violence erupts. The music is frenetic and fractured in its pulse demarcations, percussive and puissant in its sound qualities. The concluding portion reconfirms the initial one.

(The dynamic detonation of the piano part of Jørgensen's duo has led to a second version scored for cello and percussion.)

QUARTET

- *Piece* for String Quartet (1965)

Jørgensen's *Piece* depends almost solely on serial procedures. It includes, among its colors, quarter tones, slow and quick vibrato, and some strictly noise sounds.

There is a cold rigidity that surrounds this Dane's eight-minute composition. Isolated entrances in various qualities lead to a short rhythmic section. There follows more fragmentation, totally made from harmonic timbres (natural, artificial, bowed, and plucked). Oddly enough, the ending, with a dropping off of one instrument at a time until only the viola remains (thus adding a textural assist to the dynamic decrease), defines a C-major conclusion.

effective. The last two words apply to Jorrand's entire concentrated Sonata, which has a performing time of 8 1/2 minutes.

Jorrand, André

DUO

- **Sonata No. 2 for Cello and Piano**

This composer's Sonata strikes a happy balance between the old and the new, between contemporary character and familiar features. It is tough and raw with its chromatic language. It is prepped and pepped with strong and vital rhythms. Arranging these in fundamental forms produces a striking result and presents a fresh voice in 20th-century music.

The dynamic articulation of the first theme is opposite to the movement's subtitle of "Modéré" ("Moderately"). Moving over a large tonal surface, it is compared to a second idea that is of similar sizable evolvement, but more rhythmically contained. The developmental detail is concentrated and the recapitulation adheres to the temper of the subjects, not their repetition. Within the panchromatic sentences Jorrand uses sequences to punctuate and hold them in place. The "Calme" is strictly tripartite in form, both modally plain and chromatic in the first part, disturbed and passionately rhapsodic in the central part, with a compressed return to the initial portion.

"Enjoué" ("Playful") is the title for the concluding part. It is all of that, being lively and bright, sprightly and jaunty. There are nine eighth notes in the rhythmic patterns of the main theme. These are not equally divided, but arranged in four groups of two each, with a splintered eighth at the end. The resultant regular 4/4 plus 1/8 kick is metrical fun at its best and matches the thematic quality. When other passages are in regular meters such as 2/4 and 4/4 the effect is properly unsubtle and potently

Josephs, Wilfred (1927–)

DUO

- *Chacony* **for Violin and Piano (1963)**

Resemblances to the continuous variation scope of the chaconne form (Josephs uses the Old English term for the word) are present but move out of place in contemporaneous manner. The meters shift and so do the permutative settings as one section blends into the next. If anything can be said to equal the form it is the music's extrovertism which equates variational display. Withal, the B pitch (and very often its diminished-fifth move to F) serves as an important support in the structure.

The long beginning leads into harmonics for the violin and other assorted timbral qualities. In turn the music becomes quick, its dynamic quiet, and its pitches separative—all begun with the violin pizzicato. Then follow chordal supports for curved lines, a section in twice as fast speed, flowing detail, and a substantial cadenza for the violin. The preconclusion is lyrical and quiet, the ending gives flourishes for each instrument and a final pedal B in the violin over percussive seconds in the piano, as the dynamic range simmers down from *fortissimo* to *forte* to *mezzoforte* to *mezzopiano* to *piano* onto *pianissimo* and finally *pianississimo*.

TRIOS

- *Encore (on a Theme of Scott Joplin)* for Guitar, Harp, and Harpsichord, Op. 82B

A neat trick and a colorful one. The five-minute piece deserves regular program listing as well as encore placement. What Josephs has done is to take Joplin's "Maple Leaf Rag," precede it with an intro and then overlay it with material for the two other instruments.

This slick item is to be performed with "discreet" amplification. It also is to be given its theatrical touch, since the harpsichordist is to play "standing up wearing a beret."

- **Piano Trio (1974)**

A lively and resourceful use of color, but without indulging in any special effects, and an especially strong constructional impulse are to be found in Josephs's trio for violin, cello, and piano (completed in 1974 and revised in 1981).

Passacaglia shape is to be noted in the first movement. It is in allegro tempo but has linear breadth. Movement two is scherzo strung and sprung. Movement three is a seven-minute coverage of theme, seven continuously linked variations, and a coda. The finale, in its full-hearted development, can almost be considered variational as well. However, there is more integration of motival units than thematic elaboration and refurbishment.

- **String Trio (1966)**

Twelve-tone pitch use doesn't necessarily mean serial rule applies. And it doesn't in this composition for violin, viola, and cello. The opening theme in the first movement, for example, picks up all twelve pitches, but there are repetitions, and so forth, and the chromaticism should not be mistaken for serial application. Further, in two movements special timbre becomes a more unifying element than specifically controlled pitch arrangement. In both the third and fifth (final) movements sweeping arpeggios snarling behind the bridge and chains of double harmonics represent these elements.

There are further unifying factors. The percussive positivism of chordal seconds and ninths are prime points in both the second and fifth movements, and further innerrelationship exists by the horizontal spread of these pitch spans. The polyphonic detail of the first movement is also reflected in the final movement. Throughout these movements the lines are always on the move. This applies also to the Intermezzo (movement four), a kind of waltz in which the violin is mostly muted against the open timbre of the viola and cello.

Josephson, Harry D.

DUO

- *Trilogy da camera* for Flute and Piano

Musical representations of "Repartee," "Tracery," and "Filigree." The first of these is translated into a three-part realization, with the midsection rejoinder (more active, though in slightly slower tempo) surrounded by chromatic commentary. Polyphonic weave is the interlacement for "Tracery"; passagework provides the contrapuntal knitting for the final movement.

There is an underlying unity of resource in Josephson's short pieces. The wealth is also spread in regard to dedications. Movement one is for the composer's wife, the second piece is inscribed to Harriet Peacock Lejeune, and the final movement is dedicated to the American composer, Leon Stein.

Josten, Werner (1885-1963)

DUOS

- **Sonata for Cello (or Viola or Clarinet) and Piano (1938)**

In writing this work Josten threw away the book. It is a one-movement work, but that is not the unusual matter. What is concerns the contents.

The music begins with a chromatically encased, broad Adagio. It is linked to an Allegro, which gives more attention to the G-minor home tonality than the slow-paced prelude. Gutsy with cross accents, the fast music is developed and leads to a gigantic solo cello peroration (cadenza in personality) of four-dozen measures. A minute (five-measure) Adagio concludes the piece.

Josten was never an extrovert experimentalist. Nonetheless, he persistently refused to stick closely to tried (tired?) formal facts. This work is a vivid illustration of such a creative attitude.

- **Sonata for Violin and Piano (1936)**

Josten's music is of updated classic order, in clear tonality framed with modern dissonances that add vitality. The first movement's principal theme illustrates the classic décor. Not a foreign accidental intervenes, the key is purely A major; yet the piano that supports and imitates, while also in the same key, does not exactly form a tonal parallel. It digs in with free chordal choice to support the melody—this is diatonic pantonality, the free use of all tones of the key. The Adagio is like a Bach aria; a neoecclesiastical warm movement, with moving sets of thirds in the piano supporting a stimulated-by-ornaments line. A fugue forms the last movement, chromatic in the middle of its subject—classicism brought up to date again. In no place does the style change from its purity—a purity of the present built on the past.

- **Sonatina for Violin and Piano (1939)**

The opening movement is somewhat sectional, a rondo, conceived in the style of neoclassicism, containing a free interplay within tonalities. The opening dissonant chords are in the tonal polarity of E. Eventually, this norm-tone climaxes in a final E-major chord (plus attendant friction). In between, the melodic lines run in and out of focus of the tonalities they express. The writing is clear, the demarcations vagrant, yet not improvisational. Josten was a composer with polished command of his craft. This Sonatina brings reminders of the music of Paul Hindemith, but much less contrapuntally oriented.

The largesse of combining forms within one movement, further identifying such within the seal of an A–B–A, is the plan of the middle division. The Air concept was often used as a contrast to olden-day dance forms. It serves the same good deed in this instance, when it surrounds the long-short, quintupally formed jets of the Burlesca. A propulsive and variationally conceived movement completes the work. While there is more action within it than in the previous portions, Josten writes just as clearly. He changes the classic forms in his modern music, but always maintains stylistic balance.

TRIO

- **Trio for Flute, Clarinet, and Bassoon (1941)**

Only once does the leggièro quality of the semimotor rhythm let go in the Serenade. When it does, it leads to the last section, and by its single, mild, rhythmic explosion produces a texture that enhances all that went before or is to come. The free-formed *Promenade* has symmetry obtained by cohesion of germinal theme and style of writing (contrapuntal). It contains what is at first a canon in contrary motion, but which falls into imitations and other canonic driblets. The *Masquerade* is a movement of hop, skip, and jump. Throughout, the instruments have little time to breathe in this vivacious, modern cassation movement.

Joubert, John (1927–)

DUO

- *Kontakion* for Cello and Piano, Op. 69

Joubert's score bears the indication "In Memoriam K. J. (1926–1970)." He explains that the title "refers to the traditional Russian chant for the dead used in the Eastern Orthodox Church," and that "some of the material is derived from the traditional melody." A quotation of its first two phrases is made within the piano part.

Sweeping arched lines are a principal concentrate of the music, intensifying the basically slow tempo. The dynamic levels vary but ultimately reach a top point of *fortississimo.* From that point the music slows rhythmically, thins texturally, and lessens dynamically.

QUARTET

- String Quartet No. 1 in A flat, Op. 1

Joubert's neoclassic assurance is here illustrated. Tonalitywise the outer movements are in A-flat, the middle one is in the minor subdominant, enharmonically detailed, thus C-sharp. Tempo balance is achieved by way of an Allegro non troppo–Lento–Allegro sequence. Further, the outer movements are controlled by intervallic emphasis: in the first movement by ascending fifths and in the concluding movement by ascending fourths. Ternary form balances the slow movement, fugal detail and meshed polyphony highlight the finale.

However, there is no cold preaching of technical dogma in Joubert's initial opus. The range of expression is dynamic minus any romantic afflatus.

QUINTET

- *Sonata a cinque* for Recorder (or Flute), Two Violins, Cello, and Harpsichord, Op. 43

Three movements, nicely sonorous and logically designed. Movement one is lively, dogmatically rhythmic in stating its case. Sharp contrast is furnished by the middle Chaconne. The finale has been aptly described by one critic as "virtually a moto perpetuo."

OCTET

- Octet for Clarinet, Bassoon, Horn, String Quartet, and Double Bass, Op. 33

Music that is neoclassic in its outlook, with some Bartókian punch providing a fine-turned emphasis on the dramatic. Joubert uses his timbres with keen balance and with more than usual individuality assigned the double bass. Other italicizing of instrumental color pertains to the opening of the third (final) movement, with solo strength assigned the clarinet, horn, and bassoon, in turn. Further tidbits, but special and not to be overlooked, are the pair of two-measure passages in movement one for the violins, progressing in fifths in both legato harmonics and ponticello.

Syncopation intensifies the andante pace of the opening movement. Compelling robustness is found in the final Allegro, preceded by the coloristic preface mentioned above. The central movement has vivacious thrust and retains it without change of tempo throughout. Toward the end of the movement fugal detail is used.

Juon, Paul (1872–1940)

DUOS

- **Sonata for Flute and Piano, Op. 78**

The publisher (Zimmermann) includes this work in a series titled *Spätromantik (Late Romantic)*, and the editorial decision for this heading is correct. (The use of quartal harmony, especially in the first movement, might be argued as belonging in the 20th century.)

Considerable fantasy in the sonata's opening movement. The ending therefore is understandable—a march supplement and then even that fresh idea changes to a slow-tempo final pithy cadence. A darker slow movement is set in quintuple meter. The finale has a virtuosic slant including some ad lib measures and a flute cadenza. It represents music of romantic casing with some rhythmic barbed hooks.

- **Sonata in A Major for Violin and Piano, Op. 7**

Youthful enthusiasm stirs within the music. Classic methodology is blended with romantic looseness in the first movement. There, the piano anticipates the principal theme by outline in slow tempo; triadic markers are the guides for the movement's progress within a persistent diversity—the tempo changes sixteen times.

Variations, always a favorite Juon device, are utilized in the middle movement, certainly to be considered the high point of the Sonata. The six variational profiles are clearly identifiable. Examples: a minuet type in the third part, next a Chopinesque presto, and a Romanze as the fifth variant. Sixteenth-note patterns are basic to the finale. Juon offers two conclusions to his duo sonata, the original one of six-measure length, the other twice that size. There is little difference between them.

TRIOS

- *Arabesques:* **Small Trio for Oboe, Clarinet, and Bassoon, Op. 73**

Not so small—the four movements cover a performance time of seventeen minutes.

Classic allegiance is saluted here waving a romantically colored flag. The music compares the bright (parts one and especially four) with the slightly more subdued (part two) as is proper to classical sensibility. Movement three fits in as well, with its quasi Menuetto depiction. Nicely constructed and nicely packaged music.

- **Divertimento for Clarinet and Two Violas, Op. 34**

The not-so-odd background of this composer (born in Russia and studied both there and in Germany, opting to live in the latter country) can be contrasted with this very odd combination dyed with the deeper colors of tenor-average instruments. The suite product is sometimes equivalent to saying a work is in divertimento style, save that the suite can be much more serious. Juon's title makes certain that auditors realize his intentions.

The four movements are entertaining, nonponderable music. The Variations of the first movement are six in number, appearing after a long introductory thematic section. A Nachtstück (Nocturne) follows the regulative principle of dreamy writing. However, this section is texturally a quintet, since the violas are constantly playing double stops. The chords are satisfactory romantic-style observations; the color of the clarinet's low register most effective. The Exotisches Intermezzo (Exotic Interlude) is rather homespun, insistent in the use of pedal points. Lightest of all is the Ländler—the slow waltz of Austrian vintage.

- *Silhouettes*: Books I and II, for Two
  Violins and Piano, Op. 9

- *Silhouettes*: Books III and IV, for Two
  Violins and Piano, Op. 43

Eleven pieces divided into four collections and spread over two opus numbers. Juon also transcribed the total for violin, viola, and piano, using opus numbers designated as 9a and 43a.

The first three pieces are in Book I and are titled "Idylle," "Douleur" ("Sorrow"), and "Bizarrerie" ("Strange Events"). Book II begins with slowly processional music, the violins muted, described as a "Conte mystérieux" ("Mysterious Story"). Number five of the total set is a "Musette miniature" subtitled "Danse ancienne"—a minuet type that constantly stresses upbeats in all the measures. With seventeen repeats of the twelve-measure generator, the sixth piece, "Obstination," subtitled "Basso ostinato," fully lives up to its title heading. Included are strong polyphonic detail and imitation between the instruments, and a strong coda as well.

Book III begins with toccata energy in the Prélude and is followed by a large ternary piece, "Chant d'amour" ("Love Song"). The final group of pieces comprises "3 Intermezzi," "Mélancolie," and "Danse grotesque."

- *Trio caprice*: Trio No. 2 in D Major for
  Violin, Cello, and Piano, Op. 39

Although Juon subtitled his trio "nach Gösta Berling," there is no programmatic formula that is utilized. Authored by the Swede, Selma Lagerlöf (1858–1940), this novel also served as the inspirational basis for Juon's Rhapsody for piano quartet, Op. 37. It is sufficiently clear that Juon's use of generic titling (Caprice and Rhapsody) means that no story-line music is involved. (Incidentally, the score of Op. 37 does not include mention of the "Gösta Berling" background.)

However, there are many shifts in the lyrical impulses within the *Trio caprice*. The Scherzo, which connects to the previous slow movement, has a section marked Marciale, containing music of little pomposity and more descriptive of a burlesque mood. There are constant changes in the trio's final part, which substantiate the "caprice" in the title. This is in contrast to the two-subject formation and development within the first movement which emphasizes textural differences for coloration. This opening part of the trio begins with a string duet (mostly in quartet voicing, however), followed by the solo piano, and then the complete trio apparatus.

QUINTET

- **Quintet for Violin, Two Violas, Cello,
  and Piano, Op. 33**

The offbeat piano quintet formation Juon chose of two violas rather than a pair of violins provides a richer and slightly heavier timbre totality. This is matched by the infixed quality of pedal points. Within the first movement bariolage, pizzicato, double stops, drummed triplets, sustained sounds, and ostinatos are all used for the pedal anchorage. The method governs to such degree that the nickname "Pedal Quintet" would not be out of place.

Rhapsodic elements in the slow movement are responded to by triple octave-spaced spurts in the piano. The meter of the quasi Valse (third movement) continues in the last movement. It includes a Russian folk song played by the string instruments following an initial statement by the entire quintet. So much for evidence of Juon's birth and study in Russia. He then reverts to his expatriate nationalism and writes in a German romantic manner. The contrast in style effectively balances and helps to define this "two viola" piano quintet as one of Juon's best compositions.

(There is a second version of this Quintet

available, using the standard setting of two violins and one viola with the cello and piano. It is listed as Op. 33a.)

SEXTET

- **Divertimento for Piano and Wind Quintet, Op. 51**

More light chamber music is composed for winds than for any other combination. There seems to be some inattention to the fact that the colorful wind instruments are not the only means of fashioning relaxed, entertaining music. Be that as it may, Juon's work calls for the average wind quintet (flute, oboe, clarinet, bassoon, and horn) to combine with the piano in five movements that have the orderliness and attendant regard for the miscellany of divertimento design.

Two themes treated in alternation form the first movement. Then the mixed strains of Juon's Russian heritage and German training vie for attention. An Intermezzo runs in lush triadal formations; a Fantasia and another Intermezzo both show Juon's love for Brahms, while the final Rondino is pure trepakian delight.

OCTET

- **Octet for Piano, Oboe, Clarinet, Horn, Bassoon, Violin, Viola, and Cello, Op. 27a**

The Octet is considered one of Juon's most important compositions, and exists in two other versions—as a Septet for two violins, two violas, two cellos, and piano, and in a much better-known version for string orchestra, oboe, clarinet, horn, bassoon, and piano under the title of *Kammersinfonie (Chamber Symphony)*. The chamber music version is for the same combination, the strings being limited to one each of violin, viola, and cello.

Juon is no individualist, he is part of the German school that drew its solutions from the Brahms-Reger tradition; he plainly shows this in a work that rarely departs from it. There is nothing to be condemned in good imitation; not all composers can be curious for the new.

The first movement is based on the broadness of 6/4 meter (a Brahmsian favorite), with its ability to present two types of pulse—duple and triple. Juon uses and mixes both, thereby giving rhythmic activity to his most generally diatonic themes. A horn-call cadenza sounds as if Wagner had been listened to carefully. Oddly enough, however, motival transformation appears in the last movement in non-Brahmsian fashion. Use is made of the same theme that was heard in the first movement, now in foreshortened quadruple meter, thus making the tabulation of the last movement more bold and vigorous, since there is less metrical spread. The elegiac slow movement is in three-part form, contrapuntal imitations depict the end parts; while the third movement originates from the Russian quintuple rhythm so favored by the 19th-century composers of that school.

Juzeliunas, Julius (1916–)

QUARTET

- **String Quartet No. 1 (1962)**

Classical forms, firmed by tonal polarities (the outer movements are in B-flat, the central Andante sostenuto in C-sharp), provide the balance for this quartet. Juzeliunas's harmonic language is based on quartal arrangements. The vertical combinations are further colored by distinctive melodicism derived from Lithuanian music (Juzeliunas is a native of Lithuania, born in the town of Zeimelis).

The first movement is concise, sonata-outlined, with the quartal syntax providing discrete

(and the reverse, but in the minority) dissonances. The subsidiary theme adds color onto
color by discriminating glissandos and rough
pizzicato chords. While all detail is clear in the
development and recapitulation (including a
canonic snippet), the conspectus produces a
consortium of color via ostinatos, massive
chords, and thrusting arpeggiandos. Movement
two is single-themed, changed in décor, and
with highly toned manipulation, but minus
variational development. In the final dance-
driven Rondo, a cyclic arch takes place with
quotation of the second-movement theme followed by the opening movement's subject .

Jyrkiäinen, Reijo (1934–)

DUO

▪ *Varianti* for Viola and Piano (1967)

Jyrkiäinen's Darmstadt study shows in this
music of concentrated dynamism. The pithiness derives from Webern, the gestures from
intervallic distribution. But Jyrkiäinen's little
duo is not serially developed.

In the theme, half-step pitch movement is
the principal point. This is picked up in the
ostinato secundal passage for the piano and the
scurry of the viola in the first permutation.

Disjunct octave placement notwithstanding, the second variant emphasizes the theme's
basic pitch spacing. Variation three is for the
viola alone. The final section develops fast
articulations that alternate between the two
instruments (the partnered motility a parallel to
the closeness of the theme's intervallic spans).
The closing cluster chord (F–F-sharp–G–A-
flat–A) is further confirmation of the tidy formation of and relationships within Jyrkiäinen's
very short but very powerful piece.

SEPTET

▪ *Frammenti (Fragments)* for String
  Septet (Three Violins, Two Violas,
  Cello, and Double Bass) (1962)

Serialism, with typical textures and motives. In
the seven movements (matching the number of
performers) divisional identification comes
from specific color, meter, or texture. Classical
formal summations are not utilized.

Thus, part two deals with sustained materials and begins with all the instruments, save the
double bass, muted and playing without vibrato. Part three is a slithering presto, with
ponticello and pizzicato forming a "Three P's"
grouping. Wooden taps via col legno bowing
underline part five.

Only in the sense of the number of movements is the music fragmented. Totally accessible and with a firm stylistic basis, Jyrkiäinen's
septet contains solid music. It never overplays
its hand.

OCTET

▪ *Contradictions* for Eight Instruments
  (Flute, Clarinet, String Quartet,
  Guitar, and Piano) (1965)

Abstract titles fill the musical catalogues and
so do generic ones. Descriptive titles, when
they tell of true things, are always helpful and
welcome. So, this one for a mixed octet of
wind, string, and keyboard instruments.

The *Contradictions* are styled with strong
avoidance of thematic substances. Pertinent
lines and lyrical fancies are not to be heard.
Serial and rhythmic play are, with each of the
twelve sections (not numbered by the composer) adopting a different viewpoint. Coherence through contradiction, therefore.

Interestingly, there are interspersed five sections (numbers two, four, seven, nine, and
eleven) that are extremely short. In each case

Jyrkiäinen

the instrumentation of these is concentrated and unique. In the second section there are five measures for flute and violin, in the fourth section, again a total of five measures, the scoring is for flute, clarinet, and the two violins. Etc. These sections provide further formal contrariety.

Denby Richards, in his *The Music of Finland* (published in 1968), applauds the work for its interesting instrumental coloring and logical thought. True. In listing the instrumentation he substitutes percussion for the piano. False.

Kabalevsky, Dmitri (1904–87)

DUOS

- *Improvisation* **for Violin and Piano, Op. 21, No. 1**

This music was extracted by Kabalevsky from the score he composed for the film *A Petersburg Night*. Clear in form and clear in style. After some introductory sectional material, Kabalevsky touches bases with full-fledged melodic sweep. It's not difficult to identify Kabalevsky's homeland from this piece's somewhat Tchaikovskian consanguinity.

- **Sonata for Cello and Piano, Op. 71**

Passionate involvement begins at the very start, with a dramatic theme built from paired eighth notes. This rhythmic motive becomes the fundament of the third (final) movement, where toccata explosiveness takes hold. Ultimately, the first-movement theme, its time lengths doubled, forms the coda of the finale. In both of these movements there is action but never any bombast. A tightly pointed pulse encases the rhythmicity.

Movement two (Allegretto) has been described by the Soviet critic L. Raaben as "a typical Russian waltz" that "is full of inner agitation." Within there are contrastive interruptions that create "a feeling of incompleteness, of suspense and disquietude."

(The Sonata is dedicated to the great cellist Mstislav Rostropovich, with whom the composer gave the premiere of the work in Moscow on February 6, 1962.)

QUARTET

- **String Quartet No. 2 in G Minor, Op. 44**

Classical form dictates the first movement, which has the usual two themes—one in the home key, the other in the relative major. The effusive, augmented step is a paramount point in the first subject and defines the key without question. No special formal departure is made in the development section, but the ending is gauged for applause as it holds forth in triple *fortissimo* with fourteen-voice chords in the majority. Clear form, carefully plotted, offers fair novelty in the second movement. Two themes alternate diametric major and minor tonalities and are given variated treatment. The music has distinct charm through this tonal dualism, yet there is no chromaticism; everything remains distinct and succinct in each section. It is this sense of structural clarity that is Kabalevsky's primary strength. The Scherzando leggiero is lengthy, its contrasts formed by style rather than pace. Next follows a slow movement which moves directly into the concluding part, a gay and brilliant construction, its sprightliness comparable to a Haydn quartet finale.

Kadosa, Pál (1903–83)

DUOS

- *Five Short Rhythmic Studies* **for Two Violins, Op. 16d**

While most etudes are conceived as aids for study, offering specific technical problems to conquer—such as arpeggios, trills, melodic skips, intonation, and the like—the concert etude combines artistic values and pedagogical purpose. For example, the strict laboratory viewpoint of Kreutzer's studies for the violinist is a far cry from the rich objectives offered by Chopin's etudes. Concert pianists have made the latter a standard part of the repertoire, whereas no violinist would think of performing the former work in public. Kadosa not only meets the double demands required of concert studies but includes a third distinction, namely,

Hungarian folk music; and in this case the intrinsic music of the Gypsy peasants, not the second-hand brand produced by professional composers.

There is a great deal of imitative writing in all of the pieces, the only exception being the second study. The third of the set consists of two canons which are broken off after they get under way. Birhythm is a feature in the latter half of this piece, with no coincidence of bar line occurring until the final one. In contrast the first of the five studies is asymmetrical; the second is likewise, but the delineation of ostinato quarter-note double stops by the second violin gives a general impression of rigid mensural conformity. Both the fourth and fifth pieces retain one time signature each (3/4 and 2/4 respectively). Nevertheless, in these instances rhythmic rewards are forthcoming by offbeat entrances and syncopation that drags itself across the bar lines.

■ Four Duets for Two Violins, Op. 16b

A work faithful to the tenets of Gebrauchsmusik, yet concerned with a sincere creative spirit, which does not give way to merely dull music of elementary classification. Kadosa does not "write down"; he simply edits all technical problems in order to put into service a valid example of contemporary Hungarian music containing no difficulties for the performers. The first movement is designed from an eighth-note motive, while counterpoint is the entire resource of the slow movement (and the only place it is used throughout). A light Bartókian dance model serves for movement three, with the same style (this time without asymmetrical identity) employed for the last part.

■ *Improvisation* for Cello and Piano (1957)

Much more is offered here than vacuous note-spinning that has aleatoric reminders. "Improvisation" it may be, but here it is carefully (and

artistically) controlled in a slow rubato section of broad lines; then a smart rhythmic dance bit; again a slow division, this time with articulated pitch movement; and finally a more extended, rhythmic, foot-tapping conclusion.

Kadosa's material is akin to a third "generation" setting. It consists of three Romanian folk songs collected by Bartók.

■ Partita for Violin and Piano, Op. 14

In that Kadosa's music has much rhythmic charm and exploration it equates dance style particulars, and is therefore a modern link to the much older partita style and form; but in the expressed scope of the titles, confirmed by the music itself, this excellent and colorful work is a suite of miscellaneous movements. However, generic name affinity or not, the lodestar of this duet is of Hungarian twinkle, of Bartók reflections.

The Entrada has neoclassic cut, its D-major tonality progressing fan-wise through the diatonic tones of that key with fresh freedom. "In modo rustico" has primitive flavors—an assortment of chords (hunting-horn fifths), melody (pristine in movement), and rhythm (not square-cut to fit, but of seeming improvisatory pulse, picturing a closer reality to rooted folk rhythms).

Movement three has a self-explanatory title—Quasi una cadenza. This movement is split in half as first the piano, then the violin is given a chance to shine with true chamber music equality. It must be emphasized that the cadenzas are artistic, not palpable displays that go up quickly in pyrotechnical smoke.

The final Capriccio likewise indicates proper titling, especially in regard to the passionate strength of *ungarische* rubatos; the slow moving *lassu*, the quick-motioned *friss*, the brilliance of Gypsy fiddling—a honest tale of Hungarian rural society with all of its musical customs being imitated in a perfect setting. The vacillation between tempo and linear articulation is extreme, naturally capricious. There are over a dozen different ritards, twelve accelerandos, some sixteen sostenuto passages within the principal speed defined as allegro assai. Kadosa's Partita is very definitely a Hungarian music sampler.

■ *Short Suite* **for Two Violins, Op. 16e**

Kadosa uses authentic Hungarian folk materials in this work. There is no pyrotechnical meandering to be heard, no popular "Hungarian Rhapsody" is communicated. The composer is concerned only with the philosophies of true folk music. One finds that a composer can engender sufficient excitement without departing stylistically from the essential melodic turns depicted in the music of rooted Hungarian culture. Most of the melodies are taken from Bartók's collection, which proved that what Hungarian composers called national music was not so called by the people themselves. Like Bartók, Kadosa verifies that 19th-century Hungarian music is not of kinship, but only of outward reference to folk disposition.

The opening Allegro is in strict three-part form; the middle portion consists of an offbeat pizzicato ostinato by the first violin, while the second instrument plays a melody formed from a six-tone C-major scale in which B is eliminated. Movement two is a *parlando* type, with the second violin merely accompanimental, that moves without pause into the third section. The latter is formed in part from matters of rhythmic imitation.

■ **Sonata No. 1 for Violin and Piano, Op. 5**

Not the usual compounded layout for this duo. In its triproportions there are a 148-measure Triste, a 120-measure Allegrissimo, and a 74-measure Lento, which changes to Adagio.

As usual with Kadosa, a certain amount of Bartókian coinage is included. This is especially the case in the last of the three movements, which has an initial unaccompanied violin section in rubato, with the balance using figurations first colored by muted sound and later by open timbre. There are fantasy details in the first movement, all unburdened by any sense of romantic thought; a vigorous scherzo-controlled music is heard in the second movement. This part of the duo is exceedingly thin textured and is shot through with silent measures for either of the instruments.

■ **Sonata No. 2 for Violin and Piano, Op. 58**

High-powered chamber music virtuosity here, but formally under control. The Préambule is very ornamental in its lines, but the format of a sonata is clearly depicted. A Scherzo is the center piece, one that is propelled in Presto pace. The Trio of the movement has a percussive impress, filled with repetitive seventh chords.

The Finale is in four parts: a Sostenuto, of fantasy-termed material; a Vivacissimo, quasi presto that speeds in single pulses per measure; an elaborated return of the Sostenuto, followed by a rerun of the fast music. This plan offers additional formal profits since the qualities of the slow music reflect those of the Préambule and the nature of the fast music is similar to that of the Scherzo.

■ **Sonatina for Flute and Piano, Op. 56**

Kadosa's Op. 56 is structured in three connected movements. There is neat contrastive detail in the first part by quartal and triadic line movement as well as harmony. The second part starts like a slow waltz, minus any stock rhythmic support, then builds into a fast scherzando, and is completed by a return to the slow tempo. Forward drive and its maintenance mark the final part.

- **Sonatina for Violin and Cello, Op. 2c**

The routines of recitative rubato lines are presented in the first of the two connected parts of the duo. These lines alternate three times with slower-paced, quieter music. Part two is a vivacious rhythmic affair, only once interrupted with a lightly polyphonic tranquil section.

- **Sonatina for Violin and Piano, Op. 49e**

A score bright with the glow of Hungarian folk material. Pitch weights are off the beats in the first part of the opening movement; the second part follows the same rhythmic plan, comparing its dancy décor with the previous melodic rubato. Strict three-part form in movement two—a demarcative music, lean textured, further evidence of the power of Bartók's style.

Before the numbered third movement is a separate portion (minus any numbering) titled thus: (Intermezzo)—alla cadenza—. It is mostly for the violin, though the piano has a pair of measures imitative of the violin's. This is actually an introduction to the clearcut, triple-pulse music of the third movement.

- **Suite for Violin and Piano, Op. 6**

Nationalistic all the way. The Hungarian melos colors the expressive lines and dynamizes the impressive rhythms. These are the features in the jesting mood of the second of the five movements, the slow-tempo (then increased in speed), very short third movement for muted violin, and the foot-stamping, forcefully fast-paced fourth movement.

TRIO

- **String Trio No. 1, Op. 12**

Kadosa uses authentic, national material in this striking trio. He does not simply set down the folk idiom side by side with the sounds of

personal idiom but merges them to form a well-knit composition. The traditional aspect is not used as a fringe to the complete musical fabric. The result defines a composite order, of essentially concentrated primitive style but organic as a whole.

In the first movement, sectional composition is used, divided into two parts that balance each other by repetition and within which considerable attention is given fugal technique. Free form is utilized in the slow movement. Recitative passages follow in succession, colored by the use of mutes, esoteric glassy sounds (ponticello), and glissandos—all as if the nocturnal glow of a Hungarian rural district were being painted. A dance bravado covers the last movement. The ternary form of this part includes a middle section concerned with a slow-paced chorale while the outer portions are fugally prepared with Hungarian pepper. This last is not of Bachian rhythm, but a czardas disporting wildly, as is its wont, but on contrapuntal earth.

QUARTETS

- **String Quartet No. 2, Op. 25**

Music that is Bartókian in both sound and character. Moderato-moving swerves fill the first movement, constructed as a sonata. The tempo of movement two is "robust," and that it is in its scherzo contents, strictly surveyed in three parts, including a literal recapitulation, and derived from Romanian folk material. A short fantasy-proportioned slow movement and a presto finale, also shaped as a sonata, complete the quartet.

Interestingly, Kadosa is able to have plentiful rhythmic variety without resorting to a plethora of metrical changes. Movement two is in 2/4 throughout; movement four is in 3/8 throughout. Save for a single 6/8 measure, the first movement remains in 9/8. In movement three a tiny bit of metrical shift takes place, with single measures in 7/8, 4/4, and 2/4 interrupting the andante-moving lines written in 3/4 time.

- **String Quartet No. 3, Op. 52**

Some Bartók definition is indicated in the middle movement, the opening theme a strong reminder of the folk-song melodies that permeate Bartók's work. Kadosa then variates the material surrounding this opening. Further Bartók affiliation is heard in the antiphonal glissando voicing in the second of the connected variants. The outer movements are in sonata form; the first expanded by a second development section.

QUINTET

- **Wind Quintet, Op. 49a**

The assortment of materials used provides an interesting set of contrasts. In the rondo finale the "glory be" bow is to Hungarian folk music with touches of Bartók style, especially in the rhythmic end. The classical order of things surfaces in the minuet-tempo second movement. Though formally strict in its A–B–A setting, there is a decided move away from four-square blocks with a good number of five-measure phrases.

Kadosa's eclectic approach should not cause the listener to underestimate his command of clear scoring, the balancing of materials, and the use of neat harmonic diction, all very apparent in the sonata-form first movement (there is a decided Hungarian quality to the second theme) and in the ornamented fantasy moves of the slow movement.

Kaegi, Werner

TRIO

- *Miniatures* **for Oboe, Bassoon, and Harpsichord (1960)**

Honest-to-god counterpoint should not be confused with polyphony, which is actually animated harmony, tailored to fit chordal definitions. True contrapuntal behavior demands that each line maintain its individual identity while moving in meaningful association with other lines. Linear individuality, controlled so that it aurally prospers, provides textural energy. Not that harmonic counterpoint is to be scorned. It depends on the objective of a composer's style whether vertical (harmonic) strength takes over from contrapuntal reticence.

In Kaegi's piece, five of the movements are plotted so that the technique of the narrative is well-registered counterpoint for the wind instruments. The lines, of intense independence, separately float, collide, inhabit individual worlds. The harpsichord part is also separate, but it is in keyboard-instrument shop-talk form, meaning: chords, arpeggios, and small figures. This technical culture also pertains to the Fughetta (the third piece). Polyphonic to begin with, the two voices involved are freed (again, the harpsichord does not participate contrapuntally) so that strict response to the subject and imitation maintenance is annulled. The wind instruments once more follow the premise of insular strength. The effect is dynamic; the counterpoint beautifully individual.

Scoring variety is accomplished by the unaccompanied harpsichord for movement six, a prestissimo Toccata that rushes headlong in unyielding eighth notes. The preceding miniature, titled "Alea nondum jacta . . ." ("The die [is] not yet cast"), also departs from the trio formation, being a duo for the winds. Two versions are offered the players, and they can shift between them or choose either as they wish. Not much difference relates to the choice. And again, Kaegi presents his undaunted, craggy, complete counterpoint.

Kagel, Mauricio (1931–)

DUO

- *Klangwölfe (Wolf Sounds)* for Violin and Piano (1979)

The character of Kagel's avant-garde adventures in composition is such that even in works not intended for the stage theatricality is often present. (One example: *Improvisation ajoutée* for organ requires three assistants who add "business" to the playing by hand clapping, laughing, shouting, humming, and whistling.)

In this duo the violin is muted, not in the ordinary manner but by a heavy metal mute called a *Tonwolf* (thereby the title of the piece). The timbre produced by this mute is thin, nasal, and poor in harmonic overtones. Sectional disposition is made of the sound materials, beginning with rhapsodic, cadenzalike spurts. Ostinato patterns are in the majority, but each of these is subtly modified and changed as it progresses. The sense is one of detail out of focus. *Klangwölfe* is no sweet-toned madrigal, but it has, through its sequential repetitions, intense expression.

TRIO

- *Match for Three Players* (Two Cellos and Percussion) (Two Hand Cymbals, Suspended Cymbal, Suspended Sizzle Cymbal, Marimbaphone, Snare Drum, Bass Drum, Two Handle Castanets, Two Ratchets, Sistrum, Two Hand Bells, Bell, Two Jingle Bells, Flexatone, Dog Bark, Two Police Whistles, Chinese Clatter Drum, Two Dice Cases, Five Dice) (1964)

In accordance with the title, the cellists sit "as far apart from one another as possible," with the percussionist in a set-back position as the "umpire." Say what one will, this plan is simply programmatic hype for a work that illustrates raw bruitism.

Not a single sound by the cellos is in the normal category, and most of the percussion equipment is chosen for its stridulatory response. A few of the string-instrument methods of playing are: rubbing resin on wood; slapping with the fingertips, excessive vibrato (at least with a quarter-tone range); placing a fingernail on the side of or under a string; excessive pressure of the bow to obtain tone distortion; bowing where the finger is placed on a string; striking the instrument on the side, the back, and in the vicinity of the bridge; and half-registered (squawky and cracked) harmonics.

These effects are meant to destroy definite (even minutely discernible) melodic, harmonic, contrapuntal, metrical, rhythmical, and formal arrangement. *Match* is a vomiting of nightmarish noise. In this example of an eighteen-minute continuum of cacophonous yawp Kagel has no rival. And there is nothing in chamber music literature to equal it.

SEXTET

- **Sextet for Strings (Two Violins, Two Violas, and Two Cellos) (1953)**

Heavy, thick dodecaphonic music, the arguments intensified by the use of quarter tones. The individual involvement of the instruments is of volatile complexity (crucial to the style itself—technical modifications would only dissolve the dynamic of the style). There is the further element of polymetricality that is woven into the work and adds to its involutionary status. This is often of six-part total. In one place, for example, the following time signatures are used: 3+5/16 and 3/16+3/8 for the violins, 5/16 and 3/8 for the violas, and 6/16 and 3+4/16 for the cellos. However, these pulse divisions do not stay in place. Before a single measure has been completed each shifts to a different meter and no two coincide. This type of divergence leads to Kagel's warning that the Sextet can be performed without a conductor only if the players "have mastered all the problems of independent tempo and meter."

In a music of this type one cannot expect pink-pilled form, neatly packaged. The music is divided into sections with fermatas and pauses, some very short, others a bit longer. However, these are simply breathing places preparatory to continuing the interfusive action.

Kahn, Erich Itor (1905–56)

QUARTET

- *Seven Popular Songs from Brittany* for Four Instruments (Flute, Violin [or Clarinet], Clarinet, and Bassoon)

Frida Kahn has explained the background for this work. "In 1935 the Administration of the French Railroad (Chemins de Fer d'État) commissioned Erich Itor Kahn to write background music to an old saga of Brittany, *La Ville engloutie (The Engulfed City)*. For thematic material he was asked to use the folk melodies of Brittany. The story was to be narrated to the accompaniment of this music."

Kahn's intense research provided him with a huge amount of material. From it, this and three other works were produced: *Three Popular Songs* for voice and piano, *Petite suite bretonne* for chamber orchestra, and *Les Symphonies bretonnes* for large orchestra.

Although published in chronological sequence, the music is to be performed as follows: VII–VI–I–II–I–III–I–IV–V. Thus the original second and third parts of the set form trios in contrast to the principal "number one" movement, heard in third place. Kahn's music is totally simple. It is a far cry from his other works, which merge classical tradition with Schoenbergian freedom.

Kahowez, Günter (1940–)

QUARTET

- **String Quartet No. 1 (1960)**

Music that is completely involved with Bartókian stylistic force. Austrian born (in Vöcklabruck) and trained (at the Bruckner Conservatory in Linz and the Vienna Musical Academy), Kahowez imitates the Hungarian's coloristic elements and textural energy.

Regarding the former, included are the frictional pinches of grace notes; sharp chordal thrusts; the percussiveness of successive downbow attacks; various pizzicatos, including the so-called Bartók pizzicato, where the string rebounds off the fingerboard, glissandos and glides. The structuring includes asymmetry with its fluid impact, the strengths of sonorous totals (aided by special attention to open-string use in chordal combinations), and massed sound formations.

Movement one develops from three motival items, each defined by increasing rates of speed. Constant shifts apply as well to the second movement, with the paragraphing of rhapsodic detail compared to waltz projections. In the final part chordal and recitative properties in adagio are contrasted and blended and move into a molto allegro full of the choreographic frenzy that marks Bartókian fast music. A return to the slow beginning is made, followed by increases in speed that raise the tempo roof until the frenetic close. Indeed, Kahowez's music is a clone of Bartók's. Give him credit for superb imitation.

SEXTET

- *Structures for Six Instruments* (Flute [alternating Piccolo], Oboe, Clarinet, Horn, Bassoon, and Piano) (1965)

Change of style marks this Austrian composer's output. Beginning with neoclassic formations, he then turned to Bartókian language *(see above)*, and once again shifted, this time to serialism, represented by this sextet.

Each of the six pieces (most under the two-minute mark) is akin to an abstract statement, though the fifth piece has a motto that reads: ". . . ganz aufgehn können in einer Struktur" ("could completely rise within a structure"). There is no move to mix special colors into the textures. In lieu of this, two of the movements (three and five) are for reduced forces of three instruments each: number three calls for piccolo, oboe, and clarinet; number five (achieving decided timbre contrast by using the other three instruments) is for horn, bassoon, and piano.

Kai, Sesshū (1938–78)

DUOS

- **Music for Violin and Cello II (1975)**

Music by this Japanese creator wherein the aim is fixity, thereby an inert music, carefully planned but minus any emotive sense. The sounds move from one instrument to the other and sometimes the two are joined. There is no vibrato whatsoever, and there is never a connection between pitches (thus, sempre non legato!). The tempo shifts between a speed of ♩ = 60 and shorter portions paced at ♩ = 46. This alternation takes place thirteen times and then the final part of the duo is sped up a bit to ♩ = 66.

- **Music for Violin and Piano II**

Another example of Kai's style representing a music of frozen content. An abstract study of quarter notes and rests to be played in only one tempo (♩ =104), and though there are plentiful changes in dynamics, the violin is to play without vibrato throughout. A good amount of rests are within the 790 consecutive pulses of this rigid, computerlike delivery of pitches and silences.

Kalabis, Viktor (1923–)

DUOS

- **Sonata for Cello and Piano, Op. 29**

A composition of intense drama, resulting from the opposites of calmness and passion (the latter sometimes violent). Though classical structuring can be discerned—sonata, ternary, and sonata-rondo forms for the three movements—at no time does Kalabis remain satisfied with pat patterns. Balances are maintained, but sharply contrastive elements shape the structuring.

There are long lines and syncopative thrust in the Allegro moderato. A sense of declamatory song is maintained, and it continues in the opening of the Andante. Then, with firecracker impact, the speed immediately increases, the motility as well, and the cello bursts forth with *fortissimo* pizzicatos for a twenty-two-measure span, of which the last dozen are quadrupled chord sounds. And then, as suddenly, the tempo turns to Grave, with syncopated moves once again, finally calming down to a *pianississimo*. (This matches the dynamic of the sustained pitch concluding the first movement.) Movement three reverses matters by beginning dramatically, with sharp pungent rhythms, relaxes into an Adagio, returns to the vehemence, and finishes off with the Adagio. As in the previous movements, the Sonata ends softly.

- **Sonata for Trombone and Piano, Op. 32**

Kalabis is in no way an experimenter in his output. Still, the structure of this work—two movements, the second twice the length of the first—is not conventional.

The stressing of repetitive pitch particulars, rhythmicized, of course, and always articulative, is a reference point in both movements. The second movement (Allegro drammatico) is actually of huge ternary build. It begins and concludes with large, proclamatory materials. In between there is an Andante, which again makes use of repeated pitches but expands the action with activized, disjunct patterns.

The writing is trombone-flavored, made to fit the brass instrument beautifully. Let it not be thought the piano is simply supportive. It not only sustains and corroborates the trombone but has a rhythmic character throughout that gives counterpointed strength.

- **Suite for Oboe and Piano**

All the moves of the full romantic, presenting music that sings and music that principally dances. In the latter category are part one, *Der Dudelsackpfeifer kommt (The Bagpiper Appears)*, a triple-beat vivace spurred by chordal fifths; part three, *Scherzlied (Comic Song)*, vivace (molto), set in duple time; part five, another duple-pulse conception, *Die Jugend tanzt (The Youth Dances)*; and the finale (part seven), *Abschied (Farewell)*, which is not a fond affair but a very vivacious triple-beat conception.

For that matter, only one of the three even-numbered pieces is on the slow side—the waltzlike *Stelldichein (Rendezvous)* (part six). *Lied (Song)* (part two) is in alive allegretto pace, and *Sehnsuchtsvoll (Yearning)* (part four) takes a moderate course, moving constantly by a repetitive rhythmic pattern.

- **Variations for Horn and Piano, Op. 31**

Not the usual series of permutative changes on a theme. The music is so linked as almost to blend all the variational differences. Kalabis's opus can be considered as the presentation of a theme (marked by an initial rising fifth) which is developed in continuity.

A composer need not give away his variational secrets. The analytical clue here is the metronomic change of pace that coincides with subtle differences of material that eventually lead back to the theme. When it returns at the end it is softly stated and quietly pulsed.

QUARTET

- **String Quartet No. 2, Op. 19**

The outer parts (*Prolog* and *Epilog*) are in Adagio, and are developed from the same core material. In the opening part, Kalabis's habit of suddenly moving into a different (generally intense) state occurs midway.

The major part of the quartet is the central Allegro molto. That, too, has its sharply contrastive sections. A quietly delivered Andante followed by dramatic, partially rubato music interrupts the repetitively pulsed material in the central part of the movement, and toward the conclusion a part of the Andante returns. The aggressive tone of the music is apparent, even in its quieter moments. Kalabis's quartet is one of the most important produced by the contemporary Czech school of composers.

QUINTET

- *Piccolo musica da camera (Little Chamber Music)* **for Wind Quintet, Op. 27**

"Little" yes, with a performance time just over the eleven-minute mark. Three movements, with two portions of fast-paced music surrounding an Andante. The writing is generous, with sharp-pronged melody in the fast movements. Both of these are scherzo-personality conceptions, especially the first, which has sectional form. The slow movement is meditative, featuring dialogue material assigned to the flute and oboe.

NONET

- *Klasický Nonet (Classical Nonet)* **for Flute, Oboe, Clarinet, Bassoon, Horn, Violin, Viola, Cello, and Double Bass, Op. 13**

Kalabis's four-movement, nine-instrument work lives up to its title. It has fast movements at the beginning and end, with a slow movement and Scherzo within. The clean and smooth tonal writing is of a mild neoclassical quality. There isn't the slightest predilection for extremes and, in fact, Kalabis employs positive economy of gestures.

Tonal polarity is slightly used, otherwise key stability rules. The outer movements are in B-flat, the slow movement (slightly ornamental in its progress) is in E-flat, and the Scherzo is in G. No sustained originality, but certainly sustained creative efficiency.

Kalach, Jiří (1934–)

NONET

- *Chamber Music for Nine Instruments* **(Flute, Oboe, Clarinet, Horn, Bassoon, Violin, Viola, Cello, and Double Bass)**

No new fusion of formal types is to be found in this nonet. No need, what with the clear profile of thematic material and the unfussy, demarcative scoring.

The development of a single theme is the plan of the first movement. As the theme passes in review its changes are emphasized by different solo voices: violin, flute, cello, and flute again. Rondo types are used for the central slow movement and the final Allegro molto. Rhythm is a binder in both movements, blocked in its presentation. The pulsed rhythmic units sometimes become static in terms of their ostinato address. All of this is applied within a romantic syntax that remains faithful to tonality throughout.

Kálik, Václav (1891–1951)

DUO

- **Sonata for Violin and Piano (1919)**

Kálik's duo has the general tone of German romantic style with a sensitive intersplice of Czech nationalism. But there is the added point of intensity that is compelling. And there is the further matter of formal vividness, illustrated in the Fuga that begins the work. This is no simple, bare presentation of subject, fugal answer, and progress through the stipulations of the form. The music goes forward in a heavy contrapuntal manner, intertwining the materials in a sonata layout. Intensity relates to the C-minor Finale, set in fast tempo and concluding with balanced order in C major and contrastive Adagio tempo. The middle movement is a Scherzo that swings its Czech melos in polka tempo.

Kalkbrenner, Friedrich (1785–1849)

The history of music is dotted with composers who well deserve renewed examination, such as Kalkbrenner, a renowned pianist to whom Chopin dedicated his E-minor piano concerto. Like Pleyel and Clementi, his Austrian and Italian contemporaries, Kalkbrenner was a piano manufacturer as well as a composer. Another interesting fact is that Kalkbrenner was one of the first to write a piano sonata for the left hand alone.

QUINTETS

- *Grand Quintet* for Piano, Clarinet, Horn, Cello, and Double Bass, Op. 81

"Grand" in terms of the attention given to the piano; the paired strings and single wind and brass instruments are subsidiary in this conception of chamber music. The title page of the first edition stresses the matter, indicating that the quintet is "pour le Piano-Forte avec accompagnement de Clarinette, Cor, Violoncelle et Contrebasse." Of course, this is not an unexpected viewpoint from a composer who was a piano virtuoso and included the instrument in every one of the many compositions he produced (four concertos, fifteen so-

natas, seven trios, etc.).

There are three movements in this half-hour-long quintet. The Allegro risoluto is in expected sonata form. Movement two (Andante quasi adagio) is designed in a large three-part song form. The finale (Allegretto moderato) follows rondo specifications.

- *Grand Quintet* for Piano, Two Violins, Viola, and Cello, Op. 30

Kalkbrenner's quintet is evocative of the more showy side of romantic music. Knowledge and command of technique are present, but with less sustained imagery than one perceives in music of the same era. As to be expected from a piano virtuoso, the keyboard instrument predominates. The string writing is straightforward and pursues a narrow path. Only in a single place is one of the four string instruments (the cello) permitted some fancy footwork on stage. *Stürm und Dräng* mark the opening movement; the piano is the acclaimed master of the quintet combine. In the Romanza, a piano cadenza is inserted for additional spotlighting; the final portion of the opus is devoted to a Rondo, in which Kalkbrenner knits his instrumental weave more tightly than elsewhere.

Kalliwoda, Johann Wenzel (1801–66)

DUO

- *Morceau de salon* for Oboe and Piano, Op. 228

The works of this Bohemian violinist and composer, highly esteemed in his day, are seldom performed as of now. No secret genius or fancy is disclosed in his music, but certainly the *Salon Piece* is a respectable and worthy duo. It is a romantic, lyrical piece, sectionally detailed in a variational manner.

Kallstenius, Edvin (1881–1967)

QUARTET

- **String Quartet in C Minor, Op. 8**

Color Kallstenius as the "Swedish Reger." The evidence (proved by the sounds themselves): serious content, heavy texture, contrapuntal weave, chromaticized harmony, all of which recall the neobaroque splendor and the classic-romantic astuteness of the Bavarian Max Reger. Further, there is the love of variational form. In this quartet, variation is represented by the second movement, which consists of a five-measure preamble, then the theme and five variations, followed by thematic restatement.

In the opening movement, special emphasis is given the principal theme—more than generally obtains in sonata structure. It is also interesting to observe that the tone placement of the theme is weighted on the supertonic rather than the tonic. A credit of individuality must be given for the use of the cello as the soprano voice in the final chord.

The concluding movement, in rondo design, is like a fantastic march, with a tempo change marking a three-note figure whenever it appears within the theme. The length of this movement almost defeats Kallstenius, especially by his overemphasis of thematic unitarity in place of perceptive contrast.

QUINTET

- **Clarinet Quintet (Two Violins, Viola, Cello, and Clarinet), Op. 17**

Nationalism doesn't even flicker in this three-movement work. Late-romantic procedures of style cover every action of the sounds. Lightness is eliminated in favor of seriousness, even in the final (third) movement, Allegro giocoso, where it might be expected. But this music does not smile, and that finding applies to the entire quintet—some twenty minutes in length.

The thematic material is to be found in the harmonic movement of the instrumental lines. Chromaticism is plentiful and used to such an extent that one is certain the composer will turn next to atonality and/or twelve-tone style. But it is the complexity and involvement of the linear details that bring out the full intensities of this work. Recognizable counterpoint is little in comparison to the activized life of the harmonic ingredients. In the depth and focus of the line writing one finds that the whole is less impressive than its parts in this individually conceived quintet.

Kalmár, Lászó (1931–)

DUO

- **Sonata for Flute and Piano (1971)**

Music similar to prevue trailers seen in motion picture theaters. Thus: a little of this and a little of that—all athematic credits. Still, connected identification of the nine sections is clear. The first one is very slow and expressive; a Scherzando appears next. In part four the piano alone is followed by the flute alone; the same plan applies to the next portion, only the time span is larger and the pitches are connected. Part seven is very rhythmic, the final bit has the same quality as the initial bit.

QUARTET

- *Morfeo* for String Quartet (1977)

The title refers to Morpheus, the god of dreams in Roman and Greek mythology, and Orpheus, the celebrated Thracian musician of Greek mythology. A concentrated music is offered by this Hungarian composer. The materials are thin, of Webernian pomade texture, set forth in a series (in ten connected sections) of coloristic meshed webbings. These pass in review in less than five minutes.

Kalomiris, Manolis (1883–1962)

TRIO

- **Trio for Piano, Violin and Cello, Op. 22**

Kalomiris's piano trio tends to be quite sonorous because the three instruments are occupied together from start to finish. A definite national quality is certified by the inclusion of augmented steps, rhythmic and dance subtones without one whit of academic dryness.

The principal theme of the opening movement is constantly repeated in variegated manner. Monotony does not fasten itself because the excellent methods retain interest. The theme is halted only to insert a contrasting subject and is employed further to conclude the Trio; in this instance it obtains a towering effect by the use of augmented rhythm. The second movement, picturesquely titled "Transformations," is nothing more than a set of quadruple variations on a simple theme. A powerful presto tempo propels the Scherzo. This movement has a very national-sounding intermediate section in septuple meter. Though the forms chosen by Kalomiris are almost of bounded neutrality, the significant result of his Trio is as worthy as a work fashioned from a complex design.

Kaminski, Heinrich (1886–1946)

Kaminski has been called a neoclassic, neo-Gothic, neo-Lutheran, neo-Bachian, and even a neotheologian composer. Combined, all of these classification tags are correct. Kaminski was a polyphonicist, severely intent on contrapuntal arrangement; he created a product that stemmed from Wagner-Bruckner (via Bach) territories. The religious content is not of the Church, but the ponderousness is definitely a type of musical paganism that found him acceptable in Hitler's Germany after the *Kulturbolschewismus*—the elimination of all progressive music. However, later (in 1938) the Nazi's found a fault in his ancestry and performance of his music was officially forbidden.

TRIO

- ***Musik* for Two Violins and Harpsichord (or Piano) (1931)**

The entire work is controlled and bound by massive, brilliant, and uninterrupted polyphony. Further, the ascending conjunct pitches from the head of the fugue subject of movement one carry over to the third and fourth movements.

A slow and broadly conceived Praeludium introduces the Fugue in movement one. Movement two (Canon) is as intensely formalistic, with a canon at the unison between the two violins supported by the keyboard instrument with its own counterpointed detail. The Tanz (Dance) is no example of the light fantastic but is as texturally weighty as the rest of the trio. It connects with the fourth movement, which after a short introduction, moves into the concluding Fugue.

Kaminski maintains minor tonalities for three of the four movements. The outer ones are in D minor, the Canon is in A minor, and the Tanz is in D major.

QUARTETS

- ***Praeludium and Fugue on the Name Abegg* for String Quartet**

The second time the name "Abegg" has been used as the springboard for a musical work.

The initial use was by Schumann in his Op. 1, *Variations on the Name ABEGG*, for piano. The first five pitches of the theme of that piece read: A–B-flat–E–G–G, and Schumann properly dedicated the work to his friend Meta Abegg.

Kaminski's setting uses the same pitch material as the basis for development. The Prelude is moderately paced and has full-blooded partnership with solid textures. The Fugue has weight and length. It combines within its structure energy contrasted with sections of breadth, certainly far from being a bare conventional example of polyphonic style.

- **Quartet in A Minor for Piano, Clarinet, Viola, and Cello, Op. 1b**

In four movements, the last three inter-connective in that they deploy variations, four of which form the second movement; the fifth variant stands alone in third-section place as the Scherzo, and the remainder (sixth and seventh variations plus coda) depict the finale. The theme, a *Ruthenisches volkslied* (Ruthenian folk song), is announced antiphonally with four-voice harmonization in chorale style. The variants are distinct but greatly revitalized. Kaminski treats his instruments as a unit; there is no attention to foisting color on this stylistic return of baroque stolidity. The first movement shapes itself out of Bachian style, but is a modernized conception of that composer's art of polyphony

QUINTET

- **String Quintet in F-sharp Minor (Two Violins, Two Violas, and Cello)**

Linear detail and chorale lines mingle in constant juxtaposition in the opening movement, in a strongly formed contrapuntal array that highlights motival junctures and opposition. The tempos form counterprotests in the most decided and sudden shifts, with exceedingly few warnings given of changes to come by the usual dictates of ritards and accelerandos. It is akin to a musical confession, alternating fervor and humility. There are thirty-four *major* changes in the 212 measures that constitute the opening free sonata-formed movement. The effect is not only duo-subjected, but it is as though two different teams of players were replying to each other.

An ecclesiastical style is used in the slow movement. Contrasting episodes return in similar and figurated states (ever the impress of the polyphonic school in weaving counterpoints onto a theme). There are rustic overtones in the third movement, as well as Wagnerian thickness of lines and movement, in a style that departs somewhat from the austerity of the two previous sections. The objective is to relieve and contrast the polyphonistic style, but heaviness will be found. Kaminski, like so many German composers, depended on mass totality. The meters do change, however, shifting in 4/4, 3/4 combinations as well as 5/4 and 3/4, plus 3/2 (equal to 6/4). But rhythm needs clarity to unfold, else it becomes swallowed by the pluralism of moving voices.

One would expect the fugal form to be used by a composer so bent on polyphonic pugnacity. Kaminski does not disappoint. He uses that form for the final movement in the thickest of presentations. It is Bachian only in that it is strong: it is weakened by its lack of a foil. Contrast takes place only in terms of different speeds rather than voicing.

(Kaminski composed this quintet in 1916. The work was revised in 1927.)

Kaminski, Joseph (1903–72)

QUARTET

- **String Quartet**

This is a Technicolor travelogue for string quartet, including a lexicon of techniques, representing a compendium of styles. Nonetheless, the quartet will be found to be enjoyable merely for its colorfulness and its having something for everyone. It may well be that the last was the reason Kaminski's composition was awarded the Tel Aviv Municipality's "Engel" Prize in 1949.

The first movement begins with the principal dramatic theme in the viola, placed over a pedal point. The most abrasive friction is used for the second statement of the theme by constricted ninths in the two lower instruments. When the second theme enters, the second violin and viola swap sweet rejoinders in parallel thirds. This brings contrast, to be sure, but it also brings a sweeping stylistic turnabout. The form is of unitary mold. There is no direct recapitulation, merely the expansion of material.

Movement two is a set of variations, providing further free formations. Variation one treats the subject in augmentation with trill-like figurations. There, the instruments are split in terms of timbral density; the violins are muted, the viola and cello are not. Ostinatos, chunky chords, and varied patterns pitched in imitation make up the second variation. Cadenzas are found in the next part (these are marked "recitatives," but amount to the same thing). The movement concludes with an extremely fast, fancy-framed section and another one marked All' espagnola, the Spanish conception having an impressionistic patina. The movement's closing C-major chord is an unexpected touch.

A rondo system in which dance tunes predominate is employed for the finale. Wrapped within are thematic augmentation, fugato, and the cyclic device of restating the initial movement's main subject. Again, an unexpected twist is obtained by the soft dynamic conclusion in B major.

Quite a survey, indeed: diatonic and frictional harmonies, quartal and quintuple formations, homophonic and polyphonic content, imitative and canonic passages, unitary, variational, and rondo forms, and so on. It would be thought that Kaminski had covered the creative territories thoroughly. Negative! In the final movement there is additional coloristic conduct: glissandos, tremolandos, modalism, as well as scordatura! Somehow, all this technical numerosity works together. Perhaps it's the rule of "Defendit numerus" ("There is safety in numbers").

Kanitz, Ernest (1894–1978)

DUOS

- *Sonata Californiana* **for Alto Saxophone and Piano (1952)**

The regional identification is a picturesque calling card. Or creative showmanship. The three parts of this duo match sonata dictates in terms of a fast-slow-fast sequence, but otherwise the contents equate a suite.

"Sky and Water, Fragrance, Light" is frothy, with tripleted background which later changes in the recapitulation of the main theme. The music is ablaze with fast tempos. The same applies to the "Hollywood" scene, jazzy and fourthy in intervals. Within, the music contains a small march portion and a cadenza for the saxophone in recitative style. Part two (the slow movement) is a Lament, its mood a reminder of Sibelius's *Valse triste*.

- **Suite for Violin and Piano**

The suite detail of this duo is not thickly en-crusted with tradition. Although the use of a Prelude is a standard suite curtain-raiser, this one moves very fast and is governed by quartal harmonies. Likewise, rondo conclusions ob-tain a majority vote in most suite plans. Kanitz's Rondo–Finale differs a bit. It has tarantella contours, plays around with the tempo, and includes a fugato.

Movement two is a slow ("steadily glid-ing") "Vision," which observes with quartal and quinary harmonies. The remaining move-ment is a Fugue (in quasi Phrygian mode). (The pitch area for this mode is a diatonic (natural) scale with E as the starting point.)

TRIO

- **Notturno for Flute, Violin, and Viola (1950)**

Monothematic development of the initial vig-orous theme pivoted around C opens the trio. Slow-tempo music follows, ornamental in fac-ture, and containing an important pitch sweep that is announced by all three instruments in the course of the division. The final part is a mod-erately-pace section, with a presto conclusion. Kanitz's piece is always balanced with sonor-ity arrangement and harmonic conviction.

Kapp, Eugen (1908–)

DUOS

- **Sonata for Cello and Piano**

An example of this composer's romantic ideol-ogy producing a music where form and appli-cation to content are clearly proposed and where the thematic material is clear and direct and is matched by the tonalities. It will not please the virtuoso camp, but it will please listeners on the lookout for expressive music. The word is "communication," still a clean word in the 20th century.

A sonata-proportioned first movement. The middle movement is a Serenade with a decided waltz beat; the Finale is rondo typed.

Kapp seems to favor soft endings to his music. As in the piano and violin sonata *(see below)*, here each movement ends softly, though each is only in small total amount as compared to the large areas involved in the other work.

- **Sonata in C Major for Piano and Violin (1943)**

Ambitious and sincere music; sincerely tonal music, grooved with specific key slots and precise modulatory shifts. It's all been said before and more masterfully, but this does not thereby deny a work of expertise in an eclectic mild romantic sense.

That Kapp believes in his home key is ex-hibited by the fact that twenty-five measures pass in the first movement before an accidentalized pitch appears. The second sub-ject of the movement, drenched with juicy thirds, is in A major. There are digressions into C-sharp minor and C minor that alternate with the home tonality. Movement two is a fiery Scherzo in E minor. The Trio contrast is made by tempo lowering and a key shift to B-flat. A dual, rhythmically prepared cadenza preludes the recapitulation. Key clarity (C major and C minor) marks the balletic finale, introduced by a short Lento tranquillo.

Two points. It is very rare to find a title these days with the piano preceding the name of the string, wind, or brass instrument with which it is combined. Second, all three movements in the opus end softly and with sizable sustainment of the restrained dynamic level: the last four-teen measures of movement one, the conclud-ing thirty measures of movement two, and the final sixteen measures of movement three.

Kapr, Jan (1914–88)

DUOS

- *Dialogues* for Flute and Harp (1965)

Music that is a product of subtle folkloric weave in a cloth of modal and twelve-tone design. Always colorful. Always new. Two of the ten pieces are for a single instrument: in number three, the flute, and in number seven the dialogue becomes a monologue for the harp.

Most fascinating and truly unforgettable is the finale, containing wailing, crying, and gliding sounds by the flute. These are obtained by playing on the separated head of the instrument ("isolare il Capo di Flauto"). The effect is probing and of uncommon impact.

Number five of the set is dainty-dancy; number two is stimulated by bent flute sounds. The eighth dialogue is extremely colorful. It includes whispering and flutter tones for the flute and an ingenious effect for the harp, produced by small wooden paddles attached to the fingers of gloves worn by the performer.

(The first two performances of Kapr's duo took place within forty-eight hours: the première in Pilsen on November 21, 1966; the second performance in Munich on November 23.)

- Fantasie for Viola and Piano (1958)

A synthesis of various displays. Slow-tempo, chromatically festooned material is followed by a scherzando section, lightly begun, then dynamically expanded. The music relaxes and dies down and then moves into energetic command (marked at the start by unaccompanied viola). Preparing for the later recapitulatory data, some of the chromatic syntax of the beginning creeps into this section. Next comes a slow division (also specifically identified, in this case, by muted viola timbre).

At the end of the last Kapr proposes a slight return to previous material. There is a hint of the opening, then one of the scherzando portion. The latter becomes newly expanded and developed to conclude the work. The formal coalescence (which is what a fantasy music amounts to) is quite telling.

- Intermezzo for Flute and Piano (1968)

Unmetered, freely coursed music. At times a type of rhythmic regularity emerges, but it is quickly canceled. Surprisingly then, the final part of Kapr's eight-minute duo is fluidly metered and totally unisoned in its rhythms.

The various options (the result of such directions as: "fast, without regular rhythm, legato varying density through alterations of motion") are choice; it is this very caprice that offers benefits.

- Sonatina for Violin and Piano (1948)

Especially in the opening movement, Kapr is like a persuasive educator who reminds one that creative expression is the joy of retelling stories of the past with some slightly new twists. Kapr is a man of vast information. He is the generous eclectic (in both his premodernistic days, as represented here, and in the later, adventurous music, composed beginning in the 1960s).

In the tonal climate of movement one, slight bitonal drafts occur. This amalgamlike situation runs into the pair of themes that are principal in this Molto allegro e con anima movement. While both are easily recognized, dynamic and lyrical in turn, the heated surge of the former is combined with the legato vocalistic turns of the latter. In movement two the quintuple spans of the melodic line define the personality of the music.

One could call the final part (Allegro giocoso) updated Mozart in Czech clothes. Again, there is the quintuple impetus, this time transferred to a fair-size section as rhythmic contrast to the clear quarter-note totals within the other measures. It shows the art of technical balance rather than the indulgence in being a technical spendthrift.

QUARTETS

- *Rotazione 9* **for Piano, Violin, Viola, and Cello (1967)**

The title and form are explained by the concept of a rotating nine-angled crystal. As a result there are many gliding and sweeping sounds, derived from three series of melodic and harmonic elements (representing the various angles and intensities of light falling upon the crystal's planes). The incessant motility within Kapr's piece bears out the crystal's rotation.

- **String Quartet No. 3 (1954)**

Kapr as he wrote in his postromantic tonal days. Compelling music, all of it; no show-offy virtuosic attempts. Solidity is the word, and if there is any resemblance it might well be to Martinů, but even in that case Kapr's music is, in its rhythmic moments, more off the ground.

The last statement is not meant to imply that Kapr's music lacks dynamic power, of which the finale of this three-movement work, with its scoring of closeup rhythmic detail compared to passages of delicate depiction, is an example. Full development also concerns the opening (Allegro energico), which presents three themes and then proceeds to detail them in different manner on their repetitions. Movement two (Andante tranquillo) is structured from a pair of motives.

OCTET

- *Woodcuts: Four Pieces for Eight Instruments* **(Four Trumpets and Four Trombones) (1973)**

A tight packaging of timbre using eight brass

instruments: four trumpets and four trombones. The tightness carries over to the harmonic data, which involve bruising contact, but contact always of musical consequence. There's some chance throwing about—glides, and the like, but a jug of hot effects is not thrown over the auditor. Kapr's four-part music has contemporaneous meaning as it avoids all gimmickry.

Kaprál, Václav (1889–1947)

QUARTET

- **String Quartet in C Minor**

The strength here is romantic power with chunks and hunks of dramatic material, the detail splintered at times for the inclusion of strongly contrastive items. The first movement, for example, while developing a dynamic theme headed by a descent of a fourth, breaks into a declarative grave tempo with ostinato rhythmic support. It proceeds only to spin away into grave tempo again, this time for a fugato. The dualism then continues. Movement two follows suit, combining an adagio with a presto, and the juxtaposition of the two opposites is carried forward in the working out of the themes. It is all fully textured. Kaprál has no time for superficial musical repartee in his quartet.

Karadimchev, Boris (1933–)

DUO

- *Call* **for Horn and Piano**

A strong-portioned batch of brass and keyboard instrumental sound. The lines are alive with repetitive figures around which are woven short passages of incisive melodicism. There is a certain amount of sectionalism.

Karagitcheff, Boris (1879–1946)

QUARTET

- *Azerbaijan*: String Quartet No. 4

Another example drawn from the wellsprings of Soviet folk music. Karagitcheff's quartet is similar to such compositions as Lev Knipper's *Tajik Suite*, Boris Shekhter's *Turkmenia*, and Victor Bely's *Chuvash Songs*.

The exoticism of the last movement (Danses) is no primitive imitation but one of faithful artistic delineation. The grace notes, melodic turns, and augmented steps included are copies of Azerbaijan music modulations. Simplicity is represented in the middle movement, titled Chanson. The first part, Le Branle (a French group dance popular over many centuries), calls on a jogging type of rhythm to prop and pin melodies of broad character.

Kardoš, Dezider (1914–)

DUO

- Three Compositions for Violin and Piano

The first of the set is binary-formationed, with an Un poco maestoso division compared to a lusty Allegro agitato. Part two has a simple, folk-type melody that revolves with variational change. Movement three is a burlesque and zippy. Here there are bits that remind one of Bach with wrong notes.

QUARTET

- String Quartet No. 3, Op. 49

Muscular music, infused, especially in the concluding Introduzione e Finale, with Bartókian primitivism. The molto accentato content is interleafed with athletic-characterized fugal sections. The polytonal aspects of this part of the quartet are more intensely promulgated in the first movement (Preludio), which has an engaging splintery astringency.

The middle movement is a Canto lamentoso. Emphasis in this song in lamenting style is on the conjuncted impress of minor seconds, both melodic and harmonic, and in the intervallic compression within the use of glissandos. Kardoš's five-minute Canto represents significant music.

QUINTETS

- Concerto for Wind Quintet, Op. 47

Four movements with an interlock in the textural commentary. The broad moving lines of the Prelúdium (continuous in their motility) are found in the middle section of the Elégia. There, the material is different but the style and shape are the same and a still further duplication is made in the contrastive portion of the Finale.

Both the Burleska and the Finale are speedy, disjunct in outline, asymmetric in rhythmic organization. The pulse irregularity adds zip to this music, an example of a telling *jeu d'esprit*.

- Quintet for Flute, Oboe, Clarinet, Horn, and Bassoon, Op. 6

A finely turned balance of the lyrical and the dramatic is in this Slovakian composer's wind quintet. The chitchatty style all too often found in many works for winds is avoided here, without slighting the extrovert quality of the Finale.

In the Preludio the major central part is developed with an essential ascent and descent of a seventh in the theme. The outer sections are in broader tempos. The other forms are conventional but not shackled by rote conditions. There is a sizable Scherzo con Trio and then a Passacaglia. The latter has a steady momentum as it is developed, culminating in a Scherzando and then a possessive Largo in full *fortissimo*, decreasing to a very quiet coda.

Kardos, István (1891–1975)

DUOS

- *Bipartitum* **for Bassoon and Piano (1963)**

The two movements (hence the title) tend to romantic outgo, though classic forms are in control. There is also a strong Hungarian flavor (Bartókian tinges). The first part, "Serioso," leans on rondo supports; the second, "Giocoso," is a strict ternary piece with a literal recapitulation and a coda of fair size to conclude matters.

- *Scherzo variato* **for Flute and Piano**

Credit Kardos with a neat design, beginning with the nonaverage use of a forty-measure Scherzo for the subject of variational deployment. It is set in quintuple meter and its style is an aid, as the music progresses, to recall the generative source. Good-size variations are presented, employing colorful chromatic harmony. The last (third) variation concludes with a fugato.

TRIO

- *Poem and Humoresque* **for Violin, Viola, and Harp (1969)**

The two pieces are full of the neat dissonances that signal the accents of neoromantic speech. The inner conjunction of rhythmic vitality is an asset in Kardos's trio, as is the very appropriate scoring. There are substantial tuttis to obtain profitable contrasts, but thick, fatty substances are not used.

In the *Poem* there is both rhapsodic thrust and some use of imitation between the string

instruments. Vivace possibile is the tempo heading for the *Humoresque*, but in a few places the pace is slowed for a short bit and then speeded up again. This demeanor is in play for the concluding part of the piece, which recalls the vivace only in the final measure. Kardos's *Humoresque* has size and an engaging septuple meter that fluctuates in its formation so that 3+4 is mixed with 4+3 pulses and is further contrasted with an octuple setting of 3+2+3 beats within the measure.

Karel, Leon

QUARTET

- *Seascapes*: **Suite for Four Clarinets**

"Riptide" is a stream of eighth-note movement with the momentum maintained by the use of tutti textures. The same totality applies to the undulations of "Ground-Swell." In the end movement, "Whitecaps," hemiola spray whips through the quick, duple-thrusted measures.

Karel, Rudolf (1880–1945)

QUARTET

- **Piano Quartet, Op. 22**

Karel was a composer of classically healthy music, colored by his interest in the old church modes. A minor amount of native heritage permeated his work, which followed his study with Dvořák. During World War II he fought with the Czech resistance. Arrested by the Nazis in 1943, he was sent to Terezin concentration camp, where, shortly before the liberation, he died of dysentery.

The Op. 22 two-movement quartet is without doubt Karel's most important chamber work. Though the description "fragment" appears on the title page of the score, the work is an entity. There were two additional movements, unfortunately lost during an earlier critical period in Karel's life. He had been teaching in Russia, and the music disappeared during the chaotic period of the revolution.

Op. 22 was composed in 1915 (publication took place in 1926 during "peace") and the effect of the war is perceived in the first movement. It is based on a chorale, "Modlitba k Neznámému" ("Prayer for the Unknown"). In the music, which is modally styled, a variety of figurations are developed; the chorale stands out in relief, with antiphonal scoring an important factor. Balance in the Scherzo derives from a tonality shift in the center of the movement. There is no change in regard to the repetitive eighth notes that knit the music's fabric.

NONET

- **Nonet (Flute, Oboe, Clarinet, Bassoon, Horn, Violin, Viola, Cello, and Double Bass), Op. 43**

Opus number notwithstanding, Karel never finished this work. It existed in draft form at the time of his death in 1945 in a Nazi concentration camp and was completed by F. Hertl.

Karel's opus is robustly romantic. The urgency of the first movement (in G minor) almost reaches the level of Wagnerian rhetoric. While the slow movement does not move away from a similar romantic stance it shifts into chromatic cross-checking in its harmony and tends to become quite thick and crowded. The overuse of similar accompanimental figures is also crucial. (Could this be less Karel's fault and more due to posthumous editing?) A folksy finale presents matters in a very bright mood. It is totally arresting tonal music conceived with formal assurance.

Karg-Elert, Sigfrid (1877–1933)

DUOS

- ***Impressions exotiques* for Flute and Piano, Op. 134**

A distinguished set of pictorial portrayals, each sensitive, each neatly accomplished.

"Idylle champêtre" ("Rural Idyll") poetizes with exceedingly little of Karg-Elert's usual chromatic language. The "Danse pittoresque" is indeed "picturesque," first with melancholic curves, then with burlesquelike moves. Plenty of trills and twirls for "Colibri" ("Humming Bird"). The "Lotus" portrayal is long-lined, gentle and delicate. "Evocation a Brahma" is delineated with declamatory decisiveness. It builds to a tremendous climax and then subsides.

- **Sonata in B-flat Major for Flute and Piano, Op. 121**

Karg-Elert's favored two-movement total is used here. Both movements are in the sonata mold, but the second one is freely expansive and juts into both rondo and variational territories. Little matter, since the contrastive materials are clearly set forth, including scherzo and slow movement elements. Scherzo qualities also mark the second theme of the opening movement; the initial theme has pastoral contours.

- **Sonata No. 2 in B Major, for Clarinet (or Viola) and Piano, Op. 139b**

Packed tight with late-romantic detail. And also packed in terms of structuring, with only two movements, the first an expansive sonata and the second a combination of scherzo and slow movement. The syntax is fully chromatic, but there are pitch centers that control the flourish of rhetoric commanding the greater part of the music.

TRIO

- **Trio in D Minor for Oboe, Clarinet, and English horn (or Horn), Op. 49, No. 1**

This great organ virtuoso and master of organ composition turned out a fair amount of chamber music, none better than this Trio. Its odd combination is an equivalency of organ registration timbre, a subconscious transfer from Karg-Elert's most favored creative medium.

The Trio is structurally split. In its first half matters are formal, in its second part it draws from the wealth of old dances. The Introduction contains some implied imitation and is followed by a Double Fugue. Careful distinction is made between the subjects; one ascends and the other descends with grace-note decorations. The twain meeting is well accomplished. The triple-meter Sarabande moves faster than usual, is made more opulent by substituting tonal movement for dignified chordal solidity. On the other hand, the Rigaudon et Musette run true to scale. The Rigaudon begins with the usual anacrusis and is in spirited duple measure. The contrasting Musette is in brightened tonality. It drones effectively, first in the low clarinet and then reverses direction and pipes in the oboe, at the other end of the gamut.

Karkoschka, Erhard (1923–)

DUOS

- **Duet for Violin and Cello (1951)**

Dance spirit is represented in the outer movements, which are in free tonal style with G as a polarity control. Both are in the same tempo metronomically, though the essence of the first one is lusty and the quality of the other is *schwungvoll* (with élan). The ternary structure

of the finale has an interesting inverted canon as its central part. And it is a canon that rules the entire middle movement, a slowly swinging Song in duple meter that is sparked by a crisscross of pulse stresses.

- *Variationen über das Isländische Volkslied "Sumri hallar" ("Die Sonne sinkt nun") (Variations on the Icelandic Folksong "Sumri hallar" ["Now Sets the Sun"])* **for Flute and Piano (1952)**

Similar to Karkoschka's other music this piece offers a novel approach. The duo is not a single set of variations but three sets, divided into three separate movements that are, in turn, moderate, slow, and fast in tempo.

The theme is purely diatonic. Accordingly, in its presentation by the two instruments nary a chromatic pitch is heard in the opening twenty-two measures. Paramount within the theme and within all three movements is the constant inflection of metrical totals. In movement one these are 2/4, 3/4, and 4/4; in movement two these three meters are joined by 5/4; in the final movement there are but two: 6/8 and 9/8. No set patterns result; the pulse sequences are fluid. Despite the variational application the outer movements are tripartite in structure.

TRIO

- *In Triangle* **for Three Flutes (1975)**

Eleven minutes of disaccordance arrived at principally by dismembered and disfigured discursive materials. It is avant-garde music of the happy-ending kind—picturesque enough, to be sure, but totally athematic and tonally montaged.

The flutists play in three corners of the hall. Although there are a few portions that have standard notation and rhythmic cohesive stability, the greater part of the piece consists of separate sound sensations. Coincidence of lines is simply a matter of happenstance.

One section (designated "Rotation") defines imitation; another as a three-quarter-timed "Tanz" ("Dance"). However, the most positive material consists of a large section noted as "Reagieren und Improvisieren" ("Response and Improvisation"). Within are whispered sounds, sounds made without pitch (produced by vigorous fingering), chords, and other specialities outside of normal techniques. Such mutations of timbre don't smudge but actually underline the stylistic, avant-garde arrogance of Karkoschka's text.

(Another version calls for one flute and stereo tape.)

QUINTET

- **4 Aufgaben für 5 Spieler (4 Tasks for 5 Players) (1971)**

Tradition doesn't exist in this example of creative informality. Standard organizational tactics—harmony, counterpoint, rhythm, form, etc.—are absent, replaced by diagrams, charts, written instructions, free choices, and random samplings. The tabulations (five large printed pages) given the performers amount to bits and pieces. From these a fifteen-minute composition is to be made. Style, derived from a technique that establishes it, is, of course, eradicated in a production of this kind.

As in a foot race, the players are given the starting point. How the course is to be run is charted, but the routes are so improvisational that anything can (and will) occur. In this far-from-conventional unconventionality, composition is arrived at by decomposition. Naturally, no two performances will be the same.

Karkoschka's quintet can be performed by any group of five wind instruments, or any assortment of five string instruments. The combination can be mixed, but at least two of the total must be of the same type. The work consists of four parts. The first, "From Verbal Instruction," arranged in time-length segments, is a mixture of everything from hissing, voiceless whispers, and rubbing the music stands with wooden sticks to playing folk tunes in differing keys and registers and producing short, loud, shrieking sounds. And more of such assorted effectuations.

Part two is titled "Changes." In it four structures are opposed, separated and combined, changed and manipulated. Only one of the four has pitch movement; the others consist of single sounds and glissandos. The third "task" is termed "Contrary Time-Phrases." It consists of three rhythmic units: the patterns totaling ten quarter notes, thirteen eighth notes, and nine quarter notes. However, pertinent rhythmic phraseology is broken by fluctuative tempos and free interchange. The counteraction thereby cancels clarity. The final part is a "Collage" of seven themes plus one to be invented by the players. Of the seven, one is a ländler and another is an eight-measure two-part affair, which the composer properly (!) describes as containing "kitsch." Of the remainder, four are squarely tonal and the fifth is a widely leaping, ultrachromatic progression of unbalanced sounds. These are tossed around, fractioned, and combined in a madcap chronicle. Karkoschka's objective is clearly depicted in the instructions for the conclusion. Four of the performers are to play any of the "themes" they wish, with the exception of one of the tonal segments; insert silences "in and between the sections"; increase the intensity "in every respect"; and then suddenly stop.

There is no doubt that Karkoschka's *4 Aufgaben* represents a prime example of disordered ordered music. Some might classify the composition as musical dadaism.

Karlins, M. William (1932–)

DUO

- *Music* for Tenor Saxophone and Piano (1969)

A superbly crafted work, musically as well as in terms of defining the true substances of the saxophone. The prejudice against this instrument is thinning, fortunately, but musicians' anti-comments are still not negligible. A few more works like Karlins's and this instrumental bigotry will finally disappear.

Declamatory and kinetic-nervous details are found in the first movement. A slow jazz style, of genuine expressivity, marks part two, dedicated "to the Memory of Coleman Hawkins." (Hawkins, a black American jazz tenor saxophonist [1904–69], was considered the foremost performer on the instrument.) In the finale, jazz also directs some of the passages—a little dirty jazz it is, with sax growls. The main point develops into an unaccompanied cadenza.

TRIO

- *Variations on "Obiter Dictum"* for Amplified Cello, Piano, and Percussion (1965)

The theme is Karlins's—the first seventeen measures of a work for organ. There is no complacent tolerance for serial or structured systemization (a huge inventory of dull music is covered by those terms). Each of Karlins's six variations is decisively clear and yet there is no partitioning; the emotion and fantasy cohere as a solid, total, free-pitched essay. There are power bursts that are in strong contrast to the predominant, intensely tight and provocative lyricism of the amplified cello part. This music exhibits compelling creative imagination.

QUARTET

- Quartet No. 2 *(Variations and Cadenzas)* for Saxophones (Soprano, Alto, Tenor, and Baritone Saxophones) (1975)

Cogent structural balances pertain to Karlins's substantial work (the performance time is approximately 17 1/2 minutes). There are twelve variations (no theme is proposed for the permutations), divided into three groups of four. After the first and second sets there are cadenzas. In turn the cadenzas are symmetrically arranged; the first is for the two lower saxophones, the second for the two higher instruments. (In the first of these there is additional symmetry with the instrumental progress arranged baritone, tenor and baritone, tenor. The second cadenza begins with the soprano; with the entrance of the alto the entire cadenza remains a double one.)

There is, of course, considerable sonorous appeal to Karlins's virtuosic piece, but there is also the direct excitement brought by the technical distribution. The pace of the variations is kept at a moderate level until the last pair, when the speed rate moves up and in the concluding variation (finale and coda) the fastest tempo is reached. Another interesting point is the scheme of the tenth variation, which consists of four variations within the variation.

NONET

- Concerto Grosso No. 1 for Nine Instruments (Flute [alternating Piccolo], Oboe, Clarinet, Bassoon, Horn, Trombone, Violin, Viola, and Cello) (1960)

Each of the three movements has a different arrangement, the first especially referring to baroque concerto form denoted by the title of the nonet. The opening, a very slow recitativelike oboe statement, gives the tone of the movement. Later there are solo episodes for violin and flute, clarinet with viola, horn and trombone, etc. Some are short, others a bit more extended.

Movement two reduces the instrumentation to a quintet total, calling for two winds (flute and bassoon) and the string trio. The finale has a chordal introduction and moves into a very fast music. Within it, Karlins interrupts the motility for a section that is slow-pace, bleak, minus color (the strings are nonvibrato), with low-scale dynamics. When the speedy material returns with its demanding toccata-turned asymmetric detail, the contrastive impact is triple-powered.

(A version is available using augmented strings, in which case a double bass may be added to the group.)

Kárnauke, Kurt (1866–1944)

QUARTET

- **Elves' Dance for String Quartet and Triangle (ad lib)**

Four measures of introduction and the music zips off and away on light motives that move on a bed of bouncing eighth notes. The use of the triangle brightens matters, but the precisely calculated tonal balances of the dance are just as delicately resourceful without it.

Károlyi, Pál (1934–)

DUO

- **Contorni (Outlines) for Bassoon and Piano (1970)**

Bruised sonorities and a celebration of creating artistic noises. No formal straightjacket con-

strains Károlyi's duo. It begins with a violent, totally chromatic tone cluster on the piano and a four-part secundalized chord on the bassoon, and this type of scrape and stridency continues. In one place the two instruments depict a "tone rain," which constitutes a sounding of pitches in all registers in rapid succession, using great leaps and totally projected in "unsystematic confusion." Microtones on the bassoon and banging with the fist on the lowest strings of the piano are a pair of the many colors. Slow bassoon vibrato and scratching a piano string with the nails are still another pair. Etc., etc. The bassoon also provides a "tongue pizzicato," which delivers a percussive quality minus any definite pitch.

This is a music that even in its quieter moments sounds hurt and angry. This is not a music for those with delicate tastes. For flutters and whispers, light prattle and dainty outlines, they will have to seek elsewhere.

TRIO

- **Chamber Music for Two Violins and Piano**

Four parts to Károlyi's little trio, of which the first pair is titled "Two Small Pieces." These are contrasted in tempo and makeup. The first is sustained, mainly *pianissimo*, and is registered by secundal relationships; the other is likewise secundal but more frictionally textured, is pounded rhythmically, and is in the *forte* range.

Part three is a Lento, again sustained, soft in impress, and built on intervallic seconds. To confirm the title "Tritonus" for part four, the music is chockful of augmented fourths, which cover the extent of three whole tones.

Karosas, Yuosas (1890–?)

DUO

- *Sonata Jūros legenda* **for Violin and Piano**

A substantial formal depiction for this four-movement opus. Karosas shows an assured hand at interlocking the instrumental voices. It is all well sounding, well proportioned, old-style Russian-style material, with everything set perfectly in place.

In movement one there is piecemeal development. There are whole sections devoted to a specific element: triplets, double stops, harmonics. (As an example, the last covers a sixteen-measure spread.) Tripartite form is used for the simple Intermezzo. The Scherzo is dominated by across-the-bar-line duple segments set into the basic triple-pulse measures. The reverse occurs in the chaconnelike Finale, where triplet figures are spread between the duple-beat measures.

Karren, Léon

DUO

- *Sonate d'église (Church Sonata)* **for Violin and Organ (or Piano)**

Music that is not planned especially for the concert circuit but would not be out of place in that environment. The deadliness of old-fashioned oratorio-style instrumental writing, which flattens the music into dullness, is avoided, though the second of the three movements is entirely accompanimental for the keyboard instrument.

Part one is an "Offertoire," an instrumental composition played while the offering of the congregation assembled for religious worship is being collected. Its tempo is andante largo and it consists of an introduction and principal section, both in E minor; the latter is repeated, followed by a variation on the theme in E major.

The second piece is an "Elévation," music played during the Elevation of the Host in the Roman Catholic Mass. As mentioned above, the conception is solo with accompaniment, with major stress on syncopation in the melodic line. In slow tempo, of course, and the same applies to the final "Communion" (the last of the five items of the Proper of the Mass) that has the same tempo as the first piece (andante largo) but more liveliness (especially through the repetitive use of a short–long rhythmic figure).

Kartzev, Alexander (1883–1953)

QUARTETS

String Quartets

There are no misty or mystic harmonic proliferations in Kartzev's string quartets. He was a 20th-century composer of romantic music, with clear formal conditions that relate to classical functionalism. There were many Soviet composers that reacted to contemporary substances by rejection. Kartzev was one of these. His quartets have imaginative skill, warm themes, and excellent workmanship, but avoid all contacts save those that stem from the music of the Russian nationalist School by way of Misakovsky (minus any morbidity). Kartzev's quartets may not break new ground, but they have vitality.

- **String Quartet No. 1 in C Minor, Op. 11**

Kartzev's first string quartet is dedicated to Glière, with whom he studied in addition to Paul Juon and Taneiev. It thrives on syncopation: as the impetus in the principal subject of movement one; to help define the coda of that movement; as the contrastive counterpoise in the quick, second movement; again, when it denotes the slower, second theme of the finale; and in two of the free variational portions of the third movement.

The opening agitated movement is prefaced by a sustained introduction in the home tonality, which is used in part to balance the close of the movement. The second theme of the movement begins in the major dominant key but works out and away from the major tonal zone. Movement two begins as a fugal allegro but turns into a series of motival gestures. The slow portion of the work is an Intermezzo, qualified by the parenthetical inscription (quasi variazioni). This is, indeed, proper identification, for the reasoning is quite free in the five divisions within the movement, with the theme respelled at the terminal point. A fast duple-meter finale wraps up matters.

- **String Quartet No. 2 in F Major, Op. 14**

Kartzev dedicated his second string quartet, as he did his first, to one of his teachers: "To the Memory of Sergei Taneiev." No specific threnodic tone permeates the work, even with the C-sharp-minor tonality of the slow movement (which ends, as does the final F-minor movement, in the same-named major mode, in complete classical allegiance). In each of the three movements Kartzev posits two principal ideas, which he then develops and recapitulates in a changed, but fully recognizable manner. The only attention to special color are the muted instruments, which define the ternary boundaries of the middle movement's form. An additional resource is the use of augmentation, which italicizes the theme in the final movement.

Kassern, Tadeusz Zygfrid (1904–57)

DUO

- **Sonatina for Flute and Piano (1948)**

This Polish composer (Kassern became an American citizen the year before he died) never shifted from his neoclassic style. Its clarity, set within scoring that was always finely balanced and minus any sharply differentiated effects, is substantiated in this three-part work.

Alternate sections shape the first movement with fast and very slow tempo distinctions, a quadruple pulse marking the former and a broad triple meter defining the latter. Song and rondo forms are used in the other two movements.

TRIO

- **Concertino for Flute, Clarinet, and Bassoon (1935)**

The Concertino thrusts forward with rhythmic pertinence and neoclassic tooling. There is a straightforward sensibility of form relating to the fast-pace outer movements. The sustained lyricism of the middle movement (Molto sostenuto ed espressivo) provides a firm balance.

Kauder, Hugo (1888–1972)

DUO

- **Sonata for Flute and Piano (1933)**

Special scale formations are utilized in structuring the work. In the first movement the outer portions are totally within a five-pitch scale of A–B–D–E–G. Quartal and quintuple harmony support the middle section. The Andante is in the dorian mode, the material sectionally developed. Kauder indicates the final movement "is based on a scale that combines the major scale with its strict inversion." All of which places a firm tonal stamp on the music.

TRIO

- **Trio for Oboe (or Violin), Viola, and Piano (1916)**

The timbral mellowness of this combination (especially if the oboe is not substituted by a violin) would lead to the expectation of warmly styled music, and in that one would be correct. But the year of composition (1916) does not indicate the absolute imitation of Brahms that takes place. The Trio is filled with the tender simplicities and sentimentalities of that great composer; it contains the lilt of his rhythms, including in the Intermezzo the alternation of triple and duple meters (as in Brahms's C-minor piano trio). Kauder had the eclecticism that is traceable to its source. Nevertheless, his Trio, with its Viennese traits and decided predilection for vocal-style smoothness, is very satisfying music.

QUARTET

- **Quartet for Oboe, Clarinet, Horn, and Bassoon (1948)**

All three movements use the same material; in the last two there are variational developments of the first, which is a fugue. The entire work is modally styled within the orbit of D. Kauder's Quartet has the sound of plainsong. Its notation follows suit, with no bar lines rigorously denoting pulse settings, but horizontal coherencies depicted by the marking of phrase lengths. These mingle freely with and against each other in polyphony of neo-organum style.

Kauffmann, Leo Justinus (1901–44)

QUINTET

- **Quintet for Flute, Oboe, Clarinet, Horn, and Bassoon (1943)**

Typical wind quintet fare—chirpy, clear lines, uncluttered textures. And tied neatly by tonal ribbons. In this regard four of the five movements are in B-flat major, the other one in the relative minor. However, the variety of action staves off tonal monotony.

Poulenc will come to mind in the rhythmic run of the first movement. Then follows a siciliano-type movement (spelled unusually as Alla siziliana). Scherzo pep, a slow movement where in turn the horn, bassoon, and oboe have a solo stance, and a final Allegro vivace (clean-shaven Hindemith in style) represent the last three movements. Kauffmann's Quintet could just as well be titled Divertimento.

Kaufman, Jeffrey (1947–)

DUO

- *Reflections* for Clarinet and Piano

This composer's neoclassic manner, his devotion to pure instrumental music, written as a "homage" to Francis Poulenc, with tonality dynamized by fanwise spread, are all evidenced by the pithiness and the sunny nature of this duo. It is by realizing that he does not want to go beyond the fluidic limits of 20th-century classicism that Kaufman brings stylistic unity and balance to his work. Kaufman's aim is to be intelligible, and he is.

Kaufmann, Armin (1902–80)

TRIO

- **Trio for Violin, Viola, and Cello, Op. 60**

The tempo heading for the first part of Kaufmann's string trio is "fresco," and indeed the writing is "fresh." There is an introduction that ends with three measures of pizzicato ushering in a folk-flavored theme in the viola. The variants that follow are of different lengths, always linked and always of colorful content. Important to the entire structure is the ascent of a fourth, an element that is a key to the material and a support to the balance.

In contrast, the middle movement is more serious, its reflections rhapsodic, an enlargement of the alternation of quintuple- and sextuple-pulse measures. Light and balletish music, with a very swift pace covers the entire finale. For 247 measures there is no halt to the vivo tempo and no pushing away of the folk strains that identify the music's contents. Splendid inventive facility is exemplified in this work.

QUARTET

- **String Quartet No. 4, Op. 17**

At heart this Romanian composer, who changed his style several times, was a conservative who reached out a bit for modern coloration in his harmonic writing. That extension of tonality is present in this work.

Sonatina format is used in the first movement; the swirling phrase marking the principal theme is hinted at in the introduction to the movement. The comforts of scherzo expression mark the second movement. It is strictly patterned as an A–B–A plus a coda, its tempo indication is "hurried." Movement three is a Romanza with siciliano overtones, and the finale is another fast piece of music—this time the tempo heading is "furioso." A folk-tune basis is apparent in the square phrases.

Kaufmann, Serge (1930–)

QUINTET

- **Quintettino for Flute, Oboe, Clarinet, Horn, and Bassoon**

Five minutes for five movements. Piquant chordal savories. The composer's gay temperament sprinkles these pieces with admirable affinity. Delightful French-style woodwind writing in the Giocoso, Pastorale, Valse (the shortest of the group, timed at 45 seconds), Lamento, and a finale termed "Petit concert" ("small" in the title but the longest of these miniatures, with a performance time of one minute and ten seconds).

Kaufmann, Walter (1907–84)

QUINTET

- **Partita for Woodwind Quintet (1963)**

Firm neoclassic music but not coloristically or rhythmically repressed. Kaufmann provided a good mix of serious and witty data in the six movements: Prelude, Allemande, Courante, Sarabande, Menuet, and Gigue. (The original titles for these movements were in French and outlined a six-course dinner!)

Kavanaugh, Patrick (1954–)

SEXTET

- *Homage to C. S. Lewis* **for Woodwind Quintet and Alto Saxophone**

Kavanaugh's testimonial one-movement piece to the English author follows an avant-garde brand of virtuosity, and there's no mildness about it whatsoever. A number of the tricks of the style are used, including repetitive freedom and graphic notation. In the color category are wind sounds that give other than normal pitches, key clicks, "popping" or "thumping" bassoon sounds, use of multiphonics, and humming.

The big sound is paramount here, including chamberized noise. Picturesqueness is a quality avoided in the technical passion and invention of the piece.

Kay, Ulysses (1917–)

DUOS

- *Five Portraits* **for Violin and Piano (1972)**

Expanded tonalism colors the suite. This is recognizable. What is not is Kay's "enigma" without variations. Each of the movements has initials placed under the final measure in the score. They read O. D., H. S., B. J. K., I. S., and P. F. (Might the B. J. K. stand for Kay's wife, Barbara?)

Movement one is titled Scherzando, a mood portrayed in terms of asymmetrical meter and motival development. Expansive textural arrangement marks the Adagio, pertness contrasted to rubato lyricism typifies the "B. J. K." movement (Allegretto). Slow and fast music complete the work. Kay has a reputation as a neoclassicist. In this duo there is more than passing attention to postromantic style. The balanced results provide a substantially effective music.

- **Partita in A for Violin and Piano (1950)**

Polyphonic texturalism styles the Prelude. The Burlesca has both bite and controlled virtuosity. Kay's use of open strings in the double stops within the violin's line is a top-drawer use to obtain brilliance. A short Interlude is linked to the "Echo" movement, a music with the consistency of instrumental dialog.

- **Suite for Flute and Oboe (1943)**

Glowing, healthy neoclassic music. The Prelude has a kinetic quality brought by persistent sets of sixteenth-note figures. In movement two (Air) a monothematic melody, passed from one instrument to the other, floats within the measures. A pair of dances, Minuet and Gigue, make up the second half of the duo.

- *Tromba* **for Trumpet and Piano (1983)**

Tromba is well named, since the word is the Italian for "trumpet." Formal demarcation confirms the suite designation with a Prologue (a sizable one), Nocturne, and concluding "Mobile." The night-music conception is neatly colored in balanced form with the trumpet muted throughout, calling for a straight mute in the outer sections and a solotone mute in the center.

The "Mobile" is not a sonorized simulation of the Calder variety. (This is not meant to read as a negative report.) Kay's music moves around colorfully in duple beat, in allegretto tempo, and concludes with a presto burst. There, the trumpet is free and loose, with random articulation on the same D pitch for eleven continuous measures.

QUARTETS

- **Brass Quartet for Two Trumpets, Tenor and Bass Trombones (1950)**

The first movement (Fantasia) pays attention to the medium with fanfarelike jets and exciting rhythmic repetitions. The Arioso is reflective, an example of how brass instruments can portray a warmth of expression as sensitive to the ear as the winds or strings. By use of some fanfare patterns and pitch repetitions, the finale (Toccata) relates to and thereby balances the initial part of the quartet.

- **Serenade No. 2 for Four Horns (1957)**

A conservative contemporary conception, well built and well ordered, that opts for warmth of detail rather than roustabout virtuoso tactics. It is always in good taste and represents lasting art.

The outer movements of the total five are a Prelude and Epilogue. Movement two, Arietta, has inner rhythmic knitting; the same type of cohesion is applied to the fourth movement (Fantasy) by the use of a long–short-pulsed figure. Even the Toccata reflects a sensitive, firm avoidance of blare and bray by its scherzando quality.

SEXTET

- *Facets* for Flute, Oboe, Clarinet, Horn, Bassoon, and Piano (1971)

Facets is a one-movement work despite its plural title. Kay considers it a "kind of fantasy," since he examines "various aspects (or facets) of the opening motivic material." Within, one will note a tripartite form of balance with an introductory section linked to development, a lyrical division (Adagio), an episode reflecting the opening part of the work, and a final rondolike Allegro.

The instrumentalists are offered a bit of performer creativity. In one place the players each have the opportunity for random reiteration of a single given pitch, in another they can each improvise on a set of pitches. Both are exceedingly minimal in extent—Kay is not of the aleatoric school of structural freedom.

Kayn, Roland (1933–)

QUARTET

- *Spektren (Apparitions)* for String Quartet (1956)

Use of just a single untransposed tone row does not prevent a healthy state of fantasy. The constant change of tone quality and rhythmic flux of pitch arrangement erase any monotony in Kayn's piece. Textural variability is maintained—the most dense portion being the last.

Kayn does not want any peripheral sensations to blur his materials. Aside from a pair of pizzicato-sounded pitches, the entire piece is to be played without vibrato.

Kayser, Leif (1919–)

SEXTET

- *Kleine Übungen für Bläser (Small Studies for Winds)* (Three Trumpets, Three Trombones, and Tuba [ad lib])

The music of this Danish composer, who is also an ordained Catholic priest, is tonal, its gestures colored strongly with chromatic pitches. It is as if sacred and secular portrayals are combined.

Part one is in ternary form, the first and third sections vertically disposed, the second section conclusively polyphonic. Part two is a broadly paced linear statement with a fair amount of imitation. The first section of part one is then repeated.

(The composition is also performable by a "wind orchestra." Kayser does not specify the totals that may be used.)

Kazacsay, Tibor (1892–)

DUO

- **Two Duets for Oboe and English horn, Op. 113**

The first one is a Pastoral, a flowing three-part sketch with the middle section drawn on for a short coda. The second duet is titled "Dudelsackweise" ("Bagpipe Music"). A bit of the drone is simulated by successive pitches that sound D–A on the English horn. Principally, the "Dudelsack" consists of animated, whirling pitch detail.

Kâzim, Necil (1908–)

DUOS

- *Allegro féroce* for Alto Saxophone (alternating Clarinet) and Piano (1931)

To liken this piece to a "whirling dervish" is not to engage in purple prose. Actually, that description does not suffice. The words "ungagged," "delirious," and "rampant" should be added. No duo exists for a wind instrument and piano that equals the bone-crunching sonorous boulders of Kâzim's *Allegro féroce*.

The sounds are first placed in tonal forceps with cavernous clusters sharing the saxophone's heavy tone, concerned in great part with glissando. Then, in vivace, the music erupts into Turkish melorhythms placed in a 7/16 meter. The accentual division of this irregular

design is unregulated. In the middle of this the saxophone gives way to the clarinet, returning for the concluding part, wherein the top rung possible is reached in terms of dynamic intensity and speed. In exactly 2 1/4 minutes Kâzim creates what sounds like a sonorous summary of fiendish, demoniacal music.

- **Sonata for Flute and Piano (1939)**

Kâzim (sometimes known as Kâzim-Akses) concentrates his Sonata in one movement of fiercely contrasted sections, with further contentiousness within them. No ordinary contemporary sounds are these. The violently clashing sounds of Kâzim's music seem to be a conglomerate of mixed keys seething within shifting tonalities. It is not. It is the result of the use of modes Kâzim fashioned from the scale formations of old Turkish music. The preponderance of parallel sevenths, for example, should be heard as an associative stream of two different modes.

Septuple and ninefold meters are common to Turkish music. Kâzim follows suit. Contrary, however, to the common division of nine beats into three equal groups of three each, an irregular subdivision is made of two-thirds of the total divided equally into three groups of two pulses each and the remaining one-third as a group of three pulses (2–2–2–3). The Sonata begins with a quasi-athematic opening, with constant invention and elaboration, and then moves onto a slower section with a topic stated in sevenths. Then follow a tripartite Allegro in 7/8 time and the concluding section. The last is driven by sixteenth-note figuration force, with unequal division of a 9/8 meter.

Keats, Donald (1929–)

QUARTETS

- **String Quartet No. 1 (1956)**

Subtle motility conduct is a prime formal denominator in the last two of the three movements. Within the final Poco adagio there is no tempo differential. The creation of a tripartite design becomes declared by use in the middle portion of more active linear movement; a previous ceiling of eighths is lifted and thus intensified by using sixteenths. This architecture of motivity imbues the music with a unity that does not always pertain to contrastive depiction. A similar objective and rational method is used in the vigorous second movement. There, the scherzo propellation of three sounds per measure (with a number of bisected duplets as rhythmic counterpoints) is compared in the central part (again without basic tempo change) to two sounds in the same time space. This naturally produces a slower ratio within each measure's pulse. However, Keats compensates for this braking by using motility for the greater part to obtain more "action" within beats. It is achieved just as described above for the following movement: previous eighths as the fastest limit give way to sixteenths. No argument that Keats has made an excellent adaptation of matter to serve form.

While this theorem is not used to structure the opening movement, the potential of rhythmic debate is potent within the material. The music flows in an Andante, mainly in duple-listed 6/8 meter. Linear detail is paramount. It becomes sharpened, therefore, by juxtaposing triple-meter measures against the two-beat pulse arrangements. The former are never mere minor rhythmic punctuations but of seven- and eight-measure lengths so that they register with convincing clarity.

- **String Quartet No. 2 (1965)**

Keats adopts a serial-slanted attitude in this composition but is not devoted to the technique. His second quartet avoids the fixations of twelve-tone style with its hexachordic hobnobbing.

Motivic construction marks the first movement, with a contrastively opposite lyricism. Two types of percussive colorations polyphonize the structural concept: one vertical, the other horizontal. The former consists of sharp pizzicato interjections; the other of fluid pizzicato glides. The fast-paced middle movement represents the scherzo world; the basic triple-beat material counterpointed by duple sounds. Squareness vanishes as a result. In place of the usual Trio Keats uses a set of soloistic, rhapsodic adagio-tempo passages. In comparison with the dynamic of the movement's outer portions, these give a quasi-surrealistic effect. The complete disjointedness of the central section's mood is a dramatic twist of the highest order and makes the return of the principal material twice as effective. Similar fantasy rules the finale, with (in terms of a concluding movement) reverse tempo order (andante–allegro–andante). Throughout, a restless type of rhythm binds the movement. It has strong reminders of the early days of atonalism (Krenek comes to mind), and balances the introverted personality of the opening movement.

Kef, Kees (1894–1961)

DUO

- **Sonata for Clarinet and Piano (1935)**

Tonal music based on polarities, with the outer movements in E-flat and the middle one in A-flat. Kef's harmonies move about with a freeness that has both charm and appeal.

The middle movement (Largo e mesto) begins with a quasi-cadenza statement that acts not only as prelude but outlines the type of melodic flow that will follow. A rondo assortment of tempos is included in the third movement: presto, tempo di valse, and tempo di bolero. A mix, but it blends well, all in a hemiola situation of 6/8 and 3/4, with these equalized pulses freely assorted and also combined.

Keldorfer, Robert (1901–80)

DUO

- *Sonata ritmica* **for Alto Recorder (or Flute or Oboe) and Piano (1964)**

An acute example of rhythmic delineation, producing a work where form and application to content are clearly proposed and not neutralized by the special technical commitment.

Movement one is a March, but the form is framed and shaped by non-march septuple rhythm. Movement two strides like a passacaglia, moves canonically for a good part of the time, and is guided by triple meter. The fourth movement is fast-paced, conjunctly specified in pitch progress, and in several places is bound by ostinato open fifths in the piano's bass. The rhythmic denominator in this part is quintuple until the five-measure coda, which is set in sextuple pulse.

Movement three follows the Boris Blacher method of variable meters, whereby arithmetical sequence is the organizing rhythmic element. Tempoed scherzando, the meter changes in every measure beginning with measure one and continuing through nine. It then has a two-beat rest, and the sequence then runs through measures two through nine. A measure of three-beat rest follows, succeeded by a slower portion equating the movement's Trio in sextuple pulse, with the final part again a continuity of measures one through nine, with a concluding two-beat measure.

(The alternate instruments for the recorder are not noted on the score cover, the inside title page, or the first music page. The possibility of substitution is listed only on the inside cover page.)

TRIO

- **Trio for Flute, Clarinet, and Bassoon (1948)**

A Straussian quality pervades Keldorfer's wind trio. This is linked to an authoritative use of the instruments, especially in the Marcia allegra (movement one) and the concluding Fugue. This interaction does not negate music that is commanded with curvaceous phrases: in the second theme of the Marcia and in the second-movement Aria, which has juicy three-part writing. Movement three is a Menuetto, metronomically pitched fast and minus any Trio which might remove concentration from the speedy pace. In the Finale (Introduzione e Fuga) two themes are combined in the beginning part, seemingly as an anticipatory gesture to the fully polyphonic conclusion.

QUINTET

- *Music for Five Winds* **(Flute [alternating Piccolo], Oboe, Clarinet, Horn, and Bassoon) (1968)**

The basic formal problem of contrast and continuity is dealt with here in one movement, with the divisions clearly regulated by tempos. Keldorfer's music in general is fantasy-driven, though the second section (Adagio) has a three-part shape with chordal depictions surrounding the segmentalizing of phrases. The third section has scherzo outlines; the final part, animated in tempo, is stimulated by polyphonic detail.

Kelemen, Milko (1924–)

DUOS

Sonata for Oboe and Piano (1960)

Twelve-tone and serial practices shape the two movements. Quarter tones, flutter-tongued passages, harmonic sounds, tremolandos, and glissandos color the oboe part. Plucking the strings, glissandos on the strings, and short glides on the keyboard add special qualities to the piano part.

Pyramidical detail is important in the opening movement (as so often occurs in this composer's music, there is no specific tempo indication, simply the metronomic definition, which here is ♩=72). Broad scherzo depiction marks the other movement (the tempo is ♩.=76–80). Kelemen's piece is serial suavity at its best, and its style is unblemished. It represents twelve-tone music of deep commitment.

▪ Ten Fabeln (Ten Fables) for Soprano and Alto Recorders

Unusual in a double sense. Programmatic concepts are practically unknown in recorder literature, and the same applies to the avant-garde techniques that fill this score. The results offer a set of fascinating kaleidoscopic sketches.

"Die durstigen Tauben" ("The Thirsty Pigeons") is a contrapuntal duo, stimulated with flutter-tongued sounds. In "Der Mond und die Mutter" ("The Moon and the Mother") glaring multiphonics are the prime color. Free, unmetered material is combined in part three, "Zwei Schlangen" ("Two Snakes"). "Die Flamme und der Kessel" ("The Flame and the Kettle") is lit by long lines and warmed by expansive trills. Some healthy pitch bends color "Der kranke Hirsch" ("The Sick Stag"); in contrast "Die Sonne" ("The Sun") has crisp, detached pitch formations. In number seven,

"Der Alte und der Tod" ("The Old Man and Death"), there are very alive sections where the soprano instrument is to play the highest pitch possible in strident *fortissimo*. A warmer nuance covers "Die Spinne und die Trauben" ("The Spider and the Grapes"). Pitch partnership shades the conception of "Winter und Frühling" ("Winter and Spring"). Part ten, "Fledermäuse" ("Bats"), is filled with flutter-tongued sounds, tremolandos, and glissandos.

QUARTET

▪ Motion for String Quartet (1968)

Motile regularity of meter is mixed in this approximately twelve-minute work with graphic notation which frees the pulse. Within this combine there are Penderecki-type fragmented sound blocks, harsh colors, sound masses, desiccated harmonies, and sound thrusts. Free voicing is the surrogate for thematic detail. The colors are the contours.

Motion represents an avant-garde timbral urtext. These qualities include percussive sounds, not only with the wooden part of the bow but with finger action; a slow, wide vibrato as well as a rapid one; and playing very close to the bridge and directly behind it. In the field of quarter tones Kelemen introduces additional micropitch totalities by both soft and hard fluctuations of the quarter-tone sounds.

QUINTET

▪ Etudes contrapuntiques (Contrapuntal Studies) for Wind Quintet (1959)

Kelemen's set of four studies considers the matter of integrated variation by color and rhythm simultaneously, and the serial end-product is dynamic. The metrical halter is disengaged within the bar lines in this instance, but in its pertinent way, the flow is just as neatly adjusted as music based on classical-style precepts. The fluidity of Kelemen's delicate timbres makes much of the music function like an unbroken line as the sound portions pass from one instrument to the next.

Kelen, Hugó (1890–1956)

DUO

- **Three Pieces for Violin and Piano (1951)**

Hungarian sweetmeats, thoroughly soaked in folk material, are displayed in the first piece, "Sauntering," and in the third one, "Briskly." A mild kind of Leo Weiner style is applied. The middle piece is a rubato, antiphonalized "Pensive Tune (To the Memory of M. Phyllis)." No nationalistic half-truths are represented here.

Kellaway, Roger (1939–)

DUO

- *Esque* for Trombone and Double Bass **(1971)**

Cutting the light jazz bit with expertise, Kellaway opts for the subtle touch rather than the thigh-slapping approach. Combining a slide trombone with a bull fiddle may seem to be a poor choice of partnership, but it works, works very well, especially for the saucy musical strips Kellaway has put together.

Catchy title, and that's all it is supposed to be. Three movements: the first a metronomic designation ($\mathrel{} = 144$), the others are Blues and Presto.

Keller, Ginette (1925–)

DUO

- *Ébauches (Rough Sketches)* for Bassoon **and Piano (1973)**

Go around the title. Keller's five pieces, displaying coloristic fantasy, are subtle sound sketches, epigrammatic, obtaining internal coherence from stated moods. In "Vibrant," the resonances come from sweeping figures. Motility, with line against line in contrapuntal rhythmic order, is denoted in "Fluide." Fanciful disconnections: flutter-tonguing, slow glides, pedal trilling, and some improvisation are processed in "Fantasque." Part four is "Implorant," with entreatingly set phrases in the bassoon and chordal backup in the piano. Pungent phrases built around repeated pitches and sharp chords depict "Caustique."

Keller, Homer (1915–)

DUOS

- **Five Pieces for Clarinet and Bassoon**

Movement one is titled "Off in a Cloud of Dust!" but it will not interfere with the listener's following the canonic road on which the instruments travel. (The bassoon imitates the clarinet a ninth below at the distance of one measure.) The "Lullaby" is only moderately slow and there is no tune repetition.

The third piece, "Invention," is properly polyphonic. "Night Ravens" has nocturnal fantasy as well as orderly increase as the flight moves from andante to appassionata onto agitato and finally is defined as violently. The Finale has only a modicum of polyphony as the instruments cling rhythmically to each other.

- **Sonata for Flute and Piano (1953)**

Tonal substantiation with sensitive application of pitch polarity. The three short movements are set in and around E, G, and E. Formal repose follows suit, with sonata- and rondo-type outer movements. The inner Andante movement is special to the piece. It consists entirely of three-voice lines with canonic detail in the outer parts compared to, in turn, solo flute and solo piano in the middle.

QUARTET

- **Quartet for Two Trumpets, Horn, and Trombone (1951)**

Grateful and effective brass music, containing coloristic subtlety and impression. The middle movements consist of a fifteen-measure Lento of chorale outline set in quintuple meter and an Allegretto in precisely contoured A–B–A form. Lightly hedonistic music is depicted in the pair of outer movements—as expected, both are in fast tempo.

Keller, Max (1770–1855)

DUO

- **Six Pieces for Two Horns**

This Bavarian composer-organist produced a good number of masses and other sacred music but scarcely any chamber music. The horn duos (written in one day on August 31, 1829) deserve attention for their unique echo effects.

These echoes are, of course, strictly obtained by dynamic difference. Sometimes the echo is partial. Thus, in the first duet, the last four sounds of the opening four-measure phrase, heard in *forte*, are repeated by the two horns, after two beats rest, in *pianissimo*. Sometimes the echo is complete. Thus, in the second duet

measures one and three in *forte* are repeated exactly in measures two and four in *pianissimo*. The plan is constant. In the first piece, there are seven phrases with seven of the last portions echoed. In movement four the *forte* three-measure phrase is followed by the last measure repeated in *pianissimo*. This ratio of 3:1 is maintained and is then shifted to 3:3, returned again to 3:1 and completed with 3:3. Similar plans prevail in the other pieces of the set.

For the echo style to register clearly homophonic totality obtains and in some instances the two instruments proceed in absolute rhythmic unification. All very interesting, but best heard a couple of movements at a time.

Kelley, Edgar Stillman (1857–1944)

QUARTET

- **Quartet for Two Violins, Viola, and Cello, Op. 25**

Variations constitute the *total* makeup of the quartet's structure. After an introduction in Grave tempo, the theme is stated and five variations follow. Together these three parts represent movement one and are titled thus: Einleitung, Original-Thema und Variationen. Different tempos and tonalities mark the first four variations; the fifth variant is totally muted and has scherzo character.

The sixth and seventh variations, as a double variation, make up the second movement: Toccatina und Fuge, subtitled parenthetically (Dopple-Variation). A ternary totality occurs when the Toccatina returns after the Fuge. Movement three, Intermezzo, is an Adagio that constitutes the eighth of the variations.

The concluding (fourth) movement is marked Finale with the descriptive parenthetical subtitle (Triple-Variation und Coda). It is a creative *coup de maître* that deals with the remaining (ninth, tenth, and eleventh) variations. These are connected and, in turn, equate sonata form. Kelley defines them as "Haupt" ("Principal") for the ninth variant, "Seiten" ("Secondary") for the tenth variant, and "Schluss" ("Closing") for the eleventh variant. At the climax of this final movement state-of-the-art contrapuntalism is exhibited by the combination of all three variations. The close of the Quartet is identified by a recapitulation of the theme.

"Technical mastery" were the words that Arthur Shepherd, a fellow American composer, used to describe Kelley's Op. 25. Indeed, it is a distinguished contribution to the literature of American chamber music. On the other hand, Germanic compositional style never was eliminated from Kelley's music. He had spent four years (1876-1880) in Stuttgart studying composition, orchestration, piano, and organ and later lived in Berlin (from 1902 to 1910) during which time he taught piano and composition. The Germanic influence is further reflected in the use of German titles for the various sections of this, his single string quartet (composed as Op. 1 in 1880 and revised as Op. 25 in 1907).

Kelly, Robert (1916–)

DUO

- **Sonata for Tenor Trombone and Piano, Op. 19**

Music with tonal conviction, backed by triadic belief. The outer movements are in B-flat, the central one in D. Supple and subtle deviations are made, of course. (Kelly is no grim academician.)

Thematic depiction partners the healthy timbre of the trombone, and all the melodic material is of breadth and openness. Contextual succinctness is of exactitude, minus any fantasy looseness, thereby representing an innate

balance. This pertinent positiveness of purpose is shown by the pithy sixteenth-note figurations in movement one and the triple-beat creasing of the fast-pace, duple-pulse finale. A purposeful rhythmic stasis is individual to the moderately slow middle movement. Only thirteen of the total eighty-four measures do not contain the same bass-line oscillation of a pair of short–long sounds. The equilibrium between form, tonality, melody, and rhythm is apparent throughout Kelly's duo sonata.

Kelterborn, Rudolf (1931–)

DUOS

- ***Four Miniatures* for Oboe and Violin (1964)**

Twelve-tone pieces, but free of rigid development. A constant use of short rhythmic groups, of the same pitch makeup in each case, provides a merge with tonally styled procedures. A fine blend thus for these four sound impressions of five-minute length. And good color contrasts as well, with muted violin in miniature number two, and portions of plucked timbre in the fourth of the set.

- **Four Pieces for Clarinet and Piano (1970)**

The plots of three of these four pieces are concerned with cadenzalike jets of sound, as though let loose via chance improvisations. Thereby hangs the flag of success, for the constructions are strong, the material balanced without taking away the extempore-type endorsement.

The leading character in this suite is the clarinet. In numbers one and four the piano is supportive. In number three it is likewise but with some antiphonal opportunities. The clarinet describes a simpler, becalmed atmosphere in the second piece. There, the partnered treble part of the piano consists mostly of pedal snippets, while its bass line is a continuous C-sharp pedal, arranged in different rhythmic patterns.

- *Incontri brevi (Brief Encounters)* for Flute and Clarinet (1967)

Freely atonal, but with a clarity of the sonorous tissue. There are four sections and there is to be no pause between them, each marked *attacca subito*.

The tempo of the first is slow but the patterns are explosive. The tempo ($\. = 50$) is the same for the second section, but the phrases are more declamatory, though quite rhapsodic in their turns. Part three is almost three times faster, and the running patterns are principally birhythmic. The fourth part has the same tempo as part one and its contents are parallel. No romantic tunes are sung here, but the basic expressiveness places the music in the romantic category.

- *Sevenminute-Play* for Flute and Piano (1976)

The unification employed in the title is matched by the pitch compression that surrounds much of this Swiss composer's duo. The scene is set by swirling zigzag flute figures in *pianississimo* and percussive isolated accents by the piano. Flutter-tongued pitches are later used as well as portamento and glissando, but always the return is to the rhythmic eddies. Active music, indeed, but never blatant in this cadenza-personalized duo.

- Sonatine for Oboe and Harpsichord (or Piano) (1960)

Atonal style, but with some airy refinements within the four movements of the work, set forth more as a suite than a sonatine. The Recitativo e Canzona is minus meter at the start, where the free-lined oboe is heard antiphonally in contrast to the harpsichord. There is rhythmic swing in the second part of the movement. That same type of pulsed warmth surrounds the motivally structured Intermezzo. Rhapsodic content marks the Fantasia notturna. And it is again motivic style that carries the Finale. Fine credentials for atonality in this duo.

Kelterborn notes that if a piano is used it should be played to approximate the harpsichord by shifting passages an octave higher, use doublings, and the like.

TRIOS

- Five Fantasias for Flute, Cello, and Harpsichord

Structural definition is obtained in this trio by the reuse of a fundamental shape or expression. In the first of the group the recitative lines of the flute and cello are controlled in their variegation by block-chord units in the piano. In the exceedingly fast second piece swinging accompanimental formations in the piano change in sectional order within the quintuple meter: first in eighths, then in sixteenths, and finally in triplets. A secondary element is a coloristic flutter-tongued sound in the flute, used at nine different places within the forty-six-measure total.

In the fourth Fantasia motival structuring provides the balance; in the fifth of the set it is metrical unification, mainly septuple in measurement. On the other hand, in number three what is not thematically prime and is scored in a supplementary position becomes the pivotal strength of the piece. This is obtained from the cello's persistent adherence to special timbre definition by way of huge registral change, pizzicato, glissando, and harmonics.

- *Lyrische Kammermusik (Lyrical Chamber Music)* for Clarinet, Violin, and Viola (1959)

A set of five short pieces that, with its twelve-tone coverage (avoiding the locked-in basis of serialism), portrays a romantic sweetness and strength. The fires are there but they are banked.

Part one is an Elegie; the second piece (Serenata) has the strings moving against the clarinet. In the Notturno the music is haunted by *parlando* rubato. The Intermezzo is fast but restrained, and the "Nachklang" ("Reverberation") calmly concludes the suite with disjunct lines first moving against harmonic pitches and later against chords.

QUARTET

- **String Quartet No. 3 (1962)**

The middle movement of this short, three-movement work is titled Fantasia notturna, but the movements that surround it are, despite their titles (Scena I and Scena II), no less fantasia-packed. There are motival mnemonics in these outer movements. There is also considerable attention given to the timbral differences of muted and open sounds. These delicate mutations in the work bring an example of twelve-tone music touched by impressionistic qualities.

QUINTET

- **Seven Bagatelles for Wind Quintet**

Single specifics mark each of the seven pieces. Kelterborn uses contrastive material in some of the Bagatelles (in the second movement Danza, and a bit in the sixth part, a Serenata), but otherwise he maintains each concept without a recapitulation. All of it is finely tuned, with a clear melodic point of view, and balanced sonorities. The Bagatelles stay in the conserva-tive orbit of atonal style.

The opening piece is an Entrada, number three is a tenuto-pointed Notturno, and number four is a very fast Furioso with polyphonic rhythmic attention. Part five is a gentle Madrigal and the finale is a dynamically restrained Epilog.

SEXTET

- *Varianti for Six Instruments* (Flute, Clarinet [alternating Bass Clarinet], Trumpet, Violin, Viola, and Cello) (1959)

Emphasis is on specific intervals: both major and minor seconds, thirds, sixths, and sevenths. Tempo changes mark the nine sections of the sextet, with individuality of color playing a major role.

(The work can be performed with expanded strings.)

Kenins, Talivaldis (1919–)

DUO

- **Divertimento for Clarinet and Piano (1960)**

Fluid use of tonality stimulates this three-movement piece. A good supply of quartal harmonic color is included. Moderately fast and truly fast outer movements surround a ternary designed Arietta. This is music of expressive directness with more than passing attention to Hindemithian style.

Kennan, Kent (1913–)

DUOS

- *Scherzo, Aria, and Fugato* for Oboe and Piano (1949)

There is no doubt as to the formal authority of the three pieces. In the Fugato matters are regularly expressed, with a neat increase of textural weight after the first fifth of the movement. But changes are vivid in the Aria and Scherzo, which provide coloristic direction. In the Aria ornamentation gives vibrant tone to the lines. In the Scherzo squareness is cut away by the use of thirty-seven different metrical measurements in the total fifty-one measures.

- Sonata for Trumpet and Piano (1956)

Kennan's trumpet sonata (no matter what residue of previous composers' talk—mainly Paul Hindemith—will be found in his speech) breathes creative healthiness without brassy brashness. This represents fully serious and dignified writing. Sonata, ternary, and rondo designs constitute the neoclassic format.

QUINTET

- Quintet for Piano and Strings (Two Violins, Viola, and Cello) (1936)

While Kennan is addicted to the Franckian complex of quotation, parlaying one movement against the other, and using a type of roughed-up (at times) Debussy-type impressionism and a somewhat Lisztian color, his four-movement work is skillfully wrought.

The opening theme occurs constantly throughout the initial movement; it is marked on recapitulation by sweeping piano arpeggios. The theme reappears in augmentation in the closing measures of the third movement, as well as serving in several places in the last movement. These interlocked precepts are followed in the other parts of the work. The Lento, announced by a churchly theme, has the parallelisms pertinent to modality. The theme is sung recurrently, uncovered in the soprano position. An idea is taken from this movement to appear in the following one, a Vivace of triple and quadruple romping, with suggestions of Debussy, but not thereby less exciting. The final movement is patch-quilted with material stated and developed from previous sections plus new items.

Kerr, Harrison (1897–1979)

DUO

- Suite for Flute and Piano (1941)

The power and ofttimes violence of the free concatenation of dissonance surround this work. It is worth noting how efficient the lightweight tone of the flute is in portraying its role in a music of dissonant complexities. It serves up as much ginger as the many times heavier keyboard instrument. The super-refinement of friction in this Suite is a far cry from the "anything goes" of the declaration of independence sworn to by many composers in the period just after World War I. Kerr's type of the correct "wrong" note in the right place is of special and effective coherence.

The increasing grandiosity practiced by many composers went out of fashion in the early part of the current century. What remained was the true essence of musical materials. Some composers realized that by no means were either classicism or romanticism dead; only revitalization with new musical inoculations was needed. Kerr was one of these, illustrated by the neobaroque contour of his flute and piano suite.

Thus, the classical precepts of the Prelude, in which a constant figuration exists of conscious rhythmic retrogression, while the counterpointed mintings make true coin of the play between wind and keyboard instrument. The Dance mirrors minuet style. But Kerr's choreographic music has dissonant harmonies that would cause ill ease if used for utilitarian ballroom purposes. In this case the minuet style is an artistic working tool. (The matching of descending phrases by patterns that ascend is a neat gesture.) Movement three is a Recitativo—the form free, with balance established by the last measures using the initial ones in augmented values, the syntax just short of twelve-tone formations. The Toccata is of modern virtuoso order.

TRIOS

- **Trio for Clarinet, Cello, and Piano (1936)**

Stock-taking of the many component elements in musical technique shows so many types that auditors often become confused between close resemblances. To the critical ear, there are apparent differences, for example, between freely chromatic and systematized dissonance. Chromatic dissonance is an abstract concept of ordering musical sounds, almost avoiding fixed and determined themes (or, at the very least, thematic lengths as such), by its plan of motival-rhythmic arrangement expressing equally a design lacking fixed tonality, chords, and the like. It has an expressiveness of its own, not of the romantic vista. On the other hand, twelve-tone technique, so often mistaken for it, is a precise orientation of nonrepetitive tones, specified as to arrangement. Free as the development of these may be, the system stems from articulates not present in the *much* freer (and, therefore, almost despised by twelve-tone composers) methods of negated specific tonality marking the independent dissonant composition.

It is the latter technique that Kerr uses in this triple-timbre Trio. In the first movement, the theme is not one of symmetry with repose of details, but is as elastic as the harmonies and counterpoints. There is development from it, especially of a rhythmic dotted-eighth- and sixteenth-note kernel that is most often reversed. Three-part form can be traced in the slow movement. Again, a rhythmic unit drawn from the theme becomes a pinpointing identifier (a triplet of quarter notes). Fugal means are used in the compressed Scherzando. The last movement has toccatalike velocity; the chromaticism is not quite as nigrescent, though some tone clusters appear. Free tonality prevails—the final chord, for example, cadential proof, as it were, consists of D as a root combining A and E together. This is extremely mild so far as harmonic friction is concerned; but, as representative of a tonic, it is in ratio to the previous dissonance, as C major is to its dissonant relative, the dominant seventh chord.

- **Trio for Violin, Cello, and Piano (1938)**

Though there is some flirting with tonality (the work begins and ends in A minor), Kerr's piano trio (written in 1938 and revised in 1949) is tightly dissonant. In its outer Allegro movements it is rhythmically motor-driven. Within the central Grave movement there are a few places with neoromantic tinges. However, these are quickly overtaken and removed in effect by the independent dissonant style Kerr used.

Interlocking of material was another creative habit of this composer (*see below*: String Quartet). In this work material is transferred from the first movement into the following two movements, and in the final part of the work material from the preceding slow movement appears.

QUARTET

- **String Quartet (1937)**

Thematic compatibility produces an interweave that binds this quartet. The opening theme in the first violin (immediately heard successively in the cello, second violin, and viola) is the stimulant for the subject of the four variations of movement three, and, in turn, its shape is retraced for use as the theme of the final movement. Further, the principal idea in the Scherzando (movement two) is also drawn from movement one, where its birth was represented as an accompanying voice, and still further, in the Trio section of this second movement the contour of the generic theme of the quartet again appears. No happenstance for any of this; the blood relationship of the movements is proven when some of the Scherzando reappears in the final movement. All of this thematic prejudice is in favor of securing a solidity of structure.

Kerr's quartet (composed in 1937 and revised in 1940 and 1941) cannot be faulted for its construction. It is superb.

Kersters, Willem (1929–)

DUOS

- *Diagrammen (Diagrams)* **for Violin and Cello, Op. 64**

Bartókian bias, which gives Bartókian blessings, surrounds every aspect of this duo organized in five connected divisions.

The essential appropriation is heard in the rubatolike, manifold-changed quality, blended with punctuative chords and glides, of the opening. This total of nineteen measures is exactly repeated to conclude the work. The music that follows the opening section is the hair-raising, motoric kind wherein rhythm dominates the pitches and harmonies. There are 155 measures that percussively thrust throughout (even when the dynamic is low-pitched). The third part represents Bartók's "night music," though here there are no rustles or murmurs to emphasize the nocturnalized mystery of effect. Part four is a return of the fast music, resembling the previous portion, but now of different facture.

It may be unadventurous to be eclectic, but that does not deny the fact that Kersters's opus is a strong addition to the literature for violin and cello. It deserves a place next to the duos for the same pairing of string instruments by Ravel and Kodály.

- **Partita for Violin and Piano, Op. 9**

Old forms never really die. The baroque suite that was a major design in the period from about 1650 to 1750 is here presented in mid-20th-century delineation (Kersters completed his composition in September of 1956). The Partita, which is another name for the baroque suite, consisted of from three to twelve dance movements. (Of course, there are always exceptions to the rule. Jacques-Champion Chambonnières, called Champion de Chambonnières, who was born between 1601 and 1611 and died in 1672, produced a suite that comprised no less than twenty-eight dances.)

Kersters's opus of five dances begins with an Intrada. He presents the usual festive preamble the form represents with moderate pace and with declarative dynamics. Then follow an Allemande attentive to imitations; a Courante juiced with bitonality; a heavily textured Sarabande, sensitively colored, however, with harmonics and use of the full-throated G string plus the very high register of the violin; and a vivacious Gigue, peppered with ostinatos and stimulated by quartal and quintuple harmonies.

QUARTETS

- **Quartet for Clarinet, Violin, Viola, and Cello, Op. 55**

The major part of the Quartet is its central movement. Two principal ideas are contrasted and developed within it. The first has scherzo personality, with the fragmented items heard within precise metrical definition. These small ideas are developed into larger units. The build of the other subject has length and is often colored with supporting pizzicatos. Though opposite in character, the two propositions integrate cogently.

Slow-tempo rhapsodic statements are contained in the first movement. The last movement is a Chorale. It is a music of unrest, its material activated by nervous tremolando figures followed by a return to the opening mood.

- **Three Bagatelles for String Quartet, Op. 34**

Tonality freed of rigidity is the stylistic agent for this opus (also playable by string orchestra).

Each piece has directness. The first, a one-minute rhythmic item, jogs along in duple gait, but with vital septuple inserts that give spastic kicks to the music. Melodic lines kept in play with the support of tremolandos and repetitive figuration describe the middle Bagatelle. Somewhat related to the former are the ostinatos of the final piece. It is in presto. By simply slowing the speed a bit more than half its total and using the same principal theme Kersters designs the central part of the movement. A bargain method, but satisfying nonetheless.

- **Variations for Flute, Oboe, Clarinet, and Bassoon, Op. 49**

There is no one-by-one elucidative series of variations in Kersters's piece. More to the point is the projection of a variational rhapsody, a dichotomy already hinted at by the beginning of the work; the theme being squarely a twelve-tone row which precedes to a second phrase that is just as squarely bitonal.

The total thematic shape appears in several places: in long–short rhythmic statement in triple unison by the oboe, clarinet, and bassoon, and totally in quartet unison in the concluding part of the work. However, elsewhere the sounds are a survey of small developmental portions as though the variations were on these segments rather than on the theme itself. Re-survey also occurs. The first eight measures after the thematic declaration are repeated verbatim after the section that begins with the triple unison mentioned above.

- **Variations on a Theme by Giles Farnaby for Clarinet Quartet (E-flat Clarinet, Two B-flat Clarinets, and Bass Clarinet), Op. 41**

No little-by-little variational buildup in this set of six variations on a G-major Farnaby tune. (Incidentally, the score bears the following inscription under Farnaby's name:"[$\pm$1565–$\pm$1598]," a colorful means of indicating "circa." However, while c. 1565 is correct, Farnaby's death date has been proven to be in the next century, November 1640; he died in London and was buried there on November 25.)

Kersters's composition encompasses a large variety of changing textures and developments, beginning with sharply polyphonic treatment. The second variation starts as a fugato, the initial portion of the theme stands out in the third variant, and so on. There is a freely florid functionalism to the writing that avoids any sense of pedanticism in the variational treatment. To balance matters to the acute point the nine-measure thematic statement is repeated note for note at the end.

QUINTET

- **Three Rondos for Brass Quintet (Two Trumpets, Horn, Trombone, and Tuba), Op. 48**

All three pieces are as clear and as bright as the instrumental colors used. Kersters plays the brass-timbre game with directness. No fancy artifices. No complexities. All three pieces are straightforward in their rhythmic structures. There are introductory sections to the first and third pieces, and a 20th-century tang flavors the harmony.

Ketting, Otto (1935–)

DUO

- *A Set of Pieces* **for Flute and Piano (1967)**

A mastery of resource containing minute timbre tracings and declarative formations. One writer has described Ketting's work as of "completely individual style; one moment at rest, the next violent and incantatory like a summons to the dead." (One cannot accept as truth the report that Ketting has described his fifteen-minute duo as "nagging music.")

The set consists of four Epitaphs, the first three each followed by contrastive music, and then a literal restatement of *Epitaph I*. The Epitaphs are pitch frozen, a reminder of Webern. In the first one there are only three pitches for the flute: B, D-flat, and A; in *Epitaph II* there are only a pair of flute pitches: B and D. *Epitaph III* increases the total to four: A-flat, B-flat, C-sharp, and F-sharp. The piano pitch scope is larger, but fitting in proportion.

Another reminder appears in regard to the balance of the work. (These remindful considerations are only used to verbalize better the style of Ketting's music.) This time it is Varèse

that comes to mind in the ejaculatory figures that grow out of sustained detail in "Shapes and Patterns" (movement two). Movement four, "Fragments," has a huge pitch territory surveyed by the solo flute. It then links into partnership with the piano and is dropped to permit solo piano detail emphasizing tightly static chords set in rhythmic fragments. The penultimate movement (preceding the final Epitaph) is titled "Almost No Reactions." It is a flat-surfaced music, first heard in a *mezzopiano* sustained situation and later in crusty chordal soundings, set at *fortissimo* level. This is a music of expressionism, minus any exterior effects.

TRIOS

- *Small Suite* **for Three Trumpets (1957)**

Light and lucid, extroverted music, consisting of a set of five miniatures. A mini Ouverture (fourteen measures in march tempo) is followed by a trisectional Dans. Part three is an Aria with the melodic line passed from one instrument to the next. Part four is a Potpourri. The Finale ties in matters by using the first dozen measures of the Ouverture and proceeds from that point to structure a ternary piece of music.

- **Theme and Variations for Clarinet, Bassoon, and Piano (1958)**

Ketting was writing music based on strict serial principles when he was commissioned to compose this piece for the Municipality of Amsterdam. Formally and tonally the work is the direct opposite of dodecaphonic detail. Ketting decided on the stylistic shift because he felt it was a "sportsmanlike challenge" to produce a composition using traditional forms and techniques.

The theme is a Dutch folk song, " 'k Zag twee beren," and there are nine variations, within which all the duet possibilities permitted by the instrumentation are used. There is a zippy Etude for clarinet and piano (variation one); a rubato declamatory variation for bassoon and piano (number two), titled Cadens (meaing an adagio-paced Cadenza); and a neatly pert Duo for the two wind instruments. The last serves as the seventh variation.

The remaining variations are for the full trio: Number three is a mild Toccata; number four a Serenade, highlighting the piano with some sustained adjuncts in the other instruments; number five projects a lively March; variation six is a Waltz; variation seven is a fluid Pastorale; and the trio concludes with a Rumba-Finale.

Ketting, Piet (1904–84)

DUO

- **Partita for Two Flutes (1936)**

The pleasures and the beauties of neoclassicism. The lines are delicate and durable, savory and succinct.

Movement one has an unusual title: Priamel, but this is naught more than a 16th-century German spelling for the word praeambel, which defines a Prelude. A standard assortment of dances follows: Allemande, Courante, and Sarabande. A slight difference takes place in the fifth movement, where an Intermezzo is used as the Trio to the Minuet (Menuetto con Intermezzo). The closing movement is a Gigue.

TRIOS

- **Sonata for Flute, Oboe, and Piano (1936)**

Among the older composers in Holland (especially those writing in a tonal style) statistics show that polyphony dominates in their output.

This is a heritage entwined through the centuries, a continuous enthusiasm of Dutch musical creation that begins with the old Netherlands composers and marks the syntax of the modern composer. The collectivity of this exhaustive and exclusive method is illustrated by the contrapuntalism, polyrhythmicism and polytonalism in the work of Willem Pijper, many of his students and their students in turn. Ketting's Sonata is a further example. The dissonantly notched music utilizes two forms intensely concerned with contrapuntalism, namely, the chaconne and triple fugue. In addition, the freedom and boldness of toccata style embraces contrapuntalism as well. Ketting focuses his sights on the powerful thrust of moving voices. The sequence of Dutch composers' polyphonic regard remains unbroken.

In the Praeambulum the horizontal chromatic, corrugated drive of kinetic toccata power is contrasted with a short slow section. This last then combines and is engaged with the opening material. The ternary objective of the formal goal is approached by movement over very dissonant trestles of sound.

While the differences between the chaconne and passacaglia have never been satisfactorily demarcated, it has been generally assumed (based on the best Bach examples) that the former is indicated by an initial chordal presentation, which is the progenitor for the thematic derivations that follow, while the latter has a "ground bass" out of which the continuity of variational development proceeds, with more or less assertion of the theme in the bass register. In this respect, therefore, Ketting's second movement (Ciaconna) is more a passacaglia than a chaconne, but the difference really means little since the form is explicitly clear in its unfoldment. What is a bit more original is the subtraction from the usual total that marks the length of a chaconne or passacaglia theme. Ketting's ground line totals seven measures in place of eight. This theme appears almost constantly throughout the entire movement. The polyphony is of baroque strength, the variegations of manifold corroboration. Eventually the theme is moved to the piano's upper register and just after its return to the bass gamut it is heard again in higher framework, played this time by the flute. The concluding two statements of the theme are then pronounced in the bass level of the keyboard instrument.

The final movement's title (Fuga) does not tell the entire story. This very complicated movement consists of three subjects with only the first one listed in full exposition, while the second and third enter later within the continuously developed web. Ketting's polyphony is rich but thick. An important point to be noted is that the theme of the Ciaconna returns in the coda portion and thus gives the movement wider expression.

- **Trio for Flute, Clarinet, and Bassoon (1929)**

A compact, three-movement work, covering just under 51/2 minutes of performance time, and composed during the Christmas holidays of 1929. The Adagio was completed on December 23; the middle movement, Doppio movimento, was finished on Christmas Day; and the finale, Allegro, on December 27.

Melodic germ cells (a method espoused by the famed Dutch composer Willem Pijper and utilized by most of his students, including Ketting) are the structural basis for the Trio. These cells are detailed in the first three measures of the work, with a rising fifth in the bassoon, followed by an ascending third in the clarinet, and a pair of pitches (the span is an augmented second) sounded by flute fluttertonguing. From these the themes, harmonic detail, and elaboration are derived, plus the intensifying of textures and linear weights by polymetrical sections.

Keuler, Jenö (1936–)

DUO

- *Piccola partita* **for Clarinet and Bassoon (1968)**

Truly terse paragraphs. Four of them, with, for example, performance lengths of twenty and twenty-one seconds, respectively, for the third and fourth of the set.

Snappy, slightly abrasive pitch combinations; the effect is like speaking in musical slang. And a bit of descriptive matter is included. Number one has three measures of gentle music, and then five measures marked "a little perplexed," with a three measure return to the gently curved sounds. The second piece is marked *Angosciosamente* ("With anguished feeling"). *Con slancio* ("With impetuosity") is the tempo heading for the third piece. The finale is an eight-measure, legato-swerving music to be played quietly.

Keyper, Franz (c. 1756–1815)

DUO

- *Rondo Solo* **for Double Bass and Cello (or Viola)**

Note well that the instrumental pecking order in the title listing is not (as would be expected) "cello (or viola) and double bass." And well it should not be, since a considerable amount of the writing finds the "soprano" line detailed by the larger string instrument. That word "solo" in the title is not out of place either. Extreme high-register writing, double stops, and vigorous passagework deserve that description.

The rondo structuring for this music of charming virtuosity is detailed by an A–B–C–A–C–A plan.

Khachaturian, Aram (1903–78)

TRIO

- **Trio for Clarinet, Violin, and Piano (1932)**

From the start of his work, Khatchaturian was concerned with the characteristics of folk music, not only pertaining to his native Armenian region but to many others. Within his music one will find Russian, Uzbek, Ukrainian, Georgian, and Azerbaidzhanian melodies as well as Armenian ones. And so it is that the vitality and sincerity of folk music are the animated fascinations contained in this expert chamber music opus, totaling three movements.

Khatchaturian stated that his goal here had been the attempt to reproduce the sounds of native folk instruments. The choice of the clarinet results in excellent creative strategy as it stirs the embers of native intonational fires. This wind instrument is mobile and sensitive, of impressible variety, and Khatchaturian's Trio gains considerably as it draws on a fairly large segment of its total gamut. (In the first movement the clarinet imitates a zurna, a Transcaucasian wind instrument.)

Torporific music is rare from any composer who draws his working material from indigenous sources. None of the themes to be found in Khatchaturian's work are in any way a drug on the musical market. Their worth is generously set forth by excellent harmonic dress and a semi-cantillational melodic style. The first movement is rhapsodic. The second is sectional in form, yet related as a whole. Its short Allegro leads to an Allegretto with a preponderance of melodic strength gravitated off the beat; the music then becomes rhythmically agitated and develops this idea, returns to the Allegretto portion and eventually the opening. Thus a circular measured form applies in this instance. The last movement is entrancing, warmed and enriched by the main theme (announced by the clarinet alone). This is an authentic Uzbek tune, developed in perfect style that never departs from the subject's essential character. Here, Khatchaturian casts his music (and spell) by primitive quality; the sophistication of overripe harmony never intrudes and harms the integral fancy as the action of the music rises from a moderate speed to a presto and then recedes.

Khachaturian, Karen (1920–)

DUOS

- **Sonata for Cello and Piano**

The Sonata opens with an intensely contoured Recitativo; its pitch range for the cello embraces three octaves and a sixth (from the low open C string to the high A three octaves and a sixth above). The piano in this section is totally supportive, a secondary voice.

The recitando music is linked to an Invention. This term always brings to mind Bach's collection of fifteen keyboard pieces in two parts called *Inventiones* (matched by a set of fifteen pieces in three parts which he called *Sinfoniae*). But no Bachian-style documentation is here. Khachaturian's polyphonic landscape has frictioned turf, and is colored by asymmetricality, col legno and sul ponticello formations.

Movement three is an Aria also refreshed with timbre colorations—in this case pizzicato and harmonics in the music's conclusion. The finale is a dazzling Toccata. Considerable urgent ostinato octaves in the bass zone of the piano, considerable conjunct figurations for both instruments, and considerable line action in the concluding section for the cello. A crowd pleaser, certainly.

■ **Sonata for Violin and Piano, Op. 1**

A garland of 19th-century musical facts—no fancies appear in this music of semilush, semi-Tchaikovskian material. In the conclusion of the initial movement (Allegro) there is some muted sonority that follows a Recitativo portion. A little flavoring of pizzicato is used in the middle division (Andante), and the Presto finale has some folksy turns that turn into a tarantella.

Khudoley, Igor (1940–)

DUO

■ **Sonata for Cello and Piano, Op. 2**

The unfettered form of the fantasy is involved here. Still, there is an amount of structural integration: The initial Adagio returns (changed but recognizable as to relationship) at the conclusion. And the slightly jagged and open-interval music that follows the Adagio at the beginning is reflected in the latter part of the duo.

Ornamental romantic harmony is used, producing a mix of tonal poise and energy. Within this mix there is also a truly substantial section for the cello alone. Khudoley's final measures are of poetic sparseness, with the single voice of the piano in dialogue with the cello's mostly lightly plucked voice.

Kiel, Friedrich (1821–85)

Kiel's chamber music output was quite large, and discounting three small works, almost the total produced by his contemporary, Johannes Brahms. It includes two string quartets, two sets of waltzes for string quartet, a pair of piano quintets, three piano quartets, seven piano trios, four violin and piano sonatas, single sonatas

for viola and piano and cello with piano, as well as a set of Three Romances for viola and piano, and for violin and piano a *Little Suite* and a *Deutsche Reigen (German Round Dance)*.

While prolific production does not prove a composer's excellence, in Kiel's case output is matched by craftsmanship. His music has an undeniable Brahmsian cast. As such it is totally romantic. The piano quintets are probably the best of the lot and should be given their rightful place in the chamber music repertoire.

DUOS

■ **Sonata for Viola and Piano, Op. 67**

Within the romantically lyrical style of Kiel's four-movement Sonata there are both the standard structures and some points that deviate from the conventional. Kiel was no groundbreaker, but in this work he does show a desire to remove stylistic encrustations.

The thematic resource of the opening movement is concentrated. Full-scale development is made in the basic key of G minor. However, the latter part of the recapitulation and the coda of the movement are in G major. Further, the initial theme is quoted in the coda of the fourth movement.

The Scherzo stresses upbeat phrase points in its Schumannesque syntax and then has smooth four-measure melodic sequences for relationship. Its E-flat tonality moves to the subdominant point (A-flat) for the Trio section, one subdued and somewhat melancholic in its vertical progressions. Here again the interlock method Kiel used in the first movement is repeated, with a phrase from the Scherzo appearing in the last movement.

The slow movement moves far afield into B major. Diversity is certainly the objective by such tonal choice. In the finale offbeat swing of theme (again a relationship between movements, the Scherzo thematic resource being the affinitive matter of upbeats) is of G-major hunting-song-quality optimism. It is strongly opposite to the minor-key dramatic recitative for the viola that marks the middle part of the movement.

(In *Cobbett's Cyclopedic Survey of Chamber Music* Kiel's Op. 67 is listed as also scored for violin or cello and piano. In the most recent edition [published in 1972 by the Verlag Walter Wollenweber] no mention is made of such substitutions nor are parts made available for substitute instruments.)

- **Three Romances for Viola and Piano, Op. 69**

The objective here is the vigorous romantic stimulation expressed by the two instruments. There is nothing cool in these three pieces, but the intensity is controlled and the control carries over so that actually the three pieces fall into place as a totally balanced conception.

A slow-tempo first part in B-flat major is related to a slightly faster and more agitated central section in C minor; the music then returns to the initial part. To be noted is the matter of instrumental equality. Thus, the opening line for the viola is given the piano on the recapitulation and the filled-in harmonic statement of the piano at the start is reduced in content and assigned to the viola on the recapitulation. Part two is an Allegretto semplice in G major, a restrained statement compared to the previous movement. The mood of the final Romance, Allegro con passione, is confirmed by the material: urgency of melodic line and rhythmic underlining by way of the syncopative harmonic design.

Consequently, contrast but cohesion, with a tempo plan that moves in proportional increase of speed (andante–allegretto–allegro). And with tonal relationships supporting the total structure (B-flat, its submediant major [G], onto the latter's relative minor).

QUINTETS

- **Quintet No. 1 in A Major for Piano, Two Violins, Viola, and Cello, Op. 75**

Aside from the expected sonata plan, the first movement is marked by expert scoring devices. Tutti inserts give variance to the texture, and antiphonal sections add their part to the color detail. Again, scoring particulars are prominent in the second movement, where the music is mainly presented in fugal terms, the strings alone announcing the basic subject material.

Kiel's keenness for obtaining maximum timbre response in the piano quintet medium is further exemplified in the fourth movement, marked Tempo di menuetto, which includes two Trios, each different in terms of scoring, tonality, tempo, and mood. Further, the initial theme of this movement is entirely assigned to the piano, thereby balancing the opening of movement two, initiated by the four strings alone. In contrast, the second and third presentations of the principal section are covered by tutti scoring. A rondo formation is utilized for the fifth movement.

- **Quintet No. 2 in C Minor for Piano, Two Violins, Viola, and Cello, Op. 76**

The constructive principles of musical composition do not only concern a specified formal layout. The composer must derive ideas from his basic material and expand on them without destroying the unified plan and its balances. In the first movement, Kiel's presentation of sonata form proceeds almost cautiously, then catches fire in the faster tempo of the coda, where the theme is thrust forward with dramatically entwined voices. Movement two is an Arioso, the third part is an Intermezzo, and the final section is a Rondo with an Introduzione. The last has lightness of character.

Counterpoint hardly buttresses this Quintet.

Lyric poise is the lodestar of Kiel's well-wrought and sensitive music for piano with string quartet.

Kievman, Carson (1949–)

QUINTET

- *Sirocco* **for Woodwind Quintet (1975)**

No strictly run-of-the-mill writing in this case. Kievman's four-minute piece is, indeed, hot with pitch action, free of any oppressive stylistic jacket, though dusted with sound particles from beginning to end.

Huge legato phrases are initially combined—sometimes almost forty sounds are strung together in a single phrase. That type of writing returns later. Before it does there is a section of articulated sounds (some to be played "breathy, no tongue"; others to be spat out [marked "ta"]). Thus, in a copy of A–B–A format *Sirocco* fits its new demonstration into old substantiation.

This is the type of music one would expect from a composer who wrote a concerto for bassoon and fire alarm systems, with the proviso that it be played only "in buildings which meet fire department standards."

Kilar, Wojciech (1932–)

DUO

- **Sonata for Horn and Piano (1954)**

Absolutely clear designs in this colorful three-movement piece. The first is a sonata, the second (Recitativo e Arioso) is a binary concept that is run through twice, and the last is a rondo.

Fresh and smart vocabulary fill these statements. There is key mix, placement of a whole-somely diatonic melody against cluster chords, pandiatonic details, series of parallel triads in one voice going against the grain of a concentrated tonality in another voice. The asperity detailed in the grotesque finale is a delight. In the middle movement the horn proposes a cantillational quality in the Recitativo while the piano disposes of its partnership by ostinato phrases.

For once the horn stays away from the hunt and the viewing of nature scenes. This is horn music, indeed, but a type of hornistic slang. And it's very appealing.

Killmayer, Wilhelm (1927–)

QUARTETS

- **Quartet for Two Violins, Cello, and Piano (1975)**

In its repetitiveness Killmayer's differently constituted piano quartet (a second violin replacing the usual viola) represents a type of early minimalism. Still, there is greater pitch change and the style properly falls into the area of nondevelopment.

There is no metrical design, simply consecutive similarity of sound lengths. Thus, the opening consists of the cello alone playing eighty-eight quarter notes (at $\bullet$ = 60), then a triplet plus dotted eighth note, six more quarter notes, again the pithy rhythmic interruption, once more six quarter notes, the triplet alone, and then eight quarter notes. The pitch span is limited to ten. Next, fifty quarter notes, four times interrupted by triplets, are stated in unison by the strings. Section three is a repetitive set of octaves (pitched on F) by the strings with three chordal insertions by the piano.

And so it goes on. Mass sonorities in rhythmic unification. There are ten divisions in all. The ninth is a large one for the piano alone of 127 continuous quarter notes, sometimes supported by half notes. The final section is a set of six-pulse measures suddenly broken off to give the effect that the work is unfinished. One assumes that music of this neoprimitive type actually cannot have any positive conclusion.

- **Quartet for Two Violins, Viola, and Cello (1969)**

The poetic passions here reflect Webern in its aphoristic writing and reflect Orff in its rhythmic repetitions. Put together the Quartet (of single-piece, ten-minute length) is an example of cold instrumental logic. There are no metrical divisions and there is no tempo change from the beginning to the end (the metronomic indication is ♩ = 60).

Certainly, a composer of Killmayer's ability working on his score paper knows where he's at. There is no arguing that he is not fully in command of his style. But, it represents a music purposefully emotionally repressed.

Kilpatrick, Jack Frederick (1915–67)

DUOS

- **Sonata in G Minor for Violin and Piano (1947)**

Concentrated proportions and strongly tonal, urbane music. The audible logic of the materials themselves is paralleled by exact attention to standard key choices and structural arrangements.

G minor, as expected, is used for the sonata-form first movement. B-flat major is the tonality for the central movement, marked Slowly, written in the oft-used ternary formal setting, while the snappy and fast finale runs a rondo route in gay G major.

There are no great hits here but there are no errors.

- **Sonatina in E Minor for Viola and Piano, Op. 38**

Exactly tonal music, chromatically dusted, but the harmonic idiom of this composer of American Indian descent is never worn and faded. There is but one movement, and more attention is given the second theme than the initial one.

Kilpinen, Yrjö (1892–1959)

DUO

Sonata for Cello and Piano, Op. 90

Kilpinen's reputation as one of the great song composers of all time is assured. He has been called the Finnish Hugo Wolf. In the chamber music field he produced only two works: the Op. 90 cello and piano sonata, immediately followed by the Suite for Viola da Gamba and Piano, Op. 91. This minute total must be compared with Kilpinen's staggering amount of songs, which almost reached the eight-hundred mark, to realize the direction of his creativity.

The cello sonata displays the same late-romantic style lyricism as the vocal compositions. It also follows the pattern of the piano in terms of the songs, where it takes on symphonic dimensions. In the Op. 90 duo the piano is full-blooded, a perfect opposite, yet proper blend for the string instrument, which vocalizes from beginning to end. The songlike contour of the cello part is apparent when it is realized that not one chord is employed for the instrument. The use of the cello's gamut is all-embracing, but at that point color exploitation stops. Aside from some pizzicatos, the cello is a bass-baritone vocalist in the four movements. Of these the middle pair are both three part in design, the second one being the more dramatic. The outer movements have the same contrasted relationship. Movement one is direct in its sonata framework, while the finale is allegorical in tone, ambivalent in its change of tempo.

King, Robert (1914–)

DUO

▪ *French Suite* **for Cornet and Baritone**

Actually a dance suite. Further, one could well do without the *French* designation since the four dances that follow the Prelude are not exclusively of French property. The Allemande, Courante, Sarabande, and Gigue here represented all spill over specific nationalistic boundary lines. No matter. The writing is fluent, finely fixed, and gives the two instruments equal time. A further plus is the rare combination that King chose.

Kirchner, Leon (1919–)

DUOS

▪ **Duo for Violin and Piano (1947)**

Thematic unity is present, but in terms of synonymity, not set forthright by recapitulationary means or variation. Stylistic information is outlined by the piano's opening statement. This is shifted into various shapes. The tempos and rhythms are constantly free; the colors those of Webern's pointillism and Bartók's *ruvido* means (again a matter of assimilation and productivity, not imitation). There are glides and slides, played with bow and plucked by fingers, a complete exploitation of the instrumental colors and gamuts to convey this 20th-century documentation. It is music removed from system, allowed its freedom. Kirchner's Duo is a complete experience; the listener must realize that beyond technical explanation the truly important matter is the emotional contact he will receive. Few of these are musical carom

shots, but rather straight to the expressive mark.

The ending is derived from one of the units, a quasi cadenza over the piano's tone-drum roll of combined fourths, the violin moving from intervals of sixths to sevenths. The improvisational quality of the coda helps to prove the essentials of this entire work.

▪ **Sonata concertante for Violin and Piano (1952)**

In this work tonal values are integrated. This is the music's fundament without denying dissonance of dramatic impact and even atonality. The interval of a third, triadic stimuli, and conjunct moves are the principal devices used in this duo. These occur as inlays and overlays, creating the matrix on which the music rests.

One-movement design is used. In second place there is a slow-tempo section—a muted violin interlude of *recitando* contour. On either side of this Adagio are fast-paced sections, the second one a Grazioso in rondo framework that is in contrast to the initiatory dramatic music. The conclusion is almost like the opening.

The sonata lives up to its title: Concerted elements rival one another, though cooperation is fully at work. Integral cadenzas are given each of the instruments, and contrast emerges from the breadth of the violin's lines and the sense of qualified violence in the piano, making the work in effect a concerto grosso with orchestral adjuncts eliminated.

TRIO

▪ **Trio for Violin, Cello, and Piano (1954)**

In certain respects, Kirchner's work brings to mind the sensitive comment Mozart wrote in a letter three years before his death: ". . . it is better to be short and good." This control is illustrated in Kirchner's marvelously sonorous Trio. It is in only two movements: basically fast and slow.

Kirchner's music is truly his own. Similar to his other compositions, in the piano trio the use of direct, carefully measured themes is bypassed in favor of discourse and debate on specific points. A quality of consistent variation is used, with one measure dictating what the next will state. The music presents the conscious use of frictions, rhapsody, and inner agitation, brought by what the composer-author (Klaus George Roy) has described as "a sort of 'stream-of-consciousness' unfolding."

There is urgent demand in the music. The instructions *Marcato (Emphasized)* and *Molto marcato (Very emphasized)* appear often. A passage in the first movement is marked *Wild!* Thus these chromaticized cries of music that sound within a Bergian climate. The scoring is colorful and rewarding, with sizable solos and duos within the trio setting.

QUARTETS

■ String Quartet [No. 1] (1949)

Kirchner's quartet is derivative only in its nervous asymmetries; it is scarcely so as to form, or its manner of painting colors and measuring sonorities. The first movement's rhythms are exceedingly plastic, the pulse rhapsodic, and the same emboldening of the rhythm applies to the form, set in four sections. One melodic unit is important above others—that of an octave declaration. This makes its mark in three ways: repeated (at different tone levels), in the form of a subtle relationship by compression of the octave, and with attendant interpolated ornamentation. In the second movement, Adagio, the negotiation of the intervallic second is all-important—vertically, horizontally, by embellishment, and gliding chromatically.

The third movement, Divertimento, is the only symmetrical one of the entire quartet. It has the graphic design of a large Beethoven scherzo (in a tempo faster than that style, however). Though harmonies, inner pulsations, color, and vocabulary are a far cry from Beethoven, the duplication of that composer's acute sense of structural balance cannot be overlooked. (Give Kirchner a fat credit for artistic perceptiveness.)

The last movement is like a cadenza in slow motion. A rhythmic unit plays an important role, though subsidiary to the baroque outlines of the soprano voice. Its "incomplete" sextuplet (the pulse consisting of only four sounds, filled out by rests) identifies the exposition and its return in the movement. Throughout, Kirchner's keen exploration of rhythm is paramount.

■ String Quartet No. 2 (1958)

Three movements, each *attacca* into the next, each concluding with dynamically fading sound. And each movement contains the Kirchner trademarks of rhapsodically buoyant turns; rhythmical, fiorituralike patterns; and sharply shaped, asymmetric phrase lengths.

Kirchner's dissonances are not spelled out from the use of rules. Formula he does not follow in any manner, though within the shapes of the three movements there are certain returns of material that make the structure cohesive. In his consideration of form the descriptive analysis of Richard Franko Goldman is on target. According to this critic, Kirchner uses "no method but that dictated by his ear." And, importantly, Kirchner's ear never hears the outré effects that permeate so many mid- and late-twentieth-century string quartets.

■ String Quartet No. 3 and Electronic Tape (1966)

For the most part electronic sound has not been successfully combined with instruments. Because of its special texture there has been a constant, almost painful reminder of the sharp difference in timbres. Kirchner indicates that he "set out to produce a meaningful confrontation between 'new' electronic sounds and those of the traditional string quartet—a kind of dialogue-idea in which the electronics are quite integral." And he has succeeded magnificently. His quartet (quintet?) exhibits an ideal marriage of string quartet and tape sounds.

The music displays an excellent contrast and blend of the two sound-production types. The electronic tape does not frame or merely oppose; it both colors and enlarges the string spectrum. Example: The tape sound hinges to the violins and the range moves upward and outward. Here, the sonorous territory seems endless and the string quartet becomes a gigantic entity rather than four instruments punctuated or orchestrated by the tape collation.

The opus has the type of form whereby its design is made apparent by the firmly knit content. Kirchner avoids the strictly formal response, which so often is actually a formal defect. In his third quartet there is no formula, the use of which is most often just as bad as formless music. The result deserved the Pulitzer Prize given it in 1967.

Kirchner, Theodor (1823–1903)

QUARTET

- *Nur Tropfen—Ganz kleine Stücke (Just Drops—Very Small Pieces)* for String Quartet

Seven miniature pieces, some dancelike, such as the fifth of the set, an Allegro that moves like a waltz, and the seventh, which runs like a modified galop. Schumann breathes in these measures, especially in the remainder of the group, all slow in tempo, and poetic in content and in the flow of the sonorities.

Kirchner, Volker David (1942–)

QUARTET

- **String Quartet (1983)**

To paraphrase Thomas Carlyle: In every form there is innumerable meaning. Kirchner uses picturesque forms but none of the four match traditional custom.

The Mesto (Mournful) obeys a threnodic mood in its slow, first part, with consistent stepwise movement of the pitches. It then swerves into a Furioso whose only relationship to its title is again that of tight pitch movement—the lines projecting the dramatic drive of a machine in motion. The Intermezzo (Barcarola) has sway but is uneven and the pulse is broken.

Part three is a Nocturno that is neither melancholy nor languid. It has several places where it is rough and tough in sound. Elsewhere (for the greater part) the tempo is presto, within which ostinatos display metrical nervous splitting of 3+3+3 or 2+3+3 units, combined with scurrying lines that mix duple and triple pitches per beat. The finale is a Burleske. Here too the music (similar to the first movement) is divided: The first part is calmly chromatic; the second part is percussively pungent. The result is Kirchner's burlesque of a burlesque.

Kirnberger, Johann Philipp (1721–83)

DUO

- **Sonata in B-flat Major for Oboe and Basso Continuo**

Kirnberger, regarded as one of the most important theorists of his time, was less known as a composer, which is difficult to understand considering this splendid piece, which the editor,

Hermann Töttcher, describes as "a typical example of the Berlin elegant style" (that is, the gallant style *[galanter Stil]).* However, the opening movement (Adagio) is elaborately detailed and can well be considered a link to (or carryover from) the heavier and more serious baroque style (so-called *gearbeiteter Stil).* On the other hand another statement by the editor cannot be accepted. He indicates that the music "may justly be taken for a coloratura transposed for the oboe." Certainly the serious expressions found in the oboe's figurations, especially in the opening music, are far removed from such roulades.

Rondo disposition marks the middle movement (Allegro). The finale is a Menuetto con variatione. Exact measurement in this case. The double-period length of the theme is maintained in the three variations as the rhythmic action increases in each one. Complete minuet tie-up is made with a literal repeat of the theme at the end.

Kitazume, Michio (1948–)

NONET

- *Shadows I* for Nine Brasses (Three Trumpets, Three Tenor Trombones, Horn, Two Tubas) (1975)

Clustered pitch action, always short phrased. Kitazume's piece consists of short and severely demarcated ideas.

The nonet begins with trumpets alone. When the other instruments enter they emphasize sustained sounds while the trumpets continue playing dislocated figures. The next part of the work continues the stress on rhythmic bits, but all the instruments participate. This latter setting is energized by a huge amount of fluttertongued sounds. Gusto is present, none of it delicate.

Kitazume, Yayoi (1945–)

DUO

- **Sonatine for Clarinet and Piano**

Light and tuneful, tonal and affable. This is French-style music written by a Japanese composer. Indeed, nice-to-listen-to music with an Allegro in modified sonata form, a Lento that favors seventh chords, and a Rondo that favors triads. It's clean as a whistle and conceived with artistic intelligence.

SEXTET

- *Deep Blue Sky* **for Oboe, Two Violins, Viola, Cello, and Piano (1977)**

The difference between this sextet and the duo discussed above is similar to the disparity between a work like Berg's *Wozzeck* and Verdi's *La Traviata.* The clarinet and piano sonatine is superconventional while *Deep Blue Sky* is far-far-out.

From beginning to end single pitches or minute figures coalesce; the action is that of a nonthematic pitch blend into a surface of hard dissonance. And throughout, ranges are restricted, with defined pulse patterns eliminated. The piece is plotted in sections, and though some are sustained, others active, some for piano alone, and others with oboe multiphonics, the discourse is always nakedly hard-crusted as the sounds prickle and prick, sting and smart.

The title, we are told, has no bearing on the music's structure or content. Kitazume says only "that each of these three words connote a meaning that is distinct and boundless in scope."

Kjellsby, Erling (1901–76)

QUARTET

- **String Quartet No. 4**

Kjellsby does not dissent from classical formal controls in his four-movement work. And here and there, there is a bit of impressionistic quality, but it does not impare basic stylistic definition. The impressionistic sense is most evident in the second movement (Presto giocoso). This is not indicated as a scherzo, but its bouncy detail, even faster-paced central division, (entirely devoted to plucked sound), and literal recapitulation are squarely in the land of the scherzo.

The formal chain of command is clear: Movement one is a sonata, the slow movement is a ternary affair, and the finale is a rondo.

Klebanov, Dmitry (1907–)

QUINTET

- **Quintet for Piano, Two Violins, Viola, and Cello**

A big, square, piano quintet. Everything is solid and clear and emphatically tonal. Lots of pomp and celebration in the outer movements (both contain quasi marcia sections). Lots of consecutive, massively fleshed out triads. The slow (second) movement especially emphasizes this factor. Movement three is the expected Scherzo, with contrastive Trio.

Klebanov is not at all attracted to contemporary dissonance in his work (published in Moscow in 1960). He is attracted, however, to the full-blooded symphonicism of the medium. The scoring drive is unhampered. For music of this style that's the way it should be.

Klebe, Giselher (1925–)

DUOS

- **Nine Duettini for Flute and Piano, Op. 39**

Truly, "small duets." The first one consists of the piano striking a six-part chord followed by six freely separated pitches by the flute. The other movements are longer; examples: twenty-eight measures for an Allegro conception (number three), twenty-seven measures for a Con moto piece (number six).

Expressive twelve-tone depictions. Mixed in with the rhythmic explorations are some freely defined bits. The final piece is the result of extramusical stimulus, being a "Homage to Boris Blacher" (Klebe studied with Blacher between 1946 and 1951). In keeping with the "variable meters" technique Blacher developed, each of the thirty-seven measures changes meter, strictly increasing or decreasing by a single pulse.

- **Sonata [No. 1] for Violin and Piano, Op. 14**

Twelve-tone rhapsody in terms of three linked movements. The first of these utilizes a pivotal idea—a rhythmic cell of four sounds occupying a half beat and consisting of a ratio of 3:1; this is stated nine times. Movement two is ecstatic in temper, smeared with color that maintains dodecaphonic doctrine. Trills, chordal left-hand pizzicato, double harmonics, glissandos (at times, three in succession using three different strings, thus additional hues within one primary pigmentation) are included in the violin part. Extreme pedal differences, pointed up to the nth degree, mark the piano writing.

Klebe wields a soft stick. There is but one-half of a beat of *fortissimo* in the entire Sonata. Only a tidbit of *forte* is contained in the opening part, a tad more in the middle section, with none whatsoever in the final movement. In the last, the ultimate raison d'être is realized—the strongest dynamic employed is *piano*. There, Klebe's music whispers, so to speak, but in wild whispers to be sure. However, throughout the Sonata the rhythmic action is effusive, as manifold as the pitch changes.

QUARTETS

- **String Quartet, Op. 9**

Suite design is used in Klebe's Op. 9. There are six short movements, the longest of these being the second and the last. Klebe writes here in a free twelve-tone style, producing a music of chromatic tightness and tensile sound. The closing of the first movement illustrates the trend of thought—a chord of clustered sound: E-flat and E-natural at the extremes with F, G, and A-flat in between. It is this first movement that presents the quartet's basic material, akin to a sonata's exposition.

Imitation and ostinato motor drive rule the dynamically potent second movement (Vivace). Diametrical qualities are contained in the next two parts of the quartet; the first of scherzando means, using motival imitation, the second of Adagio expressivity. A concentrated peripatetic Presto follows in which the contrapuntalism is intensified. Here the music is kept under wraps until it bursts out in the last three measures. Movement six undergoes several tempo changes, each marked by different material (Molto lento–Larghetto–Moderato–Allegro vivo). The effect is one of rhapsody within rhapsody.

- **String Quartet No. 2, Op. 42**

Klebe dedicated this quartet, written in 1963, to Giuseppe Verdi to commemorate the 150th anniversary of the great Italian composer's birth in 1813. Going further, this act led to strange aesthetic comradeship. Movement three is a set of variations on a Verdi theme in which the F-major subject is dodecaphonically exercised in a dozen permutations.

Movements one and two are inlaid with change. In the first of the pair (titled Due tempi) the pace moves bluntly from Allegro to Adagio; finally, the music stays put in the fast zone. This divergency carries over to the nervous quality of the second movement (Larghetto).

Klega, Miroslav (1926–)

QUARTET

- **Concertino for String Quartet (1961)**

Klega presents his music in gracious and shapely, clear and fluent neoclassic style. There are three movements, with outer placed allegros (the first much more contrapuntal in its progressions), and a middle three-part conception that has the quality of a slowed-down gavotte.

Klein, John (1915–81)

QUARTET

- **Sonata for Two Trumpets and Two Trombones**

Brass tone color will necessarily pall much faster than the assorted values and possibilities of strings. It is for that reason that composers are wise in concentrating their chamber works for brass to avoid sprawling lengths. Klein's Sonata encompasses three movements, but its duration is much shorter, in ratio, than the same type of design for string or even wind instruments.

There is no sonata form as such in *this*

Sonata. Though the compounded set of movements generally contains at least one movement in sonata form, this is not mandatory. A number of movements in set forms put together is sufficient to depict such generic musical architecture.

The first movement is in three-part form, with the second part partially developing the material of the opening. Dissonances appear as a logical outcome of the part writing. The fugue of the last movement is preceded by a restatement of the beginning of the first movement, and the theme of that movement is wound into the latter part of the fugue itself. This forms a unity of the outer movements; somewhat that of cyclic form, more of overall balanced verification.

Klein, Richard Rudolf (1921–)

DUO

- **Sonatine in C for Soprano Recorder and Harpsichord**

No heavy make up is applied to this three-part work. Warming immediacy, tonal to the nth degree—everything is clearly textured. The central movement (Larghetto) is gently ornamented. Klein does not overload his light-faceted music.

TRIO

- **Divertimento for Three Guitars**

A score bright with interesting plan. In each part a shift in form offers the unexpected, and balance is achieved by sheer contrastive sharpness.

Movement one chugs along like a tarantella and then, without alteration of pace, changes to a different thematic basis. Movement two is trisectional: Andante–Presto–Adagio in sequence. The binding needle for the sound fabric is the use of canonic bits. The Vivace of movement three is exciting, obtained by rhythmic perpetual-motion insistence. The closing Allegretto is of light dance character.

Kleinsinger, George (1914–82)

SEXTET

- ***Design for Woodwinds*** **(Flute, Oboe [or Flute 2], Two Clarinets, Horn, and Bassoon [or Baritone Saxophone])**

A short piece in brisk tempo, with the slant of folk reaction. There is a touch of the musical-comedy score about this work, set for a sextet of flute, oboe (or a second flute), two clarinets, horn, and bassoon (a baritone saxophone may substitute for the latter, a utilitarian objective to obtain wider performance). The form is clear, that of a rondo.

Kleinsinger was brought into prominence by his *Tubby the Tuba*, a work that had its counterpart in the earlier *Peter and the Wolf*, by Prokofiev. The style of *Tubby* is matched by this chamber work's simple design.

Klengel, Julius (1859–1933)

QUARTETS

- **Theme and Variations for Four Cellos, Op. 28**

Klengel has been described as a composer who wrote in the late-nineteenth-century "Leipzig" style, combining classical and romantic aspects. The depiction fits this set of six variations on an Andante theme.

The procedure is clear and structurally definitive. For example, the character is ornamental in the first variant, rhythmically resolute in the second one, chordally positive in the fourth part, and scherzo personalized in the sixth variation. To bring balance the theme returns as the concluding part of the quartet.

- *Variations on an Original Theme* **for Four Cellos, Op. 15**

As a cellist Klengel favored that instrument in his creative work. Among the output were four concertos, a double concerto (with the violin as the other solo instrument), a work for twelve cellos titled *Hymnus*, and suites for cello and piano, cello and organ, and two cellos. (For another work for four cellos *see above*.)

There are eleven variations plus a coda in Op. 15. It is not until the final variation of the set that Klengel departs from his original thirty-two measure thematic span. Rigidity of scope, however, does not apply to the variants, each with its own, immediately recognizable profile. Especially colorful are the fifth variation (Allegretto), with antiphonal rhythmic jabs in the first and fourth cellos and the other two cellos pizzicato; variation eight, a Mendelssohnian Vivace, with three instruments supplying a pizzicato background; and the ninth variation, a Moderato in 3/8, totally in plucked timbre.

Kliuzner, Boris (1909–)

TRIO

- **Trio for Piano, Violin, and Cello (1947)**

The stylistic safe house of Soviet music is represented here (the work was completed in 1947). Kliuzner's Trio is commanded by neo-Borodin and neo-Glière procedures (for that matter, one could include Kabalevsky). Such creative obedience can't hurt and does lead to a fair success.

A short introduction in F-sharp minor (the composition is finalized in F-sharp major for standard classically oriented balance) ends in A minor and is linked to the second movement. Surging material is emphasized there with complete attention given minor tonalities. The movement begins in G minor and then shifts en route to C-sharp minor, E minor, B-flat minor, A minor, and then returns to the home key of G minor.

The slow movement (in triple pulse) reminds one of a minuet, what with its decorous demeanor, nice lilt, and flavorsome juicy thirds and sixths. As movements one and two were joined, so movements three and four. The finale is somewhat of a surprise. In place of the usual fast action, the choice is for broad melodic sweep even though the tempo is allegro.

Klosé, Hyacinthe-Eléonore (1808–80)

DUOS

- **Concert Duet No. 1 in B-flat major for Two Clarinets**

- **Concert Duet No. 2 in E-flat major for Two Clarinets**

- **Concert Duet No. 3 in F major for Two Clarinets**

Klosé is the noted pedagogue who wrote one of the most important methods for the clarinet. His *Grande méthodé pour la clarinette*, published in 1844, remains a standard teaching tool throughout the world.

Klosé the composer remains Klosé the pedagogue with a marked affinity for writing expertly for the clarinet. The musical effect is somewhat neutral and a little bit will go a long way in the concert hall. By far the best use of these duos is in the teaching studio or in the home.

All three duets are in three movements with a pair of lively movements enclosing a slow one. In the second duet the slow music is titled Romanza. Klosé uses rondos in the finales for the first two duets (the first of these subtitled Pastoral). The finale of the third duet represents the most imaginative in the entire set of nine movements. It consists of a theme and two variations, the second a swirling non-stop affair of rhythmic figurations.

Klughardt, August (1847–1902)

TRIO

- *Schilflieder: Fünf Fantasiestücke (Songs of the Reeds: Five Fantasy Pieces)* **for Piano, Oboe (or Violin), and Viola, Op. 28**

Brahmsian music, its lyrical and dramatic gambit linked to verses by the important Austrian romantic poet Nikolaus Lenau (1802–50). The Lenau text is indicated throughout the score, in sectional fashion, and is more general than directional. Klughardt's *Schilflieder* should not be considered in the program-music category. It can be heard without any reference to the textual stimulant that served the composer.

The music of the five movements projects a romantic landscape, warmly colored by the choice of the oboe and viola, with a brilliant edging applied by the piano. The writing for the keyboard instrument shows the influence of Liszt, which is somewhat confirmed by the dedication of the trio to him ("Herrn Dr. Franz Liszt in innigster Verehrung").

QUINTET

- **Quintet for Flute, Oboe, Clarinet, Horn, and Bassoon, Op. 79**

Romantic syntax merging into well-crafted tex-tures provides an agreeable example of standard-style woodwind quintet music.

The scoring is well set out for the individual instruments. In the finale (begun by an introductory Adagio and joined to the principal material in Allegro molto vivace tempo) as well as in the preceding slow movement (to be paced Andante grazioso and shaped like a minuet) attention to the separate timbres is most effective. Sonata form is used in the first movement; the second movement is an energetic scherzo type.

Klusák, Jan (1934–)

TRIO

- *Rejdovák (Czech Folk Dance)* **for Bass Clarinet, Viola, and Double Bass (1965)**

The dark-timbred scoring parallels the basal material that Klusák has used for his trio. It approximates a folk ensemble in its primitive colorative balance. To continue this idea the music has no folksy two-steps or lyric statements. Here the total chromatic embraces the score, which contains birhythmic detail and considerable nonmetrical divisions. (There are some who will state that using "dance" in the title of this trio is false advertising.)

(Klusák made another setting of his piece for bass clarinet and harpsichord.)

QUINTET

- *Music for a Fountain*: **Divertimento for Wind Quintet (1954)**

Klusák's music flows with clear neoclassic waters. Nicely warm, indeed, and never dully tepid. There is a prancing Intrada, a Menuetto, and a vivacious Rondino as parts one, three, and four. The Notturno has a slightly different cast from what one expects. In every measure the melodic line (in adagietto tempo) is propped up by tutti (though dynamically quiet) ostinato patterns. This is a "night music" that is rhythmically illustrative of earlier hours.

Knab, Armin (1881–1951)

QUARTET

- *Variations on an Original Children's Song* **for String Quartet**

The thematic basis is taken from Knab's Christmas story, *Das Lebenslicht*. It is a simple, twelve-measure G-major item and there are eight variations, all but the last run through twice.

Knab plays it close to the vest. It is not until the fifth variation that the twelve-measure total is lengthened and the key changed (to E minor). The E major of the sixth variant is the only other tonality shift. Disciplined workmanship. Knab's objective is to keep the generating melody to the fore, and that is supported throughout.

Knap, Rolf (1937–)

DUO

- *Zelomaniana* **for Oboe and Piano, Op. 2, No. 37**

There's humor in this freshly engaging short duo by the Dutch oboist-composer. (The huge total of works within one opus is a sign of creative modesty that is not followed in the music discussed here.)

A one-measure motive is basic to the piece. Other minute segments move in and then out: four measures of a canon; four measures that take off on the Beethoven Fifth's four-pitch

motive. Just before the final D-minor lightly *secco* chord an oboe cadenza is to be played "ad libitum." Also ad lib in terms of length but major to the piece are fermatas—nine of them in the first ten measures.

Knight, Morris (1933–)

TRIO

- **Cassation for Trumpet, Horn, and Trombone (1961)**

Seven sections, the first an Introduction and the last an Epilogue. Rhythmic ball-tossing figures are in "Catch"; solo colors are highlighted in the "Song for Horn" and "Trumpet Minstrel," but not at the loss of ensemble stipulations. Slippery-floor conditions exist in the glisses heard in the "Waltz for Trombone." The penultimate movement is titled "Three in Two," a nice duple-sprung tidbit.

QUINTET

- *Instances* **for Wind Quintet (1964)**

A set of pithy variations (the performance time is just over 51/2 minutes). Knight uses serial technique, but the materials produced avoid the dry and schematic. Totally colorful variants, especially viable through their rhythmic clarity.

Knorr, Ernst Lothar von (1896–1973)

DUO

- **Duo for Viola and Cello (1961)**

Symphonicism for a pair of string instruments. Knorr doesn't believe in subtle nuances—the material is laid right out in a type of formal direct fidelity.

The Praeludium is heavily textured, knitted by cello arpeggios, colored by imitations. Movement two is a Toccata with different pitch areas that are connected by a persistent rhythmic condition. These pitch centers are D, then C-sharp, and, continuing in direct sequence, B and A, with a final cadence in C.

The Largo is a large three-part statement. In the first part the viola has the thematic substance, on recapitulation the cello has it, slightly shortened. In between the instruments combine in gutsy rhythmic unison. A dynamic (Sehr schnell [Very fast]) Scherzo completes an exciting suite. No excesses or obscurities in the design. The slower-paced Trio is in fivefold meter, the instruments muted, clearly identifying its relationship to the fourfold pulse and kinetic tempo of the main body of the movement.

Knussen, Oliver (1952–)

Between 1976 and 1978 Knussen wrote three compositions, each in a different medium, described as "a triptych of chamber works." The first of these is *Autumnal* for violin and piano, Op. 14; the second, *Sonya's Lullaby*, Op. 16, is for piano; and the third is *Cantata* for oboe and string trio, Op. 15. It will be noted that the order within the group does not follow the opus chronology. The reason for this is that these pieces may be performed together or separately. In the former case the sequence indicated brings proper balance. (*See below* for commentary regarding *Autumnal* and *Cantata*.)

DUO

- *Autumnal* for Violin and Piano, Op. 14

There are two movements, and though the second is a Serenade, it is no sweet melody to be sung beneath a lady's window. *Autumnal* is dedicated to "Benjamin Britten in memoriam," and Knussen's Serenade is to be read as a nocturnal plaint, even with the tremolando plucking of the violin in "quasi mandolin" serenadish fashion. The freed twelve-tone winds that move through this music (movement one is a Nocturne) blend expressionism with impressionism. All of it represents feverish night music as much as it presents an elegiac testament.

QUARTET

- *Cantata* for Oboe and String Trio, Op. 15

Knussen sings forth in his *Cantata* for instruments but sings with twelve-tone pungency. And twelve-tone freedom. The form is additive. In the first section bimetrical and uncoordinated lines blend. Part two (the sections are all linked) is freely rhythmed but the heading, Cadenza in tempo, indicates a hybrid concept. In turn there is a nightmarish type of Corrente, frozen chordal sounds, an Agitato portion, with coloristic and improvisational detail in varied array, until the quartet ends in *pianississimo*.

SEPTET

- *Puzzle Music* for Flute (alternating Alto Flute), Clarinet, Celesta, Mandolin (alternating Guitar), Harp, and Two Percussion (Tubular Bells [or Hand Bells], Anvil, Large Baby's Rattle [or Maracas], Vibraphone [or Dulcimer], Slapstick, Guiro [largish]) (1973)

In regard to the above instrumentation, the septet can become an octet, if need be, if separate performers are used for the mandolin and the guitar. (Knussen prefers the septet arrangement.) In the percussion he indicates a preference for hand bells in place of tubular bells and the use of a dulcimer rather than a vibraphone. The anvil is not the usual one. It is to be made of copper tubing, about six inches in length and three quarters of an inch in diameter and to be "mounted on wooden holder padded with felt."

The intriguing title exemplifies showmanship in the chamber music medium. There is nothing puzzling about this stimulating 61/2-minute work, subtitled "four pieces for instrumental ensemble after John Lloyd (XVth cent.)." (Lloyd, a Welsh ecclesiastic and composer, was born c. 1480 and died in London, April 3, 1523.) The enigmatic term pertains to two of the pieces (numbers one and four), which are, in turn, solutions and instrumental settings of a pair of Lloyd's puzzle canons (also known as riddle canons). Such canons are notated in an incomplete or obscure manner, some indicated with symbolistic devices, instead of being written out in full—a sort of creative fun-and-games process. The first of the pair opens the work and was coded by Lloyd as "Iste tenor ascendit / a gradu epodoico in semitonium / et descendit in diatessaron cum diatonico." The second of the pair concludes the work and is coded *Tris*, followed by the pitches A, G, F, and E.

In contrast are the two inner movements, both contemporaneously glossed examples of Lloyd sonorously smothered by Knussen. The second piece of the set is *Toyshop Music (after "Tris la sol fa mi")*, which therefore relates to the fourth of the total set. In turn, the third piece is an *Antiphon (after "Iste tenor ascendit . . .")* and is thereby related to the opening piece.

The perfect balance and relationship thus obtained (I–III and II–IV) provide distinct contrast. This is furthered by using a different instrumentation for each of the four pieces.

NONET

- *Processionals* **for Nine Instruments (Wind Quintet and String Quartet) (1978)**

The climate of *Processionals* is totally chromatic. This style relates to the aliveness of the rhythmic particulars. It is only in the last part of the third (concluding) movement that pulsed regularity, with systemized tutti scoring, takes place.

Textural definition in three-part division occurs in the first movement. The voices build until in an ad libitum section there is instrumental explosion that reminds one of Ives and Cage, at their most extroverted stance, rolled into one. Movement two is a horn solo with a variety of supportive colors once its opening unaccompanied sustained soliloquy is concluded. The third movement surrounds a double cantus in the oboe and viola with linear data, and later a join is made with a third cantus in the horn.

The date in the title heading marks the final revision of this nonet. It was composed in 1968 (to fulfill a commission by the important Melos Ensemble). The Melos group performed the work, with the composer conducting, in London on February 11, 1969. Knussen then drastically revised the work in 1971 and again in 1978. At that time he changed the title from its original *Pantomime* to the definitive *Processionals*.

Kobayashi, Arata (1928–)

QUARTET

- **Quartet for Two Violins, Viola, and Cello (1962)**

Thematic brotherhood and a passion for cyclic construction mark the Quartet by this Japanese tonalist. But a worthy creative deed results, not merely an exhibition of technique.

A fully fashioned fugue, with subject plus accompanimental lines, opens the work. The contrastive portion is begun with snappy pizzicato and leads to a bold octave-thickened augmentation of the fugue subject. The binary plan is then run through again. Movement two is similarly an A–B–A–B structure with slow and slightly faster themes. In movement three a huge rondo concordance is exhibited, beginning with an untroubled Allegro theme linked to a dashing (related) Presto idea. The second principal theme is a Larghetto, which is a transfer of the B portion of movement two (and metronomically identical). Later a third theme enters, which is again the augmentation of the fugue subject of movement one. Indeed, a music of resource, wherein the outcome fully and thoroughly justifies the act.

Koblitz, David (1948–)

TRIO

- **Eight Three-Part Inventions for String Trio (1976)**

A neoclassic set that delights the ear with its suavity and rhythmic élan. The last is marked by "Hocket-like construction" (the composer's term), and the asymmetrical process makes this absolute music an absolute success. The second of the pieces is an Air, the melodic line in the violin, the other instruments supporting, all three muted. Number seven is also totally in muted timbre. Special color also applies to the third Invention, which is completely in plucked sound.

A charming contribution to string trio literature. (The work can also be performed with multiple strings.)

Koch, Erland von (1910–)

DUOS

- *Polska i svensk ton (Polska in Swedish mood)* **(1966) and** *Ricochet* **for Violin and Piano (1971)**

Somewhat redundant heading in the first title of this two-part piece, since the Polska is a Swedish dance. Similar in character to the Mazurka, from which it is derived, this dance of Polish origin (hence its name) moves (here swiftly) in triple time. Koch measures the style perfectly.

Ricochet has meticulous recoil with the longest sounds of tri-pitched groups shifting on and off the beat. A rewarding three-part conception, melodically and rhythmically relaxed in the center.

- *Sonatina Semplice* **for Violin and Piano (1961)**

Especially the third (final) movement—a very vivacious dance, breathes the air of Swedish folk music. Some of it infiltrates the first movement as well. In the middle, slow movement canonic process marks the second part of the main theme. A short, ternary affair, the movement's central division is indicated by tempo increase.

The *Sonatina* is totally simple and direct tonal music. But it is also a music of sensitivity.

QUARTET

- **String Quartet No. 2, Op. 28**

In the opening movement a theme of dramatic motion, chordally outlined, is compared to a smooth-lined subject, braced with rhythmic constancy. Additionally, this movement is begun and concluded with a very concentrated Adagio—sectional wires that hold the large picture in place.

Staccato and legato sound shapes are contrasted in the Scherzo. Direct formal comparison continues in the slow movement, where an expressive subject is matched to a theme of sweetness, sung in rich thirds with an Alberti bass background. In the quartet's final movement a rhythmic idea is set forth and balanced against an ascending-shaped subject in legato.

The interval of a fourth is a common strain in the composition. At times this quartal span is approached through passing tones, other times almost directly. Thus, it appears in downward degree in the second subject of movement two, upward in the initial theme of movement three, and in the final part the principal theme moves through the same quartal space. Further movement alliance is indicated by the slightly changed restatement of a part of the first movement in the last movement.

Kochetov, V.

QUARTET

- **Quartet for Two Violins, Viola, and Cello, Op. 58**

The standard four-movement totality is used in Kochetov's Quartet, composed in 1943. But there is no stodgy preoccupation in the name of pedantic accuracy. Kochetov's opus is one of sparkling romantic speech. He is thoroughly sensitive to stylistic requirements and shows as much sensitivity for coloration, formal freshness, and balance.

Three themes pass in review in the first movement, one is slow, the others are marked allegro moderato. However, in turn, the latter are contrasted by polyphonic and monophonic writing. Accentual differences are a subtle power in the scherzolike second movement. Stresses in the 2/2 theme are held to the first beat and then in a shift within the total theme

the stresses are on each half beat throughout the measure. Duo-thematic contrast serves in the slow movement, the second one using a Russian folk song, "Oh, the Fields." Metrical flux is the generative power of the finale. Most of the time the music races in quintuple meter, varying constantly from 3+2 to 2+3. Other times the quintuple measurement is combined with quartal measurement. It's all clean, clear, and zestful.

Kocsár, Miklós (1933–)

DUOS

- *Dialoghi (Dialogues)* for Bassoon and Piano (1965)

Music of rarity and quality. The bassoon is considered as a high-rank, first-class instrumental citizen, its material fresh and totally embracing the possible pitch range. In Kocsár's hands the wind instrument emerges from its oft-restricted utilitarian role into virtuoso status. This, minus its still-falsely considered limited role as a clownish instrument or best for explaining grotesque situations. Of course, Kocsár's work is not the first to depart from such a hackneyed, insular conservatism, but it is one of the best that has been created in the present century.

No emphasis is made, however, on bassoonistic gambits in place of artistic moves. The conversations between the pair of instruments are poetic and fanciful, calm and wild, suggestive and explicative. It is the kind of music one wishes to hear immediately again, being so fascinating in content.

There are five parts to the piece; the first pair are connected, and, after a pause, the last three are heard in succession. Properly conversational, no meters master the material and no bar lines punctuate it. Violence marks the second part, begun by *secco* piano data, including a repetitive figure by the keyboard instrument over which the bassoon has brilliant leaps engendered by multiple sets of notes to be played as fast as possible. The moods in this discussion shift quickly, concluded as the dialogue began, with a *fortissimo secco* passage by the piano. Number three is tranquil, sustained, and mystical. It includes soft tone clusters and vibrato that pitches a pitch into quarter-tone oscillation. The nuances are restricted. The argument in the fourth duologue reaches frenzied proportions with three counterstatements combined in a Presto possibile. The texture is magnificently dense: a single ostinato in the piano's bass, an assortment of rhythmic pressures in its mid-range, plus an argumentative counterpoint by the bassoon. Eventually, the instruments settle into repeating ad libitum three different rhythmic sets, and the section concludes with piano clusters and the bassoon's declamation—both in triple *forte*. Like the initial part of the piece the final one has a generally calm fluidity. This work of individualized impulse deserves a special place in the bassoon-piano literature.

- *Repliche (Replicas)* [No. 1] for Flute and Hungarian Cembalo (or Harpsichord) (1971)

Akin to a set of musical conversations, but one-sided since the instrumental lines do not relate one to the other, save by an occasional happenstance. Each movement connects to the next; each is marked by a contrastive tempo.

Movement one is a Sostenuto, the second is fast and energetic. Movement three is slightly faster, its mood dark and gloomy. At the end a bit of the first movement's character is quoted (but not its pitches or shape). This links to a Lento, in turn to an Allegretto vivace, and then to a Presto. Movement seven is cadenzalike but breaks away into the usual duo-planal material, with again a midget reflection of the opening Sostenuto followed by a snap Vivace conclu-

sion. The free and individual manner of the forms are partnered with the eradication of time signatures, bar lines, and metronomic controls. All very persuasive.

- *Repliche (Replicas)* No. 2 for Horn and Hungarian Cembalo (or Piano) (1976)

A clone of the first *Repliche (see above)*. There are eleven tempo sections in this case, connected and contrasted by different speeds. Part five (Allegretto) has (for the greater part) an antiphonal reasoning and therefore falls in the dialogue classification. Otherwise the formal freedom embraces individuality for each instrument.

- *Saltus hungaricus* for Flute (or Oboe or Violin) and Piano (1969)

Music that sits squarely, comfortably, and melodically in the folk class. Alternate tempos pace the suite with each movement in a positive, embraced tonality. The first is in C and the second part is in G. Both are minus a single chromatic pitch. Part three is in D with a few C-naturals, part five is in G with a few C-sharps. In between, the fourth movement is firmly in D, also without chromatic coloration.

- *Ungaresca* for Two Woodwind Instruments (Oboe and Clarinet or Flute and Clarinet or Two Clarinets) (1968)

Authentica placed in chamber music settings. Fourteen short dance items (originally many were fragments) dating from the early 18th century. These are arranged in three suites (five each in the first and third, four in the second). In a few instances a da capo is made to an earlier movement, thus: after number three there is a return to number two. However, if the entire fourteen pieces are played as a total these da capo recapitulations are to be eliminated. Kocsár dispenses with developments; he offers just the bare stuff.

TRIOS

- **Divertimento for Oboe, Clarinet, and Bassoon (1956)**

A clear and neat vehicle of meaning pervades the three movements, with differentiated tempos: a little below allegro pace, slow, and fast. The music is all composed with composure and when polyphonic is absent of fuss. The slightest simmering of native content is to be felt, but it never actually surfaces in this trio, styled by dissonant tonalism.

- **Trio for Two Trumpets and Trombone (1958)**

All too often music is so conceived that it could well be played by a number of interchangeable groups without any loss of effect. It is not that the technical scope must be limited so that brass instruments are treated more carefully than string instruments, etc. It is, rather, that the music should specifically confirm the timbre essences and individual personalities of the instruments used. This optimum condition is present in Kocsár's brass trio.

Repetitive figures, disjunctive fanfare-type thrusts, and chantlike combines mark the opening part. Conjunct lyrical phrases carry forward the slow movement; triplet rhythms are basic to the vivacious finale. The entire work illustrates musical material in absolute dovetail with instrumental content. Kocsár's Trio is music created *for* brass instruments, not music composed neutrally and then *scored for* brass instruments.

QUINTET

- **Variations for Wind Quintet (Flute [alternating Piccolo], Oboe, Clarinet, Horn, and Bassoon) (1968)**

The thematic basis is extremely rhapsodic, itself fragmented. The ten variational disclosures are connected, a mix of improvisational segments and free-wheeling repetitions of figures, having both metrical proportions as well as sections minus any pulse definition. Indeed, the sixth variation heading could describe the entire work: *Libero, quasi cadenza*. The Hungarian melos found in a considerable number of Kocsár's works is in a far different language than the post-Webernian rhetoric of this quintet.

SEXTET

- **Brass Sextet (Three Trumpets, Two Trombones, and Tuba) (1972)**

Folk-based material covering seven connected movements, each of which confirms a specific element. For example, in the first movement proportional rhythm is of prime importance (figures comprising seven eighths and five eighths in total to be translated each into duple equivalency), in the second asymmetrical differences, and in part seven sustained expressivity.

Kodály, Zoltán (1882–1967)

Bartók and Kodály are to Hungarian music what the three B's are to German music. And in their different ways the first two are as great and important as the last three.

Kodály formed, with Bartók, the core of true-principled Hungarian musical creation. Together with Bartók he collected native musical material, analyzed and described the findings. Kodály has shown how amazingly trenchant and new are the old secrets of folk sources. As is the case with Bartók, the music of Kodály is made subtle by assimilating the treasure house of folk song.

But two composers believing in similar creative gospel cannot express themselves individually unless there are differences. Rhythm is more than a clothesline on which Bartók hung his musical garments. Bartók's rhythmic plans are drawn for instruments susceptible to the supple art of mensural depiction, forming with its violent and volatile asymmetry a 20th-century "golden mean." Kodály's rhythmic demeanor is more vocal, more choral, like the naturalness of speech inflection. Kodály's nature is more melancholic than Bartók's; and the power of the first composer is of quiet strength.

No more fastidious composer exists in the field of 20th-century music. Kodály's musical glossary furnishes one of the best illustrations of authentic, national musical language. He has no intellectual artificialities; the music pours out in free style yet is as balanced as the most precise phrase that Mozart fashioned. It is a tamed music but roams freely on the tether of subtle Hungarian accent. Kodály is the Schubert of Hungarian music as Bartók is its Beethoven.

DUOS

- *Adagio* **for Violin (or Cello or Viola) and Piano (1905)**

A ternary-shaped piece that begins with a rich, soaring melody. It has very little Hungarian quantity, but contains real quality. Kodály had planned the *Adagio* as the slow movement for a sonata he never finished.

(In 1910, Kodály made the versions for cello or viola.)

- **Duo for Violin and Cello, Op. 7**

The minimal means with which Kodály is concerned here finds him employing a striking new technique, one in which he stretches the fruitfulness of the instruments to equal, at times, sonorities twice the total voices engaged. These are not effects of collateral enlargement, a substitute for a small and confined sonority, but are held subservient to the honesty of the fundamental idea of the work. They serve as specifications of tone color, weight and precisely related balances within the total formation of the composition, sensitizing and sharpening it in every instance.

Most of the first movement of Op. 7 is of broad continuity, perfectly balanced between the two instruments which often break into exultant song. No matter the extent of Kodály's rhapsodic vocalizations, the movement's form and its allied tonalities are as clear as his allegiance to Hungarian style. Equilibrium of mood and key is shown by the initial resolute theme, which is in D, compared to the tranquil second subject placed in excellent relationship by the classical dominant pivot of A. Exposition, development, and recapitulation carry forward with ever changing backgrounds. The result ushers in one of the greatest works instrumentally limited to only a violin and a cello.

Movement two (Adagio) consists of a principal theme with which a very important accompaniment—first supplemental, later integrated—is used. The Magyar feeling is more crepuscular, of dark-vested night, than heated, of meridian time, as the voices move into the contrasts of thesis and antithesis; the first more ordered in relation to the second's jubilant mood—the most persistent of all Hungarian characteristics. Oddly enough the accompanimental figure becomes transformed more than the principal theme (which incidentally partakes of a phrase length devoted to an uneven number of measures; rather ordinary to Hungarian melody, less so to the folk music of other nations). One instance of the development of this subsidiary background is its change from triplets to sixteenth notes while the cello simultaneously plays arco and pizzicato—another example of Kodály's fertile instrumentational mind as he scores for a pair of instruments with trio effect. A *parlando* introduction (arranged in antiphony) is the preamble to the final Presto, a movement in huge binary form, twice surveyed with the addition of a coda. The second portion is covered with bagpiped open fifths, while the coda rolls off a wild conclusion. Kodály's Duo displays the deep-rooted emotions of a composer who works with his own people's music and thereby understands and loves his countrymen. With such deep comprehension he makes others understand the Hungarian people as well.

■ Sonata for Cello and Piano, Op. 4

In its closest sense sonata design is typified by triple sections: exposition, development, and recapitulation. The dynamic tension of the central development division is to prove the contentions brought forward by the themes announced in the exposition, while the recapitulation concentrates and reconfirms the basic premise. Music has still to find better formal logic than the sonata form. With the broadest, "modern" outlook Kodály shows how this design may be expressed cogently by a musical journey afield yet not too far from the boundaries of classical sonata territory.

Movement one is a Fantasia. It proposes the mood of the work by dialogue and loosened rhythmic exhortations; it also sketches the composition's warmth and Hungarian manner. Movement two integrates and tightens the rhythm, sweeping along with dance motility, which confirms ("develops") the spirit of the initial part of the Sonata. At the end of the second movement the first section reappears, in a concentrated manner; thus there is formal recapitulation. Sonata terms have been fulfilled, yet this is less a sonata of two movements with semicyclic inference than it is a

work of one panel drawn in colors that complement each other.

■ Sonatina for Cello and Piano

Originally, this one-movement piece was planned to augment the Sonata for Cello and Piano, Op. 4, to a three-movement total. But matter after the fact did not prevail. Kodály wrote to the editor of the Sonatina (published by Boosey & Hawkes): "I intended to add a third movement to my Sonata in two movements, but this did not come off. My style had undergone such changes that I was unable to recapture the mood of 1909."

Nonetheless, the Sonatina has the melorhythmic turns and the melodic mannerisms that are found in Kodály's music no matter the date of creation. The principal theme is declamatory, set in fast tempo. It is always preceded by a marked rhythmic section of quasi-improvisational contour. The Sonatina represents a delightful definition of Hungarian nationalism.

TRIOS

■ Intermezzo for String Trio

Composed about 1905, published posthumously in 1976 (by Editio Musica Budapest).

The piece is plotted in ternary total; the native idiom is unmistakable.

■ Serenade for Two Violins and Viola, Op. 12

There are two facts of pronounced importance which concern this work. First, few critics will demur at the statement that just as Kodály's Duo for violin and cello forms, with Ravel's Sonata, the unsurpassed examples of compositions within such medium, that likewise this Serenade and Dvořák's Terzetto are the two superlative works in the category of string trios calling for a pair of violins and a viola. Second, it is sad to realize that with the completion of this work Kodály never returned to chamber music composition. There is no answer to this type of creative halt.

The three movements of the Serenade could well have titles affixed—these might read (based on analytical content), "Activity," "Dialogue," and "Dance." The intimate (but not introspective) style of the first movement is portrayed by a bouncing theme, activated by the allegramente (gaily) tempo. This type of subject, of fanfarelike articulation, is very predominant within Kodály's work. In this instance it is the fundamental basis of the initial movement, to which a lyrical theme gives decided contrast.

The most individual part of the trio is the middle movement. Kodály's unerring manipulation of instrumental detail is beautifully expressed as the first violin and viola converse with each other in an example rare to chamber music, one akin to operatic recitative of the boldest order. The second violin (in constant tremolo arrangement) is the sounding board on which one voice pleads with impassioned earnestness, while the other is somewhat derisive. Such declamatory writing is program music in spirit, minus detail.

The final movement is a dance. It has both vigor and repose, whipped rhythm and relaxed flow. Oppositional values make the music resplendent with authentic and constructive values. The color of pizzicato rhythm is very paramount, while some of the gentleness of this choreographic music is Mendelssohnian. In Kodály's musical philosophy there are dreams as well as stridings on the folk-dance floor.

QUARTETS

- **Gavotte for Three Violins and Cello**

Pure historical value. Found in Kodály's papers, the piece was published to commemorate the hundredth anniversary of his birth.

Working from a piano sketch plus a piano-reduction copy (which indicated the instrumentation), the short piece was edited by the Hungarian composer Ferenc Farkas. All is simplicity and all is squarely plotted: eight measures repeated, followed by sixteen measures to form the A section, a sixteen-measure contrastive section in a different key, and a da capo, as usual minus the repeated section.

- **String Quartet No. 1, Op. 2**

Although Kodály's first quartet shows great interest in the terms and turns of old Hungarian music, his characteristic method of portraying it beyond the arbitrary, classical-romantic manner is not as yet displayed. Kodály is too close to his academic study and his newly found folkloristic bona fides to rid himself so quickly of the orientations that overcoat all composers until they emerge in full maturity without such wraps. Nevertheless, Kodály's later personality is present; future possibilities and solutions are simmering.

It is important to realize that of all Kodály's chamber music works this is the only one in four movements—a sign of his early attitude in contrast to later decisions. The first two movements are derived from the cello's opening theme (a Hungarian folk song), which is defined principally with a measured dip of an intervallic fourth. This span will be heard in the Allegro that follows the quartet's introduction and in another referable theme within which it is inverted to the reverse distance of a fifth. The slow movement uses this tonal width as well in its ternary design; centered by a pair of fugatos which are then combined. Movement three (Presto) is also tripartite—a representation of a scherzo. The finale is a set of eight variations on a simple melody in a major mode. The variants are sharply contrasted. Most important and most unusual is the fourth variation. This was written by Kodály's first wife, Emma.

(In chamber music trivia this would take first prize.) It is set in 5/8 time for the greater part and is marked Allegretto.

■ **String Quartet No. 2, Op. 10**

In Kodály's second quartet the instrumental means are not novel, yet the sonorities are highly original. The speech of the four string instruments is produced from indigenous Hungarian musical dialect, which accents "open-air" intervals; its rhythms move through the Magyar slow *lasso*, the frenetic *friss*, and the *alla zoppa* of limping syncopation, its vocabulary extended by the rubatos of rural gypsy melisma. There is no better identification of Kodály's art, which conveys the subtleties of idealized musical folklore. It has all the fertile and mysterious variables that make a sensitive composer independent of scholastic calculations.

This quartet bears a relation to Kodály's first work in the same medium as does the freedom of the late Beethoven quartets to the more imitatory first half dozen. In the first quartet, Kodály examines his newly found jewels of folk song; in the second quartet the jewels are worn and glow—they form part of the décor, show the man and his personality.

Classical balance follows the use of thematic contrasts. The romantics made these more fluid; while those nationalists who freed themselves from the rather stilted practice of setting themes from folk sources in a classical framework gave their formal compounds extremely individual expression. The movements of this string quartet consist first of a moderately paced section and then the telescoping of slow and fast movements. The slow movement is unlike any other in quartet literature; it displays Kodály's penchant for having chamber music instruments seemingly converse. The reasoning of the beginning of the second movement is based on *parlando*, recitative-shaped vacillation of mood—as if portraying an un-

stated program. Nineteen times the pace shifts, within which the first violin and cello have ad libitum digressions. In the midst of this a portion in *lontano* ("distant") effect anticipates the final section. The evocative result is not a classical monologue; it is of quadripartite discourse.

The final dance section has the potent characteristics of Hungarian peasant dance music. Vivid and very forceful alternations of mood occur. The preliminary, improvisational section is one of mysticism; that which follows is dynamically sensitive. There are no superficial sensations in Kodály's Allegro. The duple-pulse rhythmic snap is constant; the essence dynamically primitive, especially an enchanting contrasting section poised on quintuple-quartal pedal points.

Koechlin, Charles (1867–1950)

Whenever Koechlin's music has been heard (most of it remains unpublished, though the total output went well over the two hundred mark), it has proven to have a specific personality of its own. Koechlin remains one of several creative figures for whom the musical world at large has not lived up to its responsibilities.

Koechlin was a creative independent. He drew from a variety of styles, choosing what best suited the idea at hand. Together with this went a Berliozian spirit of inventiveness. No matter the style, there was always the Koechlin touch, a freeing of both the lines and the rhythms within the style. No mishmash, this approach, but extremely selective creativity.

Two important factors are found within his output. One is a type of neomedievalism, formed by Palestrinian-type polyphony. The other is an open-air amiability that relates to Satie.

DUOS

- **Sonata for Flute and Piano, Op. 52**

Though Koechlin was a nonconformist in terms of design (his works evolve, are not permitted to be driven into formal enclosures), the import of tonality is not overlooked. In this Sonata, the outer movements are in E; the first in a modal point of view, the last in the diatonic. Balancing these is the central movement, set in a key a half tone higher.

Triple aspects speak of a genuine pastoral quality in the first movement, a Sicilienne in the second, and gaiety in the Final. In the latter movement, there are two strongly contrasted subjects. Each is permitted separate announcement and unfoldment; eventually they are combined.

(Programmatic detail is involved. Koechlin described the music as having been composed "on the fringe of Virgil's *Eclogues*." The first movement concerns "Tityrus, lying back beneath the shade of the spreading beech tree." Movement two pictures "And down from the high mountains taller shadows fall," and the finale represents "nymphs and huntresses in the pagan forest.")

- **Sonata for Two Flutes, Op. 75**

Totally representative of Koechlin's individuality and certainly one of his most important works. The archaic sound (although atonally pitched and pinched) is a delight to the ear, as if one were suddenly whisked centuries back. The first movement is in stanzas: twelve depictions of a chromatically interwoven line. An improvisation in scherzo style (a fantasy of whispered tone almost unreal with its figurations), is followed by the Final. This is somewhat of the dance, the last section returning to the material of the first movement. Koechlin's two flutes will haunt by their sheerly delightful sounds.

- **Sonata for Viola and Piano, Op. 53**

Although some coloristic effects used within Koechlin's Sonata for Violin and Piano *(see below)* reappear here, on the whole this duo sonata is much more dramatic, especially through the use of the heavier-toned string instrument. In the opening Adagio, the viola's lowest string is tuned down from C to B-flat, giving slightly deeper range for the first theme, which is contrasted to a type of call, used as a secondary topic. From an initial vagueness of tonality (in a shifting, dreamy type of retrospection), the movement ends in clear E-flat. This makes for an excellent preparation for the Scherzo, a dynamically agitated movement in C minor that is completed in C major, in turn bound to the slow movement (Andante [presque Adagio]). The Scherzo is like a wild ride, the rhythm ever dynamic, the ending suppressing all sound into quadruple *piano*.

What is noteworthy in the slow movement is the piano writing, a clear example of Koechlin's attitude toward this important matter. There are no limpid arpeggios, shifting harmonic figurations, as in Chopin; there is no Lisztian ornateness. The piano is used as a resonating instrument of chordal planes—vibrational harmonies in two, three, four, and five blocks. The excitement of the Final is restrained, the form exceedingly free, matching the mood of the slow movement, only in faster pace. This concluding division (Allegro très modéré mais sourdement agité) is Koechlin's paraphrase of *Sur la grève (On the shore),* the first of his *Quatre mélodies* for mezzo-soprano or baritone and piano, Op. 28.

- **Sonata for Violin and Piano, Op. 64**

Medieval polyphony in large segments is present in this Sonata, in limpid, long supple lines, together with plastic themes. Each subject is stated immediately in movements one, three, and four; in movement two it emerges later. The entire work is flexible, made of large blocks and polyharmonies, displaying luminous modality. The Sonata is picturesque (the second movement bespeaks a legendary forest; the third, a type of nocturne, but these are not actual titles, only depictions of general moods). Utter freedom is stated in a style that rhapsodizes on chordal blocks and planes. While the entire Sonata is noted in bar-line fashion, there are no time signatures (measures will sometimes have as many as fifty-six beats). Koechlin's rhapsody, however, is not merely one of willful inconsistency, but of complete comprehension. It is a work worthy of being dedicated to Gabriel Fauré (Koechlin published a biographical study of this highly important composer and a technical analysis of his works).

The first movement is calm, a serene commentary on a conjunct theme; in addition, there are triads in march motion and resonant lines helping to give support. The music moves on; there is no development, no recapitulation. Stressed in the melodic lines is an organic rising interval of a fourth inverted to quintuple descent. Opposed to this are pillowed triads. The second movement is a Scherzo, but in no sense conceived in standard form, only close to it in the matter of speed. This is program music without a program (the composer gives hints; he states, for example, to play a passage "like a distant horn"). The music comes from darkness and vagueness into light; develops by chordal play, figures, and counterpoints. The theme appears late, but by that time can hardly be considered a theme in the strict sense— merely another part of the design of this otherworld music, which, having risen to the surface, then recedes to its originating point.

The slow movement is again less thematic than a section formed on polyphony; blocked lines of triads or streams of organum float against each other—this is music devoted to free poetry rather than strict form. The Final is a rondo, the main theme a folklike tune in D major. To this is contrasted a long-scaled theme (first stated in the bass of the piano). From these, the movement develops, combines the themes, uses various "poly" techniques of tonality, modality, harmony, and rhythm. Sometimes, as many as six lines travel together. Yet all is clear, like a gigantic Gothic structure.

(In Robert Orledge's thoroughly documented study of Koechlin's life and works, he indicates the Sonata is subtitled *La nuit féerique [The Enchanted Night]*. Further, he states the first movement is "set 'in the fairy forest' and the third movement [evokes] 'night in the forest beside a large pool'." No mention of these points are in the published score.)

TRIO

- **Trio for Flute, Clarinet, and Bassoon (or Violin, Viola, and Cello; or Oboe, Clarinet, and Bassoon); Op. 92**

Koechlin was a master of contrapuntal science. (Among his many published theoretical works are separate volumes on counterpoint and fugue.) Plenty of contrapuntalism is intertwined within his huge output. Among the important compositions wholeheartedly concerned with polyphony are the *Five Chorals in Medieval Modes*, Op. 117 bis, for orchestra; an orchestral *Fugue symphonique*, Op. 121; and this wind (or string) trio.

In all instances the polyphony is of pre-Bach style, merged with natural clashes of line obstinately refusing to go the way of academic rules. Such linear strength is present in the three movements of this work. All are represented by fugues, each in increasing rates of speed (Lent [quasi adagio], Moderato sans lenteur, and Allegro con moto). The subject of the second movement is a row of thirds, followed by a descending scale line. The third fugue is the most developed, including a very exciting stretto.

QUARTETS

- **String Quartet No. 1 in D, Op. 51**

Classical proportions are conveyed in this work. All the tonalities are clear, though the part writing is very free. The first movement (in the principal D tonality) has pastorale definition. In the Scherzo, the key moves to the dominant peg, but that is the sole classical relationship, since only the spirit is that of the scherzo, the rhythms being completely asymmetrical. A binary form is used for the slow movement. In the Final, there are Haydn and Mozart touches in spirit, Koechlin's hand in formal freedom. (He described the concluding movement as a music of "incisive and virile intersections, energetic rhythms and very terse outlines.")

- **String Quartet No. 3 in D, Op. 72**

Only in the Final is the composer concerned with an ordinary model of form. That movement begins with imitative entrances of the theme, and then moves with gay demeanor in rondo form. But the first movement is more concerned with fluidity of line than with themes, development, and the like. The Scherzo points up Koechlin's determination to effectuate its spirit but not its formal considerations; rhythmic vacillation being immediately recognizable with the theme formed from 4/4, 2/4, 3/4, 6/4, and 3/4 measures. A type of Trio contrast is made by use of mutes; but the ending gets slower and slower in tempo, becomes hazier, and is enmeshed in harmonics. The days of the classical scherzo are very remote indeed. (And, even more so with the bitonality and polytonality of the harmonic plan.) Modality is the main imprint of the slow movement.

SEPTET

- **Septet for Wind Instruments (Flute, Oboe, English horn, Clarinet, Alto Saxophone, Horn, and Bassoon), Op. 165**

A divertimento that has colorful, unordinary documentation. To begin with, the scoring expands the usual wind quintet with two "extras"—English horn and alto saxophone. There are six movements, two of which are fugues. Further, the instrumentation varies. In the first movement ("Monodie") only the solo A clarinet is used, detailing long, tranquil phrases. In movement two (Pastorale) the music is for a trio of flute, clarinet, and bassoon. The remaining movements are for the full septet.

A supple scherzo shape marks the Intermezzo (movement three). Declamation (again dealing with suppleness) is involved in the fifth part, "Sérénité." The metrical disposition underlines the musical breadth with measures of 9/4, 11/4, and 12/4. Both of the fugues (movements four and six) are in 12/8 time. The tempos are contrastive, however, as are the basic qualities. Number four is a calm, legato-formed Allegretto dolce. Number six, based on a subject by Koechlin's son Yves ("Sur un thème de mon fils Yves"), is an accented, mostly bouncy Allegro, animé.

Koenig, Gottfried Michael (1926–)

QUARTET

- **String Quartet (1959)**

In a profound and intense sense, Koenig's one-piece String Quartet is serial music. However, pitch relationships and row manipulation are but one identification with twelve-tone technique. Other synthesized reasonings—and even a bit more important—are tempo variation and timbral definition. The former is no mere give-and-take of speed, but an ordering that is a strong status in the entire control of the sounds and their depiction. The latter is not simply of integrated contrast but is doubly dominant: in framing the operations of the tone sets and in their individual coloristic reasoning.

The statistics of tempo are revealing. There are no specific tempo expressions used, only precise metronomic specifications. There are, in the total 223 measures of the quartet, 57 exact speed settings; furthermore, accelerandos from a set tempo to a faster one occur 19 times; the reverse, ritardandos, from one speed to a slower one, takes place 20 times!

Koenig's timbral serialism is, naturally, a kaleidoscopic rendering. It is either layered by the instruments—example: successive measures where the first violin plays harmonics, the second violin bows sul tasto, the viola plays col legno, and the cello performs pizzicato—or it is multiassorted in each of the combined instruments. An illustration of the latter: within six beats in moderate tempo, five successive changes of color are used in the first violin, three in the viola, two in the cello, and harmonics are stated by the second violin. None of these qualities coincide, so that snarling sound opposes plucked timbre, or is in contrast to a liquified quality, etc. Dynamic differences (eight degrees from triple *piano* to triple *forte*), muted and open tone, are additional communications in this serialized color exploration. It simultaneously illuminates the pitch material, as it is projected through the varying speed sequences, and forms a superstructure on it.

Koerppen, Alfred (1926–)

TRIO

- **Serenade in F for Flute, Violin, and Viola (1952)**

More than straightforward documentation in this piece. Koerppen posits a tonal definition ("in F"), but the digressions are many. The polarity of the first movement is E-flat, the base tonal point in movement two is D, etc., so that only in the terminating division is F reached. Thus: alive and suggestive use of pantonality, with plentiful chromaticism. Further, the first twelve measures of the Einleitung (Introduction), subtitled "Stimmen der Nacht" ("Voices of the Night"), appear as a preliminary splice before the final presto ending of the concluding Marsch (March).

Koerppen's creative stance is, indeed, no unraveling of old procedures. The *Ständchen* (Serenade) is a fresh look on formal procedures. In its second part there is no tune-accompaniment endeavor. Rather, development of theme plus a full-play 21-measure cadenza depiction for the violin. Movement three is a duet for the strings titled "Zwiegespräch" ("Dialogue"). The complete inner part of this piece, in practically total duo rhythm, also suggests a controlled cadenza. Finally, the head of the march theme is identical with that of the serenade subject.

Koetsier, Jan (1911–)

QUARTETS

- *Five Miniatures* for Four Horns (1971)

Poulenc comes to mind in these stylistic, crisp portrayals. First a "Petite marche," faster than march tempo, contrasted to a "Chant sentimental," then a presto-delivered Scherzo. It is of miniature size, minus the usual Trio. Part four is a "Valse ironique," which is an excellent preparation for the short-hair spirit of the Finale.

- **Five Novelettes for Four Horns, Op. 34a**

Polished, warm, wise, and distinctive miniatures. These begin with a three-part Prélude, that has, in turn, fanfare–flowing–fanfare proportions. The "Hymne" is set vertically; the "Caprice" runs on repetitive pitches, rhythmically precise. A bell imitation follows ("Carillon"), with clear combined ringing of various sounding lengths. The finale is a vivacious "Chasse" ("Chase") that is a perfect close to the work and just as perfect material for four horns.

- *Introduction and Eight Etudes* **for String Quartet (1956)**

The formal plan would best be appreciated by members of a house string quartet who join in making music, generally on a weekly basis. However, there is no reason whatever that Koetsier's keen-witted idea should negate formalized presentation on the concert stage, with or without the reason for its make-up.

The goal of the work is to have music available for those lesser number of a quartet's team who are in the habit of being punctual at sessions. Accordingly, after the Introduction there are seven etudes, each in a different total to cover most contingencies regarding late arrival(s). These are, first, a vigorous music for two violins, then a Larghetto for viola and cello, and a third piece for the first violin and cello, followed by another duo, this one for the second violin and viola. Etude number five is the first of a set of trio formations, calling for first violin, viola, and cello. The next two are, respectively, for two violins and viola and two violins and cello. The moral of the tale is defined in part eight, a kinetic piece that occupies all four players and is therefore proof, according to the composer, of "the virtue of patience."

QUINTET

- **Quintet for English horn, Two Violins, Viola, and Cello, Op. 43**

There are a fair number of oboe quintets (oboe with string quartet), but combining the English horn with the string quartet is rather rare. A welcome entry, therefore. Within the three movements Koetsier puts neoclassic processes to good use in setting forth three vividly contrasted presentations.

A short Theme with Variations is marked by a quartal descent and ascent in the subject. This is kept up front in the three variations that follow. An Elegie forms the second movement, a fitting formal choice for inclusion in music using the poignancy of English-horn timbre. A picturesque "Böhmische Serenade" completes the piece.

Koffler, Jósef (1896–1943)

To the inhumane actions of the Nazis must be added their specific crimes against music: the burning of published music, the destruction of precious manuscripts, the torture and murder of musicians. Koffler was Jewish and was killed together with his wife and child during a street roundup of Jews in Poland.

Koffler was considered one of the best of Poland's young composers (he was only 47 when he died). His works remain, for the greater part, in manuscript, but have had performances at many international festivals. Some of his compositions are in a semi-Schoenbergian idiom (his *Third Symphony for Wind Instruments*). Some are dodecaphonic (Fifteen Variations for String Orchestra; the Trio for Violin, Viola, and Cello—*see below*).

TRIO

- **Trio for Violin, Viola, and Cello, Op. 10**

Koffler employed the twelve-tone system in only some of his works. When he used the technique it showed him to be a refined voice in the group who wrote according to the "method of composing with twelve tones." Rhythmic distinctiveness (often smudged in many dodecaphonic works) is absolute here and so is linear smoothness. Feverish (hysterical?) spreading of intervallic spans, another stubborn streak in dodecaphonic music creation, is avoided. But all this does not mean Koffler's twelve-tone opus is merely a polite creative example. It evidences, through his handling of these procedures, the prime virtue of artistry and effectiveness.

There is a further freshness in Koffler's string trio. Although a tone row is, by itself, a cyclic denominator (through use in its original form, retrograde, inversion, and inverted retrograde settings, and transposition of all four forms), here the same row at the same pitch location is used as the starting point for all three movements. There is rhythmic variance for coloration, but row repetition gives the music special cohesion.

Movement one consists of a set of connected variations, beginning with unison portrayal of the row, polyphonic expansion, and then coloristic detail: pizzicato triplets and tremolandos over a dramatic cello declaration. Then follow a thematic section for the violin joined to left-hand pizzicato punctuation and a capriccioso section portrayed in a fugal manner and earmarked throughout with glides. A canon between the violin and cello follows, the latter instrument heard in contrary motion. Some partial augmentation prefaces a bell-like variant that utilizes the special steel-blue color of harmonics in the upper and lower instruments, combined with the viola sensuously singing on its highest (A) string. The move-

ment concludes with two rhythmic variations and a reticent coda, also to be considered as a variation.

Imitation guides the entire slow movement. Its fugal dress is intensified by total muting of the instruments.

The finale (Allegro molto vivace) is speedy. It is also the lightest of all the movements in character and suitably (and expertly) designed as a rondo, marked well by the gyratory use of grace notes. The coda is underlined by the augmentation of the generating theme. As in the previous movements Koffler has proven that twelve-tone music can be written without resort to pedantic postulation. His Trio is a winner.

QUARTET

- *Ukrainian Sketches* **for String Quartet, Op. 27**

Oddly enough, Koffler's quartet was published in the Soviet Union, a rare instance of a foreign composer's publication in that country. The answer may be found in the style of the music—not a touch of atonalistic language or Schoenbergian syntax is to be found represented in the six colorful movements.

The first is held together by the use of ostinatos; the second is rhapsodic. Folk flavor imbues each of the short movements (sketches) with authenticity. Each is placed in a certain formal frame for proper viewing—for example, the third sketch. It begins as a simple eight-measure tune in light style with accentuations thrown off balance by the combination of short–long rhythms in each measure. Then follow three thematic variations in the simplest manner; a repeat of the theme plus first variation with a further (new) variant serving as the coda. The main melody receives pizzicato color background in the fourth piece—the fifth part is extremely concentrated into eight measures—these are sketches, after all. A final dancelike section ends this work of folk materials translated in the idiom of four string instruments.

Kofroň, Jaroslav

DUO

- *Bilder (Pictures)* **for Horn and Piano**

(Kofroň's suite is subtitled "Ten Little Compositions," and one is certain that performances of any grouping would meet the approval of the composer.)

The set opens with a moderately paced "Fairy Tale," followed by a twelve-measure Allegro titled "In Our Courtyard." Number three, "Under the Apple Tree," is shaded by mainly soft dynamics; number four, "New Year's Wishes," is supported by contrastive dynamics. Gentility marks "In the Evening," forwardness, of course, is depicted in the March. The horn call of a perfect fifth fills part seven, "On an Old Castle." Fast-moving figures (the horn can be muted if so desired) depict a "Mountain Creek." Relaxed and quiet atmosphere surround the "Christmas Mood" and the closing piece, "Sunday Afternoon."

Kogan, Lev (1927–)

QUINTET

- *Humoristic Suite* **for Brass Quintet (Two Trumpets, Horn, Trombone, and Tuba)**

Brass sweetmeats. Thematicism (mostly motival) is clear; ditto the story line of the five parts.

The opener is a "Little March." "The Cock and the Hen" pecks at high speed and thrice crows. Similar chordal compaction specifies "The Children Go Bathing" the natation ac-

complished at even greater speed. Once again, chordal style and high tempo are repeated in the fifth and final part, "The Gossips," the brass conversation spiced by tight harmonies. Preceding is a short movement, "The Obstinate Boy and The Obedient Girl." Active rhythm for the former and straight lines for the latter. These are combined, but the male has the last word here.

Koh, Bunya

DUO

- *Sonata festosa (Festive Sonata)* **for Flute and Piano, Op. 17**

Bunya Koh's two-instrument sonata is a sensitive, equipoised music of concentrated thought. Tone patterns in the first movement are symmetrically applied. In the beginning the sounds are pure ("white"), the B pitch withheld for a great length of time. In the center the sounds are the same with the B pitch flatted. With little exception duple pulse is employed within a rondo type of setting.

Again, particular pitch selection guides the second movement. F is entirely eliminated and the sounds B and E are used in both natural and flat form. The effect of bells and floating resonances fill this lento-tempo love song, conveyed with an open texture. Hardly any chromatic sounds color the rhythmically free, fast and gay final part of the sonata.

Köhler, Ernesto (1849–1907)

QUARTET

- *Grand Quartet* **in D Major for Four Flutes, Op. 92**

Köhler produced over one hundred works for

the flute, a few of which have kept his name in wind-music literature. His ballets and the opera *Ben Achmed* have retained their place only as biographical statistics. Born in Italy, he went to Vienna at the age of 20. Two years later he took up residence in Russia, where he became a member of the orchestra of the Imperial Ballet and later the first flutist in the orchestra of the Imperial Russian Opera House.

His intimate knowledge of the instrument makes his flute quartet a pleasure to play. The listening requirement is extremely modest and there are no challenges. Form here is formal, indeed. There are four movements in the usual fast-slow-Scherzo-moderately fast format. The first is squarely sonata in design, with exact tonic-dominant proportions for the first and second themes. The slow movement is in three-part form, similarly the Scherzo, colored a bit by strong dynamic contrasts. The finale is a Rondo.

Köhler, Hans

DUOS

- **Sonatinas for Two Flutes, Op. 96**

  - No. 1, in D Major
  - No. 2, in G Major
  - No. 3, in F Major
  - No. 4, in C Major
  - No. 5, in B-flat Major
  - No. 6, in D Major

Some would term this *Kapellmeistermusik*, what with the straightforward routines of key, form, content, phrasing arrangement, and the nothing dared or ventured. Fair enough. Still, plenty of pleasure for players if not so much for auditors.

Each of the six works is in two movements, which vary slightly in character. Number one begins with marchlike music, the second piece

starts with a legato-phrased Grazioso, the third and fifth Sonatinas commence in Adagio speed, the concluding piece begins matters in Allegro tempo. The final movements are duple-pulse Allegrettos in the majority of instances. The one exception in the group is the fourth work. There, a theme with three variations is followed by a Moderato maestoso filled with trills and figurations.

Kohn, Karl (1926–)

DUOS

- ***Encounters I* for Flute (alternating Piccolo) and Piano (1966)**

The title of Kohn's piece was chosen to indicate the occasion of its first performance, in April 1966, at the Pasadena Art Museum in California, as part of that institution's Encounter Series (in which composers presented their own music). There is a further, more pertinent cohesive matter, however. The "encounter" here is the dialogue and dramatic action between the instruments. The music has strong pace fluidity. Within its timing (5:25 minutes) there are twenty changes of tempo.

- ***Encounters II* for Horn and Piano (1967)**

Kohn's objective in this duo was to include in the music's essentially chromatic style "diatonic figurations that have been traditionally linked with the horn since its development from the 'natural' hunting horn." A parallel procedure concerned the chordal detail for the piano, with an integration "in their harmonic structure" and in terms of their doublings to "evoke reminiscences of harmonic language from the past." The representation has a range from simplicity to chromatic clusters.

Encounters II is structurally similar to the

first of the set (*see above*). The horn and piano confront and respond to each other. The course of the formal action is shaped and developed by the instruments in a dialogue that appears to unfold spontaneously.

- *Paronyms* for Flutes (Alto Flute [alternating Piccolo, Bass Flute, and Flute] and Piano) (1974)

A four-movement duo with different members of the flute family in sequential presentation. Thus: alto flute in movement one, piccolo in movement two, bass flute in movement three, and flute in the last movement. (The bass flute may be replaced by the standard flute if the larger instrument is not available.)

Three of the four pieces are derived from Kohn's *Encounters I (see above),* hence the title *Paronym*, a word cognate with another. Accordingly, a reworking and expansion of music for duo into another duo. Throughout there is an intense dramatic type of panchromaticism that creates an ongoing dramaticism within the context. There is inner contrast and there is the more direct contrast brought by the differently timbred flutes.

- *Reflections* for Clarinet and Piano (1970)

The dark colors and emotional heat of expressionism are bound in Kohn's one-movement athematic piece. Within the minute timbre tracings of the music there is a brief quote from Berg's own music for the medium (Four Pieces for Clarinet and Piano, Op. 5), and the manner in which this quote is "reflected, or bounced off, into its own course" brought the decision for Kohn's title. There is further quotation—a brief one from a Mahler symphony. It is used several times and "both clarinet and piano 'reflect' and comment on it."

QUINTETS

- **Capriccios for Flute, Harp, Cello, Clarinet, and Piano (1962)**

Not in the humorous or light-faceted category. This is a seriously formationed set of three pieces, and though not the central issue, is imbued with instrumental virtuosity that matches the formalistic side. It is not only the individual indications of spitfired flute figurations, harp registral vividness, cello cadenzas, and the like, but the instrumental interplay and interfusion that make this music virtuosically exciting.

Different aspects pertain to the three movements. The first is basically slow in tempo, of rhapsodic breadth. Movement two (Allegro) has a vertically structured quality in its outer sections, a spread (more open) character in its central, contrastive, Andante quasi adagio division. The last is a gigantic Rubato, metrically free—a fluid, flexible music that never denies the fundamental verve and fervor of its conception.

- *Little Suite* for Woodwind Quintet (1963)

Kohn's work is economical in its thinking, neoclassically typed, with open textures and tart harmonies. There is laconic humor in the dance sections (movement two is a Valse; movement three is titled, neutrally, Dance). A quiet Prelude opens the work, a Recitative and Finale concludes it. The former is pithy and proclamatory, the latter has march impetus, slowing down and decreasing dynamically in its terminal section. Movement four is a broadly paced but fantasylike Song.

SEXTET

- **Serenade for Wind Quintet and Piano (1961)**

There is a freshness and a vigorous voice expressed in Kohn's piece. The sense of freedom in the designs is apparent, and so is the panchromaticism that emphasizes the fricative intervals of seconds and sevenths. Rhapsody moves through the music, but the plots of the five movements are clear. The analytical statement by Lawrence Morton is pertinent: "The principal formal device is not development but rather the juxtaposition of related musical ideas; the music is held together by intervallic and rhythmic *elements* rather than by specific melodic or rhythmic *figures*." To a great extent the colors (the instrumental writing is full of verve and exhilaration) and densities provide a secondary supportive element for each movement.

OCTET

- *Introductions and Parodies* for Clarinet, Horn, Bassoon, Piano, and String Quartet (1967)

Two movements, the first slow and rhapsodic, giving attention to the two wind instruments and horn, with the piano and string quartet in supporting roles. Movement two begins with the string quartet alone, is basically fast-tempoed, and later returns to the initial mood.

Kohn says of the title, *Introductions and Parodies*, that it "refers to the subsequent reappearances of characteristic motifs and figurations in the various instruments, as well as to their initial entrance. Thematic materials are brought in, superimposed, recalled, and led in again throughout the work as if they were characters in a play." The *Parodies* portion is not meant to be satirical, but rather a serious reworking of material by others and one's own. From Kohn, Kohn has used a cadenzalike pas-

sage from the *Episodes* for piano and orchestra. From outside sources there appears, with substantial emphasis, the accompanying background figures and the solo arpeggios of the famous Mendelssohn violin concerto. Woven into these materials are the combine of diatonic material of past styles and the highly chromatic colorations of the present.

Kohs, Ellis B. (1916–)

DUOS

- **Duo for Violin and Cello *after Kafka's Amerika* (1971)**

An extreme rarity, illustrating the transfer of materials from the hugeness of an opera to the smallest possible chamber music unit. Sufficient problems exist in formulating such resetting, compounded by choosing minimal resources. Of course, with the composer's affirmation that the work "may be heard as 'pure' or 'abstract' music," but "it is intended to have a programmatic content, and as such it is related to the style of the symphonic poem," this squarely sets the duet into the program music area of chamber music.

The Duo parallels the opera's three acts by use of three movements. The central character, Karl ("neither hero nor antihero"), arrives in New York with other poor emigrants (the year is 1914). This is described in the opening "Arrival," with a moderately paced music that has a decided rhythmic profile. The second part of the movement concerns "Clara," a "forward and coquettish" female, described as an unfortunate encounter. This section is in triple time with both instruments muted.

Movement two consists of three parts: "Robinson and Delamarche," "The Manageress," and "Dismissal." The first depicts the two disreputable characters (the music is in unsquared septuple meter followed by polyphonic pulsations that combine 5/8 with 3/4). Karl avoids them and obtains a position as a bellboy where "he shares reminiscences of Prague and Vienna with the Manageress" (an Alla polacca section). Karl is wrongfully accused of misconduct by the Head Waiter and fired (an agitated portion mainly built on triplet rhythms).

Movement three covers the return of the dissolute pair: Delamarche, who has become the lover of a singer, Brunelda, and Robinson, who is now their servant. The first part of this movement, designated "Brunelda," is conveyed by a type of fantasy and scherzo. Karl is introduced to this menage, and Robinson "tries to tempt Karl to undertake the duties of which he" [Robinson] "has become weary." Karl avoids this ploy in the segment titled "Temptation" (the music is based on a rhythmic motive notated as two sixteenths and an eighth). The Duo ends with "Departure." Karl "finds himself again on the road, bound for an uncertain future in his new job with 'The Nature Theater of Oklahoma,' " the music beginning with cello declamation under tremolando pedalization by the violin.

- **Sonatina for Bassoon and Piano (1944)**

The three movements are structurally related. In each instance a principal subject illuminates the entire concept—in the final movement this is covered by variations on a perky theme. The development process in the preceding pair of movements is of integrative rather than permutative fashioning. By stressing the unitary thematic proposal each part of the Sonatina retains solidity and by compactness of detail remains fresh.

Kohs's *fortspinnung*—the continuation and working out of his fundamental idea—is not motivally engendered. Each subject is of complete measurement, not cellular size. In movement one the theme is stated by the bassoon, followed by eighth-note grouplets. Its next use is in rhythmic diminution paralleled by speed increase, with episodes formed from the antithesis of the eighth-note pattern. Later, both the main theme and the subsidiary eighth-note idea become augmented. In the middle movement, new, figurated material is separate from the long-line shape of the opening subject. This provides contrast, but the cogent talking point remains the theme, no matter the relationship. The vivacious Alla marcia has the requisite harmonic friction to keep its basic simple march tune up to snuff. This tonal abrasive is present in all three variations, each defined by a complete cadential halt. The Vivo coda runs down an individual type of scale, then travels up on arpeggios, moves into block chords, and signs off on a final unison.

I recall a reviewer describing Kohs's piece as "delicious." True! It is also aurally invigorating and instrumentally rewarding.

- **Sonatina for Violin and Piano (1948)**

The assertive dynamic style of the piece, with vibrant use of the violin's open strings as sonority supports, is but one of the elements that connect the three movements.

Metrical change colors the first movement, with a settling into 2/4 in the first part of the music, followed by a consistent interchange between 5/8 and 3/8 until the end of the movement. An Introduction, Theme, and set of four variations provide the formal stability for the middle movement. Unfailing vitality marks the finale, with a gridwork of syncopative ostinatos. Music of bravado and excitement.

- **Suite for Cello and Piano**

A picturesque survey that has intriguing features. "Declaration," which initiates the work, has improvisatory contours and is linked to a dodecaphonic Waltz, an illustration of how twelve-tone style can bring sensitive artistic benefits. The Trio is marked "quasi," and is acutely defined by its unaccompanied cello format.

Movement three is a twice-run-through binary-designed Sarabande. Its second portion is mostly a free inversion of the pitch direction of the initial part, the rhythms exactly duplicated. Kohs's cohesion of his material in this part is not only a neat constructive point, it is musically telling. Movement four, "Deliria," has motorized intensity, the quality having nightmarish overtones. "Deliria" is extremely fast, violently contrastive in its dynamic planes and mensural totalities. Mixed in with these is coloristic documentation: muted string sound (which in *fortissimo* roughs the ear), ponticello snarls, dusted sounds sulla tastiera, plus a constant amount of shifting between plucked and bowed timbre. The climax is made dramatic by an unexpected cello cadenza.

The finale (March) relaxes matters. It is formally strict, with a literal recapitulation and a coda which hints by its faster start that the climax is just ahead. It arrives during a seven-measure span as the music gets increasingly louder.

QUARTETS

- ## *A Short Concert* for String Quartet (String Quartet No. 2) (1948)

Herein a synthesis of a miniature concert for four string instruments, embracing not only assorted forms but varied combinations within an instrumental total of paired violins, viola, and cello. This creative currency is of fresh mintage.

Movement one is a Sonata; perky, Prokofievian in smartness, with metrical jugglery that excites the drive. The final (seventh) part is of implied programmatic detail ("Dreams: Recollections"), representative of a slow movement and representative of thoughts unstated. A *Tristan* shape flickers; an open-string statement of the second violin brings to mind the opening of Berg's violin concerto. Kohs has described the movement as "a free association of melodic frag-

ments derived from a variety of sources." Whatever these, they are otherwise not recognized and the secret (if any) remains with the composer. There is nothing secret, however, about the emotional *klang* of the music.

Between these two exterior portions is a set of five short movements, which Kohs terms a "dance suite," though one of the set is not in a dance form (titled "Farce"). The others are Forlane, Waltz, Sarabande, and Gigue. These old dances are refreshed by contemporary content that juices the forms without losing any particular of the styles involved. Save in the Forlane (and there the melodic line is completely assigned to the viola), the suite consists of varied trios, with the instruments taking turns sitting on the sidelines. The Waltz is for violin, viola, and cello with the second violin tacet; the Sarabande is a two violin and viola affair; the "Farce" is again a string trio with the first violin resting, and the Gigue is a two violin and cello combine.

- ## String Quartet [No. 1] (1940)

This is a fully contemporary piece of music, with a sensitive harmonic scheme. Additionally, it is contrapuntally strong, coloristically cohesive, and stylistically meaningful. Its importance is found in the power of its contents and the strength of its creativity.

The opening Allegro is constructed from pithy ideas. One is nervous, of zigzag pitch order, the other is marked by sustained outer pinpointing with a wide sweep in between. This plurality is exploited to the fullest, concluding in a Presto that includes the shapes of the principal ideas. A Theme and Variations follows. Its procedures are fresh. Before experiencing variation, the theme expands by textural situations. At first, it is given a pizzicato background, then bowed support; the weight scope starts with three lines, moves on to four, and reaches a point of seven- and eight-part totals. The variants are continuous, include fugato and a clever disputation wherein the quadruple meter is mixed with an implication of sexpartite pulsation. Free augmentation of the theme signifies the concluding division. Kohs knots his variation movement neatly by using the anacrusis detail pertinent to the theme as part of all the sections.

The vivid Scherzo acutely differs from the other parts of the quartet by a concentrated setting for the violins alone. Save in wind works where often instrumental elimination produces a more forceful result by such color (and textural) differential, this duo constitution is a rare instance of blending a dual medium within a single composition for strings. (The movement is so powerful and fascinating it might well be extracted and performed as a separate piece on its own.) Metrical shifts between triple and duple computation are an asset in the movement, as well as contrasts between chordal and polyphonic style, with polyharmony a pertinent factor.

In the last movement the theme announced by the cello is of primary importance. It is employed melodically, imitatively, and in augmentation. The fugue in the movement's center gives a black-white effect by its strict contrapuntalism compared to the chordal and slighter polyphonic essence in the preceding section. Further dramatic antithesis is supplied by tempos: The opening is in adagio, the fugue is in allegro. The coda is even still faster (exactly twice so). It skims along on conjunct musical footwear, similar to the hurry-scurry conclusion of Haydn's *Lark* Quartet. But, this kinetic lowering of the curtain brings reminders of Haydn only in general demeanor, of course none whatsoever in terms of style.

Kókai, Rezsö (1906–62)

TRIO

- **Serenata for Violin, Viola, and Cello (1950)**

A beautifully rich work, productively constructed, without any preordered system of arranging the tones; a continuation of the Bartók-Kodály synthesis of folk materials and art music. Certainly, a composition mainly conceived in, and imitative of, the manner of Bartók. That Kókai is a member of the Bartók alumni, maintaining and thus continuing a cogently specific tradition, does him no discredit.

The tuneful melodies (digestible, not oversweetened), the ostinatos, the native instrument imitations via appoggiatura affixtures, the syncopations, the sharp pizzicato percussions, the rubatos, the tempo flux, the consecutive use of dynamic down-bow punctuations, the grace-note attacks, and above all the rapturous rhythmical ratification are from the heritage of Bartók and worth hearing again even by proxy (and represent Bartók's style in a medium he never utilized).

Traditional forms are used for movements one and three: sonata and rondo. In the former a high point covers orchestral-like pizzicatos framing the theme. Tempo manipulation is paramount in this initial movement. Shifts between the principal pace, ritards, and accelerandos are constant. (There are some seventeen ritards alone.) In one section changes occur in every one of eight successive measures (allegro–subito andante–rallentando–subito allegro, etc.). In the rondo-designed movement alternation between the principal theme and the first episode leads to a fermata. The next episode shifts the previous primary even total of sounds per pulse to uneven groups of five. Plus a speed up of tempo, the rhythmic difference splits the movement but brings a dramatic bonus. This quintuplet setting later forms the basis for the coda.

The middle movement is, however, untraditional. Titled "Recitativo notturno e Canzone" ("Nocturnal Recitative and Song"), it achieves balance by the paradox of unbalance. The opening is for unaccompanied viola, its theme taken over by the other instruments in turn. A second theme, similarly declamatory, but more intense than the first subject, brings needed contrast. The first theme then returns, continuing free development (some hints of the second idea are included), and the movement ends with the Canzone. This portion is entirely for solo violin with viola-cello accompaniment. Most of this movement is dark and tense despite blazing and dynamically strong sections. Its strategic strength is proven by the feet-on-the-ground setting of the music that follows in the finale.

Kokkonen, Joonas (1921–)

DUO

- **Duo for Violin and Piano (1955)**

There is a conscious emphasis on variational development within the sonata formation of the first movement. Supporting a number of the sections is a different type of variational concept, with a basic rhythmic pattern changing as each new section enters. Movement two is an Intermezzo that combines the swing of a light dance (the measures in triple time) with the piquancy of a scherzo (the measures in duple time). Textural differences parallel the tempo change in the finale. In the Un poco adagio for the first half the violin is fully occupied with double stops. The idea of solidity then shifts to the piano, which combines harmonic fourths and fifths. A rondo conception guides the balance of the movement.

QUARTET

- **String Quartet No. 1 (1959)**

Kokkonen has indicated that "the key to the quartet is hidden in the first ten bars." (There are gradual pitch ascents and intervallic spans of a third in these measures.) Accordingly, "melodically and harmonically everything in the quartet in some way or other grows out of these first measures." There is no mistaking the relationships existent within the tight, conjunct moves that are principal to the three movements of the work, and it will be found that material in the opening movement becomes developed in the other movements. Still, Kokkonen's first quartet, though of intense unified pitch exploration, does not negate a classical relationship of tempo and quality between the movements.

QUINTET

- **Quintet for Piano, Two Violins, Viola, and Cello, Op. 5**

Kokkonen drives his first movement with vertical dynamic moves. Avoidance of the polyphonic stimulant is the means for an openness of texture. The Scherzo, principally in quintuple meter, is conceived in the same manner, as is the "white-note" music of the slow movement. There is some consideration of polyphony in the finale, but by and large the materials are styled as in the previous movements.

The Quintet has strong ideas without the melodies falling in the tuneful class or the solid harmonies becoming involved in more than being identified with tonal centers. Important is the use of intervallic motives as a means of unifying various themes.

Kolb, Barbara (1939–)

DUOS

- *Figments* for Flute and Piano (1967)

Assorted sound objects shape *Figments*. Though occasionally a line starts a clearly detailed linear journey, it is always interrupted to form still another of the sound objects. One is reminded of the art form of *frottages* (designs composed of rubbings of a variety of rough surfaces). Kolb's *Figments* may not have exquisite emotivity but they do have secure sensibility.

- *Homage to Keith Jarrett and Gary Burton* for Flute and Vibraphone (1976)

A "crossover" piece honoring the work of the virtuoso jazz pianist Keith Jarrett and the great jazz vibraphone soloist Gary Burton. (Jarrett also has "crossed over" in his playing, specializing in the music of Bartók.)

The music is based "on a 30-second improvisation of a tune entitled 'Grow Your Own' (an early song of Jarrett's)." Kolb made a "skeletal outline" and then wrote her music "around that of Jarrett's, creating a potpourri of Jarrett, Kolb, and reminiscences of my past." Kolb is rather modest, indicating that the duo is not to be taken too seriously, but she has produced a sensitive example of music that provides idiomatic pleasure.

TRIO

- *Solitaire* for Piano, Vibraphone, and Tape (1971)

A quiet, consonant, perpetual-motion piece that turns the vibraphone into a clangy sound by the use of echo and filter devices for the tape. There are precise performance schemes "giving variety (without chance) to each performance."

Kolinski, Mieczyslaw (1901–)

DUO

- *Dahomey Suite* for Flute (or Recorder) and Piano, Op. 31

Kolinski has always been drawn to special cultural backgrounds. His published thesis of 1930 deals with primitive music and its relationship to Samoan music. He composed the *Dahomey Suite* after listening to recordings of the music of the Dahomey tribe of West Africa made by Melville J. Herskovits.

Although there are a few chromatic tones distributed in the keyboard instrument's part, the melodic lines of the work are set in pure diatonic arrangement to fulfill Kolinski's objective: "merging African and European elements into a new stylistic element."

A single title covers the first pair of movements: "Two Dokpwe Songs to Work the Fields." In the first a drone bass and a moving line are set in rhythms to counterpoint the melody. Some ostinatos support the second part of the movement. Part three is a "Song Sung as the Body of a Dead Cult Follower is Prepared by Priests for Burial"—piano interludes extend the scope of the movement. "The Song of Illusion" has squared chordal harmonic support. Again, two movements, five and six, are partnered with a single title: "Two Tohwiyo Cult Songs." The last part of the suite is a "Story Song," marked by repetitive patterns.

Köll, Fritz (1927–)

DUO

- *Vier Concinien* for Cello (or Viola) and Piano (1966)

Thoroughly traditional material slightly updated—thus, tonal music with a good deal of chromatic inflection. Only the final movement proceeds fast. The string instrument writing lies within the first position, but Köll's set of pieces cannot be considered either academic or elementary.

Kölz, Ernst (1929–)

DUO

- *Petites nocturnes (Little Nocturnes)* for Flute (or Recorder) and Piano (1962)

A type of impressionistic process is communicated by the four pieces in this suite. At the same time, the basic idea for each conception is made prominent by repetition—developmental research is not sought. The pieces are direct and swept clean of any contrastive cobwebs that might disturb the thematic be-all and end-all.

"La Charmeuse d es serpents" ("The Snake Charmer") is filled with fourths and fifths (as are the other three movements). The initial three measures appear four times using two different scorings. "Château enchanté" ("Enchanted Castle") is described by a twirling line and arpeggiated chords. Again, four statements of the theme appear consecutively. Thematic bewitchment, one might call it.

"Pierrot" ("Clown") follows metrical buffoonery. There is a change of pulse arrangement in thirty-six of the total forty-two measures. Thematic carbon copying is used here once more as well as in the final "Grimaces,"

where there are six statements of the principal subject.

Komma, Karl Michael (1913–)

TRIO

- *Estampie* for Flute, Viola, and Harpsichord (1964)

An updating of an instrumental form from the thirteenth and fourteenth centuries. Komma's presentation is twelve tone and carefully clarified. The sections that mark the form (called *puncti*) intertwine through interval choice, motion, line fractioning, and with other procedures such as, in section four, the simultaneous use of the row in two instruments with the second of the pair proceeding at double the values of the first instrument.

In a prefatory note Komma indicates that the "Grundrhythmus" ("basic rhythm") of his piece is based on the *Kalenda maya* by Reimbautz de Vaquieras (c. 1200). (This *Estampie* is considered to be the best known example of the dance.) Although the rhythms are "abwandelt" ("modified") the performance is to be "möglichst dicht und ohne grössere Zäsuren gespielt werden" ("in a tight manner without long breaks").

There are nine sections, distinguished by scoring: flute, flute and viola, cembalo, trio, flute and viola, viola and cembalo, and the full trio again for the final three. Throughout, there is an integrated vitality that accompanies these textural differences.

Kondo, Jo (1947–)

DUO

- *Walk* **for Flute and Piano (1976)**

No light, jaunty music depicted here. Rather, tightly banded insularistic style. Save for the last couple of measures the sounds are mostly single and detached, mainly eighth notes set on and off beats, moving within an unchanged duple-pulse meter set forth "at a more or less constant *mezzo-piano* dynamic level," and in an unchanged metronomic setting of ♩ = c. 96. Pitch duality is extremely limited within the piano's part. In the six-minute length of *Walk* there are four places where breathing space is inserted in the form of performance cessation. (Kondo marks these "Stop!")

In this minimalist music, abstract detail is positively clear—so is the cancellation of any emotional debate.

(*Walk* is also available in a setting for solo piano.)

TRIO

- *Standing* **for Three Instruments of Different Families (1973)**

Kondo's trio is performable "on three different kinds of instruments, each having a completely different tone quality from the others." Though exact pitches are indicated, it is obvious this means practically zero since Kondo states if the sound indicated cannot be produced by the instrument chosen "it will be all right [to] transpose" the part. As will be realized, the given pitches are merely crutches for the objective involved: a suppression of all elements in order to obtain a static permanence of sound successions. This represents the fixity of the minimalist style.

There are 635 measures of three pulses in each, produced in a rigid metronomic state

throughout (indicated as ♩. = c. 100), always dynamically anchored at *mezzopiano* and with all pitches to be sounded in an unmodifiable staccato. The pulses are mainly heard as single eighth notes, occasionally as paired sixteenth notes. In the early part of *Standing* there are three slight halts within this "made in Japan" brand of minimalism, consisting of three, four, and two seconds, respectively.

Konietzny, Heinrich (1910–)

DUO

- *Pas de deux (Dance for Two)* **for Two Piccolos (or Two Flutes)(1968)**

Matching its dedication to two dancers, Konietzny's music is strongly rhythmic and danceable. It is also persuasive concert music. Piccolo duets are small in total, and only a very few are above musical suspicion. *Pas de deux* is one of these, with its polished craftsmanship and interesting coloristic detail.

Dissonant conjunction is the ruling premise in the opening Larghetto and the closing "Wie eine Improvisation." The latter carries out its title designation. In its give-and-take in tempo and material it is indeed "Like an Improvisation." The middle piece (Scherzetto) is, save for its final measures, a single line passed to and fro between the instruments. Hinging of the entering and departing voices creates an inner accentuation that is part of the rhythmic design.

TRIO

- *Kleine Kammermusik No. 2 (Small Chamber Music No. 2)* **for Oboe, Clarinet, and Bassoon**

All compact forms pertain. While textures are equally full in the first two movements, the first of the pair is mainly vertically disposed while the second (much slower in tempo) is horizontally constructed. A binary-designed Scherzino, bound with a pithy coda, is in third place. In balanced total with the other movements the concluding Chaconne is built on a five-measure ground with five variations.

König, Herbert (1911–)

TRIO

- *Kleine Suite (Small Suite)* **for Three Clarinets**

Tonal exactness combined with music always instrumentally clear. Light stuff but not in the lollipop category.

Imitation guides the Vorspiel (Prelude). The Menuett and the Marsch fulfill the formal requirements, though there is no contrastive Trio in either. The fourth part, Zwischenspiel (Interlude), has a modal cast; the Walzer (Waltz) is just as short, sweet, and satisfying (in a simple way).

Kont, Paul (1920–)

DUOS

- *Strohkoffer (Straw Box)*: **Suite for Violin and Piano (1951)**

A retrospective (of the 1950s) souvenir of music played in the cellar of an American bar called the Strohkoffer, where Vienna's artists and intellectuals would meet. In this nightspot Kont produced new-music concerts wherein he performed some of his own violin and piano pieces with the then unknown Friedrich Cerha, who later gained the reputation of being one of Austria's important avant-garde composers. (It was Cerha who completed Berg's unfin-

ished *Lulu* after a twelve-year stint.) Published in 1981, with a dedication to Cerha, the four-part documentation Kont produced in this Suite preserves the atmosphere of the era.

Creative innocence marks the duo's contents. (One thinks of Kont as a less robust Austrian Satie.) The only unorthodoxy represented is the simplistic soundness of the music. In the "Chinesisches Wanderlied" there is no wandering whatsoever. Five pitches are used as the melody runs in a repetitive circle, and the same chord is heard in the piano's bass within twenty-six measures of the total thirty-two. Movement two is fancifully titled "Chouncle—Valse (pour le mérite de Joh. Göthe)." This has waltz time, naturally; repetitive figures, constantly.

Part three pays tribute to Cerha, using the musical equivalents for his name. Thus, in "C–E–r–H–A's Lullaby," the lower case "r" is represented by re, or the D pitch. H is, of course, the German for the B pitch. For the conclusion there is a speedy tune that keeps chasing its tail while the piano maintains a strict left-hand–right-hand alternation of chords. Titled "Finalissimo," it's happy chase music, an example of dogmatic artlessness.

(An arrangement for solo violin and chamber orchestra, including a tenor horn and an accordion, was made of Kont's 1951 work by Cerha in 1979. Creative partnership, therefore, matched the earlier performance partnership.)

- *Three Erinnerungen (Three Recollections)* **for Two Violins (1954)**

Absolute homophony and absolute concentrated depictions. No tempos for these snapshots. The meters are quadruple (4/4), duple (2/2), and triple (3/8). But those are the only differences in the structuring, since all three items have no dynamics and all are in B-flat minor. Mind you, not a single chromatic disturbs the pitches, and in the second piece G-flat and B-flat are not used and in the third, E-flat and G-flat are eliminated. Lengths: twelve, seventeen, and nineteen measures, respectively.

Kopelent, Marek (1932–)

QUARTETS

- **String Quartet No. 3 (1963)**

A set of structures, made to contrast textures and dynamics. Within these there are timings given in seconds for small sections and durations are to be depicted by translating proportional notation within the sections. Despite this looseness the details of the work are clear, with sustained music alternating with more active materials. In length a "quartettino," since the performance time is approximately seven minutes.

- **String Quartet No. 4 (1967)**

Written entirely in proportional notation and equating a slow movement in pace and pitch progress. There is little activity within the lines, and quite often the instruments move together. Within, the twelve-pitch range is expanded to include microtones.

Kopelent has a resolute objective and presents it to the listener. He states that the work "is an introverted piece not written for an audience but for an individual listener who may find in it the strength to escape from the daily conflicts, tensions, boosting advertisements and constant benumbing of his soul. It is a deliberate musical antithesis to the composition technique of structures, colors, virtuosity, and freakish sound sources."

Köper, Karl-Heinz

QUARTET

- **Quartetto sereno** (Two Violins, Viola, and Cello) (1968)

Despite its title Köper's quartet is filled with dynamic rhythms. There is no overkill and the balances are splendid. The first movement carries its brio on the basis of a long–short figure. Movement two is a powerful Presto, scherzo punched, passacaglia formationed. The bass subject, in pizzicato, never changes, and the eight-measure span is repeated eighteen times (there is a four-measure coda). The variants above the ground bass crisscross the quintuple meter with a 1:3:3:3 rhythmic ratio. An exciting conception.

Motorized content also is contained in the fourth movement, with contrastive 2/4 and 3/8 meters. A short slow movement precedes the finale. It substitutes adagio-style reflection for textural intensity.

Koporc, Srečko (1900–65)

TRIO

- **Episodes** for Flute, Clarinet, and Bassoon

Small pieces can be blocked in with balances (such as an A–B–A scheme), single stranded (through-composed), or free detailed, relying on a specific premise to achieve constructive poise. The latter is utilized by Koporc.

Accordingly, contrapuntal conjunction and a scherzo urgency in turn mark the first pair of the *Episodes*. Fugal responsibility pertains to the third piece; a bit of inversion is used later. Koporc mixes his settings and gains thereby. Part four is also contrapuntal, but is fantasy-involved with rubato in tempo delivery intertwined with some recitative impulses. The final movement balances the contrapuntal initial one by being homophonically opposite.

These structural differences do not foist any stylistic confusion on the auditor. Koporc's music is always tonally based, chromatically engendered. (One habit must be mentioned: a fondness for glissandos. Every movement but the final one contains this coloration, even the fugal *Episode III*.)

Koppel, Herman David (1908–)

DUOS

■ *Ternio* for Violin and Piano, Op. 53a or for Cello and Piano, Op. 53b

Koppel, an important Danish composer, identifies his three-movement duet (offering a dual choice of medium) by Gallic clarity and a touch of Viennese origination. As to the latter, the theme of the first movement touches all twelve chromatic pitches, but otherwise the exposition is made from tonal and chromatically enriched datum, set forth with French-style crispness. The music motors along at an average scherzo's pace, monothematically monitored.

In movement two, Koppel reverts to primary triadic materials. The structure is a passacaglia with the eight-measure ground appearing in both the bass and the soprano at the start of the movement and repeated (with slight changes) eight times thereafter. The ground also appears in new territory as the first of the two codettas for the gay, rondo-designed final movement.

TRIO

■ *Divertimento pastorale* for Oboe, Viola, and Cello, Op. 61

The clear, traditional architecture of short forms controls the three movements. Within these there is Koppel's chromatic condiments and polyphonic partitions. Movement one is moderately fast, movement two is a Lamento, and the final part is a Scherzo. No Trio contrastive insert in the last, the principal material's profile remains unchanged.

QUARTETS

■ String Quartet No. 2, Op. 34

Koppel shapes the first movement from a rhythmic motive of equal eighth notes set in pairs of threes for pulse identification, styled separately or slurred, and elongated into melodic units of short–long or long–short shape. The entire resource of this movement stems from the rhythmic generator. It is integral and translucent in its manifold arrangement.

And another type of motivic power lights up the third movement, this time six eighths within quintuplicate meter, the first three arranged as a triplet, thus splitting the five-pulse measure into 2/5 and 3/5 totals. A cantabile idea in 4/8 (occupying the same time space as the 5/8) provides contrast. It remains subsidiary, however, when it is bimetrically combined with the stronger 5/8 rhythm.

Between these two movements is a lyrical music of breadth. The color of this part of the quartet is dark; the texture polyphonic. Still, its quiet is as dramatic as the pulsatile movement that follows.

■ String Quartet No. 3, Op. 38

Polyphony and variational development are the strengths in the first part of the quartet. The opening is indicative of the stylistic action that will be taken. In turn, the instruments enter with different material. Each is individually pronounced by separation so that the second violin theme does not begin until the eleventh measure, the viola's theme enters in the twenty-third measure, and the cello's theme is not declared until the thirty-sixth measure. Though in totality it is the first violin's theme that is given the most prominence, it is rhapsodic coil and recoil that mark the movement's development. One is reminded of Nielsen's style here.

Supple, chromatically dyed lyricism is the factor in the slow movement. Its structure is determined by the andante speed and muted timbre of the outer parts and the double speed and unmuted timbre of the central part.

A larger ternary structure holds the finale. Figuration heard in the first measure is the kernel for structural enlargement. The ending of the work is a dynamic sixteen-measure quadrupled unison for the quartet.

■ **String Quartet No. 4, Op. 77**

A rational suite structure is used. Each of the six movements is clear and personal. Further, to ensure balance of the total work the data and character of part one (lightly flowing music, scherzo tempered, set forth in totally muted timbre) are echoed in part six.

A compact ternary-designed slow movement represents the second part. Direct dynamism and a succinct scherzo spirit describe the third movement. It has hammered rhythms, cross accents, and syncopation in its supply. Part four is a Recitativo, supported by trills and tremolos. The fifth part is marked Tranquillo. However, its uneven quintuple meter is otherwise.

Fine creativity throughout. One reads Koppel's quartet score with admiration for its content.

■ **String Quartet No. 5, Op. 95**

Koppel's fifth string quartet is darker and more chromatic than his other works in the same medium. This, expectedly, carries over to cadential declarations. The first movement, an Andante of heavy and active diction, ends in a bitonal combine of C plus A-flat major.

Movement two is a Scherzo in vivace speed, set in asymmetrical arrangement. Color galore: not only by a large amount of pizzicato throughout but by the ending of a short chordal Adagio followed by a coda in poco presto tempo, with the quartet exactly divided playing plucked and bowed sounds, all wrapped in a dynamic blanket of *piano* and *pianissimo*.

A chordal slow section also prefaces the third movement (Allegro energico), which never ceases its rigorous rhythmic substantiation. Movement two concludes in C major with a D added for greater punctuation in the nine-part pizzicato chord. Movement three brings the quartet to a close with a fervent G major in three-octave unison.

SEXTET

■ **Sextet for Piano, Flute, Oboe, Clarinet, Horn, and Bassoon, Op. 36**

A forthright, though light cast of movements. Koppel does not break any new ground in this divertimentolike group of three movements.

Movement one is á la marche. Contained within it is a large secondary movement in the same tempo (Allegro moderato), but much more lyrical and in stabilized duple meter. The principal music keeps kicking off into other metrical formations, some of even total, others of uneven amount. The second movement is a Pastorale graced with grace notes and pointed with pedal points in its three-part total. Lots of ginger go-at-'em in the final allegro-paced Gajo (Gay) movement. And a good amount of it is in very alive, uneven-totaled quintuple meter. Lots of Gallic consequence in this refreshing music by a Danish creator.

Koppel, Thomas (1944–)

QUARTET

- **String Quartet No. 2, Op. 12**

Koppel's music has definite adherence to the motto that prefaces the score: "Drei Rose im Garte, / drei Tannen im Wald, / im Summer ischs lustig, / im Winter ischs kalt." ("Three roses in the garden, / three fir trees in the forest, / in summer it's happy, / in winter it's cold.") Nine movements convey flowery chromatics and arborescent murmurs, and these are contrasted with fervent ostinatos and chilly tremolandos. Rich romanticism combines here with asymmetrical settings and some aleatoric devices. Koppel doesn't mix his conceptions. Each movement maintains its single style.

Kopylov, Alexander (1854–1911)

See under **Collaborative Composers**

Les Vendredis—Set II

Kora, Toshio (1933–)

SEXTET

- **String Sextet for Two Violins, Two Violas, and Two Cellos (1978)**

There are no harmonic holds barred in Kora's substantial work. It ranges widely and rarely carries a soft stick in its probing. Totally bound in with cluster harmony and cluster polyphony, it consists of fourteen connected sections, defining (though not so indicated) three major divisions. While no A–B–A format is supposed the structural result is as clearly weighted as that found in simple ternary form.

The middle division has clear-cut metrical administration (4/4 and 3/4) and is predominantly vertically disposed. The contrastive portions in this place are polyphonically drawn, with emphasis on imitations of figures.

Surrounding this central portion are totally nonmetrical sections, all conditioned by metronomic specification. Each section speaks for itself, as it were: Fragmented isolated pitches, later joined to elongated sounds, in part one (three sharply frictioned pizzicatos indicate the end of this section). Sustained sounds, adumbrated by the pitch cohesion and colored by nonvibrato, begin the second section; these lead into graphic pizzicatos that are kicked to and fro by the polyphonic interweave. Again the section's conclusion is marked by Bartók-type pizzicato.

Having outlined so clearly his formal plan, Kora's further specifications are of immediate auditory recognition. These include parts devoted to massive legatos, hammered sixteenth-note sets, rhythmic glissandos, and disintegration of figures by lessening of totals and dynamics. In the recapitulation portion still different procedures pertain, but each is just as pertinently defined as previously. There is no slump in this structural tenacity. To close and to bring the yield of absolute balance, the ending is a retrograde setting of the beginning of the sextet.

Kora's opus was commissioned by the NHK (the Nihon Broadcasting Corporation) of Japan. It was premiered and broadcast in Japan on October 15, 1978.

Korchmarev, Klimenty
(1899–1958)

DUO

- *Three Pieces on Turkmenian Themes* for Violin and Piano

Korchmarev went to Turkmenistan in 1939. He collected a good number of native songs during his stay and from these he produced this duo, as well as the first Turkmenian ballet, *The Merry Deceiver.*

In the first piece ("Characteristic Dance") a simple thematic idea in moderato accelerates into a faster pace that occupies the balance of the movement. During this section the violin is totally concerned with double stops, occasionally punctuated with triple and quadruple stops. Even in the second piece ("Lyric Episode") this thickening of the string instrument line continues.

Korchmarev's translations are vivid. The third of the group (another Dance) is set in a 3+3+2/8 meter with two other divisions of the total eight eighth notes used as well. The writing is in the quasi-virtuosic class with fast harmonics and almost a three-dozen total of left-hand pizzicatos. This technical substantiality is not reflected in the piano part.

Korda, Viktor (1900–)

DUOS

- **Five Bagatelles for Two Horns**

Complicated writing for a pair of unaccompanied horns isn't the best approach, and Korda opts for a more optimistic, untrammeled method in his set of five pieces. Everything is refreshing, clean, pleasant, simplistic, and successful.

There are bits of imitations, especially in the first piece. Contrastive timbre with one horn

open and the other muted marks the second piece. Scherzo snap and a modified march content describe the third and fourth Bagatelles. Punchy rhythm controls and colors the allegro molto finale.

- *Variationen über ein altfranzösisches Soldatenlied (Variations on an Old French Soldiers' Song)* for Viola and Cello

The theme Korda uses is crisp and marked Alla marcia—it is introduced with lightly percussive plucked cello sound. Important to the thematic shape is the opening rising fifth, and this span will be found woven into the variants.

Korda's variations are of solid structured length. They are prefaced by two sections: "Introduktion (Quasi notturno)" and the theme, headed "Präsentation." The Introduction has a sensitive and contrastive application of dynamics, colored by pizzicato, tremolandos, and short rhythmic figures. Each variation is separate. In turn they include shifts of plucked and bowed sound; a vivacious long–short pulse setting; a totally muted, mysterious concept; and in variation four a canonic thrust. The fifth variant is a swinging setting in septuple meter, marked "Quasi serenata." The Finale is polyphonic and its concluding part shifts away into an imitation of the second variation.

QUARTET

- **Quartettino for Flute, Clarinet, Trumpet, and Horn**

Equal timbre partnership, with paired woodwind and brass instruments. Equal to neoclassical style, with the music displaying bite, spirit, and sparkle. In turn, Gemächlich (Comfortable) in tempo, then set in moderate pace, and with a final Rondo. The last has an introduction, following which it bounces away in duple pulse. Nothing heavy-handed in this score.

QUINTET

- **Divertimento for Wind Quintet**

Facile and clever music that goes beyond mere facility and cleverness. The first movement, "Preludio pentatonico," represents high-ranking invention. There are three different pentatonic pitch sets, each assigned to a specific instrument. Thus, the flute has B-flat–C–D–F–G; the oboe plays B-flat–C–E-flat–F–G; the clarinet has A–C–D–F–G; and both the bassoon and horn (similar to the flute) have B-flat–C–D–F–G. It will be noted that the scale of B-flat major exhibits the total pitch range, and these pitches in their exclusive distribution are used in a variety of melodic and rhythmic ways.

There are a pair of Scherzino movements, separated by a bouncing Burletta, a just as active Arietta, and a cheerful Capriccio built from an anapest rhythmic figure. The finale is a Passacaglia. Korda doesn't move through abstract contrapuntal territory. This one moves, and moves precipitately, at ♩ = 200, not braking for a single beat throughout its measures, which are constantly shifting between quadruple and triple totals.

Kořínek, Miloslav (1925–)

DUOS

- **Sonatina for Clarinet and Piano**

Romantic sentiments, articulated cleanly and clearly, and all ring true. The first movement is a cross between a scherzo and a waltz. A pair of themes, equal in strength, provides the material for the third movement. There is a development section that stresses the octaval spans of the initial theme, then thematic restatement, with a coda freely derived from the second theme.

The middle movement is a three-part Largo. Recitative-banked detail in the clarinet, followed by impressionistically focused material in the piano, balances both of the outer parts of the movement. The lyrical, central section is also neatly equalized by a twice-stated single phrase, the second of the pair represented with pitch changes.

- **Sonatina: Theme and Variations for Flute and Piano**

A fine sense of variational variety as well as inventive clarity is here. Tonal music, but avoiding the traps of mundane academicism.

There are three variations following the B-flat-major theme. The first is a light Scherzo; the second a slow-moving, chromatically solidified setting; and the last a lightly figurated conception. For coda purposes the theme returns.

TRIO

- **Trio for Two Oboes and English horn (1961)**

Combining a pair of oboes with an English horn provides a mellow resonance. While basically this is not removed from Kořínek's opus, the sonorities are edged a bit by the chromatic tonalism that surrounds the writing in all three movements. A pitch polarity around A controls matters.

There are other controls. The opening Scherzo is mostly three part, its middle division slowed to Andantino and shifted to a B-flat tonal area. The Variations of movement two begin with a theme that already undergoes some development. Only the first variant is separate, the other two are connected, and, in turn, hinged to the coda. Movement three presents a rhapsodically tossed Finale.

Two other controls are the fundamental syncopation within the outer movements and a quotation from movement one to set the conclusion of movement three.

Koringer, Franz (1921–)

DUO

- **Sonatine for Viola and Piano (1949)**

Neat, light-textured music. Triadic harmony involves the first movement (Allegro), quartal chording frames the second movement (Adagio), and again triads are the principal support for the homophonic, final Vivace. Simple objective is matched by simple music; everything is understandingly directed.

Korn, Peter Jona (1922–)

DUOS

- **Sonata for Horn and Piano, Op. 18**

Combining a reverence for tradition with freer neoromantic musical prose is a sort of stylistic best of two worlds. Korn's idea of sonata design is traditionally unacademic. The initial movement is of large scope, framed and set off at the outer points by muted horn and scalewise piano lines. Thus prelude balances with epilogue. In the slow movement the emphasis is on descending thematic (and melodic) substances. Linear strength including deft imitative work gives additional power.

A hybrid form is used in the final movement. This "Rondo à la gigue" is naturally fast and vivacious, its 6/8 meter almost undeviatingly maintained. Though Korn bases his primary material on horn fanfarelike data, neat legatos and syncopative contrasts are supplied. There is vigorous abundance here.

- **Sonata for Oboe and Piano, Op. 7**

Music of contemporary romantic commitment. The second movement is most representative— a Romanza. Its persuasive use of tertial harmonies projected against long lines is the exact opposite of the drypoint quality of neoclassicism. In the first movement, while there is Hindemithian influence there is no overabundance of linear demonstration. A great amount of the piano writing in the opening movement is restricted to two voices.

The final Rondo leans on syncopative drive for much of its strength and urgency. Dead center, a fugue serves as superb contrast. It also illustrates Korn's superb ability with counterpoint; the fugue combines inversion and stretto in its architecture.

Kornauth, Egon (1891–1959)

DUOS

- **Sonatine for Flute (or Violin or Viola) and Piano, Op. 46a**

Romantic delineation but with a quiet, laid-back portrayal of the style. The structures provide an entity in terms of a relaxed Rondino, the same general quality (and tempo) for an Intermezzo, and a final, slower-tempoed Siciliano. Perceptive presentations.

- **Three Pieces for Cello (or Viola) and Piano, Op. 47**

Kornauth never changed his style, and no stagnancy of conception resulted. His music, both in substance and form, always contained the healthy and warm type of materials that served the masters of the romantic school, especially Brahms and Schumann.

This meant always a continuity of line, never any episodic breaching, never any arbitrary structural quirks. These qualities are exemplified in this case by an Elegie and a Romanze. The surprise is the final piece, a Dumka. The music (in memory of Hermann v. Schmeidel) is in the tempo of a marcia funebre, becomes a bit animated, and then returns to the initial pace. Kornauth's stylistic sensitivity in matching expansive melodic lines with rhythmic stimulus is impressive.

QUARTETS

- *Kleine Abendmusik (Little Evening Music)* **for String Quartet, Op. 14**

The term *Abendmusik* generally means evening music performances, usually of a religious or contemplative character. Kornauth's suite is, of course, meant for performance at any hour, but its contents, in terms of the basic title meaning, has only one movement that might be considered of contemplative character. Further, even that movement contains a good portion that has a lightly swinging lilt. It is the third part of the work, headed "In Memory of Edvard Grieg."

Waltz and march content are depicted in the second and fourth movements, respectively. The opening part of the work has light andantino propulsion.

- *Kleine Hausmusik (Little Home Music)* **for String Quartet, Op. 41a**

Well into the 20th century, Kornauth was one of the few remaining disciples of the romantic school of composers, avidly continuing the luxuriant but intense Brahmsian viewpoint combined with the more intimate suavity of Schumann.

There isn't a single contemporary twist in this three-part piece, which won first prize in a "home music" competition sponsored by the Reichsrundfunks in Germany. Simple formal formations prevail: a two-part Sonatina, a

suavely swinging Siciliano, and a Rondino. But no academic dust blurs the constructions, including the coloristic device of harmonics to mark cadential points in the second movement, and a fourfold plan for the final movement. In the latter, ternary balances are used for parts one and three, thereby indicating a secondary stability.

QUINTET

- **String Quintet (Two Violins, Two Violas, and Cello), Op. 30**

Kornauth began his quintet in Graz, Austria, in June 1923. The second movement was completed in the same month in Switzerland, and the composition was finished in Graz in December. Accordingly, and with great rarity, the work is dedicated to a point in time—the year of 1923 ("Dem Andenken des Jahres 1923")!

And without any facetiousness, Kornauth should also have thanked Brahms. For it is that composer's style (with a bit of related Schumann) that covers the three movements.

Movement one is in sonata form. It is of substantial size, including a coda three-quarters the length of the exposition. The middle movement is also one of length, set in large song form with full romantic confidences. Rondo design is used for the finale, projected entirely in duple pulse.

NONET

- *Kammermusik (Chamber Music)* **for Flute, Oboe, Clarinet, Horn, String Quartet, and Double Bass, Op. 31**

Kornauth's nonet is not of modern experimentation, but a production of depth and beauty drawn in review from the warm richnesses of the past. The scoring method does not evoke particular instrumental colors; the nine instruments are treated elastically but in strict accordance with romantic convention wherein timbre differences are audible but as undertones to the general compactness of the total.

The theme of the first movement immediately shows the stylistic affiliation of the music with that of the 19th century. A further indication is the use of cyclic insertion. The initial theme returns later, bound in with the latter part of the third movement. This, the final movement, has more rhythmic attention given it than the other two. However, the metrical drive is not kinetic or overexuberant, but submissive to the general tone of the work—a type of warm, fall afternoon music, rather than one chilled by northern winds. The opening movement has full-scale sonata development derived from two themes, while the single subject of the Andante (movement two) proceeds in a slight variational manner.

Korngold, Erich Wolfgang (1897–1957)

One of the most interesting studies in creative retrogression (in the sense that while the late works are not immature, they never accomplished what the early ones promised) pertains to this composer. Korngold was a *Wunderkind* (as a composer, not performer), creating and having had performed a two-act ballet-pantomime at the age of 13 (the orchestration by another composer). His achievements were the subject of study at such a venerable institution as the Berlin University; orchestral works and chamber music were turned out in fair quantity before he reached the age of 15, and were performed as works worthy of men thrice in seniority. Philip Hale (one of the wisest of all American critics) raised the question in the *Boston Herald* of February 16, 1914, that if this youngster could "make such a noise at 14, what will he not do when he is 28?"

The answer, most unfortunately, is that "he did not do." Korngold's music was written,

performed, and eventually dropped out of the picture. Like so many prodigies, he never developed. His music was excellently put together, stylistically always in the Viennese manner, sprinkled considerably with derivative colors of Straussian hue. Korngold was not, with all due credit to his well-made works, original, seeking, forward-looking. He eventually came to Hollywood. That Korngold was successful in writing the average film score, which must eschew originality, forms an obvious moral to his story.

DUOS

- **Four Pieces from *Much Ado about Nothing* for Violin and Piano**

The original score Korngold wrote as incidental music for a production of Shakespeare's play consisted of fourteen numbers. The instrumentation called for a chamber orchestra including a harmonium and with the string body minus cellos. From this, five pieces were selected to form a concert composition, titled Suite from the Music to Shakespeare's *Much Ado about Nothing*, Op. 11. Still later, Korngold made a transcription of the last four numbers in the suite (the opening Overture was eliminated) for violin and piano.

Movement one, "Mädchen im Brautgemach" ("The Maiden in the Bridal Chamber"), is a lyrical, sometimes sentimental, moderately paced music, emphasizing a single theme. Movement two, "Holzapfel und Schlehwein (Marsch der Wache)" ("Dogberry and Verges [March of the Constables]"), has grotesque quality—one perceives a Mahleresque tinge to the music. Movement three is a lyrically polished, ternary-designed "Gartenscene" ("The Scene in the Garden"). The finale is titled "Mummenschanz" ("Masquerade") (sometimes translated "Mummery"). The movement is parenthetically subtitled Hornpipe. It is an apt ending to the closing words of Shakespeare's play when Benedick commands, "Strike up, pipers!"

- **Sonata for Violin and Piano, Op. 6**

It is extraordinary to realize that Korngold wrote this duo sonata in 1912, when he was only 15 years old. No slender morsel, either. The composition covers thirty-three minutes in performance. The very young composer dedicated his opus to a pair of virtuosos: Carl Flesch, the violinist, and Artur Schnabel, the pianist. The dedicatees gave the premiere performance.

There is abundant power in the thick lines of the passionate opening movement. The subjects are contrasted by direction, the first upward, the second in falling fashion; thus is relayed the subsidiary (contrastive) sense of theme as well as that of repose. The Scherzo gives an example of birthright infiltration. While the first theme is driven by the pulsatory character of the form, the second is an idealization of the Viennese waltz, delivered in fast tempo, with its off-the-first-beat accentuations holding merriment in place and maintaining the requirements of the form. There is the usual Trio, but its main body is somewhat redundant. Interestingly, the main theme of the Adagio includes both the rise and fall that define the two subjects of the opening movement. The finale runs through modified sonata form, and contains a fugato. But the *Sturm und Drang* of the Sonata ends in the opposite manner.

TRIO

- **Piano Trio, Op. 1**

Korngold began work on his piano trio in December 1909, when he was but 12 years of age. The opus was completed in April of the following year, just a month before Korngold's thirteenth birthday. The first performance followed very quickly, in Munich, in November 1910, with no less a celebrity than Bruno Walter as the pianist, the distinguished Arnold Rosé as the violinist, and Friedrich Buxbaum as the cellist.

That within the four movements there is a ringing affirmation of quasi-Straussian language does not negate crediting Korngold with the vivid conspectus of the trio. There are four movements: a sonata-styled opening, a Scherzo, a truly profound slow movement (Larghetto), and a Finale.

The commitment to rich romantic detail does not result in luxuriant orchestral textures. The scoring is superbly balanced. Harold Truscott, in a note on the trio, describes this perfectly: "One of the astonishing things about the entire work is that Korngold has written a piano part of large scope, and yet so discreet is the writing that the strings are never interfered with; everything imagined, everything that can be seen in the complex score, can be heard."

QUARTETS

- **String Quartet No. 2, Op. 26**

While it is not common to find a waltz used in chamber music, in this instance it is an undisputed novelty to find one as the utility for a string quartet's finale. When used, the waltz usually assumes the place of the scherzo, which had, in turn, replaced the minuet. Korngold's Waltz is strictly that of the gay Viennese era. As is the case with most works written in this well-known setting in 3/4 time, the title should read in the plural form. Korngold's chain of elegant dance swing eventually becomes grandiose and leads into a coda that is not in waltz tempo, though it stays within triple-pulse measurement.

Motival resources are used in the first movement. The Intermezzo is light-textured, almost Mendelssohnian in its touches. The usual chromaticism of Korngold is evinced in the Larghetto. That part of the quartet has well-directed and polished lines, but also illustrates economy of creative means.

■ **String Quartet No. 3 in D Major, Op. 34**

Korngold's usual commitment to rich romantic detail and luxuriant textures mark this four-movement work. (It was composed in 1945 but took a third of a century before it was published, by Schott, in 1978.)

The lightest quality is present in the outer sections of the third movement (Sostenuto), indicated "Like a Folk Tune." The middle portion of this E-flat-minor music shows Korngold's strong affinity for writing in the modulatory incited style of Richard Strauss. The Scherzo is full scaled, its Trio relaxed at a pace three times slower; the opening and closing movements have chromatic particulars that color the exemplary structural logic.

Korngold's quartet is "Dedicated to Bruno Walter in admiration and friendship."

■ **Suite for Two Violins, Cello, and Piano (Left Hand), Op. 23**

One for the record books. Korngold's opus is the only example extant for this combination. No tricky gimmick. The reason for the left-hand piano part is that it was written for and dedicated to the Austrian pianist Paul Wittgenstein (1887–1961), who lost his right arm in World War I and then resumed his career after developing a full-scale technique for the left hand. (Among others who wrote music especially for him were Strauss, Ravel, Britten, Schmidt, and Prokofiev.)

Dramatic variety illuminates the work. The opening Präludium und Fuge begins with a declarative solo thrust of thirty-one measures of chunky material for the piano alone; the strings then link on in unison and this leads to the Fugue. A Waltz is served up next—a joy of colorations revolving in the 3/4 time lilt with the inclusion of muted timbre, pizzicato, and a

concluding cadence set in string harmonics. The Groteske has snap, plucked sonorities, and syncopative push. There is a contrastive, lyrical Trio (the first half for the piano alone); the music is in strict three-part form with a coda. Movement four is a Lied; the conclusion is a Rondo expounded in the form of variations.

Korte, Karl (1928–)

QUARTET

■ **Second Quartet for Strings (in One Movement) (Two Violins, Viola, and Cello) (1965)**

Serially derived but free of formalistic rigidity. (Korte states that he has "always felt that aural considerations must often take precedence over serial order and as a result the quartet would be considered most unorthodox from most traditional twelve-tone points of view.")

The music moves within a variety of qualities, but its plot is firmly linked and balanced. It begins with distributed unisons, and its developments include pungent, scherzolike tactics, cadenza proportions, and aleatoric colorations. Again, to quote the composer, it is "a work of rhythmic complexity and harmonic intensity with rapidly changing moods and a strong element of sardonic humor."

QUINTET

■ *Introductions* **for Brass Quintet (Two Trumpets, Horn, Trombone, and Tuba) (1962)**

A sort of "these are what the instruments sound like" idea. Each instrument plays off stage a bit and then enters on stage while another instrument is heard from the wings. Eventually all five are front and center and produce an energetic, brass conversational piece. Music good for any type of affair, but especially youth concerts.

SEPTET

- **Matrix for Flute, Oboe, Clarinet, Bassoon, Saxophone, Piano, and Percussion (1968)**

Music of serialized sum and substance. However, no technical dry rot will be found in *Matrix*. Motival rhapsody carries the music forward, without the expressionistic coldness that pervades so many serial explanations. The balances are derived from juxtapositions of material. In this, color plays a strong role, though for the greater part the percussion is used for ictus, punctuation, and framing. The pedal roll that combines with the solo saxophone portion is, indeed, a neat bit. So is the jocularity just before the final portion of the piece. *Matrix* has the substance of real musical matter.

Kósa, György (1897–1984)

DUOS

- **Duo for Violin and Viola (1943)**

Finely balanced, but not cut to ordinary standards. Kósa's two-movement Duo sings a rhythmic tune in the first part of the work. Rolling connected figures are compared to heavier-lined voicing in which the instruments sometimes coincide rhythmically but mostly are opposed in groups of seven against four, seven against six, and six against four.

Part two announces three measures of six-part chords for the pair of instruments. From then on the statement is separated, lengthened, figurated, and spun into a set of continuous variations that range from andante to presto and back to andante. Slick!

- **Three Andersen Tales for Violin and Piano**

Reproductive imagination setting forth three stories by Hans Christian Andersen, the nineteenth-century Danish poet, novelist, and writer of fairy tales.

"Der Schweinehirt" ("The Swineherd") is in sectional form. "Die roten Schuhe" ("The Red Shoes") is described by a solo violin theme and fifteen variations, each demarcated so that identification is direct. Thus, rhythmic bounce in the first variant, energetic push in the fifth variation, violin octaves and chunky piano chords in number nine, an agitated waltz bimetrically combined with duple-pulse legato chords in the twelfth part, and a sustained, extremely soft final statement. A march concept takes care of the activities of "Der standhafte Zinnsoldat" ("The Steadfast Tin Soldier").

- **Two Bagatelles for Double Bass and Piano**

Tranquillity in the first of the pair. And phrase squareness—there are five four-measure folksong statements, the last with an extra measure of sustained pitch. Percussive induration styles the second piece, with a coda of vibrating double-bass harmonics.

TRIO

- **Trio for Two Violins and Viola (1946)**

The clue to Kósa's piece is the subtitle that appears in the score: "Máriával és Jutkával (amikor márnem lehettem velük együtt)" ("With Mary and Judith [when I was no longer together with them])." Kósa's imagery follows suit, with the sentience of a memorial piece. The music is initially restrained with wistful sadness. Ultimately it cannot be held in check and mounts dynamically into a nine-measure, triple-octave declaration, further intensified by greater speed and ascending pitch placements.

Music of this ruling is hardly expected to have a fast movement, but Kósa's Trio does, its tightly accentuated material concentrated in chordal form throughout. The hard-driven modal combinations (not even a vestige of counterpoint is implied) are restless. Chordal writing is also in the great majority in the final part, which is to be performed "in a consolatory manner." (In the second section the Trio changes into a sextet in voice total.) The deep sense of transfiguration is apparent in this touching music of hymnodic tribute.

QUARTET

- **String Quartet No. 6 (1960)**

Influences can be recognized in this five-movement quartet, and yet there is a distinct draw-off into individuality. Bartók is recognizable in the very opening, with its 15/8 meter distributed in the violins against full combination in the viola and cello of the 71/2 prime pulses. Further, the Hungarian master is imitated in the Presto all-pizzicato conclusion of movement three. And still further in the final Vivace, with its dancing five-beat concept which leads to a slower-tempo and expressive portion in 8/4 time combined with 24/8 time.

The instinctual data of Hungarian folklore wends its way through Kósa's quartet. It is never of direct quotation, but its accents and character are there. Also present is an emphasis on modal detail. Formal diversity is greatest in the interchanges of the first movement, with nine major tempo settings (the fourth one marking a recitativo that surrounds a solo viola passage with violin pizzicato over a pedal point). Movement two denotes a lament. It is stated with muted timbre, mainly five-pulse measured, chordally italicized. Presto sections are compared to the opposite speed in movement three. Modality is also very strong in the slow

(fourth) movement. No matter the differentiation of tempo shifts (the Hungarian rhapsody revisited), each movement's shape is clearly recognizable, the product of a dynamically positive creative voice.

Kosins, Martin Scot (1947–)

TRIO

- *Variations on a Theme by the Wind* for Flute, Viola, and Horn

The world of sound where action symbols principally replace standard notation and the use of precisely indicated data is extremely minimal. Indeed, in such a work the composer does take considerable risks since, as can be immediately realized, aleatoric music is a changeable (chanceable) thing, and creative perceptivity is not common among performers.

Kosins's piece bears the motto: "And now—look what the wind blew in . . . ." There are nine "Motions" in this opus. The first is a Trio, the second is "Very Viola," with the flute and horn accompanimental. The instructions for the viola are illustrative of the procedure used throughout the piece. The viola's line is to be played as written, then repeated with the insertion of nine rests, "at will; change of dynamics," and then followed with free improvisation.

Motion III is marked "Trio in the Trees"; Motion IV is called "Blues for Flute," where the wind instrument is the principal voice accompanied by the horn and viola. Motion V is titled "5's and 7's," Motion VI is "Together in the Wind." Standard notation is used for the short seventh piece, "I Remember Bela." Motion VIII—"Shapes and Sizes" requires the translation of triangles, circles, zig-zags, etc. into sound. The Finale—"Music in the Wind" is a salmagundi of pitch hunks and quotes (Tchaikovsky's Fifth Symphony, Bach's B-minor Suite for flute, etc.). Within all these are three successive cadenzas for the three instruments in turn, each instructed to play "a segment of your favorite music."

Kosma, Joseph (1905–69)

DUOS

- *Cinq chansons populaires du Languedoc (Five Popular Songs from Languedoc):* **Suite for Violin and Piano**

Tasty conceptions, nicely styled and never overstyled. In each case there is either a formal difference or a special bit of color.

"Ces maudites Montagnes" ("These Cursed Mountains") consists entirely of two-measure phrases (nine in all) with a three-measure final cadence. A four-measure introduction leads to the vivace setting of "Savez-vous ce qu'il est un . . ." ("Do you know what a . . . he is . . ."). Number three is simply titled Danse. Its fast triple beat is tinged with plucked and harmonic sounds in contrast to the bowed pitches. The fourth of the group, "Rossignolet du bois" ("Little Nightingale in the Woods") has shifting phrase lengths; the finale, "La commère" ("The Busybody"), has an infectious rhythmic push by way of sixteenth-note patterns.

- **Sonatine for Violin and Piano**

Tempo fluctuation is used very often in Kosma's piece. In the light and vivacious finale ritards lead to a full-fledged largo. The music picks up its pace and again shifts to a very slow portion, this time a grave tempo. And so it goes; later a largo and a lento cut into the vivace and the movement ends with a maestoso. All of this is not so unexpected.

The first movement (Allegro non troppo) concludes with a thematic statement in Lento.

That same tempo controls the middle movement. It lives on sequences.

QUARTET

- **Divertissement for Four Instruments (Flute, Clarinet, Bassoon, and Piano)**

Beethoven said of Ries, his protégé, that "he imitates me too much." Well, such choice is choice. The same applies to Kosma, who imitates Poulenc in this assortment of slow-fast-slow-fast music.

The varied shifts of tempo (a habit with this composer) are especially numerous in the first movement. Ostinatos are prevalent there as well as in the second movement. In the large ternary design of movement three the emphatic textural and dynamic differences provide the guide to the design. Jazzy flavor in the fourth movement.

Kostiainen, Pekka (1944–)

DUOS

- *About Five Little Bagatelles* **for Flute and Harpsichord (1972)**

Odd title, this, since there are only four pieces in the suite. Fresh miniatures with pure, two-voice, lightly biting phrases moving against the flute in the first of the set and a scherzo concept in the second piece. Number three is the longest of the group (seventy-eight measures) and is a rondo formation, including a moderate-size cadenza for the flute. Two-voice arrangement in the keyboard instrument is again used in the final (fourth) piece, this time underlining the flute's cantabile line with syncopation as well as simple figuration.

- **Sonata for Clarinet and Piano (1977)**

Many chromatic incisions with inflections of combined tonalities in this Finnish composer's duo. There is contrapuntal affinity in the opening Adagio cantabile, with motival springboarded phrases in the fast second movement. The finale is set as a trinal structure tempowise. In addition, the metrical shifts in the middle portion (Allegro) are compared to long phrases in the outer portions (Adagio).

QUINTET

- *Hommage á Prokofiev* **for Wind Quintet (1976)**

The Finnish composer's testimonial is derived from the use of the Soviet composer's opening theme (eight measures in length) from his Fifth Symphony, Op. 100 as the basis for a set of five variations. (Thematic enlargement on Kostiainen's part precedes the first actual variant.) The permutations are clearly defined by alternate fast and slow speeds.

Kotík, Petr (1942–)

TRIO

- *Music for 3* **(Viola, Cello, and Double Bass) (1964)**

Kotík, a Czech flutist and composer, dedicated his trio "in memoriam Jan Rychlík," a fellow Czech composer (1916–64). It is a composition that has a zest for the lust of force, fracas, and fulmination. There are no lines, harmonies, or recognizable forms. There are some pitches sounded, but the greatest part (almost the entire piece) is a testimonial to bruitism—the art of noises.

This is an exhibition of percussive qualities created on string instruments. Said differently, it is an example of anti-music. Consider some of the thirty performance instructions Kotík lists: Two deal with scratching sounds; another concerns placing "the hair of the bow on the reverse side of the instrument and [rolling] the wood of the bow over the hair"; six different procedures pertain to playing on the bridge, pegs, fingerboard, and tailpiece; striking, tapping, and rapping are dealt with in a set of ten explanations, etc.

Kotík's bold entry into the world of the scrappy and scratchy deserves attention because of its specialness. The beauty of the piece is its sheer ugliness, and that's special too.

Kotoński, Włodzimierz (1925–)

DUO

- *Pezzo (Piece)* **for Flute and Piano (1964)**

Two-dimensional music obtained by partnering of dissimilarities. The flute plays freely, its part is unmetered, and in some cases is noted in graphic (proportional) notation. The piano part is exactly opposite. There are four beats in each measure and the pace is marked Tempo stricto ♩ = 72. To keep matters in hand the instruments are to meet jointly at the conclusion of each eighth measure of the piano part.

Here then, a new type of counterpoint obtained by going far beyond normal birhythmic polyphony. Anticipating the need for setting an orderly stylistic stage for the linear noncoincidence the pitch substances are not involved despite the use of the total chromatic.

Kotoński

Kotschetov

TRIO

- **Trio for Flute, Guitar, and Percussion (Snare Drum, Four Tom-toms, Two Bongos, Bass Drum with Pedal, Two Cymbals, Hi-Hat Cymbals, Tam-tam, Triangle, Two Cow Bells, Four Korean Temple Blocks, and Castanets) (1960)**

A double celebration, which is the sign of the avant-garde. First, the rhythm is free, the pulse to be as irregular as possible. Second, the use of a huge amount of percussion (with a good total of different mallets required). No structural sophistication, the music is a three-banded series of events that are clearly depicted over a six- to eight-minute span and are minus any sonorous waste.

QUINTET

- **Quintet for Wind Instruments (Flute [alternating Piccolo], Oboe, Clarinet, Horn, and Bassoon) (1964)**

Sound blocks in constant motion are the principal creative compliance here. Initially, there is concentration on banded or minute cluster formations. The music then breaks away into fast, irregular, short figures, almost cadenzalike in their lack of rhythmic stability, and then returns to the long-phrased clustered properties.

Kotoński's nine-minute piece is free of metrical control. The action is directed by pulse continuity mixed in with free rhythms. To further compress the clusters microtones are used. Accordingly, harmony is a negative point in this music, while timbre tension is the affirmative matter. An affinity with electronic music style without the electronics surrounds Kotoński's wind quintet.

TRIO

- **Concertino for Flute and Two Violins, Op. 4**

This work exemplifies the type of music composed in the Soviet Union during the late 1920s. At that time all the technical and formal attainments of Western musical art were utilized in order to produce a trenchant music as an aid during the building of the socialist state. This creative policy was changed in 1932 through a decree handed down by the Council of People's Commissars that music of this type was negative—could only lead to an unhealthy development in Soviet music.

As far as dissonant music is concerned, Kotschetov's Concertino, scored for a very unusual trio formation, takes no second place. From beginning to end the harmony is tensile, set in with frictioned nails, placed, however, in very clear forms. In the Prélude there is a machinelike coldness of rhythm and for the most part the three instruments work vertically. The Arietta is bitonal, binary in form; the scoring design changes as the two portions are repeated. Kotschetov's instrumentational ability is compelling, especially in the last section of the Arietta. The Danza is rough, with mechanical ostinatos posed against a jagged melodic line. Only the Berceuse is warm and refined; there is almost a sense of Russian folk melody. The Finale-Toccata includes three fugal sections that are bisected by other related contrasts, with the coda completely one of tonal verticalism.

Notwithstanding the fact that much of this type of music has become dated, Kotschetov's trio still retains its freshness, chiefly because of its resourceful color and concentrated means.

QUARTET

- **String Quartet, Op. 58**

Kotschetov's late-period output is much more restrained, closer to tonal behavior, more academically responsive and responsible than his earlier works. Yet vestiges of the old expediencies remain. The finale of this work is illustrative. An energetic music, more than once it will remind the listener of an updated "Polovtzian" dance. Quintuple meter prevails, but with disordered order. It is not only split into 2+3 and 3+2 beats but the two formations often blend, so that pulsatile cross patterns emerge. Further, lines of quadruple-beat total travel with the quintuple, and extra excitement is thereby engendered.

The other three movements are less sensitive to contemporary rule. In the opening part an introduction begins in E minor and moves into the principal theme in the related G major. The contrasting idea is also in G major, but chromaticism expands the tonal spectrum and eventually the music moves into E major and finally returns to the E minor key of the opening. Movement two is a large Rondo; the thematic indications are oppositionally black and white, rhythmic and lyric. In the slow movement (a large tripartite division) most of the attention (and therefore development) is given to the second theme, introduced by the viola. The melody involved is not the composer's, but a Russian popular song, "Oh, You Meadow!" In the Soviet Union there was no problem with such appropriation.

Kounadis, Arghyris (1924–)

DUO

- ***Moments musicaux* for Violin and Piano (1950)**

The definition for *Musical Moments* is "lyrical pieces in Romantic style." Kounadis translates the form in terms of contemporary lyricism for the first and third pieces, with more tonal challenges offered in the second and fourth pieces. (Following the last, the first piece is repeated in full.)

Folk turns in the melody for the first of the set; the framework is made from bare fifths and ostinatos. A simple Sarabande in B minor serves for the third piece. Bitonality is the name of the technical game in the second of the set. At first, the violin proceeds in F major together with the piano's soprano while the piano's bass is in F-sharp. The middle section finds the violin in C major and the entire piano structure is in A-flat major. The final section returns to the bitonal setting of the beginning (F plus F-sharp). The fourth piece, filled with binomial rhythms of two plus three principal pulses, also indulges in polytonality.

Koutzen, Boris (1901–66)

DUO

- **Sonata for Violin and Cello (1952)**

Weighted textures, either heavy with counterpoint or harmonic action in both voices. The formal fantasy of the first and last movements parallels this style.

The center piece is an extended combination of a march type with scherzo. A germinal rhythm, an anapest, that places the strongest weight on the last of the three sounds, solidifies the music. Koutzen was a master violinist and the writing for the instruments shows his special insight, including two extremely colorful effects. One is a fifteen-measure span of double harmonics in the violin, the other is an all-pizzicato passage at the end of the movement. The latter calls for a buzzing pizzicato (that's one that even Bartók never thought of!) for the violin, together with a three-finger pizzicato for the cello.

TRIOS

- **Music for Saxophone, Bassoon, and Cello (1943)**

The abstract title of this trio is not descriptive of the milieu that the music expresses. (Significantly, *The New Grove Dictionary of American Music* lists this trio as a "Serenade.") Koutzen deemed himself a romanticist, his music slightly thick with internal action. In this composition for members of the wind and string families, an aliveness is portrayed that can best be obtained by polyphonic means. The densities do not interfere with the projection of a three-part form; observing, therein, the productivity of one tempo, but which, by augmenting or diminishing the durative values of the sounds, infers a slow-fast-slow setting.

Koutzen was awarded the first prize for this work in a contest sponsored by the American Composers' Alliance and Broadcast Music, Inc.

- **Trio for Violin, Cello, and Piano (1948)**

Music that is in both style and sound the essence of the neoromantic, represented by this Russian-American composer-violinist. Koutzen was neither inventor nor experimenter, but he was a thoughtful contemporary creator, as demonstrated by his zest for formal interplay.

There are clear-cut thematic materials in the first part of the Trio, but the developments and shape bring a fantasy glow to the music. To be noted are the thinner textures of the outer portions of the movement. Movement two is a very large trisectioned piece, in content it represents a Scherzo and Trio with recapitulation. The finale begins with a mostly four-voice statement by the strings alone. The response by the solo piano is a carbon copy in length, meter, and general content—it constitutes the first of a set of seven (unmarked) variations with a Maestoso conclusion.

QUARTET

- **String Quartet No. 2 (1936)**

The first movement's sonata order is cleared by immediate statement of theme, the requisite contrastive subject, and development, plus recapitulation. The composer's style embraces the trends of both Wagnerian elements and anti-Wagnerian dramatics. At times the shrubbery surrounding an idea makes viewing difficult, but the intention is clear. A fugato offers a defined type of contrapuntalism, providing a vivid color amid the ever-changing harmonies.

The slow movement is built on a single theme, somewhat variationally treated, including the use of augmenting its time values. The last movement stems from the preceding slow section, not only by the same intervallic impetus that marks its principal themes but by actual quotation. The contrapuntal devices are many, mixed with pure homophonic detail. To sum up, the first movement's opening returns in broadened values.

Kovàch, Andor (1918–)

DUO

- **Sonata for Viola and Piano (1951)**

Kovàch's duo sonata flirts with Hindemith in

the first movement. In its tempo progress, however, the faster-paced sections of the movement are less motoric than Hindemith's, whereas in the slower-paced divisions the relationship with Hindemith is much closer.

The three-part central movement in its middle portion, enjoys a cantillationlike contour, to be played slower and with rubato, and is completed by a moderately long viola cadenza. An unidentified folkloric theme is basic to the finale. Quartal and quintuple harmonies are the principal support. Kovàch does spread his tonalities a bit. Though the end of the work is pure C major, the first movement is signed off with a bitonal inflection and the second movement implies (by successive chords) a similar type.

TRIO

- *Musique d'automne (Autumn Music)* for **Flute, Clarinet, and Guitar (1942)**

Kovàch's seasonal representation is opposite to Swinburne's "wan with wrath" description. There are nicely colored ideas and filamented textures in the rondolike, variationally typified first movement. The third movement is tripartite, with a little march in the middle. Movement two is also three part in its construction, with a guitar ostinato backup in the outer sections. On its return, the principal theme has a different melodic partner. Truly, counterpoint clear and well defined and totally of nonscholastic context.

QUARTET

- **Quartet No. 2 for Wind Instruments (Clarinet in E-flat [or Flute], Two Clarinets in B-flat, and Bass Clarinet [or Bassoon]) (1966)**

Hindemithian profile is shadowed in Kovàch's two-movement work, the music based on the

stability of unisoned rhythmic passages and fourth spans within the linear disposition. But the data are neatly developed and the reminder of another composer does not annoy.

The most satisfactory response is obtained from the juxtaposition of polyphonic sections with forward-striding monophonic ones. Especially in the second movement Allegro, which concludes in presto, the pulse action is exhilarating. What would not be so exhilarating would be the use of the instrumental substitutions that are offered. As a clarinet quartet of three family types, the work is far more effective than would result from the inclusion of either the flute or the bassoon or both.

Kováts, Barna (1920–)

DUO

- **Sonatina for Oboe (or Recorder) and Guitar (1948)**

Equality in the instrumental plan. Although the guitar does provide the requisite rhythmic underpinning, it is not pinned down to mere accompaniment. Another credit is the sparkling rhythmic assortment: patterns of 10/8 color the second part of the first movement and a mix of 5/8 plus 3/8 paces the first half of the fourth movement, with a further mix within the 5/8 that sometimes is split into 2 + 3 pulses and other times 3 + 2.

Kováts favors large binary forms in his duo. The third movement begins as a canon but moves out of polyphonic territory midway.

Kowalski, Július (1912–)

TRIO

- *Sonatina piccola* for Piano, Flute (or Piccolo), and Cello (1979)

Music that is alive with dance decisiveness. Despite its quadruple meter, the opening movement reminds one of the dip and go of a waltz. The Scherzoso, in very fast triple pulse, fills movement two, with more sustained material in movement three. The final (fourth) movement returns to rhythmic territory, displaying the light resonance and circumstance of a march.

No overintellectuality here. Kowalski's trio has on-target tonalism and considerable repetitively pulsed figures. Tripartite forms are used throughout with strict da capo repetitions for movements two and four.

QUARTET

- Quartet for Three Cellos and Piano

Tonality is exhibited with well-placed contemporary twists. Kowalski tends to favor sectional disposition in the moderately- and slow-paced first pair of movements. There is a good and plentiful assortment of repetitive rhythmic figurations.

Movement three is a march-tempo Vivo that dances and prances as well as three cellos can, supported by a piano. Refreshing and stimulating, however.

QUINTET

- Five Inventions for Wind Quintet

"Inventions" connotes the Bach-made polyphonic form. Forget it in this case. Kowalski's fivefold set of wind quintet inventions are characterful displays. All five pieces are formed with good attention to clear designs and all move within the boundaries of contemporary tonalism. Kowalski has no compulsion to indulge in special "isms."

The first essay of the group is particularly colored by three separate paragraph markers, as it were, for the flute alone set in quasi-cadenza style. Flung lines and lyricism describe the next pair of pieces. Part four of the work is a Vivo scherzo representative, rhythmically smart and smartened further with a few flute glisses. The finale has pulsatile controlled glitter.

Kox, Hans (1930–)

DUOS

- *The Jealous Guy Plays His Tune* for Violin and Piano (1975)

A chamber music quip, flavored with jazz touches. The music runs a tight binary course and then reruns it with slight changes. Whimsical stuff.

- Sonata [No. 1] for Violin and Piano (1952)

An example (and a fine one) of Kox's early music, long before he became interested in thirty-one pitch compositions and experimented with "open-end" forms.

Twentieth-century tonalism is exemplified and there are assimilations from Stravinskian neoclassicism. The tempo sequence is fast-slow-moderately fast. In movement two (the violin is muted throughout) the recapitulation of the principal theme is colored by the addition of juicy thirds and sixths. Tightness and enunciation mark the entire duo.

- Sonata No. 4 for Violin and Piano (1966)

Dynamic spill in the first movement sufficient

to knock one in the aisles. There are appoggiatured anticipations to percussive sounds, glissandos, combined rhythmics of piano tone clusters with violin moving pitches, a ten-measure total of paired ostinatos, zooming sextuple figures, and more.

Movement two is a chromatically encased Largo. The finale is a Song con Variazioni, based on a theme by Wim Stenz. There are a half-dozen superb variations. In the first one the violin totally plucks fifths of minuscule length, in the second variation triplets are tossed about by both instruments. Variant three is a special setting of triple chords in the violin and a single line in the piano. In the fourth variation the coloristic division is again absolute: four-pitch tremolandos in the violin and thematic augmentation in the piano. Precise tutti triple voicing applies in the fifth variant, with two-part writing for the violin and again a single line in the piano. Kox marks the final variation "Jazzy." That it is. But, what must be added for descriptive actuality is the word "fugue." Truly a unique handling of the variation form.

TRIOS

- Trio No. 1 for Two Violins and Viola (1952)

- Trio No. 2 for Two Violins and Viola (1954)

Both run through the tempo ordering of fast-slow-fast. In the first work the texture is rather solid from beginning to end. Ornamentation enlarges the expressive scope of the slow movement in comparison to the optimistic openness of the outer movements.

The second Trio begins with motival development. In the Largo there is cumulative effectiveness by virtue of inward voicing set to partner a melodic line. The finale has a stimulating formal production, plus two added attractions that color the conception. The first theme is followed by a fugato, then the former returns, and so does the latter but this time its voices are inverted. Before the coda (derived from the first theme) there is a tri-rhythmic section. The first theme (in cut time) is combined with fugato elements (in 4/4 time), supported by a bass line in 3/16 time. The second speciality is the scordatura of the viola, which plays with its fourth string lowered from C to B.

QUARTET

- Four Pieces for String Quartet (in the 31-Tone Temperament) (1961)

Direct forms are used as utilities to aid realization of the enlarged pitch spectrum (see above in connection with the music of Henk Badings).

There is a free-formed Largo of sixteen measures (movement one) and the third movement is a fourteen-measure Adagio. Rondolike music is used for balancing the second movement. In the finale there is pertinent rhythmic thrust in consistent duple pulse. A short reduced-in-speed section follows (in triple meter) and then a literal rerun made of the first 117 measures with a short coda for concluding the quartet.

Koželuh, Leopold Antonín (1747–1818)

(There are other spellings used for this Bohemian composer's name: Kozeluch and Kotzeluch.)

Beethoven described him as "miserablis." However, this derisive term could not apply to his reputation as a splendid pianist. Koželuh was a prolific composer. His output included fifty sonatas and twenty-two concertos for piano, twenty-eight symphonies, eighty piano trios, three pantomimes, and twenty-five ballets.

QUARTET

- **String Quartet in B-flat Major, Op. 32, No. 1**

Rococo accord, reflective of grace and melodic elegance. No deep probing here in the three-movement sequence of an Allegro, Andantino totally played with mutes, and a final Rondo allegretto. According to the Soviet musicologist A. D. Alexeyev, there are attempts at romantic expression, but these are difficult to pinpoint—Koželuh was totally influenced by the work of Haydn and Mozart.

Kozlovskij, Alexei (1905–)

DUO

- **Sonata for Viola and Piano (1959)**

This duo finds its roots in folk music. Euphoniously dictated lines surround the predominant fifthy background in the first movement, coincidentally rhythmically set (for the greater part) in quintuple meter. The pulsed material imitates a native instrument (quasi doira). (The doira is a tambourine used in Uzbekistan and Tadjikistan in the Soviet Union.)

A good whiff of Kabalevsky infiltrates the third movement, a direct dance text. It is preceded by a short movement (Rubato assai and Sostenuto, in turn) of tonal tact that leans on ascents and descents of a fourth.

Kraehenbuehl, David (1932–)

DUOS

- *Diptych* for Violin and Piano (1953)

Kraehenbuehl indicates that the two movements may be performed as separate entities.

However, when played in succession the movements "complement each other in the same way that the fiery emotionalism of the cult of Dionysus and the lyric rationalism of the cult of Apollo complemented each other to inspire the high art of ancient Greece."

But there are actually more than two movements, since the second one is a six-part survey titled "Partita d'Apollone." And more to note. The movement begins with a Madrigale for solo piano and continues with an Allemanda for the violin alone, imitative of Bach's use of that medium. Then follow three dances: Corrente, Sarabanda, and Giga, with the duo completed by a quietly set, ornamentalized Cantilena. The dynamic level of this finale matches the close of the first movement—a "Canzona di Dionigi." This is a music within which most of the direction is forceful, a codification of healthy neoclassical writing.

- **Variations for Violin and Cello**

A neat example of concentrated music; its solidity contains no extraneous packing. Kraehenbuehl states his theme ("The Holly and the Ivy") and runs off a set of five connected variations. Within all of these, the ascending fifth that begins the theme is a formal marker.

(Originally the piece was published under the title *Variations for Two*.)

QUARTET

- *Variations on a Pavane for Krummhorns by Hermann Schein* for Clarinet Quartet (Three Clarinets and Bass Clarinet)

Johann Hermann Schein (1586–1630) was one of the earliest German composers to bring to Lutheran church music the Italian techniques of madrigal, monody, and concerto. His pavane is a broad E-flat-major statement on which

Kraehenbuehl has developed eight connected variations. Tempo does not change, though meter does. A mild contemporary covering is wrapped around the developments of the theme, with climax arrived at the final variant.

(The Variations can also be performed by multiple instruments, i.e., a clarinet choir.)

Kraft, Leo (1922–)

DUOS

- *Dualities* **for Two Trumpets (1970)**

Akin to a sampling of the formal qualities that identify the trumpet's personality. First, "Fanfares." These are presented as two types: fast and immediately slower; the sudden brake in tempo and the immediate recharge of speed set up a six-sectional plan. "March by Night" has a modified march tempo. Part three is a Polka; part four, titled "Reflection," is duo-colored, with the first trumpet playing with muted timbre. Further title definition is underlined by the canonic first half of the piece. The finale is a peppy Galop.

- *Episodes* **for Clarinet and Percussion (Five Chinese Blocks, Three Snare Drums, Two Triangles, Castanets, Maracas, Antique Cymbal, Brake Drum, Two Suspended Cymbals, and Claves (1979)**

A one-movement duo but clearly defining four sections. The first of these is a fast, rhapsodic music with no fixed meter for the clarinet and fluid meters for the percussion. Coordination of the two instruments is therefore approximate.

The very opposite (pulsewise) pertains to the balance of the piece, with meters stated precisely and in constant flux. The second section equates scherzo temper; the third is a

wide-ranging line, chromatically driven; and the fourth section is of quick, nervous denomination, concluded aptly by the snare drum, with a *fortissimo* rim shot.

- **Five Pieces for Clarinet and Piano (1962)**

Ideas are determined, lengthened, and developed in this set of pieces, each explorative of a different objective, yet all totally affiliated by the composer's basic chromatic style.

The Prelude takes matters immediately in hand, being set in a fast tempo (Kraft describes it as "tense and driving"). Part two is an Intermezzo, developed from a tone row. Dialogue marks the Capriccio (the fastest piece of the group, the metronomic indicator placed at $\b♩ = 192$). Asymmetrical conditioning excites this music, which moves into an unmetered three-voice canon toward the end. Further unmetering covers the Fantasia, which is mainly designed by antiphonal arrangement. The finale is again a driving type of music—a Tarantella.

- *Little Suite* **for Two Clarinets (1963)**

A good helping of enjoyment can be obtained from this mini suite. The Pastorale is relaxed, the tempo is flowing and the counterpoint follows suit. Part two is an Interlude (a favorite title of this composer) in which the instruments are rhythmically unified for the greater part. "Reflection" lives up to its name, with plentiful imitations. The Finale zips along in an alla breve beat with the tempo set as brisk (another favorite term in Kraft's compositions). Good balance here between homophonic and polyphonic writing.

TRIOS

- *Short Suite* **for Flute, Clarinet, and Bassoon (1951)**

Line writing is used in good amount in Kraft's four-part trio. Most direct in this manner is the "Little Fugue" (movement two). The "Morning Song" and Interlude that surround the fugue are relaxed in motion, almost casual in content. The Finale is tempoed brisk; it has an athletic quality.

- **Trios and Interludes for Flute, Viola, and Piano (1965)**

Alternative disposition of the instrumental totality is basic to the design, with the full ensemble used in parts one, three, and five, and a pair of Interludes covering parts two and four. This sets up a rondo design of color and textural proportions that can be basically coded as A–B–A–B–A. However, the use of the solo piano for the first Interlude and the flute and viola for the second Interlude lends more contrast to the design, so that the code can be revised and refined to A–B–A–C–A. Further, the statements of the Interludes are sharply opposite in tempo and mood.

The music moves in a unstressed atonal style, including canonic procedures in the second of the Trios. Kraft's blueprint is clear and so is the detail that he has placed in his structure.

QUINTET

- **Partita No. 3 for Wind Quintet (1964)**

Mostly spiky and punctuative. Kraft avoids the long line until the Finale of his five-part work (the preceding movements are Prelude, Intermezzo, "Frammenti," and Adagio). Still, in these jabs of atonal wind play there is an urgency and directness—and a firm stylistic balance.

Cadenza formations begin the "Frammenti," followed by some ad lib sustained pitches for the quintet. Later in the movement there is another cadenza spot and toward the conclusion a noncoordinated section. These add a special color to the composition.

Kraft, William (1923–)

DUOS

- *Encounters III*: *Duel* **for Trumpet and Percussion (Vibraphone, Song Bells [Optional], Glockenspiel, Tam-tam, Three Tuned Gongs, Five Temple Blocks, Five Cowbells, Three Triangles, Five Suspended Cymbals, Eight Crotales, Bongos, Snare Drum, Field Drum, Tenor Drum, and Bass Drum) (1971)**

Kraft indicates that *Encounters III* "is conceived of as a medieval battle; the trumpet represents the attacking force, the percussion the defending." With contemporary administration Kraft lets loose a colorful arsenal of material intensely picturing the creative premise. In part, what the performer chooses to play is basic to the structuring of this duo vehicle. Actually, listening to the piece without any consideration of the scenario (the movements are titled "Strategy," "Truce of God," and "Tactics") is totally satisfactory and indicates how a talented composer goes beyond self-imposed restrictions.

(For more data concerning the subtitles, *see below*: *Encounters IV*.)

- *Encounters IV: Duel* for Trombone and Percussion (Ten Crotales, Eleven Stainless-steel Bowls, Vibraphone, Nine Tuned Gongs, Timpani, Five Graded Drums [Tenor Drum, Two Timbales, and Two Bongos], Four Graduated Tam-tams, and Galvanized Tin Trash-can Lid) (1973)

A different version of *Encounters III* (for details, *see above*), with the same objectives and similar concepts dictating the titles of the movements: "Strategy" (the processes of the battle Kraft is picturing by way of musical attacks and counterattacks), "Truce of God" (referring to the medieval custom of Sabbath respite during war), and "Tactics" (battle in totality leading to denouement). Here, not only is a different brass instrument used and a larger, mostly different percussion assemblage required, but there is a tape collage of war speeches, songs, and so on (made by William Malloch). Again, as in *Encounters III*, the auditor can bypass Kraft's musical simulation of a medieval battle plan and just listen. Fantastic and fascinating duo music is thus "encountered."

The opening and closing present two quotations "played out" by the trombone in Morse code. The first of these is "make war to make peace"; the second is simply the word "peace."

- *In Memoriam Igor Stravinsky* for Violin and Piano (1974)

Sensitive detail and timbral exploration concern the three movements. In this duo Kraft is his own creative man, but one finds bound into the material old prototypes considered in a modern manner.

In movement one (a line from T. S. Eliot's *The Wasteland*, "April is the cruelest month" prefaces the score) there is fragmentation—a contemporary transfer of rhapsodic style. Similar to the two sections that follow, the music avoids final assent by the absence of a conclusive chord or the notation of a final double barline.

Part two is marked Rapidly. It is a music blanketed in a dynamic range that extends from *piano* to *pianississimo*. The few louder bits are of minor total and can be considered inner accentuations. Kraft's exhibit of perpetual-motion music has an excerpted line from Francis Thompson's *Envoy* as a prefatory motto: "Go songs, for ended is our brief sweet play."

The final portion also has a quote from Eliot—his *Four Quartets*: "Time and the bell have buried the day, / The black cloud carries the sun away." Impulsive toccata character is displayed in this case. The violin does not enter until the last half, preceded by the piano playing irregular rhythmic groups "like free hanging bells."

SEXTETS

- *Double Trio* for Piano, Prepared Piano, and Small Ensemble (Tuba, Electric Guitar, and Percussion [Timpani, Two Vibraphones, Large Tam-tam, Chimes, Cow Bells, Six Graduated Drums—Bass Drum, Tenor Drum, Field Drum, Snare Drum, and Two Bongos—Graduated Gongs, Galvanized Trash-can Lid, Five Graduated Pieces of Galvanized Iron Pipe, Wind Chimes, High-pitched Bell, Small Tam-tam, Sandpaper, Six Graduated Wood Drums and Bongos—Two Bongos, Two Temple Blocks, and Two WoodBlocks— Maraca, and Mounted Metal Rods]) (1966)

(This work is also known under the title *Double Concerto*.)

The trios divide in partnered form. The piano in Trio I is matched by the prepared piano in Trio II. The tuba (Trio I) contrasts with the electric guitar (Trio II). Both trios have percussion, one of heavy make-up, the other of light content. With this grouping, "each trio establishes its distinct image and still allows for possibilities of fusion and imitation."

In movement one the music is divided, first for Trio I then for Trio II. They are combined in the sonority sweeps of the second movement. Propulsive toccata energy is displayed in the third movement; rubato, cadenza proportions, aleatoric detail, and scherzo relationships are found in the next two movements. These culminate with a sizable prepared-piano cadenza. Then follows the Maestoso conclusion, showing, after the virtuosic variety of explosive colorations, "a grand demonstration of unity." The timbral inlays and overlays of the entire work result in an exciting sextet composition.

- *Gallery 83* **for Flute (alternating Piccolo), Clarinet (alternating Bass Clarinet), Violin, Cello, Piano (alternating Celesta), and Percussion (Vibraphone, Four Suspended Cymbals, Maraca, Crotales, Five Graduated Drums [Tenor Drum, Field Drum, Snare Drum, and Two Bongos], and Glockenspiel) (1983)**

In some respects music history repeats itself in this sextet. *Gallery 83* can be considered a dodecaphonic parallel to Mussorgsky's *Pictures at an Exhibition.* Kraft may not have had this in mind at all, but the composition does trigger such recall. Of course there are differences: a much shorter length here (only three movements) and a completely different instrumental medium. But in the descriptive sense Kraft's conception approaches the Russian's in its sensitive conveying of the style and character of three paintings. But Kraft moves far ahead of him in using one of his own paintings as the third piece in his *Gallery.*

The first is Monet's "Waterloo Bridge," which is set in a mix of impressionistic serialism. No paradox whatsoever, considering that pitch detail concerns the latter and textures the former. Part two is "Convergences" by Pollock, conveyed by instrumental threading, with a percussion section, used in ritornel fashion, important in setting a "listening" to Pollock's production. The last is a sonic translation of Kraft's "Kadinsky Variations." This is a somewhat fragmented abstract of Kraft's visual abstraction.

SEPTET

- *Cadenze* **for Violin, Viola, Flute, Oboe, Clarinet, Horn, and Bassoon (1972)**

Here the composer is partnered in both re-creation and creation by the performers. The method, as explained by Kraft: "The players must be involved with one another in various free (nondirected) interdependent areas, and in some of the cadenzas"—meaning, of course, the modus operandi of chance operations. Since the basic quality of a cadenza (there are eight in succession in Kraft's opus) has the sense of an improvisation, Kraft's decision to have performer participation in cadenza formation is quite apt.

This "eight-voice" creative counterpoint, with its contrastive degrees of color, includes some parenthetical references to other composers. Just a bit, but enough to add a flavorsome touch.

NONET

- **Nonet for Brass (Two Trumpets, Horn, Trombone, and Tuba) and Percussion (Xylophone, Glockenspiel, Deep Suspended Cymbal, Mounted Triangle Beaters, Four Graduated Drums [Tenor Drum, Field Drum, and Two Snare Drums—low and high], Vibraphone, Large Tam-tam, Chimes, Antique Cymbals or Temple Bells, Two Gongs, Large Bass Drum, Two Very Large Tam-tams, Four Graduated Suspended Cymbals, Sizzle Cymbal, Timpani, Medium Suspended Cymbal, Triangle) (1958)**

Kraft's Nonet (in six movements) is dodecaphonically detailed and developed but has unprejudiced and unconstrained individuality within the twelve-tone premise. Its colors (derived especially from four percussionists playing a huge amount of instruments) make the syntax scintillate.

Many a serial-styled piece has an impersonality while conveying a well-balanced technical order. The missing element is vitality. Kraft's Nonet has dominant singularity as well as stability, and, as is so usual with this composer (a virtuoso percussionist), the percussion writing is a constructive gem.

This is a music neither imitative nor of narrow outlook. It is twelve-tone music brought into the fullest artistic balance.

Kramer, Jonathan D. (1942–)

SEPTET

- **Septet in Four Movements for Flute (alternating Piccolo), Oboe, Bassoon, Harp, Violin, Viola, and Cello (1968)**

The characteristic manner of total-chromatic language is present. Textural totality contrasted with strong polyphony as well as fragmentation give balance and interest to the outer movements. Kramer does not indulge himself; he proposes pithiness. This is especially emphasized in movement two—a seven-measure, very slow and very Webernesque item in 2/4 meter. Almost the total chromatic is here exhibited as well, minus only one of the twelve pitches. Movement three is set in exactly the same speed and meter. Just a bit thicker but also from the Webernian orbit. It uses all pitches and totals twenty-one measures.

Further balance is confirmed by the same metronomic indication for the outer movements, both set at $\flat$ = 90. The formal exactness is matched by the materials, which are stylistically logical and conclusive. And meaningful.

Krasnov-Lapin, Georgi (1916–)

QUARTET

- **Quartet for Two Violins, Viola, and Cello**

An absorption with triple time surrounds Krasnov-Lapin's Quartet. In the opening movement it frames the inside portion, tempoed faster than the outer divisions. Oddly enough, the tempo of the beginning is andantino, while the recapitulation of this three-part movement is indicated risoluto. Keyed in G minor, the middle section, in C-sharp minor, implies a waltz profile. Movement two, in B major, swings like a minuet and is, of course, in 3/4 time; the emphasis on this pulse frame is maintained as well in the development of the material, the only change being one of tonality.

The slow movement also partakes of Krasnov-Lapin's metrical habit, with a major portion in the latter part of the movement again shadowing waltz quality. The triple-pulsed portion is underlined by a tonality shift from the movement's basic E-flat major to a half tone higher. Only the kinetic finale stays away from the Viennese-like three-beat reverberation.

Kratochvíl, Jiří (1924–)

DUO

▪ *Little Suite* **for Clarinet and Piano**

Clear images. Clear tonality. Non-involved music but consistently and irresistibly entertaining.

Each of the four movements makes its point with natural, but imaginative ideas. The Preludium fixes the clarinet line to consistent keyboard triads, its format akin to very fast waltz action. Movement two is a Passacaglia. It is formed from a six-measure basis, each in a different meter (4/8, 3/8, 4/8, 5/8, 4/8, and 7/8). The piano is totally chordal, the clarinet politely motile. A tripartite, simply cast Pastorale and a Toccata follow. No pitch restraint for the latter. Pithily peppy, both instruments charge through all the measures on a spray of sixteenth notes.

TRIO

▪ **Suite for Three Clarinets (1963)**

Good variety of forms, which sustains interest in music written in a conventional harmonic idiom. In order there are a majestic Intrada, a flowing Pastorale, and a "Motorico," where the three clarinets are joined as one in carbon-copied rhythm. No deviation from that plan in the music, sequentially driven for a total of fifty-one measures. A little imitative counterpoint colors the Notturno, which is followed by a snappy Fuga. Good show.

Krauze, Zygmunt (1938–)

QUARTETS

▪ *Polychromy* **for Clarinet, Trombone, Piano, and Cello (1968)**

The working plan presents a score of six staves with the pitches set on the lines and spaces in proportional fashion. Each stave is to be covered in precisely twenty seconds, with all the instruments playing the sounds as connected as possible and all at the same dynamic level.

There are four versions outlined to be drawn from the six-stave score. Showing how precise is this mathematical projection, the durations of the versions are to last 4:40, 4:30, 4:20, or 4:12. It is mandatory to have a stopwatch to control the presentation of Krauze's aleatoric document.

▪ **String Quartet No. 2 (1970)**

One solid chunk of pitch associations, freely chosen. The entire quartet is played in connected, sustained (legato) fashion, with interruptions of violent rhythmic portions. These have the effect of footnotes to the principal text of the work.

Pulse is eradicated in this instance through the fact that the score is totally without meter and the progress of the sounds is indicated in measures, each lasting one second in time length (the quartet totals sixteen minutes). Stylistic identification in a case of this kind equals total dynamism. Identifiable form is actually removed, replaced by cores of sonority—soft and hard. Sufficient exposure to Krauze's music for four string instruments creates an effect that is aurally mesmerizing.

▪ **String Quartet No. 3 (1982)**

Krauze's quartet illustrates minimalism applied to a motive. Here there are a pair of motives—one of these is very short and the other very long (seven times the length of the former). In the music's development a variety of presentations are made, all closely related to the basic pair.

The texture is of four-instrument total save for four solo interruptions. In turn these are for the cello, viola, second violin, and the first violin, the last concluding the composition. These color changes (the content does not change) occur at seventy-odd measure spaces.

Krebs, Johann Ludwig (1713–80)

DUO

- **Sonata No. 1 in A Major for Flute (or Violin) and Harpsichord (or Piano)**

Krebs studied with Bach for nine years and later was his assistant at the harpsichord in Bach's Collegium Musicum. His music certainly deserves to be heard on its own merits, but with these credits the lack of attention is doubly unjust.

The duo listed above is a seven-part suite. The opening Andante contrasts disjunct and conjunct figures. A triple-pulsed Allegro follows, triplet-fed with eighth-note contrasts; part three, marked Affettuoso, has the strongest rhythmic profile of the entire work. A pair of Menuettos (the first repeated after the second one has been heard), a "Plaisanterie" (the name for playful movements in 18th-century suites), and a Polonaise complete the work.

Krein, Alexander (1883–1951)

Among the Soviet composers who gave attention to the fruitful matter of Jewish music, Krein was the only one who retained full and unswerving interest in such evocations. After an initial period of romantically styled compo-

sitions, Krein turned his course almost exclusively to Jewish music, producing a pair of works for clarinet and string quartet *(see below)*. Among the few non-Jewish pieces several were in the musicopolitical category that so many Soviet composers produced either from a true inspirational basis or from a politically opportunistic objective. Among these one was based on a text drawn from the writings of Marx, Lenin, and Stalin. However, the most important part of his output, and that which made his reputation were those that had a direct Jewish slant. These include a *Jewish Capriccio* for violin and piano; a symphonic cantata, *Kaddisch*; a most successful opera, *Zagmuk*; songs; and various symphonic suites.

While some composers of denominationally designed music are restrained in their handling of the melodic materials, Krein is lavish with his Jewish themes. They do not vibrate peripherally, but sing lustily in the center of the composition's core. The stylistic result is one of proclamative-declamative intensity.

QUINTETS

- ***Hebrew Sketches*: Suite I for Clarinet and String Quartet, Op. 12**

An elegiac type of music marks the opening part. The second movement is in three sections; the outer parts are in slow tempo, the middle portion is similar to a light Hungarian-Jewish dance, with slowed-pace measures breaking into the happy tune. Krein does not divorce his music from dancelike feeling in the last movement. This part moves continually faster and faster to its conclusion.

- ***Hebrew Sketches*: Suite II for Clarinet and String Quartet, Op. 13**

In comparison to the three movements of the first suite *(see above)*, the second set has only two. These are contrasted in tempo and mood.

The first part is an antiphonal elegy of pleading character with both the dynamic range and the instrumentation, for the greater part, in thesis-antithesis style. The gay and dashing second movement is equivalent to a "freilach," a memento of happy Jewish life. Like the conclusion of the companion suite, the movement's termination is reached by faster-excited tempo.

Krein, Julian (1913–)

DUO

■ **Sonata for Violin and Piano**

The sound-stuff is easily ascertained: emancipative tonalism with neat applications of coloristic dissonance. Krein's formal models are the clear classic-romantic types, arranged in the traditional fast (sonata)–Scherzo–slow–fast sequence. The development of the first movement includes a fugato. In the Scherzo (presto in speed) the Trio division is in the same tempo but, with larger lengths of sounds, the effect is of a slower (thereby, contrasted) pace.

TRIO

■ **Trio for Piano, Violin, and Cello (1958)**

The year of composition belies the uncompromisingly romantic course of the three movements. No dainty chintzes of lightness can be found in the Trio. And a volatility of change marks the designs. Continual major tempo alterations are in the first movement, and innumerable modifications to pull back or push ahead the pace. In the variational aspects of the slow movement there are eight key shifts between the opening in F-sharp minor and the close in F-sharp major.

The last movement is a Presto that combines the personality of a scherzo and a dramatic finale. Here, too, there is continual change, commandeered by a rondo control of the form.

Krein, Mikhail (1903–76)

DUO

■ **Two Pieces for Clarinet and Piano**

A Nocturne in B-flat minor and a Scherzo in G minor. A full helping of romantic spirit is offered in this short two-part suite—the absolute minimum total to certify the use of the formal term.

The instruments are paired to sound all the lines freely and clearly. The material is completely characteristic; smooth-flowing in the first piece, lively and dancelike character in the other piece. Both display homophonic structures.

Kreisler, Fritz (1875–1962)

QUARTET

■ **Quartet in A Minor for Two Violins, Viola, and Cello**

There is a long list of music to Kreisler's credit; many of the works, indicated as violin transcriptions, were once listed under such famous names as Couperin, Boccherini, Tartini, and the like, in order to obtain an unbiased hearing for the music. Kreisler finally admitted the hoax (for that is what it was, no matter the reasons). In addition, he composed two operettas. Within chamber music denomination, however, this Quartet is Kreisler's lone representative. It is a work in which Kreisler's method is foreign to his violin tidbits, most of which imitate varying styles. The A-minor Quartet is more rhapsodic, even more educated, in a sense, though the Viennese lilt is not entirely absent.

The Fantasia begins with a solo-cello monologue and moves into the main part of the movement, spun in the triple meter so dear to Austrian composers. This introduction serves to give cyclical entity, for it reappears at the end of the work, plus a recollection of the first theme (the effect of distant relationship is further enhanced by muting three of the four instruments). The Scherzo has no Trio; in place, is the same balladry of rhapsodicism that infiltrates the entire work.

Assigned importance to introductory material, but serving for more than mere preluding, is followed in the third movement, an Einleitung und Romanze (Introduction and Romance). This section, as all others, has harmonic fluidity, yet, paradoxically has heaviness induced by chromaticism. But it does not deter warmth. The Finale has marchlike insinuations. For a work composed by a virtuoso instrumentalist, the first violin part is rather free of such musical bribery.

Krejčí, Iša (1904–68)

DUO

- *Quattro Pezzi Aggiunti* for Violin and Piano (1966)

Delightfully appetizing pieces. Within the general neoclassic format there is Poulencian wit and Milhaudian key clash. The moods are mainly on the whimsically flip side: syncopatively detailed in the first piece with a good number of grace notes, the latter also keying the fourth piece in the set. The third of the group is a Scherzino exactly outfitted with meter and contrastive Trio. Considerable block writing there as well as in the preceding Aria, the only slow-paced item.

TRIO

- **Trio for Clarinet, Double Bass, and Piano (1936)**

A good deal of grotesque glee in this Trio, its instrumental makeup extremely rare. Only the third movement is subdued, though the ostinato piano chords (mostly made up of fourths and fifths), even in their very soft dynamic, stir the waters a bit. Movement one, with its striding fourths and quartal harmony, has a snide quality. A vivacious Scherzino (second movement) and a pithy Rondino (final movement) complete the work. Both, as elsewhere, exemplify supple scoring.

QUARTETS

- **Divertimento — Cassation for Flute, Clarinet, Trumpet, and Bassoon (1925)**

Tidy neoclassicism. Everything is alert, pert, and spry. Significantly, movements one, three, and four include vivo in the tempo headings, corroborated by the metronomic indicators. Movement one is tempoed Allegretto vivo (♩ = 152), movement three, a Scherzino is marked Vivo ma non troppo (♪ = 184), and the Quasi finale is plain Vivo, minus any metronome marking. No less speedy a pace concerns the Menuetto (movement two), which is pulsed at a march rate of ♩ = 120.

- **String Quartet No. 2 in D Minor (1953)**

Neoclassical writing that is intelligent, clean, clear in feeling, and with full understanding of the style. In terms of this work, it is easy to accept the description of its composer as a "little Czech Mozart."

The D pitch is the tonal anchor for the quartet. Movements one, three, and four are in the D-minor tonality; D major is the key center for the second and fifth (final) movements. Ratification of the home key as well as the music's general dynamism is found in the opening of the Allegro feroce. A *fortissimo* rising statement in total unison appears in the first measure, reappears twice again, and is balanced by an eight-measure close also completely in unison.

Movement two is moderately paced. The Czech critic Miloslav Nedbal has described this part of the work as "especially remarkable for its broad melodies in the style of Dvořák." This type of romantic breadth in no way causes a stylistic blur. (The two-measure initial announcement by the violins reflects attention to the unison insignia that is found throughout the quartet.)

A sharply concentrated Scherzino follows. The D-minor tonality is retained in the first of the contrasting two-section Trio, with a shift to D major made in the second section. Again, a unison point is stressed—in the final measure of the movement, stated in the dominant of the home key.

Movement four is a Recitativ dedicated to the memory of the Czech painter Emil Filla. There are no unisons here, but there are a considerable number of parallelisms for three and all four instruments, which define the closest possible relationship to unison writing. Fast and faster music occupies the final part of the work. A nine-measure introduction begins in allegro, succeeded by a seventy-measure exposition in prestissimo, heard twice (classical relationship, certainly!). The development is concentrated and the unison emblem appears completely in the final six measures.

An amusing note. Despite the prestissimo in this final movement (which means the highest possible degree of speed), Krejčí requests a Più mosso (still faster)!

▪ String Quartet No. 3 (1960)

A work of expressive differences, at times punctuative and percussive, other times polyphonically rhetorical, but never anything but brilliant. Krejčí considers the four string instruments capable of powerhouse, ictus-clamped sonorities. This is exemplified by the hammered rhythms of the first movement and the massed chordal smashes in the Presto molto (Rondo) finale, which are maintained without change for fifteen measures in two places.

There are a pair of contrapuntal dispositions. In movement two an introduction leads to a fugal depiction and variational development. In movement four there is a slow-paced Chaconne. All these movements have a tensility in their drive represented either vertically or horizontally. A contrast takes place in the central third movement, a Presto molto (Scherzino).

▪ String Quartet No. 4 (1962)

In the forceful demeanor of movements one and four Krejčí's fourth quartet is a companion to his third work in the medium *(see above)*. This is the music of an angry man. A drawing in of the power (a four-measure introduction in slow tempo) and the motoric dynamism is then let loose in feroce ruggedness. And it stays that way. The finale (Rondo) has the same impingement, with a slightly thinner texture.

A melancholic mood surrounds the second movement, which begins with a fugato. Movement three (Prestissimo) is strictly three part, with a literal rerun of the initial part to close the movement. It serves to lighten the sound atmosphere with its stinging intensity.

QUINTET

▪ Wind Quintet (1964)

Not a single measure of polyphony is included in the piece. It is precise chordal unification that regulates Krejčí's five-movement work. Accordingly, one movement depicts his usual penchant for percussiveness—the initial movement, with its indicative heading: Allegro molto e feroce.

The Largo mesto has chorale quality. It is the only slow music in the work. The balance is a tripartite scherzo conception, a slightly broader balletic music, and a vivacious, quasi presto finale. Oddly enough, all three movements are set in triple meter (3/8, 3/4, and 3/8, respectively).

Krejčí, Miroslav (1891–1964)

DUO

- **Sonata for Basset Horn and Piano, Op. 81**

Chamber music for this clarinet-family instrument is exceedingly rare. Mozart and Mendelssohn are the only major composers who used the instrument. The former calls for two basset horns and bassoon in his Adagio, K. 410, and in the Adagio, K. 411, the scoring is for two clarinets and three basset horns. (For discussions of these works *see below under* Mozart.) Mendelssohn's sole use of the instrument is in a pair of Concerted Pieces, Op. 113 and Op. 114, where it is part of a trio combination with clarinet and piano (*see below under* Mendelssohn).

Mozart was quite fond of the basset horn. Two basset horns are used in his Serenade No. 10, K. 361. In the *Maurerische Trauermusik*, K. 477, one was included and later he replaced the two horns in the original scoring make-up with two additional basset horns. Four of Mozart's operas as well as his Requiem require the instrument. Otherwise, orchestrally, the only important composer to use the basset horn was Beethoven, and then but once, in his ballet *Die Geschöpfe des Prometheus*. Oddly, even though Brahms recognized its special timbre (writing to Clara Schumann he said, "I do not think any instru-

ment blends more perfectly with the human voice"), he never used the basset horn.

It was Richard Strauss who revived the instrument, including it in the scores for four of his operas. Though here and there a 20th-century composer has called on its special color (Flothuis, the Hollander; Sessions, the American), the basset horn's appearance remains, in scores of any type, a rarity.

Understandably, therefore, Krejčí's work deserves special attention and performance. It has a rich, romantic glow, its technical reflexes honed by Schumannesque procedures. The music has symphonic, narrative excitement while its colors are autumnal. Krejčí understood the capabilities and special beauties of this wind instrument and they are fully displayed throughout the three movements. The piano is an equal partner in the duo, and there, too, the instrumental writing is resonantly full and totally integrated with the wind instrument. That late-18th-century characteristics mark this Sonata is not to lower a valuation that is totally positive.

QUARTET

- **String Quartet No. 2 in G Major, Op. 7**

The formal blueprint of this work, the second of seven string quartets Krejčí wrote, was duplicated in the first of the three string quintets he composed eight years later (*see below*). A moderately paced initial vivacious portion leads into a Grave, later becomes animated, and neatly shifts to a scherzando section. From such a playful mood the music turns (after a very short silence) to an Adagio statement. This variety continues to the end. But these contrastive matters of fact are never pretentiously belabored. Throughout, there is a natural romantic flexibility that is rewarding.

QUINTET

- **Quintet [No. 1] in B-flat Major for Two Violins, Two Violas, and Cello, Op. 15**

A firm and energetic demonstration of well-proportioned romantic writing, the materials presented in sectional form so that the architecture is quite clear, even without divisional recapitulation. Still, an element is used that bobs up now and then—the use of repetitive pitch groups. These equate the means of motival manipulation.

Krek, Uroš (1922–)

DUOS

- **Solo Sonata for Two Violins (1972)**

There is strong affinity between this piece and the unaccompanied violin work that Bartók wrote for Yehudi Menuhin. First, the Hungarian's sonata is duplicated here by double strength. Second, the difficulty of Bartók's piece is likewise duplicated. Third, as titled, it is individually soloistic in equal proportions. Finally, virtuosity, of course, does not eliminate placement of Krek's "solo" work in the chamber-music category.

Bartók's motivic use will be identified in Krek's assimilation of his style. Functioning like a germ cell, the opening thrust upward and downward of the instruments keys the first movement. Contrastive portions dart in and out simply emphasizing the tightly knit structure. Movement two is in large three-part form. The mood is nocturnal—a derivative from Bartók's "night music" style. The finale is projected by vigorous triplet figures. Folk-dance material is intertwined in this part of the duo.

- **Sonata for Violin and Piano (1946)**

Krek's early style bears no resemblance to his later music, containing Bartókian mannerisms, bitonal, and secundal harmonic associations. The Sonata, composed at the age of 24, is romantic to the hilt in the outer movements, classically oriented in the Scherzo. In the first movement the tempos at the outer points are slow, thereby forming prelude and epilogue to the principal part of the movement, set in F minor. This same key is the starting point for the Finale, but with traditional obedience the music terminates in the parallel major key. The Scherzo is placed in a submediant key relationship.

- **Theme and Variations for Trombone and Piano (1970)**

No old-fashioned procedures here. Krek's approach is, first, to use a theme that is of considerable length, with wide-ranging shape, and with a patina of development already within it.

The four variations are linked. Each extracts details, pitch curves, and important intervals from the main subject, resulting in a totally integrated piece of music. Thus, the second variant uses discerptible data from the theme; the third variant is drawn from the thematic essence, its shape smoother, less rubato in rhythm and quality. The rhapsodic contour of the generating subject returns in the final variation, in which the trombone is muted.

Kremer, Clemens (1930–)

QUARTET

- ***Drei Aphorismen (Three Aphorisms)* for Two Trumpets and Two Trombones (1967)**

Compression in length is matched by harmonic

contraction in this case. Secundal counterpoint and clusters prevail. In this type of material a triad would be a musical howler. So would a unison. Kremer's maxims are delivered with stylistic soundness and they register. Each piece makes its point with pointed frictions and precise form. Each is played twice, with a short, freely conceived section heard before the repeat.

Krenek, Ernst (1900–)

DUOS

- **Five Pieces for Trombone and Piano (1967)**

Krenek has always been on the lookout for what is the "latest" being done in the compositional field, and most often he has immediately followed suit. Thus, this piece, with its total emphasis on the expanded technique of the trombone, including chordal sounds, coloristic twists, and multitudinous technical seductions. It is interesting no matter what, though totally imitative of the instrumental work of such men as Ligeti, Zimmermann, Kagel, Cage, and Bussotti. (Importantly, after producing his "sample" utilizing whatever technique was involved [chance, electronics, etc.], Krenek always returned to his serialistic world.)

Thus a music of avant-garde liberty written for the trombone virtuoso Stuart Dempster, who specializes in music containing new sounds and techniques. And plenty were included by Krenek, presumably with the aid of Dempster since the sixteen prefatory trombone instructions in the score are "by Stuart Dempster." Included are such as removing the valve slide thus making a "pop" sound, slide vibrato, muttering into the instrument, singing while playing, rolling the bell on the center section of the piano's strings. Not that the piano is left behind. In the dozen special instructions for that instrument there are glissandos, plucking and hitting the strings of the piano, and striking the wooden structure of the instrument.

A rather colorless title for the diablerie that is stuffed into the score. But the only reserved point is the title. No reticent performer will be able to cope with the spitting new technical requirements of Krenek's duo.

- **Flute Piece in Nine Phases for Flute and Piano (1959)**

Three performance choices for this work in two parts. Either part can be performed separately. If only part one is played the piano is omitted. When part two is played separately it is presented as a duo. Finally, if the entire work is played then movement one is for *both* flute and piano.

The latter setting finds the piano practically entirely percussive. The effects include hitting the lid of the keyboard with the knuckles, some one-hand clusters, and rubbing the lowest four or five strings inside the piano. For the entire work the flute lines are serially registered with free rhapsodic definition, with one section moving into the next one. Within each of the nine divisions (termed "phases") of each of the two parts there is a balanced continuity without reference to reiteration of materials.

- **Four Pieces for Oboe and Piano (1966)**

In the Four Pieces the melodic and harmonic expressionism of the Bergian type is expanded to include percussive gestures, bent oboe tones, multiphonics, and pitch glides. The blend is new though the ingredients are not.

Krenek wrote his set of pieces at the request of Heinz Holliger, the famed Swiss oboist and composer. Included for that virtuoso were such spitting new techniques as double-trilled pitches, double-trilled glissandos, and double harmonics. Quarter tones are used as well.

- *Kleine Suite (Small Suite)* for Clarinet and Piano (1924)

Not only compact in size but a sampling of neoclassic writing. The Praeludium and Air both move around a G polarity. Movement three is a mainly quartally harmonized Bourrée, which contrasts to the eleven-measure chromatically ornamented Adagio. The finale is a "Moderner" Tanz ("Modern" Dance) that reverts to harmonic polarity and moves around the C pitch. All smooth music with alert sensitivity to form and style.

- Sonata for Viola and Piano (1948)

Repetition of patterns and the rhythmic clutch of sixteenth notes create a unified basis for the first movement. Indeed, this is easily identified music of tone-row ideology. Scherzo character is employed in the middle movement, with a more flowing portion serving as contrast in the center.

The average condition of a three-movement compounded work is reversed; the end parts are in slow tempo, the fastest in between. In a way this matches the more restrained, broader tone of the string instrument employed. Within the last movement the dual elements of sustainment and release by scherzando propulsion cross each other.

- Sonata for Violin and Piano (1945)

(Though an earlier sonata for violin and piano was written in 1919, this one bears no identifying number.)

Dodecaphonic technique styles this duo. In the first movement free meters as well as polyrhythms are used. While there is rhapsodic action, the use of canon, even though in birhythmic statement, helps to solidify the shape of the movement. Song form is used in the central movement. Ever sensitive to coloration within a design, Krenek reverses the initial roles of the instruments for a short period of time in the recapitulation portion. An active finale is stimulated by a metrical plan more concentrated than the broader concepts that marked the previous two movements.

TRIOS

- String Trio (1949)

A five-movement work, with no breaks in between, in which Krenek consistently uses (and, as one writer has well described, "with complete sovereignty") twelve-tone technique. The language shows how potent this style can be in place of the overgushing conversations of the postromantic tonal elite. And it also shows how rigidity is bypassed without falsifying the style via the use of repetitive pitches to emphasize an agogic point or a rhythmic one.

The contents fully portray the formal characteristics of the separate movements involved. Thus, a thrusting Allegretto vivace, a lyrical and slightly ornate Larghetto, a motival Allegretto vivace, an Adagio, and a concluding flowing Allegretto grazioso. The first pitch of the trio is an F in the violin; the trio concludes with the same sound in tutti unison.

- Trio for Violin, Clarinet, and Piano (1946)

Twain meeting, which gives neat stylistic contrast. Movement one is freely atonal, movement two is dodecaphonic. There is a further partnership. In the latter part of the second movement a portion of the initial movement's theme is inserted. The designs used are a modified ternary one with a coda for the first movement, and a combination of variation and rondo for the second movement.

QUARTETS

■ *Country Dance* for Four Clarinets

Krenek is a noncontemporary voice in this short piece. It is very light tonal music, a bagatelle at best, but straightforward and skillfully accomplished. Two parts in the B-flat main section; two parts to the Trio in G major, then a da capo and a coda.

■ **String Quartet [No. 1], Op. 6**

In 1922, a German critic spoke of this work as being neither heaven nor hell. But contemporary ears will decide that this quartet is not described by either of those polar points, nor does it rest in between. For if hell is represented by free contrapuntalism, then the work resides there; but if such technique is projected by imaginative form, then Krenek, in his first quartet, was, at the early age of 21, residing in stratospheric regions.

Krenek's quartet is a clear presentation of firm tonal negation (i.e., atonality), so it shall swim freely. Contrapuntal means are used a great deal to grasp these free tones so that order shall prevail. There are eight connected sections in the work, each governed by clear depiction of one specific musical purpose, yet containing a generating unity by motival use. It begins with a contrapuntal movement which eventually portrays (in its chromatic shifts) the name of Bach in musical translation (aside from the A and C, which are matched with similar musical sounds, the other two letters have equivalents: H is the German for B; in the same language B is B-flat). Krenek transposes this, runs his lines to develop the small cell that shifts on a chromatic axis until it is augmented in free fashion under and over rhythmic means. A development of this material continues in the second section, the generating motive being stated distinctly. This motive will be heard again in the Adagio molto that follows, as well

as in the motor-rhythmed fugato-formed Presto. Contrapuntalism of a type more closely allied to super-late romanticism shows in the second of the slow movements that forms the fifth section; and, once more, the motive interjects to thread the sections together.

The sixth section is a nine-measure introduction to the Fuga of the seventh, but Krenek is modest with his subtitle. First, the "fugue" is a double fugue (two subjects presented separately in exposition, then combined). Next, the second subject is a sequel to the resourceful generator—augmented, but distinctly grown into contrapuntal manhood. In the first exposition, the voices reply to each other by inversion (the chromaticism of the subjects and the manner in which they are guided definitely show, in anticipation, Krenek's later decision to shift into twelve-tone technique). A heterogeneous coda and a return to the opening completes the quartet.

■ **String Quartet No. 3, Op. 20**

While Universal Edition's published score bears the indication "E-flat major," this must be considered an error. First, Krenek does not write tonally, but atonally; second, there is no indication whatsoever of a suggestion of an E-flat tonality.

In this work, Krenek writes in the fractious style common to the 1920s (the third quartet was composed in 1923). The work's ledger show free linear use, the machinistic viewpoint of the period with engine rhythms, and also the predilection of many a Viennese composer for the waltz (be it a romantic view or a twelve-tone response, the waltz appears from Brahms to Schoenberg!). This is a product similar to Krenek's first quartet, by the intermediary of atonality. The quartet has perfectly clear forms, set in a one-movement plan with distinct sections, each almost religiously concerned with a single idea or precept of technique. But sectionalism need not always lead to fantasy;

intervallic disunity can be brought into ordered arrangement by interlocked means, repetitions slightly changed, or development of one section stemming from another. Krenek's plan is huge but superbly logical.

The clusters of the opening may have been caused by the fact that Krenek began this work on a railroad trip. To a certain degree, the work reverses itself, in that the most dissonant part is at the start; save for four of the last twenty-one measures, the quartet ends in complete unison. The structuring of many a musical work is accomplished by thematic development; in this instance, the first major section develops freely along semicontrapuntal lines of two contrasted subjects (with occasional tightening by use of tutti, vertical groupings), then moves into a fugue. Having finished with this, the fugue is reworked in inversion.

The succeeding Adagio illustrates the flowery voice writing that hung on to so many otherwise nonromantic works of the period; it is subconscious action in time, in reference to previous techniques. The opening is then recalled and leads to a section that again shows the "untangling" process, for the preponderance of trills of the next Allegro (equaling suspension) resolves into a marked theme; the trills are now much less in evidence. This section is important, not only for its contrapuntal dispatchment (it contains a double canon, the antecedents of which work the intervals in opposite motion; the consequents, naturally, follow suit), but because the main theme (after a slow and fast set of almost improvisatory manner) is then developed into a Gemächliches Walzertempo. Here, the sardonic values inherent in the bite of dissonance are exemplified. The binding of the work then becomes more confirmed by a short slow and fast section leading once again to a very concise portrayal of the fugue material, in this instance not respecting fugue style but its opposite musical flesh-brother—homophony.

- **String Quartet No. 5, Op. 65**

Whether the glutted market of atonality was the cause, or whether Krenek felt he had individually exhausted its possibilities, whatever the reasons, Krenek completely changed his style in the works composed in the late twenties, moving from atonality to neoromanticism. (He would later change to a third style, the twelve-tone composition system.) Krenek, thus, became a hybrid creative personality, shifting styles (but not in any one work); the demarcation of his styles is, in fact, very severe in his output. There is full romantic allegiance to cheerful harmonic munificence, fused with the experiences founded in atonality, producing a broader-cultivated utilization of previous (19th century) means. Romantic regulations are actually a concession in the store of many an "advanced" work by Austrian and German composers; the use of Viennese rhythms, the persistent (at times) thirds and sixths are vestiges of the heritage. Krenek's return (as in this quartet) was less an about-face than it was a fuller rewelcoming. The apparent reversal is to be noted more in the *sound* of his earlier quartets, compared to this one, than in the inner essences. For the musical maxim could well be stated that once a Viennese, always a Viennese.

The opening Sonate states three themes, the characteristic repeated-tone motive used as a link and binding. These form classical-style contrasts; the second flowing compared to the marked emphasis of the first, the third denoted by pizzicato. Development and recapitulation fashion clear formal terms. A theme with ten variations forms the second movement. Each is clearly depicted in neo-Schubertian manner, not completely, however, in his harmony or style; the years have moved on. A simple Allegro, an imitative variant, and a broad Andantino lead to a fourth variation, which matches two types of rhythm for its modus operandi. After the next two variants comes a canon, and after the following pair a Chaconne; the ground bass of this appears in varied form almost throughout, forming, thereby, variation within variation. The Phantasie is in free form, being built, as the composer states, by "every new idea growing freely out of the former one." The opening measures act as a moderator, appearing occasionally in this sensuously beautiful section.

■ **String Quartet No. 6, Op. 78**

With this work, Krenek's final stylistic manner is on view. From the year 1930 on, most of his works are in the twelve-tone technique (individually portrayed by Krenek, but as rigidly in that style as all of Bach's works are in his particular polyphonic idiom). Krenek's early atonality, which had led (in some people's minds) to retrogression, now was marked by the complete leap over atonal freedom to the most direct functions of the use of tone rows, based on Schoenberg's "method of composing with twelve tones."

The row (as usual) is announced, at the beginning of this "five-movements-in-one" work, presented in assorted entrances, single and simultaneous. Motives are formed and developed. The opening, slow movement is rhapsodic, leading to an Allegro, wherein motival use is paramount; the main point of the design is formulated in the very first measure by a rhythmic propellant contrasted to a "wider," more lyrical motive. Obviously, with the premises of the functional means of twelve-tone technique, the form works from "without," in the sense that the stylistic homogeneity stems completely from the unfoldment of the row in all possible shapes and forms. The balances of the design originate from tensions, registration, and dynamics. The whole becomes quite equal to the sum of the separate parts. Or certain stress is applied to a particular rhythmic part of the motive, as in the third section, Adagio, where the rhythmic figure of two sixteenths and an eighth appear constantly, until it

is stated in quartet unison in the final measure.

A second slow movement is then followed by a Fuga a Quattro Soggetti (Fugue with Four Subjects), in which the last two are announced after the fugue is under way with a pair of subjects. Exemplifying keen structural interlocking, each of the four subjects is taken from one of the preceding movements.

Krenek has said that the sixth quartet is one of his "most uncompromising twelve-tone works produced in the years 1936 and 1937."

■ **String Quartet No. 7, Op. 96**

Serial bedrock matters of stylistic fact. Faultless technique is exhibited, but more important is the resultant eloquence.

Cohesiveness is brilliantly planned. The five movements are played without pause; the basic metronomically indicated speed is retained for the entire work. (Krenek explains that the tempos provide the "character of the individual sections and suggest appropriate modifications of tempo within the limits of the basic speed.") Thematic interlock weaves through the eighteen-minute span. (Two examples from several: The principal theme of movement two is partly derived from the second theme of movement one; the first theme of movement three is derived from the initial theme of the quartet, etc.)

Movement one is an Allegro ma non troppo, grazioso e dolce, an Adagio follows, and movement three is headed Allegro ma non troppo, ben misurato, con passione, devoted to a Fuge mit drei Themen, in Umkehrung (Fugue with Three Subjects, by Inversion). Krenek produces a polyphonic master stroke by combining the three subjects with their inversions in the final part of the movement. A short (twenty-one measures) Interlude in Andante sostenuto pace precedes the fifth movement, set in rondo form and headed Allegretto con grazia, scherzando e teneramente.

An unusual dedication marks Krenek's opus.

It reads: "Dedicated in Gratitude to the Vivifying Spirit of my American Students."

QUINTET

- *Pentagram* for Winds (Flute, Oboe [alternating English horn, ad lib], Clarinet [alternating Bass Clarinet, ad lib], Horn, and Bassoon) (1957)

Twelve-tone music, but not devoted to dark expressionistic tenancy of *Sturm und Drang* expressions. There is a casual, lightly diverting aspect to each of the four compact movements (Presto–Andante–Allegretto–Moderato allegro).

NONET

- *Symphonic Music* for Nine Solo Instruments—in Two Movements (Flute, Oboe, Clarinet, Bassoon, Two Violins, Viola, Cello, and Double Bass), Op. 11

Notwithstanding the use of "symphonic" in the title, and regardless of the fact that this work has often called on the services of a conductor, Krenek's nonet is fully in the chamber music medium.

In the galaxy of musical techniques, rhythm is the item that inlays the essential soul and characteristics of the musical idea. Thus, in the first movement, while there are the formalities of polyphony of varying types (fugato, canon, and imitations) the abstraction of the atonality is aided by the frame of the marchlike, decided motoric rhythms. The second of the movements begins with a five-voice fugue for the strings, ably contrasted by pitting against this timbral total the entrance of the four winds. Later, further definition is made by placing the smooth-running fugue against jagged rhythms. Free form is obtained by abstractions of almost hard sound; thus, an example of expressionis-

tic, introspective composition.

Kresánek, Jozef (1913–)

TRIO

- Piano Trio (1939)

The Ballade is juiced with pungent, triadic chords and with continual changes of mood, which pass through areas marked "mysterious," "animated," "furious," Valse noble, "tempestuous," and so forth. The music ends quietly after many tempo shifts additional to the dispositional differences. (One of these is an Allegro scherzando, consisting of a single 3/8 measure!)

The Burlesca is sharply rhythmic, more settled than the previous movement. The Bacchanal heaves and twists. It is not a mere succession of pulsatile turns. There is as much toccata power within the music as there is orgiastic depiction. This Slovakian composer scores with strength, but all the power is obtained from straight instrumentation. There are no gimmicked timbres.

Kreutz, Arthur (1906–91)

QUARTET

- *Quartet Venuti* (Two Violins, Viola, and Cello)

Kreutz's jazz-style string quartet pays homage to Joe Venuti, the once-starred jazz violinist (1898–1978). It was Venuti who conceived the idea of unscrewing the violin's bow, placing the bow hair underneath the strings, reattaching the hairs into the heel of the bow stick, and bowing under the strings. This made possible simultaneous contact with all four strings of the instrument rather than only the paired string contact possible by normal bowing. In this manner Venuti performed all types of full four-part harmony, which can only be approximated in broken-chord fashion with normal bowing procedure. The performers of Kreutz's opus do not have to learn the Venuti technique. They play in regular fashion, but the sounds of Kreutz's work are patterned after Venutian stylisms.

Kreutz's quartet is a bravura jazz production. The first movement (With a Fast Easy Swing) is based on a theme that is repeated in inverted form, then stated a third time in its original shape. Imitations are called on and development follows; the bowing is mostly "against the grain," thus a change of bow direction is made off the beat. Augmentation of the theme marks the coda.

The second movement (Slow and Steady) has the timbral haze and nostalgic temper of much slow-tempo jazz. Microtonal subtle glides are condiments in this tasty musical dish.

Boogie-woogie patterns are paramount in movement three (Jively). The four instruments form a clangorous group of slap plucking, including series of slurred fifths. Within the music a coloristic dualism results from the differences of right- and left-hand pizzicato. Only in the latter part of the movement is bowed sound employed. As the movement proceeds the quartet sounds get heated. This chamber music delineation of a true jam session is followed by the finale, titled à la Venuti. Save for a slow section, the music in this part is in perpetual motion, with kineticism applied to figures similar to the free variations sounded by a "licorice-stick" performer.

Kreutzer, Konradin (1780–1849)

It should be noted that this is not the Kreutzer immortalized by Beethoven by the dedication of his Sonata in A Minor for Violin and Piano, Op. 47, known as the *Kreutzer* Sonata. That

Kreutzer's forename was Rodolphe (1766–1831), and it was he who composed the famous didactic set of *40 Etudes or Caprices* that every violin student must master.

Konradin (some publications spell this "Conradin," and in at least one instance the composer is billed as "Conrad") Kreutzer's claim to fame rests on two works: the opera *Das Nachtlager von Granada (The Night Camp at Granada)* and his *Grand Septet (see below)*. Certainly, the other compositions discussed below deserve equal attention.

DUOS

- **Duet in C Major for Two Clarinets**

Clarinet duets are usually not productive of ravishing sounds, but a good number are productive of dull, academic ones. Kreutzer's contribution is absent of the second type and though not exemplifying ravishing sonorities it is a musically convincing piece—with surrogate credit to Haydn.

It has five movements. Standard forms prevail. The Moderato (third movement), preceded by an Allegro moderato and an Adagio, has a sense of variation about it. Its central portion is totally in a minor tonality, strongly coloring the music not only by its key quality but by its chordal character. A Minuet and Rondo complete the duo.

- **Sonata in G Major for Flute and Piano, Op. 35**

(This is another edition of the work *discussed below: Sonate concertante*. It has been considered separately because there are sufficient differences [beginning with the change of title] to warrant individual discussion.)

The first two-thirds of Kreutzer's duo sonata has a rugged and dramatic thrust to its diction. We have become so conditioned to music of tonal address we sometimes tend to overlook (and therefore fail to appreciate) certain subtleties a composer uses in music of standard construction.

The Andante maestoso prelude builds from a stentorian rhythmic pedal and then moves onto vigorous rhythmic passages for both instruments. That it ends in a piano cadenza is fitting. The Allegro, which is in sonata form, also has drive, derived from scalic lines and broken chord patterns.

Basically ornamental, the Andantino grazioso also has virtuosic qualities: chromatic runs in the piano, cadenza spurts for both instruments, and overall an extroverted flair. The final Rondo is rather texturally pat but does retain an active character.

- *Sonate concertante* for Flute and Piano, Op. 35

The Universal Edition 1978 publication of this work does not bear a specific tonality in the title heading, but does state in a prefatory note that it is a "new edition" of Kreutzer's Sonate concertante pour Pianoforte et Flute in G Major, Op. 35. However, it is important to emphasize that some listings of this work (confirmed by the opus number) give the tonality as F major, which it is not. (The three movements are in G, C, and G major, with a good total of G minor within the last movement.)

The duo begins with a majestic introduction, leaning heavily on the piano, which finally bursts into a short cadenza; the principal Allegro follows. More cadenzas (gratefully short) are in the middle (Andantino gracioso) movement, with the flute given equal opportunity this time. Curlicues help the motility of this movement. In the final Rondo most of the motility is derived from large amounts of successive eighth notes in the piano.

Sufficient here for good marks. The editor, Armin Guthmann, states the music has "virtuosity and cantilena as well as inventiveness." Only the last descriptive word can be termed oversell.

QUARTET

- **Quartet in E-flat Major for Clarinet, Violin, Viola, and Cello**

Correctly musical and with only a single difference from early-period Haydn string quartets. With the inclusion of the clarinet the focus of attention is given the wind instrument. It becomes the "first violin" here. A wide area of notes is assigned the clarinet, with nice rolling arpeggios and bouncy triplets in the first movement (Allegro), expansive turns of lyricism in the Andante grazioso, and controlled bounce and go in the final Rondo. The other instruments provide a strong core of support. Nice active music, all of this. It has its grace and precision without individuality.

QUINTET

- **Quintet for Flute, Clarinet, Viola, Cello, and Piano**

Of course, there is an aura of stylistic imitation in Kreutzer's piano quintet wherein two winds replace the usual pair of violins. Nonetheless, the composition does not have the museum lifelessness that marks so much music produced by the early-19th-century composers.

In the final part of the work, a Tempo di polonaise, there is energy and snap, rhythm and stimulation, especially from the piano, including a pithy cadenza. Within proper scale the same exists in the slow movement. More quintet substances are to be found in the first movement (Allegro maestoso) and in the Scherzo. Tie score, therefore, as to matters of soloism and chamber music equality.

SEXTET

- **Six Waltzes for Wind Sextet (Two Clarinets, Two Bassoons, and Two Horns)**

The set of dances that Kreutzer had published in 1809 were scored for a wind group used very often at the time for outdoor concerts. It is just as propitious for indoor listening today.

The formal process is absolute, save for a single exception. Otherwise, every phrase is of single or double eight-measure length and is always repeated. Each waltz has a contrastive Trio, with the main section repeated after the Trio. The exception is the final waltz. It has no Trio, and after the waltz portion a coda of six measures in a decreasing dynamic scale finishes the opus.

SEPTET

- *Grand Septet* **(Clarinet, Bassoon, Horn, Violin, Viola, Cello, and Bass), Op. 62**

Kreutzer's Septet is kin to Beethoven's Septet. The instrumentation is the same for both works and so are the sequence and number of movements. These begin with an Adagio leading to an Allegro, a full slow movement, a Minuet, another slower-paced movement (marked Andante as well as Maestoso), and completed by a Scherzo and vivacious finale.

The music has a good injection of Haydnesque temper, though some romantic spirits hang on to the notes. All of it is diverting as applies properly to the music's divertimento framework. Within, one hears telling expressive variety.

Kreyn, Michael (1903–)

TRIO

- **Trio for Clarinet, Bassoon, and Piano**

Tonal music without tears (and without fears, for that matter). But enriched with chromaticism that suggests rather than impales. It is a satisfying combine.

There are four movements, embracing the usual traditional overall design, the third running directly into the fourth. Of these the most developed is the initial part, set in a sensitive and darkly colored F minor. In turn, this moves to B-flat minor, then modulates continuously until the movement ends in F major in tried-and-true minor home-key mode change. A grimacing Scherzo (in G minor) stays in formal place (containing the contrasting Trio). Kreyn's "slow" movement is in moderato tempo. Though just a shade unusual in speed, it is otherwise in content. The finale is light and easy in both tone and manner. Kreyn's Trio is conservative, but is not academic.

Křička, Jaroslav (1882–1969)

TRIO

- *At Home*: **Trio for Violin, Cello, and Piano, Op. 38**

A continuous conception based on a choral: "Te Deum laudamus." The variational display moves through a Prologue, a Fugue, an Intermezzo, a Scherzo, then a second Intermezzo, and an Epilogue. The chorale generator appears in various places and its outlines are quite securely bound in with the developments. A neat balance of lyricism and dynamism is obtained.

QUARTET

- **String Quartet No. 2 in E Minor, Op. 70**

No challenge to tonality is to be found in Křička's three-movement String Quartet. The moves are late-romantic ones, but neoromantic cliché's are avoided for the greater part.

In the first movement motival development plays an important role. Color is not over-looked—there are contrastive passages that first highlight the viola and later the cello; the coda is a strong and fervent strictly chordal passage of sixteen measures.

Movement two is a set of continuous variations with the theme returning at the end. Oddly enough, sectionalism, which is related to variational technique, pertains to the third movement. There, the materials are set forth in bipartite Andante and Scherzando divisions. Included are a short waltz (with the second violin muted) and a fugue. These varieties provide an assist to the dynamic quality of the finale of the work.

Krieger, Edino (1928–)

QUARTET

- **String Quartet No. 1**

Stylistic turnabout has marked this Brazilian composer's output. His early compositions were in dodecaphonic style. Then, in 1953, he turned to neoclassicism. Nicolas Slonimsky mentions that the neoclassic works had "national allusions." This quartet is a product of the neoclassic period, but the only references to nationalistic content are the use of syncopative rhythms.

There are three movements in the standard fast–slow–fast pattern. Movement one gives special emphasis to the second theme, which is always presented polyphonically, using the device of imitation. There is rich chromaticism

in the middle movement, colored further by muted and ponticello timbres. In the final movement there is a sensitive use of linkage. Twice early in the movement and then, for a third time a little later on, a tutti chord is played twice in succession (each instrument is scored in fifths, resulting in an eleventh chord). Totally withheld thereafter, the chords are brought back in the very final measure to end the composition in a delicate *piano* dynamic.

Krieger, Johann Philipp (1649–1725)

TRIO

- *Sonate à trois* **for Two Violins and Harpsichord**

One of a set of twelve trio sonatas. Of interest are the short Adagio inserts that precede the three full-size Allegro movements. Clear, resonant, and stylish writing.

Kriens, Christian (1881–1934)

TRIO

- *Ronde des lutins (Round Dance of the Goblins)* **for Flute, Oboe, and Clarinet**

Kriens's career began auspiciously. At age 14 he made a triple debut as a pianist and as the conductor of his Second Symphony! It ended tragically, when he took his own life. In the United States (he was born in Belgium and studied in Holland) he was successful only as an orchestral violinist.

The title of this wind trio will remind one of the famous violin piece with exactly the same title, composed by Antonio Bazzini. The fiddle piece, once very popular, demands a virtuoso;

Kriens's is a bit easier to negotiate, but still requires first-class performers. Apparently, when goblins dance they dance with zip and zest!

Which is exactly the case with Kriens's depiction. Though there is one section in slow speed and another marked Grandioso, all the rest is in Prestissimo tempo, with one portion marked Più presto! Five times the principal theme is heard as the dance whirls along, precise in its precipitance. No linear involvement is made; the music is totally vertically disposed.

Kriukov, Vladimir (1902–60)

DUO

- **Sonata for Violin and Piano**

Conventional but never dull, with a touch here from, and a nod there to, Prokofiev, especially in the folk-flavored Finale. The third movement Intermezzo is expressively detailed in the key of D-flat major, with the initial presentation of the principal theme in muted violin timbre.

Indeed, it's all unsophisticated—the energetic rhapsodic curves of the first movement and the perpetual-motion drive of the Scherzo—but will not bore sophisticated ears.

Kroeger, Karl (1932–)

TRIO

- *Sonata breve* for Trumpet, Horn, and Trombone (1957)

Kroeger's neoclassic style is a robust one. It is also has a neatness of formal thought that is most convincing.

Each of the three movements has a pertinent

shape of individual identity. The first one, sonata detailed, pays special attention to the "head" of the initial theme, consisting of a pair of seventh descents with an ascending fourth in between. Included in the development is the rhythmic augmentation of the drawn-off motive by the trombone. Movement two is a Lento in ternary total. It's outer sections are in blocked form, the middle section has a polyphonic content. Vertical formations are used in the finale, rhythmically punched, with a constant shifting between triple- and duple-pulsed measures.

QUINTET

- **Partita for Brass Quintet (Two Trumpets, Horn, Trombone, and Tuba) (1963)**

A stylish and assured representation of neoclassic style. The music is healthy but not healthily academic. The Sinfonia is fast-paced and its bits of foreshortened measures add a kinetic zing to the lines. The ending, in a reduced dynamic plane, prepares for the Chorale, which also concludes softly. Movement three is a Fughetta, followed by an Interlude, moving at the slowest pace of the entire suite, rhythmically intensified in the center. It is of pithy total but of dramatic consequence. A vivacious Gigue concludes a quintet that never runs down in vitality.

Krol, Bernhard (1920–)

DUO

- **Sonata for Violin and Piano, Op. 8**

Lightly textured music that leans on neoclassic supports. The style is a hybrid that joins Rousselian line writing with Hindemithian motility.

Two elements are developed in the first movement, a pithy Presto motive that descends in half steps and a more open intervallic Allegro. The finale has conjunct action which controls the kinetic zip of the music.

Movement two is special. Plainly indicated only with a tempo (Moderato) it consists of a four-measure rhythmic idea stated by alternating plucked violin sounds and static pitched trichords in the piano. Then proceed nine variations with the piano always sounding the combined rhythmic subject and the violin producing the permutational developments. Dynamically, the total forty-one measures (four for the theme, thirty-six for the nine variations, and one additional as coda) begin *pianissimo*, move stepwise up the intensity ladder to *piano*, *mezzopiano*, etc., until *fortissimo* is reached, and then recede until the final sounds in *pianississimo*.

Kroll, William (1901–80)

QUARTETS

- **Four Bagatelles for String Quartet**

- **Four Characteristic Pieces for String Quartet**

It is not too surprising to find that one of the most important practitioners of chamber music in the United States was capable of writing aptly (if in the light manner) for the medium which occupied most of his attention. Kroll had been the first violinist of many organizations, including the quartet and sextet that bore his name, as well as the outstanding Coolidge String Quartet.

The chamber music concert encore is all too rare; it might well become more common. And when such are given, any one of these tidbits could serve equally as a movement from a well-known quartet or a special transcription. While the divisions of these works are each of short duration, their values are in reverse proportion. The sonorities are cast so beautifully that performers could do no better than to use these short suites. Listeners will enjoy their merits.

- **Four Bagatelles for String Quartet**

The generic title of Kroll's suite aptly describes all four of the short pieces. The first "Coquette" is only slightly of the salon, being a waltz stylization, sequentially arranged. "Giocoso" is of scherzo character; a Hebraic tinge infiltrates. "The Veiled Picture" pays its respects to impressionism, via pedal lines and the color of muted strings. If the four sections are performed in continuity, the last piece ("Mood") is a bit of a surprise, being of reticent quality; muted, as well, in its bacarolle sway.

- **Four Characteristic Pieces for String Quartet**

The "Little March" is on the fast side and contains a trick cadence. "Magyar," the second of the set, has typical, sustained Hungarian emotion; the Gypsy fiddler and the overdrawn slide both make their appearance. The third piece is based on a Hebrew melody (no source given) and is titled "The Ancient"; it draws on the augmented interval that holds majority place in the Orthodox Hebrew musical liturgy. "The Cossack" is in the usual three-part form of short pieces; it includes the Russian musical evocation of the steppes (as portrayed so often by the old school of composers of that country), and offers some cadenza work for the first violin. All the pieces are unabashed in their stylizations.

Krommer, Franz (1759–1831)

QUARTETS

- **Quartet in D Major for Flute, Violin, Viola, and Cello, Op. 75**

Haydnesque to the hilt, but that does not remove the freshness from this Moravian composer's wind-string quartet. There are the four usual movements. What is somewhat unusual is that the first (Allegro moderato), second (Minuetto—Allegretto), and fourth (Alla polacca) movements are almost identical in length (7 to 71/2 minutes each), while the movement that would be expected to have real length, the Adagio, is extremely short (less than 21/2 minutes).

Standard form does not, of course, take a holiday in this case. Still, the Alla polacca is much less equivalent to a polonaise and is rather more a clear, chirpy fast piece of music.

- **Quartet in E-flat for Clarinet, Violin, Viola, and Cello, Op. 69**

Neatly detailed designs with full attention to inner substances. There are three movements. The first is colored by off-strong-beat accentuations and contrasts paired eighth notes with groups of triplets. Movement two (in the subdominant key and with the odd heading Andante Allegretto) is a large binary affair. The rhythmic differences in this case help define the form's measurements. There are no secrets in the final Rondo. It bounds along, pushed by grace notes and further speeded by sparkling triplet figures.

OCTETS

- **Partitas for Two Oboes, Two Clarinets, Two Horns, Two Bassoons, and Double Bassoon (ad lib)**

- No. 4, Op. 57
- No. 5, Op. 67
- No. 12, Op. 79

(One edition of these compositions indicates the title as "Octet-Partita.")

The editor of the modern editions of these Partitas, Roger Hellyer, indicates that Krommer wrote thirteen works for this wind-instrument combination. He states that these "were published complete or in part by three different publishers in the early years of the nineteenth century." Importantly, Hellyer points out that the pieces were issued "under such titles as partita, harmonie and suite." Indicating that the octets were undoubtedly published in a different order than the sequence in which Krommer produced them, Hellyer has followed (as above) the numbering used in the Dufaut et Dubois edition, issued in Paris in the mid 1820s. Certainly a sensible decision, since this 19th-century edition was the only complete one published.

There is nothing untidy in the four movements that make up each of these works. The classic style resemblance is acute and the formats of the individual movements are almost sharply similar. Allegro-paced movements serve as the corner items, save for the finale of No. 4, which is an Alla polacca, with the inner movements pairing a Minuet and a slow-tempo representative. The Minuets, are, of course, full-scaled, with all the Trios in the same key as the principal parts of the design. In Op. 67 the Minuet follows the Adagio; in the other two works, it precedes the slow movement. Two slight tempo exceptions: In Op. 57 the Minuet whirls in unusual presto tempo; in Op. 79 the slow movement turns out to be in a tempo

Krommer used several times: Andante Allegretto (not representing a tempo change but a cross between the two noted speed rates).

Conservatism marks the use of tonalities. In all cases the home key is used for three-quarters of the opus: the outer movements and the Minuets. Thus: F major for Op. 57, B-flat major for Op. 67, and E-flat major for Op. 79. In the slow movements a key difference is revealed: C minor for Op. 67 and B-flat major for Op. 79. In No. 4 (Op. 57) the Andante cantabile is preceded by a choralish Adagio of nine measures. Both are in the key of D minor with the recapitulation of the Andante tonally reversed to D major.

Neither rare nor revealing compositions, Krommer's Partitas are consistently interesting and insightful in the handling of the instruments. In terms of instrumentational chain of command the scoring is properly proportional. The balances are splendid.

Krommer-Kramář, František Vincenc

see: Krommer, Franz

Kropfreiter, Augustinus Franz (1936–)

DUOS

- *Aphorisms* for Clarinet and Piano (1970)

Music that sits squarely, comfortably, and successfully in the dynamic class, intensely fits the instruments, and is peppered from the first row of major sevenths to the final triple set of minor seconds with substantial and sustained dissonance.

The first four pieces alternate fast and slow speeds, the final (fifth) piece uses both. Mostly

direct, epigrammatic details with unified material in each case. Some duplicates, such as measures 1–2–3 repeated in measures 10–11–12 in the first of the set, three measures carbon copied in the fourth piece and a pair of measures repeated exactly in the finale. All very convincing.

- *Colloquia (Colloquy)* (Organ Chamber Music IV) for Violin and Organ (1970)

Not only instrumental interlocution but formal integration in this three-part duo. The last ten measures of the third part are almost the same as the concluding measures of the first part. Further, affinity is secured between the opening part and the second part, either by shape similarity, slight pitch change, and exact pitch duplication, though the tempo of part two is double that of part one. On the other hand, the speed rates of the first and third parts are almost the same ($\downarrow$ = c. 52 and $\downarrow$ = c. 44).

Kropfreiter uses the total chromatic in his *Colloquia*. His textural detail is healthy; there is no heavily packed writing for the organ. Dark music for the greater part—a splendid addition to the extremely limited literature for the violin and organ.

- *Dialoge (Dialogue)* (Organ Chamber Music III) for Cello and Organ (1968)

A set of three pieces. The first is a recitative type, with the cello given most prominence. The intervallic condition is mainly disjunct, matching the chromaticism of the music, though it finally settles on D-flat. An asymmetric scherzo quality is exemplified in the second of the sequence. The intervallic situation is tighter here and aids the lucid tactility of the material. The third piece matches the first in its cello highlighting. The organ writing, which is never heavy elsewhere, is lightest of all in this concluding piece.

- **Drei Stücke (Three Pieces) (Organ Chamber Music II) for Oboe and Organ (1968)**

The adjective "concentrated" should be added to the title. The totals read: thirty-three measures in very slow tempo, forty-seven measures in a mix of march and exceedingly slow tempo, and sixty-six measures in still faster speed.

The chromatic pursuit of harmonic balance is exhibited here. And type acknowledgment. The first is "Meditative," with the instrumental lines mainly traveling in opposite motion. The third piece is "Variational," codifying a great deal of tertial spans. Piece number two is titled "Grotesk–Zwielichtig" ("Grotesque Twilight"). It shifts between lively pace and a metronomic rate four times slower. This nonuniformity is illustrated by the beginning of the piece: two measures in the first tempo, then two measures in the second tempo, again two in the first speed, followed by four in the second speed, and so on.

- **Vier Stücke (Four Pieces) (Organ Chamber Music I) for Flute and Organ (1962)**

Tart dissonances and a certain reflection of Hindemithian style, especially when counterpoint is involved. There are four movements, the first (quite fast in tempo), is mainly in triple meter; it is preceded by a quiet, pastoralelike section. A slow movement follows, its texture of special detail, with only a single line in the organ partnered to the flute's line for the first twelve and the concluding fifteen measures. Elsewhere, this type of crystal-clear conduct continues: in a good part of the lively third movement, and completely in the Sehr ruhig (Very quiet) concluding (fourth) piece. In the last the context is totally three voice.

QUINTET

- **Wind Quintet (1968)**

Chromatic emphasis marks this three-movement work (with instructions to move one movement into the next without delay), with a stated performance time of eight minutes. Examples: A theme in the opening Allegro covers ten pitches, another sweeps through all twelve. The opening statement in the slow movement (Sostenuto rubato) is made by the oboe, responded to by the other four instruments; the total pitches involved are ten. The jagged clarinet theme that announces the final part of the work (Allegro molto) covers nine pitches. Note counting is a simple matter and it bypasses the essence of the musical meaning, but it does produce the basic evidence of the style involved, especially when the harmonic plan follows suit.

Much of the fabric of the quintet is thin. Again examples are indicative. There is a rhythmic join between the flute and the bassoon that is spaced three octaves apart; less than a fifth of the total measures of the final movement involve all five instruments, whereas close to half of the total call on two or three of the quintet's voices.

The directness of the music is most decided. Only in the final cadence of the first movement is there a change of tempo. The final movement is sharply divided as to tempo rates. The first 77 measures are in $\quarternote$ = c. 168, measures 77 through 140 are set at $\dottedhalfnote$ = c. 126, and the remainder of the work (measures 141–204) are in the initial speed of the movement. These disciplines give concentrated dynamic results.

Krüger, Ulrich (1896–)

DUOS

- *Little Sonata* for Soprano Recorder (or Violin) and Piano

Some Hindemithian touches in the slow-tempo first movement. The style shifts to pristine tonalism in the three-part Pastorale and a waltz movement titled Intermezzo. A return to Hindemithian style follows in the Arioso. The awaited polyphonic moment of truth comes forth in the final movement, a Fugue.

- Sonata for English horn and Piano

A quiet, emotional quality pervades the two movements of Krüger's Sonata. While there is tempo contrast—Molto adagio and Allegro—harmonically the entire work is built from quartal and quintuple stipulations. There is more chromaticism in the first movement than there is in the other part of the work. But probity is not lessened because of the fast pace of the second movement. Even though the Allegro is in the majority, twice there are important Adagio interruptions.

TRIOS

- Trio for Oboe, Violin, and Piano

Pliant tonality surrounds the music. If not precisely personal, Krüger's music is not to be included in the dark gray hole that marks so much untonal (atonal) music.

Sonata proportions in the first movement. Three-part formation covers the middle movement, with the outer divisions in an alternating long–shorter metrical arrangement of 2/4 and 3/8. A profitable change in the finale, which is a set of five variations on a theme. The alteration consists of a scurrying Allegro portion that precedes and follows the theme and varia-tions, with a pithy slower coda following the second Allegro.

The ways of publishers are annoying at times (and composers are often silent partners to the matter). There is no mention in the publication of this Trio (issued 1968 by Hans Busch) that in the same year Krüger made a setting of the work under a different title, *Kammermusik für 7 Bläser* (flute, oboe, two clarinets, horn, and two bassoons). Nor does the septet score indicate the duo setting. What came first one does not know. A little humor enters the picture. The Trio is listed at eighteen minutes, the septet at c. nineteen minutes.

- Trio for Piano, Violin, and Cello

Vitality is expected in fast-paced movements, but sometimes the notes get in the way. Vitality needs air in which to be realized. It is here in the opening Allegro amabile, bearing down considerably on the span of a fourth, and in the concluding Allegro non troppo, where the same pitch width is in evidence. A sense of march atmosphere surrounds both movements. The central movement is far more serious, has repetitive rhythmic framework, and also adds motility via birhythmic lines in two places. Romantic lyricism here.

Krul, Eli (1926–71)

QUARTET

- String Quartet (1958)

Freely tonal, chromatically festooned music in which Krul casts his net somewhat wide in terms of form. It is a learned music, but not academic.

A Lento introduction leads into an Allegro assai that charges away in scherzo zip and uses scherzo formal nippers. The first part is repeated strictly, the Trio represented by lighter pace and shifting pulse and then the movement is concluded with a literal da capo return. A three-part, polyphonically designed music follows. Imitative points are its strengths. Contrapuntal segments are also favored in the finale, which has two surprises. The first is a recapitulative dip into the introductory material. The second is the squarely vertical disposition of the concluding measures.

Krumpholtz, Johann Baptist (1742–90)

DUO

- **Sonata in F Major for Flute and Harp (or Violin and Piano)**

Lightweight music by this harpist-composer conveyed in the set forms of a fast-paced section, a Romanze, and completed by a rondo with a Tempo di minuetto heading. Krumpholtz indicated an alternate instrumentation of violin and piano. The setting for flute and harp is, of course, more colorful.

Krützfeld, Werner (1928–)

TRIO

- *Relationen* **for Flute, Viola, and Piano**

Krützfeld treads the middle, fully firm road of serialism: neither academic nor radical. And he stays close to the road. Of the eight short pieces in this trio (averaging 151/2 measures each), the first six use the same tone row without transposition or change of the original pitch order.

Considering music of pithy content in twelve-tone style one is immediately reminded of Webern's aphoristic absorptions. However, compositional validity (call it "classical

dodecaphonicism") is present in this trio, without the use of the darting colors and fantasy that romanticize Webern's short pieces.

Kruyf, Ton de (1937–)

DUO

- **Sonatina for Flute and Piano (1960)**

Freely detailed serialism. Most of the varied shapes of the music are tightly blocked in, though in the Andantino instrumental contrasts give a textural balance. Movement two (Lento) is linked to an Allegro vivace agitated by flutter-tongued sound and sharp rhythmics projected in staccato form. A three-measure Lento concludes this darkly expressionistic duo.

QUARTET

- **Quartet for Flute, Violin, Trumpet, and Bassoon (1959)**

Serialism is mixed in with improvisation here. In movement three the viola is to improvise on six pitches over a span of six measures. Equal opportunities are offered the other instrumentalists later in the movement, and preliminary to the three concluding measures the entire quartet is involved in improvisation. Kruyf's use of twelve-tone technique is unbounded by the use of pitch repetition.

Kubelik, Rafael (1914–)

QUARTET

- **String Quartet No. 2**

Absolutely balanced in all respects, this quartet exemplifies fresh viewpoints of color and rhythm application as devices in shaping the forms of its three movements. One perceives a passionate endeavor to avoid determinate procedures. Creative clarity results. So does aural sensation.

In the Largo's white-note music (consisting entirely of half, whole, and dotted whole notes), the color effect is subtle but yet direct, obtained by timbre climate. The first thirty-nine measures of this second movement are played totally without vibrato, the remaining forty-nine measures with vibrato. Thus the effect of coolness and warmth.

Movement three is a large ternary construction. The first part proceeds fugally. On the recapitulation a different fugue subject appears (a distant cousin in resemblance to the initial one and considerably shorter). The first twenty-two measures of this portion are totally in pizzicato, the remaining twenty-one measures move into nonfugal data and serve as a vertically arranged coda. The central part of this movement represents soloism supreme. Initially, the first violin and then the cello declaim in "ad lib e rubato" manner with note lengths exactly detailed but not set within bar lines. The sonorous supports are totally fingered tremolandos in the second violin. Then follow a number of more metrically regulated measures, most of which are held in check by fermatas. These, again, are essentially expressive (deliberate) contrastive colorations in terms of a design which has polyphonic agitation surrounding it.

The first movement has splendid formal sense, based on three different stipulations. The first part (coded A in this essay) lives on scalic nourishment. Part two of the movement (noted here as B) has metrical juggling. It then settles down into a pattern of 2/4, 3/8, and 2/8. Obviously, this tightens the metrical enclosure successively by one pulse per measure (2/4 equaling 4/8). Exactly twenty times this metrical turn occurs. Differences then enter the design but the pulse variance continues. Anchoring all this are ostinatos. A tranquil section follows (indicated here as C)—suave, some-

what romantically succulent.

The three sections return but with varied synonymic relationship. Part C builds in reverse, quiets down to a sustained specification of the pitch C. Again (as in B) the measures shift from 2/4 to 3/8 to 2/8 (a further, albeit thin, relationship). Two sets of these three measures stay in C minor and four sets remain in C major to complete the movement.

Those who have seen Kubelik the conductor are aware of his sensitive application of detail, his way with color symbolism. Kubelik, the composer, follows suit.

Kubik, Gail (1914–84)

DUOS

- **Sonatina for Clarinet and Piano (1959)**

The balances of this work are as clear as the timing proportions that pertain to the piece itself, in which each movement covers four minutes, or a bit more. Kubik's harmonies and counterpoints are biting and his rhythmic continuity is asymmetric, but the solidity of updated classicism is evident. This means allegiance to triadic coloration pigmented with polyharmonic inculcations and shaded often with bitonality. It also means rhythms that are not merely of motoric drive but that are infused with American jazz.

The music illustrates cogent constructivism but is in no way scholastic. The declamatory introduction (it also serves to usher in the coda) belies the bouncy tone of the first movement proper. Its pulsative pointy sounds cover widely placed areas. The contrasting theme is no less disjunctive but curves within a legato sheath. Dynamic growth plus textural poundage form the climax of the bittersweet middle movement. In the finale Kubik displays a colorful method of contemporary fast music. Nervously articulated, the basic eighth-note pulse shifts between duple and quintuple divisioning. This free assortment represents a mid-20th-century concept of scherzo design.

(An odd matter should be mentioned. Kubik finished his Sonatina in 1959. It was published in 1971 with the dedication "In memory of Ingolf Dahl." Dahl died in 1970. Usually a composition is written *after* the death of a person, to whom it is then dedicated "in memory." Indeed, it is extraordinarily strange [and dishonest, according to this writer] to dedicate a piece *in memory* of a colleague when it was written and completed eleven years *before* his death.)

■ **Sonatina for Violin and Piano (1944)**

Without academicism of any kind, the triadal construction stands supreme in the opening movement. The factor of a consonant frame, even for dissonant unrest, is the stimulant of this movement. For example, the opening has the calm, sustained expression obtained by the jelling of thirds with and against each other. Kubik's triadal praxis is substantiated by the cadence (cadences not only mark finality but are, as well, a concentrated, aesthetic summation), which is that of *mixed* triads.

The slow movement is based upon part of the composer's incidental music for the play *They Walk Alone*, by Max Catto. In order to maintain the simplest mode of expression in connection with the use of ternary form, the main subject on its return is practically unchanged. Too much fuss in a short movement can result in serving up, conversely, much small beer.

The last movement bears out its English tempo indication (Kubik belonged to the small group of composers who believe in using one's own language for instructions to performers, but this is risky for foreign trade)—"In the manner of a Toccata: fast, briskly, with rough force." Save for a mollification of the energy, wherein the first movement's theme is recalled slightly, the music of this finale tears on vigor-

ously. The shifts of rhythm add mercurial action to the already excited kinetic form of the touch piece.

TRIOS

■ *Five Theatrical Sketches* **(Divertimento No. 3) for Piano, Violin, and Cello (1971)**

Kubik is decidedly at home among the assorted goodies that mark the divertimento design as it is considered these days. An expert instrumentator, Kubik applied his technique to the piano trio combination making it function as a mini-orchestra to maxi-effect. This bravura handling of the instruments is paralleled by a bravura creative attitude.

In the Overture (a violent and savage preamble) the cello functions mostly in violin territory, thereby making the violin, as it plays with the cello, sound tighter, trumpetlike. Kubik explained that the piece was "impregnated with a sense of tragedy. We are 'seeing' *The Tempest* or *Coriolanus*."

Movement four, "Trialogue (Fantasy-Scherzo)," is a mixture of light and heavy pitches, of delicate and ripping bowing, of vacillating rhythms and clipped lines. The pianist doubles as a percussionist, striking the edge of the instrument's console with a pencil. At times this effect is used alone; other times it is combined with normal keyboard sound. Cute and effective. So is the finale, *"Waltz and Circus March (for Fanny)."* (Fanny was the name of a little bulldog, who was "much in evidence" in the composer's studio during the composition of the piece.) The Waltz has a rhythmically irregular introduction. When it gets into swing it swings "à la Tchaikovsky." The March portion is principally pinned onto a striding, civilized type of boogie-woogie.

The Nocturne (movement two) defines its lines on contrasting octave statements and chordal positioning in the piano. The composer described the music as "sounds which paint the solitude and lonesome quality of our Middle-Western plains." In the following Intermezzo the energizing force is drawn from antiphonal presentations. Not until the midway mark is the trio apparatus used as a totality in this music that is half gay and half sad.

- **Little Suite for Flute and Two Clarinets (1947)**

Kubik's suite was written originally for three recorders (a version still retained). The folk quality is predominant, contained within very concentrated contemporary essentials. The music has the vitality to make immediate contact with audiences when performed.

A slightly modal feeling covers the "Plaintive Song," a conception in the E tonality orbit. The preceding movement (a Prelude) is a duple-paced item, designed, in most instances, so that two instruments work against the remaining one. The final Canon is a fast and lively affair. At first devoted to two voices with accompaniment, it shifts to a full three-voice canon for the middle section, then returns to the two-voice disposition, with the accompaniment overhead.

OCTET

- **Divertimento No. 2 for Eight Players (Flute [alternating Piccolo], Oboe, Clarinet, Bassoon, Trumpet, Trombone, Viola, and Piano) (1959)**

Kubik's intent is to be "diverting and gay." That he is. One will recall *Les Six* in their heyday in this music. One will also recall jugglery, animated-cartoon style, the tightly spare music of Aaron Copland (the work is dedicated to him), and the spastic nervousness of Stravinsky's *L'Histoire du soldat*.

The Overture, with just a slight silence at its conclusion, moves into a pair of Pastorales. The first of these is a bit calmer than the Overture, but retains a goodly part of its rhythmic image. The second is more flowing, but is not in the traditional rustic manner. A "Puppet Show" is described in the Scherzino movement. Secundal intervallic snap is a feature—proper to the unbuttoned Punch and Judy mood of a puppet-show scene. Movement four is a "Dialogue," for oboe and viola. The title is adhered to—the instruments never play together and it represents a neat bit of relaxation before the final "Dance Toccata." This finale balances the opening movement in tone, rhythmic tug of war, and the absence of any textural tumidity.

(Divertimento No. 1 was also written in 1959. It calls for thirteen players.)

Kubizek, Augustin (1918–)

DUOS

- **Musik für zwei Violinen (Music for Two Violins) (1952)**

Buttressed by the pointed façade of dissonant counterpoint, Kubizek's three-movement structure has imposing strength. The concentrate of two violins produces a sharp relief for the lines and results in dramatic music. There is almost a strident (fully acceptable) roughness in the work, aided by the inflexibility of the dynamics. In the speedy opening movement the *mezzoforte* is constant; in the Finale there is only slight deviation from the propelled *forte*. Only the middle portion (Arioso) is soft, and here too the level is undeviating, staying in *piano* from first to final measure.

The opening theme dominates the first movement. In movement two, a slowly striding bass in measured eighth notes supports the ornamental figuration of the neo-Bachian soprano line. The Finale is fugue-driven, marked by the use of the pungent tritone. In the limited worthy literature for paired violins, Kubizek's suite deserves a high place.

- **Sonata for Flute and Harp, Op. 24b**

A partial resetting of Kubizek's *Quartetto da camera (see below)*. Oddly, not a single mention of this transfer is made in either score. This duo transcription covers the first three of the four movements. It is clear that the polyphonic data in the finale of the four-instrument version would not be feasible in this setting and was therefore not included.

QUARTETS

- *Quartetto da camera* for Guitar, Oboe, Clarinet, and Bassoon, Op. 24a

Divertimento aspects cover this *Chamber Quartet*. Free tonalism powers the music, with fluency and variety in the formal arrangements. Especially direct are the rhythmic proportions in the first movement. In the following Scherzo the meter is set as an alternation of triple and duple pulse. In the contrastive, slower-paced Trio these are combined and the music flows in quintuple time. Rhapsody controls the quartal-punctuated slow movement; a polyphonic status exists in the final movement.

(*See above* for another setting of this work.)

- *Vergnügliche Miniaturen über eine Zwölftonreihe (Delightful Miniatures on a Twelve-tone Row)* for Violin, Clarinet, Trombone, and Bassoon, Op. 28a

Yes, charming music that covers almost ten minutes and demonstrates that twelve-tone fervor can be directed to other than dark, expressionistic territory.

In the retrograde form of the row the pitches are a whole tone lower. The inversion of the row is a fourth higher, its retrograde a fifth below. Dances are in the forefront, with a

Waltz in movement two, a Polka in movement three, and a Ländler in movement six. A March with some side-kicked metrical order follows a trio-formationed Interludium (the trombone is tacet there). The Introduction and Finale use the same material as the Interludium, and all three are unified by the same tempo, meter, and quality. Exact mathematical balance, therefore, since these three movements are, respectively, numbers one, seven, and four of the total seven.

QUINTET

- *Chamber Quintet* for Winds (Flute, Oboe, Clarinet, Horn, and Bassoon) (1955)

The succinct theorem of the outer movements is constant activity, the parts knitted tightly into the sound fabric. The same type of weave is found in the slow (fourth) movement. One is reminded of the linear weights that apply to Honegger's music. The other two movements are lighter; one a slow March that is constantly adorned with grace notes, the other a Waltz.

Kučera, Václav (1929–)

DUO

- *Duodrama* for Bass Clarinet and Piano (1967)

Percussive music for a woodwind instrument and a keyboard instrument. The chords in the harmony stay within seconds and sevenths, plus clusters. The bass clarinet part is never its usual basso profundo lyrical voice, but a vigorous sonoric abstraction— indenting, gliding, oscillating, and thrusting; the piano is a dynamic partner, including striking the strings with drum beaters. Kučera's duo begins impetuously and ends tranquilly, but even then the closing chords are not placid or sweet but percussive tone clusters.

TRIOS

- *Panta Rhei:* **Music for Flute,
    Vibraphone, and Percussion
    (Timpano, Small Drum, Three
    Tom-toms, Two Suspended Cymbals,
    Tam-tam, Three Cow Bells, Five
    Temple Blocks, Two Triangles, and
    Glockenspiel) (1963)**

A dramaturgical chamber music conception in four connected sections, totaling eleven minutes. Virtuosity is demanded on the part of all three performers; the percussionist alone handles nineteen instruments requiring five different types of beaters.

Linear activity with disjunct pitch challenges begin the trio. It proceeds to aleatoric segments, followed by music that falls in toccata territory, the pulse pertinently stoked by the percussionist (in one section this consists of thirty-one consecutive measures of eighth notes freely divided among the two cymbals and tam-tam). The fourth and concluding section is again devoted to the free relationships of aleatoric processes, colored by antiphonal dynamic crisscross.

Panta Rhei is vivid contemporary chamber music. It may lack elegance. That is not needed, since it is replaced by timbre blaze.

- *Protests:* **Chamber Cycle for Violin,
    Piano, and Timpani (1963)**

The use of the timpani requires special notice. It is a completely emancipated instrument in this trio. Gone are the days of mere rolls and simplistic punctuative backup. In this work the timpani is an extensive and expansive voice, requiring four drums, equally considered with the other instruments.

Part one of this cycle (Grave) is a slow-moving imperious and dramatic concept, built from massive quartal chords combined with and framing declarative statements. The Ritmico movement is formed from small rhythmic jets progressing to dynamic pulsatile blocks. The sounds per beat begin with triplets, move onto sixteenths and then to sextuplets. Movement three (Cantabile) emphasizes linear summary in the violin, chordal sonority in the piano, and rhythmic motility in the timpani. It is almost silky smooth in comparison to the textural thickness and exciting activity in the final part of Kučera's trio.

QUINTET

- *Diptychon:* **Music for Flute, Bass
    Clarinet, Piano, and Percussion
    (Percussion I: Glockenspiel,
    Xylophone, Vibraphone, and Bells;
    Percussion II: Timpani, Small,
    Medium, and Large Tom-toms,
    Tenor Drum, Five Temple Blocks,
    Three Wood Blocks, High and Low
    Suspended Cymbals, Tenor and
    Baritone Gongs, and Tam-tam)
    (1966)**

Two linked parts constitute this quintet. The first is titled "The Face of the World"; the second, "The Face of the People." Programmatic definition notwithstanding, there is little difference between the two parts, though the pace of the second is mostly slower at the beginning than the tempo of the first. Later into part two the pace quickens.

Free serialism is combined with types of atonal combinations, these stressing certain intervals. More to the point is the motile dynamism that is a constant. No metrical definition exists, but all notation is precise, based on lengths related to the quarter note used as the metronomic indication.

Diptychon offers a wealth of polyphony of material and instrumentation. In its make-up of unrest there is the sense of a fantasy-potpourri.

NONET

- *Dramata* **for Nine Performers (Flute [alternating Piccolo], Oboe, Clarinet, Bassoon, Horn, Violin, Viola, Cello, and Double Bass) (1961)**

A few styles are mixed into Kučera's four-part nonet program, which pictures "Tragedy," "Comedy," "Pantomime," and "Drama." The compositional instrumentalities are drawn from neoclassicism and free tonality, plus Stravinsky of the predodecaphonic days. Kučera's *Dramata* has a synthesis of these elements, though it does not provide a pertinent profile, a marked individuality. Its virtues are direct definition of the titled moods and excellent forms.

Considerable blocked scoring is used in "Tragedy." Either the strings or the winds are of composite coloration while the other group of instruments is of linear disposition. In "Comedy" the timbre tonics of staccato bassoon, piquant piccolo, and string glissando help carry out the descriptive objective. There is more fluidity in the scoring of the last two parts of the nonet. There are also considerable metrical and rhythmic allocations. None of these interfere with the matter of stabilization. This is good and interesting music.

Kuhlau, Friedrich (1786–1832)

DUOS

- **Andante and Polacca for Horn and Piano**

The F-minor Andante is rondo-shaped. Ending in the dominant, the music proceeds into the Alla polacca, which moves in bright F major. And that part, too, is rondo-shaped. A pithy, welcome, creative issue.

- *Duo brillant* **for Two Flutes, Op. 102, No. 1**

Plenty of triplets help the brilliant ongoingness of the opening movement. Nothing is hidden in Kuhlau's style; this is extrovert and light-scaled chamber music despite the intimate and concentrated medium. In contrast is the Andante cantabile, with just a touch here and there of chromaticism to color the G-major tonality. A Rondo serves for the finale, its motility aided by swirling scalic lines, both conjunct and chromatic.

- *Duo brillant* **for Two Flutes, Op. 102, No. 2**

Kuhlau usually structures his music according to traditional formulas: three movements, with fast tempos for the outer divisions and a slow movement in between. However, he departs from this occasionally, always producing interesting results.

There is no separate slow movement in this work, but there is a slow-speed portion (it totals twenty-seven measures in Adagio of 4/4 time) preliminary to the first movement proper. The Adagio is in C-sharp minor, moves to a conclusive B pitch, which marks the dominant of the E-minor tonality of the main movement, a dynamic tripleted Allegro assai con molto fuoco. Oddly enough, the same E-minor key, save for one section, serves for all portions of the following movement, Variations (on an Ancient Swedish Air). No developmental diffusion is attempted. Kuhlau makes sure that the thematic shape is always in mind, mixed with the essence of the variations. It is a simple method but it works well and fits correctly with Kuhlau's style.

- *Duo brillant* **for Two Flutes, Op. 102, No. 3**

This duo has the same metrical pulse for all

three movements. The Adagio, subtermed "melancholy" (an instruction met with often in Kuhlau's music), is in 2/4. The same time signature is used for the final Rondo (its tempo is allegretto vivace). Though the opening movement is in 6/8, its speed, Allegro vivace (the vivace for both outer movements is a further duplication) means the music will again be heard with duple-pulse impress. Kuhlau's usual Haydnesque style pertains throughout.

- *Duo brillants* **for Flute and Piano, Op. 110**

  - No. 1, in B-flat
  - No. 2, in E Minor
  - No. 3, in D

All three works are in three movements. Kuhlau did not feel the urge for spirited invention. Finding workable forms for combining the flute with piano, he proceeds to use the same mold constantly. Each duo begins with a sonata-form Allegro, with the piano first stating the theme or outlining a chordal plan from which the theme then emerges. Rondos serve for the final movements, and slow movements in three-part style occupy the center of each. All three duets are mid-Victorian in sound, and hold no technical problems.

- *Duo concertant* **for Two Flutes, Op. 10, No. 1**

Kuhlau follows his habitual formal practice in this E-minor duet, comprising three movements, with a pair of Allegros surrounding a Larghetto. But facsimile practice does not produce academic music. The part writing is neatly organized with Kuhlau's usual attention for equality between the instruments. In the slow movement the middle section of the ternary design is marked by a change of key from C major to C minor, simultaneous with more ornate stylistic gestures. A parallel tonality

shift brightens the E-minor structure of the finale, by use of an E-major portion.

- *Duo concertant* **for Two Flutes, Op. 10, No. 2**

Like the first duo in this opus, there are three movements here. However, some interesting differences are provided. The middle movement is a set of variations (Tema con variazioni) and is to be played in larghetto tempo with a significant instruction: con espressione malinconica (with melancholy expression). The variety of expressiveness obtained is noteworthy, considering the absence of a solid and true bass register and that only two homophonic, similarly timbred instruments are concerned. The second variation is made motile by unceasing syncopation; the final one is a restatement of the theme propped with tripleted accompaniment. The opening movement is a gay D-major projection; the finale an Allegretto, with Couperinesque ornamentation, set in rondo definition.

- *Duo concertant* **for Two Flutes, Op. 10, No. 3**

Kuhlau casts aside his favorite three-movement totality in this piece. It is the only work in the three-in-one opus that consists of a pair of movements, both in Allegro tempo. While speed similarity exists, monotony is canceled by metrical and qualitative differences. The first part flows in 6/8 meter, the second movement has more rhythmic issue in its 4/4 measures. The scoring scope of the music matches the qualities; both instruments in movement two cover a larger territory than contained in the previous movement. With such difference the contrastive lack of a slow movement is not felt.

- *Grand Duets* for Two Flutes,
  Op. 39, Nos. 1 and 2

The key word in the title is the descriptive "grand." In comparison with the formal concept of Kuhlau's other flute duets there is no change. He follows the three-movement scheme of two fast movements embracing a slow one—a design that has been common practice since the beginning of the 18th century. In scope, however, these duos have a broader and more detailed developmental scheme plus more modulatory coloration. In the slow movements the *idée fixe* is elaboration and ornamental figuration that adds energy to the part writing. Both finales are titled Rondo.

- *Grand Duet* for Two Flutes,
  Op. 39, No. 3

Kuhlau changes his duet format in this piece. There are four movements in place of the usual three, plus some subtle alterations in the creative approach. The opening movement, sonata styled, has scherzando qualities. Most of the power of the slow movement (Adagio con anima) is placed in the hands of the first flute. The music contains recitative properties; its tempo is a hybrid of slow pace and animation.

Kuhlau was a master of canonic technique. This was recognized by Beethoven, who paid him the compliment of calling him "Der grosse Canonier." An example of this mastery is exemplified by the third movement. Simply titled Canon, it is a bountiful achievement. The structure is precisely formed, with three-part balance, including a literal recapitulation; the contrasting Trio section is in the tonic major (the key of the movement is G minor). A good-size coda is furnished for good measure. And every portion of the music, from upbeat to conclusion, follows strict canonic procedure, the voices proceeding at an octave's distance.

The final movement is a Rondo alla polacca. This combine owes nothing to polonaise form.

It borrows, however, the principal rhythmic characteristic of the Polish dance, the dactyl pattern. The Rondo concludes one of the outstanding works in flute duet literature.

- *Grand Duets concertants* for Two Flutes,
  Op. 87

  - No. 1, in A Major
  - No. 2, in G Minor
  - No. 3, in D Major

In both the first and third works of this set Kuhlau's favorite three-movement presentation prevails. The slow movement of the first duo moves from a quiet mood into a more forceful and intense declaration. The structure is defined as tripartite when the music returns to its initial quality. As always with Kuhlau, mundane accompanimental figures are avoided, the instruments play against each other, and when one is subsidiary it retains interest in its make up. The slow movement in the third duo is quite different. It is a short Larghetto melancolico and is joined onto the finale, a duple-metered Presto assai. The concluding movement of the first duo is a Rondo alla polacca. It is of substantial length and contains a Mendelssohnian lightness. Stressed, of course, is the principal polacca rhythmic ingredient of a long and two short sounds.

The second duet is of different cut. Its opening movement is slower (Moderato assai) and more ornate than usually marks Kuhlau's first movements. There is no slow movement. Instead, an Adagio is spliced twice into the course of the second (and concluding) movement. The differences in speed and quality provide good formal showmanship.

- *Grand Sonata* for Flute and Piano,
  Op. 64

This *Grand Sonata* is one of the best and most representative of Kuhlau's compositions. Early

Beethoven style is apparent in the first movement. It is served by a simple sonata plan, with two contrasted subjects (both announced first by the piano), followed by the usual development. An ancient Danish air serves as the theme for the variations of the second section. The theme is prefaced by an introduction filled with Italian operatic levity. The variations are of the "bread-and-butter" variety, without any key change, and stay close to the theme; the third is for the piano alone; the final one includes a flute cadenza. A long and easily comprehended Haydnesque Rondo finishes the work. The suavity of the flute writing substitutes for emotive depth.

- **Introduction and Variations on a Theme from Carl Maria von Weber's *Euryanthe* for Flute and Piano, Op. 63**

Weber was Kuhlau's contemporary. Both were born in the same year, and Kuhlau outlived the German composer by only a mere half-dozen years. The use of a fellow composer's theme is always implicit homage. Thus, Kuhlau chose a Romance from the Weber opera *Unter blühenden Mandelbäumen* as his testimonial.

The introduction is majestic in tempo, ornate in style. Its G-minor key gives contrast to the G-major tonality of the theme. Six variations follow. In the first the piano is the principal protagonist. Scale lines are special to the second variation and triplet figuration to the third. In the fourth part the piano, again, holds the spotlight with an agitated and brilliant permutation. Clarity of thematic framework within the variants is constant and this pertains to the final pair of variations. The last one is the most extended of the set and is identified by octave leaps from grace notes.

- **Three Duos for Two Flutes, Op. 81**

Music squarely in the tradition of conventional forms. Each duet is in three movements, each with outer fast movements balanced in the center with a slow-tempo division. All the finales have the same Rondo title. Kuhlau controls his instruments for the greater part with harmonically directed part writing. Music that falls gently on the ear, with the most dramatic the third Duo of the set.

- **Variations on "The Last Rose of Summer" for Flute and Piano, Op. 105**

Kuhlau's choice of theme matches several others, including Beethoven (in his *Six Very Early Themes Varied* for Flute [or Violin] and Piano, Op. 105), Mendelssohn (*Fantasy on "The Last Rose of Summer"* for Piano, Op. 15), and Flotow (in his opera *Martha*).

The Irish melody is good groundwork for the bandstandish type of variational flamboyance represented. Thus: curvaceous leaps in variation two, arpeggiated groups in variation three, zippy scalic movement in variation four, pastoralish weaves plus cadenza waves in variation six. The final variant features repeated sounds and then splits away into a scherzando conclusion. All of it offers nothing genuinely new but genuine music it is, in its restricted sense.

TRIOS

- **Grand Trio concertant in G Minor for Three Flutes, Op. 13, No. 2**

Music of geniality and charm, with hop-skip-and-jump flute-weighted robustness and perennial freshness.

There are two movements both in the fast area: Allegro non tanto and Allegro con moto. The first of the pair has the usual balance of primary and secondary themes, the latter first heard in F major and when recapitulated is set in G major. In the second movement the sparkling materials include mini fanfares. Music that is a delight to play and to hear.

- *Grand Trios* for Three Flutes, Op. 86

  - No. 1, in E Minor
  - No. 2, in D Major
  - No. 3, in E-flat Major

Important works in terms of the flute tradition. Classical rhythmic structures and forms are employed, there is a minimum of padding, but in the majority the substances hold the interest. Of course, good attention is given to the flute's ability in terms of scalic runoff, repetitive tones, zooming figures, and floridity.

The E-minor opus consists of four movements, the other two Trios have three movements each. A scintillating Scherzo with a lyrical disposed Trio (but in the same tempo) highlights Op. 86, No. 1. The second movement of the second Trio is a colorful set of seven variations and coda on an "Ancient Swedish Air."

(The modern reprint of these Trios, issued by Billaudot—minus editing—errs in listing the tonality of the first Trio as G major.)

QUARTET

- *Grand Quartet* in E Minor for Four Flutes, Op. 103

Standard sonata procedure is the keynote of the work, beginning with the usual Allegro, preceded by a preliminary set of measures. The Scherzo has two Trios in different major tonalities to contrast with the minor mode cast of the Scherzo proper. Ornamentation—that great feature of flute technique—is used considerably in the slow movement. The concluding movement in rondo form is of Haydn heritage. Its coda portion is announced by a shift to a major tonality.

QUINTETS

- Quintets for Flute, Violin, Two Violas, and Cello, Op. 51

  - No. 1, in D Major
  - No. 2, in E Minor
  - No. 3, in A Major

An uncommon combination, with the string quartet section made up of paired violas in place of paired violins. In good amount, the flute takes the place of the first violin. However, the violin in Kuhlau's Op. 51 has more to do than the second violin in a string quartet of similar style, where the lion's share of material is assigned to the first violin.

Fluent and traditionally treated compositions. Four movements in each case. In movement one of the D-major Quintet there is emphasis on upbeat and off-beat entrances that shape the design. The Adagio in the same work is in ternary form, with tonality mode changes marking the sections. The Finale is duplepulsed, fast-tempoed, scherzando in feeling.

The Scherzo in the A-major opus is structured by the use of imitation. The slow movement of this work has an intensity in its central section that is a high point in Kuhlau's output; the Finale that follows exemplifies Haydn revisited.

Kuhn, Max (1912–82)

QUINTET

- *Serenata notturna*: Quintet for Flute, Oboe, Clarinet, Horn, and Bassoon

Colorfully neoromantic in its gestures. Kuhn's piece has divisions, but they are connected and eventually further solidified by cyclic inserts. The style is clear-toned in its use of chromatic harmonic language, as deft in its fluid lines as any classic conception.

The formal chart begins with variational considerations. These are then linked to a metered short cadenza for the clarinet, in turn proceeding to a Lento section and completed with exact attention to balance by a second metered short cadenza—this one for the oboe. A Rondo follows. At its conclusion a seven-measure quote from the Lento is made, five measures restated from the Rondo, and as many measures reviewed from the opening of the composition. The quintet is then completed as it began: with three announcements of an F-sharp by the horn. All this illustrates fine musical motivation—a composition clean and well-defined in its plan.

Kühnel, August (1645–c. 1700)

DUO

- **Partita for Cello and Piano**

Kühnel, a German composer, produced a total of fourteen compositions for the viola da gamba with basso continuo. This, the final work of the group, was edited by Ferenc Brodszky, with very slight alterations made in the string instrument's part and with the figured bass realized for piano. The result does not violate the original.

The Partita heading here signifies a suite formation with a Prelude and a set of dances: Allemande, Corrente, Sarabande, and Giga. All the five parts are in G minor as the basic tonality.

Kummer, Kaspar (1795–1870)

Kummer is certainly not a high-ranking composer. However, like the music of Popper, for which cellists have a special regard, and the music of Vieuxtemps, which violinists like to

play, most flutists accept the restricted scope of Kummer's compositions.

As a flutist-composer, Kummer wrote a great amount of music for the flute and its partnership with other instruments. Included are duets, trios, quartets, and quintets, as well as flute concertos and a method for the wind instrument. There is no striking originality in this output, but all the music is melodious, fun to play, and distinctly idiomatic.

Of the nine works for three flutes, those discussed below are representative examples. Clarity of form and tonality progress cover all of them. The total movements in each case are three, with a slow movement central to a pair of faster-tempo structures.

TRIOS

- **Trio in A for Three Flutes, Op. 59**

A long–short rhythmic figure is paramount in the opening Allegro non tanto. Binary form, with each part relating a legato thesis to fanfarelike articulations as the antithesis, is used in the middle movement. The finale has Mendelssohnian swing as it moves in a 6/8 Allegro. Like the first movement, this part is also marked "non tanto" (literally, "not as much," or a shade below fast tempo).

- **Trio in C for Three Flutes, Op. 53**

Possibly a subconscious result, but nonetheless excellent balance and relationship exists between the outer movements. The opening Allegro is projected by an initial theme which descends scalewise. In the Allegro vivace finale, the initial theme conjunctly drives upward. Kummer is careful to assort his meters: in the first movement it is triple, in the Andante the action is directed in flowing 6/8 time, and in the last movement the pulse is duple.

Kummer's forms are clear, neat, and in accepted molds. In the slow movement, however, the three-part design has a modified and changed format in the recapitulation. And no soprano voice dominates anywhere. All of Kummer's flute trios are scored for equal voices.

- **Trio in G for Three Flutes, Op. 24**

Straightforward form with proper thematic response marks Kummer's flute Trio. Of sharp contrasts there are none; the music flows from measure to measure with neutrality regarding dramaticism. No criticism. Three flutes used for simple tonal material cannot convey sharp thematic and mood opposition. In the final movement, made bouncy with grace notes, there is a fair amount of ostinato accompaniment.

Kupferman, Meyer (1926–)

DUOS

- *Fantasy Sonata* for Violin and Piano (1970)

Using both tone row and tonal arrangement, Kupferman not only maintains stylistic equilibrium but also obtains a contrastive force in his one-movement sonata. Basic instrumental personality is also confirmed: the violin principally sings, the piano mainly executes rhythmic plans, and horizontal and vertical regions thus are clearly identified.

The concluding part of the work is special, with the violinist whistling an extremely high E pitch and playing thereafter some quarter-tone pulsations around a sustained F-sharp.

- *Four Constellations* for Flute and Clarinet (1970)

Kupferman's stargazing identifies "Aquarius" ("Water Carrier") in a fluid, rubato manner, and "Scorpio" ("Scorpion") as an astrological

type of scherzo. "Libra" is brought to "balance" (the meaning of the name) by slow tempo and vivid registral exchange. "Sagittarius" ("Archer") is fast and rhythmically direct. In all cases the music presents pitch fancies that avoid tonal engagement.

- *The Garden of My Father's House* for Violin and Clarinet (1972)

The give-and-take of rhapsodic, almost ad lib dialogue. Principally, sustained arrangement, on one pitch or surrounding (orbiting) it with adjunct sounds set against free line elaboration. An example of the former: In measure one the C-sharp pitch in the clarinet is repeated in five different rhythms. Another, in measure seven: The violin has rhythmic patterns on an augmented octave while the clarinet freely repeats a ten-pitch figure. The dynamic planes form a counterpoint to the detail, quarter tones add a color topping to the sounds.

- *Infinities Twenty-two* for Trumpet and Piano (1967)

One of the some fifty pieces Kupferman has written based on the same tone row. *(See below* for another work, *Infinities Thirteen*, in the group.) The scope is huge. Number six is a full-length cantata on a Rimbaud text; number seventeen is for piano four hands; number eighteen is for solo harp; number twenty-five is for string orchestra, etc.

The twenty-second work is a five-part suite beginning with a sharp dialogue between the instruments ("Ritual"). This is freely metrical, as is part two, "Mode," and part four, "Turnabout." Part three, "Projectile," is in duple pulse, but the fluidity of the lines erases accentual straightforwardness and brings in a cadenza-termed sense. The finale is tempoed fast–jazz beat. Its title, "Jazz-Bond," is a play on the name of the movie hero James Bond bound in with the jazz band idea.

Kupferman

■ *Three Ideas* for Trumpet and Piano
   (1967)

One scherzoish part and a pair of slow-paced
sketches, containing some microtoned pitches
and a slight jazz overlay. The outer pieces are
of compact total, with seventeen measures of
Adagio and twenty-four measures of Lento,
respectively. The middle movement (Allegro
scherzando) has more measures but, of course,
because of its tempo, is the fastest of the set.
   No mundane approach here. The Scherzando,
save for a couple of measures, has an uneven
quintuple beat. The trumpet stays muted until
the final *Idea*, which is a contemplative bit
based on Beethoven's "Muss es sein?" motive,
which opens the finale of his last string quartet
(Op. 135).

QUARTETS

■ *Infinities Thirteen*: Quartet for Eight
   Instruments (Flute [alternating
   Piccolo and Alto Flute], Clarinet
   [alternating Bass Clarinet], Violin
   [alternating Viola], and Piano) (1965)

(*See above* under duos for another work in
Kupferman's set of *Infinities*.)
   The subtitle describes the tripling by the
flute and the two other doublings. *Infinities
Thirteen* begins with the tone row that supports
the entire set of works, but it pulls free of it
considerably. Kupferman is no hold-the-line
dodecaphonic composer; the style is not deserted but it is considered in a fluid fashion.
   There are two major divisions to the quartet.
The first is rhapsodic, fantasy-fierce, an expressionistic Bergian atmosphere is to be recognized. The second is jazz-jacketed. Within it
are sections that bring up solo timbres front and
center. The first of these is a duet for clarinet and
violin. This is linked to one for alto flute and
clarinet, and in turn, one for the solo piano. Later
the last of these solos calls for violin and piano.

Kuri-Aldana

■ **String Quartet No. 4 (1958)**

A set of variations, five in number, comprises
the first of the two parts of the work. The pace
is slow, the materials intensely conjugated and
contrasted, the twelve-tone syntax darkening
the musical prose.
   Movement two is a huge Scherzo, Bartókian
in its crushing rhythms. The Trio is severely
contrastive in mood, with flat-leveled pitch
sustainment and the use of muted timbre. It
maintains the precise definition that marks
each part of the work. This divisioning is continued to the very end. After the return to the
Scherzo's very fast material, providing a balanced tripartite division, the quartet concludes
with a modified setting of the theme used for
the variations.

QUINTET

■ **Brass Quintet (Two Trumpets, Horn,
   Tenor Trombone, and Bass
   Trombone or Tuba) (1970)**

This is twelve-tone music to the hilt, but it is
color-charmed by virtuosic throwing of the
pitches. Jazzy stuff, as well as a fugue, is
included. The brassy flashes prove that twelve-
tone passion can be combined with brashy
scoring. Stuff and fiber in this music—an impressive opus.

Kuri-Aldana, Mario (1931–)

TRIO

■ *Cantares (Songs)* for Flute, Clarinet,
   and Piano

A good number of this Mexican composer's
works are seasoned and spiced with folk materials (*Concertino mexicano* for violin and string
orchestra, *Suite ingenua* and *Villancico*,

Canción y Jarabe, both for piano, are just a few examples). Ditto for this trio.

Cantares consists of eight parts that are to be played "without a break." The collection is simply and compactly set forth and the bounty of folk detail used is never overstyled or outstyled. Various tempos in the assortment—the first section of the sixth part is a Tango. All of the music is a joy to the ears.

Kurka, Robert (1921–57)

DUOS

- **Sonata for Violin and Piano, Op. 23, No. 3**

Kurka believed in the authority, faith, and cogency of contemporary classicism. This resulted in music of melodic sweep and balance, controlled rhythm, and an emotive directness that equates eloquence. The first and third movements of the Sonata are built on sonata-allegro formations and are tonally based on G. The central movement, a ternary-structured Andante cantabile, is in the dominant key area.

- **Sonatina for Cello and Piano, Op. 21**

Decided neoclassicism runs its course through the measures of Kurka's Sonatina. The primary tonalities are balanced with F for the outer movements (the second of the pair colored with a sixth added to the tonic) and C (the dominant) for the inner portion. The last is an especially significant and beautiful movement, tempoed "Slow, but flowing," that in its ternary proportions has a constant change in harmony and texture. There is no formal austerity to this simply projected duo. The outer movements are both indicated "fast," but are cogently compared with one in a gliding triple pulse, the other in a tighter, more dynamic duple pulse.

Indeed, Kurka's work obeys structural checks and balances, but this does not interfere with a *savoir-faire* that is a delight to hear.

QUARTET

- **Moravian Folk Songs: A Little Suite for Woodwind Quartet (Flute, Oboe, Clarinet, and Bassoon), Op. 18**

Kurka always expressed a special fondness for Czech music. This is illustrated by the choices he made for this set of six short pieces.

Moderate pace for the first tune, "Jack, Jack . . . ." The second floats a bit contrapuntally in adagio tempo, titled "Why Are You So Sad, Little Girl?" A presto waltz projects "Grove, Grove, Green Grove!" Ostinato accompaniment, with the melodic part shared between the flute and the oboe, colors "There Will Be a War, There Will—But Who Will Go to It?" This adagio piece contrasts to the vivaciousness of the fifth of the set, "Katy, Come to Church! / No, I Won't, I Went Yesterday!" Although the sixth has a different title: " . . . What Did You Do?" it is a repeat of the first part of the first piece in the suite.

Kurtág, György (1926–)

DUO

- **Eight Duos for Violin and Cimbalom, Op. 4**

Stephen Walsh's comment regarding this group of pieces is on target. Walsh, one of England's most perceptive critics, says: "The great charm of these miniatures lies in the curious blend of the violin with the plangent, adenoidal twang of the cimbalom." Nothing more, but no more is needed.

Revelatory music, this. No meters, few bar lines, and those that are used mark off phrases not rhythmic pulses. Hungarian to the hilt, especially considering the cimbalom (the Hungarian dulcimer), these are akin to notated improvisations—short, *very* short, acute musical revelations.

TRIO

- *The Little Fix* for Piccolo, Trombone, and Guitar, Op. 15b

No one need state the very obvious that this combine confounds with its bold disparity of timbres. But then Kurtág is a rare independent voice and one of the great colorists among Hungarian composers. *The Little Fix* is merely another prime piece of evidence of his creative individuality.

It was first written for solo guitar and then turned into a trio. The first piece, "Fanfare in the Manner of Moussorgsky," is naturally for the trombone, and that brass instrument proclaims the lines held in place by a swerving figure in expected *forte* and in less-expected broad tempo. Chordal determination controlled by the guitar's influence is used in part two, "Hymn in the Manner of Stravinsky." The Scherzo whirls and spits out rhythms. Fifteen times the instruction at the end of a phrase is "the players suddenly become motionless." (One doesn't know who came first, but this action of inaction has been used by Lukas Foss in a number of his works. Foss uses the term "Freeze!")

There is no tempo assigned the "Nachstück" ("Night Piece"), but this is no calm Chopinesque item or Bartókian mysterious conception. It is rather more of a nightmarish bit with chain trills, constant chromatic coinage, and flutter-tongued glissandos.

QUARTETS

- *Homage to András Mihály: Twelve Microludes* for String Quartet, Op. 13

Neo-Webern music that matches that master composer in terms of concentration of detail

and length and sets up an original type of scoring climate that chills in one place and is superheated in another. Each of the twelve pieces is based (freely and fluidly) on a pitch in the chromatic scale, thus the first is on and around C, the second relates to C-sharp, and so on.

As the concept is compacted in terms of size so it is matched in terms of scoring intensity and information. And likewise the confirmation of the qualities. Thus desolate chorale sketches, scherzo dissection, and even a modal dream sequence. And all minute—less is more, indeed.

(Mihály, born 1917, is a Hungarian composer and conductor.)

- **String Quartet, Op. 1**

Webernian concentration is exhibited in the six movements of the work. The influences are not always top surface but they reflect the avant-garde as well as Bartók. Themes as such are not developed in Kurtág's work, but a fundamental concept is stated and then expanded. Thus, rhythmic fluidity (in movement two where a tenfold meter is divided 3+2+2+3), polyphony (the start of movement three is a strict canon in unison), ostinato (movement five), and so forth.

In practically every instance, a composer's Op. 1 represents sheer, bald imitation of a style. Kurtág's first opus denies such generality.

QUINTET

- **Quintet for Winds, Op. 2**

If there is any influence to be discerned it is Webern, but with the Viennese's tripulsed bits replaced by modernized Hungarian curves and pliancy. Some of the eight movements are concentrated to the ultimate: number one, Lento, with eight measures in 3/4 time; or number six, Grave, for the beginning of a thirteen-measure span, also in 3/4 time, the eleventh measure, however, is prestissimo possible and the final two measures are just a bit slower: presto. Parts two and eight are free of metrical rule. The effect is improvisation being led by the hand. Part five is totally to be an improvised bit based on certain materials that Kurtág offers for use.

Kurz, Siegfried (1930–)

QUARTETS

- **String Quartet [No. 1], Op. 27**

Movement one begins with a fugue over a pedal point, and movement two begins with a fugue minus a pedal point. There are canons of length and there are short canonic episodes in movement one. (One of the canons is related to the fugue by the use of a double pedal point riding above and below the canon in the first violin and cello.) Though there are no canons in movement two, the formal bond continues by the use there of pedal points.

The structural affinity is maintained as well in the third movement, with its pedal point bindings and its canonic actions. Marvelous color also: passages in harmonics and rows of thirteenth chords—scads of them in the concluding measures.

- **String Quartet No. 2 Op. 34**

Like so many composers, Kurz shifted from his early free tonal style to the projection of full chromaticism. Nonetheless, the second quartet is not restricted by serial boundaries but uses the twelve pitches with freedom. The prime example here is the second movement, which links an Adagio with an Allegretto and closes the movement (and the quartet) with a return to the Adagio. The movement begins with a simple motive announced by one instrument after the other, each time with a different pitch until all

twelve have been covered in the space of (significantly!) twelve measures. From that point development of this twelve-pitch material takes place.

Movement one is a stream of polyphony mainly in terms of imitative procedures. These cover all types of developmental processes, including the pyramiding of chords. Cadential points are defined by a gathering of the voices into unified rhythmic statements.

Kuss, Margarita (1921–)

DUO

- **Sonata for Violin and Piano**

Kuss avoids the academic and the buttoned-down type of tonal harmony in her duo sonata. In movement one the first subject is colored by muted timbre in the violin. In the recapitulation the initial theme is stated by a single line in the piano and entirely partnered by two-voice col legno in the violin.

Both the second and third movements use variational devices; intervallic change marking the former and principally rhythmic detail developed in the latter. The conclusion ties the work together by quoting the chordal opening of the piece with a descending-fifth figure in the violin alone heard five separate times, the final one in ritarded pace and muted sound.

Kuti, Sándor

QUARTET

- **String Quartet**

Another composer with Bartókian references, but with some differences. Ostinatos, yes. Pungent pizzicato percussions, no. Metrical change and rubato rhapsody, no. Folk integration, yes.

The Hungarian melos is sublimated. The frictions are on thin wires. The textures are as crystal clear as those of a Haydn quartet. Kuti's quartet is, indeed, special in the Bartókian syndrome. It is Bartók presented politely. This includes the pair of fastest movements (number two, an Allegro deciso, and number four, a Presto, introduced by a Grave, which later appears abridged, is then linked to a Moderato before the Presto returns, and is then concluded in Prestissimo). But there is no barbaric coagulation. Rhythmic drive is present and precipitous intensity also, but always neat. No implication is being made that Bartók is otherwise. It is just that Kuti's *ruvido* music digs in with its nails clipped and manicured.

The fast music in movement two emphasizes the principal theme, cogently identified by spans of a third and a fourth. The developments include a fugato. In the other speedy part the opening portion (in very slow tempo) points up the use of the augmented step that pigments Kuti's work throughout. This section preludes the Presto whirlwind, which includes a startling sixteen-measure passage with all four instruments playing sul ponticello—special timbre with a vengeance! Four measures of the introduction return followed by a Moderato that is a bridge of attenuated sequences, a supposed weakness that proves to be a strength, creating a tension that culminates in the return of the Presto. The other two movements (one and three) are almost relaxed in their simplicity; the latter (almost allegro in tempo) moves like a minuet. A considerable amount of imitation binds the opening movement; an Adagio, it is the only slow movement in the quartet.

Kuula, Toivo (1883–1918)

DUO

- **Sonata in E Minor for Violin and Piano (1907)**

Although the ethnic musical characteristics of his country were used by Kuula in his orchestral works, only a little bit of this authenticity filters into his chamber music. The latter is limited to but two works, a Trio (*see below*) and this Sonata.

Finnish adjuncts are noticeable in the introductory octave-depicted section of the slow movement; this section is also used later as a separate division including violin passages which imply the melos of the western section of Finland, from which part Kuula came. The last movement has, in its surcharged motor rhythm, the lightness of a Finnish folk dance—a rondo of somewhat oversupplied proportions. The first movement is the most academically formal, with the E-minor home tonality being allied respectably to its relative major key. The style of the romantic school is further exhibited by use of turbulence and suppleness, so that the subjects are well contrasted. As far as construction is concerned, the first movement is best. For the prime matter of simply establishing an individual manner of musical speech, the last two are superior. Kuula would definitely have developed if he had not died at an early age. (He was shot to death during the Finnish War of Independence.)

TRIO

- **Trio for Piano, Violin, and Cello, Op. 7**

Like Kuula's violin sonata *(see above),* his piano trio combines romantically designed mementoes with native-colored souvenirs. The Trio is of length and symphonic power. For the most part it is like a sonorous tidal wave. One technique is outstanding above all others—repetitive formations: on a single sound, based on syncopative rhythms, and from wide-ranging arpeggios.

The sombre Andante elegico has a Sibelian quality, its pathos strongly in contrast to the preceding Scherzo, which has neat contrapuntal interplay. A connection exists between the two outer movements, with a slight reminder of the opening part of the Trio drawn into the latter part of the Finale.

Kuusisto, Ilkka Taneli (1933–)

DUO

▪ **Duo for Flute and Cello (1957)**

Tonal music with some salty pitches for flavor. And that move carries over to the metrical order, which has some slight shifts that stimulate the lines.

Three movements (Moderato–Lento–Vivace) that are placidly pleasant and lighthearted, but not "light" music as the term is generally understood. Better stated: "healthy" music, the materials fitting the instrumentation.

Kuusisto, Taneli (1905–)

TRIO

▪ *Sonatine in alten Stil: Weinachtssonatine (Sonatine in Old Style: Christmas Sonatine)* **for Flute, Violin, and Piano (or Harpsichord), Op. 19**

Simple, unobtrusive tonal music, pegged quite firmly in G major for movements one (Pastorale) and two (Canzonetta). Save for two light final unison chords for the piano, the latter is a duet for the flute and violin. Movement three is a D-major Fughetta. A light-faceted trio but nonetheless planned for total balance by having a partial return of the opening movement to serve as the coda for the Fughetta, thereby concluding that movement in G major as well.

The *Christmas* heading is not explained, although the mood of the Pastorale might fit the designation.

Kvam, Oddvar S. (1927–)

DUOS

▪ *Brev (Letter)* **for Violin and Piano, Op. 31d**

A seven-minute missive. The harmonic language is characterized by fourths, with the melodic line providing broad thrusts into the chordal and rhythmic background.

If one is to read any message within the communication it is that having made his fervent point Kvam's closing is calm and dulcet.

▪ *Duo Ostinato* **for Violin and Guitar, Op. 59**

Kvam's piece (of six-minute duration) is pressed in and simultaneously stimulated by the ostinato patterns. *Patterns*, yes. Within each set there are slight pitch modifications, but whatever the boundaried shape, it does not change.

Totally uneven meters rule the pulse arrangement. First a quintuple measurement with the beats split 3+2, then an octuple setting with the eighths arranged 3+3+2, followed by a return to the quintuple total. Later the aggregate pulses are septuple and apportioned as 3+2+2. The guitar carries the ostinatos; the violin supplies the clear tonal melodic juice.

- **Sonata for Clarinet in B-flat (alternating Clarinet in A, E-flat Clarinet, and Bass Clarinet) and Percussion (Timpani, Two Conga Drums, Suspended Cymbal, Bass Drum, Tam-tam, Tenor Drum, Xylophone, Marimba, Vibraphone, Three Tom-toms, Bells [Glockenspiel], Three Tuned Water Glasses, and Snare Drum), Op. 53**

No mistaking the originality of a duo that calls for twenty-two instruments: four types of clarinet and eighteen individual percussion instruments. Better still and more important is that the music lives up to this rich instrumental inventory.

The formal patterns all contain alluring sonorities, and each of the four movements carries out its title's objective. The opening part is an "Intrata infernale," set forth by demonic swirling figures (first by the B-flat clarinet and later by the E-flat soprano instrument) and spirited ostinatos.

Movement two, "Scherzo vitale," moves in a virile prestissimo tempo. It is asymmetrically organized, begins with the tenor drum as the percussive representative, and then shifts and retains the clattered melodic vitality of the xylophone. Secundal harmony combined with conjunct clarinet lines are the principal qualities in the "Intermezzo pastorale." Defined rhythms and a fully optimistic tone pervade the "Rondo marciale." Here, as in the previous music, there is clear action. Complex calculations are not to be found in Kvam's music.

Kvandal, Johan (1919–)

DUO

- **Duo for Violin and Cello (1959)**

Neoclassic style and therefore expanded

tonalism. This reaches bitonal procedures in the finale, a zippy, duple-pulse Allegro scherzando. Both that movement and the opening one (Allegro moderato) are in regular sonata form. The middle slow movement is a ternary affair. It begins with a fairly elaborate unaccompanied cello statement. Everything is of true stylistic substance presented without compositional trickery.

QUARTETS

- ***Miniatures* for Four Violins, Op. 43**

Norwegian folklore is the principal characterization in this five-part set. The first, "Riddervise," is a majestic, march type. Part four is a "Stev," a reproduction of an ancient ballad. The finale also partakes of native flavor with a fast-paced "Dance in Rondo Form." Parts two and three are an Elegy and a Fugato.

- **String Quartet [No. 1] (1954)**

(The date of composition needs explanation. The first three movements were completed in 1946, but Kvandal did not compose the finale until 1954. No change in style resulted.)

The quartet is classically defined up to the hilt. Movement one is in sonata form. The second movement consists of a set of eleven variations. These are ornamentally developed in the first three, decidedly rhythmic in the next four, with a chordal Adagio statement as the eighth variant. Ornamentation plays the principal role in the other variations. Interestingly, the tonality, save for the tenth variation, which is in the tonic major, remains in G minor throughout. Formal positiveness continues with a scherzo plan for movement three and a combination of fugue and sonata form for the finale.

- **String Quartet No. 2, Op. 27**

Kvandal's second quartet has the stuff of a dark

drama about it. Only the second movement relaxes matters in a scherzo formation. Neoclassically styled, as is usual with this Norwegian's compositions, the quartet begins with a "Prolog" that consists of an intense introduction and a sombre passacaglia. This material becomes interlaced in the balance of the work. Both are used in succession to close the third movement, and the passacaglia becomes the initiatory statement to begin the "Epilog." There is a further inner relationship by the quotation of bits from the second movement in the finale.

QUINTETS

- **Quintet for Hardanger Fiddle and String Quartet, Op. 50**

As would be expected, the spotlight in this two-minute work is on the Hardanger fiddle, a distinctive native violin with single sympathetic strings and a low bridge that makes chord playing easy. It is rarely heard in concert conditions since its role is for playing Norwegian dance music, the performer generally embellishing the tunes and seldom playing them the same way twice.

The tuning for the first piece is G–E–B–F-sharp, for the second piece the tuning is B–E–B–F-sharp—thus the only similarity with a standard violin's tuning is the lowest string of the first piece. Taking advantage of the chordal personality of the instrument, Kvandal scores accordingly. There are hardly any places in the work where there are single pitches in the fiddle part. The first movement has bardic breadth, the second part of the Quintet is an invigorating dance.

- **Three Hymn Tunes for Wind Quintet, Op. 23b**

No pedantic chordal hymn settings are represented here. Kvandal has retained the funda-

mental melodies and worked in a sophisticated but fitting stylistic contrapuntalism. He has also carefully textured the pieces. Thus, in the central part of the ternary first setting, "Our Lord Is Faithful in Life and Death" (from Gudbrandsdalen), he alternates (save one measure for four instruments) two- and three-part writing. In turn, the first part of the binary-structured "Praise to the Lord" (from Nordfjord) is split between two-voice and three-voice lines with the second part a vertically designed statement by the entire quintet. The finale, "The Price Is Greater Than One First Did Think" (from Gudbrandsdalen), shifts between partial use of the instruments and full tutti.

Kvapil, Jaroslav (1892–1958)

DUOS

- *In Nature* for Violin and Piano

No neat pastoral but a partly contrapuntal statement in the outer parts and music of an aggressive character in between. Fine vitality and fine use of chromatic coloration.

- **Sonata in D Major for Violin and Piano (1914)**

The juices of romanticism fill classic containers in this duo. Clinging to the musical principles of the 19th century, Kvapil nevertheless made his work sound fresh and appealing.

The three movements represent sonata, large song form, and rondo, in turn. And cyclic construction is used with a bit of the slow movement's opening theme inserted in the finale.

Kyurkchiisky

QUARTET

- **String Quartet No. 5 (1949)**

Fluent and succinctly tonal, colored by the infiltration of Slovakian folk song. The music flows with nicety and without weakness, everything is clearly defined. There are no false notes or moves in this work. All of it is unsophisticated, but it will not bore sophisticated ears.

An interesting touch in the first movement is the return of the "head" of the principal theme at the conclusion in a slower tempo (Moderato at the beginning of the quartet, Adagio at the end). The Presto is right off the folk dance floor. In movement three (Lento) variational development is the key to the design. A rondo format is used for the conclusion.

Kyurkchiisky, Krasimir (1936–)

QUARTET

- **Quartet for Two Violins, Viola, and Cello (1959)**

No folksy national minority melodies are intertwined in this Quartet. The beginning shows the way things are to be—a hard-driven, aggressive, fast movement, prefaced by a slow-paced introduction. A sensitivity to color marks the entire procedure. In the introduction the instruments are muted and further dampened by the elimination of vibrato. Seven-part writing is used. Opposites are emphasized in the Allegro energico: ponticello and normal sound, *pianos* and *fortes*, and excessive vibrato. Throughout there is plenty of roughage. And some of this seeps into the Andante doloroso.

And still more follows. In the Scherzo depiction the rhythmic cells burst out and are considerably fragmented. The Trio portion is in slower pace, muted, glassy in sound (ponticello), and once again minus vibrato. Dynamism continues in the final movement, which begins with a recast of the same slow music that initiated the composition.

This hardly known composer has written a very strong string quartet. It emphasizes the bravura element partnered with timbral exploration.

A Note on the Author

Arthur Cohn combined a career of writer, violinist, composer, conductor, and music publishing executive. He was the first curator of the Fleisher Music Collection at the Free Library of Philadelphia (1934-52) and was head of the library's music department (1946-52). He then directed the serious music departments at Mills Music, MCA Music, and Carl Fischer, in New York.

He organized the Dorian String Quartet and later the Stringart Quartet which specialized in performing twentieth-century music over its six-year existence. He was the conductor of the Philadelphia Little Symphony, and for thirty-five years the musical director and conductor of the Haddonfield, New Jersey Symphony Orchestra. His guest appearances include the Philadelphia Orchestra and the National Orchestra of Mexico.

Cohn studied composition with Rubin Goldmark at the Juilliard Graduate School and his catalog of 52 compositions includes five string quartets, six orchestral suites, and a huge opus for percussion, requiring 103 instruments to be played by six performers. He was critic for the *American Record Guide, Musical Courier, Modern Music, Tempo*, and the *Rochester Times-Union. The Literature of Chamber Music* is his sixth published book.